A New Look at Modern Indian History

FROM 1707 TO THE MODERN TIMES

32nd Edition

FOOD FOR THOUGHT

Fighting corruption is not just good governance. It's self-defense. It's patriotism.
— *Joe Biden*

There is no friend as loyal as a book.
— *Ernest Hemingway*

The best way to find yourself is to lose yourself in the service of others.
— *Mahatma Gandhi*

Some books are to be tasted, others to be swallowed, and some few are to be chewed and digested.
— *Francis Bacon*

The Library of the Congress, Washington, D.C., U.S.A. Printed
Card Data-Vol. 36 A New Look At Modern Indian History
Grover, B.L. DS 463, G78
75-920179 MARC

THE SCHOOL OF ORIENTAL AND AFRICAN STUDIES,
UNIVERSITY OF LONDON
A New Look At Modern Indian History
Grover, B.L., JA 954-03/311217
www.lib.soas.ac.uk

Adelaide University, Australia,
A New Look At Modern Indian History,
by Grover, B.L.
Call No. : 954, G883S

A New Look at Modern Indian History

FROM 1707 TO THE MODERN TIMES

32nd Edition

ICS/PCS Candidates will find the book very useful both in the Preliminary and Main Examinations

B L GROVER
Formerly, Head of the Department of History
Hans Raj College, University of Delhi

ALKA MEHTA

S. CHAND
PUBLISHING
empowering minds

S Chand And Company Limited

(AN ISO 9001 : 2008 COMPANY)
RAM NAGAR, NEW DELHI-110055

S Chand And Company Limited
(An ISO 9001 : 2008 Company)

Head Office: 7361, RAM NAGAR, NEW DELHI - 110 055
Phone: 23672080-81-82, 9899107446, 9911310888 Fax: 91-11-23677446
www.schandpublishing.com; e-mail: helpdesk@schandpublishing.com

Branches

Ahmedabad	:	Ph: 27541965, 27542369, ahmedabad@schandpublishing.com
Bengaluru	:	Ph: 22268048, 22354008, bangalore@schandpublishing.com
Bhopal	:	Ph: 4274723, 4209587, bhopal@schandpublishing.com
Chandigarh	:	Ph: 2625356, 2625546, chandigarh@schandpublishing.com
Chennai	:	Ph: 28410027, 28410058, chennai@schandpublishing.com
Coimbatore	:	Ph: 2323620, 4217136, coimbatore@schandpublishing.com (Marketing Office)
Cuttack	:	Ph: 2332580, 2332581, cuttack@schandpublishing.com
Dehradun	:	Ph: 2711101, 2710861, dehradun@schandpublishing.com
Guwahati	:	Ph: 2738811, 2735640, guwahati@schandpublishing.com
Hyderabad	:	Ph: 27550194, 27550195, hyderabad@schandpublishing.com
Jaipur	:	Ph: 2219175, 2219176, jaipur@schandpublishing.com
Jalandhar	:	Ph: 2401630, 5000630, jalandhar@schandpublishing.com
Kochi	:	Ph: 2378740, 2378207-08, cochin@schandpublishing.com
Kolkata	:	Ph: 22367459, 22373914, kolkata@schandpublishing.com
Lucknow	:	Ph: 4026791, 4065646, lucknow@schandpublishing.com
Mumbai	:	Ph: 22690881, 22610885, mumbai@schandpublishing.com
Nagpur	:	Ph: 6451311, 2720523, 2777666, nagpur@schandpublishing.com
Patna	:	Ph: 2300489, 2302100, patna@schandpublishing.com
Pune	:	Ph: 64017298, pune@schandpublishing.com
Raipur	:	Ph: 2443142, raipur@schandpublishing.com (Marketing Office)
Ranchi	:	Ph: 2361178, ranchi@schandpublishing.com
Siliguri	:	Ph: 2520750, siliguri@schandpublishing.com (Marketing Office)
Visakhapatnam	:	Ph: 2782609, visakhapatnam@schandpublishing.com (Marketing Office)

© Copyright Reserved

All rights reserved. No part of this publication may be reproduced or copied in any material form (including photo copying or storing it in any medium in form of graphics, electronic or mechanical means and whether or not transient or incidental to some other use of this publication) without written permission of the copyright owner. Any breach of this will entail legal action and prosecution without further notice.
Jurisdiction : All desputes with respect to this publication shall be subject to the jurisdiction of the Courts, tribunals and forums of New Delhi, India only.

Also available in Hindi and Marathi Languages

Subsequent Editions and Reprints 1983, 84, 86, 88, 90, 92, 93, 94, 95, 97, 98, 99, 2000, 2001, 2002, 2003, 2004, 2005, 2006, 2007, 2008, 2009, 2010 (Twice), 2011 (Twice), 2012 (Twice), 2013
Thirtieth Edition 2014 (Twice), Reprint 2014, 2015, Thirty First Edition 2015, Reprint 2016 (Twice)

Thirty Second Edition 2018

ISBN: 978-93-525-3434-0

PRINTED IN INDIA
By Nirja Publishers & Printers Pvt. Ltd., 54/3/2, Jindal Paddy Compound, Kashipur Road, Rudrapur-263153, Uttarakhand and published by S Chand And Company Limited, 7361, Ram Nagar, New Delhi -110 055.

PREFACE TO THE THIRTY SECOND EDITION

We are grateful to the numerous university professors and alumni who have given us the necessary feedback for updating additional information about some topics and suggestions for inclusion of information on some recent developments. We thank all our readers who have found this book useful in the pursuit of their aims whether related to studying and preparation for examinations or otherwise. We are very specifically grateful to the senior history students, candidates preparing for the IAS examinations and various other states Civil Services Examinations.

It is relevant to mention that on the repeated demands of the students, University teachers and other aspirants, our publishers S Chand And Company Limited have brought out a Marathi version of our book '*A New Look At Modern Indian History*'.

'*Nobody can change the past, not even God*', but historians may. The British historians of Indian history have proved the truth in this statement. Early British I.C.S. administrators-cum-historians like Mountstuart Elphinstone, Alfred Lyall, W.W. Hunter, V.A. Smith et all and academic authors like H.H. Dodwell, P.E. Roberts, Percival Spear, C.H. Philips, Judith Brown et al from the British universities of Cambridge, Oxford and London displayed a racial superiority complex in narrating the British wars of conquest and aggression in India as also in their assessment of British-Indian administrative set-up organized by the ruling race. We come across catching phrases like 'Whiteman's Providential Mission, 'Blessings of British Rule in India' and 'Britain's Christian duty' in civilizing the uncivilized population in India and the world. The theme of modernization of India, under the aegis of British rule is still finding supporters in the Anglo-American universities. In fact, such writings appear an apologia for British imperial conquest of India and economic exploitation of India's vast resources. Many Indian writers like Dadabhai Naoroji, R.C. Dutt, S.N. Bannerjee, Tilak, Lajpat Rai and even some English writers like William Digby, Morris De Morris challenged the conclusions of British writers and drew attention to the "exploitative features" of British rule, of "infinite and increasing misery of Indian people" and of "aborted modernization" under British colonial rule. The debate on the theme, "British rule in India: A Blessing or a curse?" still continues.

A special feature of our book is that it mentions not only factual data about various topics but also gives information about different interpretations put forward by Western and Indian historians, with an integrated analysis. Still an additional plus feature is that at the end of every chapter *Select Opinions* of distinguished historians on the topic in question are reproduced.

Further developments have been provided in the following three Appendices:
- **Mahatma Gandhi National Rural Employment Guarantee Act (MGNREGA), 2005**
- **Delhi MCD Elections 2017**
- **Empowered Women | Empowered Nation**

The 27 Appendices provide lot of General Knowledge about Indian National Movement and Freedom Struggle, Indian Polity and Economy, current events of National and International importance etc. etc. and as such are useful for candidates preparing for the IAS and other competitive examinations. For example, in the IAS examination syllabus 'General Studies' paper is a compulsory paper both in the Preliminary and Main examinations.

We hope the students will keep liaison with us.

Hans Raj College
University of Delhi
Delhi -110 007

B L GROVER
ALKA MEHTA

Disclaimer : While the authors of this book has made every effort to avoid any mistakes or omissions and has used his skill, expertise and knowledge to the best of his capacity to provide accurate and updated information, the authors and S. Chand do not give any representation or warranty with respect to the accuracy or completeness of the contents of this publication and are selling this publication on the condition and understanding that they shall not be made liable in any manner whatsoever. S.Chand and the authors expressly disclaim all and any liability/responsibility to any person, whether a purchaser or reader of this publication or not, in respect of anything and everything forming part of the contents of this publication. S. Chand shall not be responsible for any errors, omissions or damages arising out of the use of the information contained in this publication. Further, the appearance of the personal name, location, place and incidence, if any; in the illustrations used herein is purely coincidental and work of imagination. Thus the same should in no manner be termed as defamatory to any individual.

Special Features

- Literary, Artistic and Cultural Movements
- Nehruvian Era : First Phase of Independence, 1947-64
- Nine Maps with Descriptive Notes
- Chronology of Principal Events
- Who's Who in Modern India
- Objective Type Information
- Concise Encyclopedia of Indian Freedom Struggle
- M.A. Jinnah and the Making of Pakistan
- National Symbols
- Shramev Jayate (May Day 2007)
- Prime Minister's New 15-Point Programme for the Welfare of Minorities
- Educational and Socio Economic Development of the Minority Communities 2014–15
- Department for the Welfare of SC/ST/OBC/Minorities
- Mahatma Gandhi National Rural Employment Guarantee Act (MGNREGA)
- 1-2-3 of the Nuclear Deal
- Statewise Allocation of Seats in State Legislatures
- Statewise Allocation of Seats in Parliament
- Hike in Salaries & Allowances of Members of Parliament
- Delhi Municipal Corporation Election
- Protection of Women from Domestic Violence Act, 2005
- Empowerment of Women
- Bharat Ratna Awardees

CONTENTS

The British Conquest of India: An Overview and Approach — xxvii
Triangular Struggles in North and South India — xxvii
Historical Forces and Factors for British Successes — xxvii
British Conquest of India-Accidental or Planned — xxviii
British Rule in India-A Blessing or a Curse — xxix
Select Opinions — xxx

1. Decline and Disintegration of the Mughal Empire — 1–20

Later Mughal Emperors *1*
Later Mughal Nobility *2*
Parties at the Mughal Court *2*
Role of the Sayyid Brothers in Later Mughal Politics *3*
Estimate of the Saiyid Brothers *5*
Select Opinions *5*
The Rise of New States *6*
Nizams of the Deccan *6*
Oudh *7*
Ruhelas and Bangash Pathans *7*
Bengal *7*
The Rajputs, The Jats, The Marathas *8*
Foreign Invasions from the North-West *9*
Nadir Shah's Invasion, 1738-39 *9*
Ahmad Shah Abdali's Invasions *11*
Causes of the Downfall of the Mughal Empire *12*
Select Opinions *16*
Social and Economic conditions in the Eighteenth Century *18*

2. Achievements of the Early Peshwas — 21–33

Balaji Vishwanath, 1713-20 *21*
Estimate of Balaji Vishwanath *23*
Select Opinions *23*
Baji Rao 1, 1720-40 *24*
Estimate of Baji Rao *26*
Select Opinions *26*
Balaji Baji Rao, 1740-61 *27*
Estimate of balaji Rao *29*
Select Opinions *29*
The Third Battle of Panipat, 14 January 1761 *31*

Causes of Maratha defeat *31*
Political significance of the Battle of Panipat *32*

3. Maratha Administration under the Peshwas   34–40

The Raja of Satara *34*
The peshwa *34*
The Central Administration *35*
The Provincial and District Administration *35*
Local or Village Administration *36*
Town Administration *36*
Administration of Justice *36*
The Revenue Administration *37*
The Maratha Military System *38*
Employment of foreigners *39*
Select Opinions *39*

4. Anglo-French Rivalry in the Carnatic   41–48

The First Carnatic War *41*
The Second Carnatic War *42*
The Third Carnatic War *43*
Causes for the Failure of the French *44*
Select Opinions *47*

5. The Rise of the English Power in Bengal   49–58

The Black Hole *49*
The Battle of Plassey *50*
Importanace of the Battle of Plassey *51*
Deposition of Mir Jaffar *52*
Treaty with Mir Kasim, september 1760 *52*
Mir Kasim as an Administrator *53*
Mir Kasim and the East India Company *54*
The Battle of Buxar and its importance *56*
Select Opinions on the Battle of Plassey *56*
Select Opinions on the battle of Buxar *57*

6. Career and Achievements of Dupleix   59–63

Dupleix as an Administrator *59*
Dupleix as a diplomat *60*
Dupleix as a Leader *61*
Recal of Dupleix *61*
Political ideas of Dupleix *61*
Dupleix's Place in History *62*
Select Opinions *62*

7. Clive's Second Governorship of Bengal, 1765-1767   64–69

Clive's settlement with Oudh and Shah Alam II *64*
Settlement of Bengal-The dual System *65*

Clive's justification of the Dual System 65
Evil effects of the Dual System 66
Clive's Administrative Reforms 67
Estimate of Clive 68
Select Opinions 69

8. Warren Hastings, 1772-1785   70–82

Administrative Reforms 70
Revenue Reforms 70
Judicial Reforms 71
Commercial Reforms 72
The Regulating Act and Conflict in the Council 72
The Trial of Nand Kumar, 1775 73
External Relations under Warren Hastings 74
Relations with Shah Alam II 75
Relations with Oudh 75
The Rohilla War 1774 75
The First anglo-Maratha War, 1776-82 76
The Second Anglo-Mysore War, 1780-84 79
The Affairs of Chait Singh and begums of Oudh 79
Estimate of Warren Hastings 80
Select Opinions 81

9. Administrative Reforms of Cornwallis, 1786-1793   83–91

Judicial Reforms 83
Police Reforms 85
Revenue and Commercial Reforms 85
Permanenet Settlement of Bengal, 1793 86
Cornwallis completed the work of Warrne Hastings 89
Estimated of Cornwallis 90
Select Opinions 91

10. Lord Wellesley, 1798-1805   92–101

The Subsidiary Alliance System 92
Advantages of the Subsidiary Alliance system to the Company 93
Disadvantages of the Subsidiary Alliance System to Indian States 94
Wellesley and the French Menace 95
Estimate of Wellesley 100
Select Opinions 100

11. Mysore Under Haider Ali and Tipu Sultan   102–107

The First Anglo-Mysore war, 1767-69 102
The Second Anglo-Mysore War, 1780-84 103
The Third Anglo-Mysore War, 1790-92 103
The Fourth Anglo-Mysore War, 1799 104
Administration of Tipu Sultan 104
Estimate of Tipu Sultan 106
Select Opinions 107

12. Lord Hastings and Establishment of British Paramountcy in India   108–116

    The Anglo-Nepal War, 1814-18   *108*
    Lord Hastings and the Indian States   *109*
    The Pindaris   *109*
    Hasting's Policy towards the Marathas   *111*
    Relations with the Rajput States   *113*
    The Treatment of Mughal Emperor   *114*
    Hastings' Administrative Reforms   *115*
    Estimate of hastings   *115*
    Select Opinions   *115*

13. Anglo-Maratha Struggle for Supremacy   117–125

    The First Anglo-Maratha War, 1775-82   *117*
    The Second Anglo-Maratha War, 1803-1805   *117*
    The Treaty of bassein, 31 December 1802   *118*
    The Third Anglo-Maratha War, 1817-1818   *121*
    Causes for the defeat of the Marathas   *121*
    Select Opinions   *124*

14. William Bentinck, 1828-1835   126–131

    Abolition of Sati and cruel rites   *126*
    Suppression of Infanticide and child sacrifices   *127*
    Suppression of Thugi   *127*
    Removal of humiliating distinctions in recruitment to Public Services   *128*
    Liberal policy towards the Press   *128*
    Educational Reforms   *128*
    Financial Reforms   *129*
    Judicial Reforms   *130*
    Policy towards Indian States   *130*
    Estimate of Bentinck   *130*
    Select Opinions   *130*

15. The Annexation of Sind   132–138

    The Commercial Treaty of 1832   *132*
    Auckland's policy towards the Amirs of Sind   *133*
    Ellenborough and the annexation of Sind   *134*
    Annexation of Sind sequel to the Afghan War   *137*
    Select Opinions   *137*

16. Career and Achievements of Ranjit Singh   139–146

    Early career of Ranjit Singh   *139*
    Relations with the Dogras and the Nepalese   *140*
    Relations with the Afghans   *140*
    Relations with the English   *141*
    Administration of Ranjit Singh   *142*
    Land Revenue and Justice   *143*

      Military Administration *143*
      Estimate of Ranjit Singh *144*
      Select Opinions *145*

17. The Panjab after Ranjit Singh and Anglo-Sikh Wars   147–153

      The Panjab Politics after 1839 *147*
      The First Anglo-Sikh War, 1845-46 *148*
      The Treaty of Lahore, 9 March 1846 *149*
      The Second Anglo-Sikh War, 1848-49 *150*
      The Annexation of the Punjab *151*
      Select Opinions *152*

18. Lord Dalhousie, 1848-1856   154–166

      The Second Sikh War *154*
      The Annexation of Lower Burma *154*
      The Doctrine of Lapse *155*
      Observations on The Doctrine of Lapse *157*
      The Annexation of Oudh *158*
      Lord Dalhousie's Reforms *162*
      Dalhousie's Responsibility for the Revolt of 1857 *164*
      Estimate of Dalhousie *164*
      Select Opinions *165*

19. Changes in Agrarian Structure: New Land Tenures and Land Revenue Policy   167–171

      Pre-British Agrarian Structure *167*
      British Land Revenue System and Administration *167*
      The Permanent Zamindari Settlement *168*
      The Mahalwari System *168*
      Land Settlements in North-Western Provinces and Oudh *169*
      The Ryotwari System *169*
      Thomas Munro and the Madras Settlements *170*
      Land Settlements in Bombay *170*
      Disintegration of Village Economy *171*

20. Changes in Administrative Structure and Policies under the East India Company   172–182

      Influence of contemporary British Administrative Models and Imperial Interests *172*
      The Home Government *173*
      The Governmnet of India *173*
      The Financial and Revenue Administration *174*
      Organisation of the Civil Service *176*
      Judicial Reorganisation *176*
      Changes in Economic Policy *178*
      Social Legislation and Educational Policy *179*
      Linkages between Educational Policies and British Colonial Interests *181*

21. Tribal Revolts, Civil Rebellions, Popular Movements and Mutinies, 1757-1856 — 183–186

- Revolts in Bengal and Eastern India *183*
- Revolts in South India *185*
- The Wahabi Movement *185*
- Sepoy Mutinies *186*

22. The Revolt of 1857 — 187–202

- Nature and Character of the Revolt *187*
- Rural Base of the Revolt *188*
- Causes of the Revolt *192*
- The Beginning and Spread of the Mutiny and Revolt *196*
- Causes of the Failure of the Revolt *199*
- Impact of the Revolt *200*
- Select Opinions *201*

23. Administrative Reorganisation under the Crown, 1858-1947 — 203–209

- New Administrative set-up *203*
- The Secretary of State and the India Office *203*
- The Government of India *204*
- Reorganisation of the Army *204*
- Administrative Decentralisation *205*
- Local Bodies *206*
- Economic Policy *206*
- Civil Services *207*
- Relations with Princely States *208*
- An Overview *208*

24. India Under Lytton and Ripon — 210–219

- Lytton and Free Trade *210*
- Financial Reforms *210*
- The Famine of 1876-78 *211*
- The Royal Titles Act, 1876 *211*
- The Vernacular Press Act and The Arms Act, 1878 *211-12*
- The Statutory Civil Service *212*
- Estimate of Lytton *213*
- Select Opinions *213*
- Lord Ripon's Reforms *214*
- Resolution on Local Self-Government *215*
- Educational Reforms *216*
- The Ilbert Bill Controversy 1883-84 *216*
- Estimate of Ripon *218*
- Select Opinions *218*

25. Lord George Nathaniel Curzon, 1899-1905 — 220–231

- Administrative Reforms *220*
- The Partition of Bengal, 1905 *222*

The Foreign Policy of Curzon 224
Curzon-Kichener Controversy and Resignation of Curzon 227
Estimate of Curzon 228
Select Opinions 229

26. Anglo-Afghan Relations   232–242

Circumstances leading to the First Afghan War 232
Estimate of Auckland's Policy 234
John Lawrence's Policy of Masterly Inactivity 235
Estimate of Lawrence's Policy 236
Afghan Policy under Mayo and Northbrook 238
Lytton and the Second Afghan War 238
Estimate of Lytton's Policy 240
Anglo-Afghan Relations from Ripon to World War I 242

27. The North-West Frontier   243–247

The Sind Frontier and Jacob's Policy 243
The Panjab Frontier 244
The Forward Policy 245
The Durand Agreement 246
Curzon's Policy 246

28. The Indian States   248–256

East India Company's Struggle for Equality, 1740-65 248
The Ring Fence Policy, 1765-1813 249
Policy of Subordinate Isolation, 1813-57 249
Indian States under the Crown 251
Policy of Subordinate Union, 1857-1935 251
Curzon and the Indian States 253
The Chamber of Princes 254
Policy of Equal Federation, 1935-47 255
Integration and Merger of States 255
The Reorganisation of States 256

29. History of the Growth and Development of Education in India   257–266

Early efforts to foster Oriental learning 257
Growing popularity of Western learning and Ram Mohan Roy 257
Orientalist-Anglicist Controversy 258
Charles Wood's Despatch on Education, 1854 259
The Hunter Education Commission, 1882-83 260
The Indian Universities Act, 1904 261
Government Resolution on Education Policy, February, 1913 262
The Sadler University Commission, 1917-19 262
The Hartog Committee, 1929 264
Wardha Scheme of Basic Education 264
Sargeant Plan of Education 264
Radhakrishnan Commission, 1948-49 264

University Grants Commission *265*
Kothari Education Commission, 1964-66 *265*
National Policy of Education *266*

30. The History of the Indian Press 267–272

Early History of the Indian Press *267*
The Censorship of the Press Act, 1799 *267*
Adam's Licensing Regulations, 1823 *268*
Metcalfe and Liberation of the Indian Press, 1835 *268*
The Licensing Act, 1857 *269*
The Registration, Act, 1867 *269*
Lytton and the Vernacular Press Act, 1878 *269*
The Newspapers Act, 1908 *270*
The Indian Press Act, 1910 *270*
The Indian Press (Emergency Powers) Act, 1931 *271*
The Press Enquiry Committee *272*
The Press (Objectionable Matters) Act, 1951 *272*

31. Cultural Awakening, Religious and Social Reforms 273–286

The Western Impact *273*
The Categories of Social Reform Movements *274*
The Brahmo Samaj *274*
The Prarthana Samaj *276*
The Arya Samaj *276*
The Ramakrishna Movemnet *278*
The Theosophical Movement *279*
Muslim Reform Movements *280*
The Wahabi Movement *280*
The Aligarh Movement *280*
The Deoband School *281*
Sikh Reform Movements *281*
Parsi Reform Movements *282*
Social Reform Movements in the 19th and 20th Centuries *282*

32. Lower Caste Movements in Modern India 287–291

The Changing Scenario *287*
Reactions against Brahaminical domination *287*
The Justice Party and Naicker *287*
Annadurai and the DMK *287*
Narayan Guru and the SNDP *288*
Jyotirao Phule and the Satya Shodhak Samaj *288*
Ambedkar's Dynamic Role *288*
The Mandal Commission and Reservation in Central Government Jobs *289*

33. The Growth and Development of the India National Movement 292–326

Factors Favouring Growth of Indian Nationalism *292*
Growth of Modern Political Ideas and Political Associations *297*

Political Associations in Bengal Presidency *297*
Political Assocaitions in Bombay Presidency *298*
Political Associations in Madras Presidency *299*
Trends Towards a Grand United National Political Organisation *299*
Foundation of the Indian National Congress *300*
The First Phase, 1885-1905 *301*
Assessment of the Policies of the Moderates *303*
Select Opinions *303*
The Second Phase, 1905-1919 *304*
Causes for the rise of Extremism *305*
The Objectives and Methods of the Extremist Group *307*
The Extremist Programme of Action *308*
Assessment of Extremism *309*
Select Opinions *310*
Indian Nationalists and World War I *311*
The Home Rule Movement *311*
The Revolutionary Terrorist Movement *311*
Revolutionary Activities in Maharashtra *312*
The Rand Murder at Poona, 1897 *312*
Shyamji's Krishnavarma and establishment of the India House at London
Revolutionary Movement in Bengal *313*
The Ghadr Movement *314*
Second Phase of Revolutionary Terrorism *314*
The Third Phase or the Gandhian Era, 1919-47 *316*
The Non-Cooperation Movement *316*
The Civil Disobedience Movement *318*
The Great War and the Constitutional Deadlock *318*
Assessment of Gandhi's role in India's Struggle for Independence *320*
Phases in the Political-Economic Programme of the Indian National congress *322*

34. Eminent National Leaders of India   327–338

Rammohan Roy, 1774-1833 *327*
Rammohan's Role in Modernization of India *327*
Dadabhai Naoroji, 1825-1917 *329*
Gopal Krishna Gokhale, 1886-1915 *331*
Bal Gangadhar Tilak, 1857-1920 *332*
Lala Lajpat Rai, 1865-1928 *333*
Mahatma Gandhi, 1869-1948 *334*
Estimate of Gandhi and Select Opinions *335-36*
Jawaharlal Nehru, 1889-1964 *336*

35. The Left Movements in India   339–343

Definition of the Left *339*
Circumstances favouring the growth of Left Ideologies in India *339*
The Communist Party of India *339*
Transfer of Power Negotiations and Communists Multi-National Plan *341*
The Congress Socialist Party *341*
Minor Leftist Parties *342*

36. Growth of Industrial Working Class and the Trade Union Movement   344–347

The Trade Union Movement   *344*
First World War, Left Awakening and Organised Trade Unionism   *345*
The Meerut Conspiracy Trial   *346*
Popular Governments in Provinces and Trade Unionism   *346*
Impact of the Second World War   *346*

37. Peasant Revolts and Agrarian Movements   348–354

Recuring Famines and Peasants   *348*
The Santhal Rebellion, 1855-56   *348*
Peasant Participation in the Revolt of 1857   *349*
Bengal Indigo Cultivators' Revolt, 1860   *349*
The Deccan Riots, 1875   *349*
Panjab Peasants' Discontent and the Panjab Land Alienation Act, 1900   *350*
The Indian National Congress and the Peasants   *350*
Gandhiji and Peasant Struggles   *351*
Champaran and Kaira Satyagrahas   *351*
The Mappila (Moplah) Uprising, 1921   *351*
Formation of Kisan Sabhas   *352*
Peasant Struggles on the Eve of Indian Independence   *353*

38. The Development of Famine Policy   355–358

Famines in Ancient and Medieval India   *355*
Famine under the Company's Rule   *355*
Famines under the Crown Administration, 1858 to 1947   *355*
The Orissa Famine, 1866   *356*
The Famine of 1876-78   *356*
Recommendations of the Strachey Commission, 1880   *356*
The Famines of 1896-97 and 1899-1900   *357*
Recommendations of the MacDonnel Commission   *357*
Bengal Famine of 1942-43   *357*
The Self-Sufficiency Target   *358*

39. The Growth of Local Self-Government in India   359–363

Early history of municipal institutions in India Mayo's Resolution of 1870   *360*
Ripon's Resolution of 1882   *360*
The Decentralization Commission Report, 1908   *361*
The Resolution of May 1918   *362*
Local Self-Government under Dyarchy and the Government of India Act, 1935   *362-63*

40. Growth of the Constitution under the Company's Rule   364–375

Beginnings of Company's Political Power in Bengal   *364*
The Regulating Act of 1773   *365*
The Amending Act of 1781   *367*
Pitt's India Act of 1784   *368*
The Act of 1786   *369*
The Charter Act of 1793   *369*

The Charter Act of 1813 *370*
The Charter Act of 1833 *370*
The Charter Act of 1853 *372*
The Act for the Better Government of India, 1858 *373*

41. Growth of the Representative Governmnet in India — 376–388

The Indian Councils Act, 1861 *376*
The Indian Councils Act, 1892 *378*
The Indian Councils Act, 1909 (The Minto-Morley Reforms) *381*
Select Opinions *385*
Chart showing the Growth of the Central Legislature *386*

42. The Road to Responsible Government-I — 389–399

The Government of India Act, 1919 (The Montagu-Chelmsford Reforms) *391*
Introduction of Dyarchy in the Provinces *394*
General Review of the Act of 1919 *397*
Resume-Salient Features of the Government of India Act, 1919 *397*

43. The Road to Responsible Government-II — 400–412

Circumstances leading to the passing of the Government of India Act, 1935 *400*
The Simon Commission, 1927-30 *401*
The Nehru Report, 1928 *401*
The Round Table Conferences, 1930-32 *402*
Provisions of the Act of 1935 *403*
Federal Structure at the Centre *404*
Provincial Autonomy *405*
Working of Provincial Autonomy *408*
General Observations *408*
Indian Reaction to the Act of 1935 *409*
Resume - Salient Features of the Government of India Act, 1935 *410*

44. The Transfer of Power — 413–426

The 'August Offer', 1940 *413*
The Cripps Mission, 1942 *414*
The Quit India Resolution and the August Revolt 1942 *416*
The Wavell Plan, 1945 *418*
The Cabinet Mission Plan, 1946 *420*
Attlee's Announcement, 20 February 1947 *424*
The Mountbatten Plan, 3 June 1947 *424*
The Indian Independece Act, 1947 *425*

45. Growth of Communalism and the Partition of India — 427–436

The Communal Triangle *427*
Sir Syed Ahmad Khan; Drift from Nationalism to Communalism *427*
Communalism in the Writing of Indian history *428*
The Simla Deputation (1 October, 1906) and Acceptance of the Principle of Communal Electorates *429*
Foundation of the Muslim League *430*

Congress Ministries and the Muslim League, 1937-39 *431*
The Two Nation Theory and the Demand for Pakistan *431*
The Hindu Mahasabha *432*
The Second World War and Furtherance of the Pakistan Plan *433*
Mountbatten's Plan of Partition of India *435*
Was the Partition of India Inevitable and Unavoidable? *435*
Select Opinions *435*

46. Indian Economy Under Colonial Rule — 437–452

Indian Economy on the eve of British conquest *437*
Karl Marx on Britain's Dual role in India *438*
Three Phases of Economic Exploitation *439*
The Mercantilist Phase *439*
The Drain of Wealth *440*
Deindustrialization: Decline of Indian Handicrafts *443*
Ruralization of Indian Economy *445*
Commercialization of Indian Agriculture *446*
Entry of British Finance Capital in India *447*
Rise of Modern Industry : Colonial Situation and State Policy *448*
Rise of Indian National Bourgeoisie *449*
Growth of Indian Capitalist Enterprise *449*
Impact of First World War *450*
Protection during Inter-Wars period (1918-39) *450*
Industrial Development State Policy and India Capitalist Class (1939-47) *451*
British Legacy of Poverty and Underdeveloped Economy *451*

47. The Constitution of the Indian Republic — 453–459

The Preamble *453*
Fundamental Rights and Directive Principles of State Policy *453*
Fundamental Duties *454*
The Union Executive *454*
The Supreme Court of India *456*
Government of the States *456*
An Overview of the New Constitution *457*
Select Opinions *458*

48. The Impact and Legacy of British Rule in India — 460–468

The Balance-Sheet Debate *460*
Nature of British Conquest *460*
Karl Marx on Britiain's Role in India *461*
Political Impact of British Rule in India *462*
British Impact on Law and Administration *463*
British Impact on Education, Oriental Studies and Indian Renaissance *464*
Social and Cultural Impact *465*
Economic Impact *466*
Select Opinions *467*

49. Nehruvian Era: First Phase of Independence, 1947-1964   469–483

    The Indian Independence Act, 1947   *469*
    Inauguration of Indian Independence   *469*
    End of British Paramountcy over Indian
    Princely States and Integration of States   *470*
    The fall out of Muslim League's Rejection of Cabinet Mission Plan   *470*
    Early Problems of independence   *471*
    Radcliffe's Boundary Award and the Punjab Carnage   *471*
    Problems connected with Division of Resources of Civil Government   *472*
    Problems Arising out of Division of Military Forces and Equipment   *473*
    Murder of Mahatma Gandhi   *473*
    Emergence of Nehru as the Undisputed Leader   *474*
    Parameters of Nehruvian Socialism   *474*
    Economic Dislocation   *475*
    Planning for All-round Development   *476*
    First Five-year Plan, 1955-56   *477*
    Second Five-year Plan, 1956-57 to 1960-61   *477*
    Third Five-year Plan, 1961-62 to 1965-66   *477*
    Nehru's death, May 1964   *478*
    Foreign Policy of Non-Alignment   *478*
    Relations with Neighbour-States : Pakistan   *478*
    China   *480*
    The Chinese Attack, 1962   *481*
    Nepal, Burma and Sri Lank   *481*
    Nehru's Achievements and Failures : An Overview   *482*

50. Literary, Artistic and Cultural Movements in Modern India   484–494

    Bengali Literature   *484*
    Hindi Literature   *485*
    Urdu Literature   *485*
    Tamil Literature   *485*
    Marathi Literature   *486*
    Punjabi Literature   *487*
    Art and Architecture   *487*
    Film Industry   *488*
    Theatre Associations   *488*
    Writers' Organisations   *489*
    Rabindranath Tagore   *490*
    William Radice Writes About Tagore   *490*
    Prem Chand   *492*
    Professor Alok Rai Writes About Prem Chand   *493*

APPENDICES:

General Knowledge for I.A.S. Exam. 'General Studies' Papers

I.	Karl Marx on the British Rule in India	495
II.	Karl Marx on the Future Results of the British Rule in India	499
III.	Karl Marx on the Indian Revolt	503
IV.	The Role of Classes during the Revolt of 1857	506
V.	List of Governors, Governors-General and Presidents	508
VI.	Chronology of Principal Events	510
VII.	Who's who in Modern India	519
VIII.	Activities of the Christian Missions During British Rule	523
	The Serampur Missionaries	
	Missionary Comments on Hindu Socio-religions practices	
IX.	Objective Type Information on Wars fought during Modern Indian History	525
X.	The People's Movements in the Princely States	526
	Emergence of Political Consciousness in the Princely States	
	Princely States' Role in the British Policy of 'Divide and Rule'	
	People' Movements in Some States and Princes' Reactions	
	World War II and States' Peoples' Participation in India's Freedom Struggle	
XI.	Subhas Chandra Bose and the I.N.A.	530
XII.	Concise Encyclopedia of Indian Freedom Struggle	535
XIII.	M.A. Jinnah and the Making of Pakistan	543
XIV.	National Symbols	547
	Making of the Indian National Flag	
	Dimensions of the National Flag	
	Guidelines about Hoisting of the National Flag	
	State Emblem	
	National Anthem	
	National Song	
	National Calender	
	National Animal	
	National Bird	
	National Flower	
XV.	Shramev Jayate (May Day, 2007)	555
XVI.	Prime Minister's New 15-Point Programme for the Welfare of Minorities and its Achievements	556
XVII.	Educational and Socio Economic Development of the Minority Communities	560
XVIII.	Department for the Welfare of SC/ST/OBC/Minorities	562

XIX.	Mahatma Gandhi National Rural Employment Guarantee Act (MGNREGA), 2005 – 5 years	563
XX.	1-2-3 of the Nuclear Deal...	565
XXI.	Statewise Allocation of Seats in State Legislatures	566
XXII.	Statewise Allocation of Seats in Parliament...	567
XXIII.	Hike in Salaries and Allowances of Members of Parliament	569
XXIV.	Delhi Municipal Coporation Election	570
XXV.	Protection of Women from Domestic Violence Act, 2005	571
XXVI.	Empowerment of Women	572
XXVII.	Bharat Ratna Awardees	575

LIST OF MAPS WITH DESCRIPTIVE NOTES

1. The French Wars in the Carnatic 42
2. India, 1772-85 (Warren Hastings' time) 77
3. India in 1805 [Extension of British Dominion under Wellesley (1798-1805)]... 98
4. India in 1818 (Extension of British Dominion under Lord Hastings) 120
5. Sind and the Punjab 133
6. India in 1856 (Expansion of British Dominion under Dalhousie) 159
7. Expansion of British Dominion in India, 1765-1857 160
8. The Spread of Mutiny and Civil rebellion, 1857-58 197
9. The North-West Frontier 244
10. Physical Map of India 553
11. Political Map of India 554

THE BRITISH CONQUEST OF INDIA
An overview and approach

The edifice of the Mughal central structure began to crumble in the 18th century under the weight of its own inner contradictions. Whatever the level of its military and cultural achievements, the Mughal rulers failed to create any national feeling or corporate spirit among its heterogeneous population. Revolts and desertions which were not uncommon even during the heddays of the Mughal Empire assumed alarming proportions in the 18th century when weak Mughal emperors succeeded one another in quick succession. In fact, the principle of 'survival of the weakest' became operative among the Mughal princes. The emperors became playthings in the hands of powerful and intriguing nobles. The power-hungry subhadars of Bengal, Oudh and the Deccan behaved as semi-independent rulers, sought political partners without any scruples, solicited the help of traditional enemies of the Mughal empire and even European companies in the game of territorial aggrandisement.

Nadir Shah's invasion of India in 1739 left the Mughal empire prostrate and bleeding apart from demonstrating to the world that a political vacuum was fast developing in northern India.

Triangular Struggles in North and South India. In Northern India, a triangular struggle for an empire enused between three contenders–the Mughals, the Afghans and the Marathas. The Afghans under Ahmad Shah Abdali, the Marathas under the Peshwas humbled the Mughal emperors and decimated the size of the Mughal empire; later Abdali defeated the Marathas at Panipat (1761) but withdrew from India because of internal commotion in Afghantisan. In the tragic drama, the Rohilla chiefs, the nawabs of Outh, the Jats and Rajputs played a subsidiary role but added to the political confusion. The East India Company did not take any part in the struggle for an Empire in the 18th century. However, the Indian powers weakened one another in this internecine struggle, facilitating the political ambitions of the East India Company. Hindustan was left without a strong ruler. In a typically imperialist style P. Spear sums up, "It was in this way that the British proved to be the residuary legatees of the unclaimed estate of Hindustan".

In the South too a triangular struggle for political supremacy ensued between three Indian powers– the Marathas, the Nizams and the Mysoreans. Another triangular contest between three European Companies–the Dutch, the English and the French–complicated the political scenario. The six powers entered into intrigues and conspiracies, organised plots and counterplots and formed combinations and alliances which baffled all political analysts.

The European companies added largely to the political confusion because they changed their political alliances and alignments in India at the dicates of their Home Governments in Europe. The Dutch had eliminated the Portuguese from India, Ceylon and the Spice Islands, but faced contenders in the English and the French. Finding it impossible to protect their interests in India and the Spice Islands (modern Indonesian Islands), the Dutch withdrew from India and concentrated their attention upon the Spice Islands. The residual two European power – the English and the French — fought three Carnatic wars in which the English emerged victorious. The successful English got the better of the Indian powers in the South and humbled or subordinated the Nizams, the Mysoreans and the Marathas. By the second decade of the 19th century the whole of India baring the states of Assam (in north eastern India), Punjab and Sind (in north western India) passed under direct British rule or English protectorate.

In another wave of aggressive wars the East India Company conquered Assam, Arakan and Tenasserim in 1824, Sind in 1843, Punjab in 1849 and Lower Burma in 1852. Lord Dalhousie's annexations gave the map of modern India. All the same, British imperialism continued to extend its stranglehold neighbouring contries of India in the 19th century.

Historical Forces and Factors For British Successes

The process of British conquest of various parts of India extended over a period of nearly a century. The English suffered many diplomatic failures and some military reverses but ultimately emerged victorious. A number of causes explain the victory of the British against their Indian adversaries.

First and foremost, the British were superior in arms, military tactics and strategy. The firearms used by Indian powers in the 18th century were slow firing and cumbrous and were outclassed both in quick firing and in range by European muskets and cannons used by the English. Again, European infantry could fire three times more quickly than the heavy Indian cavalry could close and fire. True, many Indian rulers, including the Nizam, the Mysoreans and the Marathas imported European arms, employed European officers to train their troops in the use of European arms. Unfortunately, Indian military officers and the rank and file never rose above the level of imitators and as such could be no match for English officers and English armies.

Secondly, the English had the advantage of military discipline. The Company ensured loyalty of sepoys by strict discipline and regular payment of salaries. On the other hand, most of the Indian rulers suffered from the chronic problem of lack of means to pay regular salaries; some of the Maratha chiefs had to divert their campaigns for collecting revenue to pay their troops. More often, the Indian rulers depended on personal retinues or mercenary soldiers who were deficient in military discipline and could mutiny or desert to the enemy when victory seemed doubtful.

Thirdly, the English had the advantage of civil discipline of the Company's servants. The Company's army was directed by men themselves under discipline without any hereditary connections or ties. Further, European military officers were given command of armies only after rigorous discipline; they were reliable as well as skilful and given overall direction of affairs. In constrast, Indian military command was usually given on caste basis to relatives whose military competence was doubtful and who could prove refractory or disloyal to subserve their personal ambitions.

Fourthly, brilliant leadership gave the English another advantage. Clive, Warren Hastings, Elphinstone, Munro, Wellesley, Lord Hastings, Dalhousie displayed rare qualities of leadership. They had the advantage of a long list of secondary leaders like Sir Eyre Coote, Lord Lake, Arthur Wellesley who fought not for the leader but for "cause and the glory of their country". The Indian side too had brilliant leaders like Haider Ali, Tipu Sultan, Chin Kulich Khan, Madhavrao Sindhia, Jaswant Rao Holkar, Nana Fadnavis, Ranjit Singh, but they more often lacked a team of second line trained personnel. Worst of all, the Indian leaders were as much fighting against one another as against the British. Their lieutenants too were notorious for desertions and for changing sides when the destiny of the leaders seemed in doubt. The Indian leaders were fighting for personal or dynastic advancement and the spirit of fighting for a higher cause or for their country was altogether absent. Percival Spear, an English writer comments, "A victory of an Indian leader was a victory for himself; victory of an English General was a victory for England".

Fifthly, the British were superior in economic resources. The East India Company never ignored their trade and commerce. Towards the end of the 18th century the Company's foreign trade crossed 10 crore dollars with an annual favourable balance of trade figure of 7.5 crore dollars. The East India Company earned enough profits in India to pay dividends to their shareholders and finance their military campaigns in India. In due course the British used their political clout to earn fabulous profits from their trade with India. England was also earning fabulous profits from her trade with the rest of the world. These national resources in money, stores and troops were available to the British in India in times of need, thanks to the advantage of superior sea power that Britain possessed.

Above all, a dynamic English people (in the vanguard of material civilisation) and motivated by a common ideal of fighting for national glorification faced a static Indian society still steeped in medieval ideals of religious complexes and altogether bereft of political nationalism of modern type. In fact, India was left far behind Europe in the race for material civilisation and thus lost her political independence.

British Conquest of India: Accidental or Planned?

Broadly, there are two theories regarding the British conquest of India. The first theory was popularized by John Seeley who maintained that the British conquest of India was made "blindly, unintentionally and accidentlly" and "in a fit of absent-mindedness". According to this view, the British came to India for trade and commerce, and had no political ambitions; they desired no territories nor wanted to squander their profits on wars, but were driven into the political troubles of India and annexed territories. The protagonists of the second theory believe that the British came to India with plans to occupy territory after territory and determined to lay the foundation of a strong and stable empire. They carried out their grand design bit by bit. The supporters of this view decry the British proclamations of peace and political neutrality as a cheap propaganda device to befool their critics.

There is an element of exaggeration in both the opposing theories. Perhaps, it will be more correct to suggest that the process of conquest of India, to begin with, was accidental but in the later stages the design of an Indian Empire gripped the imagination of both British politicians and their Indian administrators. In the 17th century, the traders of the English East India Company were lured by the fabulous profits from trade in the spices of the East. A similar motivation attracted the traders of Holland, France and other European companies. The British Flag followed the British trader. As the British conquest of India extended over a long period of a century, different circumstances and a large number of factors—quick profits, personal ambitions of individual military leaders, Governors or Governors-General, contemporary European political developments, national chauvinism etc., –contributed to the extension of British political sphere in India. Sometimes the British waged wars as a 'defensive device', at other times to save some Indian prince from some other aggressive Indian rulers like the Mysoreans or Marathas. Lord Wellesely resorted to aggressive application of the Subsidiary Alliance System to extend British dominion in India as a defensive (counter) measure against the imperialistic designs of France and Russia. From 1798 to 1818 the British motives were consciously imperialistic. Lord Hastings carried further the policy of Wellesley and treated India as a conquered rather than an acquired country. Thereafter, the British seemed to work according to a set design to conquer the whole of India, and even some neighbouring states on India's frontiers. Later Governors-General like Dalhousie annxed some states to bring them under "beneficent British Rule".

Broadly speaking, the British conquest of India was part of a world political phase when imperialistic countries of Western Europe intruded into the East in search of trade and colonies.

British Rule in India: A Blessing or a Curse?

Early European administrators and historians sought to justify the British conquest of India by declaring 18th century as a "Dark Age" in the history of India, when the Indian social system was tainted by evils of caste, child-marriage and widow burning, when Indian economy was "all stagnation" and Indian political situation presented the picture of 'chaos, confusion and political instability'. This European image of 'unchanging India' and static Indian civilisation persisted in English writings. The thrust of British argument was that India needed reforming education, good administration and long spell of beneficent British rule.

Another propaganda barrage unleased by British administrators and particularly directed at the newly-emerged middle class English educated Indian intelligentsia (the so-called collaborators of foreign rulers) was "the Blessings of British rule in India". Britain took upon itself the providential mandate of civilising the uncivilised population of the world. 'The Whiteman's Burden' carried by Englishmen was a recurrent theme in the writings of British poets, British scholars and plitician-administrators. The theme of "modernisation" of India under the aegis of British rule is still finding supporters in the Anglo-American universities. Many Indian scholars and some European writers stress the "exploitative features" of British rule, "of infinite and increasing misery" of Indian people and of "aborted modernisation" under British colonial rule.

The debate on the above two themes figures in history books and university examination papers. We reproduce here the select opinions of scholars on these two themes, leaving it to the readers to form their own judgement dispassionately.

SELECT OPINIONS

Our acquisition of India was made blindly. Nothing great that has ever been done by Englishman was done so unintentionally and so accidentally, as the conquest of India.
— *John Seeley*

John Seeley's felicitous and flatterly paradoxical expression, did not mean that the Empire had been acquired by accident, but rather, in more precise phrase of Harriet Martinean "without the national congnizance."
— *F.G. Hutchins*

The deeper reasons of intention and motive for the Company's acquisition of vast areas of territory are more obscure...... for the expansion occurred in such different parts of India at different times. In each particular situation the precise British interests at stake varied, and the perceived danger to them; as did the relative weight in decision-making of different British groups concerned in Indian affairs.
— *Judith Brown*

We conquered India by breaking all the Ten Commandments.
— *John Bright*

We British have been the most aggressive, quarrelsome, warlike, bloody nation under the sun.
— *Richard Cobden*

Since India has come under the British rule...the unfortunate Indian people have had their rights of property confiscated; their claims on justice and humanity trampled under foot; their manufacturers, towns and agriculturists beggared; their excellent municipal institutions broken up; their judicial authority taken away; their morality corrupted and their religious customs violated, by what are conventionally called the blessings of British Rule.'
— *John Dikinson*

British rule in India was comparable to a banyan tree. Under a banyan tree little or nothing can grow. The tree overshadows and kills essentially everything beneath it. The only growths that can live and thrive are the stems or slender branches sent down to the ground from the tree itself; these take root and develop; nothing else can.
— *J.T. Sunderland*

In the consolidation of political interests around communal issues, the Imperial power played on important role. By treating the Muslims as a separate group, it divided them from other Indians, by granting them separate electrorates, it institutionalized that division. This was one of the most crucial factors in the development of communal politics.
— *David Page*

The British had planned to construct an ideological citadel of Islam in the territory stretching from Turkey to China as a buffer against the surge of Communist ideology so that this would act as a ring around Soviet Russia. In order to achieve this objective, it mattered little to the British if India was partitioned, Mulsims divided or there was bloodshed among Hindus, Muslims and Sikhs. The British were netiher foes of the Hindus, nor friends of the Muslims. They set up Pakistan not as a gesture of friendship towards the Muslims, but under the compulsion of their international policies.
— *Wali Khan*

Every exponent of separatism, from Sayyid Ahmad Khan to Jinnah overstressed the negative factor and played down the positive one. All make much play of Hindu domination, majority tyranny, threats to their culture, perils of assimilation, dreaded prospects of non-Mulsim rule, a dark future in the absence of this or that etc. etc... The case for a separation on grounds of self-identification, homogeneity and national unity was not even attempted...The failures of the state of Pakistan are now seen as flaws in the idea of Pakistan.
— *K.K. Aziz*

A British government that had so much regard for Hindu sensitivities could not have accepted the final remedy of partition without the approval of the Congress...The manner in which 3 June Plan was drawn up, the way in which the actual partition took place, the injustice of the Boundary Award and Mountbatten's action in accepting accession of Kashmir all show that the essential features of the British policies had the approval of the Congress... The Muslims inherited many problems that need not have arisen at all if the British had not succumbed at every step to Congress pressure.
— *History of Freedom Movement of Pakistan*

1

DECLINE AND DISINTEGRATION OF THE MUGHAL EMPIRE

> The Mughal Empire in India was always faced with an inherent difficulty..... it could last either as a Muslim State... or by converting it into an Indian empire by admitting Hindus into unreserved partnership... and cease to be a Muslim Empire.
>
> —*History of Freedom Movement of Pakistan*

The Mughal Empire which had dazzled the contemporary world by its extensive territories, military might and cultural achievements a showed unmistakable signs of decay towards the beginning of the eighteenth century. The reign of Aurangzeb was the swan-song of the Mughal rule in India. A complex disease struck the heart of the empire and gradually spread to different parts. While nine Mughal emperors followed one another in quick succession in the fifty years following the death of Aurangzeb, many adventurers, Indian and foreign, carved out independent principalities for themselves. Mughal governors of Oudh, Bengal and the Deccan freed themselves from the control of the central government and the Hindu powers found the time opportune for assertion of their independence. Invaders from the north-west repeated their incursions in search of wealth and the European trading companies dabbled in Indian politics. Notwithstanding all these dangers, internal and external, so great had been the prestige of the empire under the Great Mughals and so strong the central structure that the dissolution was slow and a long-drawn-out process. Baji Rao I's raid of Delhi (1737) and Nadir Shah's invasion (1739) exposed the hollowness of the Mughal Empire and by 1740 the fall of the Empire was an accomplished fact.

(A) Later Mughal Emperors

Aurangzeb's death in March 1707 (at the age of 89) was a signal for a war of succession among his three surviving sons, Prince Muazzam, Muhammad Azam and Kam Bakhsh. The eldest brother got the better of the other two and defeated and killed Muhammad Azam (at Jajau, 18 June 1707) and Kam Bakhsh (near Hyderabad, 13 January 1709). Muazzam assumed the title of Bahadur Shah I. An elderly man (over 63 years of age), the new emperor was not fitted for the role of an active leader. Whether it was the outcome of statesmanship or weakness, the new emperor favoured a pacific policy. The Maratha prince, Shahu who had been in Mughal captivity since 1689 was released and allowed to return to Maharashtra. Peace was made with the Rajput chiefs confirming them in their states. However, Bahadur Shah was forced to action against the Sikhs whose new leader Banda had become a terror for the Muslims in the Panjab. Banda was defeated at Lohgarh and the Mughal forces reoccupied Sirhind in January 1711; however, the Sikhs were neither conciliated nor crushed. Bahadur Shah died on 27 February 1712. "He was the last Emperor," writes Sidney Owen, "of whom anything favourable can be said. Henceforth, the rapid and complete abasement and practical dissolution of the Empire are typified in the incapacity and political insignificance of its sovereigns."

The usual war of succession broke out again in 1712 amongst the four sons of Bahadur Shah—Jahandar Shah, Azim-us-Shan, Rafi-us-Shan and Jahan Shah. The contestants were in such indecent haste about deciding the question of succession that the dead body of Bahadur Shah was not buried for about a month. Jahandar Shah came out successful with the help of Zulfikar Khan, a prominent leader of the Irani party. Jahandar Shah (March 1712—February 1713) appointed Zulfikar Khan as his prime minister. Jahandar Shah's position was challanged by Farrukhsiyar (son of Azim-us-Shan) who with the help of the Sayyid brothers—Abdulla Khan and Hussain Ali—defeated and killed Jahandar Shah (11 February 1713). In token of gratitude, Farrukhsiyar (1713–19) appointed Abdulla Khan as his Wazir and Hussain Ali as the Mir Bakshi. Soon the emperor found the yoke of the

Sayyid brothers galling and conspired to get rid of them. However, the Sayyids proved too clever for him and with the help of Maratha troops they strangled the emperor to death on 28 April 1719. Farrukhsiyar's reign saw a victory for the Mughal arms over the Sikhs whose leader Banda Bahadur was taken prisoner at Gurdaspur and later executed at Delhi (19 June 1716). In 1717 the Emperor heedlessly granted to the English East Indian Company many trading privileges including the exemption from custom duties for its trade through Bengal.

After the execution of Farrukhsiyar, the Sayyid brothers raised in quick succession Emperor Rafi-ud-Darajat (28 February–4 June 1719), Rafi-ud-Daula (6 June–17 September 1719) and then Muhammad Shah (September 1719–April 1748). The wheel had gone full circle. The court intrigue under the leadership of Turani nobles succeeded and Hussain Ali was murdered (9 October 1720) and Abdulla Khan made prisoner (15 November 1720). During the reign of Muhammad Shah, Nizam-ul-Mulk set up an autonomous state in the Deccan, Saadat Khan carved out a state for himself in Oudh while Murshid Kuli Khan became virtually independent in Bengal, Bihar and Orissa. The Marathas under Baji Rao I raided Delhi in March 1737 and terrorised the Emperor. In 1739 Nadir Shah invaded India and left the Mughal empire 'prostrate and bleeding'.

The next Mughal emperors Ahmad Shah (1748–54) and Alamgir II (1754–59) were too weak to check the rot that had set in. Ahmad Shah Abdali from the north-west raided India several times in 1748, 1749, 1752, 1756–57 and 1759 making bold with every successive invasion. The Panjab was lost to the Afghans, while the Marathas snatched Malwa and Bundelkhand and carried on their raids in all parts of India. Shah Alam II (1759–1806) and his successors were emperors only in name, being puppets in the hands of their own nobles or the Marathas or the English. In 1803 the English captured Delhi. The fiction of the Mughal Empire was kept up by the English till 1858 when the last of the Mughal emperors Bahadur Shah Zafar was exiled to Rangoon.

(B) Later Mughal Nobility

A sinister development in the later Mughal polities was the rise of powerful nobles who played the role of 'king-makers'. Wars of succession were fought even in the hey days of the Mughal Empire but then the royal princes were the principal contestants supported by powerful *mansabdars*. In the later Mughal period the ambitious nobles became the real contenders for political power and the royal princes receded in the background. The powerful nobles and leaders of different factions used the royal princes as pawns in their game and set up and removed royal princess from the throne to suit their interests. Thus Jahandar Shah became the emperor not by his own strength but because of the able generalship of Zulfikar Khan, a leader of the Irani party. Similarly, it were the Sayyid brothers who raised Farrukhsiyar to the throne in 1713 and pulled him down in 1719 when he ceased to serve their interests. The three puppet emperors, Rafi-ud-Darajat, Rafi-ud-Daula and Mohammad Shah were raised to the throne by the Sayyids. The fall of the Sayyid brothers in 1720 came not because they had lost the confidence of the emperor but was brought about more by the Turani faction under the leadership of Nazim-ul-Mulk and Muhammad Amin Khan. And worst of all, these powerful parties were not political parties in the modern sense having different programmes for the welfare of the nation but were mere factions looking for self-advancement, more often at the cost of the nation and against the interests of the Mughal Empire.

Parties at the Mughal Court. William Irvine mentions the multiplicity of parties at the Mughal Court. Among these four were prominent—the Turanis, the Iranis, the Afghans and the Hindustanis. The first three were descendants of foreigners from Central Asia, Iran and Afghanistan who formed 'the backbone of the army of occupation'. Their number had greatly increased during the last twenty-five years of Aurangzeb's reign when he waged incessant war in the Deccan. Descendants from these foreigners held important military and civil offices in India. Among these the Turanis from Trans-Oxiana and the Afghans from Khurasan and Fars were mostly Sunnis, while the Iranis from Persia were mostly Shias. In opposition to the Mughal or Foreign Party was the Indian born or Hindustani Party.

It mostly comprised Muhammadans born in India, whose ancestors though originally foreign immigrants had settled in India for generations. This party got the support of the Rajput and the Jat chiefs and powerful Hindu landlords. The Hindus who filled almost all the subordinate civil offices naturally were ranged on their side. However, it will not be correct to assume that the political parties were based entirely on ethnic or religious groupings. As has been rightly pointed out by Prof. Satish Chandra that "slogans of race and religion were raised by individual nobles only to suit their convenience, and that the actual groupings cut across ethnic and religious divisions"[1]

The Role of Sayyid Brothers in Later Mughal Politics

The Sayyid brothers—Abdulla Khan and Husain Ali—were the most powerful factor in the Mughal court and Mughal politics from 1713 to 1720. They were the leaders of the Hindustani Party and represented the anti-Mughal and quasi-nationalist interests.

The Sayyids, the descendants of the Prophet, had for centuries settled in India, principally in the Doab and the district of Muzaffarnagar. The Sayyids were enlisted in Akbar's army and fought in many campaigns. Abdulla Khan and Husain Ali of Barha (called *Barha* probably because of the *bara* or twelve villages which they held) were descendants from Abul Farrah, a Sayyid adventurer from Mesopotamia who had settled near Patiala centuries earlier. Their father, Sayyid Miyan had served as Subahdar of Bijapur and Ajmer and later joined Prince Muazzam. In the war of succession that followed Aurangzeb's death, the two brothers fought in the vanguard of Muazzam's (Bahadur Shah) army. The emperor duly rewarded their services and raised their rank to 4,000 besides awarding the elder brother Hasain Ali the title of Abdulla Khan. In 1708 Prince Azim-us-Shan appointed Husain Ali to an important assignment in Bihar and in 1711 the same prince appointed Abdulla Khan as his deputy in the province of Allahabad. It was because of the great favours the Sayyid brothers received from Prince Azim-us-Shan that they espoused the cause of Farrukhsiyar (Azim-us-Shan's son) for the throne of Delhi in 1713. In fact it were these Sayyids who fought and killed Jahandar Shah in the battle and offered the crown of Delhi to Farrukhsiyar on a silver platter.

The grateful Farrukhsiyar on his accession as emperor appointed Sayyid Abdulla Khan as his wazir or Chief Minister with the title of Nawab *Qutb-ul-mulk, Yamin-ud-daula, Sayyid Abdullah Khan Bahadur, Zafar Jang, Sipah-salar, Yar-i Wafadar*. The younger brother, Husain Ali Khan was appointed Mir Bakshi or virtually Commander-in-chief and given the title of *Umdat-ul-mulk, Amir ul-umara Bahadur, Firoz Jang Sipah-sardar*.

Khafi Khan maintains that it was Farrukhsiyar's initial mistake to appoint Abdulla Khan as Wazir for he could never rid himself of him later on. One wonders how Farrukhsiyar could have safely done otherwise without producing a rupture with the Sayyids. An effect of the appointment of Sayyid brothers to such exalted offices was the jealousy it excited in the minds of the Turani and Irani nobles who spared no efforts to disgrace and procure the removal of these brothers.

The most active noble in the anti-Sayyid intrigues was Mir Jumla, a favourite of the emperor. Mir Jumla had the sympathy and support of Turani nobles. The timid emperor—devoid of independent judgment or strength of character—became an unwilling tool in the game of the powerful factions. The results were disastrous. The emperor heedlessly gave authority to Mir Jumla to sign his name in the exercise of the emperor's patronage. The emperor had said, "The word of Mir Jumla and the signature of Mir Jumla are my word and my signature". Abdulla Khan maintained and rightly too as Chief Minister that no *mansabs* or promotions or appointment to offices should be made without consulting him. Even Khafi Khan maintains that the Sayyid brothers were right for the emperor's delegation of his authority to Mir Jumla was contrary to all the rules of the Wazir's office.

Differences between the Sayyids and the emperor came to a head when Husain Ali requested for appointment to the subahdari of the Decean, which he proposed to exercise through a deputy. Husain Ali did not like to leave his brother exposed to the intrigues of Mir Jumla at the court. At Mir

---

1. Satish Chandra : *Parties and Politics at the Mughal Court, 1707–40*, pp 257–58.

Jumla's instance the emperor flatly refused Hussain Ali's request unless Husain Ali would personally proceed to the Deccan to assume the charge of his duties. Differences between the emperor and the Sayyids increased so much that the latter would not attend the court and made elaborate arrangements for self-defence. Outward cordiality was, however, restored through the intercession of the Queen mother and it was decided that Hussain Ali would in person assume the *subahdari* of the Deccan and Mir Jumla also would be sent out of Delhi in a similar capacity to Patna.

The emperor was not really reconciled to the patchwork. He sent several messages to Daud Khan, then Subahdar of Gujarat, to kill Husain Ali and offered him suitable reward. Husain Ali discovered the plot, engaged Daud Khan in action and killed him.

Farrukhsiyar again intrigued against Husain Ali. He sent secret messages and *firmans* to Shahu and the zamindars of the Carnatic not to obey Husain Ali. Once again Husain Ali proved too clever for the emperor. He changed his tactics in the Deccan. Far from making efforts to establish imperial authority in the Deccan he made a *rapprochement* with the Marathas and signed with Shahu the Treaty of 1719, conceding great concessions to the Marathas in return for the their active armed assistance in the struggle for supremacy going on in Delhi.

Meantime, the emperor had fallen under the influence of a Kashmiri of low origin, Muhammad Murad otherwise known as Itikad Khan. It was widely known that the emperor contemplated appointment of Itikad Khan as his Wazir in place of Abdulla Khan. Farrukhsiyar collected a large force of nearly 70,000 soldiers on the occasion of I'd-ul-fitr. Abdulla Khan fearing a *coup de main* also tried to enlist a large army. There was a strong rumour that Abdulla Khan was going to be made prisoner. The possibility of a clash between the emperor's forces and those of the Wazir was not ruled out.

Husain Ali had received news about the tense relations between his brother and the emperor. Husain Ali proceeded towards Delhi, carrying Maratha troops with him. Clash between the emperor and the Sayyids seemed inevitable. Abdulla Khan, on his part took all precautions. He won over important grandees like Sarbuland Khan, Nizam-ul-Mulk, Ajit Singh to his side by promises of rewards. When the time seemed ripe the Sayyids confronted the emperor with certain demands. Even when the emperor agreed to all their demands—surrender of all crown patronage in their hands, custody of all the forts to men of the Sayyids' choice, dismissal of Itikad Khan—so great was mutual suspicion that the Sayyids decided to take the life of Farrukhsiyar which they did on 28 April 1719.

Sayyids Pre-eminent at Delhi. After the death of Farrukhsiyar, the Sayyid brothers were complete masters of the situation at Delhi. They raised to the throne Rafi-ud-Darajat and after his death from consumption Rafi-ud-Daula. The latter died of dysentery. The 'king makers' now placed Muhammad Shah, son of Jahan Shah and a prince of 18 years on the throne. The control of the Sayyids over all matters of the state was complete. Their agents were attendants at the palace and their soldiers guarded it. The young emperor had no say in the matters of the state. Khafi Khan writes about the treatment meted out to Muhammad Shah, "All the officers and servants around the emperor were, as before, the servants of Sayyid Abdulla. When the young emperor went out for a ride, he was surrounded, as with a halo, by a number of the Sayyid's adherents, and when occasionally he went out hunting or for an excursion into the country, they went with him, and brought him back". The Queen mother wrote that "constraint used by the Sayyids was so strict that the emperor had only liberty to go to service on the Sabbath" The Sayyids greatly leaned on the support of the Hindus. One Rattan Chand, an ordinary grain-dealer, was given the title of the Raja and Abdulla Khan "reposed in him authority in all government and ministerial matters". Khafi Khan writes about Rattan Chand that "his authority extended over civil, revenue and legal matters, even to the appointment of *Qazis* in the cities and other judicial offices. All the other Government officials were put in the background, and no one would undertake any business but under a document with his seal." The two Rajput princes, Jai Singh of Amber and Ajit Singh of Jodhpur were the confederates of the Sayyids. The Marathas also supported the Sayyids. After the death of Farrukhsiyar *jizya* was once again abolished and Ajit Singh, as Subahdar of Ahmadnagar forbade the slaughter of cows there.

The Mughal Counter-Revolution and the Fall of the Sayyid Brothers. The Sayyids had reduced the Irani and Turani nobles to nobodies in politics. The pride of the Mughal race and imperial sentiments were strong cohesive forces. The leader of this counter revolution was Chin Kilich Khan popularly known as Nizam-ul-Mulk. The Sayyids had sent him out of Delhi as Subahdar of Malwa. The Nizam, calculating that a *coup d'etat* at Delhi would not be feasible, turned towards the Deccan. In the Deccan the Nizam captured the forts of Asirgarh and Burhanpur and defeated and killed Alam Ali Khan, Husain Ali's adopted son and Deputy Subahdar of the Deccan.

Meanwhile, at Delhi a conspiracy was hatched by Itimad-ud-Daula, Saadat Khan and Haider Khan. The emperor's mother and a protege of Abdulla Khan were privy to the plot. Haider Khan took upon himself to murder Husain Ali. Haider Khan presented a petition to Husain Ali, as the former was returning from the Court. As Husain Ali got busy in reading the petition, Haider stabbed him to death. Irvine comments : "In the Indian Karbala a second Hussain was martyred by a second Yazid" (8 October 1720). To avenge the death of his brother, Abdulla Khan raised a large army and tried to put another puppet, Mohammad Ibrahim on the throne in place of Muhammad Shah. However, Abdulla Khan was defeated at Hasanpur on 13 November 1720 and taken prisoner. Two years later Abdulla Khan was poisoned to death (11 October 1722).

Estimate of the Sayyid Brothers. As far as Farrukhsiyar was concerned, the Sayyid brothers were more sinned against than sinning. The constant intrigues of the emperor turned them to the point of desperation and their safety seemed to lie in the end of the emperor. The Sayyids disarmed and dislodged their opponents. They reduced the succeeding emperors to the position of *roi faineants*.

The Sayyids were Hindustani Muslims and they prided themselves on being so. They were not prepared to accept the superiority of the Turani party or be treated as a conquered, inferior or non-privileged race. It is difficult to establish as to what extent they worked for a non-Mughal monarchy and a nationalist set up against the foreign court parties.

The Sayyids followed a tolerant religious policy, reminiscent of the days of Akbar. It was under their influence that *jezia* was abolished in 1713 and after reimposition again abolished in 1719. Further, the Sayyids won over the confidence of the Hindus and gave them high posts. The appointment of Rattan Chand as Diwan is illustrative of their policy. They also won over the Rajputs to their side and transformed Raja Ajit Singh from a rebel to an ally. Ajit Singh gave his daughter in marriage to Emperor Farrukhsiyar. The Sayyids showed sympathy towards the Jats and it was on their intervention that the siege of the fort of Thuri was raised and Churaman visited Delhi in April 1718. Above all, the Marathas sided with the Sayyids and the Chhatrapati became a deputy of the Mughal emperor. The history of India would have been certainly different if the enlightened religious policy of the Sayyids had been continued by their successors in high offices.

Select Opinions

Khafi Khan, author of *Muntakhab-ul-Lubab*. Both the brothers were distinguished in their day for their generosity and leniency towards all mankind. The inhabitants of those countries which were innocent of contumacy and selfishness made no complaints of the rule of the Sayyids. In liberality and kindness to learned men and to the needy, and in protection of men of merit Husain Ali Khan excelled his elder brother, and was the Hatim suited to his day. Numbers owed their comfort to the cooked food and raw grain which he gave away. At the time of the scarcity at Aurangabad, he appropriated a large sum of money and a great quantity of grain to supply the wants of the poor and of widows... In their native country of Barha they built *sarais*, bridges and other buildings for the public benefit. Sayyid Abdulla was remarkable for his patience, endurance and wide sympathy (Elliott and Dowson, vol. vii, pp. 519–20).

Ghulam Husain Salim. There was some inequality in the merits of these two celebrated persons. It was universally acknowledged that Husain Ali Khan, the younger, was superior to his elder brother in many qualifications which bountiful heaven had bestowed on him. In actual power he excelled all the princes of his time, nay, he surpassed several that bore a character in history, for having bestowed kingdoms and crowns, and conquered empires, but neither his power nor his life was destined to endure long. If they had, it is probable that the times which we have now the mortification to behold, would not be so humiliating as they have proved, nor had the honour of Hindustan been thrown to the winds, nor the Indian nobility and gentry been reduced to that deplorable condition, to which we now see them brought. *Siyar-ul-Mutakherin* (*Briggs' translation*, p. 128).

Sidney J. Owen. It would not be easy to exaggerate the important consequence of this counter-revolution on the future fortune of India. Had not the main knot been cut by the assassination of Hussain, the Sayyids might have prevailed. And they might have established and maintained a strong government on a tolerant basis, with the support of the Indian Mussulmans and the Hindoo Princes. (*The Fall of the Mughal Empire*, p. 133).

(C) The Rise of New States

The weakening central political structure of the Mughal empire and erosion of its military strength created some sort of a political vacuum in India—tempting ambitious subahdars and powerful regional chiefs to carve out semi-independent or independent principalities for themselves; greedy foreign adventurers from across the north-western frontier repeated their incursions into India and these internal and external enemies lent a multi-dimensional character to the political confusion—all hastening the doom of the Mughal empire.

Nizams of the Deccan. The founder of the Asafjahia house of Hyderabad was Kilich Khan, popularly known as Nizam-ul-Mulk.

It was Zulfikar Khan who had first conceived the plan of an independent state in the Deccan. In 1708, through the generosity of Bahadur Shah, Zulfikar Khan had obtained the viceroyalty of the Deccan and administered it through his deputy, Daud Khan. The death of Zulfikar Khan in 1713 ended his dream. In 1713 Kilich Khan through the good offices of the Sayyid brothers obtained the viceroyalty of the Deccan. In 1715, however, Husain Ali replaced him as Subahdar of the Deccan. After the assassination of Husain Ali in 1720 fortune again smiled on Kilich Khan and he was reappointed Subahdar of the Deccan.

In 1722 the Nizam was appointed Wazir at Delhi. At the court the Nizam tried to put things in order but all his efforts were thwarted by the pleasure-loving sovereign and his flatterers. Like Clarendon at the court of Charles II of England, he urged the emperor to his sense of duty. His strict discipline provoked dislike and jealousy. Soon the Nizam felt very unhappy and set his heart on the viceroyalty of the Deccan. As Wazir he had added Malwa and Gujarat to the subahdari of the Deccan. Towards the end of 1723, on the pretext of going out on a hunting expedition, the Nizam headed towards the Deccan.

Muhammad Shah, offended at the insolence of the Nizam, appointed Mubariz Khan as full-fledged viceroy of the Deccan with instructions that he should send the Nizam dead or alive to the court. The Nizam, however, proved too strong for Mubariz Khan and the latter was killed at the battle of Shakr-Kheda (11 October 1724). The Nizam was now the master of the situation in the Deccan. Finding himself helpless, the emperor confirmed the Nizam as viceroy of the Deccan in 1725 and conferred on him the title of Asafjah.

The Nizam had difficult time in the Deccan on account of the Maratha raids. A clever politician that he was, the Nizam sought to divert Maratha energy by suggesting to the Peshwa the possibility of Maratha expansion in Northern India, a suggestion welcomed by Baji Rao I.

On more than one occasion the Nizam posed as defender of the Mughal empire. He fought against Baji Rao I but suffered defeat at Bhopal (December 1737). He also accompanied the emperor to Karnal to fight against Nadir Shah.

Decline and Disintegration of the Mughal Empire

Before leaving Delhi, Nadir Shah cautioned the emperor against the Nizam whom he "found to be full of cunning and self-interested, and more ambitious than becomes a subject". After Nadir Shah's invasion, the Nizam retired to the Deccan and further consolidated his position there.

The Nizam had all the qualities necessary for founding an independent kingdom. He was a diplomat and a benevolent ruler. He established peace and order in the Deccan, promoted agriculture and industry and endeared himself to the people.

Sidney Owen calls the Nizam a wily politician and an opportunist. He tried to put the Mughal Empire on its legs. Finding that impossible and perceiving the state hopelessly doomed, the Nizam took a boat and saved himself and some of the crew from the shipwreck.

Oudh. The founder of the independent principality of Oudh was Saadat Khan, popularly known as Burhan-ul-Mulk.

Saadat Khan was a Shia and descendant from Sayyids of Nishapur. In 1720 he was appointed the Faujdar of Biyana. He joined in the conspiracy against the Sayyid brothers and rose in the estimation of the emperor. He was amply rewarded by a grant of a *mansab* first of 5,000 and then of 7,000 as also given the title of Burhan-ul-Mulk. From 1720 to 1722 he was Governor of Agra which he administered through his deputy, Nilkanth Nagar. Soon he fell in favour at the court and was driven out of the capital and appointed as Governor of Oudh. This proved a blessing in disguise for Saadat Khan and he converted Oudh into an independent Muslim kingdom for himself. In 1739 Saadat Khan was called to Delhi to assist the empire in fighting against Nadir Shah. He fought bravely at Karnal but was taken prisoner. The dirty game he played in inducing Nadir Shah to invade Delhi recoiled on him when the invader at Delhi demanded the sum of Rs. 20 crores promised to him. Finding himself helpless, Saadat Khan took poison and ended his life in 1739.

Saadat Khan had no son. He had married his daughter to his nephew, Safdar Jang and the latter succeeded him at Oudh. Muhmmad Shah issued a *firman* confirming Safdar Jang as Nawab of Oudh. In 1748 Emperor Ahmed Shah appointed Safdar Jang as his Wazir and he and his successors came to be popularly known as Nawab-Wazirs.

In 1819 the seventh ruler of the house of Saadat Khan took the title of "the King of Oudh".

Ruhelas and Bangash Pathans. In the Gangetic valley the Ruhelas and Bangash Pathans carved out independent principalities for themselves. Daud, an Afghan soldier of fortune and his son Ali Mohammad Khan enlarged their small estate in the Bareilly district to an independent state of Rohilkhand extending from Kumaon hills in the north to the Ganges in the south. Further east, Mohammad Khan Bangash, another Afghan adventurer declared himself the ruler of Farrukhabad and later extended his sway over Allahabad and Bundelkhand.

Bengal. Murshid Kuli Khan was the founder of the independent state of Bengal. Ever since the time of Aurangzeb, Murshid Kuli Khan held the office of the Diwan and Deputy Governor of Bengal first under Prince Azim-us-Shan and later under Prince Farrukhsiyar. In 1713 Murshid Kuli Khan was appointed Governor of Bengal and in 1719 Orissa was added to his charge. Murshid Kuli was a capable administrator and Bengal made great strides in trade and commerce.

After Murshid Kuli's death in 1727, his son-in-law Shuja-ud-Din succeeded him. The governorship of Bihar was added to his charge by Muhammad Shah in 1733. After Shuja-ud-Din's death in 1739 his son Sarfaraz Khan succeeded him. In 1740, however, Alivardi Khan, the Deputy Governor of Bihar, rebelled against his master and defeated and killed Sarfaraz Khan at Gheria (10 April 1740) and seized power. Alivardi Khan obtained the emperor's consent for his usurpation by sending a present of two crores of rupees to Delhi. In 1746 the emperor asked him for money but Alivardi Khan paid no heed to it. Thus the provinces of Bengal, Bihar and Orissa were virtually lost to the empire.

Alivardi Khan did not depend upon the emperor for the defence of his provinces against the frequent raids of the Marathas. However, like the Nizam and Nawab-Wazirs of Oudh, Alivardi Khan kept up the fiction of the sovereignty of the Mughal emperor.

The Rajputs. The Rajputs alienated by the imprudent policies of Aurangzeb found in the weakness of the Mughal empire in the 18th century the right opportunity to re-establish their independence and even extend their sway in all directions. The love-hate Mughal-Rajput relationship resulted in Emperor Bhadur Shah's march towards Jodhpur and submission of Ajit Singh in 1708, followed by the formation of an anti-Mughal league by Ajit Singh, Jay Singh II and Durgadas Rathor the same year; in 1714 Hussain Ali, Commander-in-chief, again headed towards Jodhpur and forced Ajit Singh to sue for peace by giving one of his daughters in marriage to Emperor Farrukhsiyar.

In the Farrukhsiyar-Sayyid brothers tussle at Delhi, the chiefs of Jodhpur and Jaipur followed the policy of "opportune aloofness or adherence" to suit their interests. Thus to win Ajit Singh to their side, the Sayyids rewarded Ajit Singh with the governorship of Ajmer and Gujarat, a position which he held till 1721. The anti-Sayyid party appointed Jay Singh II of Jaipur as governor of Agra in 1721 and he was further given the *Sarkar* of Surat in the time of Emperor Muhammad Shah.

Thus the Rajputs at one stage controlled the entire territory extending from some 600 miles south of Delhi to Surat on the Western Coast. However, the internal dissensions prevented the Rajputs from consolidating their position and made them a prey to Maratha intervention.

The Jats. The agriculturist Jat settlers living round Delhi, Mathura and Agra had revolted against the oppressive policies of Aurangzeb. The imperialists had suppressed the revolt but the area remained disturbed. Churaman (1660–1721) the Jat leader built a strong fort at Thun and challenged Mughal authority in the region. The Mughal army under Jay Singh II, the governor of Agra, marched against Churaman in 1721, capturing his fort, Churaman committed suicide. Badan Singh (1685–1756), a nephew of Churaman, now assumed leadership of the Jats. He considerably strengthened his army and built four forts of Dig, Kumber, Ver and Bharatpur. Profiting from the paralysis that struck the Mughal empire after Nadir Shah's invasion, Badan Singh established his sway over the districts of Mathura and Agra and laid the foundation of the Bharatpur Kingdom. Ahmad Shah Abdali accepted the *fait accompli* and conferred on Badan Singh the title of *raja* with the additional epithet of 'Mahendra'. Suraj Mal (1707–63), who succeeded to the kingdom in 1756 further added to the dominion of the Bharatpur kingdom and 'for his political sagacity, steady intellect and clean vision' is remembered, as 'the Plato of the Jat tribe' and as 'the Jat Ulysses'. After Surajmal's death in 1763 the Jat kingdom gradually sank into insignificance. However, Lord Lake had to suffer humiliation when he attempted to capture Bharatpur in 1805.

The Sikhs. Guru Gobind Singh, the last of the Sikh Gurus had transformed the Sikhs into a militant sect in defence of their religion and liberties. Banda Bahadur, who assumed leadership of the Sikhs after the death of Guru Gobind Singh in 1708, waged a relentless struggle against the imperialists for eight years but found odds heavily ranged against him; he was captured and killed in 1716. The fortunes of the lowest ebb in 1716.

The invasion of Nadir Shah and repeated incursions of Ahmad Shah Abdali virtually demolished the Mughal central authority and brought about the collapse of Mughal administration in the Panjab. This political confusion gave the much sought for opportunity to the Sikh misls (brotherhoods) who brought a large part of the Panjab under their sway in the 1760s and 1770s.

The Marathas. Perhaps the most formidable challenge to Mughal authority both in the Deccan and the north came from the Marathas. Under the capable leadership of the Peshwas, the Marathas uprooted Mughal authority from Malwa and Gujarat, extended their sway over Rajputana in the 1730s and made a determined bid to fill in the political vacuum caused by the disintegration of the Mughal empire.

The Maratha position swiftly improved and at one stage in the 1750s they seemed to have established their claim as chief inheritors of the Mughal dominion till their authority was challenged by Ahmad Shah Abdali in the third Battle of Panipat (1761). The Marathas quickly recovered from the reverses suffered at Panipat and offered the most formidable challenge to the English East India Company in the struggle for political supremacy in India.

(D) Foreign Invasions from the North-West

(a) **Nadir Shah's Invasion, 1738-39.** The general deterioration in the Mughal administration was visible in the neglect of the defence of the north-west frontier. Aurangzeb had kept a vigilant eye on the defence of the north-western frontier and the Mughal provinces in that region. The Mughal province of Kabul was very well-administered and the people regularly paid the taxes. The tribal people in the north-west were pacified and regular subsidies were paid to them, the roads towards India were kept open and a constant and brisk communication of political intelligence had been maintained between Kabul and Delhi. However, after the departure of Prince Muazzam from Kabul in 1707 the administration of Kabul and Ghazni became lax. The general rot that had sapped the vitality of the empire was visible in the helpless condition of the defences of the frontier. The same jobbery, corruption and carelessness which had exposed Gujarat and Malwa to the attacks of the Marathas, exposed the north-west frontier to the ambition of Nadir Shah of Persia. Ghulam Husain, the author of *Siyar-ul-mutakherin*, writes that incapable viceroys were appointed by favouritism; the garrisons in the north-west were totally neglected; the tribal subsidies were withheld to swell the illicit gains of those in power or their dependants; and the frivolous sovereign and his like-minded ministers heard little, and cared less, about what was going on beyond the mountains. To cite an example, when the Mughal Governor of Kabul reported the threat of a Persian invasion, Khank-i-Dauran simply ridiculed the news and described it the outcome of baseless fears; when the governor reported that the salary of the soldiers had been in arrears for the past five years, evasive replies were sent to him.

Nadir Quli was born in 1688 in a Turkoman family of Khorasan. He had a stormy career in his youth. He proved the Saviour of Persia against Afghan domination. The Afghans under their leader Mahmud had snatched Kandhar from the Persians and later (1722) attacked and captured Isfahan, the capital of Persia. Nadir Kuli took upon himself the task of liberating his adopted country from the rule of the Afghans. In 1727 Nadir occupied Nishapur and turned out the Afghans from that region. Nadir acknowledged the overlordship of the Safawid Prince Shah Tahmasp and preferred to work as his Commander-in-Chief. Before long the whole of Persia was liberated from Afghan rule. The grateful Shah shared his kingdom with Nadir Kuli and allowed him to rule over half of Persia in full sovereign rights including the right to issue coins in his name. In 1736 the last of the Safawid ruler died and Nadir became the ruler of the whole of Persia and assumed the title of Nadir Shah.

Nadir Shah was greatly ambitious and sought extension of his dominions at the expense of his neighbouring countries. His first target was Kandhar. So long as Kandhar was not conquered it would remain a menace to the safety of Persia and constantly disturb the peace and prosperity of Khorasan. Moreover, without the conquest of Kandhar the full heritage of the Safawids could not be said to have come into his possession. To isolate the Afghan rulers of Kandhar, Nadir Shah entered into correspondence with Mughal emperor Muhammad Shah soliciting that Afghan fugitives might not find shelter in Kabul. Muhammad Shah gave assurances to Nadir's envoy about that. When, however, Nadir Shah conquered Kandhar in March 1738, a number of Afghan fugitives took shelter at Kabul and Ghazni. Under Nadir's strict instructions his soldiers did not violate Mughal territory and refrained from pursuing the Afghan fugitives in Kabul and Ghazni. Notwithstanding the breach of promises on the part of the Mughal government, Nadir had despatched in 1737 an imperative emissary— third of its kind—towards Delhi. Nadir's emissary was attacked and cut off at Jalalabad by the Mughal soldiers.

The indifference with which the Mughal emperor treated the envoys of Nadir Shah and the cruel treatment meted out to the last emissary was made an excuse by Nadir Shah to invade India. Besides, the Mughal emperor had insulted Nadir Shah by discontinuing the practice of exchange of ambassadors with the Persian court when Nadir ascended the throne. However, the real causes of

Nadir Shah's invasion of India are to be found in the ambition of Nadir Shah on the one hand and the apparent weakness of the Mughal Empire on the other. Nadir had heard about the fabulous wealth of India and his greed was excited. To top all, Nadir had received definite information about the wretched condition of the Mughal administration and the internal dissensions which had sapped its vitality, which belief of his was fortified by the number of letters of goodwill and invitation he had received from Indian Amirs soliciting him to invade India.

Nadir Shah entered Ghazni on 11 June 1738 and captured Kabul on 29 June. Nadir Shah, who had created for himself a reputation as a merciful enemy and liberal master, held out inducements to deserters. Nasir Khan, the Mughal governor of Kabul, surrendered without resistance and was pardoned and restored to the viceroyalty of Kabul and Peshawar on profession of loyalty to his new master. Crossing the Indus at Attock, Nadir easily defeated the governor of Lahore and treated him kindly and the latter also like Nasir Khan joined the conqueror's train on a rapid march towards Delhi.

The Battle of Karnal, 24 February 1739. Nadir's rapid advance towards Delhi alarmed the Mughal emperor. The emperor gathered an army of 80,000 and accompanied by the Nizam-ul-Mulk, Qamar-ud-Din and Khan-i-Dauran marched from the capital to confront the invader. Saadat Khan joined them soon after. The weakness of the Mughal side was soon clear from the fact that it had no knowledge of the enemy's whereabouts until Nadir's advance-guard attacked the baggage train of Saadat Khan. Further, there was neither any general plan of action nor an agreed leader. The battle of Karnal lasted only three hours. Khan-i-Dauran fell fighting in the battlefield while Saadat Khan was taken prisoner by Nadir Shah.

Nizam-ul-Mulk played the role of the peace-maker. It was agreed that Nadir would get 50 lakhs of rupees, 20 lakhs immediately and 30 lakhs in three equal instalments of 10 lakhs each payable at Lahore, Attock and Kabul respectively. The Emperor was so pleased with the services of Nizam-ul-Mulk that he conferred on him the office of the Mir Bakhsi which had fallen vacant on the death of Khan-i-Dauran.

Nadir's March to Delhi. The selfishness and mutual rivalries of the Mughal nobles played havoc at this stage. Saadat Khan, who had coveted the office of the Mir Bakhshi, was so greatly disappointed at the conferment of the post on the Nizam that he sought a meeting with Nadir and told him that he could easily secure 20 crores of rupees only if he would proceed to Delhi. Nadir had already obtained sufficient information about the state of the Mughal politics from the Nizam. During his meeting with the Nizam earlier, the Persian invader had asked him why in spite of the presence of brave men like him the Marathas had captured large territories of the empire. The Nizam had plainly told him that the court factions had created great confusion and that was why he had himself gone away to the Deccan in disgust. Now Nadir had himself tested the truth of the Nizam's observations.

Nadir Shah now decided to march to Delhi where he reached on 20 March 1739. At Delhi the *khutba* (emblem of sovereignty) was read for Nadir and coins were struck in his name. The Mughal Empire had ended, the Persian Empire had begun.

On 22 March a rumour spread in Delhi that Nadir had suddenly died. There was a popular rising in the city in which 700 of Nadir's soldiers were killed. Thereupon, Nadir gave an order for general massacre. It has been estimated that about 30,000 persons were slaughtered. On the solicitation of Muhammad Shah, Nadir ordered his men to stop the massacre.

Return of Nadir Shah. Nadir Shah remained in Delhi for about two months. He tried to collect the maximum booty from Delhi. He laid all the nobles and even the general population under contribution. Saadat Khan, the villain of the peace, was threatened with corporal punishment if he did not collect for the invader an amount of 20 crores. Helpless, Saadat Khan took poison and ended his life. Saadat Khan's successor, Safdar Jang paid two crore rupees as his part of the contribution. The booty collected by Nadir amounted to 30 crores of rupees in cash besides jewels, gold and silver plates, besides "100 elephants, 7,000 horses, 10,000 camels, 100 eunuchs, 130 writers, 200 smiths, 300 masons and builders, 100 stone-cutters and 200 carpenters". Above all, the invader carried with him the Peacock Throne of Shahjehan which alone had cost a crore of rupees. The Mughal emperor was also compelled to give a royal princess in marriage to Nadir's son, Nasir Allah Mirza.

Muhammad Shah also surrendered to Nadir Shah the Mughal provinces west of the river Indus including Kashmir and Sind. The subah of Thatta and the ports subordinate thereto were also surrendered to the invader. Besides, the Governor of the Panjab agreed to pay to Nadir a sum of rupees 20 lakhs per annum "to remove the reason for any Persian garrison being left east of the Indus".

Nadir on his part declared Muhammad Shah as Emperor of the Mughal Empire once again with the right to issue coins and have the *khutba* read in his name. Before leaving Delhi, Nadir also gave much advice to Muhammad Shah and exhorted his subjects to obey him. He also promised military support to the Mughal emperor in time of need.

(*b*) **Ahmad Shah Abdali's Invasions and the Third Battle of Panipat.** Ahmad Shah Abdali (so called because of the name of his tribe *ooloos*) was a young Afghan officer of noble lineage. Nadir Shah held high opinion about his merits and once said, "I have not found in Iran, Turan or Hind any man equal to Ahmad Shah Abdali in capacity and character." After the assassination of Nadir Shah in 1747, Ahmad Shah declared himself as ruler of Kandhar. He also issued coins bearing his name. Soon after he seized Kabul and founded the modern kingdom of Afghanistan. He enlisted a large army of 50,000. As the rightful successor of Nadir, he laid claim to Western Panjab. He invaded India five times and fought the Third Battle of Panipat in 1761.

Ahmad Shah Abdali's first invasion of India in 1748 ended in a fiasco. Abdali was not a man to be easily baulked. Early in 1749 he again crossed the frontier and defeated Muin-ul-Mulk, the Governor of the Panjab. However, he was induced to return on a promise by Muin-ul-Mulk of an annual remittance of fourteen thousand rupees. As he did not get regularly the promised tribute, Abdali invaded India the third time in 1752. Fearing a repetition of Nadir's outrages, the Mughal Emperor Ahmad Shah appeased Abdali by surrender of the Panjab and Sindh. To restore order in the Panjab which had been a prey to anarchy after the death of Muin-ul-Mulk, in November 1753 Wazir Imad-ul-Mulk appointed Adina beg Khan as Governor of the Panjab. This was, however, interpreted as interference in the affairs of the Panjab by Abdali who crossed into Indian territory for the fourth time in November 1756. In January 1757 the invader entered Delhi and plundered as far as Mathura and Agra. Before his return Abdali recognised Alamgir II as the emperor, Imad-ul-Daula as the Wazir and the Rohilla chief Najib-ud-Daula as his personal "supreme agent" and as Mir Bakhshi of the empire.

In March 1758 Raghunath Rao appeared at Delhi, expelled Najib from the capital and later overran the Panjab, appointing Adina Beg as governor of the Panjab on behalf of the Peshwa. Abdali returned to India in 1759 to avenge on the Marathas. The third battle of Panipat was fought on 14 January 1761, resulting in the total defeat of the Marathas.

Before leaving Delhi on 20 March 1761 Abdali named Shah Alam II as emperor, Imad-ul-Mulk as Wazir and Najib-ud-Daula as Mir Bakhshi. The last of Abdali's invasions came in 1767.

Ahmad Shah Abdali's invasions hastened the downfall of the Mughal Empire. The frequency of his invasions further exposed the rottenness of the Mughal Empire and created anarchy and confusion all round. So shallow was the reality of the Mughal Empire that the new Emperor Shah Alam II was not allowed to enter Delhi for twelve years and was escorted to his throne in 1772 only by the Marathas. The Rohilla leaders Najib-ud-Daula and later his son Zabita Khan and grandson Ghulam Qadir exercised undisputed power at Delhi. On 30 July 1788 Ghulam Qadir took possession of the royal palace and deposed Shah Alam and later blinded him completely (10 August 1788). It was the Maratha leader Mahadaji Sindhia who recovered Delhi for the emperor once again in October 1788. In 1803 the English captured the imperial city and Shah Alam II became a pensioner of the East India Company.

(E) Causes of the Downfall of the Mughal Empire

1. Aurangzeb's Responsibility. Although the expansion of the Mughal Empire reached its optimum point under Aurangzeb yet it only resembled an inflated balloon. The Mughal Empire had expanded beyond the point of effective control and its vastness only tended to weaken the centre. Considering the undeveloped means of communications in those days, the Mughal Empire was faced with a stupendous task far beyond the capacity of Alamgir Aurangzeb himself not to speak of his weak successors.

Whatever his compulsions, Aurangzeb sought to restore the Islamic character of the state which, he believed, had been disturbed by Akbar and his successors. His policy of religious bigotism proved counter-productive and provoked a general discontent in the country and the empire was faced with rebellions of the Sikhs, the Jats, the Bundelas, the Rajputs and, above all, the Marathas. Aurangzeb was no less stupid than his contemporary James II of England.

'The Ass
Who lost three Kingdoms for a Mass.'

Again like James II, Aurangzeb knew the art of making enemies. The imperialist designs and narrow religious policy of Aurangzeb turned the Rajputs, reliable supporters of the Imperial dynasty, into foes. The wanton destruction of Hindu temples and the reimposition of *jizyah* (1679) and other political and social indignities on the Hindus led to the rising of the Satnamis, the Bundelas and the Jats. In the Panjab the Sikhs to the last man rose against the empire paralysing Imperial administration in the province. In Maharashtra, Maratha resistance to Mughal rule assumed a national character and the whole people participated in the struggle for the defence of their religion and liberties. The Maratha guerrillas demoralised the splendid armies of Aurangzeb, broke their spirit of superiority and wore them out.

The over ambitious Aurangzeb followed the policy of aggressive imperialism towards the Shia sultanates of Golconda and Bijapur. Being a fanatical Sunni, perhaps an additional reason for his onslaught on these Deccani kingdoms was religious. However, the Deccani states of Golconda, Bijapur, Karnataka and the Marathas occasionally patched up their mutal jealousies and offered a united front to Mughal imperialism. Though Aurangzeb succeeded in reducing Bijapur (1686), Golconda (1687) and killing Sambhaji (1689), but these successes only marked the beginning of greater difficulties. The conquest of these Muslim kingdoms of the south removed the strongest local check on Maratha activities and left them free to organise resistance to Mughal imperialism.

Aurangzeb's mistaken policy of continuous war in the Deccan which continued for twenty-seven years drained the resources of the empire. These wars meant a great financial drain on the treasury and the flower of the Mughal soldiery perished in the long wars. Manucci noted in his book, *Storia Do Moger*, "Thus until this day he has not been able to accomplish the enterprise he intended (as he said) in two years. He marched carrying with him three sons, Shah Alam, Azam Tara and Kam Bakhsh, also his grandsons. He had with him much treasure, which came to an end so thoroughly during this war, that he was compelled to open the treasure-houses of Akbar, Nur Jehan, Jahangir and Shah Jahan. Besides this, finding himself with very little cash, owing to the immense expenditure forced on him, and because the revenue payers did not pay with the usual promptitude, he was obliged at Aurangabad to melt down his household silver-wares." The 'Deccan ulcer' proved as fatal to the Mughal Empire as the 'Spanish ulcer' was to prove later on to the Napoleonic Empire.

2. Weak Successors of Aurangzeb. The Mughal system of government being despotic much depended on the personality of the emperor. Under a strong monarch all went well with the administration, but the succession of a weak emperor was reflected in every field of administration. Unfortunately, all the Mughal emperors after Aurangzeb were weaklings and therefore unable to meet the challenges from within and without. Far from stemming the tide of decline they aggravated the situation by their idiosyncrasies and lax morals. Bahadur Shah I (1702–12) was over 63 at the time of his succession to the throne and was too old to maintain the prestige of the empire. He liked to appease all parties by profuse grants of titles and rewards and was nicknamed *Shah-i-bekhabar* (The Heedless King), Jahandar Shah (1712–13), the next in succession, was a profligate fool, Farrukhsiyar (1713–19) a contemptible coward, while Mohammad Shah (1719–48) spent most of his time watching animal fights. For his indifference towards public affairs and addiction to wine and woman, Mohammad Shah was nicknamed 'Rangila' Ahmad Shah (1748–54) excelled his predecessors in his sensual pursuits. His *harem* extended over a full *kos* (an area of four square miles) wherefrom all males were excluded and the emperor spent a week and sometimes a month in the company of women. In the administrative sphere Ahmad Shah did equally foolish things. In November 1753, he appointed his $2\frac{1}{2}$ year old son, Mahmud as Governor of the Panjab and in perfect keeping with the spirit named a one-year old baby, Muhammad Amin as the deputy under him. Similarly the governorship of Kashmir was conferred on one-year old Tala Sayyid Shah with a boy of fifteen as the Deputy. These appointments were made at a time when the danger of Afghan invasions was assuming alarming proportions. Such weak and imbecile emperors could hardly act as worthy custodians of public interest or maintain the integrity of the empire.

3. Degeneration of Mughal Nobility. "When gold rusts what will iron do ?", is an old adage. Following the unworthy example of the emperors, the nobles discarded hard life of military adventure and took to luxurious living. They became 'knights of romance' against 'knights at arms.' The nobles vied with one another in filling their *harems* with women drawn from a variety of races and spent most of their time in drinking bouts and gambling dens. Nobles like Bairam Khan, Muzzaffar Khan, Abdur Rahim Khan-i-Khanan, Mahabat Khan, Asaf Khan, Saidulla Khan were no longer available for the service of the state. The new nobility under the later Mughals were at best courtiers and rivalled one another in the subtle arts of finesse and flattery. At a time when the emperors ceased to be impartial judges for rewarding merit, the nobles had no incentive to fight and die for the empire. J.N. Sarkar points out in *Massir-ul-Umra* (Dictionary of Mughal Peerage) that if a nobleman's achievements were recorded in three pages that of his son usually filled a page, that of the grandson only a few lines such as 'nothing worthy of being recorded'. The senile decay that had set in the ranks of the upper classes deprived the state of the services of capable administrators and energetic military leaders.

4. Court Factions. Towards the end of Aurangzeb's reign influential nobles at the court organised themselves into pressure groups. Though these groups were formed on clan or family relationships, personal affliations or interests were the dominating factors. These groups kept the country in a state of perpetual political unrest. The Turani or Central Asian party consisted of nobles from Trans-Oxiania. During the reign of Mohammad Shah, Asaf Jah, Nizam-ul-Mulk, Qamruddin and Zakariya Khan were the principal leaders of the Turani faction, while the leaders of the Persian faction were Amir Khan, Ishaq Khan and Saadat Khan. These factions kept their own retainers who were mostly recruited from Central Asia or Persia as the case might be. Together these two factions known as 'the Mughal or Foreign Party' were pitched against the Hindustani Party whose leaders during this period were Sayyid Abdulla Khan and Sayyid Hussain Ali who enjoyed the support of the Hindus. Each faction tried to win the Emperor to its viewpoint and poison his ears against the other faction. They fought battles, upsetting the peace of the country and throwing administration to dogs. Even in the face of foreign danger these hostile groups could not forge a united front and often intrigued with the invader. The personal interests of Nizam-ul-Mulk and Burhan-ul-Mulk led them to intrigue with Nadir Shah and barter away national interests.

5. Defective Law of Succession. The absence of the law of primogeniture among the Mughals usually meant a war of succession among the sons of the dying emperor in which the military leaders of the time took sides. In the words of Erskine, "The sword was the grand arbiter of right and every son was prepared to try his fortune against his brothers". Such a system, though not commendable, was not without its advantages. It provided the country with the ablest son of the dying Emperor as the ruler. Under the later Mughals a sinister factor entered the politics of the empire bringing out the worst features of the law of succession. Now, the new principle that worked in the later Mughal period was 'the survival of the weakest.' The princes of the royal dynasty receded to the background while struggle was fought by leaders of rival factions using royal princes as nominal leaders. Powerful nobles acted as 'king-makers', making and unmaking emperors to suit their personal interests. Zulfikar Khan emerged as the 'king-maker' in the war of succession that followed the death of Bahadur Shah I in 1712. The Sayyid Brothers (Hussain Ali and Abdullah Khan) acted as 'king-makers' during 1713-20, when they raised four Imperial princes to the throne till they were removed from their position by a faction of Mir Mohammad Amin and Asaf Jah Nizam-ul-Mulk. Thus the defective law of succession weakened the bodypolitic and crippled it financially and militarily.

6. The Rise of the Marathas. Perhaps the most powerful external factor that brought about the collapse of the Mughal Empire was the rising power of the Marathas under the Peshwas. The Peshwas consolidated Maratha power in Western India and channelised the energies of the nation in an attack on the Mughal Empire. They inaugurated the policy of Greater Maharashtra and popularised the ideal of *Hindu-pad padshahi*. The ideal of Hindu Empire could only be realised at the cost of the Mughal Empire. Now the position had changed: the Marathas got on the offensive and the Mughal Emperors and their viceroys on the defensive. The tide of Maratha expansion continued to rise till it engulfed Northern India also. At one time the Marathas seemed the most powerful force in the politics of India, assuming the role of defenders of India against foreign invasions of Ahmad Shah Abdali and playing the role of 'king-makers' at Delhi as Sadashiv Rao Bhau seems to have done in 1759 and Mahadaji Sindhia in 1772. Though the Marathas were not successful in laying the foundations of a stable empire in India, they certainly played a great part in bringing about the disintegration of the Mughal Empire.

7. Military Weaknesses. There were inherent defects in the Mughal military system. The army was organised more or less on the feudal basis where the common soldier owed allegiance to the mansabdar rather than the Emperor. The soldier looked upon the mansabdar as his chief, not as an officer. The defects of this system though evident enough in the revolts of Bairam Khan and Mahabat Khan assumed alarming proportions under the later Mughal kings.

William Irvine points out that excepting the want of personal courage every other fault was found among the degenerate Mughals—indiscipline, want of cohesion, luxurious habits, inactivity, bad commissariat and cumbrous equipment. Luxury and sloth penetrated every rank of the army and the march of the spectacle of a Mughal army presented "a long train of elephants, camels, carts, and oxen, mixed up with a crowd of camp-followers, women of all ranks, merchants, shopkeepers, servants, cooks, and all kinds of ministers of luxury, amounting to ten times the number of the fighting men".

In fighting capacity the unwieldy Mughal armies were nothing more than an armed rabble. Bernier compares them to a herd of animals who fled at the first shock. The Mughal artillery was crude and ineffective against the *guerrilla* tactics of the Marathas; the Maratha fortresses which the Mughal armies could not capture despite repeated attempts easily succumbed the British arms. In 1748 the French Commander, Monsieur Paradis, with a small detachment consisting of 230 European and 700 Indian soldiers and without any guns routed a large army of the Nawab of Carnatic consisting of 10,000 men equipped with artillery and entrenched across a river. Dupleix wrote to the Company's Directors in Paris that "500 European soldiers could reduce all Moslem strongholds and provinces on this side of the Kistna."

The chief defect of the Mughal armies of eighteenth century was their composition. The soldiers were usually drawn from Central Asia and collected by the captains of companies who supplied men to anyone able to pay for them. These soldiers and their leaders came to India to make fortunes not to lose them. As such, the leaders of such armies changed sides without scruples and

Decline and Disintegration of the Mughal Empire

were constantly plotting either to betray or supplant their employers. Even the Mughal viceroys employing such troops were constantly haunted by the fear of desertion. Such hired soldiers without coherence or loyalty were unfit custodians of the interests of the Empire. What the Urdu poet Sauda wrote about Shah Alam II's time was true of later Mughal period in general.

Only forced by need does he (Mughal commander) come out of the moat (of his fort);

His Army but knows how to turn from the flight;

The infantry—afraid of the barber that shaves;

The cavalry—fall off from their beds in their sleep

If but in a dream they see their mount frisk[2].

8. Economic Bankruptcy. What ate into the vitals of the Mughal empire was the worsening economic and financial conditions which were visible in the 17th century and which steadily worsened towards the end of Aurangzeb's reign. Aurangzeb's long wars in the Deccan besides emptying the royal treasury almost ruined the trade and industry of the country. The marches of the Imperial army damaged crops in the Deccan while the beasts of burden ate away all standing crops and greenery. The Emperor ignored all complaints brought to him because of financial difficulties. Whatever little was left was destroyed by the Maratha raiders—Maratha horses were fed on standing crops and Maratha soldiers destroyed whatever property they found too heavy to be carried. The peasant gave up agriculture in disgust and many took to life of plunder and highway robbery. There was so great dislocation of normal life in the Deccan that the agents of the English and French Companies found great difficulty in procuring supplies for export to Europe.

Under the later Mughal Emperors the financial condition further deteriorated. While the outlying provinces asserted their independence one after the other and ceased the payment of any revenue to the centre, the numerous wars of succession and political convulsions coupled with the lavish living of the Emperors emptied the royal treasury to an extent that salaries of soldiers could not be paid regularly. When the emperors fell back to the uneconomic device of farming out of *Khalisah* (crown) lands and granting jagirs in payment of liquidation of arrears of pay. The crisis of the *jagirdari* was reached when the land in the country was insufficient for the total number of jagirs granted. Many a time *jagirs* were granted but the recipient had to wait for long to get actual possession of land. An aggrieved grantee sarcastically remarked that the time-gap between the grant of a *jagir* and its actual possession was long enough to turn a boy into a grey-beard person. Jagirdars in turn were so greatly under debt to money lenders that they farmed out their jagirs to them. Commenting on the poor financial condition of the Mughal nobles, the Urdu poet Sauda wrote that the mansabdars had no money to pay their retainers:

2.

پڑے جو کام اُنہیں تب نکل کے کھائی سے

رکھیں وہ فوج جو موتے پھرے لڑائی سے

پیادہ ہے سو ڈرے سرمنڈاتے نائی سے

سوار گر پڑے سوتے میں چارپائی سے

کرے جو خواب میں گھوڑا کسی کے نیچے اول

(سودا ۔ ویرانیِ شاہجہان آباد)

If you buy a horse, and take service with someone
Of your salary you will see no sign except in the world above.

Writing of the times of Alamgir II, Sir Jadunath Sarkar says that at one time the Emperor was reduced to such hard straits that for three days no fire was kindled in the *harem* kitchen and the princesses in frantic disregard of *purdhah* rushed out of the palace to the city.

Jadunath Sarkar argues that the Muslim state in India lacked a sound economic basis. The holy scriptures of the Muslims provide — or at least so the medieval Muslim scholars interpreted — that the true profession of the faithful is war. The state in India kept a huge army and was thus the greatest single employer. Peace, argues Sir Sarkar, was anaesthesia to the society and produced far-reaching economic repercussions. When the Muslim state in India under Aurangzeb reached its optimum expansion, it was no longer necessary to maintain a huge army and employ it profitably. These conditions accentuated in the eighteenth century.

9. Nature of the Mughal State. The Mughal government was eassentially a police government and confined its attention mainly to the maintenance of internal and external order and collection of revenue. The Mughals failed to effect a fusion between the Hindus and Muslims and create a composite nation. Whatever little effort was made by Akbar to weld the people into a nation was undone by the bigotry of Aurangzeb and his worthless successors. Far from reconciling the Hindus to the Mughal rule, the Mughal policies goaded them to rebellion: Many Indian chiefs looked upon the Mughal rulers as foreigners and as enemies of India and Hindu religion. The weakness of the Mughal empire in the eighteenth century gave the Marathas, the Rajputs and other Hindu communities their much awaited opportunity.

10. Invasions of Nadir Shah and Ahmad Shah Abdali. The invasion of Nadir Shah in 1739 gave a death blow to the tottering Mughal Empire. Besides depleting the Mughal treasury of its wealth, it exposed to the world the military weakness of the Empire and its utter degeneration. Turbulent elements in the country so far kept in check by the name and prestige of the Empire rose in rebellion and circumscribed the authority of the Empire. The repeated invasions of Nadir's successor, Ahmad Shah Abdali, deprived the Empire of the frontier provinces of Panjab, Sind, Kashmir etc. The Mughal authority had so greatly shrunk that in 1761 Abdali fought the battle of Panipat not against the Mughal Empire but against the Marathas who virtually controlled the whole of Northern India. For about a decade (1761–72) a virtual Afghan dictatorship under Najib-ud-daula was set up at Delhi.

11. Coming of the Europeans. With the weakness of Mughal central authority in the eighteenth century, war-lordism raised its ugly head. The European Companies also acted as warlords, and profited from the confused times. The European Companies outdid Indian princes in every sphere whether it was trade and commerce or diplomacy and war. In fact the static and stationary Indian society faced a challenge from a dynamic and progressive West. It is a sad commentary on the Mughal aristocracy that while they spent lakhs in importing European luxury articles, none ever thought of purchasing a printing press. When the Renaissance outlook had given an expansive touch to European energies the Indian people were steeped in divinism and drew sustenance from the philosophy of escapism. In fact, India was left far behind in the race for civilisation. Sir Jadunath Sarkar very aptly comments: "The English conquest of the Mughal Empire is only a part of the inevitable domination of all Africa and Asia by the European nations—which is only another way of saying that the progressive races are supplanting the conservative ones, just as enterprising families are constantly replacing sleepy self-satisfied ones in the leadership of our society."

Thus, the inherent weaknesses of the Mughal body-politic and the numerous contemporary operative causes had sapped the vitality of the Empire. When the phantom empire collapsed the surprise was not that it crumbled ignominiously, but that the end was so long delayed.

Select Opinions

J.N. Sarkar. The Mughal Empire and with it the Maratha overlordship of Hindustan fell because of the rottenness at the core of Indian society. The rottenness showed itself in the form of military and political helplessness. The country could not defend itself; royalty was hopelessly depraved or imbecile; the nobles were selfish and short-sighted; corruption, inefficiency and treachery disgraced all branches of the public service. In the midst of this decay and confusion, our literature, art and even true religion had perished. (*Fall of the Mughal Empire*, vol. iv, pp. 343–44.)

Sidney Owen. A common impression is, that... the decline and fall of the Mughal Empire were due to the degeneracy of its Sovereigns. But... it was irretrievably ruined in the reign of Aurangzeb, a monarch of great ability, energy and determination, but lacking in political insight, and a bigoted Mussulman. He struck the first morta blow by reversing Akbar's wise and generous policy of ignoring distinctions of race and religion, and reimposing the *jizya* or poll tax, on his Hindu subjects; whereby he estranged them, and turned the noblest and most warlike of them—the Rajputs, hitherto the staunchest supporters of the throne—into deadly and persistent enemies. And Shivaji and his followers not only vindicated their independence, but struck a second morta blow at the integrity of the Empire. They destroyed its military reputation. They exhausted its accumulated treasure. They spread disorder and devastation over the Deccan and beyond it... They established an *imperium in imperio*. Thus the Empire, though not dissolved, was hopelessly debilitated. The effective authority of the central government was thenceforth in abeyance... Nadir Shah, after inflicting the extremity of humiliation on the Emperor and his capital, annexed the Imperial territory west of the Indus. The dissolution of the Empire was complete. (*The Fall of the Mugyal Empire, Preface*, pp. iii-iv).

William Irvine. The more I study the period, the more I am convinced that military inefficiency was the principal, if not the sole, cause of that empire's final collapseA All other defects and weaknesses were as nothing in comparison with this... Long before it disappeared, it had lost all military energy at the centre, and was ready to crumble the pieces at the first touch. The rude hand of no Persian or Afghan conqueror, no Nadir, no Ahmad Abdali, the genius of no European adventure, a Dupleix or a Clive, was needed to precipitate it into the abyss. The empire of the Mughals was already doomed before any of these had appeared on the scene; and had they never been heard of there can be little doubt that some Maratha bandit or Sikh tree-booter would in due time have seated himself on the throne of Akbar and Shah Jahan. (*The Army of the Indian Mughals*, p. 296).

Satish Chandra. The roots of the disintegration of the Mughal empire may be found in the Medieval Indian economy; the stagnation of trade, industry and scientific development within the limits of that economy; the growing financial crisis which took the form of a crisis of the *jagirdari* system and affected every branch of state activity; the inability of the nobility to realise in the circumstances their ambitions in the service of the state and consequently the struggle of factions and the bid of ambitious nobles for independent dominion; the inability of the Mughal emperors to accommodate the Marathas and to adjust their claims within the framework of the Mughal empire, and the consequent breakdown of the attempt to create a composite ruling class in India; and the impact of all these developments on politics at the court and in the country, and upon the security of the north-western passes. Individual failings and faults of character also played their due role but they have necessarily to be seen against the background of these deeper, more impersonal factors. (*Parties and Politics at the Mughal Court*, p. 268).

Irfan Habib. Various explanations are put forward for the revolts which brought about the collapse of the Mughal Empire... Here our main concern is with what our 17th and early 18th century authorities have to say. And it will be seen that they, at any rate, put the greatest store by the economic and administrative causes of the upheaval and know little of religious reaction or national consciousness... Thus was the Mughal Empire destroyed. No new order was, or could be, created by the forces ranged against it. The period which follows does not offer any edifying spectacle: The gates were opened to reckless raine anarchy and foreign conquest. But the Mughal Empire had been its own grave-digger; and what Sa'di said of another great empire might well serve as its epitaph:

> The Emperors of Persia.
> Who oppressed the lower classes
> Gone is their glory and empire;
> Gone their tyranny over the peasant!
> (The Agrarian System of Mughal India, pp. 338–39, 351).

(F) Social and Economic Conditions in the Eighteenth Century

Despite political convulsions and instability in the 18th century, the society in general retained most of its traditional features with some changes thrown in by new environments.

Social Stratification. At the apex of the social order was the emperor closely followed by the nobility which despite hard times led a life of luxury and extravagance with great weakness for wine, women and music. At the lowest rung of the ladder was the preponderant majority of the poor agriculturist and artisan in the village. In the middle came the 'small and frugal' middle class comprising small merchants, shopkeepers, lower cadre of employees, town artisans etc. Paucity of contemporary evidence and disparities in incomes and prices in different regions of the country makes any comparison of standard of living a difficult exercise.

The institution of caste stands out a striking feature of Hindu society of the time. Caste rules prevailed in matters of marriage, dress, diet and even professions. However, economic pressures and administrative innovations introduced by the East India Company compelled some to look beyond their ancestral professions.

Place of Women in Society. Women were given a place of respect in home and society but not of equality as we understand the term today. Hindu society being mainly patriarchal (except in the Malabar and some backward areas), the will of the male head of the family usually prevailed. Though examples can be cited of Hindu and Muslim women having played significant roles in polities, administration and scholastic fields, the common woman was denied right place in society. Purdah system was common among both the Hindu and Muslim women though women of poor families out on work for livelihood could not observe it. Child marriages were common among both girls and boys though consummation usually took place after they attained the age of maturity. Dowry system was prevalent among the upper classes. Polygamy was common among ruling princes, big zamindars and men of better means though the common man contented himself with one wife. Polygamy in shocking proportions prevailed among the *kulin* families in Uttar Pradesh and Bengal. Remarriage of widows was generally looked down upon though it prevailed in some places. Surprisingly the Peshwas imposed a tax called *patdam* on remarriage of widows. The evil practice of *Sati* (of Hindu widows burning themselves on the funeral pyres of their husbands) mostly prevailed in Bengal, Central India and Rajputana among some upper castes. The Peshwas discouraged *sati* in their dominion with limited success.

Slavery. Another social evil was the prevalence of slavery. Broadly speaking, slaves could be classed into two categories—the domestic slaves and the serfs tied to the land. In the latter category the serfs were transferred with the sale of land to new masters. European travellers and administrators have testified to the widespread prevalence of slavery in India. Economic distress, famines, natural calamities, extreme poverty compelled some to sell their children for a price. The Rajputs, Khatris and Kayasthas usually kept slave women for domestic work. However, slaves in India were treated better than their counterparts in America and Europe. Slaves were usually treated as hereditary servants of the family than as menials; they were allowed to marry among themselves and the main offsprings of such marriages were considered free citizens.

Slavery and slave trade touched new dimensions with the coming of Europeans in India particularly the Portuguese, the Dutch and the English. There is mention of a court-house at Calcutta in 1752 which regularly purchased and registered slaves charging a registration fee of Rs. 4 for each entry. The European companies purchased slaves at a price ranging between Rs. 5 to Rs. 15 for a girl of 10 years, Rs. 12 to Rs. 20 for a boy of 16 and Rs. 15 to Rs. 20 for a full grown adult slave from the markets of Bengal, Assam and Bihar, and carried them to European and American markets for sale. There are reports of Europeans at Surat, Madras and Calcutta purchasing Abyssinian slaves and employing them for domestic work.

Traffic in slaves was abolished by a proclamation issued in 1789. However, rural slavery shorn of many of its classical crudities continues in India even today.

Education. The love of learning has always exercised a powerful influence on both the Hindu and the Muslim mind. However, the idea of Indian education was culture and not literacy. Vocational education according to one's *varna* or family tradition assured specialization. Both Hindu and Muslim systems of education linked learning and religion.

Centres of higher education in Sanskrit literature were called *chatuspathis* or *Tols* in Bengal and Bihar. Nadia, Kasi (Benares), Tirhut (Mithila) and Utkala (Orissa) were reputed centres for Sanskrit education. The French traveller Bernier described 'Kasi as the Athens of India', and aspirants for higher Sanskrit education flocked to its numerous institutions. Institutions for learning of higher education in Persian and Arabic were called *Madrasahs*. Persian being the court language was learnt both by the Muslims and the Hindus. Azimabad (Patna) was a reputed centre of Persian education in eastern India. Those interested in the study of Koran and Muslim theology had to acquire proficiency in Arabic.

Elementary education was fairly widespread. The Hindu elementary schools were called *pathshalas* and Muslim elementary schools were popularly known as *maktabs*. These school, were not unusually attached to temples and mosques. The students were given instruction in the three R's of reading, writing and arithmetic. Moral instruction with emphasis on truth and honesty, obedience to parents and faith in one's religion, found a place in the school curriculum. Though education was mainly popular with the higher castes, there were cases of children of lower castes attending schools. Female education received scant attention.

Arts and Literature. In the fields of arts and literature the absence of patronage at Delhi led to flight of talent to newly-established state capitals like Hyderabad, Lucknow, Murshidabad, Jaipur etc.

Asaf-ud-Daula built the Great Imambara (a building for celebration of Muharram festival) at Lucknow in 1784; the absence of any pillars or support makes it architecturally interesting. Swai Jai Singh (1686–1743) built the famous pink city of Jaipur and five astronomical observatories in India including one at jaipur, another at New Delhi and a third at Benares. At Amritsar Maharaja Ranjit Singh renovated the Sikh shrine decorating the lower half with marble and the entire upper portion was inlaid with copper surmounted with a thin plate of gold and gave it its modern name of the Golden Temple. The palace of Suraj Mal at Dig (the capital of Bharatpur) state was planned to rival in munificence the imperial palaces at Agra; work on its construction was begun in 1725 but the construction was left unfinished.

Vernacular languages like Urdu, Hindi, Bengali, Assamese, Panjabi, Marathi, Telugu and Tamil greatly developed. It was during the 18th century that the Christian missionaries set up printing presses in India and brought out vernacular editions of the Bible. Ziegenbelg, a Danish missionary composed a Tamil grammar and published a Tamil version of the Bible. Even a Tamil dictionary was compiled by these missionaries. In Bengal, the Baptist missionaries (Carey, Ward and Marshman) set up a printing press at Serampur and published a Bengali version of the Bible.

Economic Conditions. In the beginning of the 18th century the basic unit of Indian economy was still the self-sufficient and self-governing village community which produced almost all for its local needs. Its only link with the state was the payment of land revenue. While rulers and dynasties changed ceaselessly, the village communities carried on as usual. It was this 'unchangeableness of Asiatic societies' that attracted the attention of European observers and drew the cryptic remark that "they lasted when nothing else seemed to last". These village communities though factors in economic and social stability were also responsible for economic stagnation.

Town handicrafts in India had reached a high level of development and attracted world-wide markets. The cotton products of Dacca, Ahmedabad and Masulipatam, the silk fabrics of Murshidabad, Agra, Lahore and Gujarat, the fine woollen shawls and carpets of Kashmir, Lahore and Agra, the gold and silver jewellery, metal work, metal utensils, arms, shields found markets both in India and abroad.

The large-scale domestic and foreign trade brought into existence the merchant-capitalist and the development of the banking system. The emergence of *Jagat Seths, Nagar Seths* in northern India and the *Chetties* in the south with their elaborate banking houses and extensive use of hundies and other banking practices gave great fillip to trade and commerce.

These developments in the Indian economy in the 17th and 18th centuries gave some indications that some pre-conditions for a rapid growth of capitalism did exist. However, certain constraints like the existence of feudal classes (who wasted on lavish display the surplus they appropriated from the peasantry) the law of escheat (by which the property of the deceased noble was taken away by the state), the absence of correct saving habits and the use of such savings for productive purposes and, above all, the absence of politcal stability and a forward-looking state—all ill-boded for economic development on modern lines.

The presence of European trading companies in the 18th century with deep politico-economic interests added to the prevailing confusion and economic stagnation."[3]

SELECT REFERENCES

1. Chandra, Satish : *Parties and Politics at the Mughal Court*, 1707–40.
2. Habib, Irfan : *The Agrarian System of Mughal India*
3. Irvine, William : *Later Mughals*, 2 Vols.
4. Majumdar, R.C. (Ed.) : *The Maratha Supremacy* (The History and Culture of the Indian People vol. VIII.
5. Owen Sidney : *The Fall of the Mughal Empire*.
6. Sarkar, J.J. : *Fall of the Mughal Empire*, 4 Vols.
7. Richards, I.F. : *The Mughal Empire* (New Cambridge History of India)

---

3. For details see the chapter on *Indian Economy under British Rule*.

2

ACHIEVEMENTS OF THE EARLY PESHWAS

Aurangzeb's armies achieved notable successes in the Deccan in 1689 when Shivaji's son and successor Shambhuji was defeated and killed and Shahu, Shambhuji's son, taken prisoner. The Marathas were defeated but not tamed to submission. The whole Maratha nation rose in arms and the war against the Mughals became a people's war. Raja Ram, the younger son of Shivaji, carried on the struggle till his death in 1700 and thereafter his widowed queen Tara Bai who acted as regent for his minor son Shivaji II offered tough resistance to Aurangzeb. The weakness of the Mughal Empire after 1707 gave the much-needed opportunity to the Marathas. Shahu was back in Maharashtra in 1707. Maratha energy received a new fillip. The first half of the eighteenth century witnessed a considerable expansion of Maratha power both in the south and the north. The Maratha idea of a Hindu Empire was taking shape. The chief architects of this neo-imperialism were the Peshwas, the hereditary prime ministers of Chhatrapati Shahu.

Balaji Vishwanath, 1713–20

Not much is known about the early life of Balaji Vishwanath. He came from the family of Konkanastha Brahmins who are even today well-known for their intellectual acumen, industry and perseverance. His forefathers were hereditary Deshmukhs or revenue collectors of Shrivardhan in the Janjira State. Balaji Vishwanath's connections with the Angrias, the enemies of the Siddis of Janjira[1], brought him into trouble with his masters and he had to leave his homeland and settle at Saswad. Balaji's expert knowledge of revenue matters, however, stood him in good stead in seeking employment under the Maratha chiefs. He is mentioned as Sabhasad of Poona in 1696. Later he worked as Sar Subahdar of Poona (1699–1702) and Daulatabad (1704–07). During 1699–1704 Aurangzeb's forces were encamped at Poona and Khed but Balaji was not punished by the Emperor possibly because the latter thought Balaji could be useful in procuring supplies for the royal troops in the area.

The successors of Aurangzeb sought to solve the Deccan problem by releasing Shahu from Mughal captivity and thereby throwing an apple of discord in Maharashtra. Emperor Aurangzeb had carried Shahu as a prisoner in his camp during his campaigns in the Deccan. Possibly during this period Balaji found it possible to contact Shahu. He is also mentioned as mediating the release of Shahu by backdoor methods in 1705.

Shahu was released by Prince Azam Shah in 1707. Shahu's return to Maharashtra was a signal for a civil war in the land. Tara Bai, the aunt of Shahu, declared Shahu an impostor and claimed the throne of Maharashtra for her son. A battle was fought at Khed (October 1707) between Tara Bai's forces and Shahu's troops in which Balaji sided with Shahu. Shahu won the day more by the diplomacy of Balaji who won over Tara Bai's commander-in-chief Dhanaji to Shahu's side. In 1708 Senapati Dhanaji Jadhav died and Shahu appointed his son Chandrasen as the new Senapati. Chandrasen had leanings towards Tara Bai. As a safeguard against the possible treachery of Chandrasen, Shahu created the new post of *Sena-karte* (Organiser of Forces) and appointed Balaji to that post.

The fortunes of Shahu reached their lowest ebb in 1712. His Senapati, Chandrasen, deserted him and went to the side of Tara Bai; Kanhoji Angria, the Warden of the Marches on the western

---

1. The Siddis of Janjira and the Angrias of Kolaba were two strong naval powers on the western coast of India. The Siddis—a corrupt form of Sayyids—were originally sailors from Abyssinia who had taken service under the Sultans of Ahmadnagar. The Mughal annexation of Ahmadnagar and the disintegration of Maratha state after Shivaji considerably strengthened the power of the Siddis. From their island of Janjira they carried on piratical activities on the western coast. The Angrias acted as the Wardens of the west coast and manned the Maratha navy.

coast, openly declared support for the party of Tara Bai, defeated and arrested Shahu's Peshwa Bahiropunt Pingle and threatened to march on Satara; at Delhi Zulfikar Khan, Shahu's supporter at the Mughal court, had been murdered in the struggle for power politics. At this critical hour Balaji came to the rescue of Shahu and by his extraordinary skill in diplomacy saved his throne from utter failure. Balaji raised a fresh army and defeated Chandrasen Jadav. He threw disaffection in Tara Bai's camp. Above all, Balaji won over Kanhoji to Shahu's side without fighting a battle—on the one side he played upon Kanhoji's fear of the enmity of the Siddis, the British and the Portuguese, on the other hand he appealed to the national instinct of Kanhoji and impressed upon him that the Maratha *raj* was a sacred legacy of the great Shivaji and it was incumbent for the interest of the Maratha nation that their land and naval forces worked in close co-operation.

The struggle for power politics at Delhi between the rival princes and ambitious nobles brought Farrukhsiyar to the throne in 1713 and the Sayyid brothers, Hussain Ali and Abdulla Khan, as 'king-makers'. Soon the Emperor and the Sayyid brothers were at loggerheads and the court intrigues worked a full circle. In his attempt to get rid of Hussain Ali, the commander-in-chief, the Emperor sent him as the viceroy of the Deccan in 1715, at the same time instigating Daud Khan of Gujarat and even Shahu to fight against him and dispose him of. The Emperor's game was very clear to the Sayyid brothers.

In 1717 Abdulla Khan's position at the court became so precarious that he felt compelled to call Hussain Ali from the Deccan. Hussain Ali realised that if he had to remain absent from the Deccan he could not afford to antagonise the Marathas, for the Sayyid brothers were in danger of being crushed between the hostile intrigues of the Emperor in the north and the Marathas in the Deccan, Hussain Ali, thereupon, decided to secure Maratha friendship before leaving for Delhi. Shahu, who was anxious to secure the release of his mother and brother, still held as hostages at Delhi, would not miss the opportunity. The draft of a treaty was finalised and Hussain Ali promised to get the approval of the Emperor at Delhi. The main terms were:

1. That Shahu to get, in full possession, all territories known as Shivaji *Swarajya* (homeland).
2. That such other territories of Khandesh, Berar, Gondwana, Hyderabad and Karnatak, recently conquered by the Marathas to be ceded to Shahu as a part of the Maratha Kingdom.
3. That the Marathas should be allowed to collect *Chauth* and *Sardeshmukhi* from all the Mughal Subahs in the Deccan. In return for these privileges the Marathas were to place at the disposal of the Emperor a contingent of 15,000 troops and also maintain peace and order in the Deccan.
4. That Shahu would not harm anyway Sambhaji of Kolhapur.
5. That Shahu would annually pay a tribute of ten lakh rupees to the Emperor.
6. That the Mughal Emperor would release from his captivity Shahu's mother and other relations.

Accordingly, Balaji Vishwanath with a Maratha contingent of 15,000 troops accompanied Hussain Ali to Delhi. With the help of Maratha troops the Sayyid brothers removed Farrukhsiyar from the throne and the treaty was approved by the next Mughal Emperor, Rafi-ud-darajat.

Sir Richard Temple calls the gains from the treaty as constituting the Magna Carta of the Maratha dominion. The Mughal Government could no longer resist the Maratha demand for *Chauth* and *Sardeshmukhi* of the six Subahs of the Deccan. Actually the payment of *Chauth* was an open acknowledgement by the Mughals of their weak position *vis-a-vis* the Marathas in the Deccan. The Marathas had broken the loins of the Mughal army and demanded tribute which it suited their genius to take in the form of *Chauth* or one-fourth revenue of the Mughal Deccan. Shahu's possessions were recognised and legalised by the Mughal Emperor which enhanced considerably his prestige in Maharashtra. Above all, he came to be recognised as the undisputed leader of the Marathas and the pretensions of Sambhaji received a rude setback. The presence of Maratha troops at Delhi exposed to the world the weakness of the Mughal political position and the rise of a new star in the Indian firmament.

The last work of Balaji Vishwanath after his return from Delhi was to march an army against Sambhaji of Kolhapur who had created serious trouble during Balaji's absence to the north. He died on 2 April, 1720.

Estimate of Balaji Vishwanath. Balaji Vishwanath was a self-made man. From a scratch he rose to the position of the Peshwa. He is remembered today not as a brave soldier, but as a politician and a statesman. His shrewd insight into the state of politics of Maharashtra led him to espouse the cause of Shahu in prefence to that of Tara Bai or Yesu Bai. By his clever diplomacy he won over to the side of Shahu the support of Dhanaji Jadhav, Khanderao Dabhade, Parsoji and, above all, that of Kanhoji Angre. He achieved by clever moves what otherwise would have plunged Maharashtra into an endless civil war. Balaji also secured to Shahu the financial support of rich bankers like Madhaji Krishna Joshi and thus helped the state to ward off financial difficulties. His deal with the Sayyid brothers secured into the state treasury 30 lakh rupees besides the recurring gains coming in the shape of *Chauth* and *Sardeshmukhi* (*i.e.*, 35% of the revenue) from the Mughal Subahs in the Deccan. Balaji restored peace and prosperity in the land long devastated by evils of war. Above all, he tried to channelise the energies of the Marathas into the more fruitful and higher task of building a Hindu Empire.

Select Opinions

Sir Richard Temple. Balaji Vishwanath was more like a typical Brahman than any of his successors. He had calm, comprehensive and commanding intellect, an imaginative and aspiring disposition, an aptitude for ruling rude nature by moral force, a genius for diplomatic combination, and a mastery of finance. His political destiny propelled him into affairs wherein his misery must have been acute. More than once he was threatened with death for which he doubtless prepared himself with all the stoicism of his race when a ransom opportunity arrived. He wrung by power of menace and argument from the Mughals a recognition of Maratha sovereignty. He carried victoriously all his diplomatic points and sank into premature death with the consciousness that a Hindu empire had been created over the ruins of Muhammedan power and that of this empire the hereditary chiefship had been secured for his family. (*Oriental Experience*, p. 389–90).

Kincaid and Parasnis. Although Balaji Vishwanath's exploits were less brilliant than those of his more famous son, it must be borne in mind that the latter began where the former ended. The success which attended Bajirao was, in truth, the success of Balaji's prudent and far-seeing policy. It must be conceded that in the granting of lands instead of salaries to the king's officers, Balaji departed from the wise rule of Shivaji. But the fault was not the minister's but his master's. Balaji saw that Shahu had not the commanding talents and energy which had made possible the great king's concentrated dominion. Since the best was not obtainable, Balaji chose the second best and substituted for the autocracy of the king the Maratha confederacy. Such a confederacy had the seeds of weakness. Nevertheless, it made its power felt all over India and endured for more than a hundred years. Again it was to Balaji that the complicated Maratha system of collection was due. To it as much as to their victories in the field the Marathas owed the spread of their empire. (*A History of the Maratha People*, p. 222).

H. N. Sinha. Balaji Vishwanath had no other plans than creating a sphere of influence for the Marathas. He had certainly no scheme for the establishment of an empire on the ruins of the Mughal Empire, by means of conquest. His resources were not adequate for the task, and if he indulged in tha hopeless scheme, as early as 1719, he would have had little credit as a statesman. But he never indulged in such a scheme as early as that and it is a pity, that most of the patriotic historians attribute this to him. He might have considered that Mughal Empire was bound to fall into pieces in the near future, but this conviction did not blur his discretion. He worked quietly with humble beginnings, and left more ambitious schemes to be worked out by his successors. (*Rise of the Peshwas*, pp. 81–82).

Baji Rao I, 1720–40

In 1720 Chhatrapati Shahu appointed Baji Rao I, the eldest son of Balaji Vishwanath, as the Peshwa. Baji Rao was then a mere boy of 19 years but he combined youthful energy with an bald head. He had received good training in administration and diplomacy under his father.

The task before Baji Rao was really difficult. The Nizam challenged Maratha position in the south and their right to collect *Chauth* and *Sardeshmukhi* from the six Mughal provinces; part of the *Swaraja* territory was under the control of the Siddis of Janjira; Shambhuji II of the Kolhapur branch of Shivaji's family refused to recognise the superior position of Shahu and the fissiparous tendencies of many of the Maratha chiefs were a serious threat to the Chhatrapati's authority. Baji Rao approached the task with bold imagination and consummate skill and ultimately succeeded in overcoming all difficulties. He established Maratha supremacy in the Deccan and formulated the policy of the conquest of the North. With unmistakable foresight he perceived the impending collapse of the Mughal Empire and planned to use the situation to the advantage of the Marathas. He proposed to Shahu the policy of northward expansion of the Marathas in these words: "Now is our time to drive the strangers from the country of the Hindus and acquire immortal renown. Let us strike at the trunk of the withering tree, and the branches will fall off themselves. By directing our efforts to Hindustan the Maratha flag shall fly from the Krishna to Attock". Shahu was so much impressed by the wisdom of the young Peshwa that he brushed aside all conservative counsels and said: "You shall plant it beyond the Himalayas. you are, indeed, a noble son of a worthy father." Baji Rao preached and popularised the ideal of *Hindu-pad-padshahi* or Hindu Empire to secure the support of the Hindu chiefs against the common enemy, *i.e.*, the Mughal Empire.

Relations with the Nizam. Asaf Jah, Nizam-ul-Mulk, who had held the office of the viceroyalty of the Deccan during 1713–15 and 1720–21, was back again in the Deccan in 1724. Since the Nizam planned to carve out an independent kingdom for himself in the Deccan, he looked upon Maratha expansion with extreme jealousy.

The Nizam approached the problem diplomatically. Knowing full well that the Marathas were too strong to be attacked in their homeland, he sought to sow dissensions in the Maratha ranks by supporting the claims of the Kolhapur party against the claims of Shahu. While the Peshwa was away to Carnatic during 1725–26, the armies of the Nizam made a junction with the forces of Sambhaji and attacked Shahu's territories and frightened Shahu to a virtual submission. The lost position was retrieved by the Peshwa on his return when he entrapped the Nizam near Palkhed (6 March 1728) and defeated his army. The Nizam accepted the humiliating treaty of Mungi-Sivagaon agreeing to recognise the undisputed claims of Shahu to *Chauth* and *Sardeshmukhi* of the six Mughal provinces, to give up the cause of Shambhaji, to release Maratha prisoners and to restore all the territory captured by him.

The defeat of the Nizam established Maratha supremacy in the Deccan, and Maratha expansion in the south the east became a matter of time. The intrigues of Sambhaji were foiled one after the other till he accepted the position of a vassal by the Treaty of Warna (April 1731). Above all, it established Baji Rao as a great diplomat and strategist and goaded him to pursue his ambitious plans of the conquest of northern India.

Conquest of Gujarat and Malwa. Ever since the Mughal conquest of Gujarat by Akbar in 1573, the province had formed an important centre of trade between northern India and countries of East Africa and the Middle East. The Maratha incursions into Gujarat began in 1705 under the command of Khanderao Dabhade. In the negotiations between Syed Hussain Ali and Balaji Vishwanath during 1718–19, the Marathas had hoped to obtain the right to collect *Chauth* from Gujarat and had included it in the draft treaty, but the Mughal Emperor had refused to accept it. Repeated Maratha

Achievements of the Early Peshwas

inroads into Gujarat paralysed Mughal authority there and the Maratha chiefs collected *Chauth* from some districts. In March 1730 the Mughal Governor Sarbuland Khan concluded a treaty with Chimnaji, younger brother of Baji Rao I, recognising Maratha claims of *Chauth* and *Sardeshmukhi*. But the last vestige of Mughal authority was not wiped out till 1753.

The province of Malwa served a connecting link between the Deccan and Northern India. The highways of commerce as well as military routes to the Deccan and Gujarat passed through it and armies from Malwa could strike towards Rajputana or Gujarat or Bundelkhand or the Deccan. Maratha attacks on Malwa had begun in the eighteenth century when these were devised to act as a counterpoise against the Mughal attack on the mainland of Maharashtra. Balaji Vishwanath tried to secure the *Chauth* and *Sardeshmukhi* of Malwa in 1719 but without success. What could not be secured by the father by peaceful negotiations or diplomacy, the young son Baji Rao tried to secure by force. Maratha hordes under Udaji Pawar and Malhar Rao Holkar uprooted Mughal authority from Malwa. Successive Mughal governors like Sawai Jai Singh, Mohammad Khan Bangash and Jai Singh once again failed to check the tide of Maratha expansion in this direction. In 1735 the Peshwa himself proceeded to the north. The whole of Malwa passed under virtual Maratha control.

Conquest of Bundelkhand. The Bundelas, a Rajput clan, ruled over the hilly country east of Malwa, between the Jamuna and the Narmada. They had offered heroic resistance to Akbar, Jahangir and even Aurangzeb.

Bundelkhand was included in the Mughal governorship of Allahabad. Mohammad Khan Bangash on his appointment as Mughal governor of Allahabad decided to wipe out Bundela authority. The Pathan chief successfully pushed his plans and captured Jaitpur, the strongest fortress of the Bundelas and drove Chhatarsal, the Bundela leader, to great extremities.

On an appeal from Chhatarsal, a Maratha army reached Bundelkhand in October 1728. One after the other all surrendered territory was retrieved from the Mughals. Chhatarsal felt very grateful, held an open darbar in honour of the Peshwa and assigned a large part of the territory including Kalpi, Saugar, Jhansi and Hirdenagar to the Peshwa, as a jagir.

Raid on Delhi and the Battle of Bhopal. During the Maratha campaigns in northern Bundelkhand, a contingent of Maratha troops under Malhar Rao Holkar crossed the Jamuna and dashed into Oudh. Outnumbered by the superior troops of Saadat Khan, the Maratha cavalry had to fall back. The Khan sent exaggerated reports of his successess to the Mughal Court. Baji Rao decided to expose the hollowness of the Khan's claims either by wiping out Oudh forces or making a dash into the capital. By quick marches through the hilly territories of the Jats and Mewatis, Baji Rao dashed into Delhi (29 March 1737) and terrorized the Emperor. Although the Peshwa remained in the capital only for three days, yet he exposed the weakness and unpreparedness of the once mighty Mughal Empire.

At a time when the Emperor was considering a big appeasement of the Marathas, the Nizam came as the defender of the Empire. Baji Rao's successes had greatly worried the Nizam. The Maratha collection of *Chauth* and *Sardeshmukhi* from the Deccan had compromised his claims of sovereignty and reduced him to the position of virtual tributary of the Marathas. Thus the Nizam made a desperate bid to save the Mughal authority and save himself thereby. In the battle of Bhopal (December 1737), the Nizam was defeated and had to sue for peace. By the Convention of Duraha Sarai, January 1738, the Nizam promised to procure to the Peshwa,

    (*a*) The whole of Malwa.
    (*b*) The complete sovereignty of the territory between the Narmada and the Chambal.
    (*c*) To obtain a confirmation of these territories from the Emperor.
    (*d*) To pay a war indemnity of 50 lakhs of rupees.

Thus Malwa was acquired, the Nizam and the Emperor humiliated and the supremacy of Maratha arms in India established. Above all, it heralded the birth of a new Imperial Power in Northern Indian politics.

Estimate of Baji Rao. Baji Rao was great as a soldier, great as a diplomat, great as a statesman and an empire-builder. Essentially the Peshwa was a man of action, a soldier first and last. All the twenty years of his Peshwaship, Baji Rao was on the move marching, fighting and winning battles. He is remembered in Maharashtra as the fighting Peshwa, an incarnation of Hindu Energy. Baji Rao well understood the Maratha weakness in heavy artillery; he would avoid a close struggle with the enemy in the plains, but would by clever manoeuvres cut off the adversary's food supplies and thus humble him. This was the method he employed at Palkhed and Bhopal against the Nizam. The strong point of the Maratha army was its speed and mobility. Baji Rao's raid of Delhi in 1737 was a near miracle in rapid marches. Baji Rao was not only a great soldier but a skilful general and a great strategist. He carefully planned his campaigns and skilfully executed them. The skilful manner in which he entrapped the Nizam and defeated him on more than two occasions speaks for his uncommon qualities.

Baji Rao was a born leader of men. He had the discerning eye to spot out talent. It was he who picked up war leaders like the Sindhias, the Holkars, the Pawars, the Retrekars, the Phadkes, etc. Once he made his choice he reposed full confidence in his subordinates which in turn stimulated them to fruitful activity. He had the good sense to understand that the Rajputs, the Bundelas, the Jats and other Hindu communities were the natural allies of the Marathas in the struggle against the Mughals. The friendship of Sawai Jai Singh and Chhatarsal stood him in good stead.

Baji Rao was an empire-builder and the creator of Greater Maharashtra. Rao Bahadur G.S. Sardesai writes: "Shahu was no longer the petty raja of a small self-contained one race, one language kingdom, as his father and grandfather had been; he was now monarch over a far-flung and diversified dominion."[2] The Marathas spread over the Indian continent from the Arabian Sea to the Bay of Bengal and the map of India was dotted with numerous centres of Maratha power. The Indian world witnessed the shifting of political centre from Delhi to Poona.

Dr. V.G. Dighe who has made a special study of "Baji Rao and Maratha Expansion" points out the lack of foresight in Baji Rao's work in these word: "He made no attempt to mould or reform the political institutions of his state in a way that would benefit his people permanently. The feudal tendency among the Marathas, which had again raised its head after Shivaji's death, was not only not repressed, but he himself became the great military vassal of his time... The weakness of this feudal organisation made itself felt when the Maratha authority extended to the farthest confines of India."[3] Sir J.N. Sarkar, however, credits Baji Rao with great constructive foresight when he writes, "If Sir Robert Walpole created the unchallengeable position of the Prime Minister in the unwritten constitution of England, Bajirao created the same institution in the Maratha Raj, at exactly the same time."[4] Dr Dighe is rather harsh in his assessment of Baji Rao. That fissiparous tendencies subsequently appeared in the Maratha political set-up was more the responsibility of Baji Rao's successors and possibly implicit in the political situation of the times. With a rare insight he read the political situation of India and with relentless energy and uncommon foresight pursued the ideal of Hindu Empire.

Select Opinions

Richard Temple. Baji Rao was hardly surpassed as a rider and was ever forward in action, eager to expose himself under fire if the affair was arduous. He was inured to fatigue and prided himself in enduring the same hardship as his soldiers and shared their scanty fare. He was moved by ardour for success in national undertakings, by a patriotic confidence in the Hindu cause as against its old enemies Muhammedans and its new rival Europeans, then rising above the political horizon. He lived to see the Marathas spread terror over the Indian continent from the Arabian sea to the Bay of Bengal. He died as he had lived in camp under canvas among his men and he is remembered to this day among the Marathas as the fighting Peshwa, and an incarnation of Hindu energy. (*Oriental Experience*, p. 390).

---

2. R.B. Sardesai : *A New History of the Marathas*, vol. ii, p. 182.
3. V.G. Dighe : *Peshwa Baji Rao I and Maratha Expansion*, p. 208.
4. *Ibid*, Foreword, p. iii.

Kincaid and Parasins. Judged by any standard, it can hardly be denied that Baji Rao was a great man. His person was commanding, his skin fair, his features strikingly handsome... An amusing story runs that once the emperor, Mahomed Shah, curious to learn something of the appearance of the great soldier who was overrunning his dominions, sent his court artist to paint him. The artist brought back a picture of Baji Rao on horseback in the dress of a trooper. His reins lay loose on his horse's neck and his lance rested on his shoulder. As he rode, he rubbed with hands ears of corn which he ate, after removing the husks, the emperor in great alarm cried, 'Why, the man is a fiend' and at once begged the Nizam to make peace with him. Baji Rao lacked the attractive courtesy for which the other members of his house were noted. His manners were overbearing. His letters often contained censure, but never praise. Indeed he seemed rarely to have written save to reprimand a subordinate. In spite of his eminent talents he was not liked by the king and he was detested by the Deccan nobles. He was feared not loved, even by his own children. (*A History of the Maratha People*, pp. 271–72).

H. N. Sinha. Baji Rao excelled as a general. His originality of plan, boldness of execution, and eye for strategy, marked him out as a commander of no mean calibre. As Chief Minister of Shahu, he stands head and shoulders above his contemporaries in Maharashtra. In grasping the vital issues of an affair, in devising means to meet a difficult situation, and in utilizing the available resources to serve his purpose he had not a peer in Maharashtra. His foreign policy and policy of Maratha expansion were no less original than far-reaching. Therefore it has been rightly remarked that Baji Rao had the head to plan and the hand to execute. (*Rise of the Peshwas*, p. 211).

Balaji Baji Rao, 1740–61

The office of the Peshwa had virtually become hereditary in the family of Vishwanath. When Baji Rao I died in 1740, his eldest, son Balaji Rao was the next nominee of Chattrapati Shahu. Already under Baji Rao I the supreme power had passed into the hands of the Peshwa eclipsing the authority of the Chattrapati. The constitutional revolution of 1750 (Sangola Agreement) completed the process. Henceforth the Maratha king became a *roi faineant* and the Mayor of the Palace and the Peshwa emerged as the real and effective head of the Maratha Confederacy.

Balaji set in right earnest to complete the task left half-fulfilled by his father. He relentlessly worked for the expansion of Maratha power both in the north and the south. Success attended Balaji's efforts and the Maratha state reached its territorial zenith extending from 'Kattack to Attock'. Maratha war-lords ruled over extensive territories which lay interspersed throughout the Indian sub-continent. Gujarat, Malwa and Bundelkhand passed under direct Maratha administration. Maratha arms penetrated eastward into Bengal, ravaged the Carnatic, humbled the Nizam and wrested important territories from the ruler of Mysore. In the struggle for power politics at Delhi, the Maratha diplomats played a decisive role while Maratha horses quenched their thirst in the waters of the Indus.

Consolidation of Maratha position in Malwa and Bundelkhand. Malwa had been overrun by Baji Rao I's generals and *Chauth* collected from certain districts, but Maratha control was far from complete. The friendly intercession of Jai Singh with the Mughal Emperor Muhammad Shah resulted in the royal *firman* of 4 July 1741, appointing Shahzada Ahmed as the Subahdar of Malwa and the Peshwa as his deputy acting on the spot. The Peshwa in turn agreed to assit the Emperor with 4,000 troops in times of need and also not to encroach on any other imperial territory. Thus, the whole administration of Malwa including the administration of criminal justice passed under Maratha control.

Bundelkhand could prove a spearhead for Maratha attacks into the Doab and Oudh and advance eastward into Bihar and Bengal. Thus, a strong Maratha force in Bundelkhand could prove an important Maratha base in the north. Ever since Baji Rao's acquisitions of 1729, Maratha power had not made much headway in that territory. The Bundela chiefs of Datia, Chanderi, Jaitpur, Kalinjar, Panna, etc., opposed Maratha control and offered tough resistance. A Maratha force defeated the

Bundela chief of Orchha and captured Jhansi in 1742. From this time onwards Jhansi became a Maratha colony in Bundelkhand.

Extension of influence Eastward and Southward. The Maratha ruler of Tanjore was much harassed by Dost Ali, the Nawab of Carnatic. Raghuji Bhonsle of Berar sent an expedition to Carnatic to restrain Dost Ali from his nefarious plans. In a contested battle Dost Ali was killed and peace was concluded with his son. Further, Raghuji successfully conducted the siege of Trichnopoly where Dost Ali's son-in-law Chanda Sahib had taken refuge. Chanda Sahib was arrested in December 1741 and sent as a prisoner to Satara. Raghuji had his plans on Pondicherry but those did not fructify.

Raghuji further turned his attention towards the east and demanded *Chauth* from the Nawab of Bengal, Bihar and Orissa. He sent his revenue minister, Bhaskar Pant, to enforce that demand. Unable to resist the Maratha force Nawab Alivardi Khan entrapped Bhaskar Pant and had him treacherously murdered (1774). This dastardly act brought on Bengal the wrath of Raghuji who laid it waste to fire and plunder. Alivardi was compelled to surrender Orissa and agreed to an annual payment of twelve lakh rupees as *Chauth* of Bengal and Bihar (1751).

Contest with the Nizam. Asaf Jah, Nizam-ul-Mulk, died in the year 1748. The war of succession that followed among the Nizam's sons gave an opportunity to the Peshwa to liberate Khandesh and Berar from the Muslim control. No astounding successes attended the Peshwa's efforts, for the new Nizam Salabat Jang brought in the field infantry corps trained by the French General Bussy. Tired of fruitless war the Nizam surrendered western half of Berar including Baglana and Khandesh in 1752 (Treaty of Bhalki).

The outbreak of the Seven Years' War (1757–63) between the English and the French and the consequent absence of Bussy from Hyderabad gave a chance to the Peshwa who demanded from the Nizam all the region north of the Godavari and declared war. A closely contested battle was fought at Sindkhed (December 1757). The Nizam asked for peace and surrendered territory worth rupees 25 lakhs along with the forth of Naldurg. Hostilities recommended in December 1759 and the Nizam received a crushing blow at the Battle of Udgir (January 1760). The Marathas acquired territory worth sixty lakhs of rupees with the Muslim capital town of Ahmadnagar, Daulatabad, Burhanpur and Bijapur.

Maratha Entanglements in Delhi and the Panjab. The weakness of the Mughal emperors at Delhi had encouraged fissiparous tendencies in all parts of the Empire. Teh Ruhela and Pathan chiefs were planning to set up a Pathan kingdom at Delhi with the help of Ahmad Shah Abdali. The court intrigues, the Pathan-Safdar Jang differences and the repeated invasions of Ahmad Shah Abdali gave the Marathas a chance to intervene in the politics of Delhi. Terrified by the Abdali invasion of 1751, Safdar Jang solicited Maratha help and concluded an agreement with them in April 1752. He agreed to pay the Marathas 50 lakhs of rupees for protecting the Empire against external as well as internal enemies, promising to surrender the provinces of Agra and Ajmer and recognising their right to collect *Chauth* from the Panjab, Sind and the Doab. Notwithstanding this agreement the Emperor bought over the Afghan invader by the surrender of the Panjab. The agreemnt though not ratified by the Emperor whetted Maratha ambition at Delhi.

Ahmad Shah Abdali once again in January 1757 crossed the Panjab and ravaged all the territory from Delhi to Mathura, destroying temples and killing Hindus. A Maratha army from Poona was sent under the command of Raghunath Rao and Malhar Rao Holkar. Abdali left for Kabul by March 1758, while the Maratha army reached Delhi by August of the same year. Raghunath Rao reinstated the Emperor on the throne and established Maratha supremacy from the Sutlej to Benares in the east. By April 1758 Lahore was occupied and Ahmad Shah's agents were expelled from the Panjab. Very soon the whole of the Panjab passed under Maratha control.

The Maratha expansion was an open challenge to the Afghan invader. The Rohilla chief Najib-ud-Daula defied Maratha position. Dattaji Sindhia was engaged in a long drawn out siege of

Achievements of the Early Peshwas

Najib-ud-Daula near Muzaffarnagar. Meantime, Abdali crossed the Indus in 1759 and headed towards Delhi. In a vain attempt to check the invader at Thanesar and later at the crossing of the Jamuna, Dattaji Sindhia was killed. Malhar Rao's attempts to harass Abdali's troops bore no results. A strong army was sent from Poona under the command of Sadashiv Rao Bhau to check the Afghan advance. The two armies met at the historic field of Panipat and fought a battle on 14 January 1761. The Marathas lost the day and suffered heavy casualties. The Maratha dream of an empire extending over the whole of India was shattered once for all.

Estimate of Balaji Rao. Though not an equal to his father as a soldier or a politician, Balaji Rao was gifted with qualities of leadership. Taking advantage of the favourable circumstances of the times and the momentum given to Maratha expansion under Baji Rao I, he extended Maratha dominion in all directions. Under him the Maratha territory reached its zenith and the Maratha cavalry quenched their thirst in every stream that flowed between the Indus and Cape Comorin.

Balaji Rao was long remembered by the people of Maharashtra for his humane and benign administration. The administration of justice was greatly improved and civil and criminal courts became true guardians of the people's rights. The revenue administration was greatly improved and his collectors compelled to maintain regular accounts. He established a strong police force in Poona for the punishment of miscreants. The Panchayat system was reformed and made more workable. He gave attention to the development of trade, built and improved roads; trees were planted on road sides. He gave donations for religious purposes and a number of temples were built. The general condition of the people improved. For these munificent reforms Balaji Rao earned the goodwill of the people of Maharashtra. Balaji Rao made arrangements for the management of the far-flung territories won by Maratha sword.

Under Balaji Rao the ideal of *Hindu-pad-padshahi* which aimed at uniting all the Hindu chiefs under one flag received a great blow when the Holkar and the Sindhia indiscriminately ravaged the Rajputs and Raghunath Rao besieged the Jat fortress of Khumber. Thus, while at the fields of Panipat all the Muslim powers of Northern India made a common cause with Ahmad Shah Abdali, the Marathas failed to enlist the support of the Rajputs and the Jats. Balaji Rao failed to keep proper control over his subordinates and the feudal tendencies greatly undermind Maratha solidarity. In the post-Panipat period the centre of political interest shifted from the Court of Poona to Madhaji Sindhia's Court.

The third Peshwa gave undue attention to the political developments at Delhi and by his unwise moves in the Panjab brought the enmity of Ahmad Shah Abdali. During 1748–63 another power, far more formidable than the Pathans, the English East India Company was taking roots in India. The English defeated the French in the Carnatic and captured Bengal, Bihar and Orissa from Siraj-ud-Daula. The Peshwa never realised the military strength of the English nor their political ambition. Far from counteracting English plans, Balaji Rao helped the English in crushing the Maratha naval force under Tulaji Angria operating on the western coast. Thus, Balaji Rao proved myopic in his political judgement and failed to rise to the stature of a mature statesman.

Select Opinions

Kincaid and parasins. English historians have dealt scant justice to this eminent prince. And yet they of all others should have been generous to him; for, by helping to destroy Tulaji Angre and by paralysing de Bussy in the Deccan and so giving Clive a free hand in Bengal, Balaji did the English the best turn ever done to them by a foreigner. Without the real greatness of Baji Rao, Balaji was a wise and far-sighted politician. He met with rare skill and firmness the crisis caused by Tarabai's intrigues and Damaji's rebellion. He reduced to a shadow the power of the Nizam and, but for Panipat, would have added the whole of southern India to the Maratha kingdom. Occupied in the south, he never found time, while Peshwa, to go to Delhi. Had he done so, he would better have understood the Afghan menace. (*A History of the Maratha People*, p. 347).

James Grant Duff. Balaji Baji Rao was one of those princes whose good fortune, originating in causes anterior to their time, obtain, in consequence of national prosperity, a higher degree of celebrity, especially among their own countrymen, than they may fully merit. Balaji Rao, however, was a man of considerable political sagacity, of polished manners, and of great address. His measures are marked by an excessive cunning, which Brahmins in general mistake for wisdom; he practised all the arts of dissimulation, and was a perfect adept in every species of intrigue... The private life of Balaji Rao was stained with gross sensuality; but though indolent and voluptuous, he was generous and charitable, kind to his relatives, and dependants, an enemy to external violence, and to that sort of oppression which such violence implies. On the whole, he may be regarded as rather a favourable specimen of a Brahmin in power... The Maratha dominion attained its great extent under Ballaji Rao's administration; and most of the principal Brahmin families can only date their rise from that period. In short, the condition of the whole population was in his time improved; and the Maratha peasantry, sensible of the comparative amelioration which they began to enjoy, have ever since blessed the days of Nana Sahib Peshwa. (*History of the Marathas*, vol. I, pp. 409–11).

APPENDIX
The Third battle of Panipat

The causes of the third battle of Panipat lay in the decades preceding the battle. The weakness of the Mughal Empire had created some sort of a power vacuum in northern India. Ahmad Shah Abdali, who had succeeded Nadir Shah in Afghanistan, hoped to repeat the exploits of Nadir in India. The rising power of the Marathas infused with the ideal of *Hindu-pad-padshahi* coveted position and power at Delhi. The Marathas posed as defenders of the empire from internal and external dangers. In 1752 the Nawab-Wazir Safdar Jang had concluded an agreement with the Marathas offering to concede to the Marathas, among other things, the right of collecting *Chauth* from the Panjab, Sindh and the Doab in return for the Marathas defending the Mughal empire against internal and external dangers. Though the agreement was not ratified by the Emperor, it whetted Maratha appetite for territorial ambition in the North. Thus a clash between Ahmad Shah Abdali and the Marathas lay in the logic of political developments.

In 1757 Abdali had left Najib-ud-Daula as *Mir Bakhshi* at Delhi and entrusted him with the duty of protecting the Mughal emperor against the excesses of the over-bearing Wazir Imad-ul-Mulk. However, Alamgir II found Najib even worse than the wazir, for Najib treated the emperor "with a roughness unknown to the noblyborn wazir". At this stage the wazir solicited Maratha help against Najib. Raghunath Rao entered Delhi in May 1757; he restored the emperor to his position, won over Ghazi-ud-din to their side and compelled Najib to retire to his estate in Najibabad.

In March 1758 Raghunath Rao, the Maratha leader, crossed into the panjab, and drove away prince Timur, Ahmad Shah Abdali's son and agent out of the Panjab. The following months saw the Maratha authority extending up to Attock. The Marathas appointed Adina Beg Khan as Governor of the Panjab on his agreeing to pay an annual tribute of 75 lakhs of rupees. On Adina's death, Sabaji Sindhia assumed charge as Governor of the Panjab. Perhaps, it was Raghunath Rao's mistake to advance into Panjab without crushing Najib-ud-Daula or befriending Shuja-ud-Daula of Oudh or befriending the Jats and the Rajputs.

The Maratha conquest of the Panjab from the Afghans was a direct challenge to Abdali and the latter decided to accept it. Moreover, Najib Khan and the Bangash Pathans, who had entertained designs of reviving Pathan rule in India, exhorted Abdali to rescue the empire from the control of the infidel Marathas and promised all support to him. Najib-ud-Daula also used his influence and secured to Ahmad Shah Abdali the active co-operation of Shuja-ud-Daula (Nawab of Oudh), and Rohilla chiefs Hafiz Rehmat Khan, Sadullah Khan, Dundi Khan and Malla Khan. "Ahmad Shah", writes Sidney Owen, "was not only a king and a conqueror, but, as an Afghan, he sympathised with the Rohillas; and, as a devout Mussulman, he resented Maratha aggression on his co-religionists in Hindustan. The cup of his fury was full; and he resolved to bring to a decisive issue his quarrel with the Hindoo power which had thus crossed his track of conquest, ill-treated his allies, and made war on true believers."

Ghazi-ud-din's extermination of Emperor Alamgir II on November 1759 along with many others upset Abdali's administrative arrangements at Delhi. Abdali planned to chastise the wrongdoers.

The Battle of Panipat, 14 January 1761. Towards the closing months of 1759 Ahmad Shah Abdali with a large army crossed the Indus and overran the Panjab. Finding resistance impossible Sabaji and Dattaji Sindhia had to fall back towards Delhi. In the encounter that followed at Barari Ghat, some ten miles north of Delhi (on 9 January 1760), Dattaji was killed. Jankoji Sindhia and Malhar Rao Holkar also failed to check the advance of Abdali and the latter occupied Delhi.

To reassert Maratha authority in the north, the Peshwa sent Sadashiv Rao Bhau to Delhi. Bhau captured Delhi on 22 August 1760. Proceeding from Delhi on 7 October, Bhau captured Kunjpura so as to drive the invader to the north and relieve pressure on Delhi. The two armies faced each other on the battlefield of Panipat in November 1760. Both sides were handicapped for supplies and negotiated for peace. Since no meeting ground was found, the battle came on 14 January 1761. The Marathas lost the day. The Afghan victory was complete and the Maratha casualties were very heavy, estimated at 75,000 (combatants & non-combatants). "There was not a home in Maharashtra", writes J.N. Sarkar, "that had not to mourn the loss of a member, and several houses their very heads and entire generation of leaders was cut off at one stroke".

Causes of Maratha defeat. A number of factors were responsible for the defeat of the Marathas and victory of Ahmad Shah Abdali.

1. Abdali's forces outnumbered the forces under the command of Bhauji. Sir J. N. Sarkar, on the basis of contemporary records, has estimated Abdali's army at 60,000 while the Maratha combatants did not exceed 45,000.

2. Near famine conditions pevailed in the Maratha camp at Panipat. The road to Delhi was cut off by the Afghan war. There was no food for men and no fodder for the horses. The stench of the carcases of men and beasts lying uncremated and unburied made the Maratha camp a virtual hell. So desperate was the food position that on 13 January 1761 the officers and soldiers approached Bhau and said, "It is now two days that no man among us has got a grain to eat. A seer of grain cannot be had even for two rupees... Do not let us perish in this misery. Let us make a valiant struggle agaisnt the enemy and then what Fate has ordained will happen. Bhau's army lived "on the air". On the other hand, the Afghans kept their supply line open with the Doab and the Delhi region. In fact, famine conditions in the Maratha camp compelled Bhau to the precipitate action of attack.

3. While all the Muslim powers of Northern India rallied to the side of Ahmad Shah Abdali, the Marathas had to fight alone. The over-bearing attitude of the Marathas and their policy of Indiscriminate plunder had estranged not only the Muslim powers but the Hindu powers like the Jats and the Rajputs. Even the Sikhs, the deadly enemies of the Afghans, did not help the Marathas.

4. Mutual jealousies of the Maratha commanders considerably weakened their side. Bhau called Malhar Rao Holkar a dotard past his usefulness and lowered his esteem in the eyes of the army and the public. Malhar Rao angrily remarked that if these proud Brahmins of Poona (referring to Bhau) were not humbled by the enemy they would make him and other captains of the Maratha caste wash their soiled clothes. Thus, the Maratha captains were individualistic in spirit and their military tactics. The officers and the soldiers alike defied discipline and disliked team-work as the destroyer of their *elan vital*.

The campaigning, marching and discipline of Abdali's army was a direct contrast to that of the Marathas. The entire Afghan troops worked according to a single plan under strict discipline, alike in the camp and battlefield.

5. Abdali's troops were not only better organised but better equipped. While Abdali's troops used muskets, the Marathas fought mostly with swords and lances. The heavy artillery of Abrahim Khan Gardi could not prove its usefulness in hand to hand fighting. On the other hand, Abdali's swivel guns mounted on camel's back caused havoc.

6. Kasi Raja Pundit, who was not only an eye-witness of the battle of Panipat but took part in the peace negotiations with the Afghans, blames Bhauji for the defects of his character and names him as the chief cause of Maratha defeat. "Bhau began to exercise his authority in a new and offensive manner and... in all public business he showed a capriciousness and self-conceited conduct. He totally excluded from his council Malhar Rao and all the other chiefs, who were experienced in the affairs of Hindustan, and who had credit and influence with the principal people in the country; and carried on everything by his own opinion alone." Suraj Mull, the Jat Raja, advised Bhau to leave at Jhansi or Gwalior all the multitude of women and children — the families of the officers and soldiers who accompanied the army — and the extensive baggage train of luxury, as also the long train of heavy artillery. "Your troops" observed Suraj Mull, "are more light and expeditious than those of Hindostan, but the Durranis are still more expeditious than you." Malhar Rao held a similar opinion and added that "trains of artillery were suitable to the royal armies, but that the Maratha mode of war was predatory, and their best way was to follow the method to which they had been accustomed." Bhau was advised to drag out the campaign till the rains set in, and Abdali would be compelled to retreat. However, Bhau disregarded all such councils of wisdom and experience. Snubbed by Bhau, the Jat ruler abandoned his cause. Thus, the Brahmin generalissimo's arrogance and overconfidence was one chief cause of the failure of the Marathas.

Ahmad Shah Abdali, on the other hand, was probably the best General of his times in Asia and a worthy heir of Nadir Shah in capacity and spirit. Abdali's experience and maturity were great assets. In fact, Abdali's superior tactics of war and his strategy of action foiled all chances of Maratha success.

Political Significance of the Battle of Panipat. Historians have held divergent views about the effects of the battle on the fortunes of the Maratha power in India. Maratha historians hold the view that the Marathas lost nothing of political importance by it except the loss of 75,000 lives, that Ahmad Shah Abdali practically gained nothing by it and the battle led to no decisive results. G. S. Sardesai writes, "Notwithstanding the terrible losses in manpower suffered on that field by the Marathas, the disaster decided nothing. In fact, it pushed forward in the distant sequel two prominent members of the dominant race, Nana Phadnavis and Mahadji Sindhia, both miraculously escaping death on that fatal day, who resuscitated the power to its former glory. Not long after the Battle of Panipat, the Maratha power began to prosper again as before and continued to do so for forty years, until the death of Mahadji Sindhia or until British supremacy was established early in the 19th century by the Second Maratha War (1803)... The disaster of Panipat was indeed like a natural visitation destroying life, but leading to no decisive political consequences. To maintain that the disaster of Panipat put an end to the dreams of supremacy cherished by the Marathas is to misunderstand the situation as recorded in contemporary documents."

Sir J. N. Sarkar, on the other hand, maintains, "It has become a fashion with the Maratha historians to minimise the political results of the third battle of Panipat. But a dispassionate survey of Indian history will show how unfounded this chauvinistic claim is. A Maratha army did, no doubt, restore the exiled Mughal emperor to the capital of his fathers in 1772, but they came there not as kingmakers, not as the dominators of the Mughal Empire and the real masters of his nominal ministers and generals. That proud position was secured by Mahadaji Sindhia only in 1789 and by the British in 1803."

J. N. Sarkar's view seems more objective. The Maratha losses in manpower were very great. Out of the total of about one lakh persons only a few thousands escaped alive. So great was the disaster that for nearly three months the Peshwa could not get authentic details about the casualties and the fate of the military leaders. Even the Peshwa succumbed to the news of the disaster. J. N. Sarkar writes. "This battle by removing nearly all the great Maratha captains and statesmen including the Peshwa Balaji Baji Rao, left the path absolutely open and easy to the guilty ambition of Raghunath Dada, the most infamous character in the Maratha history. Other losses time could have made good, but this was the greatest mischief done by the debacle at Panipat." G. S. Sardesai counters this argument when he writes, "Panipat, in itself, brought to the Marathas a unique experience in politics and war, and heightened their national pride and sentiment as nothing else could have done. The disaster instead of damping their spirits, made them shine higher as, when a nation is on the path of advancement and progress, such ups and downs are inevitable. Such valiant soldiers as Dattaji, Jankoji, Ibrahim Khan, Sadashivrao, did not die in vain. They left their mark on the fortunes of their nation and prepared it for a greater effort such as the young Peshwa Madhavrao actually put forth. Out of death cometh life is only too true. Although one generation, the older one was cut off, the younger generation soon rose to take its place and perform the nation's service as before. The disaster was felt as personal by almost every home in Maharashtra, and every soul was stirred by it to rise to the Nation's call."

The disaster of Panipat certainly lowered Maratha prestige in the Indian political world. The Marathas who could not protect their dependants or themselves came to be looked upon as a weak reed to bank upon.

Again, the Maratha dream of an empire extending over all parts of India was irretrievably lost. True, the Marathas took the Mughal emperor under their protection and escorted him to Delhi in 1772 and again in 1789, but they never made any attempt to recover the provinces of Panjab and Multan or to play the role of the wardens of the North, West Frontier.

Sidney Owen writes that by the Third Battle of Panipat "the Maratha power was, for the time, shattered to atoms, and though the hydra-headed monster was not killed, it was so effectually scotched, that it remained practically quiescent, until great British statesmen were in a condition to cope with, and ultimately to master and disintegrate it." Certainly, the battle cleared the way for the rise of the British power in India. "It is significant," writes R. B. Sardesai, "that while the two combatants, the Marathas and the Musalmans, were locked in deadly combat on the field of ancient Kurukshetra, Clive, the first founder of the British Empire in India, was on his way to England to explain the feasibility of his dreams of an Indian Empire to the Great Commoner, Lord Chatham, then the prime minister. panipat indirectly ushered in a new participant in the struggle for Indian supremacy. This is indeed the direct outcome of that historical event, which on that account marks a turning point in the history of India."

SELECT REFERENCES

1. Dighe, V. G. : *Peshwa Baji Rao I and Maratha Expansion.*
2. Duff, Grant : *History of the Marathas, 2 vols.*
3. Kincaid and Parasins : *History of the Maratha People, 3 vols.*
4. Majumdar, R. C. (Ed.) : *The Maratha Supremacy.*
5. Ranade, M. G. : *Rise of the Maratha Power.*
6. Sardesai, G. S. : *New History of the Marathas, vol. ii.*
7. Sardesai, G. S. : *Main Current of Maratha History.*

3

MARATHA ADMINISTRATION UNDER THE PESHWAS

The Maratha administration in the 18th and early 19th centuries was a happy combination of Hindu and Mohammedan institutions. The Maratha kingdom came into existence when the Hindu and Muslim principles of government and finance had been in a process of inter-influence and interaction for some centuries. In the Maratha administrative system the basic structure was Hindu with numerous Muslim characteristics in the superstructure. Of course, the Peshwas introduced numerous changes to suit the needs of changing circumstances.

A distinct change we notice in the Maratha administrative system in the 18th century is the place that the Mughal Emperor occupied in the constitution. In the administrative system of Shivaji, the founder of the Maratha kingdom, the Mughal Emperor; even in theory does not figure at all. Under Shahu, however, we find the supremacy of the Mughal Emperor being openly acknowledged. By the Treaty of 1719 Shahu accepted a *mansab* of 10,000 from Emperor Farrukhsiyar and agreed to pay an annual tribute of ten lakh rupees to the emperor. That Shahu was sincere in his professions of loyalty to the Mughal Empire is clear from the protest which he made when a gate of the Delhi Darwaza built at Poona was built facing the north; Shahu maintained that this meant defiance and insult to the Emperor. Mahadaji Sindhia obtained from the emperor the office of *Wakil-i-multlug* for Shahu. Even Nana Fadnavis referred to the Emperor as *Prithvipati* (master of the world).

The Raja of Satara. The head of the Maratha empire was the Chhatrapati, the Raja of Satara, a lineal descendant of Shivaji. He made all high appointments. He granted *sanads* and bestowed dresses of honour on all high officials. However, the powers and prestige of the Raja declined from the time the office of the Peshwa became hereditary in the family of Balaji Vishwanath. Shahu, as long as he lived, reigned as well as ruled. Shahu's successor, Ram Raja, however, became merely a *roi faineant*. By the Sangola Agreement of 1750, the Peshwa emerged as 'the real and effective head of the state, and the Raja became 'the Mayor of the Palace'. However, the fiction of the authority of the Raja was kept up till the Maratha rule lasted in India. It should be noted that the usurpation of the authority of the Raja was silent and gradual. Scotwaring aptly remarks that "the usurpation of the Peshwas neither attracted observation nor excited surprise. Indeed the transition was easy, natural and progressive." Nonetheless, the loss of powers by the Raja was so complete under the successors of Shahu that the expenses of the Raja's household were more closely scrutinised by the Peshwa's secretariat than any other department of the state; the Raja did not have the oridinary right of appointing and dismissing his servants, and the servants were appointed and sent from Poona. Not unoften the Raja's orders were countermanded by the Peshwa. The Raja had even to request the Peshwa for grants for particular purposes.

The Peshwa. The Peshwa was originally a member of the *Ashta Pradhan* Council of Shivaji, *i.e.*, one of the eight ministers of state and probably the second in rank in the list of ministers. Balaji Vishwanath was the seventh Peshwa. It was Balaji Vishwanath who by his ability and statesmanship made the Peshwaship hereditary in his family and his son Baji Rao I made the Peshwaship pre-eminent in the Pratinidi and even eclipsed the Raja. Shahu's acceptance of Baji Rao's policy of northward expansion in the teeth of opposition of the Pratinidi further accelerated the process. The successes that baji Rao won in his policy in the north made him even stronger and in the words of Marquis of Alorna, Governor-General of Portuguese territories in India, the Raja became a mere phantom, an idol, worshipped but not always obeyed by his subjects.

As the authorized deputy of the Raja, the Peshwa exercised all the royal prerogatives, taking all policy decisions, making all high appointments and acting as the religious head of the state.

The old aristocracy like the Angrias, the Bhonsles, the Gaekwads etc. refused to recognise the Peshwa as anyone but their equal and obeyed him only as the Raja's deputy. The Angria; for example, on his visit to Poona expected the Peshwa to come two miles out of the town to receive him, to dismount on his approach and receive him on *gasha* (embroidered cloth). However the new nobility like the Sindhia, the Holkar, the Rastias etc. which had been created by the Peshwa looked upon him as their master, the giver of their bread and themselves as his children. Thus, the rise of the Peshwa to a position of pre-eminence destroyed the only bond of union, the only check to selfish individualism and set an ominous example before other chiefs like the Angrias, the Bhonsles etc. who hoped to emulate his example. "The result was", writes S. N. Sen, "that the Maratha Empire ultimately became like the Holy Roman Empire, a loose confederacy of ambitious feudal chiefs, and the Peshwa, like the Emperor, descended to the position of the head of a confederacy whose command was met with scant respect, and whose authority was confined within the territories under his direct personal rule."

The Central Administration. The Peshwa's secretariat at Poona called the Huzur Daftar was the focus of Maratha administration. It was a huge establishment having several departments and bureaux. In the words of J. Macleod the work of the Secretariat may be described thus ; "All accounts rendered to the government of the revenue and expenditure of the districts, with the settlements of them by government; the accounts of districts rendered by the hereditary district officers; and those of villages by village officers, of farms, of customs, etc., accounts of all alienations of public revenue, whether Surinjam, Inam or otherwise, of the pay, rights and privileges of the government and village officers; accounts of the strength and pay of troops and the expenses of all civil, military and religious establishments. The Rozkirds (daily registers) were registers of all revenue transactions generally, together with all grants and payments, and more particularly the accounts of all contributions and exactions, levied on foreign states — the whole of which were considered and exhibited in one comprehensive view in the Turjamas." The most important departments were the El Beriz Daftar and the Chalte Daftar. The former dealt with accounts of all sorts and was located at Poona; it maintained classified accounts from all other departments and prepared a Tarjuma — an index of the total receipt, expenditure and balance of the State's income in a year — and a Khataunis — abstract of all expenditure alphabetically arranged. The Chalte Daftar was under the direct charge of the Fadnavis. Nana Fadnavis introduced many improvements in the working of the Huzur Daftar, but under Baji rao II it fell in complete disorder.

The Provincial and District Administration. Under the Peshwas the terms Tarf, Pargana, Sarkar and Subah were indiscriminately used. However, a Subah was styled a Prant and a Tarf and a Pargana as Mahal also. The big provinces of Khandesh, Gujarat and Carnatic were under officers known as Sarsubahdars. The Sarsubahdar of Carnatic appointed his own Mamlatdars, but the Sarsubahdar of Khandesh had only the powers of general superintendence, the Mamlatdars under him rendering account direct to the central government.

Next in rank to the Sarsubahdar was the Mamlatdar who held charge of an administrative division variously styled as Sarkar, Subah or Prant. He was assisted in his work by Kamavisdar. The Mamlatdar and Kamavisdar were the representatives of the Peshwa in the district. They were men of all jobs, looking after the development of agriculture and industry, civil and criminal justice, control of local militia, the police and even arbitration in social and religious disputes. The revenue assessment of the villages in the districts was fixed by the Mamlatdar in consultation with the Patels in the villages. In case of need the Mamlatdar made available a Shibandi (militia) to assist the Patel in matters of revenue collection.

The salary and perquisites of the Mamlatdar and Kamavisdar differed from district to district keeping with the importance of the district. In Shivaji's times these posts were transferable but under the Peshwas these tended to become hereditary with its concomitants of bribery and corruption.

The Deshmukh and the Deshpande were other district officers who served as checks on the Mamlatdar and no accounts were passed unless corroborated by corresponding accounts from them. Besides, the Darakhdars — hereditary officers independent of the control of the Mamlatdar — served as checks on the district officers of every department. The Karkuns in the districts were also independent in every respect and reported direct to the central government any deviation from the normal functioning of the district administration.

The smaller administrative divisions called Mahals or Tarfs were run on the same lines as the district. The chief officer in a mahal was the Havaldar who was assisted by a Mazumdar and a Fadnavis.

Local or Village Administration. From pre-historic times the Indian village communities functioned as the units of local administration. These self-contained and self-supporting village communities enjoyed complete autonomy in their affairs under the paternal supervision of a set of government officers. The chief village officer was the Patel who performed judicial, revenue and other administrative functions. He served as a link between the village and the Peshwa's officials. The Patel's office was hereditary and could be sold and purchased; sometimes the Patel sold part of his rights and perquisites. In the latter case there might be more than one Patel in a village. The Patel did not receive any salary from the state, and his remuneration consisted of a share in every villager's produce. The Patel was the social leader of the village and had some obligations also.

The Patel was responsible for the payment of stipulated revenue from the village to the Government and was liable to be imprisoned in case of default. Further, in times of political turmoil or foreign invasion the Patel had to stand surety for the good conduct and loyalty of his co-villagers.

Next in rank to the Patel was the Kulkarni who was the village clerk and the record-keeper. Like the Patel the Kulkarni was rewarded by a number of perquisites by the villagers. Below the Kulkarni in rank came the Chaugula who assisted the Patel in his duties and looked after the Kulkarni's records. Besides, the *Bara Balutas* or twelve village artisans (Mahar, Sutar, Lohar, Chambhar, Parit, Kumbhar, Nhavi, Mang, Kulkarni, Joshi, Gurav and Potdar) rendered various services to the villagers in return for *baluta* or remuneration in kind. In some villages the *Bara Balutas* were assisted by an additional body of twelve servants called *Bara Alutas*.

Town Administration. The pattern of Maratha city administration conformed very nearly to the system that prevailed in the Mauryan times and the Kotwal's duties approximated to the duties of the Mauryan Nagaraka. The Kotwal was the chief officer in a Maratha city. His duties included disposal of important disputes, regulation of prices, maintenance of a record of persons coming in and going out of the city, arbitration in disputes relating to roads, lanes and houses and upkeep and transmission of monthly accounts to the government. Above all, the Kotwal was a Police Magistrate and at the head of the city police.

Administration of Justice. Nowhere perhaps the influence of the ancient Hindu law-givers is more perceptible than in the judicial system of the Marathas. The Maratha law was based on the old Sanskrit treatises on law like Mitakshara and Manu's Code and old customs.

The judicial officer in the village was the Patel, in the district set-up the Mamlatdar, above him the Sarsubahdar and then the peshwa, and above all the Raja of Satara who was the fountain of justice and honour. In towns the judicial duties were entrusted to the care of a Nyayadhish who was well-versed in the *shastras* and who performed judicial functions only. Thus the separation of the judicial functions from the executive was not unknown to the Marathas.

The administration of justice was very simple and well-suited to the needs of the time. There was no codified law, no set procedure for trial of cases. The emphasis was on amicable settlement of disputes. The Chhatrapati and the Peshwa acted more like patriarchs of old than modern judges.

The Panchayat was the main instrument of civil justice. The Panchayats were popularly called 'Panch-Parmeshwar' and the Panchas were often addressed as *Ma-Bap*. The decision of the Panchayat was binding on the parties. An appeal from the decision of the village Panchayat lay to the Mamlatdar who usually upheld the decision, unless the parties concerned could prove that the Panchayat was either prejudiced or corrupt. In that case the Mamlatdar could assemble a Panchayat outside the village of the disputants. In such suits the Panchayat's decision was subject to an appeal to the Peshwa.

In criminal cases the authorities were the same as in civil cases—the Patel in the village, the Kamavisdar or Mamlatdar in the district, the Sarsubahdar in the province and the Peshwa and the Chief Justice at poona above all. No regular set procedure was followed in the trial of cases. Flogging was frequently resorted to and in cases of treason against the state the instruments of torture were used. Under Shahu and Balaji Baji Rao capital punishment was unknown. For serious crimes like dacoity, murder, treason, the usual punishment was confiscation of property or imprisonment of the criminal. The main idea behind punishment was to reform the offender and not to drive him to the extreme of despair and make him a hardened criminal.

The Police. The police arrangements were satisfactory. The Metropolitan Police at Poona was a watchword of efficiency and honesty and has deserved the applause of European observers like Elphinstone and Tone. According to Elphinstone a sum of Rs. 9,000 annually was spent on the unkeep of this force which consisted of a large number of peons, horse patrols and Ramoshis. Tone writes, "It is little remarkable for anything but its excellent Police which alone employs thousand men. After the firing of the gun, which takes places at ten at night, no person can appear in the streets without being taken up by the Patrols, and detained prisoner until dismissed in the morning by the Kotwal. So strict is the discipline observed that the Peshwa himself had been kept prisoner a whole night for being out at improper hours."

The Revenue Administration. Since agriculture was the principal industry of India, land revenue formed the main source of income of the Peshwas. While Shivaji preferred a share in the actual produce of the field, the Peshwas preferred grant of land on long lease on a fixed state demand. Fixing the state demand according to the availability of irrigation facilities was as old as the days of Manu and Kautilya, but the classification of land according to fertility and actual state of cultivation was due to the Mughal influence.

To give inducements to cultivators to bring more and more land under cultivation the land newly brought under cultivation was lightly taxed. For bringing waste and rocky land under cultivation, Madhav Rao II announced that half of such land would be given in *inam* and for the remaining half rent-free concessions were offered for 20 years and a further concession in reduced taxes for another five years. In times of famines, drought or plunder of crops or failure of crops, remissions of land revenue were granted. To save the cultivator from the clutches of money-lenders the state granted *tagai* loans at low rates of interest.

The state demand as well as the mode of payment of land revenue was not uniform throughout the empire.

Thus, the revenue system of the Marathas was based on the principle of security of the taxpayer. However, the excellent system was upset by the wickedness of Baji Rao II who resorted to the system of revenue-farming to the highest bidder.

Other Sources of State's Revenue. The other sources of income of the State were the *Chauth* (25%) and *Sardeshmukhi* (10%) of the total tax collection of territories over run by the Marathas but offered the option of purchasing security by these payments. The income from the *Chauth* was traditionally divided thus — *Babti* or 25% for the Raja, *Sahotra* or 6% reserved for the Pant Sachiv, *Nadgaunda* or 3% left to the discretion of the king and *Mokasa* or 66% divided among the Maratha Sirdars for maintaining troops.

The *Sardeshmukhi* was also similarly divided. After the annexation of the territories paying *Chauth* and *Sardeshmukhi*, the remaining 65% of the revenue was called *Jagir* and was granted in varying proportions to different individuals.

The Government also derived some revenue from forests, customs and excise duties, mints etc. Permits were sold for cutting timber from forests; forest grass, bamboos, wood and wild honey were also sold. The state also granted licences for private mints to approved goldsmiths who were required to pay a royalty to the state.

The total revenue of the Peshwa's Government has been variously estimated. Lord Valentia put the revenue at Rs. 7,164,724, while Mr. J. Grant estimated it at 6 crores of rupees towards the close of the 18th century, which of course included a *Chauth* of 3 crores. Elphinstone estimated the revenue at Rs. 9,671,735 in December 1815; this figure did not included income from *Chauth*.

The Maratha Military System. The Maratha army was organised more on the Mughal model than the ancient Hindu system. The Maratha military regulations were framed on the lines of the Muslim kingdoms of the Deccan. In the Maratha emphasis on cavalry at the cost of the infantry, the methods of enlistment of troops, the mode of payment of salaries, the method of rewarding troops after conquest of a new territory, in making provisions for the dependants of the soldiers, in the branding of horses etc., we find unmistakable marks of the Mughal system. Thus both in theory and practice there was a wide departure from the ancient Hindu rules and tactics, principles and practices.

While Shivaji had mostly recruited his soldiers from Maharashtra proper, the Peshwas recruited their soldiers from all parts of India. In the Peshwa's army we find men of all races, religions and creeds — Karnatikis, Arabs, Abyssinians, Telingas, Bedars, Rajputs, Sikhs, Rohillas, Indian Christians, Shenvi subjects of Portuguese settlements in India. Thus, the Peshwa's army became heterogeneous and assumed a professional character rather than a national character. Perhaps this became inevitable as a result of the expansion of the Maratha power throughout India. Again, while Shivaji distrusted feudal levies and preferred to keep all his officers and soldiers directly under his command and paid them from his treasury, the Peshwas mainly relied on feudal levies and parcelled out the whole Maratha empire into military jagirs.

Cavalry. The mainstay of the Maratha army since the time of Shivaji had been the cavalry. Maratha leaders were granted jagirs and required to maintain a stipulated number of horsemen. The military leaders were required to bring their troops for a general muster every year. In Balaji Baji Rao's time the horses were divided into three classes: a horse worth Rs. 400 was classed as superior, the one priced Rs. 200 as middling and the one priced Rs. 100 as inferior. A horse valued at less than Rs. 100 was not counted in the muster.

The Peshwas tried to lessen the dangers of the feudal system by granting jagirs to various chiefs in the same area in the hope that their mutual jealousies would keep them as a check on one another.

Infantry. The Marathas felt the need for a strong infantry force when their empire extended beyond the Narmada. Since the Maratha talent was more suited for service in the cavalry, for its infantry regiments the Peshwas had to depend on the Rajputs, Sikhs, Rohillas, Sindhis, Arabs etc. Europeans commanded some regiments of the Peshwas' infantry. Boyd's regiment of trained infantry cost the Peshwa Rs 26,242 p.m. the Commander receiving salary at the rate of Rs. 3,000 p.m., a Captain Rs. 450, a Lieutenant Rs. 250, a Sergeant; Rs. 90, and a havaldar Rs. 15 p.m.

To induce foreigners to join the infantry, higher salaries were offered to foreigners as compared to Marathas. Thus a soldier from Arabia received Rs. 15 p.m., a Hindustani sepoy Rs. 8 p.m. while a Maratha and a Deccani only Rs. 6 p.m.

Artillery. The Maratha Artillery Department was mostly officered by Portuguese and Indian Christians. The Peshwas did set up their own factories for manufacture of cannons and cannon balls; a cannon ball factory was set up in 1765 at Ambegavan in Junnar district and one established at Poona in 1770. But for most of their requirements of the Artillery Department the Peshwas depended mostly on the Portuguese and the English. The salary of an ordinary Portuguese gunner ranged between Rs. 30 and Rs. 15 p.m.

Navy. The Angrias kept a strong fleet on the western coast but they were independent of the Peshwas. The Peshwas set up their own naval fleet. The Maratha fleet was generally used for checking piracy, collecting *zakat* from incoming and outgoing ships and safeguarding the Maratha ports.

An Admiral under Balaji Rao received a salary of Rs. 1,186 per annum besides some perquisites and possibilities of reward after a naval victory. A Sar Tandel received Rs. 10 p.m., a Tandel Rs. 7.50 and a sailor Rs. 4.50 to Rs. 5.00 p.m.

Employment of Foreigners. The Peshwas employed a large number of foreigners in their army. Challenged by European powers, superior in discipline and military skill, the Marathas tried to meet the enemy with the weapons of the enemy. To train their troops the Marathas employed English, French, Portuguese, German, Swiss, Italian, Armenian professionals in their army. They paid them very high salaries and granted jagirs for the maintenance of special battalions. However, the experience of the Marathas, like that of the Sikhs in the Panjab later on, was that these foreigners were mostly fortune-seekers and could not be expected to loyally serve their masters. To employ Englishmen and to expect them to fight against their own nationals was the height of folly. Commenting on the case with which the fort of Alighar or Koel was captured Thorn remarks, "It should here be observed that the achievement was materially facilitated by the loyal and gallant conduct of Mr. Lucan, a British officer, who had lately quitted the service of Sindhia, to avoid fighting against his country. On joining our army he undertook to lead Colonel Monson to the gate, and pointed out the road through the fort, which he effected in such a manner as to gain the particular thanks of the Commander-in-Chief, and the public acknowledgement of the government."

Estimate. The Maratha administrative system has suffered in estimation because of its comparison by British historians with the modern European set-up and not with the contemporary European standards. Such writers have described it as 'abominable' and the Maratha generals as 'robbers, plunderers and scoundrels'. An objective study would convince anyone that the Maratha administrative institutions were based on excellent set of regulations, inherited from their Hindu and Mohammedan predecessors and these left behind a legacy for the British administrative set-up. The Maratha empire certainly was not based on robbery and plunder alone, for how could it have lasted more than a century and a half unless it was based on sound principles of good government.

Select Opinions

S. N. Sen. The whole Maratha constitution was a curious combination of democracy and feudal autocracy. In fact no single term of political philosophy can be applied to it. Unable to call it a monarchy, aristocracy or democracy, Tone calls it a Military Republic. This is true only in one sense that the meanest soldier, if he had ability, could logically expect to be a Sardar of the empire. The empire itself, as Tone points out, was based, not upon confidence, but jealousy; and incapable of a comprehensive policy of national patriotism which had been the aim of Shivaji, fell to pieces when it came into conflict with a nation which combined individual self-sacrifice with national ambition. (*Administrative System of the Maratha. as*, p. 208).

S. M. Edwardes. Indeed the constitution of the Maratha Government and army was 'more calculated to destroy than to create an empire', and the spirit which directed their external policy and their internal administration prevented all chances of permanent improvement of the country over which they claimed sovereign rights. There can be no doubt that the final destruction of the Maratha political power and substitution of orderly government by the East India Company were necessary and productive of incalculable benefit to India. [H.H. Dodwell (Ed.) *Cambridge History of India*, vol. v, pp. 398–99].

SELECT REFERENCES

1. Dodwell, H. H. (Ed.) : *Cambridge History of India*, vol. v.
2. Elphinstone, M. : *Report on the Territories lately conquered from the Peshwa.*
3. Gordon, Stewart : *The Marathas, 1600–1818* (New Cambridge History of India, 1993).
4. Sen, S. N. : *Administrative System of the Marathas.*
5. Sen, S. N. : *Military System of the Marathas.*
6. Tone, W. H. : *Illustrations of some institutions of the Maratha People.*

ANGLO-FRENCH RIVALRY IN THE CARNATIC

> The struggle between Duplix and Clive in India, the defence of Arcot and the deeds which led to the founding of our Indian Empire.... all these events were part of a desperate struggle for supremacy between England and France.
>
> —J.R. Seeley

From humble beginnings in trade, the English and the French Companies were inevitably drawn into the politics of India. When the Mughal central authority weakened and the Mughal viceroy of the Deccan proved unable to protect the trade interests of the European Companies against the exactions of his subordinate officials or raids of the Marathas, the Europeans came to this firm conclusion that in order to protect their interests, they must be prepared to unsheath their sword occasionally. Steeped in the ideology of Mercantilism, the English and the French Companies looked for a huge profit margin. To secure this it was necessary to eliminate all competition of similar companies and get monopolistic control over trade. Besides, the Merchant Companies were not only interested in selling commodities dear by means of their monopoly rights, but also buying their commodities cheap. This necessitated substantial political control over the country they traded with.

In most of the European conflicts of the eighteenth century, England and France were ranged on opposite sides. India was one of the theatres of these wars. In this country, Anglo-French rivalry began with the outbreak of Austrian War of Succession and ended with the conclusion of the Seven Years' War. At the time the struggle opened in India, the headquarters of the French settlement was Pondicherry with subordinate factories at Masulipatam, Karikal, Mahe, Surat, Chandernagore and various other places; the principal settlements of the English were at Madras, Bombay and Calcutta with subordinate factories thereto.

The First Carnatic War (1746–48). The First Carnatic War was an extension of the Anglo-French War in Europe. The Austrian War of Succession broke out in March 1740. Despite the wishes and instructions of the home authorities, hostilities broke out in India in 1746. The English navy under Barnett took the offensive when it captured some French ships. Dupleix, the French Governor-General of Pondicherry since 1741, sent an urgent appeal to La Bourdonnais, the French Governor of Mauritius (Isle of France) for help. La Bourdonnais with a squadron consisting of over 3,000 men fought his way towards the Coromandel coast, defeating an English fleet on the way. Madras was now besieged by the French, both by land and sea. On 21 September 1746, the town capitulated to the French, counting among the prisoners of war Robert Clive. La Bourdonnais decided to ransom the town to the English for cash payment, but Dupleix refused to agree to this suggestion. La Bourdonnais who had been handsomely bribed by the English restored Madras to them. Dupleix disowned this rash act of La Bourdonnais and recaptured Madras. However, Dupleix's efforts to capture Fort St. David, a small English factory some eighteen miles south of Pondicherry, did not succeed. An English squadron under Rear Admiral Boscawen was equally unsuccessful in the siege of Pondicherry during June October 1748.

The First Carnatic War is memorable for the battle of St. Thome fought between the French and the Indian forces of Anwar-ud-din, the Nawab of Carnatic (1744–49). Differences arose between the French and the Nawab over the custody of Madras after its reduction in 1746. Anwar-ud-din, as the overlord of the Carnatic, had ordered the European Companies to desist from commencing hostilities within his territories and disturbing the peace of the country. Dupleix had, however, pacified him by promising to surrender Madras to him after its capture. When Dupleix showed no signs of making good his promise, the Nawab sent a force to enforce his demand. A small French army consisting of

230 Europeans and 700 Indian soldiers under Capt. Paradise met a large Indian army of 10,000 under Mahfuz Khan at St. Thomé on the banks of the river Adyar and defeated it. The victory of Capt. Paradise amply demonstrated the superiority of disciplined European troops against the loose Indian levies.

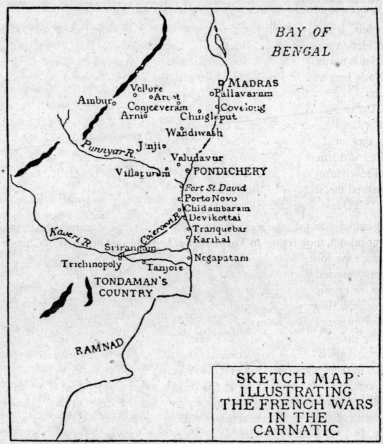

The First Carnatic War came to end with the termination of hostilities in Europe. The Treaty of Aix-la Chapelle (1748) brought the Austrian War of Succession to a conclusion. Under the terms of this Treaty, Madras was handed back to the English much to the disgust of Dupleix.

The first round of the struggle was a drawn one. On land the French superiority had been clearly displayed. Dupleix had given ample proof of his extraordinary skill and diplomacy. The English had failed to defend Madras and unsuccessfully conducted the land-cum-sea operations against Pondicherry. Nevertheless, this war had adequately brought out the importance of naval power as an important factor in Anglo-French conflict in the Deccan.

The Second Carnatic War (1749–54). The First Carnatic War had whetted the political ambition of Dupleix. He had acquired a good taste for oriental warfare. He sought to increase his power and French political influence in Southern India by interfering in local dynastic disputes and thus to outmanoeuvre the English. Malleson rightly sums up the position thus: "With ambition aroused, mutual jealousy excited, the temptation of increased dominion knocking at their doors, what had they (Europeans) to do with peace". The much sought for opportunity was provided in the disputed succession to the thrones of Hyderabad and Carnatic. Nizam-ul-Mulk, Asaf Jah, who had converted his viceroyalty of the Deccan into an independent kingdom of Hyderabad died on 21 May, 1748. He was succeeded by his second son, Nasir Jang (1748–50). His claim was, however, contested by his nephew, Muzaffar Jang, a grandson of the late Nizam. In the Carnatic, the right of Nawab Anwar-ud-din was disputed by Chanda Sahib, son-in-law of the former Nawab Dost Ali. The two conflicts were soon merged into one and in the following years we witness the spectacle of many political alliances and counter-alliances being formed in quick succession.

Dupleix, who saw in this fluid political situation an opportunity to advance his political schemes, decided to support the candidature of Muzaffar Jang for the Subahdarship of the Deccan and Chanda Sahib for the Nawabship of Carnatic. The English inevitably found themselves ranged on the side of Nasir Jang and Anwar-ud-din. Astounding successes attended the plans of Dupleix. The combined armies of Muzaffar Jang, Chanda Sahib and the French defeated and killed Anwar-ud-din at the battle of Ambur near Vellore in August 1749. Nasir Jang lost his life in the encounter of December 1750. Muzaffar Jang became the Subahdar of Deccan and amply rewarded the services of his benefactors. Dupleix was appointed governor of all the Mughal territories south of the river Krishna. The Nizam surrendered some districts in the Northern Circars to the French. Further, at the request of the new Subahdar, a French army under an able officer Bussy was stationed at Hyderabad. The stationing of this army ensured the security of the French interests there. Chanda Sahib became the Nawab of Carnatic in 1751. Dupleix was at the height of his political power.

The anti-climax for the French was not late in coming. Mohammed Ali, the son of the late Nawab Anwar-ud-din, took refuge in Trichinopoly. The repeated attempts of Chanda Sahib and the French to reduce the fortress failed. The English were not inactive. The successes of Dupleix had very much compromised the position of the English. In 1751 Robert Clive, who earlier had failed to provide effective reinforcement to Mohammed Ali at Trichinopoly, suggested a countermove to Governor Saunders. He proposed that a surprise attack be made on Arcot, the capital of the Carnatic, in a bid to divert pressure on Trichinopoly. He rightly calculated that Chanda Sahib must rush to save his capital. The plan was well conceived. Rober Clive with a force of only 210 men stormed and captured Arcot in August 1751. A large force of 4,000 men diverted by Chanda Sahib from Trichinopoly to Arcot failed to retake the town. Robert Clive's outlay resisted the onslaughts of his enemies and successfully sustained the famous siege for fifty-three days (September 23 to November 14) "immortalized and somewhat exaggerated in the glowing words of Macaulay". The capture of Arcot encouraged the English to push their schemes with greater vigour and demoralised the French and Chanda Sahib. In 1752 a strong English force under Stringer Lawrence relieved Trichinopoly. The French force outside Trichinopoly surrendered to the English in June 1752. Chanda Sahib was treacherously killed by the Raja of Tanjore.

The French disaster at Trichinopoly sealed the fate of Dupleix. The Directors of the French Company dissatisfied with the political ambitions of Dupleix and the ruinous expense these involved decided to recall him. In 1754 Godeheu replaced Dupleix as the Governor-General of the French possessions in India. In January 1755, a provisional peace treaty was concluded between the two Companies in India.

The second round of the conflict also proved inconclusive. On land the superior English generalship had been demonstrated when their candidate Mohammed Ali was installed the Nawab of Carnatic. The French were, however, still strongly entrenched at Hyderabad where French soldier-diplomat Bussy had obtained further grants from the new Subahdar Salabat Jang (Muzaffar Jang had lately been killed in an accidental skirmish in February, 1751). Important districts of Northern Circars yielding an annual revenue of thirty lakh of rupees were ceded to the French Company. In this struggle the French predominant position in the Deccan Peninsula was definitely undermined. The English now had an edge over the French.

The Third Carnatic War (1758–63). Like the First Carnatic War, this conflict between the English and the French in India was an echo of the struggle in Europe. The outbreak of the Seven Years' War in Europe ended the short peace between the European Companies in India. In April 1757, the French Government sent Count de Lally who reached India after a voyage of twelve months in April 1758. In the meantime the English had defeated Siraj-ud-duala and captured Bengal in 1757. The conquest of Bengal placed at the disposal of the English the immense riches of Bengal and with that financial stick they could beat the French effectively in Southern India.

Count de Lally captured Fort St. David in 1758 and sanctioned a hasty and misconceived attack on Tanjore to exact an outstanding payment of 56 lakhs rupees from that ruler[1]. The campaign ended in failure damaging French reputation seriously. Lally's next move was to besiege Madras, but the appearance of a strong English naval force before Madras compelled Lally to abandon the siege. Lally then summoned Bussy from Hyderabad. This was a capital mistake of Lally. Bussy's recall from Hyderabad weakened French position in that capital. The English fleet under the command of Pocock defeated the French fleet under D'Ache thrice and compelled him to retire from the Indian waters. The English command of the sea left the field open for them and the final victory was no longer in doubt. A staggering blow was struck at the French at Wandiwash (1760) by Sir Eyre Coote. Bussy was taken prisoner. The French in January 1761 ignominiously retreated to Pondicherry. Pondicherry after a blockade of eight months capitulated to the English. Mahe and Jinji were lost by the French in quick succession. Thus was rung down the curtain to the drama of Anglo-French rivalry in the south. Undoubtedly the French position in India was lost beyond redemption.

The third and the final round of the struggle proved decisive. Pondicherry and some other French settlements were no doubt returned to the French by the Treaty of Paris (1763) but these were never to be fortified. The French political cause in India was doomed for good.

Causes for the Failure of the French

The French position which at one time dazzled the Indian world by its political successes was destined to end in humiliation and failure. Among the various causes responsible for the defeat of the French and the victory of the English, the following few deserve special mention:

French Continental Preoccupations. The continental ambitions of France in the 18th century considerably strained her resources. The French monarchs of the time were fighting for "natural frontiers" for their country which meant acquisition of new territories towards the Low Countries, extension of the frontier to the Rhine and towards Italy. Such expansionist schemes involved that country deeper and deeper into the political muddle of Europe, taxed her energies and kept her constantly at war with the states of Europe. France cared more for a few hundred square miles of territory on her frontier to bigger stakes in North America or India. France attempted simultaneously the difficult task of continental expansion and colonial acquisitions. This divided her resources and made her unequal to the task in facing her adversaries. It was the misfortune of France that she gained almost nothing on the continent and lost her colonial possessions also. England, on the other hand, did not covet an inch of European territory. A part of Europe, England felt herself apart from it. England's interests in Europe were mainly confined to the maintenance of a balance of power in that continent. England's ambition was mainly colonial and in this single-minded objective she came off with flying colours. She won the struggle both in India and North America and worsted off France in both these regions.

Different Systems of Government in England and France. French historians have rightly attributed the failure of France in the colonial struggle to the inferior system of the government prevalent in France as compared to the English system of government. The French government was despotic and depended on the personality of the monarch. Even under Louis XIV, the *Grand Monarque*,

---

1. Some accounts put this figure at 70 lakhs.

the system was showing serious cracks. The numerous wars that Louis XIV waged sapped the vitality of the state, ruined her financial resources and made French power look like an inflated balloon. The deluge followed close on his death. His weak and sensual successor, Louis XV frittered away the resources of France upon his numerous mistresses and other favourites like dancers and hair-dressers. England, on the other hand, was ruled by an englightened oligarchy. Under the rule of the Whig Party, England took great strides towards a constitutional set-up, reducing the British realm into "a sort of a crowned republic." The system showed considerable vitality and grew from strength to strength. Alfred Lyall emphasises the rottenness of the French system of Government when he writes: "India was not lost by the French because Dupleix was recalled, or because La Bourdonnais and D'Ache both left the coast at critical moments or because Lally was headstrong and intractable. Still less was the loss due to any national inaptitude for distant and perilous enterprises in which the French have displayed high qualities... It was through the short-sighted, ill-managed European policy of Louis XV, misguided by his mistresses and by incompetent ministers, that France lost her Indian settlements in the Seven Years War."[2]

Differences in the Organisation of the two Companies. The French Company was a department of the state. The Company had been launched with a share capital of $5\frac{1}{2}$ million livres out of which the monarch subscribed $3\frac{1}{2}$ million livres. Its directors were nominated by the king from the shareholders and they carried on the decisions of two High Commissioners appointed by the Government. Since the state guaranteed dividend to the shareholders, the latter took very little interest in promoting the prosperity of the Company. So great was the lack of public interest that from 1725 to 1765 the shareholders never met and the Company was managed as a department of the state. Under these circumstances the financial position of the French Company progressively deteriorated. At one stage the resources of the Company dwindled to such a low ebb that it had to sell its trading rights to a group of merchants from St. Malo for an annual payment. From 1721 to 1740 the Comapany traded on borrowed capital. Constantly propped up by subsidies from the royal treasury, the Company was kept going by monopoly of tobacco and gambling in lotteries. Such a company was ill-equipped to support the ambitions of Dupleix or finance his expensive wars. The English Company, on the other hand, was an independent commercial corporation. While this Company could not remain altogether unaffected by the political upheavals in England, the interference of the government into its day-to-day affairs was very little. Whoever controlled the administration in England, the King or Parliament, there was great interest in the ruling circles for the well-being of the Company. Compared to the French Company, the English Company was financially sounder, its trade was far more extensive and business methods better. The directors of the English Company always emphasised the importance of trade. With them trade came first and politics later on. The English Company earned enough to finance its wars. It has been estimated that during 1736–1756, the total sales of the English Company amounted to £ 41,200,000 as compared to the total sales of Indian goods in France which were approximately £ 11,450,000 during the same period. Financially the English Company was so rich that at one time it was in danger of being regarded as a milch cow by the Government of England. In 1767 the English Company was asked to pay £ 400,000 a year to the British treasury. There was even talk of using the surplus funds of the Company in liquidating the national debt of England. When Dupleix inaugurated the policy of making political gains to compensate for the declining profits of the French Company he took the first step towards its decline.

Role of the Navy. The events of the Carnatic Wars amply demonstrate how the fortunes of the two Companies waxed and waned with their strength on the seas. During 1746, French successes on land followed her naval superiority along the Coromandel coast. True, the English naval power did not

---

2. Alfred Lyall : *Tue Rise and Expansion of British Dominion in India*, p. 117

assert its superiority during the few years following 1748, more because England and France were officially at peace. Dupleix's astounding successes were won during 1748–51 when the English navy was temporarily out of action. The naval superiority of England during the Seven Years, War placed Count de Lally at a grievous disadvantage and he could not hope to repeat the exploits of Dupleix. The retirement of French fleet under D'Ache from the Indian waters left the field clear for the English and their final victory was no longer in doubt. During the Austrian War of Succession French maritime strength was so greatly reduced that, according to Voltaire, she was left with no warships during the Seven Years' War. Pitt the Elder made the maximum use of the superiority of England on the high seas. Superior naval force enabled the English East India Company to keep open her communications with Europe, cover her operation on land in the Carnatic by supplying reinforcements from Bombay and Calcutta and cut off and isolate French force in the Carnatic from the rest of the world. Superior maritime strength proved to be England's most powerful weapon in the struggle for colonial supremacy. Even if other factors were equally proportioned navy would have the casting vote.

Impact of English Successes in Bengal. The English conquest of Bengal in 1757 was undoubtedly of great significance. Besides enhancing the political prestige of the English Company, it placed at its disposal the vast resources in wealth and manpower of Bengal. The financial resources of the English Company considerably improved. At a time when Count de Lally was ill at ease as to how to make payments to his troops. Bengal sent not only troops but supplies to the Carnatic. The Deccan was too poor to finance the political ambition of Dupleix or military schemes of Count de Lally. True, Bussy had obtained the cession of the Circars from the Nizam, but there is no evidence of any remission of funds to Southern India except the lakh and a half of rupees sent by Bussy to Lally in 1758.

Decidedly the power of superior finance was on the side of the English. V. A. Smith emphatically declares: "Neither Bussy nor Dupleix singly, nor both combined, had a chance of success against the government which controlled the sea routes and the resources of the Gangetic valley. It is futile to lay stress upon the personal frailties of Dupleix, Lally or lesser men in order to explain the French failure. Neither Alexander the Great nor Napoleon could have won the empire of India by starting from Pondicherry as a base and contending with the power which held Bengal and command of the sea".[3] "Dupleix", writes Marriott, "made a cardinal blunder in looking for the key of India in Madras; Clive sought and found it in Bengal".[4]

Respective Leadership compared. The superior political leadership and military generalship of the English in India stand in striking contrast to that of the French. Perhaps Dupleix and Bussy were in no way inferior to Clive; Lawrence and Saunders. The comparison ends there. Dupleix and Bussy could do everything but enthuse the French with their own spirit; they had to depend on incompetent subordinates. Count de Lally who came to India at a critical moment was headstrong and of a violent temper. He looked upon the Company's servants of Pondicherry as a set of dishonest rogues whom he hoped to set right by threats and punishment. He so greatly alienated his compatriots that they openly rejoiced when the English defeated him. The English, on the other hand, were lucky in procuring the services of capable commanders and very many servants far superior to any of the subordinates of Dupleix and Bussy. Writes Malleson: "The daring of Lawrence, the dogged pertinacity of Saunders and his Council, the vigour and ability of Calliaud, of Forde, of Joseph Smith, of Dalton, and of many others, stand out in striking contrast to the feebleness, the incapacity, the indecision of the Laws, the D'Anteuils, the Brenniers, the Maissins and others whom Dupleix was forced to employ".[5]

---

3. V.A. Smith : *Oxford History of India*, p. 482
4. J.A.R. Marriott : *The English in India*, p. 55.
5. G.B. Malleson : *History of the French in India* (1868), p. 567

Responsibility of Dupleix. Dupleix notwithstanding his political brilliance cannot escape the responsibility of damaging the position of the French in India because his complete absorption in political intrigues blinded him to some very important aspects of the contest. He showed comparative indifference towards the trading and financial problems of the French Company. Consequently the French trading activity even otherwise not very sound began to decline rapidly. Moreover, at times he was indiscreetly reckless about finances and thus ruined the prospects of his well-conceived political plans. It is rather intriguing that a man of Dupleix's imagination should display such an utter lack of imagination in believing that the policy he had adopted in the Deccan was politically expedient. The English would not easily accept Dupleix's new position as governor of all the Mughal territories south of the river Krishna (a title conferred on him by Muzaffar Jang in 1751). Further, he failed to grasp the fact that the Anglo-French conflict in India was merely a projection of the clash of political and imperial ambitions of the two countries in Europe and the New World. In addition, Dupleix suffered from such an overweening self-confidence that he did not appraise his superior authorities in paris even about some of the serious military and naval setbacks suffered by the French in India. Thus, if he did not get timely reinforcements from France the fault was greatly his.

It must not be forgotten that India was one of the many theatres of the world-wide struggle between England and France for colonial supremacy and that the English, on a general summation proved to be superior cotenders.

Select Opinions

Alfred Lyall. The two primary conditions of success, whether commercial or military, in India were the establishment of strong *points d'appui* on the coast, and the maintenance of a naval force that could keep open communications with Europe; but the English had gained the preponderance at sea, while the French had now lost their footing on land. The causes of their failure are to be found, not in the ill-luck or incapacity of individuals (for that might have been repaired), but in the wider combination of circumstances that decided against France her great contest with England at that period. (*The Rise and Expansion of British Dominion in India*, p. 110).).

H.H. Dodwell. The principal cause which had contributed to this complete victory (of the English) was certainly the relentless pressure of sea-power. Although the French fleet was never destroyed, yet the cumulative effect of the three actions which were fought established an irresistible superiority, such as later in 1783 Suffren had just established when the news of peace robbed him of the fruits of victory. While the English received supplies of food and money from Bengal, recruits of men from Europe, and grain from their northern settlements, the French could receive nothing but what came to them laboriously by land. The first were constantly strengthened, the second was constantly weakened. And this enabled Coote to establish his military superiority over Lally in the field and to hem in within the walls of Pondicherry. (*The Cambridge History of India*, vol. v, pp. 164–66).

P.E. Roberts. The causes of great historical events are wrought deeper into the woof of things. A later and truer view relegates the land campaigns (though here there is some exaggeration in the contrary direction) to the dominion of 'obscure operations' and believes that the control of the sea was all-important. Captain Mahan, the chief exponent of this theory, has made a very weighty contribution to naval history, but as the history of Europeans in India was not his main subject he has been inclined to underrate other factors contributing to this particular question. A wide and impartial survey will give to each and all of them their proper place, and will attribute a full share of credit to the masterful genius displayed alike in peace and war by Rober Clive. (*History of British India*, pp. (127–28).

---

5. G.B. Malleson : *History of the French in India* (1868), p. 567.

SELECT REFERENCES

1. Dodwell, H. H. (Ed.)   : *Cambridge History of India*, vol. v.
2. Dodwell, H. H.   : *Dupleix and Clive.*
3. Lawrence   : *Narrative of Anglo-French Conflicts*
4. Malleson, G. B.   : *History of the French in India.*
5. Spear, P.   : *Oxford History of Modern India*, 1740–1975.
6. Thompson and Garratt   : *Rise and Fulfilment of British Rule in India.*

5

THE RISE OF THE ENGLISH POWER IN BENGAL—PLASSEY AND BUXAR

> The system, of a "sponsored" Indian State, controlled but not administered, was the one Clive had in mind for Bengal.
>
> –P. Spear

The first English factory in Bengal was established at Hugli in 1651 under permission from Sultan Shuja, second son of Emperor Shahjehan and then Subahdar of Bengal. The same year, much pleased with the services of Mr. Boughton in curing a royal lady, the Subahdar granted the Company the privileges of free trade throughout Bengal, Bihar and Orissa for a nominal lump sum payment of Rs. 3,000. Soon after English factories sprang up at Kassimbazar, Patna and other places in the province. In 1698 the English obtained from Subahdar Azim-us-Shan the zamindari of the villages of Sutanuti, Kalikata and Govindapur, the present site of Calcutta, on payment of Rs. 1,200 to the previous proprietors. In 1717 Emperor Farrukhsiyar confirmed the trade privileges granted by earlier Subahdars of Bengal, besides according permission to the Company to rent additional territory around Calcutta.

In 1741 Alivardi Khan, the Deputy Governor of Bihar under Nawab Sarfaraz Khan, rose in revolt, killed the Nawab in a battle and to fortify his position as the new Subahdar of Bengal got a confirmation from Emperor Muhammad Shah by payment of a large sum of money. Alivardi Khan's rule of fifteen years was spent in fighting the Maratha menace which assumed alarming proportions during this period. Taking advantage of the Maratha incursions into Bengal, the English obtained the Nawab's permission to dig a ditch and throw up an entrenchment around their settlement of Fort William. Alivardi Khan's attention was drawn to the developments in the Carnatic where the European Companies had usurped all power and he was urged to expel the Europeans from Bengal before they struck roots there. The Nawab likened the Europeans to bees who would make him honey if left in peace but would sting an intruder to death. Before long the evil prognostications were to come out true!

Alivardi Khan died on 9 April 1756 and was succeded by his grandson, Siraj-ud-daula. The new Nawab besides facing rival claimants to the throne like Shaukat Jang of Purnea and Ghasiti Begum of Dacca had serious apprehensions about the designs of the English. Anticipating another round of Anglo-French struggle in Europe and its extension to India, the English had begun to strengthen the fortifications of Fort William and mounted guns on the walls of the fort. Besides, the English gave offence to Siraj-ud-daula by indirectly lending support to the claims of Ghasiti Begum besides giving asylum to political offenders from Bengal. Siraj-ud-daula's repeated pleadings with the English to desist from their nefarious projects only evoked evasive replies. Finding his authority flouted in his own dominions, Siraj-ud-daula launched the offensive against the English. Philip Woodruff's[1] argument that plunder was the main motive behind the Nawab's attack on Fort William hardly stands the test of careful scrutiny. Fort William was besieged on 15 June 1756 and surrendered after a feeble resistance of five days. Governor Roger Drake and other important citizens escaped through the back door down the river Hooghly. The Nawab placed Calcutta under the charge of Manik Chand and returned to Murshidabad.

The Black Hole. Mention may be made here of the much propagated Black Hole Episode. Following the normal practices of war, English prisoners at Calcutta which included some women and

---

1. Philip Woodruff: *The Men Who Ruled India*, vol. i, P. 95.

children were lodged in a prison room of the fort. The number of prisoners is given out as 146 and the dimensions of the prison room as 18 feet long by 14 feet 10 inches wide. So the story goes, that out of the 146 white prisoners shut up on 20th June only 23 survived the next morning when the prison room was opened, the rest having trampled one other down for places near the window. Excessive heat and suffocation took a heavy tool.

Siraj-ud-daula has been painted as a monster of cruelty and directly responsible for the tragic happenings. J. Z. Holwell, one of the survivors of the Black Hole and the prime author of the story, did not mention the names of the victims. Probably the number of victims was far less. And they were kept in the guard-room or prison of Fort William itself. Further, it was a subordinate officer of the Nawab who had shut up English prisoners into that prison room, for which the Nawab himself was in no way directly responsible. The casualties were thus, in no way, due to malice or callous nature of the Nawab. The Nawab's fault lay in that he did not punish the guard responsible for the tragedy. Nor did he show any tenderness to the survivors. The prisoners fell victims to the summer solstice. The incident was considered so insignificant as not to deserve any mention at the hands of the contemporary Muslim historian Ghulam Hussain, the author of *Siyar-ul-Mutakherin*. However, the East India Company's authorities used the episode as a propaganda device to malign the Nawab and won support of the British public opinion for the war of aggression which it was to wage almost uninterruptedly for the terrible retribution that followed it.

The Battle of Plassey. When the news of the capitulation of Calcutta reached Madras, the authorities there immediately decided to direct an army which had been built up to fight against the French towards Calcutta. The command of the expedition was given to Robert Clive who had recently returned from England. Clive was urged to do his work as rapidly as possible for the Madras authorities wanted their troops back in Madras for defence against the impending French attack. The expedition sailed on 16 October 1756 and reached Bengal on 14 December. Manik Chand, the Nawab's officer in-charge of Calcutta, was bribed and he surrendered Calcutta to the English after making a show of resistance. In February 1757, the Nawab made peace with Clive by the Treaty of Alinagar (Calcutta renamed so after Siraj-ud-daula captured it) restoring to the English their former privileges of trade, granting permission to fortify Calcutta and promising compensation for the losses suffered by the English.

The wheel had gone a full circle. Now the English were on the offensive. Taking advantage of the disaffection among the Nawab's officers, Clive arranged a conspiracy in which Mir Jaffar (the Commander-in-Chief of the Nawab's army), Rai Durlabh, Jagat Seth (an influential banker of Bengal) and Omi Chand, an intermediary, joined. It was planned to make Mir Jaffar the Nawab who in turn was to reward the services of the Company and pay compensation for the losses suffered by them earlier.

The English had given great offence to the Nawab by capturing the French settlement of Chandernagore in March 1757. At a time when the Nawab feared an Afghan invasion from the north and a Maratha invasion from the west, the English force under Clive proceeded towards Murshidabad to fight against the Nawab. On 23 June 1757 the rival forces faced each other on the battlefield of Plassey, a mango grove 22 miles south of Murshidabad. The English army consisted of 950 European infantry, 100 European artillery, 50 English sailors and 2,100 Indian sepoys. The Nawab's large army of 50,000 was commanded by the treacherous General Mir Jaffar. An advance party of the Nawab's troops led by Mir Mudan and Mohan Lal got the better of the English troops and forced Clive to withdraw his forces behind the trees. A stray shot from the English side, however, killed Mir Mudan. Siraj-ud-daula summoned his army officers and sought their advice. Mir Jaffar played upon the fears of the Nawab and counselled a withdrawal of the army behind the entrenchment. Further, the Nawab was advised to retire from the battlefield leaving the control of operations to his Generals. The card was well played. The Nawab retired to Murshidabad followed by 2,000 horsemen. The little band of Frenchmen who held out were soon overpowered by Clive's troops. Mir Jaffar merely looked on. Clive won the day and received a message of congratulations from Mir Jaffar. Mir Jaffar reached Murshidabad on 25th and proclaimed himself the Nawab of Bengal. Siraj-ud-daula was captured and put to death. Mir Jaffar rewarded the services of the English by the grant of the zamindari of 24-Parganas besides a personal present of £234,000 to Clive and giving 50 lakh rupees in reward to army and naval officers. The Company was compensated for the losses suffered at Siraj-ud-daula's capture of Calcutta. All French settlements in Bengal were surrendered to the English. It was also understood that British merchants and officials would no longer be asked to pay duties on their private trade.

Importance of the Battle of Plassey. The battle—rather the rout of Plassey—was hardly important from the military view-point. It was a mere skirmish. The total casualties were 65 on the Company's side and 500 in the Nawab's army. The English army showed no military superiority either in manoeuvres or startegy of the battle. It was desertion in the Nawab's camp that gave Clive the victory. After Mir Mudan's death treacherous commanders held the field. If Mir Jaffar and Rai Durlabh had remained faithful the outcome of the battle would have been different. It was treason that drove the Nawab from the battlefield, it was treason that made Clive the victor.

Perhaps it was in the game of diplomacy that Clive excelled. He played on the fears of the Jagat Seths, worked up the ambition of Mir Jaffar and won a victory without fighting. K. M. Pannikar believes that Plassey was a transaction in which the rich bankers of Bengal and Mir Jaffar sold out the Nawab to the English.

The battle of Plassey is important because of the events that followed it. Plassey put the British yoke on Bengal which could not be put off. The new Nawab, Mir Jaffar, was dependent on British bayonets for the maintenance of his position in Bengal and for protection against foreign invasions. An English army of 6,000 troops was maintained in Bengal to help the Nawab maintain his position. Gradually all real power passed into the hands of the Company. How hopeless was the position of Mir Jaffar is clear from the fact that while he wanted to punish Diwan Rai Durlabh and Ram Narayan, the deputy governor of Bihar, for disloyalty, the English held his hand. Mr. Watts, the British Resident at Murshidabad, held considerable influence. Ghulam Hussain Khan, the Muslim historian, noted that English recommendation was the only sure way to office. Very soon Mir Jaffar found the English yoke galling and intrigued with the Dutch to oust the English from Bengal. Clive thwarted this design and defeated the Dutch at Bedara (November 1759). When Mir Jaffar refused to read the writing on the wall, he had to give place to Mir Kasim, a nominee of the Company, in 1760.

The battle of Plassey and the subsequent plunder—for there was not much difference then between fair trade and plunder—of Bengal placed at the disposal of the English vast resources. The first instalment of wealth paid to the Company immediately after Plassey was a sum of £800,000, all paid in coined silver. In the graphic language of Macaulay, "the fleet which conveyed this treasure to Calcutta consisted of more than a hundred boats." Bengal then was the most prosperous province, industrially advanced and commercially great. "The immense commerce of Bengal", wrote Verelst in 1767, "might be considered as the central point to which all the riches of India were attracted. Its manufactures find their way to the remotest part of India." The vast resources of Bengal helped the English to conquer the wars of the Deccan and extend their influence over Northern India.

A great transformation came about in the position of the English Company in Bengal. Before Plassey the English Company was just one of the European Companies trading in Bengal and suffering various exactions at the hands of the Nawab's officials. After Plassey the English Company virtually monopolised the trade and commerce of Bengal. The French never recovered their lost position in Bengal, the Dutch made a last bid in 1759 but were humbled. From commerce the English proceeded to monopolise political power in Bengal.

Plassey proved a battle with far-reaching consequences in the fate of India. "There never was a battle." writes Malleson, "in which the consequences were so vast, so immediate and so permanent." Col. Malleson certainly overstates the case when he writes that it was Plassey which "made England the great Mohammadan power in the world; Plassey which forced her to become one of the main factors in the settlement of the burning Eastern Question; Plassey which necessitated the conquest and colonisation of the Cape of Good Hope, of the Mauritius, the protectorate over Egypt." Nevertheless, the battle of Plassey was an important event in the chain of developments that made the English the masters of India.

Eric Stokes, a modern writer, describes "The Plassey Revolution as the first English eassy in private profiteering on a grandiose scale". The consequences of Plassey shaped the form of British overrule and the modes of cultural contact.

Deposition of Mir Jaffar. Though Mir Jaffar had played the disgraceful role of 'Colonel Clive's jackal', he failed to meet the heavy demands for money made on him by the Company. This brought about his ruin.

Plassey had brought about a gradual tansformation in the character of the Company. It did not remain merely as a trading Company but also became a military Company possessing a considerable landed property which could only be maintained by arms. In the context of the then politics, military control was synonymous with political control. Thus, the Company had to play the role of commercial-cum-military-cum-political body. A clear change is perceptible in the English attitude as to the proper way the Nawab's government should function, especially when the Company's interests were involved.

Wherefrom were the funds to come for meeting the new responsibilities of the Company and its growing army? All that Mir Jaffar had agreed to pay was a sum of 1 lakh of rupees per month while the army was in active operations. The Company also derived an annual income of 5 to 6 lakh rupees from the lands around Calcutta, ceded to the Company by Mir Jaffar. Further, the Nawab had assigned to the Company for a period of two years (April 1758 to April 1760) certain portions of the districts of Burdwan and Nadia. But the income from these sources was found inadequate. Worst of all, the Nawab could not make the stipulated payments and always fell in arrears. By 1760 Mir Jaffar was in debt to the Company to the tune of 25 lakhs. For the financial year 1760 (beginning from 1 August) the Company's estimated expenditure was—18 lakhs for the military, a contribution of 10 lakhs for the Madras Council (engaged in war with the French), apart from the amount necessary for the Company's commercial investment. Against this the estimated amount available was only $37\frac{1}{2}$ lakhs of rupees among others included 25 lakhs due from the Nawab as the fullfilment of his debt.

Though Mir Jaffar was charged by Holwell (officiating Governor from February to July 1760) for harbouring anti-English activities, of intriguing with the Dutch or of working in collusion with Shahzada Ali Gauhar (later Shah Alam II) the Nawab's main 'crime' was his 'poverty, which was extreme.' As late as August 1760, Governor Vansittart suggested to Colonel Caillaud that he would continue to support Mir Jaffar's administration if the Nawab could be brought round to the cession of Burdwan and Nadia to the Company expected to yield an annual income of Rs. 50 lakhs per annum. Mir Jaffar failed to see the writing on the wall.

Treaty with Mir Kasim, September 1760. The situation seemed ripe to Mir Kasim, son-in-law of Mir Jaffar, and he did not let go the opportunity. A person of consummate political skill he pushed forward his claim for Nawabship by strong professions of attachment to the English cause. Above all, Mir Kasim promised to take measures immediately to relieve the financial distress of the Company. On 27 September 1760, a treaty was signed between Mir Kasim and the Calcutta Council which provided:

(i) For all charges of the Company and its army and provisions for the field etc., Mir Kasim agreed to cede to the Company the districts of Burdwan, Midnapur and Chittagong;

(ii) The Company would get half the share in the *chunam* trade of Sylhet;

(*iii*) Mir Kasim promised to pay a sum of rupees five lakhs towards financing the Company's war efforts in Southern India;

(*iv*) **It was agreed that Mir Kasim's enemies** *were the Company's enemies* **and his friends the Company's friends; and**

(*v*) The Company promised not to allow the tenants of the Nawab's territory to settle in the lands of the Company and *vice versa*.

Thus the Company was saddled with the responsibility of assisting the new Nawab with its army and was not expected to interfere in the general administration of the Nawab.

To give effect to the Treaty, Vansittart and Caillaud proceeded to Murshidabad on 14 October 1760. Finding his palace surrounded by the Company's army, Mir Jaffar decided to resign in favour of Mir Kasim. Mir Jaffar preferred to reside at Calcutta on a pension of Rs. 1,500 p.m. grudgingly sanctioned by the new Nawab Mir Kasim. Thus Mir Jaffar was paid back in his own coin. He had betrayed Siraj-ud-daula in 1757, he was betrayed by Mir Kasim in 1760.

On becoming the Nawab of Bengal Mir Kasim heavily bribed the 'king-makers'. Mr. Vansittart received Rs. 500,000, Mr. Holwell Rs. 270,000, Mr. McGuire Rs. 180,000 and 5,000 gold mohurs, Mr. Summer Rs. 240,000, Mr. Smith Rs. 134,000, Major Yorke Rs. 134,000 and Colonel Caillaud Rs. 2000,000 among others all totalling Rs. 29 lakhs. Thus in the process of solving the Company's financial difficulties the members of the Calcutta Council enriched themselves.

Mir Kasim as an Administrator. Mir Kasim was the ablest Nawab among the successors of Ali Vardi Khan. Already he had given a proof of his administrative ability as the *faujdar* of Rangpur and Purniah. He transferred his capital from Murshidabad to Monghyr. Probably he wanted to start at the new capital with a clean slate, away from the atmosphere and intrigues of Murshidabad. The Nawab also wanted to be at a safe distance from Calcutta so that he might be less under the supervision and interference of the Company.

Mir Kasim also sought to recognise and modernise his army on the European pattern. Arrangements were made for the manufacture of fire-locks and guns at Monghyr. The Nawab had to safeguard himself against Shahzada Ali Gauhar who was still in Bihar and was a constant source of danger to the position of Mir Kasim. Moreover, Mir Kasim had plans for the expansion of his territory northward at the expense of the Nepalese.

Mir Kasim also sought to suppress the refractory zamindars of Bengal and Bihar who had on several occasions defied the authority of the old Nawab. These anti-state rebellions might become the focal points for malcontents in the state. Ramnarayan, the Deputy Subahdar of Bihar, was banking on English support for defince of the Nawab's authority. Ramnarayan had never accepted Mir Jaffar's accession to power and it was only Clive's intervention that had saved him from Mir Jaffar's anger. Encouraged by the English, Ramnarayan arrogated to himself the position of an independent ruler. His loyalty to Mir Kasim also was suspect. In spite of repeated reminders from the Nawab, Ramnarayan did not submit the accounts of the revenues of Bihar. Mir Kasim could not tolerate the open defiance of his authority. Fortified with the support of Governor Vansittart, Mir Kasim suspended Ramnarayan and later dismissed him and put him to death.

Mir Kasim also turned his attention towards the improvement of the finance of the state. Old officers who had misappropriated funds were heavily fined. Some new cesses were levied. An additional tax of $1\frac{1}{2}$ annas or 3/32 part of the original crown rents was imposed. He also collected *Khajiri-jama*, which had hitherto been concealed. The author of *Siyar-ul-Mutakherin* has paid rich tribute to Mir Kasim for his administrative achievements. He writes, "In unravelling the intricacies of affairs of government and especially the knotty mysteries of finance; in examining and determining private differences; in establishing regular payment for his troops and for his household; in honouring and rewarding men of merit and men of learning; in conducting his expenditure exactly between the extremities of parsimony and prodigality; and in knowing intuitively where he must spend freely and where with moderation,—in all these qualifications, he was an incomparable man indeed and the most extraordinary prince of his age."

Mir Kasim and the East India Company. The Company had thought that they had found in Mir Kasim an ideal puppet. He seemed capable of improving the finances of the province and in a better position to meet the heavy demands of the Company. In fact, the Company looked for a capable yet timid ruler. Warren Hastings, who had supported the revolution of 1760 at Murshidabad wrote about Mir Kasim, the new ruler, as "a man of understanding, of an uncommon talent for business and great application and perseverance....... His timidity, the little inclination he had ever shown for war, with which he has been often reproached, would hardly have disqualified him for the Subahship, since it effectively secured us from any design that he might form against our Government, and disposed him the easier to bear the effects of that superiority which we possessed over him...... since a spirit superior to that of a worm when trodden upon could not have brooked the many daily affronts which he was exposed to from the instant of his advancement to the Subahship".

Mir Kasim, however, belied the expectations of the Company. He could not fit in the game of imperialism. Harry Verelst, Governor of Fort William in Bengal (1767–69) and author of the book entitled *A View of the Rise, Progress and Present State of the English Government in Bengal* analysed the causes of conflict between the Company and Mir Kasim under two headings—'immediate' causes and the 'real' causes. According to Verelst while the immediate cause was the inland trade but the real cause was the Nawab's political ambition. "It was impossible that Meer Cossim should rest the foundation of his government upon our support. Self-defence taught him to look for independence". Following Verelst's analysis, Prof. H. H. Dodwell and Dr. Nand Lal Chatterji have drawn a distinction between the political ambition of the Nawab and the problem of inland trade. Prof. Dodwell writes, "The dominating fact of the situation was that the interests of the English and the Nawab were irreconcilable. There could be no stability in affairs so long as the Nawab fancied himself an independent governor and the English claimed privileges wholly inconsistent with that independence". Dr. Chatterji writes, "The dispute in regard to the duties on private inland trade was neither the sole, nor even a principal cause of his war with the English. He had wider and more ambitious designs, when he finally determined to go to war" and further, "There is no doubt that the Nawab had, from the beginning, aimed at establishing his complete independence of the English, and he patiently strove to break the supremacy which they had obtained after the revolution of 1757. His object was to establish an independent and unfettered 'Subahdari' in Bengal by reducing the extraordinary power and influence of the European traders".

A closer examination of the available evidence, however, suggests that Mir Kasim was not working for political independence. Nowhere do we find him seeking to get back the three assigned districts or to question the Company's monopoly in saltpetre trade or their share in the *chunam* trade of Sylhet. He did not seek independence but only sought to limit the fast-expanding encroachments of the English on his jurisdiction. He merely sought the observance of the treaties in letter and spirit. The abuses of inland trade, which were multiplying year after year, not only decimated the financial resources of Mir Kasim but more and more circumscribed his political authority. The methods of the English traders and their *gomastahs* were a growing menace to his political authority. These English agents and their *gomastahs* not only injured the people but would bind and punish the Nawab's officers. Macaulay wrote, "Every servant of a British factory was armed with all the power of his master, and his master was armed with all the power of the Company". The Company's agents would often hold a court under a tree and award punishments to natives that suited their fancy. What Mir Kasim really wanted was restoration of the jurisdiction of his courts over the *gomastahs* in cases of dispute. The English knew well that their illegitimate trade involved coercion of the natives, and the *gomastahs* were the instruments of that coercion. To subject the *gomastahs* to the jurisdiction of country courts was bound to weaken the foundation of their illegitimate trade. Thus, it was not Mir Kasim's desire for independence which generated the crisis but the efforts of the English to overstep their political and legal rights that drove Mir Kasim to the point of desperation.

Mir Kasim's clash with the Company came over the regulation of inland duties. Vansittart defined inland trade as "the trade from place to place in the country, in the articles of the produce of the country". The right of the Company—granted to it by Farrukhsiyar's firman of 1717—to carry on their export and import trade free of any custom duties was never in question. What the Nawab objected to was the misuse of the Company's *dastak* (a Pass-Chit or permit signed by the President of Calcutta Council which exempted the goods specified from payment of duties) by which the Company's servants indulged in inland private trade without payment of any duties. Nay, even more. The Company's servants sold the Company's dastak to Indian merchants for a commission. Besides, the arrogance of power led the Company's servants to flout the authority of the Nawab, disgrace his officials and plunder the people. Mr. Ellis, a hot-headed agent of the Company at Patna, ordered the arrest of an Armenian merchant who had purchased a small quantity of saltpetre (for which the Company enjoyed monopoly rights) for the use of the Nawab. On another occasion Mr. Ellis sent two Company's soldiers to search the Monghyr fort in search of two deserters from the Company's army.

The Company's servants were not content with carrying on trade free of inland duties. The duty-free trade simply meant buying cheap in an otherwise competitive market. The Company's servants used coercive methods to get things at cheaper rates. Mir Kasim pleaded with the Governor of the Company for justice and reason. He wrote to the Governor in May 1762:

> "And this is the way your gentlemen behave; they make a disturbance all over my country, plunder the people, injure and disgrace my servants... In every Pergunnah, every village and every factory, they buy and sell salt, betel nut, ghee, rice, straw, bamboos, fish, gunnies, ginger, sugar, tobacco, opium and many other things, and many more things I can write and which I think it is needless to mention. They forcibly take away the goods and commodities of the peasants, merchants etc. for a fourth part of their value, and by way of violence and oppression they oblige the peasants to give five rupees for goods which are worth but one rupee; and for the sake of five rupees they bind and disgrace a man who pays a hundred rupees in land-tax, and they allow not any authority to my servants... The officers of every district have desisted from the exercise of their functions and by being deprived of any duties I suffer a yearly loss of nearly twenty-five lakhs of rupees..."

Abuses of inland trade had greatly decimated the Nawab's revenue and made the position of his Indian subjects helpless. All negotiations for a peaceful settlement proved unavailing because of the rigid stand taken by the Company's authorities. Governor Vansittart and Warren Hastings, another member of the Council, met the Nawab at Monghyr and concluded a compromise agreement with him. The Nawab admitted the English traders to a share in the inland trade provided they paid 9% duty on the prime cost of commodities. It was also agreed that the Nawab alone would be competent to grant the legal *dastak*. What was more important, the Nawab's ultimate authority in the settlement of disputes about the trade was accepted. Unfortunately, the majority at the Calcutta Council repudiated the agreement. "The narrow-sighted selfishness of commercial cupidity", comments H. H. Wilson, "had rendered all Members of the Council, with the two honourable exceptions of the Vansittart and Hastings, obstinately inaccessible to the plainest distates of reason, justice and policy". In fact, the members of the Calcutta Council, most of whom participated in inland trade, welcomed a clash with Mir Kasim and his deposition more so because that would provide them with an opportunity to receive large presents from the new incumbent.

Mir Kasim took the drastic step to abolish all inland duties, thus placing the Indian merchants on the same footing as the English. The Nawab was perfectly justified in this move. Vansittart and Warren Hastings believed, "The Nawab has granted a boon to his subjects and there are no grounds for demanding that a sovereign prince should withdraw such a boon or for threatening him with war in the event of refusal". The majority of the members of the Governor's Council wanted to compel the Nawab to tax his subjects, for in that case alone the English merchants could misuse the *dastak* to their advantage. Thus, the Calcutta Council wanted to deny to Mir Kasim the right to rule his people with justice and economy. Mr. Ellis, the Chief at Patna, provoked hostilities by an attack on the Patna town.

H. H. Dodwell rightly points out that the war between the Nawab and the Company was "a war of circumstances rather than intentions". While the Nawab wanted to rule in his own right the English demanded extrordinary privileges which were wholly inconsistent and irreconcilable with the Nawab's independence. In fact, the Nawab was fighting against the march of events and against a force far stronger than himself. The question at issue was not of moral rights but of superior might. Mir Kasim's fault was that he incorrectly judged the political situation.

Mir Kasim was more sinned against than sinning. He had betrayed Mir Jaffar, his father-in-law, in the lure for Nawabship. However, his sins recoiled on him. The superior authority of the English always stood like a Damocles' sword over his head. The continuous English interference made his Nawabship ineffective and ridiculed his position in the eyes of his countrymen. Mir Kasim realised that he had been entangled in a trap. He became desperate and challenged the Company but was defeated. Mir Kasim had to atone for his sins not only by losing his Nawabship but spent the rest of his life in abject misery as a homeless wanderer (died, 7 June 1777).

The Battle of Buxar (1764) and its Importance. The war between Mir Kasim and the Company broke out in 1763. In the series of encounters that followed, Mir Kasim was worsted. He escaped to Oudh and organised a confederacy with the Nawab of Oudh and the Emperor in a final bid to oust the English from Bengal. The combined armies of the three powers numbering between 40,000 to 60.000 met an English army of 7,072 troops commanded by Major Munro at the battlefield of Buxar on 22 October 1764. Casualties on both sides were heavy. The English won the day.

The battle of Buxar was a closely contested battle in which the losses of the English numbered 847 killed and wounded while on the side of the Indian powers more than 2,000 officers and soldiers were killed. If the victory of Plassey was the result of British conspiracy and diplomacy, the same can hardly be said of Buxar. Mir Kasim had made adequate preparations for the conflict and the Nawab of Oudh had mustered his best soldiers in the field. Evidently it was a victory of superior military power.

Buxar confirmed the decisions of Plassey. Now English power in Northern India became unchallengeable. The new Nawab of Bengal was their stooge, the Nawab of Oudh a grateful subordinate ally, the Emperor their pensioner. The whole territory up to Allahabad lay at their feet and the road to Delhi open. Never after Buxar did the nawabs of Bengal or Oudh ever challenge the superior position of the Company; rather the years following witnessed the tightening of English grip over these regions.

If the battle of Plassey had made the English a powerful factor in the politics of Bengal, the victory of Buxar made them a great power of Northern India and contenders for the supremacy of the whole country. The English now faced the Afghans and the Marathas as serious rivals in the final struggle for the Empire of Hindustan. If Plassey had imposed the European yoke on Bengal, the victory of Buxar riveted the shackles of bondage.

The battle of Buxar proved to be a decisive struggle with far reaching political consequences in the destiny of India.

Select Opinions on the battle of Plassey

G. B. malleson. There never was a battle in which the consequences were so vast, so immediate and so permanent. From the very morrow of the victory the English became virtual masters of Bengal, Bihar and Orissa. During the century which followed, but one (no) serious attempt was made to cast off the yoke virtually imposed by Plassey, whilst from the base it gave them, a base resting on the sea and with proper care, unassailable, they were able to extend their authority beyond the Indus—their influence amongst people of whose existence even Europe was at that time profoundly ignorant. It was Plassey which made England the greatest Muhammadan power in the world; Plassey which forced her to become one of the main factors in the settlement of the burning Eastern question; Plassey which necessitated the conquest and colonisation of the Cape of Good Hope, of the Mauritius, the protectorship over Egypt; Plassey which gave to the sons of her middle classes the finest field for the development of their talent and industry the world has ever known to her aristocracy unrivalled opportunities for the display of administrative power; to her merchants and manufacturers customers whose enormous demands almost compensate for the hostile tariffs of her rivals, and alas! even of her colonies; to the skilled artisan remunerative employment; to her people generally a noble feeling of pride in the greatness and glory of the empire of which a little island in the Atlantic is the parent stem, Hindustan the Noblest branch; it was Plassey which, in its consquences, brought consolation to the little island for the loss of America. (*The Decisive Battles of India*, pp. 67–68)

P. E. Roberts. A comparison of the position in 1756 with that in 1760 reveals beyond all possibility of cavil the magnitude of his achievement. In 1756 the British in Bengal, though the most prosperous European community in that province of the Empire, were regarded merely as a body of merchants with one rich settlement, a few territorial rights in the villages round Calcutta, and some upcountry agencies or factories at Cossimbazar, Dacca, Balasore, Jagdea and Patna... By 1760 the position was entirely altered. The British were supreme in Bengal. The French and Dutch were impoverished and reduced; their military and political power was gone. The titular Nawab of the province was little more than the creature and protege of the Company. British influence extended outwards from Calcutta through Bengal and Bihar to the southern boundary of Oudh. The possession of this rich country also completely altered the English position in Madras. (*History of British India*, p. 142)

N. K. Sinha. The Bengal Revolution of 1757 repeated some of the attitudes of the Revolution of 1740. It has been said that the battle of Plassey was the reply of divine justice to the battle of Giria which in secular terms might mean beginning of a succession of evils. A band of foreign adventurers—Persian, Central Asian and Afghan soldiers of fortune—thronged the Court at Murshidabad. They formed the main strength of the Nawabs... The conspiracy of 1757 resembled that of 1739–40. But circumstances in 1757 were so very different from those in 1740. Alivardy could ultimately get rid of the Afghan mercenaries. The conspirators at Plassey depended very much upon the aid of a foreign power. This proved to be their undoing. (*The History of Bengal*, pp. 5–6)

Select Opinions on the Battle of Buxar

G. B. Malleson. Whether regarded as a duel between the foreigner and the native, or as an event pregnant with vast permanent consequences, Buxar takes rank amongst the most decisive battles ever fought. Not only did the victory of the English save Bengal, not only did it advance the British frontier to Allahabad, but it bound the rulers of Awadh to the conqueror by ties of admiration, of gratitude, of absolute reliance and trust, ties which made them for the ninety-four years that followed the friends of his friends and the enemies of his enemies. (*The Decisive Battles of india*, p. 208)

Alfred Lyall. The eventual and secondary consequences of the battle of Buxar were very important. The success of the English brought the emperor into their camp, intimidated the Vizier, carried the armed forces of the Company across the Ganges to Benares and Allahabad, and acquired for them a new, advanced and commanding position in relation to the principalities north-west of Bengal, with whom they now found themselves for the first time in contact. By this war the English were drawn into connexion with upper India, and were brought out upon a scene of fresh operations that grew rapidly wider. (*The Rise and Expansion of British Dominion in India*, pp. 147–48)

SELECT REFERENCES

1. Chatterjee, N. L. : *Mir Qasim*
2. Dodwell, H. H. (Ed.) : *Cambridge History of India*, vol. v.
3. Lyall, Alfred : *Rise and Expansion of the British Dominion in India.*
4. Malleson; G. B. : *The Decisive Battles of India.*
5. Roberts, P. E. : *History of British India.*
6. Thompson and Garrett : *Rise and Fulfilment of British Rule in India.*
7. Muir, Ramsay : *Making of British India.*
8. Sharma, S. R. : *Making of Modern India.*

6

CAREER AND ACHIEVEMENTS OF DUPLEIX

Joseph Francis Dupleix was born in 1697. He was the son of a wealthy Farmer-General of Taxes and Director-General of the Company of the Indies. His father's influence worked in getting Dupleix a high post at Pondicherry in 1720. Here Dupleix made a great fortune by indulging in private trade then permitted to servants of the French Company in India. A drastic change in the constitution and personnel of the French Company at home caused great frictions and misunderstandings at Pondicherry about the activities of Dupleix and the Directors suspended him from service in December 1726. Dupleix remained in India and appealed to the Home Authorities, who reconsidered the entire case and to compensate Dupleix for the injustice he had suffered, appointed him Governor of Chandernagore in 1730. In 1741 Dupleix was named as the Director General of French Colonies in India in succession to Dumas, a position which he held till 1754. The same year the Mughal Emperor conferred on Dupleix the title of Nawab, and honour which greatly increased the prestige of Dupleix among the Indian princes. In 1750 Muzzaffar Jang, the Subahdar of Deccan invested Dupleix with the title of Nawab of all the territories between the river Krishna and Cape Comorin including Carnatic.

Dupleix was a great administrator, a skilful diplomat, a born leader of men and, above all, combined keen political insight with a broad vision.

As an Administrator. As the Governor of Chandernagore Dupleix gave ample proof of his qualities as an administrator. He understood the power of trade. He invested his personal fortune in trade, advanced loans to his compatriots, induced Indian merchants to settle in Chandernagore and opened trade communications with provinces in the interior of India. Further, he opened trade negotiations with countries in the Persian Gulf, with China and even Tibet. Soon the decaying and lifeless colony of Chandernagore was humming with activity. Its population multiplied and economic prosperity was marked. Chandernagore became the most flourishing European settlement in Bengal.

Dupleix's unusual successes at Chandernagore attracted the notice of the Directors at home who nominated him as Governor-General of Pondicherry in succession to Dumas in 1741. Now Dupleix's genius could find full play. Dupleix found Pondicherry suffering from the after-effects of the Maratha invasion; land there had not been cultivated while famine had decimated the population; rival candidates for the nawabship of Carnatic had created chaotic conditions in the Carnatic; there were strong rumours of an impending Anglo-French conflict while the fortifications of Pondicherry were in a hopeless condition. Above all, the Directors at home, very much alive to the importance of French colonies in North America, had in a despatch of 18 September 1743 pressed upon him the necessity of drastic economies in expenditure and ordered suspension of all outlay on account of buildings and fortifications. Dupleix rose equal to the occasion. He reduced public expenditure in teeth of opposition of his Council and balanced income and expenditure. He put a cut on salaries and suppressed corruption among the subordinate officers. However, that part of the Directors' communication which had ordered suspension of all expenditure on fortifications, Dupleix decided to disobey. The man on the spot, Dupleix alone knew that to abandon the plans of fortification was to court ruin. He strengthened the defences of Pondicherry, spending a large amount from his personal funds. He also took all practicable steps to develop the trade of the colony and made it the emporium of commerce of Southern India.

Dupleix's defiance of the orders of the Directors earned him not censure but praise. His self-reliant measures so greatly improved the situation that the Directors wrote to him in the despatch of 3 November 1746 : "The promptitude with which the town of Pondicherry has been enclosed on the side facing the sea has given us real pleasure. We are under a great obligation to you on that account...

We have seen with not the less satisfaction all the measures you have taken, both to provide, notwithstanding your poverty, cargoes for the ships, the sailing of which we had announced to you".[1] The impact of the master's touch was felt in all spheres of administration.

As a Diplomat. The account of the first two Carnatic wars is replete with the skill of Dupleix as a diplomat. Dupleix excelled all his contemporaries in the game of politics. With an uncommon insight into the political situation of the Deccan, he visualised and sought to devise the methods by which ultimately the European conquest of India was to be carried out. The events of the first Carnatic war indicate how Dupleix used the political situation in the Carnatic to his advantage. At the outbreak of the war, Dupleix feared a blockade of Pondicherry by the English Commander Barnett, who had been specially sent by the English Ministry to the Coromandel Coast. As a defensive measure, Dupleix at once appealed to the Nawab of Carnatic to forbid the English into waging war in his territories. The Nawab saw a clear logic in his request and informed the English Governor Morse that he would not permit the English to attack the French settlements. It was a diplomatic victory for Dupleix. When Dupleix supported by the naval squadron led by La Bourdonnais decided to besiege Madras, he in turn informed the Nawab that he would hand over Madras to him after its reduction. After the capture of Madras Dupleix hesitated surrender of the town on the plea that the fortifications must first be demolished. The Nawab, however, grew impatient and threatened action against the French but was defeated at St. Thomé (1746). The victory of St. Thomé gave to Dupleix an approximation of his strength and the general supremacy of disciplined European troops over Indian forces, a realisation from which Dupleix fully profited. Again, when Dupleix learnt that the Admiral La Bourdonnais had decided to ransom Madras to the English, he implored him against that course of action in a language that establishes him a diplomat *par excellence*. After citing examples from history that promises made under certain circumstances had never been considered binding, he added, "In the name of God, in the name of your children, of your wife, I conjure you to be persuaded of what I tell you. Finish as you have begun, and do not treat with an enemy who has no object but to reduce us to the most dire extremity... Let us then profit by our opportunity, for the glory of our monarch and for the general interests of a nation which will regard you as its restorer". The Home Authorities had also given their ruling that the position of the Governor-General was superior to that of La Bourdonnais, the Commander of the Navy. As such Dupleix was perfectly justified in not recognising the compact entered into between La Bourdonnais and the English hostages, for it was contrary to his directions and therefore *ultra vires*.

The events of the first Carnatic War had greatly raised the prestige of Dupleix and established him as a shrewd diplomat, conclusions which the course of the second Carnatic war amply confirmed. Dupleix's main purpose was enhancement of political influence. It was he who indicated by his example how Europeans could profit by espousing the claims of rival claimants. Taking advantage of disputed succession both at Hyderabad and Carnatic (1748) Dupleix decided to support the cause of Muzzaffar Jang for Hyderabad and Chanda Sahib for Carnatic and secured many great concessions from both. His candidates emerged successful. In 1751 Dupleix's power reached its zenith. After Muzzaffar Jang's death the new Subahdar Salabat Jang owed his position to the French, and was virtually their nominee. In fact, the entire country between the Vindhyas and the Krishna came under the control of the French General Bussy. A French army was permanently stationed at Hyderabad at the expense of the Subahdar. South of the river Krishna, Dupleix was personally proclaimed the Nawab of Carnatic, a title conferred by the Subahdar of the Deccan and confirmed by the Mughal Emperor.

One may be intrigued at the fact that with all his skill in diplomacy, Dupleix's plans ended in smoke. The chief flaw in the machine was that Dupleix himself was not a man of action. He was not a soldier. He could plan a campaign, could direct his lieutenants what to do but could not lead an army

---

[1]. Quoted by Malleson in *Rulers of India series* : *Dupleix*, p. 42.

in the battlefield. In this sphere Dupleix was inferior to Lawrence or Clive or Dalton. The repeated attempts to capture Trichnopoly (during 1752–1753) failed because Dupleix's commanders like Monsieur Law and Maniville failed to translate his schemes into action.

As a Leader. Dupleix was a born leader of men. By his commanding personality be inspired confidence in his subordinates who put faith in his superior judgement. When orders came for the recall of Dupleix, many senior officers decided to tender their resignations in protest. When Bussy decided to resign his service and retire to France, Dupleix exhorted him to stay at the post of duty. Pussy wrote in reply, "Your departure to Europe is a thunderbolt which has confounded and alarmed me. You, who are leaving export me to continue to serve the nation and to support a work which as on the brink of destruction. Do you sincerely believe I shall not be enveloped in the same disgrace as yourself ? The blow is perhaps deferred, or suspended only to be struck with greater force. But however that may be, I have ever considered it my duty to defer to your counsels and to follow your reasoning".

Recall of Dupleix. Modern British historians hold the view that the English had no hand in the recall of Dupleix in 1754. However Dodwell supports the view of Colonel Malleson that the English ambassador at Paris was instructed to inform the Foreign Minister of France that the policy of Dupleix was injurious to the trading interests of both the Companies. The failure of Dupleix's plans to capture Trichnopoly drove the French Directors to the same conclusion. Dupleix was made the scapegoat for all French failures and held responsible for the prolonged war between the two nations in India. One, however, wonders how the English Governor Saunders was anyway less responsible for the war. The propaganda of the English viewpoint that the continuance of Dupleix in office was the main obstacle in the relations between the two Companies at last carried conviction with the French Directors and they recalled Dupleix.

Whatever the reasons and circumstances for the recall of Dupleix, it cannot be denied that his recall proved ruinous for the cause of the French in India. Writes Malleson, "We cannot but marvel at the blindness, the infatuation, the madness that recalled Dupleix".[2] The replacement of Dupleix by Godeheu did not mean a complete reversal of his policy, but his successor was hardly a worthy custodian of French interests against mounting odds. At time when Dupleix had detached from the English side all their allies, *i.e.*, the Marathas, the Raja of Tanjore and even the ruler of Mysore, orders came from home for his recall. Whether Dupleix could have utilised his diplomatic genius to full advantage remains a big "if" of history. Malleson certainly overstates the case when he says that "if Dupleix had been able to continue in India for another two years, the rich heritage of Bengal would have fallen to France instead of his rivals".[3]

Political Ideas of Dupleix. There is divergence of opinion among historians as to the exact nature of the political ideas of Dupleix. Some scholars led by Major Malleson and Henri Martin believe that Dupleix was a pioneer among Empire builders and credit him with a well thought-out plan for the conquest of India, which failed because the French Government did not give him full support and let him down. Major Malleson gives credit to Dupleix of having been "the first to grasp the necessity of establishing European predominance in Hindustan... to show practically how that predominance could be established and maintained".[4] Martin in his book *Histoire de France* writes that "Dupleix had seen Asia, like America and the whole world, destined to submit to the law of the European races... Dupleix was determined to give India to France... His plan was as much prudent in respect of means as audacious in respect of the final objective".[5] On the other hand, Alfred Martineau, another biographer of Dupleix, believes that Dupleix had no plans for empire building in Asia until 1749 or perhaps before

---

2. Col. Malleson : *History of the French in India*, p. 416.
3. *Ibid*, p. 416.
4. *Ibid*, p. 414.
5. Martin : *Historie de France*, vol. xv, p. 308.

1750. It were the unexpected successes of 1750 that opened a new vista of political ambition before him and his political ideas took a definite shape. According to Martineau the chief motive that led Dupleix formulate the plan for a French colonial empire in India was financial necessity. He writes, "Constantly embarrassed in his trading operations by the delay or insufficiency of funds coming from France, he came slowly to the idea that the only means to get rid of such embarrassments was to find money in India, without waiting for funds from Europe and without having to seek the assistance of bankers. That made it necessary to have fixed territorial revenue, the collection of which could be assured only by the exercise of a political power. This was first conceived and later developed in the mind of Dupleix the idea of creating for our advantage a sort of colonial empire in India".[6] Prof. Dodwell and P. E. Roberts find much truth in this viewpoint. Martineau believes that the wrong judgement and blind obstinacy of Dupleix were mainly responsible for his fall. Prof. Dodwell maintains that Dupleix had dissipated his resources and flung his nets too wide and therefore his policy lacked the elements of permanent success. He did not keep the French Government fully informed of his political plans, while the resources of the French Company in India were inadequate. "Like the Deccan," writes Dodwell, "Carnatic was too poor. It was ruinous to dispute it against another European power. His schemes and policy demanded a wealthier province than either Carnatic or the Deccan for their realisation."[7] Above all, the superior naval power of England proved a deciding factor.

Place in History. Dupleix stands as a very striking figure in Indian history. His claims to greatness and honour cannot be denied. P. E. Roberts writes, "Dupleix raised the prestige of France in the East for some years to an amazing height; he won a reputation among Indian princes and leaders that has never been surpassed and he aroused a dread in his English contemporaries which is at once a tribute to his personal power, a testimony to his sagacity".[8] Above all, Dupleix deserves to be remembered in Anglo-Indian history for he was the first who worked at methods which proved a guide to the English in the conquest of India. It was Dupleix who first made extensive use of disciplined troops, who first discovered the illusions of Mughal military greatness, who first thought of the plan of permanently stationing European troops at native courts at Indian expense, who first dabbled in Indian politics to European advantage and first, above all, who built the rudiment of a European Empire in India. G. B. Malleson writes, "The effect of his schemes survived him. The ground he had so well watered and fertilised, the capabilities of which he had proved, was almost immediately after his departure occupied by his rivals with immense results".[9]

Given the resources of an affluent Company like the English East India Company and the backing of a progressive nation like the English nation Dupleix would certainly have done better than any of his contemporaries in India. The drive, the resourcefulness and political imagination displayed by Dupleix might have been equalled but never surpassed in the annals of Western colonisation of the East.

Select Opinions

Lord Macaulay. The man who first saw that it was possible to found an European empire on the ruins of the Mogul monarchy was Dupleix... He clearly saw that the greatest force which the princes of India could bring into the field would be no match for a small body of men trained in the discipline, and guided by the tactics of the West. He also saw that the natives of India might, under European commanders, be formed into armies, such as Saxe or Fredric would be proud to command. He was perfectly aware that the most easy and convenient way in which an European adventurer could exercise sovereignty in India, was to govern the motions, and to speak through the mouth of some glittering puppets dignified by the title of Nawab or Nizam. The arts both of war and policy,

---

6. Martineau : *Dupleix et l' Inde Francaise*, vol. i, p. vi.
7. H.H. Dodwell : *Cambridge Shorter History of India* (Indian edition), p. 425.
8. P.E. Roberts : *History of British India* (1938), p. 119.
9. G.B. Malleson : *Dupleix* (1889), p. 161.

which a few years later were employed with such signal success by the English, were first understood and practised by this ingenious and aspiring Frenchman. (*Historical Essays*, pp. 310–11).

M. Xavier Raymond. England has been much admired and often cited for having resolved the great problem of how to govern, at a distance of 4000 leagues, with some hundreds of civil functionaries and some thousands of soldiers, her immense possessions in India. If there is much that is wonderful, much that is bold and daring, much political genius in the idea, it must be admitted that the honour of having inaugurated it belongs to Dupleix, and that England, which in the present day reaps from it the profit and the glory, has had but to follow the path which the Genius of France opened out to her. (*L' Univers Pittoresque,* vol. ii, *L'Inde*).

G. B. Malleson. There was a market resemblance in features and in genius between Napoleon and Dupleix. Each was animated by unbounded ambition, each played for a great stake; each displayed in their final struggles, a power, a vitality, a richness of resource and genius such as compelled fear and admiration... Their names still remain, and will ever remain to posterity as examples of the enormous value, in a struggle with adversity, of a dominant mind and directed by a resolute will. (*Dupleix*. p. 159).

Alfred Lyall. We may regard Dupleix as the most striking figure in the short Indian episode of that long and arduous contest for transmarine dominion which was fought out between France and England in the eighteenth century, although it was far beyond his power to influence the ultimate destiny of either nation in India, and although the result of his plans was that 'we accomplished for ourselves against the French exactly everything that the French intended to accomplish for themselves against us' (Clive). It is certain, moreover, that the conception of an Indian Empire had already been formed by others besides Dupleix, and that more than one clearheaded observer had perceived how easily the whole country might be subdued by an European power. (*The Rise and Expansion of British Dominion in India*, pp. 101–02).

SELECT REFERENCES

1. Dodwell, H. H. : *Dupleix and Clive.*
2. Dodwell, H. H. (Ed.). : *Cambridge History of India,* vol. v.
3. Malleson, G. B. : *Dupleix* (*Rulers of India series*).
4. Malleson, G. B. : *History, of the French in India.*
5. Sen, S. P. : *The French in India.*

CLIVE'S[1] SECOND GOVERNORSHIP OF BENGAL
(May 1765 to February 1767)

Clive ranks as the Conquistador of British India, rather than a major-Anglo-Indian Statesman.
–P. Spear

When the news of the victory of Buxar reached England, the general opinion in London was that the man who had laid the foundations of the Company's political power in Bengal should be sent again to consolidate it. Thus Clive was sent out to India as Governor and Commander-in-Chief of the British possessions in Bengal.

On reaching Calcutta Clive found that the whole political system of Northern India was in a melting pot. The administration of Bengal was in utter disorder. The lust for riches with all the attendant civils had debased the character of the Company's servants adversely affected the trade of the Company and resulted in the oppression of the people.

Political Settlements

Settlement with Oudh. Clive's first and foremost task was to settle and define relations with the defeated powers. He proceeded to Oudh and met Shuja-ud-Daula, the Nawab Wazir of Oudh, at Allahabad and concluded with him the Treaty of Allahabad (16 August 1765). By this treaty Shuja-ud-Daula was confirmed in his possessions on the following conditions:—

(*i*)   That the Nawab surrenders Allahabad and Kora to Emperor Shah Alam;

(*ii*) That he agrees to pay Rs. 50 lakhs to Company as war indemnity;

(*iii*) That he confirms Balwant Singh, zamindar of Benaras, in full possession of his estate.

Further, the Nawab entered into an offensive and defensive treaty with the Company binding him to render gratuitous military help to the Company in time of need and the Company to help the Nawab with troops for the defence of his frontier on the latter agreeing to pay the cost of its maintenance.

Settlement with Shah Alam II. By the second Treaty of Allahabad (August 1765) the fugitive Emperor Shah Alam was taken under the Company's protection and was to reside at Allahabad. He was assigned Allahabad and Kora ceded by the Nawab of Oudh. The Emperor in turn issued a *firman* dated 12 August 1765 granting to the Company in perpetuity the Diwani of Bengal, Bihar and Orissa in return for the Company making an annual payment of Rs. 26 lakhs to him and providing for the expenses of the *Nizamat* of the said provinces which was fixed at Rs. 53 lakhs.

Clive's political settlements showed considerable understanding of the realities of the situation. He did not annex Oudh for it would have placed the Company under an obligation to protect an extensive land frontier open to attacks from two strong powers of the time—the Afghans under Ahmad Shah Abdali and the Marathas. The friendly treaty with Oudh made the Nawab a firm friend of the Company and created Oudh into a buffer state. Thus Shuja-ud-Daula was turned into a grateful ally bound to the Company by ties of self-interest. Clive's settlement with Shah Alam also showed considerable practical wisdom. He ruled out the march to Delhi as 'a vain and fruitless project'. He

---

1. Robert Clive born, 1725; enters Company's service as writer, 1742; Captain in the army, 1751; Governor of Bengal, 1757–60; leaves for England February 1760; second term as Governor of Bengal, 1765–67; died 1774.

made the Emperor a pensioner and thereby a useful 'rubber stamp' of the Company. The Emperor's *firman* legalised the political gains of the Company in Bengal.

Settlement of Bengal—the Dual System. Clive's solution of the political tangle of Bengal was the setting up of the infamous Dual System whereby the Company acquired real power while the responsibility for administration rested on the shoulders of the Nawab of Bengal.

In the hey days of the Mughal Empire the two principal officers of the Central government in a province were the Subahdar and the Diwan. The Subahdar looked after the *Nizamat* functions, *i.e.*, military defence, police and administration of criminal justice, while the Diwan was the chief financial officer and in charge of revenue affairs, besides being responsible for the administration of civil justice in the province. The two officers served as a check on each other and were directly responsible to the Central government. After the death of Aurangzeb the Mughal central authority weakened and Murshid Kuli Khan, the Nawab of Bengal, exercised both the *Nizamat* and *Diwani* functions.

The *firman* issued by Emperor Shah Alam an 12 August 1765 granted the Diwani functions to the Company in return for an annual payment of Rs. 26 lakhs to the Emperor and providing for the expenses of the *Nizamat* (fixed at Rs. 53 lakhs). Earlier in February 1765, Najm-ud-Daula was allowed to succeed as Nawab of Bengal (after the death of his father Mir Jaffar) on the condition that he practically surrendered the *Nizamat* functions, *i.e.*, the military defence and foreign affairs of the province entirely into the hands of the Company and the civil administration to the care of a Deputy Subahdar to be named by the Company and not removable without their consent. Thus, the Company acquired the *Diwani* functions from the Emperor and the *Nizamat* functions from the Subahdar of Bengal.

At this time the Company was neither willing nor able to undertake the direct collection of revenue. For the exercise of *Diwani* functions, the Company appointed two Deputy Diwans, Mohammad Reza Khan for Bengal and Raja Shitab Roy for Bihar. Mohammad Reza Khan also acted as Deputy Nazim. Thus the whole administration, Nizamat as well as Diwani, was exercised through Indian agency, though the actual power rested with the Company. This system of government came to be remembered as Dual System or Dyarchy, *i.e.*, rule of two, the Company and the Nawab. In actual practice the Dual System proved a sham, for the East India Company exercised all political power and used the Indian agency merely as an instrument for their purposes.

Clive's Justification of the Dual System. Clive was fully conscious of the fact that all power had passed into the hands of the Company and nothing was left to the Nawab except the name and shadow of authority. "This name", wrote Clive to the Select Committee. "this shadow, it is indispensably necessary we should seem to venerate". Clive gave his reasons for the new set up:

Firstly, open assumption of authority would have brought the Company in its true colours and might have achieved the miracle of uniting some Indian princes against the Company and thus embroil them in war;

Secondly, it was very doubtful whether the French, the Dutch or the Danes would readily acknowledge the Company's subahship and pay into the hands of their servants the duties on trade or the quit-rents of those districts which they had long possessed by virtue of Imperial *firmans* or grants from former Nawabs of Bengal;

Thirdly, open assumption of political power could create complications in England's diplomatic relations with France, Holland, Portugal or Sweden and might urge those powers to join in an anti-British front the like of which Europe saw later during 1778–80 (the American War of Independence);

Fourthly, the Company did not have at its disposal trained personnel to take over and run effectively the work of administration. Clive wrote to the Court of Directors that even "three times the present number of civil servants would be insufficient" for that purpose. The few servants of the Company that could be available for the task of administration were ignorant of Indian practices, languages and customs;

Fifthly, the Court of Directors were opposed to the acquisition of the territories for that might interfere with their trade and profits. The Directors were more interested in commerce and finance than territorial acquisitions; and

Lastly, Clive well understood that open assumption of political power of Bengal might move the British Parliament into interfering with the affairs of the Company.

Evil Effects of the Dual System. The scheme of government devised by Clive proved ineffective and unworkable and created anarchy and confusion in Bengal. It failed from the very moment of its inception.

(*a*) **Administrative breakdown.** Owing to the impotence of the *Nizamat*, the administration of law and order virtually broke down and the administration of justice was reduced to a farce. While the Nawab had no power to enforce law and provide justice, the Company on their part disavowed all responsibility for administration. In the countryside the dacoits roamed freely and the *Sannyasi* raiders reduced the government to a mockery. The whole administration from top to bottom was unscrupulous and corrupt. Blinded by their cupidity, the Governor and members of the Council could not choose honest Indians as their functionaries. The Indian servants of the Company followed the bad example of their masters. In this vitiated atmosphere, the people of Bengal suffered. Sir George Cornewall declared in the British House of Commons in 1858, "I do most confidently maintain that no civilised government ever existed on the face of this earth which was more corrupt, more perfidious and more rapacious than the government of the East India Company from 1765 to 1784".

(*b*) **Decline of Agriculture.** Bengal, once the granary of India was laid waste. The land revenue was annually farmed out to the highest bidder. The tax collectors or contractors had no permanent interest in the land and they rack rented the cultivators. The Bengali peasant suffered from the evils of over-assessment, harshness of collection and was subjected to the worst exactions by government officials. William Bolts, a servant of the Company, wrote that the peasants were "chastised by the officers of the revenue, and not unfrequently have by those harpies been necessitated to sell their children in order to pay their sents, or otherwise obliged to fly the country". Thus many cultivators ran away to jungles or joined the ranks of the robbers. In 1769 Richard Becher, a servant of the Company, wrote to the Directors, "It must give pain to an Englishman to have reason to think that since the accession of the Company to the *Diwani* the condition of the people of this country has been worse than it was before... this fine country which flourished under the most despotic and arbitrary government, is verging towards its ruin..." Then came the famine of 1770 which produced untold miseries and took a heavy tool of life. "The scene of misery that intervened" observed a servant of the Company in 1770, "and still continues, shocks humanity too much to bear description. Certain it is, that in several parts the living have been fed on the dead". During the famine land revenue was collected with severity and even extortion practised, while the servants of the Company added to the misery of the people by trading and profiteering in essential articles of foodstuff.

(*c*) **Disruption of Trade and Commerce.** Agricultural depression adversely affected the trade and commerce of the country. By the *firman* of 1717 issued by Emperor Farrukhsiyar the Company had been granted the privileges of trading duty-free in Bengal. This concession authorised the President of the Company at Calcutta to issue *dastaks* or pass chits exempting the goods mentioned in it from duty, stoppage or even inspection. If its legitimate use worked against the interests of the country, its misuse ruined the country merchants and traders. The Company's servants virtually monopolised the internal trade of Bengal and would undersell the Indian merchants in the local markets. Clive himself referred to these abuses in the course of a speech in the House of Commons when he said that the Company's merchants traded not only as merchants but as sovereigns and had "taken the bread out of the mouths of thousands and thousands of merchants, who used formerly to carry on the trade, and who are, now reduced to beggary".

(*d*) **Ruination of Industry and Skill.** The weaving industry of Bengal received a rude setback. The Company used political power to discourage the silk industry in Bengal, for the silk fabrics of

Bengal competed with silk fabrics manufactured in England in the English markets. In 1769 the Court of Directors sent orders to the Bengal authorities urging them to encourage the manufacture of raw silk and discourage the weaving of silk fabrics. Thus the silk winders of Bengal were compelled to work in the Company's factories. To save themselves from such oppression and compulsion many silkwinders of Bengal cut off their thumbs. It was no longer profitable for the weaver to weave much when he could not keep the gains of his labour. William Bolts, a contemporary, wrote about the various and innumerable methods of oppressing the poor weavers which were duly practised by the Company's agents or *gomastahs* in the country, such as by fines, imprisonments, floggings, forcing bonds from them etc. Bolts mentions that the black *gomastahs* (agents) did not obtain the consent of the poor weaver, but invariably forced him to sign the contract and receive advance money. Should the weaver refuse to accept the contract he was usually tied in his girdles and flogged. Further, these *gomastahs* registered a large number of weavers in their books and did not permit them to work for any other; sometimes the weavers were transferred from one merchant to another like so many slaves. "The roguery practised in this department", writes Bolts, "is beyond imagination; but all terminates in the defrauding of the poor weaver; for the prices which the Company's *gomastahs*, and in confederacy with them the *Jachendars* (examiners of fabrics) fix upon the goods, are in all places at least 15 per cent, and in some even 40 per cent less than the goods so manufactured would sell in the public bazar or market upon free sale".[2] By monopolising the internal trade of India, the Company's servants forced up the prices of raw material like cotton and silk to the disadvantage of Indian producers. The artisans no longer found their traditional occupations profitable and deserted them. Thus Indian industry languished.

(*e*) **Moral Degradation.** Moral degradation also set in the Bengal society. The farmer realised that the more he laboured the more he would have to pay to the revenue-farmers and government officials would work no more than was absolutely necessary for the bare needs of his family. Similarly, the weaver who could not keep all the reward of his hard work did not give his best to his work. The incentive for work being no longer there, the society became static and showed unmistakable signs of decay.

Administrative Reforms. Clive had the resolution of a task-master and the boldness of a dictator. The soldierly qualities of decisive action were amply displayed in his administrative reforms.

(*a*) **Civil Reforms.** The transformation of the Company into a political body had called for administrative reforms. The three revolutions of Bengal (1757, 1760 and 1764), had enriched the governors and councillors and demoralised the servants of the Company from top to bottom. The general desire to 'get-rich quick' had vitiated the whole atmosphere. Bribery and corruption were rampant and acceptance of presents was carried to extreme limits. The servants of the Company indulged in private trade and misused the Company's *dastak* to seek exemption from payment of internal duties. The servants of the Company put self-advancement above the interests of the Company.

Clive compelled the servants of the Company to sign 'covenants' prohibiting acceptance of presents. He forbade the servants of the Company from indulging in private trade and made payment of internal duties obligatory.

To compensate the servants of the Company for their low salaries and loss of income from cessation of private trade, Clive sought to regulate and regularise the control of internal trade. A Society of Trade was formed in August 1765 with monopoly of trade in Salt, Betelnut and Tobacco. All the production and import of these goods into Bengal was purchased by this Society and then sold at selected centres to the retailers. The profits from this trade were to go the superior servants of the Company on a graduated scale, the Governor to receive £17,5000 per annum out of the profits, a member of the Council and a Colonel in the army to get £ 7000, a Major's share was £ 2000 and so on the lower ranks to receive in a descending scale.

---

2. William Bolts : *Considerations on Indian Affairs* (1772), pp. 193-94.

The evils of private trade had raised the prices of ordinary commodities of life and the people of Bengal suffered. Clive sought to abolish plunder by the individual servants of the Company only to put the plundering activities of the Company's servants on a collective basis. The Society of Trade made the matters worse for the people. The Court of Directors disallowed the mostrous scheme in 1766. Clive decided to abolish the Society in January 1767 but the work of the Society was not actually wound up till September, 1768.

(*b*) **Military Reforms.** As early as 1763 the Court of Directors had sent orders for reduction of the double *bhatta* (field allowances) paid to military officers in Bengal. Due to one or the other reason the enforcement of the order was deferred to until Clive's arrival. The double *bhatta* originally granted on active service was continued by Mir Jaffar in times of peace also. The practice had continued since then and *bhatta* was considered by military officers as a part of their salary. Thus the allowance of Bengal army officers was twice as high as of corresponding officers in the Madras army. The Directors sent orders that the *bhatta* be brought on par with the *bhatta* of Madras army Clive issued orders that with effect from I January 1766 double allowance would be paid only to officers on service outside the frontiers of Bengal and Bihar.

The white brigades stationed at monghyr and Allahabad decided to organise resistance to Clive's orders by deciding to resign their commissions *en mase*. They calculated that the possible advance of the Marathas would coerce Clive. One of them even planned the assassination of Clive. Clive was not daunted by these threats. He rose to the occasion, accepted all resignations and ordered the arrest and trial of all ring leaders. Further, he promoted non-commissioned officers, even mercantile agents, and called all available troops from Madras. Clive's resolution proved effective and the White Mutiny was quelled.

Estimate of Clive. Robert Clive may justly lay claim to be the true founder of British political dominion in India. He correctly read the intricacies of the political situation of the time and struck boldly and in the right direction. He outdid his French adversary Dupleix and achieved more permanent results. His successful conduct of the siege of Arcot (1751) turned the seales against the French in the Carnatic. In Bengal he won the battle of Plassey (1757) against Siraj-ud-daula and reduced the new Nawab Mir Jaffar to the position of a mere puppet of the English. With the resources of Bengal the English conquered South India and routed their only political rival in India, the French. Above all, he transformed a mere trading body that the East India Company was into a territorial power with the role of 'king-maker' in Bengal. Coming back to Bengal in 1765, Clive consolidated the gains of the Company and regulated the foreign relations on a secure basis. Clive fully deserved the praise of Burke that "he settled great foundations".

Percival Spear in a recent study of Clive and his work in India points out that the British empire in India would have come into existence even without Clive, though in a different way and over a different time span. He concludes that "Clive was not a founder but a harbinger of the future. He was not a planner of empire but an experimenter who revealed something of the possibilities. Clive was the forerunner of the British Indian empire".[3]

Clive's weakness for money and Machiavellian methods found critics even in England and he was charged for these in the British parliament. He exacted illegal presents and set a bad precedent for his successors who in order to enrich themselves engineered revolutions in Bengal (1760 and 1764). Clive joined in the general plunder of Bengal by organising the Society of Trade. In devising the scheme of Dual Government in Bengal Clive's paramount consideration was establishment of English power and not welfare of the people. The whole of Bengal was reduced to the position of an estate of the East India Company. Sardar K. M. Pannikar very aptly remarks that during 1765–1772 the Company eastablished a 'robber state' in Bengal and plundered and looted Bengal indiscriminately. During this period British Imperialism showed its worst side in India and the people of Bengal suffered greatly.

---

3. Percival Spear : *Master of Bengal* : *Clive and his India* (1975), p. 199.

Clive failed to rise to the heights of a statesman. He proved to be a man of insight rather than foresight and his administrative settlement bequeathed a crop of difficulties to his successors. If the main justification of British rule in India was, as we are often told, the establishment of peace and order in this distracted land, then Clive can claim no share in this lofty work, for his various expedients only added to disorders in India.

Select Opinions

Lord Macaulay. Clive, like most men who are born with strong passions and tried by strong temptations, committed great faults. But every person who takes a fair and enlightened view of his whole career must admit that our Island, so fertile in heroes and statesmen, has scarcely even produced a man more truly great either in arms or in Council... From his first visit to India dates the renown of the English arms in the East... With the defence of Arcot commences that long series of Oriental triumphs which closes with the fall of Ghazni... From Clive's second visit to India dates the political ascendency of the English in this country... Such an extent of cultivated territory, such an amount of revenue, such a multitude of subjects, was never added to the dominion of Rome by the most successful proconsul... From Clive's third visit to India dates the purity of the administration of our Eastern Empire- (*Historical Essays*, pp. 375–76).

Alfred Lyall. Clive was high-spirited, courageous, indefatigable man, to whom above all others the English are indebted for the foundation of their empire in India... His daring and his sagacity, his singular talent for politics and his genius for war, produced in Lord Clive a rare combination of masculine qualities exactly fitted to the circumstances of his time in India. (*The Rise and Expansion of British Rule in India*, p. 178).

P. E. Roberts. As a soldier Clive was a great leader of man, but Pitt's famous description of him as a heaven born general is hardly appropriate. 'There is little trace', says Sir Charles Wilson truly, 'of skilful combination in his plans, and on some occasions he appears to have neglected the most obvious military precautions. To seek the enemy and, on finding him, to attack with headlong valour seems to have been his guiding principle, and his successes were due rather to his personal intrepidity, and his power of inspiring large masses of men with confidence, than to studied plans or dexterous manoeuvres'. (*History of British India*, pp. 165–66).

Nandalal Chatterji. Clive endeavoured to correct the abuses in the Company's civil and military services, but his reforms were temporary expedients. The changes he introduced did not solve any problem, and only served to worsen the situation. So far as the civil service was concerned, the covenants could not be fully executed, and the scandalous evils of presents and private inland trade remained practically uncorrected Clive's gold currency proved a disastrous failure and it made the matter worse by further aggravating the scarcity of silver. His exclusive trading company, formed for the benefit of the senior covenanted servants in opposition to the Company's repeated orders, was an utterly venal project which could not strike at the root of the evil of private inland trade. Having started with the laudable resolution of cleansing the *Augean Stable*, Clive ended by making the confusion worse confounded. The system which he laid down and the course which he followed were characterised by a short-sighted opportunism which reveals his failure to rise to the heights of a statesman. (*Clive as an Administrator*, p. 92).

SELECT REFERENCES

1. Chatterji, Nanda Lal : *Clive as an Administrator.*
2. Forrest, G. W. : *Life of Lord Clive*, 2 vols.
3. Macaulay, Lord : *Historical Essays : Lord Clive.*
4. Malleson, G. B. : *Life of Lord Clive.*
5. Spear, Percival : *Master of Bengal : Clive and his India.*

WARREN HASTINGS[1], 1772–85

The appointment of Warren Hastings as Governor of Bengal in 1772 opens a new chapter in the history of the East India Company. The Company had decided to recognise the *fait accompli*, tore the mask of Mughal sovereignty and rule Bengal by the right of conquest. The task before Warren Hastings was really herculean. He had to give Bengal a workable system of administration and to transform a company of merchants ignorant of the customs and habits of the Indian people into administrators. Above all, he had to rehabilitate the finances of the Company and develop its commerce. The reforms of Warren Hastings may be grouped under the following headings:—

Administrative Reforms. The Court of Directors decided to end the Dual System of administration set up by Clive and in 1772 required the President and Council to 'stand forth as the Diwan' and take over charge for the entire care and management of the revenues of Bengal, Bihar and Orissa. Warren Hastings dismissed the two Deputy Diwans, Mohammad Reza Khan and Raja Shitab Rai. The Governor and the Council formed the Board of Revenue and the Company appointed its own officers called Collectors to manage revenue affairs. The treasury was removed from Murshidabad to Calcutta. Thus the entire internal administration was transferred to the servants of the Company and the Nawab deprived of even an ostensible share in the government. However, the Nawab still lived in a state of sovereignty. Hastings also reorganised the household of the Nawab of Bengal and appointed Munny Begum, the widow of Mir Jaffar, as the guardian of the minor Nawab Mubarak-ud-daula. The allowance of the Nawab was reduced from 32 lakhs to 16 lakhs. Further, Hastings redefined relations with the Emperor. He stopped the payment of 26 lakhs of rupees annually paid to Emperor Shah Alam since 1765. The districts of Allahabad and Kora assigned to the Emperor by Clive in 1765 were also taken back and sold to the Nawab of Oudh for 50 lakhs of rupees. Though the motivating force was economy, the plea put forward was that the Emperor had accepted the protection of the Marathas. Evidently the treatment meted out to the Emperor was harsh and an *ex-parte action*. The Emperor was never warned of the consequences of his dealings with the Marathas. Warren Hastings' action was a breach of a solemn promise and remains morally and legally indefensible.

Revenue Reforms. The system of land revenue administration devised by Akbar and the great Mughal Emperors had broken down in the early eighteenth century and what the Company inherited was only confusion. Baden Powell remarks that "some theory or practice of revising the assessment, some customary period for such revision might have been expected, but none was left us".

In order to work out a satisfactory system of land revenue administration, Warren Hastings resorted to the devise of experimentation and tried to evolve a system by the proverbial method of trial and error.

(*a*) In 1772 Warren Hastings made a five-year settlement of land revenue by the crude method of farming out estates to the highest bidder. Acting on the presumption that the zamindars were mere tax-gatherers with no proprietary rights, in the settlement of 1772 no preference was given to them and in fact in certain cases they were actually discouraged from bidding.

In 1773 changes were made in the machinery of collection. The Collectors who had been found to be corrupt and indulged in private trade were replaced by Indian Diwans in the districts. Six

---

1. Born 1732; entered E.I. Company's service as writer, 1750; Resident at Cossimbazar; member, Calcutta Council, 1761–64; member, Madras Council, 1769–72; Governor of Bengal, 1772–74; first Governor-General of the Company's territories in India, 1774–85; died, 1818.

Provincial Councils were set up to superwise the work of Indian Diwans. The overall charge rested with the Committee of Revenue at Calcutta. The trend of Hastings' mind was towards centralization and he desired to ultimately centralise all functions into the hands of the Committee at Calcutta.

The quinquennial settlement was a miserable failure and the peasants suffered greatly. Most of the revenue-farmers were mere speculators, had no permanent interest in the land and therefore tried to extort the maximum sum from the cultivators by way of land revenue. The officers of the East India Company themselves participated in the bidding through their servants or *banias*. Even Warren Hastings himself was not free from this greed; there is the case of a grant registered in the name of a ten-year old son of Kuntu Baboo, an Indian servant of Warren Hastings. Further, the land had been over-assessed and the state demand fixed very high. Added to it was the harshness in the method of collection. The result was that many revenue contractors fell in heavy arrears, many had to be arrested for default and the ryot deserted the land.

(b) After the expiry of the quinquennial settlement in 1776, Warren Hastings reverted to the system of annual settlement on the basis of open auction to the highest bidder. Preference was given to the zamindars in making the settlement. Some changes were made in the machineray of collection in 1781.[2] The Provincial Councils were abolished. The Collectors were reappointed in the districts but were to have no power in the settlement of revenue. The *Qanungos* too were reappointed. The entire work of supervision was concentrated in the hands of the Committee of Revenue at Calcutta.

We may say that Warren Hastings failed to devise a satisfactory system of land revenue settlement. His bias towards centralisation worked against an effective system of land revenue collection or acquisition of detailed knowledge regarding revenue matters. In 1782 Sir John Shore declared that "the real state of the districts is now less known and the revenue less understood than in 1774". Warren Hastings left behind him "a dark trail of misery, insurrection and famines". How unsatisfactory the land revenue policy was may be clear from Cornwallis' remarks in 1789 that "one-third of the Company's territory in Hindustan is now jungle, inhabited only by wild beasts".

Judicial Reforms. Better success attended Warren Hastings' efforts in judicial matters. Before Hastings the judicial system in Bengal was summary and unsatisfactory. The zamindars decided civil and criminal cases and the systems of arbitration was very popular. Verelst commented : "Every decision is a corrupt bargain with the highest bidder...Trifling offenders are frequently loaded with heavy demands and capital offences are as often absolved by the venal judge". The interference of Englishmen or their agents in the interior had made matters worse; they very often interfered with the native judicial courts and even acted as judges. Since the acquisition of Diwani in 1765 the civil jurisdiction had passed into the Company's control and was exercised by the Deputy Diwan.

Warren Hastings tried to build up a framework of justice after the Mughal model. In 1772, a Diwani Adalat and a Faujdari Adalat were set up at the district level. The Diwani Adalat was presided over by the Collector who was competent to decide all civil cases including those concerning personal property, inheritance, caste, marriage, debts etc. In case of Hindus, the Hindu law was applicable, in case of Muslims the Muslim law. The Diwani Adalat could decide cases involving sums up to Rs. 500 above which appeals lay to the Sadar Diwani Adalat at Calcutta presided over by the President and two members of the Supreme Council assisted by Indian officers.

The District Faujdari Adalat was presided over by Indian officers of the Company who decided cases with the assistance of Qazis and Muftis. The Collector, a European officer, was authorised to exercise some control and supervision over the Faujdari Adalat (*i.e.* to see that the evidence was

---

2. Warren Hastings could not work out his original idea of employing only Indian officers in the districts and confining the Company's servants to Calcutta. Penderal Moon maintains that all the ex-members of the Provincial Councils had to be provided with jobs and there were many fresh recommendations from London. Thus Warren Hastings was compelled to re-employ the Company's servants as Collectors in the districts and some as judges of diwani adalats. (Penderal Moon : *Warren Hastings and British India*, p. 253).

duly submitted and weighed and the verdict passed was fair and impartial and given in open court). The Mohammadan law was followed in the Faujdari Adalat. This Adalat could not award death sentence or order confiscation of property for which the confirmation of the Sadr Nizamat Adalat was necessary. Appeals from the Faujdari Adalat lay to the Sadr Nizamat Adalat presided over by the Deputy Nazim assisted by the Chief Qazi and the Chief Mufti and three Maulvis. The President and Council supervised the proceedings of this Court.

The Regulating Act of 1773 provided for the setting up of a Supreme Court at Calcutta competent to try all 'British subjects'. However in Calcutta and its subordinate factories the Court exercised jurisdiction over all persons, Indian or European. Outside Calcutta complaints or suits against or between Indians could be heard by the said Court only with the consent of the parties. In the Supreme Court the English law was administered while the Sadr Diwani Adalat, Sadr Nizamat Adalat and other courts at the district level decided cases according to Muslim and Hindu laws supplemented by regulations framed by the President and the Supreme Council in their legislative capacity. The jurisdiction of the Supreme Court and other courts often clashed. To remove possibility of friction between the Supreme Court and Sadr Diwani Adalat and Sadr Nizamat Adalat, in October 1780 Warren Hastings appointed Impey, Chief Justice of the Supreme Court, as Superintendent of Sadr Diwani Adalat at a salary of Rs. 5,000 p.m. The Court of Directors disallowed this appointment and Impey had to resign in November 1782. Thus the dualism in the legal system continued throughout the Company's rule in India.

Warren Hastings attempted to codify Muslims and Hindu laws. A translation of the Code in Sanskrit appeared in 1776 under the title of 'Code of Gentoo Laws'. William Jones and Colebrooke published Colebrooke's *Digest of Hindu Law* in 1791. Attempts were also made to translate *Fatwai-i-Alamgiri* into English.

Commercial Reforms. Warren Hastings sought to clear the bottlenecks in the internal trade of Bengal. The various customhouses in the zamindaries were suppressed. Henceforth only five custom-houses at Calcutta, Hughli, Murshidabad, Dacca and Patna were to be maintained. The duties were lowered to $2\frac{1}{2}$%, payable by all merchants, Europeans and Indians alike. He checked the misuse of *dastak* or free passes signed by the Company's officers exempting from duties the goods of the servants of the Company indulging in private trade. Steps were also taken to check the exploitation of the weavers by the Company's agents. He made efforts to develop trade relations with Bhutan and Tibet.

In short, by these various reforms Warren Hastings gave an administrative framework to Bengal. He, however, gave no place to the sons of the soil in the positions of trust and responsibility, perhaps a necessary concomitant of foreign rule.

The Regulating Act and Conflict in the Council

The Regulating Act of 1773 vested the administration of British territories in India in the hands of a Governor-General assisted by a Council of four members. The Governor-General was to preside over meetings of the Council, but the decision of the majority was to bind the whole, the Governor-General having merely a casting vote in case of an equal division. Three members formed the quorum. The Governor-General and the Councillors were named in the Act. Warren Hastings was named as the first Governor-General and Clavering, Francis, Monson and barwell as the four Councillors. At the time of his appointment barwell was in India, already in the service of the Company. The other three Councillors reached India in October, 1774.

The new Councillors set out from England with a strong prejudice that Warren Hastings was corrupt and so was the entire government of the Company in Bengal. Of the Triumvirate— Clavering, Francis and Monson —Francis was undoubtedly the ablest and the most ambitious. His ambition was to replace Warren Hastings or to succeed him. Differences between this Triumvirate and the Governor-

General supported by Barwell began the very day the new Councillors reached Calcutta. They complained of inadequate reception which they described as "mean and dishonourable" and attributed motives to Warren Hastings for not providing even a guard of honour at their arrival. This was an inauspicious beginning. At the very first meeting of the Council the new Councillors wanted to discuss the past excesses of Warren Hastings' administration. They demanded all papers pertaining to the transaction with the Nawab Wazir of Oudh at Benaras and all correspondence with Middleton, the English Resident at Lucknow, to be laid at the Council table. Further, they wanted to discuss the Company's involvement in the Ruhela War. On the refusal of Warren Hastings to produce the necessary papers, the Majority decided the recall of Middleton from Lucknow, denounced the Ruhela War as 'unjust and impolitic' and ordered for the recall of the Company's troops from Rohilkhand. The Triumvirate by virtue of their majority in the Council approved the appointment of Bristow as the British Resident at Lucknow and concluded a new treaty with the Nawab of Oudh. By the treaty of Fyzabad, the new Nawab Asaf-ud-daula (who had succeeded his father in January 1775) was required to increase the monthly subsidy for the use of the Company's brigade from Rs. 210,000 to Rs. 260,000 as also to cede to the Company in perpetuity the zamindari of Benares. The Triumvirate also attacked the Quinquennial Settlement of land revenue made in 1772 and charged Warren Hastings for having overestimated the rents which could not be paid by the bidders. Francis produced before the Council a plan for a Permanent Settlement of land revenue in Bengal. The Majority also criticised Hastings' creation of new criminal courts of justice and passed a resolution restoring to the Nawab all the rights of the Nizamat. Mohammad Reza Khan was reinstated as the Naib-Suba. The Majority also differed with the Governor-General over questions of foreign policy and criticised his interference in the internal disputes of the Marathas and interpreted it as the desire of the Governor-General to extend the Company's territories.

For nearly two years, from October 1774 to September 1776 the Majority in the Council usurped all authority in their hands. On 5 September 1776 Monson died which gave Warren Hastings majority in the Council. Reporting the matter to Lord North, Hastings wrote, "It has restored to me the constitutional authority of my station". With only three members of the Council left and Barwell on his side and his own casting vote. Warren Hastings regained effective control in the Council. However, the storm had not blown over. In a moment of disgust in March 1775 Warren Hastings had written to his London agent, Colonel Macleane, to tender his resignation. Hastings' desire was conveyed to the Court of Directors in October 1776. In November 1776 Mr. Edward Wheler was appointed by the Court of Directors to fill the vacancy caused by Hastings' resignation and Clavering was appointed as the new Governor-General to succeed Hastings. With the death of Monson in September 1776, Hastings had changed his mind and he sent instructions to his agent at London accordingly. The Court of Directors' orders reached India on 14 June 1777 and Clavering took oath as Governor-General on 20 June 1777. Hastings, however, refused to hand over to Clavering maintaining that his agent at London had exceeded his powers. The matter was referred to the Supreme Court which upheld Hastings' point of view.

Hastings had gained majority in the Council after September 1776 but it was not the end of his troubles. The new Councillor, Mr. Wheler sent out in place of Monson was due to reach India towards the end of 1777. However, Edward Wheler was not a man of strong character and there was every fear of his becoming 'the echo of Francis'. Luck again favoured Hastings, for Clavering died on 30 August 1777. Even this did not mark the end of conflict in the Council. Francis continued his opposition to Hastings. Early in 1780 a reconciliation was reached between Francis and Hastings but it proved short-lived. The two fought a duel in which Francis was injured by a pistol shot. The conflict did not end till Francis' departure for home in December 1780. Some years later Hastings wrote, "My antagonists sickened, died and fled".

The Trial of Nand Kumar, 1775. The story of the conflict in the Council and discomfiture of Warren Hastings and Barwell encouraged Nand Kumar, who had some old grouse against Warren

Hastings, to bring some charges of corruption and nepotism against the Governor-General. On March 14, 1775 Francis produced a letter from Nand Kumar before the Council which charged Warren Hastings of having accepted R. $3\frac{1}{2}$ lakhs as gratification from Munny Begum for appointing the latter as guardian of the minor Nawab, Mubarak-ud-daula. A few days later, Nand Kumar offered to appear before the Council to substantiate the charges. Warren Hastings refused to recognise the right of the Council to sit in judgement on him and dissolved the Council in a huff, Warren Hastings decried Nand Kumar as 'the basest of mankind,' 'a wretch' and as coming from 'the dregs of the people'. Warren Hastings' action lent suspicion to the whole case and convinced the Trio about the truth of Nand Kumar's charges. The Trio sought the advice of the law officers for the recovery of the amount from Warren Hastings.

Meantime, Warren Hastings and his friends planned a counter-offensive against Nand Kumar. On 19 April 1775, one Kamal-ud-din brought charges agaisnt Nand Kumar and Fowke for having coerced him to sign a petition containing various allegations against Hastings and Barwell. The case was referred to the Supreme Court. A more sensational charge against Nand Kumar was filed by Mohan Prasad, a pleader, acting on behalf of the executor of a banker named Balaki Dass (deceased) alleging that a certain Jewels Bond purporting to be signed by Balaki Dass and to be an acknowledgement by him of a debt due to Nand Kumar was a forgery. On 6 May 1775, Nand Kumar was arrested for forgery and hanged by a majority decision of a European jury.

Critics of Warren Hastings and Impey have described the trial and execution of Nand Kumar as "a judicial murder" and have accused Warren Hastings and Impey to have acted in collusion. Macaulay believed that Warren Hastings was the real prosecutor and wrote that 'only idiots and biographers (reference to Gleig's *Memoirs of Warren Hastings*) doubt that Warren Hastings was not the real prosecutor'. In this context the comments of Mr. Chambers, one of the four judges of the Supreme Court, are revealing. He wrote, "I argued against the general unfitness of punishing forgery with death in this country. My arguments on this head were overruled in private as they had been in public. The credit of Nand Kumar's evidence against the Government was thus not only invalidated. It was destroyed entirely by taking the witness not only out of the way but out of the world". Apologists of Warren Hastings like J.F. Stephen contend that the prosecution of Nand Kumar for forgery in 1775 was a mere coincidence and that Warren Hastings had no hand in the trial and ultimate punishment of Nand Kumar. One, however, cannot escape the conclusion that Nand Kumar was punished on weak evidence and the temper of the Chief Justice—Impey was a close friend of Warren Hastings—played the decisive part. True, the law of England provided for capital punishment for forgery, but the same had never been applied in Calcutta. A few years earlier the Mayor's Court in Calcutta which followed the English criminal law and pardoned a prominent Bengali, who was sentenced to death for forgery. Thompson and Garratt describe the whole affair as "a scandalous travesty of decency" while P.E. Roberts attributes it to "an error of judgment" on the part of the judges and the sentence of death as "miscarriage of justice". Evidently, the punishment accorded to Nand Kumar was excessive and even unjust because no Indian law prescribed death penalty for forgery.

External Relations Under Warren Hastings

In his dealings with Indian ruling powers, Warren Hastings faced a very complicated and explosive political situation. Clive's political arrangements had begun to crumble one after the other. The Marathas had recovered from the losses they suffered at Panipat and were once again making a bid for the supremacy of Northern India. The Emperor had accepted the protection of the Sindhia. The friendship with Shuja-ud-daula, the Nawab of Oudh, had considerably loosened. In the South, Hyder Ali was adopting an aggressive mood and was preparing to take revenge on the Company. All these difficulties Warren Hastings had to face at a time when England faced a hostile coalition of European powers ranged on the side of the revolting American colonies.

1. Relation with Emperor Shah Alam II. The Marathas under the capable and experienced leadership of Mahadaji Sindhia and Jaswant Rao Holkar had consolidated their position in Northern India. After overrunning Rajputana, defeating the Jats, expelling the Rohillas from the Doab, the Marathas captured Delhi in February 1771. The same year they escorted the Emperor to his throne in Delhi. In reward for their services the Emperor handed over to the Marathas Allahabad and Kora which Clive had given to him in 1765.

Warren Hastings decided to throw off the mask and stop the payment of the annual tribute of Rs. 26 lakhs to 'the king of shreds and patches'. He maintained that the Company did not get the *Diwani* by the Emperor's 'piece of paper' but by the best of all titles, *i.e.*, power. Later, Hastings sold Allahabad and Kora to the Nawab of Oudh for Rs. 50 lakhs.

2. Relations with Oudh. Clive had sought to create Oudh as a buffer state for the territories of the Company. Every year the Nawab had asked for the help of the Company's troops without payment of extra expenses which meant heavy loss of the Company. In short, the relations with the Nawab were very unsatisfactory and he was looked upon with suspicion.

Warren Hastings felt the clear need of re-defining relations with the Nawab of Oudh or alternatively the latter might join the Marathas for the partition of Rohilkhand or might even succumb to a Maratha-Rohilla combination. Hastings personally proceeded to Banaras and concluded the Treaty of Banaras (1773) with the Nawab. By this treaty, Allahabad was handed over to the Nawab for Rs. 50 lakhs. The Nawab agreed to increase the subsidy of the Company's troops from Rs. 30,000 a month to Rs. 2,10,000 a month for one brigade when called for service. Further, a secret clause provided that in case the Nawab asked for the help of the Company's troops against the Rohillas he would pay a further sum of Rs. 40 lakhs to the Company. Warren Hastings defended the Treaty of Banaras before the Council thus—discontinuance of the Emperor's allownace, a safe frontier, a compact state of Oudh, financial gain and the alliance between the Marathas and the Nawab of Oudh rendered impossible.

3. The Rohilla War, 1774. Both the Rohilla Chief and the Nawab of Oudh feared the Maratha attack. Early in 1772 the Marathas defeated Zabeta Khan and occupied all his territories of Rohilkhand. Hafiz Rehmat Khan, the Rohilla leader feared the Maratha attack and concluded a treaty with the Nawab of Oudh (17 June 1772) promising to pay forty lakh rupees to the Nawab for his help in defending Rohilkhand against possible Maratha attack. As expected, the Marathas headed towards Rohilkhand in the spring of 1773 but retraced their steps when they found the forces of the Company and Oudh ranged on the opposite side. The Maratha danger was warded off and the Nawab demanded the promised sum of forty lakhs of rupees from the Rohilla Chief which the latter evaded.

In February 1774, the Nawab of Oudh decided to invade Rohilkand with a view to its annexation. The Nawab feared a Rohilla-Maratha combination against Oudh. The time seemed opportune for the Nawab's plans. The Maratha danger had receded for the time being following dissensions in the Maratha camp after the death of Peshwa Madhav Rao. Further, the Nawab had lately won over the Emperor and Zabeta Khan to his side. On the strength of the treaty of Banaras, the Nawab sought the help of the Company's troops which were lent against the Rohillas. Rohilkhand was invaded and the decisive battle fought at Miranpur Katra (April 1774). Hafiz Rehmat Khan died in action. Rohilkhand except for the small remanent of Rampur State was annexed to Oudh and 20,000 Rohillas banished from the country.

Warren Hastings, conduct has been subjected to severe censure for participation in the

Rohilla war. Burke criticised the landing of the Company's troops against the Rohillas who had given no offence to the Company and spoke of bartering 'the lives and liberties of a free people' to the Nawab of Oudh. Macaulay has charged Hastings with looking on callously while the Rohilla 'villages were burnt, their children butchered, and their women violated'. Young Palk at Patna talked of 'hiring the troops to the country powers'. Colonel Pearse called the operations 'un-British', while Colonel Alexander Champion wrote of the 'destruction and devastation', the 'banditti' of the Nawab, the cries of the 'widow and the fatherless'. Many Rohilas were banished from the territories and barbaric treatment meted out to the family of Hafiz Rehmat Khan. Apologists of Warren Hastings' policy like Sir John Strachey[3] defend Hastings' conduct on the ground that while concluding the Treaty of Banaras, Hastings believed that the occasion for helping the Nawab against the Rohillas would never arise. To commit the Company to a course of action in the hope that the occasion for the same would never come is a sad commentary on Warren Hastings' political judgment. Again, it is contended that General Sir Robert Barker was present at the time of the treaty between Hafiz Rehmat Khan and the Nawab of Oudh. The mere presence of the British General could not mean that the Company became the 'guarantor' for the treaty. Further, Sir John Strachey's plea that the Rohillas deserved expulsion from that territory because they had forcibly established their rule some twenty-five years earlier over the Hindu population of Rohilkhand loses all force when we consider that the Nawab of Oudh had as bleak a right to rule over Oudh as the Rohillas had over Rohilkhand—both had usurped Mughal authority and assumed virtual independence in the early years of the eighteenth century. Penderal Moon comed to the conclusion that the Rohilla war was not marked by any special atrocities or inhumanity towards the Rohillas, for the Nawab would not wish to see the country he had to annex extensively ravaged and plundered. Mr. Moon believes that the entire controversy about alleged atrocities arose because of the malice of Philip Francis, who was out to discredit Warren Hastings[4]. It seems the vehemence of the critics and the apologists of Warren Hastings has clouded an objective assessment. From the viewpoint of the people of Rohilkhand the rule of the Nawab of Oudh proved more oppressive than that of the Rohillas.

Warren Hastings' motives for participation in the Rohilla war were a mixture of sound strategy and mercenary considerations. Warren Hastings wanted to include Rohilkhand in the Company's defensive line. Defending his conduct in the British House of Commons, Warren Hastings talked of the 'defensive war' against Rohilkhand. A note from his diary of 1773 refers to "the indirect advantages which were to be drawn from it than from any great opinion of the expedition itself". In his anxiety to procure the Nawab of Oudh's consent to the Treaty of Banaras, Warren Hastings committed the Company to participation in the possible invasion of Rohilkhand. It is abundantly clear that Warren Hastings' whole conduct was motivated by political considerations and mercenary gains resulting from the treaty with Oudh rather than the righteousness of the Rohilla War The 'moral' aspect of the whole affair hardly entered into Hastings' calculations.

4. The First Anglo-Maratha War, 1776–82. While Warren Hastings had won some laurels by concluding a subsidiary alliance with Oudh and the Madras Government distinguished themselves by strengthening their influence over Carnatic and the Northern Sarkars, the President and Council of Bombay felt belittled for no achievement in the field of political or territorial aggrandisement because of the powerful Maratha confederacy in the area. The Bombay authorities cast their longing eyes on the territories on the Western Coast, coveted the ports of Salsette and Bassein and hoped to attain political ascendancy at Poona. The dissensions at Poona gave them the much needed opportunity for profitable intrigue.

---

3. Sir John Strachey: *Hastings and the Rohilla War*, 1892.
4. Penderal Moon : *Warren Hastings and British India*, p. 129.

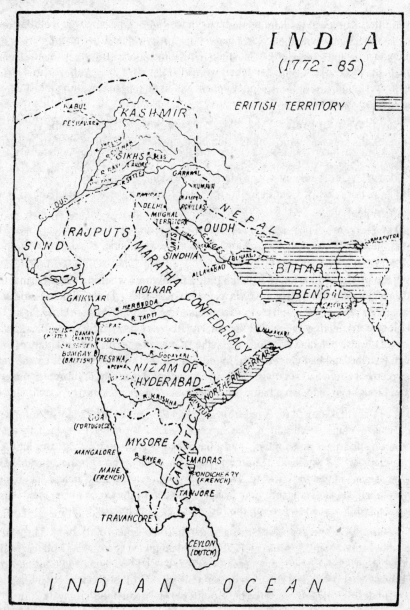

Descriptive Note on Political Condition of India during 1772–1785. (Warren Hastings' time)

Extent of E.I. Company's Territories—In 1785 the British dominion in India extended over Bengal, Bihar and Orissa (the last-mentioned comprising only a small area around Midnapure), Banaras and Ghazipur (acquired from the Nawab of Oudh by the Treaty of Faizabad in 1775), Northern Sarkars, port of Salsette (acquired from the Marathas by the Treaty of Purandhar in 1776) apart from the harbours of Madras, Bombay and some minor ports.

Mughal Territory—The old Mughal Emperor Shah Alam II exercised nominal sovereignty over Delhi and adjoining areas but had accepted the protection of the Maratha chief Mahadaji Sindhia, the latter wielding considerable influence at Delhi.

Oudh—Oudh was an autonomous state in Northern India committed to an offensive-defensive alliance with the E.I. Company since 1765. The Nawab of Oudh's dependence on the Company's troops for defence of his territories was evident from the Treaties of Banaras (1773) and Faizabad (1775) whereby he transferred his sovereignty over Banaras to the E.I. Company apart from agreeing to pay an increased subsidy for the Company's troops stationed in Oudh.

North-Western India— The Sikh *misls* controlled territories in the cis-Sutlej and trans-Sutlej areas. Muslim Chiefs ruled in North Western Punjab, at Multan, Sindh and Kashmir.

Maratha Confederacy— The Maratha confederacy controlled the whole of Western India, major parts of Central India from Delhi to the borders of Hyderabad state and from Gujarat in the West to Cuttack in the east.

The Deccan— The Nizam ruled over the autonomous state of Hyderabad; Mysore was ruled by Hyder Ali; Tanjore and Travancore were under Hindu rulers.

Internal dissensions overtook Maharastra following the death of the fourth Peshwa Madhav Rao (1772) and murder of the fifth Peshwa Narayan Rao (1773). The claims of Madhav Rao Narayan (the posthumous son of Narayan Rao) were disputed by Raghunath Rao the uncle of Narayan Rao). Finding himself ineffective against the Council of Regency headed by Nana Phadnavis, Raghunath Rao solicited English help and concluded with the Bombay Government the Treaty of Surat (1775). In Raghunath Rao the Bombay Government found a pliant tool and hoped to set up at Poona the type of Dual Government Clive had set up in Bengal. An English expeditionary force occupied Salsette and Bassein and fought an indecisive battle with the Poona forces at Arras.

The Calcutta Council received from Bombay the copy of the Treaty of Surat with Raghunath Rao after actual operations had started. The Supreme Council strongly condemned the war as 'impolitic, dangerous, unauthorized and unjust', and questioned the wisdom of the Bombay Government's attempt to conquer the whole of Maratha Empire for a man who appeared incapable of affording effectual assistance in the undertaking. The Supreme Government at Calcutta sent Colonel Upton to Poona who concluded the Treaty of Purandhar (1776) whereby the Company retained Salsette, accepted a war indemnity but agreed to give up the cause of Raghunath Rao.

A turn in European politics changed the political situation in India. The American War of Independence broke out in 1775 and by 1778 France had joined against England in a bid to average the losses suffered earlier. A French adventurer, Chevalier de St. Lubin reached Poona and greatly alarmed the Governor-General. Warren Hastings ordered the seizure of all French settlements in India, sent a large force under Goddard to reinforce the Bombay army, treated the Treaty of Purandhar as a 'scrap of paper' and sanctioned operations against the Marathas. A British force sent by the Bombay Government heading towards the Western Ghats suffered an ignominious failure and signed the humiliating Convention of Wadgaon (1779) by which the Company was required to give up all advantages gained by the Treaty of Purandhar.

In 1781, Captain Popham recovered British prestige by defeating the Sindhia in a number of skirmishes and capturing Gwalior. Sindhia was brought round to an understanding with the Company on the latter's promise to allow him to prosecute his designs in and around Delhi. Thus the Sindhia acted as a mediator and by the Treaty of Salbai (May 1782) the war with the Marathas was concluded on the basis of mutual restitution of each other's territories. The Company gave up Bassein and other territories captured since the Treaty of Purandhar, but retained Salsette and the Elephanta Island. The English gave up the cause of Raghunath Rao and recognised Madhav Rao Narayan as the Peshwa.

The Treaty of Salbai merely established *status quo ante bellum*. From the Company's viewpoint, it saved her prestige and territories in times of great crisis although it landed her in considerable financial difficulties. Further, it gave the Company a free hand to deal with the Mysorean ruler. On the other hand, the war had amply demonstrated Maratha strength and potential and thus forbade a policy of twenty years' peace towards them.

5. The Second Anglo-Mysore War, 1780–84. In his attempt to safeguard India against French designs, Warren Hastings ordered the seizure of all French settlements in India including the port of Mahe (1779) on the Malabar coast which Hyder Ali regarded as within his jurisdiction. Hyder Ali contended that it was his duty to protect the port against any possible French attack. The Governor-General, however, feared that the port of Mahe might be used by the Mysorean ruler to receive help from the French against the Company. Further, the English gave offence to Hyder Ali by marching an English force across a part of his territory without permission, in order to take Guntur in the Northern Sarkars.

Hyder Ali came to a common understanding with the Marathas, won over the Nizam to his side, secured promises of French help and in July 1780 attacked the Carnatic and captured Arcot, defeating and annihilating the Company's troops under Sir Hector Munro sent to fight against him. The Company was at war with the Marathas and Hyder Ali simultaneously and worsted off on both fronts. "By the summer of 1780", writes Alfred Lyall, "the fortunes of the English in India had fallen to their lowest watermark". The energetic policy of the Governor-General, however, saved the situation. An army was sent from Calcutta under Sir Eyre Coote who defeated Hyder Ali (reinforced by 3,000 French troops under Bussy) in the battles of Porto Novo (1781) and Arni (June 1782). The Marathas were detached from the Triple Alliance by a compromise with the Sindhia. The French help under Admiral Baille de Suffren reached India in 1782, but the English fleet under Hughes proved equal to the occasion and prevented the French from supplying large reinforcements to the Mysore ruler. Luckily for the English, Hyder Ali died in December 1782. The struggle was continued by his able and ambitious son, Tipu. In July 1783, however, reached the news of the end of the American War of Independence. Suffren, thereupon, sailed back for Europe leaving Tipu to fight his battles. Lord Macartney, the Governor of Madras, decided on peace which was concluded by the Treaty of Mangalore in March 1784 on the basis of mutual restitution of each other's territories and return of prisoners of war. The struggle ended in a draw.

The Affairs of Chait Singh and Begums of Oudh. Wars against the Marathas and the Mysore ruler so greatly strained the financial resources of the Calcutta Government that Warren Hastings resorted to transactions that formed the main arround of his subsequent impeachment in England. The Raja of Banaras, Chait Singh, was originally a feudatory of Oudh. On the death of Nawab Shuja-ud-daula of Oudh in 1775, his son Asaf-ud-daula succeeded him. The Company took advantage of this change and forced the new Nawab to accept a new treaty in May 1775 by which Banaras was transferred to the Company. Chait Singh thus became a vassal or the Company. The Treaty of 1775 also provided that Chait Singh would annually pay to the Company 22 lakhs of rupees. The Treaty specifically laid down that beyond the stipulated tribute "no demand shall be made upon him by the Hon'ble Company, of any kind, or on any pretence whatsoever, nor shall any person be allowed to interfere with his authority or to disturb the peace of his country". Financial stringency drove Warren Hastings to questionable methods. In 1778 he demanded an additional 5 lakhs rupees from Chait Singh as a war levy. The demand was repeated in 1779 and again in 1780. In 1780 the Raja sent two lakhs of rupees as a bribe to Warren Hastings to avert further demands. This, however, did not deter Warren Hastings from demanding the extra subsidy and a contingent of 2,000 cavalry. The Raja wrote an apologetic letter to the Governor-General and procrastinated. Warren Hastings resolved to punish the Raja and imposed on him a fine of Rs. 50 lakhs. Hastings was determined to plunder Chait Singh. "His plan", in the graphic language of Macaulay, "was simply this, to demand larger and larger contributions till the Raja should be driven to remonstrate, then to call his remonstrance a crime, and to punish him by confiscating all his possessions". Hastings personally proceeded to Banaras. The Raja received the Governor-General at Buxar and placed his turban at Hastings' feet. The Governor-General refused to discuss the matter till he had reached Banaras. Reaching Banares, Warren Hastings placed Chait Singh under arrest. The soldiers of Chait Singh could not withstand the indignities heaped on their ruler and rose in rebellion which, of course, was easily suppressed. Chait Singh was replaced by his nephew Mahip Narayan, a minor on an annual payment of Rs. 40 lakhs instead of the usual Rs. 22 lakhs. The new Raja was reduced to the position of a mere pensioner of the Company.

Apologists of Warren Hastings' policy base their defence on the ground that Chait Singh was a mere zamindar and the sum of 22 lakhs of rupees he paid annually was land revenue and not tribute; as such Chait Singh was liable to pay war contributions. The argument is hardly tenable for by the agreement of 1775 the Company had specifically agreed not to demand any extra money beyond the stipulated amount of 22 lakhs of rupees per annum. Moreover, if Warren Hastings decided to collect a war levy from zamindars, it should not have been levied on Chait Singh alone. Whatever might have been the status of Chait Singh, one cannot but argue that Warren Hastings' conduct was impolitic, merciless and vindictive and his political judgment was clouded by the long strife in the Council and successful wars against the Indian-ruling princes. The sad commentary on the whole affair is that Warren Hastings could not obtain the wealth of Chait Singh on which he had set his heart for financing the Company's wars; rather he burdened the Company's treasury with an additional cost of the minor war agains Chait Singh. Apart from monetary considerations the exercise of despotic power coupled with anger and arrogance had thrown Hastings off his balance.

Disappointed at Banaras about wealth Warren Hastings had hoped to obtain, he turned his attention towards Oudh. Asaf-ud-daula, the Nawab of Oudh, owed the Company about Rs. 15 lakhs for the subsidiary force that had been stationed in Oudh, even against the wishes of the Nawab. Pressed for payment, Asaf-ud-daula suggested that he might be allowed to take possession of the vast treasure of the Begums, the wives of his late father. Earlier on the intercession of the British Resident, the Nawab had received from the Begums a sum of £ 560,000 on the guarantee from the Calcutta Council that no further demands would be made on the Begums. The hint was sufficient for Warren Hastings and he instructed Mr. Middleton, the British Resident in Oudh, to allow no "negotiations or forbearance, but prosecute both services until the Begums are at the entire mercy of the Nawab". British officers goaded the reluctant Nawab in coercing the Begums to dislodge 105 lakhs of rupees, the amount which was mostly paid to the Company in discharge of the Nawab's debt.

Sir Alfred Lyall describes Warren Hastings' conduct as 'unworthy and indefensible' and adds: "The employment of personal severities, under the superintendence of British officers, in order to exact money from women and eunuchs is an ignoble kind of undertaking".

Estimate of Warren Hastings. Warren Hastings is a very controversial figure in modern Indian history. He raped, despoiled and conquered India and showed the British aggressive side to India. Macaulay talked of his hard heart and lax principles when he wrote, "The rules of justice, the sentiments of humanity, the plighted faith of treaties were in his view as nothing when opposed to the immediate interests of the state. His only steadfast principle was that Might is Right. He left behind a dark trail of misery, desolation and famines in Bengal, Banaras and Oudh". Philip Francis reported that once a flourishing and rich India was reduced to 'beggary and ruin'. However, his contribution to the cause of British dominion was really great. At a time when the overseas possessions of Great Britain witnessed rebellion, defeat or humiliation, in India the British position remained unharmed. Warren Hastings saved the Company's position in the face of great difficulties. In this field of administrative reforms he laid the foundations where the superstructure was raised by Cornwallis.

If Warren Hastings despoiled India, he enriched it also. He was a man of literary tastes. He patronised Oriental learning. Himself he was an earnest student of Indian literature, knew Persian and Arabic and could speak Bengali. He wrote the introduction to the first English translation of the Gita by Charles Wilkins. Under his inspiration European scholars like Wikins, Halhed and Sir William Jones attempted to study Indian classical literature and prepared the way for the development of the work of British Orientalists in India. Wilkins invented the cast printing for Bengali and Persian characters. He also translated the Gita and Hitopadesha in English. Nathaniel Brassey Halhed published a Sanskrit Grammar in 1778. Sir William Jones laid the foundation of the Asiatic Society of Bengal in 1784 with the purpose of "enquiring into the history, civil and natural, the antiquities, arts, sciences and literatures of Asia".

Warren Hastings' weakness for money was perhaps as great as Clive's. He accepted bribes of Rs. 2 lakhs from Chait Singh of Banaras and Rs. 10 lakhs from the Nawab of Oudh at a time when he extorted money from the Raja and the Nawab on the plea of Maratha wars. Mr. Moon has estimated that the various presents he accepted amounted to about 30 lakhs of rupees. Warren Hastings made a thorough use of his patronage in India to bribe the Directors at home and thus maintained himself in office even when the Home Government was dissatisfied with his policies. In 1780 the House of Commons passed a resolution for the recall of Hastings, but Hastings played his card. He won over the Court of Proprietors by showing great favours to their sons and nominees. He won over Sulivan, the Chairman of the Court of Directors, by the grant of an opium contract to his son, which the latter sold for £ 40,000. Further Warren Hastings created numerous posts and increased the cost of civil establishments of the Company from £ 251,533 in 1766 to £927,945 in 1784.

Warren Hastings' harsh, despotic and arbitrary acts roused the conscience of the English and he was impeached by the parliament. The trial began in 1788 and lasted till 1795. Despite Burke's[5] scathing criticism of Warren Hastings' policies in India the spirit of hero-worship prevailed in the British parliament and Hastings was acquitted of all charges for he had furthered the interests of his country in India. He was made a member of the Privy Council and an annuity of £ 4,000 was sanctioned for him. Moved by the same spirit, Professor Dodwell terms the trial of Warren Hastings as tragic and adds: "The one supremely great man whom England sent to rule India was checked in every action either by opposition in his own Council, or by hostility of the home Government or by the provisions of the worst piece of legislation which ever passed the British Parliament regarding India. If Burke had wished to impeach anyone, he would have done well to choose his old enemy Lord North, the author of the Regulating Act, rather than Warren Hastings, its unhappy victim".[6] V.A. Smith's judgement is more balanced when he writes: "His few errors, so far as they were real, were those of a statesman exposed to imminent peril and beset by embarrassments so complex that fallible human judgement was bound to err occasionally". Percival Spear puts the balance sheet thus: "The achievement of Hastings is an established fact; his character remains something of an enigma"[7]. In judging Warren Hastings we may perhaps not lose sight of the hard fact that an absolute moral code can hardly be applied in case of architects of empires, for when was an empire built without any criminality.

Select Opinions

Lord Macaulay. Those who look on Warren Hastings' character without favour or malevolence will pronounce that in the two great elements of all social virtue, in respect for the rights of others, and in sympathy for the sufferings of others, he was deficient. His principles were somewhat lax. His heart was somewhat hard. But while we cannot with truth describe him either as a righteous or as a merciful

---

5. Burke called Hastings a 'weasel and a rat', 'a fraudulent bullock-contractor' and 'a Captain-General of Inequity'.
6. H.H. Dodwell; *Cambridge Shorter History of India*, 1958 edition p. 465.
7. Percival Spear; *Oxford History of Modern India*, p. 70.

ruler, we cannot but regard with admiration the amplitude and fertility of his intellect, his rare talents for command, for administration, and for controversy, his dauntless courage, his honourable poverty, his fervent zeal for the interests of the State, his noble equanimity, tried by both extremes of fortune and never disturbed by either. (*Historical Essays*, pp. 488–89).

A.M. Davies. To outward appearances Warren Hastings had done no more than justify his retention of his post and the trust reposed in him, by bringing the Company safely through a great crisis with its territories intact and resources unimpaired. Actually however, he had achieved immeasurably more and to estimate what that more was we have only to recall the extent of British power in India at the beginning of his administration and to compare it with what it was at the end. On the one hand, two weak footholds on the coast at Madras and Bombay, undisputed but undefined authority over the vast, chaotic famine-stricken province of Bengal, a weak alliance with one native state, no friends, no security, bankrupt finances, demoralized officers, incompetent leaders. And on the other hand, an empire in being that had conclusively proved itself to be the most powerful state in India, an empire that was built on secure foundations, buttressed with treaties and alliances, doubly strong because it had gained the respect and goodwill of no small part of the Indian world, and that only required a continuance of the same able statesmanship to become the paramount power. The contrast is a fair measure of Hastings' achievement.

Penderal Moon. Looking back at Hastings' career in the light of history, we can see that the ultimate effects of his actions were almost exactly the reverse of what he himself intended. By rescuing from bankruptcy and chaos the Company's Government in Bengal and then bringing it safely through the critical years of war he made possible and indeed ultimately inevitable: (i) the extension of British dominion over the whole of India; (ii) the reduction of such Indian rulers as survived to the status of mere puppets; and (iii) the establishment in India of an essentially British administration. He himself desired none of these things. The first he saw to be possible, but disclaimed all wish for its realisation; the second and third he unceasingly deplored and resisted; yet after his thirteen years rule in Bengal nothing could prevent them coming to pass. He built, perhaps better than he knew, yet worse than he intended. (*Warren Hastings and British India*, pp. 334–35).

Alfred Lyall. Warren Hastings showed a genius for pioneering administration that would have won him distinction at any epoch of our Indian history. His fortune brought him forward in the transitional period between Clive and Cornwallis, when the confusion of new conquest was still fermenting and when the methods of irregular, unrecognised rulership had been discountenanced but not discontinued, when the conscience of the nation demanded orderly government before it had become altogether practicable. It is no wonder that among the sundry and manifold difficulties of such a period a man of his training and temper should have occasionally done things that are hard to justify and easy to condemn, or that his public acts should have brought him to the verge of private ruin. For he was undoubtedly cast in the type, so constantly recurrent in practical history, of the sons of Zeruiah and he very nearly earned their historical reward. (*Warren Hastings*, pp. 234–35).

SELECT REFERENCES

1. Feiling, Keith : *Warren Hastings.*
2. Macaulay, Lord : *Warren Hastings* (*Historical Essays*).
3. Moon, Penderal : *Warren Hastings and British India* (*Teach Yourself History Library series*).
4. Weitzman, Sophia : *Warren Hastings and Philip Francis.*
5. Woodruff, Philip : *The Men Who Ruled India*, vol. I.

ADMINISTRATIVE REFORMS OF CORNWALLIS,[1] 1786–93

In 1786 the Court of Directors sent Cornwallis, a nobleman of high rank and aristocratic disposition, to India to carry out the policy of peace outlined in Pitt's India Act and to reorganise the administrative system in the country. Cornwallis was specially charged with the duty of finding out a satisfactory solution of the land revenue problem, establishing an honest and efficient judicial machinery and of reorganising the commercial department of the Company. In India Cornwallis took up the threads of the administrative system devised by Warren Hastings and built a superstructure which remained substantially in force till 1858.

Judicial Reforms. The first impulse of Cornwallis was towards concentration of authority in the district in the hands of the Collector. This trend was also in line with the instructions of the Court of Directors who had enjoined economy and simplification. In 1787 the Collectors in-charge of districts were made judges of Diwani Adalats, were given more magisterial powers and empowered to try criminal cases with certain limits.

Further changes were made in the field of criminal administration during 1790–92. The District Faujdari Adalats presided over by Indian judges were abolished and in their place four circuit courts, three for Bengal and one for Bihar, were set up. These circuit courts were presided over by European covenanted servants who decided cases with the help of Qazis and Muftis. These courts toured the districts twice a year and tried persons committed by the city magistrates. Further, the Sadr Nizamat Adalat at Murshidabad so far presided by a Mohammedan judge was replaced by a similar court set up at Calcutta comprising the Governor-General and members of the Supreme Council assisted by the Chief Qazi and two Muftis.

Cornwallis Code. Cornwallis' judicial reforms took the final shape by 1793 and were embodied in the famous Cornwallis Code. The new reforms were based on the principle of separation of powers. Under the influence of the eighteenth century French philosophers, Cornwallis sought to separate the revenue administration from the administration of justice. The Collector was the head of revenue department in a district and also enjoyed extensive judicial and magisterial powers. Cornwallis rightly believed that concentration of all powers in the hands of the Collector in the district retarded the improvement of the country. How could the Collector acting as a judge of the Diwani Adalat redress the wrongs done by him as collector or assessor of revenue? Thus neither the landlords nor the cultivators could regard the Collector as an impartial judge in revenue cases. The Cornwallis Code divested the Collector of all judicial and magisterial powers and left him with the duty of administration of revenue. A new class of officer called the District Judge was created to preside over the District Civil Court. The District Judge was also given magisterial and police functions.

A gradation of civil courts was set up. The distinction between revenue and civil cases was abolished and the new Diwani courts were competent to try all civil cases. At the lowest rung of the ladder were the Munsiffs' courts presided over by Indian officers and competent to decide cases involving disputes up to 50 rupees. Next came the courts of Registrars presided over by European officers which tried cases up to 200 rupees. Appeals from both these courts lay to the District or City Courts. District Judges presided over District Courts and decided civil suits with the assistance of

---

1. Charles Cornwallis, first marquis born 1738; surrender before American forces at Yorktown, Oct. 1781; Lord Lieutenant of Ireland, 1798–1801; Governor-General of India, 1786–93 and 1805; died 1805.

Indians well-versed in law. Above the District Courts were the four Provincial Courts of Appeal at Calcutta, Murshidabad, Dacca and Patna. These courts were also to supervise the working of District Courts and on the basis of their report the Sadr Diwani Adalat could suspend the District Judges. In certain cases it had original jurisdiction also. These courts presided over by English Judges heard appeals in suits involving disputes up to 1,000 rupees. Next in order of gradation came the Sadr Diwani Adalat at Calcutta presided over by the Governor-General and his Council which heard appeals from Provincial Courts in cases involving over 1,000 rupees. Appeals lay to the King-in-Council in disputes involving more than £ 5,000. Regulations also laid down the procedure to be followed in these courts and also the qualifications of Indian officers attached to these courts. The Mohammedan law was administered in respect to Mohammedans and Hindu law in respect to Hindus.

Even the European subjects in the districts were made amenable to the jurisdiction of the local civil courts. Europeans intending to reside in the districts away from Calcutta were not given licences until they agreed to submit themselves to the jurisdiction of the district civil courts. Further, Government servants were made answerable before the civil courts for the acts done by them in their official capacity. Thus Cornwallis proclaimed the principle of Sovereignty of Law in India.

Important changes were introduced in the field of criminal administration. The District Faujdari Adalats presided over by Indian officers were abolished. The District Judge was given magisterial powers to order the arrest of criminals and disturbers of peace. The petty cases were decided by the District Judge himself while for serious offences he committed the culprits to the four circuit courts. The provincial circuit courts of appeal which heard appeals in civil cases also worked as criminal circuit courts. The judges of these circuit courts toured their divisions twice a year and decided criminal cases with the assistance of Indian Qazis and Muftis. These courts could pass sentences of death or life imprisonment subject to the confirmation of the Sadr Nizamat Adalat which was the highest court of appeal in criminal cases. The Governor-General enjoyed the general power of pardon or commutation of punishment.

Reform of Criminal Law. If Warren Hastings had asserted the right of the Company's government to interfere with the administration of law, Cornwallis maintained that the Company had the right to reform the criminal law itself. The Mohammedans take their criminal law to be divinely ordained.

During 1790–93 Cornwallis introduced certain changes in the criminal law which were regularised by a Parliamentary Act of 1797. In December 1790 a rule was framed for the guidance of Mohammedan law officers that in all trials of murder they were to be guided by the intention of the murderer either evident or fairly inferable and not by the manner or instrument of perpetration. Further, in cases of murder, the will of the heir or kindred of the deceased were not to be allowed to operate in the grant of pardon or in the demand of compensation money as a price of blood. Again, the usual punishment of amputation of limbs of body was replaced by temporary hard labour or fine and imprisonment according to circumstances of the case. Regulation IX of 1793 amended the law of evidence by providing that 'the religious persuasions of witnesses shall not be considered as a bar to the conviction or condemnation of a prisoner'. Thus non-Muslims could give testimony against Muslims in criminal cases—not permitted so far according to the Muslim law of evidence.

Observations on Judicial Reforms. The judicial system set up by Cornwallis was based on the principle of equity and Western conception of justice. Codified secular law took the place of the religious law or personal law of the ruler or his local agent. The sovereignty of law was proclaimed in unmistakable terms. Even Government officials, for acts done by them in their official capacities, could be tried in the courts. However, in its immediate effects the Cornwallis Code produced many undesirable effect. The novel, unfamiliar and elaborate code was so complicated that the common man could not profit by it. Justice proved very expensive and gave opportunities to a man of means to wear out the uneducated and the poor man. False witnesses were produced. Falsehood, chicanery and deceit began to yield dividends. Litigation greatly increased. Law courts proved insufficient and could not cope with the increased work resulting in great delay in the disposal of justice. Above all, the traditional judicial functionaries like the Panchayats, Zamindars, the Qazi, the Faujdar, the Nazim etc. were replaced by European judges ignorant of the customs and habits of Indians. In 1817 Munro commented that nine-tenths of the European judges knew as little of India as if they had never left Great Britain.

Police Reforms. To supplement and implement the judicial reforms important changes were introduced in the police administration. In Calcutta itself a state of near lawlessness prevailed and ruffians and bad characters went unpunished. In many streets people passed after sunset only at the peril of their lives. "The outskirts of Calcutta had more the appearance of a jungle than an inhabited town," remarked a Police Superintendent. Even the Police Superintendents were corrupt. The Regulation of 1791 defined the powers of the Police Superintendent. To induce the police officials to act honestly and with promptitude Cornwallis raised the salaries of all police officers and offered good rewards for the discovery and arrests of burglars and murderers.

In the districts the zamindars were deprived of all police powers and they were no longer to be considered responsible for robberies committed in their estates unless their complicity could be proved. The English magistrates were given control of the district police. Each district was divided into areas of 400 square miles and each area placed under the charge of a Police Superintendent assisted by an establishment of constables.

Revenue Reforms. Cornwallis reorganised the Revenue Department. In 1787 the province of Bengal was divided into fiscal areas and each placed under a Collector. The number of Collectorships was reduced from 36 to 23. The old Committee of Revenue was renamed as the Board of Revenue and charged with the duty of superintending the work of the Collectors. Till the year 1790 the old system of annual settlements was continued. In 1790 Cornwallis with the approval of the Court of Directors decided to recognise the zamindars as the owners of land subject to the annual payment of land revenue to the state. A ten-year settlement was made with the zamindars in 1790 on the basis of 89% of the rental. In 1793 the decennial settlement was declared permanent and perpetual.

Commercial Reforms. Cornwallis found corruption rampant in the Commercial Department. While the Company's goods were not infrequently sold at loss in Europe, the Company's servants made huge profits in the goods they sent to England on their personal accounts. Ever since the establishment of the Board of Trade at Calcutta in 1774, the Company had procure goods through European and Indian contractors. These contractors usually supplied goods at high prices and of inferior quality. The members of the Board of Trade rather than checking the malpractices of the contractors were often found to be in league with them by accepting bribes and commissions. Cornwallis remarked that "the warehouses at Calcutta were a sink of corruption and iniquity". Cornwallis reduced the strength of the Board of Trade from eleven to five members. The method of procuring supplies through contracts was given up and the method of procuring supplies through Commercial Residents and Agents begun. These Commercial Residents made advances to the manufacturers and settled prices with them. The Company started getting supplies at cheaper rates. In 1788 Cornwallis wrote to the Court of Directors: "I do not even conceive there is a single agent employed in it who ventures to state an article beyond the terms actually advanced by him. I therefore regard that Department as clear, and as now furnishing the investment intelligently and attentively provided at its genuine and fair cost, without any charge upon it but what has been actually expended as necessary". Thus Cornwallis put the Commercial Department of the Company on a footing on which it remained so long as the Company traded.

Suppression of Bribery, Corruption and Evils of Private Trade. Himself Cornwallis was above the greed for money that has tarnished the names of Clive and Warren Hastings. Cornwallis forbade the Company's employees the acceptance of bribes or presents or indulgence in private trade.

He required each officer to declare his property under oath before he left India. He enforced this rule even though he had to dismiss some high officials. Cornwallis could do nothing with the infamous creditors of the Nawab of Carnatic but he prevented the further spread of this evil among the Company's servants.

Cornwallis' approach to the problem was basic. He realised that the low salaries of the Company's servants tempted them to supplement their meagre income by corrupt or illegal methods. Responsibility, he held, must be paid for or the public official would abuse his trust. He decided to raise the salaries of the employees of the Company. A Collector was to get a salary of Rs. 1500 per mensem with an additional allowance of 1% on total revenue collected. District officials were provided with European assistants on good salaries. Cornwallis wrote to the Court of Directors in 1786, "It is not by a moderate addition to the salaries of a few necessary and important offices, but by the suppression of useless places and by preventing ruinous bargains and collusive contracts that the situation of our finances can be materially affected".

Cornwallis resisted the recommendations of even the Prince of Wales. Once he wrote to Viscount Sydney, the Secretary of State : "Lord Ailesbury has greatly distressed me by sending out Mr. Risto recommended by the Queen, but I have too much at stake, I cannot desert the only system that can serve the country even for sacred Majesty".

Europeanisation of Administrative Machinery. Cornwallis suffered, like most of his countrymen in later years, from the evil infection of racial discrimination. He had a very low opinion about Indian character, ability and integrity. He regarded every native of Hindustan to be corrupt. He sought to reserve all higher services for the Europeans and reduce Indians to the position of hewers of wood and drawers of water. The doors of covenanted services were closed to Indians. In the army, Indians could not rise above the position of Jemadars or Subedars and in civil services not above the status of Munsiffs or Sadr Amins or Deputy Collectors. According to Sir John Shore : "The fundamental principle of the English had been to make the whole Indian nation subservient, in every possible way, to the interests and benefits of ourselves. The Indians have been excluded from every honour, dignity or office which the lowest Englishman could be prevailed upon to accept".

Considering the condition of administrative services in contemporary England or the notoriously lax morals of the servants of the Company in India one marvels at Cornwallis' conclusions. While he sought to improve the honesty of higher services by increasing their emoluments, he never thought of applying the same methods to Indian administrative personnel. Cornwallis, it seems, was very much prejudiced against Indians. He put the official seal on the policy of racialism which bedevilled Anglo-Indian relations till British rule lasted in India.

Permanent Settlement of Bengal, 1793

At the time of his appointment Cornwallis was especially directed to devise a satisfactory solution of the land revenue system in Bengal which should ensure the Company's interest as well of the cultivators. The first essential for a satisfactory approach to the problem was a thorough enquiry into the usages, tenures and rents prevalent in Bengal. Prolonged discussion followed in which the leading part was taken by Sir John Shore, the President of the Board of Revenue, Mr. James Grant, the Record Keeper and the Governor-General himself. The discussion centred round three vital questions: With whom was the settlement to be made—the zamindars or the actual tillers of the soil? What would be the state's share in the produce of land? Should the settlement be for a term of years or permanent?

What was the position of the zamindar? Was he to be considered merely as an hereditary tax-gatherer with no proprietary rights or was he the owner and proprietor of land.[2] On this point John

Shore and James Grant held opposite views. John Shore maintained that the zamindar was the owner of land subject to the payment of annual land revenue to the state. As such the zamindar could bequeath the entire land to his children, sell it or mortgage it. This was the position in the later Mughal times, maintained Shore. James Grant, on the other hand, maintained that the state was the owner of all land in the country, the zamindar was just the rent-collecting agent and as such could be discarded at the will of the state. Cornwallis, who himself was an English landlord, accepted the viewpoint of John Shore. Cornwallis' conclusion was very much affected by what was practicable. The Company's servants did not possess sufficient administrative experience to make a direct settlement with the ryot. The system of farming estates to the highest bidder had been tried for long with undesirable consequences. Thus, Cornwallis decided to make a settlement with the zamindars.

What was to be the basis for the revenue settlement? James Grant maintained that the settlement should be made on the basis of the highest Mughal settlement, namely, that in force in 1765. Shore argued that in the Mughal times there was great discrepancy between the assessed amount and the revenue actually collected and that arrears were very often written off. Ultimately it was decided that the settlement was to be made on the basis of the actual collections of the year 1790-91 which were put at Rs. 2,68,00,000.

For what period was the settlement to be made? About this Shore and Cornwallis held different views. Shore held the view that considering the absence of proper survey or demarcation of estate boundaries and limited means of assessment, the settlement should be made for an initial period of ten years. Cornwallis wanted to declare the settlement permanent and perpetual. He held the view that a ten-year period was too limited to induce any zamindar to clear away the jungles or introduce other permanent improvements in the land. The Court of Directors gave sanction to the view of Cornwallis.

The Settlement. The zamindars were recognised owners of land and a ten years' settlement was made with them in 1790. In 1793 the decennial settlement was declared permanent and the zamindars and their legitimate successors were allowed to hold their estates at that very assessed rate for ever. The state demand was fixed at 89% of the rental, leaving 11% with the zamindars as their share for their trouble and responsibility.

Observations on the Settlement. Contemporary opinion claimed a number of advantages for the Permanent Settlement:

Financially, the Permanent Settlement secured a fixed and stable income for the state and the state could depend upon that income, monsoons or no monsoons. Further, it saved the Government the expenses that had to be spent in making periodical assessments and settlements.

Economically, it was claimed that the Permanent Settlement would encourage agricultural enterprise and prosperity; waste land would be reclaimed and the soil under cultivation would be improved; the zamindars would introduce new methods of cultivation like better rotation of crops, use of manure etc. Thus the Settlement would create conditions for the development of the fullest power of the soil. This in turn would create a contented and resourceful peasantry.

Politically, Cornwallis expected that the Permanent Settlement should create a class of loyal zamindars who would be prepared to defend the Company at all costs because their rights were guaranteed by the Company. Thus the Permanent Settlement secured for the government the political support of an influential class in the same way as the Bank of England had for William III after 1694.

---

2. In early times the idea of absolute ownership of land did not exist in India. All classes connected with the land possessed certain rights. The cultivator possessed the right to cultivate the land and enjoyed security of tenure on the condition of payment of more or less definite share of produce to the overload.

   In the 18th century in most parts of India land had no market value. This was mostly due to poor yield from the land and absence of security. The Company started the 'search for the landlord' in an attempt to approximate the Indian to the English land system. There might have been no desire to change the Indian system but ignorance and the assumption that there must be definite ownership of land in a particular individual led Cornwallis to the drastic decision to recognise the zamindar as the owner of land.

The zamindars of Bengal stood loyal during the great rebellion of 1857. Seton Karr commented that the "political benefits of the settlement balance its economic defects".

Socially, the hope was expressed that the zamindars would act as the natural leaders of the ryot and show their public spirit in helping the spread of education and other charitable activities.

Lastly, the Permanent Settlement of Bengal set free the ablest servants of the Company for judicial services. Further, it avoided the evils normally associated with the temporary settlements, the harassment of the cultivator, the tendency on the part of the cultivator to leave the land to deteriorate towards the end of the term to get a low assessment etc.

Disadvantages. Whatever little economic or political purposes the Settlement might have served during its first few years, it soon turned into an engine of exploitation and oppression. It created "feudalism at the top and serfdom at the bottom". Many of the advantages claimed proved to be illusory.

Financially, the state has proved to be a great loser in the long run. The advantages of a fixed and stable income were secured at the great sacrifice of any prospective share in the increase of revenue from land. Even when new areas of land were brought under cultivation and the rents of the land already under cultivation had been increased manifold, the state could not claim it legitimate share in the increase. The state demand fixed in 1793 remained almost the same even in 1954.

The Permanent Settlement retarded the economic progress of Bengal. Most of the landlords did not take any interest in the improvements of the land but were merely interested in extracting the maximum possible rent from the ryot. The cultivator, being under the constant fear of ejectment, had no incentive to improve the land. The zamindars did not live on the estates, but away in the cities where they wasted their time and money in luxury. Thus, the zamindars became a sort of 'distant suction pumps' sucking the wealth of the rural areas and wasting it in the cities. Besides, a host of intermediaries grew up between the state and the actual cultivator. This process of sub-infeudation sometime reached ridiculous proportions, there being as many as 50 intermediaries. All the intermediaries looked to their profits and the ryot was reduced to the position of a pauper. In this context it may be worthwhile to quote the view of Carver who wrote: "Next to war, famine and pestilence, the worst thing that can happen to a rural community is absentee landlordism".

Politically, the Permanent Settlement did fit in the game of the Company and the zamindars along with other vested interests became the favourite children of Imperialism. However, the British Administration gained the loyalty of the few at the cost of the alienation of the masses. Besides, the system divided rural society into two hostile classes, namely, the zamindars and the tenants.

Socially, the Permanent Settlement stands condemned. By recognising the absolute right of ownership of the zamindars the Company sacrificed the interests of the peasants whether of property or occupancy. In a way the peasants suffered from a double injustice, first by surrendering their property rights and secondly by being entirely left at the mercy of the zamindars who rack-rented them. True, the Government attempted rectification and passed tenancy legislation (Bengal Rent Acts of 1859 and 1885) to protect the interests of the ryot, but the zamindars evaded the protective legislation. The growth of pupulation resulting in an excessive pressure on land played into the hands of the zamindars and they not infrequently ejected the ryot. In fact, the peasant was reduced to the position of a serf.

In the beginning the zamindars themselves were in great difficulty. The state demand was pitched very high[3]. Added to this over-assessment was the harshness in the method of collection of revenue. The zamindars were required to deposit the revenue in the government treasury by the sunset of the last day fixed for the purpose failing which the lands were confiscated and auctioned.

---

3. In contemporary England the Land Tax was between 5 and 10 per cent of the rental. The Company's land revenue collections in 1793 amounted to £ 2,680,000, whereas the last Muslim ruler of Bengal, Mir Qasim, had realised only £ 8,17,553 in 1764. (R.C. Dutt : *Economic History of India*, Indian edition, vol. i, Preface, pp. xxv–xxvi).

This 'sunset' law created great hardships and deprived many zamindars of their land for temporary difficulties. During 1797–98 estates worth 17 per cent of the total revenue of Bengal were sold for nonpayment of the state demand in time. The 'sunset' law created so great insecurity that at one time no bidders were coming forth. The frequent changes in the ownership of land affected adversely the condition of the cultivators.

We might say in conclusion that a temporary settlement for 40 or 50 years, renewable again and again, would have secured all the objectives Cornwallis had in view. It was hardly a wise policy measure to bind posterity for all times. If some Indian nationalists like Romesh Dutt gave their unqualified support to the policy of Permanent Settlement it was partly due to the fact that they themselves came from a class which was the beneficiary from the Settlement of Bengal and partly due to the fear that the control of the bureaucracy would be worse than that of the zamindars. In the twentieth century the economic insufficiency and social injustice of the settlement became very glaring. Besides, it was found against the tenets of political or social justice. The Government of Free India has tried to set right the wrong done by Cornwallis. The West Bengal Acquisition of Eastates Act, 1955, has abolished zamindari by paying compensation to the zamindars at a huge expense to the public exchequer.

Cornwallis Completed the Work of Warren Hastings. In his administrative reforms, Cornwallis built a superstructure where the foundations had been laid by Warren Hastings. Cornwallis gave to India the basic administrative set-up that continued without many changes for long.

In 1772, Warren Hastings had initiated the policy of assuming direct responsibility for the government of Bihar and Orissa and of administering revenue affairs and cognate matters through the Company's own agency. The Dual System set up by Clive in 1765 was brought to an end and the Company assumed sovereign functions. This constitutional process was carried further by Cornwallis by his judicial and police reforms.

Warren Hastings had felt greatly aggrieved at the prevalence of bribery and corruption among the servants of the Company. He sought to check the 'get rich-quick' mentality of the Company's servants by forbidding them to indulge in private trade or accept presents and compelled them to sign covenants. At the same time Warren Hastings sought to give them adequate salaries. Financially handicapped by the numerous wars that Warren Hastings had to fight, he sought to compensate the members of the Committee of Revenue by 1% commission on the net revenue realised. Cornwallis was in a better position to effect reforms in this direction. He enjoyed the confidence of both the Court of Directors and Henry Dundas, the President of the Board of Control. Placed in happier circumstances, Cornwallis improved the pay scales and allowances of all the senior servants of the Company. At the same time Cornwallis required each officer of the Company to declare his property on oath before he left India and enforced his orders even though he had to dismiss some high officers. Thus, Cornwallis made a determined bid to improve the notoriously lax morals of the European servants of the Company. However, Cornwallis failed to apply the same corrective in the case of the Indian employees of the Company. Evidently, racial prejudice coloured his vision.

In solving the knotty problem of land revenue administration Cornwallis greatly profited from the various experiments of Warren Hastings. In 1772, Warren Hastings had made a quinquennial settlement but fell back to the system of annual settlements after 1776. In the beginning Warren Hastings regarded the zamindars as merely tax collectors and discouraged them from bidding in the settlement of 1772. By 1776, however, he clearly realised that the zamindars alone possessed the requisite local knowledge about land matters and in all subsequent settlements he gave preference to the zamindars. Cornwallis acted on the presumption that the zamindars were strongly entrenched in the country and a satisfactory settlement could only be made with them. In 1790, he made a decennial settlement with the zamindars of Bengal which he declared permanent in 1793. Thus we find that in devising a satisfactory revenue policy both Warren Hastings and Cornwallis groped in darkness and in the absence of actual survey and classification of land success eluded both. A more satisfactory system was devised by Munro in Madras.

In improving the judicial system also Cornwallis proceeded on the lines indicated by Warren Hastings. Warren Hastings set up a rudimentary judicial system by setting up Faujdari and Diwani Adalats at the district level supervised by the Sadr Nizamat and Sadr Diwani Adalats. Cornwallis improved and elaborated the systems by setting up an hierarchy of courts both for civil and criminal cases. In the district the Munsif's Court disposed of petty civil cases followed by the Registrar's Court and the Zilla Court. Appeals from the Zilla courts lay to the four Provincial Courts. The Sadr Diwani Adalat comprising the Governor-General and members of the Supreme Council was the highest court of appeal in India. Appeals could also be made to the Privy Council in England in certain cases.

In 1772, Warren Hastings had made the Collector in charge of the Diwani Adalat leaving the Faujdari Adalat to be presided over by Indian officers. The Collector (*i.e.*, the European Officer), how-ever, was given the power of superintendence over the Faujdari-Adalat. In 1780, Warren Hastings vested English judges of the Civil Courts with magisterial powers. It was left to Cornwallis to take the next step and appoint European officers of Faujdari Adalats also.

The separation of revenue administration from civil jurisdiction, the most important feature of the Cornwallis Code of 1793, was also begun by Warren Hastings. In the reorganisation of 1781 Warren Hastings had appointed the Collectors in the districts but they were given no powers to try civil cases. The judges of the new Civil Courts tried all civil cases, besides acting as magistrates, with power to commit criminals for trial to Faujdari Courts. Evidently, the division of powers was far from complete for the Collector still decided revenue cases and the jurisdiction of the Collector and the Civil Judge clashed. Nevertheless, a separation between revenue and judicial functions was emerging. The Cornwallis Code of 1793 separated the revenue administration from the administration of justice. The Collector henceforth was to be the revenue-collecting officer of the district while the judicial, magisterial and police functions were left to the charge of the District Judge. It may be added in this connection that the Cornwallis system did not work for long and the Collector's power greatly increased and he became the '*Maa Baap*' of the district and the real local representative of the provincial government.

In the matter of the substitution of English criminal law for Mohammedan law Cornwallis went only a little further than Hastings. Warren Hastings had proceeded very cautiously for, he believed that, the English standard could not be applied to India. However, he had used his executive authority to moderate excessive punishments awarded to dacoits and their families by the Indian officers according to the Mohammedan law. Cornwallis went a step further when in many cases he substituted English criminal law for the Mohammedan law. The Cornwallis Code of Civil Procedure was greatly based on the earlier codes under Warren Hastings.

Estimate of Cornwallis. Cornwallis was not as brilliant as Warren Hastings or Wellesley. "But", writes Aspinal, "he possessed many qualities of mind and heart which inspired confidence in others: devotion to duty, modesty, perseverance, moderation, the art of conciliation, willingness to accept the advice of those who possesed a more expert knowledge of a subject than himself". Cornwallis was lucky in having a band of able and experienced assistants like John Shore, James Grant, George Barlow etc. In the field of administrative reforms the record of Cornwallis' achievement is impressive. He has left his imprint on the administrative system and his methods of administration came to be remembered by the dignified name of the 'Cornwallis System' or the 'System of 1793'. In many respects his system of administration began to be regarded as 'perfect and infallible' and even claimed some sacrosanctity. The Court of Directors recognised his services by sanctioning him a pension of £ 5,000 for twenty years.

Cornwallis sought to solve Indian problems by anglicization of the Indian administration. He introduced British principles and planted British institutions in India so evident from the settlement of land tenures and the judicial and police arrangements made.

From the viewpoint of India some of Cornwallis' methods were unfortunate. By Europeanising the higher services in India and denying the Indian people of share in those he inaugurated a policy which was continued by almost all Governors General till the British rule in India lasted. Further, Cornwallis sought to implant English institutions in India. His judicial reforms were modelled after the English law and code of the time which itself was imperfect. Gleig's comments are very appropriate when he says that Cornwallis sought "to make everything as English as possible in a country which resembles England in nothing". Unfortunately Cornwallis did not introduce in India the English ideas of civil liberty and social equality.

Select Opinions

W.S. Seton-Karr. No one... would place Cornwallis on the same platform as Wellesley or Dalhousie or would compare him for ability, vigour and energy to that servant of the East India Company who from a writer became Governor-General and was rewarded by a diadem. But there was nothing common place about Cornwallis...In his contempt for jobbery, his determination to place the Company's servants, whom he transformed from merchants to administrators, above the reach of temptation, in his anxiety to protect native rights and interests, in constructive ability and in tenacity of purpose, he may challenge a comparison with some of the most eminent men who have ruled India. (*The Marquis of Cornwallis*, pp. 193-94).

L.M. Penson. Although the policy that Cornwallis came to enforce in 1786 was new, it was not wholly new. In every direction Cornwallis built on foundations already laid or begun to be laid by his predecessors, and especially by Hastings. It was the emphasis rather than the principle that was new ; but the principles were now clearly stated, and the strength of the home government was used to enforce them. Every aspect of reform was foreshadowed in the work or in the projects of Hastings, and hence the solidarity of the work of Cornwallis. Yet even when all allowance has been made, much credit must be given to Cornwallis himself ... He possessed great qualities and stood for important principles. Above all, he was beyond reproach, upright and honest. He had not to fear a sudden decline in favour ; he had no pettiness of ambition ; he was not a time - server ; and he left behind him a tradition of service which was of lasting value in Indian administration. Loyalty and integrity there had been before, but it was a loyalty to the Company and an integrity in the Company's affairs. Cornwallis was a public servant who upheld national and not private traditions. His service was to the Crown and not to the people over whom he ruled, and he thus embodied fitly the new spirit of Indian rule.

Thompson and Garratt. Cornwallis' main task throughout his term was to reinstate British reputation. He was 'the first honest incorruptible Governor India ever saw, and after his example, hardly any Governor has dared to contemplate corruption'. Hastings is widely credited with reforming the administration ; as a matter of fact, he achieved practically nothing in this respect, after a first spurt of early promise of some success. Nearly all the esteem now given to him on this head should go to his infinitely less known successor. It is the greatest possible tribute to what Hastings at any rate intended, as well as to the cruel reality of his limitations, that Cornwallis, who had such immense trouble undoing his jobs, always spoke tolerantly of him, and with increasing forgiveness. (*Rise and Fulfilment of British Rule in India*, pp. 171-72).

SELECT REFERENCES

1. Aspinall, A. : *Cornwallis in Bengal.*
2. Dodwell, H.H. : *Cambridge History of India*, vol. v, chapters XXV-XXVI.
3. Dutt, R.C. : *Economic History of India*, vol. 1.
4. Ross, Charles : *The Correspondence of Morquess Cornwallis.*
5. Seton - Karr, W.S. : *The Marquis of Cornwallis and the Consolidation of British Rule.*

Lord Wellesley, 1798-1805

> In the hands of Clive and Warren Hastings, the Subsidiary System was a defensive instrument to safeguard the Company's possessions; in the hands of Wellesley, it was an offensive device, with which to subject independent State to British control.
>
> —*P. Spear*

Richard Colley Wellesley, better known as Marquess Wellesley, succeeded Sir John Shore as the Governor-General of India in 1798. Earlier he had held office as Lord of the British Treasury and a Commissioner of the Board of Control. At the time of his appointment as Governor-General, Wellesley was thirty-seven years of age, still full of energy and in the prime of his youth.

Wellesley had failed to make an impression in English political life for he did not find the sphere where his genius could work. "You want a wider field; you are dying of cramp", remarked a contemporary. The political situation in India offered him that wider field, that necessary sphere of action where his abilities found ample opportunities for display.

Wellesley had a clear vision of the mission before him. He wanted to make the Company the supreme power in India, to add to its territories and to reduce all the Indian states to a position of dependence on the Company. Wellesley gave up the policy of peace and non-intervention and inaugurated the policy of war, more war and further wars. He acted on the theory that the only alternative to retrogression would be aggrandisement and the policy of non-intervention would only strengthen the enemies of the Company. In his forward policy he was backed by the War Ministry in England. He adopted a very high-handed and offensive attitude towards Indian rulers. He described himself as a Bengal tiger, and was always looking for a prey. He was agoistic and held an unusually high esteem for his own views and sentiments. He could not understand any other political system than the one known in Western Europe and he made no secret of his views that he considered the annexation of Maratha territories as the greatest blessing that could be conferred on the people of India. He could not understand why the Marathas should refuse to come under the mild regimentation of a 'beneficent power' that had come all the way from Europe to India. While he described his policy as 'just and reasonable,' 'temperate and moderate', he talked of the Maratha political system in very low terms and described Maratha policies as 'perverse', 'full of intrigue' and 'duplicity'.

The Subsidiary Alliance System

The Subsidiary Alliance System was used by Wellesley to bring Indian states within the orbit of British political power. The system served the double purpose of asserting British supremacy in India and at the same time of saving India from the menace of Napoleon. The system played a very important part in the expansion of the Company's dominions and many new territories were added to the Company's possessions.

Alfred Lyall mentions four stages in the Company's participation in Indian wars. In the first stage, the Company undertook to lend its troops to a friendly Indian prince to assist him in his wars, as for instance, the Treaty with the Nizam (1768). In the second stage, the Company's troops took the field on their own account with the assistance of an Indian ally who made common cause with them. The next stage was reached when the Indian ally was not to supply men but money. The Company undertook to raise, train and equip an army under English officers and render available to the ally a fixed number of troops on receiving a sum of money towards the cost of these troops, as for instance in the Treaty with Hyderabad (1798). The final stage was the next logical step. The Company undertook to defend the territories of an Indian ally and for that purpose stationed a subsidiary force in the

Lord Wellesley

territory of the state. The Indian ally was asked not to pay money but surrender territory from the revenues of which the expenses of the subsidiary force were to be met, as for instance the Treaty with the Nizam (1800).

Wellesley did not invent the Subsidiary System. The system existed long before him and was of an evolutionary growth. Dupleix was perhaps the first who had lent European troops to Indian princes at the expense of the latter. The English also adopted this system. Ever since the governorship of Clive the system had been applied with more or less insight by almost every Governor and Governor-General of India. Wellesley's special contribution was that he greatly developed and elaborated the system and applied it in the case of almost every Indian state. The earliest subsidiary treaty negotiated by the Company was with the Nawab of Oudh in 1765 by which the Company undertook to defend the frontiers of Oudh on the condition of the Nawab defraying the expenses of such defence. A British Resident was also stationed at Lucknow. The first time the Company insisted that the subsidiary state should have no foreign relations was in the treaty with the Nawab of Carnatic concluded by Cornwallis in February 1787. Later Sir John Shore in the treaty with the Nawab of Oudh (21 January 1798) insisted that the Nawab was not to hold communications with or admit into his service other European nationals. The demand for surrender of territory in commutation of cash money was the next logical step. Usually the monetary demands of the Company for the upkeep of the subsidiary force were so heavy that the Indian states, whose revenues shrank or expanded according to the monsoon, were not in a position to meet those and usually fell in arrears. Wellesley therefore made it a general rule to negotiate for the surrender of 'territory in full sovereignty' for the upkeep of the subsidiary force.

A typical Subsidiary Treaty was negotiated on the following terms and conditions:

(a) The Indian state was to surrender its external relations to the care of the Company and was to make no wars. It was to conduct negotiations with other states through the Company;

(b) A bigger state was to maintain an army within its territories commanded by British officers for the 'preservation of public peace' and the ruler was to cede territory in full sovereignty for the upkeep of that force; a smaller state was required to pay tribute in cash to the Company;

(c) The state was to accept a British Resident at its head-quarters;

(d) The state was not to employ Europeans in its service without the consultation of the Company;

(e) The Company was not to interfere in the internal affairs of the state; and

(f) The Company was to protect the Indian state against foreign enemies of 'every sort or kind'.

Advantages to the Company. 1. The Subsidiary System was the Trojan-horse-tactics in Empire building. It disarmed the Indian states and threw British protectorate over them. The Governor-General was present by proxy in every Indian state that accepted the subsidiary alliance. Thus it deprived the Indian princes of the means of prosecuting any measure or of forming any confederacy against the British.

2. It enabled the Company to maintain a large standing army at the expense of Indian princes. According to Wellesley himself, "By the establishment of our subsidiary forces at Hyderabad, and Poona, with the Gaikwar, Daulat Rao Sindhia and the Rana of Gohud, an efficient army of 22,000 men is stationed within the territories, or on the frontier of foreign states, and is paid by foreign subsidies. That army is constantly maintained in a state of perfect equipment, and is prepared for active service in any direction at the shortest notice. This force may be directed against any of the principal states of India without the hazard of disturbing the tranquillity of the Company's possessions, and without requiring any considerable increase to the permanent military expenses of the Government of India."

3. The stationing of the Company's troops in the capitals of the Indian princes gave the English the control of strategic and key positions in India without arousing the jealousy of other European nations.

4. By this system the Company threw forward her military considerably in advance of its political frontier and thus kept "the evils of war...at the distance" from the sources of her wealth and power. In case of actual war the theatre of war was always away from the Company's territories and this saved her territories from the devastations that usually accompany wars.

5. The subsidiary System helped the Company to effectively counteract any possible French moves in India. The Company required the subsidiary ally to dismiss all Frenchmen from his service.

6. The Company became the arbiter in inter-state disputes. All avenues of direct contact between Indian states and foreign powers were closed.

7. The officers commanding the subsidiary force were very well paid. The British Residents wielded considerable influence in the affairs of the Indian states. This placed great patronage into the hands of the Company's authorities in India.

8. The Company acquired 'territories in full sovereignty' from Indian states and expanded her dominions in India. By the treaty of October 12, 1800, the Nizam surrendered to the Company all the territories acquired by the Nizam from Mysore in 1792 and 1799. In 1801, the Nawab of Oudh was made to surrender half of his dominions comprising Rohilkhand and Lower Doab.

A British writer humorously compared the Subsidiary alliances to "a system of fattening allies as we fatten oxen till they were worthy of being devoured".

Disadvantages to Indian States. The Subsidiary System proved demoralising for the Indian princes and evil for the people of those states.

1. An Indian state by accepting disarmament and surrendering foreign relations accepted a subordinate position and virtually lost her independence. Sir Thomas Munro pertinently remarked that "a state purchased security by the sacrifice of independence, of national character—and of whatever renders a people respectable".

2. The British Residents interfered into the day-to-day administration of the states to the extent that the normal functioning of administration was rendered impossible. " I can therefore have no doubt," wrote Munro, " that the Subsidiary System must everywhere run its full course, and destroy every government which it undertakes to protect."

3. The Subsidiary System supported every weak and oppressive ruler and deprived the people of any possible remedy against misrule. Sir Thomas Munro testified : "The usual remedy of a bad government in India is a quiet revolution in the palace, or a violent one by rebellion, or foreign conquests. But the presence of British force cuts off every chance of remedy, by supporting the prince on the throne against every foreign and domestic enemy."

4. A state which accepted the subsidiary alliance courted financial bankruptcy. The subsidy demanded by the Company—usually one-third of the annual revenue of the state—was so heavy that the state fell in arrears. The officers of the subsidiary force were paid high salaries and lavish funds were spent on equipment, for the expense came out of the revenues of the state. The ruler taxed the people heavily and impoverished the country. Even when territory was demanded in commutation of subsidy the Company's demand was put very high. Wellesley wrote to the Secret Committee of the Board of Directors about the deal with the Nizam : "In commutation of 40 lakhs a country rated at the annual value of 62 lakhs of rupees was taken away in full sovereignty in the Nizam's case."

Karl Marx very aptly summed up the effects of the subsidiary alliance system : "As to the native states, they virtually ceased to exist from the moment they became subsidiary to or protected by the Company. If you divide the revenue of a country between two governments, you are sure to cripple the resources of one or the administration of both...the conditions under which they are allowed to retain their apparent independence are, at the same time, the conditions of permanent decay, and of an utter inability of improvement." Even Munro wrote, " that the simple and direct mode of conquest from without is more creditable both to our armies and to our national character, than that of dismemberment from within by the aid of a subsidiary force."

Among the states that accepted the Subsidiary Alliance were the Nizam of Hyderabed (September 1798 and 1800), the Ruler of Mysore (1799), the Raja of Tanjore (October 1799), the Nawab of Oudh (November 1801), the Peshwa (December 1801), the Bhonsle Raja of Berar (December 1803) the Sindhia (February 1804), the Rajput states of Jodhpur, Jaipur, Macheri, Bundi and the Ruler of Bharatpur.

Wellesley and the French Menace

Wellesley sailed for India in 1797, the darkest year in English history. The First Coalition of European powers against France had been shattered. Napoleon Bonaparte had conquered Egypt and Syria and was seriously meditating an invasion of India. In 1798, Napoleon hoped to mass about 100,000 men on the Euphrates and invade India. A keen student of the campaigns of the past, Napoleon had read about Alexander's triumphant march from Alexandria to India and wanted to repeat those exploits. Later in 1801 Napoleon made an alliance with Czar Paul of Russia and drew up a plan for the invasion of India. It was proposed to send a French army of 35,000 men under General Massena *via* Ulm, the Danube, the Black Sea to Astrakhan. At Astrakhan a Russian army comprising 35,000 soldiers was to join the French army and the united armies were to invade India *via* Herat, Farrah and Kandhar. During this period England was engaged in a life and death struggle against French and had good experience of the might of Napoleon on land. England was fighting for her existence. England very well realised the implications of a defeat at the hands of Napoleon. It would mean the ruin of her commerce which brought her wealth and financed the political set up in the country which in turn secured the enjoyment of that wealth.

Today it seems that Napoleon's plans of the conquest of the East were fanciful, but contemporaries did not regard it as such. The Secret Committee of the Court of Directors had written to Wellesley in a despatch of 13 June 1798 : "Our Empire in East has ever been an object of jealousy to the French and we know that their former Government entertained sanguine hopes of being able to reach India, by a shorter passage than round the Cape of Good Hope, and we have no doubt that the present Government would risk a great deal and even adopt measures of the most enterprising and uncommon nature, for the chance of reducing, if not annihilating, the British power in that quarter of the world." General Stuart wrote to Henry Dundas in 1800 thus : "Bombay is our natural emporium...with the Red Sea, which has acquired a new degree of political importance since the attempt of the French to reach India through Egypt...The design is in itself practicable and would have most likely succeeded, had the Turks either been in alliance with the French or the enemy pushed on immediately after he had reached Cairo."[1] There was the possibility of the French using their colony of Mauritius as a spearhead of their attack on the Western coast of India, considering that it was not practicable for the British navy to patrol all the harbours effectively. Besides, the French navy could make a determined bid for supremacy, though temporary in the Indian Ocean, the way they had done during the American War of Independence. In this connection Arthur Wellesley wrote in 1802 : "We have seen the French navies contend with those of Great Britain and an opinion had frequently been advanced by those who are in the habit of considering these questions that during this war the navy of France would have been as formidable as her army if it had not been for the continental contest, which rendered the land service more necessary."[2]

---

1. Owen : *Selection from Wellesley's Despatches*, p. 577.
2. *Ibid.*, p. 87.

Wellesley was not to take any risks. He had rightly understood Napoleon's maxim : 'Impossible is a word to be found in the dictionary of fools.' Tipu Sultan of Mysore, 'the ancient native enemy of the Company', was in correspondence with French authorities and planned to turn out the English from India. The same day Wellesley landed in Calcutta, the envoys of Tipu reached back Mangalore on their return from Mauritius bringing with them a frigate and some French soldiers and further promises of help. In Napoleon's plans on India, Tipu saw the right opportunity for taking revenge on the English. He had planted the 'flag of Liberty' at Seringapatam, styled himself 'Citizen Tipu' and entered into an offensive and defensive alliance with the French. Tipu was making elaborate preparations alliance with the French. Tipu was making elaborate preparations for a war with the Company. The Nizam of Hyderabad being deserted by the English after his defeat at Kharda (1795) at the hands of the Marathas, had employed the French Commandant Monsieur Raymond and had organised a corps of 14,000 men with his help. The Maratha chieftain Mahadaji Sindhia very well understood the enmity between the English and the French and had employed Count de Boigne and later on Monsieur Perron to train a Maratha army which then stood at 8,000 infantry and 8,000 cavalry. The Sindhia had granted the revenues of the Ganga-Jamuna Doab for the upkeep of the French officers and their soldiers. Since the Sindhia could not maintain full and effective control over his mercenary captains or their regular troops, these French officers could serve as an instrument of Napoleon. Holding Delhi and Agra as they did, they could launch an offensive against Bihar and Bengal. Wellesley referred to Monsieur Perron's 'independent state' and could not tolerate a French colony in the heart of Hindustan. Wellesley also viewed with considerable concern the employment of European and French officers by Ranjit Singh of the Panjab. A contributory factor was the contemplated invasion of Zaman Shah from the north-west.

Wellesley set out in right earnest to combat French danger to Britain's position in the East.

1. With his usual enthusiasm Wellesley mobilised the English community in Bengal and urged them to contribute liberally towards the war funds. He succeeded in collecting £ 120, $785 - 3s - 1\frac{1}{2}d$ from Bengal alone and remmitted it to England as war contribution. Besides, many Europeans offered themselves for service in any campaign against Napoleon.

2. Wellesley came to the conclusion that the best way to safeguard India against the hostile designs of Napoleon was to make the Company the arbiter of the Indian political world and place the Indian states beyond the influence of the French. George Barlow, Secretary to government, summed up Wellesley's policy in 1803 thus : "It is absolutely necessary for the defeat of these (*i.e.* French) designs that no native state should be left to exist in India which is not upheld by the British power or the political conduct of which is not under its absolute control." In other words, the Company sought to tame not only the actual but even the potential allies of France. He forced Indian princes to accept subsidiary alliances. An Indian State which accepted the subsidiary alliance had to accept disarmament, expel Frenchmen and other Europeans from his service, surrender her external ralations and accept the superior position of the East India Company. Besides, the subsidiary alliance system enabled the Company to maintain a large standing army at the expense of Indian states. In 1798, Wellesley offered the Nizam the choice of immediate fighting or acceptance of the subsidiary alliance. The weak and vacillating Nizam reluctantly accepted the subsidiary alliance in September 1798. He had to dismiss his French-trained troops. The French officers of the Nizam's army were sent as prisoners to Calcutta and then deported to Europe. A subsidiary force of six battalions commanded by British officers was stationed at Hyderabad at the expense of the Nizam. Wellesley succeeded in rooting out French influence from Hyderabad. Next Wellesley turned his attention towards Tipu Sultan of Mysore, who had solicited French support in his plans to throw out the English from India. Wellesley calculated that a French invasion *via* the Red Sea could only be possible after the middle of 1799 and he decided to deal with Tipu before that time. On the refusal of Tipu to accept the subsidiary alliance war began in February 1799 and was over by May of the same year. Tipu was killed in fighting. The territories of

Mysore state were reduced in size and handed over to a prince of the old Hindu dynasty who accepted the subsidiary alliance. A very dangerous foe in the south was removed and, above all, the Company got command over the sea coast of the lower peninsula. French mischief from the side of Malabar Coast was rendered impossible. A resolution of the House of Commons thanked Wellesley "for counteracting with equal promptitude and ability the dangerous intrigues and projects of the French particularly by destroying their power and influence in the Deccan, whereby he has established on a basis of permanent security the tranquillity and prosperity of the British Empire in India."

Wellesley next turned his attention towards the North planning to secure for the Company the position of arbiter of Northern India also. The state of Oudh had greatly degenerated and Oudh could no longer serve as a buffer against a possible French invasion. In 1801, Wellesley forced the Nawab into the acceptance of a large subsidiary force and surrender to the Company for its upkeep Rohilkhand, the northern districts of the Doab. Next, Wellesley turned his attention towards the Marathas, the only power of importance left in India which was independent of British protection. The French officers in the army of the Sindhia could serve as instruments of Napoleon. Besides, Maratha possessions along the western coast left them open to French influence and possibility of French infiltration from that corner could not be ruled out. The defeat and death of Tipu had been likened "to the loss of his right arm" by the Peshwa. Wellesley's offer of subsidiary alliance was turned down. However, internal dissensions in the Maratha camp drove Peshwa Baji Rao II into the trap of the Company in December 1802 when the Peshwa signed a subsidiary treaty. A British subsidiary force was stationed at Poona. The Sindhia and the Bhonsle Raja felt humiliated and made war with the English but were defeated. Both the Bhonsle Raja and the Sindhia accepted subsidiary alliances and surrendered important territories to the Company. Thus Wellesley succeeded, in the words of Lord Lake, "in the great and glorious work of destroying the last nests of French scoundrels in India" and thereby saving Britain's "great and flourishing possessions from the claws of the rapacious tyrant, the First Consul" (*i.e.*, Napoleon).

3. Wellesley advocated a carefully calculated strategy for the defence of India. To prevent Goa from falling into the hands of the French, Wellesley garrisoned Goa in 1799 by arrangement with the Portuguese. In 1801, England and Denmark were on opposite sides. Wellesley at once occupied the Danish settlements in Bengal, namely Tranquebar and Serampore. About Serampore Wellesley wrote to Henry Dundas : "Its vicinity to the seat of Government in Bengal rendered it peculiarly obnoxious; adventurers of every nation, Jacobins of every description swarm at Serampore and it is the asylum of all our public defaulters and debtors."

4. Wellesley sought to encircle Indian powers by acquiring the maritime provinces of Gujarat, Malabar and Cuttack, and thus preventing any French military help reaching the Indian princes. Wellesley put the surrender of the Malabar coast as one of the main pre-conditions for friendly relations with Tipu. Similarly, during the war with the Marathas, the English quickly occupied the harbour of Broach and the forts of Champaner and Pawangarh. Wellesley was very well alive to the importance of Gujarat when he wrote of "the facility which the possession of the sea-port of Broach afforded to Sindhia, of improving his military establishment, by the accession of French or other European officers, of military supplies and stores etc. and even a body of French or other European troops". Similarly by the acquisition of Cuttack, very much coveted by Wellesley, the English besides linking their territories of Bengal and Madras would effectively cut off any communication between the Raja of Nagpur and the French.

5. In 1799, Wellesley sent a British envoy, Mehdi Ali Khan, to the court of the Shah of Persia to counter French intrigues in that country. Later he sent John Malcolm with lavish presents to the Shah's court. Malcolm reached Tehran in November 1800 and concluded a treaty with the Shah whereby the latter agreed not to allow the French to settle in his dominions and to expel and extirpate them if anywhere they had formed a settlement.

Descriptive Note on Extension of British Dominion under Wellesley

(i) After, the Fourth Anglo-Mysore War (1799) Wellesley annexed the South Kanara coast, Wynaad in the south-east, Coimbatore and Darupuram in the south-east besides Seringapatam.

(ii) By a revised subsidiary treaty forced on the Nizam (12 October 1800) the latter ceded to the Company the districts of Bellary and Cuddapah.

(iii) By a treaty (10 November 1801) forced on the Nawab-Wazir of Oudh, the Company acquired Rohilkhand, Furrukhabad, Mainpuri, Etawah, Kanpur, Fatehgarh, Allahabad, Azimgarh, Basti and Gorakhphur.

(iv) After the Second Anglo-Maratha War (1802-3) the Company's territorial gains included the Upper Doab (territory between the Ganges and the Jamuna), all territories north of the Rajput States of Jaipur, Jodhpur and Gohud, the part of Broach, the fort of Ahmednagar besides the district of Cuttack in Orissa.

(v) Wellesley took over the administration of Tanjore (25 October 1799), Surat (March 1800) and Carnatic (31 July 1801).

Extent of E.I. Company's Territories

In 1805 the Company's dominion extended along the whole sealine of India from the Sind frontier at the mouth of the Indus down the western coast up to Cape Comorin and thence northeastward along the Bay of Bengal to the frontier of Burma. In Northern India the Company's political jurisdiction extended from Bengal to the desert bordering upper Sind and Panjab. The princely states of Oudh, Nagpur, Gwalior, Indore, Baroda, Hyderabad, Mysore, Travancore and others had all accepted the protection of the East India Company.

The Maratha Confederacy. The Maratha chiefs controlled major part of Western India, ruled over extensive territories in Central India apart from exercising general control over the Rajput states.

North-Western India. Sikh *misls* ruled over extensive territories on both sides of the river Sutlej. Ranjit Singh was emerging as a powerful ruler in the Punjab. Muslim chiefs ruled over north-western Punjab, Multan, Kashmir and Sind.

6. Wellesley proposed the despatch of an expedition against the French naval base at Mauritius, but the British Admiral Rainier, who was in command of the British squadron, refused to co-operate on the ground that he could not act without express orders from the Crown. Even the Court of Directors did not favour the proposal. Wellesley also urged the Home Authorities to sanction an attack upon the Dutch possessions of Batavia and the Cape Colony (the Dutch at that time were the allies of France).

7. In 1800, Wellesley sent an expedition of Indian troops under General David Baird to Egypt to fight against Napoleon. From the Red Sea the army marched across the desert and reached Rosetta on the shores of the Mediterranean. On his arrival there General Baird found that the French force had already surrendered and the French danger had been averted for the time being. The Indian force returned back to India in 1802.

8. By the Treaty of Amiens (1802) between Napoleon and England, England restored Pondicherry to the French. Bonaparte used this opportunity to send military officers to this settlement to negotiate with Emperor Shah Alam II through the French officers in the service of the Sindhia. Monsieur Perron and his forces controlled the Mughal Empire and could wield his nominal authority. At one time Napoleon seriously meditated sending a French force to India to save the Emperor from his enemies. Lord Wellesley saw in French designs a possibility of further mischief. In 1803, Lord Lake captured Delhi and Agra and took the Emperor under the company's protection and gave him a liberal pension.

Thus by his energetic and well-planned policy Wellesley succeeded not only in sefeguarding India against possible French designs but in considerably adding to British dominions in India. At a time when empires in Europe were crumbling like houses of cards before the might of Napoleon, in the East Wellesley kept the British flag high. As to the methods he employed to achieve his objective, Alfred Lyall comments: "As a matter of fact Wellesley was applauded and supported in measures ten times more high-handed and dictatorial than those for which Warren Hastings had been impeached a dozen years earlier". It seems the British temper had greatly changed due to the continuous war against Revolutionary France and Napoleon.

Estimate of Wellesley's Achievements. According to Sidney J. Owen, Wellesley converted the British Empire *in* India to the British Empire *of* India. From one of the political powers in India, the Company became the supreme power in India and claimed the whole country as its sole protectorate. From Wellesley's time onwards the defence of India was the Company's responsibility.

There was considerable expansion of British dominion in India. In 1798 there was no land route linking the three Presidencies without a person having to pass through foreign territories of Indian princes ; then the only unchecked link was by sea. In 1805 there was a direct land route linking Calcutta with Madras and Madras with Bombay. The Imperial cities of Delhi and Agra together with the contiguous tracts on both sides of the Jamuna passed under British administration; Rohilkhand was ceded by the Nawab of Oudh: important tracts of Bundelkhand, Cuttack, valuable tracks in Gujarat, strategic territories along the western coast were added to Company's territories. The addition of these territories along with the acquisition of Surat, Tanjore, Carnatic and cession of territories by the Nizam gave a new shape to the three Presidencies. British superiority in India was amply demonstrated, the unquestioned proclamation of British Paramountcy was a question of time and the next logical step.

While opinions will continue to differ on whether the 'French intrigues' were a real danger to British position in India or were merely made a convenient excuse by Wellesley for pursuing schemes of aggression, whetheres, Maratha-French combinations were the causes or effects of Wellesley's aggressive policy, one thing is certain that Wellesley's methods were far more high-handed and dictatorial than those for which Warren Hastings had been impeached by the British Parliament a dozen years earlier. During that interval the temper of the English nation had greatly changed. Embittered by the strenuous struggle against Revolutionary and Napoleonic France the British Liberal tradition of Burke and Fox had receded to the background and the Parliament condoned all methods, however objectionable, only if those buttressed British prestige in India.

Select Opinions

P.E. Roberts. Wellesley was one of the greatest of British rulers of India. Only Clive, Warren Hastings and Dalhousie can challenge comparison with him, and in actual achievement he outdistanced them all. He came to India at an auspicious time for one who wished to play a great part, when the policy of non-interference and neutrality was on the point of breaking down, and he seized the tide of his opportunity at the flood. He had great chances and made the most of them. His own imperious will, wide and bold political grasp of facts, and gorgeous imagination swept onward to a more ambitious view of British Dominion than had hitherto been entertained. It was afterwards realized that the change he inaugurated was in any case inevitable. But while others shrank from it even when they saw it coming, Wellesley went boldly forth to anticipate and to meet it. He saw that Great Britain could no longer play any but the predominant part in India. (*History of British India*, pp. 243-44).

Henry Beveridge. Wellesley saw clearly that the British in India had advanced too far to recede, and that no alternative was left except either to gain the whole or lose the whole. The idea of becoming stationary was an absurdity. If they did not advance, they must lay account with being driven back. If they repudiated the empire placed within their reach, some other power would certainly seize it. Marquess Wellesley saw this from the first, and having made his choice in favour of domination, pursued it on system with consummate ability and brilliant success. The legality, wisdom and even the justice of some of his measures are very questionable, but the House of Commons undoubtedly did right when...it declared that Wellesley had been actuated by an ardent zeal for the service of his country, and an ardent desire to promote the safety, interests and prosperity of the British Empire in India. (*A Comprehensive History of India*, vol. II, pp. 802-3).

Alfred Lyall. Whereas up to his time the British government had usually dealt with all states in India upon a footing of at least nominal political equality, Lord Wellesley revived and proclaimed the imperial principle of political supremacy. All his views and measures pointed towards the reconstruction of another empire in India, which he rightly believed to be the natural outcome of our position in the country, and the only guarantee of its lasting consolidation. (*The Rise and Expansion of British Dominion in India*, p. 269).

Philip Francis. We never pretended to be thoroughly afraid of our safety until in effect we had no enemy left and literally nothing to fear...Nothing can be more simple than the principle, nor more effectual than the operation of this subsidiary treaty. If once you can persuade the Nizam, the Peshwa or any other native prince, for whom you happen to have a particular friendship, that his Government is in danger and that his person is not safe without your assistance, the business is done. A British army is on the frontier ready to march the moment the treaty is signed, enters his country, takes possession of his capital and secures him in his palace. If he should happen to be a short-sighted, narrow-minded person or not sufficiently quick in accepting these proofs of your friendship, there are various ways of convincing him. Sword in hand is the shortest. If you follow the agents of Lord Wellseley and the armies of Britain you will find them in the centre or in the remotest corner of the Peninsula, carrying slavery and desolation into countries and exacting tributes from peoples, whose names are hardly known in England, and then we revile the peoples of India as if they were the aggressors, as if they were the invaders, and as if there could be no repose or security for the British establishment as long as any native power in that immense continent was left in a state of independence. We go into their country to charge them with lawless ambition and we rob them of their property in order to convict them of insatiable avarice.

SELECT REFERENCES

1. W.H., Hutton,   : *Marquess Wellesley* (Rulers of India series).
2. Owen, S.J. (Ed)   : *Selection from Wellesley's Despatches*, 2 vols.
3. Roberts, P.E.   : *India under Wellesley.*
4. Torrens, W.M.   : *Marquess Wellesley.*

11

MYSORE UNDER HAIDAR ALI AND TIPU SULTAN

> Tipu Sultan's failure.. was a tragedy for him...and a tragedy for the sub-continent for his defeat meant the end of the first round of the struggle for Freedom.
> — *History of the Freedom Movement of Pakistan*

Eighteenth century India provided very favourable circumstances for the rise of military adventurers both in the north and the south. One such soldier of fortune, Haidar Ali (born 1721) started his career as a horseman and rose to the position of the ruler of Mysore. The process of usurpation of royal authority of the Wodeyar[1] ruler Chik Krishnaraj started during 1731-34 when two brothers. Devraj (the Commander-in-chief) and Nanjaraj (the Controller of Revenue and Finance) controlled real power in the state. The quadrangular conflict for supremacy in the Deccan among the Marathas, the Nizam, the English and the French East India Companies dragged Mysore in the game of adventurous politics. The repeated incursions into Mysorean territories of the Marathas in 1753, 1754, 1757 and 1759 and of the Nizam in 1755 and the heavy financial demands made by the invaders rendered the Mysore state financially bankrupt and politically a fertile ground for military exploits at the hands of powerful neighbouring states. Devraj and Nanjaraj unable to rise to the occasion had to give place to a man of superior military talent, sound diplomatic skill and unquestioned qualities of leadership. By 1761 Haider Ali was the *de facto* ruler of Mysore.

Haider Ali prepared himself to meet the challenges of the time. A well-disciplined army with a strong and swift cavalry wing was necessary to meet the challenges of the Marathas, an effective artillery wing along could counter the French-trained Nizami armies. He was also aware of the superior Western know-how in arms manufactures. With French help Haidar Ali set up an arsenal at Dindigul and also profited from the Western methods of training an army. Above all, he learnt the art of permutation-combination at the diplomatic chessboard and tried to out-manoeuvre his adversaries in the game.

During 1761-63 Haider Ali conquered Hoskote, Dod Bellapur, Sera, Bednur etc. and subjugated the poligars of south India.

The Marathas who had recovered fast from the Panipat debacle (1761) under Peshwa Madhav Rao frequently raided Mysore territory and defeated Haidar Ali in 1764, in 1766 and again in 1771 compelling Haidar to buy off the Marathas as also to surrender some important territories to them. Quick to take advantage of political confusion at Poona after the death of Peshwa Madhav Rao in 1772, Haidar Ali during 1774-76 not only recovered all the territories earlier surrendered to the Marathas but acquired Bellary, Cuddapah, Gooty, Kurnool and important territories in the Krishna-Tungabhadra Doab.

The First Angle-Mysore War (1767-69). Blinded by their easy successes in Bengal the English concluded a treaty with Nizam Ali of Hyderabad (1766) and in return for the surrender of Northern Circars committed the Company to help the Nizam with troops in his war against Haidar Ali. Haidar already had territorial disputes with the ruler of Arcot and differences with the Marathas. Suddenly Haidar found a common front of the Nizam, the Marathas and the Nawab of Carnatic operating against

---

1. The chiefs of Mysore were feudatories of the Vijaynagar kingdom. In 1612 king Venkata II permitted Raja Wodeyar to assume the title of Raja of Mysore. The Wodeyars considerably expanded their dominion during the 17th century. The succession of Immadi Krishnaraja in 1732 as ruler of Mysore amidst an explosive Deccani politics marked the beginning of the decline of the Wodeyar dynasty.

him. Undaunted, Haidar played the diplomatic game, bought the Marathas, allured the Nizam with territoral gains and together with the latter launched an attack on Arcot. After a see-saw struggle for a year and a half, Haidar suddenly turned the tables on the English and appeared at the gates of Madras. The panic-stricken Madras Government concluded the humiliating treaty on 4 April 1769 on the basis of mutual restitution of each other's territories and a defensive alliance between the two parties committing the English to help Haidar in case he was attacked by another power.

The Second Anglo-Mysore War (1780-84). The treaty of 1769 between Haider Ali and the English Company proved more in the nature of a truce and Haidar Ali accused the Company of not observing the terms of the defensive treaty by refusing to help him when the Marathas attacked Mysore in 1771. Further, Haider found the French more helpful in meeting his military demands for guns, saltpetre and lead than the English. Some French military hardware naturally found its way to Mysore through Mahe, a French port on the Malabar coast. The outbreak of the American War of Independence and French alliance with the American colonists made Warren Hastings extremely suspicious of Haidar Ali's relations with the French. Under the circumstances the English attempt to caputure Mahe which Haidar considered to be under his protection, was a direct challenge to Haidar Ali.

Haidar Ali arranged a joint front with the Nizam and the Marathas against the common enemy—the English East India Company. In July 1780 Haidar attacked Carnatic and captured Arcot, defeating an English army under Colonel Baillie. Meanwhile the English detached the Marathas and the Nizam from the side of Haidar. Undaunted, Haidar boldly faced the English but suffered a defeat at Porto Novo (Nov. 1781). The following year Haidar inflicted a humiliating defeat on the English army under Col. Braithwaite ; Braithwaite was taken a prisoner. Haidar died on 7 December 1782, leaving the task unfinished to his son, Tipu. Tipu continued the war for another year, but absolute success eluded both sides. Tired of war, the two sides concluded peace by the Treaty of Mangalore (March 1784) on the basis of mutual restitution of each other's territories. The second round of the struggle too proved inconclusive.

The Third Anglo-Mysore War (1790-92). British imperialism, true to its very nature, considered every peace treaty as a breathing time for another offensive against Tipu. Acting against the letter and spirit of the policy of peace and non-expansion loudly proclaimed in Pitt's India. Act (1784), Lord Cornwallis worked on the anti-Tipu suspicions of the Nizam and the Marathas and arranged a Triple Alliance (1790) with them against Tipu. Convinced of the inevitability of a war with the English, Tipu had sought the help of the Turks by sending an embassy to Constantinople in 1784 and again in 1785 and on to the French king in 1787.

Tipu's differences with the Raja of Travancore arose over the latter's purchase of Jaikottai and Cranganore from the Dutch in Cochin state ; Tipu considered the Cochin state as his tributary state and thus considered the act of the Travancore Raja as violation of his sovereign rights. He decided to attack Travancore in April 1790. The English, itching for a war, sided with the ruler of Travancore (vide their earlier treaty of 1784) and declared war against Tipu. At the head of a large army Cornwallis himself marched through Vellore and Ambur to Bangalore (captured in March 1791) and approached Seringapatam. The English captured Coimbatore only to lose it later. Supported by the Maratha and Nizam's troops the English made a second advance towards Seringapatam. Tipu offered tough resistance but realised the impossibility of carrying further the struggle. The Treaty of Seringapatam (March 1792) resulted in the surrender of nearly half of Mysorean territory to the victorious allies. The British acquired Baramahal, Dindigul and Malabar while the Marathas got territory on the Tungabhadra side and the Nizam acquired territories from the Krishna to beyond the Pennar. Tipu had also to pay a war indemnity of over three crores of rupees. Tipu lost heavily in this round of strength and could only save his kingdom from total extinction by preparation and planning which seemed beyond his resources. Cornwallis summed up the Company's gain: "We have effectively crippled our enemy without making our friends too formidable".

The Fourth Anglo-Mysore War (1799). The East India company's policy in India alternated wars with spells of peace for recuperation of their resources. The arrival of imperialist Lord Wellesley as Governor-General in 1798 in the backdrop of Napoleonic danger to India augured ill for the maintenance of status quo. Wellesley was determined to either tame Tipu to submission or wipe out his independence altogether. The *modus operandi* was the Subsidiary Alliance System. The charge against Tipu Sultan of planning intrigues with the Nizam and the Marathas or sending emissaries to Arabia, Zaman Shah of Afghanistan or Constantinople or the French in the Isle of France (Mauritius) or the Directory at Versailles were convenient excuses to force down the desired end. Tipu's explanation that only "40 persons, French and of a dark colour, of whom 10 or 12 were artificers and the rest servants paid the hire of the ship, came here in search of employment" did not satisfy Wellesley. The operations against Tipu began on 17 April and with the fall of Seringapatam on 4 May 1799 brought to a close the history of Mysore's independence. Tipu died fighting bravely. The members of Tipu's family were interned at Vellore. The English annexed Kanara, Coimbatore, Wynead, Dharpuram besides the entire sea coast of Mysore. Some territories were given to the Nizam. A boy of the earlier Mysore Hindu royal family was installed on the *gaddi* of Mysore and a Subsidiary Alliance was imposed.

Administration of Tipu Sultan

The only system of government known to the Indian sub-continent at that time was despotism and Tipu's system could not be different. The Sultan was the embodiment of all civil, political and military authority in the state. He was his own foreign minister, his own commander-in-chief and acted as the highest court of appeal in his kingdom.

In spite of the absence of any constitutional checks on his authority, Tipu Sultan did not behave like an irresponsible despot. He displayed a high sense of duty to his office and believed that his subjects "constitute a unique trust held for God, the Real Master." He took great care to work for the welfare and happiness of the people.

The Central Administration. Tipu Sultan's zeal for innovation and improvement prompted him to introduce a number of changes in the system of government he inherited from his father. H.H. Dodwell gives Tipu the credit of being the first Indian sovereign who sought to apply the western methods to his administration. Each department was put under the charge of a chief assisted by a number of subordinate officers who constituted a Board. The decisions in the department were taken after full discussion where members enjoyed the right to dissent. The decisions were taken by a majority of votes and the minutes of the meetings were recorded. However, the final decision in all important matters rested with the Sultan.

There was no office of the Wazir or Prime Minister in Tipu's administration. The seven principal departments each under a *mir asif* was directly responsible to the Sultan. The seven departments were the Revenue and Finance Department (Mir Asaf Cutchehri), the Military Department (Mir Miran Cutchehri and the Zumra), the Commerce Department (Malikut-Tujjar Cutchehri), the Marine Department (Mir Yam Cutchehri) and the Treasury and Mint Department (Mir Khazain Cutchehri). Besides there were some minor departments like Post & Intelligence Department, the Public Buildings Department, the Cattle Department etc.

The Provincial and Local Administration. After 1784 Tipu divided his kingdom into seven provinces called *asafi tukris*. Later the number of provinces was increased to 17. The two principal officers in a province were the *asaf* (Civil Governor) and the *faujdar* (Military Governor) and the two were expected to act as a check on each other. The provinces were further divided into districts and further down there were a number of villages in each district. The traditional village *panchayats* provided the infrastructure for local administration.

Land Revenue. By and large Tipu continued the revenue system of Haidar Ali but introduced greater efficiency into it. He tried to establish direct relationship between the Government and the cultivator by discouraging the jagirdari system, resumption of unauthorised *inam* (rent free) lands and confiscation of the hereditary land rights of the poligars (zamindars).

The Government employed the method of inducement-cum-compulsion to bring more land under cultivation. The *Amil*, incharge of the district, toured his district and sanctioned taqavi (advances of money) loans to the needy peasants to purchase ploughs and extend cultivation. Further, if the *Amil* found that in a household there were a number of men and a few ploughs, he would urge the head of the family to acquire more ploughs; in case of defiance and if the *Amil* was satisfied that in a village there was more ground fit for cultivation (say, of sugarcane) than under actual plough then, as a penal measure, the *Amil* could charge the land tax cultivated on the basis of all cultivable land and not the land under actual cultivation.

The land revenue demand of the state ranged from 1/3 to 1/2 of the total produce, depending on the fertility of the land and availability of irrigation facilities. In 1792 the state's income from revenue was over two crores which was reduced to nearly one-half after the treaty of Seringapatam, 1792 (when he had to surrender half his kingdom to the E.I. Company and her allies). To make up for this loss in income, in 1765 Tipu increased the assessment by 37½% over pre-1792 rates.

Trade and Commerce. In the fashion of European powers Tipu also realised that a country could be great only by developing its trade and commerce. He promoted both foreign and inland trade and imposed tight Government control over it.

Realising the importance of trade with the Persian gulf and Red Sea regions, he sought to establish commercial factors and stationing commercial agents at Muscat, Ormuz, Jeddah, Aden etc. He even planned to establish commercial relations with Pegu and China. A Commercial Board was established and the Regulations of 1793-94 set forth the general duties of the officers in the department. He declared government monopoly of trade in sandalwood, betelnut, pepper, cardamos, gold and silver bullion, foreign export of elephants etc. Similarly, for conduct of inland trade the Government acquired monopoly rights for purchase of the ryot's share of production of some specified articles, like sandalwood and black pepper. A number of factories were set up in the Mysore state which manufactured a wide range of articles ranging from war ammunition, paper, sugar, silk fabrics, small tools and fancy goods.

Asok Sen believes that the principal aim of Tipu's trade policy was of making the government 'the chief merchant of his dominions' and the trader was to enrich the treasury. Economic activity came to be directly subordinated to political and military interests and were not compatible with the long-term interests of trade and industry, nor with the preparation of society and economy for the making of an industrial revolution under the aegis of capitalism.[2]

Military Administration. Compulsion of circumstances required the Sultan to give his maximum care to the raising and maintenance of an efficient military force. Tipu Sultan's infantry was disciplined after the European model with Persian words of command. He did employ French officers to train his troops and raised a French corps also but unlike the Nizam and the Sindhia never allowed French corps to develop a pressure group value. In fact the number of French troops in his army gradually declined till it stood at only 20 Europeans in 1794 and after the fall of Seringapatam in 1799 stood at merely 4 officers and 45 non-commissioned officers and privates.

The strength of Tipu's army varied in accordance with the military requirements and resources available. On the eve of the Third Anglo-Mysore War Tipu's military forces comprised 45,000 regular infantry and 20,000 horse besides some irregular force. In 1793 after Tipu had surrendered half his territory to the English and their allies, his army was estimated to be 30,000 regular infantry, 7,000

---

2. Barun De. (Ed.), *Perspectives in Social Sciences* I. p. 95.

cavalry, 2000 artillery besides 6,000 irregular cavalry.

Both Haidar Ali and Tipu realised the importance of a naval force but could not rise to the level of their main adversary, the East India Company. Whatever ships Haidar Ali had built were destroyed by Sir Edward Hughes when he entered Bangalore in 1780.

The English occupation of Tipu's Malabar possessions in the Third Anglo-Mysore war drew the Sutan's attention to the need for an effective naval task force. In 1796 Tipu set up a Board of Admiralty and planned for a fleet of 22 battleships and 20 large frigates. Three dockyards at Mangalore Wajidabad and Molidabad were established. However, his plans did not fructify and he found his resources unequal to the potential and resources of the English. It was probably realising this factor when he remarked, "I can ruin their resources by land but I cannot dry up the sea".

Estimate of Tipu Sultan. Born on 20 November 1750 to Haider Ali and Fatima after many prayers, the child was given the name of Tipu Sultan. Thus Sultan was a part of his name by which he was known both as a prince and a ruler. He received all the scholastic education of a Muslim prince and could freely converse in Arabic, Persian, Kanarese and Urdu. He know horse riding, shooting and fencing and was in possession of excellent health. He despised the use of palanquins and described them as fit only for use of women and invalids. Tipu Sultan possessed an energetic mind free from 'Eastern apathy or Eastern conservatism'. He was eager to learn and showed proper appreciation of the Western sciences and Western political philosophy. He actively supported the proposal of the French soldiers at Seringapatam to set up a Jacobin Club in 1797 and ordered a salute of 2,300 cannons, 500 rockets to celebrate the occasion. He is also reported to have planted the "Tree of Liberty" at Seringapatam, enrolled himself as a member of the Jacobin Club and allowed himself to be called Citizen Tipu.

As an administrator and ruler Tipu was successful and earned the praise of his adversaries. Lieutenant Moore noted, "When a person travelling through a strange country finds it well cultivated, populous with industrious inhabitants, cities newly founded, commerce extending, towns increasing and everything flourishing so as to indicate happiness he will naturally conclude it to be under a form of government congenial to the minds of the people. This is a picture of Tippoo's country. Even Sir John Shore commented that the peasantry of Tipu's dominions were well protected and their labours encouraged and rewarded. Tipu also won the confidence and loyalty of his soldiers. In times when desertions by military commanders was not uncommon. Tipu's troops displayed discipline and fidelity that earned the notice of his contemporary European observers also.

Wilks remarks that "Haidar was born to create an empire, Tipu to lose one" seems correct in retrospect of history but does scant justice to the capabilities of Tipu and does not take into full account the heavy odds he faced. Tipu's boldness and spirit of innovations have been described as great negative points. While Haidar had maintained the fiction of the sovereignty of the Wodeyar dynasty till he lived, Tipu assumed the title of the Padshah in 1787[3], issued coins in his name, had Arabic names substituted for Hindu ones in the cyclic years and months and issued a new calendar. Tipu's innovations were not merely changes but improvements introduced by a mentally alert monarch.

The imperialist writers' depiction of Tipu as a 'monster pure and simple' and a bigoted monarch is obviously biased. Tipu's fanaticism has been over-played. It is true he crushed the Hindu Coorgs and the Nairs but he did not spare the Muslim Moplahs when they defied his authority. The discovery of Sringeri Letters reveals that in response to a request from the chief priest of the Sringeri temple, Tipu sanctioned funds for repair of the temple and installation of the image of goddess Sarada (after it had been damaged in a Maratha raid of 1791). The Sultan never interfered with worship in the Sri Ranganatha, the Narasimha and the Ganga-dharesvara temples situated within the Sernigapatam fort.

---

3. Mohibbul Hasan, *History of Tipu Sultan*, p. 7.

Tipu Sultan stands out as a fascinating personality in the history of South India. Brave and daring he stuck to his self-respect and spurned Wellesley's offer of a Subsidiary Alliance. He preferred a hero's death to the tame existence of a band-wagon of Western imperialism. His great misfortune was that he was pitted against the imperial giants who had both the will and capacity to buldoze the whole of India. His life and darings enthuse more the modern Indian mind than the host of other Indian princelings.

Select Opinions

Mohibbul Hasan. Tipu has been regarded by some writers as the first Indian nationalist and a martyr for India's freedom. But this is a wrong view arrived at by projecting the present into the past. In the age in which Tipu lived and ruled there was no sense of nationalism or an awareness among Indians that they were a subject people. It will, therefore, be too much to say that Tipu waged war against the English for the sake of India's freedom. Actually he fought in order to preserve his own power and independence, (*History of Tipu Sultan*, p. ix)

Asok Sen. The hypothesis...was formulated as an inquiry into the economic directions of Tipu Sultan's Mysore, of the suitability of his policies and measures for economic growth and modernization...Whether in respect of agriculture, or that of trade and industry, Tipu's means of striking an advance could not go beyond the elaborate manipulations of statecraft which continued and even accentuated the stranglehold of politics and bureaucracy on the processes of appropriation and use of economic surplus. Thus with all his originality of will and purpose, Tipu Sultan had little success in setting forth a course of change significantly different from the general experience of 18th century crisis of Indian politics and society where 'Public Life' tended over and over again to become a system of plundering (*A Pre-British Economic in India of Late Eighteenth Century : Tipu Sultan's Mysore*)

Alfred Lyall. It may be truly said that the stars in their courses fought against Tippu...He had no political ability of higher sort ; still less had he any touch of that instinct which had occasionally warned the ablest and strongest Asiatic chiefs to avoid collision with Europeans. He was swept away by a flood that was overwhelming far greater States than Mysore, that had taken its rise in a distant part of the world, out of events beyond his comprehension and totally beyond his control and that was now running full in the channel which carried the English, by a natural determination of converging consequences, to supreme ascendancy in India. (*The Rise and Expansion of the British Dominion in India*, p. 243).

SELECT REFERENCES

1. Forrest, Denys : *Tiger of Mysore—the Life and Death of Tipu Sultan.*
2. Gupta, Subbaraya : *New Light on Tipu Sultan.*
3. Hasan, Mohibbul : *History of Tipu Sultan.*
4. Kareem, C.K. : *Kerala under Haidar Ali and Tipu Sultan.*
5. Sheik Ali, B. : *English Relations with Haidar ali.*
6. Sinha, N.K. : *Haidar Ali.*
7. Wilks, M. : *Historical Sketches of South India in an Attempt to Trace the History of Mysore.*

Lord Hastings and Establishment of British Paramountcy in India

If Lord Wellesley had established the Company's military ascendancy in India, Lord Hastings sought to impose British paramountcy in this country. If Wellesley had succeeded in expelling the French and defeating his Indian opponents, Hastings succeeded in establishing in unmistakable terms the political sovereignty of England over the whole of India. In fact Hastings completed the fabric of British dominion in India almost exactly as his great predecessor had planned it.

The Anglo-Nepal War, 1814–16. The first problem Hastings had to face in India was a war with the Gurkhas of Nepal. The Gurkhas from Western Himalayas had wrested the control of Nepal from the successors of Ranjit Malla of Bhatgaon in 1768. A hardy people, the Gurkhas began to expand their dominion beyond the mountains. Checked in the north by the Chinese, they pushed forward towards the ill-defined frontiers of Bengal and Oudh. The English occupation of Gorakhpore district in 1801 had brought the Company's frontier co-terminous with the territory of the Gurkhas. The dispute between the Company and the Nepalese arose out of the latter's occupation of the districts of Butwal (north of Basti district) and Sheoraj (further east of Butwal). The English reoccupied the districts without an open conflict.

In May 1814 the Gurkhas once again attacked the three police stations of Butwal. Lord Hastings took it as a challenge to the Company's authority and resolved to launch an offensive against the Gurkhas along the whole frontier from the Sutlej to the Kosi.

Hastings who also held the office of the Commander-in-Chief of the army planned the campaign. A large army of 34,000 soldiers was mustered against the Gurkha army of 12,000. The campaigns of 1814–15 were a dismal failure. General Gillespie's attack on the mountain fortress of Kalanga failed, the General losing his life in action. Gillespie's successor, Major-General Martindell also suffered an ignominious defeat before the stronghold of Jaitak. The English prestige suffered a great set back.

Undaunted, the English renewed their efforts. Colonels Nicholls and Gardner succeeded in capturing Almora in the Kumaon hills in April 1815. While General Ochterlony wrested the fort of Malaon from Amar Singh Thapa in May 1815.

The fall of Malaon induced the Gurkhas to open negotiations for peace. However, Hastings' exorbitant demands hardened the attitude of the Gurkhas and the war party came in ascendancy in Nepal. Hostilities commenced again. David Ochterlony, now in supreme command, advanced into the heart of Nepal and inflicted a defeat on the Nepalese at Makwanpur on 28 February 1816. Finding further resistance difficult, the Gurkhas accepted the Treaty of Sagauli in March 1816. The Governor-General was content with a moderate treaty and did not press his demands. In fact both sides had a taste of each other's strength and were in an accommodating mood.

The Treaty of Sagauli, 1816. The Company's gains were not unimportant. The Gurkhas surrendered to the Company the districts of Garhwal and Kumaon, including a great portion of the Tarai. The Tarai boundary was marked by pillars of masonry. The Gurkhas agreed to accept a British Resident at Kathmandu and permanently withdrew from Sikkim. For a loan of a crore of rupees obtained from the Nawab of Oudh during the war, the English handed over a part of the Tarai in the Rohilkhand pargana to the Nawab.

The north-west frontier of the Company was pushed up to the mountains. The English obtained the sites for the hill stations and summer capitals of India—Simla, Mussoorie, Ranikhet, Landour and

NainiTal. Besides the route for communications with the remoter regions of Central Asia was opened. By a separate treaty with the Raja of Sikkim on 10 February 1817 the Company handed over to the Raja a part of the territory lying between the Mechi and the Tista rivers. This gave the Company an effective barrier on the eastern frontier of Nepal.

The friendship between Nepal and the English subsisted till the British rule lasted in India, nay, has even survived that. The Gurkhas, one of the finest class of soldiers in the world, were too glad to serve as mercenaries for the English army. Actually three battalions of the Gurkha soldiers were formed by Ochterlony even before the end of the war. The Gurkhas ready to fight for any side capable of giving them a good living considerably strengthened the Company's army and helped in the expansion of its dominion in India.

Lord Hastings and the Indian States. Before coming to India, the Earl of Moira had been a great critic of 'forward policy'. In a debate in the House of Lords on 11 April 1791, he had questioned the wisdom of the policy of war against Tipu Sultan of Mysore by observing that "a scheme of conquest, for the extension of territory, was not only held generally as an improvident act, but particularly so in India". He further described the Mysore war as 'a subject of depreciation and regret'. He was equally vehement in criticising the war policy of Wellesley.

Although a critic of the 'war policy' of Wellesley, Hastings was essentially different in political outlook from men like Barlow. Commenting on the policy of his predecessors he observed, "Our first plan was to avoid meddling with the native powers. The second was to control them all, and we have since attempted partially to revert to the first after having taken one half of the powers of India under our protection, and made the other half our enemies". He proposed to end this anomalous and unsatisfactory state of affairs in India. Further, he clearly saw the growing menace of the Pindaris and the necessity of maintaining peace in the country. He did not believe in an expensive system of defence against the Pindari raids. He desired their complete suppression. If extirpation of the Pindari danger meant war with the Marathas, he would not desist from it. Hastings also realised that the existence of independent Maratha rulers like the Sindhia, the Bhonsle and the Holkar was inconsistent with British position in India. The indpendence of the Marathas must be destroyed if the Company was to become the arbiter of the dentiny of India. In February 1814 Hastings noted in his Private Journal, "Our object ought to be to render the British Government paramount in effect, if not declaredly so. We should hold the other states vassals in substance if not in name".

Thus, Hastings' objective in India was three-fold : (a) to suppress the Pindaris, (b) to destroy the independence of the Maratha chiefs and make them accept the Company's supremacy, and lastly (c) to bring under the Company's protection all harmless states.

The Pindaris. The etymology of the word Pindari is variously explained. The most popular explanation is that the word Pindari is of Marathai origin meaning 'consumer of *pinda*' a fermented drink. In the 18th and 19th centuries the word was used to describe the hordes of cruel marauders whose main occupation was loot and plunder.

The origin of the Pindaris is lost in obscurity. They were first heard of in 1689 during the Mughal invasion of Maharashtra. During the time of Baji Rao I they were referred to as irregular horsemen attached to the Maratha army, serving without pay and receiving in lieu thereof licence to plunder. After the battle of Panipat in 1761, the Pindari leaders settled chiefly in Malwa and served as auxiliaries of Maratha chiefs like the Sindhia and the Holkar, and the Nizam ; they came to be designated as Sindhia Shahi Pindaris, Holkar Shahi Pindaris and Nizam Shahi Pindaris. Malhar Rao Holkar gave one of the Pindari chiefs a golden flag ; in 1794 the Sindhia granted them lands in Narbada valley which they extended soon by "conquests from the Grassias or original independent landlords in their neighbourhood". Malcolm had in view their connection with the Marathas when he wrote, "Condemned from origin to be the very scavengers of the Mahrathas their habits and character took, from the first, a shape suited to the work they had to perform". As the power of the Marathas declined the

Pindaris became a body by themselves frequently engaged in devastating the territory of the very chiefs whom they professed to follow.

The weakness of the Mughal central authority, the corruption of weak and expiring states, the repeated plundering raids of the Marathas created conditions in India in which the Pindaris rose 'like masses of putrefaction in animal matter'. The chaotic political condition in many parts of India deprived large number of people of their peaceful occupations. The life of plunder offered an easier means of livelihood than honest labour. The Pindari ranks swelled during the Governor-Generalship of Wellesley when a large body of professional soldiers were disbanded by the subsidiary allies of the East India Company. The Pindaris spread misery all round and many hardy peasants were impelled to join their ranks. The Pindaris thus formed 'not a particular force but a system fed and nourished by the very miseries they created'.

The Pindaris did not come from any particular area or believe in any particular religion. They were a heterogeneous element drawn from the ranks of disbanded soldiers, fugitives from justice, idle, profligate and unscrupulous men both from Hinduism and Islam. The prospect of rich plunder was the only tie of cohesion among the members of a Pindari party. Their mode of warfare was a peculiar one. They avoided pitched battles with regular armies. When on march, they carried no baggage of any description and supported themselves and their horses on the grain and provision which they plundered. Their favourite weapons were long bamboo spears ; some used fire-arms also. Their chief merit was their speed. "The celerity of their marches was not more remarkable than their secrecy. It was scarcely possible to gain information of their movements till they had completed". Like swarms of locusts they destroyed and left waste whatever province they visited. British writers like Malcolm, Princep, Duff, Tod and Thornton have given detailed accounts of the plundering raids of the Pindaris.

In the early 19th century the chief Pindari leaders were Chitu, Wasil Muhammad and Karim Khan. The Pindaris gradually extended the area of their operations, organising raids in the Company's territories. In 1812 the Pindaris plundered the British districts of Mirzapur and Shahabad. In 1815 they raided the Nizam's dominions, and in 1816 plundered the Northern Sarkars.

Lord Hastings decided to take stern action against the Pindaris. The Court of Directors also authorized action. Hastings improved the Company's diplomatic position by concluding agreements with the Maratha chiefs, the Rajput princes and the ruler of Bhopal, getting promises of help against these robber bands.

British writer like V.A. Smith, P.E. Roberts and S.M. Edwards have popularised the myth that the Pindari marauders, the Afghan free-booters and the Maratha chiefs were in league with one another and Daulat Rao Sindhia was the 'nominal sovereign' of the Pindaris. The problem, therefore, before the Governor-General was not only to encircle the Pindaris, but also to check the attempts of the Maratha chiefs to break through to their assistance ; and that the prescience of the Governor-General was fully justified, for 'the hunt of the pindaris became merged in the third Maratha war'. Recent researches have proved that the population in the Maratha territories even was not safe from the depredations of the Pindaris and that Daulat Rao Sindhia himself employed his troops to suppress the Pindaris. In the summer of 1815 the Sindhia entered into a definite agreement with the Pindaris whereby the latter agreed to give up the policy of plunder and to live on the lands allotted to them by the Sindhia. Edmonstone, Vice-President of the Governor-General's Council, asserted that the Sindhia was sincere in his desire to suppress the Pindaris and to dissociate himself from their activities. It seems Hastings was keen on war with the Sindhia. He noted in his Private Journal on 23 December 1816: "It is far better if the Sindhia be resolved to risk his existence for the support of the Pindaris." In fact, Hastings did not really desire the Sindhia's co-operation in his campaign against the Pindaris. On the other hand, he desired war against the Sindhia and found in the campaign against the Pindaris the right opportunity to provoke him to it.

With his plan to suppress the Pindaris and defeat the Marathas in one sweep, the Governor-General collected a large army of 1,13,000 men and 300 guns. Hastings himself took the command of the Northern Force and entrusted the charge of the Deccan Army to Sir Thomas Hislop. By the end of 1817 the Pindaris were driven across the Chambal and by January 1818 their organised bands were destroyed. Karim Khan surrendered himself to Malcolm and was given a small estate in the Gorakhpur district. Wasil Mohammad took refuge in the Sindhia's camp and the latter handed him over to the English. In captivity at Ghazipur, Wasil Mohammad committed suicide. The other Pindari leader, Chitu, escaped for safety to the forests where he was devoured by a tiger. Thus ended the Pindari menace. In 1824 Malcolm wrote, "The Pindaris are effectually destroyed, that their name is almost forgotten." Duff wrote, "The Pindharees thus dispersed, without leaders, and wothout a home or a rendezvous, were afterwards little heard of though flying parties were seen in the Deccan until the termination of the war with the Peshwa."

Hastings' Policy Towards the Marathas. It was Hastings' main objective to make the Company the Paramount Power in India. The independence of the three Maratha rulers—the Sindhia, the Bhonsle and the Holkar—had to be destroyed before the Company could become the arbiter of the destinies of India. Since this object could not be achieved by negotiations, Hastings was prepared for war.

The chaotic state of affairs in the territories of the Maratha chiefs greatly facilitated the task of Hastings. The Raja of Berar was probably the weakest of the three Maratha chiefs. After the death of Raghuji Bhonsle on 22 March 1816, his imbecile son, Parsoji succeeded to the *gaddi*. The Dowager Rani, Buka Bai's claim or appointment as Regent was disputed by the young Raja's cousin, Appa Sahib, who considered himself as the next successor to the *gaddi* of Nagpur. The British Resident Mr. Jenkins, saw in these dissensions the ripe opportunity to force a subsidiary alliance on the state. Appa Sahib in his keenness to get British support offered very favourable terms, even more favourable than the Company had got by the treaties of Bassein and Hyderabad. The Treaty of Nagpur signed on 27 May 1816 had, as Jenkins pointed out, more of the protective element and less of equality and reciprocity in it. By this treaty a subsidiary force of six battalions of infantry, a regiment of cavalry and a company of European artillerymen were stationed at Nagpur. The subsidy to be paid by the state was fixed at 7½ lakhs of rupees per annum. Besides, the Raja agreed to surrender his foreign affairs to the care of the Company. This treaty was of great advantage to the Company because a strategic control over Nagpur was of immense advantage both for defence and offence. In the words of Malcolm, "In the actual condition of India, no event could be more fortunate than the subsidiary alliance with Nagpur. It struck a serious blow at the power of the Maratha Confederacy".

Peshwa Baji Rao II, after accepting the subsidiary alliance by the Treaty of Bassein on 31 December 1802, had found the British stranglehold too galling. The more he tried to recover his independence of action the more he found his efforts thwarted by the British. The Company compelled the Peshwa, much against his will, to accept the Six Articles of Agreement (7 July 1812) whereby the Southern Jagirdars were confirmed in their territories. The Peshwa's claims over the Gaekwar of Baroda, a feudatory of the English sparked off another trouble in 1814. At the suggestion of the Company, the Gaekwar sent his Chief Minister Gangadhar Shastri to Poona to negotiate with the Peshwa. The Peshwa's claim for tribute from Kathiawar and Baroda amounted to over a crore of rupees, while the Baroda Government put up counter-claims. No settlement was reached. On his way back, Gangadhar Shastri was murdered at Nasik on 14th July 1815, at the instance of Trimbakji (the Chief Minister of the Peshwa). Mountstuart Elphinstone, the British Resident, demanded the arrest of Trimbakji. The Peshwa procrastinated but surrendered Trimbakji on 25th September, and the latter was lodged in the Thana jail. From the jail, Trimbakji escaped in October 1816. By this time Hastings was free from the Nepal war. He urged Elphinstone to demand the surrender of Trimbakji within a stated period, to be fixed by the Resident and also demand adequate securities for future good behaviour. Should the Peshwa refuse to submit to the proposed restrictions, he was to be treated an enemy and war declared against him. The Governments of Madras and Bombay and the British Resident at Hyderabad were asked to be ready with troops in case of need. On 7 May 1817, the British Resident presented to the Peshwa a demand for the surrender of Trimbakji within a month and surrender of the forts of Raigarh, Simhagarh and Purandhar as pledges for the fulfilment of the agreement. The wretched Peshwa vacillated between fight, resistance and submission. Meanwhile, Colonel Smith surrounded Poona with his troops and the forts were also occupied by the English. On 13th June 1817, the Peshwa made an abject submission and accepted a new Treaty of Poona by which among other things :

(a) The Peshwa accepted the dissolution of the Maratha confederacy ;

(b) The Peshwa was not to hold any communication with other powers except through the British Resident ;

(c) The Peshwa renounced his claims over the Gaekwar for an annual payment of four lakhs of rupees ;

(d) The Peshwa ceded to the Company the fort of Ahmadnagar and also transferred his rights over Bundelkhand, Malwa and Hindustan to the Company ; and

(e) The Peshwa agreed to admit in his dominion any number of additional troops the Company's Government might think necessary and also to permit them to pass through any part of his territory.

The treaties of Nagpur and Poona conferred distinct political and military advantages on the Company. The Maratha confederacy was finally dissolved and this constituted a milestone in the establishment of British paramountcy in India.

The Treaty with the Sindhia, 5 November 1817. In September 1817, Lord Hastings arrived with a big force at Kanpur. He put forward definite conditions for acceptance before the Sindhia, non-acceptance of which was to mean his being treated as an enemy. The Sindhia accepted a humiliating treaty in Novemebr 1817 under which :

(1) The Maharaja agreed to provide 5,000 troops of cavalry to fight against the Pindaris ;

(2) The Sindhia was not to increase his army, which during the operations against the Pindaris was to occupy the positions allotted to it by the Company ;

(3) British garrisons were to be stationed into the Sindhia's forts of Asirgarh and Hindia, which were to be restored to the Sindhia after the termination of the action against the Pindaris ;

(4) The lands in the possession of the Pindaris were to be restored to their rightful owners ; and

(5) The Sindhia agreed to the abrogation of Article 8 the Treaty of 1805 by which the Company's Government had been precluded from entering into alliances with the States of Rajputana.

The treaty practically disarmed the Sindhia and gave the Company great advantages in their action the Pindaris. Moreover, the Company had proved the stronger of the two and the Sindhia had to accept humiliating terms. All the same, the Sindhia's relations with the Company were of 'amity and friendship' and constitutionally and theoretically he was still independent.

The Maratha chiefs though humbled were not reconciled to the loss of their independence. There were secrect moves for concerted action under the leadership of the Peshwa. On 5th November 1817, the British Residency at Poona was attacked and burnt. The British troops repulsed and defeated the Peshwa's large army at Khirki (5th November). Brigadier-General Smith occupied Poona on 13th November and the Peshwa escaped for life. The Peshwa was chased from place to place. Two more defeats at Koregaon (1 January 1818) and Ashta (20 February) sealed the fate of the Peshwa.

The Nagpur troops under Appa Sahib (who had succeeded to the *gaddi* a year earlier by murdering Parsoji Bhonsle) declared war against the English on 26th November 1817. The Council of Regency for Holkar also gave a call for war against the foreigner Appa Sahib was humbled at Sitabaldi

(26th November) and the Holkar's army was defeated at Mahidpur by Hislop on 21 December 1817.

Hastings' Political Settlements with the Marathas. Hastings decided to dispose of both Baji Rao II and the Peshwaship. By a proclamation issued in the name of the British Government, Eliphinstone declared the annexation of Baji Rao's dominions to the British possessions. He also announced the intention of placing Pratap Singh, the Raja of Satara, a lineal descendant of Shivaji 'at the head of an independent sovereignty of such an extent as may maintain the Rajah and his family in comfort and dignity'. Baji Rao II was given a pension of eight lakh rupees a year and allowed to settle at Bithur near Kanpur under British control.

The Holkar signed the Treaty of Mandasor on 6 January 1818. He had to surrender to the Company all his territories south of the Narmada including Khandesh ; he confirmed Amir Khan's (Nawab of Tonk) independence and the latter's engagements with the British. The Holkar also renounced his claims over the Rajput states and over parganas in possession of Zalim Singh of Kota. He also agreed to receive a British subsidiary force in his dominion, to submit all foreign disputes to British arbitration and to surrender his foreign relations to the care of the Company. Lastly, the Company's government was not to permit the Peshwa to exercise any sovereignty over the Holkar. The Holkar was hardly eleven years old. Tantia Jog was appointed as the Chief Minister. Indore thenceforward became the capital of the State.

The settlement made about the Bhonsle's dominions was equally harsh. All the Bhonsle's territories north of the Narmada were annexed to the British dominion. Raghuji Bhonsle III, grandson of Raghuji II, was accepted as the Raja over a mulcted State. Since the Raja was an infant, the British Resident assumed charge of the Government. Even the district administration in the state was put under European officers. The British control was so complete that even the Raja's household, all departments of the state including Mint and Treasury were placed under British supervision.

The Sindhia was compelled to sign another agreement in June 1818. The Maharaja ceded to the Company the town and district of Ajmer and gave up his claim over the fort of Islamnagar in favour of the Nawab of Bhopal, as desired by the Company. The Sindhia without fighting accepted British supremacy. He recognised British ascendancy as an accomplished fact. He maintained a British contingent on a permanent basis. He voluntarily retired from Rajputana and also agreed to the Company's mediation between himself and his tributaries. Though technically still independent, the Sindhia had come as much under British influence as the Holkar or the Nawab of Oudh.

The Maratha wars resulted in the realisation in full measure of Hastings' aim and ambition. Not only was the Maratha power completely uprooted but vast territories were added to the Company's possessions.

Relations with the Rajput States. Lord Wellseley had concluded an agreement with the Rajput state of Jaipur but it had been cancelled under Cornwallis and Barlow under instructions from the Home authorities. By its treaty with the Sindhia on 23rd November 1805, the Company had pledged itself not to enter into treaties with the Rajput states. Further, by Declaratory Articles published by Barlow, British protection was withdrawn from the Rajput states. Thus, the Maratha chiefs exercised a varying degree of control over the chieftains of Rajputana and levied tribute.

Lord Hastings' idea to form a confederacy of Indian states under the leadership of the Company required the vassal states to perform two duties, *viz.*, (*i*) to submit for settlement all their disputes through the arbitration of the Company ; (*ii*) to furnish all their forces at the call of the Paramount Power at any time. Determined to establish British paramountcy in India, Hastings compelled the Sindhia to accept a treaty in November 1817 whereby the clause precluding the Company from entering into engagements with the Rajput states was abrogated.

Hastings looked upon the Rajput states as "our natural allies and the natural enemies of the Marathas". By taking the Rajput states under its protection, the Company could not only check the extension of the power of the Sindhia, the Holkar and Amir Khan but also would get immense strategic advantages for its military and political position in Central India. Hastings wrote, "The establishment of our influence over those States would interpose strong barriers between the Sikhs and those Powers which might be expected to aid them".

Charles Metcalfe, the British Resident at Delhi, was entrusted with the duty of negotiating alliances with the three big Rajput states of Udaipur, Jaipur and Jodhpur as also to bring the smaller states of Kota, Bundi, Karauli within the ambit of the Company's political system. Agreements were also signed with the small principalities of Banswara, Dungarpur and Pratapgarh (the offshoots of the House of Udaipur) and also with the states of Bikaner and Jaisalmer.

Charles Metcalfe gave assurances to the Rana of Marwar that the Company had no desire to interfere into the internal affairs of the state nor any intention to enter into separate agreements with the feudatories of the state. The Rana was prevailed upon to sign a the feudatories of the state. The Rana was prevailed upon to sign a Treaty on 6th January 1818 on the basis of perpetual friendship defensive alliance, protection and subordinate co-operation. Article 8 of the treaty laid down that the Jodhpur state would furnish a contingent of 1,500 horsemen for the service of the Company's Government and whenever necessary place all the forces of the state under the overall command of the Company. Further, the state was required to pay an annual tribute of Rs. 1,08,000 per annum to the Company.

The ruler of Udaipur raised objections to the use of terms like supremacy, 'subordinate co-operation'. Metcalfe catered to the susceptibilities of the Rana and signed a treaty on 13th January 1818. The Rana was not required to render any horsemen for service but had to pay a tribute amounting to one-fourth of the revenue of the state for five years and thereafter at 3/8 ths of the revenue. The treaty with the Rana of Udaipur greatly boosted the morale of the Company, for the Ranas of Udaipur had never surrendered their independence to any power, not even the Mughals, in so definite, formal and effectual terms.

The Raja of Jaipur was the last to capitulate. Metcalfe threatened to conclude separate agreements with the nobles subordinate to the state of Jaipur if the Raja did not accept a treaty. On 2nd April 1818, the Raja was brought round to the acceptance of a treaty on terms similar to those accepted by the Rana of Mewar. The tribute payable was fixed on a sliding scale for the first six years.

Hastings' treaties with the Rajput states were rather harsh and contained more humiliating terms than those imposed on the Sindhia or other Maratha states. These conditions look particularly harsh when we consider the fact that these states were not hostile to the Company and had a great tradition of chivalry behind them. Tod sympathised with them and earnestly wished "for the restoration of their former independence". Even the Court of Directors was moved and orders were drafted in 1829 for revising the humiliating clauses precluding these chieftains from communicating with their peers ; there was a proposal for modifying the articles relating to the payment of tribute and for withdrawal of Political Agents from their states. However, these proposals were never seriously taken up.

The Company's demand for a fixed tribute was justified on the plea that it was the state's share towards the cost of their defence. Moreover, it was a demonstration of the Company's paramountcy and subordinate position of the states. Thus, the independence of Rajput states was swept away in a strong tide of British imperialism.

The Treatment of the Mughal Emperor. So far the assertion of the Company's sovereignty has been spasmodic and incomplete. Hastings who had established the complete ascendancy of the Company over the Indian States was jealous of the place of honour and dignity which the Mughal Emperor enjoyed. Till then the governor-General's address to the Emperor was in the form of an *Arzdasht* (petition) to the Emperor who addressed the Governor-General as "our specially regarded servant, our honoured son, and the deserving object of our royal regard etc. Further, the Governor-General's seal bore the phrase 'the servant of the Emperor'. During his tour of Northern India Hastings refused to wait on the Emperor unless he waived all ceremonial implying supremacy over the Company's dominions and met him on a status of equality. Hastings' protest had the desired effect on Emperor Akbar II who received Hastings' successor, Lord Amherst in 1827 on a footing of equality and without the ceremonial to which Hastings had objected. However, till 1835 the Company's coins carried the stamp of Emperor Shah Alam.

Hastings' Administrative Reforms. Though Hastings' genius was more suited for war, yet his Governor-Generalship saw some important civil and administrative reforms being carried out. The Governor-General was lucky in having a band of very capable administrators in Sir John Malcolm, Sir Thomas Munro, Mountstuart Elphinstone Jenkins and Charles Metcalfe.

Thomas Munro who became Governor of Madras in 1820 established the Ryotwari system of land tenure in Malabar, Canara, Coimbatore, Madura and Dindugal. The settlement was made directly with the ryot, the actual tiller of the soil. The ryot was considered the owner of the soil with rights of sale and transfer. The cultivator became the direct payer of land revenue without the interposition of the zamindar or the village community.

Elphinstone who became the Governor of Bombay in 1819 and was charged with the responsibility of settling the districts acquired from the Peshwa combined the Ryotwari with the Mahalwari system in Bombay. Under it the rights and rent of each cultivator was fixed after survey. The farming of the village was entrusted to the care of a Patil for a number of years.

In the North-Western Provinces (roughly modern U.P.) the Mahalwari system was introduced. Under Regulation VII of 1822 land revenue settlements were made with the representatives of each village community or *mahal*, leaving the adjustment of the share of each individual cultivator to be settled among themselves.

Hastings somewhat modified the judicial system set up by Cornwallis. In the Bengal Presidency Cornwallis' laudable system of separating the judiciary from the executive was modified and henceforth the Collector could hold the office of the magistrate also.

Lord Hastings relaxed press restrictions abolishing pre-censorship of the press. However, the Government laid down some general rules for the guidance of newspaper editors with a view to prevent the publication of news likely to affect the authority of the Government or prove injurious to the public interest.

Estimate of Hastings. Though in his sixtieth year at the time of arrival in India, Hastings proved to be pre-eminently a man of action. He planned and carried through extensive strategical operations, fought twenty-eight battles and won a hundred and twenty fortresses. Though a great critic of Wellesley's policy, he was 'destined to complete the fabric of British dominion in India almost exactly as his great predecessor had planned it.' All rival states looking for equality of status with the Company were humbled and the unquestioned Paramountcy of the British in India was established. Thus, Hastings' Governor-Generalship marks an important milestone in the expansion and consolidation of British dominion in India.

Select Opinions

J.S. Mill. The administration of the Marquess of Hastings may be regarded as the completion of the great scheme of which Clive had laid the foundations, and Warren Hastings and Marquess of Wellesley had reared the superstructures. The crowing pinnacle was the work of Lord Hastings and by him was the supremacy of the Empire in India proper finally established. Of the soundness of the work no better proof can be afforded than the fact that there has been no international warfare since his administration. Rajputs, Maratha and Mohammedans have remained at peace with one another under the shade of British power. The wars in which the latter had been engaged have carried that power beyond the boundaries of Hindustan, but no interruption of internal tranquillity from the Himalayas to the sea has been suffered or attempted.

M.S. Mehta. Lord Hastings came just about midway between Wellesley and Bentinck, not only in point of time, but also in personal character. These two distinguished pro-consuls were two distinct types, and stood for two kinds of ideals in public administration. Although Hastings belonged wholly neither to one nor to the other, he shared the attributes of both...Compared to Wellesley, Hastings was of a milder nature. He had all the gentleness and also the weakness of moderate-minded people. He was imperialistic in his outlook, without being of a predatory mentality. He possessed considerable ability, although his judgement was not always reliable. He was essentially a militarist, but at the same time there was in him a conciliatory spirit, which did not make him a ruthless conqueror. By nature and personal conviction he was not as interfering Governor-General, as Wellesley would certainly have been had the latter lived in Hastings' time. (*Lord Hastings and the Indian States,* pp. 260–61).

Major Ross of Bladensburg. The scheme for producing the pacification of India was not Hastings' conception, but having approved of its merits, he adopted it as his own, and, more fortunate than his great predecessor (Wellesley), he was able to take large and comprehensive measures to bring it to a successful conclusion...The Indian continent was reduced to order, the irregularities in the Company's territories were gradually removed, its possessions were consolidated, and the paramount position of England was assured. The settlement which the Marquess of Hastings made has been modified, but it has never been undone ; his work was thorough, far-reaching and comprehensive. Modern India is largely based upon the results which he attained. The period of his administration forms an era in the history of our advance in the East, which marks the end of a halting policy and the dawn of a new order, when Great Britain finally assumed undivided responsibility for, and supreme control over, the Empire of Continental India. (*Marquess of Hastings*, p. 218).

P.E. Roberts. Lord Hastings was less precipitate than Lord Wellesley, less harsh to errant native rulers, and he did not proceed against them till his case was very strong. He was an able administrator, a hard and conscientious worker, a good judge of men, and his name and fame deservedly rank only just below the greatest in the rolls of Governors-General. (*History of British India*, p. 291)

SELECT REFERENCES

1. London, P. : *History of Nepal.* 2 vols.
2. Malcolm, John : *The Political History of India.*
3. Marchioness of Bute (Ed.) : *The Private Journal of Marquess of Hastings.*
4. Mehta, M.S. : *Lord Hastings and the Indian States.*
5. Princep, Henry : *History of the Political and Military Transactions in India during the Administration of Marquess of Hastings,* 2 vols.
6. Ross Major : *The Marquess of Hastings.*

ANGLO-MARATHA STRUGGLE FOR SUPREMACY

On the ruins of the Mughal Empire had been built the empire of the Marathas and the same set of circumstances had whetted the political ambition of the English East India Company. Both operated in their own spheres. While the Marathas had proved stronger than other Indian princes, the English Company emerged successful over the European trading companies in the country. Towards the last quarter of the eighteenth century, the two powers so far pursuing their schemes of conquest in their respective spheres, were brought face to face, into clash and conflict. The Maratha power waned before the rising power of the English Company.

The First Anglo-Maratha War, 1775-82. The first phase of the Anglo-Maratha struggle was brought about by the inordinate ambition of the English and accentuated by the internal dissensions of the Marathas. The Bombay Government hoped to set up in Maharashtra the type of Dual Government Clive had set up in Bengal, Bihar and Orissa. The mutual differences of the Maratha leaders gave to the Company the much sought of opportunity. The fourth Peshwa Madhav Rao died in 1772, the fifth (Narayan Rao) succumbed to the intrigues of his uncle Raghunath Rao, another claimant for the *gaddi*. The birth of a posthumous son to Narayan Rao drove Raghunath Rao to the point of desperation and he signed with the Bombay Government the Treaty of Surat (1775) hoping to gain the coveted *gaddi* with the help of English subsidiary troops. However, the British attempt proved premature. In the war that followed fortune wavered on both sides till the two parties realised the futility of the struggle by concluding peace at Salbai (1782) on the basis of mutual restitution of each other's territories. It proved a drawn struggle. Both sides had a taste of each other's strength which ensured mutual respect and peace for the next twenty years.

The Second Anglo-Maratha War, 1803-1806. The second phase of the struggle was intimately connected with the circumstances created by the French menace to India. Wellesley who came to India as Governor-General in 1798 was an imperialist to the backbone and believed that the only possible way to safeguard India against French danger was to reduce the whole of India to a position of military dependence on the Company. He relentlessly pursued that objective by the infamous Subsidiary System of alliances. The Marathas refused all offers of the Governor-General for acceptance of the subsidiary alliance, but were driven into Wellesley's trap by their internal differences and criminal self-seeking.

In March 1800 Nana Fadnavis, the Chief Minister at Poona, died. "With him", remarked Colonel Palmer, the British Resident at Poona, "departed all the wisdom and moderation of the Maratha Government". Nana had well understood the inherent danger of English intervention in Maratha affairs and declined all overtures for a subsidiary alliance from Wellesley. Freed from Nana's vigilance, Baji Rao's worst qualities found a free play. With his fondness for intrigue, the Peshwa sought to keep up his position by putting the Maratha chiefs one against another. However, Baji Rao was caught in the net of his own intrigues. Both Daulat Rao Sindhai and Jaswant Rao Holkar sought pre-eminence at Poona. The Sindhia prevailed at first and the Peshwa passed under his virtual control. On 12 April 1800, the Governor-General advised the Resident at Poona to exert his 'utmost endeavours to engage' the Peshwa to conclude a secret treaty with the Company offering British help in turning out the Sindhia from the Deccan.. The Peshwa did not accept the offer and in May the Resident reported that 'no consideration but that of unavoidable and imminent destruction will induce his (Peshwa's) assent to the admission of a permanent subsidiary British force into his dominions'.

Events took a serious turn at Poona. In April 1801 the Peshwa brutally murdered Vithuji, the brother of Jaswant Rao Holkar. This brought the Holkar with a large army in the field against the Peshwa and the combined troops of the Peshwa and the Sindhia were defeated on 25 October 1802 at Hadapsar, near Poona. The Holkar placed Vinayak Rao, son of Amrit Rao, on the *gaddi* of the Peshwa. Baji Rao II fled to Bassein and on 31 December 1802 signed a treaty of 'perpetual and general alliance' with the English.

The Treaty of Bassein, 31 December 1802

(*i*) The Peshwa agreed to receive from the Company 'a permanent regular native Infantry, with the usual proportion of field pieces and European artillery-men attached, and with the proper equipment of war-like stores and ammunition'— to be permanently stationed in his territories;

(*ii*) The Peshwa agreed to cede in perpetuity to the Company territories yielding an income of 26 lakhs of rupees. The territories surrendered were to be in Gujarat ; territories south of the Tapti ; territories between the Tapti and the Narbada and some territory near the Tungabhadra;

(*iii*) The Peshwa also surrendered the city of Surat ;

(*iv*) The Peshwa agreed to give up all claims for *chauth* on the Nizam's dominions and also agreed not to resort to arms against the Gaekwar ;

(*v*) The Peshwa agreed to the Company's arbitration in all differences between him and the Nizam or the Gaekwar ;

(*vi*) The Peshwa undertook not to keep in his employment Europeans of any nation at war with the English ; and

(*vii*) The Peshwa also agreed 'neither to commence nor to pursue in future any negotiations with any power whatever' without giving previous notice and entering into mutual consultation with the East India Company.

Importance of the Treaty. The importance of the Treaty of Bassein in the building up of British supremacy in India was variously estimated by the politician of the day. Lord Castlereagh, the President of the Board of Control, in a minute entitled 'Observations on the Treaty of Bassein' criticised the political wisdom of the policy and believed that Wellesley had exceeded his legal authority. He characterized the policy as 'critical and delicate' and thought that it was "hopeless to attempt to govern the Maratha Empire through a feeble and perhaps disaffected Peshwa". He apprehended that the Treaty would involve the English "in the endless and complicated distractions of that turbulent Maratha Empire".

Castlereagh's contentions were answered by Major-General Wellesley and in October 1804 John Malcolm prepared a rejoinder. Lord Wellesley believed that by the Treaty "the Company obtained for the first time something like a rational security for the improvement and continuance of the peace of India. A new power was thrown into the weight of its own scale ; a lawful rights was established to interfere in the preservation of the Peshwa's authority, whenever it should be attacked ; the intrigues of the foreigners were excluded from his capital...Our own military resources were considerably increased without expense to the Company ; the army of the Peshwa likewise became bound at our call on every occasion of emergency..." The treaty was more than a mere defensive alliance, as it was described. The Governor-General himself wrote in 1804 that the flight of the Peshwa from Poona "seemed to hold out a very favourable opportunity for establishing in the most complete manner the interests of the British Power in the Maratha Empire".

True, the Treaty of Bassein was signed with a 'cypher' but it gave great political advantages to the English. The paramount British influence was established at Poona. The head of the Maratha Confederacy had accepted a position of dependent relationship on the Company with its natural corollary that the other Maratha chiefs (member of the Maratha Confederacy) were reduced to a similar position of subordination to the Company— a relationship which they had feared and would not accept without a fight.

By surrendering his foreign policy to the care of the Company, the Peshwa had made the Company responsible for every war in which the Peshwa's Government might be involved. Thus, the treaty made the Company arbiter in the disputes between the Peshwa and other Maratha chiefs and the Peshwa and other Indian rulers.

A specific clause in the treaty provided for the Company's mediation in all cases of disputes between the Peshwa and the Nizam. Thus, the Peshwa virtually surrendered all his claims over the Nizam. This marked the achievement of another object of Wellesley's policy, namely, that the state Hyderabad definitely passed under the Company's protection.

The Treaty of Bassein also put the Company in a very advantageous position in case of war with the Marathas or any other Indian or foreign rivals. The Company's subsidiary troops were encamped at the capitals of the four Indian powers—at Mysore, Hyderabad, Lucknow and Poona. From these four militarily focal points the Company's troops could spread and meet any opponent.

The Treaty of Bassein did not establish the Company's political supremacy in India but certainly was an important milestone in that direction. Thus Sidney Owen's remark that "the treaty by its direct and indirect operations gave the Company the Empire of India" merely contains the exaggeration of a true political phenomenon.

The national humiliation was too much for the Marathas. The Sindhia and the Bhonsle challenged British power, while the Gaikwar and the Holkar kept aloof. Quick blows dealt by Arthur Wellesley in the Deccan and by Lord Lake in Northern India shattered Maratha power and the two chiefs accepted humiliating treaties. By the Treaty of Deogaon (17 December 1803) the Bhonsle Raja ceded to the Company the province of Cuttuck and whole of the territory west of the river Warda. The Sindhia concluded the Treaty of Surji-Arjangaon (30 December 1803) by which he surrendered to the Company all his territories between the Jamuna and the Ganges, all territories situated to the north of the principalities of Jaipur, Jodhpur and Gohud besides the fort of Ahmednagar, the harbour of Broach and his possessions between the Ajanta Ghat and the river Godavri. Both the princes also accepted British Residents at their courts.

In April 1804 Holkar was drawn into a conflict with the Company. Some hasty and uncalculated moves on the part of the Company's Generals gave an initial advantage to Jaswant Rao Holkar, but his defeat was never in doubt. Meantime, Wellesley had been called back from India by the Home authorities and a change in policy in India was contemplated. It was Sir George Barlow who concluded with Holkar the Treaty of Rajpurghat (25 December 1805) by which the Maratha chief gave up his claims to places north of the river Chambal, over Bundelkhand, over the Peshwa and other allies of the Company.

In the second round of the struggle the Maratha power had been shattered though not completely annihilated. The English conquest of Delhi, apart from other gains, considerably enhanced their prestige and put them in the forefront of the Indian political scene.

Descriptive Note on Political Condition of India in 1818

Lord Hastings not only completed but consolidated the policy of Wellesley. British supremacy in India was established beyond doubt and the Company claimed the Paramount right of intervention in the interests of the security and tranquillity of the Indian people.

Extension of Company's Dominion under Hastings

(i) After the Anglo-Nepalese war (1814-16), the Gurkha ruler surrendered to the East India Company the provinces of Kumaon and Garhwal apart from surrendering some more territories in the Tarai. Thus the Company acquired sites for development of hill stations like Simla, Mussoori, Ranikhet, Landour and Nainital.

(ii) After Maratha defeat in the Third Anglo-Maratha war (1817-18). Lord Hastings abolished by a proclamation the Peshwaship. The entire dominion belonging to the Peshwa in western India was acquired by the East India Company and merged in the Bombay Presidency. The Company also acquired the Peshwa's political rights over Bundelkhand, Malwa and Hindustan.

(*iii*) The Maratha chiefs like the Sindhia, the Bhonsle and the Holkar ceded important territories north and south of the Narbaba besides Khandesh and Ajmer.

Within the natural boundaries of India bounded by the ocean and the mountains, the British sovereign influence extended from Assam in the east to the river Sutlej and the upper Sind desert in the west and from the Himalayas in the north to Cape Comorin in the south.

Establishment of British Paramountcy was a settled fact of the Indian political scene and Indian states were reduced to the position of 'Subordinate Isolation'.

The Third Anglo-Maratha War, 1817-1818. The third and the final phase of the struggle began with the coming of Lord Hastings as Governor-General in 1813. He resumed the threads of aggressive policy abandoned in 1805 and was determine to proclaim British Paramountcy in India. The breathing time that the Marathas had got after Wellesley's recall in 1805 was not utilized by them for strenghthening their power, but wasted in mutual conflicts Hastings' moves against the Pindaris transgressed the sovereignty of the Maratha chiefs and the two parties were drawn into a war. By carefully calculated moves the English forced humiliating treaties on the Raja of Nagpur (27 May 1816), the Peshwa (13 June 1817) and the Sindhai (5 November 1817). Exasperated the Peshwa made the last bid to throw off the British yoke. Daulat Rao Sindhia, Appa Sahib of Nagpur, Malhar Rao Holkar II also rose in arms. The Peshwa was defeated at Khirki, Bhonsle's army routed at Sitabaldi and Holkar's army crushed at Mahidpur. The entire Maharatha force was routed by superior military power of the Company. Baji Rao's possession of Poona and its districts were merged in the Bombay Presidency, while the other princes were confined to greatly reduced territories in subordination to the Company.

Causes for the Defeat of the Marathas

While the Marathas proved superior to the various Muslim powers that rose on the ruins of the Mughal Empire, they were inferior to the English in material resources, military organisation, diplomacy and leadership. In fact, a static eastern people steeped in medievalism could not successfully contend with the dynamic English nation rejuvenated by the forces of the Renaissance, fortified with the latest military weapons and saturated in Machiavellian methods of statecraft.

1. Inept Leadership. The character of the Maratha state being despotic the personality and character of the head of the state counted for much. In the absence of a settled constitution, the state descended into a terrible engine of oppression in the hands of worthless and selfish leaders. Peshwa Baji Rao II and Daulat Rao Sindhia, who controlled the supreme government at Poona, by their misdeeds brought the doom of the empire built by the efforts of Baji Rao I and his successors. Baji Rao II had a criminal stain in his character. Besides driving many loyal sirdars into the enemy's camp, Baji Rao himself moved into the Company's camp when he signed the Treaty of Bassein (31 December 1802) accepting the subsidiary system of alliance. Thus, he bartered away Maratha independence for his selfish ends which even unfortunately, were not fully realised. Daulat Rao Sindhia was an unworthy successor of Mahadaji Sindhia. He was indolent and a lover of luxury even at the cost of public business. Broughton wrote about him, "This light-hearted prince is by no means insensible to the embarrassment of his affairs...But these things affect him for an hour. A tiger, or a pretty face, an elephant fight or a new supply of paper-kites have each sufficient attraction to direct his chagrin.."[1] Sardesai writes about these two leaders thus : "Their misdeeds brought the Poona court and society to such a moral degradation that no one's life, property or honour was safe. People even in distant parts of the land had to suffer terrible misery through misrule, oppression, plunder and devastation. The sirdars and jagirdars, particularly of the southern Maratha country were so completely alienated

---

1. Broughton : *Letters from a Maratha Camp.* p. 123.

that they rushed for escape into the arms of the English".[2] Perhaps Jaswant Rao Holkar was the ablest and most enterprising of Maratha leaders, but he too had unbalanced mind bordering on insanity.

The total absence of first rate personalities was an important cause of the fall of the Marathas. Unfortunately most of the eminent leaders died towards the end of the eighteenth century. Mahadaji Sindhia in February 1794, Haripant Phadke in June 1794, Ahalya Bai Holkar in August 1795, Peshwa Madhav Rao II in October 1795, Tukoji Holkar in August 1797 and Nana Fadnavis in March 1800, succeeded by weaklings and imbeciles like Baji Rao II, Daulat Rao Sindhia, Jaswant Rao Holkar and the lot. On the other hand, the East India Company was lucky in having the services of able persons like Elphinstone, John Malcolm, Colonel Colins, Jonathan Ducan, Arthur Wellesley (later on the conqueror of Napoleon), Lord Lake and above all Richard Wellesley.

2. Inherent Defects of Maratha State. Jadunath Sarkar contends that there were inherent defect in the character of the Maratha state and at no time any concerted attempt had been made at well-thought-out organised communal improvement, spread of education or unification of the people either under Shivaji or under the Peshwas. The cohesion of the peoples of Maratha state, argues Sarkar, was not organic, but artificial, accidental and therefore precarious. The religio-national movement which had worked in the destruction of the Mughal Empire in the seventeenth century had spent itself in the process of expansion of the Maratha Empire. The defects of the Maratha state though very evident in the heydays of the Empire became glaring in the nineteenth century when they had to contend with a European power organised on the best pattern of the West.

3. Absence of Stable Economic Policy. The economic policy of the Maratha state was hardly conducive to a stable political set-up. During the long wars against Aurangzeb, the Maratha people had been uprooted, the peasants had given up cultivation and joined the profession of the soldier. Even after the withdrawal of the Mughals from Maharashtra, the Maratha people tried to live on the sword, now fighting and plundering the Mughals in their provinces of Gujarat, Malwa, Bundelkhand etc. Under the early Peshwas the wars of the state were financed by the plunder of the territories conquered and by collection of *chauth* and *sardeshmukhi* from dependent territories. Thus, the Maratha Empire subsisted not on the resources of Maharashtra, but on the tribute levied from newly acquired territories. When the Maratha Empire reached its optimum point of expansion such new sources of income dried up, while it cost the state the co-operation of the princes from whom the tribute was exacted. The later Maratha leaders made the matters worse by civil wars, thereby ruining the economy of Maharashtra. Wellesley wrote, "They have not left a stick standing at the distance of 150 miles from Poona ; they have eaten the forage and the grain, have pulled down the houses and have used the material as firewood and the inhabitants are fled with their cattle."[3] A terrible famine visited the Deccan in 1804 taking a very heavy toll of life. The Maratha chiefs were reduced to such straits that they had to mortgage most of their territories to bankers. Thus the Maratha leadership failed to evolve a stable economic policy to suit the changing needs of time. In the absence of any industry or foreign trade openings, fighting was the only lucrative opening for the youth. War became the 'national industry' of the Marathas and recoiled on the economy of the state.

4. Weakness of Maratha Political Set-up. Even in its heydays, the Maratha Empire was a loose confederation under the leadership of the Chhatrapati and later the Peshwa. Just as the Peshwa usurped the power of the Chhatrapati, the subordinate 'war lords' usurped the authority of the Peshwa. Powerful chiefs like the Gaikwar, the Holkar, the Sindhia and the Bhonsle carved out semi-independent kingdoms for themselves and paid lip-service to the authority of the Peshwa. When the Poona Government weakened after the disaster of Panipat, the feudal units fell apart and even weakened each other by internal conflicts. Malet wrote about the Maratha confederacy, "The seeds, however, of domestic dissensions are thickly and deeply sown in the Maratha system (if system it may be called)

---

2. Sardesai : *Main Currents of Maratha History*, pp. 161-62.
3. Gurwood : *Wellington's Despatches*, vol. i, p. 508.

and it is perhaps as good a security as any that their neighbours can have that the whole of its parts composed as it now is, cannot be brought into cordial coalition." There was irreconcilable hostility between the Holkar and the Sindhia, while the Bhonsle Raja of Nagpur claimed the kingship of the Maratha Empire. Not unoften the Maratha chief took sides against each other, much to the detriment of the nation and the state. In the war of succession (1743–50) between Madho Singh and Ishwari Singh for the *gaddi* of Jaipur after the death of their father Raja Singh, the Sindhia and the Holkar took opposite sides. Mutual jealousies prevented the Maratha sirdars from offering a united front to the East India Company. In 1803 when the Sindhia and the Bhonsle went to war against the English Company, Jaswant Rao Holkar kept aloof waiting the outcome of the conflict. In 1804 Holkar himself was drawn into a conflict with the Company and single-handed could not meet the challenge. Thus, the absence of a corporate spirit among the Maratha chiefs considerable weakened their ranks.

5. Inferior Military System of the Marathas. In military strength the Marathas were no match for the English. Though not lacking in personal prowess and valour, the Marathas were inferior to their opponents in organisation of the forces, in war weapons, in disciplined action and effective leadership. The centrifugal tendencies of divided command and improper organisation account for much of the Maratha failures. Treachery in the Maratha ranks played havoc. Fortescue in his *History of the British Army* points out that at the battle of Assaye Pohlam's artillery brigade betrayed the master ; had Pohlam's brigade done its duty, the position of the British would have been in great jeopardy. Again, Monsieur Perron, the Commander-in-Chief, was a mere adventurer whose chief motive was to take all his ill-gotten wealth out of India. He resigned on the eve of the Second Maratha War. His successor, Monsieur Louis Bourquin, was merely a cook in Calcutta about whom Compton says that "there is no more contemptible character among the military adventurers of the Hindustan than Bourquin, cook, pyrotechnist and poltroon." The mercenary soldiers of the Marathas had no higher motive than of personal interest ; loss of a battle meant at worst a temporary loss of employment to them.

Arthur Wellesley's contention has been greatly developed by Sir Alfred Lyall in his book *Rise and Expansion of British Power in India* to prove that the abandonment of the guerilla system of warfare was a cardinal mistake of the Marathas. Thomas Munro, an authority on the military affairs of the time, pointed out that the victories which Holkar won against Monson were because of 'marches' and convoys rather than of battles and 'sieges'. It is further contended that the neglect of cavalry on the part of the Sindhia and concentration on artillery and infantry affected adversely the mobility of the army, depriving it of the chief advantage it had possessed against the armies of the Mughals. The argument has been carried too far. One wonders how the Sindhia could keep his control over the far-flung empire by keeping a band of guerillas, particularly when he had to fight pitched battles against desperate enemies in the deserts of Rajputana. Perhaps the Maratha fault lay not in abandoning the guerilla system of warfare, but in inadequate adoption of the modern techniques of warfare. The Marathas neglected the paramount importance of artillery. Mahadaji Sindhia deserves the credit of trying to fight the enemy with the enemy's weapons. His battalions were trained on the European model and factories were set up for the manufacture of fire-arms, but these departments were entirely in the hand of foreigners whose loyalty in times of need was always in doubt. The Poona Government also set up an artillery department, but it hardly functioned effectively. The importance of powerful artillery we realise when we consider how British artillery easily reduced many Maratha forts which had baffled the Mughal armies under Aurangzeb. Undoubtedly, the best results could have been achieved in a coordinated development of all the three wings of the army, viz., infantry, cavalry and artillery.

6. Superior English Diplomacy. The English were superior to the Marathas in the game of diplomacy. Before actual operations would start the Company would take care to win allies and isolate the enemy diplomatically. The absence of unity among the Maratha chiefs considerably simplified the task of the British. In the Second Maratha War the English won over the Gaekwar and the Southern Maratha Jagirdars to their side, while the Peshwa was their ally by the Treaty of Bassein. These diplomatic gains gave to the Company supply bases at Poona and in Gujrat and enabled them to take quick offensive against the Sindhia's territories of Ahmednager and Broach. Similarly, the friendship of the Southern Maratha Jagirdars ensured to the Company the line of communication between the British army and their supply base at Seringapatam.

7. Superior English Espionage. The Marathas were careless about military intelligence. The Marathi historian Sardesai points out that while every British officer who toured their country used his eyes and afterwards his tongue and pen, and while a number of Britishers could speak and understand Maratha, the Marathas knew nothing about England, about the British system of Government, about their settlements and factories in India and outside, their character and inclinations, their arms and armaments, perhaps even Nana Phadnavis did not at all possess such details and the Marathas were woefully ignorant.

As against this, the Company's spy system was perfect. The Company's Residents in the courts of Indian princes supplied all sorts of information to the Company's secretariat. In 1803 when the Second Maratha War broke out the Company possessed knowledge of the potentialities of their foe, their strength and weaknesses, their military methods or want of method and, above all, an understanding of the dissensions in the Maratha confederacy. C.W. Malet while stationed at Surat collected detailed information about the families of Sindhia and Holkar. Palmer wrote in December 1798, "I consider it as the duty of every British subject in this country, however situated, to contribute to the utmost of his power, to the stock of general information". That the Holkar did not participate in the Second Maratha War commencing in 1803 and the Gaekwar remained aloof from all subsequent Maratha conflicts was all calculated by Wellesley and partially a success of his diplomacy.

8. Progressive Outlook of the English. While the Europeans had been emancipated from the shackles of the Church and Divinism and were devoting their energies to scientific inventions, extensive ocean voyages and acquisition of colonies, the Indians were still wedded to old dogmas and notions. If the ideal of our upper classes wars performance of rituals, the lower classes were fascinated by the Bhakti cult preached by Nanak, Kabir, Chaitanya and others. Baji Rao II cared more for religious merit and distributed gifts among Brahmins to earn religious merit and gave very little attention to mundane matters of the state. J.N. Sarkar points out that growth of orthodoxy and Brahmin-Maratha differences sapped the vitality of the state. G.W. Forrest in his *Maratha series* writes that "the jealousy which from various causes ever subsists between the Maratha chiefs and the Brahmins would prevent the union of the whole empire which must be most formidable to the rest of India." Thus, the entire Indian outlook was medieval and not modern.

We might say that when the English attacked the Marathas, the latter were already past the prime of their power. The Maratha power had lost its early vigour and momentum. Thus the English attacked a 'divided house' which started crumbling at the first push.

Select Opinions

S.N. Sen. The decline and fall of the Maratha military power was due firstly to the revival of feudalism after the death of Sambhaji, which caused disunion and dissension from which Shivaji had tried to save his people ; secondly, to the rejection of Shivaji's idea of racial amity on a religious basis in favour of the principle of personal aggrandisement which led to the denationalisation of the Maratha army, and thirdly and lastly, to the failure of the Maratha leaders to keep pace with the scientific progress in other parts of the world, to learn and assimilate what others had to teach and improve upon what they had learnt. In Europe there was steady progress from feudalism to national monarchy and from national monarchy to democracy ; in Maharashtra the process was reversed by the Peshwas, and the result was decline, decay and fall of the Maratha empire.

V.V.S. Khare. The Marathas did not possess any national sentiment. The internal jealousy and selfish treachery among them triumphed over the public interest. While individually the Marathas were clever and brave, they lacked the corporate spirit so essential for national independence. The scientific spirit of enquiry and improvement was entirely absent among them. They neglected to develop artillery as the main support of defence. The pernicious system of allowing lands in lieu of pay for military service proved ruinous. After the death of Madhavrao I no capable leader appeared in Maharashtra. The Marathas as a race lacked the virtue of discipline and methodical pre-arrangement. The British were past masters in the art of the diplomacy and the Marathas could not stand against them.

Sir Thomas Munro (wrote on 12 August 1817). When I consider the weakness of the native states and the character of the chiefs under whose sway they now are, I see little chance of a protracted resistance from them. They have not force to turn our armies and lengthen out the contest by a predatory invasion of our territories. They may run ahead for a few days but will have no time to rest or plunder. They will be exhausted and overtaken. It is not that they want resources, that they have not men and horses, but that there is no one amongst them possessed of those superior talents which are necessary to direct them to advantage. There is so little system or subordination in native government that much more energy is required under them than under the more regular governments of Europe, to give full effect to their resources. Daulatrao Sindhia was never formidable even in the height of his power. The great means which he possessed were lost in his feeble hand. The exertions of Holkar against Lord Lake were still weaker than those of Sindhia. The power of Holkar's as well as Sindhia's government has so much declined since that time (1805), that it is scarcely credible they would venture to oppose us. The superiority of our Government is so great that the event of any struggle is no longer doubtful.

SELECT REFERENCES

1. Dodwell H.H. : *Cambridge History of India*, vol. V.
2. Duff, Grant : *History of the Marathas*, 2 vols.
3. Joshi, V.V. : *Clash of Three Empires*.
4. Sardesai, G.S. : *Main Currents of Maratha History*.
5. Sardesai, G.S. : *New History of the Maratha People*.
6. Gorden, Stewart : *The Maratha* (New Cambridge History of India).

WILLIAM BENTINCK, 1828-35

I shall govern in name, but it will be you who govern in fact

— *Bentinck to Jeremy Bentham*

William Cavendish Bentinck succeeded Lord Amherst as Governor-General of India and took charge of Indian administration in July 1828. Bentinck began his career as an Ensign in the army, but soon rose to the position of a Lieutenant-Colonel. In 1796 he became a Member of Parliament. He fought with distinction against the forces of Revolutionary and Napoleonic France in Northern Italy. In consideration of his military experience, he was appointed Governor of Madras in 1803 to counter possible French designs in the Deccan. In 1806 some Madras regiments stationed at Vellore mutinied against the orders of the Commander-in-Chief forbidding them to use their caste-marks or wear earrings. The Vellore Mutiny was suppressed but the Court of Directors abruptly terminated Bentinck's services.

In 1828 Bentinck was selected to succeed Lord Amherst as Governor-General. Bentinck was a true Whig, inspired by the same ideals which characterised the ruling classes in the Era of Reform in England. While in command of English troops in Sicily in 1812, William Bentinck had encouraged the Sicilians to adopt a constitutional government on the English model. In the eulogistic language of Macaulay, inscribed on Bentinck's statue at Calcutta, William Bentinck "infused into Oriental Despotism the spirit of British freedom ; who never forgot that the end of government is the welfare of the governed ; who abolished cruel rites ; who effaced humiliating distinctions ; who allowed liberty to the expression of public opinion ; whose constant study it was to elevate the moral and intellectual character of the people committed to his charge". Undoubtedly, Bentinck took effective steps to root out social evils like *sati* and infanticide, established law and order in the country by suppressing the *thugs*, gave a larger share to the Indians in the subordinate services, expressed noble sentiments regarding the liberty of the press and took vital decisions regarding the educational system in India. He, however, did nothing to liberalize the administration or extend the blessings of political liberty to India to deserve the great praise Macaulay has showered on him. The Company's government remained as despotic as ever. P.E. Roberts is very correct when he remarks that "the famous statement represents rather the pious aspirations of the Governor-General and the ultimate tendency of his policy, than anything actually achieved".

Abolition of Sati and Cruel Rites. No previous Governor-General of India had ever tackled social problems with greater courage than Bentinck did. He tried to reform Hindu society by abolition of the cruel rite of *sati* and suppression of infanticide. He crushed the gangs of assassins called *thugs* and made peaceful living possible.

The term *sati* literally means 'a pure and virtuous woman'. It is used in the case of a devoted wife who contemplates perpetual and uninterrupted conjugal union with her husband after life and as a proof thereof burns herself with the dead body of her husband. The belief that the dead need company and victuals in their journey to far off Paradise was prevalent among many primitive peoples, and it was customary to bury, with the body of a chief, his drinking bowls horses, dogs and even his favorite wives and concubines. Probabily this practice was brought to India by the Indo-Scythian invaders. In India its popularity was due to a false sense of conjugal duty sanctioned by society and religion, though the motivating urges were economic and moral.

Some enlightened Indian princes had taken steps to abolish this cruel practice in their dominions. Emperor Akbar had attempted to restrict it. The Marathas had forbidden it in their dominions. The

Portuguese at Goa and the French at Chandernagore had also taken some steps towards its abolition. The East India Company had however, adhered to its declared policy of non-interference into the social and religious customs of the people of India. Early British Governors-General like Cornwallis, Minto and Lord Hastings had taken some steps to restrict the practice of *sati* by discouraging compulsion, forbidding administration of intoxicating drugs to the sorrow-stricken widows, putting a ban on the burning of pregnant women or widows below 16 years of age and, above all, making compulsory the presence of police officials at the time of sacrifice, who were to see that no compulsion was used. These restrictions, however, proved inadequate and unsuccessful.

Enlightened Indian reformers led by Raja Rammohan Roy urged William Bentinck to take necessary steps and declare the practice of *sati* illegal. The loss of his sister-in-law by *sati* had stirred Rammohan Roy to action and he had published a number of pamphlets condemning the practice. His arguments were supported by many of the progressive Indian newspapers and the conscience of the nation had been awakened. William Bentinck provided the necessary legislative corrective. He collected relevant facts and figures about *sati* cases, obtained the views of army officers, of the Judges of Nizamat Adalat, of the Superintendents of Police of the Lower and Upper Provinces and came to the conclusion that there was no danger of mutiny or civil commotion. Regulation No. XVII of December 1829 declared the practice of *sati* or of burning or burying alive of widows illegal and punishable by the criminal courts as culpable homicide. The Regulation of 1829 was applicable in the first place to Bengal Presidency alone, but in 1830 was extended in different forms to Madras and Bombay Presidencies.

No public disorders followed the enactment. A few orthodox Bengalis vainly made an appeal to the Privy Council against Government's interference in their religious customs. Counter-petitions were sent to the King by Rammohan Roy and Devendranath Tagore and William Bentinck was thanked for what he had done.

Suppression of Infanticide and Child-sacrifices. The practice of killing infant girls prevailed among some Rajput tribes. Many dubious methods were used to destroy female children ; some neglected to suckle the child, others administered poisonous drugs (mostly opium) through the nipple of the mother's breast, still some dare-devils put the girl in a sack and threw it into a river. Infanticide was found to be prevalent among some Rajput tribes in the province of Banaras, among the Jharija Rajputs of Cutch and Gujarat and cases were also reported among the Rathors of Jaipur and Jodhpur and even the Jats and Mewatis were not immune from this evil practice. Although infanticide had been declared illegal by Bengal Regulation XXI of 1795 and Regulation III of 1804, the inhuman practice still continued. William Bentinck took vigorous steps to suppress this immoral and inhuman practice.

William Bentinck's attention was also drawn to the ritual of offering child sacrifices at special occasions in Saugar island in Bengal. Bentinck issued prompt orders to stop this evil practice.

Suppression of Thugi. Another great reform to the credit of William Bentinck is the suppression of thugs. The thugs, *i.e.*, cheats were a sect of hereditary assassins and robbers who lived by preying upon innocent and defenseless travellers. A more appropriate name for thugs was *pansigar*, derived from the scarf and noose used by the thugs to strangle their victims.

However remote the origin of *thugi* the organisation found a very congenial atmosphere for growth during the period of decay and downfall of the Mughal Empire when all police arrangements broke down and public roads became insecure. Petty officials of small states in Central India, unable to effectively deal with thugs, made common cause with them and gave them protection in return for a share in the spoils. The thugs were particularly active in the entire area from Oudh to Hyderabad and in Rajputana and Budelkhand.

The thugs belonged to both the Hindu and Muslim religions and worshipped the Hindu goddeses like Kali, Durga or Bhawani, to whom they offered the heads of their victim as sacrifices. The thugs were hardened criminals who subordinates their conscience by their perverse reasoning. They believed that *thugi* was a preordained means of livelihood for them and their victims were ordained to die at their hands. They had a very disciplined organisation. If some were expert stranglers, others were adept-in quick disposal of the dead bodies, still others good spies and informants. They had their own code of words and signs. For the beginners a course of apprenticeship was provided and initiation as a master thug was done amidst religious ceremonies. So efficient was the organisation of the thugs that not even a single case of failure ever came to the notice of the Government.

The strength of a thug gang varied from a single thug to as many as 400 thugs. Usually the victim was a single individual, but sometimes a dozen men were murdered at the same time.

While there could be some difference of opinion about the abolition of *sati*, the public opinion solidly supported the Government measures to suppress *thugi* in 1830. The operations against the thugs were put in the charge of Colonel William Sleeman. The rulers of Indian states were invited to co-operate in this task. Colonel Sleeman arrested as many as 1,500 thugs and sentenced them to death or imprisonment for life. *Thugi* on an organised scale ceased to exist after 1837, although individual bad characters continued their nefarious activities.

Removal of Humiliating Distinctions in Recruitment to Public Service. In matters of recruitment to public services, William Bentinck sought to efface the humiliating distinctions between Europeans and Indians introduced by Cornwallis and upheld by subsequent Governors-General. Fitness was now laid down as the criterion for eligibility. Section 87 of the Charter Act of 1833 provided that no Indian subject of the Company in India was to be debarred from holding any office under the Company "by reason of his religion, place of birth, descent and colour". It is believed that this Charter clause was inserted at the instance of Bentinck. Though the immediate effect of this clause was very little, it laid down a very important and healthy principle.

Liberal Policy towards the Press. Bentinck's policy towards the press was characterised by a liberal attitude. He believed the press to be a safety-value for discontent. The reduction of *bhatta* and other financial measures were subjects of severe criticism and even abuse in the press. His minute embodying the decision to impose some restrictions on the press contain his views. It runs thus : "The Adjutant General of the Madras Army, who was at that time at Calcutta, described the angry feelings and language so loudly expressed here, and all the signs of the times, to be precisely similar to those which prevailed before the Madras mutiny, and he anticipated a similar explosion...The Mutiny did take place at Madras though there was not a shadow of liberty belonging to the press there...My firm belief is that more good than harm was produced by the open and public declaration of the sentiments of the army. There was vent to public feeling and the mischief was open to public view; and the result is so far confirmatory of the opinion here given that no overt act took place." He, however, drew a distinction between discussion of a proposal and clamour against and censure of a final decision given by the Supreme Authority. Nor could he tolerate Government officials making use of official information to criticise the act of Government. He therefore, favoured a prohibitory order banning all further discussion on the question of *bhatta*. In reply to a joint petition of the Indian and European journalists of Calcutta seeking the abolition of all restrictions on the press, Lord William Bentinck's Government assured the petitioners that "the unsatisfactory state of laws relating to the press had already attracted the notice of His Lordship in Council and he trusts that in no long time a system will be established which, while it gives security to every person engaged in the fair discussion of public measures, will effectively secure the Government against sedition and individuals against calumny." In March 1835 William Bentinck was compelled to resign owing to ill health and its was left to his devoted lieutenant and successor Charles Metcalfe to remove the restrictions from the Indian press.

Attempts to Elevate the Moral and Intellectual Character of Indians—Educational Reforms. perhaps the most significant and of far-reaching consequences were Bentinck's decisions about education in India. As early as 1825 Elphinstone had wirtten that the only effective path to social reform and the only remedy for social abuses was education. The 'Macaulayian System' of education has profoundly affected the moral and intellectual character of the people of India.

Bentinck's Government defined the aim of education in India and the medium of instruction to be employed. How were the govenment grants for education to be spent? Were government subsidies to be spent for the encouragement of Oriental languages and Indian literature or for instruction of Indians Western sciences and literature and through the medium of English? The members of the Committee of Public Instruction were divided into two groups of equal strength : the Orientalists led by Hayman Wilson and Princep Brothers and the Occidentalists or Anglicists led by Sir Chrles Trevelyan and supported by Indian liberals like Raja Rammohan Roy. Bentinck appointed Macaulay as the President of the Committee. Macaulay gave a definite turn to the controversy. He set forth his views in the famous minute dated 2 February 1835 in which he ridiculed Indian literature. Were public funds to be spent, wrote Macaulay, to teach 'medical doctrines which would disgrace an English farrier, astronomy which would move laughter in girls at an English Boarding school, history abounding with kings thirty feet high and reigns 30,000 years long, geography made up of seas of treacle and seas of butter......Are we to teach false history, false astronomy, false medicine, because we find them in company with a false religion." He contended that the vernacular languages contained neither literary value nor scientific information and that "a single shelf of a good European library was worth the whole native literature of India and Arabia." He further wrote, "What the Greek and Latin were to the contemporaries of More and Ascham our tongue is to the people of India." In making his recommendations Macaulay had planned to produce a class of persons who would be "Indian in blood and colour, but English in taste, in opinions, in morals and intellect" and expressed the hope in one of the letters to his father that "if our plans of education are followed up, there will not be a single idolater among the respectable classes in Bengal 30 years hence."

Macaulay's views were accepted and embodied in a Resolution of March 7, 1835, which decreed that English would be the official language of India in the higher branches of administration. Since then English language, English literature, English political literature and English natural sciences have formed the basis of higher education in India.

Financial Reforms. The heavy drain of Burmese War had depleted the treasury of the Company. In 1828 public expenditure far exceeded the revenue. In the words of Charles Metcalfe, "The Government which allows this to go on in time of peace deserves any punishment." With an eye on the Charter debates, the Home authorities had enjoined on Bentinck the policy of peace and economies in public expenditure.

Bentinck appointed two committees, one military and one civil, to make recommendations for effecting economy in expenditure. Under special instructions from the Court of Directors, Bentinck reduced the *bhatta, i.e.* extra or additional allowance paid to military officer. The new rules decreed that in case of troops stationed within 400 miles of Calcutta one-half *bhatta* would be allowed. Thus, a saving of £ 20,000 a year was effected. The allowances of civil servants were also reduced.

The Government adopted better measures for the collection of land revenue in Bengal. The land revenue settlement of the North Western Provinces (modern U.P.) carried on under the supervision of Robert Merttins Bird yielded better revenues. Expenditure on the costly settlements in the Straits of Malacca was reduced. Further, Bentinck employed Indians wherever possible in place of high-paid Europeans.

Opium trade was regularised and licensed. In future opium could be exported only through the port of Bombay, which gave the Company a share in the profits in the shape of duties.

The net result of these economies was that the deflicit of one crore per year that Bentinck inherited was converted into a surplus of 2 crores per year by 1835. He had also stimulated the economy by encouraging iron and coal production, tea and coffee plantations and irrigation schemes.

Judicial Reforms. The Provincial Courts of Appeal and Circuit set up by Cornwallis were burdened with excessive duties and usually arrears accumulated. The judicial procedure followed in these courts was cumbersome and often resulted in delays and uncertainties. William Bentinck abolished these courts, transferring their duties to magistrates and collectors under the supervision of Commissioner of Revenue and Circuit. For the convenience of the public of Upper Provinces (present-day U.P.) and Delhi, a separate Sadr Nizamat Adalat and a Sadr Diwani Adalat were set up at Allahabad and the residents of these areas were no longer under the necessity of travelling a thousand miles to file their appeals at Calcutta.

Persian so far had been the court language. Bentinck gave the suitors the option to use Persian or vernanculars in filing their suits. In higher coruts Persian was replaced by English as the court language. Qualified Indians were appointed in junior judicial capacities of Munsiffs and could rise to the position of Sadr Amins.

Policy towards Indian States. In deference to the wishes of the Court of Directors, Williams Bentinck followed the policy of non-interference into the affairs of Indian states as far as possible. Despite disorder and anarchy in Jaipur resulting in an attack on the British Resident, Bentinck refused to interfere. At the request of the new Nizam, Nasir-ud-daula, who succeeded his father to *gaddi* in 1829, the British officers were removed from Hyderabad. A similar policy of non-intervention was followed towards the states of Jodhpur, Bundi, Kota and Bhopal even when there were strong reason for interference.

Bentinck, however, departed from the policy of non-intervention and annexed Mysore (1831), Coorg (1834) and central Cachar (November 1834) on the plea of misgovernment.

Bentinck was alive to Russian advances in Central Asia. To demonstrate the solidarity of Indian powers, he concluded a 'treaty of perpetual friendship' with Ranjit Singh, and a commercial-cum-political treaty with the Amirs of Sind. He also supported the claims of Shah Shuja on the throne of Kabul.

Estimate of Bentinck. The seven years of Bentinck's administration gave a period of respite from an almost continous policy of wars and annexations. Historians like Thornton described the period from 1828-35 as 'blank of achievements' and the Governor-General having "done less for the interest of India and for his own reputation than any who had occupied his place since the commencement of the nineteenth century, with the single exception of Sir George Barlow". The Duke of Wellington had a very poor opinion of Bentinck both as a soldier and administrator. Notwithstanding all this criticism, we can say that far from loosening British hold on India, Bentinck played a very great part in consolidating British authority by his policy of internal reforms. In all fairness, however, it may be said that it was no object of Bentinck's policy to facilitate the development of self-governing institutions which came later due to quite different developments. Thus Macaulay's eulogistic language showers on Bentinck more praise than he deserves. In the history of India Bentinck's name will be long remenbered for the introduction of a number of social and administrative reforms which had played a great part in modernizing India.

Select Opinions

Lord T.B. Macaulay (Text of inscription on Bentinck's statue at Calcutta, composed by Macaulay):

To

William Cavendish Bentinck

Who during seven years ruled India with eminent integrity and benevolence ;

Who place at the head of a great empire, never laid aside the simplicity and moderation of a private citizen ;

Who infused into Oriental despotism the spirit of British freedom ;

Who never forgot that the end of the government is the happiness of the governed ;

Who abolished cruel rites ;

Who effaced humiliating distinctions ;

Who gave liberty to the expression of public opinion ;

Whose constant study was to elevate the intellectual and moral character of the nation committed to his charge ;

This Monument was erected by men

Who, differing in race, in manners, in language and religion, Cherish with equal veneration and gratitude the memory of his wise, reforming and paternal administration.

P.E. Roberts. Bentinck was a true Liberal of his day, thoroughly in accord with the ideals that inspired the era of Catholic emancipation and Parliamentary reform. His personal habits were simple, and he intensely disliked the state that is generally considered necessary for the position he occupied. In this respect, as well as in his philanthropic care for the peoples of India, economy in administration and earnest desire to preserve peace, he may be compared with that other essentially Liberal Governor-General among his successors, the Marquis of Ripon...He was undoubtedly the first Governor-General openly to act on the theory that the welfare of the subject peoples was a main, perhaps the primary duty of the British in India, though this conception had already inspired great administrators, such as Elphinstone and Munro. (*History of British India*, pp. 300-01)

Thompson and Garratt. The arrival of Lord William Bentinck marked the beginning of a new era in numerous ways. His seven years' rule proved a peaceful interlude between two periods of severe and costly campaigning, and thus made it possible to achieve reforms which were long overdue..He consolidated and reorganised the administration which since the time of Cornwallis had been hastily adapted to the newly-conquered countries. His own instincts were those of a Liberal reformer. He believed in peace, retrenchment and reform, in free competition, free trade and a strictly limited sphere of State action. In Sir Charles Metcalfe he had an admirable chief of staff who supplied the local knowledge and some of the driving force behind the reforms. These touched nearly every side of Indian life and formed the basis of the paternal government of the Victorian era. Bentinck initiated new policies in the spheres of finance, justice, and education. (*The Rise and Fulfilment of British Rule in India*, p. 317).

Grenville. Bentinck is a man whose success in life has been greater than his talents warrants, for he is not right-headed, and has committed some great blunders or other in every public situation in which he has been placed, but he is simple in his habits, popular is his manners, liberal in his opinions and magnificiently hospitable in his mode of life. These qualities are enough to ensure popularity.

SELECT REFERENCES

1. Bary, Theodore de : *Sources of Indian Tradition.*
2. Bearce, George D. : *British Attitudes Towards India.*
3. Boulger, D. : *William Bentinck* (Rulers of India series).
4. Roselli, J. : *Lord William Bentinck.*
5. Spear, P. : *Oxford History of Modern India.*
6. Stokes, Eric : *The English Utilitarians and India.*
7. Taylor, Meadows : *Confessions of a Thug.*

15

THE ANNEXATION OF SIND

> We have no right to seize Sind, yet we shall do so and a very advantageous, useful, humane piece of rascality it will be.
>
> —*Sir Charles Napier*

With humble beginnings in trade the English power had been expanded by arms and diplomacy and the glittering bubble must expand, or it will burst. The cupidity of the Directors, the ambition or avarice of their agents in India coupled with the Englishman's insolence of superiority and the inherent craving for aggrandisement made collision with the Indian princes inevitable, and conquest a corollary of that collision. The same logic of events which brought the rest of India under British rule operated in the case of Sindh also.

Sind in the eighteenth century was ruled by the Kallora chiefs. In 1771 a Baluch tribe of the Tralpuras descended from the hills and settled in the plains of Sind. Hardy men and excellent soldiers, very soon the Talpuras acquired great influence and usurped power. In 1783 Mir Fath Ali Khan, the leader of the Talpuras, established complete hold over Sind and the Kallora prince was exiled. Mir Fath Ali Khan who claimed a vague suzerainty over Sind was confirmed in his dominions by the Durrani monarch and forced to share the country with his brothers. When he died in 1800, those brothers, popularly known as 'Char Yar' divided the kingdom among themselves, calling themselves the Amirs or Lords of Sind. Soon after these Amirs extended their dominion on all sides, took Amarkot from the Raja of Jodhpur, Karachi from the chief of Luz, Shaikarpur and Bukkar from the Afghans.

As early as 1775 the East India Company had established a factory at Thatta, then a town of considerable commercial importance, but it had to be abandoned in 1792 because of fiscal impositions and the prevailing political unrest. Fear of French designs prompted Lord Minto to send British mission to Kabul, Persia, Lahore and Sind. A treaty of 'eternal friendship' was signed with the Amirs in 1809 providing for mutual intercourse through envoys and the Amirs promised not to allow the French to settle in Sind. The treaty was renewed in 1820 with the additional article which excluded the Americans from Sind. It also settled border disputes between the two parties on the side of Cutch where the Company's frontier and the frontiers of Sind met. Soon after the commercial and navigational value of the Indus attracted the attention of the Company's authorities. It was in pursuance of commercial motives that in 1831 Sir Alexander Burnes, under orders from Lord Ellenborough, then President of the Board of Control, was sent for the exploration of the Indus under pretence of carrying presents to Ranjit Singh at Lahore.

The Baluchis could scent the game of the English. When Burnes first entered the Indus, a Baluchi soldier said; "The mischief is done, you have seen our country". A Seiad commented : "Alas ! Sind is now gone since the English have seen the river which is the high road to its conquest".

In 1832 William Bentinck sent Colonel Pottinger to Sind to sign a new commercial treaty with the Amirs. Simultaneously Lieutenant Del Host was sent to survey the course of the Lower Indus. Pottinger signed a treaty with the Amirs of Sind on the following terms :

1. A free passage for English travellers and merchant through Sind, and the use of the Indus for commercial pursuits ; but not vessel of war was to come by the said river nor military stores to be conveyed by the above river or roads of Sind.

2. No English merchant was to settle in Sind, and travellers and visitors were required to have passports.

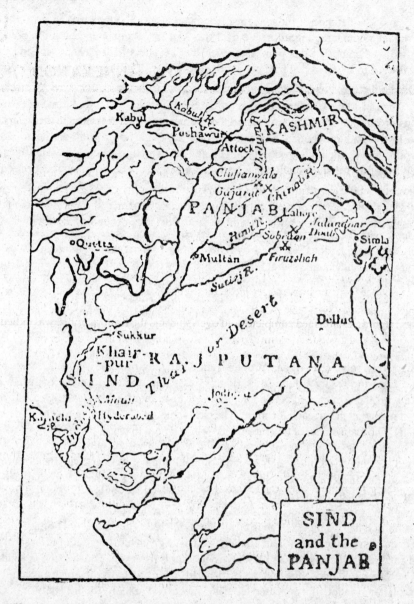

SIND and the PANJAB

3. Tariff rates were to be announced and no military dues or tolls to be demanded. The Amirs agreed to alter the tariff rates, if found too high.
4. The Amirs agreed to put down, in concert with the Raja of Jodhpur, the border robbers of Cutch.
5. The old treaties of friendship were confirmed and the contracting parties agreed not to look with the eye of covetousness on the possessions of one another.

The details of tariff rates were settled by a supplementary commercial treaty of 1834. Colonel Pottinger was stationed as Company's Political Agent in Sind. Soon the Company put up a claim for a share in the tolls collected at the mouth of the Indus.

The designs of Ranjit Singh on Sind provided the East India Company with an excuse to throw a cordon round Sind. At the Rupar meeting between Ranjit Singh and William Bentinck (1831), the latter refused to discuss any proposal for the partition of Sind. Lord Auckland looked upon Sind from the larger problem of the defence of India against Russian designs. To counter Russian plans Auckland wanted to obtain a counteracting influence over the Afghans. Ranjit Singh was too powerful to be coerced in the furtherance of this plan. However, the weakness of the Amirs of Sind offered too tempting a reward to be missed. Thus, consolidation of British influence in Sind was considered a necessary preliminary to plans on Afghanistan.

Ranjit Singh had taken Rojhan, a town on the Sind frontier, and at one time even meditated a regular invasion of Sind. The Company seized this moment to offer protection to the Amirs. Pottinger was sent to Hyderabad to negotiate a new treaty offering British protection on the condition of the Amir accepting the Company's troops in his capital to be maintained at the cost of the Amir or alternatively promise British mediation in return for concessions. The Amirs neither desired nor asked for foreign aid and told Pottinger : "We have relinquished the Sikhs, and we will do again". Pottinger then told the Amirs that Ranjit Singh would be let loose, perhaps aided, to pursue his designs on Sind. Reluctantly the Amirs agreed to a treaty in 1838 by whcih theAmirs accepted the Company's mediation in their dispute with the Sikhs, and secondly, accepted a British Resident at Hyderabad, who could move freely anywhere he liked escorted by British troops. Thus, the Amirs virtually passed under British protection. Lieutenant-General Sir W.F.P. Napier writes : "This treaty by which a loaded shell was placed in the palace of the Ameers to explode at pleasure for their destruction, was abstractedly, an unjust oppressive action".[1] P.E. Roberts writes : "Under Auckland and his cabinet of secrataries British policy in India had fallen to a lower level of unscrupulousness than ever before, and the plain fact is that the treatment of Sind from this time onward, however expedient politically, was morally indefensible".[2]

To effectively solve the Afghan problem, the Company brought round the Sikh ruler to the signing of a Tripartite Treaty in June 1838. By this treaty Ranjit Singh accepted British mediation for his dispute with the Amirs, and Shah Shuja agreed to relinquish his sovereign right on Sind on condition of receiving the arrears of tribute. The exact amount of the tribute was to be determined by the Company. The main object of this machinery was to obtain finances for the Afghan adventure and obtain so much of the Amirs' territory as would secure a line of operations agisnt Afghanistan through Sind. Casting all scruples to the wind, Colonel Pottinger was sent with the draft of a treaty to the Amirs with the direction to persuade or compel the Amirs to pay the money and also consent to the abrogation of that article of the Treaty of 1832 which concerned the non-conveyance of military stores through the roads and rivers of Sindh. The Amirs produced declaratory articles showing that Shah Shuja himself had exempted them from all claims in 1833. The Amirs told Pottinger : "It is a joke to call it a demand from the King (Shah Shujah). You have given him bread for the last five and twenty years, and any strength he has now or may have hereafter is from you. The demand is yours". Colonel Pottinger, however, told the Amirs that the British had "the ready power to crush and annihilate them, the will to call it into action, if it appeared requisite, however, remotely, for the safety or integrity of the Anglo-Indian empire or frontier." Under threat of superior force, the Amirs accepted a treaty in February 1839 by which a British subsidiary force was to be stationed at Shikarpur and Bukkar and the Amirs of Sind were to pay rupees three lakhs annually for the maintenance of the Company's troops. Further, the Amirs were not to have any negotiations with foreign States without the knowledge of the Company's government; to provide store-room at Karachi for military supplies; to abolish all tolls on the Indus and to furnish an auxiliary force for the Afghan war if called upon to do so. The British Government in return pledged itself not to meddle with the internal rule of the Amirs either generally or in respect of their separate possessions and to protect them from foreign aggression. Even when the negotiations were going on, the Company's troops captured Karachi and retained it, regardless of

---

1. W.F.P. Napier : *The History of General Charles Napier's Conquest of Sind*, p. 31.
2. P.E. Roberts, : *History of British India* p. 326.

The Annexation of Sind

the treaty which was immediately altered and sent to the Amirs for signatures 'who objected, implored and finally gave way, by fixing their seals to the revised documents'.

During the Afghan war, the Amirs of Sind, in the words of T. Archbold, "found themselves saddles with the general liability to help the British forces; parts of their territory had been taken from them, obviously for ever ; they had to contribute in varying proportions a large amount of money, instead of the old tribute, in order to maintain troops in their midst whom they did not want ; and their independent position was gone for ever, because they had now come definitely within the sphere of British influence". Even then the Amirs faithfully carried out the terms of the treaties imposed on them, but instead of getting reward for their fidelity were charged with hostility and disaffection against the British government.

Lord Ellenborough succeeded Auckland as Governor-General in 1842. In his dealing with the Amirs of Sind, the new Governor-General proved to be even more unscrupulous than Lord Auckland. According to V.A. Smith, "Ellenborough was eager to find a pretext for the annexation of that country, and it was not long before his search was rewarded...he deliberately provoked a war in order that he might annex the province...the desire to obtain control of the great waterway seems to have been the leading motive of the annexationists in the time of Lord Auckland as well as that of Lord Ellenborough". Ellenborough laboured hard to regain the prestige of the English which had suffered during the Afghan war. In justification of his policy, he wrote to the Duke of Wellington : "The Amirs, too, had been strangely misled as to the real circumstances under which we retired from Afghanistan. They believed us beaten".

In September 1842 Sir Charles Napier replaced Major Outram as the Company's Resident in Sind. Napier was given full civil and military authority and placed in charge of all the troops of Upper and Lower Sind. According to V.A. Smith, "Napier who was bent on annexing the province, pursued a bullying policy, always assuming that the Government of India was at liberty to do what it pleased without the slightest regard to treaties." If Ellenborough said, "I cannot enter upon our right to be here at all, that is Auckland's affair", Sir Napier said, "I cannot go into arguments. I am not Governor-General. I am only one of his commanders."[3] Sir W. Butler in his biography of Sir C. Napier writes that "no man ever longed for a mistress more than this man longed for war". Napier announced that the charges against the Amirs had been proved. Amir Rustum of Khairpur was charged with entering into secret intercourse with foreign States contrary to treaty and hostile to the British ; maltreatment of British public servants ; obstructing the navigation of the Indus; illegal imprisonment of British subjects etc. Against Nasir Khan of Hyderabad the charges were—assembling of troops to attack Sher Mohammad of Mirpur on a boundary dispute under British arbitration; delaying transfer of Shikarpur when he heard of the disasters in Afghanistan; secretly coining base money to defraud the British Government in the payment of tribute ; exacting illegal tolls and obstructing the navigation of the Indus; preventing his subjects from settling and trading in the British cantonment at Karachi etc. Above all, these two Amirs were charged with a secret offensive and defensive alliance against the Company.

Lord Ellenborough, placed in a dangerous position by the Afghan disasters, proposed a new treaty to the Amirs as security for the future, but containing also a demand of territory as a punishment for past transgressions. Outram was sent as a Commissioner to Sind to negotiate the details of the new treaties. By new treaties the Amirs were required to cede important territories in lieu of tribute, to provide fuel to the steamers of the Company navigating the Indus and surrender the right of coining money. The English Company was to coin money for the Amirs and the new coins were to bear on one

---

3. C. Napier said, "It is not for me to consider how we came to occupy Sind, but to consider the subject as it now stands. We are here by right of treaties entered into by the Amirs, and therefore stand on the same footing as themselves ; for rights held under treaty are as sacred as the right which sanctions that treaty." (Quoted by Sir W.F.P. Napier, *op. cit.*, p.. 81).

side the effigy of the Queen of England. Meantime a succession dispute at Khairpur gave Napier the opportunity to interfere. Napier supported the claims of Ali Murad, brother of the old Mir Rustum in prference to the claims of Mir Rustum's Napier's intention was to have only one governing chief in each province, instead of many. This would simplify the Company's political dealings with the princes. Mir Rustum, however, abdicated in favour of his son and took to flight. From the flight of Mir Rustum may be dated the commencement of the Sindian war. The Amirs of Upper Sind fled to the desert and to Lower Sind, there to raise the banner of revolt in conjunction with their cousins of Hyderabad. The Amirs had reluctantly accepted the new treaties, but Napier suspected that the Amirs were preparing for war. When Napier repeated the Governor-General's orders to disband the armed bands, the Amirs replied, "There are no bands, we are all submission." Napier was not convinced and was eager to commence hostilities in winter, fearing the rigours of the hot weather ahead. He proceeded to capture Imamgarh situated in the heart of the desert and approached only by vague uncertain tracks. The fortress was captured in January 1843. Napier's acts of aggression drove the Baluchis to the point of desperation. They planned to murder Major Outram and were prepared to fight to the bitter end. In February 1843 Napier defeated a Baluchi army at Miani and won another victory at Dabo, six miles from Hyderabad the following months. By April the whole of Sind had capitulated. The *Punch* carried a cartoon wherein Napier announces the news to Lord Ellenborough in the phrase "*peccavi*, I have Sind". The Amirs were made captives and banished from Sind. Napier accepted £ 70,000 as a sort of booty from the plunder of Sind; a sum of £ 3,000 was offered to Qutram which he refused to accept. Writing in 1857 Lieutenant-General Sir W.F.P. Napier eulogised the achievements of Charles Napier in these words : "He thus gave to the Anglo-Indian Empire a shorter and safer frontier on the West, with the command of the Indus, opening a direct commercial way to Central Asia, and spreading through that vast country a wholesome terror of the British arms"[4] and further that "to remove such brutal treacherous tyrants (the Amirs) was worthy of England's greatness. The conquest of Sind is, therefore, no iniquity. The glory of the achievement is a pure flame kindled on the altar of justice."[5] Lord Ellenborough paid rich tribute to Napier for "having added a province, fertile as Egypt to the British Empire."

The annexation of Sind has met with universal condemnation both at the hands of politicians and historians. Even Outram disagreed with Napier's policy and wrote to him : "I am sick of your policy ; I will not say yours is the best, but it is undoubtedly the shortest—that of the sword. Oh, I how wish you had drawn it in a better cause!"[6]. *The Times of London* described the whole business "rotten throughtout." *The Bombay Times* wrote : "Alas ! that this man bears the name of Englishman : Alas ! that he is born in the glorious age of Wellington, which he disgraces". Henry Lawrene wrote: " I do not think that Government can do better than restore it to the Amirs." Even the conqueror of Sind, Napier himself was not convinced of the righteousness of annexation. In his diary he noted : "We have no right to seize Sind, yet we shall do so, and a very advantageous, useful, humane piece of rascality it will be." Robert Peel, the Prime Minister of England, described the conquest as full of 'precipitate and unjust proceedings which would discredit the 'name and character' of the British authorities. Though convinced of the unjustness of the annexation of Sind, the Home authorities did not reverse the decision of the Govenment of India. Mr. Gladstone, the Liberal leader, said some years later that "the mischief of retaining was less than the mischeif of abandoning Sind,"

Historian Innes wrote that the case for annexation of Sind was more or less deliberately manufactured, while Edward Thorton believed the annexation to have been effected without 'fair pretence', and that the Amirs of Sind "owed us nothing, and they had inflicted on us no injury, but it suited our policy to reduce them to vassalage and they were thus reduced". Ramsay Muir has equally pointed in his criticism when he writes : "Sind is the only British acquisition in India of which it may

---

4. *Ibid.*, p. 267.
5. *Ibid.*, p. 285.
6. Quoted by V.A. Smith in *Oxford History of India*, p. 685.

fairly be said that it was not necessitated by circumstances ; and that it was therefore an act of aggression".

Percival Spear, a modern apologist of British imperialism, regards penetration of Western influence synonymous with British imperial expansion in India ; he labels the annexation of Sind as 'the least creditable' and 'fascist' but argues that Sind could not for ever remain isolated from the world and, adds further, that it was not in her own best interests that she should do so.[7]

Annexation of Sind sequel to the Afghan War. Charles Napier believed that the Sindian war was not isolated event, but "the tail of the Afghan storm". P.E. Roberts elaborates the same view when he writes : "The conquest of Sind followed in the wake of the Afghan war and was morally and politically its sequel". The unattractive and barren land of Sind assumed great importance for the Company's authorities because of its strategic value in building up the defences of India against possible Russo-Persian designs on India. In a letter to the British Resident, Pottinger, on July 26, 1833, Lord Ackland wrote : "You will in the first place state to the Amirs that, in the opinion of the Govenor-General, a crisis has arrived at which it is essentially requisite for the security of British India, that the real friends of that Power should unequivocally manifest their attachment to its interest ; and you will further apprise them that a combination of the Powers to the Westward, apparently have objects in views calculated to be injurious to our Empire in the East, has compelled the Governor-General to enter into a counter-combination for the purpose of frustrating those objects."[8]

Perhaps it was inexpedient and unjust to invade Afghanistan, but that invasion in the eyes of Ellenborough and many Englishmen made it expedient, though unjust, to coerce the Amirs of Sind. Ranjit Singh would not give a passage through the Punjab to the Company's army of invasion of Afghanistan. The weakness and richness of the Amirs of sind offered advantages which the unscrupulous Government of Aukland would not overlook. Thus, the Amirs were coerced to provide finances for the Afghan adventure and also military cantonments and other facilities in their territories for the passage of the Company's troops. Treaty after treaty was forced on the Amirs to meet the changing Afghan situation. The failure of the Afghan adventure put the Govenment of India under the necessity of increasing vigilance about the frontier problem. Thus it was found inxpedient to abandon the military cantonments of Khairpur, Bukkar, Sukkar and Karachi. Lord Ellenborough wrote to the Duke of Wellington on 22 March 1843 : "I hardly know how I could have accomplished the object of retaining possession of a commanding position upon the Lower Indus without a breach with the Amirs. We could hardly have justified our remaining at Karachi; we could not have justified our remaining at Bukkar, after the termination of the war with Afghanistan, without a new treaty...". Moreover, the British prestige had greatly suffered. In India there was universal despondency and such a great terror of the Afghans that it was scarcely possible to find resources for remittance to the British Generals in Afghanistan. There were stirrings at Gwalior and Saugor and spreading unrest in the whole of Bundelkhand. Some Madras regiments were on the verge of mutiny. In short, the fear of England's power and belief in her invincibility had been shaken. To demonstrate England's strength and to re-establish her prestige, Ellenborough sanctioned the conquest of Sind. Elephinstone has rather bluntly put it : "Coming from Afghanistan, it put one in mind of a bully who has been knocked in the street and went home to beat his wife in revenge".

Select Opinions

H.H. Dodwell. Viewed broadly, the annexation of Sind seems comparable with the assumption of the Carnatic. In both cases advantage was taken of foolish and hostile conduct to secure a considerable political advantage. Ellenborough, like Wellesley, was more concerned to consolidate and strengthen

---

7. P. Spear, *Oxford History of Modern India*, p. 165.
8. Quoted in *Cambridge History of India*, v., p. 525.

the position of the East India Company than to make benevolent gestures in the idle hope that others would follow so futile an example. (*The Cambridge Shorter History of India*, p. 668).

W.A.G Archbold. The judgement that has held the field hitherto has been hostile ; from 1844 when a writer in the *Calcutta Review* said : "The real cause of this chastisement of the Ameers consisted in the chastisement which the British had recieved from the Afghans", till the recent verdict in the *Cambridge Modern History*. But the truer view will be more like that of Outram's great apologist: "In the light of subsequent history it may even be argued that Outram's policy of the trust in the Ameers would have proved less wise than Napier's policy of vigilant coercion" : assuming for the moment that such were the respective policies of the two men...And yet the whole transaction has been thought to bear a colour of injustice which may rightly be ascribed to some of its parts, and the plea of the happiness of the people, who gained enormously by the change, has not been held sufficient to justify what happened. [H.H. Dodwell (Ed.), *The Cambridge History of India*, p.p. 538-39).

SELECT REFERENCES

1. Colchester, Lord : *History of the Indian Administration of Ellenborough.*
2. Dodwell, H.H. : *Cambridge History of India*, vol. v.
3. Khera, P.N. : *British Policy towards Sind.*
4. Lambrick, H.T. : *Sir Charles Napier and Sind* (Oxford 1952).
5. Napier, N.F.P. : *The Conquest of Sind.*
6. Young, Keith : *Sind in the Forties.*

16

CAREER AND ACHIEVEMENTS OF RANJIT SINGH

The weakness of the Mughal authority and the Afghan invasions of Ahmad Shah Abdali had created general confusion and anarchy in the Punjab. Ahmad Shah Abdali claimed the Punjab as a part of his dominion although his governors exercised hardly any other function of government except collection of revenue. The successors of Ahmad Shah could not keep control over the Punjab and the province became a 'no man's land'. These political conditions were conducive to the rise to power of Sikh misls (military brotherhoods with democratic set-up) under Sikh chieftains which held extensive territories in the Panjab. The important misls numbered twelve and one of these was the Sukarchakyia misl which controlled the territory between the Ravi and the Chenab.

Ranjit Singh was born at Gujranwala on 2 November 1780 in the house of Mahan Singh, the leader of the Sukarchakyia misl. His father died when Ranjit Singh was mere boy of 12. Ranjit Singh like Akbar showed an early grasp of political affairs. From 1792 to 1797 a Council of Regency consisting of Ranjit's mother, his mother-in-law and Diwan Lakhpat Rai controlled the actual affairs of the misl. In 1797 Ranjit Singh overthrew the Regency and took over the actual administration in his hands.

When Ranjit Singh assumed leadership of the Sukarchakyias, his authority extended over a few districts of the Rachna and the Chaj Doab. North of Sutlej the Bhangi misl was the most powerful and ontrolled extensive areas from the Jhelum and then down the river besides the actual control of Lahore and Amritsar. Another important misl was of the Kanheyas which ruled over the territories north of Amritsar. The Ahluwalia misl controlled the Jullundur Doab. South of the river Sutlej the Phulkian chiefs of Patiala, Nabha, Kaithal ruled over scattered territories extending from the Sutlej to the Jamuna. Afghan chiefs who usurped the authority of the Kabul Govenement ruled over Kasur, Multan, Attock, Peshawar, Bannu, Dera Ismail Khan, Kashmir etc. Zaman Shah, the grandson of Ahmad Shah Abdali, considered himself the rightful ruler of the Punjab and led a number of invasions to assert his authority.

Luckily for Ranjit Singh, the important misls were in a state of disintegration towards the close of the eighteenth century. The struggle for power politics also engulfed Afghanistan in a civil war from which the country did not recover for three decades. Ranjit Singh fully exploited the political situation to his advantage and by following a ruthless policy of 'blood and iron' carved out for himself a kingdom in the central Panjab.

In return for the services rendered to Zaman Shah Abdali during the latter's invasion of Punjab (1798), the Afghan ruler authorised Ranjit Singh to occupy Lahore and rule it on behalf of the Afghan suzerain. Ranjit Singh lost no time in ousting the Bhangi sirdars from Lahore, which he occupied in 1799. The occupation of Lahore considerably enhanced the prestige of Ranjit Singh. Emboldened, Ranjit Singh snatched Amritsar from the Bhangis in 1805[1]. The control of Lahore and Amritsar (the former the political capital of the Panjab and the latter the religious capital of the Sikhs) put Ranjit Singh in the forefront of the political life of the Panjab. The following few years saw the establishment of his authority over entire territory from the Sutlej to the Jhelum. Latif sums up the process thus : "The old Sikh confederacies had either all been swept away by his systematic usurpations and grasping policy or like the Phulkians and the Nihangs had sought the protection of a power greater than his by settling east of the Sutlej. The Kanhayia, Ramgarhia and Ahluwalia Misls ranged themselves under his banner and took pride in following him to the battlefield".

---

1. Cunningham, Griffin and Latif mention 1802 as the date of Ranjit Singh's attack on Amritsar. However, Sohan Lal, the Court diarist of Ranjit Singh, records 1805 as the year of conquest of Amritsar.

Ranjit Singh's great desire was to become the ruler of the entire Sikh people and with that objective in view he wanted to bring the Cis-Sutlej (Malwa) territories under his control. To achieve that objective the Maharaja organised three expeditions. In 1806 he marched an army of 20,000 men and advanced up to Patiala. He captured Doladhi and exacted tribute from Sahib Singh of Patiala. On his way back he conquered Ludhiana, Dakha, Raikot, Jagraon and Ghumgrana. Next year the Maharaja again crossed the river Sutlej and sucessfully arbitrated in the dispute between the Raja of Patiala and his wife, Rani Aus Kaur. On his arrival in Patiala, Ranjit Singh was given a warm welcome and offered rich presents. The Maharaja on his return journey exacted tribute from the Rajas of Kaithal, Kalsia besides conquering Naraingarh, Wadni, Zira, Kot Kapura and other territories. The Sikh chiefs of the Cis-Sutlej states felt the heavy hand of the Maharaja and decided to seek British protection. Consequently Raja Bhag Singh of Jhind, Bhai Lal Singh of Kaithal and Sardar Chen Singh, the Diwan of Patiala, waited on a deputation on Mr. Seton, the British Resident at Delhi. The same year Metcalfe who had come to Lahore to negotiate a treaty with Ranjit Singh urged upon the ruler of Lahore to give up all claims on the Cis-Sutlaj states. Undaunted, the Maharaja again crossed the Sutlej in 1808 and captured Faridkot, Malerkotla, and Ambala. By the Treaty of Amritsar (1809), however, Ranjit Singh accepted the East India Company's greater right over the Cis-Sutlej territories.

Relations with the Dogras and the Nepalese

At the time Ranjit Singh was extending his sway over the plains of the Panjab, the Dogra Chief, Sansar Chand Katock, with his headquarters at Kangra wanted to extend his influence over the Apline Panjab. In 1804 Sansar Chand descended from the hills and advanced up to Bajwara and Hoshiarpur. However, an advancing army sent from Lahore defeated Sansar Chand and captured Hoshiarpur for the Maharaja. Checked in the plains, Sansar Chand tried to extend his dominion over the neighbouring hill states. Threatened by Sansar Chand, the hill chief of Kahlur (who held territories on both sides of the Sutlej) sought the help of the Gurkhas of Nepal. A Gurkha army under Amar Singh Thapa besieged Kangra. Unable to meet the challenge single-handed Sansar Chand solicited Ranjit Singh's help, agreeing to surrender the fort of Kangra as the price for military assistance. A Sikh army under Diwan Mohkam Chand got the better of the Gurkhas and defeated them and foiled all their plans of expansion in this direction. Kangra was annexed by the Maharaja and Sansar Chand passed under Sikh protection. The enraged Gurkhas solicited British help against the Maharaja, but again suffered a diplomatic setback. Later the Gurkhas were engaged in a conflict with the English (1814-16) and had to surrender hilly tracts to the Company. In 1834 Raja Golab Singh captured Ladakh. Later in his career when the Maharaja's relations with the Company became strained, he accepted a Nepalese mission in May 1837 at Lahore and even Gurkha soldiers were enlisted in the Maharaja's army.

Relations with the Afghans

The Panjab formed a part of the Afghan dominion under Ahmad Shah Abdali. After Abdali's death in 1773 with the exception of Multan, Kashmir, the trans-Indus tracts and a few other pockets, the Sikh misls established their hold in central and eastern Punjab. Fortunately for Ranjit Singh the successors of Ahmad Shah weakened themselves in their internal conflicts and this turn of political events in Afghanistan acted and reacted on the condition in the Panjab and greatly facilitated the rapid growth of Ranjit Singh's dominion.

Shah Shuja, grandson of Ahmad Shah Abdali, occupied the throne of Kabul in 1800, but was finally ousted from power by his brother Shah Mahmud in 1809. Shah Mahmud has succeeded with the help of powerful Barakzai Sirdars, Fateh Khan and Dost Mohammad. These Barakzai brothers played the role of 'king-makers and usurped authority in Kashmir and Peshawar.

In his efforts to recover the throne of Kabul, Shah Shuja solicited Ranjit Singh's help and came to Lahore. Here Ranjit Singh took from Shah Shuja the famous *Koh-i-noor* diamond. In fact, the Maharaja wanted to make use of Shah Shuja's name and conquer Multan, Kashmir and other Afghan provinces east of the Indus. Shah Shuja, however, escaped from Lahore and sought the Company's protection at Ludhiana. In 1831 in another bid to recover the throne of Kabul, Shah Shuja sought the Maharaja's help. Ranjit Singh offered to help Shah Shuja if the latter would send his heir-apparent to attend on the Maharaja with an auxiliary force, agree to ban cow-slaughter in Afghanistan and deliver to him the gates of the temple of Somnath. Shah Shuja refused to accept these preposterous proposals which would reduce him to the position of the Maharaja's vassal. The Company also did not encourage the plan. In 1835 Ranjit Singh concluded a treaty with Shah Shuja, waiving the pre-conditions he had laid down in 1831. Shah Shuja, however, agreed to recognise the Maharaja's claims over the Afghans territories on the right bank of the Indus. Fearing Shah Shuja's motives and British moves, Ranjit Singh thought it prudent to annex Peshawar in 1834. Dost Mohammad, who had by then occupied the throne of Afghanistan, in a bid to recover Peshawar from the Sikhs, organised a crusade against Ranjit Singh and at the head of a large army of 40,000 tribesmen besieged Peshawar. The Sikhs proved too strong for him and Hari Singh Nalwa, the Marshal of Sikh Forces, defeated the Afghans and captured Jamrud. Thus, the entire territory east of the Khyber pass passed under the sway of Ranjit Singh, although his control over the tribal tracts was rather tenuous.

Relations with the English

Ranjit Singh's ambition to acquire the Cis-Sutlej territories brought him face to face with another expanding power in the Indian sub-continent, the English East India Company. As early as 1800, the English, fearing an Afghan invasion of India under Zaman Shah, had sent Munshi Yusaf Ali to the court of Ranjit Singh with the request that the Maharaja should not join Zaman Shah in case he invaded India. In 1805 Jaswant Rao Holkar hotly pursued by Lord Lake came to Amritsar and solicited Ranjit Singh to make a common cause against the English. Ranjit Singh at that time was busy in his plans of expansion towards the west and, therefore, did not think it prudent to incur the hostility of the English. The Maharaja read selfish motives in Holkar's moves and would have nothing to do with him; he, rather, described Holkar as a *pukka huramzada* (great bastard). On January 1, 1806, Ranjit Singh signed a treaty of friendship with General Lake agreeing to force Jaswant Rao Holkar to leave Amritsar. General Lake, in turn, promised that the English would never form any plans for the seizure and sequestration of Ranjit Singh's possessions and property.

Alarmed by the prospects of joint Franco-Russian invasion of India, in 1807 Lord Minto, the Governor-General (1807-13), sent Charles Metcalfe to Lahore to negotiate a friendly treaty with Ranjit Singh. The Maharaja offered to accept Metcalfe's proposal of an offensive and defensive alliance on the condition that the English would remain neutral in case of a Sikh-Afghan war and would recognise him the sovereign of the entire Panjab including the Malwa (Cis-Sutlej) territories. The negotiations did not fructify because Charles Metcalfe was not authorized by his Government to recognise the Maharaja's plans on Cis-Sutlej states. Meantime, the Napoleonic danger somewhat receded (because of the Spanish revolt) and the English attitude stiffened. The English Commander David Ochterlony made a show of force, marched an army to Ludhiana and finally in February 1809 issued a Proclamation declaring "the Cis-Sutlej states to be under British protection, and that any aggressions of the chief of Lahore would be resisted with arms." Fearing that the jealous Panjab chiefs might not transfer their allegiance to the British, the Maharaja agreed to sign the Treaty of Amritsar (25 April 1809) with the Comapny on the following terms :

(1) "Perpetual friendship shall subsist between the British Government and the state of Lahore; the former shall be considered, with respect to the latter, to be on the footing of the most favoured powers and the British Government will have no concern with the territories and subjects of the Raja to the northward of the river Sutlej.

(2) "The Raja will not maintain in the territory which he occupies on the left bank of the river Sutlej more troops than are necessary for the internal duties of that territory nor commit or suffer any encroachments on the possessions or rights of the chiefs in its vicinity.

(3) "In the event of violation of any of the preceding articles, or of a departure from the rules of friendship, this treaty shall be considered null and void."

The Treaty of Amritsar was important for its immediate as well as potential effects. In its immediate effects it checked one of the most cherished ambitions of Ranjit Singh to extend his rule over the entire Sikh nation, living east or west of the river Sutlej. By accepting the river Sutlej as the boundary line for his dominions and the Company's, the Maharaja compromised his cherished political ideal besides suffering territorial and economic losses. According to Cunningham the treaty with the Company gave Ranjit Singh a *carte blanche* so far as the region to the west of Sutlej was concerned; with the disappearance of all danger, for the time being, from the English, the Maharaja directed his energies towards the west and captured Multan (1818), Kashmir (1819) and Peshawar (1834). In its ultimate effects the treaty showed the weak position of Ranjit Singh *vis-a-vis* the Company. The British were brought close to the frontier of the Lahore kingdom and this brought the danger of war nearer. Besides, the treaty gave the Company a degree of control over Ranjit Singh's relations with the neighbouring states of Sind, Bahawalpur and Afghanistan.

The relations from 1809 to 1839 clearly indicate the weak position of the Maharaja. The Company forestalled the moves of Ranjit Singh on Sind. In 1831 Alexander Burnes was sent to the Court of Lahore. Burnes travelled *via* Sind to Lahore. In October 1831, William Bentinck met Ranjit Singh at Rupar and both parties professed friendship for each other. William Bentinck rejected all proposals of the Maharaja for the partition of Sind. At the time the Rupar meeting was being held, Colonel Pottinger, the British Agent in Sind, concluded a commercial treaty with the Amir of Hyderabad and the Mahraja was told that the treaty was of a purely commercial nature. Ranjit Singh could see the British game, but was not prepared for a showdown with the Company. Thus, Ranjit Singh was checked in the guise of material utilitarianism. The fear of Russian advances in Central Asia led the English to occupy and later build a cantonment at Ferozepur in 1835. The stationing of British troops at that strategic town worried Ranjit Singh but his protest went unheeded.

To thwart Russian intrigues in Afghanistan, the Company decided to remove from the throne of Kabul Dost Mohammad, the unfriendly Amir of Afghanistan, and instead put Shah Shuja as the ruler. Ranjit Singh was asked to join in the project. The Maharaja himself was indifferent to the Russian danger; rather he feared British designs and encirclement of his territories. However, the threats of the British Agent, Macnaghten, that the expedition would be undertaken whether Ranjit Singh joined or not brought Ranjit Singh round to the signing of the Tripartite Treaty on June 26, 1838. The Maharaja, however, refused to give passage to the British army through his territories.

Ranjit Singh's relations with the English Company were characterized by an inferiority complex. The rising tide of British imperialism posed a serious threat to the Maharaja's dominions. The Maharaja was conscious of his weak position, but took no step to organise a coalition of Indian princes or maintain a balance of power in the country. He just postponed the evil day by grudgingly yielding at every step. He proved to be a poor statesman in this respect. N.K. Sinha writes : "In the last decade of his career Ranjit Singh is a pathetic figure, helpless and inert...He feared to expose the kingdom he had created to the risk of war and chose instead the policy of yielding, yielding and yielding."

Administration of Ranjit Singh

The only system of government known to the Indian subcontinent at that time was despotism. Ranjit Singh had neither the necessary intellectual training nor the inclination to make bold innovations in the system of government. The Maharaja was the embodiment of all civil and political authority in the state. Ranjit Singh, however, was a benevolent despot and looked to the welfare of the people. He considered himself as a servant of the Khalsa or the Sikh Commonwealth and acted in the name of the Khalsa. He even designated his government 'Sarkar-i-Khalsaji' and struck coins in the name of Guru Nanak and Guru Govind Singh.

Although the Maharaja was the pivot of the administration, yet there was a Council of Ministers to help him in the task of administration. He divided the kingdom into provinces, each under a Nazim. A province was further sub-divided into districts, each under the charge of a Kardar. At the village level the Panchayats functiond effectively.

Land Revenue and Justice. The main source of income of the state was land revenue which was collected with great severity. The state demand was fixed between 33% and 40%, depending on the fertility and richness of the soil. Sir Lepel Griffin is correct in his judgement when he says that the Maharaja "Squeezed out of the unhappy peasant every rupee that he could be made to disgorge" but took care not "to kill the goose that lay the golden egg". The Maharaja was anxious to safeguard the interests of the peasantry and issued instructions to the marching armies not to destroy standing crops or damage them in any way. To the sons of the peasantry, the Sikh army provided ample opportunities for employment.

The administration of justice was rough and ready. There was no hierarchy of courts as we find today. The administration of justice was more of a local than a national concern. The local officers decided cases according to local custom. An Adalat-i-Ala was set up at Lahore which probably heard appeals from the district and provincial courts. Excessive fines were imposed on the criminals, of course depending on the means of the offenders. Even the most heinous crime could be forgiven in return for money payment. Justice was thus looked upon as a source of income to the state.

Military Administration. Ranjit Singh gave his maximum care to the maintenance of an efficient army. If he had built a kingdom out of atoms with the help of armed strength, a strong army was necessary to maintain its frontiers. Besides, faced with enemies on all sides, an efficient army was a necessity. Ranjit Singh's genius was best displayed in the organisation of an excellent fighting army.

Ranjit Singh realised the essential weakness of Indian armies. Irregular levies, poorly equipped and without proper training could hardly meet the challenges of the times. The Maharaja decided to build an army on the pattern of the army of the Company and recruited French officers to drill and discipline the troopers. Due emphasis was laid on the organisation of the artillery department. Workshops were set up at Lahore and Amritsar for the casting of heavy guns and the manufacture of shot and powder. Ranjit Singh adopted the system of 'Mahadari' or monthly payment of salaries to soldiers and officers, and gave care to the equipment and mobilisation aspects of the army.

A Model Army or Fauj-i-Khas was raised in 1822 by General Ventura and Allard. The special brigade had its own emblem and used French words of command in drill. The normal strength of this Model Army consisted of four battalions of infantry, three regiments of cavalry besides the artillery wing. Ilahi Baksh headed the artillery department of Fauj-i-Khas.

A special feature of Ranjit Singh's army was the employment of Europeans in the service of the state. At one time there were 39 foreign officers drawn from different nationalities of the world, namely, Frenchmen, Germans, Americans, Greeks, Spaniards, Russians, Scotch, Englishmen and Anglo-Indians. The Maharaja gave these European officers all types of inducements to settle in the Punjab. Outstanding among these European officers were Ventura, Allard, Court, Gardner, Avitable. General Ventura headed the Infantry Department of Fauj-i-Khas, Allard was in charge of Cavalry, while Court and Gardner reorganised the Artillery Department. These European officers rose to high positions in the civil administration, for example, General Ventura was for some time Governor of Derajat and Avitable became Governor of Peshawar in 1837.

It has been estimated that in 1835 the strength of Ranjit Singh's army stood at 75,000 which included about 35,000 regularly trained, disciplined and equipped troops. Ranjit Singh's army proved an effective fighting force which got the better of the Afghans, the Gorkhas and the Dogras and even baffled the British in the two Sikh wars.

Estimate of Ranjit Singh. Ranjit Singh stands out as a fascinating personality in Indian history. Though ugly in physical appearance (Baron Hugel described him as the most ugly and unprepossessing man he saw throughout the Panjab), Ranjit Singh had an impressive personality. Fakir Aziz-ud-din, the Foreign Minister of Ranjit Singh, on an enquiry from an English officer as to which eye of the Maharaja was blind, replied: "The splendour of his face is such that I have never been able to look close enough to discover". Ranjit Singh was loved by the people of the Panjab, Hindus and Muslims alike. If Ranjit Singh looked upon the Sikhs as his colleagues and co-religionists, he respected learned men of other religions also. Once the Maharaja wiped off the dust from the feet of a Muslim mendicant with his long grey beard.

Lepel Griffin calls Ranjit Singh "the beau ideal of a soldier–strong, spare, active, courageous and enduring". Brave like a lion, Ranjit Singh led his armies and often fought in the forefront like a common soldier. He was thoroughly conversant with the various arts of war. He always planned his campaigns well in advance. While leading his campaigns against the tribesmen of the North-West frontier region, he always engaged the tribesmen in the plains and took care not to follow them in their hills. Victor Jacquement, a French visitor to the Court of Ranjit Singh, compares Ranjit Singh with Napoleon Bonaparte. True, Ranjit Singh used Machiavellian methods, the policy of 'force and fraud' to gain his ends, but he was never cruel and blood-thirsty. Rather, he treated the vanquished with kindness and consideration. According to Baron Von Hugel: "The sole aim of Ranjit Singh is the preservation and extension of his unlimited power; and though his ambitious mind considered all means perfectly allowable to this end he has never want only imbued his hands in blood. Never perhaps was so large an empire founded by one man with so little criminality."

As a ruler Ranjit Singh showed deep solicitude for the welfare of the people. He took adequate care to safeguard the interests of the common man against official oppression. It is said that a box was affixed outside his palace in which his subjects could lodge their complaints. The key of this box was personally kept by the Maharaja. He also paid personal visits to various parts of the country to acquaint himself with the actual state of affairs. Men of all communities enjoyed the benefits of his mild and merciful administration. Faqir Aziz-ud-din, a Muslim, was his Foreign Minister and was greatly trusted by the Maharaja. Jamadar Khushal Singh, the Dogra Brothers, and Teja Singh occupied very high positions in the lahore Darbar. Dhian Singh Dogra was the Prime Minister and enjoyed the title of 'Raja'. Above all, Ranjit Singh gave to the people of the Panjab the blessings of peace, the like of which they had not seen in the past one hundred years.

It is difficult to regard Ranjit Singh as a constructive statesman. The kingdom he had so assiduously built up disintegrated within a decade of his death, and the Maharaja himself cannot escape the responsibility for that. He had so greatly concentrated all administration in his hands that his disappearance from the scene caused not a 'vacancy' but a 'void' and the entire structure began to crumble. Beside, Ranjit Singh failed to subordinate the army to the civil authority. So long as he lived his personal influence kept the army under control, but after his death the army got out of control, dabbled in politics and reduced the civil government to a mere non-entity. Again, unlike Shivaji, Ranjit Singh did not breathe into the hearts of the people any sentiment that could keep them together after his death. Perhaps Shivaji's successors were as incapable as Ranjit Singh's successors, but the history of Maharashtra after the death of Shivaji is quite different from the history of the Panjab after the Maharaja's death. Nowhere is Ranjit Singh's shortsightedness more apparent than in his dealings with the English. Realising fully well that the English were throwing a cordon round his kingdom and fully cognizant of British expansionist designs, he bided his time and avoided a conflict. On several occasions, he thought of going to war with the British, but his courage always failed him. The Maharaja left the inevitable task of fighting with the English to his weak and incompetent successors.

Notwithstanding his shortsighted policy Ranjit Singh occupies a high place in Indian History. The memory of this hero is still cherished by the people of the Panjab. Summing up the achievements of Ranjit Singh, Cunningham writes: "Ranjit Singh found the Panjab a warring confederacy, a prey to the factions of its chiefs, pressed by the Afghans and the Marathas, and ready to submit to English supremacy. He consolidated the numerous petty states into a kingdom, he wrested from Kabul the fairest of its provinces, and he gave the potent English no cause of interference". He rolled back the tide of invasion from the north-west and extended his sway up to the North-western Khyber Pass. Above all, he left behind a tradition of strength and it is here that history enthuses posterity.

Select Opinions

J. D. Cunningham. Ranjit Singh found the Panjab a waning confederacy, a prey to the factions of its chiefs, pressed by the Afghans and the Marathas, and ready to submit to English supremacy. He consolidated the numerous petty states into a kingdom, he wrested from Kabul the fairest of its provinces, and gave the potent English no cause for interference. He found the military array of his country, a mass of horsemen, brave instead, but ignorant of war as an art, and he left it mustering fifty thousand disciplined soldiers, fifty thousand well-armed yeomanry and militia, and more than three hundred pieces of cannon for the field. His rule was founded on the feelings of a people but it involved the joint action of the necessary principles of military order and territorial extension. (*History of the Sikhs*, p. 222)

N. K. Sinha. The one great external cause of Ranjit's failure is found in his relations with the British Government. Very early in his career he had entered into a treaty with the British Government. But in almost all cases, as Bismarck has put it, a political alliance means a rider and a horse. In this Anglo-Sikh alliance, the British Government was the rider and Ranjit was the horse. The English limited Ranjit's power on the east, on the south and would have limited him on the west if that were possible. Evidently a collision between his military monarchy and British Imperialism was imminent, Ranjit Singh, the Massinissa of British Indian history, hesitated and hesitated forgetting that in politics, as in war, time is not on the side of the defensive. When the crash came after his death under far less able men, chaos and disorder had already supervened and whatever hope there had been when he was living, there was no more when he was dead. In his relations with the British Government Ranjit Singh is seen at his worst. He never grandly dared. He was all hesitancy and indecision. (*Ranjit Singh*, pp. 191-92)

Lepel Griffin. The Sikh monarchy was Napoleonic in the suddenness of its rise, the brillancy of its success, and the completeness of its overthrow. Like his contemporary, Napoleon Bonaparte, the Maharaja of Lahore failed to found a lasting dynasty on the ruins of the petty States, Rajput, Muhammadan and Sikh, which he in turn attacked and destroyed. His victories had no permanent result; his possessions, like a faggot of sticks, bound together during his lifetime by the force of his imperious will, fell as under the moment the restraining hand was severed. His throne and the tradition of his power and greatness passed into the hands of incompetent successors, who allowed the ship of the State to drift on to the rocks in irremediable wreck... As Ranjit Singh had sown, so was the harvest. The father had eaten sour grapes and the children's teeth were set on edge. The kingdom founded in violence, treachery and blood did not long survive its founder. Created by the military and administrative genius of one man, it crumbled into powder when the spirit which gave it life was withdrawn; and the inheritance of the Khalsa passed into the hands of the English. (*Ranjit Singh* pp. 9-10, 218-219.)

G. L. Chopra. That Ranjit Singh was a 'State in person' is more particularly true of him than of several other despots known to history. Hence his death was certain to bring a rapid paralysis of the central authority in the kingdom. His court also... was composed of diverse elements and conflicting interests; and the harmonious co-operation of its members was only possible under his own unifying authority. His ministers were mostly favourites and adventures, who had never been allowed to exercise much personal initiative, and were always taught to reflect in their actions the sole will of their monarch. Consequently when that monarch died their efforts were directed to individual gain and advantage rather than to collective benefit; while the absence of any competent successor revealed the inherent weakness of all states based on personal absolutism. (*The Panjab As a Sovereign State*)

SELECT REFERENCES

1. Chopra, G. L.   : *The Panjab as a Sovereign State.*
2. Cunningham, A.J.D. : *History of the Sikhs.*
3. Griffin, L.   : *Ranjit Singh.*
4. Latif, M.   : *History of the Panjab.*
5. Singh, Khushwant   : *The Sikhs.*
6. Sinha, N. K.   : *Ranjit Singh.*

THE PANJAB AFTER RANJIT SINGH AND ANGLO-SIKH WARS

Notwithstanding Ranjit Singh's great personal achievements, he failed to found a stable Sikh state in the Panjab. He was a despot and established military rule in the Panjab. As is usually the case with one man's rule, after Ranjit Singh's death the military set-up exploded in fierce but fading flames and in the process was consumed the edifice of the Sikh state so assiduously built by Ranjit Singh. Ranjit Singh's death caused not a vacancy but a void and the entire structure was submerged. Anarchy and confusion reigned supreme and gradually all real power passed into the hands of the Khalsa army. Ranjit Singh had left a large standing army of 40,000 soldiers which proved to be a great drain on the resources of the state. Within five years of Ranjit Singh's death the strength of the army increased three-fold and it became an unbearable burden on the shrinking resources of the state. When the soldiers could not be paid their salaries, they got out of control, frequently interfered in politics and bargained with rival royal claimants for salary increases. The soldiers formed their own Panchayats (advisory councils) and decided whether or not to proceed on particular expeditions irrespective of what the civil authority ordered. The army everywhere got the upper hand, assumed the role of 'king-makers' and eclipsed the civil authority. Besides, the powerful rival factions and jealous jagirdars held in check by the strong hand of Ranjit Singh got out of control and converted the Panjab into a veritable arena for power politics. The incompetent and worthless sons of Ranjit Singh, the legitimacy of many of whom was doubtful, could not check the rising forces of disorder. A modern critic ably sums up the positions thus: "They (rival factions) were the brains behind the intrigues, the army was the power, and claimants to the throne were the pawns". The history of the Panjab in the years following the death of Ranjit Singh was thus the history of plots and counter-plots, murders and assassinations, of desertions and treachery—all undermining the very stability of the state.

Ranjit Singh suddenly died of a paralytic stroke in June 1839. He was succeeded by his imbecile son, Kharak Singh. Dhian Singh continued to hold the post of the Wazir. The new Maharaja was an opium-eater and an unworthy ruler. Soon the powerful cliques of the Sindhanwalia sirdars (Chet Singh, Atar Singh, Lehna Singh and their nephew Ajit Singh) and the Dogra brothers (Dhian Singh, Golab Singh and Suchet Singh) brought anarchy and confusion to the Panjab. Chet Singh, a favourite of the Maharaja, was murdered by Wazir Dhian Singh's hirelings on 8 October 1839 in the palace before the very eyes of the Maharaja. Soon Kharak Singh was put in prison and his son Naonihal Singh proclaimed the Maharaja with Dhian Singh as the Wazir. Perhaps Naonihal Singh was the ablest among Ranjit Singh's successors. He restored law and order in the state, sent an army to reduce the hill states of Mandi and Suket, captured Ladakh and parts of Baltistan and kept a strict watch on the activities of the jealous English. Fortune, however, did not spare him long for the Panjab. On November 5, 1840, Kharak Singh died in prison and the reign of Naonihal Singh ended the same day. Returning home from the cemetery after performing the funeral rites of his father, the youthful prince was grievously hurt by the fall of an archway of the Lahore fort. Naonihal Singh did not survive the accident.

After the death of Naonihal Singh, the Dogras and the Sindhanwalias assumed the role of 'king-makers', espoused the cause of rival claimants and enlisted the support of the army by promises of increased salaries to the soldiers. The Sindhanwalias supported the claims of Mai Chand Kaur, the mother of Naonihal Singh who wanted to govern as regent on behalf of the expected child of her deceased son, Naonihal Singh. The Dogras supported the claims of Sher Singh, another son of Ranjit Singh. Sher Singh emerged successful with the help of the Sikh army and was proclaimed the Maharaja in January 1841. Dogra Dhian Singh became the Wazir and the Sindhanwalia sirdars took refuge with the British. Sher Singh, in a bid to conciliate the Sindhanwalia sirdars, recalled them and showered great favours on them. In September 1843 Ajit Singh Sindhanwalia treacherously shot dead the Maharaja and also killed Dhian Singh. Dhian Singh's son Hira Singh enlisted the support of the army by promises of increased salaries and avenged the death of his father by putting to death Sindhanwalia sirdars, Lehna Singh and Ajit Singh.

In September 1843 Dalip Singh, a minor son of Maharaja Ranjit Singh was proclaimed the Maharaja with Rani Jindan as regent and Hira Singh Dogra as Wazir. Raja Hira Singh himself fell a victim to a court intrigue and was murdered on 21 December 1844. The new Wazir, Jawahar Singh, the brother of Rani Jindan, soon incurred the displeasure of the army and was deposed and put to death in September 1845. Lal Singh. a lover of Rani Jindan, won over the army to his side and became the Wazir in September 1845. Teja Singh was the new Commander of the forces.

The First Anglo-Sikh War, 1845-46. The English were closely watching the happenings in the Panjab and cast longing eyes on the fertile plains on the other side of the Sutlej. As early as May 1838 W. G. Osborne had written: "One course to pursue on Ranjit Singh's death is the instant occupation of the Panjab by an overwhelming force and the establishment of our north-western frontier on the Indus. The East India Company has swallowed too many camels to strain at this gnat." In 1840 Auckland remarks: "With many of our statesmen and with all our soldiers there is a strong impatience for the possession of the Panjab." However, the British involvement in the Afghan muddle delayed action on the part of the Company. In 1841 Sir Willian Macnaghten wrote to Lord Auckland "the desirability of crushing the Singhs, macadamizing the Panjab and annexation of Peshawar". The failure of the Afghan adventure lowered British prestige and they wanted to demonstrate their strength at the cost of the Amirs of Sind and the Panjab. Lord Ellenborough regarded the annexaion of the Panjab 'a question of time' and wrote to the Queen on the need of reducing the Sikh power to ineffectiveness. To the Duke of Wellington, Ellenborough wrote in October 1843: "The time cannot be far distant when the Panjab will fall into our management... I do not look to this state of things as likely to occur next year, but as being ultimately inevitable." In another letter to the Duke written in February 1844, Lord Ellenborough penned: "I earnestly hope that we may not be obliged to cross the Sutlej in December next. We shall not be ready so soon... I am quietly doing what I can to strengthen and equip the army."

Lord Hardinge, a soldier of great repute, succeeded Lord Ellenborough in 1844. The new Governor-General took vigorous measures to strengthen the Company's military position. The strength of the Company's army in the Punjab was increased to 32,000 with 68 guns and additional reserve force of 10,000 men at Meerut. Besides, 57 boats were brought from Bombay for making pontoon bridges over the Sutlej. The commander actually gave training to his soldiers in bridge-throwing. The Sikh soldiers on the other side of the Sutlej saw all this and drew their own conclusions. The Company's troops in Sind were well-equipped and kept in readiness for any possible march on Multan. The Company's contention that the preparations were of a defensive nature and calculated to meet possible eventualities of an attack from the Sikhs was clearly hypocritical, considering the chaotic state of affairs in the Panjab.

The appointment in 1843 of Major Broadfoot as Company's Agent at Ludhiana for dealing with the affairs of the Sikhs, worsened Anglo-Sikh relations. An energetic and hot-headed man, Major Broadfoot made the impolitic declaration that all cis-Sutlej possessions of Lahore Darbar were under British protection equally with Patiala and other chiefships and liable to escheat on the death or deposition of Maharaja Dalip Singh. The high-handed manner in which he interfered in the affairs of the priest-like Sodhis of Anandpur (a fief of Lahore Darbar) caused great concern at Lahore. Besides, the border incidents near Ferozepore and Multan did not leave the issues in doubt and precipitated matters.

P. E. Roberts and Percival Spear lay undue stress on the explosive situation at Lahore and try to shift the responsibility for the war on the shoulders of the ruling clique and the unmanageable Khalsa army. Spear writes, "If the army could not be controlled it must be disbanded or its energies diverted in war. No one dared to attempt the former and so the latter was the only recourse".[1] Roberts writes in a little more effective language that Rani Jindan dreaded the absolute and capricious power of the Khalsa army and "found her only hope of security in urging it on to challenge British supremacy. Either it would spend its super-abundant energy in a career of conquest and the sovereignty of Hindustan would pass to the Sikhs, or it would be shattered in the conflict and she could then make her own peace with the offended British nation... This—the main feature of the Sikh war—must constantly be borne in mind."[2]

At the time of the Anglo Sikh conflict, selfish and traitorous persons controlled the government at Lahore and the Khalsa army was without a General or at any rate without one supreme controlling mind.

The British moves and preparations seemed to denote to the Sikh army "a campaign, not of defence but of aggression and it decided that if the English wanted war they would have it on their own territory." Consequently Sikh troops crossed the Sutlej, between Hariki and Kasur on 11 December 1845 and took offensive against the English troops commanded by Sir Hugh Gough. On 13th December Henry Hardinge, the Governor-General, made his declaration of war proclaiming that the possession of Maharaja Dalip Singh on the left of the British bank of the Sultej was confiscated and annexed to the British territories. Lal Singh, the Commander-in Chief of Sikh troops, played the traitor and sent a message to the English, as reported by Captain Nicholson, that "he would show his good wishes by keeping back his force for two days from joining the Infantry or Regulars, and had marched them today back to Assul, and would tomorrow to Hariki, if I would consider him and the Bibi Sahib (Rani Jindan) our friends." Four battles were fought at Mudki, Ferozeshah, Buddewal and Aliwal but did not decide the issue. The final battle of Sobraon (10 February 1846) proved decisive. Due to the treachery of Lal Singh and Teja Singh, who gave all information regarding the trenches to the English, the battle resulted in great slaughter of the Sikh troops. An English army crossed the Sutlej, occupied Lahore and dictated peace terms in the very capital of Ranjit Singh on 9 March 1846. The treaty was concluded on the following terms:

1. The Maharaja renounced "for himself, his heirs and successors, all claims to, or connection with, the territories lying to the south of the river Sutlej."

2. The Maharaja ceded to the Company "in perpetual sovereignty, all his forts, territories and rights in the Doab, or country, hill and plain situate between the rivers Beas and Sutlej."

3. The Company demanded a war indemnity of Rs. $1\frac{1}{2}$ crores. The Lahore Darbar being unable to pay the amount demanded, agreed to transfer to the Company "in perpetual sovereignty as equivalent for one crore of rupees all hill forts, territories, rights and interests, in the hill countries, which are situated between the rivers Beas and Indus, including the provinces of Kashmir and Hazarah." The remaining 50 lakhs of rupees the Lahore Darbar agreed to pay on or before the ratification of the treaty.

4. The Maharaja further agreed to "disband the mutinous troops of the Lahore army, taking from them arms" and limiting the regular army to 20,000 infantry and 12,000 cavalry.

5. The Maharaja agreed "never to take or retain, in his service, any British subject, nor the subject of any European or American state without the consent of the British Government." Further free passes were to be allowed to the British troops through Lahore territories.

6. The minor Dalip Singh was recognised as the Maharaja with Rani Jindan as Regent of the State and Lal Singh as the Wazir.

---

1. P. Spear : *The Oxford History of Modern India*, p. 171.
2. P. E. Roberts : *History of British India*, p. 334.

7. Sir Henry Lawrence was named as the British Resident at Lahore. The Company was not to interfere in the internal administration of the Lahore state.

According to a supplementary treaty concluded on 11 March 1846, at the request of Wazir Lal Singh and others a British force was to remain at Lahore till the close of the year 1846 for protecting the person of the Maharaja and Lahore citizens during the reorganisation of the Sikh army. The Lahore fort was vacated for the English army and the expenses for the maintenance of the Company's troops were to be defrayed by the Lahore darbar.

The Panjab was not annexed in February 1846. The argument that the Panjab was not annexed in deference to the memory of Ranjit Singh, a friend of the Company, may be dismissed as childish. Some British historians popularised the view that Lord Hardinge followed the policy of "experimental forbearance". A close study of the events and developments suggests that annexation of the Panjab would have created very difficult problems for the British. The Khalsa army had been defeated, but not annihilated; there still were 25,000 Sikh soldiers at Lahore and Amristar and 8,000 of them at Peshawar. Besides, every Sikh peasant knew the use of arms. Thus the possibilities of guerilla warfare could not be ruled out. There was also a deficit in the Indian treasury and the hot season was ahead. A moderate and conciliatory policy, thus, seemed the best under the circumstances. The Governor-General, however, took vigorous steps to weaken the Lahore state 'to such an extent that its absorption was a matter of time'. Territorially the Punjab state was reduced in size, militarily enfeebled and financially crippled. The real game of the English is clear from Lord Hardinge's letter dated 23 october 1847 to Henry Lawrence in which he wrote : "In all our measures taken during the minority, we must bear in mind that by the Treaty of Lahore, March 1846, the Panjab never was intended to be an independent state ... In fact, the native prince is in fetters, and under our protection and must do our bidding".

The Second Anglo-Sikh War, 1848-49. The few months following the treaty of Lahore greatly disillusioned Rani Jindan and Lal Singh and revealed to them the true intentions of the English. They soon began to resent the Resident's control. When the Resident asked the Lahore darbar to surrender Kashmir to Raja Gulab Singh, Lal Singh indirectly encouraged Imam-ud-din, the Darbar's Muslim Governor there, to resist. An English forces proceeded to Kashmir and captured it. Lal Singh was found guilty of complicity in the affair, was tried by a Court of Inquiry presided over by the British Resident, found guilty and exiled. The administration of Lahore darbar was entrusted to a Council of Regency consisting of Fakir Nur-ud-din, Teja Singh, Sher Singh and Dina Nath.

The year 1846 was fast coming to a close and time was coming (as stipulated in the treaty of 1 March 1846) for the withdrawal of British troops from Lahore. Lord Hardinge planned to control the Lahore administration for some years more in the name of the minor Maharaja. The Resident urged some influential sirdars to petition the Company for the retention of her troops at Lahore during the minority of the Maharaja. These sirdars were won over by promises of reward and threats of severe action. Consequently a new treaty was signed at Bhyrowal on 22 December 1846, which provided for the stationing of British troops at Lahore for the protection of the Maharaja and preservation of the peace of the country. The Lahore darbar agreed to pay Rs. 22 lakhs per annum for meeting the expenses of the British force. During the minority of Dalip Singh (which was to last till 1854) the actual administration was vested in the British Resident assisted by a Council of eight chiefs. Thus, the British Resident became the virtual ruler of the Panjab with unlimited civil and military powers and the sirdars were reduced to the position of executive officers. When Maharani Jindan resented the usurpation of all powers in the hands of the Resident, her turn also came. On August 2, 1847 the Governor-General issued a proclamation which read thus: "The Governor-General of India who feels the interest of a father in the education and guardianship of the young prince" thought it "absolutely necessary to separate the Maharaja from the Maharani, his mother". The Maharani was removed to Sheikhupura and her allowance arbitrarily reduced to Rs. 48,000 per annum.

Lord Hardinge was succeeded by Dalhousie as Governor-General in January 1848. At that time the strength of the British army in the north-west stood at 70,000 soldiers with 9,000 in the Lahore state. The new Governor-General was a great imperialist and an avowed annexationist. He did not believe in 'half measures' and was strongly of the opinion that the British Government should "not put aside or neglect such rightful opportunities of acquiring territory as may from time to time present themselves."

The immediate occasion for the Company's invasion of the Punjab was provided by the revolt of Mul Raj, the Governor of Multan. In 1846 at the suggestion of the British Resident, Mul Raj was asked to pay twenty lakh rupees as *nazrana* and surrender all land north of the Ravi to the Lahore darbar. In addition it was decided to raise the revenue of Multan by about one-third for three years. Unable to continue under the new harsh conditions imposed on him Mul Raj tendered his resignation in December 1847. He was asked to continue till alternative arrangements were made. The new British Resident, Fredrick Currie on his arrival at Lahore in March 1848 sent Kahan Singh Mann as the new Governor of Multan on a fixed salary of Rs. 30,000 per annum and two British officers accompanied the new Governor to assist him in the take-over. The rude and over-bearing behaviour of Vans Agnew and Lieutenant Anderson so greatly irritated the people of Multan that they rose in rebellion and compelled Mul Raj to assume their leadership. The two British officers were murdered. Multan was all ablaze. Soon this fire spread to other parts of the Panjab and developed into a national rising. Chattar Singh, the Sikh Governor of Hazara, revolted in August. Sher Singh, Chattar Singh's son, who had been sent by the Lahore darbar to besiege Multan, crossed over to the side of the rebels with his entire army. The Sikhs also purchased the friendship of the Afghans by the cession of Peshawar. A desperate attempt was made to shake the British yoke.

The Company's Government delayed action against the rebels of Multan because of the approaching summer season and prompted by the desire to allow the rebellion to take the status of a Sikh rising and then take effective and final decision regarding the fate of the Panjab. In October 1848, Dalhousie wrote: "The task before me is the utter destruction and prostration of the Sikh power, the subversion of its dynasty and the subjection of its people. This must be done promptly, fully and finally." In the proclamation of war he said: "Unwarned by precedents, uninfluenced by example, the Sikh nation has called for war and on my word, Sirs, they shall have it with a vengeance."

A large British army under Lord Gough crossed the Ravi on 16 November and fought an indecisive battle at Ramnagar. Multan surrendered in January 1849 and the Sikhs suffered a defeat at Chillianwala a few weeks later. The final and decisive battle was won by the English at Gujrat, and the whole of the Panjab lay prostrate at their feet.

Three courses were open to Dalhousie—(*i*) The reversion to *status quo* with a greater degree of British control under the nominal sovereignty of the Maharaja, (*ii*) annexation of Multan only and punishment of Mul Raj, and (*iii*) annexation of the whole of the Panjab. Dalhousie decided to annex the Panjab. He did not believe in the maintenance of 'sham royalties' and 'titular dignitaries.' He was convinced that all real power must pass into British hands, whether that power was exercised through British officials in the name of the Maharaja or through direct annexation. In the former case, Dalhousie argued that "it would be a mockery to pretend that we have preserved the Panjab as an independent state." Such an arrangement, he argued, would be a breeding ground for constant intrigues. "There never will be peace in the Panjab", Dalhousie said, "as long as its people are allowed to retain the means and the opportunity of making war. There never can be now any guarantee for the tranquillity of India, until we shall have effected the entire subjugation of the Sikh people and destroyed its power as an independent nation."

Sir Henry Lawrence, the former British Resident at Lahore, contended that annexation might perhaps be just but would be inexpedient. John Lawrence described the annexation not only just, but maintained that its expediency was both undeniable and pressing. In protest Sir Henry Lawrence tendered his resignation, but withdrew it later on at the suggestion of Lord Hardinge, the former Governor-General of India. Lord Hardinge wrote to Henry Lawrence: "The energy and turbulent spirit of the Sikhs are stated by one section of politicians here as ground for not annexing. In my judgement this is the agrument which would dispose me if I were on the spot to annex." In the words of William Hunter, "The victory of Sobraon in 1846 gave to Lord Hardinge the right of conquest; the victory of Gujrat in 1849 compelled Lord Dalhousie to assert that right." On March 29, 1849, came the proclamation from the Governor-General which ran thus: "The kingdom of the Panjab is at an end and that all the territories of Maharaja Dalip Singh are now, and henceforth, a portion of the British Empire in India." Dalip singh was given a pension of £50,000 per annum and sent to England for education. The administration of the Panjab was entrusted to a Board of Commissioners.

Major Evans Bell described the annexation of the Panjab as inexpedient and avoidable and maintained that "the annexation of the Panjab was no annexation, it was a sacred breach of trust." There is much truth in Bell's contention. Ever since the treaty of Bhyrowal (22 December 1846) the Resident was the internal ruler of the Panjab and exercised all civil and administrative powers in the name of the minor Maharaja. It was the Sikh army and not the Maharaja or the Council of Regency which had risen in rebellion. As the Regent for the Maharaja, it was the bounden duty of Fredrick Currie, the British Resident, to suppress the rebellion of Mul Raj or the Sikh army. Since the Maharaja could not be held responsible for the rebellion, it was evidently unjust to deprive him of his kingdom on that plea. The English Company through the Resident was acting as the guardian of the minor Maharaja and when it annexed the kingdom of the ward it was evidently a sacred breach of trust. Dalhousie's announcement that he 'considered the state of Lahore to all intents and purposes to be directly at war with the British Government greatly puzzled Fredrick Currie, the British Resident at Lahore, who was the administrator of the Panjab. Dalhousie was, however, up for a higher game and determined to annex the Panjab on one or the other plea.

Select Opinions

Evans Bell. Dalhousie violated treaties, abused a sacred trust, threw away the grandest opportunity ever offered to the British Government of planting solid and vital reform up to the northern limits of India; and by an acquisition as unjust as it was imprudent, weakened our frontier, scattered our military strength and entailed a heavy financial burden upon the Empire. That, I believe, will be the verdit of posterity and history upon the transactions which have just passed under our review. (*The Annexation of the Panjab and the Maharajah Duleep Singh*, pp. 136-37).

Ludlow. Dalip Singh was an infant, his minority was only to end in 1854. We were his declared protectors. On our last advance into his country we had proclaimed (18 November, 1848) that we came to punish insurgents and to put down all "armed opposition to constitued authority." We fulfilled that pledge by annexing his whole country within six months. On the 24th March 1849 the kingdom of the Panjab was declared to be at an end; the child, our protege, was pensioned off, all State property confiscated to the Company, the celebrated diamond, the *Koh-i-Noor* surrendered to the Queen. In other words, we 'protected' our ward by taking his whole territory from him... Having once recognized and undertaken to protect Dalip Singh, it was a mockery to punish him for the faults of his subjects. As between us and him in putting down insurrection, we were simply fulfilling our duty towards him. No such act on the part of his subjects could give us any title against him. Fancy, if you can, a widow lady with a houseful of mutinous servants who turn out and attack the police. The police knock them on the head, walk into the house, and kindly volunteer to protect the mistress against any violence on their part. A quarrel again breaks out, the truncheons are again successful, and the inspector now politely informs the lady that her house and the estate on which it stands are no longer her own, but will be retained in fee simply by the police; that on turning out she will receive an annuity equal to about one and six pence in a pound of her rental, and that she must hand over for the use of the Chief Commissioner her best diamond necklace. Is this an exaggerated version of our conduct towards that innocent boy Dalip Singh, now grown into a Christian gentleman? (*British India*, vol. ii, p 166).

SELECT REFERENCES

1. Banerjee, A. C. : *Anglo-Sikh Relations*
2. Bell, Evans : *Annexation of the Punjab*
3. Cunningham, J. D. : *History of the Sikhs*
4. Latif, M. : *History of the Panjab*
5. Mahajan, Jagmohan : *History of the Panjab*

18

LORD DALHOUSIE, 1848-56

> I have laboured to harness to India's bullock-cart civilisation three great engines of social improvement—Railways, Uniform Postage and Electric Telegraph.
>
> —*Lord Dalhousie*

Earl of Dalhousie was appointed the Governor-General of India in 1848 to succeed Lord Hardinge. Son of a Scot nobleman, Dalhousie was well known for his mastery of details and capacity for work. Earlier he had served as President of the Board of Trade in the Ministry and acquired reputation as a capable and conscientious officer. Aristocratic and despotic by disposition, he was well fitted for the new job. He was 36 years of age when he came to India as Governor-General.

Eight years of Dalhousie's rule are full of important events in every field. He is regarded as one of the greatest Governors-General of India and his contribution to the building up of the British Empire in India is very great. If there occurred any possibility of annexing an Indian state, Dalhousie did not miss it. Innes says: "His predecessors had acted on the general principle of avoiding annexation if it could be avoided; Dalhousie acted on the principle of annexing if he could do so legitimately." His annexations were both of 'war' and 'peace'. His annexations of war based on 'the right of conquest' were those of the Panjab and Pegu and of 'peace' came by the application of the Doctrine of Lapse and included among others of Oudh, Satara, Jaitpur, Jhansi and Nagpur. In the field of social and public reforms Dalhousie's contributions are equally great, as by those he laid the foundations on which modern India has been built up.

Annexations: Through Conquests

(*i*) **The Second Sikh War and the Annexation of the Panjab, 1849**. The revolt of Mul Raj, the Governor of Multan, had created a serious situation. Two British officers, Vans Agnew and Lieutenant Anderson had been murdered by Multan sepoys. The Sikh Governor of Hazara had raised the banner of revolt. The Sikhs won over Dost Muhammad, the Amir of Afghanistan, by the cession of Peshawar. The Panjabis rallied in large numbers under the banner of Mul Raj and the rebellion developed into a national war in the Panjab. Lord Dalhousie decided in favour of a final war and declared: "Unwarned by precedents, uninfluenced by example the Sikh nation has called for war and on my word, Sirs, they shall have it with a vengeance."

On November 16, 1848, the British armies under Lord Gough crossed the frontier. Bloody encounters were fought at Ramnagar, Chilianwala and Gujrat. The Sikh cause collapsed. Lord Dalhousie decided in favour of annexation arguing that "there never will be peace in the Panjab as long as its people are allowed to retain the means and the opportunity of making war. There never can be now any guarantee for the tranquility of India, until we shall have effected the entire subjugation of the Sikh people and destroyed its power as an independent nation." By the proclamation of 29 March 1849, the Panjab was annexed. Maharaja Dalip Singh was pensioned off and the British took over the administration of the Panjab. Politically, for the British this annexation was expedient and beneficial, as it carried the British frontiers to its natural boundaries and placed the famous passes of the North-West under the protection of the English. But Dalhousie had no legal or moral justification to annex the Panjab. Evans Bell calls it a 'violent breach of trust.' The British Resident, according to the Treaty of Bhyrowal, was the trustee of Maharaja Dalip Singh's territories and if there was any disturbance or rising, it was his responsibility, and not that of the Maharaja.

(*ii*) **The Annexation of Lower Burma or Pegu, 1852**. After the Treaty of Yandaboo 1826, a large number of British merchants had settled on the southern coast of Burma and Rangoon. These British merchants often complained of ill treatment at the hands of the Governor of Rangoon. Two British Captains, Sheppard and Lewis were heavily fined by the Burman Government on some specific charges brought against them. The British merchants sent a petition to Lord Dalhousie and this petition provided the desired opportunity. Dalhousie who was determined to maintain British prestige and dignity at all costs remarked: "An insult offered to the British flag at the mouth of the Ganges should be resented as promptly and fully as an insult offered at the mouth of the Thames." He deputed Commodore Lambert of H. M. Frigate 'Fox' to Rangoon to negotiate for redress of grievances and demand compensation. The despatch of warships for purposes of negotiating peace was an unusual measure denoting that the issue would be settled by sword rather than by civilised methods of negotiations and parleys. Lambert adopted a very provocative line of action by capturing one of the Burman King's ships. War ensued in which the Burmese were defeated. Dalhousie who had already made up his mind to annex Lower Burma on account of the threatening advance of America and France in the Eastern seas, issued a proclamation on December 20, 1852, annexing Pegu. Arnold says: "The Second Burmese War was neither just in its origin nor marked by strict equity in its conduct or issue." Dalhousie justified it by saying that "it was demanded by sound views of general policy".

Lord Ellenborough believed that 'the two insults' could be settled amicably. Benjamin Disraeli likened it to the Afghan expedition, both motivated by the exaggerated ambition to extend India to its illusory natural frontiers. Liberal leaders like Cobden and Bright described the annexation 'a very serious evil'. *The London Times* commented that the maintenance of British prestige in India did not require fresh annexations. Lord Aberdeen, the British Prime Minister, avowed ignorance about the whole affair and said that he did not know how to judge it. However, the imperial sentiment prevailed and the policy of imperial consolidation went space unchecked.

(*iii*) **Sikkim.** The Raja of Sikkim, a small state lying between Nepal and Bhutan, was charged with the offence of maltreating and imprisonment of two English doctors. In 1850 some outlying districts of the state including Darjeeling were annexed by Lord Dalhousie.

The Doctrine of Lapse — Annexations of 'Peace'

No account of Dalhousie's work of imperial consolidation can be complete without a mention of the Doctrine of Lapse. Some important Indian states were annexed by the enforcement of the Doctrine. The Doctrine of Lapse can be better understood in the context of Dalhousie's declared conviction that the old system of ruling through "Sham royalties" and "artificial intermediate powers" resulted in the misery of the people. In fact, his logical and straight Scottish mentality wanted to tear the mask of Mughal sovereignty and dispossess Indian princes who pretended to be descendants of the Mughals.

According to Dalhousie, there were three categories of Hindu states in those days in India:

(*i*) Those states which were not tributary and which were not and never had been subordinate to a paramount power.

(*ii*) Hindu princes and chieftains which were tributary and owed subordination to the British Government as their paramount power in place of the Emperor of Delhi or the Peshwa, etc.

(*iii*) Hindu sovereignties and states which had been created or revived by the *sanads* (grants) of the British Government.

Reviewing his policy in 1854, Lord Dalhousie explained that "in states covered by class I we have no right to their adoptions, In the class II the rulers have to require our assent to adoption which we have a right to refuse. But which policy would usually lead us to concede. In the principalities of the III class I hold that succession should never be allowed to go by adoption".

The East India Company had acquired the position of supreme power in India after the fall of the Maghal Empire and the defeat of the Maratha confederacy. Dalhousie maintained that "the British government in the exercise of a wise and sound policy is bound not to put aside or neglect such rightful opportunities of acquiring territory or revenue as may from time to time present themselves, whether they arise from the lapse of subordinate states by the failure of all heirs of every description whatsoever, or from the failure of heirs natural where the succession can be sustained only by the sanction of the government being given to the ceremony of adoption, according to Hindu law."

Dalhousie recognised the right of the adopted son to succeed to the personal property of the chieftain, but drew a distinction between succession to private property and succession to the royal *gaddi*: in the latter case, he held, that the sanction of the Paramount Power must be obtained. The Paramount Power could refuse 'adoption' in case of states covered by categories II and III and declare the states having passed back or 'lapsed' to the supreme authority. In such cases the 'Right of Adoption' was substituted by the Paramount Power's 'Right of Adoption' was substituted by the Paramount Power's 'Right of Lapse'. The power that gives, it was argued, could also rightfully take it away.

Dalhousie did not invent the doctrine. As early as 1834 the Court of Directors had laid down that in case of failure of lineal successors the permission 'to adopt' was an indulgence that "should be the exception, not the rule, and should not be granted but as a special mark of favour and approbation." Few years later in 1841, the Home authorities decided in favour of a uniform policy and directed the Governor-General "to persevere in the one clear and direct course of abandoning no just and honourable accession of territory or revenue while all existing claims of right are at the same time scrupulously respected". It was in pursuance of the policy thus laid down that Mandavi state was annexed in 1839, Kolaba and Jalaun in 1840 and the titular dignity of the Nawab of Surat abolished in 1842.

Dalhousie's contribution was that he uniformly applied this Doctrine of Lapse and did not ignore or neglect any opportunity in consolidating the territories of the East India Company. He steadily enforced the principles previously laid down. Mr. Innes has summed up the position thus: "His predecessors had acted on the general principle of avoiding annexation if it could be avoided; Dalhousie acted on the general principle of annexing if he could do so legitimately". It may be added that the over-zealous Governor-General treated some states as 'dependent principalities' or 'subordinate states' which rightly were protected allies'. Dalhousie's decision, therefore, had to be reversed by the Court of Directors in case of the old Rajput state of Karauli.

The states actually annexed by the application of the Doctrine of Lapse under Lord Dalhousie were Satara (1848), Jaitpur and Samhbalpur (1849), Baghat (1850), Udaipur (1852), Jhansi (1853) and Nagpur (1854).

Satara. Satara was the first Indian state to be annexed. In 1848 the Raja of Satara, Appa Sahib died without leaving a natural son. He had, however, adopted a son some days before his death but without the consent of the East India Company. Lord Hastings after destroying the Maratha power in 1818 had conferred this principality of Satara on Pratap Singh, the representative of the house of Shivaji and in his 'sons and heirs and successors'. In 1839 the Prince had been deposed and replaced by his brother Appa Sahib. The Bombay Council headed by Sir George Clerk advised against the annexation. Lord Dalhousie decided to regard it as 'dependent principality' and declared the state annexed. The Court of Directors approved Dalhousie's decision; "We are fully satisfied that by the general law and custom of India, a dependent principality like that of Satara, cannot pass to an adopted heir without the consent of the Paramount Power; that we are under no pledge, direct or constructive, to give such consent; and that the general interests committed to our charge are best consulted by withholding it". In the House of Commons Joseph Hume described the annexation as a victory of 'might over right' but the House of Commons acquiesced in the annexation.

Sambhalpur. Raja Narayan Singh, the ruler of the state, died without adopting a son. The state was annexed in 1849.

Jhansi. The Raja of Jhansi had been originally a vassal of the Peshwa. After the defeat of Baji Rao II, Lord Hastings in 1818 had concluded a treaty with Rao Ramchand, constituting "him, his heirs and successors" hereditary rulers of the territory on terms of 'subordinate co-operation'. After the death of the Raja in 1835, the East India Company recognised a grand-uncle, Raghunath Rao, to succeed to the principality. The old Raja died a few years later. Another successor Gangadhar Rao, from the royal family, was recognised in 1838. In November 1853 the ruler died without leaving a male heir and the state was declared escheat. The claims of the adopted son were disregarded.

Nagpur. This large Maratha state comprised an area of 80,000 square miles. In 1817 Lord Hastings had recognised an infant descendant of the Bhonsle family, Raghuji III as the Raja. The British Resident, Sir Richard Jenkins, acted as the Regent for ten years till 1830, when the boy came of age and the administration was transferred to him. The Raja died in 1853 without adopting an heir to the throne. The claims of the Rani to adopt a son were set aside and the state was annexed. The personal possessions of the late Raja were declared to be 'fairly at the disposal of the Government' on the plea that those were purchased out of state revenues. Then followed the spoliations of the Nagpur Palace, the sale by auction of the jewels and furniture of the Bhonsle's palace, a sum of £ 200,000 being realised by the ignominious sale.

Observations on the Doctrine of Lapse. 1. During the rise and expansion of the British domination in India, the East India Company from time to time had given assurances that not only the rights and privileges of the Indians but their laws, habits, customs and prejudices would be respected. The right of adoption has always been a great religious ceremony and greatly prized by the Hindus. Under the Mughals and the Peshwas the recognition of the supreme power was usually obtained by the payment of a *nazrana* or succession duty. Lord Dalhousie revived an obsolete custom and used it for imperial purposes. The Doctrine of Lapse, like the taxation during the 'personal rule' of Charles I, was the revival of a feudal law and looked like an 'act of spoliation under the garb of legality'.

2. The line of demarcation between 'dependent states' and 'protected allies' was very thin and amounted to hair splitting. In any case of disputed interpretation the decision of the East India Company was binding and that of the Court of Directors final. There was no supreme court to give impartial verdict on the questions of right and wrong.

3. Lord Dalhousie broke with precedent and was on many occasions guided by imperial considerations. Even Lee-Warner admits that with regard to Satara and Nagpur "imperial considerations weighed with him... they were placed right across the main lines of communication between Bombay and Madras and Bombay and Calcutta."

4. The Court of Directors withheld their sanction to the annexation of Karauli on the ground that the state was a 'protected ally' and not a 'dependent state.' Similarly, Baghat and Udaipur were returned to their respective rulers by Lord Canning.

Dalhousie was an annexationist. He applied the Doctrine of Lapse to achieve his aggressive ends. Where the 'doctrine of lapse' could not be applied, as in the case of Oudh, he annexed it on the pretext of 'good of the governed'. Rulers of Indian states believed that their states were annexed not by the applicaton of the Doctrine of Lapse, but due to the 'lapse of all morals' on the part of the East India Company. " Whatever might have been the facts", writes P. E. Roberts, "the natives did undoubtely believe that the existence of all native principalities was threatened" and the extinction of all states was regarded to be a question of time only. Actions were conclusive proof of Dalhousie's intentions. In fact, Dalhousie's Doctrine of Lapse was a part of his imperialist policy and was based on the old doctrine of 'Might is Right'.

Abolition of Titles and Pensions. Some titular sovereignties were swept away. After the death of the Nawab of Carnatic in 1853, Dalhousie concurred with the Madras authorities in not recognising anyone as his successor. This decision of the Governor-General was partially reversed in 1867. The Raja of Tanjore died in 1855, survived by two daughters and sixteen widows. The regal title was abolished. Dalhousie's plan to abolish the regal title of the Mughal Emperor after the death of Bahadur

Shah II (then 70 years of age) and stoppage of the pension of twelve million rupees per annum was not approved by the Court of Directors. The annual pension of eight lakhs of rupees paid to the ex Peshwa Baji Rao II was not transferred to his adopted son after the former's death in 1853. It was contended that the pension had been allowed to Peshwa Baji Rao II for his lifetime only, and so could not pass on to his adopted son, Nana Sahib.

The Annexation of Berar, 1853. The Nizam of Hyderabad had failed to pay to the East India Company the stipulated sum for maintaining an auxiliary force in Hyderabad. His debts had greatly accumulated. In 1853 the Nizam was compelled to code to the East India Company the cotton-producing area of Berar and certain adjoining districts calculated to yield a revenue of about fifty lakhs for the maintenance of the Hyderabad contingent.

The Annexation of Oudh, 1856. Oudh was another important Indian state annexed by Lord Dalhousie. This state first came into contact with the British as early as 1765, when its Nawab was defeated at Buxar. Oudh lay then at the mercy of the British but Clive decided not to annex it. He restored Oudh to the Nawab but made him part with the districts of Kora and Allahabad. When Wellesley came to India, he forced a new treaty (1801) on the Nawab and made him part with half of his dominions comprising Rohilkhand and the Lower Doab. After that, the Nawab became increasingly dependent on the Company for external defence and maintenance of internal law and order and shut his eyes to the welfare of the people, who groaned under the misrule of the Nawab's officers and the Company's trade agents.

William Bentinck, least ambitious and most humane of Governor-General, sent a warning to the Nawab asking him to improve his administration. Even when authorized by the Court of Directors to assume the administration of the state, William Bentinck decided against annexation. Lord Auckland in 1837 signed a fresh treaty with Nawab Muhammed Ali Shah by which he reserved for the East India Company "the right to intervene in the internal affairs of Oudh if gross and systematic oppression, anarchy and misrule should hereafter at any time prevail within the Oudh dominions, such as seriously to endanger the public tranquillity." This treaty, however, was disallowed by the Court of Directors and was, therefore, regarded as a 'dead letter'. In 1847 Lord Hardinge sent another warning to the Nawab.

By the middle of the nineteenth century the British opinion in India was ripe for the annexation of Oudh. In fact, mid-Victorian imperialists believed that Britain alone had the capacity for good government, that Indians had to be governed, that Oudh had, therefore, to be annexed. *The London Times* had given expression to the same sentiment when it referred to the Indians "as the very small people" which "a very great people has gone across the earth and taken possession of." In the accomplishment of this task Dalhousie was not to be deterred by sentimental respect for Indian loyalty or even respect for earlier treaties.

The main excuse for annexation of Oudh was the continuation of misrule there. The fundamental fact that British intervention had been greatly instrumental for misrule was ignored. Sir Henry Lawrence summed up the situation: "The facts furnished by every writer on Oudh affairs all testify to the same point, the British interference with that province has been so prejudicial to its court and people as it has been disgraceful to the British name." The charge of misgovernment was a convenient pretext to annex Oudh. According to Prof. K. K. Datta, "The existence of the ill-governed state of Oudh, almost in the centre of the rapidly expanding British Empire in India, could not but appear to the architects of the latter as a gross anachronism, which should be removed as quickly as possible to facilitate their own task".

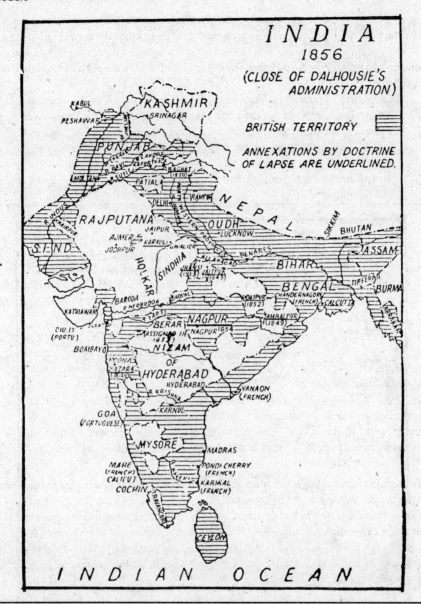

Descriptive Note on Expansion of British Dominion under Dalhousie

(i) After the Second Anglo-Sikh war (1848-49) Panjab was annexed to the Company's dominion.

(ii) In 1850 the Sikkim ruler was compelled to cede to the Company the Sikkim Terai and the lower course of the Tista river.

(iii) After the Second Anglo-Burman war (1852), Dalhousie acquired Lower Burma (Pegu).

(iv) In 1853 a new treaty was forced on the Nizam of Hyderabad compelling him to cede Berar to the Company.

(v) By application of the Doctrine of Lapse, Dalhousie annexed the States of Satara (1848), Jaitpur, Sambhalpur (1849), Baghat (1850), Udaipur (1852), Jhansi (1853) and Nagpur (1854).

(vi) In 1856 Oudh was annexed on the pretext of misgovernment.

Dalhousie's annexations added between a third and a half to the territorial size of British India of 1848. In the north-west the British became the Warden of the Passes, in the north the boundaries of British India became contiguous to Tibet and the Chinese empire, in the south-east the British controlled the entire coast line on both sides of the Bay of Bengal. Within the Indian sub-continent, the British Indian empire touched its 'natural frontiers' bounded by the ocean and the mountains.

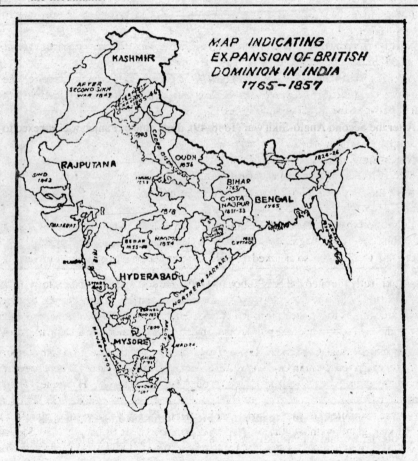

Descriptive Note on the Expansion of British Dominion in India (1765—1857)

12 August 1765—Emperor Shah Alam II granted to the East India Company the *Diwani* of Bengal, Bihar and Orissa.

Territorial Gain from Anglo-Mysore Wars. After the Third Anglo-Mysore war (1790-92), the English acquired Malabar on the west, Dindigul and the surrounding districts in the south and Baramahal districts in the east.

Lord Dalhousie

After the Fourth Anglo-Mysore war (1799), the English annexed the South Kanara coast, Wynaad in the south-west, Coimbatore and Darapuram in the south-east besides Seringapatam itself.

Gains from Treaties with the Nizam. By treaty of 12 October 1800, the Nizam surrendered to the East India Company all the territories he had acquired from the Mysore State after the second and third Mysore wars.

In 1853 the Nizam ceded Berar to the East India Company.

Gains froms Anglo-Maratha Wars. After the Second Anglo-Maratha war (1802-3) the East India Company's acquisitions included the Upper Doab (territory between the Ganges and the Jamuna), all territories north of the Rajput states of Jaipur, Jodhpur and Gohud besides Broach, Ahmednagar fort and the district of Cuttack in Orissa.

After the Third Anglo-Maratha war (1817-18), the Peshwa's entire dominions were acquired, all Maratha territory north and south of the Narbada river besides some minor other gains.

North-Western India. In 1809 the East India Company declared its protectorate over all cis-Sutlej states.

After the First Anglo-Sikh war (1845-46), the East India Company acquired the Jullundur Doab (territory between the river Beas and the Sutlej) besides all hill territory situated between the Sutlej and the Indus.

After the Second Anglo-Sikh war (1848-49), the whole of Panjab was annexed to the Company's dominion. Sind was annexed in 1843.

North-Eastern India. After the First Anglo-Burmese war (1824-26), the English gains included Assam, Arakan and the coastal strip of Tenasserim.

After the Second Anglo-Burmese war (1852) the English annexed Lower Burma (Pegu).

Expansion through the Doctrine of Lapse. Dalhousie annexed Satara (1848), Jaitpur and Sambhalpur (1849), Baghat (1850), Udaipur (1852), Jhansi (1853) and Nagpur (1854).

In 1856 Oudh was also annexed by Dalhousie on the pretext of misgovernment.

Dalhousie skillfully planned the annexation of Oudh. He sent special officers to investigate the charges of misrule in Oudh, wrote lengthy reports about the rottenness of government there and won over the Home authorities to his viewpoint. Thus fortified by the approval of the Home authorities and having won the tacit approval of the public opinion in England, Dalhousie acted with promptitude.

In 1848 Colonel Sleeman was sent as Resident to Lucknow. Sleeman wrote lengthy reports about the prevalence of misgovernment in Oudh. Colonel Sleeman, however, did not favour annexation but favoured increasing control of the administration through European agency. He wrote: "Were we...to annex or confiscate Oudh or any part of it, our good name in India would undoubtedly suffer; and that good name is more valuable to us than a dozen Oudhs... Here the giant's strength is manifest, and we cannot 'use it like a giant' without suffering in the estimation of all India". In 1854 Sleeman was replaced by Outram. Outram also reported that the administration in Oudh was rotten and the lot of the people was miserable. Three possible courses were debated in the Governor-General's Council, viz.,

1. To force the Nawab to abdicate and annex the state;

2. To retain the Nawab and his dignity, but to take all actual administration of the state into the hands of the Company for ever; and

3. The British Resident at Lucknow to assume charge of actual administration for a limited time.

The general opinion in the Governor-General's Council was in favour of annexation. Properly tutored by the exaggerated reports of Dalhousie, the Court of Directors gave their verdict in favour of annexation and ordered Lord Dalhousie to accomplish the task before laying down his office. Dalhousie acted with promptitude. He asked Nawab Wajid Ali Shah to sign the abdication. On his refusal, the state was annexed by a proclamation on February 13, 1856. Dalhousie's justification was : "The British Government would be guilty in the sight of God and man. If it were any longer to aid in sustaining by its countenance an administration fraught with suffering to millions". Some Conservative Directors of the Company had serious misgivings about the wisdom of this policy. A censure motion was brought in the General Court of the East India Company which described the annexation of Oudh as one of the worst example of Indian spoliation in the history of British rule in India. John Shepherd, a Director of the Company, commented that the annexation would be 'as liable to destroy the liberties of Indians so as to promote their rights and welfare. Indian opinion regarded the annexation of Oudh as a 'gross violation of material faith' and unwarranted by international law. Some writers have described this annexation as *Dacoitee in Excelsis*.

Lord Dalhousie's Reforms[1]

Administrative Reforms. Several reforms touching almost every department of administration were introduced by Lord Dalhousie. This great imperialist took care to consolidate the gains of the East India Company. To relieve the Governor-General for his wider responsibilities, Bengal was placed under the charge of a Lieutenant-Governor. For the newly acquired territories, he introduced the system of centralised control. This was known as 'Non Regulation' system. Under this system he appointed a Commissioner over a newly acquired territory who was made directly responsible to the Governor-General.

Military Reforms. Dalhousie's annexations had extended British India from Bengal in the east to the Panjab and Sind in the west. The dreams of an Asiatic Kingdom had been realised. A strategic control of these extensive areas necessitated better distribution of the troops. Thus the headquarters of the Bengal Artillery were shifted from Calcutta to Meerut, the permanent headquarters of the army were gradually shifted to Simla and this process was completed in 1865. The hill station of Simla grew increasingly important and became the seat of the Government of India for a major part of the year.

Dalhousie foresaw danger in the great numerical increase of the Indian army particularly during the Second Anglo-Sikh War. He proposed reduction in the strength of the Indian element in the army which despite some reduction stood at 2,23,000 men in 1856, as against 45,000 Europeans. He impressed upon the Home authorities the necessity of increasing the strength of European soldiers in India so that an equipoise could be kept between the British and Indian troops. He described the European force in India "as the essential element of our strength." Three regiments were added to the army. He protested against the despatch of two European regiments for service to China and Persia.

A new 'Irregular Force' was created in the Panjab under the direct control of the Panjab administration and with a separate system and discipline. Gorkha regiments were raised and their strength continually added to. These regiments proved of great value to the British during the crisis of 1857-58.

Educational Reforms. In Lord Dalhousie's time a number of important reforms were introduced in the field of education. In 1853 the Thomasonian system of vernacular education was recommended for the whole of the North-Westen Provinces, Lower Bengal and the Panjab with such modifications as their various circumstances might be found to require. Similar instructions were sent to the Bombay and Madras authorities.

In July 1854 Charles Wood, the President of the Board of Control, addressed to the Government of India his famous education despatch known as "Wood's Despatch" which provided for the creation of "a properly articulated scheme of education from the primary school to the university." Wood's despatch was very comprehensive and in the words of Lord Dalhousie "left nothing to be desired". It

---

1. For Karl Marx's views on the contemporary and future Political and Social Results of British Rule in India see Appendices A and B.

laid the foundations on which the modern education system has been built up. It recommended Anglo-Vernacular schools throughout the districts, Government colleges of higher grade in important towns and a University in each of the three presidencies of India. The 'infiltration theory' was abandoned. Voluntary efforts in the field of education were to be aided by grants-in-aids from the state; such grants were to be sanctioned subject to certain rules and on condition of proper government inspection. A Director of Public Instruction was to be appointed in each province who aided by inspectors was to organise and control education at the level lower than the University.

Examining universities on the model of the London University were to be set up at Calcutta, Bombay and Madras. These universities were to award degrees in token of acquirement of knowledge. Chairs were to be created for the instruction in Law and Civil Engineering. The first three universities in India were established in 1857.

Teaching of both the Vernaculars and English was to be encouraged, but English was thought to be the best vehicle for instruction of Western philosophy and sciences. An Engineering college was established at Roorkee.

Railway Development. Under Dalhousie British dominion in India was bound together by iron lines. Strategic railway lines were planned to facilitate internal communication for the defence of India. The broad outlines of the scheme were laid down by Lord Dalhousie in his famous Railway Minute of 1853 which formed the basis for the future railway extension in India. The first railway line connecting Bombay with Thane was laid down in 1853. The following year a railway line was built from Calcutta to the Raniganj coal-fields. A few miles of railway line were also built in the Madras Presidency. By 1856 various routes were being surveyed and constructed.

The railway lines were not built out of the Indian exchequer but by private enterprise. Besides relieving the Indian exchequer of the expense it could not have borne, it gave the English capital and enterprise a chance of investment. Subsequently railway lines in India were mostly built by public companies under a system of 'Government guarantee' on the lines indicated by Lord Dalhousie.

Besides encouraging trade and facilitating commerce and annihilating distances the railways have gone a long way in uniting India. As early as 1865 Sir Edwin Arnold wrote: "Railways may do for India what dynasties have never done—what the genius of Akbar the Magnificent could not effect by Government, nor the cruelty of Tipu Sahib by violence—they may make India a nation".

The Electric Telegraph. Dalhousie may be regarded as the Father of Electric Telegraph in India. O'Shanghnessy was appointed the Superintendent of the Electric Telegraph Department in 1852. Obstacles seemed insurmountable, but were overcome by the untiring zeal and energy of O'Shanghnessy. Nearly 4,000 miles of electric telegraph lines were constructed connecting Calcutta with Peshawar, Bombay and Madras and other parts of the country. In Burma a line was laid down from Rangoon to Mandalay. The Telegraph Department proved of great assistance during the great Rebellion of 1857-58. "It is that accursed string (the telegraph) that strangled us", acclaimed a rebel at the time of his execution.

Postal Reforms. The basis of the modern postal system also was laid down under Lord Dalhousie. As a result of the findings of an expert commission, a new Post Office Act was passed in 1854. Under the new system a Director-General was appointed to superintend the work of Post Offices in all the Presidencies ; a uniform rate of half an anna per letter, irrespective of the distance over which it might be sent, was introduced; postage stamps were issued for the first time. As a result of these reforms the Post Office which had so far been a drain on the treasury became a source of revenue. The social, administrative, financial and educational developments resultant from the extension and improvement of this system speak volumes for Dalhousie's desire for promoting the material progress of India.

Public Works Department. Before Lord Dalhousie the construction of Public Works had been a part of the job of the Military Board. A separate Public Works Department was set up for the first time and large amount of funds began to be spent on works of public utility. Irrigational works were undertaken on an extensive scale. The main stream of the Ganges Canal was completed and declared open on April 8, 1854; the Ganges Canal was described 'as a work which stands unequalled in its class and character among the efforts of civilised nations'. Construction work connected with the Bari Doab Canal in the Panjab was taken in hand. Many bridges were constructed and the work on the Grand Trunk Road was taken up with more enthusiasm.

Commercial Reforms. Ports of India were thrown open to the commerce of the world. Free-trade principles were becoming a passion with Englishmen of the mid-nineteeth century. The harbours of Karachi, Bombay and Calcutta were developed and a large number of light-houses were constructed.

Indian agriculture received special attention. The digging of canals, the development of railway facilities and construction of works of public utility ushered in a new commercial era. Indian resources particularly of cotton, flax and tea were developed to supply raw material for the mills of Lancashire and Manchester, importing in return cheap manufactured goods from England. Indian trade began to be more and more dominated by Englishmen.

Dalhousie's Responsibility for the Revolt of 1857. A storm had been gathering in India for a number of years. It burst out in 1857, a year after Lord Dalhousie left India. Dalhousie's policy, however, justified and legitimate it might have been, had caused great disquietude among the Indian Princes. The Ruling Princes, in the words of V. A. Smith, "knew nothing about subtle distinctions of 'dependent' and 'subordinate' states..... They simply saw that principality after principality was escheated and annexed for one reason or another, so that no ruler of a native state felt safe..... the pace was too fast and the cumulative effect of the transactions was profoundly unsettling". The Doctrine of Lapse disregarded the customs and prejudices of the Indian people. It broke away from precedents and gave new interpretations to outdated and outmoded doctrines.

V. A. Smith blames Lord Dalhousie for lack of foresight. Smith writes: "The outgoing Governor-General certainly had not the slightest prevision of the storm that was to break the next year in May, and had not made any arrangements to meet it... he must share with his predecessors the censure due for permitting the continuance of a most dangerous military situation in India. He had not taken any precautions to protect the enormous store of munitions at Delhi, which was left in the hands of the native army, or to secure the essential strategical position of Allahabad. Whatever thought was devoted to military preparation in India was directed to the Panjab. Everywhere else the old haphazard distribution of the troops continued and nobody in authority, military or civil, seems to have realized the obvious perils incurred". T. R. Holmes absolves Dalhousie of reponsibility for the weak military condition of the East India Company and blames the Commander-in-Chief for his failure to remedy the indiscipline in the army and for his neglect to safeguard Delhi and Allahabad. T. R. Holmes, on the other hand, believes that the rebellion that broke out in Oudh was "due not to annexation, but to the harshness with which the Talukdars were treated"; the excesses committed in Jhansi are attributed "to the failure of Havelock's earlier attempts to relieve the Residency." Holmes credits Dalhousie for his wise policy and constructive administrative work and says : "By the construction of roads and telegraphs, and by the administration which he bestowed upon the Panjab, he contributed much to the power by which the Mutiny was quelled."

It must, however, be stated that Dalhousie's annexations and escheats worsened the situation. He went too far and too fast. His ruthless and injudicious policy provided leaders like the Rani of Jhansi, Nana Sahib, Tantia Tope, etc., who channelised the prevalent discontent and proved the brain behind the movement once the soldiers had mutinied. Responsibility for the Rebellion of 1857–58 partly rests on the shoulders of Lord Dalhousie.

Estimate of Dalhousie. Sir Richard Temple says: " As an imperial administrator, Dalhousie has never been surpassed and seldom equalled by any of the illustrious men whom England has sent forth to govern India." Marshman writes: "He exhibited perhaps the finest example which ancient or modern history affords, of what can be accomplished for the benefit of mankind by an enlightened despot acting upon a large theatre."

Sir William Wilson Hunter has summed up Dalhousie's work in three words — conquest, consolidation and development. His annexations gave the map of modern India. Annexation of the Panjab pushed the dominion of the East India Company to the hills in the North-West and British officers became the Warden of the Passes; the annexation of Sikkim territory brought Indian boundaries contiguous to Tibet and the Chinese empire and the acquisition of Lower Burma extended British authority along the coast from Chittagong to Rangoon. The work of internal territorial consolidation was achieved by annexation of a number of Indian states. Dalhousie's conquests and annexations added nearly a quarter million square miles to the East India Company's dominions, adding between a third and a half to the territorial size of British India of 1848. His reforming activities extended to every branch of administrative development. By his far reaching schemes of railways, roads, canals and public works he launched India on the road to become a manufacturing and mercantile India. Dalhousie also proved an active modernizer. He laid the foundations of and indicated the lines on which modern India was to be built.

Dalhousie, however, had the defects of his qualities. He cared very little for moral values and plighted word. While dealing with the Panjab, he cared more for the end than for the means. He also paid no need to the feelings and prejudices of Indians while dealing with the Indian states. Thus Dalhousie proved to be a ruthless imperialist and was greatly responsible for creating unrest all round and the Rebellion of 1857 too.

Select Opinions

Lee-Warner. Three commanding figures stand out in the annals of Indian history. The first of these, Warren Hastings, created the British administration of Bengal... The second, the Marquis of Wellesley, conceived and created the political system by which the Native Sovereignties lying outside British India were included in one empire of India under the control of the paramount power. Lord Dalhousie brought into harmony the work of his two great predecessors. He consolidated the scattered territories under the Company's direct rule, carrying the British frontier across the Indus and the Irrawaddy and enlarged the sphere of foreign interests by throwing the aegis of British protection over Baluchistan, and entering into an alliance with Afghanistan. He removed formidable obstacles to the moral and material development of a continent, linking together British provinces by annexation of states, sweeping away phantom royalties and connecting all portions of the empire by railway and telegraphs. He gave to the administrative system the shape which it still preserves, the centralising imperial control over postal and other communications but permitting freedom to the local administrations in other directions. By him were laid the foundations of the legislative assemblies and the departments of education. (*The Life of the Marquis of Dalhousie*, Vol. ii, p. 416)

Ramsay Muir. Dalhousie was a man of immense ability and energy, untiring energy, inflexible will, absolute honesty of purpose and real devotion to the greatness of his own country. For sheer force of personality two only among the long line of governors deserve to be compared with him—Warren Hastings and Wellesley. He was a greater man than Wellesley, because he took a far deeper view of the problems of government, he was a lesser man than Hastings, because he lacked Hastings' generous humanity, his power of reading the minds of his colleagues and understanding the point of view of the millions whom he so resolutely laboured to serve. (*The Making of British India*, p. 337).

P. E. Roberts. The great traits of Dalhousie's character are no longer in dispute. He was inspired with a noble and vivid ideal for duty, which drove him on to sacrifice his health and comfort recklessly... His minutes and dispatches are masterpieces of eloquent English, lucid statement and merciless logic. He was a supremely able judge of character... On the other hand, he had defects of his qualities. He possibly attempted to do more than any one man, however able, could do. There was not much field left to his subordinates except to carry out his rather imperious will. Though he freely supported men with whom he was in complete agreement, he was somewhat intolerant of original ideas. It is only fair to remember that there was an opposition in India to many tendencies of his policy and not a factious opposition only. but one based on reasoned principles. Men like Henry Lawrence, Low, Sleeman, and Outram, while freely admitting his splendid qualities, considered that he would have done better to pay more heed to native feelings and prejudices even at the cost of sacrificing some of his most valuable reforms. (*History of British India*, pp. 357–58).

SELECT REFERENCES

1. Anonymous : *Dacoitee in Excelsis or the Spoliation of Oudh.*
2. Arnold, Edwin : *The Marquess of Dalhousie*, 2 vols.
3. Hunter, W. W. : *Dalhousie* (Rulers of India series)
4. Lee-Warner, W. : *The Life of Dalhousie*, 2 vols.
5. Pannikar, K. M. : *Introduction to the Study of the Relations of Indian States with the Government of India.*

19

CHANGES IN AGRARIAN STRUCTURE : NEW LAND TENURES AND LAND REVENUE POLICY

The new land systems (zamindari and ryotwari) made mobile land and the peasant, and left the way open for the growth in power of the moneylender and the absentee landlord.

— D. & A. Thorner

The British imperial rulers of India unleashed far-reaching changes in Indian agrarian structure. New land tenures, new land ownership concepts, tenancy changes and heavier state demand for land revenue triggered of far-reaching changes in rural economy and social relationships. The Government policies ushered in a new era of distorted modernisation.

Pre-British Agrarian Structure. Since the times of Manu village communities in India functioned as units of local-self government and land revenue administration. In the pre-capitalist stage of Indian economy, the idea of absolute ownership of land did not exist. All classes connected with land possessed certain rights. The cultivator possessed the right to cultivate and enjoyed security of tenure on the condition of payment of more or less fixed share of produce of the year to the overlord. The Patil or the village head-man acted as the *mamlatdar* or the collector (and magistrate and head farmer also) and passed on the state demand of land revenue (which varied form 1/6th to 1/3rd of the rental value) to the ruler or the nawab. The internal village arrangement connected with cultivation, allotment of the same categories of land to certain categories of cultivators, provision of irrigation facilities, allocation and collection of land revenue from individual cultivators etc., were settled by the Patil in consultation with the village Panchayats according to local customs and practices.

British Land Revenue System and Administration. The British conquerors of India sought to derive the maximum economic advantage from their rule in India. British industrial and mercantile interests (by advocating Free Trade principles) prevented the East India Company from raising any substantial revenue from high custom tariffs. The Company's government in India had, therefore, to rely on land revenue as the principal source of income for the State. As such land revenue matters received the maximum care of the new colonial rulers.

Early British administrators of the East India Company considered India as a vast estate and acted on the principle that the Company was entitled to the entire economic rent, leaving to the cultivators merely the expenses of cultivation and wages of their labour. Village communities were disregarded. In almost all parts of the Company's territories the early administrators resorted to the 'farming' of land revenues. Exessive land revenue demands proved counter-productive. Agriculture began to languish, large areas went out of cultivation and famines stared the people in the face. This necessitated some serious thinking, both in India and England, about land revenue matters. Some policy decisions emerged from serious deliberations.

New Land Tenures. The words land tenure (tenure is derived from the Latin word *teneo* i.e. to hold) are used to refer to the conditions on which land is held by the zamindar/cultivator from the state or the cultivator from the landlord. Broadly speaking, the English adopted three types of land tenures in India viz., the Zamindari tenure, the Mahalwari tenure, and the Ryotwari tenure. Permanent zamindari settlements were made in Bengal, Bihar, Orissa, Benares Division of the U.P., Northern Carnatic and roughly covered 19% of the total area of British India. The Mahalwari tennure was introduced in major portions of the U.P., the Central Provinces, the Panjab (with variations) and covered nearly 30% of the area. The Ryotwari settlements were made in major portions of Bombay and Madras Presidencies, in

Assam and some other parts of British India covering roughly 51% of the area. The British rulers adopted[1] various forms of land tenure in India.

The Permanent Zamindari Settlement. The zamindari system was a creation of the British rule and many non-economic considerations entered into its acceptance. The system was known by different names like *Jagirdari, Malguzari, Biswedari* etc. Under the Permanent Settlement system the State's land revenue demand was settled once for all while in other zamindari tracts the land revenue was revised after a fixed number of years ranging from 10 to 40 years.

Under the zamindari system, the zamindar (many of whom had been merely revenue collectors) was recognised as the owner who could mortgage, bequeath and sell the land. The State held the zamindar responsible for the payment of land revenue and in default thereof the land could be confiscated and sold out.

The State's land revenue demand was fixed very high. In Bengal, for example, the State demand was fixed at 89% of the rental, leaving only 11% with the zamindar. Mr John Shore gives us the following figures of revenue collection for the 4 years (1762–65).

		Actual collection
Mir Kasim's Administration	1762-63	Rs. 64.6 lakhs
Mir Jafar's Administration	1763-64	Rs. 76.2 lakhs
–Do–	1764-65	Rs. 81.7 lakhs
First year of Company's Diwani	1765-66	Rs. 147.0 lakhs
Company's collection for	1790-91	Rs. 268 lakhs

From the above figure it is clear that in the very first year of the Company's *diwani* the revenue collection increased by almost 80% over the collection for the previous year. By the year 1790-91, the Company's revenue collection figure stood at Rs 268 lakhs which was nearly double the collections of 1765–66.

A snag in the Permanent Settlement of Bengal was that while the State's land revenue demand was fixed, the rent to be realised by the landlord from the cultivator was left unsettled and unspecified. This resulted in rack-renting and frequent ejections of tenants from their traditional holdings. The Bengal Rent Acts of 1859 and 1885 provided some relief to cultivators. Some scholars believe that the much praised tenancy legislation was primarily enacted to keep the countryside quiet.

The Mahalwari System. Under this system, the unit for revenue settlement is the village or the mahal (*i.e.*, the estate). The village land belongs jointly to the village community technically called 'the body of co-shares'. The body of co-shares are jointly responsible for payment of land revenue, though individual responsibility is also there. If any co-sharer abandons his land it is taken over by the village community as a whole. The village community is the owner of village 'common land' including the forest land, pastures etc.

---

1. Recent researches have cast doubt on the thesis put forward by Eric Stokes (*The English Utilitarians and India,* Oxford 1959) and G. D. Bearce (*British Attitudes Towards India,* Oxford 1961) that contemporary ideological attitudes fashionable in England, to a noticeable degree, guided the British administrators in India in their policies. The current view seems to have veered round Baden Powell's analysis that the land revenue systems adopted by the British in India were essentially practical adaptations to local circumstances and that they had to be so, emphasised Baden Powell, if they were to work at all. (*The land Systems of India,* Oxford 1892). According to this view the acceptance of the 'big landlord' settlement in Bengal, the individual peasant landholder system in Madras and Bombay Presidencies, the Mahalwari system in U. P. were acceptance of the prevailing systems in those areas with minor variations.

The Indian view point – both nationalist and Marxist – regards British land revenue systems and settlements in India geared to subserve the interests of a colonial economy (see Morris D. Morris and others : *Indian Economy in the Nineteenth Century* : *A Symposium,* Delhi, 1969).

Changes in Agrarian Structure

Land Settlements in North-Western Provinces and Oudh. The North-Western Provinces and Oudh (roughly modern U.P.) came under British rule at different times. In 1801 the Nawab of Oudh surrendered to the Company the districts of Allahabad, and adjoining areas called the 'Ceded Districts'. After the Second Anglo-Maratha War the Company acquired the territory between the Jamuna and the Ganges called the 'Conquered Provinces'. After the last Anglo Maratha War (1817-18), Lord Hastings acquired more territories in Northern India.

Henry Wellesley, the first Lt Governor of the Ceded Districts, made a land revenue settlement with the zamindars and farmers for three years fixing the State demand higher by 20 lakh rupees during the very first year over the Nawab of Oudh's demand, to which another burden of rupees 10 lakhs was added before the third year was out. The incidence of the Company's land revenue demand was still higher if we keep in view another factor. While the Nawab's revenue collection varied according to the actual production in a year, the Company's demand was realised with a rigidity unknown in India before. Similar land revenue settlements were made for the conquered provinces.

The Regulation of 1822. Holt Mackenzie, the Secretary to the Board of Commissioners, recorded his Minute of 1819 emphasising the existence of village communities in Northern India. He recommended a survey of land, preparation of record of rights in land, settlement of land revenue demand village by village or mahal by mahal and collection of land revenue through the village headman or Lambardar.

Regulation VII of 1822 gave legal sanction to the above recommendations. Thus the land revenue settlements were made on the basis of 80% of the rental value, payable by the zamindars. In cases where estates were not held by the landlords but by cultivators in common tenancy, the State demand was allowed to be fixed at 95% of the rental.

The system broke down because of the excessive state demand and harshness in its working and collection of land revenue.

Regulation IX of 1833 and Land Settlements by Merttins Bird. The Government of William Bentinck made a thorough review of the scheme of 1822 and came to the conclusion that the scheme had caused widespread misery and failed under the weight of its harshness. Prolonged consultations resulted in the passing of the Regulation of 1833 which provided for simplification of the procedure for preparing estimates of produce and of rents and introduction of the system of fixing average rents for different classes of soil. For the first time the use of field maps and field registers was prescribed.

The new scheme worked under the supervision of Merttins Bird, remembered as the Father of Land Settlements in Northern India. Under the new scheme land in a tract was surveyed, showing field boundaries and the cultivated and uncultivated land. Then the assessment for the whole tract was fixed followed by setting down the demand for each village, leaving to the *mahal* powers to make internal adjustments. The State demand was fixed at 66% of the rental value and the Settlement was made for 30 years.

The Settlement work under the scheme begun in 1833 was completed under the administration of James Thomson (Lt. Governor, 1843–53).

Even the 66% rental demand formula proved to be harsh and unworkable. Consequently Lord Dalhousie felt the need for issuing fresh Directions to Settlement Officers. Under the revised Saharanpur Rules of 1855 the State revenue demand was limited to 50% of the rental value.

Unfortunately, the Settlement officers evaded the new rules in practice. They interpreted the 50% rental value to mean one-half of the "prospective and potential" rental of estates and not the "actual rentals". Thus the system fell heavily on the agricultural classes and created widespread discontent which found full vent during the Revolt of 1857–58.

The Ryotwari System. Under this system every 'registered' holder of land is recognised as a proprietor of land and is held responsible for direct payment of land revenue to the State. He has the right to sub-let his land holdings, to transfer, mortgage or sell it. He is not evicted from his holdings by the Government so long as he pays the State demand of land revenue.

Land Settlements in Madras. In Madras Presidency, the first land revenue settlements were made in the Baramahal district after its acquisition by the Company in 1792. Capt. Read assisted by Thomas Munro fixed the State demand on the basis of 50% of the *estimated produce* of the fields, which worked out to be more than the whole economic rent. The same system was extended to other parts.

The first assessments were very severe and caused widespread misery.

Thomas Munro and the Madras Settlements. Thomas Munro (Governor 1820–27), realised the unfairness of the early settlements. He extended the ryotwari system to all parts of the province (except the permanently settled areas) on the basis of 1/3rd of the gross produce of the holdings, which too unfortunately absorbed nearly the whole of the economic rental. The State demand was fixed in money and had no connection with the actual yield of the holding or the prevailing prices in the market.

Munro's land settlements operated for nearly thirty years and caused widespread oppression and agricultural distress. The peasantry sank deeper in poverty. He fell in the clutches of the *chetty* (moneylender) for payment of land revenue. The machinery of collection was very oppressive and torture was normally resorted to for collection of State dues. In the British Parliament members asked questions about the vile practices of torture which included preventing defaulter from taking his meals or attending to calls of nature, tying a man down in a bent position, making a man sit with brickbats behind his knees, tying defaulters by their back hair or tying by the hair to a donkey's or buffalo's tail, placing a necklace of bones or other degrading materials round the necks etc. etc.

In 1855 an extensive survey and settlement plan was decided upon on the basis of 30% of the gross produce. Actual work began in 1861. The Rule of 1864 limited the State demand to 50% of the rental, but these instructions remained more on paper and never became actual facts of administration. The terrible Madras famine of 1867-78 revealed the real state of the Madras peasantry.

Land Settlements in Bombay. In Bombay Presidency too the Company decided in favour of the Ryotwari system with a view to the elimination of landlords or village communities which could intercept their profits.

Elphinstone's and Chaplin's Reports. Elphinstone, Governor of Bombay 1819-27, submitted a detailed 'Report on the Territories Conquered from the Peshwa' in October 1819. He emphasised two important features of the Maratha Government, (*a*) the existence of village communities as units of local administration and (*b*) the existence of *mirasi* tenture (*mirasdars* were hereditary peasant proprietors who cultivated their own fields and paid land-tax at fixed rates to the State). Chaplain, the Commissioner of the Decan, submitted two reports in 1821 and 1822, referring to the past practices in revenue settlements and making some valuable suggestions.

Regular survey of the land was conducted by Pringle during 1824-28. The State demand was fixed at 55% of the net produce. Unfortunately, most of the surveys were faulty and the estimate of produce of fields proved to be erroneous. All this resulted in over assessment and oppressions of the peasantry. In disguest many cultivators deserted their fields and large tracts of cultivable land went out of cultivation.

Wingate's Survey and the Ryotwari Settlement in Bombay. In 1835 Lt. Wingate of the Engineers Corps was appointed the Superintendent of Survey. He submitted a report in 1847 which was jointly signed by H. C. Goldsmid, Capt. Davidson and Capt. Wingate.

Broadly speaking, the State land revenue demand for a district was first determined on the basis of 'the past history of the District' and 'past condition of the people' (*i.e.* their paying capacity). Then the total district demand was distributed among the fields. The earlier system of equitable basis of field produce was substituted by a geological basis of assessment. Further, the assessment was placed upon each field instead of the holdings of a cultivator, so that each cultivator could give up any field he liked or take up other fields which might have remained unoccupied. The settlement was made for 30 years.

The new assessment was more or less based on guess work and erred on the side of severity.

Resettlement work began after 30 years. It was taken up in 1866. Because of the American Civil War (1861-65) the demand for Bombay cotton temporarily pushed up the prices. This temporary boom gave an opportunity to the Survey officers to push up the assessment by 66% to 100%, without giving any right to the cultivators to appeal to a court of law.

The Deccan witnessed Agrarian riots in 1875. The Government responded by the enactment of the Deccan Agriculturists' Relief Act, 1879 by providing relief against the moneylenders, but did nothing to restrain the excessive State demand — the root of all evils.

The two great evils of the Ryotwari system in Bombay were over assessment and uncertainty. Further, there was no provision for an appeal to the court of law against over assessment. The collector informed the cultivator of the rate at which his land had been assessed in future with the warning that if he chose to retain it on the new terms, he could; if he did not choose, he could throw it up.

Disintegration of Village Economy. The overall impact of the East India Company's revenue systems and excessive state demand coupled with the new judicial and administrative set-up turned Indian rural economy upside down with the village Panchayats deprived of their two main functions — land settlements, judicial and executive functions – and the Patel merely acting as a Government official charged with the duty of revenue collection, the old politico-economic-social framework of village communities broke down. The introduction of the concept of private property in land truned land into a market commodity. Changes came in social relationships. New social classes like the landlord, the trader, the moneylender, and the landed gentry shot into importance. The class of rural proletariat, the poor peasant proprietor, the sub-tenant, and the agricultural labour multiplied in number. The climate of cooperation gradually gave place to the system of competition and individualism. The prerequisites of the capitalist development of agriculture were created. Further, new modes of production, introducton of money economy, commercialization of agriculture, better means of transport and linkage with the world market added a new dimension to Indian agriculture and rural economy.

SELECT REFERENCES

1. Baden-Powell, B. H. : *The Land Systems of British India*, 2 vols.
2. Dutt, R. C. : *Economic History of India*, 2 vols.
3. Stokes, Eric : *The English Utilitarians and India.*
4. Stokes, Eric : *The Peasant and the Raj*
5. Morris D. Morris : *Indian Economy in the Nineteenth Century: A symposium.*

CHANGES IN ADMINISTRATIVE STRUCTURE AND POLICIES UNDER THE EAST INDIA COMPANY

> The government of an exclusive company of merchants is perhaps the worst of all governments for any country whatever.
>
> — *Adam Smith*

C.P. Ilbert[1] has rightly observed that the history of development of British power in India falls into three periods *viz.*, (*i*) From the beginning of the 17th century to 1765 when the East India Company was a trading corporation existing on the sufferance of the Indian powers and in rivalry with other European trading companies; (*ii*) From 1765 to 1858 the Company acquired and consolidated its dominions and shared its sovereignty with the British Crown and gradually lost its mercantile privileges and powers; (*iii*) The third and the last period started from 1858 when the remaining powers of the East India Company were transferred to the Crown.

The English East India Company's merchants came to India for trade and the obvious motive was to earn maximum profits. However, the stiff competition from other European merchant companies – the Dutch East India Company and the French East India Company—limited their trade and profits. A way out was to eliminate European rival companies from the Indian trade. This led the English Company to wage wars against the Dutch and French companies in which struggle the English Company won convincing victory by 1763. Thereafter, the English Company acquired virtual monopoly over India's foreign trade. However, even this achievement did not satisfy the ambition of the English Company. Their next target was to acquire control of political power in India so that they could control and direct the economy of India and use it for maximizing their profits.

As the English Company was transformed from a purely commercial body into a commercial-cum-political body, it was realised that it could not hold and govern territories effectively unless it evolved a suitable system of administration.

The administrative and legal system developed by the Company in India could not evolve in a vacuum. The Company's authorities had to accept the existing Indian administrative structure and gradually introduce necessary changes. Judith M. Brown, an Oxford University scholar, has asserted that in the 18th century the British "were in a real sense prisoners of the sub-continent they had conquered" and it was only in the late 18th century and early 19th century that the process of "change and continuity" began.

Influence of Contemporary British Administrative Models and Imperial Interests

As the British Crown had emerged as the Paramount Power in India, the intellectual currents and administrative models of England were bound to affect the pattern of administrative system in India. For example, the ideas of 'Utilitarianism' connected with the names of Jeremy Bentham, David Ricardo, J. S. Mill had become popular and found acceptance in Britain in the period known as the Age of Reform. These 'Utilitarian' ideas on how to govern and control India particularly in matters of form of government, taxation and administration of justice etc. were reflected in the structure of the Indian administrative system. The Evangelical missionary zeal also carried weight with many administrators. Another motivating trend was the interests of the British merchants and manufacturers. In this context, it must be emphasised that the British imperial interest in India changed from time to time in consonance

---

1. C. P. Ilbert was the Law Member of Lord Ripon's Executive Council (1880-84). He is well known for the Ilbert Bill Controversy and his book, *The Government of India* (Clarendon Press, 1898).

with the economic developments in Britain. For example, up to 1815 the Company's main thrust was to accept the existing Indian institutions and administrative apparatus, for the main motive was to maximize the agricultural surplus. In other words, there was no imperative need for evolution of a uniform administrative structure or even a modern judicial system. However, after 1815, the development of the Industrial Revolution in England transformed the economy and society of Britain. Hence-forth, the British industrialist lobby looked for a market for their industrial products and also looked upon India as a source of supply of raw material like cotton, jute etc., and even opium and food products for export and mercantile profit. Hence, arose the need for a greater penetration into Indian economy and society and further control over Indian trade not only with Britain but with the rest of the world also. These factors explain the impulse for changes in the administrative and legal system and also for drastic changes in the administrative and legal system and also for field of Indian economy.

The process of making changes in administrative structure and policies to subserve British colonial interests continued after 1858 also when India passed under direct Crown rule.

Broadly speaking, the entire administrative structure of the East India Company— the Home Government in London, the Government of India, the Financial and Revenue administration, organisation of the Civil Service, judicial reorganisation, changes in economic policy, Social legislation and Educational policy — all were planned and changes were introduced in these fields from time to time to make British rule in India durable as also draw the maximum economic advantage from British Colonial rule in India.

The Home Government: The Company's administrative business in London was managed by a committee of 24 Directors (known as the Court of Directors) who were elected annually by a body of share-holders popularly known as the Court of Proprietors. The Court of Directors further constituted from amongst its own members, a number of committees which carried out the day to day business of the Company in London. In due course, the powers and privileges of the Company were first confirmed and supplemented, then supervised and regulated and later curtailed by the Crown and successive acts of Parliament.

The Government of India: C.P. Ilbert has traced the origin of the Company's authority in India to a two-fold source. It was derived (*i*) party from the British Crown and Parliament and (*ii*) partly from the Great Mughals and other Indian rulers. In England, the powers and privileges of the East India Company were confirmed by various Charter Acts and other Parliamentary legislation like the Regulating Act (1773), the Ameding Act (1781), the Pitt's India Act (1784) and the Act For Better Government of India (1858).

In India, concessions were granted by Indian princes and sometimes concessions were wrested from them under military and political pressures which made the Company and the Crown partial territorial sovereignty in India. In 1639, the chief of Wandiwash gave the Company the permission to govern Madras with the right to build a fort and mint money. Subsequently, the nawab of Carnatic and the Mughal authorities surrendered all authority over Madras to the Company. In 1668, King Charles II of England through a Charter transferred to the Company the port and island of Bombay (which the king had received in dowry in 1661, when he married princess Catherine of Braganza of Portugal) for an annual rent of £10 only. In Bengal, the Company obtained from Subahdar Azim-us-Shan the zamindary of the three villages of Kalikata, Sutanuti and Govindpur (the present site of Calcutta) on Payment of Rs 1200/- to the previous proprietors. In 1717, emperor Farruksiyar issued a *firman* authorizing the Company to rent additional territory around Calcutta. After the Black Hole incident (20th June, 1756), the Company's expeditionary force surrounded Calcutta and in February 1757 compelled Nawab Siraj-ud-daula to restore Fort William to the Company with permission to fortify it as also permit them to coin money.

The factories and affairs of the Company on the east and west coasts of India, and in Bengal were administered at each of its principal settlements at Madras (Fort St. George), Bombay and Calcutta

(Fort William) by a President (or Governor) and a Council consisting of the senior servants of the Company. Power was exercised by the President and Council collectively, and orders were issued in accordance with the decision of the majority. The three 'Presidencies' were independent of one another and answerable directly to the Court of Directors in London.

In early 1770s the East India Company faced financial bankruptcy and in August 1772 applied to the British Government for a loan of a million pounds. This gave the British Parliament the opportunity to enquire into the affairs of the Company and regulate them. As such, the Regulating Act 1773 was passed which limited the influence of the Court of Proprietors and provided for election of Court of Directors for a period of 4 years (hitherto the election was held every year) and further required the Directors to lay before the British Treasury in London correspondence relating to India dealing with revenues and to submit to Secretary of State all information dealing with civil and military administration.

The Regulating Act also provided for appointment of a Governor-General assisted by four councillors for management of affairs of Bengal Presidency and to exercise some powers over the Presidencies of Bombay and Madras.

The Pitt's India Act, 1784 further extended the British Parliament's control over management of the East India Company. In England, Board of Control (Commissioners for the affairs of India) was instituted headed by the Chancellor of Exchequer to further tighten the control over the Company's administrative set-up in London. The Board had access to all papers and instruments of the Company. In India, the number of members of Governor General's Council was reduced from 4 to 3, out of which one was to be the Commander-in-Chief of the Company's forces in India. In 1833, a fourth member known as the Law Member was added to the Council.

In 1813, the British parliament passed the Charter Act of 1813 by which it deprived the Company of the monopoly of trade with India except the trade with China and the trade in tea. By the Charter Act of 1833 the Company was asked to close its commercial bussiness as early as possible and to administer Indian territories in 'trust for His Majesty, his heirs and successors.'

In India, the Charter Act of 1833 brought about legislative centralization by drastically depriving the Governments of Madras and Bombay of power of legislation. Such arrangments continued till the company's rule in India lasted till 1858.

The Financial and Revenue Administration : After the Company's victories in the battles of Plassey and Buxar, it emerged as commercial-cum-military-cum-political power in Bengal and henceforth used its new position of strength to maximize its profits in India. Gradually, the British ambition to conquer the whole of India took shape which required a large army for conquest of various parts of India and the consolidation of the empire. All this ambitious programme required lot of funds which could only be obtained by resort to a well-planned and thorough exploitation of India's economic resources.

Land revenues had been the traditional source of income of the state in India. Judith M. Brown has aptly remarked "Land revenue had been the financial foundation of Mughal raj; it was to be crucial to the British raj well into the twentieth century". Other sources of income included customs and excise duties, opium and salt trade, monopolies, tributes received from Indian states, income from forests, provincial rates, stamps, registration etc. etc.

Land Revenue Policy : As income from land revenue amounted to more than half of the gross income of the state and there seemed a scope for its enhancement, the early British administrators gave their maximum care to the land revenue matters. The colonial rulers of India made far-reaching changes in land revenue tenures, apart from introducing new land ownership concepts, tenancy laws and making heavier state demand of land revenue. Broadly speaking, three types of land tenures were adopted *viz.*, the Zamindari tenure, the Mahalwari tenure and the Ryotwari tenure. Permanent Zamindari settlements were made in Bengal, Bihar, Orissa, Benaras division of modern U.P., northern Carnatic in the 18th century. In the 19th century the colonial rulers realised that the Permanent Settlement system blocked all future increases in land revenue receipts. Hence, the Mahalwari system was devised under which the state's land revenue demand was fixed for a number of years ranging from 10 to 40 years. This system was introduced in U.P., Central Provinces (roughly modern Madhya Pradesh) and the Punjab (with variations). A still more flexible system from the state's point of view was the Ryotwari System under which the settlements were made with the 'registered holders of land' (recognised as proprietors of land) and made responsible for direct payment of land revenue to the state. In this system all intermediaries– like the zamindars– between the state and the raiyat (*i.e.*, cultivator) were eliminated. This system offered chances of still better collection of land revenue for the state. The Ryotwari settlements were introduced in major portions of Bombay and Madras Presidencies, in Assam and some other parts of India covering roughly 51% of the area.

R.C. Dutt[2] has given the following figures about the steady increase in the revenue from the land tax:

1817-19 -	£12,363,634
1827-28 -	£13,754,703
1837-38 -	£11,853,975
1847-48 -	£14,437,254
1857-58 -	£15,317,911

In 1858-59, the land revenue alone accounted for half of the Government's total revenue.

The overall impact of the East India Company's land revenue system based on excessive state demand in addition to rigidity in collection of land revenue (even in times of partial failure of rains) coupled with a new and corrupt judicial and administrative set-up turned Indian rural economy upside down. The zamindars might have gained in certain areas, but the actual tillers of the soil suffered heavily and were pushed below the poverty line. Rural under development and backwardness is a legacy if British colonial rule.

Salt : The East India Company had the monopoly of trade in salt. The Government realised a large revenue from salt manufactured in Company's territory and imposed a heavy duty on salt manufactured in Indian Native states and imported into British territory. Salt was manufactured along the Coromandel and Malabar coasts by solar evaporation. Salt was manufactured by owners of the salt pans under licence from the Government, to whom they delivered the salt at prices fixed by the Company's government. The government sold the salt to wholesalers at a fixed price. The monopoly price was originally fixed about Rs. 7 per 100 lbs of salt, but was subsequently raised very substantially.

Bengal imported most of its salt requirements from the U.K. although the Madras government had surplus salt to export to Bengal, in spite of the fact that the salt imported from the U.K. was brought at a much higher price. The import of British salt into Calcutta increased from 502,616 maunds in 1845–46 to 1,850,762 maunds in 1851–52.

The high salt duty was the most obnoxious tax and its incidence was felt by the poorer sections of society. In 1850, the Madras Board of Revenue calculated that the poor labour nearly spent one month's wages every year to buy 18 lbs of salt per head needed for a family of six members.

The net revenue of the Company derived from salt-manufacture rose from £800,000 in 1793 to nearly £1,300,000 in 1844.

Opium : If the obnoxious salt duty yielded 7% of the total revenue of the state in 1858-59, the deadly opium duty added 17% of the total revenue in the same year.

---

2. Dutt, R.C. *The Economic History of India*, vol. II p. 108.

Opium was grown in British territories of Benaras and Patna and in some Indian states. The East India Company had the monopoly of opium trade grown in Benaras and Patna which it sold at a profit of more than 200 per cent. The governments of Bengal and Bombay also realised substantial revenue from transit duties. Another agonizing aspect of the opium trade was its forcible introduction in the market of Canton for sale in Chinese markets.

Organisation of the Civil Service : The organisation of an efficient Civil Service which worked according to set rules, in contrast to the personal rule of the monarch in pre- British times, was another feature of the administration of the English East India Company.

In the early days of the Company, the senior and junior merchants, factors and "writers" performed commercial as well as administrative functions. The Court of Directors exercised the patronage of nominating their favourites and not unoften their sons and those of their friends as Civil Servants. There are cases of civil posts being sold. Warren Hastings created highly paid posts which increased the cost of administration but did not improve efficiency or remove corruption. Lord Cornwallis took steps for Europeanization of the services. He further raised the pay scales of civil officials but did nothing to improve the method of selection and training of Civil Servants. Lord Wellesley took the first step for training of Civil Servants when he founded the fort William College, in Calcutta in November 1800 where the Civil Servants of the Company were to receive training in the literature, science and languages of India. The college did not find the favour of the Court of Directors and was continued merely as a language school for Bengal Civil Servants till 1854. In England, the Company in 1806 established the East India College at Haileybury for imparting a two years' training to the young officers appointed for service in the East.

The doors of the Company's Civil Servants were closed to Indians. However, the Charter Act of 1833 carried clause 87 which sought to remove colour bar in matter of appointments to Civil Services. All the same, in actual practice no Indian was appointed to Higher Civil Services. Even the famous Queen Victoria's Proclamation of 1858 which contained an assurance that "our subjects of whatever race or creed, be freely and impartially admitted to office in our service", did not materially change the policy of keeping the Civil Service of the Company as a close preserve of the British nationals. As a sop to Indian sentiments and to give a semblance of racial equality in Civil Services, the Company created the posts of Deputy Collector and Deputy Magistrate to which some Indians could hope to rise.

Judicial Reorganization : The English Indian Company acquired territories in India through various processes. The island of Bombay was obtained through cession in full sovereignty from the British Crown in 1868. On the Coromandal coast, the English Company acquired Madras and adjoining territories granted to it permanently and irrevocably by the nawab of Carnatic. In Bengal, the situation was very complex because of the Dual authority of the *diwani* system. Emperor Shah Alam II's firman granted to the Company in 1765 the Diwani of Bengal, Bihar and Orissa. As such, the Company was responsible for the Diwani functions only which included administration of civil justice also. The nawab of Bengal exercised the Nizamat functions which meant maintenance of law and order and administration of criminal justice.

The laws made for Bombay provided for religious toleration, trial by jury and the establishment of a Court of Judication. In 1718, the jury system was abolished and the appeals were to be made to the Governor and Council and the judges included a Hindu, a Muslim, a Parsi, a Portuguese and the Company's employees. In 1726, the Court of Directors sought the permission of the king of England to establish Mayor's Court; consequently three Mayor's Courts composed in each case of the Mayor and nine aldermen were established at Fort William (Calcutta), Madras and Bombay for trial of disputes between employees within these town and the dependent factories.

In the early stages of British conquest of India, the Company's authorities found not a unified but a diverse judicial system, Hindu and Muslim, operating in different parts of the country. Broadly

Changes in Administrative Structure and Policies Under the East India Company

speaking in pre-British India, the judicial set-up was a mix of Hindu law of the Shastras and Muslim Koranic law supplemented by customary law supported by the rulling power. The European merchant companies which established their factories and plantations in India could not easily accept the Muslim criminal law which provided for the amputation of limbs of the body or stoning of criminals as penalties; nor could they accept the principle that the evidence of an infidel (kafir) could not be recognised against a Mohammadan (the faithful) or that there should be a privileged law for the Brahmin alone. With the rise of national states in Europe, the concept of territoral and public law had developed in European national states. The European merchants companies had to apply a uniform legal system in the territories under their control. It was Warren Hastings who organised a rudimentary framework of the judicial system by setting up Diwani and Faujdari Adalats at the district level; appeals from these adalats could be made to the Sadar Diwani Adalat and Sadar Nizamat Adalat at Calcutta. However, it was Lord Cornwallis who improved and elaborated the system by setting up an hierarchy of courts, both for civil and criminal cases. In the district, at the lowest rung of the ladder were the Munsiff's Courts presided over by Indian officers competent to decide cases involving disputes up to 50 rupees; next came the Registrars' Courts presided over by European officers which tried cases upto 200 rupees; appeals from these courts lay to the District or City Courts. Appeals from District (Zilla) Courts lay to the four Provincial Courts. Next in order of gradation were the Sadar Diwani Adalat and Sadar Nizamat Adalat. In certain Diwani cases appeals could also be made to the Privy Council in England. The Cornwallis Code of 1793 gave the final shape to the judicial system which continued without many changes for long.

An Overview

The Rule of Law: The British deserve the credit for having introduced in India the modern concept of the rule of law. This meant the end of arbitrary authority exercised by the earlier rulers of India. A person could now know his rights and privileges and a set procedure was laid down for asserting them. However, in actual practice many instances of interference with the rights and provileges of the individuals took place. All the same, an opportunity was provided for bringing officers guilty of breach of law to the court.

(*ii*) **Equality before Law :** In the eyes of law all men were considered equal, irrespective of their religion, caste or class. This meant the end of the earlier practice of varying the law according to the class and status of the person, say between a Brahmin or a non-Brahmin or between a zamindar and a peasant. Henceforth, under British administration, the humblest of the humble could move the court for his legitimate rights. In actual practice, however, the principle of equality before law was violated when laws became complicated and beyond the grasp of uneducated poor masses; they had to engage lawyers who charged excessive fees and preferred to work for the rich; in addition, the prevalence of corruption in the administrative machinery and the police worked against the rights of the masses.

(*iii*) **Recognition of Personal Civil Law.** The Company's authorities recognised the rights of the various Indian communities — Hindu, Muslim, Parsi or Christian — to be judged by law of their community, particularly in matters connected with marriage, adoption, of joint family matters like succession and partition of property.

(*vi*) **Growth of trained judicial officers and professional lawyers :** In pre-British times, the landlords and the rulers played a notable role in deciding judicial disputes. In contrast, under Company's rule, written law (and later codified law) promoted confidence in the judicial system. The emergence of a professional class of lawyers trained to defend the rights of their clients augured in the modern system if judicial administration (of course, with all its limitations).

The Company's judicial system was praised because it was based on the principle of sovereignty of law, introduction of codified secular law and Western concept of justice. However, it produced many undesirable effects. The novel, unfamiliar and elaborate system was beyond the comprehension of the common man who could not hope for quick and cheap justice. Falsehood, chicanery and deceit began to yield dividends. Litigation increased and the professional lawyers exploited the uneducated persons involved in judicial disputes. Worst of all, the appointment of English judges saturated with racial complex and ignorant of Indian customs and habits proved very biased in disputes involving Indians vs Europeans and Anglo-Indians. All the same, it served the interests of the Company's authorities in collection of land revenue and other taxes and also in maintenance of law and order.

Changes in Economic Policy : During 1600-1757 the East India Company was merely a trading body which purchased Indian goods like cotton and silk cloth, handicrafts, spices etc. which it sold abroad in England and other foreign countries at a profitable price. Since India's demand for foreign goods was very limited, the Company mostly paid in gold and silver for purchase of Indian goods. Since the Company's trade was beneficial to India, the Indian rulers saw no objection in permitting the foreign companies in setting up their 'factories' (*i.e.,* godowns) in India. Rather, the British manufacturers urged the British Government to impose restrictions on the free import of Indian manufactures into England. After 1700, the British Government passed laws prohibiting the wear or use of printed or dyed Indian cloth.

The East India Company's victories in the battles of Plassey (1757), and Buxar (1764) brought about a change in the pattern of Company's trade with India. In 1765, Emperor Shah Alam II was forced to grant the *Diwani* of Bengal, Bihar and Orissa to the Company which become a source of great surplus income for the Company. In 1765 Lord Clive estimated the total revenue of Bengal at 4 millions which after defraying all administrative expenses would leave a net surplus income at £1,650,000. The quantum of surplus income increased year after year due to increase in rate of land revenue demand and ruthless method of collection of land revenue from the farmers. The 'surplus revenue' from Bengal was used by the Company as its 'investment' to purchase Indian goods for export from India. Obviously, the export of Indian good increased year after year but India as a country did not receive any imported goods or bullion in return. Hence, the process of 'drain of wealth' from India started.

The latter half of the 18th century witnessed the beginning of Industrial Revolution in England. A new capitalist class emerged which through the support of the ruling Whig Party brought about another shift in Company's economic policy in India. The powerful British industrial lobby exercised, considerable influence on the politics of England and it crusaded for abolition of the Company's monopoly rights of trade with India. Their efforts were successful when the Charter Act of 1813 abolished the Company's monopoly of trade with India except in tea and trade with China. The final blow was struck by the Charter Act of 1833 when the Company's monopoly of trade in tea and of trade with China was abolished and the Company was directed to close its commercial business as early as possible.

The rising British industrial class received a psychological boost from the writings of Adam Smith (1723-90), who is remembered as the father of the science of political economy. In his famous book *Wealth of Nations* (1776), he advocated that the policy of *laissez-faire* (free trade) helped in the economic development of all nations. It was under the impulse of this thinking that the British parliament passed the Charter Acts of 1813 and 1833 which abolished the monopoly rights of the East India Company in India and the East Indies. Further, the markets of India were thrown upon to British products almost free of all duties.

As far as India was concerned, Imperial Britain followed the policy of one way free trade *i.e.,* while Indian markets were thrown upon to British industrial products without any custom duties, British authorities imposed high custom duties on import of Indian hadicraft goods like cotton and silk fabrics. H.H. Wilson, the co-author of James Mill in *The History of India* has summed up the injustice of the discriminating treatment meted out to Indian trade by imperial Britain thus:

> "Had this not been the case, had not such prohibitory duties and decrees existed, the mills of Paisley and Manchester would have been stopped in their onset, and could

scarcely have again set in motion, even by the power of steam. They were created by the sacrifice of the Indian manufacture. Had Indian been independent, she would have retaliated, would have imposed prohibitive duties upon British goods, and would thus have preserved her own productive industry from annihilation. This act of self-defence was not permitted her, she was at the mercy of the stranger. British goods were forced upon her without paying any duty and the foreign manufacturer employed the arm of political injustice to keep down and ultimately strangle a competitor with whom he could not have contended on equal terms".

One cannot avoid the conclusion that in spite of all pious platitudes expressed by the British Government and Governor-General of India, the main thrust of Britain's economic policy in India was thorough economic exploitation of India. India was gradually transformed into an agrarian appendage of industrial Britain and in return providing a ready market for absorbing British manufactured products.

Social Legislation and Educational Policy : Till the English victories in the battles of Plassey (1757) and Buxar (1764), the Company was merely a trading body and could not possibly take interest in the social and educational fields. However, the various Christian missions—which had sometimes preceded and more often followed European Companies' trading activities in India– did comment on the Hindu and Muslim communities, social practices and religious beliefs. For example, some Baptist missionaries in a pamphlet entitled " Addresses to Hindus and Mohamedans" referred to Mohamed as a false prophet and denounced Hinduism as 'a mass of idolatry, superstition and ignorance'. The thrust of the missionary activities was to convert Hindus and Muslims to Christianity. The foreign-funded Missions also tried to allure the backward and weaker sections of Indian society by opening charity centres like dispensaries, orphan houses and even schools which provided free food, clothes and free education of Indian children.

The concept of British government's responsibility for the welfare of the Indian people they ruled emerged during the Dual System of government in Bengal 1765–1772 when the servants of Company, from the Governor to the lowest clerk, indulged in an "open and unashamed plunder" of Bengal, Bihar and Orissa. In 1769, Richard Becher, a servant of the Company wrote to the Court of Directors, "It must give pain to an Englishman to have reason to think that since the accession of the Company to the Diwani (1765) the condition of the people of this country has been worse than it was before... this fine country which flourished under the most despotic and arbitrary government, is verging towards its ruin", Willian Bolts, a contemporary writer in his book *Consideration on Indian Affairs* referred to the roguery and oppression practised against the weavers. Even the great contemporary economist Adam Smith referred to the Company's *"plundering"* role in India and even labelled the Court of Proprietors as the board "for appointment of plunderers of India". In 1772, Lord North, the British Prime Minister appointed two committees, a Select and a Secret Parliamentary committee to probe into the working of the Company in India. Both the committees recommended that trade must be separated from law and sovereignty *i.e.,* the sovereignty of the Parliament must be asserted in the governance of India. In other words, by the following Regulating Act of 1773 the British Crown accepted powers and responsiblity (though partial) for administration of the Company's territories in India and the process countinued under subsequent Pitt's India Act and other Charter Acts.

In 1808, the Court of Directors sent a despatch to Lord Minto (Governor-General 1807–13) reiterating the Company's policy of non-interference in the socio-religious beliefs of the people living in the Company's territories. The obvious instruction to the Governor-General was to restrain the Christian Missions from their proselytizing activites. The Charter Act of 1813 struck a different note when it lifted all restrictions on the entry of missionaries of the U.K. into India. In addition, some of the Company's servants — both civil and military — began propagation of England's 'Christian Duty' in India in the field of both social and religious reform.

A new pro socio-religious thrust came with the change of political and intellectual environment in contemporary England. The Tory party was out and the progressive Whig party (referred to as the Liberal party after 1834) came into power under the leadership of Lord Grey. The Benthamities (Philosophical Radicals) and Humanitarian became active in the matter of reform of abuses, old and new, both in England and her overseas colonies including India. In England, the Age of Reform began with the enactment of first Parliamentary Reform Act (1832), Abolition of Slavery (1833), the Factory Act (1833), the New Poor Law Act (1834), followed by Municipal Reform Act and the Education Act.

The Court of Directors gauged the progressive mood of the Parliament and could hope for renewal of the Charter of Company due in 1833 only if it could present the pro-reform postures and policies of the East India Company in India. As such, the Court of Directors advised Lord William Bentinck (Governor-General, 1828–35) to act fast and remove the most conspicious abuses in Hindu society. Thus (in the environment of reform) Regulation XVII of 4 Dec., 1829 declared practice of *Sati* illegal in Bengal Presidency and in 1834 its operation was extended to Madras and Bombay presidencies; Infanticide had already been declared illegal by Bangal Regulations of 1795 and 1804 but its strict enforcement was given due attention. The question of Widows' Remarriage was carried out by Act of 1856 which legalized marriage of widows and declared issues from such marriages as legitimate. Attention was also given to education of women.[3] The process thus started was carried out under the Crown administration after 1858.

Changes in Education Policy : Both the European and Indian Social reformers believed that social evils in society could not be eradicated by legislation alone. A sound system of modern education alone could create awareness about deficiencies in our outdated and irrational social practices and generate the urge for efforts to bring about equality between man and woman and a better deal for children in society. The Medieval system of education in India was mostly based on study of religious scriptures and philosophical thought and texts were crammed rather than understood; as such the spirit of enquiry, scientific outlook and rationalism did not develop much in India.

The Western Christian Missions were pioneers in the field of introduction of Modern system of education in India. The first printing press in India was set up by the Portuguese Christian Missionaries at Goa in 1556. The missionaries of various European countries also set up school and published several literary works. The Danish missionaries even published a Tamil dictionary. All the same, it must be mentioned that the efforts of the Christian missionaries were directed towards using education, not as an end in itself, but as means to evangelization.

As explained earlier, the English Company's authorities did not accept responsibility for the education of the people living in Company's administrative territories in the 18th century. All the same, the Company's government set up the Calcutta Madras (1781), followed by a Sanskrit College (1792) at Benaras. However, a body of reformers in Bengal, who no doubt admitted the value of Oriental learning, but believed that better results could be achieved through a knowledge of English language and Western literature available in English. The most conspicuous among them was Raja Rammohan Roy, who joined hands with David Hare and with the help of Sir Edward Hyde East, (the Chief Justice of Bengal) founded in March 1817 the Hindu College at Calcutta. Another, extreme pro-Western wing popularly known as Young Bengal Group crusaded for the acceptance of the West in toto *i.e.* Western thought, social values, great veneration for Christianity and in general a great disgust for Eastern culture and Indian religions.

It is believed that under the pressure of missionary lobby in England, the British Parliament, while renewing the Charter of the Company, inserted a provision in the Charter Act 1813 that the Company would set apart annualy a sum of rupees one lakh for the encouragement of education amont the inhabitants of the British territories in India.

---

3. For details of social reforms see Chapter XXXI.

Orientalist-Anglicist Controversy : Till 1823, the educational clause of the Charter Act of 1813 remained unimplemented. However, in 1823 a General Committee of Public Instruction was set up to take charge of government educational and utilise the educational grants. Unfortunately, the ten members of the General Committee of Public Instruction were divided into equal groups, viz., the Orientalists (who advocated the utilisation of funds for promotion of oriental subjects) and the Anglicists (who crusaded for the cause of Western Sciences and Western literaure through the medium of English langulage). The stalemate continued till Lord William Bantinck, the Governor-General appointed G.B. Macaulay as the Chairman of the Committee. Macaulay's famous minute dated 2 February, 1835 advocated the Anglicists' point of view. Lord William Bentinck's government passed a resolution on 7 March 1835 which declared the Government's orders that henceforth government funds would be utilised for "promotion of European literature and science" through the medium of English language. A further Government notification of 1838 made it clear that henceforth no funds would be made available for oriental learning.

Wood's Education Despatch of 1854 : In 1854 Sir Charles Wood, President of the Board of Control and later the first Secretary of State for India, sent a comprehensive Despatch on Education to the Government of India in which he recommended "a property articulated scheme of education from the primary school to the University" for the whole of British India. The Despatch reiterated that (a) the aim of education in India was to be diffusion of European languages (b) through the medium of both English and Indian languages. In brief, it recommended medium of instruction to be vernacular languages at the primary level, followed by Anglo-vernacular schools at the middle and high school levels and education through the English medium at College and University levels. It also recommended the setting up of universities at Calcutta, Bombay and Madras on the model of the London University.

Linkages between Educational Policies and British Colonial interests: The British imperial authorities (the Home Government in London and the Company's authorities in India) favoured the Western System of education through the medium of English language out of administrative compulsions. Apart from this aspect, the moral, political and commercial considerations also favoured the Macaulayian system of education.

As the British Empire in India expanded its territories, the administrative needs of the Company also increased. In the Revenue and Judicial departments, the clercial and middle level of staff was required to have apart from knowledge of Persian and vernaculars, a working knowledge of English language. Besides the salaries paid to India employees were a fraction of the salaries at which European staff could be available.

The moral considerations were linked with the spread of Christianity. Alexander Duff considered education as the soundest weapon for attracting heathens to Christianity. G.B. Maucaulay shared Duff's ideas when he wrote to his father: "No Hindu who has received English education ever remains attached to his religion. It is my firm belief that if plans of education are followed up, there will not be a single idolator among the respectable classes in Bengal thirty years hence".

Macaulay's hope that the spread of Western knowledge would win converts to Christianity did not materialize though some converts from upper classes were made. In fact, Duff and Macaulay failed to understand the flexibility and profundity of Hinduism.

Politically, the newly-educated Western educated class — whether in Government service or in the new professions of lawyers, engineers, doctors, teachers etc.— unconsciously or consciously become supporters of British rule in India, for their interests were linked with the continuation of British rule in India. Thus, Macaulary's dream of creating a class of persons who would be "Indians in blood and colour, but English in taste, in opinion, in morals and intellect" did materialize. These "Brown Englishmen" believed that India's progress was inexorably linked to the continuation of British rule.

The British commercial community both in Calcutta and in Britain became strong supporters of the cause of anglicization of education in India. The English-educated Indian middle class not only helped in exploitation of India's natural resources but became the great consumers of British goods from neckties to shoes. G.B. Macaulay in a speech in the House of Commons in 1833 emphasised the economic advantage thus:

"The mere extent of empire is not necessarily an advantage... It would be, on the most selfish view of the case, far better for us that the people of India were well-governed and independent of us, than ill-governed and subject to us; that they were ruled by their own kings, but wearing our broadcloth, and working with our cutlery, than that they were performing their *salaams* to English Collectors and English Magistrates but were too ignorant to value or too poor to buy English manufactures."

SELECT REFERENCES

1. Griffiths, P. : *The British Impact on India.*
2. Kaye, Sir John : *Administration of the East India Company.*
3. Mishra, B.B. : *The Central Administration of the East India Company.*
4. Stratchey, Sir John : *India, its Administration and Progress.*

Tribal Revolts, Civil Rebellions, Popular Movements and Mutinies, 1757–1856

The century after 1757 witnessed a number of popular mobilizations, revolts and mutinies against foreign rule and its attendant evils. The pinch of the loss of independence, foreign intrusion into local autonomy, introduction of administrative innovations, excessive land revenue demands dislocation of economy was felt in different regions of India at different points of time and as such caused disturbances mostly of a local nature.

Revolts in Bengal and Eastern India

The Sanyasi Revolt. The establishment of British rule in Bengal after 1757 and the new economic order it brought spelt ruin on zamindars, peasants, and artisans alike. The famine of 1770 and the callousness on the part of the Company's stooges was seen as a direct impact of alien rule. The restrictions imposed on visits to holy places estranged the *sanyasis*. The *sanyasis*, with a tradition of fighting against oppression, espoused the popular cause and organised raids on the Company's factories, state treasuries and valiantly fought against the Company's armed forces. Only after prolonged military action could Warren Hastings contain *sanyasi* raids.

Chuar and Ho Risings. Famine, enhanced land revenue demands and economic distress goaded the Chuar aboriginal tribesmen of Midnapur district to take up arms. The Rajas of Dhalbhum, Kailapal, Dholka and Barabhum organised a revolt in 1768 and followed a scorched-earth policy. The disturbed conditions continued till the end of the century.

The Ho and Munda tribesmen of Chhota Nagpur and Singhbhum had their own scores to settle. They challenged the Company's forces in 1820–22, again in 1831 and the area remained disturbed till 1837.

Kol Risings. The Kols of Chhotanagpur resented the transfer of land from Kol headmen (Mundas) to outsiders like Sikh and Muslim farmers. In 1831 the Kol rebels killed or burnt about a thousand outsiders. The rebellion spread to Ranchi, Singhbhum, Hazaribagh, Palamau and western parts of Manbhum. Order could be restored only after large-scale military operations.

Santhal Risings. The Santhals of Rajmahal hills resented the ill-treatment at the hands of revenue officials, oppression of the police and exactions of the landlords and the money-lenders. The Santhals rebelled in 1855 under the leadership of Sidhu and Kanhu, declared the end of the Company's rule and declared themselves independent. Extensive military operations brought the situation under control in 1856. The Government pacified the Santhals by creating a separate district of Santhal Parganas.

The Ahoms' Revolt. The Ahom nobility in Assam accused the Company's authorities of non-fulfilment of pledges of withdrawal from their territory after the conclusion of the Burman war. The attempt of the English to incorporate the Ahoms' territory in the Company's dominion sparked off a rebellion. In 1828 the Ahoms proclaimed Gomdhar Konwar as their king and planned a march to Rangpur. The superior military power of the Company aborted the move. A second revolt was planned in 1830. The Company followed a pacific policy and in 1833 handed over upper Assam to Maharaja Purander Singh Narendra and a part of the kingdom was restored to the Assamese Raja.

Khasi Rising. The East India Company occupied the hilly region between Jaintia in the east and Garo hills in the west. The English also planned a military road to link up the Brahmaputra valley with Sylhet and brought a large number of Englishmen, Bengalis and other labour to complete the project.

Tirat Singh, the ruler of Nunklow, resented the intrusion into his territories, won over the support of the Garos, the Khamptis and Singhpos in a bid to drive away the lowland strangers. The insurrection developed into popular revolt against British rule in the area. The superior English military force suppressed the revolt in 1833.

Pagal Panthis' and Faraizis' Revolts. Pagal Panthis, a semi-religious sect founded by Karam Shah, lived in the northern districts of Bengal. Tipu, the son and successor of Karam Shah, was inspired both by religious and political motives. He took up the cause of the tenants against the oppressions of the zamindars. In 1825 Tipu captured Sherpur and assumed royal power. The insurgents spread their activities to the Garo hills. The area remained disturbed in the 1830s and 1840.

The Faraizis were followers of a Muslim sect founded by Haji Shariatullah of Faridpur in Eastern Bengal. They advocated radical religious, social and political changes. Shariatullah's son Dadu Mian (1819–60) took upon himself to expel the English intruders from Bengal. The sect supported the cause of the tenants against the exactions of the zamindars. The Faraizi disturbances continued from 1838 to 1857. Most of the Faraizis joined the ranks of the Wahabis.

Revolts in Western India

Bhil Risings. The Bhils, an aboriginal tribe, live in the Western Ghats with their strongholds in Khandesh. During 1817–19 the Bhils revolted against their new masters, the English East India Company. The Company's authorities alleged that the revolts had been encouraged by Peshwa Baji II and his lieutenant Trimbakji Danglia. Agrarian hardships and fear of the worst under the new regime were their apprehensions. Several British detachments ruthlessly crushed the revolt. However, the Bhils were far from being pacified. Encouraged by the British reverses in the Burman war, the Bhils under their leader Sewram again revolted in 1825. The trouble erupted in 1831 and again in 1846 signifying the popular character of the discontent

Koli Risings. The Kolis, living in the neighbourhood of the Bhils, also resented the imposition of British rule and dismantlement of their forts. The new order of administration set up by the Company caused widespread unemployment. The Kolis rose in rebellion in 1829, in 1839 and once again during 1844–48.

The Cutch Rebellion. Anti-British sentiments prevailed in the Cutch and Kathiawar areas. The struggle between the Cutch ruler, Rao Bharmal and the pro-**Jhareja** chiefs was at the root of the trouble. In 1819 a British force defeated and deposed Rao Bharmal in favour of his infant son. The actual administration of Cutch was committed to the care of a Council of Regency under the superintendence of the British Resident. The administrative innovations made by the Regency Council coupled with excessive land assessment caused deep resentment. The news of the English reverses in the Burman war emboldened the chiefs to rise in revolt and demand the restoration of Bharmal. Extensive military operations had to be undertaken. The trouble erupted again in 1831. The company's authorities were compelled to follow a conciliatory policy.

Waghera Rising. The Wagheras of Okha Mandal resented the impositions of foreign rule from the very beginning. The exactions of the Gaekwar of Baroda supported by the British Government compelled the Waghera chief to take up arms. The Wagheras carried on inroads into British territory during 1818–19. A peace treaty was concluded in November 1820.

Surat Salt Agitation. Surat had a long history of opposition to unpopular measures. The raising of salt duty from 50 paise to one rupee in 1844, caused great discontent among the people. Soon the anti-Government spirit turned into a strong anti-British spirit. Some Europeans were attacked. Faced with a popular movement the Government withdrew the additional salt levy. Similarly in 1848 the Government's decision to introduce Bengal Standard Weights and Measures had to be withdrawn against the people's determined bid to resort to boycott and passive resistance.

Ramosi Risings. The Ramosis, the hill tribes in the Western Ghats, were not reconciled to British rule and the British pattern of administration. In 1822 their leader Chittur Singh revolted and plundered the country around Satara. There were eruptions again during 1825–26 and the area remained disturbed till 1829.

The deposition and banishment of Raja Pratap Singh of Satara in September 1839 caused widespread resentment in the area and a chain of disturbances occurred during 1840–41. Narsingrao Dattatraya Petkar collected a sizable number of troops, captured the fort of Badami and hoisted the flag of the Raja of Satara. A superior British force restored order in the area.

Kolhapur and Savantvadi Revolts. The hardships caused by administrative reorganisation in the Kolhapur state after 1844 caused deep resentment. The *Godkaris* (the hereditary military class which garrisoned Maratha forts) were disbanded. Faced with the spectre of unemployment the *Godkaris* rose in revolt and occupied the forts of Samangarh and Bhudargarh. Similarly, the simmering discontent caused a revolt in Savantvadi.

Revolts in the South India

The Revolt of the Raja of Vizianagaram. The East India Company acted in a very high-handed manner after acquisition of the Northern Sarkars in 1765. It demanded a present of three lakhs from the Raja apart from ordering him to disband his troops. On the Raja's refusal, his estate was annexed. This was a signal for a revolt in which the Raja received full support of his people and his troops. The Raja lost his life in a battle in 1794. Wisdom dawned on the Company's authorities who offered the estate to the deceased Raja's son and also reduced the demand for presents.

Similarly the *poligars* of Dindigul and Malabar took up arms against the evils of the English land revenue system. During 1801–5 the *poligars* of the Ceded Districts and North Arcot revolted against the Company. Sporadic risings of the *poligars* in the Madras Presidency continued up to 1856.

Diwani Velu Tampi's Revolt. In 1805 Wellesely imposed a subsidiary alliance treaty on the ruler of Travancore. Resentful of the harsh terms imposed on the State, the ruler did not pay the subsidy and fell in arrears. The overbearing attitude of the British Resident caused deep resentment and Diwan Vela Tampi raised the banner of revolt with the support of the Nair battalion. A large British force had to be deployed to meet the situation and restore peace.

THE WAHABI MOVEMENT

The Wahabi movement offered the most serious and well-planned challenge to British supremacy in India from 1830s to 1860. Syed Ahmad of Rae Bareli (1786–1831), the leader of this movement in India was influenced by the teaching of Abdul Wahab (1703–87) of Arbia, but even more by the preaching of the Delhi saint Shah Waliullah (1702–62). Syed Ahmed condemned all accretions to and innovations in Islam and advocated a return to the pure Islam and society of Arabia of the Prophet's times. The Wahabi movement was basically a revivalist movement.

For the achievement of the desired objectives, Syed Ahmad looked for (*a*) the right leader, (*b*) a proper organisation and (*c*) a safe territory wherefrom to launch his *jihad*. Syed Ahmad was acclaimed as the desired leader (the *Imam*), a country-wide organisation with an elaborate secret code for its working under four spiritual vice regents (*Khalifas*) was set on foot and Sithana (in *Darul-Islam*) in the North-Western tribal belt was at Patna though it had its missions in Hyderabad, Madras, Bengal, Uttar Pradesh and Bombay.

Since *Dar-ul-Harb* (The world of Kafirs) was to be converted into *Dar-ul-Islam* (The world of Islam) a *jihad* was declared against the Sikh kingdom of the Panjab. Peshawar was captured in 1830, but lost to the Sikhs the following year with Syed Ahmad losing his life in action. After the overthrow of the Sikh ruler and incorporation of the Panjab into the East India Company's dominion in 1849 the sole target of the Wahabis' attack became the English dominion in India.

During the Revolt of 1857 the Wahabis played a notable role in spreading anti-British sentiments but their exact participation in anti-British military activities has not been identified so far.

The British rulers of India viewed the potential danger of the Wahabis' base of operations from Sithana in the background of a possible war between Great Britain getting involved in a war with Afghanistan or Russia. In the 1860s the Government launched a multi-pronged attack by organising a series of military operations on the Wahabi base of operations in Sithana (aided and abetted by the frontier tribesmen) while in India a number of court cases for sedition were registered against Wahabis. The movement lost its vitality though the Wahabi fanatics continued to help the frontier hill tribes in their encounters with the English in the 1880s and 1890s.

The Wahabi movement was a movement of the Muslims, by the Muslims and for the Muslims and aimed at the establishment of *Dar-ul-Islam* in India. At no stage did it assume the character of a nationalist movement. Rather it left behind a legacy of isolationist and separatist tendencies among the Indian Muslims.

SEPOY MUTINIES

The East India Company needed a large army to pursue its plans of territorial aggrandizement in India. Its demands for recruits increased as its plans for expansion outside the boundaries of India and for imperial purposes took shape. However, the sepoys found that their pay, allowances and terms of service worsened as they conquered more and more territories for their masters. Further, the sepoys shared all the discontent and grievances—social, religious and economic—that afflicted the civilian population.

1764—A battalion of Munro's army at the battlefield of Baksar deserted to Mir Kasim.

1806—Mutiny at Vellore in protest against interference in the social and religious practices of the sepoys. The sepoys unfurled the flag of the ruler of Mysore.

1824—47th Native infantry unit mutinied when ordered to proceed to Burma without adequate overseas allowances.

1825—The Grenadier Company in Assam mutinied.

1838—An Indian regiment at Sholapur mutinied for nonpayment of full *bhatta*.

1844—34 N. I. and 64th regiment joined by some others refused to proceed to Sind without old pecuniary benefits.

1849–50—There was mutinous spirit in the Company's army of occupation in the Panjab. The regiment at Govindgarh mutinied in 1850.

SELECT REFERENCES

1. Datta, K. K.   :   *Anti-British Plots and Movement before 1857.*
2. Datta, K. K.   :   *Santhal Rebellion.*
3. Majumdar, R. C. (Ed.) :   *British Paramountcy and Indian Renaissance,* vol. IX.
4. Chaudhuri, S. B.   :   *Civil Disturbances under British Rule, 1757–1857.*

THE REVOLT OF 1857

> It was far more than a mutiny...... yet much less than a first war of independence.
>
> —*Stanley Wolpert*

> At the time many British people preferred to see the events largely as a military mutiny—understandably as any wider interpretation would have cast doubts on the nature of the *Raj*.
>
> —*Judith Brown*

The record of the East India Company had been of ever increasing conquest and commercial exploitation. The greed of the Englishman knew no limits. The cumulative effect of British expansionist policies, economic exploitation. and administrative innovations over the year had adversely affected the position of all—rulers of Indian states, sepoys, zamindars, peasants, traders, pundits, moulvies etc., excepting, of course, the Western educated class in towns who owed their 'position' to the Company's Government. The Lucknow Proclamation pinpointed that British rule had endangered all the four things dear to Hindus and Muslims alike—religion, honour, life and property. The resentment of the Indians had found expression in a number of mutinies and insurrections from time to time in different parts of the country; to mention only a few, the mutiny at Vellore in 1806, at Barrackpore in 1824, at Ferozepur in February 1842 closely followed by the mutiny of 7th Bengal Cavalry and 64th Regiment, 22nd mutiny of 22nd N.I. in 1849, of the 66th N.I. in 1850, the 38th N. I. in 1852 etc., the Bareilly rising of 1816, the Kol insurrection of 1931–32, the 1848 revolt of the Rajas of Kangra, Jaswar and Datarpur, the Santhal rising of 1855–56 etc., which arose out of a wide range of political, economic and administrative causes. The simmering discontent burst out into a violent storm in 1857 which shook the British empire in India to its very foundations.

Nature and Character of the Revolt

Historians have held divergent view about the nature of the outbreak of 1857, British historians like Kaye, Malleson, Trevelyan, Lawrence, Holmes have painted it as 'a mutiny' confined to the army which did not command the support of the people at large. A similar view was held by many contemporary Indians like Munshi Jiwan Lal, Moinuddin (both eye-witnesses at Delhi), Durgadas Bandyopadhyaya (eye-witness at Bareilly), Sir Syed Ahmad Khan (Sadr Amin at Bijnor in 1857) among many others. Others described it as a 'religious war against the Christians' or ' a racial struggle for supremacy between the Black and the White.' Still others described 'a struggled between Oriental and Occidental civilization and culture'. A few described it the result of ' Hindu-Muslim conspiracy to overthrow the British rule'. Some Indian nationalists have called it a well-planned national struggle and as 'the first war of Indian independence'.

Sir John Lawrence and Seeley thought it to be a Sepoy's Mutiny and nothing more. Sir John Seeley describes the Revolt of 1857 as a 'wholly unpatriotic and selfish Sepoy Mutiny with no native leadership and no popular support'. According to him, it was a rebellion of the Indian sepoys against the constituted government of the day. Some Indian states, it is conceded, also joined in the revolt but these were states which nursed a grievance because of the annexation policy of Lord Dalhousie. The British Government, as the constituted authority of the land suppressed the revolt and restored law and order. The interpretation is unsatisfactory. Unquestionably, the Revolt began as a military rising, but it was not everywhere confined to the army. Even the army as a whole did not join the revolt, and a considerable section fought on the side of the government. In fact the rebels came from almost every section of the population. In Oudh it enjoyed the support of the masses and so also in some districts of Bihar. In the trials of 1858–59 thousands of civilians, along with the soldiers, were held guilty of rebellion and punished.

It is difficult to agree with L. E. R. Rees that the Revolt was 'a war of fanatic religionists against Christians.' During the heat of the rebellion the ethical principles underlying the various religions had little influence on the combatants. Both sides quoted their religious scriptures to cover their combatants. Both sides quoted their religious scriptures to cover their excesses over the other party. The Christians ultimately won but not Christianity. The Hindus and Muslims were defeated but not their respective religions. True, Christianity like Western science has influenced the Indian mind but the Christian missionaries had no astounding success in the work of proselytization.

Nor was it 'a war of races, a struggle between the White and the Black. True, all the Whites in India, whatever their nationality, were ranged on one side, but not all the Blacks. As Captain J.G. Medley point out : "In fact (counting the camp-followers) for every white man in camp there certainly twenty black ones". In the British war-camps Indians served as cooks and looked after the comforts of the soldiers. It were the black palanquin-bearers who carried the white wounded soldiers out of the danger zone. Leaving the non-combatants out of account there was a high proportion of Indian soldiers in the Company's army that took part in the suppression of the rebellion. To be more correct, it was a war between the Blacks rebels on one side and the White rulers supported by other Black on the other side.

Some English historian led by T. R. Holmes popularized the view that the Revolt of 1857 was a conflict between civilization and barbarism.' The explanation smacks of narrow racialism. During the rebellion both the Europeans and the Indians were guilty of excesses.[1] If the Indians were guilty of the murder of European women and in some cases children in Delhi, Kanpur and Lucknow, the record of the British was equally tarnished by dark deeds which were no less and barbaric that those of the Indians. Hodson indulged in indiscriminate shooting at Delhi. Neill took pride in the fact that he hanged hundreds of Indians without any trial whatsoever. Around Allahabad there was hardly a single tree which was not used as a gallows for unfortunate peasants. At Banaras even the street urchins were caught and hanged. Russell, the correspondent of *The Times,* mentions that Muslim noblemen were sewn alive in pig-skin and pork was forced down their gullets. In fact, vendetta took the better of men on both sides. No nation or individual which indulges in such horrible atrocities can claim to be civilised.

Sir James Outram and W. Tayler described the outbreak as the result of Hindu-Muslim conspiracy. Outram held "it was a Mohammedan conspiracy making capital of Hindu grievances". The explanation is inadequate and unsatisfactory.

Benjamin Disraeli, a contemporary conservative leader in England, described it 'a national rising'. He contended that the so-called Mutiny was 'no sudden impulse but was the result of careful combinations, vigilant and well-organised, on the watch for an opportunity... the decline and fall of empires are not affairs of greased cartridges... such rebellions are occasioned by adequate causes and accumulation of adequate causes.'

Early national leaders, looking for ideals to arouse national consciousness among the people, reinterpreted the uprising of 1857 as a people's revolt and its leaders as national heroes gifted with the vision of a free India. The lead was taken by V. D. Savarkar who in his book *The Indian War of Indpendence,* published in London in 1909, described it " a planned war of national independence" and tried to prove that the rising of 1826–27. 1831–32, 1848, 1854 were rehearsals of the great drama played in 1857. Later national leaders further developed the theme of the popular character of the

---

1. For Karl Marx's observations see Appendix C.

Revolt and cited it as a shining example of the perfect accord and harmony between the Hindus and the Muslims in the fight for freedom from British yoke[2]. In 1957 the people of India celebrated the centenary of the events of 1857 with the fervour and enthusiasm as if it was a war of independence.

Recently two distinguished Indian historians, Dr. R. C. Majumdar and Dr. S. N. Sen, have made an exhaustive study of all available records, official as well as non-official. The two scholars differ in their interpretation of the events of 1857–1858. Both the scholars, however, agree that the uprising of 1857 was not the result of careful planning nor were there any master minds behind it. The mere fact that Nana Sahib went to Lucknow and Ambala in March-April 1857 and the struggle started in May of the same year cannot be regarded as evidence that he planned it. The view that Munshi Azim Ullah Khan and Rango Bapuji prepared the plans for the uprising is untenable. Azim Ullah Khan and gone to London to plead before the Court of Directors the right of Nana Sahib for the pension paid to Baji Rao II. On his way back he visited Turkey and met Omar Pasha on battlefield of Crimea. Rango Bapuji was sent to London to secure the rendition of Satara. The fact that both had been in London on missions cannot be regarded as pointing to their participation in the conspiracy. Even the story of the circulation of messages through *chapatis* or lotus flowers does not prove anything. During the trial of Bahadur shah efforts were evidence collected did not convince even the British officers. In fact, the course of the trial made it clear that the uprising was as much a surprise to Bahadur Shah as to the British.

Again, both Dr. Majumdar and Dr. Sen agree that in middle of the nineteenth century Indian nationalism was in an embryo from. "India in the first half of the nineteenth century" asserts Dr. Sen, "was a geographical expression". In 1857 the Bengalis, the Panjabis, the Hindustanis, the Maharastrians, the Madrasis never realised that they belonged to the same nation. The leader of the, Rebellion were no 'national' leaders. Bahadur Shah was no 'national' king. He was compelled by the soldiers to assume their leadership. Nana Sahib raised the banner of revolt only after his envoy in London had failed to get for him the pension of Baji Rao II. Even after the revolt had begun he declared that he would come to terms with the English if only pension was sanctioned. The trouble in Jhansi was over the right of succession and annexation. The Rani's slogan was *"mera Jhansi, deyugi nahin."* No doubt, the Rani died a hero's death, but at no stage did she indicate that her cause was the cause of the nation. The Nawab of Oudh, a worthless debauchee, could never aspire to national leadership. The taluqdars of Oudh fought for their feudal privileges and for their king, not for any national cause. Most of the leaders were mutually jealous and messes was no better. The majority of the people remained apathetic and neutral. The movement failed to enlist popular support except in Oudh and Shahabad district of Bihar. Nationalism, as it is understood today, had yet to come.

R. C. Majumdar gave his analysis of the revolt of 1857 in his book entitled *The Sepoy Mutiny and the Revolt of 1857*. Subsequently he elaborated some of his arguments in the chapters he contributed to the Bhartiya Vidya Bhavan's *British Paramountcy and the Indian Renaissance,* vol. ix. The main trust of Majumdar's argument is the uprising of 1857 was not a war of independence. He maintains that the Revolt took different aspects at different places. In some regions (like large parts of Madhya Pradesh and the Panjab) it was a mutiny of sepoys joined later by disgruntled elements eager to take advantage of anarchy; in other area (like the U. P., some parts of Madhya Pradesh and western parts of Bihar) the mutiny of sepoys was followed by a general revolt in which apart from the soldiers, civilians, particularly the dispossessed rulers of Indian states, landlords, tenants and others took part; in still other parts of the country (like Rajasthan and Maharashtra) the civil population sympathised with the rebels but kept themselves within bounds of law and did not take part in overt acts of rebellion.

---

2. The struggle of 1857 took a national and racial but not a communal turn. In the fight for freedom, Hindus and Muslims stood shoulder to shoulder. Their common effort was to liberate themselves from the British yoke. (Maulana A. K. Azad's Foreword in S. N. Sen's *Eighteen Fifty Seven*, p. xviii).

R. C. Majumdar stresses the point that the most important elements who fought against the British were the sepoys. The sepoys had their own grievances, similar to those which had led them to local mutinies on many previous occasions. He contends that the sepoys were mostly inspired by the desire of material gain than any political or even religious considerations. The sepoys at Delhi, Bareilly and Allahabad indulged in plunder and loot and both Europeans and Indians were their victims. These soldiers inspired a sense of dread and terror rather than that of sympathy and fellow-feeling among the people. The sepoys at Delhi refused to fight unless their salaries were paid. Dr. Majumdar comes to the conclusion that " there is nothing in the conduct or behaviour of the sepoys which would justify us in the belief or even assumption, that they were inspired by love for their country of fought against the British with the definite idea of freeing their motherland."

Dr. Majumdar, however, underlines another facet of the Revolt of 1857. He maintains that its national importance was indirect and posterior. He writes: "It has been said that Julius Caesar dead was more powerful than when he was alive. The same thing may be said about the Mutiny of 1857. Whatever might have been its original character, it soon became a symbol of challenge to the mighty British power in India. It remained a shining example before nascent nationalism in India in its struggle for freedom from the British yoke, and was invested with the full glory of the first national war of independence against the British."

Dr. S. N. Sen believes that the rising of 1857 was a war of independence. He contends that revolutions are mostly the work of a minority, with or without the active sympathy of the masses. Such was the case with the American Revolution of 1775–83 and the French Revolution. A very large percentage of American settlers remained loyal to the British crown and about 60,000 of them emigrated to Canada after the war was over. Similarly, in Revolutionary France there many royalists. Dr. Sen contends that when a rebellion can claim the sympathies of the substantial majority of the population, it can claim a national character. Unfortunately in India the majority of the people remained disinterested and even apathetic. The Rebellion of 1857 cannot be invested with a national character. However, it was not merely a military and even apathetic. The Rebellion of 1857 cannot be invested with a national character. However, it was not merely a military rising. Dr. Sen comes to the conclusion: "The Mutiny became a revolt and assumed a political character when the mutineers of Meerut placed themselves under the King of Delhi and a section of the landed aristocracy and civil population declared in his favour. What began as a fight for religion ended as a war of independence for there is not the slightest doubt that the rebels wanted to get rid of the alien government and restore the old order of which the king of Delhi was the rightful representative."

Another Indian scholar, Dr. S. B. Chaudhuri, in his book *Civil Rebellions in the Indian Mutinies, 1857–59* has confined his attention to the detailed analysis of the civil rebellions which accompanied the military insurrection of 1857. Dr. Chaudhuri maintains that the revolt of 1857 can be bifurcated into two sub-divisions, mutiny and rebellion. He believes that the outburst of 1857 was the coming together of two series of disturbances, the military and the civil, each provoked by independent grievances. Dr. R. C. Majumdar, however, maintains that the outbreaks before 1857, whether civil or military, were "a series of links following one single chain—the isolated ebullitions which culminated in the great conflagration of 1857."

The Marxist interpretation of the Revolt of 1857 as the struggle of the soldier-peasant democratic combine against foreign as well as feudal bondage which failed because of feudal betrayal goes off the mark. There seems to have been no ideology or programme behind their revolt except local grievances or anti-British sentiments.

An Overview

There are as many interpretations of the Revolt of 1857 as there are writers on it.

There is a broad general consensus among historians that in the middle of the 19th century conception of nationality—if nationalism is taken in the modern sense—was in embryo, Prof. S. N. Sen remarks that Indian in 1857 was "a geographical expression" and the Bengalees, the Punjabis, the

Hindustanis, the Maharastrians and the people in the south did not realise that they belonged to the same nation.

Was the Mutiny and Revolt of 1857 a War of Independence? Pt. Jawaharlal Nehru wrote: "Essentially it was a feudal outburst headed by feudal chiefs and their followers and aided by the widespread anti-foreign sentiment."[3] Nehru refers to the rural base of the Revolt and points out that even the feudal chiefs were unorganised and had no constructive ideal or community of interests[4]. The rulers of princely States as a whole kept aloof or helped the British, fearing to risk what they had acquired or managed to retain. Prof. R. C. Majumdar argues that some segments of Indian society in many parts of India fought against the British, but their motives seems to have material interest and religious considerations and in very few individual cases the rulers were moved by the disinterested and patriotic motive of freeing the country from the yoke of imperial British rule. Majumdar concludes : "It is difficult to avoid the conclusion that the so-called First National War of Independence of 1857 is neither First, nor National nor War of Independence".[5]

Prof. S.N. Sen looks upon the events of 1857 in the broader perspective and argues that revolts and revolutions are mostly the work of minority, with or without the active sympathy of the masses as it happened during the American War of Independence or even the French Revolution. Following this logic, Sen concludes : "What began as a fight for religion ended as a War of Independence for there is not the slightest doubt that the rebels wanted to get rid of the alien government and restore the old of which the King of Delhi was the rightful representative."[6]

Western scholars particularly from the Universities of Cambridge, Oxford and London followed by scholars from the U.S.A. and Australian Universities labelled the revolt of 1857 as ' The Mutiny of 1857' (*i.e.*, a military outbreak). This interpretation is the outcome of the British imperial bias. A recent British historian, Dr. Judith M. Brown has admitted the existence and **persistence of this when she writes. "At the time many British People** preferred to see the events largely as a military mutiny—understandably, as any wider interpretation would have cast doubts on the nature of their *raj*— 'a mutiny complex' does seem to have become part of the British picture of India"[7] Prof. F.G. Hutchins, a U.S.A based historian expresses a similar opinion when he writes: "The uprising of 1857 was termed a mutiny by the British because they wished to emphasise its treasonous nature and in addition to convey the impression that it was confined to the Indian troops of the British Army. It is clear, however, from recent scholarly researches that while it began as a military mutiny, the uprising quickly assumed the character of a popular rebellion."[8]

---

3. Nehru, Jawaharlal : *The Discovery of India*, p.301 (London, 1946)
4. **Rural Base of the Revolt.** Recent studies in Indian agrarian society have thrown interesting sidelights on the rural on the rural participation in the Revolt of 1857. S.B. Chaudhuri put forward the thesis that the rural areas rose as one man and the principal cause was the loss of land rights to the urban moneylender and trader under pressure of British land revenue system. Eric Stokes disagrees with this view and on the basis of some regional studies comes to the conclusion that violence and rebellion were often the fiercest and the most protracted where land transfers were low and the hold of the moneylender the weakest.

    Eric Stokes believes that in rural areas the Revolt of 1857 was essentially elitist in character. He maintains that the major agrarian violence did not come from peasant group but from traditionally superior class communities for whom British rule had meant loss of political influence and relative economic deprivation. The mass of the population, believes Stokes, appear to have played little part in the fighting or at most tamely followed the behest of its local caste leadership. Not that the entire rural elite was on the side of the rebels; rather it too reggedly split down the middle with the result that even within the same district peasant proprietors or magnates reacted in quite opposite directions. In Meerut district, for example, while the Jats of Hapur pargana fought on the British side, the Jats in Baraut and Barnawa parganas (on the other side of the Hindon river) fought against the British forces and sent supplies to the rebels at Delhi.

5. Majumdar, R.C: *History and Culture of the Indian People*, Vol. IX, p-625
6. Sen, S.N. : *Eighteen Fifty-seven*, p.411 (The Publication Division, Ministry of Information and Broadcasting, Delhi 1957)
7. Brown, Judith M. : *Modern India*, p.86 (Oxford University Press, 1994)
8. Hutchins, F.G. : The Illusion of Permanence, p.79 (Princeton University press, 1967)

Prof. Stanley Wolpert, an American historian strikes a slightly different stance when he writes about the Revolt of 1857. "It was far more than a mutiny..... yet much less than a first of independence".

Whatever the nature of the Revolt of 1857, it soon become a symbol of challenge to the British imperial rule in India. During our freedom Struggle, our leaders and people in general drew inspiration from some of the heroic events of 1857. Undoubtedly, the Revolt of 1857 became a turning point in Modern Indian History.

Causes of the Revolt

The Anglo-Indian historians have greatly emphasised the importance of military grievances and the greased cartridges affair as the most potent causes which led to the great rising of 1857. But modern Indian historians have established beyond that 'the greased cartridge' was not the only cause, nor even the most important of them. The causes of the Rebellion lay deeper and are to be found in the history of the hundred years of British rule from the Battle of Plassey (June 1757) to the rebellion of Mangal Pandey when on March 29, 1857, he murdered an English Adjutant. The greased cartridge and the Mutiny of soldiers was merely the match-stick which exploded the inflammable material which had gathered in heap on account of a variety of causes political, social, religious and economic.

Political Causes. The East India Company's policy of 'effective control' and gradual extinction of the Indian native states took a definite shape with the perfection of the Subsidiary Alliance System under Lord Wellesley. Its logical culmination was reached under Dalhousie who threw all codes of morality and political conduct to the winds and perfected the infamous Doctrine of Lapse. Dalhousie's annexations and the Doctrine of lapse had caused suspicion and uneasiness in the minds of almost all ruling princes in India. The right of succession was denied to the Hindu Princes. The guarantee of adoption to the throne "did not extent to any person in whose veins the blood of the founder of the dynasty did not run". The distinction between 'dependent states' and "protected allies' was very thin and looked more alike hair-splitting. In case of disputed interpretation, the decision of the East India Company was binding and that of the Court of Directions final. There was no Supreme Court to give an impartial verdict on questions of right and wrong. While the Panjab, Pegu, Sikkim had been annexed by the 'Right of Conquest', Satara, Jaipur, Sambhalpur, Baghat, Udaipur, Jhansi and Nagpur were annexed by the application of the Doctrine of Lapse. Oudh was annexed on the pretext of " the good of the governed". Regal titles of the Nawabs of Carnatic and Tanjore were abolished and the pension of Peshwa Baji Rao II's adopted son was stopped. The Indians held that the existence of all states was threatened and absorption of all states was a question of time. The common belief current was that annexations were not because of the Doctrine of Lapse, but due to the 'Lapse of all Morals' on the part of the East India Company. That the fears of the people were not without foundation is clear from the correspondence of one of the architects of British India, Sir Charles Napier, who wrote: "Were I Emperor of India for twelve years.... no India prince should exist. The Nizam should no more be heard of ... Nepal would be ours..." Malleson has rightly stated that the policy of Dalhousie and the utterances and writings of other high officials had created ' bad faith and Indians got the feeling that the British were 'playing the wolf in the garb of the lamb'.

The Muslim feelings had been grievously hurt. Bahadur Shah II, the Mughal Emperor, was an old man and might die any moment. Lord Dalhousie who was not in favour of retaining an *imperium in imperio* had recognised the succession of Prince Faqir-ul-Din, but imposed many strict conditions on him. After Faqir-ud-Din's death in 1856, Lord Canning announced that the prince next in succession would have to renounce the regal title and the ancestral Mughal palaces in addition to the renunciations agreed upon by Prince Faqir-ul-Din. These acts greatly unnerved the Indian Muslims who thought that the English wanted to humble the House of Timur. In the words of Alexander Duff : "The Mohammadans have for the last hundred years not ceased to pray, like privately in their house and publicly in their mosques throughout India for the prosperity of the House of Timur or Taimurlane, whose lineal representative is the titular emperor of Delhi. But the prosperity of the House of Timur, is their estimation, undoubtedly implies neither more nor less than downfall of the British power, and the re-establishment of their own instead. In their case, therefore, disaffection towards the British Government with an intense longing for its speedy overthrow is sedulously nurtured as a sort of sacred duty which they owe alike to their faiths and the memory of their ancestors."

The 'absentee sovereigntyship' of the British rule in India was an equally important political factor which worked on the minds of the Indian people against the British. The Pathans and the Mughals who had conquered India had, in course of time, settled in India and become Indians. The revenues collected from the people were spent this very country. In the case of the British, the Indians felt that they were being ruled from England from a distance of thousands of miles and the country was being drained of her wealth.

Besides, the policy of *Pax-Britanncia* pursued by the British during the past four decades had led to the disbanding of Pindaris, Thugs, and irregular soldiers who formed the bulk of the native armies. These people had lived mostly on plunder, and when deprived of the means of livelihood by the British, they formed the nucleus of antisocial elements in different areas. When in 1857, there occurred some disturbances they swelled the ranks of the rebels.

Administrative and Economic Causes. The annexation of Indian states produced startling economic and social effects. The Indian aristocracy was deprived of power and position. It found little chance to gain the same old position in the new administrative set-up, as under the British rule all high posts, civil and military, were reserved for the Europeans.

In the military services, the highest post attainable by an Indian was that of a Subedar on a salary of Rs. 60 or Rs. 70 and in the civil services that of Sadr Amin on a salary of Rs. 500 per month. The chances of promotion were very few. The Indians thought that British were out to reduce them to 'hewers of wood and drawers of water."

Sir Thomas Munro, pleading for the employment of Indians, wrote in 1817, "Foreign conquerors have treated the natives with violence, and often with cruelty, but none has treated them with so much scorn as we; none has stigmatized the whole people as unworthy of trust, as incapable of honestly and as fit to be employed only where we cannot do without them. It seems to be not only ungenerous, but impolite, to debase the character of the people fallen under our dominion..." Despite the recommendations contained in the Charter Act of 1833, the policy had remained more or less the same.

The administrative machinery of the East India Company was 'inefficient and insufficient'. The land revenue police was most unpopular. Many districts in the newly-annexed states were in permanent revolt and military had to be sent to collect the land revenue. In the district of Panipat, for example, 136 horsemen were maintained for the collection of land revenue, while only 22 were employed for the performance of police duties. At the out-break of the Rebellion, Sir Henry Lawrence is reported to have remarked: "It was the Jackson, the John Lawrence, the Thomason, the Edmonstones who brought India to this." In the land revenue settlement newly acquired territories, the English administration had eliminated the middleman by establishing direct contact with the peasants. The land revenue settlement of North-Western Provinces was described as "a fearful experiment... calculated so as to flatten the whole surface of society." Many talukdars, the hereditary landlords (and tax-collectors for the Government) were deprived of their positions and gains. Many holders of rent-free tenures were dispossessed by the use of a *quo-warranto*—requiring the holders of such lands to produce evidence like title-deeds by which they held that land. Large estates were confiscated and sold by public auction to the highest bidders. Such estates were usually purchased by speculators who did not understand the tenants and fully exploited them. It was Coverly Jackson's policy of disbanding the native soldiers and of strict inquiry into the titles of the talukdars of Oudh that made

Oudh the chief centre of the Rebellion. The Inam Commission appointed in 1852 in Bombay confiscated as many as 20,000 estates. Thus, the new land revenue settlements made by the East India Company in the newly-annexed states drove poverty in the ranks of the aristocracy without benefiting the peasantry which groaned under the weight of heavy assessments and excessive duties. The peasants whose welfare was the chief motive of the new revenue policy did not like the passing of the old ways. They fell in the clutches of unprincipled moneylenders; they often visited their dispossessed landlords and with tears in their eyes expressed their sympathy for them. The taluqdars of Oudh were the hardest hit. In the words of Asoka Mehta: " Out of the 25,543 villages included in their estates at the time of the annexation of the kingdom, 13,640 paying a revenue of Rs. 35,06,519 were settled with taluqdars, while 11,903 villages paying Rs 32,08,319 were settled with persons other than taluqdars... the taluqdars had lost half their villages, some had lost their all." The ruthless manner in which the Thomasonian system was carried into effect may be clear from the resumption of the revenue of free villages granted for the temple Lakshmi in Jhansi.

British economic policies in India worked against the interests of Indian trade and industry. The East India Company used its political power to destroy Indian handicrafts and industry and developed it into an appendage of a foreign exploitative system. Writing in 1853 Karl Marx, a very shrewd observer, very aptly remarked: "It was the British intruder who broke up the Indian hand-loom and destroyed the spinning-wheel. England began with depriving the Indian cottons from the European market; it then introduced twist into Hindustan and in the end inundated the very mother country of cotton with cottons"[9]. The ruination of Indian industry increased the pressure on agriculture and land, which lopsided development in turn resulted in the pauperization of the country in general.

Social and Religious Causes. Like all conquering people the English rulers of India were rude and arrogant towards the subject people. However, the English were infected with a spirit of racialism. The rulers followed a policy of contempt towards the Indians and described the Hindus as barbarians with hardly any trace of culture and civilisation, while the Muslims were dubbed as bigots, cruel and faithless.

The European officers in India were very exacting and over-bearing in their social behaviour. The Indian was spoken as *nigger* and addressed as a *suar* or pig, an epithet most resented by the Muslims. Even the best among them like Bird and Thomason insulted " the native gentry whenever they had the opportunity of doing so".

European officers and European soldiers on their hunting sprees were often guilty of indiscriminate criminal assaults on Indians. The European juries, which alone could try such cases, acquitted European criminals with light or no punishment. Such discrimination rankled in the Indian mind like a festering sore.

It may be easy to withstand physical and political injustices but religious persecution touches tender conscience and forms complexes that are not easy to eradicate. That one of the aims of the English in Indian was to convert the Indians to Christianity is clear from the speech of Mr. Mangles, the Chairman of the Directors of the East India Company, in the House of Commons: "Providence has entrusted the extensive empire of Hindustan to England in order that the banner of Christ should wave triumphant from one end of India to the other. Everyone must exert all his strength that there may be no dilatoriness on any account in continuing in the country the grand work of making all Indians Christians," Major Edwards had openly declared that "the Christianization of India was to be the ultimate end of our continued possession of it." Vir Savarkar has pointed that the superior military and civil officers used to abuse the very names of Ram and Mohammad and prevail upon the sepoys and

---

9. For the full text of Marx's article see Appendix A.

the civilians to embrace the Christian faith. Sepoys were promised promotions if they accepted the True Faith. The missionaries were Given ample facilities and the American Missionary Society at Agra had set up an extensive printing press. Idolatry was denounced, Hindu gods and goddesses ridiculed, Hindu superstitions dubbed as ignorance. Sir Syed Ahmed Khan mentions that "it has been commonly believed that government appointed missionaries and maintained them at its own cost." The Evangelical opinion was voiced by Lord Shaftesbury who believed that the failure to Christianize India was the cause of the whole trouble.

The Religious Disabilities Act of 1850 modified Hindu customs; a change of religion did not debar a son from inheriting the property of his heathen father. Stranger rumours were current in India that Lord Canning had been specially selected and charged with the duty of converting the Indians to Christianity. In this surcharged atmosphere even the railways and steamships began to be looked upon as indirect instruments for changing their faith. The telegraph was regarded as 'the accursed string' and the rebels once said that 'it was this accursed string that strangled them". In the words of Benjamin Disraeli : "The Legislative Council of India under the new principle had been constantly nibbling at the religious system of the native. In its theoretical system of national education the sacred scriptures had suddenly appeared in the schools". The Indian mind was getting increasingly convinced that the English were conspiring to convert them to Christianity. The activities of Christian *padris* and efforts of Dalhousie and Bethune towards woman education made Indians feel that through education the British were going to conquer their civilisation. Even 'education offices' set up by the British were styled as *shaitani daftars*.

Military Causes. Since the Afghan adventure of Lord Auckland, the discipline in the army had suffered a serious set back Lord Dalhousie had written to the Home authorities that "the discipline of the army from top to bottom officers and men alike, is scandalous". The Bengal Army was " a great brotherhood in which all the members felt and acted in union", and service in the army was hereditary. Three-fifth of the recruits of the Bengal Army were drawn from Oudh and the North-Western Provinces and most of them came from high caste Brahmin and Rajput families who were averse to accepting that part of the army discipline which treated them on par with the low caste recruits. Sir Charles Napier had no confidence in the allegiance of 'high caste mercenaries'. During the Governor- Generalship of Lord Dalhousie three mutinies had occurred in the army—the mutiny of the 22nd N. I. in 1849, of the 66th N. I. in 1850, and the 38th N. I. in 1852.

The Bengal Army sepoys reflected all the feelings of the civil population of Oudh. In the opinion of Maulana Azad, the annexation of Oudh "marked the beginning of a rebellious mood in the army generally and in the Bengal army in particular... it gave a rude shock to the people... they suddenly realised that the power which the Company had acquired through their service and sacrifice was utilised to liquidate their own king".

The extension of British dominion in India had adversely affected the service condition of the sepoys. They were required to serve in area away from their homes without the payment of extra *bhatta*. The sepoys yearned for the good old days when the Indian rulers used to crown their meritorious deeds by bestowing jagirs and other prizes upon them whereas their victories in Sind and the Panjab had brought worse days for them. In 1824 the sepoys at Barrackpore had refused to serve across the seas in Burma and the 47th regiment had been disbanded. In 1844 four Bengal regiments had refused to moved to Sind till extra *bhatta* was sanctioned.

In 1856 Canning's government passed the General Service Enlistment Act which decreed that all future recruits for the Bengal army would have to give an undertaking to serve anywhere their service might be required by the Government. The Act did not affect old incumbent, but was unpopular because service in the Bengal army was usually hereditary. Moreover, those soldiers who had been sent in the army of invasion of Afghanistan during 1839–42 had been sent in the army of invasion of Afghanistan during 1839–42 had not been taken back in the folds of the caste. Sepoys declared unfit for foreign service were not allowed to retired with pension, but were to be posted for duty at cantonments.

The privilege of free postage so long enjoyed by the sepoys was withdrawn with the passing of the Post Office Act of 1854 Besides, the disparity in numbers between European and Indian troops had lately been growing greater. In 1856, the Company's army consisted of 238,000 native and 45,322 British soldiers. This disproportion was rendered more serious by the defieiency of good officers in the army, most of whom were employed in administrative posts in the newly annexed states and the frontier. The distribution of the troops was also faulty, Moreover, disasters in the Crimean war had lowered the general moral of the British soldiers. All these factors made the Indian soldiers feel that if they had struck at that hour, they had reasonable chances of success. So they were waiting only for an occasion which was provided by the 'greased cartridge' incident. The greased cartridges did not create a new causes of discontent in the army, but supplied the occasion when the underground discontent came out in the open. In 1856 the Government decided to replace the old-fashioned musket, 'Brown Bess' by the 'Enfield rifle'. The training for the use of the new weapon was to be imparted at Dum Dum, Ambala and Sialkot. The loading process of the Enfield rifle involved bringing the cartridge to the mouth and biting off the top paper with mouth. In January 1857 a story got currency in the Bengal regiments that the greased cartridge contained the fat of pig and cow. At once a denial was issued by the military authorities without investigating into the matter. Subsequently enquiries proved that "the fat of cows or oxen really had been used at Woolwich arsenal" (V. A Smith). Assurances of superior officers and slight concessions proved of no avail. The sepoys become convinced that the introduction of greased cartridges was a deliberate move to defile their religion. It was argued that the East India Company was playing the part of Aurangzeb and it was but natural that sepoys should play the part of Shivaji.

The Beginning and Spread of the Mutiny and Revolt. The refusal of the sepoys to use the greased cartridges was regarded by the authorities as an act of insubordination and punished accordingly. On 29 March 1857 the sepoys at Barrackpore refused to use the greased cartridge and one Brahmin sepoy, Mangal Pandey, attacked and fired at the Adjutant. The 34 N. I. regiment was disbanded and sepoys guilty of rebellion punished. At Meerut, in May 1857, 85 sepoys of the 3rd Cavalry regiment on their refusal to use the greased cartridge were court-martialled and sentenced to long terms of imprisonment. On 10th May the sepoys broke out in open rebellion, shot their officers, released their fellow sepoys and headed towards Delhi. General Hewitt, the Officer Commanding at Meerut, had 2,200 European soldiers at his disposal but did nothing to stem the rising tide.

Delhi was seized by the rebels on 12th May 1857. Lieutenant Willoughby, the officer-in-charge of the magazine at Delhi, offered some resistance, but was overcome. The palace and the city were occupied. Some European inhabitants of Delhi were shot dead. Bahadur Shah II was proclaimed the Emperor of India. The loss of Delhi was a serious loss of prestige to the English.

Very soon the rebellion spread throughout Northern and Central India at Lucknow, Allahabad, Kanpur, Bareilly, Banaras in parts of Bihar, Jhansi and other places. Fortunately for the English, the Indians rulers remained loyal and rendered valuable services in the suppression of the rebellion. India south of the Narbada remained practically undisturbed.

The Revolt of 1857.

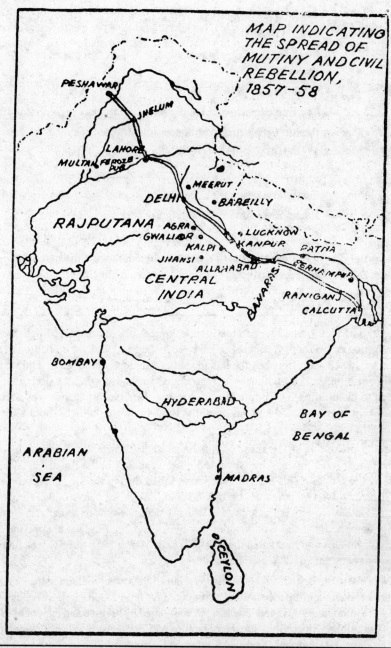

Descriptive note on the Spread of Mutiny and Civil Rebellion during 1857–58.

2 February 1857	— Mutiny of the 19th Native Infantry at Berhampur.
10 May 1857	— Mutiny of Sepoys at Meerut.
11–30 May 1857	— Outbreaks in Delhi, Ferozepur, Bombay, Aligarh, Etawah, Bulandshahr, Nasirabad Bareilly, Moradabad, Shahjehanpur and other stations in U.P.
	The Mughal Emperor proclaimed as the Emperor of India
June 1857	— Mutinies at Gwalior, Bharatpur, Jhansi Allahabad, Faizabad, Sultanpur, Lucknow etc.,

	The civil rebellion spreads through the Indo-Gangetic plain, Rajputana, Central India and some parts of Bengal.
July 1857	— Mutinies at Indore, Mhow, Saugar and certain places in the Panjab like Jhelum sialkot etc.
August 1857	— Civil rebellion spreads throughout Saugor and Nerbudda districts.
September 1857	— The English recapture Delhi : further outbreaks in Central India.
October 1857	— Revolt spreads to Kotah State.
November 1857	— The rebels defeat General Windham outside Kanpur.
December 1587	— Sir Colin Campbell wins the battle of Kanpur.
	— Tantia Tope escapes.
March 1858	— Lucknow recaptured by the English.
April 1858	— Jhansi falls to the English. Fresh rising in Bihar led by Kunwar Singh.
May 1858	— The English recapture Bareilly, Jagdishpur and Kalpi.
	Indian rebels begin guerilla warfare Rohilkhand.
July-December 1858	— English authority re-established in India.

The recapture of Delhi could be of great psychological importance and English efforts were directed towards that end. Troops from the Punjab were rushed and took their position to the north of Delhi. Though resistance was offered by the Indian soldiers. In September 1857 Delhi was recaptured by the English, but John Nicholson, the hero of the siege, was badly wounded during the operations and succumbed to his injuries. The Emperor was arrested. Terrible vengeance was wrecked on the inhabitants of Delhi. Two sons and a grandson of the Emperor were publicly shot by Lieut. Hodson himself.

The rebellion broke our at Lucknow on 4th June. Henry Lawrence, the British Resident, the European inhabitants and a few hundred loyal sepoys took shelter in the Residency. The Residency was besieged by the Indian rebels and Sir Henry was killed during the siege. The command of the besieged garrison devolved on Brigadier Inglis who held out against heavy odds. The early attempts of Havelock and Outram to recover Lucknow met with no success. Some relief came in November 1857 when Sir Colin Campbell, the new Commander-in-Chief, sent from England entered the city with the help of Gorkha regiments and evacuated the Europeans. In March 1858 the city was finally reduced, but guerilla activity continued till September of the same year.

Kanpur was lost to the British on 5th June 1857. Nana Sahib was proclaimed the Peshwa. General Sir Hugh Wheeler, commanding the station, surrendered on June 27. Some Europeans, men women and children, were murdered. At Kanpur Nana Sahib was joined by his able and experienced Lieutenant, Tantia Tope. The military operations for the recapture of Kanpur were closely associated with the recovery of Lucknow. Sir Campbell occupied Kanpur on December 6. Tantia Tope escaped and joined the Rani of Jhansi.

In the beginning of June 1857 the troops at Jhansi mutinied Rani Lakshmi Bai, the widow of the late Raja Gangadhar Rao, was proclaimed the ruler of the state. After the loss of Kanpur, Tantia Tope joined the Rani. Sir Hugh Rose recaptured Jhansi by assault on 3rd April 1958.

The Rani of Jhansi and Tantia tope marched towards Gwalior where they were hailed by the Indian soldiers. The Sindhia however, decided to remain-loyal to the English and took shelter at Agra. Nana Sahib was proclaimed the Peshwa and plans were chalked our for a march into the South. Gwalior was recaptured by the English in June 1858, the Rani of Jhansi died fighting clad in soldier's uniform on the ramparts of the fort. Tantia Tope escaped southward; in April 1859 he was captured by one of Sindhia's feudatory who handed him over to the British to be hanged.

At Bareilly Khan Bahadur Khan had proclaimed himself the Nawab Nazim. In Bihar a local zamindar Kunwar Singh of Jagdishpur raised the banner of revolt. At Banaras a rebellion had been organised which was mercilessly suppressed by Colonel Neill who put to death all rebels, suspected and even disorderly boys. By July 1858 the rebellion had been almost completely suppressed.

Causes of the Failure of the Revolt

1. The Revolt of 1857 was localized, restricted and poorly organised. The Bombay and the Madras armies remained loyal. India south of the Narbada was very little disturbed. Sind and Rajasthan remained quiet and Nepal's help proved of great avail in the suppression of the Revolt. Dost Mohammad, the ruler of Afghanistan, remained friendly. The Punjab was effectively controlled by John Lawrence. The worst affected area were Western Bihar, Oudh, Rohilkhand, Delhi, and the territory between the Chambal and the Narbada.

2. The resources of the British Empire were far superior to those of the rebels. Luckily for the British the Crimean and the Chinese wars had been concluded by 1856, and British troops numbering 1,12,000 poured into India from all parts of the world. About 3,10,000 additional Indian soldiers were recruited in India. The Indian soldiers had very few guns and muskets and mostly fought with swords and spears. On the other hand, the European soldiers were equipped with the latest weapons of war like the Enfield rifle about which Nana Sahib said: "The blue cap kills before they fire". The electric telegraph kept the Commander-in-Chief informed about the movements of the Indian rebels and their strategy. A concerted plan was formed to suppress the Rebellion. Russell, the Correspondent of *The Times* of London, summed up the advantages of the electric telegraph thus: "Never since its discovery has the electric telegraph played so important and daring a role as it now does in India; without it the Commander-in-Chief would lose the effect of half his force. It has served him better than his right arm". Considering the vast resources of the British Empire and her naval superiority, it may be said that even if the English had been driven back to the coastal areas or into the sea, before long she would have reconquered India by her superior military strength.

3. The revolt of 1857 was mainly feudal in character carrying with it some nationalistic elements. The feudal elements of Oudh, Rohilkhand and some other parts of Northern India led the rebellion; other feudal prices like the Rajas of Patiala, Jhind, Gwalior, Hyderabad helped in its suppression. European historians have greatly praised Sir Dinkar Rao, the Minister of Gwalior, and Salar Jang, the Wazir of Hyderabad, for their loyalty. In the movement of crisis Canning said: "If the Sindhia joins the Mutiny, I shall have to pack off tomorrow,". Canning acted very wisely when he gave solemn assurances to the Indian princes and thus won over their support. The Indian princes were amply rewarded after the suppression of the Rebellion. The districts of Berar were restored to the Nizam and his debts remitted. Nepal was rewarded by the cession of some Oudh territory. The Sindhia, the Gaikwar and the Rajput princes also received some rewards or concessions.

4. The Revolt was poorly organised. The leader of the Revolt were not lacking in bravery, but were deficient in experience, organising ability and concerted operations. Surprise attacks and guerilla tactics could not win them their lost independence. The various commissions and boards appointed by the Government of India and provincial governments after the suppression of the rebellion could not find any plan behind the rebellion or any scheme on which the movement was launched. The trial of Bahadur Shah II proved that the rebellion was as much a surprise to him as to the British.

5. The rebels had no common ideal before them except the anti-foreign sentiments. Bahadur Shah II was declared the Emperor at Delhi, while at Kanpur and Gwalior Nana Sahib was proclaimed the Peshwa. Hindu-Muslim differences lay dormant against the common enemy, but were not dead. The peasants and the inferior castes showed no active sympathies; the soldiers in the Bombay and Madras armies were recruited from the lower castes and they remained loyal.

6. The East India Company was fortunate in having the services of men of exceptional abilities in the Lawrence brothers, Nicholson, Outram, Havelock, Edwards etc, They fought the toughest battles in the initial stages of the Revolt and controlled the situation till reinforcements were received from abroad.

Impact of the Revolt

The Revolt of 1857 though completely suppressed had shaken the British rule in India from its very foundations. Lord Cromer once remarked: "I wish the Young generation of the English would read, mark, learn and inwardly digest the history of the Indian Mutiny: it abounds in lessons and warnings". The techniques of controlling India though well established by '1857 were confirmed and uniformly acted upon thereafter. The reactionary and vested interests were well protected and encouraged and became pillars of British rule in India: the policy of divide and rule was deliberately pursued and made the main prop of British control; tight European control over key positions both in the civil and military administration was maintained.

(1) The control of Indian administration was transferred from the East India Company to the Crown by The Government of India Act 1858. In the words of Sir H.S. Cunningham the change was 'formal' rather than 'substantial'. Sir Henry Rawnnson director of the Company who favoured abolition of the Company correctly summed up the significance of the change: "The one great result will be a change of name, which may enable us to condone the past—the immediate past—and to set out from a fresh starting point into a fresh career of empire." In India the same sort of Governor-General and the same military and civil service continued as before. In Britain the Act of 1858 provided for the appointment of a Secretary of State for India, who was to be assisted by an Advisory Council of fifteen: Eight members to be nominated by the Crown and seven members at first to be selected by the Court of Directors and afterwards by co-option by the Council itself. Thus the former directors of the Company sat on the India Council. No new policy was inaugurated. Rather, in the proclamation of 1 November 1858 the Queen announced a continuation of the Company's policies.

Ever since 1784 the Crown through the Board of Control had exercised considerable influence over Indian affairs and, in fact, had the deciding voice in all major issues. The Act of 1858 ended the dualism in the control of Indian affairs and made the Crown directly responsible for management of Indian affairs.

(2) The Queen's announcement declared against any desire for "extension of territorial possessions" and promised "to respect the rights, dignity and honour of native princes as their own", while general amnesty was granted to "all offenders, save and except those who have been or shall be convicted of having directly taken part in the murder of British subjects". The Indian states had served as "breakwaters to the storm which would otherwise have swept over us in one great wave" and to preserve them as the bulwark of the Empire became a cardinal principle of British policy. The Taluqdars of Oudh who had joined in large numbers in the rebellion were reinstated and confirmed in their estates subject to promises of loyalty and future good behaviour. In the words of Pt. Nehru, these taluqdars took pride in calling themselves the 'Barons of Oudh' and became one of the pillars of British rule. Thus feudal and reactionary elements became the favourite children of imperialism.

(3) The Proclamation of 1858 contained an assurance that "our subjects, of whatever race or creed, be freely, and impartially admitted to office in our service, the duties of which they may be qualified by their education, ability and integrity duly to discharge". To give expression to this pledge the Indian Civil Service Act of 1861 was passed, which provided for an annual competitive examination to be held in London for recruitment to the Covenanted Civil Service. Unfortunately, the detailed rules framed for the conduct of this examination had the effect of keeping the higher services a close preserve of the Englishman.

(4) The Indian Army had been mainly responsible for the crisis of 1857. It was thoroughly reorganised and built up on the policy of 'division and counterpoise'. The Army Amalgamation

Scheme of 1861 transferred the Company's European troops to the services of the Crown. The European troops in India were constantly renovated by periodical visits to England in what came to be known as the 'linked-battalion' scheme. The strength of European troops in India was increased from the pre 1857 figure of 45,000 to 65,000 and the number of Indian troops reduced from the pre-1857 figure of 238,000 to 140,000. All Indian artillery units (with the exception of a few mountain batteries) were disbanded. The general formula followed was that in Bengal Presidency the proportion between the European and Indian troops should be 1: 2. while for Bombay and Madras Presidencies it should be 1 : 3 Besides the policy of counterpoise of natives against natives was to be followed which was explained by the Report of the Panjab Committee on Army Organisation, 1858, in these words: "To preserve that distinctiveness which is valuable, and which while it lasts makes the Mohammedan of one country fear and dislike the Mohammedan of another, corps should in future be provincial, and adhere to the geographical limits within which differences and rivalries are strongly marked". All big posts in the army and the artillery departments were reserved for the Europeans. In the fifty years following the Rebellion of 1857 no Indian soldier was thought fit to deserve the King's commission and a raw English recruit was considered superior to an Indian officer holding the Viceroy's commission.

(5) It was increasingly realised that one basic cause for the Revolt of 1857 was the lack of contact between the ruler and the ruled. Sir Bartle Frere, in his famous Minute of 1860, urged 'the addition of the native element' to the Legislative Councils. The association of Indians in the task of legislation, it was believed, would at least acquaint the rulers with the sentiments and feelings of the Indians and thus provide an opportunity for avoidance of misunderstandings. Thus, a humble beginning towards the development of representative institutions in India was made by the Indian Councils Act of 1861.

(6) The emotional after-effects of the Revolts were perhaps the most unfortunate. Racial bitterness was perhaps the worst legacy of the struggle. *The Punch* cartooned the Indian as a subhuman creature, half gorilla, half-negro who could be kept in check by superior force only. The agents of imperialism in India dubbed the entire Indian people as unworthy of trust and subjected them to insults, humiliation and contemptuous treatment. In the words of Jawaharlal Nehru: "Imperialism and the domination of one people over another is bad, and so is racialism. But imperialism plus racialism can lead only to horror and ultimately to the degradation of all concerned with them". The entire structure of the Indian government was remodelled and based on the idea of a master race. This neo-Imperialism was justified by the philosophy of the Whiteman's-burden and the civilising role of England in India. The gulf between the rulers and the ruled widened and erupted occasionally in political controversies, demonstrations and acts of violence.

(7) The Revolt of 1857 ended an era and sowed the seeds of new era. The era of territorial aggrandisement gave place to the era of economic exploitation. For the British, the danger from the feudal India ended for ever; the new challenge to British Imperialism came from progressive India fed on the philosophy of John Stuart Mill and British liberals of the nineteenth century.

Select Opinions

R. C. Majumdar. It would thus appear that the outbreak of the civil population in 1857 may be regarded as a war of independence only if we take that term to mean any sort of fight against the British. But, then, the fight of the Pindaris against the English and the fight of the Wahabis against the Sikhs in the Panjab should also be regarded as such. Those who demur to it should try to find out how much the rebels in 1857 were prompted by motives of material interest and religious considerations which animated, respectively, the Pindaris and the Wahabis, and how much by the disinterested and patriotic motive of freeing the country from the yoke of foreigners. Apart from individual cases, here and there, no evidence has yet been brought to light which would support the view that the patriotic motive of freeing the country formed the chief incentive to the general outbreak of the people... It is difficult to avoid the conclusion that the so-called First National War of Independence of 1857 is neither First, nor National, nor War of Independence. (*British Paramountcy and Indian Renaissance,* vol. IX, pp. 624–25).

S. N. Sen. The Mutiny was inevitable. No dependent nation can for ever reconcile itself to foreign domination. A despotic government must ultimately rule by the sword though it might be sheathed in velvet. In India the sword was apparently in the custody of the Sepoy Army. Between the Sepoy and his foreign masters there was no common tie of race, language and religion...The Mutiny was not inevitable in 1857 but it was inherent in the constitution of the empire. (*Eighteen Fifty Seven,* p. 417)

Maulana Abul Kalam Azad. The question naturally arises if the uprising was a result of a nationalist upsurge alone. The answer cannot be an unqualified affirmative if nationalism is understood in its modern sense. There is no doubt that the participants were moved by patriotic considerations, but these were not strong enough to provoke a revolt. Patriotism had to be reinforced by an appeal to religious passion before the People arose.... As I read about the events of 1857 I am forced to the sad conclusion that Indian national character had sunk very low. The leaders of the revolt could never agree. They were mutually jealous and continually intrigued against one another. They seemed to have little regard for the effects of such disagreement on the common cause. In fact, these personal jealousies and intrigues were largely responsible for the Indian defeat. (*Eighteen Fifty Seven* Foreword, pp. XIV–XV)

S. B. Chaudhuri. First War of Independence it certainly was, as in the whole canvas of the recorded history of India it would be difficult to find a parallel to this gigantic anti-foreign combine of all classes of people and of many provinces of India. There was never a war in India lasting continuously for more than a year and simultaneously in all the regions which had for its objective the abasement and ejectment of the alien rulling power. (*Theories of the Indian Mutiny*).

Eric Stokes. 1857 stands firmly in a historical continuum. Not of course that it was the direct product of social forces blowing off the political crust but rather fortuitous conjuncture that laid these forces bare. Like 1848 in Europe—despite obvious disparities—it was an uprising *sans issue* that could catch a society moving into the early stages of modernisation. (*The Peasant and the Raj,* p. 39).

SELECT REFERENCES

1. Chattopadhyaya, H. P : *The Sepoy Mutiny, 1857.*
2. Chaudhuri, S. B. : *Civil, Rebellion in the Indian Mutinies, 1857–59.*
3. Chaudhuri, S. B. : *Theories of the Indian Mutiny.*
4. Chaudhuri, S. B. : *English Historical Writings on the Indian Mutiny, 1857–59.*
5. Embree, A. T. : *1857 in India.*
6. Joshi, P. C. (Ed.) : *Rebellion, 1857.*
7. Majumdar, R. C. (ed.) : *British Paramountcy and Indian Renaissance (The History and Culture of the Indian People, Vol. IX)*
8. Majumdar, R. C. : *The Sepoy Mutiny and the Revolt of 1857.*
9. Sen, S. N. : *1857.*
10. Sengupta, K. K. : *Recent Writings on the Revolt of 1857___A Survey (ICHR, 1975).*
11. Stokes, Eric : *The Peasant and the Raj.*

Administrative Reorganization Under the Crown, 1858–1947

> The Revolt of 1857 led not to the downfall but to the consolidation and permanence of our empire in the East.
>
> —*The Saturday Review, London*

> All experience teaches us that where a dominant race rules another the mildest form of government is a despotism
>
> —*Sir Charles Wood, Secretary of State for India, 1859–66.*

It is a historic truism that the basic changes in a colony's polity, economy, social and administrative structure are not determined by the needs and interests of the colony but by the aspirations and interests of the Imperial power. After 1857 many rival Western imperial and capitalist countries and even the USA and Japan posed a serious challenge to Britain's political and trade position in the colonies and semi-colonies and in the international market. Besides, in the latter half of the nineteenth century inside Britain a capitalist lobby had emerged as a strong force in the British parliament in foreign policy and international trade. All this changed scenario impelled Britain to make vigorous efforts to consolidate its control over India. As such, changes in administrative structure and policies became inevitable. However, administrative changes were not introduced in one lot but in phases—all designed to put British rule in India on a "rock of granite".

New Administrative Set-up

All sections of political opinion in England came to the conclusion that the East India Company's economic and administrative policies were largely responsible for the widespread discontent among different segments of Indian society which had erupted in the Revolt of 1857. The British Government also got alarmed and took the decision to end the Company's rule in India. The Government also decided to put Indian administration under the direct rule of the Crown.

The British parliament passed the Government of India Act, 1858, which transferred the government, territories and revenues from the Company to the Crown. The Act also declared that India was to be governed by and in the name of the Sovereign and also authorised the appointment of an additional Principal Secretary of State and created the Council of India. Immediately after Queen Victoria issued a proclamation to the Princes, Chiefs and people of India notifying that she had taken upon herself the government before administered in trust for her by the Company. The Queen appointed George (Lord Canning) to be the first Viceroy.

A further development about the Crown's position in India was made in 1876 when the Sovereign was empowered by an act of parliament to assume the title of Empress of India (or *Kaiser-i-Hind*) and a proclamation to that effect was made in a Darbar held at Delhi on 1 January, 1877. Since that time it became customary in India, to use the title 'Queen Empress' and 'King Emperor'.

The Secretary of State and the India Office

Under the Act of 1858, the Secretary of State (a British minister for Indian Affairs) became the Constitutional advisor of the Crown in all matters relating to India. The Secretary of State was to be assisted by the India Council consisting of 15 members appointed at first for life but later for periods of 10 to 15 years. The establishment of the Secretary of State-in-Council was commonly known as the

India office. The Council was divided Committees each under a Secretary, an Assistant Under Secretary with a staff of clerks. The other Departments of the India Office were those of the Accountant General, the Registrar, Superintendent of Records and the Director of Funds. The Medical Board, the Legal Advisor and Solicitor to the Secretary of State may also be mentioned. It should be noted that the salary of the Auditor and his assistants as well as the salaries, pensions and other charges of the entire establishment of the India Office were paid out of the revenues of the Government of India.

The Government of India

The Act of 1858 did not make any important changes in the administration of India, but the Governor General as representing the Crown became known as the Viceroy. The designation 'Viceroy' although it was most frequently used in ordinary parlance had no statutory authority and had never been used by parliament. This title of Viceroy was frequently employed in Warrants of Precedence, in the statutes of Indian Orders, and in public notifications, appeared to be one of ceremony and was most appropriately used in connection with the State and social functions of the Sovereign's representative for the Governor General was the sole representative of the Crown in India. The salary of the Viceroy was fixed at rupees 2½ lakhs per annum.

The Executive Council of the Governor General consisted of 4 members. A fifth member was added in 1861 and permission for appointment of 6th member made in 1874. For legislative purposes only, the Indian Council Act, 1861 expanded the Viceroy's Executive Council by addition of 'not less Act, 1861 expanded the Viceroy's Executive Council by addition of 'not less than 6 and more than 12' "additional" members. The Indian Council Act, 1892 carried further this system by increasing the strength of "additional" members from not less than 10 and not more than 16 members, The Indian Councils Act, 1909, The Government of India Acts, 1919 and 1935 further expanded the Legislative Councils but the real powers remained in the hands of the Governor General.

As for the relations between the Secretary of State and the Governor General were concerned, the Secretary of State often acted as the "Grand Mughal". The Secretary of State in very clear language told Lord Mayo:

"The principle is that the final control and direction of the affairs of India rest with the Home government and not with the authorities appointed and established by the Crown, under parliamentary enactment, in India itself."

The laying of direct cable line between England and Indian in 1870, and the introduction of stream vessels and the opening of the Suez Canal enabled the Secretary of State to tighten his control over Indian affairs. An offshoot of the centralization of all effective authority in London was an indirect increase in the hold of British industrialists, merchants and bankers over the economic policy of India. In reality, the new administrative set-up after 1858 remained, as before 1858, a foreign despotism. This was not a chance development but the result of a deliberate conviction and policy as is evident from the speech of Charles Wood at the time of moving the Indian Councils Bill, 1861 in the British Prliament when he said:

"All experience teaches us that where a dominant race rules another the mildest form of government is a **despotism**".

Reorganization of the Army

As the sepoy revolt at Meerut on 10th May had heralded the Mutiny and Revolt of 1857 and shook the very foundations of British rule in India, the reorganisation of the army received the maximum attention of the Home authorites. Sir John Lawerence, the Chief Commissioner of the Punjab, who had organised the English recapture of Delhi in September, 1857 wrote, "Among the defects of pre-mutiny army, unquestionably the worst and one that operated most fatally against us, was the brotherhood and homogeneity of the Bengal Army and for this purpose the remedy is counterpoise of the Europeans, and secondly of native races."

Another factor which brought the army in great focus was the fact that in the second half of the 19th century Britain was spreading its tentacles over the whole of Africa and Asia and in reality emerged as the biggest imperial power in the world "where the sun never set." Britain had perforce to fight against other imperial powers like France, Germany, Russia, Italy etc. Thus, the Indian army was strengthened and used (a) for the defence of India's borders as also (b) for the defence and expansion of British empire elsewhere in the world (e.g., Indian army was sent to Crimea, China, Newzealand for defence of British imperial interests).

The major changes introduces were:

(a) The East India Company's European forces were amalgamated with those of the Crown. The infantry became regiments of the line; the Bengal, Madras and Bombay artillery and the corresponding corps of Indian Engineers were amalgamated with the Royal Artillery and Royal Engineers.

(b) The strength of the European troops in India was increased from the pre-1857 figure of 45,000 to 65,000 and the number of Indian troops reduced from the pre-mutiny figure of 2,38,000 to 1,40,000.

(c) In Bengal presidency the proportion between the European and Indian troops was fixed at 1 : 2 while for Bombay and Madras Presidencies it was to be 1 : 3.

(d) A distinction between martial and non-martial races was made. The native troops from the Punjab, Nepal and the North and the North-West were declared as martial races and soldiers from these areas were recruited in large numbers.

(e) Various steps were taken to encourage regional loyalties among the soldiers, so that they may not unite on national considerations.

As a result of the army reorganization, defence expenditure increased and accounted for 25% to 30% of the total Central and provincial governments revenues in India. Even a memorandum of the India Office dated 3rd February, 1908 pointed out that while Great Britain spent 22%, the dominions 3% and the colonies 4%, India was forced to contribute over 33% of its annual revenue on defence. In fact, the Public Debt of India multiplied not for the benefit of the Indian people but for satisfying the greed of Imperial Britain.

Administrative Decentralisation

The Charter Act of 1833 passed by the British parliament had brought about legislative centralization in the Company's territories in India. The Governments of Bombay and Madras were drastically deprived of their powers of legislation and left only with the right of proposing to the Governor-General-in-Council projects of laws which they thought expedient.

The Indian Council Act, 1861 reversed the trend of legislative centralisation and made a beginning towards legislative decentralization when the Act restored legislative powers of making and amending laws to provinces of Bombay and Madras, with the reservation that in certain matters the Governor-General's prior approval had to be obtained. Legislative Councils were set up in Bengal and Bombay in 1862, in U.P. in 1886, in Punjab in 1894, Western Bengal and Assam in 1905 and the process was continued as and when new provinces were created. The powers of provincial Legislative Councils were enlarged by the Indian Councils Act, 1892. The process so begun was carried further by the Indian Councils Act, 1909. The Government of India Act 1919 introduced 'dyarchy' in the provinces and, the Act of 1935 introduced 'provincial autonomy.'

The policy of financial devolution was initiated by Lord Mayo and continued further by Lord Lytton Ripon. In 1877 the provincial governments were given the control of expenditure on financial services like excise, land revenue reforms, law and justice etc., and also handed over some specified sources of revenue (e.g., excise, license fee etc.) from their respective provinces. In 1882 the system of giving fixed grants to the provinces was stopped and instead the system of 'Divided Heads' was introduced i.e., income from subjects like Excise, Stamps, Forests. Registration was divided in equal proportion among the Central and Provincial governments. The system of 'Divided Heads' remained operative till it was modified by the Government of India Act, 1919.

Local Bodies

The policy of legislative and financial decentralization inaugurated in 1861 made possible the development of Local self-government in the form of Municipalities and District Boards. The need for municipal measure was recognised and Acts were passed for Bengal in 1864 and 1868, for Madras in 1865, for Punjab in 1867 and the North-Western provinces (modern U.P.) in 1868.

In 1870 Lord Mayo's Government while introducing the system of provincial finance emphasized the need for development of self-government and strengthening of municipal institutions. As a follows-up measure new Municipal Acts were passed for Madras in 1871; for Bombay, Bengal and the North-Western Provinces, the Punjab and the Central Provinces in 1873, and for Burma (then a part of India) in 1874. These Acts widened the sphere of municipal usefulness and extended the elective principle. However, the election procedure was not brought into practical operation in many places. It was Lord Ripon's government which through a Resolution in 1881–82 extended the election principle and local self-government. Acts were passed in 1883–84 which greatly altered the constitution, powers and functions of municipal bodies. Even a private citizen was eligible for contesting the office of the Chairman of a municipality, a position which had hitherto been filled by the executive officer. The Decentralization Commision Report, 1908, recommended development of District Boards, Sub-District Boards and Village Panchayats. The Montfort Report, 1918, recommended "There should be as far as possible, complete popular control in local bodies and the largest possible independence for them of outside control." The Government of India Act, 1935, which introduced provincial autonomy, gave a further impetus to development of institutions.

The unfortunate part of the development of local self-institutions was the racial bias of the Anglo-Indian bureaucracy and their distrust about the competence of Indians to manage their own affairs even in local bodies. Lord Curzon's government passed the Calcutta Corporation Act, 1899, which reduced the strength of elected members in the Calcutta Corporation. Even on the eve of Indian independence, the local bodies functioned more as departments of the Government rather than any local self-government bodies.

Economic Policy

The economic policy under the British Crown rule in India was subservient to the larger interests of Great Britain. In other words, Great Britain used her political control over India for thorough economic exploitation of India's vast resources. However, the *modus-operandi* for economic exploitation changed with changing times. The character of 'drain of wealth' from India which operated on Mercantilist principles under the East India Company underwent a change under the Crown and took the form of exploitation through the policy of forced *laissez-faire*, that is, free trade; at a later stage it took the form of British India Finance Capitalism.

In the latter half of the 19th century many European countries imposed high custom duties to protect their indigenous industries against dumping of British industrial products. To compensate British industry for its loss of markets if Europe, the British Government forced the Government of India to adopt the policy of free trade and open Indian markets for unlimited sale of British industrial goods. Later, British Finance Capital entered India in a big way and made an iron grip over Indian industry, trade and commerce. Under the slogan of modernization of India, British Capital, was employed in the extension of railway lines (more for strategic defence purposes and also for better infiltration of British products into remote areas of India), development of iron and coal mines and intensive cultivation of plantation industry of tea, coffee, jute, indigo etc. The ports were developed and British owned steam companies carried on India's international trade. In short, Britain's financial, economic and industrial activities were interlocked in the race for thorough economic exploitation of India's recourses.

Every section of Indian society barring the small comprador class was hard hit by Britain's economic policies.

The Land Tenure and Land Revenue policy of the British Indian Government divided the agricultural class into two rival camps—the zamindar class versus the tenant and agricultural labour. Further, the Government's excessive land revenue demand strengthened the money-lending class which emerged as the new parasite class in rural India. The new judicial system introduced by the British also became an instrument of exploitation of the poor and illiterate classes. In short, the rural masses were pushed below the poverty line.

The fate of the industrial worker was no better under the Crown rule. Unable to complete with the British industrial products available in the Indian market, the Indian industrialist tried to economize which took the form of payment of inadequate wages to the worker, long hours of work and even employment of child labour in factories. No doubt, the Trade Union Movement began in India with two organisations of the All India Trade Union Congress (AITUC) in 1920 and the All India Trade Union Federation in 1929, but these organisations functioned as appendages of national and international political parties.

The educated middle class faced racial discrimination in the sphere of higher civil and military services. The facilities for higher technical education remained inadequate.

For the country in general, the situation—whether it was in the field of industrial development or modernization of agriculture—was that of underdevelopment. Indian nationalist leaders like Dadabhai Naoroji, M. G. Ranade, G. V. Joshi and R. C. Dutt strongly criticised the economic policies of the Indian Government, Naoroji's famous book *Indian Poverty and un-British Rule in India* held British policies responsible for the 'growing poverty of India' and accused Britain of "bleeding India white". J. L. Nehru used more blunt language when he wrote, "British and Indian economic interests conflict all along the line". The logical corollary of this statement was that only India's freedom from British colonial rule could improve the economic position of India.

Civil Services

Lord Cornwallis began the process of Europeanization of higher services in India. Since the Court of Directors made all appointments to the Indian Civil Services through nominations, no Indian ever got a chance. The Charter Act of 1833, under Section 87, provided that no Indian subject of the Company in India was to be debarred from holding any office under the Company "by reason of his religion, place of birth, descent and colour." In actual practice no Indian ever got appointment to the C. C. S. (later renamed I. C .S.).

In 1853, an act of Parliament threw open appointments to the I. C. S. through open competition. The first competitive examination was held in 1855. Though the doors were open to Indian aspirants, very few Indians got the chance because of numerous handicaps:

(a) The I.C.S. examination was held in London only with no examination centre anywhere in India.

(b) The syllabus for the examination suited more the English youth. The examination was heavily based on the knowledge of Greek, Latin and English.

(c) The maximum Age limit for candidates was lowered from 23 years to 22 years in 1860, further lowered to 21 years in 1866 and later lowered to 19 years. After considerable agitation by Indian nationalists, the age limit was fixed between 22 to 24 years in 1906.

Not only were the higher services virtually closed to Indians, even in the higher grades of Minor Services Indians were discriminated against. In the latter category the competitors were the Eurasians popular known as Anglo-Indians. In some services like the Survey of India, the Indian Salt Department, the Excise and Post Office Departments, the educational qualifications required from Anglo-Indian and domiciled Europeans were fixed lower than required from Indian candidates. For long the P. W. D. Railways (Engineering), Telegraph (Engineering), The Railway (Stores) Departments were considered to be the close preserve of the Anglo-Indian community.

Relations with Princely States

The Indian prices like many other feudal elements in Indian society stood by the British Government during the Revolt of 1857. Lord Canning openly recognized their pro-British role when he remarked, "If the Sindhia joins the Mutiny today, I shall have to pack off tomorrow." The princes of Patiala, Jind, Gwalior, Hyderabad greatly helped the Government in the suppression of the Revolt.

After 1857, the British Government and the Government of India identified the Indian princes and the Zamindars as the vested interests who benefited from the continuation of British rule in India. Thus, these elements became the main prop of British rule under the Crown.

The Queen's proclamation of 1858 promised "to respect the rights, dignity and honour of native princes as their own.' The princes were amply rewarded when the Government abandoned the policy of the Doctrine of Lapse and the annexation of Indian states. Henceforth, the new policy was to punish the princely rulers for mismanagement but not to annex their states. For example, in 1874 Malhar Rao Gaekwad of Baroda was accused of misrule and attempts to poison the British Resident; he was deposed from the *gaddi* after a mock trial but the state was not annexed; instead, another member of the Gaekwad family was put on the *gaddi*. The immunity from annexation was given to the Indian States but various measures brought about the complete subordination of the Indian princes to the Paramount Power. Lord Canning declared in 1862 in unambiguous language, "The Crown of England stood forth as the unquestioned Ruler and Paramount Power in all India." Lord Canning granted 140 sanads or 'instrument of grant of adoption' to Hindu and Muslim princely rulers. By the Royal Titles Act, 1876, passed by the British parliament, Queen Victoria assumed the title of Empress of India-British-India, and princely India. A Government notification in August 1891 read, "The Paramount Supremacy of the former (the Crown) presupposes and implies the subordination of the latter (Indian princes)." Under the Crown rule, the British Crown regulated the status and salutes of Indian princes in all matters of ceremonial. The Government of India also encroached upon the internal sovereignty of the Indian princes in matters of extension of railways, irrigation canals, telegraphs, construction of strategic railways etc. The Indian princes lost their international status. None of them enjoyed even an iota of external sovereignty. Lord Curzon, the die-hard imperialist, even put restrictions on the foreign trips of Indian princes.

During World War I and II the Indian princes stood by the Government of India and placed all their resources at the disposal of the Crown. In the Last decade of India's Freedom Struggle, the British Government used the Indian princes as a counterpoise to nationalist aspirations. However, for all their loyalty to the British Crown, Prime Minister Attlee's announcement of 20th February 1947 and Mountbatten Plan of 3 June 1947 simply emphasized the lapse of British paramountcy in India and the Indian states were left to face the new scenario of Free India and Free Pakistan.

An Overview

In spite of all the tall claims made by the British politicians and imperial school of British historians that Great Britain ushered in India a new era of progress and modernisation—through consolidation of political unity, establishment of peace and internal stability, organisation of an all-India administrative system, development of economic infrastructure by developing rapid means of transport and communications, inflow of Foreign Finance Capital etc. etc.— in 1947 presented the picture of an under developed country. Rather, it will be more correct to say that many of our present day problems—politically-loaded casteism, regional chauvinism, religious fundamentalism, communalism, reservation quotas in legislative bodies, government and university services for Scheduled Castes, Scheduled Tribes and the O.B.Cs—have their roots in the divide and rule policies followed by the Government of India during a century of Crown Rule in India.

SELECT REFERENCES

1. Dharma Kumar (Ed.) : *The Cambridge Economic History of India.*
2. Dodwell, H. H. (Ed.) : *The Cambridge History of India a Vol. VI.*
3. Griffiths, P. J. : *The British Impact on India.*
4. Gopal, S. : *British Policy in India, 1858–1905.*
5. Grover, B. L. : *Curzon and Congress (I.C.H.R. 1995).*
6. Ilbert; C. P. : *The Government of India.*
7. Metcalf, T. R. : *Ideologies of the Raj (New Cambridge History of India).*
8. Spear, Pecival : *The Oxford History of India.*
9. Strachey, John : *India, its Administration.*

India Under Lytton and Ripon

The Viceroyalties of Lytton and Ripon prepared the soil of British India for nationalism, the former by internal measures of repression......, the latter indirectly as a result of the European community's rejection of his liberal humanitarian legislation.

—S. A. Wolpert

Lord Lytton, 1876–80

Lord Lytton was a nominee of the Conservative Government of Benjamin Disraeli and was appointed with a special eye to the Central Asian developments. Mr. Disraeli's first letter to Lytton indicated the task the Viceroy was to perform: "The critical state of affairs in Central Asia demands a statesman, and I believe if you will accept this high post you will have an opportunity, not only of serving your country, but of obtaining an enduring fame." Lord Lytton, who on an earlier occasion had refused the governorship of Madras on account of his bad health, was tempted to accept the post of the Viceroy as ' a high and glorious command, which it would be a dereliction of duty to disobey'. Lytton took over charge from Lord Northbrook at Calcutta in April 1876. Lytton was a diplomat by profession and had served the British Foreign Office in many capacities. He was a reputed poet, a novelist and an essayist and known in the literary world as 'Owen Meredith'. Till 1876 Lytton had no experience of administration nor any acquaintance with Indian affairs.

Lytton and Free Trade. Free trade had become a passion with the ruling circles of England, more so because it suited the interests of an industrially advanced country that England was at that time. The Lancashire cotton manufacturers were jealous of the new cotton mills that were springing up at Bombay and wanted to prevent India from developing competitive industries; they attacked the import duties on cotton goods levied in India. The Conservative Government, fully aware of the importance of the Lancashire vote, moved a resolution in the House of Commons on 11 July 1877 which runs thus: "That in the opinion of this House, the duties now levied upon cotton manufactures imported into India, being protective in their nature, are contrary to sound commercial policy, and ought to be repealed without delay, so soon as the financial condition of India will permit." Lord Salisbury, the Secretary of State for India, forwarded the said resolution to the Indian Government urging it to repeal the cotton duties. Notwithstanding the poor financial condition of India caused by famine, Lytton abolished import duties on twenty nine articles including sugar, sheetings, drill and some other varieties of cloth though all the members of the Viceroy's Executive Council were arrayed against him like "all the elephants of Porus." Even Lord Salisbury had second thoughts and told Lytton that hurried action might give impression of heedlessness. The Manchester Chamber of Commerce was, however, not satisfied with the pace and urged the abolition of the 5% *ad valorem* duty on all varieties of cotton cloth. The Viceroy accepted in principle the desirability of abolishing all import duties, but wanted to wait till the lean financial years were over. However, in 1879 the duties on the coarser kinds of imported cotton were removed and the Viceroy had to use his constitutional powers to overrule the majority in his Council. Lord Salisbury, the Secretary of State, approved of the Viceroy's action although the India Council was equally divided, seven voting for and seven against. Thus the claims of Indian administration were subordinated to the necessities of English politics.

Financial Reforms. The policy of financial devolution begun under Lord Mayo was continued. Another step forward was taken in that direction. The Provincial governments were given the control of the expenditure upon all ordinary provincial services including land revenue, excise, stamps, law and justice, general administration etc. For the discharge of the newly transferred services, the provincial governments were not given any increase in their fixed grants, but handed over some specified sources of revenue (*e.g.*, law and justice, excise, licence fee) from their respective provinces. It was also provided that any surplus above the estimated income was to be shared equally with the Central Government, the latter on its part undertaking to meet half of any deficit. It was hoped that the system would give the provinces an effective inducement to develop the revenue resources collected in the provinces, which would also improve the financial position of the government as a whole.

Sir John Strachey, the Finance Member of the Viceroy's Council, also took steps to equalize the rates of salt duties in the British provinces. He also negotiated with the Indian princes for surrender of their rights of manufacture of salt in return for compensation. Thus inter-state smuggling of salt came to an end and the salt duties began to yield more revenue to the government.

The Famine of 1876–78. A severe famine ravaged India during 1876–78. The areas worst affected were Madras, Bombay, Mysore, Hyderabad and some parts of Central India and the Panjab. The famine-affected area was estimated at 257,000 square miles, with a population of more than 58 millions. Many villages were depopulated and large tracts of territory went out of cultivation. Romesh Dutt has estimated that five million people perished in a single year[1]. The Government made half-hearted efforts to help the famine-stricken. The Government famine machinery was inadequate and ineffective and the unwisdom of the policy was amply clear. In 1878 a Famine Commission was appointed under the presidency of Richard Strachey to enquire into the whole question of famines and grant of famine relief. The Commission disfavoured the grant of gratuitous help and wanted such a relief to be limited to the impotent poor. It urged that able-bodied persons should be provided employment on wages sufficient to maintain them in health. Further, it urged for the creation of a Famine Fund in every province. As a part of the preventive programme, the Commission recommended the construction of railway and irrigation works. Thus were laid down the principles on which the Government of India based its subsequent famine policy.

The Royal Titles Act, 1876. The British Parliament passed the Royal Titles Act, investing Queen Victoria with the title of Kaiser-i-Hind or Queen Empress of India. The bill was ridiculed by the Liberals in England and coldly received in India. However, a grand darbar was held at Delhi on 1 January 1877 to announce to the people and princes of India the assumption of the title. Unfortunately, the darbar was held at a time when several parts of the country were in the grip of a severe famine. The Government of Lytton spent millions on pomp and pageantry when millions were dying of hunger and starvation. "The Royal Titles Act and the Delhi Darbar", writes R.G. Pradhan, "drove an under-current of national humiliation among the people of India". A Calcutta journal adversely commented that Nero was fiddling while Rome was burning. In a way, the darbar proved a blessing in disguise. Lala Lajpat Rai writes: "The darbar reduced the chiefs of India from the position of allies to that of feudatories, but it quite unconsciously and against the intentions of its author raised in theory the status of the Indian subjects of the Queen to that of citizens of the British Empire... The darbar marked the beginning of the movement which filled the educated Indian with the idea of obtaining his rightful place in the Empire. He became articulate and began to assert himself. He raised the cry of India for Indians' and claimed his country as his own."[2]. It was after the vast assemblage of 1877 that S. N. Banerjee thought in terms of organising an association of Indians to voice their grievance and work for their rights. He had drawn his own lessons from the event.

The Vernacular Press Act, March 1878. The unpopular policies of Lytton and the Government's apathy towards the suffering of the people drove discontent among the masses. In the Bombay Presidency, records William Wedderburn, agrarian riots were followed by gang robberies and attacks on moneylenders. The simmering discontent came to the surface and the government

---

1. Romesh Dutt, *The Economic History of India*, vol. II (1960 ed.) p. 319.
2. Lajpat Rai, *Young India*, p. 124.

policy began to be openly criticised in the vernacular press. Alarmed at the rapid growth of seditious writings, Lytton decided on a repressive policy. In March 1878 the Vernacular Press Act was put on the statute books. Act IX of 1878, an Act for the Better Control of Publications in Oriental Languages, empowered a magistrate to call upon the printer and publisher of any vernacular newspaper to enter into a bond undertaking not to publish anything likely to excite feeling of disaffection against the government or antipathy between persons of different races, castes or religions among Her Majesty's subjects. The magistrate could also demand security and forfeit it, if it contravened the regulations. If the offence re-occurred the equipment was liable to be seized. No appeal against the magistrate's action could be made to a court of law However, vernacular newspapers could get exemption from the operations of the act if the printer submitted proofs of the paper to a Government Censor.

Sir Erskine Perry, a member of the India Council, described the bill as "a retrograde and ill-conceived measure, injurious to the future progress of India" and commented that no imperial legislator could forge a more powerful weapon for extirpating an obnoxious press. S.N. Banerjee described the act as 'a bolt from the blue'. The worst feature of the Act was the discrimination between 'the disloyal native press' and 'the loyal Anglo-Indian press'. The Gagging Act, as it was nicknamed, apparently succeeded in making the vernacular press submissive, but drove the discontent underground. It was an unwise step to 'smother the rising flames of discontent blocking the chimney'.

The Arms Act, 1878. Another repressive measure of Lytton's administration was the Indian Arms Act. Act XI of 1878 made it a criminal offence to keep, bear or traffic in arms without licence. The panalties for contravention of the Act were imprisonment for a term which may extend to three years or with fine or with both and in case of concealment or attempt at concealment to a term which may extend to seven years or with fine or both. The worst feature of the act, however, was the racial discrimination it introduced. Europeans, Anglo-Indians and some categories of government officials were exempted from the operation of this Act. The Act put the official seal upon the already patent fact that Indians were no longer to be trusted.

The Statutory Civil Service. The Charter Act of 1833 had declared all offices in India open to merit irrespective of nationality or colour. The Charter Act of 1853 had provided for the holding of a competitive examination in London for recruitment to higher services under the Company. In 1864 Satyendra Nath Tagore was the first Indian to qualify for the covenanted service. The Act of 1870 had made it clear that one-fifth of the recruits to the covenanted service should be Indians even without a competitive examination, but it took the government ten years to frame rules to implement this decision.

Very few Indian could enter the sacred precincts of the Indian Civil Service. The difficulties facing young Indian aspirants were very great. During 1862–75 only 40 Indians had competed, out of which a mere 10 were successful. The European bureaucracy in India advocated a total closure of the doors of the I.C.S. to Indians and those already employed to be got rid of by paying compensation. Lord Lytton recorded in a confidential minute: "No sooner was the Act of 1833 passed then the Government began to devise means for practically evading the fulfilment of it. We have had to choose between prohibiting them and cheating them and we have chosen the least straight forward course... I do not hesitate to say that both the Government of England and of India appear to me up to the present moment unable to answer satisfactorily the charge of having taken every means in their power of breaking to the heart words of promise they have uttered into the ear."

Lytton proposed the straightforward course of closing the Covenanted Civil Service to Indians and instead to create 'a close native service' to meet the provisions of the Act of 1870. The idea did not find favour with the Home authorities. Lord Cranbrooke, the secretary of State, thought that the legislation to separate the black from the white sheep into two distinct flocks was not feasible and savoured of discrimination. Lytton then proposed the plan of the Statutory Civil Service in 1878–79. According to the rules of 1879, the Government of India could employ some Indians of 'good family and social standing' to the Statutory Civil Service on the recommendation of the provincial governments and subject to the confirmation of the Secretary of State, provided the number of such appointments did not exceed one-sixth of the total appointments made to the Covenanted Service in a year. The Statutory Civil Service was not to have the same status and salary as the Covenanted Service. The Statutory Service, however, did not prove popular with Indian public and had to be abolished eight years later. The Secretary of State did not agree to Lytton's proposal of closing the Covenanted Service to the Indians altogether. However, steps were taken calculated to discourage Indians from competing for the said examination by lowering the maximum age from 21 to 19 years. Since the examination was held only in London, young Indians had to face insurmountable difficulties. "Throughout India", writes S. N. Banerjee, "this was regarded as a deliberate attempt to blast the prospects of Indian candidates for the Indian Civil Service."

The Second Afghan War. Lytton provoked a senseless war with the Afghans with a view to establish a 'scientific frontier' towards the north-west. The adventure proved a failure, while the government had squandered millions extorted from the poor ryot.

Estimate. Lytton undoubtedly was a man of ideas. It was he who favoured the idea of forming a separate North-West Frontier Province under the direct supervision of the Central Government. It was left to Curzon to give a practical shape to this proposal. Lytton's plan for the formation of an Indian Privy Council of Indian Princes was subsequently endorsed by the Montford Scheme of reforms and the Chamber of Princes came into existence in 1921. Lytton had also proposed putting India on the gold standard. Further, the recommendations of the Famine Commission of 1878 formed the basis for the subsequent famine administration of the Government in India.

Lytton must be judged a failure as a ruler of India. H. C. E. Zacharias points out the names of Lord Lytton and Lord Curzon as the two Viceroys who have done more harm to India and to England's position in India than any other men that can be named. Marquess of Hartington (afterwards Duke of Devonshire) said in the British Parliament that Lytton was the very reverse of what an Indian Viceroy should be. Lytton's unpopular and repressive policy drove discontent among the masses. The unrest became widespread and was becoming dangerous. A deep distrust characterized the relations of the rulers and the ruled. According to Blunt, " the state of things at the end of Lord Lytton's reign was bordering upon revolution". Lytton's reactionary policy was greatly responsible for the beginning of counteraction of the part of the Indians. If, however, the ultimate justification for British rule in India, as Philip Woodruff thinks, was the reaction it provoked and the political life it stung into India, then Lytton may share due credit with others in the making of modern India. In the evolution of political progress bad rulers are often a blessing in disguise and so was Lytton. His repressive policy stirred the Indian community into life. Taken in this light, Lytton proved to be a benefactor of India, without intending it to be.

Select Opinions

V. A. Smith. Lytton's reputation has been obscured by the lack of an adequate biography; by certain foreign peculiarities of manner and habits which offended conventional opinion; and, above all, by reason of the bitter partisan controversies aroused by his Afghan policy, executed by him under the instructions of Lords Beaconsfield and Salisbury. The equally venomous criticism of the Vernacular Press Act further discredited him in popular opinion. Those causes have prevented Lord Lytton from attaining the 'enduring fame' promised by the Prime Minister, and perhaps may be said to have left a general impression that he was a failure as a ruler of India. If such an opinion exists it is based upon insufficient grounds. The best parts of his internal policy were of permanent value, and served as the basis of development effected by his successors; while the most essential measures of his Afghan policy, by which I mean the occupation of Quetta and the securing of the Kurrum valley either remained undisturbed, or, if reversed for a time, had to be reaffirmed a few years later. (*The Oxford History of India*, p. 747–48.)

P. E. Roberts. No Viceroy in modern times has been subjected to fiercer criticism than Lytton... His Afghan policy was.. indeed a calamitous and unrighteous blunder, and on that head alone Lord Lytton's claims to statesmanship are justly forfeit. The great loss of life in the famine of 1878–80, the measures taken to limit the freedom of the press, the miscalculation in the estimates of the war charges, all these things naturally gave ground for criticism. Yet no one can read Lord Lytton's minutes and dispatches without realising that he was a man of more than ordinary gifts. Though often hasty and impulsive, he brought some new and fruitful conceptions into the field of Indian politics. Many of his unrealized ideas only failed of realization because they were before their time. He advocated the introduction of a gold standard into the monetary system of India. He suggested the creation of a north-west frontier province under the direct control of the government of India. He proposed the formation of an Indian Privy Council of the ruling chiefs.. He tried to stop the tendency to pass too lenient sentences on Europeans who had assaulted their Indian servants. (*History of British India*, p. 460).

S. Gopal. Of real achievement Lytton could show little. He had sound impulses on such matters as the official attitude to the subject race and the employment of Indians in the civil service. His famine administration was efficient, and the gross error in the financial estimates in the last year of the viceroyalty was not a substantive one. Yet on the whole Lytton's domestic policy was irrelevant. He believed in symbol and ceremony, exalted the feudal princes and sought to terrorize the middle classes of Bengal, when in fact the areas of political sensitivity were Bombay and the Western Deccan. It was his adventurism in foreign policy which turned the viceroyalty to ashes. He was eager in 1879 to annex a major portion of Upper Burma. However, he restrained his ardour, especially as his enthusiasm was not shared by the Home government and he was being criticised at that time for his forward policy in Afghanistan. There he acted as a runaway horse. Lytton's policy could have been vindicated only by success; but this, to the surprise of few, was denied him. He had fought with a sword but no shield ; and he paid the price. (*British Policy in India*, pp. 127–28)

Lord Ripon. 1880–84

George Fredrick Samuel Robinson, first Marquess of Ripon, was born in 1827. He began his public career in 1849 as attached at the Brussels Legation. In 1852 he entered the House of Commons on the Liberal Party ticket and in 1859 became Under Secretary for India. From 1861 to 1863 he was Under -Secretary for India and then was Secretary of State for India during 1866–68. In 1874 he accepted the Roman Catholic religion. During 1868–74 Ripon was a member of Gladstone's Cabinet and was responsible for such legislation as the Irish Church Act, the Education Act and the Ballot Act. In 1880 he was appointed the Viceroy of India.

In 1880 the Liberal Party came to power in England under the leadership of Gladstone. Gladstone, the chief devotee of Liberty in Europe, explained his policy towards India thus: "Our title to be in India depends on a first condition, that our being there is profitable to the Indian natives; and on a second condition, that we can make them see and understand it to be profitable". Gladstone chose Ripon to carry out this policy. Ripon was an honest man with a broad outlook. He was a true Democrat. In 1852 Ripon wrote in a pamphlet entitled "The Duty of the Age" that Democracy was determined by two factors. First, that every man so far as he is a man has a claim to share in the government of his country, in all its duties, responsibilities and charges, and secondly, that self-government is the highest and noblest principle of politics, the safest foundation on which the state can rest. The sincerity of purpose is clear from his first public pronouncement in Calcutta when he said: "Judge me by my acts and not by my words". A true liberal of the Gladstonian era, Ripon's whole political outlook was the very antithesis of his immediate predecessor. He was inspired with a sense of mission and duty towards India. His principal measures bear the stamp of humanitarianism. He took some steps towards liberalizing the administration in India.

India was in a state of fermentation—political, social and religious—when Lord Ripon came to India. Lytton's unpopular measures had driven discontent among the masses and India was bordering on revolution. Ripon tried to heal the wounds of India and apart from undoing most of the unpopular acts of Lytton, took some positive and constructive steps for the good of the Indians. It was he who formulated the policy of local self-government and thereby laid the foundations of representative institutions in India.

Repeal of the Vernacular Press Act, 1882. The obnoxious Press Act of 1878 was repealed by Act III of 1882 and newspapers published in vernacular languages were allowed equal freedom with the rest of the Indian press. This wise action of Ripon tried to undo the wrong done by Lytton and went a long way in conciliating public opinion. Of course, the Government retained the Sea Customs Act of 1878 which authorised the Post Office authorities to search and seize any vernacular writing of a seditious nature.

The First Factory Act, 1881. To improve the lot of factory labourers, the Government of Ripon passed the first Factory Act which sought to regulate and improve the condition of labour in Indian factories. The Act was applicable in case of factories employing 100 or more hands. The Act prohibited the employment of children under the age of seven, limited the number of working hours for children below the age of twelve and required that dangerous machinery should be fenced. Inspectors were apppointed to supervise the implementation of these measures. The Act though limited in its scope opened a new phase in the industrial history of India.

Financial Decentralization, 1882. Lord Ripon continued the policy of financial devolution inaugurated under Lord Mayo. As the first experiments in financial decentralization worked well, the Government of Ripon decided to increase further the financial responsibilities of the provinces. The sources of revenue were divided into three classes, *viz.*, Imperial, Provincial and Divided.

(*i*) **Imperial Heads.** Revenue from Customs, Posts and Telegraphs, Railways, Opium, Salt, Mint, Military Receipts, Land Revenue etc., went wholly to the Central Government and the Central expenditure was to be met out of this income.

(*ii*) **Provincial Heads.** Income from subjects of local nature like Jails, Medical Services, Printing, Roads, General Administration etc. was to go entirely to provincial governments. As the income from the transferred heads was not ordinarily sufficient for provincial requirements, the Central Government made good the deficiency in provincial income by a grant of fixed percentage of the land revenue which otherwise remained an Imperial subject.

(*iii*) **Divided Heads.** Income from Excise, Stamps, Forests, Registration etc., was divided in equal proportion among the Central and Provincial Governments. The division of expenditure of these heads generally followed the incidence of the corresponding heads of receipts.

The Resolution of 1882 introduced the system of quinquennial settlement with the provinces.

The chief merit of the new system was that it gave the provincial governments a direct interest in Divided Heads raised within their jurisdiction. The system also harmonised the financial interests of the Central and Provincial Governments which now shared not only the receipts but also the expenditure on certain heads. Financial settlements with the provinces were revised in 1887, 1892 and 1897. The system of Divided Heads begun by Ripon remained operative till it was modified by the Reforms of 1919.

Resolution on Local Self-Government, 1882. Perhaps the most noble work of Ripon was the Government Resolution on Local Self-Government. Ripon set at work the municipal institutions of the country, for there, as he said, began the political education of the people. The development of Local Government was advocated not with a view to efficiency of administration, but as an instrument of political and popular education.

Local Boards were to be developed throughout the country. In the rural areas the Governor-General desired that smallest administrative unit—the sub-division, the taluka or the tehsil—should form the maximum area under a Local Board. In towns the Municipal Committees and City bodies to form the local board. Local bodies were to be charged with definite duties and entrusted with suitable sources of revenue. Ripon desired that provincial governments should apply in case of local bodies the same principle of financial decentralization which Lord Mayo had introduced towards them. The local boards, both urban and rural, must everywhere have a large preponderance of non-official members, and the system of election wherever local circumstances permitted. The official interference was to be reduced to the minimum and "the Government should revise and check the acts of local bodies, but not dictate to them". Chairmen of these local bodies should not be officials, but elected by the local bodies themselves. Of course, official executive sanction should be neccessary in certain cases, such as the raising of loans, undertaking works costing more than the prescribed sum imposition of taxes in other than the authorised forms, the alienation of municipal property, framing of rules and bye-laws etc.

In pursuance of the above resolution Local Self-Government Acts were passed in various provinces during 1883–85. The Madras Local Boards Act of 1884 gave the work of lighting and cleaning of streets, education, water supply and medical aid to local bodies. Similar acts were passed in the Punjab and Bengal.

Resolution on Land Revenue Policy. Ripon disfavoured the proposal which had been before the government for twenty years, of establishing a permanent settlement of the land revenue on the model of Bengal througout India. In 1793 Lord Cornwallis had by the Permanent Settlement of Bengal transformed tax-collectors (zamindars) into landlords and placed the ryot at their tender mercy. Ripon sought to modify the 'Permanent Settlement' of Bengal even by proposing to give the ryot an assurance of permanence and security, while at the same time committing the government not to make any further enhancement of land revenue except on the ground of rise of prices. The zamindars of Bengal opposed the measure, the peasants of Bengal did not support it for they feared that the Anglo-Indian bureaucracy would be worst than the zamindars. Ripon's proposals did not find favour with the Secretary of State.

Educational Reforms. In 1882 an Education Commission was appointed under the Chairmanship of Sir William Hunter to review the progress of education in the country since Wood's despatch of 1854 and to suggest measures for further implementation of the policy laid therein. The Commission emphasised the State's special responsibility for the expansion and improvement of primary education. It recommended that primary education may be entrusted to the care of the newly established Municipal and District Boards under the vigilant supervision and control of the government. As far as secondary education was concerned, the general principle was laid down that there should be two divisions of courses, one of literary education preparing students for Entrance Examination of the University and the other of a practical character opening commercial and a vocational careers. The Commission noted with satisfaction the system of grants-in-aid and urged its extension for secondary and higher education. A general principle was laid down that government should withdraw as early as possible from the direct management of secondary schools. The commission also drew the attention of the Government to the inadequate facilities for female education outside the presidency town and made suggestions for its spread. The Commission did not make any recommendations regarding University education for it was not in its terms of reference.

Most of the recommendations of the Commission were accepted by the Government. The last quarter of the nineteenth century witnessed an unprecedented growth of schools in the country, mostly through private philanthropic activity.

The Ilbert Bill Controversy, 1883–84. Sir C.P. Ilbert was the Law Member of the Viceroy's Council. At the instance of the Viceroy he introduced a bill popularly known as the LIbert Bill, in the

Legislative Council on 2 February 1883. The Bill sought to abolish at once and completely "every judicial disqualification based merely on race distinctions".

Before 1857 there were two separate systems of law and jurisprudence in the Company's territories. The first was the Mohammadan law administered in the rural areas by the Company's courts based on the *de jure* authority of the Mughal Emperor. The second was the English law administered in the Presidency towns by the Supreme Court. Most of the Governor-General had felt that it would be unfair to submit Englishmen in India to Mohammadan law, and as such, except in the Presidency towns, no Indian judge could try criminal cases involving European British subjects. Indian judges, however, could try all civil cases even when Europeans were a party to a dispute. This dual system of law and courts was abolished in 1861 when the Indian Penal Code of the year gave a uniform criminal law to the country and High Courts were established in the provinces. However, disparity between Indian and European judges continued. The Ilbert Bill sought to correct this anomaly and give equal powers to Indian and European judges.

Mr. Behari Lal Gupta, a Presidency Magistrate of Calcutta, wrote to Sir Ashley Eden, Lieutenant Governor of Bengal, that while officiating as Presidency magistrate he had exercised judicial powers which he had to forfeit on being appointed to a more responsible post in the mofussil. This invidious discrimination between the Indian and European members of the Covenanted Civil Service naturally undermined the authority of the Indian judges. The proposed Bill sought to establish equality between the English and Indian judges.

The Bill was most unpopular with the European community in India. Englishmen, particularly of the planters' class, ill-treated and even on occasions beat their Indian servants to death. Those Englishmen were tried by English judges who usually let them off with no or very light punishment. To defend their special Privileges the European community organised a Defence Association and collected a fund of Rs 150,000. They carried on propaganda both in India and London. They argued, "Shall we be judged by the Nigger? Shall he send us to jail? Shall he be put in authority over us? Never! It is impossible! Better that British rule in India should end than that we should be obliged to submit to such humiliating laws". They thought that the Viceroy had launched an attack on his own countrymen. They hurled abuses at him and passed resolutions urging the British Government to racall him before the expiration of the period of his office. There were possibilities of racial riots breaking out in Calcutta. Some Europeans of Calcutta organised a conspiracy to overpower the sentries at the Government House, arrest the Viceroy and push him in a steamer and deport him to England. The tea-planters of Assam formed a conspiracy to kidnap the Viceroy who was scheduled to visit their province for a hunt. In London, *The Times* attacked the policies of Ripon. Even the Queen doubted the wisdom of the Viceroy's proposed Bill.

Ripon bowed before the storm of agitation and a compromise was reached in 1884 which virtually surrendered the very principle for which the bill had been introduced. The amended Bill was enacted on 26 January 1884, which provided that European British subjects, when brought to trial before a District Magistrate or Sessions Judge, whether European or Indian, were to have a right to claim trial by a jury of twelve, at least seven of whom must be Europeans or Americans. If in the mofussil districts, no jury could be formed, the magistrate was to transfer the case to such other court as the High Court might direct.

Rendition of Mysore. On the charge of misgovernment Lord William Bentinck had annexed the State of Mysore in 1831. Later on it came to the knowledge of the government that the reports of oppression in Mysore were greatly exaggerated. However, the Company's authorities refused to reverse the decision. Ripon decided to correct the wrong done in 1831 and restored the administration of the state to the adopted son of the deposed Raja who had died in 1866. The Instrument of Transfer which laid down conditions on which Mysore was restored to the Maharaja indicated the changed nature of relations between the Paramount Power and the Indian princes.

Resignation of Ripon. In the summer of 1882 Gladstone had willingly sanctioned the occupation of Egypt. A contingent of Indian troops was sent to Egypt and the burden of the Imperial war fell partly on the Indian Exchequer. Ripon launched a strong protest against this gross injustice. Ripon felt that his mission in India had failed. The Ilbert Bill greatly disillusioned him. He resigned before the term of his Viceroyalty was over and returned to England a defeated man.

Estimate of Ripon. Florence Nightingale called Ripon 'the Saviour of India' and his rule the beginning of a golden age in India. Arnold White, on the other hand, thought that Ripon had "opened the door to the loss of India". Ripon was very popular with the Indians who long remembered him as 'Ripon the Good and Virtuous'. In his presidential address at the Indian National Congress session at Lahore in 1909, Pandit Madan Mohan Malviya said: "Ripon was the greatest and the most beloved Viceroy whom India has known. He was loved and respected by educated Indians as I believe no Englishman who has ever been connected with India, except the Father of the Indian National Congress, Mr. Allan Octavian Hume and Sir William Wedderburn, has been loved and respected. Ripon was loved because he inaugurated that noble scheme of local self-government... because he made the most courageous attempt to act up to the spirit of the noble Proclamation of 1858, to eradicate race distinctions, and to treat his Indian fellow subjects as standing on the footing of equality with their European fellow subjects.... because he was a God-fearing man... and believed in the truth of the teaching that righteousness exalteth a nation... because he was a type of the noblest of Englishmen, who have an innate love of justice and who wish to see the blessing of liberty which they themselves enjoy extended to all their fellowmen." One of the last acts of Ripon in 1909 was to vote for the Minto-Morley Reforms in the House of Lords. He died in 1909.

Unfortunately, for India and Ripon the best measures of Ripon—local self-government, substitution of merit for patronage and jobbery in filling posts in the higher branches of subordinate services, the Ilbert Bill—were defeated by the Indian bureaucracy. Very little was done in the sphere of local self-government or as Blunt puts it: "Poor little acts were passed allowing native communities to mend their own roads, provided the Commissioner does not think them incapable of doing so." Perhaps the outcome of Ripon's efforts was little, Ripon is remembered not that he had been able to do much, but as Surendra Nath Banerjee puts it, for "the purity of his intentions, the loftiness of his ideals, the righteousness of his policy, and his hatred of racial disqualifications."[3] Repon's doings, though unsuccessful, raised hopes and aspirations which marked the beginning of political life in India.

Select Opinions

P. E. Roberts. Lord Ripon was indeed of a different stamp from the typical Viceroy, and in his whole political outlook was the very antithesis of his immediate predecessor. He was a true Liberal of the Gladstonian era, with a strong belief in the virtues of peace, *laissez-faire,* and self-government... Among men of Indian race who had received an education on English lines there was growing up a strong and altogether natural desire to play a more active part in the administration of their country, and to introduce into the East those conceptions of constitutional and representative government with which their newly acquired western knowledge made them, in theory at any rate, acquainted. With these aspirations Lord Ripon heartily sympathised, and he was determined to take some forward steps in the direction of liberalizing the Indian Government. (*History of British India.* pp. 463–64)

S. Gopal. Ripon was a man of no high intellectual or administrative ability, and there was little in his Indian record which raised him above the rank of mediocrity. Yet, paradoxically, his term has become one of the great peaks of British Indian History. Thinking Indians were persuaded by the events of those four years that there were men in high places in Britain who regarded dominion as a trust and were willing to exert themselves to fulfil that trust... Ripon was sure in his mind that it was the

---

3. S. N. Banerjee : *A Nation in the Making,* p. 64

growing class of educated Indians to whom responsiblity should gradually be transferred. 'To overlook and despise these men, to regard them as people to be "kept down" is to the height of political folly.' The unspectacular expansion of local self-government and plans to raise the age of recruitment to the civil service were his methods of increasing the participation of these educated Indians in government; and neither proved fruitful. But the tension created by the careless decision to me grant powers of criminal jurisdiction to Indian judges over European British subjects in the country districts floodlighted the political ideas and beliefs of the Viceroy, and did more than any other event after 1857 to make British rule unacceptable to politically concious Indians. They realized too that British statesmen by themselves could achieve little, for they would always be confronted by the blind yet powerful antagonism of the Birish community in India. If Indians were some day to be free, they would themselves have to strike the blow, 1883 saw the beginnings of Indian political organisation and nationalist endeavour (*The Viceroyalty of Lord Ripon*).

SELECT REFERENCES

1. Balfour, Lady Betty : *The History of Lytton's Indian Administration.*
2. Blunt, W. S. : *India under Ripon*
3. Gopal, S. : *The Viceroyalty of Lord Ripon.*
4. Wolf, Lucien : *The Life of Lord Ripon.*

LORD GEORGE NATHANIEL CURZON
1899–1905

> I believe the Congress is tottering to its fall, and one of my greatest ambitions while in India is to assist it to a peaceful demise.
>
> —*Curzon to Secretary of State*

The appointment of Lord Curzon as Viceroy of India in succession to Lord Elgin II was the fulfilment of the life-long dream of Curzon. While at Eton he had written about the allurements and demands of an Indian Viceroyalty and believed that he was born to hold that post. He knew more about India and Indian problems in 1899 than any other Viceroy at the time to his appointment. He had been to India before a number of times and had earlier travelled across Korea, China, Japan, Ceylon, Afghanistan, Samarkand, Tashkent and Persia and acquainted himself with problems connected with India's defences. He had written three books on Asian problems. It was said that Curzon knew more about India than any living man of the times, yet he thought that he had a lot to learn, for he once said: "The East is a University in which the scholar never takes a degree."

For a dutiful and conscientious Viceroy the task was really great. The famine of 1896–97 and the following bubonic plague had created problems, Revenues were declining. Changing times called for a thorough overhauling of the administrative machinery. Far more serious was the political climate in the country' renascent India was questioning the very right of the British to rule India. The problem of India's defences assumed new dimensions in the age of rising European imperialism.

Administrative Reforms

Curzon had a clear-cut conception of the task before him. He was convinced of the necessity and urgency of a thorough reform of the entire administrative machinery. In the course of a conversation in London in July 1904 he said that "epochs arise in the history of every country when the administrative machinery requires to be taken to pieces and overhauled and readjusted to the altered necessities or the growing demands of the hour." There was scarcely a department of government or a branch of the service which escaped his crusading zeal for reform. He aimed at 'efficiency' of administration and the trend of his mind was towards 'officialization' and 'centralization.' He showed scant consideration for the feelings and aspirations of the people and hoped to build British rule in India on a "rock of granite." Curzon's method was to appoint an expert commission to probe into the working of a department and then enact necessary legislation.

(1) **Police Reforms.** In 1902 a Police Commission was appointed under the presidentship of Sir Andrew Frazer to enquire into the police administration of every province. The report of the Commission submitted in 1903 was described by Curzon thus : "No more fearless or useful report had ever been placed before the Government of India." The report described the police force as "far from efficient, defective in training and organisation, inadequately supervised corrupt and oppressive" and emphasised its failure to secure the confidence and co-operation of the people. Among the various recommendations of the Commission were increase in salaries of all ranks of the police, increase in the strength of police force in all provinces, setting up of training schools both for officers and constables, direct recruitment in place of promotion in higher ranks, setting up a provincial police service, creation of a Central Department of Criminal Intelligence under a Director with subordinate departments in the provinces, etc., etc.

Most of the recommendations of the Commission were accepted and implemented. This meant an increase of expenditure on the Police Department from £2,117,000 in 1898 to £3,212,189 by 1908–9.

(2) Educational Reforms. Curzon found fault with the existing system of education, lamented the deterioration of standards and growth of indiscipline. He believed that educational institutions had become factories for the production of political revolutionaries. In 1902 a Universities Commission was appointed to enquire into condition of universities in India and to recommend proposals for improving their constitution and working. In the words of S.N. Benerjee, the report of the Commission "convulsed educated India from one end of the country to another." On the basis of the recommendations of the Commission, the Indian Universities Act (1904) was passed. The Act sought to increase official control over universities by limiting the number of fellows and increasing the nominated element over elected fellows. The Government was vested with the authority to veto the regulations passed by the Senates. Conditions for affiliation of private colleges were made strict and periodical inspections by the Syndicate made compulsory. The universities were also desired to take active part in the promotion of study and research. In the words of H.C.E. Zacharias : "The Act of 1904 certainly left the India University to be an institution meant not for the fostering of love of learning but for the providing of efficient hurdles in a race after job."[1]

(3) Economic Reforms. Curzon's administration passed legislation relating to Famines, Land Revenue, Irrigation, Agriculture, Railways, Taxation, Currency etc.

The famine and drought of 1899–1900 had affected wide areas in south, central and western India. More than 10 lakh persons died in British India alone. A Famine Commission was appointed under the presidency of Sir Anthony Macdonnell to enquire into the results of famine operations. The commission reported that the relief distributed was excessive and undue emphasis was laid on gratuitous measures. It recommended payment by 'task work' for the able-bodied and laid down rules for dealing with the fodder famine.

The Land Resolution of 16 January 1902 outlined the aim of greater elasticity in revenue collection and the policy of reduction of assessment in cases of failure of crops. If there was to be any increase in the land revenue demand at the time of settlement, it was to be graduated.

In 1901 a Commission was appointed under the chairmanship of Sir Colin Scott Moncrieff to investigate into the whole question of Irrigation. The Commission recommended an additional expenditure of $4\frac{1}{2}$ crores of rupees on irrigation spread over 20 years. The work on the Jhelum canal was completed and the digging of the Upper Chenab, the Upper Jhelum and the Lower Bari Doab canals taken in hand. Further, the Punjab Land Alienation Act (1900) put restrictions on the transfer of land from agriculturists, to non-agriculturists, while the Co-operative Credit Societies Act (1904) sought to provide cultivators with loans at cheap rates of interest. Besides, for the improvement of Indian agriculture and livestock and encouragement of scientific methods of cultivation, an Imperial Agriculture Department under an Inspector-General was set up.

A new Department of Commerce and Industry was established to look after the entire industrial and commercial interests in India. This department looked after Posts and Telegraphs, Factories, Railway Administration, Mines, Ports, Marine etc.

The Indian Coinage and Paper currency Act of 1899 made the British sovereign legal tender in India at the rate of Rs. 15 to a sovereign. India was put on a gold standard. However, the plan did not work well. Ultimately the Gold Exchange Standard Plan was evolved under which the Government was to give rupees in return for gold, and gold for rupees only in case of foreign remittances.

Curzon gave special attention to the development of railways. The existing lines were improved while work on new lines was taken in hand. It is said that Lord Curzon actually built a far greater

---

1. H.C.E. Zacharias : *Renascent India,* p. 137.

mileage of railway lines than any other Viceroy had done so far. Mr. Thomas Robertson, a railway expert, was invited from England to give advice on the working and administration of railways. The expert found the condition of railways unsatisfactory and recommended a 'root-and-branch reform' of the entire railway system. He urged that railway lines should be built "more as commercial enterprises than they have been in the past." He also recommended the setting up of a Railway Board to look after all matters connected with Railway administration, control of State owned lines, supervision of Company owned lines and other cognate matters.

(4) **Judicial Reforms.** Curzon also aimed at improvement of the judicial set-up. The number of judges of the Calcutta High Court was increase to cope with increased work. He also increased the salary and pension benefits of the judges of the High Court as well as subordinate courts. Above all, the Indian Code of Civil Procedure was revised. However, nothing substantial was done to improve the procedure followed or delay caused in the decision of cases.

(5) **Army Reforms.** From the very beginning of British rule in India the army had performed the double task of protection from external dangers as well as helped in the maintenance of peace within the country. Russian activities in Central Asia and the completion of the Tashkent Railway alarmed the Government of India and worried them about the north-west defences.

The work of the reorganisation of the army was mostly the work of Lord Kitchener, the Commander-in-Chief in India from 1902 to 1908. The Indian army was grouped into two commands— the Northern Command with its headquarters at Murree and striking point as Peshawar and the Southern Command with its headquarters at Poona and striking point at Quetta. In each division there were to be three brigades, two of native battalions and one of British battaliorn. Every Brigadier was to be responsible for the efficiency of his brigade. A training college for officers on the model of Camberley College of England was set up at Quetta. Better arms were supplied to the British troops. Above all, every battalion of the army was subjected to a severe test called. 'The Kitchener Test". The reorganisation of the army naturally meant an increase in expenditure on this department.

(6) **Calcutta Corporation Act, 1899.** In the name of efficiency Curzon sought to undo the noble work done by Lord Ripon in the field of local self-government. The Calcutta Corporation Act reduced the strength of elected members, thereby giving the British element a difinite majority both on the Corporation and on its various committees. In fact the Corporation was reduced to the position of "an Anglo-Indian house". The Indian members resented the change and 28 members resigned in protest. Curzon remained undeterred and was so happy with his doing that at a banquet in 1903 he said that he would like to become the Mayor of Calcutta after his retirement from the office of Viceroyalty.

(7) **Ancient Monuments Act, 1904.** A keen student of history and deeply interested in archaeology he passed an Act to repair, restore and protect the historical monuments in the country. A sum of £ 50,000 was sanctioned for carrying on the repair of historical buildings in India. He even put pressure on the Indian states to preserve the rich heritage of India in the Ajanta-Ellora Caves, at the Sanchi Stupa etc. He urged the provincial governments to open museums for the safe custody of rate objects, thus Curzon paid his homage to "the poets, artists and creators of the past."

The Partition of Bengal, 1905

A masterpiece of Curzon's internal policy was the partition of Bengal into two provinces of Bengal proper and Eastern Bengal and Assam in 1905. Efficiency of administration demanded the re-arrangement of boundaries between Bengal and Assam.

The province of Bengal at that time comprised Bangal, Bihar and Orissa with an area of 189,000 square miles and a population of 80 millions. Non-Bengalis of Bihar and Orissa numbered 21 millions. Curzon described the partition as 'a mere readjustment of administrative boundaries'. It was explained that the eastern districts of Mymensingh and Backergange divisions were notorious for lawlessness and crime and the police arangement was unable to cope with the situation. The Lieutenant-

Governor who was in charge of the extensive areas could not properly look after these extensive areas. Besides, there had been historical precedents of the creation of separate administrative units, as the setting up of North-West Provinces in 1865 and separation of Assam under a High Commissioner in 1874.

In 1904 Curzon went on a personal tour of Eastern Bangal and by October 1905 the proposal of partition took a final shape. The new province of Eastern Bangal and Assam was to include Assam and the divisions of Dacca, Rajshahi and Chittagong with an area of 106,540 square miles and a population of 31 million people, out which 18 millions were Mohammedans and 12 millions Hindus. The headquarters of the new province was Dacca. The province was put under the charge of a separate Lieutenant-Governor. Western Bengal—Bihar and Orissa inclusive—was left with an area of 141,580 square miles and a population of 54 millions out of which 42 millions were Hindus and 9 million Mohammedans.

The opposition to the partition of Bengal was great and Vocal. The Bengal intelligentsia took it to be a subtle attack upon the growing solidarity of Begali nationalism, an attempt to undermine the traditions, history and language of the Bengalis. The nationalists pointed out that the scheme was devised to divide the people on the basis of religion and to put the Muslims against the Hindus. That this explanation was not without foundation was clear from the declaration of the Lieutenant-Governor of Eastern Bengal that of his two wives, the Mohammedan wife was his favourite. Even Lord Curzon during his tour of Eastern Bengal explained that one object of the partition proposal was to create a Mohammedan province where Islam could be predominant and its followers in ascendancy. Evidently, the Mohammedans of Eastern Bangal were won over by visions of political and material advantages awaiting them in a Muslim majority province.

Far more offensive was the manner in which the proposal of partition was carried out in the teeth of public opposition. The Viceroy described the popular agitation as 'partly unscrupulous and partly misinformed,' while Sir Andrew Fraser, the Lieutenant-Governor, attributed the agitation to vested interests of two professional classes, the Calcutta Bar who feared a setback to their work due to the creation of a separate High Court at Dacca and the Calcutta journalists who feared the possibility of new newspapers being published from Dacca. Lord Morley, the new Secretary of State, declared in 1905 that the partition was a 'settled fact'.

It was suggested to the Government that united Bengal could be placed under a Governor with a separate executive council as in Madras and Bombay. The Viceroy turned down the proposal as unsatisfactory . "Government by one man", wrote Curzon to the Secretary of State in a letter dated 28 January 1904, "is infinitely better than Government by three men if it can be so managed. What we want in India is personal knowledge of localities and personal touch with the people. This can only be gained by the familiarity of the Head of the Administration with the places and people under his charge. With a triumvirate as ruling power this is quite impossible, and Bombay and Madras are both, in my view, illustrations that the weak points are in excess of the merits of the system". Probably the best solution could be, what was done six years later, the separation of non-Bengali speaking parts of Bihar and Orissa from Bengal proper.

Sentiment on both sides clouded the real issue and poisoned the political atmosphere. The partition was forced at a psychological moment, the year of Japan's victory over Russia. The Indian opinion was utterly disregarded. Gokhale in a speech at Benaras in 1905 said: "The Viceroy had made up his mind. The officials under him had expressed approval. What business had the people to have an opinion of their own and to stand in the way? To add insult to injury, Lord Curzon described the opposition to his measures as 'manufactured'—an opposition in which all classes of Indians, high and low, uneducated and educated, Hindus and Mohammedans, had joined, an opposition than which nothing more intense, nothing more widespread, nothing more spontaneous, had been seen in the country in the whole of our political agitation." Curzon made it a prestige issue and decided not to yield to pressure. Bengali youth accepted it as a challenge to their nationalism and pledged to undo it. Surendra Nath Banerjee became the leader of the opposition and the popular slogan was "Surrender Not Banerjee"

Recent researches have proved that Curzon's main motives were political and machiavellian. The partition of Bengal was a strong weapon in Curzon's armoury to undermine the solidarity of politically advanced Bengalis and at lessening the political influence of Calcutta in Indian affairs. In a private confidential letter to the Secretary of State on 17 February 1904, Curzon wrote, "The Bengalis, who like to think themselves a nation, and who dream of a future when the English will have been turned out and a Bengali Babu will be installed in Government House, Calcutta, of course bitterly resent any disruption that will be likely to interfere with the realization of this dream. *If we are weak enough to yield to their clamour now, we shall not be able to dismember or reduce Bengal a gain* and you will be cementing and solidifying, on the eastern flanks of India, a force already formidable and certain to be a source of increasing trouble in future."[2]

The partition of Bengal, whatever its justification from the administrative viewpoint, was a cardinal blunder of Curzon. It embittered Indo British relations. It created a branch between Muslims and Hindus for the Muslims thought that they had been deprived by the Hindus of the opportunities possible from a Muslim majority province. However, the partition and the resultant agitation gave a great fillip to the nationalist movement. The annulment of the partition in 1911 gave India a 'sense of power', besides inculcating love for *Swadeshi*.

The Foreign Policy of Curzon

Right from the time of Warren Hastings and Wellesley the question of suitable land frontiers had agitated the minds of the British administrators in India as well as the Home authorities in England. Curzoo, however, Looked upon the problem of frontiers from a fresh angle. A keen student of geo-politics, Curzon gave to the problem of frontiers a 'scientific' basis and developed British India into what Mr. K. M. Pannikar calls an 'Empire' claiming to be heard in its own right, often forcing Home authorities into policies with which it was not in full agreement and considerably influencing British policy towards Asiatic countries Curzon's general foreign policy towards Asiatic countries —Arabia, Persia, Afghanistan, Tibet and as far eastwards as Siam—is abundantly clear from what Curzon once said about Britain's position towards the North-Western areas: "We do not want to occupy it but we cannot afford to see it occupied by our toes we are quite content to let it remain in the hands of our allies and friends; but if rival and unfriendly influences creep up to it and lodge themselves right under our walls, we are compelled to intervene because a danger would thereby grow up that might one day menace our security."

The Persian Gulf. Britain's special interest in the Persian Gulf dates from the seventeenth century when she occupied important stations in the area. British Residents in the Gulf acted as arbiters in the quarrels of the chiefs on the Arabian coasts, British navy suppressed piracy and enforced peace between warring chief-tains from Aden to Baluchistan. Although England did not aim at any colonial empire in this area she would not tolerate the territorial interests of any other great power in that area.

In the last quarter of the nineteenth century European nations were competing with one another in the race for more and more colonies and 'spheres of influence'. Russia was thrusting southward and looked for a port in the Persian Gulf France was looking for a coaling station in the area, Germany was working on a plan to extend her Berlin-Bagadad Railway project to the Gulf and even Turkey was keen to re-establish her suzerainty over Kuwait,

---

2. For details see B. L. Grover's *A Documentary Study of British Policy Towards Indian Nationalism*, 1885–1909.

In 1892 M. Deloncle declared in the French Chamber of Deputies that England's claim "to keep order by herself in the Persian Gulf" and to be " sovereign arbiter of all disputes between the Arab, Persian and Turkish chiefs" of the Gulf was exercised "in a form European diplomacy had never recognised". In 1898 M. Ottavi, the French Consul at Muscat, secured from the Sultan of Oman the coaling station of Bunder Jissah, a harbour five miles South of Muscat. Curzon sent Colonel Meade supported by a British cruiser under Admiral Douglas to Oman and under threat of military action the Sultan revoked the concession to the French. England also thwarted all attempts of Russia, Germany and Turkey to gain vantage positions in the Gulf or challenge British position in that quarter. On 5 May 1903. Lord Lansdowne, the British Foreign Secretary, in a speech in the House of Lords gave an unequivocal declaration of England's policy: "I say it without hesitation; we should regard the establishment of a naval base or of a fortified post in the Persian Gulf by any other Power as a very menace to British interests, and we should certainly resist it by all the means at our disposal. Curzon's personal visit to the Gulf escorted by a naval flotilla during November-December 1903 demonstrated to the world England's position of importance in the Gulf and Curzon's view expressed before his appointment as Viceroy: "I should regard the concession of a port upon the Persian Gulf to Russia by any Power as a deliberate insult to Great Britain, as a wanton rupture of the *status quo,* as an international provocation to war, and I should impeach the British Minister, who was guilty of acquiescing in such a surrender, as a traitor to his country".

Curzon also thwarted Russian intrigues in the Perso-Afghan dispute about Seistan. On the strength of an old treaty of 1857, whereby both Persia and Afghanistan had agreed to settle their differences through the good offices of the British Government, Curzon despatched in 1902 Sir Henry MacMahon who arbitrated to the satisfaction of both the parties.

Tibet. As early as 1774–75 Warren Hastings has sent George Bogle as the Company's envoy into Tibet to develop trade relations with that country. A second envoy was sent in 1783 for the same purpose. The priestly hierarchy of Tibet joined by the Chinese Resident there foiled all such attempts. In 1866 the consent of the Chinese, who claimed suzerainty over Tibet, was obtained for the despatch of a mission, but the plan fell through. The Tibetan-Sikkim dispute over common boundary brought matters to the point of hostilities. A Sino-British convention of 1890 demarcated the boundaries; it also considered questions pertaining to trade between India and Tibet which took the shape of a definite agreement by 1893. However, no actual trade resulted from this agreement for the Tibetans refused to accept this Convention and China which claimed suzerainty over Tibet could not enforce it.

At the time of Curzon's arrival in India the relations with Tibet had reached the point of deadlock. The Chinese suzerainty over Tibet was ineffective. The Viceroy's letters to the Dalai Lama were returned unopened. Above all, the Russian influence at Lhasa was increasing and alarmed Curzon. A Russian national, Dorjieff had won the confidence of the Dalai Lama and brought to Tibet Russian arms and ammunition.[3]

Curzon who had tried to forestall Russian influence towards the North-West in Afghanistan and Persia could not remain indifferent to the Russian advances in Tibet. Rumours were also afoot about a secret Sino-Russian agreement for establishment of a Russian protectorate over Tibet. The protests of the Russian ambassador in London against the contemplated despatch of a special mission to London against the contemplated despatch of special mission to Tibet by the Government of India lent further suspicion to Russia's designs in that quarter.

---

3. So great was the dread of Russian influence that in 1902 Lord Lansdowne reminded the Russian Government that if there were "any display of Russian activity in that country we should be obliged to replay by a display of activity not only equivalent to but exceeding that of Russia.

In 1903, with the permission of Home authorities, Curzon sent Colonel Younghusband with a small Gorkha contingent on a special mission to Tibet to "oblige Tibetans to come to an agreement". The Tibetans refused to negotiate and offered non-violent resistance. Younghusband pushed his way reaching Gyantse on April 11 and Lhasa on 3 August 1904. The Dalai Lama fled away from the capital leaving the charge of administration in the hands of senior officials. Younghusband dictated terms on 7 September 1904 which provided that Tibet would pay an indemnity of Rs. 75 lakhs at the rate of one lakh rupees per annum. As a security for the payment, the Indian Government was to occupy the Chumbi valley (territory between Bhutan and Sikkim) for 75 years. Provision was also made for opening trade marts at Yatung, Gyantse and Gartok. The Tibetans were also to respect the frontiers of Sikkim. Further clauses provided that Tibet would not grant any concessions for railways, roads, telegraphs etc. to any foreign state, but give Great Britain some control over the foreign affairs of Tibet.

Mr. Brodrick, the Secretary of State, charged the Government of India with disregard of his instructions in that the huge indemnity demanded was 'in defiance of his express instructions' and occupation of the Chumbi valley for 75 years 'as disobedience of orders. Meantime Lord Lansdowne gave assurances to Russia that no occupation or protectorate or even interference in the internal affairs of Tibet was intended. The Government of India defended the position of Younghusband but admitted an 'error of judgement' on its part. On the insistence of the Secretary of State and true to the pledge given to Russia the treaty was revised reducing the indemnity from Rs. 75 lakhs to Rs. 25 lakhs and providing for the evacuation of the Chumbi valley after three years. The valley was actually evacuated in january 1908.

Critics of Curzon's policy hold that the Younghusband mission just gratified the imperialist tendencies of the Viceroy and that no permanent results followed. Only China gained out of the whole affair because the Anglo-Russian Convention of 1907 provided that the two great powers would not negotiate with Tibet except through the intermediary of the Chinese Government. It must, however, be said that Curzon's vigorous and determined approach counteracted all Russian schemes in Tibet—a great concern of the Viceroy.

The North-West Frontier. Curzon followed 'a realistic and commonsense policy towards the tribesmen of the north-west frontier. He would have nothing to do with the 'elastic and pliable adjectives' of Lawrence's Policy or Forward Policy or surrender to the 'paralysing influence of these labels'. He said: "Let our new frontier policy be called by any name that men chose. Only let it be based not upon obsolete political formulas, but upon up-to-date commonsense". In the light of past experience Curzon hoped to draft a code of frontier policy which could with consistency, and without violent interruptions, be applied to the whole line of north-west frontier from the Pamirs to Baluchistan. Accordingly he followed the policy of 'withdrawal of British forces from advanced positions, employment of tribal forces in defence of tribal territory concentration of British forces in British territory behind them as a safeguard and a support and improvement of communications in the rear." Regular British troops were withdrawn from advanced position in the tribal area like Gilgit, the Khyber, the Kurram and the Waziri country and the task of the defence of these advanced posts entrusted to tribal militia (like Khyber Rifles, Kurram Militia etc.) trained and commanded by British officers. As support to these tribal levies, mobile columns of British troops were station at strategic stations like Malakand, Dargai, Peshawar, Kohat Bannu etc., to rush for support whenever and where ever neccessary. Communications in the rear were developed as a support to this new policy and a number of strategic railway lines were laid down. Besides, at a Darbar held at Peshawar in April 1902 and largely attended by the tribal chiefs, Curzon assured the chiefs of the peaceful and non-aggressive aims of British policy but at the same time warned them of the consequences of violating the frontier. Curzon crowned his policy by the creation of a new North-West Frontier Province consisting of the settled districts of Hazara, Pashawar, Kohat, Bannu, Dera Ismail Khan and the trans-border tracts lying between the administrative frontier and the Durand Line.

Curzon claimed all success for his frontier policy. Speaking in March 1904, Curzon referred to the past five years as unmarked by a single expedition on the entire North-West Frontier and the total loss of only 109 men for maintenance of peace in the area. Curzon had in mind the expeditions undertaken during 1894–98 with tremendous expenditure and loss in lives. Speaking in the House of Lords in 1908, Curzon said: "If anybody and been disposed to doubt the success of the scheme of frontier policy which has now been inexistence for ten years, his doubts must have dispelled, and I hope that we shall now hear no more of the wild-car schemes for advancing into tribal territories, annexing upto the border, and driving roads through the tribal country."

Curzon's policy was, however, not without its shortcomings. Lord Minto wrote to the Secretary of State that "neither the border police nor the levies have been capable of filling the position from which the troops were withdrawn" while Prof. Dodwell comments that "when the Khyber Rifles developed a habit of shooting their Adjutants, the outside world heard nothing of it".

Curzon-Kitchener Controversy and Resignation of Curzon. In the Vicereoy's Executive Council there used to be two members representing the Military Department—the Commander in-Chief who was the executive head of the army in India and the Military Member (an ordinary Executive Department and adviser to the Governor-General on military matters.

Lord Kitchener who came to India as Commander-in-Chief in 1902 objected to this cumbrous department machinery and desired an end to this dual control of military affairs. In fact Kitchener wanted the abolition of the office of the Military Member of the Viceroy's Executives Council and all functions regarding military administration to be entrusted to the care of the Commander-in-Chief. Curzon strongly opposed this proposal maintaining that the proposal, if accepted, "would subvert the military authority of the Government of India as a whole and substitute for it a military autocracy in the person of the Commander-in-Chief."

The matters came to a head when in February 1903 Mr. Edmond Ellis, the Military Member, modified the plan submitted by the Commander-in-Chief for the Tibet mission. Kitchener took offence at it and said, "While I am Commander-in-Chief nobody is going to have a word in criticism of my proposals and no department which renders this possible shall exist". Kitchener was in full battle array.

A change in the Government in England in 1902 had brought A. J. Balfour as Prime Minister and St. John Brodrick as the new Secretary of State. The new Government apprehensive of a war with Russia was not inclined to support the "dual system" and was more likely to support Kitchener. After great deliberations the Home Government suggested a compromise. The position of the Military Member was not abolished but he was reduced to the position of a Military Supply Member whose duties were more of a civilian than of a military nature. All purely military functions of the Department were transferred to the Commander-in-Chief. Curzon was urged to accept the compromise. Sharp differences, however, arose over the appointment of the new Military Supply Member; Curzon proposed the name of Sir Edmund Barrow while Kitchener claimed the right to be consulted in the appointment of the Military Supply Member. The Secretary of state did not approve of the name of Edmund Barrow maintaining that the Secretary of State was the final authority in making appointments to the Viceroy's Executive Council. Curzon took it as lack of confidence in him and tendered his resignation in August 1905.

In England Balfour and Brodrick sought to create the impression that Curzon sought to usurp the authority of the Secretary of State and his resignation was due to his differences on matters of foreign policy with the Home Government. Brodrick was certainly guilty of travesty of facts. The real cause of the conflict lay not so much in differences on principles but in personal animosity between two dominating personalities—Curzon and Kitchener. Kitchener though a very popular soldier was "too ferocious' in manners with great capacity for intrigue. Lord Eisher observed that "to achieve a purpose Kithener is Ignatius Loyala and Juggernaut" while Milner pointed out, "I do not think Kitchener has ever distinguished between fighting, shall we say, the Mahdi and fighting his own colleagues and countrymen". A great tactician, Kitchener got the better of Curzon. Thus Curzon was out-manoeuvred by Kitchener and Brodrick with Balfour as a willing accomplice. Even Ripon expressed his unhappiness at the victory of Kitchener and wrote, "The military element is triumphant, the civil element is discredited. This is a great misfortune."

Estimate of Curzon. Curzon was a great imperialist. How great importance he attached to the Indian connection is clear from what he said in 1898: "India is the pivot of our Empire... If the Empire loses any other part of its Dominion we can survive, but if we lose India the sun of our Empire will have set." He believed that British supremacy in India was intended to endure and he did his best to make it impregnable. Speaking in 1909 at the classical Association he said: "It will be well for England, better for India, best of all for the cause of progressive civilization in general if it be clearly understood from the outset that... we have not the smallest intention of abandoning our Indian possessions, and that it is highly improbable that any such intention will be entertained by our posterity."

Curzon's foreign and domestic policies were motivated by the urge to make the British position in India impregnable. He tried to keep India as a close preserve for Britain and save her from the onslaught of rising European imperialism on the more to get more and more colonies. He succeeded in checking the infiltration of Russian, German and French influence into the Persian Gulf and took adequate precautions to save India's North-Western and Northern Frontier against Russian designes. In his internal policies he tried to overhaul the entire administrative machinery and make it more efficient to subserve the interests of the ruling power. He made painstaking studies of Indian problems of every kind, appointed numerous commissions to collect data and indicate directions of policies. In his educational reforms he aimed at greater official control of universities and limitation of private efforts in the field; in his famine policies he aimed at perfection of the government machinery of famine relief rather than studying the root causes of famines and take preventive measures; in his economic policies relating to irrigation, land revenue, agriculture, railways, taxation and currency he aimed at greater efficiency rather than the improvement of the lot of the people. Curzon had a fetish for efficiency. This virtue of efficiency became a vice in India because it was, as Rabindranath Tagore puts it, 'untouched by hand', *i.e.,* the human element was missing. Mr. Montagu very aptly compared Curzon "to a motor driver who spent all his energies and time in polishing up the different parts of his machine, but drove it not because he never knew where to drive to."

If a man in public life is to be judged by his work, Curzon must be admitted a failure as a statesman. His attitude of lofty superiority and contempt for the opinions of the Indians and everything Indian undermined the wisdom of his reforms. He insulted the Indians and injured their deepest feelings. At the Calcutta University Convocation he said: "We have hardly learned how to light the lamp of the soul... We have to save the rising generation from walking into false paths and guide them to right ones." On another occasion he described the Bengalis as cowards, windbags, unpracticable talkers and mere frothy patriots. He refused to meet the President of the Indian National Congress and characterised their activities as the letting off of 'gas'; he looked upon their resolutions with contempt, because, as he said, nothing had ever come out of them.

Curzon by his impolitic utterances and imperialist designs brought political unrest in India to a bursting point. In the early years of the twentieth century India witnessed widespread anarchism and political commotion. Cases of violence increased and young enthusiasts put implicit faith in the cult of the bomb. The responsiblity for this widespread political unrest must greatly rest on the shoulders of Curzon. Apologists of Curzon's policies like Lovat Fraser assert that the indian agitation and development of national sentiment was the outcome of the general wave of resentment against European domination manifest at that time throughout Asia and that the Indian nationalists took advantage of the excitement created by Curzon's policies to propagate their views, Fraser believes that popular movement, "would have spread with almost or much incendiary rapidity, if the universities had been left alone, if Bengal had remained one and indivisible, if indeed, Lord Curzon had never been born."

Curzon was perhaps the ablest Viceroy that England had till then sent to rule over India. In India Curzon became the most hated person. Like James II of England Curzon knew the art of making enemies. By his closed-mined approach he even antagonised the conservative and loyalist elements in India. If he aimed at strengthening the foundation of British rule in India, the succeeded only in undermining British position in India. It was Curzon's greatest misfortune that he could not understand the people over whom he ruled. He could not appreciate the hopes and aspirations of the Indians. Gokhale compared Curzon with Aurangzeb and said: "We find the same attempt at a rule excessively centralized and intensely personal, the same strenuous purpose, the same overpowering consciousness of duty, the same marvellous capacity for work, the same sense of loneliness, the same persistence, in a policy of distrust and repression, resulting in a bitter exasperation all round... He does not believe in what Mr. Glaodstone used to call the principle of liberty as a factor a human progress. He has no sympathy with popular aspirations, and when he finds them among a subject among a subject people he thinks he is rendering their country a service by trying to put them down." Philip Woodruff comments that even when Curzon gained a point by intellect and industry, he lost another by doing the right thing in the wrong way.[4] Possibly there could be no meeting ground between Curzon's policies and Indian aspiration. Lala Lajpat Rai puts it thus : "India aimed at self-government and freedom, Curzon aimed at prolongation of their period of bondage. We wanted to be assertive and self-reliant, he wanted us to be submissive and under permanent control and tutelage. We wanted an extension of representative government, Curzon did his best to discredit the institutions that had been granted and to set back the hand of the clock."[5]

In many respects Curzon can be compared with Dalhousie. Both possessed sharp intellect, relentless energy, considerable drive and persistence in a decided course. Both were authoritarian in temperament, ruthless in their ways and wanted to achieve too much as too great a pace. If Dalhousie gave a raw deal to Princely India, Curzon treated with scorn the nationalist elements and both sowed the wind leaving to their successors to reap the whirlwind.

If both Curzon and Dalhousie possessed great administrative talent and played a notable role in modernising India, both displayed lack of statesmanship and left a rich legacy of difficulties for their successors. Their Governor-Generalships are today remembered not so much for what they achieved as for what occurred in opposition to them.

Bad rulers are very often a blessing in disguise. Curzon's imperialistic policies provoked reaction which in turn stung political life in India. Out of his tyranny was born a stronger sense of nationhood. Taken in this light Curzon proved to be a benefactor of India without intending to be a benefactor of India without intending to be so.

Select Opinions

Earl of Ronaldshay. It is sometimes asked how it was that Curzon, with all his genius for administration and the varied powers which compelled universal admiration, failed to appreciate the significance of—still more to sympathise with—the rapid growth of national self-consciousness which, especially in Bengal, was taking place before his eyes? The answer is undoubtedly to be found in the deep-rooted convictions which he entertained as to the nature of Great Britain's task in India. He was not one of those who held that India had been won by sword and must be held by the sword. But he was most emphatically amongst those who believed that the destinies of the Indian peoples had

---

4. Philip Woodrufff : *The Men Who Ruled India, vol.* II, p. 194.
5. Lajpat Rai ; *Young India,* p.168

been entrusted by Providence to British keeping. "To me", he declared speaking of British rule in India at the Guildhall in the summer of 1904, "it is the greatest thing that the English people have done or doing now; it is the highest touchstone of national duty".... And it was more than anything else his openly expressed assumption that it was in him, as the representative of the race chosen by God for its loftier standards—administrative, cultural and moral-to be His instrument in leading India along the road to higher things, that reposed the sole right of speaking for Indian peoples that earned for him the dislike of the educated classes. The more thoughtful among the Indian Nationalist showed a subtle appreciation of his point of view. "His idea clearly is to strengthen England's hold on India and to establish her here as India's permanent overlord, yet at the same time to secure some sort of autonomy subject to this overlordship for the Indian Government as representing the interests of the Indian people." And they gave point to their analysis by contrasting Lord Curzon's aims with the policy of Ripon. "Lord Ripon's ideal was to secure, by slow degrees, autonomy for the *Indian people.* Lord Curzon's is to secure it for the *Indian Government,"* (*The Life of Lord Curzon,* vol. II. pp. 417–21)

Lovat Fraser. The real causes of unrest in India—I am now alluding to Anarchism—had no more connection with the Viceroyalty of Curzon than they had with the moon. They sprang from that quickening of new aspirations which swept throughout Asia as a result of the victories of Japan... It has often been complained against Curzon that while he instilled new strength into British rule, he did nothing to satisfy the aspirations of Indians for a larger share in the control of their own affairs. The complaint is quite legitimate, and is entitled to an answer. The particular work which Lord Curzon went to India to do did not include an enlargement of liberties, such as now been granted. It was a work which presented many more difficulties than he had anticipated; he undertook many reforms which he had never originally contemplated; and during the whole of his second period of office he was intermittently engaged in a serious conflict which could not have been foreseen. Had he been able to complete the full term he had projected, had his pathway been peaceful towards the end, it is my belief, and that of men who were intimately associated with his Viceroyalty, that he would have come to realise the desirability of rounding off his labours by some substantial concession to the aspirations of educated Indians. It would have been the natural and coping-stone of his work, (*India Under Curzon And After,* pp. 461–65)

P. E. Roberts. While men may legitimately differ as to Lord Curzon's statesmanship and as to the ultimate effect of his general policy upon the destinies of the people he was called upon to govern, there can hardly be any question as to the high ideals that inspired him, or of the devotion to duty which, in the teeth of much ill-health, domestic sorrow, and physical pain, drove him on to the end of his course... Lord Curzon's name will stand amongst the foremost of those that make up the illustrious role of the Governors General of India. (*History of British India,* pp. 556–57)

Michael Edwardes. Curzon left India believing that he had failed. He had instituted great reforms, but had been unable to see them to fulfilment. He was convinced, however, that the failure had been due to people, not to ideas—and in a sense he was right... The British were no longer sure of their mission. When the poets and the imperialists were shouting most loudly about duty and responsibility, the British people refused to listen. In fact, Britain's own 'native race' the working class—who had themselves been exploited as a result of imperialists' interest in foreign parts—were now declaiming their own slogans, demanding democracy and a voice in their own destiny. The imperial vision was to be eclipsed by a new vision of reform at home. Curzon had always despised democracy as much as he did the Indian intellectual but it was to be the often unconscious alliance between the British working class and a small minority of Indians which, in the end, was to separate India from the British Empire and begin the slow and often painful march to freedom for all colonial peoples of the world. Curzon had unfortunately failed in his desire to bring back 'the vitality of the unexhausted purpose', but the purpose had been dead for over half a century and no one could have raised it from the tomb.

S. Gopal. The best assessment of Curzon's personality as Viceroy would seem to be his own comment on his ablest civil servant, Anthony MacDonnell: 'a strange creature—by far the most capable administrator that we have in this country, but destitute of a ray of human emotion.' (*British Policy in India*, p. 227).

R. C. Majumdar. Lord Curzon's conception of a Viceroy was that of a benevolent autocrat. But in the judgment of his career by the Indians, the scale weighed heavily in favour of autocracy against benevolence. Lord Curzon's career in India also illustrates another characteristic of imperial statesmen of British, namely, the wide gap between profession and practice... In view of all that was said and done by Lord Curzon, it is hardly a matter of surprise that his administration, as a whole was regarded with great disfavour by the Indians. His attitude was most reactionary and repressive in respect of the educated classes in India. There were four fields in which they had been steadily making their influence felt, but in all of them Curzon's policy sought to put them back. He fettered the press by the Official Secrets Act, placed higher education under official control, took away the self-government in city Corporations—granted a quarter of a century ago—abolished competition for high offices, and made everything dependent upon the pleasure of officials. He explained away the Queen's Proclamation and evidently thought that it was not to the interest of the Englishmen that educated classes should be more and more associated with the government of their country. (*British Paramountcy And Indian Renaissance*, Part II, pp. 406–7)

SELECTED REFERENCES

1. Dilks, David : *Curzon in India*, 2 vols.
2. Frazer, Lovat : *India Under Curzon and After.*
3. Gopal, S. : *British Policy in India.*
4. Grover, B. L. : *A Documentary Study of British Policy Towards Indian Nationalism.*
5. Grover, B. L. : *Curzonian Policies and the Great Nationalist Debate.*
6. Releigh, Sir T. : *Lord Curzon in India.*
7. Ronaldshay, Lord : *Life of Lord Curzon*, Vol. ii.

26

ANGLO-AFGHAN RELATIONS

The problem of Imperial defence and the search for a scientific frontier towards the north-west brought the English into contact and clash with the Afghans. The danger from the Afghans and Afghanistan ended with the end of the eighteen century. Zaman Shah who had once contemplated an invasion of India in the days of Sir John Shore and Wellesley had been blinded in the internal conflicts of Afghanistan and had taken refuge at Ludhiana as a pensioner of the East India Company. The Napoleonic fear in the early years of the nineteenth century and later Russian designs and advances in Central Asia kept the Government of India in a state of disquietude. This Russophobia gives the clue to the nature and character of Anglo-Afghan relations in the nineteenth century.

After the death of Timur Shah Durrani in 1793 a civil war broke out among his 23 sons. The Barakzai sirdars, Fateh Khan and Dost Mohammad, played the role of 'king-makers' and ultimately usurped the throne of Kabul. Shah Shuja, a grandson of Ahmad Shah Abdali (who ruled Kabul from 1803 to 1809), was defeated and obliged to take shelter at Ludhiana in 1816 as a pensioner of the East India Company. A number of royal weaklings succeeded but ultimately gave place to Dost Mohammed who was elected chief by an assembly of sirdars and proclaimed Amir by the Chief Mulla in 1826. Dost Mohammad occupied Kabul and Ghazni. Enemies surrounded him on all sides. Outlying provinces asserted their independence while Peshawar was lost to the Sikhs in 1834.

Circumstances Leading to the First Afghan War, 1839–42

Auckland's Afghan Policy. At the time Auckland came to India as Governor-General in 1836, there were alarming reports from Teheran about Russian advances. Russian ambition in Central Asia dates from the acquisition of Georgia in 1801. The Russo-Persian wars of 1811–13 and 1826–28 greatly humbled Persia and she was compelled to surrender important territories round the Caspian Sea to Russia besides being forbidden to keep armed vessels in that sea. Russian influence replaced British influence in Persia and thwarted an English scheme for the establishment of a new route by the Euphrates river to India.

The increased Russian influence in Persia after the Treaty of Turkomanchai (1828) alarmed English mind about possible Russian design on India. Experts in England raised the cry of 'India in danger'. Mr. McNeill, the British Minister to Persia, wrote in 1836 that a 'Russian Regiment at her farthest frontier post, on the western shore of the Caspian, is actually farther from St. Petersburg than from Lahore, a thousand miles on each side.' There was a search for a 'scientific frontier'. The passes of the north-west seemed to hold the keys to the gateway of India. It was felt that Afghanistan should be under the control of a friendly prince. The politicians of the day felt that the fall of Herat meant, for both political and geographical reasons, the removal of the last barrier on any possible march to India. The Shah of Persia further alarmed the English mind by threatening Herat at Russia's instigation. Dost Mohammad seemed somewhat indifferent towards Herat's defences.

The Russian danger seemed real. What steps could be taken? Both Lord Palmerston, British Foreign Secretary, and Auckland, who had been colleagues earlier in the ministries of Lord Grey and Lord Melbourne, advocated a Forward Policy and thought in terms of bringing Afghanistan within their political ambit. Palmerston wrote to Melbourne: "By taking the Afghans under our protection and in garrisoning, if necessary, Herat, we shall regain our ascendancy in persia. British ascendancy in Persia gives security in the eastwards to Turkey and tends to make the Sultan more independent and to place the Dardanelles more securely out of the grasp of Czar Nicholas". The Court of Directors held similar views when they wrote to Lord Auckland in June 1836 that 'the time has arrived at which it would be right for you to interfere decidedly in the affairs of Afghanistan. Such an interference would doubtless be requisite, either to prevent the extension of Persian dominion or Russian influence".

Dost Mohammad, the Amir of Afghanistan, was anxious for English friendship and sent a congratulatory letter to Auckland on the latter's appointment as Governor-General. Dost Mohammad, however, made his friendship conditional on British diplomatic help in recovering Peshawar from the Sikhs. Auckland replied in a cold and frigid manner, asserting neutrality in the Sikh-Afghan dispute and wrote:" It was not the practice of the British Government to interfere in the affairs of the independent states". In desperation Dost Mohammad turned to Russia and Persia for help in recovering Peshawar.

In September 1837 Auckland sent Capt. Alexander Burnes to Kabul nominally on a commercial mission, but in reality to judge the political conditions there. Burnes reported from Kabul that "the Amir was entirely English in views" but insisted that British diplomatic pressure should be exerted on Ranjit Singh to restore Peshawar to the Afghans. Auckland was adamant and wrote to Burnes: "Dost Mohammad must give up all hopes of obtaining Peshawar; that in keeping the peace between Lahore and Kabul, the Government of India was rendering him service of highest value, and as a consequence Dost Mohammad must conclude no alliance with foreign powers on pain of British displeasure". Despaired of all help from the English, Dost Mohammad received a Russian envoy, Capt. Viktevitch at Kabul, with marked favours. Burnes' mission failed and he left for India on 26 April, 1838. Meanwhile a Persian force laid siege of Herat in November 1837 and threatened its defences.

After the failure of Burnes' mission, two broad alternatives were left to Lord Auckland viz., either to abandon all plans on Afghanistan and confine defensive measures to the line of the Indus or to invade Afghanistan, with or without the help of Ranjit Singh, dethrone the unfriendly Amir, Dost Mohammad, and entrust the country to some friendly prince, say Shah Shuja.

The Government of Auckland decided upon a 'forward policy' and signed a Tripartite treaty (June 1838) with Shah Shuja and Ranjit Singh. The treaty provided that Shah Shuja would be reinstated on the throne of Kabul with the armed assistance of the Sikhs. The Company was to remain in the background 'jingling the money bag'. In return Shah Shuja bound himself to conduct his foreign relations with the advice of the English and the Sikhs; he further recognised the Maharaja's claims over the afghan territories on the right bank of the Indus and also gave up his sovereign rights over the Amirs of Sind in return for a large sum of money. Preparations were made on a large scale for the invasion of Afghanistan and an army of invasion was assembled at Ferozepur.

Meanwhile the whole political situation changed. The despatch of a British expeditionary force to Karrack in the Persian Gulf so greatly alarmed the Shah of Persia that he raised the siege of Herat on September 9, 1838. Moreover, under diplomatic pressure from England, the Russian government recalled its envoy from Kabul. So the original irritants which had stirred Auckland to activity ended.

Auckland, however, decided to proceed with his plan of the invasion of Afghanistan. His mind was set at establishing a permanent barrier against the schemes of aggression from the north-west frontier. He believed that he had gone too far to countermand his plans without damaging the prestige of the English. Moreover, the isolation of Dost Mohammad offered an additional reason for teaching the Afghans a lesson. Accordingly, an English army under the command of Sir John Keane marched through the Bolan Pass, captured Kandhar and Ghazni and entered triumphantly into Kabul in August 1839. Dost Mohammad surrendered in 1840 and was sent as a prisoner to Calcutta. Shah Shuja was proclaimed as the Amir of Afghanistan.

The stupidity of the entire plan became evident before long. Shah Shuja was unacceptable to the people of Afghanistan and could be maintained in his position with British armed help alone. Auckland decided upon withdrawal of British troops, though a small garrison was left in Kabul under the command of General Elphinstone. Soon the Afghans rose in rebellion. Alexander Burnes was murdered in November 1841. On 11, December 1841, Macnaghten signed a humiliating treaty with

Akbar Khan, son of Dost Mohammad, agreeing to surrender his arms and evacuate Afghanistan. Dost Mohammad was to be released and Shah Shuja given the option of remaining in Afghanistan or proceeding to India with the British troops. Macnaghten fell a victim on 23 December 1841. The retreat from Kabul began in January. General Elphinstone along with his entire army of 4,500 and 12,000 camp followers was murdered in January 1842. Shah Shuja himself was assassinated in April 1842. Lord Ellenborough who succeeded Auckland in February 1842 decided upon evacuation of all British troops from Afghanistan. The grandiose plan exploded like a balloon.

Estimate of Auckland's Policy. The Afghan policy of Auckland has been subjected to universal condemnation. J. J. Mcleod Innes described the Afghan war as " the most unqualified blunder committed in the whole history of the British in India".

(1) Morally, the war was unjustified. In reply to a congratulatory letter from Dost Mohammad in 1836, Auckland himself had written to the Amir of his Government's neutrality in the Sikh-Afghan dispute over Peshawar in that "it was not the practice of the British Government to interfere in the affairs of other independent states". Afghanistan was an independent state and Dost Mohammad its acknowledged ruler. As such Dost Mohammad was perfectly in entering into negotiations with Persia or Russia uninfluenced by British interests.

(2) Politically, the policy was inopportune and an outcome of misdirected activity. There could be some justification for the invasion of Afghanistan before September 9, 1838 when the Russo-Persian danger seemed real. However, after the Persians had raised the siege of Herat, the imminent danger to India's defences disappeared. Again, the decision to support Shah Shuja was unfortunate. This prince was unpopular with the Afghans, particularly because he had come there with the help of the infidel Sikhs and the Englishmen. One Afghan chieftain met the advancing British troops in 1839 and told the commander: "If Shah Shuja is really a king, and come to the kingdom of his ancestors, what is the use of your army and name ? You have brought him by your money and arms into Afghanistan, leave him now with us Afghans and let him rule us if he can". In the words of historian Kaye, Shah Shuja's entry into Kabul was "more like funeral procession than the entry of a king into the capital of his restored dominion." With sullen and saddened faces the Afghans watched the parade of British strength. Very soon it became clear to the English that Shah Shuja could only be maintained on his throne with the help of British bayonets and at considerable expense to the Government of India. The best course under the circumstances would have been an admission of failure and a compromise with Dost Mohammad, the most popular ruler. The persistence in a wrong course only ended in a disaster, considerably damaging British prestige.

(3) The main object of Auckland to erect a permanent barrier in the north-west by installing a friendly prince on the throne of Afghanistan could not be realised. Dost Mohammad was released and the Afghans welcomed him as the Amir. The friendship and goodwill of the Afghans could not be won, rather the Anglo-Afghan animosity deepened, which in turn encouraged the Persians and the Russians in their expansionist plans.

(4) Lord Auckland and Lord Palmerston took an over-nervous view of Russian danger and decided to fight the shadow while the actual enemy was some thousand miles away. Benjamin Disraeli questioned in the British Parliament: "Why it was necessary to create a barrier for our Indian Empire? When he looked at the geographical position of India he found an empire separated on the east and west from any power of importance by more than 2,000 miles of neutral territory bounded on the north by an impassable range of rocky mountains, and on the south by 10,000 miles of ocean. He wanted to know how a stronger barrier, a more efficient frontier could be secured than this which they possessed." In November 1839 a Russian expedition against the Khanate of Khiva had ended in a great failure. Disraeli described the war as having been proclaimed without reason and prosecuted without responsibility.

(5) The judgment of all those who were competent to speak on Indian affairs was towards condemnation of the policy. Bentink, Elphinstone, Wellesley all decried the Afghan adventure. The Duke of Wellington had warned that any attempt to settle a government in Afghanistan would be "a perennial march into that country," Sir Henry Fane, the Commander-in-Chief, had advised in 1837, "Every advance you might make beyond the Sutlej to the westward, in my opinion, adds to your military weakness... If you want your Empire to expand, expand it over Oudh or over Gwalior and the remains of the Maratha Empire. Make yourself completely sovereign of all within your bounds. But let alone the far west."

(6) One political crime inevitably leads to another. The passage of British troops through Sind and the occupation of Shikarpur, Bukkar and Karachi were a gross violation of the Treaty of Perpetual Friendship concluded with the Amirs of Sind. Such interference resulted in the usurpation of the authority of the Amirs, and ultimately to war and annexation of Sind.

J. A. R. Marriott described the Afghan policy of Auckland "a compound of folly, and ignorance and arrogance", though only the opening chapter of a long story.

John Lawrence's Policy of Masterly Inactivity

The second chapter of Anglo-Afghan relations opens with the Governor-Generalship of Lord Ellenborough and ends with the Viceroyalty of Lord Northbrook. As opposed to the policy of misdirected war and activity, it has been called the policy of Masterly Inactivity. This policy of Masterly Inactivity was a direct outcome and a reaction to the disasters of the first Afghan war. The policy is very much associated with the name of John Lawrence because it was during his viceroyalty that the time came for its application and the outlines of this policy came to be sharply defined.

The term 'Masterly Inactivity' was coined by J.W.S. Wyllie in an article which he contributed on Lawrence's Afghan policy to the January 1867 issue of *The Edinburgh Review*. Since then the phrase has been used to support or criticise the Afghan policy of different Governors-General. The choice of the phrase is unfortunate and has given rise to considerable controversy and misrepresentation. Some have taken it to mean a policy of military inactivity coupled with severance of all diplomatic activity.

The phrase 'Masterly Inactivity' does not correctly explain the Afghan policy of Lawrence. His policy was not based on indifference towards Afghan affairs and ignorance about Russian ambitions in Central Asia, but was based on the principle of non-interference in the internal affairs of Afghanistan and watchfulness towards happenings in that corner of the world. R.B. Smith, Lawrence's biographer, has very appropriately summed up Lawrence's policy thus: "Sir John Lawrence's foreign policy was a policy of self-reliance and self-restraint, of defence not defiance, of waiting and watching that he might be able to strike harder and in the right direction, if the time for aggressive action should ever come".

Lawrence's policy was an outcome of practical common sense and intimate knowledge of the frontier problem. John Lawrence had been the Commissioner of the Panjab till 1859 and had first hand knowledge about the arid terrain of Afghanistan and the Afghan passion for independence. As such, Lawrence was not likely to be swayed by passing sentiments or influenced by military adventurers. He opposed the Forward Policy of occupying military stations like Quetta or stationing of a British Resident at Kabul or supporting one or the other pretender to the throne of Kabul for, as he argued, such a policy would mean going half way to meet the proposed danger; would incur the displeasure and even enmity of brave and patriotic Afghans; draw an English army away from the natural frontier of an almost impassable river (the Indus) and mountains to a frontier surrounded by enemies on all sides besides involving the Government of India in huge military expenditure. Lawrence, therefore, decided upon a policy of non-intervantion into the affairs of Afghanistan. He convinced the Afghans that he did not covet an inch of their territory, would not interfere in their domestic feuds and wars of succession, would recognise any *de facto* ruler whosoever and wherever he might be, would never force a British envoy on the rulers of Afghanistan, but would be willing to help a successful prince with money and arms to enable him to stabilize his position or meet any foreign danger.

Russophobia had been the dread of all Indian governments. What was Lawrence's solution of this danger? At one stage Lawrence believed that Russia might prove a safer neighbour than the wild tribes of Central Asia. During 1844-53 Anglo Russian relations were cordial and Czar Nicholas I made more than one attempt to seek a friendly agreement with England in regard to their relations in Central Asia. England, however, cold-shouldered the Czar's overtures. The Crimean War (1854–56) saw the two countries at war and humiliation of Russia. Checked in the Near East, Russian expansionism found a new vent in Central Asia. In 1864 the Russians occupied Chimkent, in 1865 Tashkent and in 1867 the new province of Russian Turkestan was constituted with General Kaufmann as its first Governor-General. In 1868 Samarkand, the capital of the Khanate of Bokhara, capitulated to the Russians.

Lawrence refused to take an alarmist view of these developments and decided to follow the policy of *laissez-faire* into the affairs of Afghanistan. He expressed his views thus: "I feel no shadow of a doubt that if a formidable invasion of India from the west were imminent, the Afghans *en-masse*, from the Amir of the day to the domestic slaves of the household, would readily oppose it" and that he was firmly convinced that the first invaders of Afghanistan, whether British or Russian, would be received as foes while the next would be welcomed as friends and deliverers. Thus, Lawrence advocated that a strong force of British troops should be kept ready on the Indian frontier to meet all eventualities and secondly, that Russia should be told through British diplomatic channels that her advance beyond a particular point in Central Asia would mean war between the two countries in all parts of the world.

Dost Mohammad, the Amir of Afghanistan, died in 1863. Before his death he had named his son Sher Ali as his successor. However, a war of succession ensued among his 16 sons, the main contestants being Afzal, Azim and Sher Ali. In 1864 Lawrence recognised Sher Ali as the ruler of Afghanistan. In 1866 Sher Ali lost Kabul then and now Kandhar to Afzal. Lawrence now recognised Afzal as ruler of Kabul and Kandhar and Sher Ali as ruler of Herat. An October 1867 Afzal died and his younger brother Azim Khan succeeded him. The Government of India decided to recognise the *fait accompli* and recognized Azim Khan as the Amir of Kabul. In September 1868 Yakub Khan, Sher Ali's son defeated Azim Khan and Abdur Rehman and recaptured Kabul and Kandhar. Lawrence once again recognised Sher Ali as the Amir of Afghanistan. Lawrence refused to be embroiled in the dynastic wars of Afghan princes and did not give any military assistance to Sher Ali during 1865–67 or to Azim Khan in 1868.

A slight modification is seen in Lawrence's policy during 1867–68. His policy of non-interference rested on the fulfilment of two conditions, namely, that the peace on the frontier was not disturbed and that no condidate in the civil war sought foreign help. In case any party sought Russian or Persian help then Lawrence would counter that more by assisting the ruler of Kabul with moderate supply of arms and subsidy to keep his position. As Sher Ali had established himself on the throne of Kabul, Lawrence tried to cultivate friendship with him and in 1868 offered him a present of £ 60,000 and 3,500 stands of arms.

Estimate of Lawrence's Policy. (1) Lawrence's policy has been defended by some and criticized by others. It is claimed that every reasonable advantage was gained by remaining passive. At the Khyber Pass meeting between Lawrence and Dost Mohammad, the latter had apprised Lawrence of the nature of Afghan politics and advised a policy of non-interference. Lawrence, it is maintained, had no idea of doing away with the wish of an old friend who had rendered many services during the crisis of 1857. Besides, the Government of India was committed to a policy of non-interference by the Anglo-Afghan Treaty of 1855. Lawrence felt that it was the right opportunity to impress on the Afghan people the British policy of non aggression and disinterestedness.

(2) It is maintained that a policy of interference would have defeated the very purpose in view by driving the Afghans into the camp of Persia and Russia. Any forward moves on the part of the Government of India would have involved military campaigning in Afghanistan amidst a hostile population and at a great cost to the English. Lawrence was fully convinced that the first invaders of Afghanistan, whether British or Russian, would be received as enemies while the next would come as helpers and deliverers. Besides, any moves on the part of the British coould have evoked countermoves on the part of the Russians. Mr. Wyllie puts the same argument thus: "Lawrence lulled the wakeful Anglophobia of Russian generals and disarmed their inconvenient propensity to meet supposed plots of ours in Afghanistan by counter-plots of their own in the same country."

(3) Lawrence was not blind to Russian expansionist designs in Central Asia. Besides advocating the maintenance of a strong force on the Indian side of the frontier to meet all possible eventualities. He sought to check Russian intrigues in Central Asia through diplomatic channels in Europe. He suggested "a clear understanding with the Government of St. Petersburg as to its objects and designs in Central Asia, and that it might be given to understand that it cannot be permitted to interfere in the affairs of Afghanistan or those of any state which lies contiguous to our frontier."

(4) The *laissez-faire* policy of Lawrence has been criticized on the ground that it indirectly encouraged wars of succession and consequent unrest in Afghanistan. "Critics of the policy of *laissez-faire*", says P. E. Roberts, "could say with some truth that such action was a direct encouragement to successful rebellion, that British approval of an Afghan chieftain's claims swung automatically with the gale of superior force like the vane of a weather-cock, and that no ruler of Afghanistan could set much store by recognition which was transferred so lightly from one rival to another." Mr. Wyllie has ably demolished this argument. "In the first place", he writes, "the nomination of Sher Ali by his father though binding on the Barakzai family, gave him not a little of claim to our recognition. No such being as Dost Mohammad's heir could have any existence for the British Government until the voice of the chiefs and people should have ratified the deceased Amir's choice. Secondly, anything that the Indian Government then or subsequently did or refrained from doing had no more effect in rousing or quelling the force of Amir Khan's revolutionary ambition, than it could have upon the motion of the planets in heaven."

(5) Again, critics point out that uncalled for interference is one thing but to refuse help to a friendly prince when he begs for it in return for valuable services is quite another thing. Lawrence refused all help to Sher Ali in 1865, when that prince was in difficulty and in dire need of it. Had Lawrence helped him, it would have resulted in a speedy triumph of Sher Ali-in the war of succession. Sher Ali would have naturally reciprocated the friendly gestures of the Government of India. Lawrence, however, gave him a present of £ 60,000 and some arms only after Sher Ali came out successful in the war of succession in 1868. Sher Ali interpreted this gesture as an outcome of Russian fear at Calcutta. Thus this belated gift did not earn Lawrence the goodwill and friendship of Sher Ali.

(6) If one main object of Lawrence's policy was the establishment of friendly relations with the Amir of Afghanistan, it is contended, Lawrence did not succeed in that. Sher Ali regarded the English policy as 'cold-blooded and selfish' and remarked that "the English look to nothing but their own interests and bid their time." Thus, it is held, many of the troubles of Sher Ali were due to lack of British help and recognition. Lord lawrence, however, held the view that the misfortunes of Sher Ali were "mainly due to the defects of his character and were the natural consequence of his rule. At one time he was capricious, insolent and headstrong; on other occasions when energetic and prompt decision was essential he would give no orders and would not allow others to act".

(7) Prof. Dodwell points out that Lawrence's plan to check Russian advance in Central Asia through European diplomatic channels was Utopian in principle and rather unpracticable. This approach indicated Lawrence's weakening in his policy of 'Masterly Inactivity'. "Lawrence seems wholly to have ignored", remarks Prof. Dodwell, "the point that unless England could entrench herself so

strongly in Central Asia as to convince Russia of the futility of movements in that direction, an agreement in Europe could only be reached by subordinating English to Russian interests on the continent", or as Curzon pointed out: " Russia would be able to keep England quiet in Europe by finding occupation for her in Asia.'

It may be said in conclusion that though all the possible advantages could not be gained by Lawrence's policy, it decidedly was a better alternative to the Forward Policy followed by Auckland and Lytton. It was a policy of restrained activity and an outcome of keen insight into the difficult problem. The wisdom of the policy can be best judged when we look to the results which came out with the reversal of policy.

Mayo and Northbrook. The policy of Lord Mayo (1868–72) was "no reversal but a continuation and development" of the Afghan policy of Lawrence. In 1869 Sher Ali was given a second gift of £ 60,000. Alarmed by Russian advances in Central Asia, Sher Ali asked for a defensive alliance with the English and for a definite treaty, a fixed subsidy and an unqualified support for his dynasty in all emergencies. Mayo refused to enter into any such engagement. In 1873 the Khanate of Khiva fell to the Russians and Sher Ali endeavoured to convince Lord Northbrook (1872–76) that "the interests of the Afghan and the English governments are identical, and that the frontier of Afghanistan is in truth the frontier of India". The Liberal Government of Gladstone in England instructed Northbrook to inform the Amir that the English "would maintain their settled policy in favour of Afghanistan if the Amir abides by their advice is external affairs."

Lytton and the Second Afghan War, 1878–80

With the arrival of Lytton as Viceroy of India in 1876, a change in the policy towards Afghanistan was perceptible. Lytton was a nominee of the Conservative Government of Benjamin Disraeli (1874–80). Under Disraeli the vague and wavering policy of the Liberals was replaced by a spirited foreign policy. Disraeli's foreign policy was of 'proud reserve', of having 'scientific frontiers' and safeguarding 'spheres of influence'. He wanted to check Russia's expanding power both in Europe and Asia. "Both in the East and West', Disraeli said, "our object is to have prosperous, happy and contented neighbours'. Such matters, it was argued, could not be settled in a day. "You cannot settle them as you would pay a morning visit", Disraeli once said. Relations with Afghanistan could no longer be left ambiguous. "One hand", said Lytton, "washes another, and it is time for the Amir to show us some of his soap".

Lytton was sent to India with definite instructions to conclude "a more definte, equilateral and practical alliance" with the Amir of Afghanistan. Now the boot was on the other foot. Lytton offered to Sher Ali all the terms he had asked of Lord Mayo and Northbrook, namely, a definite treaty, a fixed subsidy, support against Russia and acknowledgement of Sher Ali's younger son, Abdulla Jan, as the next successor to the throne of Afghanistan in preference to the elder son, Yakub Khan, In return Sher Ali was asked to accept a British Resident at Kabul.

Lytton looked for an opportunity to open negotiations with the Amir of Afghanistan. The assumption by the Queen of the title of Kaisar-i-Hind provided the needed opportunity. Lytton announced that a complimentary mission under Sir Lewis Pelly would be sent to Kabul to announce the news to Sher Ali. Sher Ali politely refused to receive such a mission and gave the following reasons for that:

(a) Sher Ali maintained that political questions had been sufficiently discussed at the Simla Conference (July 1873) and therefore was no urgency or necessity of sending a mission;

(b) Permitting a British mission to visit Afghanistan, the Amir could not refuse the same concession to Russia;

(c) The Afghans are self willed and greatly prize their honour. The arrival of British mission would injured their feelings and, under the circumstances, the Amir could not guarantee the safety of the British envoy; and

Anglo-Afghan Relations

(d) If the British mission put forward some proposal unacceptable to him, even the existing relations would worsen.

In fact, the Amir of Afghanistan wanted to keep the friendship of his powerful neighbours, Russia and England, and not to estrange either. He was equally anxious to keep both at an arm's length.

Lytton regarded the Amir's reply as constituting "a contemptuous disregard" of British interests and tried the 'policy of threats'. The Mohammedan Agent of the Government of India, Atta Mohammad at Kabul was asked to inform Sher Ali that the position of Afghanistan between Russia and Great Britain resembled that "of an earthen pipkin between two iron pots", that if Sher Ali remained a friend the military power of England " could be spread round him as a ring of iron, and if he became an enemy, it could break him like a reed". "There was nothing that prevented England" Sher Ali was told, "from coming to an understanding with Russia which might have the effect of wiping Afghanistan out of the map altogether."

Lytton had lost all faith in the policy of "masterly inactivity" and his mind was working towards an ambitious 'forward policy'. He wrote to Lord Salisbury, the Secretary of State, "The Amir is satisfied that there is nothing more to be got out of us, that there is nothing much to be feared from us... he thinks his northern neighbour more formidable, and further "that a policy of passive expectation has been tried with great patience for many years past and I cannot find that it has been productive of a single result that is not eminently unsatisfactory". Lytton actually started preparations for military operations. Quetta was acquired from the Khan of Kelat by the Treaty of Jacobabad (December 1876), a British Agency was established at Gilgit, a boat bridge was constructed at Khoshalgarh and British officers were sent to the Afghan border to study strategic positions.

The Russian factor precipitated the crisis. The Anglo-Russian relations in Europe were brought to a crisis following the defeat of Turkey in the Russo-Turkish war (1877–78) and the Treaty of San Stefano which practically liquidated European Turkey and greatly increased Russian influence in the Balkans. Under threat of war from England and other European powers, Russia agreed to submit the terms of the Treaty of San Stefano before a conference of great powers held at Berlin (June-July 1878) and presided over by the German Chancellor, Bismarck. As a counter-stroke to British policy in Europe, the Russian Government sent General Stolietoff as the Russian envoy of Kabul. The idea was to exert diplomatic pressure on England and extract concessions at the Berlin Conference. Baron de Staal, Russian ambassador to London in the seventies, explained Russian policy in Central Asia in these words; "Great historical lessons have taught us that we cannot count on the friendship of England and that she can strike at us by means of continental alliances while we cannot reach her anywhere. No great nation can accept such a position. In order to escape from it the Emperor Alexander II, of everlasting memory, ordered our expansion in Central Asia, leading us to occupy today in Turkestan and the Turkestan steppes a military position strong enough to keep England in check by the threat of intervention in India". General Stolietoff pushed his way towards Kabul on 22 July 1878 despite Sher Ali's requests and protests. The Russian Government threatened to support the candidature of Abdur Rehman, a nephew of Sher Ali and a Russian pensioner at Tashkent, if Sher Ali offered any resistance to the Russian envoy's entry into Afghanistan. Immediately after the signing of the Treaty of Berlin, the Russian Government instructed General Stolietoff not to commit Russia to any agreement. Further, the Afghan government told Ghulam Mohammad, Lytton's emissary at Kabul that as soon as servants of Russian mission lying ill got well the mission would be dismissed. Thus, the great irritant that worried Lytton was removed.

Lytton was stunned. He could not understand how after accepting a Russian envoy at Kabul, Sher Ali could refuse a similar concession to England. Accordingly, Lytton announced in August 1878 the despatch of a British envoy of high rank, General Sir Neville Chamberlain to Kabul. The mission proceeded up to Jamrud. However, at the Khyber Pass Faiz Mohammad, the officer commanding the Afghan troops told Chamberlain that armed resistance would be offered if he proceeded further. Anglo-Afghan relations reached the point of deadlock, Lytton's envoy was stopped at Ali Masjid. The mission was dissolved. Lytton wrote to the Home authorities : "Sher Ali is not only a savage, but a savage with a touch of insanity. His feelings towards us are of bitter enmity... If by war or at the death of Sher Ali—the opportunity of dismembering Afghanistan came—the earlier opportunity should not be lost upon". The situation somewhat eased when the Russian Government withdrew their envoy from Kabul. Two alternatives were now open to Lytton, viz., either to wait for sometime and then renew friendly negotiations with Sher Ali or to invade Afghanistan and dictate terms to the Amir now that the Russian help was no longer available to Afghanistan.

Lytton decided on the invasion of Afghanistan. An ultimatum was sent to Sher Ali, demanding a 'ful and suitable' apology and a promise to accept permanent British Resident at Kabul, failing compliance Afghanistan was to be invaded. Hostilities commenced on the expiry of the ultimatum date on 20th November 1878. A large British army, numbering between 30,000 to 40,000 marched into Afghanistan through the Khyber, the Peiwar and the Bolan Passes. All opposition crumbled very soon and Sher Ali fled into Russian Turkistan, where he died on 21 February 1879. A peace treaty was signed with Yakub Khan, the eldest son of Sher Ali, at Gandamak 26 May 1879 on the following terms:

(a)   Yakub Khan agreed to the stationing of a permanent British Resident at Kabul with agents at Herat and other places in the frontier ;

(b)   The Amir agreed to conduct his foreign policy with the advice of the Government of India;

(c)   The Amir agreed to the British control of the Kurram and Mishni Passes and such other frontier territory as was demanded by the 'forward school' of British strategists, i.e., the administration of the districts of Kurram, Pishin and Sibi; and

(d)   In return the Government of India agreed to give the Amir all support against foreign aggression and an annual subsidy of six lakhs of rupees.

The Treaty was hailed as securing 'a scientific and adequate frontier' for the Indian Empire. The Viceroy boasted that "the Afghans will like and respect us all the more for the thrashing we have given to Sher Ali", The British victory, however, was short-lived. The British Resident at Kabul, Major Cavagnari, was murdered like Alexander Burnes on 3 September 1879. British troops marched for the second time into Afghanistan and recaptured Kabul and Kandhar. Yakub Khan abdicated and took shelter in the British camp declaring that he would rather be a grass-cutter with the British than attempt to rule the Afghans; he was taken prisoner and sent to Dehra Doon. The English Commander found Kabul 'much more Russian than English, the officers arrayed in uniforms of Russian pattern'. Lytton chalked out plans for the dismemberment and disintegration of Afghanistan. In April 1880 Gladstone won at the polls in England. Lytton resigned and was succeeded by Marquess of Ripon. Meantime, Abdur Rehman, a nephew of the Sher Ali, appeared on the scene and was recognised as the Amir of Afghanistan by Ripon also. The policy of disintegration of Afghanistan was given up and that of a 'buffer state accepted again.

Estimate of Lytton's Policy. (1) The Afghan policy of Lord Lytton has been universally condemned both on moral and political grounds. Lytton showed a lamentable ignorance about the Afghan character and tried to coerce a people who prize their independence above everything else. Perhaps Lytton himself was as capricious and wilful as Sher Ali whom he wanted to snub. Lytton refused to take the lessons of history.

(2) V. A. Smith described Lytton's Afghan policy as "carefully thought out and skilfully executed, with one exception... the stationing of a permanent British envoy at Kabul was a step practically certain to result in disaster." Smith points out that the acquisition of Kalat gave the English the strategic position at Quetta commanding the road to Kandhar; the subsequent developments effected by construction of strategic railways and other methods were rendered possible by the policy pursued by Lord Lytton. It may be said that the only achievement of the 'gigantic gamble' was

the acquisition of Quetta and that too was acquired by a separate understanding with the Khan of Kelat in December 1876, two years before the commencement of the Afghan War.

(3) If Lytton had succeeded in forcing a British envoy on the Afghans, it would certainly have evoked the Russians to action and intrigue to counter British advances. This would have involved the building up of British armies at Kabul at considerable expense and would have drawn the Government of India deeper into the Afghan muddle.

(4) It is contended that Lytton inherited a position of extreme difficulty and that Russian invasion of India was thought to be somewhat real and was "a common topic of conversation in every assemblage of chiefs between Tabriz and Peshawar". It may be said that Lytton took an over-nervous view of the situation when he thought that nothing short of war could stave off Russian action. Lord Salisbury had pointed out the essential weakness of Russian position and advised the use of large-scale maps.

(5) It is contended that Lytton was merely a puppet in hands of the Imperialist Prime Minister Benjamin Disraeli who controlled the strings from London, Disraeli deplored the policy of 'Masterly Inactivity' and admired Lytton's policy. Lytton, however, precipitated matters, and that was perhaps his real blunder. After the failure of Neville Chamberlain's mission, the control of events virtually passed into the hands of the Viceroy, "the man on the spot', and instead of exercising restraint, Lytton precipitated war. Perhaps, the best course could be to demand the withdrawal of the Russian agent at Kabul directly from St. Petersburg. This was the course which Benjamin Disraeli advocated, as is clear from his letter to Lord Cranbrook of 26 September 1878. "Lytton was told", wrote Disraeli, "to wait until we had received the answer from Russia to our remonstrance.... He disobeyed us... He was told to send the mission by Kandhar. He has sent it by the Khyber and received a snub which it may cost us much to wipe away." Again, Disraeli wrote to Lord Salisbury on 3 October 1878: "If Lytton had only been quiet and obeyed my orders, I have no doubt that, under the advice of Russia, Sher Ali would have been equally prudent." Added to it were the comments of Lord Salisbury that the Viceroy was "forcing the hands of the Government.... unless curbed, he would bring some terrible disaster." These comments of Benjamin Disraeli and Salisbury, written before the disaster occurred, constitute the most conclusive condemnation of Lytton's action. Disraeli, however, refused to let down the Viceroy and this loyalty to a colleague brought the Afghan disaster.

(6) Lytton had all along been a great critic of the 'Inactivity' policy of his predecessors in India and of Gladstone. About Gladstone he wrote, "Gladstone has played the game of Russia in England to perfection and the Czar ought to give him a pension." In fact, Lytton was convinced of the inevitability of war with Russia. On 8 November 1876 he wrote to Salisbury, "So far as India is concerned, no event could be so fortunate as a war with Russia next spring" He was convinced that England was stronger than Russia in Central Asia and even thought of taking the offensive and raising the Muslim Khanates of Central Asia against Russia. Salisbury all along advised Lytton to prevent " the muskets going off of themselves" and urged him "to resist military seducers if they are besetting your virtue." Salisbury believed that 'a Kandhar' next year "a more mischievous policy than inactivity." After the spring of 1878, Cranbrook succeeded Salisbury as Secretary of State for India, and Lytton got a freer hand in following a 'forward' policy. Lytton more than anyone else was responsible for the disastrous war.

(7) Lytton's policy rested on two props—either control of the foreign relations of Afghanistan through a British Resident at Kabul or failing that to dismember and disintegrate Afghanistan. Abdur Reham, "the ram caught in the thicket" proved to be no better than Sher Ali. After so much of expenditure in blood and treasure Afghanistan was restored to the same position as before the Second Afghan War. The demand for a British Resident at Kabul was given up. Lytton's policy smacked of failure from the outset and it failed miserably. Later events showed the fallacy of Lytton's supposition that every Afghan chief was a secret friend of Russia. Rather it became clear that they were no more friends of Russia than of Britain; they were in fact friends of Afghan independence.

Anglo-Afghan Relations from Ripon to World War I

Russia's expansionist designs continued unabated even after the Second Afghan War. Fortified by a secret treaty with Germany and taking advantage of England's difficulties in Sudan, the Russians occupied Merv (a place 150 miles south-west of the Oxus and only 200 miles from Herat) in 1884. This occupation was a direct violation of the assurance given by the Russian Foreign Minister to the British Government that Merv lay outside the sphere of Russian influence. The two countries, England and Russia, agreed to the appointment of a joint commission to delimit the northern frontier of Afghanistan. Before the Boundary commission could complete its work, the Russians brought matters to a crisis by occupying Panjdeh, a station one hundred miles south of Merv, in March 1885. Even the Liberal Government of Gladstone was stirred to action and Gladstone declared: "We know that the attack was a Russian attack; we know that the Afghans suffered in life, in spirit and in repute; we know that a blow was struck at the credit and authority of the Sovereign, our protected ally, who had committed no offence... we must do our best to have right done in the matter". The Government called reservists and the Parliament passed a vote of credit for military preparations. The crisis was averted by the Russian cession of Zulfikar Pass to Afghanistan.

Russia, however, continued her advance southwards an east-wards and annexed the Pamirs in 1895, by Anglo-Russian convention of 1895, signed at Petersburg, Russia recognised the river Oxus as the southern boundary of her empire. Thus the Russian advance towards Herat was checked. After 1895 Russia turned her attention towards the Far East and was soon involved in war with Japan. It was the Anglo-Russian Entente of 1907 which established cordial relations between the two countries in all parts of the world. Regarding Afghanistan it was agreed that the Russian Government recognised Afghanistan 'as outside the sphere of Russian influence' and further bound themselves not to send any agent to Kabul and also to conduct their political relations with Afghanistan through the intermediary of Great Britain. Britain, on her part, agreed not to change the political status of Afghanistan or use her influence against Russia. Both countries were to have complete equality of commercial opportunity in Afghanistan.

Oddly enough the two countries, England and Russia, had not consulted Afghanistan in the matter. Amir Habibullah refused to signify his assent to the agreement between England and Russia. Anglo-Afghan relations once again reached a breaking point. Provoked by the German agents, the Amir crossed the Indian frontier during the First World War, but was defeated, a peace treaty was concluded in 1921, which affirmed Afghanistan's right to manage her external relations. In 1922 ambassadors were exchanged between Kabul and London.

SELECT REFERENCES

1. Chakravarty, S. : *From Khyber to Oxus.*
2. Gopal, S. : *British Policy in India.*
3. Kaye, J.W. : *History of the War in Afghanistan.*
4. Pal. Dharam : *Administration of Lord Lawrence.*
5. Prasad, Bisheshwar : *The foundations of India's foreign Policy.*
6. Shukla, R. L. : *Britain, India and the Turkish Empire.*
7. Smith, Bosworth R. : *Life of Lord Lawrence.*
8. Trotter, L. J. : *The Earl of Auckland.*

27

THE NORTH-WEST FRONTIER

The hilly barren tracts lying between the Indus and Afghanistan and extending from the Pamirs in the north to the shores of the Arabian sea in the south and varying in width constituted the North-West Frontier of India. This 1,200 miles long belt of territory has offered an almost impenetrable barrier to all the invading armies from the north-west except when they came by the five passes of Khyber, Kurram, Tochi, Gomal or Bolan. North of the Khyber Pass high mountains make the area insurmountable while the south of the Bolan pass the territory of Baluchistan is protected by a dreary desert. Thus the only vulnerable land frontier has been between the Khyber and Bolan passes, *i.e.,* between Peshawar and Quetta.

Nature is unkind to the people of this area. There is very little rain and little vegetation. A popular local proverb runs thus—"O God, when thou hadst created Sibi and Dadhar, what object there was in conceiving hell". Another local saying current is that when God created the world, he dumped the rubbish on the frontier. Since the middle ages these hilly tracts have been inhabited by hardy and fanatical Muslim tribesmen who live on petty trading and plunder of the neighbouring fertile fields of the Panjab. During the winter months the Pathans of this area come to the Panjab to sell dry fruits and medicinal herbs and retire back to their territory by April. The plundering raids are organised from April to November when no hostages remain in the plains. Further, this frontier area was the rallying ground for disgruntled Muslims from India, deserters from the Indian army and robbers and dacoits.

This frontier area has presented both an international and local problem of enormous complicity and difficulty to all Indian governments since the time of Imperial Mauryas. The annexation of Sind and the Panjab brought the frontier of the Company coterminous with the territory of the Baluchis and the Pathans. The policy of the Government of India towards these frontier tribes was not a uniform and settled policy. Nor was it a policy of 'non intervention' in the tribal affairs, as was asserted in the Indian Legislature in February 1921. The policy as well as the methods of handling frontier problems varied from time to time and in different parts of the long frontier. Fear of Russian expansionist designs in Central Asia and desire to settle the government in Afghanistan prompted some Viceroys like Lytton, Lansdowne and Curzon to the building of strategic roads and railways and even annexation of strategic tribal areas. The only settled aim of frontier administration was the desire to reach a 'scientific frontier', the term being invested with different connotations at different times.

Sir. Charles Napier, the conqueror and first administrator of Sind, also arranged to protect the 150 miles of Sind frontier from the inroads of Bugtis, Dombkis, Jakranis and Baluchis by building strategic forts on the frontier, and garrisoning them with troops; besides the inhabitants of the frontier tracts were supplied with arms for their own defence. These measures met with little success and disorder reigned supreme, for the British subjects in the frontier tracts far from resisting the raiders very often joined them in plunder of the interior. Under Napier's successor, Bartle Frere as Commissioner of Sind and Major John Jacob as the sole Political Agent of Upper Sind the 'Napier System' was changed. Jacob disarmed British subjects on the frontier for they were suspected of helping the intruders. The forts on the frontier were dismantled. Jacob covered the country with a network of roads and canals and organised two regiments of Irregular Horse to chastise the offending tribesmen. Jacob's method consisted in vigilant patrolling of the frontier areas and keeping in readiness mobile columns to meet eventualities, recognition of the Khan of Kalat as head of all the Baluchi tribes and full support to him in punishing offending individuals or tribes. Such was the Sind frontier system.

Claiming all success for the system, Bartle Frere once said: "Can anyone believe that human nature changes where the Sind frontier meets the Panjab".

The Panjab frontier presented more difficult problems. The frontier was long and extremely mountainous and could not be defended by Jacob's methods. While the Baluchi chiefs bordering the Sind frontier were comparatively speaking loyal and obedient to hereditary chiefs, the Pathans of the northern frontier were not. For about a quarter century the sole aim of the Panjab frontier administration was to have a quiet frontier to protect their subjects and to keep trade routes open. John Lawrence directed the Deputy Commissioners of frontier districts to convince the tribesmen that they had no intention of interference in their affairs. However, if there were any inroads from across the frontier, the Panjab administration sent troops into the tribal territory to punish not only the individual offenders by the whole tribe and rather indiscriminately. Thus, for about a quarter century hardly any British official crossed the border into tribal country although tribesmen were allowed to trade within British borders.

The second phase of the Punjab frontier policy was an attempt to solve the problem by trying to 'civilise' the tribesmen. Hospitals were opened in the tribal territory, agricultural land on this side of the frontier given to peacefully-disposed tribesmen, trade fairs organised on the frontier and

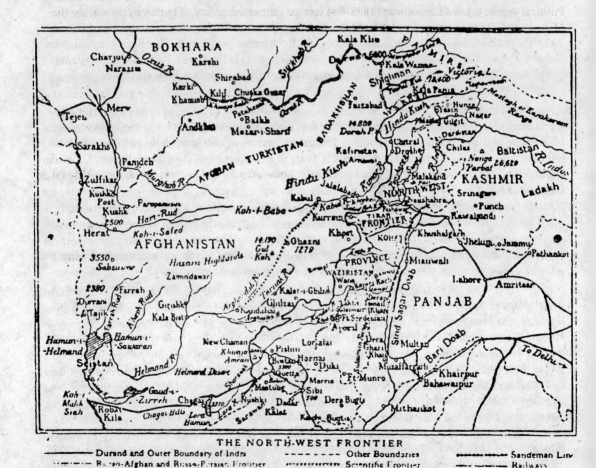

THE NORTH-WEST FRONTIER

various avenues of employment provided in the army and police force. At the same time, an effective force was used to punish offending tribes. Coercion took the form of fines, blockades and punitive expeditions. This policy of "butcher and bolt" meant destruction of their crops, burning of tribal villages and blowing up of their defensive towers. Fines were collected from the offending tribes as compensation for property plundered. These methods of persuasion-cum-force did not prove very successful. The tribesmen remained as turbulent as ever before.

With the arrival of Lytton in 1876 the policy of Masterly Inactivity gave place to a Forward Policy. The search for a 'scientific frontier' led the Government to interfere in the tribal area and occupation of strategic stations all along the frontier. This resulted in a uniform policy along the Panjab and Sind frontier. Major Sandeman was appointed Agent to the Governor-General in Baluchistan. In relation to Baluchistan the policy of 'non-intervention' gave place to the policy of 'conciliatory intervention'. Lytton wrote on 23 March 1877 : "If it be conducive to British interests, as we have no doubt it is, to influence the tribes and the people who live beyond our border, we must be in contact with them. It is by the everyday acts of earnest, upright English gentlemen that lasting influence must be obtained, not by spasmodic demonstrations...." In 1876 Quetta was acquired from the Khan of Kalat. The same year the districts of Hazara, Peshawar and Kohat were grouped into the Commissionership of Peshawar and the three southern districts of Bannu, Dera Ghazi Khan and Dera Ismail Khan into the Commissionership of Derajat. In February 1877 Baluchistan was created into a Political Agency. Lord Lansdowne (1888–94) carried further the policy of Lytton by displacing the Maharaja of Kashmir, extention of British control over Bori and Zhob valleys, occupation of Hunza and Nagar in the Gilgit valley and finally in compelling the Khan of Kalat to resign in 1892. In 1892 Kurram Agency was formed, and during 1895–96 Malakand, Tochi and Wana Agencies were formed.

These forward moves of the British Government created serious apprehensions in the mind of the Afghan ruler, Abdur Rehman. To conciliate him and to delimit the boundary into spheres of influence, Lord Lansdowne sent Sir Mortimer Durand on a mission to Kabul in 1891. By the Durand Agreement (1893) the Amir's subsidy was increased from twelve to eighteen lakh rupees per annum; he was also allowed to import arms and ammunition at discretion. The Amir on his part agreed not to interfere into the affairs of Khyber Afridis, the Waziris and tribes inhabiting Swat, Bajaur, Dir and Chitral. The same year the Government of India announced a formal protectorate over Gilgit and Chitral.

The Durand Agreement established friendly relations with the Amir of Afghanistan. However, the frontier did not become more peaceful, rather there were greater chances of collision with the uncivilised tribes. In the words of C. C. Davies: "The new boundary line was not based upon sound topographical data, for during the process of demarcation, it was discovered that certain places marked on the Durand map, did not exist on the actual ground. Many ethnic absurdities were perpetrated.... The tribesmen were not consulted before 1893... Perhaps the Amir's consent was purchased by the increase of his subsidy to eighteen lakhs of rupees and by the recognition of his right to import munitions of war." Even the Amir of Afghanistan was apprehensive of British designs. He said: "Though England does not want any piece of Afghanistan, still she never loses a chance of getting one and this friend has taken more than Russia has." The years following the Durand Agreement were a period of great disturbances in the whole tribal area. The British Agent was besieged in Chitral fort, the British forts at Chakdarra and Malakand were attacked and the Mohmand, Orakzai and Afridi tribesmen rose in rebellion. Even the Amir of Afghanistan assumed the title of *Zia-ul-millat wa-ud-din* and declared a holy war against the British. In 1895 the Liberal Government of Lord Rosebury ordered the evacuation of Swat, Bajaur and Chitral. The change in the British Government and coming into power of Lord Salisbury resulted in a reversal of policy and Chitral was not evacuated. During 1898–99 punitive expeditions were dispatched against the Mohmands and the Afridis. At least 40,000 troops were employed in these operations. The tribesmen submitted, but the casualties on the British side were heavy. British troops were dispersed in a number of forts built in the tribal area.

Curzon's Policy. On his arrival in India in 1899, Curzon found more than 10,000 British troops stationed beyond the frontier in the tribal area. Curzon was a widely travelled man and had made a close study of the geography of Asia and its political and economic problems. Added to this well-informed mind was the strong will and determination of the new viceroy.

Under Curzon the frontier policy was revised and a new system came into operation. He followed a 'realistic and common sense' policy towards the tribesmen. He would have nothing to do with the 'elastic and pliable adjectives' of Masterly Inactivity or Forward Policy or surrender to the "paralysing influence of these labels." He said: "Let our new frontier policy be called by any name that men choose. Only let it be based not upon obsolete political formulas, but upon up-to-date commonsense." In the light of past experience Curzon hoped "to draft a code of frontier policy which could with consistency, and without violent interruptions, be applied to the whole line of North-Western frontier from the Pamirs to Baluchistan." Curzon's policy may be summed up as a policy of 'military concentration as against diffusion, and of tribal conciliation in place of exasperation.'

(*i*) Curzon ordered the withdrawal of British regular troops from advanced positions in the tribal territory, from the Khyber, the Kurram valley, the Waziri country and Gilgit. Troops were retained at Chitral out of imperial considerations, while the protection of Gilgit was placed under the charge of the Government of Jammu and Kashmir.

(*ii*) The defence of tribal tracts was left to bodies of tribal levies trained by British officers and required to act as militia in defence of their own native valleys and hills. Recruitment to local militias like the Khyber Rifles, the Kurram Militia, the Waziristan Militia also solved the unemployment problem in these areas.

(*iii*) The local militia was supported by mobile columns of regular British troops concentrated at strategic stations like Malakand, Dargai, Peshawar, Kohat, Bannu, Dera Ismail Khan, etc.

(*iv*) To support the new policy, Curzon developed communications in the rear. To support the Malakand garrison a railway was built from Nowsherra to Dargai; Peshawar was connected with Jamrud by rail, and further to Landikotal by road. In Baluchistan, the construction of Quetta-Nushki railway was taken in hand.

(*v*) In April 1902 a great Darbar was held at Peshawar attended by 3,000 persons and many tribal chiefs. Curzon assured the tribal chiefs of the peaceful intentions and non-aggressive aims of British policy. At the same time he warned that "if you dart out from behind the shelter of the door to harass and pillage and slay, then you must not be surprised if we return quickly and batter the door in." Addressing another assemblage of Baluchi chiefs, he remind them of their responsibility to check lawlessness in their area. Referring to the murder of some Englishmen by the Ghazis he said: "If we could lift the *purdah* of the future world and see what fate has attended these murders, I do not think there would be many future Ghazis on the Pathan frontier or in Baluchistan." The tribesmen understood that the Viceroy meant what he said.

(*vi*) Allowances were sanctioned for different tribes to be paid at regular intervals to induce them to keep roads and passes open and to maintain peace and tranquillity on the frontier.

(*vii*) Curzon created a new North-West Frontier Province comprising the five settled districts of Hazara, Peshawar, Kohat, Bannu and Dera Ismail Khan and the trans-border tracts lying between the administrative frontier and the Durand Line. Ever since the annexation of the Panjab in 1849, the administration of the frontier was the responsiblity of the Panjab Government. As early as 1877 the Seceretary of State had expressed the view that the circumstances under which the frontier had been made the responsibility of the Panjab Government were obsolete. Lytton suggested the formation of a huge frontier province extending from Hazara in the north to the Arabian Sea. Curzon who brought an expert knowledge to bear on the problem saw the anomalous nature of the administrative arrangement and wrote to Shelburne in April 1900: "The Government of India, realising its own ignorance, but not realising that it was duplicating the danger, has placed between itself and the frontier, the Panjab Government, which knows even less and which has for 20 years been an instrument of procrastination and obstruction and weakness. I hope that one of the great reforms of my time will be removal of this danger." In 1901 the new North-West Frontier province was created and put in charge of a Chief Commissioner who was placed directly under the control and supervision of the Government of India. To avoid the confusion of names, the old North-Western Provinces was renamed the United Provinces of Agra and Oudh.

Curzon claimed all success for his frontier policy. Speaking on 30 March 1904, Curzon referred to the past five years as 'unmarked by a single expedition on the entire North-West Frontier' and the total loss of only 109 men in the maintenance of peace in the area. Curzon had in mind the 42 punitive expeditions organised during 1850–90, with great expenditure and loss in lives. During the seven years of Curzon's administration only £ 248,000 were spent on the frontier military operations as against £ 4,584,000 during 1894–98. Speaking in the House of Lords in 1908 Curzon said: "If anybody had been disposed to doubt the success of the scheme of frontier policy which has been in existence for ten years, his doubts must have been dispelled, and I hope we shall now hear no more of the wildcat schemes for advancing into tribal territories, annexing up to the border, and driving roads through the tribal country."

Curzon's policy, however, was not without its shortcomings. Lord Minto wrote to the Secretary of State that "neither the border police nor the levies have been capable of filling the position from which the troops were withdrawn", while Prof. Dodwell comments that "When the Khyber Rifles developed a habit of shooting their Adjutants the outside world heard nothing of it." The largescale importation of arms and ammunition into the tribal area revolutionized the nature of warfare. During 1908–09 the Afridi, the Mohmand and Mahsud tribes rose in rebellion, aided and abetted by the Afghans. Punitive expeditions had to be sanctioned, Curzon's system entirely broke down.

The Montagu-Chelmsford report recommended the association of an advisory council to assist the Chief Commissioner. The Indian Statutory Commission recommended for the creation of an elected Legislative Council and grant of representation to the North-West Frontier Province in the Central Legislature. In 1932 the province was raised to the status of a Governor's province and Sir Ralph Griffith appointed the first Governor.

SELECT REFERENCES

1. Bellow, H. W. : *North-West Frontier and Afghanistan.*
2. Davies, C. C. : *The Problem of the North-West Frontier.*
3. *Report of the North-West Frontier Committee* (Bray Committee), 1921.
4. Woodruff, Philip : *The Men Who Ruled India,* vol. i.

28

THE INDIAN STATES

The British and the Princes needed one another; India's need for either was highly doubtful.

F. G. Hutchins

The Indian states numbered no fewer than 562 and covered a total area of 712,508 square miles. These states included some big like Hyderabad (as large as Italy) with a population of 14 millions and an annual revenue of 8.5 crores of rupees and tiny states like Bilbari with a population of 27 persons and an annual income of Rs. 8 only. It has been estimated that 202 states had each an area of less than 10 square miles, 139 less than 5 square miles each while 70 states had each an area not exceeding one square miles.[1] Generally speaking, the Indian states were "the inaccessible and less fertile tracts of the Indian peninsula." In the process of conquest, the East India Company acquired important coastal tracts, the valley of the great navigable rivers accessible from the sea and such tracts which were rich in agricultural products and densely populated by prosperous people.

The making of Indian states was largely governed by the same circumstances which led to the growth of the East India company's power in India. Many Indian states as independent or semi-independent principalities came into existence in the later Mughal period. The East India Company became a political power during the same period, profiting from the weakness of the Mughal central authority. Many states like Hyderabad, Oudh, and Rajput states were not conquered or annexed by the English but accepted the Company's supremacy. Some states notably the Rajput states of Central India had for centuries resisted the Mughals and later the Marathas and were saved from extinction by British intervention. Some states were created by the British in the process of the overthrow of Maratha Confederacy.

A retrospective examination of the relations between the British and the Indian states suggests the following broad stages:[2]

(1) East India Company's Struggle for equality with Indian states, 1740–65.

(2) The Policy of Ring Fence, 1765–1813.

(3) The Policy of Subordinate Isolation, 1813–57.

(4) The Policy of Subordinate Union, 1857–1935.

(5) The Policy of Equal Federation, 1935–47.

The Company Struggles for Equality, 1740–65

Prior to 1740 the East India Company was a commercial body with very little political ambition. The political ambitions of the Europeans in India may be dated from 1740, when Dupleix started dabbling in Indian politics and dreamed of laying the foundation of a French dominion in India. For the defence of their commercial interests, the English followed the example of Dupleix and signalled their political identity by the capture of Arcot in 1751. In 1757 the English won the battle of Plassey and became the political force behind the nawabs of Bengal. The Company became a ruling power after the Emperor, Shah Alam II granted it the *Diwani* of Bengal, Bihar and Orissa in 1765. Till 1765 the

---

1. Figures for 1941.
2. Sir William Lee Warner in his book *The Native States of India* (London, 1910) has mentioned three epochs in British Relations with Indian States viz, (*i*) The Policy of Ring Fence down to 1813, (*ii*) The Policy of Subordinate Isolation, 1813–57, and (*iii*) The Policy of Subordinate Union from 1857 onwards. Since the book was published in 1910, Lee-Warner's analysis was intended to cover the period up to 1910.

Company stood in relation to the Indian state in a position of subordination and was striving for a status of equality with them.

The Policy of Ring Fence or Buffer State, 1765–1813

Warren Hastings' wars against Mysore and the Marathas were fought with the objective of establishing an equality of status with the Indian rulers. This period also saw the emergence of the policy of creating buffer states around the Company's territories. The idea was purely that of defence of the frontiers of the Company. Broadly speaking, it was the policy of defence of their neighbours' frontiers for safeguarding their own territories. The chief danger to the Company's territories. was from the Afghan invaders and the Marathas. To safeguard against these dangers, the Company undertook to organize the defence of the frontiers of Oudh on the condition that the Nawab would defray the expenses of the defending army. The defence of Oudh constituted the defence of Bengal at that time.

With the arrival of Wellesley, the Company's relations with the Indian states underwent a change. Wellesley sought to reduce the Indian states to a position of dependence on the Company in fact if not declaredly so. He aimed at bringing the Indian states within the ambit of British political power and military protection. On 12 July 1803 George Barlow wrote: "No native state should be left to exist in India which is not upheld by the British power or the political conduct of which is not under its absolute control." This policy may be described as the extension of the policy of 'ring fence'. Wellesly described his policy as purely defensive and pacific, for he felt compelled to extend the British dominions to counteract the designs of France. The rulers of Hyderabad, Mysore, Oudh and other lesser states accepted the Subsidiary Alliance System. The defeat of the Marathas in 1803 and Holkar in 1805 virtually established the supremacy of British power. The Subsidiary System was the Trojan-horse tactics in Empire-building.

The Policy of Subordinate Isolation, 1813–57

The wars of Lord Hastings (1813–23) opened a new stage in the relations of the East India Company *vis-a-vis* the Indian states. The Imperial idea grew and the theory of Paramountcy began to develop. In February 1814 Hastings noted in his diary: "Our object ought to be to render the British Government paramount in effect. If not declaredly so." The treaties that he concluded with the Indian states were not on the basis of reciprocity and mutual amity, but imposed the obligation on the part of the Indian states to act in subordinatte cooperation with the British Government and acknowledge its supremacy. Thus, the Indian states surrendered all forms of external sovereignty to the East India Company. The states, however, retained full sovereignty in internal administration.

The decades following the retirement of Lord Hastings saw the rapid increase of the influence of the Company in the internal administration of the states. The British Residents were usually the organs of communication between the Government of India and the rulers of Indian states. Gradually their influence and power increased. Mountstuart Elphinstone explained his work as Resident thus— –intelliegence work, reporting situation of native Raja's armies and palace intrigues, performing military duties. As early as 1805 Cornwallis wrote to Lord Lake that "unless the British Residents exercised a power and an ascendancy that they ought not to exercise native governments would be immediately dissolved." With the assertion of the Company's Paramountcy and adoption of the policy of 'subordinate cooperation' under Lord Hastings down to 1857 "the Resident ministers of the Company at Indian courts were slowly but effectively transformed from diplomatic agents representing a foreign power into executive and controlling officers of a superior government." Lord Hastings himself noted in his private journal: "Instead of acting in the character of ambassador, he (the Resident) assumes the functions of a dictator; interferes in all their private concerns, countenances refractory subjects against them and makes the most ostentatious exhibitions of his exercise of authority". Raja Chandu Lal during his administration in Hyderabad took his orders from the Resident, Colonel Low, Colonel Walker acted as an administrator. Resident when he helped the Gaekwar to collect revenue from the feudal chiefs. Colonel Macaulay wrote to the Raja of Cochin: The resident will be glad to learn that on his arrival near Cochin the Raja will find it convenient to wait upon him." Henry mead, a journalist, wrote before 1857: "The whole functions of the government were carried on in most cases by the Resident in fact, if not in appearance. The titular monarch sighed in vain for the personal freedom enjoyed by his subjects. The Resident at Travancore was a savant and the Raja built an observatory and maintained men of science. The Raja of Mysore maintained stud horses, race horses, organised gold cups and presented heavy purses because the Resident was a lover of sports of turf".

The Charter Act of 1833 metamorphosed the character of the Company. The Company was asked to wind up its commercial business. It assumed political functions in fact and name. A radical change followed in the policy towards the Indian states. The Company adopted the practice of insisting on its prior sanction and approval in all matter of succession in states. Later they found it practicable to advise the princes on the choice ministers.

The policy of annexation of states whenever and wherever possible was laid down by the Court of Directors in 1834. The policy was reiterated with emphasis in 1841 when the Court of Directors issued a directive to the Governor-General "to persevere in the one clear and direct course of abandoning no just and honourable accession of territory or revenue". The Governors-General of this period were frankly annexationists. Annexations were made to acquire new territories and new sources of revenue on the plea of failure of natural heirs or misgovernment. The Company as the supreme power had the right to withhold sanction for 'adoption' of heirs and the states in such cases 'lapsed back' to the Supreme Power. The Supreme authority which gave, it was argued, had the right to take back also. As to the problem of misgovernment in native states, the Company itself was to be greatly blamed. The Subsidiary System was full of evil consequences for the rulers of the Indian states. "Wherever the Subsidiary System is introduced", wrote Munro, "the country will soon bear the marks of it, in decaying villages and decreasing population". "If ever there was a device for insuring mal-government", wrote Sir Henry Lawrence in 1848, it is that of a native Ruler and Minister both relying on foreign bayonets and directed by a British Resident. Even when all these are able, virtuous and considerate, still the wheels of government could hardly move smoothly. Each of the three may work incalculable mischief, but no one of them can do good if thwarted by others". Karl Marx wrote in 1853: "As to native states, they virtually ceased to exist from the moment they became subsidiary to or protected by the Company. If you divide the revenue of a country between two governments, you are sure to cripple the resources of one or the administration of both... the conditions under which they are allowed to retain their apparent independence are, at the same time, the conditions of permanent decay and an utter inability of improvement". William Bentinck annexed Mysore (1831), Cachar (1832), Coorg (1834), and Jaintia (1835). Auckland annexed Karnul, Mandavi (1839), Kolaba and Jalaun (1840). Dalhousie annexed about half a dozen Indian states including big states like Nagpur, Satara and Oudh.

Even after the establishment of the East India Company's undisputed supremacy in 1818, the policy of the East India Company *vis-a-vis* the Indian states was "chaotic, indefinite and contradictory." "The authorities of the East India Company" writes K.M. Pannikar, "were wavering with every passing fancy as to whether the rulers were zamindars, feudatories, tributaries or independent sovereigns; and each Governor-General and each Resident held and enforced his own views." Sometimes a Governor-General followed earlier precedents, at other times created new precedents. While a good number of Indian states were annexed, some states like Khairpur in 1832, Bahawalpur in 1833, Kashmir in 1846 were assured of the Company's policy of non-intervention into the internal affairs of their states Prof. Dodwell very aptly sums up the position thus: "Besides the rights vested by treaty in the Company, there had arisen, under no sanction but that of superior power on the one side and reluctant acquiescence on the other, a body of precedents relating to successions and to interference in the internal administration of the states. Together these constituted the Company's paramountcy—undefined, undefinable, but always tending to expand under the strong pressure of political circumstances."

INDIAN STATES UNDER THE CROWN
The Policy of Subordinate Union, 1857–1935

The assumption of direct responsibility by the British Crown in 1858 provided an occasion for better definition of the relations between the Government of India and the Indian states. The Queen's Proclamation, however, confirmed the existing anomalies:

"We hereby announce to the native princes of India, that all treaties and engagements made with them by or under the authority of the East India Company are by us accepted, and will be scrupulously maintained, and we look for the like observance on their part."

Yet the years following the Proclamation of 1858 marked a vital transformation in the relations between the Indian states and the Government of India.

The Queen's Proclamation announced the abandonment of the policy of annexation. The Doctrine of Lapse was buried deep in the soil. An assurance was given that the Crown desired "no extension of present territorial possessions." The change in policy was due to the loyal attitude of the ruling princes during the Revolt of 1857–58 which had amply demonstrated that the princes could be used as breakwaters to future possible storms in India[3]. Lord Canning gave practical shape to the new trend by granting 140 *sanads* or 'instruments or grants of adoption' to Hindu and Muslim princes. Lord Lansdowne issued 17 more *sanads*. The new policy was to punish the ruler for misgovernment and if necessary to depose him but not to annex the state (*e.g.*, in 1874 the Gaikwar was removed from the *gaddi* for charges of misgovernment, but the state was not annexed). The change in policy was welcomed by the princes.

This immunity from the policy of annexation was obtained at great cost and lowering of the status of the Indian princes. Under the East India Company the sanction of the Governor-General was necessary only in case of failure of 'natural heirs'. After 1858, the fiction of the authorities of the Mughal Emperor came to an end and the Crown stood forth as the unquestioned ruler and paramount power in India. As such, all successions had to regularly seek the sanction of the Crown. The Central Government wrote to the Chief Commissioner of Central Provinces in 1884: "The succession to a native state is invalid until it receives in some form the sanction of the British authorities." The ruler did not inherit the *gaddi* as of right, but as a gift from the Paramount Power. The Indian prince was granted possession and administration not sovereignty and his continuation as ruler was conditional on his loyalty to the British Crown. Normally every ruler was formally installed on the *gaddi* by the British Agent. The British Government also acted as the guardian of a minor prince and arranged for administration of the state during minority.

Further, the fiction of the Indian princes standing on a status of equality with the Crown as sovereign independent states finally came to an end. Canning referred to the rulers of Indian states as "feudatories and vassals" and to the Crown as " the unquestioned ruler and Paramount Power in India." Again, he wrote: " There is a reality in the suzerainty of the sovereign of England which has never existed before and which is not only felt but eagerly acknowledged by the chiefs." Paramountcy was not only a historical fact but a legal principle capable of interpretation and expansion, The Royal Titles Act of 1876 put the final seal on the new relationship by proclaiming the Queen as Kaiser-i-Hind, *i.e.*, Queen Empress of India.[4] At the time of rendition of Mysore in 1881, the position of the new prince was made conditional on his remaining "faithful in allegiance and subordination to the Crown."

---

3. Lord Canning wrote on 30 April 1860 : 'It was long ago said by Sir John Malcolm that if we made all India into zillahas (or British districts) it was not in the nature of things that our Empire should last fifty years; but that if we could keep up a number of native states without political power, but as royal instruments, we should exist in India as long as our naval supremacy was maintained. Of the substantial truth of this opinion, I have no doubt and the recent event have made it more deserving of our attention than ever."

The conditions on which the Indian prince was restored in Mysore became a set of principles which were applied in case of all Indian states. A Government notification dated 21 August 1891 declared: "The paramount supremacy of the former (the Crown) presupposes and implies the subordination of the later (Indian princes)."

The Crown also exercised the right to regulate the status and salutes of the Indian princes in all matters of ceremonials. Just as the Mughal Emperor before 1858 granted titles and honours, the Crown awarded titles and decorations to Indian princes.

The Government of India exercised the right to interfere in the internal sphere of Indian states, partly in the interests of the prince himself, partly in the interests of the welfare of the people of the state and partly to secure proper conditions for British subjects or foreigners in the state and partly in the interests of India as a whole. In a minute of 1860, Canning wrote: "The Government of India is not precluded from stepping in to set right such serious abuses in a native government as may threaten any part of the country with anarchy or disturbance, nor from assuming temporary charge of a native state when there will be sufficient reason to do so. Of this necessity the Governor-General-in-Council is the judge, subject to the control of Parliament". In 1867 the Nawab of Tonk, Mohammad Ali Khan was charged with complicity in an attack on the relations of his tributary, the Thakur of Lawa. The Nawab had to resign in favour of his son. Similarly, in 1870 the ruler of Alwar was deposed and a Council of Regency was setup. In 1875 the Gaekwar of Baroda was charged with an attempt to poison the British Resident. In addition, the Gaekwar had refused to introduce changes in administration on the lines suggested by the British Resident. A Commission of Enquiry was appointed. Although the charges against the ruler could not be proved yet the Gaekwar was removed from the *gaddi* on the score of mal-administration. In 1884 a British Resident was forced on the Maharaja of Kashmir and in 1889 the Maharaja was forced to resign in favour of a Council of Regency. Again, in 1891 the Government of India interfered in the turbulent affairs of Manipur. The ruler and the Senapati were exiled. The removal, trial and sentence of Jubraj of Manipur, writes Sydney Low, was not an 'unquestioned right' as Lee Warner puts if, but " an act of prerogative justified by necessity than a legal power vested in the Government of India." In 1892 the Khan of Kalat was deposed for mismanagement of the state.

The British were further helped in their encroachments on the internal sovereignty of the Indian princes by the pressure of irresistible currents of history and by force of circumstances. Developments of an all-India character compelled the rulers of Indian states to fall in line with the Government of India's policy. The development of modern means of transport and communications, of a public press and all India public opinion all worked in that direction. The rulers were required to aid economic schemes for the welfare of the whole country, to cede land and jurisdiction thereto for extension of railways, irrigation canals, telegraphs, post offices, construction of strategic roads. Further, the states were required to assist in military plans and provide all facilities for movement of the Indian army.

The Government of India exercised complete and undisputed control over the external and international affairs of the Indian states. The government of India could declare war, neutrality or peace for the Indian states. The Bulter Committee remarked: "For international purposes, state territory is in the same position as British territory and state subjects are in the same position as British subjects."

The period also saw the growth of 'political practice' and 'usage' which further circumscribed the rights of Indian princes. Under the impress of changing circumstances, the Crown exercised powers which exceeded the most liberal interpretation of treaties. Rather than abrogate the old treaties or seek for revision of those, the Government resorted to the less provocative devise of 'constructive

---

4. Lytton thought that Royal Titles Act marked the beginning of "a new policy by virtue of which the Crown of England should henceforth be identified with the hopes, the aspirations, sympathies and the interests of a powerful native aristocracy".

interpretation' of the old treaties. In the words of N. D. Varadachariar: "The treaties began to be regarded as guides of political conduct rather than sources of legal right." Thus grew up the Political Department under the Viceroy. In other words, a body of case law grew up.

Curzon and the Indian States. Lord Curzon stretched the interpretation of old treaties to mean that the Indian princes in their capacity as servants of the people should work side by side with the Governor-General in the scheme of Indian Government. He adopted a policy of patronage and "intrusive surveillance.' He issued a circular desiring Indian princes to devote their energies not in pursuit of pleasures but "in the welfare of their subjects and administration." He put restrictions on their trips to Europe. Long absence from India was to be regarded as dereliction of duty.[5] Curzon went to the length of declaring at Bahawalpur in 1903 that the relationship between Indian states and Government of India "was neither federal nor feudal but tended to a type not based on treaty. It represents a series of relationships that have grown up between the Crown and the Indian princes under widely differing historical conditions, but in process of time had gradually conformed to a single type."

The new trend seemed to reduce all the Indian states to conform to a single type, whether they were treaty states or enjoying varying degrees of authority. All the states were uniformly dependent on the British Government and were considered as having become integral parts of the Indian political system. Lord Reading removed the misconceptions of the Nizam when he wrote to the latter that "the title Faithful Ally which your Exalted Highness enjoys has not the effect of putting your government in a category separate from that of other states under the paramountcy of the British Crown."

Policy of Subordinate Union — the Chamber of Princes

From 1905 onwards the Government of India followed a policy of cordial co-operation towards the Indian states. The growth of political unrest in British India put the Government of India on the defensive and the Government thought it expedient and prudent to utilise the support of Indian princes to counter progressive and revolutionary developments. The Government of India and the Indian princes formed "common front to preserve their positions and privileges." The government of India no longer feared the Indian princes, individually or jointly. Thus, the policy of Subordinate Isolation gave place to the policy of Subordinate Union.

As early as 1876 Lytton had suggested the formation of an Indian Privy Council of Chiefs of great Indian states to confer with the Governor-General on matters of common interest. The idea did not find favour with the authorities in England. Similar schemes of Lord Curzon for a Council of Ruling Princes and of Minto for an Imperial Advisory Council proved abortive. During the First World War, Lord Hardinge often called the Indian Princes for joint consultations on matters of Imperial Defence. Lord Chelmsford carried the scheme of conferences further by utilising them for the purpose of discussing general questions affecting the states as a whole. The authors of Montagu-Chelmsford Reforms favoured the formation of a Council of Princes and made definite suggestions in the matter. These recommendations formed the nucleus for the formation of the Chamber of Princes, formally inaugurated in February 1921.

For purposes of representation in the Chamber of Princes, the Indian states were divided into three categories :

(*i*)   109 states which enjoyed full legislative and jurisdictional powers were represented directly.

---

5. One chief reacted to Curzon's circular by saying "We are supposed to be chiefs, but we are treated as worse than paid servants." The circular was not strictly enforced.

(*ii*) 127 states which enjoyed limited legislative and jurisdictional powers were represented by 12 members chosen from among themselves.

(*iii*) Remaining 326 states which could better be classed as jagirs or estates or feudal holdings.

The chamber of Princes was merely an advisory and consultative body. It had no concern with the internal affairs of individual states nor could it discuss matters concerning the existing rights of states or their freedom of action."[6]

Working of the Chamber of Princes. The Indian Princes thus became the favourite children of British Imperialism and in fact were "collectively recognized as an independent constituent of the Empire". The princes, however, were worried about the uninterrupted and continuous growth of "Political Practice" and the concept of Paramountcy. On the request of the Princes, a Codification Committee was appointed as early as September 1919 to codify 'Political Practice' and define limits of the concept of Paramountcy. While accord was reached on minor issues like settlement of boundary dispute, payment of compensation to states for land taken for railways, irrigation, navigation, defence and other purposes, the larger problem of the extent of the sovereignty of the Paramount Power could not be settled.

Lord Reading's statement that extension of Paramountcy was based "not only upon treaties and engagements but existed independently of them" further alarmed the Indian princes.[7] At a time when proposals for the future constitutional reforms of India were being discussed, the Indian Princes urged Lord Irwin of the necessity of having the nature of relationship between the states and the Supreme Power properly examined and clearly defined. In 1927 the Government appointed the Indian States Committee, popularly known as the Butler Committee (from the name of its chairman Sir Harcourt Butler) to investigate the relationship between the Paramount Power and the Indian states. The Indian Princes engaged a distinguished lawyer, Sir Leslie Scott, to present their viewpoint before the Committee. Scott argued that as each state was originally independent so each remained independent except to the extent to which any part of the ruler's sovereignty was transferred to the Crown. In other words, Scott pleaded that residuary powers rested with the Indian states.

The Butler Committee made the following points:

(1) On the question of Paramountcy and development of Political Practice, the Committee reported: "Paramountcy must remain paramount, it must fulfil its obligations, by defining and adopting itself according to the shifting necessities, of the time and the progressive development of states" and further that "usage lights up the dark corners of treaties."

(2) The states were bound by treaties with the Crown and the states should not be handed over without the rulers' prior consent to an Indian Government in British India responsible to an Indian Legislature.

---

6. The King Emperor in his proclamation outlined the jurisdiction in these words: "My Viceroy will take its counsel freely in matters relating to the territories of the Indian states generally and in matters that affect these territories jointly with British India or with the rest of my Empire. It will have no concern with the internal affairs of individual states or their rulers or with the relations of individual states to my government, while the existing rights of the states and their freedom of action will be in no way prejudiced or impaired."

7. The Chancellor of the Chamber of Princes complained of the extensive authority exercised by officers of the Political Department: "The Ruler and his administration are regarded as under the Orders of Political Officer... The Princes of India frankly recognize the right of the Crown under the treaty relationship to assert its authority for the correction of gross injustice or flagrant misrule. But we are clearly of opinion that such an obligation does not confer a right upon the agents of the Government of India to interfere at their own discretion with the internal administration of the state." As early as 1875 the Prince of Wales had spoken of the "rude and rough manner of these English political officers."

(3) The Viceroy, not the Governor-General-in-Council, was to be the Crown agent in dealing with the states.

The Indian Princess were surprised at the concept of Paramountcy being left undefined. Nevertheless the hydra-headed creature was fed on usage and Crown prerogative and 'the implied consent' of the Princes.

Policy of Equal Federation, 1935–47

The Indian Princes were invited at the Round Table Conferences during 1930–32. In the Federal structure proposed for the whole of India by the Government of India Act 1935, the Indian states were to be allotted 125 out of 375 seats in the Federal Assembly and 104 out of 260 seats in the Council of States. The Federation of India was to come into existence only when rulers of states representing not less than one-half of the total population of the states and entitled to not less than half of the seats (*i.e.*, 52) allotted to the states in the upper chamber of the Federal Legislature agreed to join the Federation.

The Solicitor-General explained the position thus: "The whole principle of the Federation is that the Ruler shall remain ruler of his state and his subjects shall, therefore, remain his subjects, the Ruler undertake to see that the provisions of the Act are enforced in that state."

Prof. Rushbrook William, the Chief Adviser of the Indian Princes at the Round Table Conference wrote in 1930: "The rulers of the Native States are very loyal to their British connection... The situation of these feudatory states, checkboarding all India as they do, are a great safeguard. It is like establishing a vast network of friendly fortresses in debatable territory. It would be difficult for a general rebellion against the British to sweep India because of this network of powerful loyal native states". Lee-Warner wrote about 'the steadying influence' of the Indian princes in the proposed Federal set-up. He wrote: "What is it we have most to fear? There are those who agitate for independence for India, the right ro secede from the Empire altogether... It becomes important, therefore, that we should get what steadying influence we can against this view... There will be approximately 33 per cent of the princes who will be members of the Legislature, with 40 per cent in the Upper chamber... With that influence in the federated legislature I am not afraid in the slightest degree of anything that may happen, even if the Congress managed to get the largest proportion of votes."

The Federation never came into existence for the requisite number of states did not agree to join it.

The Congress successes in the elections of 1937 had repercussion on the states where agitation started for civil liberties and responsible government. On December 3, 1938 Mahatma Gandhi declared that the awakening in the states was due to the 'time spirit' and that there could be no half way house between total extinction of the states and full responsible government. The outbreak of the Second World War in September 1939 finally shelved the federal scheme.

Integration and Merger of States

During the Second World War, India witnessed hectic political activity. The Indian National Congress adopted the policy of non co-operation. The British Government made various efforts to break the deadlock—Cripps' Proposal (1942), Wavell's Plan (1945), the Cabinet Mission Plan (1946) and finally Attlee's announcement (20 February 1947). The future of the Indian states figured in all constitutional discussions. Cripps declared that the British Government did not contemplate transferring the Paramountcy of the Crown to any other party in India. The Princes worked on various schemes to form a union of their own with full sovereign status — a Third Force in the Indian political set-up. The Nawab of Bhopal, as Chancellor of the Chamber of Indian Princes, expressed the hope that the British Govenment would not leave the states 'as a sort of no man's child' and would treat their problem on the same basis as a major communal issue. Attlee's announcement of 20 February 1947 and

Mountbatten's Plan of 3 June 1947, however, emphasised that with the lapse of Paramountcy, Indian states would be free to join any dominion they liked, India or Pakistan. Lord Mountbatten refused to recognize any state or combination of states as separate dominions.

In the National Provisional Government, Sardar Patel headed the States Ministry and appealed to the sense of patriotism of Indian princes and urged them to join the Indian Union on the basis of the surrender of three subjects of Defence, Foreign Affairs and Communications. By 15 August 1947 as many as 136 jurisdictional states acceded to the Indian Union. Kashmir signed the Instruments of Accession on 26 October 1947, Junagadh and Hyderabad in 1948. Portuguese enclaves of goa, Daman were annexed in December 1961.

Many small states which were too small for a modern system of administration were merged with the adjoining provinces, i.e., 39 states of Orissa and Chattisgarh became part of either Orissa or Central Provinces; Gujarat states were merged with the Bombay province. A second form of the integration of states was the formation of units into centrally-administered areas. In this category came the states of Himachal Pradesh, Vindhya Pradesh, Tripura, Manipur, Bhopal, Bilaspur and Kutch. A third from of the integration of states was the formation of states-unions. Thus came into existence the United States of Kathiawar, United States of Matsya, the Union of Vindhya Pradesh, Madhya Bharat, the Patiala and East Panjab States Union (PEPSU), Rajasthan and United States of Cochin-Travancore.

The Reorganisation of States

The reorganisation of the provinces of India on linguistic lines had been one of the demands of the Indian National Congress during the struggle against the British. In Free India the question of reorganisation was forced by the fast and death of Sriramulu who had wanted the creation of a Telugu State of Andhra Pradesh. The linguistic state of Andhra was created in 1953. In 1954 the Government of India appointed a Commission to examine objectively and dispassionately the question of the reorganisation of the states of the Indian Union "so that the welfare of the people of each constituent unit as well as the nation as a whole is promoted." The three members of the Commission were Mr. Fazl Ali (Chairman), Pandit Hridayanath Kunzru and Sardar K. M. Pannikar.

The Commission submitted its report in September 1955 and recommended 16 states and three centrally administered areas for the Indian Union. The states of Travancore-Cochin. Mysore Coorg, Saurashtra, Kutch, Madhya Pradesh, Bhopal, Vindhya Pradesh, Ajmer, Tripura, Himachal Pradesh, PEPSU were to cease to be separate units in the scheme of reorganisation. The distinction between Part 'A', Part 'B' and Part 'C' states was to end.

The States Reorganisation Act, 1956 passed by the Union Parliament provided for the setting up of 14 states and 6 Union Territories. In 1961 Bombay State was bifurcated to form the two states of Maharashtra and Gujarat. In 1962 the state of Nagaland and in 1966 the state of Haryana were created. Today the 28 States of the Indian Union are Andhra Pradesh, Arunachal Pradesh, Assam, Bihar, Goa, Gujarat, Haryana, Himachal Pradesh, Jammu and Kashmir, Karnataka, Kerala, Madhya Pradesh, Maharashtra, Manipur, Meghalaya, Mizoram, Nagaland, Orissa, Panjab, Rajasthan, Sikkim, Tamil Nadu, Tripura, Utter Pradesh, West Bengal, Chattisgarh, Uttranchal, Jharkhand besides 7 Union Territories.

SELECT REFERENCES

1. Lee-Warner : *The Native States of India (1910).*
2. Majumdar, R. C. : *British Paramountcy and Indian Renaissance.* Part I. vol.IX.
3. Menon, V. P. : *Story of the Integration of the Indian States (1956).*
4. Pannikar, K. M. : *Introduction to the Study of the Relations of Indian States with the Government of India (1927).*
5. Varadachariar : *Indian States in the Federation.*
6. *Indian States Committee Report (Butler Committee) 1928–29.*

History of the Growth and Development of Education in India

During the eighteenth century the Hindu and Muslim seats of learning languished. The numerous political convulsions in the country created abnormal conditions hardly conducive to intellectual pursuits both in teachers and pupils. The loss of political power deprived the native schools of learning of their public endowments. In a letter to the Court of Directors dated 21 February 1784, Warren Hastings referred to the decayed remain of schools in every capital town and city of Northern India and the Deccan.

The East India Company became a ruling power in Bengal in 1765. Following the example of contemporary English Government, the Court of Directors refused to take on itself the responsiblity for the education of the people of India and decided to leave education to private effort. However, the Indian officers of the East India Company urged the Court of Directors to do something for the promotion of learning. Some half-hearted efforts were made by the Company's Government to foster oriental learning. Warren Hastings, himself an intellectual, set up the Calcutta Madrasa in 1781 for the study and learning of Persian and Arabic. In 1791 the efforts of Jonathan Duncan, the British Resident at Benares, bore fruit and a Sanskrit College was opened at Benares for 'the cultivation of the laws, literature and religion of the Hindus.' These early attempts for the education of the people in oriental languages met with little success. It was found that there were more teachers than students. The Christian missionaries the attempts to revive an out-of-date system of education and advocated the teaching of Western literature and Christian religion through the medium of English. The Serampore missionaries, in particular, were very enthusiastic for the spread of education. Mention may be made of the Fort William college set up by Lord Wellesely in 1800 for the training of the civil servants of the Company, in the languages and customs of India. The College published an English-Hindustani Dictionary, a Hindustani grammar and some other books. The Court of Directors ordered the closure of the college in 1802.

The Court of Directors made a humble beginning towards the development of education in India in 1813 when the Charter Act (1813) provided for an annual expenditure of one lakh of rupees "for the revival and promotion of literature and the encouragement of the learned natives of India, and for the introduction and promotion of a knowledge of the sciences among the inhabitants of the British territories." Administrative needs of the Company required Indians well-versed in the classical and vernacular languages. In the Judicial Department Indians conversant with Sanskrit, Arabic or Persian were required to sit as assessors with English judges and expound Hindu or Muslim law from Sanskrit or Persian or Arabic books. Besides, the knowledge of Persian and vernaculars was valued in the Political Department for correspondence with rulers of Indian states. The clerical staff in the revenue and commercial departments had contacts with uneducated masses and for them knowledge of vernaculars was a must. However, for higher grade of staff in the Company's services, knowledge of English as well as vernaculars was essential.

Growing Popularity of Western Learning and Ram Mohan Roy. The main factor which tipped the scale in favour of English language and Western literature was the economic factor—Indians wanted a system of education which could help them to earn their livelihood.[1] Progressive

---

1. Mr. Shore, the judge at Fatehgarh (modern U.P.) wrote in 1834 : "At present few, if any, would learn English as long as it leads to no office or emolument."

Indian elements also favoured the spread of English education and Western learning. Raja Ram Mohan Roy protested against the Government's proposal to strengthen the Calcutta, Madras, the Benares Sanskrit College and establishment of more oriental colleges in Bengal. He wrote to Lord Amherst in 1823 that Sanskrit education could "only be expected to load the minds of youth with grammatical niceties and metaphysical distinctions of life which are of little or no practical use to their possessors or to society. The pupils will there acquire what was known two thousand years ago, with the addition of vain and empty subtleties since then produced by speculative men." He added. "Youths will not be fitted to be better members of society by the Vedantic doctrines which teach them to believe that all visible things have no real existence, that as father, brother, etc... have no real entity, they consequently deserve no real affection and therefore the sooner they escape from them and leave the world the better." Advocating the importance of modern scientific learning, he wrote, "The Sanskrit system of education would be the best calculated to keep the country in darkness, if such had been the policy of British Government. But as the improvement of the native population is the object of the Government, it will consequently promote a more liberal and enlightened system of instruction, embracing Mathematics, Natural Philosophy, Chemistry, Anatomy with other useful sciences." The protests of Raja Ram Mohan Roy did not go unheeded. The Government agreed to encourage the study of English as well as Oriental languages. A grant was sanctioned for the Calcutta Hindu College set up in 1817 by enlightened Bengalis, which imparted instruction mainly in English language and emphasised the study of Western humanities and sciences. The Government also set up three Sanskrit Colleges one each at Calcutta, Delhi and Agra. In addition, funds were set apart for the translation of European scientific works into Oriental languages.

Orientalist-Anglicist Controversy. The General Committee of Public Instruction consisted of ten members. Within the Committee there were two groups, the Orientalist led by H.T. Prinsep who advocated the policy of giving encouragement to Oriental literature and the Anglicist or the English Party which favoured the adoption of English as a medium of instruction. The equal division of parties in the Committee made it extremely difficult for it to function effectively. Stalemates in the meetings of the Committee were frequent. Ultimately both the parties in the committee submitted their dispute to the Governor-General-in-Council for orders. As a member of the Executive Council, Macaulay wrote his famous Minute on educational policy dated 2 February 1835 and placed it before the Council. Macaulay favoured the viewpoint of the Anglicist Party. He showed great contempt for Indian customs and literature when he said that "a single shelf of a good European library was worth the whole native literature of India and Arabia." Regarding the utility, importance and claims of English language he wrote: "Whoever knows that language has ready access to all the vast intellectual wealth which all the wisest nations of the earth have created and handed in the course of ninety generations... In India, English is the language spoken by the ruling class. It is spoken by the higher class of natives at the seats of Government. It is likely to become the language of commerce throughout the seas of the East." Macaulay cited the examples of European Renaissance and case of Russia and dilated upon " the great impulse given to the mind of a whole society—of prejudice overthrown, of knowledge diffused, of task purified, of arts and sciences planted in countries which had recently been ignorant and barbarous." Possibly, Macaulay aimed to create a class of persons who should be "Indian in blood and colour, but English in tastes, in opinions, in morals and in intellect.". In other words, he sought the production of brown Englishmen" to fill the lower cadres in the Company's administration.

The Government of Lord William Bentinck in the Resolution of 7 March 1835 accepted the viewpoint of Macaulay that, in future, the object of the Company's Government should be the promotion of European literature and sciences, through the medium of English language and in future all funds were to be spent for that purpose.

The 'Macaulayian system' was a systematic effort on the part of the British Government to educate the upper classes of India through the medium of English language. Education of the masses was not the aim of Macaulay. "It is impossible for us" wrote Macaulay in 1835, " with our limited means to attempt to educate the body of the people." He rather put implicit faith in the 'infiltration theory'. He believed that the English educated persons would act as a 'class of interpreters' and in turn enrich vernacular languages and literature and thus the knowledge of Western sciences and literature would reach the masses. Thus a natural corollary of Macaulay's theory was the development of vernacular languages as ancillary to the teaching of English.

Hereafter the Government made half-hearted efforts to develop vernacular languages and the development of literature in these languages was left to the genius and needs of the people who spoke these languages. In the North-West Provinces (modern U.P.) Mr. James Thomason, Lieutenant-Governor during 1843–53, made efforts to develop a comprehensive scheme of village education through the medium of vernacular languages. The smaller English schools were abolished and English education confined to colleges. In this village school useful subjects like the mensuration, agricultural science etc., were taugh throught the medium of vernaculars. Above all, a Department of Education was organized for the inspection and improvement of indigenous schools. The motivating force behind Thomason's plan was to train personnel for employment in the newly set up Revenue and Public Works Departments of the province.

Sir Charles Wood's Despatch on Education, 1854. Sir Charles Wood, the President of the Board of control in the coalition ministry of Earl of Aberdeen (1852–55), was a true product of the Palmerstonian era of English history. He was a firm believer in the superiority of English race and institutions and sincerely believed that these institutions could serve as a useful model for the world Charles Wood showed a larger vision about education than most of the zealous educationists in India. In 1854 Wood prepared his comprehensive despatch on the scheme of future education in India. The despatch came to be considered as the Megna Catra of English education in India. The scheme envisaged a co-ordinated system of education on an all-India basis, The main recommendations may be summarised thus:

(1) It declared that the *aim* of Government's educational policy was the teaching of Western education. "The education which we desire to see extended in India" wrote Wood in the despatch, "is that which has for its object the diffusion of the improved arts, science, philosophy and literature of Europe, in short of European knowledge".

(2) As to the *medium of instruction,* it declared that for higher education English language was the most perfect medium of education. It also emphasised the importance of the vernacular languages, for it was through the medium of the vernacular languages, that European knowledge could infilter to the masses.

(3) It proposed the setting up of vernacular primary schools in the villages at the lowest stage, followed by Anglo-Vernacular high schools and an affiliated college at the district level.

(4) It recommended a system of grants-in-aid to encourage and foster private enterprise in the field of education. This grants in-aid was conditional on the institutions employing qualified teachers and maintaining proper standards of teaching.

(5) A Department of Public Instruction under the charge of a Director in each of the five provinces of the Company's territories was to review the progress of education in the province and submit an annual report to the Government.

(6) Universities on the model of the London University were proposed for Calcutta, Bombay and Madras. The constitution of the University provided for a Senate, a Chancellor, a Vice Chancellor and Fellows—all to be nominated by the Government. The universities were to hold examinations and confer degrees. A university might set up professorships in various branches of learning.

(7) The despatch emphasised the importance of vocational instruction and the need for establishing technical schools and colleges.

(8) Teachers' Training Institutions on the model then prevalent in England were recommended.

(9) The despatch gave frank and cordial support for fostering the education of women.

The new scheme of education was a slavish imitation of English models. Almost all the proposals in the Wood's Despatch were implemented. The Department of Public Instruction was organised in 1855 and it replaced the earlier Committee of Public Instruction and Council of Education. The three universities of Calcutta, Madras and Bombay came into existence in 1857. Mostly due to Bethune's efforts girls schools were set up on modern footing and brought under the Government's grant-in-aid and inspection system.

The ideals and methods advocated in Wood's Despatch dominated the field for about five decades. The same period also witnessed a rapid Westernization of the educational system in India. The indigenous system gradually gave place to the Western system of education. Most of the educational institutions during this period were run by European headmasters and principals under the Education Department. The missionary enterprise played its own part and managed a number of institutions. Gradually private Indian effort appeared in the field.

The Hunter Education Commission, 1882-83. In 1882 the Government appointed a Commission under the chairmanship of W.W. Hunter to review the progress of education in the country since the Despatch of 1854. Another reason for the appointment of the Commission was the propaganda carried on by the missionaries in England that the education system of India was not carried on in accordance with the policy laid down in Wood's Despatch. The resolution appointing the Commission instructed the Chairman so to reorganise education in India that "the different branches of public instruction should, if possible, move forward together and with more equal step than hitherto. The principal object, therefore, of the enquiry of the Commission should be the present state of elementary education throughout the Indian Empire and the means by which this can be extended and improved". The Commission was not "to enquire into the general working of the Indian universities". Thus the Commission mostly confined its remarks to secondary and primary education. It visited all the provinces and passed no fewer than 200 resolutions. Its main recommendations were:

(*i*) It emphasised the State's special care for the extension and improvement of primary education. "Primary instruction" declared the Commission, "should be regarded as the instruction of the masses through the vernacular, in such subjects as will best fit them for their position in life". While private enterprise was to be welcomed at all stages of education, primary education was to be provided without reference to local co-operation. The Commission recommended the transference of the control of primary education to the newly set up District and Municipal Boards. The local boards were empowered to levy cess for educational purposes.

(*ii*) For Secondary education, the principle was laid down that there should be two divisions—one, a literary education leading up to the Entrance Examination of the University and the other of a practical character preparing students for commercial and vocational careers.

(*iii*) The Commission recommended that an all-out effort should be made to encourage private enterprise in the field of education. To achieve that objective, it recommended the extension and liberalization of the grants-in-aid system, recognition of aided schools as equal to Government, institutions in matters of status and privileges etc. The Government should withdraw, it was recommended, as early as possible from the direct management of secondary and collegiate education.

(*iv*) The Education Commission drew attention to the inadequate facilities for female education outside the Presidency towns and made recommendations for its spread.

The twenty years following the report of the commission saw an unprecedented growth and expansion of secondary and collegiate education[2]. The marked feature of this expansion was the participation of Indian philanthropic activity. A number of denominational institutions sprang up in all parts of the country. Interest was kindled in Indian and Oriental studies apart from the pursuit of Western knowledge. Another development of the period was the setting up of the teaching-cum-examining universities. The Punjab University was founded in 1882 as 'the supreme literary, supreme teaching and supreme examining body", The Allahabad University was set up in 1887.

The early years of the nineteenth century was a period of growing political unrest and controversies in educational policies. Political developments acted and reacted on educational developments. The official view was that educational expansion had not proceeded on the right lines, that quality had deteriorated under private management, there was lot of indiscipline in schools and colleges and that educational institutions had become factories for the production of political revolutionaries. All these unhealthy developments were attributed to unregulated rapid expansion under irresponsible private enterprise. Nationalist opinion admitted the lowering of standards but emphasised that the Government was not doing its duty to liquidate illiteracy.

In his characteristic zeal improvement of all branches of administration, Curzon sought to reconstruct education in India. He deprecated the 'too slavish imitation of English models' and Macaulay's colossal blunder in erecting an 'inverted pyramid' and prejudice against Indian vernaculars. He referred to the poor quality of teachers who were 'merely the purveyors of certain articles to a class of purchasers' and found fault with the examination-ridden system of education. His motives were mainly political and only partly educational. Curzon justified the increase of official control over education in the name of quality and efficiency, but actually sought to restrict education and discipline educated mind towards loyalty to the Government. The nationalist mind saw in Curzon' policies an attempt to strengthen imperialism and sabotage development of nationalist feelings.

The Indian Universities Act, 1904. In September 1901 Curzon summoned the highest educational officers of the Government throughout India and representatives of universities at a round table conference at Simla. The Conference opened with a speech by the Viceroy in which he surveyed the whole field of education in India. "We have not met here" he said, "to devise a brand new plan of educational reform which is to spring fully armed from the head of the Home Department and to be imposed *nolens volens* upon the Indian public". Later developments were to prove the hypocrisy behind this assertion. The Conference adopted 150 resolutions which touched almost every conceivable branch of education. This was followed by the appointment of a Commission under the presidency of Sir Thomas Raleigh on 27 January 1902 to enquire into the condition and prospects of universities in India and to recommend proposals for improving their constitution and working. Evidently, the Commission was precluded from reporting on primary or secondary education. As a result of the report of the recommendations of the Commission the Indian Universities Act was passed in 1904. The main changes proposed were as under:

(1) The universities were desired to make provision for promotion of study and research, to appoint university professors and lecturers, set up university laboratories and libraries and undertake direct instruction of students.

2.			1881–82	1901–02
	1.	No. of Secondary Schools	3,916	5,124
	2.	No. of pupils in Secondary Schools	214,077	590,129
	3.	No. of Arts and Professional Colleges	72	191
	4.	No. of pupils in Colleges	—	23,009

(2) The Act laid down that the number of Fellows of a university shall not be less than fifty nor more than a hundred and a Fellow should normally hold office for a period of six years instead of for life.

(3) Most of the Fellows of a university were to be nominated by the Government. The elective element at University of Calcutta, Madras and Bombay was to be twenty each and in case of other universities fifteen only.

(4) The Governor control over the universities was further increased by vesting the Government with powers to veto the regulations passed by the Senate of a university. The Government could also make additions or alterations in the regulations framed by the Senate and even frame regulations itself over and above the head of the Senate.

(5) The Act increased university control over private colleges by laying down stricter conditions of affiliation and periodical inspection by the Syndicate. The private colleges were required to keep a proper standard of efficiency. The Government approval was necessary for grant of affiliation or disaffiliation of colleges.

(6) The Governor-General-in-Council was empowered to define the territorial limits of a university or decide the affiliation of colleges to universities.

The Nationalist opinion both inside and outside the Legislative Council opposed the measure. Mr. G. K. Gokhale described the bill 'a retrograde measure' which cast unmerited aspersion on the educated classes of the country and was designed to perpetuate "the narrow, bigoted and inexpensive rule of experts." The Sadler Commission of 1917 commented that the Act of 1904 made 'the Indian universities among the most completely governmental universities in the world'. Indian opinion believed that Curzon sought to reduce the universities to the position of departments of the State and sabotage development of private enterprise in the field of education. Ronaldshay, Curzon's biographer, admits that "the changes actually brought about were small and out of all proportion either to the time and thought which the Viceroy had devoted to them or to the violence of the opposition with they had been assailed... In its broad outline the system of higher education remained much as it has been before."[3] However, a good outcome of Curzon's policy was the sanction in 1902 of a grant of Rs. 5 lakhs per annum for five years for improvement of higher education and universities. The Government grants have become a permanent feature ever since then.

Government Resolution on Education Policy, 21 February 1913. In 1906 the progressive State of Baroda introduced compulsory primary education throughout its territories. Nationalist opinion could see no reason why the Government of India could not introduce compulsory primary education in British India. During 1910–13, G. K. Gokhale made heroic efforts in the Legislative Council urging the Government to accept the responsiblity for compulsory primary education.

In its Resolution of 21 February 1913, the Government of India refused to recognise the principle of compulsory education, but accepted the policy of the removal of illiteracy. It urged the provincial governments to take early steps to provide free elementary instruction to the poorer and more backward sections of the population. Private effort in this direction was also to be encouraged. Regarding secondary education, the Resolution stressed the need for improvement of quality of schools. As far as university education was concerned, the Resolution declared that a university should be established for each province and teaching activities of the universities should be encouraged.

The Sadler University Commission, 1917–19. In 1917 the Government of India appointed a Commission to study and report on the problems of Calcutta University. Dr. M.E. Sadler, Vice-Chancellor of the University of Leeds, was appointed its Chairman. The Commission included two

---

3. The Earl of Ronaldshay : *The Life of Lord Curzon,* vol, ii, p.194.

Indian members, namely Sir Asutosh Mukerji and Dr. Zia-ud-din-Ahmad. While the Hunter Commission had reported on problems of secondary education and the University Commission of 1902 mainly on the different aspects of university education, the Sadler Commission reviewed the entire field from school education to university education. The Sadler Commission held the view that the improvement of secondary education was a necessary condition for the improvement of university education.

The Commission reported that an effective synthesis between college and university 'was still undiscovered when the reform of 1904 had been worked out to conclusion' and the foundation of a sound university organisation had not been laid down. Further, it reported that 'the problems of high school training and organisation were unresolved. Although the Commission reported on the conditions of Calcutta University, its recommendations and remarks were more or less applicable to other Indian universities also. The following were the main recommendations:

1. A twelve-year school course was recommended. After assessing the Intermediate Examination, rather than the Matriculation, the students were to enter a university. The Government was urged to create new type of institutions called Intermediate colleges. These colleges could either be run as independent institutions or might be attached to selected high schools. For the administration and control of Secondary Education, the Commission recommended the setting up of a Board of Secondary and Intermediate Education.

The idea behind these recommendations was, on the one hand, to prepare students for the universities, and to relieve the latter of a large number of students quite below any university standard and, on the other hand, to offer a sound collegiate education to students who did not propose, and should not be encouraged, to proceed to universities.

2. The duration of the degree course after the Intermediate state should be limited to three years. For the needs of abler students provision was to be made for Honours courses as distinct from the Pass courses.

3. The Commission recommended less rigidity in framing the regulations of universities.

4. The old type of Indian university, with its large number of affiliated and widely scattered colleges, should be replaced by centralized unitary-residential-teaching autonomous bodies. A unitary teaching university was recommended for Dacca to lessen the rush of numbers at the colleges of Calcutta University. Further, colleges in the mofussil should be so developed as to make it possible to encourage the growth of new university centres by concentration of resources for higher education at a few points.

5. It stressed the need for extension of facilities for female education and recommended the establishment of a special Board of Women Education in the Calcutta University.

6. The necessity of providing substantial facilities for training of teachers was emphasised and desirability of setting up the Departments of Education at the University of Calcutta and Dacca.

7. The University was desired to provide courses in applied science and technology and also to recognise their systematic and practical study by award of degrees and diplomas. The universities were also to provide facilities for training of personnel for professional and vocational colleges.

Seven new universities came into existence during 1916–21, namely Mysore, Patna, Banaras, Aligarh, Dacca, Lucknow and Osmania. In 1920, the Government of India recommended the Sadler Report to provincial governments.

Education under Dyarchy, 1921–37. As a result of the Montagu-Chelmsford Reforms of 1919, the Department of Education was transferred to the control of popular ministers in the various provinces. The Central Government ceased to take direct interest in educational matters and the Department of Education in the Government of India was amalgamated with other departments. Above all, the Central special grants for education liberally sanctioned since 1902 were discontinued. Financial difficulties prevented the provincial governments from taking up ambitious schemes of educational expansion or improvement. Despite all these handicaps there was considerable expansion of education, mostly by philanthropic effort.

The Hartog Committee, 1929. The quantitative increase of education inevitably led to deterioration of quality and lowering of standards. There was considerable dissatisfaction with the educational system. The Indian Statutory Commission appointed an report on the development of education. The main findings of the Hartog Committee were as follows:

1. It emphasised the national importance of primary education, but condemned the policy of hasty expansion or attempt to introduced compulsion in education. The Commission recommended the policy of consolidation and improvements.

2. For secondary education, the Commisssion reported that the system was dominated by the Matriculation Examination and many undeserving students considered it the path to university education. It recommended a selective system for admission and urged the retention of most of the boys intended for rural rural pursuits at the Middle Vernacular School stage. After the Middle Stage students should be diverted to diversified courses leading to industrial and commercial careers.

3. The Commission pointed out the weaknesses of university education and criticised the policy of indiscriminate admission which led to lowering of standards. It recommended that "all efforts should be concentrated in improving university work, in confining the university to its proper function of giving good advanced education to students who are fit to receive it and, in fact making the university a more fruitful and less disappointing agency in the life of a community."

Wardha Scheme of Basic Education. The Government of India Act 1935, introduced provincial autonomy and popular ministries started functioning from 1937. The Congress party came into power in seven provinces. The Congress party set at work to evolve a national scheme of education for the country. In 1937 Mahatma Gandhi published a series of articles in his paper, *The Harijan*, and proposed a scheme of education called Basic Education, better-known as the Wardha Scheme. The main principle of Basic Education is 'learning through activity'. The Zakir Husain Committee worked out the details of the scheme and prepared detailed syllabi for a number of crafts and made suggestions concerning training of teachers, supervision, examination and administration. The scheme centred round 'manual productive work' which might cover the remuneration of the teachers. It envisaged a seven year course through the mother tongue of the students. The outbreak of the war in 1939 and the resignation of Congress Ministries led to the postponement of the scheme. It was left to the National Government to take up the work after 1947.

Sargeant Plan of Education. In 1944 the Central Advisory Board of Education drew up a national scheme of education, generally known as the Sargeant Plan (Sir John Sargeant was the Educational Advisor to the Government of India) This plan envisaged the establishment of elementary schools and high schools (junior and senior basic schools) and introduction of universal free and compulsory education for children between the ages of 6 and 11. A school course of six years was to be provided for children between the ages of 11 and 17. The high schools were to be of two types: (*a*) academic and (*b*) technical and vocational school with different curricula. The plan also recommended the abolition of the Intermediate course and the addition of an extra year each at the high school and the college stage.

The Sargeant Scheme envisaged a 40-year educational reconstruction plan for the country, which was reduced to 16 years by the Kher Committee.

Radhakrishnan Commission, 1944–49. In November 1948 the Government of India appointed a Commission under the chairmanship of Dr. Radhakrishnan to report on university education in the country and suggest improvements. The important recommendations of the report submitted in August 1949 were as follows:

1. Twelve years of pre-university educational course.

2. The working days at the university should not be less than 180 in the year exclusive of examination days. These working days should be divided into three terms each of 11 weeks' duration.

3. Higher education to have three main objectives : General Education, Liberal Education and Occupational Education. The first of these was to be specially emphasised for its importance has not been adequately recognised so far. More attention should be paid to subjects, such as Agriculture, Commerce, Education, Engineering and Technology, Law and Medicine. The existing engineering and technical institutes should be looked upon as national assets and steps taken to improve them.

4. A university degree should not be considered as essential for the administrative services.

5. As three years are required to qualify for the first degree, it is not desirable that the work during the period should be judged by a single examination. As far as possible, examinations should be held subject-wise at different stages.

6. The examination standards should be raised and made uniform in all the universities and university education placed on the 'concurrent list'.

7. The scales of pay of the university teachers should be raised.

8. A University Grants Commission should be set up to look after university education in the country.

University Grants Commission. In pursuance of the recommendation of the Radhakrishnan Commission, the University Grants Commission was constituted in 1953. The Commission was given an autonomous statutory status by an Act of Parliament in 1956. Most of the matters connected with the University education including the determination and co-ordination of standards and facilities for study and research have been committed to the care of this body. The Central Government annually places at the disposal of the University Grants Commission adequate funds from which grants are made to different universities and development schemes are implemented.

Kothari Education Commission, 1964–66. An Education Commission under the Chairmanship of Dr. D. S. Kothari was appointed by the Government of India in July 1964 to 'advise Government on the national pattern of education and on the general principles and policies for the development of education at all stages and in all aspects.' Distinguished educationists and scientists from the U.K., U.S.S.R. were associated while the UNESCO Secretariat made available the services of Mr. J. F. Mc Dougall who served as Associate Secretary of the Commission.

The Commission recognised that education and research are crucial to the entire development and progress of a country—economic, cultural and spiritual. It condemned the rigidity that characterised the existing system and emphasised the need for flexibility in educational policy to suit the changing circumstances. It expressed the hope that the Report would provide some basic thinking and framework for taking the first step towards bringing, what it called, an educational revolution in the country.

The Report made recommendations touching various sectors and aspects of education, the principal among those being :

1. Introduction of work-experience (which includes manual work, production experience, etc.) and social service as integral parts of general education at more or less all levels of education;

2. Stress on moral education and inculcation of a sense of social responsibility. Schools should recognise their responsibility in facilitating the transition of youth from the world of school to the world of work and life;

3. Vocationalisation of secondary education;

4. The strengthening of centres of advanced study and the setting up of a small number of major universities which would aim to achieve highest international standards;

5. Special emphasis on the training and quality of teachers for schools;

6. Education for agriculture and research in agriculture and allied sciences should be given a high priority in the scheme of educational reconstruction; and

7. Development of quality and pace-setting institutions at all stages and in all sectors.

National Policy on Education

Largely based on the recommendations of the Kothari Commission, in 1968 the Government of India adopted a resolution on education which stressed (*i*) free and compulsory education up to the age of 14; (*ii*) improved status and emoluments of teachers; (*iii*) adoption of the three-language formula and development of regional languages; (*iv*) equalisation of education of science and research; (*v*) development of education for agriculture and industry; (*vi*) improvement on quality and production of inexpensive textbooks; and (*vii*) investment of 6% of national income in education.

New Education Policy, 1986

The aim of New Education Policy is to transfer a static society into one vibrant with a commitment to development and change. The long-term programme and strategy consists of:—

1. Increase in literacy rate from the present 36% of the population to 56% by 2000 A. D.

2. Universalisation of Elementary Education.

3. Vocationalisation of Higher Secondary Education. The target is to bring 10% of school children within its preview by 1990 and 25% by 1995.

4. Improvement of Higher Education and to train motivated manpower to new challenges inherent in modernisation and globalization of economy.

5. Education should have special relevance and the curricula should be so devised to imbibe in the students the noble principles and ideals enshrined in our Constitution viz.; (*a*) pride in the national heritage (*b*) commitment to principles of secularism and social justice (*c*) devotion to the cause of unity and integrity of the country (*d*) firm belief in principle of international understanding.

SELECT REFERENCES

1. Basu, Aparna : *Growth of Education and Political Development in India, 1898–1920.*
2. Dayal, B. : *The Development of Modern Indian Education (1953).*
3. Mukherjee, S. N. : *History of Education in India (1957).*
4. Nurullah and Naik : *Histoty of Education in India During British Period (1956).*
5. *Report of the Radhakrishnan Commission on University Education, 1949.*
6. *Report of the Kothari Education Commission, 1966.*

THE HISTORY OF THE INDIAN PRESS

Broadly speaking, the functions of the press are to convey government policies to the public, keep government informed of public needs and reaction to government policies and keep the public and government informed of events and happenings at home and abroad. Each of these functions developed as the need for it was felt.

The history of the Indian press begins with the coming of the Europeans. The Portuguese were the first European nation who brought a printing press to India and the first book published in India was by the Jesuits of Goa in 1557. In 1684 the English East India Company set up a printing press in Bombay. For about a century no newspapers were published in the Company's territories because the Company's servants in India wished to withhold the news of their malpractices and abuses of 'private trading' from reaching London[1].

The first attempts to publish newspapers in India were made by the disgruntled employees of the East India Company who sought to expose the malpractices of private trade. In 1776 William Bolts[2], being censured by the Court of Directors for private trading, resigned his service under the Company and announced his intention to publish a newspaper and made it known that he had in his possession "in manuscript many things to communicate which most intimately concerned every individual." The official quarters at once reacted and Bolts' scheme ended in embryo. It was left to James Augustus Hickey to publish the first newspaper in India entitled *The Bengal Gazette or Calcutta General Advertiser* in the year 1780. For his outspoken criticism of Government officials and scurrilous attacks on the Governor-General and the Chief Justice, Hickey's press was seized in 1782. The following years saw the appearance of new publications like *The Calcutta Gazette* (1784), *The Bengal Journal* (1785), *The Oriental Magazine of Calcutta or Calcutta Amusement* (1785), *The Calcutta Chronicle* (1786). *The Madras Courier* (1788), *The Bombay Herald* (1789) etc. The promoters of these new publications profited from Hickey's bitter experience and avoided clash with the authorities.

The circulation of newspapers during this early period never exceeded a hundred or two hundreds. These journals usually aimed to cater to the intellectual entertainment of the Europeans and Anglo Indians. There was hardly any danger of public opinion being subverted in India. What really worried the Company's officers in India was the apprehension that these newspapers might reach London and expose their misdoings to the Home authorities. In the absence of press laws, the newspapers were at the mercy of the Company's officials. The Government sometimes enforced pre-censorship, sometimes deported the offending editor for anti-government policies.

The Censorship of the Press Act, 1799. Lord Wellesley imposed censorship on all newspapers. Apprehending a French invasion of India and engaged in the struggle for supremacy in India, might have the effect of weakening his influence *vis-a-vis* his Indian adversaries or the French. The Censorship of Press Act, 1799, imposed almost wartime restrictions on the press. The regulations required: and

    (a) The newspaper to clearly print in every issue the name of the printer, the editor and the proprietor ; and

---

1. Cowper commented on the 'get-quick-rich' pursuits of the Company's servants :
   It is not seemly nor of good report
   That thieves at home must hang, but he that puts
   Into his overgorged and bloated purse
   The wealth of Indian provinces, escapes. (Cowper in '*The Task*')
2. Author of the book *Considerations on Indian Affairs* (1772).

(b) The publisher to submit all material for pre-censorship to the Secretary to the Government.[3]

Breach of these rules was punishable with immediate deportation. In 1807 the Censorship Act was extended to cover journals, pamphlets and even books.

Relaxation of press restrictions came under Lord Hastings. The Governor-General tried to put his liberal ideas in practice and succeeded in establishing in India some of the progressive views which were gaining ground in England. In 1818 pre-censorship of the press was dispensed with. However, the Government laid down some general rules for the guidance of newspaper editors with a view to prevent the discussion of topics likely to affect the authority of the Government or injurious to public interests.[4] The Governor-General refused, much against the wishes of the members of his Council and particularly John Adams, to cancel the licence of James Buckingham, the editor of *The Calcutta journal or* deport him.

The Licensing Regulations, 1823. The appointment of John Adams as acting Governor-General in 1823 gave him the opportunity to give a practical shape to his reactionary views. Press Regulations of 1823 proved more stringent than any that had been in force earlier. The new regulations required:

(a) Every printer and publisher to obtain a licence for starting a press or using it.

(b) The penalty for printing and/or publishing any literature without the requisite licence was Rs. 400 for each such publication or imprisonment in default thereof. Magistrates were authorised to attach unlicensed presses.

(c) The Governor-General had the right to revoke a licence or call for a fresh application.

From the arguments supporting the ordinance and its subsequent application, it is clear that Adams' regulations were directed chiefly against newspapers published in the Indian languages or edited by Indians. Raja Ram Mohan Roy's *Mirat-ul-Akbar* had to stop publication. After Adams' regulations only three Bengali and one Persian newspapers continued publication in Calcutta. J. S. Buckingham was also deported to England.

The Liberation of the Indian Press, 1835. Lord William Bentinck adopted a liberal attitude towards the Press. Although Adams' press regulations were not revoked, considerable latitude of discussion was given to the press, Indian as well as Anglo-Indian. It was, however, left to Charles Metcalfe, officiating Governor-General (1835–36) to repeal the obnoxious ordinance of 1823 and earn the epithet of 'Liberator of the Indian Press'. Lord Macaulay, a true Whig, supported the case for a free press in India. He argued that since the Government possessed unquestionable powers of interference whenever the safety of the state was in danger, it was therefore unnecessary to keep the offensive form and ceremonial of despotism in times of peace. A new Press Act requied a printer and publisher to make a declaration giving a true and precise account of the premises of publication. It was open to a printer and publisher to cease to function as such by a similar declaration to that effect. The result of this liberal press policy which continued unchanged till 1856 was the rapid growth of newspapers all over the country.

---

3. The Secretary, in turn, had been instructed not to permit publication of any information regarding military movement of troops, ships, stores or specie, all speculation in regard to relations between the Company or any Indian power or information likely to cause alarm or dissatisfaction among residents in the Company's territories.
4. Editors were required not to publish news concerning (a) the doings of the Court of Directors or other public authorities in England connected with the Government of India; to avoid remarks on the conduct of the Members of the Governor-General-in-Council or Judges of the Supreme Court or political transactions of local administration; (b) Discussions likely to create alarm or suspicion among the native population ; (c) Republication from English or other newspapers of passages coming under any of the above heads; and (d) Private scandals or personal remarks on individuals tending to excite dissensions in society.

The Licensing Act, 1857. The emergency caused by the Rebellion of 1857 led the Government to reimpose restrictions on the press. Act No. XV of 1857 reintroduced licensing restrictions in addition to the existing registration procedure laid down by the Metcalfe Act. The Act prohibited the keeping or using of printing presses without a licence from the Government and the Government reserved the discretionary right to grant licences or revoke them at any time. The Government was also empowered to prohibit the publication or circulation of any newspaper, book or other printed matter. The act was an emergency measure and its duration was limited to one year. Charles Metcalfe's statute, however, continued in force.

The Registration Act, 1867. The Press and Registration of Books Act XXV of 1867 replaced Metcalfe's Act of 1835 pertaining to registration of printing presses and newspapers. The Act was of a regulating nature and not a restriction on printing presses or newspapers. By this Act every book or newspaper was required to have printed legibly on it the name of printer and publisher and the place of printing. Further, within one month of the publication of a book a copy of the book had to be supplied free of charge to the local government. This Act was amended in 1890 and again in 1914, 1952, and 1953.

Act XXVII of 1870, an Act to amend the Indian Penal Code, was passed which contained a sedition section.[5] The revolt of the Wahabis (1869–70) alarmed the Government and impelled it to arm itself with wider powers to deal effectively and promptly with seditious writings and speeches. Later on this section was incorporated in the Indian Penal Code as Section 124-A.

The Vernacular Press Act, 1878. An unfortunate legacy of the Rebellion of 1857 was the growth of the spirit of racial bitterness among the rulers and the ruled. As a result the European press in India after 1858 was always ranged on the side of the Government in all political controversies. The vernacular press, which had developed and grown[6] on an unprecedent scale since 1857 became more vocal and increasingly critical of governmental policies. This in turn created a strong public opinion critical of the imperialist acts of Lord Lytton. The terrible famine of 1876–71 which took a toll of over six million souls and the lavish expenditure on the Imperial Darbar at Delhi in January 1877 made the public opinion and the press restive. Lytton on his part considered the newly rising intellectual class in India as 'a deadly legacy from Macaulay and Metcalfe' and tried to stifle their views.

The Vernacular Press Act 1878 was designed to 'better control' the vernacular press and to empower the Government with more effective means of punishing and repressing seditious writings. The Act empowered

(1) a District Magistrate with the previous permission of a Local Government to call upon the printer and publisher of any vernacular newspaper to enter into a bond undertaking not to publish anything likely to excite feelings of disaffection against the government or antipathy between persons of different races, castes and religions among Her Majesty's subjects. The magistrate could further require a publisher to deposit security and to forfeit it if the newspaper contravened the regulation. If the offence reoccurred, the press equipment could seized.

---

5. Section 5 of Act XXVII of 1870 reads as follows: "Whoever by words, either spoken or intended to be read, or by signs or by visible representation or otherwise, excites or attempts to excite feelings of disaffection towards the Government established by law in British India, shall be punished with transportation for life or for any term, to which fine many be added or with imprisonment for a term which may extend to three years, to which fine may be added or without fine."

6. In 1878 there were 62 vernacular papers in the Bombay Presidency, 60 in the North-West Provinces, Oudh and Central Provinces, 28 in Bengal and 19 in Madras. It was calculated that there were probably more than a lakh readers of such papers.

(2) The magistrate's action was final no appeal could be made to a court of law.

(3) A vernacular newspaper could get exemption from the operation of the Act by submitting proofs of the paper to a government censor.

The act came to be nicknamed Gagging Act. The worst feature of the Act was that it discriminated between the English press and the Vernacular press and no right of appeal to a court of law was given. Under the Act, proceedings were instituted against *The Som prakash, The Bharat Mihir, The Dacca Prakash, The Sahachar* and a few other newspapers. The Act suceeded in its objective and the tone of the vernacular press became submissive and the vernacular newspapers of the period showed very little originality in thinking and more often largely borrowed from the English press.

Lord Cranbrook, the new Secretary of State, objected to the pre-censorship clause of the Act on the ground that the censors would have to be Indians and that they would have to, in point of fact, re-write the newspapers. Consequently in September 1878 the pre-censorship clause was deleted. At the suggestion of the Secretary of State, a Press Commissioner was appointed charged with the duty of supplying authentic and accurate news to the press.

The Vernacular Press Act was repealed in 1882 by the Government of Lord Ripon. Ripon, the nominee of the Liberal Government of Gladstone, held the view that the circumstances which justified the Act of 1878 no linger existed.

The misery caused by the famine of 1896–97 and the bubonic plague led to discontent in the Deccan and there were cases of violence. The newspaper press played its part in the political controversies. By Act VI of 1898, Section 124 of the Penal Code was restated and amplified and a new Section 153-A was added. Similarly, Section 505 of the Penal Code was amended to punish statements which might lead to public mischief, cause disaffection among the armed forces or induce a person to commit an offence against the state.

The Newspapers Act, 1908. The disaffection created by the unpopular acts of Lord Curzon resulted in the growth of an Extremist Party in the Indian National Congress and led to acts of violence. The newspapers of the time often commented adversely on the Government policies. The Government followed a repressive policy and enacted the Newspapers (Incitement to Offences) Act, 1908. According to this Act:

(*a*) The magistrates were empowered to confiscate printing presses, property connected thereto of newspapers which published objectionable material which served as incitement to murder or acts of violence ;

(*b*) The Local Government was empowered to annul any declaration made by the printer and publisher of an offending newspaper made under the Press and Registration of Books Act, of 1867; and

(*c*) The newspaper editors and printers were given the option to appeal to the High Court within fifteen days of the order of forfeiture of the press.

Under the Newspapers Act of 1908, the Government launched prosecutions against nine newspapers and confiscated seven presses.

The Indian Press Act, 1910. The Government further sought to strengthen its hands by the Indian Press Act of 1910 which revived the worst features of Lytton's Press Act of 1878. The Act empowered the Local Government to demand at the time of Registration security of not less than Rs. 500 and not more than Rs. 2,000 from the keeper of a printing press or publisher of a newspaper and to forfeit the security and annual the declaration of Registration of an offending newspaper. The Government could allow fresh Registration and may demand a security of not less than Rs. 1,000 and not more than Rs. 10,000 and forfeit the fresh security and annul the fresh declaration of Registration as well as confiscate the Press and all copies of such newspapers, books etc., if the newspapers persisted in publishing objectionable material.[7] The aggrieved party could appeal to a Special Tribunal of the High Court against orders of forfeiture within two months. Further, the printer of every newspaper was required to supply to the Government free of charge two copies of each issue of the newspaper published. The Act gave powers to the Chief Customs Officer to detain all imported packages which contained objectionable material.

Under the Act action was taken against 991 printing presses and newspapers. Out of these 286 were warned, in 705 cases heavy securities were demanded. During the first five years of the Act the Government confiscated securities amounting to about five lakh rupees.

During the First World War, 1914–18, the Defence of India Rules were promulgated. The executive used the new powers not only for war purposes but also for purposes of repression of political agitation and free public criticism.

In 1921 a Press Committee was appointed under the chairmanship of Sir Tej Bahadur Sapru, then Law Member of the Viceroy's Executive Council, to review the working of press laws. On the recommendations of the Committee, the Press Acts of 1908 and 1910 were repealed.

The Indian Press (Emergency Powers) Act, 1931. The swift turn of the political movement in the thirties and the civil disobedience movement launched by Mahatma Gandhi moved the Government to issue a fresh Press Ordinance in 1930 'to provide for the better control of the Press.' This Act revived the provisions of the Press Act of 1910. In 1931 the Government enacted the Indian Press (Emergency Powers) Act which gave sweeping powers to the provincial governments in suppressing the propaganda for the civil disobedience movement. Section 4 (1) of the Act sought to punish "words, signs or visible representations which (*a*) incite to or encourage or tend to incite to or to encourage, the commission of any offence of murder or any cognizable offence involving violence, or (*b*) directly or indirectly express approval or admiration of any such offence, or of any person, real or fictitious, who has committed or is alleged or represented to have committed any such offence."

In 1932 the Press Act of 1931 was amplified in the form of the Criminal Amendment Act of 1932. Section 4 was made very comprehensive and expanded to include all possible activities calculated to undermine the Government's authority.

---

7. Section 4(1) of the Act gives detailed information about what constituted objectionable material. Any publication containing "any words, signs or visible representations which are likely or may have a tendency, directly or indirectly, whether by inference, suggestion, allusion, metaphor, implication or otherwise:

   (*a*) to incite to murder or to any offence under the Explosive Substances Act, 1908, or to any act of violence, or

   (*b*) to seduce any officer, soldier or sailor in the Army or Navy of His Majesty from his allegiance or his duty, or

   (*c*) to bring into hatred or contempt His Majesty or the Government established by law in British India or the administration of justice in British India or any Native Prince or Chief under the suzerainty of His Majesty or any class or section of His Majesty's subjects in British India, or to excite disaffection towards His Majesty or the said Government or any such Prince or Chief, or

   (*d*) to put any person in fear or to cause annoyance to him and thereby induce him to deliver to any person any property or valuable security, or to do any act which he is not legally bound to do, or to omit to do any act which he is legally entitled to do, or

   (*e*) to encourage or incite any person to interfere with the administration of the law or with maintenance of law and order, or

   (*f*) to convey threat of injury to a public servant, or to any person in whom that public servant is believed to be interested, with a view to inducing that public servant to do an act or to forbear or delay to do any act connected with the exercise of his public functions.

During the Second World War (1939-45), the executive exercised exhaustive powers under the Defence of India Act. Pre-censorship was reinforced, the Press Emergency Act and the Official Secrets Act were amended and at one time the publication of all news relating to the Congress activities declared illegal. The special powers assumed by the Government during the war ended in 1945.

The Press Enquiry Committee. In March 1947 the Government of India appointed a Press Enquiry Committee and charged it with the duty of examination of the press laws in the light of the fundamental rights formulated by the Constituent Assembly of India Among the recommendations of the Committee were the repeal of the Indian Emergency Powers Act of 1931, amendments in the Press and Registration of Books Act, modification in Sections 124-A and 153-A of the Indian Penal Code, repeal of the Indian States (Protection against Disaffection) Act, 1932 and the Indian States (Protection) Act, 1934.

The Press (Objectionable Matters) Act, 1951. The new Constitution was adopted in January 1950. In 1951 the Government felt compelled to seek amendment of Article 19(2) of the Constitution and enactment of the Press (Objectionable Matters) Act. The new Act was more comprehensive than any earlier legislation affecting the press. It replaced the Central and State Press Acts which had been in operation till then. The Act empowered the Government to demand and forfeit security and demand further security from presses and newspaper for publication of 'objectionable matter'. The Government could also declare certain publications forfeited, prohibit transmission by post of objectionable documents, to seize and destroy unauthorised newspapers and to seize and forfeit unauthorised presses. The aggrieved owners of newspapers and printing presses were allowed the right to demand trial by jury. The Act remained in force till 1956.

The All-India Newspapers Editors Conference and the Indian Federation of Working Journalists opposed the Act and urged the Government to institute a comprehensive enquiry into the working of the Indian Press. The Government yielded to the demand and in 1952 appointed the Press Commission under the presidency of Sir justice G.S. Rajadhyaksha. The commission which submitted its report in August 1954 recommended among other things the setting up of an All-India Press Council, the system of price-page schedule for newspapers, banning of crossword puzzle competitions, a strict code of advertisements by newspapers, and drew the Government's attention to the desirability of preventing concentration in the ownership of Indian newspapers. In recent years the Central Government has passed the Delivery of Books and Newspapers (Public Libraries) Act, 1954; The Working Journalists' (Conditions of Service) and Miscellaneous Provisions Act, 1955; The Newspaper (Prince and Page) Act, 1956, The Parliamentary Proceedings (Protection of Publications) Act, 1960 etc., etc.

SELECT REFERENCES

1. Barns, Margarita : *The Indian Press (1940).*
2. Gates, Reed : *The Indian Press Year Book (Annual).*
3. Ghose, H. P. : *The Newspaper in India* (1952).
4. Lovatt, Pat : *Journalism in India* (1928).
5. *Report of the Press Commission*, 3 parts (published by Manager of Publications, New Delhi).

CULTURAL AWAKENING, RELIGIOUS AND SOCIAL REFORMS

No reformation is possible without a renaissance.

—*G.W.F. Hegel*

The Western Impact. The impact of British rule on Indian society and culture was widely different from what India had known before. Most of the earlier intruders who came to India had settled within her frontiers, were absorbed by her superior culture and had become one of the land and its people. However, British conquest was different. Eighteenth century Europe had experienced novel intellectual currents and created the Age of Enlightenment. A new spirit of rationalism and enquiry had given a new dynamism to European society. The development of science and scientific outlook had affected every aspect of activity—political, military, economic and even religious. In contrast to Europe, which was in the vanguard of civilisation in the 18th century, India presented the picture of a stagnant civilisation and a static and decadent society. Thus, for the first time, India encountered an invader who considered himself racially superior and culturally more advanced.

For some time it seemed that India was completely bowled over by new Western ideas and Western values in life. It seemed that India had lagged behind in the rase for civilisation. This produced diverse reactions. Some English-educated Bengali youth (known as Derozios) developed a revulsion against Hindu religion and culture, gave up old religious ideas and traditions and deliberately adopted practices most offensive to Hindu sentiments, such as drinking wine and eating beef. More mature minds led by Rammohan Roy were certainly stimulated by Western ideas and Western values but refused to break away from Hinduism; their approach was to reform Hindu religion and society and they saw the path of progress in an acceptance of the best of the East and the West. Another current was to deny the superiority of Western culture and prevent India from becoming a colourless copy of Europe; they drew inspiration from India's past heritage and reinterpreted it in the light of modern rationalism. This neo-Hinduism preached that Europe had much to learn from India's spiritualism.

The new scientific outlook, the doctrine of rationalism and humanism particularly impressed the English-educated class. The Indian leaders, stimulated by the new knowledge, sought to reform Hinduism from within and sought to purge it of superstitious beliefs and practices. Idolatry, image worship, practice of pilgrimages came up for close scrutiny and consequent reform.

The new concept of secularization was born. The term secularization implies that what was previously regarded as religious was no longer regarded as such. The magic wand was moved by rationalism *i.e.*, the emergence of a tendency to regulate individual religious and social life in accordance with the principles of reason and to discard traditional beliefs and practices which cannot stand the test of modern knowledge. This approach brought a great change in the concept of 'pollution and purity' which formed an integral part of traditional Hindu religion. The educated persons could see no logic behind labelling certain forbidden vegetables such as garlic, ginger, onion, beetroot as impure; rather food value of vegetables received more importance. Further, domestic rituals underwent a change. For example, the attainment of puberty by girls was no longer an occasion for elaborate rituals; it began to be looked upon as a natural stage in the process of growth. Urbanisation, modernisation, new trends in eating at tables and restaurants promoted new outlook and erosion of orthodox way of living.

The ferment of ideas gave an expansive touch to Indian culture. A spirit of renaissance pervaded the whole country. Indian intellectuals closely scrutinized the country's past and found that many beliefs and Practices were no longer of any use and needed to be discarded; they also discovered that many aspects of India's cultural heritage were of intrinsic value to India's cultural awakening. The result was the birth of many socio-religious reform movements touching almost every segment of Indian society.

Two Categories of Reform Movements. The reform movements fall in two broad categories: *One,* Reformist movements like the Brahmo Samaj, the Prarthana Samaj and the Aligarh movement, *Two,* Revivalist movement like the Arya Samaj, the Ramakrishna Mission and the Deoband movement. Both the reformist and revivalist movements depended on a varying degree on an appeal to the lost purity of the religion they sought to reform. The only difference between one reform movement and the other lay in the degree to which it relied on tradition or on reason and conscience.

Another significant aspect of all the reform movements was their emphasis on both religious and social reform. This link was primarily due to two main reasons. (*a*) Almost every social custom and institution in India derived sustenance from religious injunctions and sanctions. This meant that no social reform could be undertaken unless the existing religious notions which sustained the social customs were also reformed. (*b*) Indian reformers well understood the close interrelation between different aspects of human activities. Rammohun Roy, for example, believed that religious reform must precede demand for social reform or political rights.

The Brahmo Samaj (The Society of God)

The Brahmo Samaj was the earliest reform movement of the modern type which was greatly influenced by modern Western ideas. Rammohan (1774–1833) was the founder of Brahmo Samaj. He was a very well-read man. He studied Oriental languages like Arabic, Persian and Sanskrit and attained proficiency in European languages like English French, Latin, Greek and Hebrew. His extensive studies freed his mind from the bigotry that characterised Bengali.

Although Rammohan Roy was a man of versatile genius, the governing passion of his life was religious reform. At a time when the Bengali youth under the influence of Western learning was drifting towards Christianity, Rammohan Roy proved to be the champion of Hinduism. While he defended Hinduism against the hostile criticism of the missionaries, he sought to purge Hinduism of the abues that had crept into it. At the early age of fifteen he had criticised idolatry and supported his viewpoint by quotations from the Vedas. He re-interpreted Hindu doctrines and found ample spiritual basis for his humanitarianism in the Upanishads. He started a campaign for the abolition of *sati*, condemned polygamy and concubinage, denounced casteism, advocated the right of Hindu widows to remarry. He rejected Christianity, denied the divinity of Jesus Christ[1], but accepted the humanism of Europe Thus, Rammohan Roy sought to effect a cultural synthesis between the East and the West. Even today he is recognised as the forerunner of Modern India and a great path-finder of his century, for he embodied the new spirit of enquiry, thirst for knowledge, broad humanitarianism–all to be achieved in the Indian setting. In the words of Dr. Macnicol: "Rammohan Roy was the herald of new age" and the fire he kindled in India has brunt ever since.

Rammohan Roy accepted the concept of one God as propounded by the upanishads. For him God was shapeless, invisible, omnipresent and omnipotent, but the guiding spirit of the universe and omniscient. In August 1828, Roy founded the Brahmo Sabha which was later renamed Brahmo Samaj. The Trust Deed executed in 1830 explained the object of the Brahmo Samaj as "the worship and adoration of the Eternal, Unsearchable, Immutable, Being who is the Author and Preserver of the Universe". The Samaj declared its opposition to idol worship and "no graven image, statue or sculpture, carving, painting, picture, portrait or the likeness of anything was to be allowed in the Samaj building. There was no place for priesthood in the Samaj building. There was no place for priesthood in the Samaj nor sacrifices of any kind were allowed. The worship was performed through prayers and

---

1. *The Precepts of Jesus*, published in 1820.

meditation and readings from the Upanishads. Great emphasis was laid on "promotion of charity, morality, piety, benevolence, virtue and strengthening of the bonds of union between men of all religious persuasions and creeds"

It should be clearly understood that Rammohan Roy never intended to establish a new religion. He only wanted to purge Hinduism of the evil practices that had crept into it. Roy remained a devout Hindu till the end if his life and always wore the sacred thread.

From the beginning the appeal of the Brahmo Samaj had remained limited to the intellectuals and educationally enlightened Bengalis living in the towns. The orthodox Hindus led by Raja Radhakant Deb organised the Dharma Sabha with the object of countering the propaganda of Brahmo Samaj. The early death of Rammohan in 1833 left the Brahmo Samaj without the guiding soul and a steady decline set in.

It was left to Debendranath Tagore (1817–1905) to infuse new life into the Brahmo Samaj and give the theist movement a definite form and shape. Tagore joined the Samaj in 1842. Earlier, Tagore headed the Tattvabodhini Sabha (founded in 1839) which was engaged in search of spiritual truth. The informal association of the two Sabhas gave a new strength in membership and purpose to the Brahmo Samaj. Tagore worked on two fronts. Within Hinduism the Brahmo Samaj was a reformist movement, outside he resolutely opposed the Christian missionaries for their criticism of Hinduism and their attempts at conversion. Tagore condemned idol worship, discouraged pilgrimages, ceremonials and penances among the Brahoms. Under his leadership branches of the Samaj were established in various towns and the Brahmo message spread in the countryside of Bengal.

Keshab Chandra Sen joined the Brahmo Samaj in 1858. Soon after Tagore appointed him the Acharya of the Brahmo Samaj. The energy, vigour and persuasive eloquence of Keshab popularised the movement and the branches of the Samaj were opened outside Bengal, in the U.P., the Panjab, Bombay, Madras and other towns. In Bengal itself there were 54 branches in 1865. However, Keshab's liberal and cosmopolitan outlook brought about a split in the Samaj. Under Keshab's influence the Samaj began to cut itself from Hindu moorings; henceforth religious scriptures of every sect and every people including the Christians, Muslims, Parsis began to be read in the Brahmo Samaj meetings. On the social front, Keshab spoke against the caste system and even advocated intercaste marriages. To Debendranath these developments looked too radical and by virtue of his position as the sole trustee of the dismissed Keshab from the office of the Acharya in 1865. Keshab and his followers left the parent body in 1866 and formed the *Brahmo Samaj of India*. Debendranath's Samaj henceforth came to known as the *Adi Brahmo Samaj*.

A further split in Keshab's Brahmo Samaj of India came in 1878. Some close disciples of Keshab began to regard Keshab as an incarnation. This was not liked by his progressive followers. Further, Keshab began to be accused of authoritarianism. All along Keshab Chandra had advocated a minimum age for marriage of Brahmos, but did not follow his own precepts. In 1878 Keshab married his thirteen-year old daughter with minor Hindu Maharaja of Cooch-Bihar with all the orthodox Hindu ceremonials. He justified his action on the plea that such was the will of God and that he had acted on intuition. Most of Keshab's followers felt disgusted and set up a new organisation called the *Sadharan Brahmo Samaj*.

The Brahmo Samaj has played a notable role in the Indian Renaissance. H.C.E. Zacharias writes: "Rammohan Roy and his Brahmo Samaj form the starting point for all the various Reform Movements—whether in Hindu religion, society or politics—which have agitated Modern India". The intellectual mind which had been cut off its moorings by the Christian propaganda found a way out in the Brahmo Samaj. In the field of religious reform the main significance of Brahmo Samaj lay not in what it retained of traditional Hinduism but what it discarded of the old beliefs of Hinduism. It's overall contribution may be summed up thus: (*i*) it discarded faith in divine *Avatars;* (*ii*) it denied that any scripture could enjoy the status of ultimate authority transcending human reason and conscience; (*iii*) it denounced polytheism and idol-worship; (*iv*) it criticised the caste system; (*v*) it took no definite stand on the doctrine of Karma and transmigration of soul and left it to individual Brahmos to believe either way.

In matters of social reform. Brahmo Samaj has influenced Hindu society. It attacked many dogmas and superstitions. It condemned the prevailing Hindu prejudice against going abroad. It worked for a respectable status for woman in society—condemned *sati*, worked for abolition of *purdah* system, discouraged child marriages and polygamy, crusaded for window remarriage, provision of educational facilities etc. It also attacked casteism and untouchability though in these matters it attained limited success.

The Brahmo Ideas in Maharashtra or the prarthana Samaj

The Brahmo ideas spread in Maharashtra where the Paramahansa Sabha was founded in 1849. In 1867, under the guidance of Keshab the Prarthana Samaj (Prayer Congregation) was established in Bombay. In Bombay the followers of Prarthana Samaj never "looked upon themselves as adherents of a new religion or of a new sect, outside and alongside of the general Hindu body, but simply as a movement within it"[2]. Apart from the worship of one God, in Western India the main emphasis has been on social reform, upon 'works' rather than 'faith'. They believed that the true love of God lay in the service of God's children. Their approach was not confrontation with Hindu orthodoxy, but they relied on education and persuasion.

In the field of social reform the focus was on four objects: (*i*) Disapproval of caste system, (*ii*) Raising the age of marriage fo both meals and females, (*iii*) Window remarriage, (*iv*) Women education.

The prominent leaders of the Samaj were Justice Mahadev Govinda Ranade (1842–1901), R.G. Bhandarker (1837–1925) and N.G. Chandavarkar (1855–1923). The Depressed Classes mission, the Social Service League and the Deccan Education Society have done creditable work in the field of social and educational reforms.

A number of Brahmo Samaj centres were opened in the Madras State. In the Panjab the Dayal Singh Trust sought to implant Brahmo ideas by the opening of Dayal Singh College at Lahore in 1910.

The Arya Samaj

The Arya Samaj movement was an outcome of reaction to Western influences. It was revivalist in form though not in content. The founder, Swami Dayanand, rejected Western ideas and sought to revive the ancient religion of the Aryans.

Mulshanker (1824–83) popularly known as Dayanand was born in a Brahmin family living in the old Morvi state in Gujarat. His father, a great Vedic scholar, also assumed the role of the teacher and helped young Mulshankar acquire good insight into Vedic literature, logic, philosophy, ethics etc. Dayanand's quest for the truth goaded him to *yogabhyas* (contemplation or communion) and to learn yoga it was necessary to leave home. For fifteen years (1845–60) Dayanand wandered as an ascetic in the whole of India studying *Yoga*. In 1875 he formally organised the first Arya Samaj unit at Bombay. A few years later the headquarters of the Arya Samaj were established at Lahore. For the rest of his life, Dayanand extensively toured India for the propagation of his ideas.

Dayanand's ideal was to unite India religiously, socially and nationally— Aryan religion to be the common religion of all, a classless and casteless society, and an India free from foreign rule. He looked on the Vedas as India's 'Rock of Ages', the true original seed of Hinduism. His motto was 'Go back to the Vedas'. He gave his own interpretation of the Vedas. He disregarded the authority of the

---

2. Zacharias : *Renascent India,* p.43.

later Hindu scriptures like the Puranas and described them as the work of lesser men and responsible for the evil practices of idol worship and other superstitious beliefs in Hindu religion. Dayanand condemned idol worship and preached unity of Godhead. His views were published in his famous work *Satyartha Prakash* (The True Exposition).

Dayanand launched a frontal attack on the numerous abuses (like idolatry, polytheism, belief in magic, charms, animal sacrifices, feeding the dead through sraddhas etc.) that had crept into Hindu religion in the 19th century. He rejected the popular Hindu philosophy which held that the physical world is an illusion (*maya*), that man's soul is merely a part of God, temporarily separated from God by its embodiment in the illusory mask of the body and that man's object, therefore, was to escape the world where evil existed and to seek union with God. Against this belief, Dayanand held that God, soul and matter (*prakriti*) were distinct and eternal entities and every individual had to work out his own salvation in the light of the eternal principles governing human conduct. In rejecting monism, Dayanand also dealt a severe blow at the popular belief in pre-determination. The swami contended that human beings were not playthings of fate and as such no one could avoid responsibility for his actions on the plea that human deeds were predetermined. Dayanand accepted the doctrine of *karma*, but rejected the theory of *niyati* (destiny). He explained that the world is a battlefield where every individual has to work out his salvation by right deeds.

Dayanand challenged the dominant position of the Brahmin priestly class in the spiritual and social life of the Hindus. He ridiculed the claim of the priests that they could act as intermediaries between man and God. The swami asserted every Hindu's right to read and interpret the Vedas. He strongly condemned the caste system based on birth, though he subscribed to the Vedic notion of the four-varuna system in which a person was not born in any *varuna* (caste), but was identified as a Brahmin, Kshatriya, Vaishya or Shudra according to the occupation he followed. The swami was also a strong advocate of equal status between man and woman; he pleaded for widow remarriage and condemned child marriages. In a sarcastic language he described the Hindu race as "the children of children".

It should be clearly understood that Dayanand's slogan of 'Back to the Vedas' was a call for revival of Vedic learning and Vedic purity of religion and not revival of Vedic times. He accepted modernity and displayed patriotic attitude to national problems.

The creed and principles of the Arya Samaj first defined at Bombay in 1875 were revised at Lahore in 1877. The Ten Principles were approved by Dayanand and have remained unaltered to this day. The Principles are: (1) God is the primary source of all true knowledge. (2) God who is All-truth, All-knowledge, Almighty, Immortal, Creator of universe, alone is worthy of worship. (3) The Vedas are the books of true knowledge. (4) An Arya should always be ready to accept truth and abandon untruth. (5) All actions must conform to *dharma*, that means after due consideration of right and wrong. (6) The principle aim of this Samaj is to promote the world's well-being, material, spiritual and social. (7) All persons should be treated with love and justice. (8) Ignorance should be dispelled and knowledge increased. (9) Everybody should consider his own progress to depend on the uplift of all others. (10) Social well-being of mankind should be placed above the individual's well-being.

Perhaps the most phenomenal achievement of the Arya Samaj has been in the field of social reform and spread of education. The Samaj based its social programme entirely on the authority of the Vedas, of course conditioned by rationalism and utilitarianism. The Arya Samaj's social ideals comprise, among others, the Fatherhood of God and the brotherhood of man, the equality of sexes, absolute justice and fairplay between man and man and nation and nation and love and charity towards all. The Arya Samaj lays great emphasis on education and enjoins on all Arya Samajists to endeavour "to diffuse knowledge and dispel ignorance". The D.A.V. institutions spread over the length and breadth of the country are a standing proof of the educational achievements of the Samaj. The nucleus for this movement was provided by the Anglo Vedic School established at Lahore in 1886. The education imparted in D.A.V. Institutions combines the best of the modern and classical Indian studies. The orthodox opinion in the Arya Samaj which stands for the revival of Vedic ideal in modern life set up the Gurukula Pathsala at Hardwar in 1902.

The Arya Samaj movement gave "proud" self-confidence and self-reliance to the Hindus and undermined the belief in the superiority of the White Race and Western culture. As a disciplined Hindu organisation, it has succeeded in protecting Hindu society from the onslaught of Islam and Christianity. Rather, the Samaj started the *shudhi* movement to convert non-Hindus to Hinduism Further, it infused a spirit of intense patriotism. The Samaj always remained in the forefront of political movement and produced leaders of the eminence of Lala Hans Raj, Pandit Guru Dutt and Lala Lajpat Rai. Dayanand's political slogan was 'India for the Indians'.

While the Brahmo Samaj and the Theosophical Society appealed to English educated elite only, Dayanand's message was for the masses of India also. The Arya Samaj movement has taken deep roots in the Panjab, Haryana, the Uttar Pradesh, Bihar and Rajasthan.

The Ramakrishna Movement

The didactic rationalism of the Brahmo Samaj appealed more to the intellectual elite in Bengal, while the average Bengali found more emotional satisfaction in the cult of *bhakti* and *yoga*. The teachings of Ramakrisna Mission are based on ancient and traditional concepts amidst increasing Westernization and modernisation. The Ramakrishna Mission was conceived and founded by Swami Vivekananda in 1897, eleven years after the death of Ramakrishna.

Ramakrishna Paramahansa (1834–86) was a poor priest at the Kali temple in Dakshineswar near Calcutta. His thinking was rooted deeply in Indian thought and culture, although he recognised the Truth in all religions. He considered and emphasised that Krishna, Hari, Rama, Christ, Allah are different names for the same God. Unlike the Arya Samaj, Ramakrishna Mission recognizes the utility and value of image worship in developing spiritual fervour and worship of the Eternal Omnipotent God. However, Ramakrishna put his emphasis on the essential spirit, not the symbols or rituals. He stood for selfless devotion to God with a view to the ultimate absorption in Him. This spirituality and compassion for suffering humanity inspired those who listened to him.

It was left to Swami Vivekananda (Narendranath Datta, 1862–1902) to give an interpretation to the teachings of Ramakrishna and render them in an easily understandable language to the modern man.

Vivekanand emerged as the preacher of neo-Hinduism. He attended the Parliament of Religions held at Chicago in 1893 and made a great impression by his learned interpretations. The keynote of his opening address was the need for a healthy balance between spiritualism and materialism. He envisaged a new culture for the whole world where the materialism of the West and the spiritualism of the East would be blended into a new harmony to produce happiness for mankind.

The swami decried untouchability and the caste system. He strongly condemned the touch-me-not attitude of Hindus in religious matters. He regretted that Hinduism had been confined to the kitchen. He frowned at religion's tacit approval to the oppression of the poor by the rich. He believed that it was an insult to God and humanity to teach religion to a starving man. Once he said, "Him I call a Mahatma whose heart bleeds for the poor, otherwise he is a Duratma. So long as millions live in hunger and ignorance I hold every man a traitor who while educated at their expense, pays not the least heed to man". Thus, Vivekanand emphasised the fundamental postulate of his Master that the best worship of God is through service of humanity. In this way he gave a new social purpose to Hinduism.

Ever since its inception the Ramakrishna Mission has been in the forefront of social reform in the country. It runs a number of charitable dispensaries and hospitals, offers help to the afflicted in times of natural calamities like famines, floods, epidemics.

Vivekanand never gave any political message. All the same, through his speeches and writings he infused into the new generation a sence of pride in India's past, a new faith in India's culture and a rare sense of self-confidence in India's future. He was a patriot and worked for the uplift of the people. "So far as Bengal is concerned' writes Subhas Bose "Vivekanand may be regarded as the spiritual father of the modern nationalist movement.

The Theosophical Movement

The Theosophical Society was founded by Westerners who drew inspiration from Indian thought and culture. Madame H.P. Blavatsky (1831–1891) of Russo-German birth laid the foundation of the movement in the United States in 1875. Later Colonel M.S. Olcott (1832–1907) of the U.S. Army joined her. In 1882 they shifted their headquarters to India at Adyar, an outskirt of Madras. The members of this society believe that a special relationship can be established between a person's soul and God by contemplation, prayer, revelation etc. The Society accepts the Hindu beliefs in re-incarnationtion, *karma* and draws inspiration from the philosophy of the Upanishads and Samkhya, Yoga and Vedanta school of thought. It aims to work for universal Brotherhood of Humanity without distinction of race, creed, sex, caste or colour. The Society also seeks to investigate the unexplained laws of nature and the powers latent in man. The Theosophical Movement came to be allied with Hindu Renaissance.

In India the movement became somewhat popular with the election of Mrs. Annie Besant (1847–1933) as its President after the death of Olcott in 1907. Early in her life Mrs. Besant lost all faith in Christianity, divorced her husband, an Anglican clergyman, and came in contact with theosophy (1882). In (1889) she formally joined the theosophical Society. After the death of Madame Blavatsky in 1891, Mrs. Besant felt lonely and decided to come to India. Mrs. Besant was well acquainted with Indian thought and culture and her approach was Vedantic as is very evident from her remarkable translation of the *Bhagvat Gita*. Madame Blavatsky's main emphasis had been on the occult than spiritualism. Mrs. Besant found a bridge between matter and mind. Gradually Mrs. Besant turned a Hindu[3], not only in her views but also in her dress, food, company and social manners. In India, under her guidance, Theosophy became a movement of Hindu Revival.

Talking of the Indian problem, Annie Besant once said: " The Indian work is, first of all, the revival, strengthening and uplifting of the ancient religions. This has brought with it a new self-respect, a pride in the past, a belief in the future, and as an inevitable result, a great wave of patriotic life, the beginning of the rebuilding of a nation." Besant laid the foundation of the Central Hindu College in Benares in 1898 where both the Hindu religion and Western scientific subjects were taught. The College became the nucleus for the formation of Benares Hindu University in 1916. Mrs. Besant also did much for the cause of female education. She also formed the Home Rule League on the pattern of the Irish Home Rule movement.

The Theosophical Society provided a common denominator for the various sects and fulfilled the urge of educated Hindus. However to the average Indian the philosophy of Theosophical Movement seemed rather vague and deficient in positive programme and as such its impact was limited to a small segment of the westernised class.

---

3. A legend got great currency that Mrs. Annie Besant was a pure Brahmin in her previous birth and as such could give a competent exposition of the Hindu *Shastras*.

Muslim Reform Movements

If Hindu mind had responded to Western influences with a desire to learn, the first reaction of the Muslim community was to shut themselves in a shell and resist Western impact.

The Wahabi Movement

The earliest organised Muslim response to Western influences appeared in the form of the Wahabi Movement (which may more aptly be called the Walliullah Movement). It was essentially a revivalist movement. Shah Walliullah (1702–62) was the first Indian Muslims leader of the 18th century who expressed concern at the degeneration which had set in among Indian Muslims. He voiced his anguish at the ugly departures from the purity of Islam. His contribution to the Muslim reform movement was twofold. (*a*) He urged the desirability of creating a harmony among the four schools of Muslim jurisprudence which had divided the Indian Muslims. He sought to integrate the best elements of the four schools. (*b*) He emphasised the role of individual conscience in religion. He held that in cases where the Qoran and the Hadis could be liable to conflicting interpretations, the individual could make a decision on the basis of his own judgement and conscience.

Shah Abdul Aziz and Syed Ahmed Barelvi popularized the teachings of Walliullah but also gave them a political colour. They aimed at creating a homeland for the Muslims. The beginning was made by a *Fatwa* (ruling) given by Abdul Aziz declaring India to be *dar-ul-harb* (land of the kafirs) and the need to make it *dar-ul-Islam*. The campaign was initially directed against the Sikhs of the Punjab. After the British annexation of the Panjab in 1849, the movement was directed against the British. The movement was Crushed by the superior military force of the British in the 1870s.

The Aligarh Movement

A legacy of the Revolt of 1857 was the official impression that the Muslims were the arch conspirators in 1857–58. The Wahabi political activities of 1860s and 1870s confirmed such suspicions. However, a wind of change was perceptible in the 1870s. W.W. Hunter's book *The Indian Musalman* made a vigorous plea for reconciling and "rallying the Muslims". Round the British government through thoughtful concessions. A section of the Muslim community led by Syed Ahmed Khan was prepared to accept this stance of official patronage. These Muslims felt that the Muslims community would forgo its rightful share in the administrative services if they shut themselves in a shell and resist modern ideas.

Sir Syed Ahmed Khan's (1817–98) name stands out conspicuous among the Muslim reformers of the nineteenth century. Born in Delhi in 1817 in a respectable Muslim family, he received education in the traditional Muslim style. He was in the judicial service of the Company at the time of the Rebellion of 1857 and stood loyal to the Government. He retired from service in 1876. In 1878 he became a member of the Imperial Legislative Council. His loyalty earned him a knighthood in 1888. Syed Ahmed tried to modernize the outlook of the Muslims. He tried to reconcile his co-religionists to modern scientific thought and to the British rule and urged them to accept services under the Government. In this objective, he achieved great success.

Sir Syed also tried to reform the social abuses in the Muslim community. He condemned the system of *piri* and *muridi*. The *pirs* and *faqirs* claimed to be followers of the Sufi school and passed mystic words to their disciples (*murids*). He also condemned the institution of slavery and described it un-Islamic. His progressive social ideas were propagated through his magazine *Tahdhib-ul-Akhlaq* (Improvement of Manners and Morals).

In his masterly work *Commentaries on the Qoran,* Sir Syed criticised the narrow outlook of traditional interpreters and gave his own views in the light of contemporary rationalism and scientific knowledge. His emphasis was on the study of Koran. The word of God, he said, should be interpreted by the work of God which lies open before all to see.

In the field of education, Sir Syed opened the M.A.O. College at Aligarh in 1875, where instruction was imparted both in Western arts and sciences and Muslim religion. Soon Aligarh became the centre of religious and cultural revival of the Muslim community. The school became the nucleus for the formation of the Muslim University in 1920.

The Deoband School

The orthodox section among the Muslim ulema who were the standard bearers of traditional Islamic learning organised the Deoband Movement. It was a revivalist movement whose twin objectives were: (*i*) to propagate among the Muslims the pure teachings of the Koran and the Hadis and (*ii*) to keep alive the spirit of *jihad* against the foreign rulers.

The ulema under the leadership of Muhammad Qasim Wanotavi (1832–80) and Rashid Ahamad Gangohi (1828–1905) founded the school at Deoband in the Saharanpur district of the U.P. in 1866. The object was to train religious leaders for the Muslim community. The school curricula shut out English education and Western culture. The instruction imparted was in original Islamic religion and the aim was moral and religious regeneration of the Muslim community. In contrast to the Aligarh movement which aimed at welfare of the Muslim community through Western education and support of the British Government, the Deoband school did not prepare its students for government jobs or worldly careers but for preaching of Islamic faith. It was for its religious instruction that the Deoband school attracted students not only from all parts of India but from the neighburing Muslim countries also.

In politics, the Deoband School welcomed the formation of the Indian National Congress in 1885. In 1888 the Deoband ulema issued a religious decree (*fatwa*) against Syed Ahmed Khan's organisations 'the United Patriotic Association, and 'The Muhammaden Anglo-Oriental Association'. Some critics observe that the Deoband ulemasi' support did not stem from any positive political philosophy or any opposition to British Government but was mainly influenced by their determination to oppose Sir Syed Ahmed's activities.

The new Deoband leader Mahmud-ul-Hasan (1851–1920) sought to impart a political and intellectual content to the religious ideas of the school. He worked out a synthesis of Islamic principles and national aspirations. The Jamiat-ul-Ulema gave a concrete shape to Hasan's ideas of protection of the religious and political rights of the Muslims in the overall context of Indian unity and national objectives.

Sikh Reform Movements

The rationalist and progressive ideas of 19th century also influenced the Sikh community. In 1873 the Singh Sabha movement was founded at Amritsar. Its objective was twofold. It planned to bring to the Sikh community the benefits of Western enlightenment through moden education. It also countered the proselytizing activities of the Christian missionaries as well as Hindu revivalists. The Sabha opened a network of Khalsa schools and colleges throughout the Punjab.

The Akali movement was an offshoot of the Singh Sabha movement. The Akali movement aimed to liberate the Sikh gurdawaras (temples) from the control of corrupt *mahants* who enjoyed the support of the government. In 1921 the Akalis launched a non-violent, non-cooperation satyagraha movement against the *mahants*. The Government resorted to repressive measures but had to bow before popular opinion and pass the Sikh Gurdawaras Act in 1922, which was later amended in 1925.

The Akali movement was a secretarian or a regional movement but not a communal movement. The Akali leaders played a notable role in the national liberation struggle though some dissenting voices were heard occasionally.

Parsi Reform Movements

The Parsi community could not remain unaffected by the wind of change that swept India. In 1851 a group of English-educated Parsis set up the Rahnumai Mazdayasnan Sabha or Religious Reform Association for the object of "the regeneration of the social condition of the Parsis and the restoration of the Zoroastrian religion to its pristine purity". Naroaj Furdonji, Dadabhai Naoroji, K.R. Came were in the forefront of the movement. The newspaper *Rast-Gofter* (Truth-Teller) propagated the message of the Association. Parsi religious rituals and practices were reformed and Parsi creed redefined. In the field of social reform, attention was focussed on improvement of lot of Parsi women in society like removal of *purdah* system, raising the age of marriage and education of women. Gradually the Parsis emerged as the most Westernised section of Indian society.

An Overview

The various reform movements gave the much needed confidence to educated Indians who had been demoralized and uprooted from their moorings by propaganda of western cultural superiority. These reform movements reassured Indians about the greatness of their ancient religions and their rich cultural heritage. The intelligentsia got a new identity which was badly needed.

The reform atmosphere helped Indians to discard many obsolete rites and practices and adjust their religious beliefs to the new environment of rationalist and scientific thought. Above all, a new secular and nationalist outlook also developed.

The reform movements suffered from some retrograde features also. Many reformists desired and worked for social uplift within he framework of imperialism and openly preached loyalty to the British. Again, these reformists held Western society as an ideal while combating inadequacies of their own. Another limitation was that most of these reform movements confined their activities to upper and middle classes in towns, leaving out of purview the backward classes and countless millions living in India's villages. Still another negative aspect was the growth of religious chauvinism. The over-emphasis on superiority of one's own religion and social set-up generated narrow communal outlook. The Imperial rulers were quick to take advantage of this communal divide and used it to weaken the Indian national movement.

Social Reform Movements in the 19th and 20th Centuries

The same set of circumstances—the impact modern education, rational, humanitarian and scientific approach to life—which ushered in—both in action and reaction—reform movements in religion were largely responsible for social reform movements in the 19th and 20th centuries Rammohan Roy, a pioneer in modern religious reform movements in India, was also the Morning Star of modern social reform movement in the country. Social reform became an integral part of religious reform in India and this was equally true of Brahmo Samaj, Prarthana Samaj, Arya Samaj, Ramakrishna Mission, Theosophical Society in Hinduism as also among the Muslims, the Parsis and the Sikhs.

C. H. Heimsath in an excellent analysis of the Hindu social reform movements has indicated three distinct phases in the history of social reform in India, *viz.*, first phase of individual revolt and reform together with strong religious links from Rammohun to the early 1880s; the second phase was marked by the elevation of social reform movement to a national plane as exemplified by the efforts of Behramji Malabari and the Indian National Social Conference; the third stage began when social reform was indentified with a regeneration of the traditional spirit of the nation and is popularly associated with the activities of 'extremist' leaders of the early 20th century. To it may be added the fourth phase under the leadership of Mahatma Gandhi when social reform became a main plank in the all round regeneration of Indian society.

The social reform movement in India have aimed at uprooting social evils, and inculcating in men and women the spirit of sacrifice for the general good of the society. The first and foremost social problem that attracted enlightened opinion was the need for a *better deal for women* in society, in the abolition of the cruel rites of *sati* and infanticide, in the condemnation of child marriage and polygamy and popularization of widow remarriage, in the abolition of *purdha*, in provision of educational facilities for women and economic openings to make them self-supporting and finally an equal share for women in the political life of the country by enfranchisement. Another social evil that was a major concern of the English educated and Hindu intelligentsia was the *caste restrictions* in Hindu society and the *degrading position of the lower castes* especially the untouchables. Of these two great evils, those connected with the position of women received greater attention in the 19th century, while the problems of the untouchables (Harijans) came in sharp focus in the 20th century because of its political overtones.

Sati. The term *sati* literally means a 'pure and virtuous woman'. It was applied in case of a devoted wife who contemplated perpetual and uniterrupted conjugal union with her husband life after life and as proof thereof burnt herself with the dead body of her husband. Enlightened Indian rulers like Akbar, the Peshwas had imposed restrictions on its performance. Though the East India Company broadly adhered to its declared policy of noninterference with the social customs of the people, yet early Governors-General like Cornwallis, Minto and Lord Hastings had taken some steps to restrict the practice of *sati* by discouraging compulsion, forbidding administration of intoxicating drugs to the sorrow-stricken widows, putting a ban of the *sati* of pregnant women or widows below the age of 16 years and, above all, making compulsory the presence of police officials at the time of sacrifice who were to see that no compulsion was used. However, these restrictions proved inadequate and achieved limited success.

Enlightened Indian reformers led by Rammohan Roy launched a frontal attack on the evil of *sati*. With an eye, to the coming Charter debates in the British Parliament and anxious to get a renewal of its charter for another 20 years by presenting a creditable image of its activities in India, the Court of Directors encouraged William Bentinck to enact legislation to suppress *sati*. Regulation XVII of December 1829 declared the practice of *satis*. or burning or burying alive of widows illegal and punishable by criminal courts as culpable homicide The Regulation of 1829 was applicable in the first instance to Bengal Presidency alone, but was extended in slightly modified forms to Madras and Bombay Presidencies in 1830. Thus, the evil practice of *sati* on any scale was wiped out though stray cases might have occurred here and there.

Infanticide. Another horrible and cruel rite particularly common among the Bengalis and the Rajputs was of killing their infant daughters at birth, taking female children to be a great economic liability. Further, if the parents could not arrange marriage for their daughters, it was considered a social disgrace and a violation of religious injunctions. Some socially backward tribes followed the practice of killing their infant daughters at their birth; this was done by the mother by deliberately neglecting the feeding of a female child to administering poisonous drugs to the child through the nipples of the mother's breast. Maharaja Dalip Singh, son of Ranjit Singh, mentions that "he had actually seen when he was a child at Lahore, his sisters put into a sack and thrown into the river".

Enlightened British and Indian opinion was unanimous in condemning infanticide. When persuasion alone could not help, the Bengal Regulations XXI of 1795 and III of 1804 declared infanticide illegal and equivalent to committing a murder. Pressure was exerted through Political Residents and Agents in Indian states to eradicate this evil rite. As a precautionary measure, the Government of India passed an Act in 1870 making it compulsory for parents to register the birth of all babies and providing for verification of female children for some years after birth, particularly in areas where the custom was resorted to in utmost privacy.

Widow Remarriage and Prohibition of Child marriage. The lot of women in society could not be improved merely by the negative steps of suppression of *sati* and infanticide but by positive action in popularizing widow remarriage and raising the age limit for marriage of girls. The Brahmo Samaj debated the question of widow remarriage and popularized it among the Brahmos. The efforts of Pt. Ishwar Chandra Vidyasagar (1820–91) Principal of Sanskrit College, Calcutta, deserve special mention. He dug up old Sanskrit references and proved that Vedic texts sanctioned widow remarriage. He sent a petition signed by 987 persons to the Government of India urging it for legislative action. His efforts were rewarded when the Hindu Widows' Remarriage Act (Act XV of 1856) legalised marriage of widows and declared issues from such marriages as legitimate. However, in Bengal the widow remarriage reform achieved very limited success.

In Western India, Prof. D. K. Karve took up the cause of widow remarriage and in Madras Veeresalingam Pantulu made herculean efforts in the same direction. Prof. Karve started his career as a teacher in a Girls' School at Bombay and seven years later in 1891 became a Professor at Fergusson College. In the meantime he became a widower. He refused to marry a teenager and married a Brahmin widow in 1893. Karve devoted his life to the uplift of Hindu widows and became the Secretary of the Widow Remarriage Association. In 1899 he opened a Widows' Home in Poona with the object of giving high-caste widows an interest in life by providing them openings in the profession of teachers, doctors and nurses and making them, at the same time, self-supporting. He crowned his work by setting up an Indian Women's University at Bombay in 1916.

Legislative action in prohibiting child-marriage came in 1872 when by the Native Marriage Act (propularly known as Civil Marriage Act) marriage of girls below the age of 14 and boys below 18 years were forbidden. However, this act was not applicable to Hindus, Muslims and other recognised faiths and as such had very limited impact on Indian society. B. M. Malabari, a Parsi reformer of the 19th century, started a crusade against child marriage and his efforts were crowned by the enactment of the Age of Consent Act (1891) which forbade the marriages of girls below the age of 12. The Sharda Act (1930) further pushed up marriage age and provided for penal action in marriages of boys under 18 and girls under 14 years of age. A improvement was made by the Child Marriage Restraint (Amendment) Act, 1978 which raised the age of marriage for girls from 15 to 18 years and for boys 18 to 21.

Education of Women. Hindu society in the 19th century suffered from false religious illusions that Hindu scriptures did not sanction female education that education of girls wrought wrath of gods leading to their widowhood.

The Christian missionaries, whatever their motive, were the first to set up the Calcutta Female Juvenile Society in 1819. However, the celebrated name of J.E.D. Bethune, President of the council of Education, will always be remembered with respect. In 1849 he founded a Girls' School in Calcutta. Pt. Ishwar Chandra Vidyasagar also did a lot in popularizing the cause of female education and was associated with no less than thirty-five girls' schools in Bengal. In Bombay the students of Elphinstone Institute became the spearhead of the movement for women education and founded the Students Literary and Scientific Society. Charles Wood's despatch on Education (1854) laid great stress on the need for female education. In the broad perspective, women education became a part of the general campaign for amelioration of the plight of women in society.

Abolition of a Slavery. Slavery of the Greek or Roman or American negro type did not exist in India. Slavery in India was more akin to what may be termed as bonded-servant, bonded-labour type and slaves in India were treated in a humane manner unknown to Western countries. In this context the observation of the Committee of Circuit deserves to be quoted. It reads, "The ideas of slavery, borrowed from our American colonies, will make every modification of it appear in the eyes of our contrymen in England a horrible evil. But it is far otherwise in this country; here slaves are treated as children of the families to which they belong and often acquire a much happier state by their slavery than that could have hoped for by the enjoyment of liberty." If in northern India slaves generally served as domestic servants, in south India slaves were mostly employed in cultivation. Of course, European slave-owners in India treated their slaves in the same inhuman manner characteristic of Western slave-owners.

Slavery was abolished in the British empire in 1833 and a cause was inserted in the Charter Act of 1833 requiring the Governor-General-in-Council to abolish slavery in India as soon as it could be safely and conveniently carried out. Act V of 1843 declared slavery illegal in India and all existing slaves were emancipated without any compensation to the slave-owners. The Penal Code of 1860 also declared trade in slavery illegal. Bonded-labour in one or the other form, however, lingers on in India even now.

Social Reform in the 20th Century

The history and course of social reform movement in the 20th century is marked by the coming into existence of a number of social organisations both at the all-India and provincial levels. The Indian National Social Conference founded in 1887 by M.G. Ranade had limited objectives and achieved limited success. In 1903 the Bombay Social Reform Association was founded and in Madras Mrs. Anni Besant set up the Hindu Association. In September 1932 the All-India Anti-Untouchability League was founded, later renamed as Harijan Sevak Sangh. Further, the social reform movement lost its exclusive male and upper caste basis and orientation; women themselves crusaded for an equal status in society and organised the first All India Women's Conference in 1926 while the lower castes founded All India Depressed Classes Association (March 1918) and All India Depressed Classes Federation.

Though many social evils like drinking, beggary etc., received the attention of social reformers in the 20th century, the twin problems of improvement of the lot of women and Depressed Classes received greater attention partly because of the dynamic leadership of Gandhiji and partly due to the political overtones of the problem of Depressed Classes.

Attacking the *purdah* system among women Gandhiji said, "The sight of the screen made me sad. It pained and humiliated me deeply... Let us not live with one limb completely or partially paralysed... Let us tear down the *purdah* with one mighty effort." The All India Women's Conference also denounced *purdah*. Gandhiji appealed to women to come out of the *purdah* and participate in the nationalist struggle by picketing and spinning. In the Civil Disobedience Movement, launched by Gandhiji in 1930 women participated and courted arrest in large numbers to evoke a comment from a foreign observer that if the Civil Disobedience Movement accomplished nothing else but the emancipation of women in India, it would have fully justified itself.

When the Muslim League obtained separate electorates and taunted the Hindu that the Depressed Classes were not part of the Hindu community but constituted a separate community deserving represenatation in its own rights, the political ambition of the Depressed Classes was touched and they realized their bargaining potential in the fast changing political scene. The Indian National Congress and Hindu social organisations saw the political-cum-social aspect of the problem of lower castes and made some determined efforts to keep them within the fold of Hinduism. In 1928 the Indian National Social Conference adopted a resolution that "the present caste system is a great obstacle to the unification of the Hindu society, and therefore resolves that its abolition should be expedited by (a) encouraging true inter-dining, (b) promoting intercaste marriages, and (c) removing untouchability and all disabilities arising therefrom wherever they exist." Gandhiji organised the Harijan Sevak Sangh with headquarters at Delhi which has done some useful work. Dr. B. R. Ambedkar, a politically-conscious leader of the Depressed classes, was not satisfied with these half-hearted moves and blamed the Harijan Sevak Sangh as a wing of the Congress with the "real aim of ensuring the Untouchables and to make them the camp-followers of the Hindus and the Congress". In 1945 Dr. Ambedkar criticised Gandhiji in his famous book, *What Congress and Gandhi have done to the Untouchables* and advised his fellow untouchables to embrace Buddhism.

The Constitution of the Indian Republic has abolished 'untouchability' and forbidden its practice in any form, while reservation of seats for Scheduled Castes and Scheduled Tribes in the Lok Sabha and State Vidhan Sabhas, apart from reservation of seats for them in the services, are steps in the right direction. Caste disabilities are fast crumbling under the new democratic set up and economic pressures and the Scheduled Castes are increasingly playing their due role in the national life.

SELECT REFERENCES

1. Ahmad, Aziz : *Islamic Modernism in India and Pakistan.*
2. Heimsath, C. H. : *Indian Nationalism and Hindu Social Reform.*
3. Jones, Keneth : *Arya Dharma : Hindu Consciousness in the 19th Century.*
4. Narain, V. A. : *Social History of India—The Nineteenth century.*
5. Natrajan, S. : *A Century of Social Reform in India.*
6. Parekh, Manilal : *Brahmo Samaj.*
7. Ranade, M. G. : *Religious and Social Reforms.*
8. Sarkar, Sumit : *Bibliographical Survey of Social Reform Movements in the 18th and 19th Centuries (I.C.H.R., 1975).*
9. Zacharias, H. C. E. : *Renascent India.*
10. Jones, Kenneth : *Socio-Religious Reform Movements in British India (New Cambridge History of India, 1994)*

THE LOWER CASTE MOVEMENTS IN MODERN INDIA

There are certain things which cannot be mended but only ended. Brahmanical Hinduism is one such.

—*Ramaswamy Naicker*

In medieval times the Indian religious reformers mostly attracted their followers from the lower castes. In contrast to this the socio-religious reform movements of the 19th century were mostly pioneered by the Upper Caste Hindus who condemned the cast system and untouchability. Unfortunately both these challenges though conceived in the spirit of enlightened social regeneration achieved marginal success.

The Changing Scenario. A number of circumstances in the 19th and 20th centuries created class consciousness among the lower castes who took upon themselves to struggle for caste equality. Their efforts resulted in the organisation of various lower caste movements in South India and Western India. The British Policy of Divide and Rule, the growth of Western system of education, the introduction of a common Indian Penal code (1861) and Code of Criminal Procedure (1872), the extension of the railway network (where every Indian could buy ticket of any class and occupy any seat available), the growth of national conciousness and the popularity of the modern political thought based on equality and social egalitarianism created a social and political climate in which the caste system could not be defended. The leading lights among the Lower Castes themselves organised caste movements.

Reactions against Brahminical Domination. In South India, the lower caste movements were a direct revolt against the Brahmanical domination in the Madras Presidency. It is interesting to note that in 1916 a spokesman of the lower castes pointed out that out of the 15 members of the All India Congress Committee from Madras Presidency only one was a non-Brahmin. Some of the lower caste leaders propagated that the Dravadians were the original inhabitants of India while the Aryans were the immigrants into India and they had brought the evil institution of the caste system with them.

The Justice Party and Naicker. In 1917 Sri P. Theagaraya and Dr. T.M. Nair organised the first Non-Brahminical organisation called South Indian Liberal Federation, which later came to be popularly known as the Justice Party. In 1937, Ramaswamy Naicker (1879-1973) was elected the President of the Justice Party. Naicker was a crusader for social equality and fought against the evil of untouchability. He denounced Hinduism as an instrument of Brahmanical control the laws of Manu as inhuman, the puranas as fairy tales. He ridiculed Hindu gods and godesses and concluded. " There are certain things which cannot be mended but only ended. Brahmanical Hinduism is one such." Naicker condemned religion as superstition and opposed imposition of Hindi on the Dravadians. Quick-tempered as he was, Naiker tarred caste name-boards on hotels, cutting off the holy thread of Brahmins, beating of deities with chappals and breaking of idols. His followers called him a Thanthai (father) and Periyar (Great Soul).

Annadurai and the D.M.K. Naicker's follower and friend C.N. Annadurai (1909-1969) carried further the Dravadian movement. Anna (elder brother) came from a weaver community of Kancheepuram. In 1944, the Justice Party was renamed Dravida Kazhagam (Dravadian Federation). In September 1949 the party split and under Anna's leadership Dravida Munnetra Kazhagam (Dravadian Progressive Federation) came into existence. In 1962 Anna was elected to the Rajya Sabha. In the 1967 General Elections the DMK Party formed the first DMK Government in Tamil Nadu with Annadurai as the Chief Minister. Anna was not against unity of India, but demanded greater autonomy for states. In the words of M. Karunanidhi. "Anna was a Statesman and a Scholar, a literateur and a social reformer, a mass leader and a friend of the poor. Anna will be ever remembered specially as the maker of new Tamil Nadu"

Narayan Guru and the SNDP

In the State of Kerala, another leader of the Ezhava Caste (the untouchable caste), Shri Narayan Guru (1854-1928) established the SNDP (Sree Narayana Dharma Paripalana Yogam) in Kerala and at many places outside Kerala. Narayan and his associates launched a two-point programme for the uplift of the Ezhavas. Firstly, to give up the practice of untouchability with respect to caste below their castes. As a second step, Narayan Guru built a number of temples which were declared open to all castes. He also simplified rituals regarding marriage, religions worships and funerals Narayan Guru achieved notable success in transforming the untouchable groups into a backward class. He Openly criticised the Congress and Mahatma Gandhi for their lip-sympathy towards the lower castes. He criticised Gandhiji for his faith in *Chaturvarna,* which , he maintained, is the parent of the caste-system and untouchability. He pointed out that the difference in castes is only superficial and emphasised that the juice of all leaves of a particular tree would be the same in content. He gave a new Slogan "One religion, one caste and one god for mankind"

Jyotirao Phule and the Satya Shodhak Samaj

In Western India, Jyotirao Govindrao Phule (1827-90) struggled for the lower castes. Jyotiba was born at Poona in 1827 in a Mali caste (his family members supplied flowers, garlands etc., to the Peshwa's family and came to be called Phule).

Some incidents of Brahmanical arrogance changed the outlook of Jyotiba. Once Jyotiba was scolded and insulted by a Brahmin for his audacity in joining a Brahmin marriage procession. The Brahmins also opposed Jyotiba in running a school for the lower castes and women. The Brahminical pressure compelled Jyotiba to close the school ; under upper caste pressure Gobindrao turned Jyotiba and his wife from leaving his family house.

Jyotiba believed that the Brahmin under the pretext of religion, tyrannzied over other castes and turned them into their slaves. Jyotiba was ever critical of the Indian National Congress Leaders for their neglect of the interests on the weaker sections. He maintained that the Congress could not be called truly national unless it showed general interest in the welfare of the lower and backward castes.

In 1873, Jyotiba started the Satya Shodhak Samaj (Truth Seeking Society) with the aim of securing social justice for the weaker sections of society. He opened a number of schools and orphanages for the children and women belonging to all castes. He was elected as a member of the Poona Municipal Committee in 1876.

Jyotiba's publications include *Dharma Tritiya Ratiya Ratna* (Exposure of the Puranas), *Ishara* (A Warning), *Life of Shivaji,* etc. In 1888, Jyotiba was honoured with the title mahatma.

Ambedkar's Dynamic Role

B.R. Ambedkar (1891-1956) was another crusader in the cause of the uplift of the lower castes. Bhim Rao was born on 14 April 1891 in a Mahar (Hindu untouchable) caste at Mhow. Bhimrao married Rambai of his own caste in 1905; she died in 1935. In 1948, Bhimaro married a second time Dr. Sharada Kabir who came from a Saraswat Brahmin family of Bombay.

Ambedkar graduated from Elphinstone College, Bombay; later he did his M.A. and Ph. D., from Columbia University. In 1923, he was called to the Bar.

In July 1924, Ambedkar started an organisation in Bombay called 'Bahishkrit Hitkarni Sabha' for the moral and material progress of the untouchables. He resorted to methods of agitation and launched *Satyagraha* to establish civic rights of the untouchables to enter the Hindu temples and draw water form public wells.

In 1930 Ambedkar entered national politics. He demanded separate electorates for the untouchables. He was nominated as a delegate of the three around Table Conferences in London (1930-32). The Communal Award announced by the British Prime Minister on 17 August 1932 provided for separate electorates for the Depressed Classes. This upset Gandhiji who went on fast unto death; a final compromise popularly known as the Poona Pact (24 Sept., 1932) provided for reservation of seats for the Depressed Classes in the general constituencies.

In desperation, Ambedkar opposed the National Congress's demand for independence and wanted British rule in India to continue to safeguard the interest of the lower castes. In April 1942, he founded the Scheduled Caste Federation as an all India party. Later, he announced that Scheduled castes would leave Hindu fold altogether. He along with many followers embraced Buddhism.

On the eve of independence, Ambedkar was nominated by the Congress Party as a member of the Constituent Assembly. His contribution in framing and piloting the Indian Constitution and the Hindu Code Bill are well recongnised. Today, Ambedkar is remembered as the emancipator of the lower castes.

The new Constitution of Indian Republic has accepted the Principle of Equality for all Indian citizens and has abolished untouchability. The Untouchability (offences) Act 1955 spells out the punishment to be awarded for offences under this Act.

The Mandal Commission and Reservations in Central Government Jobs

The Constitution of India (Part XVI) mentions "special provisions relating to certain classes." Apart from listing special provisions for the Scheduled Castes, Scheduled Tribes and Anglo-Indian community (which took the form of reservations in the Lok Sabha, Legislative Assemblies of States, in Services and Posts and Education and Grants etc.), it also (vide Article 340 of the Constitution) makes a provision for appointment of a Commission to investigate the conditions of socially and educationally backward classes, popularly known as Other Backward Classes (O.B.C.) within the territory of India.

In 1953, the President of India appointed a Commission under the Chair manship of Kaka Saheb Kalelkar with the following terms of reference:-

(a) *To determine the test by which any particular class or group of people can be called 'backward'.*
(b) *To prepare a list of such backward communities for the whole of India.*
(c) *To examine the difficulties of backward classes and to recommend steps to be taken for their amelioration.*

In 1955, the Kalelkar Commission submitted its report to the Government for its consideration The Government, on its part, considered the Commission's recommendations as very vague and not to be of much practical value; as such no action was taken on the report.

Another commission popularly known as the Mandal Commission was appointed to look into the grievances of the Backward classes. The Chairman of this Commission was Mr. B.P. Mandal.

The Mandal Commission submitted its report in August, 1980. The report supported the system of caste-based reservations, identified over 450 backward classes, comprising 52% of the country's population and further recommended reservation of 27% of the seats in academic institutions and jobs in Government organisations for these classes. This recommended reservation quota was in addition to the existing 22.5% jobs quota reserved for the Scheduled Castes and Scheduled Tribes.

The Mandal Commission report had been gathering dust in the Home Ministry for 10 years when in August, 1990, Mr. V.P. Singh, then Prime Minister of Indian of the National Front Government, accepted the recommendation of the Mandal Commission and committed his Government to its implementation. He announced that 27% of the jobs in the Central Government and Public Sector Undertaking will be reserved for the socially and educationally backward classes popularly known as the O.B.C.

Narsimha Rao Government which assumed office in 1991 referred the Mandal Commission Report to the Supreme Court for its opinion. The Apex Court found no constitutional incongruity in the recommendations of the Mandal Commission Report. However, the Apex Court recommended that the "creamy layer" among the O.B.C. may be excluded from the reserved quota.

In 1993, Narsimha Rao's Government finally took a decision accepting reservation of vacancies in Central Government Civil post central financial institutions and Public Sector Undertaking to the extent of 27% for the O.B.C. subject to the exclusion of the socially advanced persons/sections known as the "cremy layer". The Government notification spelt out the following rules for the exclusion the 'cremy layer" as applicable to the son(s) and daughter(s) of :

(a) Person holding constitutional positions,

(b) Parents either of whom is a class I officer,

(c) Parents both of whom are class II officer,

(d) Parents either or both of whom is or are in the rank of Colonel and above in Army or hold equivalent positions in the Navy, Air Force and the Para-Military Forces,

(e) Families owning irrigated land which is equal to or more than 85% of the ceiling in terms of irrigated area as laid down by the State Land Ceiling Laws,

(f) Persons having gross annual income of Rs. 1 lakh or above or possessing wealth above the exemption limit as prescribed in the Wealth Tax Act for a period of there consecutive years.

Income from salaries or agricultural land shall not be included."

In the first phase, the benefit of reservation has been extended to the castes and communities which are common to the lists of the Mandal Commisssion Report as well as the State Government Lists. The lists of the Other Backward Classes in respect of 18 States which have provided reservations in the State services for the O.B.C. nemely, Andhra Pradesh, Assam, Bihar, Goa, Gujrat, Haryana, Himachal Pradesh, Karnataka, Kerala, Madhya Pradesh, Maharashtra, Orissa, Punjab, Rajasthan, Tamil Nadu, Tripura, U.P. and West Bengal have been published in the Gazette of India. The O.B.C. lists of Union Territories of Pondicherry, Dadra and Nagar Haveli and Daman and Diu and Delhi were notified by the Central Government during 1994-95. Other State Government and Union territory Administrations are identifying the O.B.Cs. to enable the Central Government to provide the benefit of reservations.

An Overview. The Government decisions on the Mandal Commission report have been welcomed as well as condemned in the country. In has been hailed as step towards establishment of an egalitarian society, which was the aim of the founding fathers of the Indian Constitution.

Mr. N. A. Palkhiwala, a noted jurist condenmed the Mandal Commission report, for 'it is bound to encourage casteism, the very factor Dr. Ambedkar tried hard to obliterate'. Commenting on V.P. Singh's remarks that he can now die in peace as the Mandal Report has been cleared by the Supreme Court Palkhiwala remarked, "He may die in peace, but India will not live in peace for centuries to come."

The process of identifying the O.B.C. is an unending process and is kept open. The Government also set up on 14th August, 1993, a National Commission for Backword Classes as a permanent body for entertaining, examining and recommending upon requests for inclusion and complaints of under-inclusion in the lists of O.B.C. class citizens. This provision is likely to be exploited by certain section of the O.B.C. and their political mentors.

The system of reservations tends to become endemic in the body-politic, as has been the case with the reservations for the Scheduled Castes and Scheduled Tribes. The Constitution provided for reservations for these classes initially for a period of 10 years, and after every 10 years the reservation period has been extended for a further period of 10 years, again and again. This is likely to be the case for the job reservation quotas for the O.B.Cs.

The politics of caste and reservation is likely to become a festering wound in the Indian body-politic.

SELECT REFERENCES

1. Annadurai, C.N.   : *Nadum Yedum.*
2. Keer, Dhananjaya   : *Dr. Ambadkar : Life and Mission.*
3. Baker, C.J.   : *The politics of South India.*
4. Smith, D.E.   : *South Asian Politic and Religion*

THE GROWTH AND DEVELOPMENT OF THE INDIAN NATIONAL MOVEMENT

Indian nationalism was the child of the British Raj, and British authorities blessed its cradle.

— R..Coupland

Nationalism is really only anti-colonialism.

— A.d. Smith

The year 1885 marks the beginning of a new epoch in Indian History. In that year an all-India political organisation was set on foot under the name of the Indian National Congress. The Indian mind became increasingly conscious of its political position. A retrospective examination of the National Movement suggests three broad stages in its development. In the first stage of its existence (1885–1905), the vision of the Indian National Congress was dim, vague and confused. The movement was confined to a handful of the educated middle class intelligentsia who drew inspiration from Western Liberal and Radical Thought. During the second stage (1905–1918), the Congress came of age and its aim and scope were considerably extended. It aimed at an all-round uplift of the people—social, cultural, economic and political. Swaraj or self-government was the goal on the political front. Some progressive elements within the Congress adopted Western revolutionary methods to liquidate Western Imperialism. The final stage (1919-47) was dominated by the objective of *Purna Swaraj* or complete independence to be achieved under the leadership of Mahatma Gandhi by the characteristically Indian method of non-violent non-cooperation.

(A) Factors Favouring Growth of Indian Nationalism

Stimulus-Response Debate. Traditional Indian historiography explains rise and growth of Indian nationalism in terms of Indian response to stimulus generated by British Raj through creation of new institutions, new opportunities, resources etc. In other words, Indian nationalism grew partly as a result of colonial policies and partly as a reaction to colonial policies.

The growth of Indian national consciousness in the latter half of the nineteenth century was not to the liking of British colonial rulers. At first, British scholars and administrators denied the existence of any feeling of nationality in India. In 1883 J.R. Seeley described India as mere 'geographical expression' with no sense whatever of national unity. In 1884 John Strachey, an ex-Indian civil servant told the alumni of Cambridge University, "This is the first and most essential thing to learn about India—that there is not, and never was an India". He further forecast that India will never become a united nation.

When the closing decade of the 19th century and first decade of the 20th century demonstrated that nationalism had grown and was gaining strength, British scholars struck a new posture. The authors of the Montford Report claimed credit that British rule was the harbinger of nationalist upsurge in India ; it wrote, "The politically-minded Indians...are intellectually our children. They have imbibed ideas which we ourselves set before them and we ought to reckon it to our credit. The present intellectual and moral stir in India is no reproach but rather a tribute to our work". R. Coupland in a more forthright language wrote "Indian nationalism was the child of the British Raj." Coupland forgot to mention that Indian nationalism was an unwanted child of the Raj whom it refused to feed at birth and sought to strangle it subsequently. It would be more correct to say that Indian nationalism was partly the product of a world-wide upsurge of the concepts of nationalism and right of self-determination initiated by the French Revolution, partly the result of Indian Renaissance, partly the offshoot of modernisation initiated by the British in India and partly developed as a strong reaction to British imperial policies in India.

1. Impact of British Rule. British colonial rulers followed modern methods political military, economic and intellectual—to establish and continue their stranglehold over India and for fuller economic exploitation of India's resources. A dose of modernisation was an essential concomitant of the colonial scheme of administration and this modernisation—distorted though it was—generated some developments and one of these was growth of Indian nationalism.

2. Political Unity of India. Imperial Britain conquered the whole of India from the Himalayas in the north to Cape Comorin in the South and from Assam in the east to the Khyber Pass in the west. They created a larger state than that of the Mauryas or the great Mughals. While Indian provinces were under "direct" British rule, Indian states were under "indirect" British rule. The British sword imposed political unity in India. Common subjection, common institutions, common laws began to shape India in a common mould. Despite imperial efforts to sow communal, regional and linguistic dissensions, pan-Indianism grew. The establishment of political unity fostered the spirit of one-mindedness.

3. Establishment of Peace and Administrative Unification of India. After the chaotic conditions of 18th century (partly created by the aggressive wars waged by European trading companies), the British rulers established peace and orderly government in India. British scholars take pride in the fact that *Pax Britannica* brought prolonged peace and order for the first time in India.

The British also established a highly centralised administrative system in India. Percival Griffiths refers to the impersonality of British administration to be its most important characteristic *i.e.* the fundamental character of administration did not change with the change of top-administrators like Secretaries of State and Viceroys (as had been the case with all previous empires in India). Further, administrative Unification had important effects in many other fields. A highly trained professional, Indian Civil Service managed the district administration in all parts of India. A unified judicial setup, codified civil and criminal law rigorously enforced throughout the length and breadth of the country imparted a new dimension of political unity to the hitherto cultural unity that had existed in India for centuries. In the words of Edwyn Bevan, the British Raj was like a steel-frame which held the injured body of India together till the gradual process of internal growth had joined the dislocated bones, knit up torn fibres, and enabled the patient to regain inner coherence and unity.

4. Development of rapid means of transport and Communications. The necessities of administrative covenience, considerations of military defence and urge for economic penetration and commercial exploitation were the drives behind planned development of modern means of transport. A network of roads linked one province with another and the metropolitan centers with *mofussil* areas.

For more than anything else the development of railways have unified the country. The construction of railways began in India in the 1850s and by 1880 some 8500 miles of rail track had been built, extending to 25000 miles by 1900. Apart From many other advantages, the railways have facilitated the growth of nationalism. As early as 1865 Edwin Arnold wrote, "Railways may do for India what dynasties have never done— what the genius of Akbar the Magnificent could not effect by government, nor the cruelty of Tipu Saheb by violence, they have made India a nation".

The development of the modern postal system and the introduction of electric telegraph in the 1850s helped to unify the country. A cheep $\frac{1}{2}$ anna uniform postage rate for inland letters and still cheaper rates for transmission of newspapers and parcels brought about a transformation of newspapers and parcels brought about a transformation in the social, educational, intellectual and political life of the people. National literature could be circulated through the post offices that operated in every nook and corner of the country. The electric telegraph brought about a revolution in the speedy transmission of messages. Thus, the modern means of communications enabled people living in different parts of

India to maintain regular contacts with one another and thus promoted the cause of nationalism. In fact, modern political organisations like the Indian National Congress, the All-Indian Trade Union Congress, the All-India Kisan Sabha, the All-India Muslim League could neither have come into existence nor could function on a national scale without the facilities provided by modern railways motor buses or the communication facilities provided by the Post and Telegraph Department.

5. Introduction of Modern Education. The introduction of modern system of education afforded opportunities for assimilation of modern Western ideas which in turn gave a new direction to Indian political thinking. Sir Charles E. Trevelyan, T.B. Macaulay and Lord William Bentick (then Governor General) took a momentous decision in 1835 when they inaugurated the system of English education in India. Asked to give his opinion about the possible effect of English education upon the probable maintenance of the British Government in India, Trevelyan argued before the Indian Committee of the House of Lords in 1835 that "the British raj in India could not last for ever. It was bound to die one day, either at the hands of those Indians who subscribed to the indigenous model of political change or at the hands of those who had been educated in English and subscribed to the new British model of political change. If it was to die at the hands of the latter, it would take a long time and the severance of the British connection with India would be neither violent nor harmful to Britain, for cultural and commercial bonds would continue". Macaulay struck a different note though the end-result he envisaged was not very different. In the course of a speech before the House of Commons in 1833, Macaulay said, "It may be that the public mind of India may expand under our system until it has outgrown that system, that by good government we may educate our subjects into a capacity for better government; that having become instructed in European language, they may, in some future age demand European institutions".

The English system of education though conceived by the rulers in the interests of efficient administration opened to the newlyeducated Indians the floodgates of liberal European thought The liberal and radical thought of European writers like Milton Shelley, Bentham, Mill, Spenser, Rousseau and Voltaire inspired the Indian intelligentsia with the ideals of liberty, nationality and self-government and made clear to them the anachronism of British rule in India.

The newly-educated class usually adopted the professions of junior administrators, lawyers, doctors, teachers etc. Some of them visited England to receive higher education. While in England they saw with their own eyes the working of political institutions in a free country. On their return to India, these persons found the atmosphere cringing and slavish with the total denial of basic rights to citizens. These 'vilayat-returned' Indians with the ever-expanding English educated class formed the middle class intelligentsia. This English educated intelligentsia, somewhat conscious of political rights, found that despite the promises contained in the Charter Act of 1833 and the Queen's Proclamation of 1858 the doors of higher services remained closed to the Indians. This realisation drove discontent and frustration among them and this discontent proved infectious. Men like Surendranath Banerjee, Manmohan Ghose, Lalmohan Ghose, Aurobindo turned nationalists only after the doors of the coveted services were closed to them. These intelligent and well-informed persons formed the nucleus for the newly-arising political unrest and it was this section of the society which provided leadership to the Indian political association.

The spread and popularity of the English language in all parts of India gave to the educated Indians a common language—a lingua franca—through the medium of which they could communicate with one another and transact their conferences and congresses. In the absence of such a lingua franca it would have been very difficult for the Bengalis, the Panjabis, the Tamilians, the Maharastrians etc., to come on a common platform or organise a movement of an all-India character.

6. Emergence of a Modern Press. The emergence of the modern press both English and Vernacular was another offshoot of British rule in India. It were the Europeans who set up printing presses in India and published newspapers and other cheap literature. Gradually the Vernacular press came into existence and developed on the Western pattern. In spite of the numerous restrictions imposed on the press by the colonial rulers from time to time Indian journalism made rapid strides. The latter half of the 19th century saw an unprecedented growth of Indian-owned English and Vernacular newspapers. In 1877 there were about 169 newspapers published in vernacular languages and their circulation reached the neighbourhood of 100,000.

The Indian press has played a notable role in mobilising public opinion, organising political movements, fighting our public controversy and promoting nationalism. Newspapers like the *Indian Mirror, the Bengalee, the Amrita Bazar Patrika, Bombay chronicle, the Hindu Patriot, the Mahratta, Kesari, Andra Prakasika, The Hindu, Indu Prakash, Kohinur* etc. in English and different Indian languages exposed the excesses of British Indian administration apart from popularizing among the people the ideas of representative government, libery, democratic institutions, home rule and independence. It may be no exaggeration to state that the press became the mirror of Indian nationalism and the primary medium of popular public education.

7. Rise of the Middle Class Intelligentsia. British administrative and economic innovations gave rise to a new urban middle class in towns. The new class readily learnt English for it promoted employment and gave a sence of prestige. This class, prominent because of its education, new position and its close ties with the ruling class came to the forefront. P. Spear writes, "The new middle class was a well-integrated all-India class with varied background but a common foreground of knowledge, ideas and values ... It was a minority of Indian society, but a dynamic minority....It had a sense of unity of purpose and of hope". This middle class proved to be the new soul of modern India and in due course infused the whole of India with its spirit. This class provided leadership to the Indian National Congress in all its stages of growth.

8. Influence of Historical Researches. Historical researches in ancient Indian history conducted mostly by European scholars like Max Muller, Monier William, Roth, Session etc. opened new vistas of India's rich cultural heritage. In particular, the excavations conducted by archaeologists like Marshall and Conningham created a new picture of India's past glory and greatness no less impressive than that of ancient civilisations of Greece and Rome. The scholars praised the Vedas and Upanishads for their literary merit and excellent analysis of the human mind. The theory put forward by European scholars that the Indo-Aryans belonged to the same ethnic group of mankind from which stemmed all the nations of Europe gave a psychological boost to educated Indians. All these gave a new sense of confidence to the educated Indians and inspired them with a new spirit of patriotism and nationalism.

9. Impact of Contemporary European Movements. Contemporary strong currents of nationalist ideas which pervaded the whole of Europe and South America did stimulate Indian nationalism. A number of national states came into existence in south America on the ruins of the Spanish and Portuguese empires. In Europe the national liberation movements of Greece and Italy in general and of Ireland in particular deeply stirred the emotions of Indians. Educated Indians touring Europe were greatly impressed by these nationalist movements. We find Surendranath Banerji delivering lectures on Joseph Mazzini and the "Young Italy" movement organised by him. Lajpat Rai very often referred to the campaigns of Garibaldi and the activities of Carbonaris in his speeches and writings. Thus, European nationalist movement did Lend strengh to the developing nationalism in India.

10. Progressive Character of Socio-Religious Reform Movements. In the 19th century educated-Indians began to examine afresh their religious beliefs and customs and their social practices in the light of new knowledge of Western science and philosophy which thay had acquired. The result was various religious and social reform movements in Hindu religion like the Brahmo Samaj, the Prarhana Samaj, the Arya Samaj, the Ramakrishna Mission, the Theosophical Society. Similar movements reformed Muslim, Sikh and Parsi societies also.

In the religious sphere the reform movements combated religious superstition, attacked idolatry, polytheism and hereditary priesthood. In the social sphere, these movements attacked the caste system, untouchability and other social and legal inequalities, these movements were progressive in character for they sought recognisation of society on democratic lines and on the basis of ideas of individual equality, social equality, reason, enlightenment and liberalism.

Most of the religious societies had no political mission, all the same whosoever came under their influence rapidly developed a sence of self-respect and spirit of patriotism. Since many reform movements drew their inspiration from India's rich cultural heritage, these promoted pan-Indian feelings and spirit of nationalism.

11. Racialism. One unfortunate legacy of the Rebellion of 1857 was the feeling of racial bitterness between the rulers and the ruled. The *Punch* cartooned Indians as half-gorilla, half-negroes. The Anglo-Indian bureaucracy developed an attitude of arrogance and contempt towards the Indians. They somehow came to the conclusion that the only argument that worked effectively with the Indians was superior force. Thus, Europeans developed their own social code of ethics and worked out the theory of a superior race. The Indians were dubbed as belonging to an inferior race and no longer worthy of any trust. The Indians were frequently referred to as a nation of liars, perjurers and forgers. The Anglo-Indian lobby produced books, races particularly the English. This narrow approach evoked a reaction in the Indian mind and put the educated-Indians on the defensive.

12. Economic Exploitation. The impact of British rule on the Indian economy was disastrous. Jawaharlal Nehru has summed up the Indian viewpoint when he writes, "The economy of India had....advanced to as high a stage as it could reach prior to the Industrial Revolution" but "foreign political domination ... led to a rapid destruction of the economy she had built up, without anything positive or constructive taking its place", the net result being "poverty and degradation beyond measure". The general object of British policies—even though claimed to be social welfare by some British scholars—was a systematic destruction of traditional Indian economy.

The sharp reaction to discriminatory British economic and fiscal policies gave rise to economic nationalism in India. In the first half of the nineteenth century Britain was in the vanguard of Industrial Revolution and needed cheap raw material and a market for her industrial products. Interests of imperial Britain required that Indian economy policies of India in all fields–agriculture, heavy industry, finance, tariffs, foreign capital investment, foreign trade, banking etc—were all geared to the preservation of the colonial economy.

In spite of British intentions to the contrary, modern capitalist enterprise made a beginning in India in the 1860s. This development alarmed the British textile manufacturers who started clamouring for revision of Indian tariff rates to suit their sectional interests. The classic example is the controvery over Cotton Duties which were frequently shuffled at the lobbying of British capitalists. The £-Re-exchange ratio was also manipulated to the disadvantage of Indian industry and foreign trade. All these developments made it clear that whenever British economic interests clashed with Indian economic development, the latter had be sacrificed.

The extravagant civil and military adminstration, the denial of high posts to Indians, the ever-mounting "Home Charges", the continuous drain of wealth from India resulted in stagnation of Indian economy. The cumulative effect was increasing misery for the people. Periodical famines became a regular feature of Indian economic life. During the second half of the 19th century 24 famines visited various parts of India taking an estimated toll of $28\frac{1}{2}$ million souls. What is worse is that even during the famine times, export of foodgrains from India continued.

Indian nationalists developed the "theory of increasing poverty in India" and attributed it to Britain's anti-India economic policies. They tagged poverty and foreign rule. This psychology developed a hatred for foreign rule and love for Swadeshi goods and Swadeshi rule. The spirit of nationalism received a powerful stimulus in the process.

13. Lord Lytton's Reactionary Policies. The short-sighted acts and policies of Lord Lytton acted like catalytic agents and accelerated the movement against foreign rule. The maximum age limit for the I.C.S. examination was reduced from 21 years to 19 years, thus making it impossible for Indians to compete for it. The grand Delhi Darbar of 1877, when the country was in the severe grip of famine, solicited the remark from a Calcutta journalist that 'Nero was fidding while Rome was burning.' Lytton put on the statute book two obnoxious measures—the Vernacular Press Act and Indian Arms Act (1878). Lytton's unpopular acts provoked a great storm of opposition in the country and led to the organisation of various political associations for carrying on anti-Government propaganda in the country.

14. The Ilbert Bill Controversy. The Ilbert Bill controversy raised passions on both sides which did not easily subside. Ripon's Government sought to abolish 'judicial disqualification based on race distinctions' and the Ilbert Bill sought to give Indian members of the Covenanted civil Service the same powers and rights as their European colleagues enjoyed. The Bill raised a storm of agitation among the members of the European community and they all stood united against the bill. Ripon had to modify the bill which almost defeated the original purpose. The Ilbert Bill controversy proved an eye-opener to the Indian intelligentsia. It became clear to them that justic and fairplay could not be expected where the interests of the European community were involved. Further, it demonstratred to them the value of organised agitation.

(B) Growth of Modern Political Ideas and Political Associations

Associations, like cricket, were British innovation and, like cricket, became an Indian craze.

—*Anil Seal*

Western domination of India generated certain forces—some as a result of its impact and some as a reaction to it—which ultimately challenged Western imperialism. As early as 1833 Lord Macaulay, in the course of a speech before the House of Commons, had explained the implications of his educational policy: "It may be that the public mind of India may expand under our system until it has outgrown that system, that by good government we may educate our subjects into a capacity for better government ; that having become instructed in European language, they may, in some future age demand European institutions." One important effect of the introduction of Western culture in India was the growth of Modern Political concepts like nationalism, nationality, political rights etc. The Indian sub-continent witnessed the growth of political ideas and political organisations hitherto unknown to the Indian world. And it were political associations which heralded 19th century India into modern politics. What distinguished these new political associations from earlier religious and caste associations of the country were the secular interests that bound together the new classes.

Political Associations in Bengal Presidency. Raja Rammohan Roy was the pioneer of political movement in India. He was greatly influenced by Western ideas. He was a widely-read man. His extensive studies had freed his mind from bigotry that characterized an average Bengali. His sympathies in the domain of politics were cosmopolitan and his heart went in sympathy for popular movements all over the world. In 1821 the Raja celebrated in Calcutta the establishment of a constitutional government in Spain.

Rammohan Roy was the first Indian to focus the attention of the Englishmen on the grievances of India and to ask for remedial measures. He demanded liberty of the press, appointment of Indians in civil courts and other higher posts, codification of law etc. It was generally believed that some of the beneficent provisions in the Charter Act of 1833 were due to his lobbying in England.

The task of organising political associations was, however, left to the associates of Rammohan Roy. The first such association called "Bangabhasha Prakasika Sabha" was formed in 1836. The association discussed topics connected with the policy and administration of the Government and sought redress by sending petitions and memorials to the Government.

In July 1838 the "Zamindary Association" more popularly known as the "Landholders' Society" was founded to safeguard the interests of the landlords. Although limited in its objectives, the Landholders' Society marks the beginning of an organised political activity and use of methods of constitutional agitation for the redressal of grievances. The Landholders' Society of Calcutta cooperated with the British India Society founded by Mr. Adams in London in July 1839.

In April 1843 another political association under the name of the Bengal British India Society was founded with the object of "the collection and dissemination of information relating to the actual condition of the people of British India...and to employ such other means of peaceful and lawful character as may appear calculated to secure the welfare, extend the just right, and advance the interests of all classes of our fellow subjects". However, the Landholders' Society and the Bengal British India Society did not flourish well and on 29 October 1851 the two associations were merged into a new one named the British Indian Association. This Association was dominated by members of the landed aristocracy and its primary objective was safeguarding their class interests. However, the Association struck a liberal note and when the time came for the renewal of the Charter of the East India Company it sent a petition to the Parliament praying for establishment of a separate legislature of a popular character, separation of judicial from executive functions, reduction in the salaries of higher officers, abolition of salt duty, *abkari* and stamp duties etc. The prayers of the Association were partially met and the Charter Act of 1853 provided for the addition of six members to the Governor-General's Council for legislative purposes. The British Indian Association continued its existence as a political body down to the 20th century even though it was over-shadowed by the more popular Indian National Congress.

By 1870s there were signs of change inside Indian society. In the Presidency towns higher education was well established and the members of the new professions were acquiring status and developing new ambitions. A new elite had grown in all the Presidencies whose aspirations and status were roughly comparable. These were good development for the formation of more popular and broad-based associations. In September 1875 Babu Sisir Kumar Ghose founded the Indian League with the object of "stimulating the sense of nationalism amongst the people" and of encouraging political education. Within a year of its foundation, the Indian League was superseded by the Indian Association founded on 26 July 1876 by Ananda Mohan Bose and Surendranath Banerjee. The Indian Association hoped to attract not only "the middle classes" but also the masses, and therefore kept its annual subscription at Rs. 5 as opposed to the subscription of Rs. 50 p.a. fixed by the British Indian Association. Soon the Indian Association became 'the centre of the leading representatives of the educated community of Bengal.'

Lytton's unpopular measures whipped up political activity in India. A regulation of 1876 reduced the maximum age for appearing in the Indian Civil Service examination from 21 to 19 years. Since the examination was held only in London, young Indians had to face innumerable difficulties. The Indian Association took up this question and organised an all-India agitation against it, popularly known as the Indian Civil Service Agitation. Surendranath Banerjee went on a whirlwind tour of northern India in May 1877 and visited Benaras, Allahabad, Kanpur, Lucknow, Aligarh, Delhi, Meerut, Amritsar and Lahore. At certain centres he visited, new political organisations to act in concert with the Indian Association of Calcutta were set up. Next year, Banerjee went on a similar mission to the Presidencies of Bombay and Madras.

Political Associations in Bombay Presidency. While to the Bengali Hindus the English might have appeared as deliverers from the tyrannical rule of the Muslim nawabs, in Maharashtra the British were looked upon as foreign tyrants who had displaced indigenous rulers. Commenting on the nature of British rule, Shri Bhaskar Pandurange Tarkhadkar wrote in the *Bombay Gazette* in 1841, "If I were to give you (the English) credit for your having saved us from the Pindaris and Ramosis, your trading system stands in the way which has indeed more effectually emptied our purses in a few years than the predatory excursions of these tribes could do in some five or six hundred years. In short, it must be acknowledged that your progress in cunning and craftiness has kept pace with your advancement in knowledge and wisdom."

On the lines of the British India Association of Calcutta, on 26 August 1852 was founded the Bombay Association with the object of 'memorializing from time to time the Government authorities in India or in England for the removal of existing evils, and for the prevention of proposed measures which may be deemed injurious or for the introduction of enactments which may tend to promote the general interests of all connected with this country". The Bombay Association sent a petition to the British Parliament urging the formation of new legislative councils to which Indians should be also represented. It also condemned the policy of exclusion of Indians from all higher services, lavish expenditure on sinecure posts given to Europeans. However, the Bombay Association did not survive for long.

The reactionary policies of Lytton and the Ilbert Bill controversy caused political commotion in Bombay. The credit for organisation of the Bombay Presidency Association in 1885 goes to the popularly called brothers-in-law—Mehta, Telang and Tyabji, representing the three chief communities of Bombay town. At Poona the Poona Sarvajanik Sabha was established in 1867 with the object of serving as a bridge between the Government on the one hand and the people on the other. The Bombay Presidency Association and the Poona Sarvajanik Sabha worked in close collaboration.

Political Association in Madras Presidency. A branch of the British Indian Association of Calcutta was set up at Madras under the name of the Madras Native Association. The Madras Association also sent petition to the Parliament on the eve of the passing of the Charter Act of 1853 making demands similar to that of the British Indian Association and the Bombay Association right from its inception was worked by some officials, possessed very little vitality, had hardly any hold upon the public mind and languished into obscurity after 1857.

Political trends similar to other presidencies were at work in Madras Presidency also. A number of small local associations came into existence during the viceroyalty of Ripon. The Madras Mahajana Sabha was formed in May 1884 to co-ordinate the activities of local associations and 'to provide a focus for the non-official intelligence spreading through the Presidency.' At its conference held on 29, 31 December 1884 and 1-2 January 1885 the Sabha demanded expansion of legislative councils, representation of Indians in it, separation of judicial from revenue functions etc.

Trends Towards a Grand United National Political Organisation. Although the idea of a common political organisation for the whole country was as old as the first stirrings of constitutional politics in India, it took decades to ferment and materialize. The East India Association founded in London in October 1866 had hoped to set up branches in Calcutta and Bombay and claimed to work for "the public interest and welfare of the inhabitants of India generally." In 1877 the Poona Sarvajanik Sabha had urged the representatives of Bombay and Bengal to work together and the following year sent a deputation to Calcutta "to hold a conference with the representatives of the native press and the political associations in Calcutta for the interchange of ideas." There were protests all over India over the imposition of the Licence Tax (1878) and abolition of Cotton Duties (1879). In the 1880s certain developments gradually pushed the hesitant leaders of the various regional associations to common and concerted action. Various schemes were in the air. In 1882 there was a plan for a national meeting. The Indian Association of Calcutta had plans to hold a national conference. In 1883 Telang went from Bombay to Calcutta to arrange for 'more political concert' between Calcutta and Bombay. There was a plan to form a Federation of the Native Press, a scheme to start a National Newspaper, a plan to set up an Indian Constitutional Reform Association.

During 1883-84 the various local associations in the presidency towns were forging towards unity. In Calcutta the Indian Association, the British Indian Association, the National Mohammedan Association and the Indian Union had worked together to call the National Conference. During November-December 1884 there were spontaneous demonstrations throughout India to mark Ripon's departure from India. These demonstrations marked a spirit of organisation which India had never known before, commented the editor of *The Times of India*.

The Foundation of the Indian National Congress

It will not be correct to trace the genesis of the Indian National Congress to the efforts of a single individual like A.O. Hume or assume that it appeared as a sudden efflorescence. The various political organisations in different parts of India and the ferment of ideas had prepared the ground and the foundation of the Indian National Congress in 1885 was only a visible embodiment of that national awakening.

The efforts of the Indian Association of Calcutta and its leader Surendranath Banerjee in organising the Indian National Conference deserve special mention. In December 1883 met the first Indian National Conference to which representatives drawn from all the major towns of India were invited. Shri. Ananda Mohan Bose, the President, expressed the hope that the Conference would prove to be the first stage in the formation of a National Parliament. The second National Conference met at Calcutta during the X-mas week of 1885. However, the Indian National Conference was soon eclipsed by the more popular and more representative Indian National Congress.

It was left to Mr. Hume, a retired official of the Government of India, to give a practical and definite shape to an organisation of an all-India character. W.C. Bonnerjee popularized the view that the idea of the Indian National Congress was a product of Lord Dufferin's brain, that he suggested it to Mr. Hume who undertook to work it out. Dufferin's idea was to have a political organisation though which the Government could ascertain the real wishes of the people and thus save the administration from any possible political outburst in the country. Lala Lajpat Rai maintained that the Indian National Congress was organised to serve as a 'safety-valve' for the growing unrest in the country and strengthen the British Empire. "The idea was," writes Lala Lajpat Rai, "not only to save the British rule from any danger that threatened it but even to strengthen it...the redress of political grievances and political advance of India was only a by product and of secondary importance."

Whatever might have been the motive of Lord Duffering and Mr. Hume, it cannot be denied that Mr. Hume was a true liberal and 'deadly earnest' about the necessity and desirability of a political organisation. Mr. Hume's open letter to the graduates of the Calcutta University is revealing. He wrote, "Scattered individuals however capable and however well-meaning, are powerless singly. What is needed is union, organisation and well-defined line of action and to secure these an association is required," Hume asked for fifty volunteers to join in a movement to promote the mental, moral, social and political regeneration of the people of India. Mr. Hume secured the sympathy and support of the Government officials and public men in India and England for the Indian National Congress. Thus the movement was a child both of England and India.[4]

Recent researches have proved that Allan Hume was an enlightened imporialist. He was alarmed at the growing gulf between the rulers and the ruled. Hume saw with considerable misgivings the establishment of the Indian National Conference in 1883 by S.N. Banerjee, 'a dismissed government servant' of 'advanced political views' who had done much to popularize the ideas and teachings of Italian nationalists like Mazzini and Garibaldi. Hume decided to by-pass this Indian National Conference and instead organise 'a loyal and innocuous' political organisation. And Hume did succeed in organising the Indian National Congress and made it, at least in the beginning' a forum for pro-British and anti-Russian propaganda.[5]

In 1885 met the first Indian National Congress at Bombay under the presidency of Shri Womesh Chandra Bannerjee.

---

4. Philip Woodruff : *The Men Who Ruled India*, vol. ii, p. 176.
5. B.L. Grover : *A Documentary Study of British Policy Towards Indian Nationalism*, p. 11.

The Growth and Development of the Indian National Movement

First Phase, 1885-1905

(Period of Moderate Politics or Tea-Party Politics or Political Mendicancy)

The national leaders like Dadabhai Naoroji, P.M. Mehta, D.E. Wacha, W.C. Bannerjee, S.N. Banerjee who dominated the Congress policies during this period were staunch believers in liberalism and 'moderate' politics and came to be labelled as Moderates to distinguish them from the neo-nationalists of the early 20th century who were referred to as Extremists. The Moderate leaders explained their political outlook as a happy combination of liberalism and moderation. Believers in the spirit of liberalism, they worked to procure for Indians freedom from race and creed prejudices, equality between man and man, equality before law, extension of civil liberties, extension of representative institutions etc. As to their methods, M.G. Ranade explained, "Moderation implies the conditions of never vainly aspiring after the impossible or after too remote ideals, but fairness."[6] Thus the Moderate leaders were convinced believers in the policy of gradualism and constitutionalism.

During this period the Congress was dominated[7] by the affluent middle class intelligentsia, men of legal, medical, engineering, literary pursuits and journalists. The ideas and methods of this middle class held the field and governed the character of the national struggle. The educated middle class was enamoured of titles and services under the state and by its training and culture had isolated itself from the masses. The delegates to the Congress sessions were mostly drawn from the cities and had hardly any real contact with the masses. Sir Pherozeshah Mehta once explained : "The Congress was indeed not the voice of the masses, but it was the duty of their compatriots to interpret their grievances and offer suggestions for their redress."

The Congress had been founded by A.O. Hume after consultations with Lord Dufferin (Viceroy, 1884–88). The congress leaders were full of admiration for British history and culture and spok of the British connection as 'providential'. It was their cardinal faith that British rule in India was in the interest of the Indians. As such they looked upon the British Government not as an antagonist but as an ally ; in the course of time, they believed, Britain would help them to acquire the capacity to govern themselves in accordance with the highest standards of the West. In 1886, Dadabhai Naoroji presiding over the Calcutta session of the Congress dwelt at length on the 'Blessings of British Rule' and his remarks were cheered by the audience. Mr. Hume moved a resolution for three times three cheers for Her Most Gracious Majesty the Queen Empress and a further resolution for long life of the Queen. Ananda Mohan Bose as Congress President (1898) declared, "The educated classes are the friends and not the foes of England—her natural and necessary allies in the great work that lies before her." Thus, it was generally believed that the chief obstacle in the path of India's progress was not British colonial rule but the social and economic backwardness of the Indian people and the reactionary role of the Anglo-Indian bureaucracy.

The Moderate leaders stood for the maintenance, reather strengthening of the British Empire. This approach was the outcome of their apprehension that anarchy and disorder would reappear in India if British Government was superseded. In their eyes British rule was the embodiment of Peace and Order in the country and as such British rule was indispensable in India for a long time to come. Gokhale explained this viewpoint when he said, "Whatever the shortcomings of bureaucracy. and however intolerable at times the insolence of the individual Englishman, they alone stand to-day in the country for order; and without continued order, no real progress is possible for our people. It is not

---

6. *Quoted in M.R. Palande (ed.) : Source Material for a History of the Freedom Movement in India,* vol. ii, pp. 848-9.
7. In Marxist parlance, the Congress was dominated by the progressive bourgeois-landlord-rich farmer combine and its ideological representatives, the educated middle class.

difficult at any time to create disorder in our country—it was our position for centuries—but it is not so easy to substitute another form of order for that which has been evolved in the course of a century". The Moderates sincerely believed that India's progress could be possible only under the supervision of the British. Hence their loyalty to the British Crown. Badr-ud-din Tyabji, the third Congress President, declared that nowhere among the millions of Her Majesty's subject in India were to be found "more truly loyal. nay, more devoted friends of the British Empire than among these educated natives". Thus, the Moderates would do nothing to weaken the Empire. Loyalty to the Crown was their faith, one important article of their political religion.

Most of the Congress leaders of the period believed that the British people were just, righteous and freedom-loving. They were further convinced that the British people meant justice to be done to India. If Indians had certain grievances, these were only due to the reactionary policy of the British bureaucracy in India or ignorance of the British people about these grievances. As such the nationalist leaders believed that all they had to do was to prepare their case and present and plead it before the British Parliament and nation and their grievances would be redressed and justice done. As a natural corollary the Congress leaders put great emphasis on Congress propaganda in England. A British Committee of the Indian National Congress was set up in Londen which published a weekly ournal *India* to present India's case before the British public. Dadabhai Naoroji was never tired of telling the Congress leaders: "Nothing is more dear to the heart of England—and I speak from actual knowledge—than India's welfare ; and, if we only speak out loud enough and persistently enough, to reach that busy heart, we shall not speak in vain." Thus, with a view to educating the English people about the real needs of India, in 1890 a decision was taken to hold a session of the Indian National Congress in London in 1892, but owing to the British elections of 1891 the proposal was postponed and afterwards never revived.

During the period under review, the Congress demanded a few concessions and not freedom for the nation. True, Lokamanya Tilak used the word *Swaraj* or self-government towards the last decade of the nineteenth century but it did not become popular nor did it figure in the official resolutions of the Congress. Presiding over the Poona Congress in 1895, Surendranath Banerjee declared that the Congress had never asked for "representative institutions for the masses but "representative institutions of a modified character for the educated community, who by reason of their culture and enlightenment, their assimilation of English ideas and their familiarity with English methods of Government might be presumed to be qualified for such a boon." Congress resolutions generally demanded expansion of Legislative Councils with enlarged powers and more representation of Indians in them ; representation of Indians in the Secretary of State's Council, Viceroy's Executive Council and Governors' Executive Councils; more opportunities for Indians in the Civil Service; holding of simultaneous examinations in India as well as England; broadening of the basis of civil liberties; reduction of military expenditure and more expenditure on development of education; separation of judiciary from executive work in District administration; enquiry into the backward economic and industrial condition of the country; improvement of the lot of Indians in South Africa and the Empire generally etc. These demands were always worded in prayerful and apologetic language and the Congress was wedded to the use of constitutional methods.

Official attitude towards the Congress. Despite its moderate methods and its emphasis on loyalty to the British Crown the Indian National Congress failed to evoke sympathetic response from the Government. In the beginning, however, the official attitude was of outward neutrality. It was in this spirit that Lord Dufferin gave a garden party to the delegates attending the second Congress session (1886) at Calcutta, taking care to explain that the invitation was not to representatives of the Congress but to 'distinguished visitors to the capital' ; in 1887 the Governor of Madras gave facilities to the organisers of the third session of the Congress at Madras. However, the official attitude stiffened after 1887. The publication of Congress pamphlets like 'A Tamil Congress Catechism', 'A conversation between Moulvi Farrukh-ud-in and one Ram Buksh of Kambakhtpur' which condemned despotic system of government and absentee landlordism brought about the open hostility of the Government. The officials encouraged reactionary elements like Sir Syed Ahmed Khan and Raja Sheo Prasad of Benares to organise the United Indian Patriotic Association to counter Congress propaganda. Further, Lord Dufferin challenged the very national charater of the Congress and dubbed it as representing only 'a microscopic minority' and Congress demands as 'a big jump into the unknown'. In 1890 Government employees were forbidden from participating in its deliberations or attending its meetings. Lord Curzon was more categorical in his pronouncements when he said that the Congress was 'tottering to its fall' and one of his greatest ambitions in India was 'to assist it to a peaceful demise'.

Assessment of the Policies of the Moderates (1885-1905). The achievements of this period were decried by the Radical otherwise called Extremist leaders of the early twentieth century. The policy of the Moderate leaders or the 'Old Guard' was criticised as 'political mendicancy'. Lala Lajpat Raj wrote : "It was at best an opportunist movement. It opened opportunities for treacheries and hypocrites. It enabled some people to trade in the name of patriotism."[8]

A big charge against the moderates was their loyalty to the Crown. It may be mentioned that the Moderate leaders belived that India lacked some of the essential elements which constituted a nation and British rule kept them together. As such they did not see any alternative to British rule in the foreseeable future. Their patriotism, therefore, demanded that they should be loyal to the British *raj*, for any termination of British rule was likely to be harmful to Indian national interests. B.C. Pal, then a Moderate leader, said in 1887, "I am loyal to the British Government because with me loyalty to the British Government is identical with loyalty to my own people and my own country...I am loyal to the British Government, because I love self-government."

In all fairness it must be said that men like Dadabhai Naoroji, Sir Pherozeshah Mehta, Sir Dinshah Wacha, Gopal Krishna Gokhale, Surendra Nath Banerjee etc. were the most progressive elements in Indian society and true patriots. They desired all-round progress and modernisation of India—social reform, modern education, industrial and economic development of India. They earnestly wished the betterment of Indian society and worked to lessen the harshness of British rule. Their main achievement was the appointment of a Public Service Commission in 1886 which caused disappointment and the enactment of the Indian Councils Act of 1892 which did not modify the basic constitution. Further, their efforts resulted in a resolution of the House of Commons (1893) for simultaneous examination for the I.C.S. in London and India and appointment of the Welby Commission on Indian Expenditure (1895). In addition, they did a lot of spadework. Their methods–the use of prayers, press and protests–brought about political maturity.

Perhaps, the greatest service of the Moderate leaders was rendered when they assessed the economic impact of British rule on India. They focussed public attention on the fact of *Indian poverty* and explained that this poverty was largely due to the colonial exploitation of India's economic resources by Britain. The Drain Theory popularized by Dadabhai Naoroji, Dutt, Wacha and others was an open indictment of Britian's economic role in India. This Drain Theory was used as a convenient stick by the Extremist leaders to malign and spit British rule in India.

Select Opinions

Gopal Krishna Gokhale. Let us not forget that we are at a stage of the country's progress when our achievements are bound to be small, and our disappointments frequent and trying. That is the place which it has pleased. Providence to assign to us in this struggle, and our responsibility is ended when we have done the work which belongs to that place. It will, no doubt, be given to our countrymen of future generation to serve India by their successes; we, of the present generation, must be content to serve her mainly by our failures. For, hard though it be, out of these failures the strength will come which in the end will accomplish great tasks.

---
8. Lajpat Rai : *Young India*, p. 156.

Pattabhi Sitaramayya. We cannot blame them for the attitude they adopted as pioneers of Indian political reform any more than we can blame the brick and mortar that is buried six feet deep in the foundation and plinth of a modern edific. They have made possible the superstructure, storey by storey, by colonial self-government, Home Rule within the Empire, *Swaraj* and on the top of all, complete independence.

Bipan Chandra. The period from 1858 to 1905 was the seed time of Indian nationalism; and the early nationalists sowed the seeds well and deep. Instead of basing their nationalism on appeals to shallow sentiments and passing emotions, or abstract right of freedom and liberty, or on obscurantist appeal to the past, they rooted it in a hard-headed and penetrating analysis of the complex mechanism of modern imperialism and the chief contradictions between the interests of the Indian people and British rule. The result was that they evolved a common political and economic programme which united rather than divided the different sections of the people......In spite of their many failures the early nationalists laid strong foundations for the national movement to grow upon and that they deserve a high place among the maker of modern India.

Second Phase, 1905—1919
(Rise of Extremism or Radical Politics)

The closing decade of the 19th century and early years of the 20th century witnessed the emergence of a new and younger group within the Indian National Congress which was sharply critical of the ideology and method of the old leadership. These 'angry young men' advocated the adoption of *Swaraj* as the goal of the Congress to be achieved by more self-reliant and independent methods. The new group came to be called the Extremist Party in contrast to the older one which began to be referred to as the Moderate Party.

The process of split in the Congress Party began when Lokamanya Tilak clashed with the Moderates (also called *Sudharaks*) over the question of Social Reforms. In July 1895 Tilak and his group ousted Ranade and Gokhale from the control of Poona Sarvajanik Sabha. Gokhale organised a separate political association called 'The Deccan Sabha'. There was no love lost between Tilak and Gokhale. Tilak outmanoeuvred Gokhale from national politics over the 'apology affair'[9] and Gokhale was labelled a *Kacha* reed *i.e.* spineless fellow who could be brow-beaten by the Government.

Tilak was made of a different stuff than most of the Congress leaders. He was forthright in his criticism of the Government and its policies and was prepared to make sacrifices to get wrongs redressed. He was the first Congress leader to suffer several terms of imprisonment for the sake of the country. As early as 1882, for criticising in strong language the treatment meted out to the Maharaja of Kolhapur, the Government tried and sentenced Tilak to four months' imprisonment. Again, in 1897 Tilak was charged with 'exciting feelings of disaffection to the British Government' and sent to jail for 18 months' R.I. At the Congress session at Amraoti (Dec. 1897) the supporters of Tilak made an attempt to push a resolution demanding the release of Tilak. The Moderate leaders who controlled the Congress did not permit it. Similarly, the Moderates foiled the attempt of martyrdom at the Congress session at Madras (Dec. 1898). At the Lucknow session of the Congress (Dec. 1899). Tilak's attempt to move a resolution condemning Governor Sandhurst's administration of Bombay was also blocked

---

9. While in England in 1897 Gokhale wrote a letter to the *Manchester Guardian* on 2 July 1897 condemning the behaviour of Plague Commissioners at Poona. This letter coupled with the speech on the same subject which Gokhale delivered in London, alarmed the Secretary of State, who in turn wrote to the Governor of Bombay ordering an enquiry into the affairs. On his return to Bombay Gokhale was asked by Lord Sandhurst to substantiate the charges against the Plague Commissioners. Gokhale found himself cornered. He offered an unqualified apology to the Government and publicly admitted that he had been misinformed.

by the Moderate leaders on the plea that the matter was of provincial interest and could not be discussed at the National Congress. It was because of ideological differences with Tilak and his Group that the Moderate leaders were determined to keep Tilak and Congressmen of his line of thinking out of all positions of power and responsibility in the Congress and never gave him a chance to become the Congress President.

CAUSES FOR THE RISE OF EXTREMISM

The dissatisfaction with the working of the Congress had been expressed by Bankim Chandra Chatterjee when he described the Congressmen as "place-hunting politicians". Aurobindo Ghose wrote a series of articles during 1893-94 entitled 'New Lamps for Old' wherein he described the Congress as being out of contact with the 'proletariat', its character as 'unnational' and its work as 'failure' and added : "Yet more appalling was the general timidity of the congress, its glossing of hard names, its disinclinations to tell the direct truth, its fear of too deeply displeasing our masters". He thought that the Congress was 'dying of consumption.'

Among the cause and circumstances that helped in the growth of Extremism the following deserve special mention :

1. Recognition of the True Nature of British Rule. The efforts of the early nationalist leaders paved the way for the development of the next stage of the nationalist movement. By their painstaking studies and writings the early nationalist leaders had *exposed the true nature of British Rule in India.* They conclusively proved by elaborate statistical data that British rule and its policies were responsible for the economic ruin of India and her deepening poverty. Dadabhai Naoroji, for example, exposed the exploitative nature of British rule in India and proved that Britain was 'bleeding India white' and the constant 'drain of wealth' from India was directly responsible for India's economic miseries. He characterized British rule in India as 'a constant and continuous' plunder. Nationalist leaders like Ananda Charlu, R.N. Mudholkar, D.E. Wacha, G.K. Gokhale, Madan Mohan Malaviya too exposed the exploitative nature of British rule in India. R.C. Dutt and G.V. Joshi, examined thread-bare the true nature of British Land Revenue policy while S.N. Banerjee explained at length the big gap between the professed aims and practised policy of the Government of India in matters of recruitment to public service. The second session of the Congress (Calcutta, 1886) brought a resolution on increasing poverty of India and this resolution was affirmed year after year at subsequent Congress sessions. The 'proverty verging on starvation' of fifty millions of the population was described by the Congress as due to the most extravagant civil and military administration, mounting Home Charges, discriminating tariff policy (as evident from the frequent changes in the Cotton Duties and Sugar Duties etc.) shortsighted land revenue policy, indifference to technical and industrial development of India and exclusion of the sons of the soil from a share in the Higher and Minor services. Scholarly writings of nationalist leaders like Ranade's *Essays in Indian Economics* (1898), Dadabhai Naoroji's *Indian Poverty and un-British Rule in India* (1901), R.C. Dutt's *Economic History of India* (1901) were the arsenals from which the new leaders shot their arrows at the British rule in India. Thus the Extremist ideology was a natural and logical next step in the development of Indian political thinking.

2. Reaction to Increasing Westernization. The new leadership felt the stranglehold of excessive Westernization in Indian life, thought and politics—Christianity and utilitarianism (visible in the teachings of Brahma Samaj) were a challenge to Indian religion and thought; the materialistic and individualistic Western civilization was eroding the values of Indian culture and civilization ; and the merger of Indian national identity in the British Empire was being attempted.

The intellectual and emotional inspiration of the new leadership (Extremists) was Indian. They drew inspiration from Indian spiritual heritage, they appealed to heroes of Indian history and hoped to revive the glories of ancient India. The writings of Bankim, Vivekananda and Swami Dayanand appealed to their imagination. Though Bankim, in the beginning, had written in Bengali and on Bengal (*Anandamath,* published in 1880), by 1886 he had emerged an Indian and dreamed of a united India under the leadership of a superman like Lord Krishna (video *Krishna Charitra* Part 1, 1886). Bankim saw in Lord Krishna a *Karamyogin* i.e. a man of action who fought evil and stood for righteousness. He saw in Lord Krishna a good soldier, a clever strategist and a successful empire-builder, at Kurukshetra war Lord Krishna deliberately worked for the destruction of petty states and for the emergence of *dharmaraja*. The main *mantra* of Bankim, 'Service to the Motherland' now acquired an added significance. Vivekanand a great Vedantist, gave new confidence to the Indians in India's past heritage. He exhorted his compatriots to realize the value of their rich cultural heritage. He gave a feeling of self-confidence to the youth and gave them a new mission–to conquer the West with India's spirituality– Swami Dayanand exploded the myth of Western superiority. By referring to India's rich civilization in the Vedic Ages, when Europe was steeped in ignorance, Dayanand gave a 'new confidence' to the Hindus and undermined the current belife in the superiority of the White races over the Brown or Black. Dayanand's Political message was 'India for the Indians'.

3. Dissatisfaction with the Achievement of the Congress. The younger elements within the Congress were dissatisfied with the achievements of the Congress during the first 15-20 years and were disgusted with the cold and reactionary attitude of the Government. They had lost all faith in the British sense of justice and fairplay. They were strongly critical of the methods of peaceful and constitutional agitation, popularly nicknamed of 3 Ps–Petition, Prayer and Prostest—and described these methods as 'political mendicancy'. They became impatient with the slow, almost negligible achievements during the first fifteen years and advocated the adoption of European revolutionary methods to meet European imperialism.

On his return from England in 1905 Lala Lajpat Rai told his countrymen that the British democracy was too busy with its own affairs to do anything worthwhile for India, that the British press was not likely to champion their aspirations and that it was very difficult to get a hearing in England. He exhorted the people that if they really cared for their country, "they would have to strike a blow for freedom themselves, and they should be prepared to give unmistakable proof of their earnestness."[10]

The younger generation of Congressmen (also called Nationalists or Extremists) had nothing but disgust for the Old Guard. According to them the only 'political religion' of the Congress was— loyalty to the Crown ; their only 'political aim'–to improve their chances of getting seats in the central / provinicial legislatures or judicial services or acquiring titles etc.; their only 'political activity'— excessive speechyfying and attending Congress session towards December-end every year. The Moderate leaders were accused of limiting the range of their activities for the benefit of the middle class intelligentsia and limiting the membership of the Congress to the middle class—for fear of losing their leadership if the masses joined the movement. Thus the Moderate leaders were accused of 'trading in the name of patriotism'. Tilak described the Congress as 'a Congress of flatterers'[11] and Congress session 'a holiday recreation[12] while Lajpat Rai dubbed Congress meeting 'the annual national festival of educated Indians.' Both Tilak and Lajpat Rai believed that the Congress had no constructive activity. Tilak affirmed : "We will not achieve any success in our labours if we croak once a year like a frog."

4. Deteriorating Economic Condition of India. The economic miseries of the closing years of the 19th century provided a congenial atmosphere for the growth of extremism in Indian national activity. The terrible famines of 1896–97 and 1899–1900 coupled with the bubonic plague which broke out in Maharashtra took a heavy toll of life. The Government relief machinery was inadequate, slow-moving and badly organised. Tilak criticised the callous and over-bearing Government Plague

---

10. Lajpat Rai : *Young India, p. 170.*
11. Ram Gopal : *Lokamanya Tilak,* p.130.
12. *Ibid,* p. 207.

Commissioners who caused more harm than good. He thundered that fear and anxiety was the cause of the disease and that "plague is less cruel to us than the official measures".[13] Riots broke out in the Deccan and the Government tried to stifle public opinion and suppress lawlessness. These events revealed to the Indians their plight of utter helplessness. Even recurring famines were attributed to the antinational policy followed by the Government. In his presidential speech in 1903 Lal Mohan Ghose referred to the Durbar of 1903 and said : "Nothing could seem more heartless than the spectacle of a great Government imposing the heaviest taxation upon the poorest population in the world, and then lavishly spending the money so obtained over fire-works and pompous pageants, while millions of the poor were dying of starvation".[14]

5. **Contemporary International Influences.** Events outside India exercised a powerful influence on the younger generation. The humiliating treatment meted out to Indians in British colonies, especially in South Africa, created anti-British feelings. Further, nationalist movements in Egypt, Persia, Turkey and Russia gave Indians new hopes and new aspirations. Indian nationalists gained more confidence and drew inspiration from Abyssinia's repulsion of the Italian army (1896) and Japan's thumping victory over Russia (1905). If Japan could become a great power on its own, what—but for the British grip—was holding India back. The spell of European invincibility was broken.

6. **Curzon's Reactionary Policies.** Cutzon's seven-year rule in India which was full of 'missions, omissions and commissions' created a sharp reaction in the Indian mind. Curzon refused to recongnise that India was a 'nation' and characterized their activity as the 'letting off of gas'. He insulted Indian Intelligentsia and talked very low of Indian character ; at the Calcutta University Convocation Curzon said, "Undoubtedly truth took a high place in the codes of the West before it had been similarly honoured in the East, where craftiness and diplomatic wile have always been held in high repute." The Calcutta Corporation Act, the official Secrets Act and the Indian Universities Act created great resentment in India. The Delhi Durbar held in 1903, coming at a time when India had not fully recovered from the devastating efects of the famine of 1899-1900 was interpreted as 'a pompous pageant to a starving population.'

7. **The Partition of Bengal.** The worst and most-hated aspect of Curzon's administration was the partition of Bengal into two provinces of Bengal and Eastern Bengal and Assam in 1905.

The partition forced in teeth of Bengali opposition and protests from the Indian National Congress (in 1904) showed the contemptuous disregard Curzon and the Home authorities had for Indian public opinion. It was abundantly clear that the partition of Bengal was a machiavellian devise to divide the people on the basis of religion and to put the Muslims against the Hindus. The uttar disregard Curzon showed for public opinion gave ample evidence, if any evidence was still needed, that the Moderates' policy of 'petitions, prayers and protests' was barren of results.

The Objectives and Methods of the Extremist Group

The new turn in Indian politics found expression in two forms—(i) The formation of the Extremist Group within the Congress, (ii) the growth of Terrorism or Revolutionary movement in the country at large.

Four prominent Congress leaders—Lokamanaya Tilak, Bipin Chandra Pal, Aurobindo Ghose and Lala Lajpat Rai—defined the creed of the new group, gave articulate form to its aspirations and guided its operations. Tilak gave the slogan to the new group when he said "*Swaraj* is my birthright and I shall have it." Tilak explained :

> '*Swaraj* or self-government is essential for the exercise of *Swadharma*. Without *Swaraj* there could be no social reform, no industrial progress, no useful education, no fulfilment of

---

13. *Ibid.*, p. 137.
14. *Congress Presidential Addresses* (Natesan & Co., Madras) vol. i.p. 62.
15. *Report on the Twentieth Congress*, 1904, Resolution xiv.

the national life. That is what we seek, that is why God has sent us into the world to fulfil Him.'

B.C. Pal elaborated the demand of the new party thus :

"It is not *reforms,* but *re-form,* which is the new cry in the country. It is the abdication of the right of England to determine the policy of the Indian Government, the relinquishment of the right of the present foreign despotism to enact whatever law they please to govern the people of the country, the abandonment of their right to tax the people according to their own sweet will and pleasure, and to spend the revenues of the country in any way they like."

Aurobindo Ghose described "Swaraj as the fulfilment of the ancient life of India under modern conditions, the return of the *Satyuga* of national greatness, the resumption by her of her great role of the teacher and guide, self-liberation of the people for final fulfilment of the Vedantic ideal in politics, this is the true Swaraj for India."[16] Aurobindo emphasised : "Political freedom is the life breath of a nation ; to attempt social reform, educational reform , industrial expansion, the moral improvement of the race without aiming first and foremost at political freedom, is the very height of ignorance and futility".

Lajpat Rai bemoaned : "A subject people has no soul, just as a slave can have none...A man without a soul is a mere animal. A nation without a soul is only a dumb driven cattle." Thus, *Swaraj* was the first requisite for a nation and reforms or good government could be no substitute for it.

It should be clearly understood that the Nationalists' (Extremists') demand for *Swaraj* was a demand for "complete freedom from foreign control and full independence to manage national affairs without any foreign restrants. The *Swaraj* of the Moderate leaders was merely a demand for colonial self-government within the Empire. The methods employed by the two groups (Moderates and Extremists) were different in their tempo and approach. While the Moderates had infinite faith in the efficacy of constitutional agitation and in appealing to the British sense of justice and fairplay, in holding annual conferences, making speeches, passing elaborate resolutions and sending deputations to England, the Extremists had no faith in the 'benevolence' of the British public or parliament, nor were they convinced of the efficacy of merely holding conferences. Tilak explained his conviction, "We will not achieve any success in our labours if we croak once a year like a frog." The Nationalists also affirmed their faith in Passive Resistance, mass agitation and strong will to suffer or make self-sacrifices. The new leadership sought to create a passionate love for liberty, accompanied by a spirit of sacrifics and a readiness to suffer for the cause of the country. They strove to root out from the people's mind the omnipotence of the ruler and instead give them self-reliance and confidence in their own strength. B.C. Pal explained the strategy thus :

"Untrained in the crooked ways of civilised diplomacy, they had believed what their rulers had said, either of themselves or of their subjects, as gospel truth. They had been told that people of India were unfit to manage their own affairs and they believed it to be true. They had been told that the people were weak and the Government was strong. They had been told that India stood on a lower plane of humanity and England's mission was to civilise the 'semi-barbarous natives'. The Nationalists School took upon themselves to expose the hollowness of all these pretensions. They commenced to make what are called counter-passes in hypnotism, and at once woke the people to a sence of their own strength and an appreciation of their own culture."[17]

The Extremist Programme of Action. The Extremists advocated Boycott of Foreign goods, use of Swadesh goods, National Education and Passive Resistance.

---

16. Aurobindo : *Bande Matram,* 3 May 1908.
17. B.C. Pal : *The Spirit of Indian Nationalism,* p. 42.

Economic boycott of British-made goods and use of Swadeshi or home-made products was designed to encourage Indian industries and provide the people with more opportunities for work and employment. Lala Lajpat Rai explained that the original idea behind boycott of British goods was to cause pecuniary loss to the British manufacturers and thus secure their sympathy and help for getting the partition of Bengal annulled. Soon it was discovered that economic boycott might prove a powerful weapon against economic exploitation by the foreigners. Further, it proved a most effective weapon for injuring British interests in India. Besides, it was believed, the newly-rising Indian manufacturing class would liberally provide funds for the Congress and thus strengthen it. Lajpat Rai summed up : "We desire to turn our faces away from Government House and turn them to huts of the people. This is the psychology, this is the ethics, this is the spiritual significance of the boycott movement."

A National Scheme of Education was to replace the boycott of Government-controlled universities and colleges. The Extremists tried to enlist the students in their service. When the Government threatened to take disciplinary action against the students, the national leaders advocated national universities independent of Government control. Guroodas Banerjee headed the Bengal Council of National Education. Bengal National Collage was established at Calcutta and a large number of national schools sprang up in East Bengal. In Madras the Pachaiappa National College was set up. In the Panjab the D.A.V. movement made considerable headway.

Tilak preached non-cooperation. In 1902 at Poona he said, "You must realise that you are a great factor in the power with which the administration of India is controlled. You are yourselves the great lubricants which enable the gigantic machinery to work so smoothly. Though down-trodden and neglected, you must be conscious of your power of making the administration impossible if you but choose to make it."

The Extremists also encouraged co-operative organisations. Voluntary associations were set up for rural sanitation, preventive police duties, regulation of fairs and pilgrim gatherings for providing relief during famines and other national calamities. Arbitration Committees were set up to decide civil and non-cognizable disputes. The object of the co-operative movement was explained by B.C. Pal thus :

"To create in the first place a strong civic sentiment in the people with the help of co-operative organisations for the furtherance of the common good, and thus to train them gradually for the longer and heavier responsibilities of free citizenship, and in the next place to cover the whole country with a network of active political organisations which would place the leaders in direct and living touch with the people, and enable them to bring from time to time, the irresistible pressure of organised public opinion to bear upon the government, helping thereby the gradual expansion of popular rights."

Assessment of Extremism. In any assessment of what popularly known as 'extremist' thought and politics one must not lose sight of the fact that is was not a consistent political philosophy. Advocates of extremism ranged from active revolutionaries at one end to secret sympathizers of revolutionary activities, to those who were opposed to all violent methods at the other end. Further, its top leaders—Aurobindo, Tilak, Pal and Lajpat Rai—differed in their emphasis on political ideals and practical course of action. Even the views of individual leaders underwent change with changing circumstances. For example, Tilak's conception of 'Swaraj' meant some sort of self-government while Aurobindo conceived of 'Swaraj' as 'complete independence' from foreign rule, Further, Tilak's revolutionary fervour somewhat mellowed towards the end of his political career and he showed signs of cooperation with the government, while Aurobindo's concept of 'complete independence' was transformed into 'human unity' and 'world union' in his later career. However, it must be stated that all extremist leaders were one in realising the evils of foreign rule and in demanding some degree of independence from colonial stranglehold. Extremism was, in fact, an attitude of mind and a practical strategy to meet a particular situation.

The extremists talked of democracy, constitutionalism and progress and talked of broadening the social base of the national movement. Most of them represented the urban lower middle class and aimed at spreading the Congress message to the people. They spoke, wrote and edited newspapers in vernacular languages and thus succeeded in conveying their meassage to a larger audience.

The extermists well understood and highlighted the negative role of Britain in India. They saw clearly the clash of interest between the British rulers and Indian national interests. Thus the main focus of their politics was (a) to get a larger share for Indians in the administration of their country and (b) to end Britain's economic exploitation of India. They also realised that these objectives could not be realised without pressure tactics and some sort of direct action. Hence the Moderates' philosophy of co-operation gave place to non-cooperation and resistance to unjust acts of the government. Thus the Extremists gave new slogans to the Indian nationalist movement—'non-cooperation, passive resistance, mass agitation, self-reliance, descipline of suffering' etc. The Extremists transformed patriotism from 'an academic pastime' to 'service and suffering for the nation'.

Socially speaking, the rise of the Extremist ideology proved to be a reactionary development. In contrast to the Moderates (who were modernists and enlightened in matters of social reform) the Extremists became revivalists and obscurantists in matters of social reforms. Tilak's opposition (for whatever reasons) to the Age of Consent Bill (which proposed to raise the age of consummation of marriage for girls from 10 to 12 years), his association with Anti-Cow-Killing societies, his organisation of the Ganesh Festival (1893) as a national festival projects him as the leader of Hindu orthodoxy and Hindu nationalism. Similarly, Lala Lajpat Rai and B.C. Pal, though ardent advocates of social reform spoke of Hindu nation and need for protection of Hindu interests at political levels. Though the revivalist dimension of Extremist politics was mainly directed against the foreign rulers, it developed an unhealthy inter-relationship between religion and politics apart from encouraging communalism and Muslim separatism.

The policy of the Extremists yielded good dividends. The partition of Bengal was annulled in 1911 which gave a new self-confidence and self-assurance to Indian nationalists. The aim of 'Swaraj' though denied by Lord Morley was no longer looked upon as a revolutionary demand and the shock of the First World War was required to compel the British Government to Proclaim self-government institutions as the goal of constitutional development in India.

Select Opinions

B.G. Tilak. Two new words have recently come into existence with regard to our policies, and they are *Moderates* and *Extremists*. These words have a specific relation to time and they, therefore, will change with time. The Extremists of to-day will be Moderates of tomorrow, just as the Moderates of to-day were Extremists of yesterday.

Daniel Argov. Both the moderates and the extremists came from the middel class, both were reacting to British rule and both voiced Indian grievances. The moderates claimed social equality and a share in the British Government of India on the grounds that they were British subjects; the extremist demanded social equality and political emancipation as their birthright. The moderates appealed to Englishmen in England and placed their reliance on English history and English political ideas ; the extremists drew sustenance from India's heritage and appealed to Indians by invoking religious patriotism. The moderates emphasised the need for political apprenticeship under the providential guidance of British rule; the extremists rejected the idea of England's providential mission in India as an illusion. They disparaged the constitutional agitation of the moderates as "mendicancy", and their stress on apprenticeship as an acceptance of unending political servitude. Instead, they called for self-reliance and self-apprenticeship through Swadeshi, Boycott and Passive-Resistance. In contrast, the moderates stressed that their constitutional agitation was practical statesmanship, that emotional idealism was fraught with peril, that rashness was not courage, that British rule would not come to end becouse of Boycott and above all, the removal of British rule would result in chaos and anarchy.

Indian Nationalists and World War I

The Indian National Congress was under the control of the Moderates when the First World War broke out in 1914. The Indian National Congress decided to support the British war efforts, both as a matter of duty and in a spirit of bargaining to get concessions.

However, a section of Indian leadership believed that no concessions could be possible unless popular pressure was brought to bear upon the government. Hence the need for a real mass movement and the formation of the Home Rule League.

Home Rule Movement. In 1915 Mrs. Annie Besant announced her decision to establish a Home Rule League at Madras on the model of the Irish Home Rule League. In 1916 Tilak organised his own Home Rule League at Poona. Both the Leagues worked in unison and aimed at the achievement of self-government for India. The Leagues' objective was to educate the people and provide the congress demand for self-government with the support and strength of a nation united in knowledge of itself and its single aim. The Home Leagues functioned independently as the Congress could not adopt a radical programme as that. The Home Leagues aimed to pressurize the British public for granting self-government to India.

The Lucknow Session, 1916. The Lucknow session of the Congress is memorable for it marked the re-union of the Moderate and Extremist parties after the Surat Split (1907). The union became possible with the deaths of Gopal Krishna Gokhale and Ferozeshah Mehta in 1915. Tilak and Mrs. Annie Besant dominated the Lucknow session.

Another noteworthy development was the Congress League Pact (1916) for acceptance of a united scheme of constitutional reforms. The resultant efforts produced the Congress League Scheme and the 'Nineteen Memorandum' to give concrete shape to political thinking in the country. This combined activity and the psychology created by the war culminated in the Declaration of 20 August 1917 by the Secretary of State, Lord Montagu in the British Parliaments. In 1918 the Montagu-Chelmsford Reforms were announced and in 1919 the Government of India Act passed by the British Parliament.

The Act of 1919 did not satisfy national aspirations. This dissatisfaction coupled with the repressive policies followed by the government gave new turn to the nationalist movement. Mahatma Gandhi emerged as the new leader and gave a new direction and new dimension to the nationalist movement.

The Revolutionary Terrorist Movement

The Revolutionary terrorist movement was largely the out-come of the same set of causes which gave rise to the Extremist wing in nationalist politics. Only the revolutionaries wanted quicker results and discounted the value of persuasion (popularized by the Moderates) and low-grade pressure (advocated by the Extremists). The revolutionaries believed that alien rule was destructive of all that is worthwhile in national life—political liberties, religious freedom, morality and Indian culture. Though it is difficult to pin point the political philosophy of the revolutionary terrorists in different parts of India, but their one common aim was—Freedom of the Motherland from British rule.

As to the methods, the revolutionaries believed that Western Imperialism could only be ended by Western methods of violence. Hence the advocacy of the cult of the revolver and the bomb. The revolutionaries formed secret societies, recruited the young and thused them with higher values of bold Action and Sacrifice for the cause of the country; they distributed arms, taught their members the use of arms and even the manufacture of bombs. By assassination of European officials, they sought to demoralise the official class, paralyse the administration and uproot the enemies of Freedom—both foreign and Indians. To finance their projects, they even condoned acts of murder, dacoities, looting of banks, offices and even train derailments.

Revolutionary Activities in Maharashtra. The authors of the Sedition Committee Report, 1918, observed the first indications of revolutionary movement in India in Maharashtra and among the Chitpavan Brahmins of the Poona district. These Brahmins were descendants of the Peshwas (chief ministers under Chhatrapati Shahu and later rulers of Maharashtra). It was the Peshwa rule (the Chitpavan government) which was overthrown by the East India Company under Lord Hastings. These Brahmins kept their love and devotion to *Swaraj* and a certain discontent and longing for a return to power naturally remained.

B.G. Tilak's (a Chitpavan Brahmin) inauguration of the Ganapati festival in 1893 and the Shivaji festival in 1895 injected some pro-Swaraj and anti-British bias in the politics of Maharashtra.

The Rand Murder at Poona, 1897. The first political murder of Europeans was committed at Poona on 22 June 1897 by the Chapekar brothers (Chitpavan Brahmins) Damodar and Balkrishna. The target of attack was Mr. Rand, President of the Plague Committee at Poona, but Lt. Ayerst was shot accidentally. The provocation was the tryanny of the Plague Committee on sending soldiers to inspect houses of civilians for plague-afflicted persons. Tilak in his newspaper *Mahratta* had written "Plague is more merciful to us than its human prototypes now reigning in the city". The Chapekar brothers were caught, convicted and hanged. The authorities also implicated Tilak and prosecuted him for seditious writings against the British Government ; Tilak was awarded 18 month of R.I. Although the nationalist opinion then and national historians thereafter have defended Tilak, but a more objective view would suggest that Tilak's writings and speeches did preach and justify resort to violence and inspired the young Chapeker brothers. Consider, for example, his writing in the *Kesari* on 15 June 1897, "Srimat Krishna's advice in the *Gita* is to kill even our own teachers and our kinsmen. No blame attaches to any preson if he is doing deeds without being actuated by a desire to reap the fruits of his deeds...God has not conferred upon the foreigners the grant inscribed on a copper-plate of the kingdom of Hindusthan...Do not circumscribe your vision like a frog in a well ; get out of the Penal Code and enter the extremely high atmosphere of the *Srimat Bhagavad Gita* and consider the actions of great men."

Shyamji Krishnavarma and Establishment of India House at London. Krishnavarma, a native of Kathiawar in Western India, had studied at Cambridge University and qualified for the Bar. After his return to India, he served in several Indian states but felt thoroughly disgusted with the overbearing attitude of Political Residents. He decided to work for India's liberation from British oppression and chose London as the centre of his activities. In 1905 Krishnavarma set up the India Home Rule Society popularly known as the India House ; he also published a monthly journal, *The Indian Sociologist* to espouse Indian causes. He also instituted six fellowships of Rs. 1,000 each for qualified Indians visiting foreign countries. Very soon the India House became a centre of Indian activities in London. A group of Indian revolutionaries including V.D. Savarkar, Hardayal and Madan Lal Dhingra became members of the India House.

V.D. Savarkar, a young graduate from Fergusson College, Poona, availed of Krishnavarma's fellowship offer and left for London in June 1906. Earlier at Nasik, Savarkar had set up an association called Mitra *Mela* which in 1904 had been merged into the secret, society called *Abhinav Bharata* after Mazzini's *Young Italy*. The band of young enthusiasts made India House a centre for pro-India and anti-British propaganda. In May 1900 the India House celebrated the golden jubilee of the Indian revolt of 1857 and V.D. Savarkar described it as a war of independence. Savarkar's views were published the following year in his book entitled. *The Indian War of Independence,* 1857. Another pamphlet entitled "Grave Warning" was widely distributed in London and copies sent to India.

In 1909 Madan Lal Dhingra shot dead Col. Willliam Curzon Wyllie, political A.D.C. to the India office.

The British authorities were swung into action. Madan Lal was hanged. Savarkar arrested and deported to India where he was sentenced to transportation for life. Shyamji left London and settled in Paris. Thus the activities of the India House at Londan had to be wound up.

On 21 December 1909 Mr. Jackson, the unpopular District Magistrate of Nasik, was shot dead. The Abhinav Bharat Society at Nasik had members at various places in Western India. The Ahmedabad Bomb Case (November 1909), the Satara Conspiracy (1910) were other cases of terrorist activities in Western India.

Revolutionary Movement in Bengal. The beginning of revolutionary activities in Bengal is traced to the work of *bhadralok* class. P. Mitra organised a secret revolutionary society under the name of *Anushilan Samiti*. The partition of Bengal and the Indian offensive through Boycott of British goods and Swadeshism stirred the political consciousness of Bengal to an extent hitherto unknown. Soon the original goal of the annulment of the Partition of Bengal got enlarged into the attainment of Swaraj.

In 1905 Barindra Kumar Ghose published the *Bhavani Mandir* (indicating a detailed plan for organising a centre of revolutionary activities) followed by the publication of *Vartaman Rananiti* (Rules of modern warfare). The *Yugantar* (New Era) and *Sandhya* preached anti-British ideas. Another pamphlet *Mukti Kon Pathe* (Which way lies Salvation) exhorted the Indian soldiers to supply arms to revolutionaries. The youth of Bengal was exhorted to worship Bhawani as the manifestation of *Shakti* and to acquire mental, physical, moral and spiritual strength. The emphasis was on *Karma* and Action.

Revolutionary activities resulting in acts of violence began in 1906 when some robberies were planned to finance the plane of revolutionaries. In 1907 unsuccessful attempts were made to kill the : Lt. Governors of Eastern Bengal and Bengal.

The Muzaffarpur Murders and the Alipore Conspiracy Case. On 30 April 1908 an attempt was made to murder Mr. Kingford, the Judge of Muzaffarpur (now in Bihar) who earlier as chief Presidency Magistrate had awarded severe punishments to some youngmen for trivial offences. Prafulla Chaki and Khudiram Bose were carged with the duty of bomb-throwing. The bomb was by mistake thrown on the carriage of Mr. Kennedy, killing two ladies. Prafulla Chaki and Bose were arrested ; Chaki shot himself dead while Bose was tried and hanged.

The Government searches for illicit arms at Maniktala Gardens and elsewhere at Calcutta led to the arrest of 34 persons including the two Ghose brothers, Arobindo and Barindra who were tried in the Alipore Conspiracy case. During the trial Narendra Gosain, who had turned approver, **was shot dead in jail.** In February 1909 the Public Prosecutor was shot dead in Calcutta and on 24 February 1910 a Deputy Superintendent of Police met the same fate while leaving the Calcutta High Court.

B.G. Tilak lauded the Bengal terrorist for their higher aims. In the *Kasari* of 22 June 1908 he wrote "There is considerable defference between the murders of 1897 and the bomb outrage of Bengal...Their (Chapekar brothers) aim was specially directed towards the oppression consequent upon the plague, that is to say, towards the particular act. The Bengali bomb party had of course their eyes upon an extensive plain brought into view by the partition of Bengal."

The Rowlatt Committee report put the number of dacoities at 110 and attempts at murder over 60 cases in Bengal alone during 1906–17.

Revolutionary Movement in other Provinces. The educated classes in the Panjab were affected by revolutionary ideas. The Panjab Government's proposals for modification of tenures in the Chenab Canal Colony and the Bari Doab had spread widespread discontent among the rural masses. The Government of India acted promptly by vetoing the Canal Colony legislation and arresting and deporting Lajpat Rai and Ajit Singh under provisions of Regulation III of 1818. Ajit Singh was released after 6 months and later fled to Persia. Lal Chand Falak and Bhai Parmanand were arrested and sentenced to various terms of imprisonments.

In December 1912 a bomb was thrown on Lord Harding on his state entry in Chadni Chowk, Delhi, Killing his attendants.

Bihar, Orissa and the U.P. were scenes of the Muzaffarpur and Nimez murders and the Benares Conspiracy case though these provinces were comparatively less affected by revolutionary movement.

The Ghadr Movement. Hardayal, an intellectual giant and a fire-brand revolutionary from the Panjab, was the moving spirit behind the organization of the Ghadr Party on November 1913 at San Franscisco in the U.S.A. He was actively assisted by Ram Chandra and Barkatulla. The party also published a weekly paper, the *Ghadr* (Rebellion) in commemoration of the Mutiny of 1857. The *Ghadr* in its premier issue asked the questions : What is our name ? Mutiny. What is our work ? Mutiny. Where will mutiny break out ? In India. The Ghadr Party highlighted the point that Indians were not respected in the world abroad because they were not free. Consequent upon complaints made by the British representative, the U.S. authorities launched proceedings against, Hardayal, compelling him to leave the United States.

With the outbreak of World War I Hardayal and other Indians abroad moved to Germany and set up the Indian Indepedence Committee at Berlin. The Committee planned to mobilise Indian settlers abroad to make all efforts—send volunteers to India to incite rebellion among the troops, to send explosives to Indian revolutionaries, and even organise an invassion of British India—to liberate the country.

The *Komagata Maru* case created an explosive situation in the Panjab. One Baba Gurdit Singh chartered a Japanese ship *Komagata Maru* for Vancouver and sought to carry 351 Sikhs and 21 Panjabi Muslims to that town. The Canadian authorities refused permission to the ship to land and the ship returned to Budge Budge, Calcutta on 27 September 1914. The inmates of the ship and many Indians believed that the British government had inspired the Canadian authorities. The Government of India ordered all the passengers to be carried direct by train to the Panjab. The already explosive situation in the Panjab worsened with a band of fresh malcontents. Large-scale political dacoities were committed in the Jullundur, Amritsar, Ludhiana districts of the Panjab. The Lahore Conspiracy trials revealed that Panjab had come 'within an ace of widespread bloodshed.'

The Government of India unleashed repressive legislation to meet revolutionary activities : The Prevention of Seditious Meetings Act (1907), The Explosive Substances Act (1908), The Indian Criminal Law Amendment Act (1908), The Newspaper (Incitement to Offences) Act, 1908, The Press Act, 1910 and, above all, the obnoxious multi-fanged Defence of India Rules, 1915.

A temporary respite in revolutionary activities came with the close of World War I when the Government released all political prisoners arrested under the Defence of India Act. Further, the discussions about the new scheme of constitutional reforms (Government of India Act 1919) also created an atmosphere of conciliation and compromise. More so, Gandhiji's emergence on the national scene with promise of big achivements through non-violent methods also halted the pace of violent revolutionary activities.

Second Phase of Revolutionary Terrorism. The virtual failure of the Non-Cooperation Movement and the gloom that descended on the nationalist scene again created conditions calling for bold and terrorist revolutionary activities. The old *Anusilan* and *Yougantar Samitis* reappeared in Bengal and revolutionary organisations erupted in almost all important towns of Northern India. A new development was, however, the feeling that better results could be achieved only through an all-India organisation and better coordination. Hence a meeting of revolutionaries from all parts of India was called at Kanpur in October 1924. The Kanpur meeting was attended by old-timers like Sachindranath Sanyal, Jogesh Chandra Chatterjee and Ramprasad Bismil and youngsters like Bhagat Singh, Shiv Varma, Sukhdev, Bhagwati Charan Vohra and Chandrashekhar Azad. The deliberation resulted in the setting up of the Hindustan Republican Association subsequently (September 1928) reorganised as the Hindustan Socialist Republican Association or Army (H.S.R.A.) with provincial unit in Bengal, Bihar, the U.P., Delhi, the Panjab and even Madras.

The HSRA had a three-fold objective (a) to rouse the consciousness of the people of India to the futility of the Gandhian methods of non-violence, (b) to demonstrate the need and desirability of Direct Action and Revolution in order to achive complete independence, (c) ideologically inspired by the Russian Revolution and the Socialist thought, the Association hoped to substitute British imperialism in India by a federated Republic of the United States of India. The terrorists also introduced a novelty in their methods to finance their activities. Henceforth they decided not to plunder private individuals but to make government treasuries alone as the target of their dacoities.

On 9 August 1925 the U.P. revolutionaries successfully carried out the dacoity on the Kakori-bound train on the Saharanpur, Lucknow railway line. The subsequent trial-proceeding in the Kakori Conspiracy case evoked wide sympathetic echoes in the press and the case was also the subject of a resolution in the U.P. Legislative Council. The leader Ramprasad Bismil embraced the gallows with the slogan 'I wish the downfall of the British Empire' and Roshanlal with the slogan "Bande Matram" on their lips. A band of Panjabi revolutionaries led by Bhagat singh shot dead Mr. Saunders (17 December 1928), the Assistant Superintendent of Police, Lahore to avenge the fatal assault on Lala Lajpat Rai during the anti-Simon Commission demonstrations (30 October 1928). The police unleashed a reign of terror on the Lahore civilians and the general public reaction was that while the revolutionaries eseaped after daring acts, the public had to suffer the consequences of their doings. To efface this impression, the Panjab unit of the H.S.R.A. decided to send two volunteers to commit a crime and court arrest. It was in pursuance of this decision that Bhagat Singh and Batukeshwar Datta threw a bomb in the Central Assembly on 8 April 1929 ; they had no intention to kill anybody but just wanted to demonstrate in the fashion of the French anarchist-martyr Vaillant that : "It takes a loud noise to make the deaf hear." Since capital punishment could not be awarded in the Assembly Bomb Case the Government combined it with the Lahore Conspiracy Case. The Saunders Murder case) and sentenced Bhagat Singh, Raj Guru and Sukhdev to capital punishment ; they were executed in the Lahore jail on 23 March 1931 and their dead bodies cremated at Hussainiwala off Ferozepur. In Bengal, Surya Sen masterminded the Chittagong Armoury Raid (April 1930) and declared himself the President of the Provisional Independent Government of India. The revolutionaries demonstrated their valour but without much tangible success. Surya Sen could not for long escape the long arm of the police and was arrested and hanged in early 1933.

Another lull in both the revolutionary and non-violent activities came during the political negotiations preceding the enactment of the Government of India Act 1935 and the halting imperialist manoeuvres during 1935–39. The stage of another crisis was reached when the Government of India unilaterally involved India in World War II without consulting Indian opinion. The failure of the Cripps Mission (April 1942), the Quit India Resolution (14 July 1942), the arrest of Gandhi (9 August 1942) was a signal to revolutionary minds to settle old scores. The popular Revolt of 1942 was a struggle in which both the Gandhites and the Revolutionaries made a joint though unsuccessful effort to shake off foreign rule. A new brand of revolutionaries became active under the leadership of Subhash Chandra Bose who sought to uproot British imperialism from India by an armed invasion from abroad under the banner of the I.N.A.

Were the revolutionaries seditionists and enemies of society or true patriots, martyrs and freedom-fighters ? — the question will be defferently answered by the imperial historians and Indian writers. Equally difficult it is to answer the question of the measure of real success achieved through revolutionary terrorist methods. Though the Ghandhites and the Indian National Congress disapproved of Terrorist methods they were not unaware of the spirit of selfless service to the Motherland that inspired the young revolutionaries. Even Ghandhiji appreciated Bhagat Singh's patriotism, his courage and deep love for Indian humanity and observed : "Our heads bend before Bhagat Singh's bravery and sacrifice." The All India Congress Committee, too, observed 18 August 1929 as "Political Sufferers Day" all over India...Further, the second phase of revolutionaries was not merely romanticist and revivalist but gave a socialist orientation to the movement. Above all, the slogan of *Inquilab Zindabad*

(Long Live the Revolution) under which the Gandhites fought the struggle was first popularised by the revolutionaries.

In India today, the freedom revolutionaries are remembered as martyrs who laid down their lives for the cause of the Motherland.

> The nation will remember its martyrs
> By honouring their tombs as places of pilgrimage.[18]

The Third Phase[19] or the Gandhian Era, 1919-1947
(Aim of Swaraj through Non-Violent Non-Cooperation)

During the period the object of the Congress was the attainment of *Swaraj* by all legitimate means within the Empire if possible and without it if necessary. On 31 December 1929 came the unequivocal declaration that *Purna Swaraj* or Complete Independence was the goal of the Congress.

The period was dominated by the personality of Mahatma Gandhi who introduced new ideas into Indian politics. Gandhi deprecated the policy of violence and underground plots but preached open and active resistance to injustice. He advocated the adoption of the policy of *Satyagraha* (literally persistence in Truth), *i.e.*, non-violent non-cooperation towards a government which did not look to the interests of the governed and was high handed and oppressive. The Congress movement gradually became a mass movement. The Congress organisation was considerably stregthened and its constitution made more democratic. The aim of the Congress was the all round improvement of India society. Gandhi used to explain his programme for strengthening India by pointing to the five fingers of his hand, exhorting the people to practise five virtues—spinning, removal of untouchability, sobriety (non-consumption of alcohol or opium), Hindu-Muslim amity and equility for women. The five virtues were to be achieved through non-violent methods.

The Great War of 1914-18 gave a big shock to imperialism by advocating the principle of self-determination. During the war, the Congress gave ample demonstration of loyalty. Mahatma Gandhi showed great enthusiasm and urged the Gujarati peasants to join the army and 'think imperially', if they aimed to win *Swaraj* Gandhi's loyalties earned him the epithet of "Recruiting Sergeant of the Government" and a medal for his services in the war

The Non-Cooperation Movement, 1920-22. The events of the year 1919 greatly disillusioned Gandhi and from a cooperator he turned a non-cooperator. The passing of the Rowlatt Acts

---

18. शहीदों की चिताओं पर लगेंगे हर बरस मेले ।
    वतन पर मरने वालों का यही बाकी निशां होगा ।।

19. Adopting Marxist postulates some scholars have viewed the development and progress of the nationalist movement during this phase in a different light. According to them, the most important development during this period was the unholy alliance between the Indian industrial bourgeoisie and the top Congress coterie under the leadership of Gandhi. The Indian industrial bourgeoisie which had gained considerable strength during the First World War started supporting the Indian National Congress ; the Congress policy of Swadeshism and Boycott of foriegn goods particularly suited it and promoted its class interests. "Thusd" asserts A.R.Desai "from 1918 the Indian industrial bourgeoisie began to exert a powerful influence in determining the programme, policies, strategies, tactics and forms of struggle of the Indian nationalist movement led by the Congress of which Gandhi was the leader." Another important development was the emergence of new social forces in the rise of the industrial working class and the Kisan Sabhas, their political awakening and their direct participation in the nationalist movement as independent political units. These new development which stemmed from Indian industrialization and modernization also revealed the inner contradictions, and evolving tensions and antagonism. The workers' interests lay in fighting not only foreign imperial and capitalist interests but also indigenous capitalists and exploiters. However, the Indian National Congress increasingly became the party of the Indian Bourgeoisie.

The Growth and Development of the Indian National Movement

(abridgement of court procedure in trial of political cases and giving the Executive extensive powers to arrest and detain persons without trial), the Jallianwalla Bagh tragedy (where General Dyer fired at a peaceful crowd killing and wounding thousands) and the Khilafat wrongs gave a new turn to Indian politics.

In support of the Khilafat movement Gandhi inaugurated the Non-cooperation campaign with a bang on 1 August 1920. At its Nagpur session (December 1920) the Congress approved and ratified the policy of Non-violent Non-cooperation towards the unjust Government. The Nagpur session is also memorable for the new Congress Constitution that was adopted. The Congress aim of Swaraj was reaffirmed but now explained to mean "self-government within the empire if possible and outside if necessary". Further, the earlier emphasis on the use of "constitutional means" was substituted by "all peaceful and legitimate methods". The Congress party was organised on modern lines with local Congress Committees at the grass-root village level through sub-divisional, district and provinicial committees with the All India Congress Committee of 350 members at the apex; a Working Committee of 15 was to act as the chief executive. The new Congress constitution really marked the beginning of Gandhian era in Indian politics.

The Khilafat Committee and the Congress agreed upon the triple purpose of Non-Cooperation– satisfactory solution of the Khilafat question, redressal of the Panjab wrong and attainment of Swaraj.

As to the Non-cooperation course of action, the Khilafat Committee in its 6 June 1920 meeting outlined four stages of non-cooperation viz., resignation of titles and honorary posts, resignation from civil services under the Government, resignation from Police and Army services and finally Non-Payment of taxes. The Indian National Congress outlined a seven-item programme of Non-Cooperation viz, (1) surrender of titles and honorary offices, (2) refusal to attend Government durbars and official function, (3) boycott of Government-or Government-aided schools and colleges, (4) boycott of British courts, (5) refusal of all classes to offer themselves for service in Mesopotamia (6) boycott of elections to provincial and central assembly election, and (7) boycott of foreign goods. On the constructive side, people were urged to develop the spirit of discipline and self-sacrifice, to set up national educational institutions, decide their disputes through mutual arbitration, take to hand-spinning, hand-weaving and use of *Swadeshi* goods. Gandhi toured the whole country to whip up enthusiasm of the people. Wherever Gandhi went he gave an impression to each individual that unless he non-cooperated with the Government he would delay *Swaraj*. In 1921 about 30,000 persons courted arrest. Much against the wishes and instructions of Gandhi, the movement led to a serious mob violence at Chauri Chaura in U.P. where a police station was burnt and a number of police officials were killed. Gandhi at once suspended the non-cooperation movement in February[20] 1922 and declared that *Swaraj* had 'stunk in his nostrils' and that without adequate discipline and restraint on the part of the people the movement had proved to be a 'Himalayan blunder'. Gandhi advised constructive work to the people.

Dissatisfied with Gandhi's policies, C.R. Das and Motilal Nehru founded the Swaraj Party. The Swaraj Party adovocated the programme of 'Council entry'. They hoped to wreck the functioning

---

20. Marxist writers, like many nationalists, blame Gandhi for paralysing and demoralising the non-cooperation movement, but explain Gandhi's motivations through their standardized concepts and propositions. They decry Gandhi's petty bourgeois reformist-pacificism capsuled in the innocent-seeming term non-violence. They see the phraseology of non-violence as only a cover, conscious or unconscious, for class interests and maintenance of class exploitation. R.P. Dutt particularly refers to the Midnapor and Guntur No-Rent and No-Tax campaigns where the peasants withheld the payment of rent to the zamindars and taxes to the Government. This development, argues Dutt, revealed the inner contradictions in the Non-Cooperation movement. Alarmed at these threatening developments the Indian bourgeoisie interests associated with Gandhi decided to stay their hands and called off the struggle by the Bardoli decision of the Congress Working Committee on 12 Febuary 1922—leaving the mass movement prostrated and in shambles.

of Legislative Council by a policy of 'uniform continuous and consistent obstruction'. In the elections of 1923, the Swarajists secured an absolute majority in Bengal and the Central Provinces and by their tactics made it impossible for the ministers to function. Gradually the Swarajists. drew towards Gandhiji and his policy of direct action.

To report on the working of the constitution set up by the Government of India Act 1919, the British Government announced the appointment of the Simon Commission in 1927. Lord Birken head justified the exclusion of Indians from the Simon Commission (1927-30) on the plea that there were vital differences among the various Indian political parties and challenged them to produce an agreed constitution and submit it to the Parliament for consideration. The Indians accepted the challenge and the All Parties Conference which met in 1928 appointed a sub-committee presided over by Motilal Nehru to draft a constitution. The committee produced the famous Nehru Report which advocated a constitution based on the principle of responsible government for India on the lines of self-governing dominions within the British Empire. At its Lahore session (29-31 December 1929) the Congress adopted the resolution of Complete Independence for India as its goal. Nehru hoisted the tricolour flag of Indian independence on 1 January 1930.

The Civil Disobedience Movement, 1930–34

Gandhiji who had re-entered active politics in 1928 gave the call for a Civil Disobedience Movement in 1930. The C.D.M. differed from the earlier Non-Coperation Movement (1921-22) in that while the N.C.M. sought to bring the working of the Government, to a stand still by not cooperating with the administration, the C.D.M.aim at paralysing the administration by performance of specific illegal acts. The Mahatma himself started the C.D.M. by breaking the obnoxious Salt laws. On March 12, 1930, Gandhi led by 78 followers started from Sabarmati Ashram on the famous Salt March to Dandi Beach to manufacture illegal salt. Subhash Bose compared the Salt March to Napoleon's March to Paris on his return from Elba. Mr. Brailsford, an English journalist, described the Dandi March as 'the kindergarten stage of revolution' and ridiculed the notion that 'the King Emperor can be unseated by boiling sea water in a kettle'. *The Statesman* of Calcutta sarcastically commented that Gandhi could go no boiling sea water till Dominion Status was attained. The imperialists, however, had miscalculated the moral effects of the civil disobedience movement. Soon the number of volunteers offering *Satyagraha* increased and the number reached 60,000 or even more.

Rapprochement was effected by the famous Gandhi-Irwin Pact (5 March 1931) and the Viceroy declared that Dominion Status was the goal of India's constitutional development. The Civil Disobedience movement was provisionally suspended and Gandhi attended the Second Round Table Conference to discuss the scheme of constitutional reform for India. He returned home towards the end of 1931 greatly disappointed and talked of resuming civil disobedience movement. In January 1932 the Government struck again, arrested Gandhi and other Congress leaders and declared the Congress an illegal organisation. However the C.D.M. gained more popularity and more than 1 lakh persons courted arrest. In 1933 Gandhi confessed failure of the movement and resigned his membership of the Congress and confined his work to the uplift of the Harijans. Nevertheless the years 1928-34 had greatly changed the Congress movement by giving it greater unity, self-confidence, pride and determination. Above all, the Congress became a movement of the masses.

The Great War and the Constitutional Deadlock. The outbreak of the Second World War in September 1939 and the Allied Powers' declaration that they were fighting to save the world for democracy greatly raised the hopes of Indian nationalists. The Congress urged the Government to declare their war aims in clear terms. The British Prime Minister declared that the war aim was self-preservation while another minister announced that Britain's aim in joining the war was to win it. The British Government involved India into war without consulting the people of the country. The Viceroy assumed emergency powers under the Defence of India Rules. Unsatisfied with the Government of India's policies, the Congress ministries resigned in October 1939. In August 1940, the Viceroy announced the famous 'August Offer' proposing the expansion of the Viceroy's Executive Council to constitute it as a War Advisory Council for the purpose of associating Indians in the task of the prosecution of the war. As far as the Congress demand for self-government was concerned, the 'Offer' held the promise to set up after the war a body representative of Indian people to devise the framework of a new constitution for India. The Congress rejected the 'August Offer' as unsatisfactory. On the top of it came Churchill's declaration that Atlantic Charter did not apply to India and that he had not become the Prime Minister of England to preside over the liquidation of the British Empire. The entry of Japan in the war and their remarkable success against, what they called, A.B.C.D. Powers (America, Britain, China and the Dutch) posed a real danger to the safety of India's defences. The shock of Japan's victories in the Far East impelled England to soften her attitude towards India and in March 1942 the British War Cabinet sent Sir Stafford Cripps with new constitutional proposals. The Cripps Plan held the promise of Dominion Status and for that purpose a Constituent Assembly representing the people from British India and Indian States was to be set up after the war : to placate the demands of the Muslim League, the provinces and Indian States were to be given the right to remain out of the proposed federation and form a separate dominion. During the war the Viceroy was to hold all powers in consultative co-operation with the Indian representatives. Thus, the 'Cripps Proposals held promises for the future' with no immediate concessions. The Congress rejected the offer as unsatisfactory. Gandhi described the 'Cripps Offer' as a post-dated cheque, to which someone added the words 'on a failing bank'.

Driven to frustration, in August 1942 the Congress adopted the Quit India Resolution demanding the immediate setting up of a National Government and end of British rule. The Government acted with great promptitude by arresting the top Congress leaders. Rendered leaderless, the people burst out in acts of violence. Repression and coercion descended on India like the London fog. About a thousand persons were killed in police firings while the number of those wounded ran into thousands. In 1944 Gandhi was released and the Quit India Resolution was withdrawn.

In June 1945 Lord Wavell called the representatives of the Congress and the Muslim League at a conference at Simla to discuss a new plan for breaking the constitutional deadlock. The communal impasse wrecked the new proposals. In September 1945, Mr. Attlee, the British Prime Minister, made the historic announcement recognising India's right to independence. A Cabinet Mission comprising Lord Pethick-Lawrence, Sir Stafford Cripps and A.V. Alexander was sent to India in 1946 to discuss with the leaders of Indian opinion the framing of a new Indian constitution. The Cabinet Mission rejected the demand of the Muslim League for a separate sorverign state of Pakistan as impracticable, but tried to meet the wishes of the Muslim League half-way by recommending the grant of great autonomy to the provinces with the additional option to form separate groups with their own executives and legislatures. Only the three subjects of Foreign Affairs, Defence and Communications were reserved for the Union Government and residuary powers were to rest with provinces. The Muslim League found the plan unacceptable and observed 16 August 1946 as Direct Action Day. The League's action was the signal for the beginning of communal riots in Bengal which gradually engulfed the whole of India. Nevertheless, an Interim National Government under the leadership of Pandit Jawahar Lal Nehru was formed at the Centre and the Constituent Assembly held its first session on 9 December 1946.

On February 20, 1947, Prime Minister Attlee announced in the House of Commons the decision of His Majesty's Government to hand over power to the people of India by 30 June 1948 at the latest agreement or no agreement among the various political parties. In March 1947, Mountbatten replaced Wavell as Viceroy of India. Mountbatten came to the conclusion that the only solution of the constitutional impasse was the partition of the country and he won over the Congress leaders to that viewpoint. The Indian Independence Act of 1947 provided for the setting up of the two independent dominions of India and Pakistan with effect from 15 August 1947.

Assessment of Gandhi's Role[21] in India's Struggle for Independence. Gandhi emerged as a new Messiah in Indian politics in 1919 and completely dominated Indian Politics down to 1947. How complete was Gandhi's influence in Indian politics should be clear from Jawahar Lal's assessment. Writing in 1945 Nehru wrote, "Gandhiji's influence is not limited to those who agree with him or accept him as a National Leader, it extends to those also who disagree with him and criticize him...To the vast majority of Indian's people he is the symbol of India determined to be free, of militant nationalism, of a refusal to submit to arrogant might, of never agreeing to anything involving national dishonour. Though many people in India may disagree with him on a hundred matters, though they may criticize him or even part company from him on some particular issue, at a time of action and struggle when India's freedom is at stake they flock to him and look up to him as their inevitable leader'[22]

Mahatma Gandhi was an heir to the political traditions of both the Moderates and the Extremists and attempted not only a synthesis of the best in their thinking but gave it a more practical and dynamic turn. The dichotomy between social and political work which had divided the Moderate and the Extremist leaders no longer worried Gandhi, for his emphasis was that politics should be made an agent for social change. His concept of *Swaraj* was that of Ram Rajya or Kingdom of God on earth which worked for the benefit of the masses. The early nationalist leaders like M.G. Ranade, Dadabhai Naoroji, R.C. Dutt, and even Tilak, Lajpat Rai and B.C. Pal spoke at length about the poverty of the masses and Britain's exploitative role in India but hardly did anything for the amelioration of the lot of the poor masses. Gandhi made it clear that the Congress represented the dumb, semi-starved millions scattered over the length and breadth of India and he initiated practical steps to better their social and economic lot. His emphasis on eradication of untouchability, uplift of the Harijans, setting up of Udyog Sangh (Village Industies Association), the Cow Protection Association, the Talimi Sangh (the Basic Education Society), revival of Khadi industry and adoption of hand-spun and hand-woven cloth as the national uniform were all calculated to improve the lot of the poor masses living in the villages.

As a fighter for India's freedom, Gandhi had no peer. He was a saint-politician who employed moral means for the attainment of political ends. He used 'soul-force' against brute force. Through his plotical compaigns of Non-cooperation Movement of 1920-22, Civil Disobedience Movement of 1930–34, the Individual Civil Disobedience Movement of 1940-41 and the Quit India Movement of 1942-45 Gandhi tried to convince (pressurize ?) the alien rulers to see the justness of India's cause. He used legal and extra-legal methods but never immoral or dishonest means to achieve his objectives. Fearlessly launching the policy of 'unadulterated non-cooperation' with the imperial power of Britain, Gandhi wrote on 24 May 1942, "Leave India in God's hands, in modern parlance' to anarchy and that anarchy may lead to internecine warfare for a time or to unrestrained dacoities. From these a true India will arise in place of the false one we see". Gandhi would accept no argument—old or new—for continuance of British rule in India. Replying to the argument that Britain alone could defend India against Japanese

---

21. Marxist dialecticians have viewed Gandhi's role differently. R.P. Dutt, for example, refers to Gandhi's personal idiosyncrasies and capacity for dishonest quibbling and lebels him as 'the ascetic defender of property" the mascot of the bourgeoisie' and in actual achievement-statistics as 'the Jonah of revolution', 'the general of unbroken disasters' and 'the best guarantee of the shipwreck of any mass movement which had the blessing of his association' Gandhi is also viewed as the rising hope of the bourgeoisie (as also of imperialism) and capable of unleashing the pressure of a mass movement or the mere threat of a mass movement just enough to extract the most favourable terms for the Indian bourgeoisie from British imperialism, at the same time fully capable of saving India from revolutionary mass movement. In 1934 Gandhi resigned from the membership of the Congress but (it is alleged) operated from behind the scenes. During 1939-40 and again in 1942 Gandhi, the Generalissimo of the Congress, again assumed direct leaderdhip only to prove 'a heavy liability for the Indian national movement.'

22. J.L.Nehru : *The Discovery of India*, p.422.

aggression, Gandhi wrote on May 1942, "The presence of the British in India is an invitation to Japan to invade India. Their withdrawal removes the bait. Assume, however it does not free India will be better able to cope with the invasion". On 14 July 1942 the Congress Working Committee passed the 'Quit India' resolution, demanding that "British rule in India must end immediately" and affirming its view that freedom of India "was neccessary not only in the interest of India but also for the safety of the world and for the ending of Nazism, Fascism, Militarism and other forms of imperialism, and the aggression of one nation over another."

What were the effects of Gandhi's political campaigns Gandhian methods and techniques rich dividends. Not only was the hatred for slavery and love for freedom firmly planted in the Indians mind but the imperial rulers also came to realize that British rule in India was wrong and unjust. The ruling circles in Britain realized that Gandhi and the Congress could arouse the masses against the Government at any time and make its functioning difficult and he could repeat this performance whenever he liked. On the basis of his conversation with Winston Churchill, George VI noted in his diary on 28 July 1942, "He (Churchill) amazed me by saying that his colleagues and both, or all three parties in Parliament were quite prepared to give up India to the Indians after the war. He felt they had already been talked in to giving up India. Cripps, the Press and the U.S. public opinion have all contributed to make their minds up that our rule in India is wrong and has always been wrong for India".[23] Thus Gandhian methods convinced the rulers that transfer of power into Indian hands was inevitable and it could no longer be delayed.

Gandhi was a unique national figure. He combined in himself the role of a prophet, a Hindu religious reformer, a social reformer and a nationalist fighting the struggle for Indian independence for the humanity in general he had the message of non-violence and *ahimsa*; he wanted to purge Hindu religion of its dogmas and superstitions ; he worked for a new social order of social equality bereft of the evils of castism and untouchability ; as a nationalist he became a symbol of democracy, individual and national freedom.

The impact of 'Gandhi's personality on Hindu-Muslim relations and unity of the country has been variously assessed. Penderel Moon blames Gandhi for a rapid Hiduising of the Congress which proved injurious to the cause of Indian unity. He writes : "This Hinduising of the national movement, which Gandhi's leadership promoted and symbolised, was injurious and ultimately fatal to Hindu-Muslim unity...At the more conscious level of political bargaining he can be blamed for repeated failure to come to terms with leaders of Muslim opinion. His Congress colleagues must share the blame and, of course blame also attaches to the Muslim politicians and, to some extent, to the British who at a crucial time showed little interest in bringing the parties together. But the largest share of responsibility for the failure to reach an agreement that could have preserved Indian unity appears to fall on Gandhi and the Congress–though it was they who most desired to preserve it."[24]

Mohit Sen, an Indian communist, writes : "As in the case of Tilak, the criticism is made that the language of Gandhiji, his prayer meetings, his insistence on non-violence and the rest helped to spread communalism or at least brought grist to the mill of the communalists. This appears to be unbalanced criticism. The main result of the work and preaching of Gandhiji was the partial turning of the awakened Hindu masses to secularism and nationalism and from communalism and casteism. He did not succeed completely by any means, as the partition tragedy only too grimly showed. Nevertheless, more than any other single individual on a massive scale he was able to place a picture of a secular India and of communal unity. The fact that India chose to remain a secular republic is in a large measure due to him. The Hindu communalist felt at an enormous disadvantage in compating him since it was impossible to contest the "Indianness" or the "Hinduness" of the man or to dispute that

---

23. J.W. Wheeler : *King George VI : His Life and Reign*, p. 703.
24. Penderel Moon : *Gandhi and Modern India*, pp. 276.

what he was telling the people sprang from the very depths of the traditions of India.

The grateful Indian nation paid its tribute to Gandhiji's memory through the resolution passed by the Indian Parliament on 24 December 1969. It reads:

"That this House, on the occasion of the centenary year of Mahatma Gandhi, pays its respectful tribute to the memory of the Father of the nation, who led the country to Swarajya by non-violent means, who infused a new spirit into the massess, who uplifted the teaming milions of the oppressed and the downtrodden, who awakened the national conscience of the people, and who inspired the people with a spirit of dedication and service; places on record its deep gratitude to that Apostle of Ahimsa who crusaded of peace, justice and equality and gave the strife-ridden world the message of universal brotherhood and humanism; and rededicates itself to promote the high ideals of Truth, non-violence and service to the nation and to humanity, for which the Mahatma lived and sacrificed his life."

RESUME

PHASES IN THE POLITICO-ECONOMIC PROGRAMME OF THE INDIAN NATIONAL CONGRESS

A significant development in the second half of the 19th century India was the spread of English system of education which in its turn became the channel for growth of political consciousness, nationalism, self-government, civil rights etc. This new system of education brought into existence a middle class intelligentsia which largely voiced the public opinion in India and became the spokesman of New India.

Demand for Moderate Concessions (1885-1905). During the first two decades of the Indian National Congress (1885-1905) the Congress did not demand Swaraj, but asked only for some constitutional concessions and administrative reforms like equal opportunities for Indians in the ICS. Most important was the emphasis on individual liberties and extension of the Rule of Law. On the economic front, the Congress leaders discovered the inherent contradictions in British and Indian economic interests. At the second Congress Session (1886) at Calcutta, a resolution was passed on "increasing Indian Poverty" which was attributed largely to British discriminatory economic policies towards India. From this basic realisation, the theory of Drain of Wealth from India gradually emerged.

Demand for Swaraj (1906). During the first decade of the 20th century the aim of the Congress was spelt out to be the "attainment of Swaraj" (though the full connotations of the word Swaraj were not spelt out). The economic aspect became very relevant when the Swadeshi Movement was launched with the programme of Economic Boycot of British-made goods, use of Swadeshi or home-made products to encourage Indian industries and provide Indian people with more opportunities for work and employment. Thus, Swadeshism was not only an economic or a social or a political movement but it became an all-comprehensive movement extending to the entire spectrum of national life.

Mahatma Gandhi and Beginning of Mass Nationalism. The Indian expectations of getting the right of self-determination after World War I were belied by the constitutional fraud *i.e.* the Government of India Act (1919) and the policy by blind repression followed by the Government of India after the enactment of the Rowlatt Act in 1919. The post-war economic depression coupled with the Government's manipulation of £-Re-exchange ratio brought bad days for the common man. Jawaharlal Nehru summed up the situation of all-round gloom thus: "We seemed to be helpless in the grip of some all-powerful monster; our limbs were paralysed, our minds deadened. The peasantry were servile and fear-ridden; the industrial workers were no better. The middle classes, the intelligentsia, who might have been beacon-light in the enveloping-darkness, were themselves submerged in this all-prevailing gloom".

The Jallianwala Bagh Tragedy (13th April 1919) and the following reign of terror unleashed in the Punjab coupled with the Khilafat Issue compelled the Hindus and Muslims to organise a joint front against the repressive policies of the British Government in India. The Non-cooperation Movement (1920-22) brought the rural masses also in the Freedom Struggle. Even students and women participated in the National Movement. All this made the Congress a movement of the masses. Henceforth, the Congress became a genuine revolutionary organisation.

Demand for *Purna Swaraj* (1929). An unequivocal definition of Swaraj came from the Congress Session held at Lahore in December 1929. It declared: "Swaraj in Article I of the Congress Constitution shall mean complete independence". On the midnight of 31st December 1929 the Congress Tricolour Flag of Indian Independence was unfurled by the Congress President, Pt. Jawaharlal Nahru at Lahore. The Salt Satyagraha (March-April 1930) and the Civil Disobedience Movement (1930-34) that followed demonstrated not only to Indians but to the whole world that the final liquidation of British Imperial rule in India could not be delayed for long.

The Emergence of Left Ideology. The 20's and 30's of the 20th century witnessed the development of the Left ideologies and a powerful Socialist trend developed in the nationalist movement. The Communist party of India came into existence. The Socialist ideas influenced national leaders like Jawaharlal Nehru, Subhas Chandra Bose, a large number of socialist-minded groups and individuals. Within the Congress Party socialist ideas made a dent and the Congress Socialist Party was organised in 1934. It may be no exaggeration to state that throughout the 1920's, 1930's, and 1940's the youthful elements (including the revolutionaries) were, greatly influenced by socialist ideas.

The Karachi Session of the Congress (1931). The socialist radicalism found reflection in the 45th session of the All India Congress held at Karachi (29–31 March) under the presidentship of Sardar Vallabbhai Patel.

"The Karachi Congress passed the following resolution on Fundamental Rights and Duties and Economic Programme:

This Congress is of opinion that to enable the masses to appreciate what "Swaraj," as conceived by the Congress, will mean to them, it is desirable to state the position of the Congress in a manner easily understood by them. In order to end the exploitation of the masses, political freedom must include real economic freedom of the straving millions. The Congress therefore, declares that any constitution which may be agreed to on its behalf should provide, or enable the Swaraj Government to provide for the following:

Fundamental Rights and Duties. Every citizen of India has the right of free expression of opinion, the right of free association and combination, and the right to assemble peacefully and without arms, for purposes not opposed to law or morality.

Every citizen shall enjoy freedom of conscience and the right freely to profess and practise his religion, subject to public order and morality.

The culture, language and script of the minorities and of the different linguistic areas shall be protected.

All citizens are equal before the law, irrespective of religion, caste, creed or sex.

No disability attaches to any citizen, by reason of his or her religion, caste, creed or sex, in regard to public employment, office of power or honour, and in the exercise of any trade or calling.

All citizens have equal rights and duties in regard to wells, tanks, roads, schools and places of public resort, maintained out of State or local funds, or dedicated by private persons for the use of the general public.

Every citizen has the right to keep and bear arms, in accordance with regulations and reservations made in that behalf.

No person shall be deprived of his liberty nor shall his dwelling or property be entered, sequestered, or confiscated, save in accordance wih law.

The State shall observe neutrality in regard to all religions. The franchise shall be on the basis of universal adult suffrage.

The State shall provide for free and compulsory primary education.

The State shall confer no titles.

There shall be no capital punishment.

Every citizen is free to move throughout India and to stay and settle in any part thereof, to acquire property and to follow any trade or calling, and to be treated equally with regard to legal prosecutions or protection in all parts of India.

Labour. The organisation of economic life must conform to the principle of justice, to the end that it may secure a decent standard of living.

The State shall safeguard the interests of industrial workers and shall secure for them, by suitable legislation and in other ways, a living wage, healthy conditions of work, limited hours of labour, suitable machinery for the settlement of disputes between employers and workmen, and protection against the economic consequences of old age, sickness and unemployment.

Labour to be freed from serfdom and conditions bordering on serfdom.

Protection of women workers, and specially, adequate provision for leave during maternity period.

Children of school going age shall not be employed in mines and factories.

Peasants and workers shall have the right to form unions to protect their interests.

Taxation and Expenditure. The system of land tenure and revenue and rent shall be reformed and an equitable adjustment made of the burden on agricultural land, immediately giving relief to the smaller peasantry, by a substantial reduction of agricultural rent and revenue now paid by them, and in case of uneconomic holdings, exempting them from rent so long as necessary, with such relief as may be just and necessary to holders of small estates affected by such exemption or reduction in rent, and to the same end, imposing a graded tax on net incomes from land above a reasonable minimum.

Death duties on a graduated scale shall be levied on property above a fixed minimum.

There shall be a drastic reduction of military expenditure so as to bring it down to at least one half of the present scale.

Expenditure and salaries in civil departments shall be largely reduced. No servant of the State, other than specially employed experts and the like, shall be paid above a certain fixed figure, which should not ordinarily exceed Rs. 500 per month.

No duty shall be levied on salt manufactured in India.

Economic and Social Programme. The State shall protect indigenous cloth; and for this purpose pursue the policy of exclusion of foreign cloth and foreign yarn from the country and adopt such other measures as may be found necessary. The State shall also protect other indigenous indusries, when necessary, against foreign competition.

Intoxicating drinks and drugs shall be totally prohibited, except for medicinal purposes.

Currency and exchange shall be regulated in the national interests.

The State shall own or control key industries and services, mineral resources, railways, waterways, shipping and other means of public transport.

Relief of agricultural indebtedness and control of usury—direct and indirect.

The State shall provide the military training of citizens so as to organise a means of national defence apart from the regular military forces.

The Faizpur Congress Session (December 1936). On the political front the Congress reiterated the "entire rejection of the Government of India Act, 1935", and put forward the demand for a Constituent Assembly elected by adult suffrage. It also resolved that this Congress demand should be supported by "a mass agitation outside to enforce the right of the Indian people to self-determination."

Agrarian Programme: A resolution was passed to draw up an All-India Agrarian Programme. It reiterated that "the most important and urgent problem of the country is the appalling poverty, unemployment and indebtedness of the peasantry" and expressed the Congress conviction that the final solution of this problem involves the removal of British Imperial exploitation and a radical change in the antiquated and repressive land tenure and revenue systems."

As an interim measure a 13 point programme was suggested which demanded substantial reduction in rent and revenue, exemption from rent on uneconomic holdings, lowering of canal and irrigation rates, fixity of tenure, relief in rural debt; provision for a living wage for agricultural labour and, above all, recognition of Peasant Unions; introduction of cooperative farming, wiping out of rent arrears etc.

The New National Agenda

The 1930s and 1940s witnessed a multidimensional thrust for removal of India's backwardness—social, economic, political and even cultural. The Congress Election Manifesto for 1937 elections and later of 1945-46 elections were indicative of the multidimensional approach to pull India out of backwardness.

After Indian Independence (1947) although India has made great progress on the socio-economic front yet Mahatma Gandhi's ideal of "wiping off every tear from every eye" remains a distant dream.

SELECT REFERENCES

1. Argov, Daniel : *Moderates and Extremists in the Indian Nationalist Movement.*
2. Chandra, Bipin : *The Rise and Growth of Economic Nationalism.*
3. Gallagher, J.A. et al : *Locality, Province and Nation.*
4. Grover, B.L. : *A Documentary Study of British Policy Towards Indian Nationalism.*
5. Low, D.A. (Ed.) : *Congress and the Raj.*
6. Majumdar, R.O. : *History and Culture of the Indian People, vols. X, XI.*
7. Mclane, J., : *Indian Nationalism and the Early Congress.*
8. Mehrotra, S.R. : *The Emergence of the Indian National Congress.*
9. Sarkar, Sumit : *The Swadeshi Movement in Bengal.*

10.	Seal, Anil	:	*The Emergence of Indian Nationalism.*
11.	Strokes, Eric	:	*The Peasant and the Raj.*
12.	Tripathi, Amales	:	*The Extremist Challenge.*
13.	Wolpert. S.A.	:	*Tilak and Gokhale.*
14.	Brown, Judith M.	:	*Gandhi's Rise to Power, 1915-22.*
15.	Brown, Judith M.	:	*Gandhi and Civil Disobedience, 1928-34.*
16.	Desai, A.R.	:	*Social Background of Indian Nationalism.*
17.	Dutt, R.P.	:	*India Today.*
18.	Tara Chand	:	*History of Freedom Movement in India.*

34

EMINENT NATIONAL LEADERS OF INDIA

Rammohan Roy, 1774-1833

Rammohan Roy is popularly remembered as 'the Father of the Indian Renaissance', 'a peak in the panorama of modern coming culture and civilisation', 'a prophet of humanism', 'a progenitor and Father of Modern India.' Commenting on the Renaissance in India initiated by Rammohan Roy, Prof. J.N. Sarkar described it as "the beginning...of a glorious dawn, the like of which the history of the world has not seen elsewhere...truly a Renaissance, wider, deeper and more revolutionary than that of Europe after the fall of Constantinople."

Rammohan Roy was born in a Bengali Brahmin family at Radhanagar in 1774. His ancestors were landholders and had seen service under the nawabs of Bengal and were recipients of titles. Rammohan received his early education in his home town and acquired some proficiency in Bengali, Persian and Sanskrit. In the 1790s he travelled in northern India and spent some time in the Himalayas where he seemed to have acquired some knowledge of Buddhist doctrines. His liberal education gave Rammohan a good grounding in Hinduism, Buddhism and Islamic theology and prepared his mind for a comparative study of all religions.

In 1803 Roy accepted service under the East India Company and was attached to Digby as Diwan taught Roy English and introduced him to Western liberal and rationalist thought. In 1814 Rammohan retired from service and settled in Calcutta and embarked on a glorious career of public service and reform. In 1815 Rammohan founded the Atmiya Sabha to propagate the monotheistic doctrines of Hinduism.

Indian society had variously reacted to Western culture. At one end was the Old Order—represented by India princes and religious fanatics–who saw all evils in Western thought, values and British policies in India. At the other end were Bengali Radicals–popularly referred to as the 'Young Bengal' group, the first generation of the English-educated youngmen—who had all praise for Western thought, social values, great veneration for Christianity and a general disgust for Eastern Culture and Indian religions. Rammohan Roy followed a middle path between these two extreme groups. He had all praise for Western rationalism, scientific outlook, humanitarianism but refused to turn a blind eye to Indian culture and Indian religions. Roy sharply reacted to the propaganda and abusive language used by Christian missionaries about Indian cultures and religion and wrote in the *Bengal Harkaru* "If by the Ray of Intelligence which the *Christian* says we are indebted to the English, he means the introduction of useful mechanical arts, I am ready to express my assent and also my gratitude, but with respect to *Science, Literature or Religion,* I do not acknowledge that we are placed under any obligation. For by a reference to History it may be proved that the world was indebted to *our ancestors* for the first dawn of knowledge, which sprang up in the East, and thanks to the Goddess of Wisdom, we have still a philosophical and copious language of our own, which distinguishes us from nations who cannot express scientific or abstract ideas without borrowing the language of foreigners."

Rammohan's Role in Modernization of India

Rammohan's mind was set at a synthesis of the best in the East and the West in the Indian setting. He is truly remembered as the modernizer of India because his multifarious activities—his efforts towards social and religious reforms, his zeal for the spread of Western system of education, his advocacy of civil rights, liberty of the press, support for constitutional movements in the world—all played a part in promoting in India a liberal, cosmopolitan and modern outlook.

In the field of social reform, Rammohan can be justly called the Morning Star of social reformation in India. His great objective was to get a better treatment for women in society. The efforts he made for the abolition of the barbarous and inhuman custom of *sati* are too well known to be detailed here. He was far in advance of his contemporaries when he defended women's rights to remarriage and pleaded for change in the law of inheritance of property in favour of women. Roy advocated prohibition of polygamous marriages and child marriages. Above all, he well realized that women could not hope to get a status of social equality with men unless they received opportunities for education. Hence, Roy became a strong supporter of women education.

Rammohan launched a frontal attack on another evil of Hindu society—casteism. He realized that the caste system had reduced the social organism to a purely biological function and impeded growth of unity and solidarity among the Indian people. He wrote, "The distinction of castes, introducing innumerable divisions and subdivisions among them (Hindus) has entirely deprived them of patriotic feeling...we have been subjected to such insults for about nine centuries, and the cause of degradation has been...our division into castes which has been the source of want of unity among us." Roy suggested the adoption of the Saiva form of marriage to remove all discrimination of caste and race.

Rammohan's attitude towards religion and religious matters was utilitarian and he has been assessed as 'a religious Benthamite'. He judged different religions not so much from the point of view of the 'basic truth' in them but from their social usefulness. His emphasis was on the ethico-religious thought common to all religions of the world. That is why he emphasised the unity underlying all religions. His practical mind found expression in the foundation of the Brahmo Samaj. The aim of the Brahmo Samaj was something to which all religions could subscribe, namely the worship and adoration of the Eternal, Unsearchable and Immutable Being, who is the Author and Preserver of the universe'. Keshab chandra Sen explained Rammohan's creed as contained in the trust deed for the Brahmo Samaj thus : "The Brahmo Samaj was established to bring together the peoples of the world, irrespective of caste, creed' and country, at the feet of the One Eternal God."

In matters of development and spread of education, Roy's emphasis was on the growth of English educaion in India. Here Roy's view was that liberal education of the Wesern type alone could help remove 'the darkness of ignorance' and help in the progress of society ; further English education alone could enable Indians to take part in the administration of the country and public activities for the benefit of the people. Fortified with this conviction Roy wrote in a forthright language to Lord Amherst in December 1823, "The Sanskrit system of education would be the best calculated to keep this country in darkness, if such had been the policy of the British legislature. But as the improvement of the native population is the object of the Government, it will consequently promote a more liberal and enlightened system of instruction, embracing Mathematics, Natural Philosophy, Chemistry, Anatomy, with other useful sciences, which may be accomplished with the sums proposed by employing a few gentlemen of talent and learning educated in Europe and providing a college furnished with necessary books, instruments and other apparatus".

As far his political ideas, Roy accepted British rule as a *fait accompli* and believed that it would work as a 'regenerative force' for the advancement of India. In this matter Rammohan was a forerunner of the Indian Liberal thinkers of the 19th century. He explained his conviction to Victor Jecquemont : "India requires many more years of English domination so that she might not have many things to lose, while she is reclaiming her political independence". It was in this spirit that Rammohan advocated European colonisation of India. It was Roy's political faith that British rule, British tutelage alone could launch India into the modern world of rational thought, civil and political liberty and a highly civilised free country of the world.

Roy did not ask for responsible government, but did demand wide-ranging administrative reforms like a better judicial system separation of executive from judicial functions, wider share for Indians in the services and, above all, liberty of the press.

Roy's passionate love for freedom had cosmopolitan sympathies and he made no secret of his views. For example, when the Holy Alliance Powers (the despotic group of powers comprising Czarist Russia, Austria and Prussia) crushed the popular movement in Naples, the Raja's heart was so greatly depressed that he cancelled an evening engagement with Mr. Buckingham and wrote to him, "From the late unhappy news I am obliged to conclude that I shall not live to see liberty universally restored to the nations of Europe and Asiatic nations, especially those that are European colonies". Again, in 1821 the Raja celebrated in Calcutta the establishment of a constitutional government in Spain. Brajendranath Seal has correctly pointed out that Rammohan pointed the way to the solution of the larger problem of international culture and civilisation in human history and became a precursor...a prophet of coming humanity."

An Assessment of Rammohan's Work. Critics have pointed out that Roy's successes in the matter of social and religious reforms were limited. Again, Prof. Hiren Mukerjee has pointed out the ineptness of the comparison between the Indian Renaissance of 19th century and European Renaissance of 15th century which changed the face of Europe and the world. Rammohan did indeed attempt to effect a synthesis between the cultures of the East and West, but it was a synthesis of the lower order. "The true synthesis" as Prof. Susobhan Sircar has pointed out "lies in the fusion of two opposites into a third higher entity which supersedes the earlier stages of development. Where is that higher third in our renaissance ?"

It must be pointed out that like great men of all ages, Rammohan was greater for what he was than for what he achieved. Conceding the limitations imposed by the age which Rammohan lived, he was certainly a man of vision who rose gloriously above his contemporaries.

Select Opinions

Rabindranath Tagore. Rammohan was the only person in his time...to realize completely the significance of the modern age. He knew that the ideal of human civilization does not lie in isolation of independence, but in the brotherhood of inter-dependence of individuals as well as nations. His attempt was to establish our peoples on the full consciousness of their own cultural personality, to make them comprehend the reality of all that was unique... in their civilization, and simultaneously to make them approach other civilisations in the spirit of sympathetic co-operation.

Sumit Sarkar. Rammohan's achievements as a modernizer were thus both limited and extremely ambivalent. What is involved in this estimate is not really his personal stature, which was certainly quite outstanding ; the limitations were basically those of his times—which marked the beginning of a transition, indeed, from the precapitalist society, but in the direction, not of full-blooded bourgeois modernity, but of a weak and distorted caricature of the same which was all that colonial subjection permitted.

Barun De. Rammohan's political and economic ideas merit veneration only by those who worship the history of Indian's liberalism. Yet, it is also possible to place them in the stark perspective of the failure of the Indian liberal bourgeoisie to solve the problem of mass poverty, which has been created by the imperialism from which Rammohan could hardly break away. This is a perspective which is as dark as that of 18th century India against which Rammohan has been glorified by Brajendranath Seal, Rabindranath Tagore, Susobhan Chandra Sarkar and others. In the last resort, the *Harkaru* had a point in 1832, when it said about his evidence to the House of Commons Committee : "One must be hammer or anvil in this world" says an old Spanish proverb, "Rammohan Roy, it is clear, belongs to the hammers and...is taken for the anvils."

Dadabhai Naoroji, 1825–1917

Dadabhai Naoroji reverentially remembered as the Grand Old Man of India was associated with the Indian National Congress right from its inception. In the words of Pattabhi Sitaramayya, Naoroji began "his connection with the Congress from its very outset, continued to serve it till the evening of his life, and took it through the whole gamut of evolution, from the humble position of being a people's organ seeking redress of administrative grievances to that of a National Assembly working for the definite object of attaining *Swaraj*".

Dadabhai Naoroji was born at Khadak (Maharashtra) in the house of a poor Parsi priest. He studied at the Elphinstone College where he was acclaimed by an English Professor as "the promise of India". He started his career as an Assistant Professor of Mathematics and Natural Philosophy in his old *Alma Mater,* but in 1855 left the teaching Profession and proceeded to London as a partner in a Parsi firm. In 1862 he left the Camas and started his own business, but was not very successful. In 1869 he returned to Bombay. In 1873 he accepted the office of the Diwan of Baroda, but left it in disgust. He was elected to the Bombay Municipal Corporation and later the Town Council. In 1892 he had the signal honour of being the first Indian to become a Member of the House of Commons on the Liberal Party's ticket from Finsbury. He was President of the Indian National Congress thrice, in 1886, 1893 and 1906.

From his early life Dadabhai was active in taking steps for the social and political advantage of his countrymen. He founded *Dnyan Prasarak Mandali* and founded a Girls High School at Bombay. The credit for establishing the Bombay Association in 1852, the first political association of its type in the Bombay Presidency, also goes to Dadabhai. During his stay in England, from 1855 to 1869, he spared no efforts in educating British public on Indian affairs through the London Indian Association and the East India Association. These services of his in England made him a national hero in the eyes of his countrymen.

In politics Dadabhai was conscious of the numerous benefits that India derived from British rule in India and pledged "loyalty to the backbone" to the British crown and desired "the permanent continuance" of British rule in India (Calcutta session, 1886). As the Congress movement passed the period of adolescence, it demanded Swaraj. Although Tilak was the first to raise the slogan 'Swaraj is my birthright and I shall have it,' the credit for demanding Swaraj from the Congress platform for the first time goes to Dadabhai Naoroji. Delivering his Presidential address at the Calcutta session of the Congress (1906) Naoroji said, "We do not ask for favours, We want only justice. Instead of going into any further divisions or details of our rights as British citizens the whole matter can be comprised in one word Self-government or Swaraj like that of the United Kingdom or the Colonies.' Naoroji had faith in British sense of Justice and fairplay. "The day, I hope," he said "is not distant when the world will see the noblest spectacle of a great nation like the British holding out the hand of true fellow citizenship and of justice" and again in 1906, "Indians are British citizens and are entitled to and claim all British citizens' rights."

Dadabhai exposed the exploitive nature of British rule in India. He was the first Indian to draw the attention of the Indians as well as the British public to the drain of wealth from India to Great Britain and the resulting poverty of the Indians. In his monumental book *Poverty and un-British Rule in India* published in 1901, he piled up statistics to prove his thesis. In a letter to J.T. Sunderland in 1905, he wrote, "The lot of India is a very sad one. Her condition is that of a master and a slave ; but it is worse: it is that of a plundered nation in the hands of constant plunderers with the plunder carried away clean out of the land. In the case of plundering raids occasionally made on India before the English came the invaders went away and there were long intervals of security during which the land could recuperate and become again rich and prosperous. But nothing of the kind is true now. The British invasion is continuous and the plunder goes right on, with no intermission and actually increases and the impoverished Indian nation has no opportunity whatever to recuperate."

C.Y. Chintamani paid Naoroji a rich tribute when he wrote, "The public life of India has been adored by a galaxy of brilliant intellects and selfless patriots, but there has been in our time none comparable with Dadabhai Naoroji," while G.K. Gokhale said, "If ever there is the divine in man, it is in Dadabhai." Dadabhai was a unique figure in Indian history, verily an Indian Gladstone.

Gopal Krishna Gokhale, 1866-1915

Gopal Krishna Gokhale was a follower of Mahadeva Govind Ranade, popularly known as the Socrates of Maharashtra. "Never had a guru", writes Dr. Zacharias, "a more apt pupil than Ranade in Gokhale." Like his master Ranade, Gokhale was a strong believer in the policy of moderation and sweet reasonableness. Gokhale was Gandhiji's guru.

Gopal Krishna Gokhale was born on 9 May 1866 in a Maratha Brahmin family at Kolhapur. After graduation in 1884, Gokhale joined the Deccan Educational Society founded by Ranade. He served the society for twenty years in various capacities as a school-master, a professor and Principal of Fergusson College, Poona. He also edited the Quarterly Journal of the Poona Sarvajanik Sabha.

Gokhale made his first appearance at the Congress platform at the Allahabad session in 1899. In 1897 he along with Mr. Wacha was selected to give evidence before the Welby Commission on Indian Expenditure. In 1902 he was elected to the Bombay Legislative Council and later to the Imperial Legislative Council. In the Council, Gokhale made his mark as an eloquent and persuasive speaker. He possessed the knack of saying of the hardest thing in the gentlest language. In the Legislative Council Gokhale greatly criticised the Indian official finance and spoke with considerable insight on the annual budgets. He attacked the Salt Tax and proved with facts and figures how a basket of salt costing 3 pies was sold at 5 annas. He also exposed the hollowness of the British pretensions in the matter of appointment of Indians to higher services. Commenting on the Government's open declaration in 1894 that "the highest posts must for all time to come be held by Europeans", Gokhale said that "the pledges of equal treatment which England has given us have supplied us with a high and worthy ideal for our Nation and if these pledges are repudiated, one of the strongest claims of British Rule to our attachment will disappear." He worked as Joint Secretary of the Indian National Congress and later in 1905 presided over the Berares session. In 1906 he went to England to educate the British public about the situation created by the Partition of Bengal and played a great part, officially and unofficially, in the formulation of the Minto-Morley Reforms of 1909. In 1910 Gokhale was again elected to the Imperial Legislative Council. He also served as a Member of the Indian Public Service Commission (1912–15) and urged it to increase the share of Indians in higher services. During 1910–13 Gokhale made heroic efforts in the Imperial Legislative Council for the introduction of free and compulsory education throughout India.

In his political philosophy Gokhale was a true liberal. He was a staunch believer in moderation and sweet reasonableness. He was firmly convinced that regeneration of the country could not be achieved "amid a hurricane of political excitement." He appealed to the better nature and sense of fairplay of the English public. He believed in purity of aims and purity of actions. It were really these principles that attracted Gandhi who became Gokhale's political pupil.

Gokhale clearly saw the reactionary role of the Anglo-Indian bureaucracy. Commenting on the rules framed in India for representation to the Imperial Legislative Council under the Act of 1892 he said, "I will not say that they have been deliberately so framed as to defeat the object of the Act of 1892, but I will say this, that if the officer who drafted them had been asked to sit down with the deliberate purpose of framing a scheme to defeat that object, he could not have done better."

Gokhale played the difficult role of an intermediary between the rulers and the ruled. He interpreted popular aspirations to the Viceroy and the Government's difficulties to the Congress. This, on occasions, made him unpopular with both. The Extremists in the Congress found fault with his moderation and dubbed him a 'faint-hearted Moderate,' while the Government on occasions charged him with holding extremist views and being 'a seditionist in disguise'. On 31 October 1907, Minto

---

1. B.L. Grover: *A Documentary Study of British Policy Towards Indian Nationalism.* p. 246.
2. *Ibid.*, p. 245.

wrote to Morely about Gokhale, "As a party-manager Gokhale is a baby...he is always whining just like the second-rate Irishmen, between Dan O'Connell and Parnell".[1] Morely distrusted him and described him as a "turning fork."[2] Gokhale put forward his views in a very candid language, "The Englishman who imagines that India can be governed much longer on the same lines as in the past, and the Indian who thinks that he must seek a destiny for his country outside this Empire, of which now, for better or worse, we are a part–both alike show an inadequate appreciation of the realities of the present situation."

In 1905 Gokhale laid the foundation of the Servants of India Society with a view to "the training of national missionaries for the service of India, and to promote, by all constitutional means, the true interests of the Indian people". This society has trained social workers of the stature of V. Srinivas Shastri, G.K. Devadhar, N.M. Joshi, Pandit Hirdaya Nath Kunzru and is a standing monument to the spirit of service of society whose true embodiment was Gopal Krishna Gokhale.

Mrs. Sarojini Naidu called Gokhale a rare combination of "the practical, strenuous worker and the mystic dreamer of dreams".

Bal Gangadhar Tilak, 1856–1920

Tilak reverentially remembered by Indians as Lokamanya and the 'Uncrowned King of India' played a leading part in popularizing the cult of patriotism and making the Congress movement broadbased.

Tilak was born in a Maratha Brahmin family at Ratnagiri. After taking a degree in Law in 1879, Tilak planned in collaboration with Agarkar the establishment of institutions to impart cheap education to the people. In January 1890 the Poona New English School was founded. He was also associated in the formation of the Deccan Educational Society and the foundation of the Fergusson Collage, Poona.

Tilak was the first nationalist leader who sought close contact with the masses and was in this respect a forerunner of Gandhiji. With that object in view Tilak started *akharas, lathi* clubs and Anti-Cow-Killing Societies. The Shivaji and Ganapati festivals were started to inculcate among the people the spirit of service to the nation. He also started two newspapers entitled *"The Maharatta'* (English) and '*Kesari'* (Marathi) to propagate his views.

Again, Tilak was the *first* Congress leader to suffer several terms of imprisonments for the sake of the country, an example emulated by Gandhiji and others. For criticising in strong language the treatment meted out to the Maharaja of Kolhapur, the Government tried Tilak and sentenced him to four months' imprisonment in 1882. In 1897 he was charged with instigating the murders of Mr. Rand and Lt. Ayerst and sent to jail for 18 months R.I. Again, in 1908 Tilak for commenting on the Muzaffarpur Bomb case was tried for sedition and sent to Mandalay jail for six years. Tilak emerged from these trials with an unbroken spirit and a stronger patriot.

Tilak played a leading role in organising, in collaboration with Lala Lajpat Rai and B.C. Pal, the Nationalist Party (the Extremist Party) against the weak-kneed party of the Old Guard (otherwise called The Moderates). If the birth of Extremism in Indian politics, as Mrs. Annie Besaint puts it, began with the outbreak of plague and excesses of the officials in 1897, then the credit for bringing about a transformation in Indian politics belongs to Tilak. His 'extremist' views caused a split in the Congress at Surat in 1907 and Tilak was considered as the 'arch-offender' for the split. Even Lord Montagu told Chintamani that there was only one genuine extremist in India and that was Tilak.

Tilak was the *first* again to openly declare the demand for *Swaraj*. "*Swaraj* is my birthight", he said, "and I shall have it." It was mostly due to his efforts and those of his associates that the Congress resolution at Calcutta (1906) demanding Self-Government, Boycott and National Education was passed. Tilak was not satisfied with the type of responsible government prevalent in the self-governing Dominions within the Empire. He demanded *Swaraj*. The Congress session at Nagpur in

1920 demanded *Swaraj* and authorized the use of 'all peaceful and legitimate means' for its attainment. Thus, Tilak's stand was vindicated immediately after his death in August 1920.

Tilak believed in service and sacrifice and had the courage to defy the authority of the Government. It was mostly due to his efforts that the Congress from being the admirer of the Government turned into a great critic of the British Empire.

The Anglo-Indian bureaucracy thought Tilak a seditionist and Sir Valentine Chirol called him the 'Father of Unrest in India.' Tilak sued Chirol for defamation and went to England in this connection. Although the case was lost, it opened his eyes to the real character of British rule in India.

Tilak favoured a policy of responsive co-operation. During the First World War, he urged the people to co-operate with the British Government. In return he expected the British Government to come forward with a reciprocal gesture and announce Home Rule for India. Disappointed, Tilak set up the Home Rule League at Poona in 1916. Tilak was not satisfied with the Government of India Act, 1919. He died in August 1920.

Tilak has been described as an Extremist in politics but a Moderate in matters of social reform. He did oppose the Age of Consent Bill, not because he did not see the necessity of social reform but because he believed that a foreign government should not legislate about social reform. He contended that social changes could better be brought about by educating public opinion.

Tilak was a scholar of eminence. His books *The Arctic Home of the Vedas* and *Gita Rahasya* are a testimony to his scholarship.

Dr. Pattabhi Sitaramayya has compared Gokhale and Tilak thus, "Tilak and Gokhale...were both patriots of the first order. Both had made heavy sacrifices in life But their temperaments were widely different from each other. Gokhale was a 'Moderate' and Tilak was an 'Extremist' if we may use the language in vogue at the time. Gokhale's plan was to improve the existing constitution ; Tilak's was to reconstruct it. Gokhale had necessarily to work with the bureaucracy; Tilak had necessarily to fight it. Gokhale stood for co-operation wherever possible and opposition wherever necessary ; Tilak inclined towards a policy of obstruction. Gokhale's prime concern was with the administration and its improvement; Tilak's supreme consideration was the Nation and its upbuilding. Gokhale's ideal was love and service, Tilak's was service and suffering. Gokhale methods bought to win the foreigner, Tilak's to replace him. Gokhale depended upon others' help, Tilak upon self-help, Gokhale looked to the classes and the intelligentsia, Tilak to the masses and the millions. Gokhale's arena was the Council Chamber; Tilak's forum was the village *mandap*. Gokhale's medium of expression was English; Tilak's was Marathi. Gokhale's objective was Self-Government for which the people had to fit themselves by answering the tests prescribed by the English; Tilak's objective was Swaraj which is the birthright of every Indian and which he shall have without let or hindrance from the foreigner. Gokhale was on a level with his age; Tilak was in advance of his times."[3]

The selfless patriotism, indomitable courage and fierce determination of Tilak opened a new chapter in the history of the freedom movement in India.

Lala Lajpat Rai, 1865-1928

Lajpat Rai popularly known as the Sher-i-Panjab (The Lion of the Panjab) was a philanthropist, a social reformer and a true nationalist. If Sri Aurobindo Ghose was the prophet, B.C. Pal the hot-gospeller, Tilak the supreme strategist of Neo-Nationalism then Lala Lajpat Rai was the standard of the revolt against the 'mendicant policy' of the old Guard.

Lajpat Rai was born in 1865 in a family of Aggarwals of Ludhiana. He took a degree in Law and set up practice at Hissar. Soon after he moved to Lahore and was drawn in the whirlwind of politics. At Lahore he came under the influence of Mahatma Hans Raj, 'a silent man of singular

---

3. Pattabhi Sitaramayys : The History of the Congress. 1935 edition, pp. 165-66.

austerity and devotion in life. A true and dedicated Arya Samajist, Lajpat Rai was associated in the foundation of the D.A.V. College, Lahore. He was a fearless journalist and founded and edited *The Panjabee*, *The Bande Matram* and the English weekly *The People*. Lajpat Rai suffered various terms of imprisonments for the sake of his country.

In politics Lala Lajpat Rai was inclined towards 'extremism'. He was one of the trio—Bal, Pal and Lal—who organised the Extremist Group in the Congress. He along with Gokhale went to England in 1905 to educate the English public about the problems and aspirations of Indians. He returned home a greatly disappointed man and told his countrymen that the British Government was too busy with its own affairs to do anything for India, that the British Press was not likely to champion their aspirations and that it was very difficult to get a hearing in England. He told his countrymen that if they really cared for their Motherland "they would have to strike a blow for freedom themselves and they should be prepared to give unmistakable proof of their earnestness". In 1907 his name was proposed by Tilak for the Presidency of the Surat Congress but he withdrew his name. In 1914 he went to England and later to the U.S.A. to espouse India's case and create an opinion against imperialism. In 1920 he was elected to preside over the special session of the Congress (Calcutta, September 1920). At first Lajpat Rai was not in favour of the policy of non-cooperation but later on fell in line with Gandhiji. He along with many others protested against the withdrawal of the Non Cooperation Movement in 1922. This resentment found expression in the formation of the Swaraj Party which was organised by Lajpat Rai, C.R. Dass and Motilal Nehru. Lajpat Rai entered the Central Legislature as a Swarajist.

Lajpat Rai was a true nationalist. He had the fighting spirit and pride in his Motherland characteristic of a true Arya Samajist. A staunch believer in Hindu-Muslim unity, Lajpat Rai was not prepared to sacrifice Hindu interests in any policy of undue appeasement of other minorities. This led him to co-operate with Pandit Madan Mohan Malaviya in organising the Hindu Sangathan movement. In 1928 Lajpat Rai led a demonstration against the Simon Commission when it visited Lahore. He succumbed to the injuries he received from the brutal lathi charge on the procession. He died a martyr on 27 November 1928.

Lajpat Rai desired an all-round uplift of the masses—educational, social, economic and political—and tirelessly worked for the attainment of this objective. He was a true embodiment of earnestness, spirit of self-denial and self-sacrifice.

Lajpat Rai was man of true vision. He played a leading part in freeing the minds of his countrymen from 'the fear of offending the false gods' that had by force or fraud taken possession of their bodies and souls. Mahatma Gandhi described Lajpat Rai's death as the setting of a great planet from India's solar system.'

Mahatma Gandhi, 1869-1948

Mahatma Gandhi lovingly remembered as Bapu (Father of the Nation) so completely dominated the Indian scene from 1919 to 1948 that this period is rightly called the Gandhian era in Indians history. An Apostle of Peace and Non-violence, Gandhiji's message has a universal appeal and is exercising profound influence on humanity in general.

Mohandas Karamchand Gandhi was born on 2 October 1869 at Porbander in Western India. After qualifying for the Bar in England in 1891, Gandhi returned to India and set up practice at Rajkot and later at Bombay. In 1898 he received an offer from an Indian firm in South Africa and reached there. In South Africa, Gandhi protested against the discriminating treatment meted out to Indians, formed the Natal Indian Congress and suffered imprisonment. He also protested against the Asiatic (Black) Act and the Transvaal Immigration Act and started his non-violent civil disobedience movement. The South African Government had to heed to the voice of reason and in 1914 repealed most of the obnoxius acts against the Indians. In 1915 Gandhi returned to India and in admiration of his services to his countrymen began to be called Mahatma. The next four years he spent in studying the Indian situation. In 1917 Gandhi mobilised the peasants of Champaran in north Bihar against the exploitation of European indigo-planters. The Jallianwala Bagh Tragedy and the Rowlatt Act (1919) made Gandhi very unhappy and he hurled himself in the mainstream of Indian politics. **He described the British Government 'satanic'** and started his policy of non-cooperation. He launched non-cooperation in 1920, civil disobedience in 1930 and 1940 (Individual Civil Disobedience). In August 1942 he called upon the British to 'Quit India' and was arrested once again.

Gandhi's Message of Truth (Satya) and Non violence (Ahimsa). A true devotee of Truth, Gandhi maintained that God is Truth and Truth is God and further that God is Love (of humanity) and Love is God. Gandhi's love for truth was derived from Hinduism while for his belief in non-violence he was indebted to Buddhism, Jainism and Christianity. Thus the basic element in Gandhian creed was rooted in Hinduism with branches in all religions.

Mahatma Gandhi made *Satya* and *Ahimsa* as the basis of the new social order that he envisaged. He advocated the freedom of the whole world–freedom from violence, freedom from cupidity and aggressiveness, freedom from passions and ambitions that have destroyed nations. Freedom for India was to be won through Non-violence and Non-cooperation with the evil-doer. Non-violence, maintained Gandhi, is the law of our species, as violence is the law of the brute. In *Young India* Gandhi wrote, "The *rishis*, who discovered the law of non-violence in the midst of violence were greater geniuses than Newton. They were themselves greater warriors than Wellington Having themselves known the use of arms, they realised their uselessness, and taught a weary world that its salvation lay not through violence but through non-violence". An essential prerequisite of the policy of *Satyagraha* (literally persistence in Truth), held Gandhi, is fearlessness. He wanted to uproot from the minds of the people the all-pervasive, all-oppressing, all-strangling fear–fear of the C.I.D., of the police, of the jail and of the officials. In place of fear the people were asked to cultivate the spirit of **selfsacrifice and conscious-suffering for righteous cause. Explaining his policy Gandhi wrote, "Non-cooperation is not a movement of brag, bluster of bluff. It is a test of our sincerity. It requires solid and silent self-sacrifice"** Non-violence was its essential concomitant as "in its dynamic condition it means conscious-suffering. It does not mean meek submission to the will of the evil-doer, but it means the pitting of one's whole soul against the will of the tyrant." The basic object of Satyagraha was to convert the evil-doer. The Satyagraha movement was directed against the system–exploiting imperialism of the British–and not the British people individually or collectively. At the root was the conviction that human nature being essentially good it will assert itself, the tyrannical heart will melt at the sight of suffering and the scales of ingorance, selfishness will fall and virtue and justice will prevail.

Gandhi's Constructive Programme. Under Gandhi's leadership there was considerable expansion of the consructive activities of the Congress. He sought not only political freedom for India but also material, social and moral welfare of the masses. With that end in view he started the Gram Udyog Sangh (Village Industries Association), the Talimi Sangh (Basic Education Society) and the Cow Protection Association. He sought the cessation of exploitation in society not through socialisation of land and capital but through decentralisation in the economic sphere. He sought encouragement of cottage industries. Khadi is the symbol of the economic programme of Gandhi.

Gandhi also worked for social improvement of the masses. He desired abolition of all type of inequalities–inequalities based upon birth, caste, wealth etc. He worked for the **uplift of the untouchables**, whom he called Harijans (children of God). He condemned social evils of intemperance and worked strenuously for equality for women and Hindu-Muslim unity.

On 30 January 1948, a Hindu fanatic who considered Gandhi principally responsible for the partition of India shot him dead.

Estimate of Gandhi. Though unkind critics have called Gandhi as 'a philosophical anarchist' for his defiance of constituted authority and the imperialists like Lord Linlithgow called Gandhian methods as 'a form of blackmail'. Gandhi himself pursued the path of Truth (as he saw it) and kept up the purity of means in the achievement of his objectives. Gandhi had openly announced that he would wait for 300 years to get freedom than employ any objectionable means to achieve it. Undoubtedly, it was mostly due to the influence of Gandhian ideas that terrorism was kept in check and freedom for the country achieved without much violence and bloodshed.

Steeped in idealism, many of Gandhi's ideas were divorced from realism. His philosophy of 'the *charkha*, the bullock-cart and self-sufficient village' has not prevented modern India from largescale industrialisation and great expansion of the public sector. Again, Gandhi's idea of the rich becoming the 'trustees' of the poor seems unworkable. He had no faith in socialism or communism but these seem popularisms of today.

Gandhi's resort to large-scale disobedience and defiance of constituted authority has left a bad legacy behind. It has provided a convenient cloak to the unscrupulous and the anti-social elements to defy the constituted authority in free Indian in the name of Satyagraha. This has spread the habit of disorder–an unhealthy trend in modern Indian politics.

Though Gandhi was a strong advocate of Hindu-Muslim unity yet it was during the Gandhian era of Indian politics that Hindu-Muslim differences assumed new proportions. Under Gandhi's leadership the Congress showed a marked disposition towards Hinduism. In his writings and speeches Gandhi often employed language, imagery and symbolism derived from Hindu sources (*e.g.*, he desired Ram Rajya for India). This did cause reaction in the Muslim mind. Although the blame for fomenting Hindu-Muslim dissensions must lie on the shoulders of opportunistic, Muslim leadership and British imperialists yet Gandhi cannot be altogether exonerated from the blame.

Perhaps, Gandhi's greatest failure lay in that he could not prevent what he 'shuddered to think' and what he called 'the vivisection of India'. It seems Gandhi lost control over the events and the masses and the partition of India and the murders of 1946-47 seemed to give the impression that his teachings had been lost on his own countrymen.

Select Opinions

Acharya Kriplani. The Mahatma is more right when he is wrong than we are when we are right...Many of us are correct in our little correctnesses and are small in the process. But the Mahatma was incorrect in many things and yet correct in the sumtotal and big in the very inconsistencies. In the end he seldom or never came out at the wrong place.

Rabindranath Tagore. Great as Gandhi is as a polititician, as an organiser, as a leader of men, as a moral reformer, he is greater than all these as a man, because none of these aspects and activities limits his humanity. They are rather inspired and sustained by it. Though an incorrigible idealist and given to referring all conduct to certain pet formulae of his own, he is essentially a lover of men and not of mere ideas.

Arnold Toynbee. The gereration into which I happen to have been born has not only been Hitler's generation in the West and Stalin in Russia it has also been Gandhi's in India; and it can already be forecast with some confidence that Gandhi's effect on human history is going to be greater and more lasting than Stalin's or Hitler's.

Jawaharlal Nehru, 1889–1964

A great leader of the Gandhian era, Jawahar Lal Nehru ranks next to Gandhi in the galaxy of freedom fighters. In fact, apart from Gandhi if there was any person whose life was the history of the country's struggle for freedom, it was Jawahar Lal's. After India achieved independence in 1947 Nehru so completely dominated the Indian political scene up to his death in 1964 that during this period India was Nehru and Nehru was India.

Son of another freedom fighter Motilal Nehru, Jawaharlal was born at Allahabad on 14 November, 1889. Being the only son of an affluent lawyer, Nehru was sent to England for studies.

After qualifying for the Bar in 1912. Nehru returned to India. He made his first appearance at the Congress platform as a delegate to the Bankipore session in 1912. He came in close contact with Gandhiji during the non-cooperation movement in 1921. He suffered nine terms of imprisonment totalling over nine years. In 1923 he was elected General Secretary of the Congress and presided over Congress session in 1929, 1939, 1946 and every session from 1951 to 1954. In 1946 Nehru headed the Interim Government and was the First Prime Minister of Free India, a position which he held till his death in 1964.

In his political philosophy Nehru was a true disciple of Gandhi and fully subscribed to his doctrine of non-violence. Gandhi had full faith in Nehru and made no secret of his belief that after his death. Nehru would be his heir and would keep up his faith in non-violence and lead the nation along its path.

Nehru found nationalism too narrow an ideology for his broad humanitarian outlook. He was a true internationalist and expressed sympathy and support for the suppressed humanity against imperialism and colonialism. He lent moral support to liberal movements in Africa, Asia and South America and sympathised with peoples of all creeds and countries. An ardent believer in world peace Nehru was a strong advocate of the U.N.O. During numerous international crises like the Suez Canal, Korea, Laos, the Congo, Vietnam, Arab-Israeli conflict, Nehru strove hard for return of peace and made available his good offices.

In the economic field Nehru was a socialist and stressed the need for economic planning. He headed the National Planning Committee appointed by the Congress in 1939. After independence he was the Chairman of the Planning Commission and it was mostly due to his influence that socialistic pattern of society was accepted as the goal of economic planning in India.

Nehru stood for the modern scientific outlook and advocated adoption of scientific and technological method for the advancement of India. On numerous occasions he presided over the All India Science Congress. The C.S.I.R. (Concil of Scientific and Industrial Research) centres in various parts of the country are a standing monument to his foresight.

Being the first Prime Minister of India–who exercised unquestioned authority and received unstinted public support for seventeen long years–Nehru was the pace-setter in many spheres of national activity. Nehru's great emphasis on secularism, socialism and democratic processes for the attainment of national objectives has taken root in Indian way of thinking and has provided positive patterns for the development of India.

A prince among freedom fighters, Nehru caught the imagination of the masses and continued to hold their affection till be lived. Perhaps, Nehru's greatest contribution to the nation is his daughter, Mrs. Indira Gandhi, who with rare imagination and manly determination has pursued the national objectives spelt out by Mahatma Gandhi and Jawaharlal Nehru.

Select Opinions

Jawaharlal Nehru. I have become a queer mixture of the East and West, out of place everywhere, at home nowhere. Perhaps my thoughts and approach of life are more akin to what is called Western than Eastern, but India clings to me, as she does to all her children, in innumerable ways ; and behind me lie, some-where in the subconscious, racial memories of a hundred, or what-ever the number may be, generations of Brahmins. I cannot get rid of either that past inheritance or my recent acquisitions. They are both part of me, and though they help in both the East and the West, they also create in me a feeling of spiritual loneliness not only in public activities but in life itself. I am a stranger and alien in the West, I cannot be of it. But in my own country also, sometimes, I have an exile's feeling.

If I were given the chance to go through my life again, with my present knowledge and experience added, I would no doubt try to make many changes in my personal life ; I would endeavour to improve in many ways on what I had previously done, but my major decisions in public affairs would remain untouched. Indeed, I could not vary them, for they were stronger than myself, and a force beyond my control drove me to them.

Michael Brecher. Along with his international outlook was a vision of a renascent Indian sociey to follow independence, a land in which the timeless ills of poverty and disease would be eradicated or at least alleviated...The twin vision of Jawaharlal Nehru made him the voice of Indian youth and of a whole generation of intellectuals. This was his third contribution to the nationalist movement, to enlist the active support of the young Westernized intelligentsia and young men generally for the Congress cause...Indeed, but for him there can be little doubt that young nationalists in the early thirties would have turned to the Communist Party in large numbers...The purity of his public life, his honesty, and his aversion to corruption served as a bastion in a movement which, like all movements, was affected by different motives and impulses.

Perhaps his great defect is indecision...Closely related to these defects is the tendency to yield to pressure. This was true in the years before Independence when Nehru frequently gave way to Gandhi and the Right Wing...It has also been true since Independence Nehru is a bad judge of character. He is also blinded by past loyalties and previous service of colleagues with the result that he retains them in high party and governmental positions after they no longer merit this trust and influence. Loyalty often outweighs sound judgement.

These weaknesses are the weaknesses of a giant. For Nehru is a giant, both as man and statesman. If political greatness be measured by the capacity to direct events, to rise above the crest of the waves, to guide his people, and to serve as a catalyst of progress, then Nehru surely qualifies for greatness.

S. Gopal. Jawaharlal Nehru played a decisive role in the history of the twentieth century as a leader of the Indian people, as representative of the new mood of Asia, and as a spokesman of the international conscience.

SELECT REFERENCES

1. Brecher, M. : *Nehru : A Political Biography.*
2. Fisher, L. : *Life of Gandhi.*
3. Gandhi, M.K. : *My Experiments with Truth.*
4. Gopal, S. : *Jawaharlal Nehru : A Biography.*
5. Joshi, V.C. (ed.) : *Ram Mohan Ray and the Process of Modernization in India.*
6. Karmarkar, D.P. : *Bal Gangadhar Tilak.*
7. Masani, R.P. : *Dadabhai Naoroji.*
8. Nehru, J.L. : *Autobiography.*
9. Paranjpe, R.P. : *Gopal Krishna Gokhale.*
10. Rai, Lajpat : *Unhappy India.*

THE LEFT MOVEMENTS IN INDIA

> The Soviet Republic enjoys tremendous popularity among all the Eastern peoples...for the reason that in us they see an unswerving fighter against imperialism.
>
> —V.I. Lenivn

Definition of the Left. The terms *Left* and *Right* were first used as political terms in France during the French Revolution to distinguish the pro-Revolutionaries (the Left) from the anti-Revolutionaries (the Right). The terms acquired a wider connotation after the Industrial Revolution and the rise of Socialist and Communist thought.

Circumstances favouring growth of Left ideologies in India. Leftism in India grew out of the special politico-economic circumstances prevailing in India towards the end of the First World War and was inextricably intertwined with the mainstream of the nationalist movement. These circumstance swere:

(*a*) The First World War brought in its train crippling financial burdens, rising prices of necessities of life, famine conditions and manipulative profiteering–all exposing the evils of imperialist-capitalist domination.

(*b*) The romantic appeal of the revolutionary ideas of Marx coupled with the reflected glory of the new regime in the U.S.S.R. fired the imagination of the Indian intellectuals, political leaders, the terrorists and even the workers and made them conscious of a new ideology loaded with a socio-economic content.

(*c*) Gandhiji's slogan of Swaraj and Swadeshi and his attempt to carry the message to every nook and corner of India gave a new orientation to the political movement. Even the workers and peasants were drawn into the mainstream of national life. The new development provided a fertile ground for inauguration of an organised and ideologically inspired socialist movement.

(*d*) A volatile section of the new generation of educated middle class with the spectre of unemployment staring them in the face had lost faith in the 19th century liberalism and all that it stood for and was attracted towards individualistic terrorism or the new revolutionary socialist ideology.

(*e*) A section of the radicals felt unhappy with the 'weak and watery reformism' of Gandhi, labelled him as the leader of the 'forces of reaction' and saw his cult of non-violence as an obstructive element in the development of a real revolutionary mass struggle against British imperialism and its indigenous allies. These radicals also questioned the exclusive emphasis on Swaraj without a socio-economic dimension.

The Left Movements

Left movements in India developed into two main streams :

(*a*) Communism which functioned as a branch of the International Communist Movement and was by and large controlled by the Comintern and

(*b*) the Congress Socialist Party which functioned as left wing of the Indian National Congress and drew inspiration from the philosophy of Democratic Socialism. Both these movements drew support from the anti-imperialist sentiments prevalent in India.

The Communist Party. Towards the end of 1920, M.N. Roy and other Indian emigres at Taskhent announced the formation of the Communist Party of India. In India on 1 September 1924, Satyabhakta in a press note released immediately after the conclusion of Kanpur Conspiracy trial announced that he had formed the C.P.I. with himself as the Secretary.

The history of the Communist movement can be divided into five distinct phases :—

First phase : the Period of 'There Conspiracy Trials'. After receiving thorough training at Moscow at the Communist University for Toilers of the East and assured of adequate financial support from Moscow, the first band of Communist revolutionaries crossed into India only to find themselves accused of organising a conspiracy against the King Emperor. The movement picked up somewhat only after the Communist Party of Great Britain took upon itself to supervise and energies the movement in India. One of its emissaries, Philip Spratt arrived in India in December 1926 and organised a number of unions, edited newpapers and launched some youth and front organisations. Four Workers' and Peasants' parties were organised in Bengal, Bombay, the Panjab and the U.P. In December 1928 the All India Workers' and Peasants' Party came into exisence. During 1928–29 the Communist Party organised a series of industrial strikes at Bombay.

The Communist movement during this period attracted notice by its being involved in conspiracy trials thrice, viz. the Peshawar Conspiracy Trial (1922–23), the Kanpur Conspiracy Trial (1924) and the Meerut Conspiracy Trial (1929–33). The Meerut Trial which continued for over three and a half years and ended with the conviction of 27 persons (half of them being nationalists or trade unionists) made martyrs of the Communists. The anti-British stance of the Communists gained for them sympathy of the nationalists. The Congress Working Committee set up a Central Defence Committee, sanctioned a sum of Rs. 1,500 and the defence case was pleaded by eminent nationalists like J.L. Nehru, K.N. Katju and F.H. Ansari. Gandhiji visited the prisoners in the jail in 1929 and expressed sympathy for the Communist leaders. In that atmosphere of unreserved sympathy for the Communists, the Congress members of the Central Legislative Assembly successfully opposed the enactment of the Public Safety Bill (1928)–a bill directed against the Communists in India. The long drawn out trial also provided a handy opportunity to the Communist leaders to make politically-loaded propaganda speeches that received wide coverage in the nationalist press. By 1934 the Communist movement in India acquired some respectability and Communist ideology may be said to have been established in this country.

In July 1934 the CPI was declared an illegal organisation.

Second Phase : The Period of Political Wilderness. At a time when the nationalist movement under Gandhiji's leadership made giant strides forward in arousing the masses against imperialist stranglehold, the CPI suffered from both organisational and ideological articulation. Receiving its cue from the decisions of the Communist International of 1928, the CPI attacked both the right wing and the left wing in the Indian National Congress. It were the times when the Congress had boycotted the simon Commission (1928), adopted the resolution on Purna Swaraj (Dec. 1929), and launched the Civil Disobedience Movement (1930–31, 32–34). The CPI sought to steal the thunder from the Congress popularity by attempting to project the triangular character of the contest (the people's struggle not only against foreign imperialism but also against Indian, exploiters). It attacked the petty-bourgeois-nationalist leadership of Gandhiji and charged him with acting as the tool of imperialism and thereby betraying the revolutionary struggle of the masses. It even denounced the Congress Left wing as a counter-revolutionary force and 'a dangerous obstacle to the victory of Indian nationalism'. This tactical approach proved to be totally unrealistic and the Communists found themselves thrown adrift from the political mainstream.

Third Phase : Communists and the Anti-Imperialist United Front Plan. Taking policy of directions from the deliberations of the Seventh Congress of the Communist International (Moscow, 1935) R.P. Dutt and Ben Bradley published their thesis entitled *The Anti-Imperialist People's Front in India* in March 1936. Dutt-Bradley labelled the Indian National Congress as merely the united front of the Indian people in the nationalist struggle. They advised the Communists to join the Indian National Congress, utilise its solid party organisation, strengthen the left-wing within the Congress (C.S.P.) and oust the reactionary right-wing elements. The Communists, the CSP and the Trade Unionists planned to organise a *Front Populaire* on the basis of a common minimum programme. The Communist leadership failed to take advantage of the favourable circumstances or broaden the social base of their movement and the popular front never came into existence. All the same, profiting from the tide of rising mass upsurge and quickening allround political activity in the latter half of the 1930's, the Communists emerged from their political quarantine and found again a place among the radical elements in Indian politics.

Fourth Phase : The Second World War and the Communist Somersault. When the Second World War broke out the Indian Communists, under advice from the Comintern leaders, continued their United Front Policy against all types of Imperialism (including Fascism and Nazism). Rather, the Communists scored a point over the Indian National congress with the latter's initial vacillation and pro-British attitude of leaders like Gandhiji. By September 15, 1939 the Congress too described the war as an imperialist war.

The Indian Communists, however, found themselves in a very false position when in June 1941. Hitler attacked the Soviet Union, the Fatherland of Socialism. The Communists in India staged a right-about turn and relabelled the war as a 'people's war' and announced full support for the Allied-Russian war effort. The Government of India rewarded the CPI by declaring it a legal organisation in 1942. The Communists extended all possible support and even acted as British "spies" in suppressing the popular revolt of 1942. This sudden shift in the Communist policy evoked strong condemnation in nationalist circles and clearly demonstrated that the CPI's policy decisions were dictated by outside and international wire-pullers.

Fifth phase : The Transfer of Power Negotiations and Communists' Multi-National Plan. During the period the CPI's posture was pro-Muslim ; it sought to further widen Congress-League alienation and encourage all separatist elements and work for the division of India into a number of sovereign states. Its strategy was to tighten control over at least one such state and to make it as a base for the liberation of the rest of India. Unfortunately, However, the Muslim League spurned the idea of an alliance with the Communists. The CPI, therefore, stood as a discredited organisation.

In 1942 the CPI adopted a resolution declaring India to be a multi-national state and identifying as many as 16 Indian "nations". In 1946 they put forward before the Cabinet Mission a plan for division of Indian into 17 separate sovereign states on the model of the Balkans or the U.S.S.R. By 1947 the Communist movement in India had lost whatever place it had in Indian politics and the CPI was in complete disarray.

When national emancipation from British imperialism was the dominant instinct of the people, the CPI's extra-national loyalties and exclusive dependence on European models made it a suspect organisation. In fact the Communists' concept of Proletarian Internationalism could not be reconciled with India's national aspirations. Further, Marxism's basic articles of faith in 'class antagonism' and 'violence' are alien to Indian tradition. However, Marxist-Leninist philosophy, shorn of its extra-national loyalties, has some relevance to independent India. The yawning gap between the rich and the poor and the under-developed condition of Indian economy are favourable climatic conditions in which Marxist Socialism can take root in India and serve as the beacon-light for the down-trodden masses.

The Congress Socialist Party. The Congress Left wing emerged as a 'rationalist revolt' against the mysticism of Gandhism on the one hand and dogmatism of Communism on the other. Their ideological inspiration came from Marxism and Democratic Socialism and they stood for anti-imperialism, nationalism and socialism. Subhash Chandra Bose explained that the Congress Leftists were not only anti-imperialists but they also desired reconstruction of national life on a socialist basis. For the achievement of their goal they had to fight on two fronts : (*a*) light foreign imperialism and its Indian allies, (*b*) fight the milk-water nationalists (the Rightists) who were prepared for a deal with Imperialism. In other words, they stood for complete independence and Socialism ; they wanted Swaraj not for the classes but for the masses.

The disillusionment with Gandhian ideology and technique of nationalist struggle when Gandhi suddenly announced the withdrawal of the Non-Cooperation Movement in 1922, when the nation stood on the verge of a popular revolt. Gandhi played a similar card when he suspended the Civil Disobedience Movement in 1931 and called it off in 1934 and advised Congressmen to resort to individual *satyagraha*. The left-wing came to the conclusion that dogmatic adherence to the theory of Non-Violence 'was unsustainable' and based on 'slippery foundations.'

In July 1931 J.P. Narayan, Phulan Prasad Varma and others formed the Bihar Socialist Party. The Panjab Socialist Party came into existence in September 1933. The All India Congress Socialist Party was formally started in October 1934 with a constitution and a specific 15-Point Programme.

The Congress Socialist Party was not a rival political organisation to the Congress but was launched "to work within the Congress, to strengthen it, to mould and shape its policies. All the same, the Right-wing of the Congress labelled Congress Socialists as 'internationalists' and thus undependable for the struggle for national liberation. The Communists branded the Congress Socialists as Social Fascists and 'fake socialists'. The Congress Socialists hit back by describing the Indian Communists as 'satellites of the U.S.S.R.', as 'social-chauvinists' and charged them 'with betraying socialism and distorting Marxian dialectics'.

The CSP condemned the Government of India Act 1935 as an anti-people united front of imperialism and the forces of national reaction and was critical of the Congress Party's acceptance of office in the provinces in 1937. It was because of the Socialist pressure that the Congress Election Manifesto of 1936 contained a programme for the removal of the socio-economic grievances of the people.

The CSP disagreed with the Congress offer of conditional help for British war effort as it maintained that the war was a conflict between the partners of imperialism for repartition of the world. The Congress socialists wanted the Congress to wage a revolutionary mass struggle for independence. They supported the Quit India Movement and took a leading part in organising the Revolt of 1942.

The CSP was not in favour of a negotiated settlement for the transfer of power but advocated the need for a revolutionary struggle to destroy edifices of imperialism, feudalism and communalism in India.

The Congress Socialists described the Muslim League 'in league with Britain' and Jinnah as traitor to his country and tool of the imperialists. They hoped for Hindu-Muslim unity not on the basis of temporary pacts or agreements but "by laying emphasis on the economic issues which equally affected the Hindu and Muslim masses of the country".

The CSP described the Partition of India as an act of surrender by the Congress leadership and admitted its own failure and that of the wider revolutionary movement in working out an alternative and positive policy.

Minor Leftist Parties

The Communist movement in India served as a nursery for the growth of many minor leftist parties during 1939-40. Most of these leftist parties centred around personalities and became near-defunct after the central figure disappeared.

The Forward Bloc. After losing the leadership contest with Gandhi, Subhash Chandra Bose formed the Forward Bloc in March 1939. The Bloc accepted the creed, policy and programme of the Congress but was not bound to have confidence in the Congress High Command. It sought to rally all anti-imperialist, radical and progressive groups under one banner. It played a role in organising the Left Consolidation Committee.

Bose opposed the Congress attitude of co-operation with the British war effort and went abroad to seek military help for the liquidation of imperialism in India. In 1947 the All India Forward Bloc described the transfer of power as a bogus transfer and alleged that the frightened bourgeois had entered into partnership with British imperialism to defeat the mass struggle.

Revolutionary Socialist Party. The terrorists of the early 20th century provided the nucleus for the organisation of this party which was launched in 1940. It stood for violent overthrow of British imperialism and establishment of Socialism in India. Ideologically the R.S.P. was closer to C.S.P. than the Communist party. In the Gandhi-Bose tussle, the R.S.P. supported Subhash Chandra Bose. The R.S.P. refused to support the allied war effort even after the U.S.S.R. had joined the Allies. The party described the transfer of Power and Partition as a "back-door deal between the treacherous bourgeois leadership of the Congress and Imperialism".

Other Minor Parties. The Bolshevik Party of India was established in 1939 by N. Dutt Mazumdar, the Revolutionary Communist Party was launched by Saumyendranath Tagore in 1942 and the Boshevik-Leninist Party was announced in 1941 by a group of Trotskyite revolutionaries like Indra Sen and Ajit Roy. Each of these was a dissident Communist group and claimed to be the fittest party for leading the Indian Revolution.

M.N. Roy, the pioneer of the Communist movement in India organised the Radical Democratic Party in 1940 after his complete disillusionment with Marxism. He veered round to the view that the Indian Revolution could not be brought about by the proletariat alone but only under the leadership of a multi-class party.

SELECT REFERENCES

1.	Lakhanpal, P.L.	:	*History of the congress Socialist Party.*
2.	Masani, M.R.	:	*The Communist Party of India.*
3.	Sharma, B. S.	:	*Political Philosophy of M.N. Roy.*
4.	Sinha, L.P.	:	*Left Wing in India.*
5.	Overstreet, G.D. and Windmiller, M.	:	*Communism in India.*
6.	Weiner, Myron	:	*Political Parties in India.*
7.	Balabushevich, V.V. & Dyakov A.M.	:	*A Contemporary History of India, 1918–55*

Growth of Industrial Working Class And the Trade Union Movement

> Indian labour leaders did not emerge from the ranks of labour. Instead the leaders came from India's uppermost strata or even from abroad. These leaders were usually affiliated with one or another political party, and carried their political quarrels along with them.
>
> —*D. & A. Thorner*

The foundation of modern industries in India was laid between 1850 and 1870. Lord Dalhousie's Railway Minute of 1853 started the process of the introduction of machinery into the locomotion of India. The thousands of hands employed in construction of railways were harbingers of modern Indian working class. The development of ancillary industries directly or indirectly connected with railways became inevitable. The coal industry developed fast and employed a large working force. The first cotton mill was set up in Bombay in 1854 and the first jute mill started working at Calcutta the same year. The tea industry also greatly developed. The number of working hands employed in textile mills increased from 74,000 in 1886 to 195,000 in 1905, the working force in jute industry multiplied from 27,494 hands in 1879–80 to 154,962 in 1906, while the coal mines employed 75,749 in 1904.

The Indian working class suffered from all forms of exploitation—low wages, long working hours, unhygienic conditions in factories, employment of child labour and absence of all amenities—from which the labour force has suffered in the early stages of industrialisation and capitalism in England and the West *plus* the evils of a rapacious colonial rule.

The colonial situation, however, gave a distinctive touch to Indian working class movement. The Indian working class had to face two basic antagonistic forces—an imperialist political rule and economic exploitation at the hands of both foreign and native capitalist classes. Under these compulsive cricumstances the Indian working class movement became intertwined with the political struggle for national emancipation.

The Trade Union Movement. A trade union may be defined as "a continuous association of wage-earners for the purpose of maintaining or improving the conditions of their working lives". Political motivations and ideologies influenced the Indian trade union movement and were in turn influenced by its increased strength.

The twin aspects of the Indian Trade Union movement—labour organisation for industrial bargaining and its ideological orientation—should be viewed in the larger background of the naionalist struggle against imperialism and the emergence of politically-inspired opposing International Labour organisations.

Early History. Ironically the first ever demand for regulation of the condition of workers in factories in India came from the Lancashire textile capitalist lobby ; apprehending the emergence of a competitive rival in the Indian textile industry under conditions of cheap and unregulated labour, they demanded the appointment of a commission for investigation into factory conditions. The first commission was appointed in 1875 although the First Factory Act was not passed before 1881. The Act prohibited the employment of children under the age of 7, limited the number of working hours for children below the age of 12 years and provided that dangerous machinery should be fenced. Under similar extraneous pressure from British textile interests the Factory Act of 1891 was passed which limited the working day to 11 hours with an interval of $1\frac{1}{2}$ hours for women labour , increased the minimum and maximum ages of children from 7 and 12 years and 14 years Similar circumstances resulted in the enactment of factory acts for jute industry in 1909 and 1911. The opening decade of the 20th century also gave the first ever demonstration of the emerging political consciousness among the Indian working class ; the Bombay workers went on a political six-day strike over the conviction and inprisonment of Lokamanya Tilak in 1908—a development which elicited Lenin's comments that "the Indian proletariat has already matured sufficiently to wage a class-conscious and political mass struggle".

First World War, Left Awakening and Organised Trade Unionism. The First World War and its aftermath brought a period of soaring prices, unprecedented profiteering for the industrialists but miserably low wages for the workers. The average dividend paid by the jute mills during 1915-24 was 140% (420% in 1919), while the average wage of workers in the industry was only £12 p.a. Similarly the cotton mill industry paid an average dividend of 120% (the highest being 365%).

The emergence of Mahatma Gandhi on the national scene also marked a determined bid to broad-base the nationalist movement and mobilisation of the workers and the peasants for the national cause. It was felt that the workers should be organised into a national Trade Union and drawn into the vortex of the struggle for independence. At almost the same time the October Revolution in Russia and the formation of the Comintern was a open call to the workers of the world to combine to dispossess the capitalists and institute a Proletarian Revolution. The setting up of the League of Nations' Agency I.L.O. (International Labour Organisation) gave an international complexion to the labour problem.

The initiative in organising a Trade Union on the national basis was taken by the nationalist leaders and the All-India Trade Union Congress (AITUC) was founded on 31 October 1920. The Indian National Congress President of the year, Lala Lajpat Rai, was elected its President. The national leaders kept close association with this Trade Union and nationalist leaders like C.R. Das, V.V. Giri and later on Sarojini Naidu, J.L. Nehru and Subhash Bose presided over its annual sessions. By 1927 the number of trade unions affiliated to the AITUC increased to 57 with a total membership of 1,50,555. To begin with the AITUC was influenced by social democratic ideas of the British Labour Party. Despite some Socialist leanings the AITUC remained, by and large, under the influence of moderates like N.M. Joshi who believed that the political activities of labour organisations should not go beyond agitation for the amelioration of their economic grievances. Gandhian philosophy of non-violence, Trusteeship and class-collaboration had great influence on the movement and strike was a weapon rarely employed. The Trade Union Act of 1926 recognised trade unions as legal associations, laid down conditions for registration and regulation of trade union activities, secured their immunity, both civil and criminal, from prosecution for legitimate activities but put some restrictions on their political activities.

The rise of the Communist movement in India in the 1920s lent a militant and revolutionary content to the Trade Union movement. The 4th Congress of the Communist International sent a message to the AITUC not to be content with 'fair day's wages for a fair day's work' but to fight for the ultimate goal of overthrow of capitalism and imperialism. Further, the Indian Communists were urged to organise the Trade Union movement 'on a class basis and purge it of all alien basis'.

During 1926-27 the AITUC was divided into two groups called 'the reforming' and 'the revolutionary' groups also labelled as the Geneva-Amsterdam group' and the 'Moscovite group', the former wanting AITUC to be affiliated to the International Federation of Trade Unions (IFTU) with headquarters at Amsterdam and the latter desiring affiliation with the Red Labour Union (R.I.T.U.) organised from Moscow. The Communist thinking seemed to carry greater influence. During 1928 the country witnessed unprecedented industrial unrest. The total number of strikes was 203 involving no less then 506,851 people and the total number of working days lost was 31,647,404. These strikes were inspired more by political ideas than immediate economic demands. The Communist journal *Kranti* thundered, "There is no peace until capitalism is overthrown". On the question of affiliation to an international labour body too the Communist viewpoint prevailed and the AITUC was affiliated to the

Pan-Pacific Secrertariat and to the Third International at Moscow. In protest the moderate group under Joshi's leadership withdrew from the AITUC and formed the All India Trade Union Federation in 1929.

Alarmed at the increasing strength of the Trade Union movement and its control under extremist hands, the Government of India sought to contain its activities by legislative restrictions. A Public Safety Bill was introduced in the Legislative Assembly in 1928 but could not get majority support and had to be issued in the form of an ordinance in 1929. The Trade Disputes Act (1929) provided, among other provisions, for compulsory appointment of Courts of Enquiry and Conciliation Boards for settling industrial disputes, made strikes illegal in public utility services (like Postal Service, Railways, Water and Electricity Departments) unless each individual worker planning to go on strike gave an advance notice of one month to the Administration and, above all, forbade trade union activities of coercieve or purely political nature and even sympathetic strikes.

The Meerut Conspiracy Trial. In March 1929 the Government of Lord Irwin arrested the principal leaders of the working class movement and brought them to Meerut for trial. The principal charge against the 31 trade union leaders was of "conspiring to deprive the King of his Sovereignty of India". The trial lasted $3\frac{1}{2}$ years and resulted in the conviction of Muzaffar Ahmed, Dange, Joglekar, Spratt, Bradley, Usmani and others to various terms of transportation or rigorous imprisonment. However, the Meerut trial (1929-33) attracted world-wide publicity and drew symphathetic comments from Prof. instein, H.G. Wells, Harold Laski and even President Roosevelt. In 1933, the Joint Council of the British Trade Union Congress and Labour Party described it as "a judicial scandal". In Indian it brought the Leftists and the Rightists together and a broad-based Central Defence Committee defended the case.

The Meerut trial dealt a 'heavy immediate blow' to the working class movement and weakened the political role of the working class in the national struggle that followed—as had been the intention of imperialism.[1]

During the Non-cooperation Movement (1930–34) the Government struck hard at the workers and resorted to large-scale arrests, victimization through repression, legislation and appointment of commissions. These developments drove home to the union leaders the lesson of unity. The Congress Socialist Party founded in 1934 also worked for unity between the moderate and radical trade unions. During 1935-36 the three trade union organisations viz., AITUC, the Red Trade Union Congress and the National Federation of Trade Unions worked towards unity though the merger was not formalised before April 1938.

Popular Governments in Provinces and Trade Unionism. The formation of Congress ministries in six provinces in 1937 gave a fillip to trade union activities and the number of trade unions increased to 296 by 1938. The Congress ministries showed a sympathetic attitude towards the workers' demands. The most successful strike during this period was of Kanpur workers strike which continued for 55 days and involved 10,000 workers. The Government appointed the Kanpur Labour Enquiry Committee under the chairmanship of Babu Rajendra Prasad. The Congress governments in Bihar, Bombay, the U.P. and the C.P. also appointed Labour Enquiry Committees which made liberal recommendations for improvement of the lot of workers. Some beneficial legislations like the Bombay Industrial Disputes Act (1938), the Bombay Shop Assistants Act (1939), the C.P. Maternity Act (1939), and the Bengal Maternity Act (1939) were enacted.

Impact of the Second World War. The Second World War brought another era of rising prices and lagging behind wages. The year 1940 witnessed many strikes. More so because the Trade Unions could not remain indifferent to political developments. In September 1940 the AITUC adopted a resolution disavowing any sympathy for imperialism or fascism. It resolved that "participation in a

---

1. R. P. Dutt : *India Today,* pp. 391-92.

war, which will not result in the establishment of freedom and democracy in India, will not benefit India, much less will it benefit the working class."

M.N. Roy, the Communist-turned-Radical Democratic leader seceded from the AITUC and formed a pro-Government union called the Indian Federation of Labour ; the Government responded by sanctioning a grant of Rs. 13,000 p.m. to the loyal organisation. The section of the AITUC under Communist influence also showed a pro-Government stance after the Soviet Union joined the war on the side of the Allied Powers. During the 'Quit India' movement in August 1942 the nationalist wing of the AITUC suffered the most, the Communist wing having declared in favour of the official Labour-Management-Government conciliation formulae.

In spite of the Communists getting thoroughly discredited and isolated for their pro-British stance, the nationalist leaders failed to capture the leadership of the AITUC. Consequently in 1944 national leaders led by Sardar Vallabbhai Patel organised the Indian National Trade Union Congress. Thus the advent of independence saw the polarization of Trade Unionism on the basis of political ideology.

SELECT REFERENCES

1. Bradley, B.F. : *Trade Unionism in India.*
2. Chowdhury, S.R. : *Leftist Movements in India, 1917-47.*
3. Dange, S.A. : *On the Indian Trade Union Movement.*
4. Lakhanpal, P.L. : *History of the Congress Socialist Party.*
5. Masani, M.R. : *The Communist Party of India.*
6. Overstreet and Windmiller : *Communism in India.*
7. Sinha, L.P. : *Left Wing in India.*
8. Weiner, Myron : *Party Politics in India—The Development of a Multi-Party System.*

37

PEASANT REVOLTS AND AGRARIAN MOVEMENTS

> Before 1920 peasant revolts emerged from the peasants themselves, with some of them focussing around local charismatic leaders. After 1920 peasant revolts tended to come under the guidance of regional, national or urban-based political movements,
>
> —Kathleen Gough

An important impact of British rule on rural India was the far-reaching changes in Indian agrarian structure. The old agrarian system gradually collapsed under new administrative innovations. The new land tenures created new types of land ownerships. New social classes emerged in rural India. Land became a marketable commodity. The excessive state land revenue demand and exactions of the zamindars drove the peasant into the clutches of the moneylender and the trader. Absence landlordism, parasitical intermediaries, the avaracious moneylender—all combined to push the peasant deeper into the depth of poverty. A massive process of pauperization and proletarianization began and created a new category of agricultural proletariat. The peasant had to face oppression at the hands of not only foreign but indigenous exploiters and capitalists also.

In the 19th century peasant mobilisations were in the nature of protests, revolts and rebellions primarily aimed at loosening the bonds of feudal exploitation ; they protested against enhancement of rent, evictions, usurious practices of moneylenders ; their demands included occupancy rights, commutation of produce rent into money rent etc. In the absence of class consciousness or proper organisations the peasant revolts did not develop a political matrix. In the 20th century, however, we witness the emergence of class consciousness and formation of peasant organisations like the Kisan Sabhas. In the decade preceding the advent of independence the Kisan Sabhas increasingly came under the spell of left political parties like the Congress Socialist Party and the Communist Party of India.

Recurring Famines and Peasants : The most prominent fact of Indian history during the second half of the 19th century was the recurrence of famines and large-scale starvation deaths of workers and peasants. During this period 24 famines, big and small, affected various parts of the country and took an estimated toll of 28.5 million souls. The great famines of 1876–78, 1896–97 and 1899–1900 and the large-scale mortality revealed the cumulative effect of oppressive land policies. Scarcity and famine conditions created law and order problem in the countryside, striking terror into the hearts of not only the rural rich but the townsmen and even the local officials. The Famine Commissions of 1880, 1898 and 1901 made recommendations which revealed that by and large the famine relief system was "devised not so much with any laudable philanthropic sentiments as by the anxiety of the government to protect the institution of property and stave off the growing threat to the established order."[1]

The Santhal Rebellion, 1855-56. The Santhals, a peaceful and unassuming agricultural people, originally belonged to Manbhum, Barabhum, Hazaribagh, Midnapur, Bankura, and Bribhum areas. The Permanent Settlement of Bengal (1793) handed over the land which they had cultivated for centuries to the zamindars. The excessive rent demands of the zamindars compelled these peaceloving people to leave their ancestral homes and settle in the plains skirting the Rajmahal hills. With great industry they cleared the forests. Once the land was made suitable for cultivation the greedy zamindars of the adjoining areas laid claim to the proprietionship of the soil. The moneylenders, mostly from

---

1. N. G. Ranga and Swami Sahajanand Saraswati, *History of Kisan Movement,* quoted by A. R. Desai in *Peasant Struggles in India,* p. 49.

Bengal and upper India, started their usurious practices. "The Santhal", reported a writer in the *Calcutta Review*, "saw his crops, his cattle, even himself and family appropriated for a debt which ten times paid remained and incubus upon him still". worst still, the Santhal found the police, the revenue and court *amlas* all ranged behind the moneylender and all combining to practise extortions, oppressive exactions and forcible dispossession of his property and land.

The Santhals' main grouse was against the "civilised people" from Bengal and upper India, but they turned against the Government when they found that instead of remedying their grievances, the Government officials not only protected the oppressors but participated in their economic oppression. In June 1855, under the leadership of two brothers, Sidhu and Kanhu, the Santhals announced "their intention to take possession of the country and set up a Government of their own". They cut off postal and rail communications between Bhagalpur and Rajmahal. The Santhals proclaimed the end of the Company's rule; the regime of their Subah had commenced. The troops were alerted and military operations began. Unable to face the Company's musketry, the rebels took shelter in the thick jungles and carried on their struggle. A British force under major Burrough suffered a humiliating defeat. However, in February 1856 the rebel leaders were arrested and the rebellion suppressed with great brutality. The government tried a pacification by creation of a separate district of Santhal Parganas.

Peasant Participation in the Revolt of 1857. No uniform pattern of peasant participation in the disturbed areas can be discerned. However, in most of Oudh and Western U.P., the peasant forgot the oppressive hands of the local zamindars and joined the local feudal leadership in a bid to uproot foreign imperialism. Canning's announcement of confiscation of proprietary rights in the soil was meant to punish those who had taken active part against the Government. However, after the revolt, for tactical considerations the British Indian government decided to maintain the landed classes as the social buttress of the British raj. The post 1857 settlement was made with the taluqdars of Oudh, restoring most of the land to them; rather the position of the taluqdars was strength end by conferring on them some magisterial and revenue powers. The interests of the occupancy peasants were ignored and the Chief Commissioner even refused to extend the provisions of the Bengal Rent Act of 1859 to Oudh. Rather, the peasants of some areas like the Meerut division were made to pay some additional cesses as a punitive impost for participation in the revolt.

Bengal Indigo Cultivators' Revolt, 1860. The revolt was directed against British planters who behaved like feudal lords in their estates. The revolt enjoyed the support of all categories of the rural population including the zamindars, moneylenders, rich peasants and even karamcharis of indigo concerns.

Right from the beginning of the 19th century many retired officers of the East India Company and some upstarts who had earlier been slave traders in America acquired land from Indian zamindars in Bihar and Bengal and began large-scale cultivation of indigo. These planters committed great abuses and oppressions on the cultivators in the process of forcing them to grow indigo crop under terms which were the least profitable to them. In April 1860 all the cultivators of the Barasat subdivision and in the districts of Patna and Nadia resorted to, what may be called, the first general strike in the history of Indian peasantry. They refused to sow any indigo. The strike spread to Jessore, Khulna, Rajsthan, Dacca, Malda, Dinajpur and other places in Bengal. Faced with such solid unity and determination and apprehending a great agrarian uprising, the Government ordered a notification to be issued enjoining on the police to protect the ryot in the possession of his lands, on which he was at liberty to sow any crop he liked, without interference on the part of the planter of anyone else. The planter could, if he liked, move the civil court for breach of contract. An Indigo Commission was also appointed in 1860. Its recommendations were embodied in Act VI of 1862. The Bengal indigo planters developed cold feet and gradually moved out to Bihar and Uttar Pardesh.

The Deccan Riots, 1875. The Deccan peasants uprising was directed mainly against the excesses of the Marwari and Gujarati moneylenders.

A combination of adverse circumstances—excessive government land revenue demand, slump in the world cotton prices at the end of the American Civil War—pushed the Deccan peasants Deeper in the morass of indebtedness. The evergreedy Marwari and Gujarati moneylenders, adept in the art of manipulation of their accounts and the peasants' illiteracy and habit of signing any bond without having a proper knowledge of its contents were at the root of the trouble. The civil courts invariably gave verdicts in favour of the usurious moneylenders who obtained decrees of evictions against the peasants.

The trouble started in village Kardeh in Sirur taluka in December 1874 when a Marwari moneylender Kalooram obtained a decree of eviction against Baba Saheb Deshmukh, a cultivator in debt to him for Rs. 150. The callous attitude of the moneylender in pulling down the house aroused the wrath of the villagers. The entire Poona district was ablaze by June 1875. The peasants attacked the moneylenders' houses, shops and burnt them down. Their chief targets were the bond documents, deeds and decrees that the moneylenders held against them. The rising spread to most of the talukas of Ahmadnagar district. The police assisted by the military was swung into action. By June 1875 nearly a thousand peasants were arrested and the uprising completely suppressed. The struggle had a popular base for the Government could not get trustworthy evidence against the rebels. The Government appointed the Deccan Riots Commission to investigate into the causes of the uprising. The ameliorative measure passed was the Agriculturists' Relief Act of 1879 which put restrictions on the alienation of the peasants' lands and imposed some restrictions on the operations of the Civil Procedure Code in that the peasant could not be arrested and sent to civil debtors' jail for failure to pay debts.

Punjab Peasants' Discontent and the Punjab Land Alienation Act, 1900. Rural indebtedness and large-scale alienation of agricultural land to non-cultivating classes was a countrywide phenomenon in rural India during the last quarter of the 19th century. Faced with peasant uprisings in Bengal and Maharashtra the Government could not wait for a similar rebellion in the Punjab before it would act. The communal complexion of the Punjab rural situation and the martial character of the Sikhs called for an early effective action.

As early as 1895 the Government of India addressed a circular to the provincial governments suggesting the advisability of imposing restrictions on alienation of agricultural land. The famines of 1896-97 and 1899-1900 resulting in large-scale distress brought the matter in sharp focus. The Panjab Land Alienation Act, 1900 was passed "as an experimental measure" to be extended to the rest of the country if it worked successfully in the Punjab. The Act divided the Punjab population under three heads *viz.*, the agricultural classes, the statutory agriculturist class (those who though not belonging to the agricultural class long settled interests in the land) and the rest of the population including the moneylenders. Restrictions were imposed on the sale and mortgage of the land from the first category to the other two categories, though members of the second and third category could sell or mortgage land as they pleased.

The Punjab peasant was also given partial relief against oppressive incidence of land revenue demand by the Government extending the Saharanpur Rules to the Punjab whereby the state land revenue demand was not to exceed 50% of the annual rental value of land.

The Indian National Congress and the Peasants. The Indian National Congress, to begin with at least, worked as a joint venture of British imperialists and the Indian bourgeoisie and could not be expected to champion the cause of the oppressed peasants. The Congress year after year passed resolutions on the existence of Indian poverty but the methods it suggested smacked of class interest; it asked for extension of Permanent Settlement to different parts of India and restrictions on over assessment where Permanent Settlement could not be introduced, Indianisation of public services, State help for industrialization, abolition of salt tax etc. but never officially demanded tenancy reforms in Bengal, Bihar, Orissa, Assam, Madras, the U.P., the C.P. or the Panjab. R.C. Dutt's *Open's Letters to*

Curzon on famines and land assessments in India were, consciously or unconsciously, more calculated to espouse the interests of the Indian landlords than the Indian peasants. Curzon's sarcastic dig at R.C. Dutta that the Government had done more to protect the tenants from the rapacity of the zamindars than the Indian National Congress remained unanswered.

Gandhiji and Peasant Struggles. Gandhiji's entry into Indian politics marked a change into the politico-economic life of India. In his anxiety to broaden the social base of the Congress he carried his message to the villages and sought to involve the peasants in the nationalist struggle.

Champaran and Kaira Satyagrahas. The European indigo planters of Champaran, a district in the north-western part of Bihar, practised all types of oppressions on the local Bihari peasants not very dissimilar from the earlier malpractices of planters in Bengal Gandhiji assisted by Rajendra Prasad and others started an open enquiry into the real condition of the peasants. He taught the peasants of Champaran the virtues of Satyagraha which consisted in open, disciplined, non-violent non-cooperation with injustice against the indigo planters. The Government of Bihar took offence at Gandhian moves and prohibited them from pursuing their enquiry and arrested Gandhiji. Later the Government developed cold feet and appointed an Enquiry Committee (June 1917) with Gandhi as one of the members. The ameliorative enactment, the Champaran Agrarian Act freed the tenants from the special imposts levied by the indigo planters Unfortunately, however, the Congress leaders did not follow up the matter to its logical conclusion by freeing the Champaran peasants from the excessive rents charged by the zamindars and exorbitant interest rates charged by the moneylenders.

The Kaira (Kheda) campaign was chiefly directed against the Government. In the spring of 1918 crop failures and drought brought misery to the peasants of Kaira in Gujarat. The Bombay Government, however, insisted on its pound of flesh in the form of land revenue. The land revenue rules provided for remission of land revenue if the crop yield was less than 25% of then normal. the cultivators claimed that to be the case which the Government officials denied. Gandhiji organised the peasants and enlisted the support of all classes. Peasants in large numbers offered Satyagraha and suffered imprisonment for defying unjust laws. The Satyagraha lasted till June 1918. The government had to concede the just demands of the peasants. Judith Brown has estimated that the government did collect nearly 93% of the assessment.

The Champaran and Kaira struggles established Gandhiji as the leader of the masses and opened the eyes of the educated kisans to the political possibilities of peasants' mass-action.

The Mappila (Moplah) Uprising, 1921. The Muslim leaseholders (kanamdars) and cultivators (verumpattamdars) of South Malabar (kerala state) were popularly known as Moplahs. They were mainly converts to Islam from the lower caste Hindus like Tiyya. Some of them were descendants of the Arabians Muslims who had settled during the 8th and 9th centuries on the Malabar Coast. The Moplahs mostly took to agriculture and worked tenants ro *jemis* (bonded labour) of Hindu landlords. In the 19th century the Moplah agrarian grievances (which centered round excessive land revenue demand, insecurity of land tenure, renewal fees and extra landlord exactions) resulted in as many as 22 outbreaks between 1836 and 1894 (in talukas or south Malabar) in which the rebels killed numerous police and government officials and some Hindu landlords. In the 19th century the British rulers always branded Moplah peasants' strikes as communal outbursts and suppressed the rebels.

Since most of the landlords belonged to Hindu upper castes like Namboodri and Nair and most of the Moplahs were Muslim converts fom Hindu lower castes, the Moplah outbreaks assumed the dimensions of a class conflict with religious overtones. Many Moplahs believed that the cruel landlords merited death and it was a religious virtue to kill oppressive landlords (who also happened to be *kafirs* i.e. non-believers) even though they might have to become *shahids* (martyrs); in the latter case they would go straight to heaven. Thus, acts of violence helped a Moplah to wipe out the source of injustice and at the same time ensure for himself a place in paradise. Seen in this light, what religion provided was justification, not a motive to violence.

The Moplah rebellion of 1921 stemmed from twin grievances of the Moplah Muslim, peasantry (continued landlord oppression) and British government's anti-khilafat policies. In April 1920 Malabar District Congress held at Manjeri struck a pro-peasant stance and passed resolutions demanding tenancy reforms.

Soon after many tenants' associations were formed at Kozhikode and other places. The reader should remember that during 1920-21, the Congress under Gandhiji's leadership and the Khilafat Movement under Ali Brothers had joined hands for redressal of Indian grievances.

In 1921 the Moplah peasants' movement and the Khilafat movement got inextricably merged into one. The Khilafat movement become a world-wide protest movement of the Muslims against the harsh treatment meted out by the victorious Allied Powers to the Sultan of Turkey (the Khalifa of the Muslim community) and the dismemberment of the Turkish empire. The Indian Muslims under the leadership of the Ali Brothers whipped up anti-British hysteria and created a rebellious mood against the Government. The volatile Moplahs declared Ali Musaliar, a highly respected priest and a local Khilafat leader, as the Raja and Khilafat flags were unfurled over government buildings in the Ernad taluka of south Malabar.

The immediate provocation for the revolt was provided by E.F. Thomas, the district magistrate of Ernad taluka, who on 20 August 1921 raided a mosque at Tirurangadi in a bid to arrest Ali Musaliar. Soon the rebellion spread to Walluvanad and Ponnani talukas. From the months of August to September 1921 the British writ did not run in these areas, for the rebels had killed some European officers, blocked the roads, cut off telegraph lines, uprooted railway lines and destroyed many Government buildings.

In October 1921 the Government authorities sent a strong contingent to deal with the rebellion. Surrounded on all sides, the desperate Moplahs misled by rumours and suspecting Hindu complicity with the government resorted to inhuman killing of innocent Hindu men, women and children. By the end of the year 1921 the government crushed rebellion resulting in the killing of 2,337 Moplahs and wounding another 1652, though the unofficial figure put the number of casualities at 10,000. In addition, about 3000 Moplahs were sentenced to transportation for life to the Andaman jails.

The Moplah rebellion was ruthlessly crushed, which so greatly demoralised the community that thereafter they dared not take part in any peasant revolt or national political activity till the British rule lasted in India.

Formation of Kisan Sabhas. A section of the kisan leadership saw the inner contradictions in Congress agrararian policy. The peasant movements lanuched by the Congress were primarily aimed at seeking relief against escessive government land revenue demand and were thus solicitous for the interests of the zamindars and landed magnates. The Congress was virtually indifferent to inter-agrarian relations i.e. relations between landlords on the one hand and tenants, cultivators and agricultural labour on the other hand under Permanent Settlement and in ryotwari areas the relations between the rich farmer and sharecroppers or landless labour. The propaganda of the Communists and other left parties created class consciousness among the peasants and provided the nucleus for the formation of Kisan Sabhas.

In the 1920s Kisan Sabhas were organised in Bengal, the Panjab and the U.P. In 1928 the Andhra Provincial Ryots Association was formed. However, the first All India Kisan Sabha was formed at Lucknow on 11 April 1936. The Kisan Sabha explained its objective of "securing complete freedom from economic exploitation and achievement of full economic and political power for peasants and workers and all other exploited classes." It also demanded a moratorium on debts, abolition of land revenue and rent from uneconomic holdings, reduction of land revenue and rent, licensing of moneylenders, minimum wages for agricultural workers, fair prices for sugarcane and commercial crops and irrigation facilities. It also envisaged abolition of zamindari and vesting of land in the tiller of the soil. All these objectives were to be achieved by proper organisation and active participation in the national struggle for independence.

The Kisan Sabhas launched anti-settlement agitation against zamindari 'zulum' in Andhra Pradesh. In U.P. and Bihar heroic struggles were launched against zamindars' exploitation. In 1936 agitation started against Bakasht (self-cultivated land) movement in Bihar. Bakasht was zamindar's khas land which was cultivated by tenants on condition that they would pay a certain portion of the produce as rent to the land owner. The zamindars sought to bring more and more land under this category in a bid to prevent tenants from claiming occupancy rights. There was largescale eviction of tenants on one or the other plea in 1937. The Kisan Sabha organised the evicted tenants and they offered satyagraha, thereby preventing others from cultivating land. Violent clashes occurred resulting in many casualties. The All India Kisan Sabha organised a Bihar Kisan Day on 18 October 1937 against police repression on satyagrahis.

The growth of Kisan Sabhas also worked as a pressure on the Indian National Congress. The Congress struck a radical Posture in agrarian programme at its karachi and Faizpur sessions. The Faizpur Congress adopted resolutions on the need for reduction of rent and revenue abolition of fedual dues and levies, fixity of tenure, moratorium on debts and need for statutory provisions for ensuring living wage and suitable working conditions for the agricultural labourers.

Popular Ministries in Provinces and Peasant Movements. The peasants hoped for much from popular provincial governments formed in 1937 but faced disillusionment. To focus attention on their demands nearly 20,000 peasants gathered outside the Bihar Legislative Assembly on 23 August 1937, the opening day of the Assembly shouting slogans : "Give us water, we are thirsty ; give us bread, we are hungry : remit all our agricultural loans ; down with zamindars and save us from oppression." The Kisan leaders expected much from the new government and sought to persuade the Congress to adopt some measures for the cause of the peasants. The Restoration of Bakasht Land Act and Bihar Tenancy Act in 1938 afforded some relief to the tenants' but evictions continued. The Government also made tenants' holdings transferable without prior consent of zamindars, and reduced the *salami* rates ; rents were reduced by nearly 1/4th on an average etc. However, the Kisan leaders wanted the Congress to establish Kisan raj which meant abolition of zamindari and distribution of land among the landless. The zamindar-backed Congress government in Bihar could not legislate for zamindari abolition. The performance of Congress ministries in the Central Provinces and Bombay was equally unsatisfactory. The Bengal government's ambiguous land ligislation resulted in widespread eviction of tenants.

Radical elements in the Kisan Sabha advocated a break with the Congress accusing it of pro-zamindar policies. However, in the name of keeping up a united front against foreign imperialism, the Congress leaders succeeded in keeping the Congress and the Kisan Sabha together. In disgust Swami Sahajan and resigned from the Kisan Sabha in 1945. His exit marked the leginning of the complete control of the Communists over the Kisan Sabha.

Peasant Struggles on the Eve Indian Independence. In the decade preceding the advent of independence three significant peasant struggles, namely, Tebhaga Movement in Bengal, the Telengana outbreak in Hyderabad state and the Varlis revolt in Western India deserve mention. The Tebhaga movement was a protracted peasant struggle involving lower stratum of tenants such as bargardars (share-croppers), adhiars and poor peasants etc. against not only the zamindars but a section of the rich peasants (jotedars), against moneylenders, traders and the British bureaucracy. The Bargardari Bill introduced by Suhrawardy's government afforded some relief to rent-paying tenants. The insurrection in Telengana during 1946–51 was launched in the territory of the Nizam's state of Hyderabad against intense exploitation and oppression of landlords, moneylenders, traders and the Nizam's officials. It may be mentioned that the Nizam's crown lands and those of his aristocracy accounted for nearly one-third of his vast dominions on which more than 20 lakh poverty-stricken peasants worked for their living. The movement was linked with the States people movement under the leadership of the Praja Mandal and had the sympathy of the Congress, the Arya Samaj and the linguistic demand for a Vishal Andhra state. The role of the Communist party in organising the peasants was very significants. The entry of Indian troops in Hyderabad and the state's accession to the Indian Union did not end the struggle. The vestiges of feudalism continued intact. The peasants of Telengana and the adjoining areas of Madras state continued their struggle under Communist leadership and many an official and landlord either fled away or were murdered. The movement was withdrawn in October 1951 with the change in tactics by the Communists in India. The revolt of the Varlis, tribal people in Western India, not far away from Bombay, was a struggle against exploitation of forest contractors, moneylenders, rich farmers and landlords on the tacit support of the British bureaucracy. The Kisan Sabha took up their cause and launched a struggle in May 1945. The police oppression failed to terrorize the Varlis. The Varlis increasingly came under the influence of the Communist Party.

On the morrow of independence, India inherited an antiquated agrarian system which called for drastic structual changes and a dynamic tiller-oriented infrastructure for agricultural development. The 46 years of independence seem to have belied such hopes.

SELECT REFERENCES

1. Blyn, G. : *Agricultural Trends in India, 1891–1947.*
2. Desai, A.R. : *Peasant Struggles in India.*
3. Dhanagare, D.N. : *Agrarian Movements and Gandhian Politics.*
4. Natrajan, L. : *Peasant Uprising in India.*
5. *Report of Congress Agrarian Reforms Committee, 1949.*
6. Sen, S. : *Agrarian Relations in India.*
7. Whitcombe, E. : *Agrarian Conditions in Northen India.*

The Development of Famine Policy

Famines in Ancient and Medieval India. Even during the Hindu period of her history India did not enjoy absolute immunity from famines. But judging from the infrequency of allusions to these calamities in the ancient Sanskrit works and from the testimony of foreign travellers, it would not be incorrect to say that famines were an exceptional occurrence in ancient India. When they did occur, adequate relief measures were undertaken by the state. Kautilya in his *Arthasastra* mentions among other relief measures the revision of taxes, emigration, the granting of money and grain from state funds, construction of artificial lakes, tanks, wells etc. and the importation of grain from other places. During the Mohammendan period there were several famines and scarcities, the most severe occurring in the reigns of Mohammad Tughlak, Akbar, Shah Jahan and Aurangzeb. In spite of vigorous measures adopted by the emperors the famines took a heavy toll of life.

Famines Under the Company's Rule

During the rule of the East India Company India suffered in one part or another from twelve famines and four severe scarcities. The first of these was the dreadful Bengal famine of 1769–70 which claimed a third of the population of the province. No relief measures worth the name were undertaken by the state. Rather, the Company servants made large profits by buying up rice and retailing it at high prices. The years 1781 and 1782 were years of scarcity in Madras; in 1784 a severe famine afflicted the whole of Northern India. During the Madras famine of 1792 the state opened relief works for the famine-stricken. The Famine Commission of 1880 noted that "till the end of the 18th century the position of the British in India was not such as either to create any sense of general obligation to give relief or to supply sufficient means of affording it".

During the 1803 famine in North-Western Provinces and Oudh (now Uttar Pradesh) the state granted remissions of the revenue gave loans and advances to landowners, offered a bounty on all grain imported into Benares, Allahabad, Kanpur and Fatehgarh. The Guntur Famine of 1833 took away a heavy toll of life; in that 2 lakh persons died out of a total population of 5 lakhs. In 1837 there was a severe famine in Upper India. Public works were opened at several centres. However, the work of relieving the helpless and the infirm was left in the hands of the charitable public.

Under the East India Company no attempt was made to formulate any general system of famine relief or prevention. However, the provincial governments and district officers tried various experiments to afford relief to famine-stricken areas such as the storage of grain by the Government, penalties on hoarding, bounties on imports, advancing loans for sinking of wells etc.

Famines Under the Crown Administration, 1858 to 1947

The transfer of power from the Company to the Crown and the economic developments of the latter half of the 19th century like the extension of railways and other means of communications and transport, growth of overseas trade changed the complexion of the problem. The state also realised its responsibility for expansion of irrigation facilities, enactment of agrarian legislation and adoption of preventive measures as well as formulation of famine relief policy to meet possible famines.

Under the Crown there were ten severe famines besides a large number of scarcities. The first famine occurred in 1860–61 in the area between Delhi and Agra. This was the first occasion on which poor-houses were used as a means of affording relief and it was the first time when the authorities thought fit to enquire into the causes, area and intensity of the famine as well as took measures to cope with the distress. Colonel Baird Smith was deputed for this purpose but his report did not lead to any formulation of general principles of relief.

The Orissa Famine, 1866. The drought of 1865 followed by a famine the following year affected Orissa, Madras, Northern Bengal and Bihar. The calamity was most severe in Orissa, hence the name the 'Orissa Famine.' The Government officers though forewarned took no steps to meet the approach of the calamity and when it came looked helpless. The Government adhered to the principles of free trade and the law of demand and supply. The Government did provide employment to the able-bodied, leaving the work of charitable relief to voluntary agency. Since voluntary agency did very little, the famine took a heavy toll of life. It was estimated that 13 lakh persons died in Orissa alone.

The Orissa calamity proved a turning point in the history of Indian famines for it was followed by the appointment of a Committee under the chairmanship of Sir George Campbell to report on the matter. The Committee made recommendations which in some measure anticipated those of the Royal Commission of 1880. The old doctrine that the Public was responsible for the relief of the helpless was abandoned. The Government was expected to borrow money in order to afford finance for building of railways and canals. Further, the district officers were made responsible for saving all preventable deaths.

In 1868 a severe famine visited Northern and Central India. The worst affected areas were Rajputana and Central India. The Government took action to relieve distress but the relief given was not commensurate with the magnitude of the distress and there was considerable loss of life.

The Famine of 1876–78. The great famine of 1876–78 was perhaps the most grievous calamity experienced since the beginning of the 19th century. It affected Madras, Bombay, Uttar Pradesh and the Panjab. The famine affected area was estimated at 257,000 sq. miles with a population of more than 58 millions. Many villages were depopulated and large tracts of territory went out of cultivation. R.C. Dutt has estimated that 5 million persons perished in a single year. The Government made half-hearted efforts to help the famine-stricken. The government famine machinery was inadequate and ineffective and the unwisdom of the policy was amply clear. The Government refused to recognise its responsibility for saving human lives and "the task of saving life, irrespective of cost, is on which is beyond their power to undertake, and that in the interest of the distressed population itself, as well as of the taxpayer generally, The Government of India was bound to adopt precaution against indolence or imposition."[1]

Recommendations of Strachey Commission, 1880. In 1880 the Government of Lytton appointed a Commission under the presidency of Sir Richard Strachey to formulate general principles and suggest particular measures of a preventive or protective character. The Commission recommended the adoption of the following basic principles:

(1) Employment on works must be offered before the physical efficiency of applicants had been impaired by privation. Wages paid should be adjusted from time to time to provide sufficient food for a labourer's support.

(2) It should be the duty of the state to provide gratuitous relief to the impotent poor and listed the category of persons entitled to receive it. The relief provided could take the form of supply of raw grain or money or cooked food might be provided on condition of residence in a poor-house or a relief camp. For the distribution of gratuitous relief the distressed tracts should be divided into circles and each circle placed under a competent officer.

(3) Supplies of food in the distressed areas should be carefully watched. However, the Government must trust private trade in supply and distribution of food and prohibit export of grain only if a became reasonably certain that action was necessary to conserve the resources of India as a whole.

---

1. *Report of Famine Commission,* 1901.

(4) The Commission made suggestions in regard to suspensions and remissions of land revenue and rents.

(5) The cost of famine relief should be borne by the provincial governments. However, Central assistance was to be made available whenever necessary.

(6) In times of excessive drought facilities should be provided for migration of cattle to grassy forest areas where abundant pasturage was available.

The Government accepted in general the Commission's recommendations and steps were taken to find new resources for the creation of a Famine fund to meet extraordinary charges. In 1883 the provisional Famine Code was formulated which formed a guide and a basic for the various Provincial Famine Codes which were subsequently formulated. The first chapter of these codes prescribed precautions to be taken in ordinary times. The second gave instructions to be followed when a relief campaign seemed imminent. Districts might be declared by provincial governments either scarcity or famine areas. The remaining chapters described the duties of all concerned when the famine actually began. The droughts in different provinces between 1883 and 1896 afforded opportunities of testing and revising the provincial codes.

The Famine of 1896–97. Between 1880 and 1896 there were two famines and five scarcities, all of them of a more or less local character. The great famine of 1896–97 affected almost every province, though in varying degrees of intensity, the total population affected was estimated at 34 millions. The relief operations were conducted with a fair measure of success except in the Central Provinces where the death rate rose very high. Extensive relief operations were undertaken and in many parts of the country people were relieved in their own homes. The total cost of relief was estimated at 7.27 crores. A commission presided over by Sir James Lyall, ex-Lt. Governor of the Panjab, adhered largely to the views expressed by their predecessors in 1880 suggesting some alterations which were designed to impart greater flexibility to the maxims then adopted.

The Famine of 1899–1900. Closely following the calamity came the famine of 1899–1900. It affected an area of 189,000 sqmiles and a population of 28 millions. The authorities failed and in some cases refused to open relief works in the early stages of the famine, and when they were opened such vast numbers came on them that the system almost completely broke down in many cases. The relief expenditure came to Rs. 10 crores.

Recommendations of MacDonnell Commission. Lord Curzon appointed a Commission under the presidency of Sir Anthony MacDonnell. It submitted its report in 1901 in which it summarised accepted principles of relief, suggesting variations wherever necessary. The Commission emphasised the benefits of a policy of "moral strategy", early distribution of advances for purchase of seed and cattle and sinking of temporary wells. It also advocated the appointment of a Famine Commissioner in a province where relief operations were expected to be extensive. It also emphasised enlistment of non-official assistance on a larger scale and preference in particular circumstances of village works to the large public works which had hitherto been the backbone of relief schemes. The Commission also stressed the desirability of better transport facilities, opening of agricultural banks, improvement of irrigation facilities and vigorous measures to foster improved methods of agriculture.

Most of the recommendations of the Commission were accepted and before Curzon left India he had taken various measures to prevent and combat famine.

Between 1901 and 1941 a large number of famines and scarcities of a local character occurred, those of 1906–07 and 1907–08 being the more serious.

Bengal Famine of 1942–43. The Great Bengal Famine of 1942–43 took a heavy toll of life. The root cause of the famine lay in a series of crop failures that Bengal experienced from 1938 and in the conditions created by the Second World War. The normal import of rice from Burma stopped and trade and movement of foodgrains was dislocated because of controls and nearness of Bengal to the theatre of war in the East. This famine might be called "more man-made than an act of God". Man exploited the situation created by Nature and War.

Relief measures were belated and inadequate. The dealy in facing the problem of relief and the non-declaration of the famine were bound up with the unfortunate war propaganda policy of "no shortage". Relief expenditure was at one stage limited on financial grounds. Above all, the Central Government showed a callous disregard for the misfortunes of Bengal and wanted the Provincial Government of Bengal to undertake and organise famine relief.

The Self-Sufficiency Target. It is evident that famines in India are frequently occurring calamities. The present food situation in the country is a mere extension of the famine problem that has been with us for long. The complexion of the problem has changed as a result of the momentous changes in the political and economic field since 1947, but the basic issue–the failure of supply to keep pace with the growing demand for food–remains the same. Increasing population coupled with improved standard of consumption of foodgrains among the poor classes have added to the complexity of the problem. The National Government put 'self-sufficiency' in foodgrains as the immediate goal of our agricultural policy. But the country even after the successful completion of five Five-Year Plans finds itself more distant from that goal today than it was at the beginning of the First Five-Year Plan. Now the emphasis has shifted from meeting a famine when it occurs to avoiding its visitation. The "Green Revolution" propped under the leadership of Smt. Indira Gandhi has somewhat lessened the complexity of food problem and the target of self-sufficiency is nearly achieved.

SELECT REFERENCES

1. Anstey, Vera.   :   *Economic Development of India.*
2. Bhatia, B.M.   :   *Famines in India.*
3. Digby, William   :   *Prosperous' British India.*
4. Dutt, R.C.   :   *Economic History of India, 2 vols.*
5. Dutt, R.C.   :   *Famines in India.*
6. Loveday, A.   :   *History and Economics of Famines in India.*
7. Ray, S.C.   :   *Economic Causes of Indian Famines.*

39

GROWTH OF LOCAL SELF-GOVERNMENT IN INDIA

> When municipal and local boards were formed in most of the provinces after 1882, economy was the cue...The new system was casting wider nets to find collaborators for the Raj.
>
> —*Anil Seal*

Local Self-Government means the management of local affairs by such local bodies as have been elected by the people living in that particular locality. The importance of local self-government has been emphasised by political thinkers and administrators of all ages. It was Tocqueville who said that "town meetings are to liberty what primary schools are to science". Inaugurating the Conference of Provincial Local Self-Government Ministers in August 1948, Pandit Jawaharlal Nehru said, "Local Self-Government is, and must be, the basis of any true system of democracy. We have got rather into the habit of thinking of democracy at the top and not so much below. Democracy at the top will not be a success unless it is built on this foundation from below."

Local bodies are constituted on two different principles. One is that local bodies enjoy extensive powers to act anyway they like for the good of the community unless circumscribed by law in any sphere of activity. The other principle is that local bodies cannot go beyond the specific functions defined for them in the various acts and statutes. In Germany local bodies are constituted on the first principle, while in the U.S.A. and the U.K. the second principle operates. In India local bodies have developed on the pattern of the U.K.

Municipal government functioned in India in the time of the Imperial Mauryas, but in the sense in which it is understood today, it is an offshoot of the British rule. It was in the presidency towns that local bodies first came into existence. In 1687 the Court of Directors ordered for the setting up of a corporation in Madras. The Corporation, composed of British and Indian members, was empowered to levy taxes for building a guildhall, a jail, a school house for meeting the expenses of municipal staff and for "such further ornaments and edifices as shall be thought convenient for the honour, interest security and defence of the town and its inhabitants." The experiment proved premature for the inhabitants resisted the payment of direct taxes. As such no projects could be taken in hand. The Mayor sought the permission of the authorities to levy an octroi duty (and indirect taxes people had been accustomed to pay in India since time immemorial) in a bid to find founds for scavenging. The Charter of 1726 provided for the setting up of a Mayor's Court to supersede the corporation. The powers of the Mayor's Court were more judicial than administrative. Similar Mayor's Courts were set up in Bombay and Calcutta.

The Charter Act of 1793 put the municipal institutions on a statutory basis. The Governor-General was empowered to appoint Justices of Peace in the presidency towns. These Justices of Peace were given powers to levy taxes on houses and lands to meet the cost of police, scavenging and repair of roads. A house tax at the rate of 5% of the rental value was imposed in the presidency towns. Between 1840 and 1853 the rate-payers were given the right to elect members of corporations, but the process was reversed in 1856 when all executive power, in the Bombay town, was concentrated in the hands of a nominated commissioner. A similar procedure was followed in Madras and Calcutta. Further attempts to introduce the elective element were made in 1872, 1876 and 1878.

Outside the presidency towns the beginning of municipal institutions is to be traced from the Bengal Act of 1842. The Act was passed to enable "the inhabitants of any place of public resort or residence to make better provision for purposes connected with public health and convenience." The Act was of a permissive nature and a municipal institution could be set up in a town only after 2/3 of the householders had requested for that. Under this Act a Municipal Board was set up in one town only, and here too when the householders were called upon to pay direct taxes, they not only refused but prosecuted the Collector for trespass when he went round to collect taxes. A great step forward was taken in 1850 when an Act was passed applicable to the whole of British India. This Act authorised municipal bodies to levy indirect taxes. The Act, however, was of a voluntary nature. The North-Western Provinces (modern U.P.) and Bombay took advantage of this Act and municipal committees were set up in several towns. The publication of the Royal Army Sanitary Commission Report in 1868 gave further fillip to the development of municipal institutions. The report, though primarily dealt with army affairs, drew attention of the Government to the insanitary conditions in the towns. In the years following a number of municipalities were set up in every province. In the Punjab and Central Provinces elected elements were also introduced in local bodies.

In rural areas a parallel development of local institutions was taking place. The Sind Administration by the Act of 1865 authorised local bodies to levy rates in the shape of a cess of one anna in a rupee on land and *sayer* (miscellaneous) revenue as also a tax on stamps. The Government of Madras and Bombay followed suit. In 1866 the Madras Government authorised the levy of a road cess at the rate of $3\frac{1}{4}$% of the annual rental of land. The Bombay Government by Act III of 1869 provided for the creation of a local fund committee in each district under the presidency of the Collector of the district concerned; these committees levied certain cesses and looked after public health, education and other local needs of the people.

Mayo's Resolution of 1870. The Indian Council Act of 1861 inaugurated the policy of legislative devolution and Mayo's Resolution of 1870 on financial decentralization was its natural corollary. Administrative convenience and financial stringency prompted the Imperial Government to transfer to the control of provincial governments certain departments of administration which, among others, included education, medical services and roads. Here we find the beginnings of local finance. The provincial governments were authorized to resort to local taxation to balance their budgets. Of course the meagre resources of the provincial governments were supplemented by an annual grant from the Imperial Government. Lord Mayo's Resolution emphasised : "Local interest, supervision, and care are necessary to success in the management of the funds devoted to education, sanitation, medical relief, and local public works. The operation of this Resolution in its full meaning and integrity will afford opportunities for the development of self-government, for strengthening municipal institutions, and for the association of Natives and Europeans to a greater extent than heretofore in the administration of affairs."

The various provincial governments passed municipal Acts to implement the policy outlined. The Bengal District Board Cess Act, 1871 was the first step towards provision of local self-government in rural Bengal. Similar acts were passed in Madras, North-Western Provinces and the Punjab.

Ripons' Resolution of 1882. Ripon's viceroyalty saw the liberalization of administration in every sphere. The Resolution of 1882 stands out as a landmark in the development of local self-government. Reviewing the progress in the field since Mayo's resolution of 1870, the Government of Ripon noted with satisfaction that a large income from local rates and cesses had been secured and in some provinces the management of this income had been freely entrusted to local bodies and that municipalities had increased in number and usefulness. However, it was felt that there was a greater inequality of progress in different parts of the country than varying local circumstances seemed to warrant, that many services admittedly adapted for local management were still reserved in the hands of provincial governments while the expenses for 'watch and ward' (police maintenance) were a great burden on the resources of the municipalities. The government of Ripon desired the provincial government to apply in case of local bodies the same principle of financial decentralization which Lord Mayo's Government had begun towards them. The provincial governments were asked to unbertake a careful survey of provincial, local and municipal finances with a view to ascertain :

(a) What items of receipt and charge could be transferred from provincial to local heads for administration;

(b) What re-distribution of items was desirable, in order to lay on local and municipal bodies those which were best understood and appreciated by the people; and

(c) To consider ways of equalizing local and municipal taxation throughout the Empire.

On receipt of detailed reports from provincial governments, the Imperial Government adopted the Resolution of 1882 which marks the effective beginning of local self-government in India. The development of local bodies was advocated not only with a view to improving the administration, but as an instrument of political and popular education. Local boards were to be developed throughout the country and charged with definite duties and entrusted with suitable sources of revenue. For rural areas, Taluka Boards or District Boards were to be set up. These local bodies were to have non-official majorities coupled with a general system of election wherever local circumstances permitted. Official interference was to be reduced to the minimum and exercised to revise and check the acts of local bodies but not to dictate policies. Of course, official executive sanction was necessary in certain cases, such as raising of loans, alienation of municipal property, imposition of new taxes, undertaking works costing more than a prescribed sum, framing rules and bye-laws etc.

In pursuance of this Resolution many Acts were passed between 1883 and 1885 which greatly altered the constitution, powers and functions of municipal bodies in India. Unfortunately, however, the bureaucracy did not share the liberal views of the Viceroy and thought that the Indians were unfit for self-government. The closing decades of the nineteenth century was a period of Imperialism, and the high priest of that creed, Lord Curzon, actually took steps to increase official control over local bodies.

The Decentralization Commission Report, 1908. The entire subject of local self-government was reviewed by the Royal Commission on Decentralization and important recommendations made touching almost every sphere of local administration. The report of the Commission is still a guiding star for state governments. The Commission pointed out the lack of financial resources as the great stumbling block in the effective functioning of local bodies. Sir Herbert Risley, the Home Secretary to the Government of India, put on record : "I think it must be admitted that the resources of district boards and district municipalities are not sufficient to enable them to work up to the modern standards of local administration. In municipalities that is most conspicuously the case in respect of schemes of water supply and drainage, the advantages of which, especially of the former, are now pretty generally realised. Similarly in some rural areas in Bengal the old sources of water supply have fallen into disrepair and the district boards are approached with demands far beyond their financial resources. In other parts of the same province the silting up of old channel and changes of levels are believed to cause malarial fever, and large schemes of drainage are advocated which the local bodies are unable to carry out."

The Commission laid emphasis on the development of Village Panchayats and Sub-District Boards. It recommended that the Village Panchayats should be entrusted with more power likes (a) summary jurisdiction in petty civil and criminal cases; (b) incurring of expenditure on village scavenging and minor village works; (c) construction, maintenance and management of village schools; (d) management of small fuel and fodder reserves etc. Above all, for proper functioning of Village Panchayats, these should be given adequate sources of income and the interference of district officers should be circumscribed.

The Commission greatly emphasised the importance of Sub-District Boards and recommended that these should be established in every taluka of tehsil and should be the principal agencies in rural board administration. They did not desire to place Sub-District Boards entirely under the control of a District Board for the whole district. The scheme suggested envisaged separate spheres of duties and separate sources of revenue for Sub-District Boards and the District Boards.

Regarding municipalities, the Commission urged the withdrawal of existing restrictions on their powers of taxation and also stoppage of regular grants-in aid from provincial governments except for undertaking large projects such as those concerning drainage or water supply. It suggested that municipalities might undertake the responsibility for primary education and, if willing, for middle vernacular schools, otherwise the government should relieve them of any charges in regard to secondary education, hospitals, famine relief, police, veterinary works, etc.

The Government of India Resolution of 1915 contained the official views on the recommendation of the Decentralization Commission. The Resolution referred to "the smallness and inelasticity of local revenues" and "the difficulty of revising further forms of taxation". Thus, most of the recommendations of the Commission remained on paper and the condition of local bodies continued to be where it wat left by Lord Ripon.

The Resolution of May 1918. The historic announcement of 20 August 1917 declared that the future direction of constitutional advance was towards grant of responsible government to the people on India and the first step towards the progressive realisation of that ideal was to be in the sphere of local self-government. The Montford Report suggested : "There should be, as far as possible, complete popular control in local bodies and the largest possible independence for them of outside control."

The Government of India Resolution of 16 May 1918 reviewed the entire question of local self-government in the light of the announcement of 20 August 1917. In order to give effect to the new policy outlined, the Resolution suggested that local bodies should be made as representative as possible of the people, their authority over the matters entrusted to them should be real and not nominal, that all unnecessary official control should be checked and local bodies allowed to learn by their mistakes. The Resolution in general endorsed the recommendations of the Decentralization Commission in entrusting the municipal boards with greater powers to vary the rate of taxation, in giving them a more free hand in regard to their budget, in greater control of services paid for by local bodies etc.

Regarding village panchayats, the Rosolution stated that local bodies should not be looked upon as mere mechanical adjuncts of local self-government but as associations designed to develop village corporate life on the basis of the intimacy existing between the inhabitants who had not only common civic interests but were also kept together by ties of tradition and of blood. The provincial governments were urged to make an effective beginning towards development of village panchayats.

Under Dyarchy. With the coming into force of the Government of India Act 1919 local self-government became a 'transferred' subject under popular ministerial control. The Government of India no longer issued any instruction to provincial governments and each province was allowed to develop local self-institutions according to provincial needs and requirements. Under the Scheduled Taxes Rules, the taxes which could be imposed by local bodies were separated from those which fell within the competence of provincial governments. The Indian ministers, however, could not do much work in the sphere of local self-government for lack of funds, since finance was a 'reserved' subject under the charge of an Executive Councillor.

The Simon Commission reporting in May 1930 referred to the wide financial powers exercised by local bodies. It, however, observed that village panchayats had not shown any marked progress except in the U.P. Bengal and Madras. The Commission suggested the retrograde step of increasing the control of provincial governments over local bodies in the interest of greater efficiency and quoted the example of England where "by numerous administrative devices, by inspection, by audit, by the giving of grants-in-aid on conditions ensuring efficiency and by insisting on standards of competence in the municipal staff, the local Government Board and its successors, the Ministry of Health have steadily raised the standard of administration in local authorities." Reporting on the poor financial condition of local bodies, the Commission adversely commented on the reluctance of the elected members to impose local taxes and stated that generally speaking, the management of finances of local bodies had deteriorated since the introduction of the Reforms of 1919 and this laxity could not be adequately corrected by inadequate powers of audit possessed by provincial governments.

The Government of India Act 1935 and after. By the Government of India Act 1935 provincial autonomy was introduced which gave further impetus to the development of local institutions. Popular ministries controlled finance and could make available adequate funds for development of local bodies. The demarcation of taxation between provincial and local finance which prevailed since the Reforms of 1919 was done away with. Practically in every province new Acts were passed giving more functions to local bodies. However, the financial resources of local institutions and their powers of taxation remained more or less the same as in the days of Ripon. Rather, after 1935 certain new restrictions were placed on the powers of local bodies to levy or enhance terminal taxes on trades, callings and professions and municipal property. The provincial governments seemed to have ignored the liberal policy of granting wide powers of taxation to local institutions as recommended by the Decentralization Commission. At the time of India's independence, the control of provincial governments over local bodies in matters of new proposals for taxation, for reduction or abolition of existing taxes were subject to the prior approval of the provincial governments.

The attainment of independence in 1947 and the greater emphasis on the building of democracy from the bottom upwards raised new hopes. The Directive Principles of State Policy (Article 40) of the New Constitution enjoins on State Governments the desirability of organising village panchayats and endowing them with such powers and authority as may be necessary to enable them to function as units of self-government. The Local Finance Enquiry Committee report submitted in 1951 drew attention to the desperate financial plight of the local bodies and made detailed suggestions for assigning certain new sources of revenue to them and giving them independent powers of taxation. The Report goes on to say that local bodies "can attain financial responsibility only by the exercise of such powers and having to bear the consequences of their errors." The Committee deplored the policy of habitually protecting local bodies against themselves and expressed the hope that "with the grant of larger powers will come an increased realisation of responsibility and the growth of informed public opinion will constitute a check which will prove more effective than official intervention."

SELECT REFERENCES

1. Dodwell, H.H. : *Cambridge History of India, vol. vi.*
2. Hart, S.G. : *Introduction to Self-Government in Rural Bengal.*
3. *Local Finance Enquiry Committee Report, 1951.*
4. Masani, R.P. : *Evolution of Self-Government in Madras.*
5. *Royal Commission on Decentralization Report, 1909.*

GROWTH OF THE CONSTITUTION UNDER THE COMPANYS RULE

The Charter giving a twenty years lease to the East India Company was considered by the natives of India as farming them out.

—*Halliday*

The acquisition of the *Diwani* of Bengal by the East India Company in 1765 provides the key to the development of the British Indian Constitution.

On August 12, 1765 Clive secured from Shah Alam II, the powerless and effete Mughal Emperor, a *firman* granting to the English Company the *Diwani* of Bengal, Bihar and Orissa, stipulating in return to pay the Emperor an annual subsidy of 26 lakhs of rupees. The Nawab of Bengal became a mere pensioner : the Company was to pay him annually a fixed sum of 53 lakhs of rupees for the support of the *Nizamat*. Clive thus established a Double Government in theory, with the Company as *Diwan,* and the Nawab as *Nazim.* But the Nawab, having lost all independent military or financial support for his executive actions, became in fact a mere figurehead.

According to Clive's arrangement, the Company left to the Deputy Diwans Mohammad Reza Khan for Bengal and Raja Shitab Rai for Bihar, the functions of *Diwan i.e.,*—land revenue and customs collection, and administration of civil justice. The deputy newab was to administer Bengal really in the interest of the Company while maintaining a fiction of the sovereignty of the Mughal Emperor and the formal authority of the nawab.

Thus, though the assumption of the *Diwani* is important as marking the formal recognition of the English position in Bengal, it left that position very anomalous. The actual conduct of government was still in the hands of Indian administrators, at a distance from the Company's headquarters though under its control. The establishment of this 'masked system' was a sign of the Company's unwillingness to recognise that it had ceased to be a mere trading body and become a ruling power. The primary object of this arrangement was to bolster up the finances of the Company which had suffered from the maintenance of armies without incurring the burden of formal and avowed dominion.

In England, the aspect of the arrangement which attracted chief attention was the immense wealth which the Company was expected to derive from the revenues of Bengal, estimated at £ 4,000,000 per annum. Some, including Pitt, held even then that the Crown should take over the governmental authority which the Company had now assumed, but this view was held by few and the first intervention of Parliament in the affairs of the Company in 1767 took the form merely of a demand for a share of the plunder to the extent of £ 400,000 per annum.

The system of government associated with the name of Clive continued under his successors Verelst (1767-69) and Cartier (1769-72). Under the system, the Nawab was relegated to the position of a figurehead, the administration was in the hands of the Deputy Nawab, a nominee of the Company and the English Resident at the Durbar decided every matter of importance. In that arrangement a fatal divorce of power from responsibility was inherent which caused most of the scandals and abuses speedily to make their appearance. In the first place, the abuses of private trade reached a greater height than ever before. The reason for it is not far to seek. The Indian administrators in that arrangement were open to illegitimate pressure, and unable to restrain the misconduct of the Company's servants. In the second place, the demands of the Company for increase of revenue led to gross oppression of the peasantry. the collection of the revenue from land was entrusted to zamindars who though theoretically removable had in most cases become hereditary and in some cases represented ancient princely families powerful zamindars often paid very little especially when the government was weak and could not force them or could be bribed to let them off lightly. When the Company found its revenue shrinking and demanded increase from the Indian revenue officers, the result was severe oppression in some districts, the whole burden of which fell upon the peasantry. An attempt was made by Verelst, to check high-handedness and venality by appointing English Supervisors for the *Diwani* lands, but it was found in the days of Cartier that they only made confusion more confounded and corruption more corrupt. What was really lacking was a principle of government adequate to the substance. During the seven years that the Dual System was in operation, the Company was on the verge of bankruptcy and had to ask to be excused from paying the sum of £400,000 p.a. demanded by Parliament while its servants were flourishing exceedingly. The sad state of affairs at last roused the British Government to make an effort to introduce some order into the affairs of the Company in India.

(A) The Regulating Act of 1773

Circumstances Leading to the Act. The first association of the British with the work of administration under what is called the system of Dual Government (1765 to 1772) is a discreditable and shameful page of British history, which has been summed up in a contemporary Muslim history, the *Siyar-ul Mutakherin*, thus : "The new rulers paid no attention to the concerns of the people and suffered them to be mercilessly oppressed and tormented by officers of their own appointing." Then came the famine of 1770 in Bengal which was one of the most appalling disasters in the recorded history of India. The Company was not responsible for the famine but it and its agents were largely to blame for a complete collapse of government. W.E.H. Lecky describes the plight of the people in the following words : "Never before had the Indians experienced a tyranny which was so skilful, so searching and so strong..."

During the twelve years preceding Warren Hastings' administration the servants of the Company thronged back to England loaded with wealth and what was strongly suspected of being the plunder of Bengal. The incursion of these 'Nabobs' with their lavish notions and orientalized habits into the aristocratic circles of the time is one of the most striking social phenomena of eighteenth century England. Contemporary memoirs and letters reveal the mingled contempt, envy and hatred with which they were regarded. While the servants of the Company were making huge profits, the Company itself was on the verge of insolvency.

It was an ill-chosen moment for the Company to go bankrupt, especially when it had so few friends, being hated by all and sundry. Yet that is what it contrived to do.

A blind folly had for some time past possessed the Directors and shareholders of the Company. In 1769 when the Company was in debt to the tune of £6 millions, a dividend of $12\frac{1}{2}$ % was decleared, though the Directors had to conceal facts and falsify accounts. When news reached England of the famine in Bengal and Haider Ali's successful onslaught into the Carnatic, the Company's stock showed a spectacular decline and before long rumours got abroad of the Company's true financial position. The Directors in sheer desperation applied to the Bank of England for a loan of £1,000,000.

The fat was really in the fire when the Directors of the bankrupt Company applied to the Government for relief ; for in doing so, they signed the death warrant of their Company's independence. The opportunity to turn its distress to the advantage of the State and especially of its Royal Head was too good for the resurrected Tories to miss. Lord North with secure majorities in both Houses of Parliament prudently referred the application to Parliament. A Select Committee was appointed to enquire into the Company's affairs. This Committee was presided over by General Burgoyne who in proposing a resolution for the appointment of the Committee declared : "The most atrocious abuses that ever stained the name of civil government called for redress...if by some means sovereignty and law are not separated from trade, India and Great Britian will be sunk and overwhelmed never to rise again."

Certainly, the conduct of the Directors supplied abundant food for speculation. In March of that year (1772) they had declared another dividend of $12\frac{1}{2}$% in August they asked the Government for of loan of £ 1 million. The discrepancy was so glaring that it caused the House of Commons to appoint a second (Secret) Committee to investigate the reasons for it. Why should a Company go bankrupt, members pertinently asked, when its servants were returning to England with their pockets bulging with gold. It was an interesting question.

In the spring of the following year the Committees of Enquiry issued their reports. As expected these were highly condemnatory. Two Acts of Parliament were passed. The first granted the Company a loan of £ 1, 400,000 at 4% interest on certain conditions. The second was the important Regulating Act. The Regulating Act was not passed without opposition in Parliament. The bill was fiercely opposed by the Company and its friends.

Provisions of the Regulating Act. The Act remodelled the constitution of the Company both in England and in India. In England the right of vote in the Court of Proprietors was raised from £ 500 to £ 1,000. It was provided that the Court of directors, hitherto elected every year, was henceforth to be elected for four years. The number of Directors was fixed at 24, one-fourth retiring every year. The Directors were required to "lay before the Treasury all correspondence *from* India dealing with the revenues and before a Secretary of Stage everything dealing with civil and military administration." Thus, for the first time the British Cabinet was given the right of controlling Indian affairs, although the right was imperfect.

In Bengal a collegiate government was created consisting of a Governor-General (President) and four members of the Council. The vote of the majority was to bind the Council, the Governor-General having a casting vote when there was an equal division of opinion. Three members of the Council formed a quorum. The first Governor-General (Warren Hastings) and Councillors (Philip Francis, Clavering, Monson and Barwell) were named in the Act. They were to hold office for five years, and could be removed earlier only by the King on the recommendation of the Court of Directors. Future appointments were to be made by the Company. The Governor-General-in-Council were vested with the civil and military government of the Presidency of Fort William in Bengal. They were to superintend and control in certain matters the subordinate Presidencies of Madras and Bombay.

The Act empowered the Crown to establish by charter a Supreme Court of Judicature, consisting of a Chief Justice and three puisne judges. The Supreme Court was to be a Court of Equity and of Common Law, a Court of Admiralty, and Ecclesiastical Court. All the public servants of the Company were made amenable to its jurisdiction. All British subjects in Bengal, European and Indian, could seek redress in the Supreme Court against oppression ; the Supreme court could also entertain suits, actions and complaints against persons in the Company's service or any of His Majesty's subjects. The Court could determine all types of cases and grant redress through all the methods then in vogue in English judicial procedure. The Court was given both original and appellate jurisdiction. Following the British custom, the Court heard these cases with the help of a jury of British subjects. The Supreme Court was constituted in 1774 with Sir Elijah Impey as Chief Justice and Chambers, Lemaister and Hyde as the Puisne judges.

The Regulating Act laid down the fundamental principle of honest administration by providing that "no person holding or exercising any civil or military office under the Crown shall accept, receive or take directly or indirectly any persent, gift, donation, gratuity or reward, pecuniary or otherwise."

Liberal salaries were provided for the Governor-General (£ 25,000), each member of the Council (£ 10,000), the Chief Justice of the Supreme Court (£ 8,000) and for each puisne Judge (£ 6000) a year.

Assessment of the Act. The Act appointed a Governor-General but shackled him with a Council that might reduce him to impotence as was actually the case with Warren Hastings from 1774 to 1776 when he was almost uniformly outvoted in the Council. The Act established a Supreme Court of Justice but made no attempt accurately to define the field of its jurisdiction, sefecify the law it was to administer or draw a line of demarcation between its functions and those of the Council The Act was a compromise throughout and intentionally vague in many of its provisions. It did not openly assert the soverignty of the British Crown or invade the titular authority of the Nawab of Bengal. The Act had "neither given the state a definite control over the Company nor the Directors a definite control over their servants, nor the Governor-General a definite control over his Council nor the Calcutta Presidency a definite control over Madras and Bombay." The Act was based on the theory of checks and balances. In actual practice it broke down under the stress of Indian circumstances and its own inherent defects. Hence the chief defects of the new system inaugurated by the Act were : (a) the unworkable relations which it established between the Governor-General and his Council,(b) the anomalous relations between the new Supreme Court administering English law, and the country courts already existing in Bengal. The Council and the Court were ranged in two hostile camps set against each other on the borderland of debatable jurisdictions. The Governor-General-in-Council could make no laws that the judges did not condescend to notice. There was the serious lacuna in the Act of a supreme legislative authority nearer than England to arbitrate in these quarrels and to mark off the proper sphere of the executive and judicial departments, (c) The insufficient authority of the Governor-General-in-Council over the other Presidencies. In all these respects the system broke down completely when put to operation.

Importance of the Act. It must be said for the Regulating Act that it was the first serious attempt made by a European power to organise government in a far-off country inhabited by a civilised people. There were no European colonists here as in North American administration among whom could easily work the type of institutions functioning in the mother country. Unlike South America again Indian territories of the East India Company did not represent an undeveloped country. Thus "the Regulating Act tried to sail in an unchartered sea. It left the details of administration in India to the devices of the Company. It tried, however, to organise an honest and efficient supreme authority in Bengal, at Madras and at Bombay. To provide against the abuse of their powers by the servants of the Company, it set up a Supreme Court of Judicature at Calcutta. In England no public servant was then above the law, he was accountable for whatever he did to ordinary courts. The Act in short was a well-meant attempt to introduce a better system of government but being designed in ignorance of the real nature of the problem it was a total failure and only added to Hastings' difficulties instead of strengthening his hands."

The Regulating Act was in operation for eleven years till it was superseded by the Pitt's Act of 1784. Warren Hastings was the only Governor-General who had to administer India under it.

(B) The Amending Act of 1781

Certain remedial and supplementary legislation followed the Regulating Act. One such measure was the Amending Act of 1781. This Act exempted the actions of the public servants of the Company done by them in their official capacity from the jurisdiction of the Supreme Court. The question of the jurisdiction of the Supreme Court was settled. This Court was to have jurisdiction overall the inhabitants of Calcutta and was to administer the personal law of the defendant. The Act also provided that the Supreme Court must take into consideration and respect the religious and social customs and usages of the Indian while enforcing its decrees and processes. The Government was also to keep these in view while making rules and regulations. The Act further provided that appeals could be taken from the Provincial Courts to the Governor-General-in-Council that was to be the final Court of Appeal except in those civil cases which involved a sum of £ 5,000 or more. In the latter category of cases the appeal could be taken to the King-in-Council. Lastly, it was laid down in the Act of 1781 that the rules and regulations made by the Governor-General-in-Council were not to be registered with the Supreme Court. Formerly the Supreme Court under the Regulating Act registered and published such rules and regulations probably with the intention that in doing so the Court could pronounce upon the legality or otherwise of those measures being or not being repugnant to the laws and customs of England.

The Act of 1781 thus effected important changes in the system inaugurated by the Regulating Act. The Act of 1781 asserted in unmistakable terms the need of strengthening the Government, the importance of an unimpeded machinery of revenue collection, and regard for the religious and social customs and usages of the Indians in the making of the laws and their execution.

(C) Pitt's India Act, 1784

Circumstances Leading to the Passing of the Act. In 1781 as in 1772, both a Select and a Secret Committee were appointed to go into the affairs of the Company. The former (the Select Committee) investigated the relations between the Supreme Court and the Council in Bengal, the latter (the Secret Committee) the causes of the Maratha War. The voluminous reports they presented were freely used as arsenals for weapons against the Company by party orators in Parliament. Parliamentary interference in the affairs of the Company was obviously once again called for, especially when the Directors of the Company were obliged openly to confess that the war had beggared them and to apply to the State for another loan of a million pounds. After a measure drafted by Dundas, Chairman of the Secret Committee, had been rejected, Fox introduced his India Bill in Parliament. The measure was really inspired by Burke and, behind him, by Philip Francis. This bill sought to transfer all the political and military powers of the Company to a Board of Seven Commissioners to be nominated in the first instance by Parliament and afterwards by the Crown, and all its commercial powers to a subordinate body of nine Assistant Directors who were ultimately to be nominated by the holder of East India stock, though they too in the first instance were to be appointed by Parliament. The bill if it had been passed would in effect have swept aside the Company as a political power and brought all political appointments under the control of a commission which was to be appointed in the first instance by Parliament and afterwards by the Crown. The chief advocates of this measure had ten years earlier opposed North's Act as an intolerable invasion of the right of property. The feature of the Bill upon which the Opposition seized was the surrender of the immensely valuable patronage of India to the Ministry or the Crown and Pitt thundered against it as the most desperate and alarming attempt at the exercise of tyranny that ever disgraced the annals of any country. The Bill, however, was passed in the House of Commons by large majorities only to be rejected in the House of Lords through the intervention of George III. The Bill was thrown out and the Ministry— the coalition of Fox and North—resigned. It may be observed in passing that for the first and the last time a British Ministry was wrecked on an Indian issue. Pitt came into power and in January 1784 he moved for leave to bring in his India Bill and leave was granted ; even the second reading was taken but the Bill was not destined to be put on the statute book for the new Ministry had to resign. Pitt's new Parliament met in May 1784. Following the lines laid down in his Bill of January, the new Bill was finally carried in the House of Commons in July, and in the House of Lords in August 1784. Fox, throughout the session, continued to refer to the superior merits of his own Bill. Pitt had taken the precaution of neutralising the opposition of the English Company with the result that the measure was introduced in parliament fortified and recommended by the consent of the Company. In essentials Fox's and Pitt's measures were on the same lines except that the latter did not touch the patronage of the Company. Pitt himself pointed out that while Fox's India Bill ensured a permanency of men, his Bill ment a permanency of system.

Provisions of the Act. The Act of 1784 introduced changes mainly in the Company's Home Government in London. It greatly extended the control of the State over the company's affairs. While the patronage of the Company was left untouched, all civil, military and revenue affairs were to be controlled by a Board popularly known as the Board of Control, consisting of the Chancellor of the Exchequer, one of the principal Secretaries of State and four members of the Privy Council appointed by the King. A Secret Committee of three Directors was to be the channel through which important orders of the Board were to be transmitted to India. The Court of Proprietors lost the right to rescind, suspend or revoke any resolution of the Directors which was approved by the Board of Control.

In India, the chief government was placed in the hands of a Governor-General and Council of three. The Governor-General was still left liable to be over-ridden by the Council but as the number of Councillors was reduced to three, he, by the use of his casting vote, could always make his will predominate if he had one supporter. Beyond this the Act of 1784 did not go. This defect was met in the Act of 1793, whereby the Governor-General was empowered to disregard the majority in Council provided he did so in a formal way accepting the responsibility of his own action. Under the Act of 1784 the Presidencies of Madras and Bombay were subordinated to the Governor-General and Council of Bengal in all matters of diplomacy, revenue and war. Last but not the least, only covenanted servants were in future to be appointed members of the Council of the Governor-General. The experiment of appointing outsiders had proved calamitous.

Observations on the Act. Pitt's India Act of 1784 brought about two important changes in the constitution of the Company. First, it constituted a department of state in England known as the Board of Control, whose special function was to control the policy of the Court of Directors, thus introducing the Dual System of government by the Company and by a Parliamentry Board which lasted till 1858. The Board of Control had no independent executive power. It had no patronage. Its power was veiled; it had access to all the Company's papers and its approval was necessary for all despatches that were not purely commercial, and in case of emergency the Board could send its own draft to the Secret Committee of the Directors to be signed and sent out in its name. The Act thus placed the civil and military government of the Company in due subordination to the Government in England. The Court of Directors retained their patronage and their right of dismissing their servants. The head of the Board was at first one of the Secretaries of State without special salary, but after 1793 a special President of the Board was appointed and this officer was ultimately responsible for the government of British India until he was succeeded in 1858 by the Secretary of State for India. Pitt's India Act thus settled the main lines of the Company's Home and Indian Government down to 1858.

Secondly, the Act reduced the number of members of the Executive Council to three, of whom the Commander-in-Chief was to be one. It also modified the Councils of Madras and Bombay on the pattern of that of Bengal.

Among the most striking provisions of the Act was the prohibition not merely of all aggressive wars in India but of all treaties of guarantee with Indian Princes like those with the nawabs of Carnatic and Oudh on the ground that "to pursue schemes of conquest and extension of dominion in India are measures repugnant to the wish, the honour and the policy of this nation." But this declaration was more honoured in breach than in observance in subsequent years. In fact the Act was a very skilful measure bearing all the marks of a political compromise. Burke admitted that it was "as able and skilful a performance for its own purposes as ever issued from the wit of man." Pitt, as Sir Courtney Ilbert has pointed out, has done two things: (*a*) he had avoided the charge of conferring patronage on the Crown, and (*b*) the appearance of radically altering the Company and the Government in England.

(D) The Act of 1786

In 1786 Pitt brought another bill in the Parliament relating to India in a bid to prevail upon Cornwallis to accept the Governor-Generalship of India. Cornwallis wanted to have the powers of both the Governor-General and the Commander-in-Chief. The new Act conceded this demand as also gave him the power to override his Council in extraordinary cases on his own responsibility.

(E) The Charter Act of 1793

In 1793, the Company's commercial privileges were extended for another twenty years. The power which had been specially given to Cornwallis on his appointment to override his Council was extended to all future Governors-General and Governors. The control of the Governor-General over the Presidencies of Bombay and Madras was emphasised. During the absence of the Governor-General from Bengal, he was to appoint a Vice-President from the civilian members of his Council to act for him. When he went over to Bombay or Madras he was to supersede the local Governor as the head of the administration. The Commander-in-Chief was not to be a member of the Governor-General's Council *ipso facto*. Regarding Home Government, the first-named Commissioner of the Board of Control was to be its President. The two junior members need no longer be members of the Privy Council. All the members were in future to be paid salaries not out of the State Exchequer but out of the Indian revenues. This practice continued up to 1919.

(F) The Charter Act of 1813

By 1813 when renewal of the company's charter was due, there were elaborate discussions about the justification of the commercial privileges enjoyed by the Company. The extent of the Company's territories in India had so much expanded that it was considered to be well-nigh impossible for it to continue as both a commercial and a political functionary. Moreover, Englishmen demanded a share in the trade with India in view of the new economic theories of *laissez faire* and the Continental System introduced by Napoleon which had closed the European ports to British trade. The Englishmen, therefore, demanded the termination of the commercial monopoly of the Company.

By the Charter Act of 1813 the Company was deprived of its monopoly of trade with India but it still enjoyed its monopoly of trade with China and the trade in tea. Subject to these restrictions the Indian trade was thrown open to all Englishmen. The shareholders of the Company, naturally enough, opposed tooth and nail this move though they did not stand to lose much by this decision as they were granted a dividend of $10\frac{1}{2}\%$ out of the revenues of India. The Act continued to the Company for a further period of twenty years the posession of the territories and revenues "without prejudice to the undoubted sovereignty of the Crown...in and over the same." It is to be noted that the constitutional position of the British territories in India was thus explicitly defined for the first time. Separate accounts were to be kept regarding commercial transactions and territorial revenues. By the Act of 1813, the power of superintendence and direction of the Board of Control was not only defined but also enlarged considerably. What makes the Charter Act of 1813 important is that it contained a clause providing for a sum of one lakh of rupees annually to be "set apart and applied to the revival and improvement of literature and the encouragement of the learned natives of India and for the introduction and promotion of a knowledge of the sciences among the inhabitants of the British territories in India." As an enunciation of the principle of State responsibility for education this famous clause deserves to be remembered as one of the most significant British pronouncements relating to India.

(G) The Charter Act of 1833

Circumstances Leading to the Act. The twenty years intervening between the Charter Acts of 1813 and 1833 witnessed great changes in England. The Industrial revolution had great impact on the country ushering in the Machine Age which revolutionized the methods of production. Cheap products of the new machines and their export overseas widened the outlook of the people. Money flowed in giving birth to a new spirit of independence. Class consciousness gave a new tone to British politics. A new class of intelligentsia emerged to take up cudgels on behalf of the labourer. Writers echoed the significance of the New Age in their works.

In 1830 the Whigs came into power and opened the way for the triumph of the liberal principles. The gospel of the Rights of Man was openly preached. The great Reform Act was passed in 1832 though after a tussle. The dignity of mankind was given due recognition and the doctrine of *laissez-faire* was being widely accepted. Reforms were in the air.

It was in this atmosphere of reform and liberal ideas that the Parliament was called upon to view the Charter of the Company in 1833. There were not a few then in Parliament who advocated that the Company should be wound up and that the Crown should take over the administration of India. But this view was not shared by the majority in Parliament and that body agreed with Macaulay that the Company's rule in India had to be contiuned though on a different basis. Macaulay was the Secretary to the Board of Control and James Mill, the renowned historian and a disciple of Bentham, occupied a high position at the India House. Their influence is clearly discernible in the Charter Act of 1833.

Provisions of the Act. The Act gave another lease of life to the Company for twenty years to administer Indian territories "in trust for His Majesty, his heirs and successors." The Company lost its monopoly of China trade. It was also asked to close its commercial business as early as possible.

However, the interests of the share-holders were safeguarded by guaranteeing them a dividend of 10.5% per annum till the Company's stock was purchased a the £ 200 per cent at some future date.

Henceforth, all restrictions on European immigration into India and acquistition by them of land and property in India were removed. This clause removed the legal barrier on the European colonization of India.

The Act centralised the administration of India. The Governor-Gereral of Bengal became the Governor-Gereral of India. The Governor-General-in-Council was given the power to control, superintend and direct the civil and military affairs of the Company. Bombay, Madras and Bengal and other territories were placed under the complete control of the Governor-General-in-Council. All revenues were to be raised under the authority of the Governor-General-in-Council who was to have complete control over the expenditure also. In short, all powers, administrative and financial, were centralised in the hands of the Governor-General-in-Council.

The Act also brought about legislative centralisation. The Governments of Madras and Bombay were drastically deprived of their powers of legislation and left only with the right of proposing to the Governor-Gereral-in-Council projects of the laws which they thought expedient.

The Act enlarged the Executive Council of the Governor-General by the addition of the fouth member (Law Member) for legislative purposes. The fourth member was expected to give professional advice regarding law-making. He was entitled, in theory, to sit and vote at meetings of the Council only for the purpose of making laws. At the suggestion of the Directors, Macaulay, who was the first holder of the post, was in practice admitted to all the meetings. A Law Commission was constituted with the purpose of consolidating, codifying and improving Indian laws.

Of the general provisions in the Act, the most important was Section 87 which provided that "no Indian or natural-born subject of the Crown resident in India should be by reason only of his religion, place of birth, descent, colour or any of them, be disqualified for any place of office or employment under the Company." According to the Directors, the object of this provision "is not to ascertain qualification, but to remove a disqualification." The meaning of the enacment we take to be that there shall be no governing caste in British India ; that whatever other test of qualification may be adopted, distinction of race or religion shall not be there...Fitness is henceforth to be the criterion of eligibility." There is no denying the fact that it was a momentous decision which ended the ill-conceived and short-sighted policy introduced by Cornwallis. In actual practice, however, very little was done to give effect to this pious provision. The high civil and military services remained shut to the Indians. They could hold only minor jobs. Keith writes in this connection : "This excellent sentiment (expressed in Section 87 of the Act of 1833) was not of much practical importance since nothing was done, despite the views of Munro, Malcolm, Elphinstone, Sleeman and Bishop Herber, to repeal the provision of the Act of 1793, which excluded any but covenanted servants from occupying places worth over £ 500 a year."[1] This continued exclusion of Indians from higher branches of services was greatly resented by them and in course of time this declaration in the Act of 1833 became the sheet-anchor of political agitation.

The Act 1833 enjoined the Government of India to take measures for amelioration of the condition of slaves and ultimate abolition of slavery in India. By Act V of 1843 slavery was abolished in India.

Observations on the Act of 1833. The Act of 1833 undoubtedly brought about important and far-reaching changes in the constitution of India. The Company was relieved of its monopoly of tea trade in India and of the trade with China, thus completing the work of the Charter Act of 1813 The Company having lost its commercial privileges could now concentrate on administration. As pointed out by Marshman : "The separation now effected of the functions of the State from all commercial speculations serves to give more elevated tone to the views and policy of the Court of Directors, and to impart a more efficient character to their administration." The provision for the codification of law was of great consequence. Before 1833 laws were "so imperfect that in many cases it was quite impossible to ascertain what the law was." There were several types of laws enforceable in India. It was a difficult question at times to decide as to which law was applicable in a particular case. The Act of 1833 authorised the Governor-General to appoint Indian Law Commissioners to study, collate and codify various rules and regulations prevalent in India.

The provisions concerning the abolition of slavery and the throwing open to all, irrespective of religion, place of birth, descent and coloure services in India are other commendable features of the Act. The Act might have been passed before "empty benches and in uninterested audience" of the House of Commons, but that does not minimise the importance of the said Act.

(H) The Charter Act of 1853

As the time approached for the renewal of the Company's Charter there was a growing demand that the Double Government of the Company in England should be ended. The demand was made for good reasons, *viz.*, that the Court of Directors had outlived its usefulness and that the existence of the Court of Directors and the Board of Control only resulted in unnecessary delay in the despatch of business and undue expenditure. An application putting forward this demand was actually sent by the Presidencies in India urging the appointment of a Secretary of State with a Council to handle all business relating to India.

It was also felt that the existing legislative machinery under the Charter Act of 1833 was inadequate. Voice was also raised against the Governor-General of India continuing also as the Governor of Bengal, for it was feared that so long as he combined these functions he could not be free from a bias in favour of Bengal. Besides, great territorial and political changes had taken place since the Charter Act of 1833. Sind and the Punjab had been annexed to the Company's territories in 1843 and 1849 respectively. A number of Indian states besides Pegu in Burma had fallen victims to Dalhousie's policy of ruthless annexation. The newly acquired territories had to be constitutionally provided for. Then there was the demand for the decentralisation of powers and for giving the people of India a share in the management of their own affairs for which there was some support in England too. Lord Derby, for instance, brought home to Parliament in April 1852 that "it is your bounden duty in the interest of humanity, of benevolence and of morality and religion, that as fast as you can do it safely, wisely and prudently, the inhabitants of India should be gradually entrusted with more and more of superintendence of their own internal affairs." It was under these circumstances that the British Parliament was called upon to renew the Charter of the Company in 1853. The parliament had in the preceding year appointed two Committees to go into the affairs of the Company and on the basis of their reports the Charter Act of 1853 was framed and passed.

Provisions of the Act. The Act renewed the powers of the Company and allowed it to retain possession of Indian territories "in trust for Her Majesty, her heirs and successors' not for any specified period as the preceding Charter Acts had done but only "until Parliament should otherwise provide." The Act provided that the salaries of the members of the Board of Control, its Secretary and other officers would be fixed by the British Government but would be paid by the Company. The number of the members of the Court of Directors was reduced from 24 to 18 out of which 6 were to be nominated by the Crown. The Court of Directors was dispossessed of its power of patronage as services were thrown open to competitive examinations, in which no discrimination of any kind was to be made. A committee with Macaulay as its President was appointed in 1854 to enforce this scheme. The Court of Directors was empowered to constitute a new Presidency or to alter the boundaries of the existing ones to incorporate the newly-acquired territories. This provision was made use of to create a separate Lieutenant-Governor-ship for the Punjab in 1859. The Act also empowered the

---

1. A.B. Keith, *A Constitutional History of India*, p. 135.

Crown to appoint a Law Commission in England to examine the reports and the drafts of the Indian Law Commission which had by then ceased to exist, and recommended legislative measures.

In India, the separation of the executive and the legislative functions was carried a step further by the provision of additional members for purposes of legislation. The Law Member was made a full member of the Governor General's Executive Council and this Council while sitting in its legislative capacity was enlarged by the addition of six members, namely, the Chief Justice and a puisne judge of Calcutta Supreme Court and four representatives, one each from Bengal, Madras, Bombay and the North-Western Provinces. The provincial representatives were to be civil servants of the Company with not less than ten years' standing. The Governor General was empowered to appoint two more civil servants to the Council though this power was never actually exercised. The procedure of the Council was to be on the lines of the British Parliament. Questions could be asked and the policy of the Executive Council could be discussed, though the Excutive Council retained the power to veto a bill of the Legislative Council. Discussion in the Council became oral instead of in writing, bills were referred to Select Committees instead to a single member and the legislative business was conducted in public instead of in secret.

Observations on the Act. The Act was a compromise between two conflicting views. Those who favoured the retention of the Company's territorial authority were satisfied by the provision that the Company should continue to govern India in trust for the Crown until Parliament should other wise direct. Those who wanted the substitution of Crown control for that of the Company found to their satisfaction that the number of Directors was reduced from 24 to 18 of whom 6 were to be nominees of the Crown and that the quorum was fixed at 10 so that when the meetings of the Court were thinly attended, the nominees of the Crown were able to have a majority. The Directors lost their patronage.

In its actual working, the newly-formed Legislative Council threatened to alter the whole structure of the Indian Government. Contrary to the intentions of the framers of the Act, the Legislative Council had developed into an Anglo-Indian House of Commons, questioning the Executive and its acts and forcing it to lay even confidential papers before it. It had refused to submit legislative projects to the Secretary of State before their consideration in the Council and had even refused to pass legislation required by the Secretary of State (or the Court of Directors before 1858). On the other had, it asserted its right to independent legislation. The spirit of independence displayed by the Legislative Council under the Act of 1853 from the very beginning disturbed its author, Sir Charles Wood, President of the Board of Control. To remove doubts on the subject he declared : "I do not look upon the Legislative Council as some of the young Indian do as the nucleus and beginning of constitutional parliament in India." But Dalhousie pointed out that he had not "conceded to the Legislative Council any greater power than the law clearly confers upon it." It may, however be said that Wood "was neither the first nor the last legislator to fail in limiting the consequences of a Bill to his intentions." All said, the creation and functioning of the Legislative Council made the Act of 1853 an important constitutional measure of the nineteenth century.

The one glaring defect of the Act, however, was the continued exclusion of the people of the land with the work of legislation and one could condemn this in the words of Sir Bartle Frere : "The perilous experiment of continuing to legislate for millions of the people with few means of knowing except by rebellion, whether the laws suit them or not."

(I) The Act for the Better Government of India, 1858

Circumstances Leading to the Act. The Charter Act of 1853 had clearly laid down that the Company was to retain the territories and the revenues in India in trust for the Crown not for any specified period as preceding Charter Acts had provided but only until Parliament should otherwise direct. The door was thus left open for the Crown to step in any time and take over the administration from the hands of the Company. The crisis of 1857-58 gave a fillip to the demand that a trading company should not be allowed to continue as a political power. This time this demand could not possible go unheeded and when reorganisation took place after the crisis "it furnished an opportunity for transferring control from the Company to the Crown in appearance as well as reality."

Lord Palmerston while introducing a Bill for the Better Government of India in the House of Commons in February 1858 pointed out: "The principle of our political system is that all administrative functions should be accompanied by ministerial responsibility—responsibility to Parliament, responsibility to public opinion, responsibility to the Crown; but in this case the chief functions in the Government of India are committed to a body not responsible to Parliament, not appointed by the Crown, but elected by person who have no more connection with India than consists in the simple possession of so much India stock." So, according to Palmerston, the first defect of the Company's rule was its utter irresponsiblity. Another defect pointed out was the cumbrous, complex and irrational nature of the system of Double Government. Palmerston's Bill went through the second reading but before it could become law the ministry changed and Palmerston was thrown out. Lord Derby, with Disraeli as the Chancellor of Exchequer, succeeded. Disraeli introduced a new India Bill but it was ridiculed by Palmerston who was now in the opposition. The Act for the Better Government of India as passed was based on a series of resolutions passed by Parliament. It received the Royal assent on August 2, 1858.

Provisions of the Act. The Act laid down that "India shall be governed by and in the name of the sovereign through one of the principal Secretaries of State (Secretary of State of India), assisted by a Council of 15 members." The Secretary of State received the powers so long enjoyed by the Court of Directors and the Board of Control. Thus the sytstem of 'Double Government' introduced by Pitt's India of 1784 was finally abolished. Of the 15 members of the Council of the Secretary of State, 8 were to be appointed by the Crown and 7 by the Court of Directors. The Act provided that at least half of these members must have served in India for not less than ten years and they must not have been away from that country for more than ten years at the time of their appointment. The vacancy among the Crown nominees would be filled up by the Crown, while among those elected by the Directors would be filled up by the Council by election. The members would continue in office during good behaviour and would be removed only on petition, to the Crown by both the Houses of Parliament. The Council was to be advisory, in most cases the initiative and the final decision remained with the Secretary of State. The Governor-General received the title of Viceroy. He became the direct representative of the Crown. His prestige, if not his statutory authority, was increased. The Act divided the patronage between the Crown, the Secretary of State in Council and the authorities in India. Appointments to the Covenanted Civil Service were to be made by open competition under the rules laid down by the Secretary of State with the help of Civil Service Commissioners. The Act declared the Secretary of State for India as a corporate body who could sue and be sued in England and in India.

Observations on the Act. It has been rightly observed that the assumption of the Government of India by the Crown in 1858 was 'rather a formal than a substantial change'. The Crown, as we have already noticed, had been steadily increasing its control over the Company's affairs since the beginning of its territorial sovereignty. The main rules under which India was governed before the passing of the Act of 1858 were already those of the British parliament. As pointed out in John Stuart Mill's petition on Indian affairs, the British Government had long possessed the decisive voice and was thus 'in the fullest sense accountable for all that has been done and for all that has been forborn or omitted to be done'. The British administrators, including the Governor-General, though nominally the servants of the Company's Board of Control, knew in the heart of their hearts that in reality they were answerable to the British Cabinet with its Indian Minister who was the President of the Board of Control and through them to Parliament. Beginning from the Regulating Act, a series of statutes (of 1784, 1793, 1813, 1833, and 1853) had progressively reduced the powers of the Court of Directors, till they had become just nominal.

The Charter Acts of 1813 and 1833 had explicitly declared the sovereignty of the Crown over the territories acquired by the Company and the Charter Act of 1853 frankly declared that the Company was to hold the territories and the revenues of India in trust for the Crown till it was determined otherwise. The number of Directors, under the Act of 1853, was reduced from 24 to 18 of whom 6 were to be nominees of the Crown. The choicest flower in the bunch was indeed taken away when the Directors were deprived of their power of patronage. The result was that the Company had for all intents and purposes ceased to take an effective part in the machinery of government but was, according to Ramsay Muir, "only a superfluous fifth wheel." The Company, in other words, had been dead as a political power long before 1858, but its skin was still preserved as though it was still alive. All that the Act of 1858 did was to give a decent burial to that corpse.

It may sound paradoxical but nevertheless it is true that the control of Parliament over Indian affairs slackened from the very time it acquired it. The plain fact of the matter was that when power was in the hands of the Board of Control and the Court of Directors, Parliament asserted its authority. But when the Board of Control and the Court of Directors were replaced by the Secretary of State for India who was responsible to Parliament, the latter was satisfied. It was satisfied because it got what it wanted to get, and having got it, it neglected to exercise the power of continuously controlling and criticising Indian administration. Another reason was that the Secretaries of State for India were far abler men than the members of the Board of Control had been. The quick means of communication between India and England made Indian news available in England much more swiftly than ever before. Parliament was content with leaving the Secretary of State alone to act as he pleased. The Secretaries of State managed the affairs of India efficiently and there were no occasions for Parliament to give any directions to them or interfere in their work. Moreover, from 1857 to 1915, British politicians and parties had their hands full with affairs of their own and they had neither the inclination nor time to study Indian problems. The intricacy and vastness of the Indian problems made it hardly worthwhile to pursue them even as a hobby. As the most brilliant Englishmen had entered the Indian Civil Service and were carrying on the administration of India efficiently, it was thought both ungenerous and unnecessary, from the British point of view, to criticise them. Thus, developed the theory of trusting the man on the spot and supporting him and leaving him alone. The Secretary of State backed the Governor-General and the letter in turn the Governors and so on and so forth. The members of Parliament realised that nothing was to be gained by interfering in Indian affairs. Thus, the interest of Parliament in Indian affairs slackened right from the time it assumed control in appearance and reality in 1858.

SELECT REFERENCES

1. Banerjee, A.C. : *Indian Constitutional Documents,* vol. c.
2. Ilbert, C. : *The Government of India* (1922).
3. Keith, A.B. : *Constitutional History of India.*
4. Keith, A.B. : *Speeches and Documents on Indian Policy,* vol. i.
5. Mukerjee, P. : *Indian Constitutional Documents,* vol. i.
6. Singh, G.N. : *Landmarks in Indian Constitutional and National Development.*

41

GROWTH OF THE REPRESENTATIVE GOVERNMENT IN INDIA

(A) The Indian Councils Act, 1861

Circumstances leading to the Act. The Act of 1858 exclusively introduced changes in the Home Government. So far as India was concerned, it did not touch the administrative set-up in India. There was a strong feeling that sweeping changes in the constitution of India were called for after the great crisis of 1857-58, especially in the direction of establishing closer contacts with Indian public opinion. The crisis had clearly brought home the fact that "the perilous experiment of continuing to legislate for millions with few means of knowing except by rebellion whether the laws suit them or not" must be done away with. Sir Bartle Frere, Governor of Bombay, summed up this point of view aptly by pointing out: "Unless you have some barometer or safety-valve in the shape of a deliberative council, I believe, you will always be liable to very unlooked for and dangerous explosions." These sentiments were also voiced by prominent Indian like Syed Ahmed Khan who opined that one of the major causes of the crisis of 1857-58 was the want of contact between the rulers and the ruled. The question of giving representation to Indians in the Legislative Councils was even mooted in 1858 but then the view prevailed that if such representation was slight it would not serve any purpose, if on the other hand it was liberal it would be ascribed not to any sense of fairness on the part of the British Parliament but to the fear which the crisis had produced in their minds. So the question of associating Indians with the work of legislation was put off till things had settled down.

There were other reasons which necessitated changes in the constitution of India. By the Charter Act of 1833 legislation had been centralised. The Legislative Council (at the Centre) had alone the power to legislate for the whole of the country. It dealt with all legislative matters, great and small. It was in the nature of things ill-fitted to do its job on account of its ignorance of the conditions prevailing in different parts of the vast country. Nor had the Council the will or the time to seek out certain common legislative standards applicable to all parts of the country.

In the next place, the working of the existing Legislative Council, set up by the Charter Act of 1853, left much to be desired. The Council had become a sort of a debating society or a Parliament on a small scale. It had arrogated to itself all the functions and privileges of a representative body. It adopted all the formalities of parliamentary procedure in the making of laws such as three readings and reference to committees which all caused delay. Trying to act as an independent legislature, it sometimes stopped supplies, and did not work entirely according to the wishes of the Home Government. It embarrassed the Indian Government by calling for information on a variety of subjects including secret matters. All this the authorities in England desired to correct. After an exchange of views between the Home Government and the Government of India, the first Indian Councils Act was passed in 1861.

Provisions of the Act. In the first place, the Act added to the Viceroy's Executive Councils a fifth member who was to be 'a gentleman of legal profession, a jurist rather than a technical lawyer'. Secondly, the Act empowered the Governor-General to make rules for the more convenient transaction of business in the Council. This power was used by Lord Canning to introduce the portfolio system in the Government of India. Up to that time the theory was that the Government of India was a government by the entire body of the Executive Council; so all business and all official papers had to be brought to the notice of the members of the Council. This system was very cumbrous and inconvenient. Canning now divided the departments of Government between the members of the

Council. Thus were laid the foundations of Cabinet Government of India, each branch of the Administration having its official head and spokesman in the Government, who was responsible for its administration and its defence. Under the new system the routine matters of administration were disposed of by the member in-charge; the more important matters were placed by the member concerned before the Governor-General and decided in consultation with him. Only matters of general policy now came before the Executive Council as a whole. The decentralisation of business undoubtedly made for efficiency and was described by John Stuart Mill "as one of the most successful instances of the adaptation of means to ends which political history had yet to show."

Thirdly, for purposes of legislation, the Viceroy's Executive Council was expanded by the addition of not less than six and not more than twelve 'additional' members, who would be nominated by the Governor-General and would hold office for two years. Not less than half of these members were to be non-officials. No statutory provision was made for the addmission of Indians but in practice some of the non-official seats were offered to 'natives of high rank'. The function of the Legislative Council at the Centre so created was strictly limited to lagislation : it would have no control over administration or finance or right of interpellation. It was the answer to the attempt made by the Legislature created by the Charter Act of 1853 to transform itself into 'an Anglo-Indian House of Commons'.

Fourthly, the Act restored the legislative powers of the making and amending laws to the provinces of Madras and Bombay. However, no laws passed by the provincial councils were to be valid until those received the assent of the Governer-General. Further, in certain matters (e.g. Currency, Posts and Telegraphs, naval and military matters) the prior approval of the Governor-General was made obligatory. Legislative Councils were established in Bengal, the North-Western Provinces (now called Uttar Pardesh) and the Punjab in 1862, 1886 and 1897 respectively under a provision in the Act of 1861.

Fifthly, the Governor-General was empowered, in cases of emergency, to issue, without the concurrence of the Legislative Council, ordinances which were not to remain in force for more than six months.

Observations on the Act. The main interest of the Act lay in the gradual construction and consolidation of the mechanical framework of the government. The three separate presidencies were brought into a common system; the lagislative and administrative authority of the Governor-General-in-Council was asserted over all the provinces and extended to all their inhabitants; and the principal of recognising local needs and welcoming local knowledge was admitted, so that local councils were created or re-created and a few non-official and even Indian members were introduced for the purposes of advice.

The Act by vesting legislative powers in the Governments of Bombay and Madras and by making provision for the institution of similar legislative councils in other provinces laid the foundations of legislative devolution culminating in the grant of autonomy to the provinces by the Government of India Act, 1935. It should, however, be understood that by the Act of 1861 no attempt was made to demarcate the jurisdiction of the Central and Local legislatures as in federal constitutions. The Governor-General's Council could legislate for the whole of India, and the provincial council for the whole of the province, with the reservation that before doing so in respect of certain matters the Governor-General's sanction had to be obtained.

The character of the legislative councils established by the Act of 1861 left much to be desired. The legislative councils could not possibly be called true legislature either in composition or in functions. The councils were merely committees for the purpose of making laws–committees by means of which the executive government obtained the advice and assistance in their legislation and the public derived the advantage of full publicity being ensured at every stage of the law-making process. While the Government enacted the laws through its Council, the public had a right to make itself heard and the executive was bound to defend its legislation. True, the *ex-officio* and the official members were in a majority and every official legislation could be sure of the majority in its favour. This was all the more easy because the nominated non-official members were always in a minority, were reluctant to attend the sessions of the Council and were always in a hurry to depart. All the same it will not be correct to describe the laws made in the legislative councils as in reality the orders of government. The laws were enacted in a manner which ensured publicity and discussion, were enforced by the courts and not by the executive and could not be changed but by the same deliberate and public process as that by which they were made and could even be enforced against the executive or in favour of individuals when occasion required.

The functions of the new councils were strictly limited to legislation. They were expressly forbidden to transact any business except the consideration and enactment of legislative measures before them. The councils could not entertain any motion except a motion for leave to introduce a Bill or having reference to a Bill actually introduced. The councils could not inquire into grievances, call for information or examine the conduct of the executive. The acts of administration could not be impugned nor were they to be defended in such assemblies. Thus the conduct of administration including all matters connected with finance remained under the exclusive purview and control of the wholly official Executive Councils.

The Act of 1861 in no way established representative government in India on the model prevalent in England or England's White Colonies; in the functioning of the House of Commons or the colonial Representative Assemblies there were no limitations on the discussion of financial matters and taxation as provided for in the Act of 1861. Regarding this, Sir Charles Wood, the Secretary of State, while introducing the Bill made it clear that Her Majesty's Government had no intention to introduce a representative law-making body in the normal sense of words. Mr. Wood likened the functions of the proposed Legislative Councils to those of the *durbar* of an Indian rular where the nobles expressed their opinion but the ruler was not bound by their advice.

(B) The Indian Councils Act, 1892

Circumstances leading to the passing of the Act. The growth of the Indian Constitution after the Act of 1861 is largely the story of political disaffection and agitation alternating with Council reform. The reforms grudgingly conceded were always found inadequate, occasioned disaffection and evoked demand for further reforms. It is true of all subsequent Acts passed by the British Parliament relating to India, namely the Acts of 1892, 1909, 1919 and 1935. In each case the story is in its broad outline practically the same.

The Legislative Council created by the Act of 1861, naturally nough, failed to satisfy the aspirations of the people of the land. The element of non-officials, negligible as it was, did not even represent the people. It consisted of either big zamindars, retired officials or Indian princes, none of whom could claim to understand the problems of the people.

During the second half of the nineteenth century nationalism began to grow in India. A number of factors contributed to this growth. The setting up of universities at Culcutta, Madras and Bombay in 1857 spread education bringing nationalism in its wake. The use of English by the educated people brought them closer to one another. The repressive policy pursued by the British Government after quelling the Rebellion of 1857 created feelings of hatred against it. The members of the Indian Civil Service were arrogant and haughty and the gulf between them and the people considerably widened. Lord Lytton's administration added to the bitterness of the people against the Government. The twin acts repression—the Vernacular Press Act and the Indian Arms Act—passed in 1878 greatly exasperated the feelings of the people. The administration of Laytton was accused of emasculting Indian manhood to further British imperialistic aims. The fierce cotroversy between the Government of England and the Government of India regarding the abolition of 5% cotton duties opened the eyes of Indians. Nothing more had so clearly demonstrated the hollowness and insincerity of the British professions of justice and fairplay than the abolition of cotton duties in which case the interests of the Indian merchants were sacrificed for the sake of Lancashire manufacturers. Then came the Ilbert Bill controversy. All these events highlighted the fact that justice could not be expected from the English rulers where their own interests were involved. It was under these circumstances that the Indian National Congress was founded in 1885. The initial objective of the Congress was to mobilise public opinion in India, to ventilate the grievances of the people and to press for reforms in a constitutional but nonetheless in an emphatic manner. In its very first session, the Congress passed the following resolution : "This Congress considers the reform and expansion of the Supreme and exsisting Local Legislative Councils by the admission of a considerable proportion of elected members (and the creation of similar councils for the North-Western Provinces and Oudh and also for the Punjab) essential; and holds that all budgets should be referred to these Councils for consideration, their members being moreover empowered to interpellate the Executive in regard to all branches of administration." Similar resolutions were passed at the subsequent sessions of the Congress.

In the beginning the attitude of the British Government was friendly and sympathetic towards the Congress but by 1888 that attitude changed. Lord Dufferin in that year made a frontal attack on the Congress by dubbing it as representing only 'a microscopic minority' and Congress demands as 'a big jump into the unknown'.

Though Lord Dufferin thus tried to belittle the importance and representative character of the Congress he was too astute a statesman not to realise the significance of the movement launched by the Congress and he secretly sent to England proposals for liberalising the Councils. He also appointed a Committee of his Council to prepare a plan for the enlargement of Provincial Councils, for the enhancement of their status, the multiplication of their functions, the partial introduction in them of the elective principle and the liberalisation of their general character as political institutions. At the same time he declared in plain words that it should not be concluded that he was contemplating to set up a parliamentary system after the British model. He repudiated strongly any such intention on his part.

The report of the Committee together with Lord Dufferin's own views was sent to the authorities in England proposing changes in the composition and functions of the Councils with the main aim "to give a still wider share in the administration of public affairs to such Indian gentlemen as by their influence, their requirements and the confidence they inspired in their own countrymen, are marked out as fitted to assist with their counsel the responsible rulers of the country."

The Conservative Ministry in England at the instance of Lord Cross, Secretary of state for India, introduced in 1890 a bill in the House of Lords on the basis of these proposals but the measure proceeded at a snail-slow speed and was passed only two years later as the Indian Councils Act.

Provisions of the Act. The Act dealt exclusively with the powers, functions and composition of the Legislative Councils in India. With regard to the Central Legislature, the Act provided that the number of 'additional' members must not be less than ten or more than sixteen (subject to the approval of the Secretary of State in Council, the Governor-General was to make regulations under which the nomination of the additional members was to be made). The increase was described as 'a very paltry and miserable addition'. But Curzon defended it on the ground "that the efficiency of a deliberative body is not necessarily commensurate with its numerical strength...large bodies...do not promote economical administration but are apt to diffuse their force in vague and vapid talk." The Act also provided that two-fifths of the total members of the Council were to be non-officials. These non-officials were partly nominated and partly elected.

The principle of election was conceded to a limited extent. In two respects the rights of the members of the Legislatures were increased. They were entitled to express their views upon financial statements which were henceforth to be made on the floor of the Legislatures, although they were not empowered to move resolutions or divide the House in respect of any financial question. Secondly, they were empowered to put questions within certain limits to the Government on matters of public interest after giving a six days' notice.

In regard to the Provincial Legislatures, the Act enlarged the number of 'additional' members to not less than eight or more than twenty in the case of Bombay and Madras. The maximum for Bengal was also fixed at twenty but for the North-Western Province and Oudh the maximum was fixed at fifteen. In their functions the members of the Provincial Legislatures secured the right of interpellation of the executive in the matters of general public interest. They could also discuss the policy of the Government and ask questions, which, however, as in the case of the centre, required a six days' previous notice. And their questions too could be disallowed without assigning any reason.

The Principle of Election under the Act. The significant feature of the Indian Councils Act of 1892 was the principle of election which it introduced, though the word 'election' was very carefully avoided in it. In addition to the officials, the Central Legislature was to have elected non-officials whose number was to be five and who were to be elected one each by the non-official members of the four Provincial Legislatures of Madras, Bombay, Bengal and the North-Western Provinces and one by the Calcutta Chamber of Commerce. The other five non-officials were nominated by the Governor-General. In the case of the Provincial Legislatures, the bodies permitted to elect members were Municipalities, District Boards, Universities and the Chambers of Commerce. The method of election, however, was veiled. The 'elected' members were officially declared as 'nominated' though after taking into consideration the recommendation of the bodies described above. These bodies met to make 'recommendations' to the Governor-General or Head of the Provincial Government. The person favoured by the majority was not described as 'elected', but recommended for nomination. The clause in question in the Act read as follows: "It will be possible for the Governor-General to make arrangements by which certain persons may be presented to him, having been chosen by election, if the Governor-General should find that such a system can properly be established."

Observations on the Act. The Indian Councils Act of 1892 was undoubtedly an advance on the Act of 1861 and it was as it should have been. The Act of 1892 widened the functions of the legislatures. The members could ask questions and thus obtain information which they desired from the executive. The financial accounts of the current year and the budget for the following year were presented to the legislatures, and the members were permitted to make general observations on the budget and make suggestions for increasing or decreasing revenue or expenditure. As the functions of the legislatures were widened they attracted the country's best talent. Eminent Indian leaders like Gopal Krishna Gokhale, Asutosh Mookerjee, Rash Behari Ghosh and Surendra Nath Banerjee found their way in the Lagislatures. Their eloquence and political wisdom amply demonstrated the parliamentary capacity and patriotism of the educated Indians. Moreover, the size of the Legislatures both at the Centre and in the Provinces was enlarged. In case of the Centre the maximum and minimum of additional members and the element of non-officials therein were raised by four in each case as compared to the Act of 1861. The Councils in Bombay, Madras and Bengal had a maximum of twenty additional members under the Act of 1892. Of these, nine were officials, four nominated non-officials and seven elected. The electing bodies in the provinces were District Broads and Municipalities (grouped together into electoral colleges for this purpose), Universities and Chambers of Commerce.

This recognition of the principle of election, veiled though it was in the Act of 1892, was a measure of considerable constitutional significance. A beginning was made though the goal of the representative government was yet a far cry.

There were, however, certain defects and shortcomings in the Act of 1892 by reason of which the Act failed to satisfy Indian nationalists. The Act was criticised at successive sessions of the Indian National Congress. Critics pointed out that the system of election in the Act was a roundabout one. "The so-called right of election to the Legislatures enjoyed by the local bodies and by other electorates amounted merely to nomination by these bodies, but it was up to the government to accept them or reject them." Then, the functions of the Legislative Councils were strictly circumscribed. The members could not ask supplementary questions. Any question could be disallowed and there was no remedy against it. The Councils did not get any substantial control over the budget. The rules of election were unsatisfactory. Certain classes were over-represented while others did not get any representation at all. In the case of Bombay, out of six seats two were given to European merchants but none to the Indian mercantile community. Again, two seats were assigned to Sind but none to Poona and Satara. According to Gokhale : "The actual working of the Act manifested its hollowness. Bombay Presidency was given eight seats. Two of them were assigned by the Government of India in thier rules to the University of Bombay and the Municipal Corporation. The Bombay Government gave two seats to the European Mercantile Community, one seat to the Sirdars of the Deccan, one to the Zamindars of Sind and only two seats to general public." In his Presidential address delivered in 1893 at the Lahore session of the Congress, Dadabhai Naoroji observed : "By the Act of 1892 no member shall have the power to submit or propose any resolution or divide the Council in respect of any such financial discussion or in answer to any question asked under the authority of this Act or the rules made under this Act. Such is the poor character of the extent of the concession made to discuss finances or to put questions. Rules made under this Act shall not be subject to alterations or amendment at meetings for the purpose of making laws and regulations. Thus , we are to all intent and purposes under an arbitrary rule."

In conclusion we may say that despite the fact that the Act of 1892 fell far short of the demands made by the Congress it was undoubtedly a great advance on the existing state of things. By conceding the principle of election of representatives and giving the Legislature some control over the Executive, the Act did pave the way for the introduction of parliamentary responsible government in India.

(C) The Indian Councils Act, 1909
(The Minto-Morley Reforms)

Circumstances leading to the passing of the Act. The Indian Councils Act of 1892 failed to meet the legitimate wishes of the Congress and Lokamanya Tilak condemned the weak-kneed policy of the Congress in these words : "Political rights will have to be fought for. The Moderates think that these can be won by persuasion. We think that these can be won by pressure." The continuing economic exploitation by the alien rulers led to the energetic thesis by patriots like R.C. Dutt, Dadabhai Naoroji and others contending that the impoverishment of the country was the direct result of a deliberate and systematic policy of the foreign rulers who naturally wished to encourage "Home" manufacture at the expense of the local industry and trade.

Another factor that caused keen and active discontent was that educated Indians were not given any share, much less their due share in the Government services and the administration. Lord Curzon's imperianst and strong policies and attitudes added fuel to the fire and intensified bitterness of the intelligentsia against alien domination. A born bureaucrat and effciancy-monger, Curzon had no sympathy for the aspirations of the sons of the soil but acted autocratically, brushing aside and ignoring all reactions of the Indians. He completely officialised the Calcutta Corporation, giving it a European majority by reducing total membership by a third, through his infamous Act of 1899. A similar policy was pursued towards the Indian Universities five year later, which took away the autonomy of these Universities, and in the same year (1904) the Official Secrets Act greatly extended the scope of the term "sedition". But the climax was reached by the infamous Partition of Bengal in 1905 which was considered to be "a subtle attack on the growing solidarity of Bengali nationalism." The Bengalis felt "humiliated, insulted and tricked" and resorted to a vigorous agitation to get the wrong undone.

There were other causes of discontent. Indian overseas and specially in South Africa were being subjected to humiliation and indignities galore simply because they were Indians, or perhaps members of an enslaved race. This fanned national resentment and the people of India began to feel that it was vain and futile to hope for improvement in the conditions and treatment of Indians in the British colonies and overseas possessions unless and until they were free in their own homeland.

The closing years of the nineteenth century witnessed the horrors of famine and bubonic plague, bringing distress and misery to thousands of people. The people blamed the British Government for their plight and they detested even the well-intentioned governmental measures to stay the spread of infection of plauge as an intentional violation of their privacy.

The press in the country which was free since 1882 took ample notice of all these factors and was extremely critical of the British administration, so much so that Minto had to write to Morley thus: "I am afraid we must consider seriously how to deal with the native press, for in many cases the utterances of newspapers are outrageous." Nor did the platform in this respect lag behind. The famous trio, Bal Gangadhar Tilak, Bipin Chandra Pal and Lala Lajpat Rai, thundered about in the country and electrified the whole atmosphere.

Still another factor which fostered the rise and growth of 'extremism' in the country was the tremendous and shattering blow to the prestige of the White Man in the East by the Oriental dwarf, Japan, defeating in 1904-5 that Occidental giant, Russia—a case of David overthrowing Goliath. All over Asia this led to a new awakening and a new hope that what had been done to the Russian Bear might also be done to the British Lion in India. The same thing had earlier been done, on a smaller scale, by Abyssinia's victory over Italy at Adowa in 1896.

Under these circumstances 'extremism' grew apace despite repressive measures by the Government, and the Indian National Congress was split into camps—the Moderates and the Extremists. The split took place at Surat in 1907. The moderates still clung to the idea of adopting constitutional means to gain their objective. To the Extremists, on the other hand, the end justified all means. They took recourse to boycott (mainly of foreign trade goods but also of Government services, titles and honours), to the Swadeshi movement, to educational institutions of the national type and to terrorist methods.

In the meantime another important development had taken place. While the Congress was growing stronger as the exponent of the demand for national freedom, the Muslims generally kept themselves aloof from it. According to Coupland, "the indifference, if not antagonism" of the Muslims towards the nationalist movement was due to their "relative backwardness in education, coupled with the knowledge that they were only about one-quarter of the Indian population as a whole." Their 'indifference', at its intial stage, was gargely due to the policy advocated by Sir Syed Ahmed Khan. It gradually became something like 'antogonism' when the British bureaucracy, alarmed at the growing influence of the Congress as a mighty nationaliser', deliberately adopted a policy of 'divide and rule.' The first official manifestation of this policy may be noticed in Lord Minto's reply to a deputation of Muslim leaders led by the Agha Khan on October 1, 1906. He promised them not only separate communal representation but also representation much in excess of their population of account of "their services to the Empire". The die was thus cast and the foundations of Muslim communalism were laid.

If the Indian Councils Act of 1892 was passed to take the wind out of the sails of the Congress movement, that of 1909 was taken into hands by the Indian Government to rally to its side the Moderates in the Indian National Congress and the Muslims in order to buttress the authority of British bureaucracy.

The time was now opportune for introducing further reforms for Lord Morley, the radical disciple of Gladstone had now become the Secretary of State for India in the Liberal Cabinet. Both Lord Morley and Lord Minto found themselves in full agreement as to the desirability of some further political advances. Minto had by this time felt that the permanence of the British administration in India "dapends upon a sound appreciation of the changing conditions which surround it." There was a lengthy correspondence between the Secretary of State and the Viceroy on the subject. While the latter was still framing his proposals, a Committee of the Executive Council of the Viceroy had studied the subject and the Government of India sent a despatch to England embodying its proposals. Minto now wrote to the Secretary of State : "The time is getting on, and we must arrange a plan of campaign as to our reforms, not only as to the nature of the reforms themselves but as to how and when we are to launch them." Morley sent back the proposals to be referred to the Local Governments in India for public criticism. In the light of all this, the Bill was drafted, and after the approval of the Cabinet, passed by the Parliament in February 1909, to become the Indian Councils Act of 1909.

Earlier in August 1907 two Indians—K.G. Gupta and Syed Hussain Bilgrami—were made members of the Secretary of State's India Council. In India, on 24 March 1909, Mr. Sytendra Sinha was appointed member of the Viceroy's Executive Council.

Provisions of the Act. The size of the Legislatures, both at the Centre and in the Provinces, was enlarged and so were their functions.

Central Legislature. The number of 'additional' members here was now raised at the maximum to 60. The Legislature was thus to consist of 69 members of whom 37 were to be officials while the remaining 32 non-officials. Of the officials, 9 were to be the *ex-Officio* members, namely the Governor-General, seven ordinary members (Executive Councillors) and one extraordinary member, while the remaining 28 were to be nominated by the Governor-General. Of the 32 non-officials, 5 were to be nominated by the Governor-General while the remaining 27 were to be elected. For the elected members, it was declared that the territorial representation did not suit India and that "representation by classes and interests is the only practicable method of embodying the elective principle in the constitution of the Indian Legislative Councils." Thus, of the 27 elected members, 13 were to come from the General Electorates, consisting of the non-official members of the legislatures of Bombay, Madras, Bengal and United Provinces, each of which would send two members (= 8) ; and the non-official members of the legislatures of the Central Provinces, Assam, Bihar and Orissa, the Punjab and Burma, each of which would send one member (= 5). Of the remaining 14, twelve were to come from class Electorates ; six of them coming one each from the Landholders' constituencies in the six provinces of Bombay, Madras, Bengal, Bihar and Orissa, United Provinces and the Central Provinces; and six being returned by the separate Muslim constituencies—one each from Madras, Bombay, United Provinces and Bihar and Orissa (= 4) and two from Bengal. The remaining were to be returned from the Special electorates, one each from the Bengal and Bombay Chambers of Commerce.

Provincial Legislatures. The membership of the Lagislative Councils of the different provinces as enlarged under the Act of 1909 was as follows : Burma, 16 ; Eastern Bengal and Assam, 41, Bengal, 52; Madras, Bombay and United Provinces, 47 each ; and Punjab, 25. The Act provided for non-official majorities in the provinces. However, this did not mean non-official elected majorities, as some of the non-officials were to be nominated by the Governors and through these the official control over the Council was retained. In Madras, for example, the number of the non-officials was 26, while that of the officials 21. Of the non-officials, however, only 21 were to be elected, while the remaining five were to be nominated by the Governor. As these nominated members always sided with the Government, the officials were 'in a manner of speaking in the majority'. The same was true of all other provinces.

The elected members in the Provincial Legislatures were to be returned by different constituencies. In Bombay, for instance, out of the 21 elected members, 6 were to be returned by the Special electorates consisting of the Bombay Corporation and the Bombay University etc., 8 were to be returned by the General electorates consisting of District Boards and Municipalties etc. and the remaining 7 were to be returned by Class electorates consisting of Muslims (returning 4) and the Landlords (returning 3).

The membership of the Executive Councils of Bengal, Madras and Bombay was raised to 4 and the Government was empowered to constitute similar Councils for the Lieutenant-Governors as well.

Functions of Legislative Councils. The functions of the Legislative Councils, both at the Centre and in the Provinces, were also enlarged. Now the members were given the right of discussion and asking supplementary questions, the Member in-charge for the latter being authorised to demand time, if he could not furnish the information asked for on the spot. Detailed rules were laid down concerning the discussion of budgets in the Central Legislature. Members, though not empowered to vote, were empowered to move resolutions concerning additional grants to the Local Governments, any alteration in taxation, on a new loan, which might have been proposed in the financial statement or the explanatory memorandum. The financial statement, it was further provided, before its submission in the Council, had to be referred to its Committee consisting of the Finance member (Chairman) and non-officials and nominated members on a 50 : 50 basis.

Rules were also laid down concerning discussion of matters of general public interest. Members could discuss these matters, moving resolutions on them and could also vote, though the President was empowered to disallow the whole or a part of such resolutions, without assigning any reason. Nor was the Government obliged to accept such resolutions, even if passed, whether concerning public interest or concerning financial statements.

There were, however, certain subjects which the members could not discuss under the Act. They could not discuss the foreign relations of the Government of India and its relations with the Indian Princes, a matter under adjudication of a court of law, expenditure on state railways, interest on debt etc.

Observations on the Act. The Reform of 1909 afforded no answer and could afford no answer to the Indian political problem.[1] Narrow franchises, indirect elections, limited powers of the Legislative Councils made a hotch-potch of representative government. The real power remained with the Government and the Councils were left with no functions but criticism.

The Reforms created new problems in Indian politics. One such problem was the introduction of separate electorates for Muslims, by which, according to Jawaharlal Nehru, a "political barrier was created round them, isolating them from the rest of India and reversing the unifying and amalgamating process which had been going on for centuries...The barrier was a small one at first, for the electorates were very limited, but with every extention of franchise it grew and affected the whole structure of political and social life like some canker which corrupted the entire system." For the so-called political importance of the Muslims, they were accorded not only separate communal representation but also representation much in excess of their population on account of their "services to the Empire." The matter could not possibly rest there. Other communities in the country not only resented this invidious distinction but also claimed to have rendered "better services to the Empire" than the Muslims and yet had not been shown any special consideration. The Sikhs thus fought for their rights and special representation was also conceded to them in 1919. It was a signal for other communities to intensify their agitation. Thus the Harijans, the Indian Christians, the Europeans and the Anglo-Indians also got separate representation by the Act of 1935. The national unity forged through centuries was thus shattered with one blow. "The Minto-Morley Reforms have been our undoing", observed Mahatma Gandhi. They, indeed, stabbed the rising democracy, as K.M. Munshi pointed out. According to the Report on Indian Constitutional Reform (1918) : "It (the system of communal electorates) was opposed to the teachings of history. It perpetuated division of creeds and classes which meant the creating of camps organised against each other and taught them to think as partisans and not as citizens. It stereotyped existing relations and was a very serious hindrance to the development

---

1. *Report on Indian Constitutional Reforms* (Calcutta, 1918), p.52.

of self-governing principle." Lord Morley was right when he wrote to Lord Minto that in granting separate electorates " we are sowing dragon's teeth and the harvest will be bitter."

There were other reasons for the dissatisfaction of the people of India with the Reforms of 1909. What the people had demanded was that responsible government should be set up in the country. But all that they had got was "benevolent despotism" tempered by a remote and only occasionally vigilant democracy. While introducing the Bill in Parliament Lord Morley had made it absolutely clear that he had no intention of setting up "a Parliamentary system in India." To the newly-born nationalistic forces in the country this declaration was quite irritating.

In their actual working the Reforms created much confusion. While parliamentary forms were introduced, no responsibility was conceded. This led to thoughtless and irresponsible criticism of the Government. Indian leaders made Legislatures as the platform for denouncing the Government. The feeling that they would not have to shoulder responsibility made them irresponsible in their attitude.

The system of election introduced by the Act was so indirect that the representation of the people at large became a process of infiltration through a series of sieves. The people elected members of local bodies, which elected members of an electoral college, which in turn elected members of the provincial legislatures, who in turn elected members of the Central Legislature. As pointed out by the authors of the Montford Report of 1918 : " There is absolutely no connection between the supposed primary voter and the man who sits as his representative on the Legislative Council, and the vote of the supposed primary voter has no effect upon the proceedings of the Legislative Council. In such circumstances, there can be no responsibility upon and no political education for the people who nominally exercise a vote. The work of calling into existence an electorate capable of bearing the weight of responsible government is still to be done."[2]

The Reforms of 1909 gave to the people of the country "the shadow rather than the substance." They granted influence and not power. It left responsibility for government on one set of men while rapidly transferring power to another set of men. It created a situation eminently calculated to exasperate the executive and legislature with each other and thereby threw the British Government and the Indian community at large into a posture of mutual antagonism.

Select Opinions

Report on Indian Constitutional Reforms, 1918. The Morley-Minto Reforms of 1909 in our view are the final outcome of the old conception which made the Government of India a benevolent despotism which might as it saw fit for purpose of enlightenment consult the wishes of its subjects...The Government is still a monarch in *durbar*, but his councillors are uneasy, and not wholly content with his personal rule ; and the administration in consequence has become slow and timid in operation. Parliamentary usages have been initiated and adopted in Councils up to the point where they cause the maximum of friction, but short of that at which by having a real sanction behind them they begain to do good. We have at present in India neither the best of the old system, nor the best of the new. Responsibility is the savour of popular government, and that savour the present Councils wholly lack.

H.C.E. Zacharias. The essence of these Reforms lay in conceding what at once was evacuated of all meaning. Thus the elective principle of democracy was adopted ; yet at the same time antidemocratic communal representation was added. The official majority was done away with ; but the elected members remained in a minority. The membership was considerably enlarged ; but an emphatic disclaimer was issued simultaneously that the new Council in no way meant the introduction of a parliamentary system. The Council of India and even the Viceroy's Executive Council were opened to some very few select Indians ; but the liberal aspect of admitting Indians, to the arena of

---

2. *Idid.*, p.54.

government, could in no way disguise the fact that real power remained safely in British hands. Yet, when all this is said, it must be pointed out that in many respects the Act of 1909 was an improvement on that of 1892, though in one respect, namely, the introduction of communal electorate, it was worse.

R. Coupland. The Act of 1909 brought the constitutional advance begun by the Act of 1861 to the threshold of representative government...Yet the idea that this development was comparable with what had happened in England or the Colonies was firmly rejected at each of its stages by all the British statesmen and officials concerned. The Legislative Councils were still regarded as *durbar* rather than as parliaments ; and in 1909 no less than in 1892 both the authors of the measures of advance and their critics, Liberals as well as Conservatives, declared as categorically as Macaulay in 1833 that India was not qualified for a parliamentary system.... "If it could be said", Morley told the House of Lords, "that this chapter of reforms led directly or necessarily to the establishment of a parliamentary system in India, I for one would have nothing at all to do with it"...Another letter to Minto reveals that Morley's attitude was not wholly negative. "Not one whit more than you do I think it desirable or possible or even conceivable, to adapt English political institution to the nations who inhabit India. Assuredly not in your day or mine. But the *spirit* of English institutions is a different thing, and it is a thing that we cannot escape even if we wished...because British constituencies are the masters, and they will assuredly insist—all parties alike—on the spirit of their own political system being applied to India." But Morley left the problem there. He made no positive suggestion as to how in fact the spirit of British institutions could be separated from their form and animate an autocratic government.

Chart showing the Growth of the Central Legislature

The following table shows the growth of the Central Legislature both in size and functions since the Regulating Act.

Note. The figures denoting the size do not include the Governor-General and the Commander-in-Chief who were *ex-officio* members.

Act	Size	Composition	Functions
1773	4	Members of the Governor-General's Council	No distinction between Executive and Legislative functions.
1781	4	—do—	—do—
1784	3	—do—	—do—
1786	3	—do—	—do—
1793	3	—do—	—do—
1813	3	—do—	—do—
1833	4	3 Members of the Governor-General's Executive Council 1 Law Member	Empowered to make laws for all the territories, Bombay and Madras having lost their right to make their own laws.
1853	10	4 Members of the Executive Council (Law Member now a full member) 1 Chief Justice of the Calcutta Supreme Court. 1 puisne judge of the Calcutta Supreme Court.	Legislation was for the first time treated as a special function of the Government requiring special machinery and special processes. The Legislature assumed the role of a miniature representative

Growth of Representative Government in India

		4 Representatives one each from Bengal, Madras, Bombay and North-Western Provinces.	assembly.
1858	10	—do—	—do—
1861	17	5 Members of the Executive Council (the fifth member was now added). Not less than 6 and not more than 12 "additional" members nominated by the Governor-General. Not less than half of these members were to be non-officials. No provincial representation now.	Function advisory and limited to legislation only. No financial discussion possible.
1892	22	6 Members of the Executive Council. Not less than 10 and not more than 16 'additional' members (officials 6, nominated non-officials 5, Elected non-officials were to be returned thus : by the Calcutta Chamber of Commerce 1 ; by the non-officials in four Provincial Councils. 4); Provincial representation re-introduced.	Empowered to discuss the annual financial statement under certain restrictions. Members could address questions to Government on matters of public interest but could not censure the Executive or move a resolution of non-confidence against it. No supplementaries were allowed.
1909	69	Governor-General +1 Extraordinary Member +7 Members of the Executive Council. 60 'Additional' members Break-up of 60 Additional Members	Empowered to move resolutions. To ask supplementaries. To discuss the Budget but the Government could not be censured or defeated.

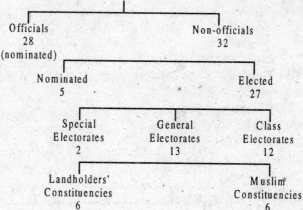

SELECT REFERENCES

1. Banerjee, A.C.   : *Indian Constitutional Documents* (1961 edition), Vol. II.
2. Coupland, R.   : *The Indian Problem* (1833-1935).
3. Keith, A.B.   : *Constitutional History of India.*
4. Keith, A.B.   : *Speeches and Documents on Indian Policy*, Vol. II.
5. Sharma, S.R.   : *The Constitution of India.*

42

THE ROAD TO RESPONSIBLE GOVERNMENT—I

The Government of India Act, 1919
(The Montagu-Chelmsford Reforms)

The Montford Reforms...were only a method of further draining India of her wealth and of prolonging her servitude.

—*Mahatma Gandhi*

Circumstances leading to the passing of the Act. The Minto-Morley Reforms were passed not with the intention of establishing a parlimentary system in India but with the opposite intention of buttressing the authority of the British bureaucracy by rallying to its side the Moderates and the Muslims. This view is clear from the speech made by Lord Morely in the House of Lords on February 23, 1909. He observed : "There are, I take it, three classes of people we have to consider in dealing with a scheme of this kind. There are the Extremists who nurse fantastic dreams that some day they will drive us out of India..... The second group nourishes no hopes of this sort, but hopes for autonomy or self-government of the colonial species and pattern, and then the third section of this classification asks for no more than to be admitted to co-operation in our administration, and to find a free and effective voice in expressing the interests and needs of their people. I believe that the effect of the Reforms has been, is being and will be to draw the second class who hope for colonial autonomy into the third class who will be content with being admitted to a fair and full co-operation." Actually the Reforms of 1909 did not satisfy, much less please, any section of the people.

The Indian National Congress, shorn of its left wing, expressed its dissatisfaction at "(*a*) the excessive and unfairly preponderant share of representation given to the followers of one particular religion, (*b*) the unjust, invidious and humiliating distinctions made between Muslims and non-Muslims in the matter of electorates, the franchise and the qualifications of the candidates, (*c*) the wide, arbitrary and unreasonable disqualifications and restrictions for candidates seeking election to the Councils, (*d*) the general distrust of the educated classes, (*e*) the unsatisfactory composition of the non-official majorities in the Povincial Councils, rendering them ineffective and unreal."

Certain circumstance, both internal and external, led to discontentment among the Muslims also. A proof of it is to be found in the modification of the constitution of the Muslim League. In March 1913 its goal was laid down to be "the promotion among Indians of Loyalty to the British Crown, the protection of the rights of the Muslims and, without detriment to the foregoing objects, the attainment of the system of self-government suitable to India." As the Muslims could not come to a settlement with the British Government in regarded to the condition on which a Muslim University was to be founded at Aligarh, the former felt greatly hurt, as also at the annulment of the partition of Bengal in 1911. Certain outside events also led to a deterioration of Anglo-Muslim relations in the country. The hostile attitude of England towards Turkey in the Turco-Italian War (1911-12) was viewd with dismay by the Muslims in India. The Balkan Wars of 1912-13 were considered by them as a great conspiracy of the Christan Powers against Turkey, "the Sword of Islam". These were "represented as a struggle between the Cross and the Crescent". This estrangement of the Muslims with British Government had one salutary effect, namely, that it brought the Hindus and the Muslims closer. At a largely attended public meeting at Lucknow, Muzar-ul-Haque, a prominent Muslim leader, said : "The anti-Congress Mussulman is fast becoming an extinct species and will have soon to be searched for in some archaeological museum." The Congress League reapprochement resulted in the Lucknow Pact (1916).

The Extremists who according to Morley "nurse fantastic dreams that some day they will drive us out of India" continued their activities through organisations established both in India and abroad. The Ghadr movement in the Panjab and the *Komagatamaru* incident in Bengal were only two examples of their terrorist activites.

So great was the discontent among the people of India with the Minto-Morley Reforms that the British Government had to resort to repressive measures to suppress the rising tide of discontent. The Indian Press Act of 1910, the Seditious Meetings Act of 1911 and the Criminal Law (Amendment) Act of 1913, were all aimed towards this end. The Defence of India Act of 1915 which provided for the trial of revolutionary offenders by a strong bench without appeal and for the internment of suspects was a particularly obnoxious measure.

Although the outbreak of the war in Europe in August 1914 had no immediate connection with the defence of India yet as a part of the British Empire, the country automatically became involved in it. Once in the war, India made ungrudging contribution to the war effort. Not only did the country furnish the sinews of war—men and munitions—she took up responsibility for one hundred million pounds of the war debt. As the war went on "the affirmation of the moral values in the war, and the emergence of the doctrine of self-determination, deeply influenced Indian public opinion. If the war was being fought to make the world safe for democracy. it was hoped that it would at least put India on the road to self-government. If self-determination was to be applied to the politicallydormant Arabs in the Turkish Empire, it was asserted, it should be applied to Indians as well."

Under the circumstances, the question of further constitutional reforms did not brook delay. A patent proof of the wide awakening of the Indians at this stages was that they themselves formulated various schemes for reforms for the consideration of the Government. Among those who put forward different schemes for the reforms were the nineteen members of the Central Legislature, including Mr. Jinnah, Srinivasa Shastri and Surendra Nath Banerjee, who in a Memorandum submitted in 1916, observed : "What is wanted is no merely good government or efficient administration, but government that is acceptable to the people because it is responsible to them." In December, 1916 a joint scheme prepared by the Congress and the Muslim League, the outcome of the Lucknow Pact, was put forward.

Montagu's Statement of 20 August 1917

Just five weeks after assuming office on August 20, 1917, Montagu, the new Secretary of State made a statement in the House of Commons regarding the goal of British Government in India. he announced :

> "The policy of His Majesty's Government, with which the Government of India are in complete accord, is that of the increasing association of Indians in every branch of the administration and gradual development of *self-governing* institutions with a view to the progreassive realisation of *responsible* Government in India as an integral part of the British Empire. They have decided that substantial steps in this direction should be taken as soon as possible....I would add that progress in this policy can only be achieved by successive stages. The British Government and the Government of India, on whom the responsibility lies for the welfare and advancement of Indian peoples, must be judges of the time and measure of each advance, and they must be guided by the co-operation received from those upon whom new opportunities of services will thus be conferred and by the extent to which it is found that confidence can reposed in their sense of responsibility."

The authors of the Montford Report regarded this declaration as "the most momentous utterance ever made in India's chequered history" which marked "the end of one epoch and the beginning of a new one". It was a declaration of belief in the philosophy of liberalism. It was based on the idea that 'liberty alone fits men for liberty'. The Declaration eased the tense Indian atmosphere for the time being at least.

There was, however, a section of people in India to whome the declaration failed to satisfy. It was argued that no definite time was prescribed, by which India would reach her goal. Nor was there any standard laid down, by which one could decide whether a certain stage for further reforms had been reached or not. It was indeed insulting to india, it was pointed out, that the British were to the sole judge to decide whether India was capable of a particular set-up or not.

The Secretary of State came to India in November 1817 and discussed his scheme of reforms with the Viceroy, Lord Chelmsford, and some eminent British civil servants and Indian politicians of all shades of opinion. A committee was appointed consisting of Sir William Duke, Earl of Donoughmore, Bhupendra Nath Basu and Charles Robert (The M.P. Who had put the question in the Commons in reply to which the Secretary of State had made the Declaration) which together with the Viceroy, helped Montagu to prepare the draft of a reform scheme which was published in July 1918 and is called the Montagu-Chelmsford (the Montford) Report on the basis of which the Government of India Act 1919 was drafted.

The Government of India Act, 1919

Preamble. The Act laid down in its Preamble the principles on which the reforms were to be progressively carried out in India. These principles were more or less the same as embodied in the Declaration of August 20, 1917. An analysis of the Preamble brings out of the following points : (1) British India is to remain an integral part of the British Empire. (2) Responsible Government in British India is the objective of the declared policy of Parliament. (3) Responsible Government is capable of progressive realisation only. (4) In order to achieve Responsible Government, it is necessary to provide for two things: the increasing association of the Indians in every branch of administration and the gradual development of self-governing institutions. (5) Concurrently with the development of self-governing institutions in the provinces, it is expedient to give to provinces in provincial matters the highest measure of independence of the Government of India, which is compatible with the due discharge by the latter of its own responsibilities.

The significance of the Preamble was that what already declared by Montagu was now given a definite legal shape. The sovereignty of the British Parliament over India was reasserted and the country was told in clear terms of the basis of the future British action.

Main Provisions of the Act

A. Changes in the 'Home' Government. The Secretary of State for India who used to be paid out of the Indian revenues was now to be paid by the British Exchequer, thus undoing an injustice dating from 1793. Some of his functions were taken away from him and given to the High Commissioner for India who was to be appointed and paid by the Government of India. This new functionary acted as the agent of the Governor-General-in-Council. He was to be incharge of the Stores Department, the Indian Students Department, etc. The control of the Secretary of State was reduced in the provincial sphere in India in so far as Transferred Subjects were concerned but his control over the Centre remained as complete as before.

The curtailment of the powers and functions of the Secretary of State was done, it appears, in deference to the wishes of the Congress which had passed a resolution at the 1916 session that "India must be government from Delhi and Simla and not from Whitehall and Downing Street." The Act, however, met these wishes in a very small way.

B. Changes in the Government of India : On the Excutive Side. The Act did not introduce responsible government at the Centre though Indians were to have greater influence there. The number of Indians in the Governor-General's Executives Council was raised to there in a Council of eight. The Indian members were entrusted with departments like that of Law, Education, Labour, Health and Industries.

The new scheme of Government envisaged a division of Subjects into the Central List and the Provincial List. A List of Central subjects was drawn up which were to be administered by the Governor-General-in-Council. Those subjects which were of national importance or which related to more than one province, such as Foreign Affairs, Defence, Political Relations, Posts and Telegraphs, Public Debt, Communications, Civil and Criminal Law and Procedure, etc., were included in the Central List, while others which were only of provincial importance, such as Public Health, Local Self-Government, Education, Medical Administration, Land Revenue Administration, Water Supply, Famine Relief, Law and Order, Agriculture, etc., were included in the Provincial List. Any subject not specially transferred to the provinces was a Central subject.

Comments on the Changes on the Executive side. The changes introduced in the Executive Council at the Centre left much to be desired. Though a step was taken towards increasing association of Indians by raising their strength to three in a council of eight, yet the departments assigned to them were comparatively unimportant. Nor were these members made responsible to the Legislative. Placed as they were, they could not but be the yes-men of the Viceroy.

The division of subjects into two lists left much to be desired. The division was not clear-cut or based upon proper considerations. Critics point out that while subjects like Commerce and law regarding Property were placed in the Central List, important subjects like Excise and laws regarding Land Tenure were given to the Provinces. Although all subjects in the Provincial List were provincial for purposes of administration, that was not the case for purposes of legislation. Certain portions of them in regard to which uniformity in legislation was considered desirable were made "subject to legislation by the Indian Legislature." These were borrowing and taxing powers of local self-governing bodies, supplies and irrigation, industrial matters including factories, electricity, etc.

The chief executive authority still remained with the Governor-General, who was a representative of the Crown and was constantly in correspondence with the Secretary of State for India. He exercised full control over his Councillors and enjoyed vast powers over the country. Thus the wishes of the people of the country in respect of the appointment, powers and functions of the Governor-General were ignored in the Act.

Changes on the Legislative side. The Act set up a bicameral legislature at the Centre in place of the Imperial Council consisting of one House. The two Houses now were to be the Council of State and the Central Legislative Assembly.

The Council of State which was to be the Upper House was to consist of 60 members, 26 of whom were to be nominated by the Governor-General and 34 were to be elected, introducing therby an elected majority. The 26 nominated members were to consist of 20 officials and 6 non-officials, while of the 34 elected members, 20 were to be elected by General constituncies, 10 by the Muslims, 3 by the Europeans, and 1 by the Sikh constituencies. The Council of State was renewed partially every year, though a member held his seat for five years. Its President was to be nominated by the Viceroy and its members were called "Honourable". Women were not entitled to become its members. The governor-General could address the House, and he could summon, prorogue or dissolve the House.

The franchise was extremly restricted. Only those paying an income tax on the minimum income of Rs. 10,000 a year or those paying a minimum land revenue of Rs. 750 a year were entitled to vote. In addition, the other qualifications were that either a person must be on the Senate of a University or he must have some past experience in some Legislative Council of India, or he must be title-holder. Out of the entire population of India in 1920 of 24 crores not more than 17,364 persons possessed the requisite qualifications for a vote.

The Legislative Assembly which was to constitute the Lower House was to consist of 145 members, of whom 41 were to be nominated and 104 elected. Of the 41 nominated members, 26 were officials and 15 non-officials. Of the 104 elected members, 52 were to be returned by the General constituencies, 32 by the Communal constituencies 30 by the Muslims and 2 by the Sikhs), and 20 by the Special constituencies (7 by the landholders, 9 by the Europeans and 4 by the Indian Commercial community).

The life of the Assembly was to be three years but it could be extended by the Governor-General. It is to be noted that the last Assembly elected in 1936 was dissolved after ten years.

The franchise here was much restricted though as compared to Council of State it was not so high. The minimum qualifications were that either a person must be an occupant or an owner of a house of the minimum annual rental value of Rs. 180, or he must be paying the municipal tax of Rs. 15 a year, or must be paying an income tax on an income of not less than Rs. 2,000 a year or he must be paying a land revenue of at least Rs. 50 a year. The number of persons who thus became entitled to vote stood at 909,874 in 1920.

The distribution of seats among the different provinces was made on the basis of their so-called importance and not on the basis of their population. For instance, both the Panjab and Bihar and Orissa were granted 12 seats each though the population of the Panjab was only $\frac{2}{3}$ of that of Bihar and Orissa. The reason was the military importance of the Panjab. Bombay and Madras were granted 16 seats each though the population of Bombay was only half of that of Madras. The reason here was the commercial importance of Bombay.

Powers of the Central Legislature. The Central Legislature, constituted of the above-mentioned two Houses, was supposed to have been given very wide powers. It could legislate for the whole of British India, for the Indian subjects and servants of the Government, whether inside or outside the country. It could repeal or amend any law already existing in the country. The members were given the right to move resolutions and motions for adjournment of the House, to consider urgent questions of public importance immediately. They had the right to ask questions and supplementaries. Short-notice questions could also be asked. The members enjoyed the right of freedom of speech.

There were, however, certain restrictions imposed on the Legislature. In certain cases, previous sanction of the Governor-General was required for the introduction of a bill such as (*a*) Amendment or repeal of an existing law or an ordinance of the Governor-General, (*b*) Foreign relations and the relations with the Indian States, (*c*) Discipline or maintenance of the military, naval and the air forces, (*d*) Public debt and public revenue and (*e*) Religion, religious rites and usages of the people. Further, if the Governor-General felt that and bill or a part of it affects the safety or tranquillity of British India or any part thereof, he could prevent its consideration.

If on the advice of the Governor-General the Legislature refused to pass a law, the Governor-General could pass it himself, subject to the sanction of the Crown. He could make and promulgate ordinances in cases of emergency which could last for six months and which had the same force of law as a law passed by the legislature. His assent was essential for the enactment of law passed by the legislature. Thus we see that the vetoing power of the Governor-General was real and was actually exercised.

With regard to the budget, it was laid down in the Act that the Government would submit proposals for appropriation in the shape of demands for grant in the Legislative Assembly. Certain items were subject to the vote of the Assembly, others were open for duscussion and some could not even be discussed much less voted upon.

Observations on the Changes Introduced by the Act at the Centre. There is much truth in the statement that the Act of 1919 introduced *responsive* and not *responsible* government at the Centre. No vote of no-confidence by the Legislature could turn out the members of the Executive Council of the Governor-General and as such they were irremovable. But that did not mean that they could ride roughshod over the wishes of the Legislature. In fact, they did respond to the wishes of the Legislature and through it to the wishes of the people. Some of the members of the Legislature were put on the standing committees such as that of Public Accounts and Finance and here they got considerable opportunity to influence the governmental policy. Moreover, they could expose the Government by putting it questions, supplementaries and moving motions of adjournment. They could also reject the budget and move and pass resolutions against the Government. The large elected majority in the Assembly, if not heard to, could make things hot for the Government. Even the most irresponsible Executive Councillors could not afford to ride the high horse and domineer over the Legislature. They had to respond to the wishes of the members of the Legislature as a rule.

Provincial Government (Introduction of Dyarchy)

Changes on the Executive side. The most significant changes made by the Act of 1919 were in the field of provincial administraion. One of the principles enunciated by the Montford Report was: "The provinces were the domain in which the earlier steps towards the progressive realisation of responsible government should be taken. Some measure of responsibility should be given at once and our aim is to give complete responsibility as soon as conditions permit. This involves at once giving the provinces the largest measure of independence, legislative, administrative and provincial, of the Government of India which is compatible with the due discharge by the latter of its own responsibilities." The preamble to the Act reiterated this principle.

To give effect to this principle, the Act introduced what is called Dyarchy in the Provinces. Under this system, the subject to be dealt with by the Provincial Government were divided into two parts: Reserved and Transferred subjects. The Reserved subjects were administered by the Governor with the help of the members of the Executive Council who were nominated by him and who were not to be responsible to the Legislature while the Transferred subjects were administrered by the Governor acting with ministers appointed by him from among the elected members of the Legislature and who were to be responsible to the Legislature and were to hold office during his pleasure. The right of interference enjoyed by the Secretary of State in Council and the Governor-General-in-Council in the Transferred subjects were very much restricted. The Reserved Departments, however, were subject to the direction, control and supervision of the Governor-General-in-Council as well as the Secretary of State for India in Council.

The Reserved subjects were: Land Revenue, Famine Relief, Justice, Police, Pensions, Criminal Tribes, Printing Presses, Irrigation and Waterways, Mines, Factories, Electricity, Gas, Boilers, Labour Welfare, Industrial Disputes, Motor Vehicles, Minor Ports, Excluded Areas and Public Services. On the Transferred side, the Ministers advised the Governor in respect of Education (other than European and Anglo-Indian Education), Libraries, Museums, Local Self-Government, Medical Relief, Public Health and Sanitation, Agriculture, Co-operative Societies, Veterinary Department, Fisheries, Public Works, Excise, Industries, Weights and Measures, Control of Public Entertainments, Religious and Charitable Endowments, etc. The law did not require meetings of all ministers together to take decisions on all Transferred subjects. The Governor dealt with each minister individually. On matters of common concern, particularly on the allocation of the revenues, there was joint consultation between the Reserved and Transferred halves of the Government, the Governor presiding and having the last word of the subject with him.

Changes on the Legislative Side. The Act also introduced chages in the Provincial Legislatures, called Legislative Councils; their size was increased, their total membership varying from province to province. Of the total number of the members of a Provincial Council, at least 70% were to be elected, while not more than 20% were to be officials, the remaining were to be nominated non-officials. The figures for the various provinces were as follows:

Province	Elected members	Officials	Nominated Non-officials	Total
Madras	98	11	23	132
Bombay	86	19	9	114
Bengal	114	16	10	140
United Provinces	100	17	6	123
Panjab	71	15	8	94
Bihar and Orissa	76	15	12	103
Central Provinces	55	10	8	73
Assam	39	7	7	53
North-West Frontier Province	39	7	7	53

The system of election introduced for the Provincial Councils was direct, the primary voters electing the members. However, high property qualifications, the communal and class electorates and special weightage to certain communities figured in the provincial franchise.

The functions of the Provincial Councial were also enlarged. The members enjoyed the right and freedom of speech, the right to move resolutions, the right to ask questions and supplementaries, the right to initiate legislation concerning any provincial subject, though every bill passed required the approval of the Governor. The members could reject the budget, though the Governor could restore it, if necessary.

Observations on the Changes made in the Provincial Government. Dyarchy was introduced in the provinces on April 1, 1921, and continued in operation till April 1937, though it ceased to function in two provinces for some time during this period—in Bengal from 1924 to 1927, in the Central Provinces from 1924 to 1926.

During its operation, the limitations and defects of Dyarchy came to the surface. To enumerate them :

1. The division of administration into two halves each independent of the other is opposed to political theory and practice of governments. The actual division of subjects under the two heads of Reserved and Transferrred was illogical and irrational, the result being that neither a Minister, nor an Executive Councillor could work independently of the other. Thus, while Agriculture was a Transferred subject, Irrigation was kept as Reserved, though the two for obvious reasons cannot be separated. Take another case : Industry was Transferred, while Water, Power Factories and Mines were kept as Reserved. Examples can be multiplied of such incongruities in the division of subjects.

2. It was not possible at times to have unity of purpose between the two branches of administration. For instance, when there was agitation in regard to the Sikh Gurdwaras, the aim of the Member in charge of law and Order, which was a Reserved subject, was to introduce certain legislative measures to meet the situation, but this he could not do, as the legislation in this connection could be introduced only by the Minister in-charge of Religious Endowments, which was a Transferred subject.

3. At times there was such a confusion that the authorities could not decide whether a particular subject belonged to one department or the other. C.Y. Chintamani, a Minister of U.P., thus relates an experience : in 1921, an enquiry was started in the Department of Agriculture on the question of the fragmentation of holdings. When the Report was submitted in the following year, all of a sudden it was discovered that the question should have been handled by the Revenue Department, to which the matter was now referred. But here too, when the question had engaged the attention of the Revenue Department for two years, it was discovered that the subject after all belonged to the Co-operative Department.

4. There was no love lost between the two halves of the Government. The ministers were the representatives of the people while the members of the Executive Council belonged to the bureaucracy. Friction between them was inevitable. At times the Ministers and the Executive Councillors condemned one another in public. As a rule, the Governor backed the members of the Executive Council against the Ministers.

5. The position of the Ministers was weak in another way. They had to serve two masters, namely, the Governor and the Legislative Council. A Minister was appointed by the Governor and dismissed at his will. He was responsible to the Legislature for the administration of his department. He could not retain his office if the Legislature passed a vote of no confidence against him. From the point of view of practical politics, the Ministers cared more for the Governor than the Legislature. There were no strong parties in the Provincial Legislatures. The result was that no Minister had a majority to back him in office. He had always to depend upon the backing and support of the official bloc in the Legislature and this he could only get if the Governor was happy with him. It is not surprising therefore that the Ministers always looked up to the Governor and were dependent upon him. The result was that the Ministers sank to the position of glorified secretaries and were always at the beck and call of the Governors.

6. The Governors did not encourage the principle of joint responsibility amongst the Ministers. The latter never worked as a team. They were at times pitched against one another. In 1928, Feroz Khan Noon, a Punjab Minister, publicly criticised and condemned the action of his Hindu colleague.

7. In most important matters, the Ministers were not even consulted, as for instance in the case of Gandhi's arrest. The repressive policy against the non-cooperation movement was planned and executed but the Ministers were neither consulted nor did they even know what actually the Government was planning to do. They, in the words of C.R. Dass, "were only dumb spectators, who could neither speak nor say anything."

8. A Minister did not have the required control on the services under his own department. His own Secretary had a weekly interview with the Governor and therefore his opinion carried greater weight than that of the Minister. Whenever there was a difference of opinion between the Minister and his permanent Secretary or between the Minister and the Commissioner of a Division or the head of a department, the matter had to be referred to the Governor, who always supported the officials against the Minister. As pointed out by P. N. Masaldan : "The carrying out of the policy laid down by the Ministers was largely left to the services over which the Ministers had no control. It was, for the Ministers, a case of holding responsibility without corresponding authority."

9. The appointment, salary, suspension, dismissal and transfer of the members of All-India Services was under the control of the Secretary of State for India. These persons continued to be under the control of the Secretary of State even if they held charge in the Transferred departments. They, in consequence, did not care for the Ministers. The Ministers had no power to choose officers of their own liking when vacancies occurred in their departments.

10. All the so-called nation-building departments were transferred to the Ministers but they were given no money for them. The result was that the Ministers had to depend upon the sweetwill of the Finance Member. As a member of the bureaucracy, the Finance Member had little sympathy with the aspirations of the people as represented by the Ministers. He cared more for the needs of the Reserved departments, than for the Transferred departments. The Finance Member could always put a spoke in the wheeel when money was demanded for the Transferred departments and thus thwart the schemes and projects for those departments put up by the Ministers.

Apart from the limitations and defects in the system of Dyarchy as enumerated above, there were still other hindrances in the way of its successful working. The poltical atmosphere in the country was surcharged with suspicion and distrust on account of terrible happenings in the Panjab and elsewhere, and the attitude of the British Government towards Turkey. The monsoon failed in

1920 and added to the misery of the people. Slump also came in the market with the result that the finances of both Central and Provincial governments were upset as also the favourable balance of trade of India. Under the Meston Award, the Provincial Governments were required to make certain annual contributions to the Government of India. The Government of India insisted upon its pound of flesh from the provinces which themselves were in financial difficulties. The financial crisis in the provinces and the atmosphere of suspicion and distrust boded ill for the successful working of the new constitution.

General Review of the Act of 1919. The Act of 1919 had three major defects from the nationalist point of view, namely, (*a*) The absence of even partial responsible government at the Centre, (*b*) The consolidation of 'separate electorates'. Although the Montford Report had declared that communal 'separate electorates' was 'a very serious hindrance to the development of the self-governing principle, yet 'separate electorates' came to be a permanent feature of the Indian political life. (*c*) The introduction of dyarchy in the provinces was too complicated to be smoothly worked.

Nevertheless, somethings can be said in favour of the Act. The Act undoubtedly made a new departure. For the first time in the history of British rule it provited for transfer of power, even though the transfer was halting and the power extremely limited. As Coupland says: "The Act crossed the line between legislative and executive authority. Previous measures had enabled Indians increasingly to control their legislatures but now their Government...Now Indians were to govern, so to speak, on their own... as leaders of the elected majorities in their legislatures, and responsible to them."

Though dyarchy has been condemned out of hands, it would be wrong to say that dyarchy brough no constitutional progress. Dyarchy was, probably, the best transitional mechanism that appeared after a prolonged examination of alternatives.

RESUME

Salient Features of the Government of India Act, 1919

World War I quickened the pace of nationalist development in India. The loudly-proclaimed Allied Leaders' announcement that they were fighting against the Germans to defend democracy and to provide to every nation, big or small, the right to determine its own form of government. The Indian nationalists took these statements at their face value and demanded that the right of self-determination should be applied to India also.

As a sop to Indian nationalist demands and for world propaganda purposes. Lord Montague, the Secretary of State, announced in the House of Commons on 20 August 1917 the goal of constitutional advance in India to be 'the gradual development of self-governing institutions with a view to the progressive realisation of responsible government as an integral part of the British Empire', making it absolutely clear that the British authorities would determine the stages and timing of such advance.

The Montford Report (1918) laid down a fourfold formula to implement the policy in the first stage, *viz.,*

(*i*) Introduction of complete popular control in local bodies (municipalities, talukas, district boards, etc.);

(*ii*) Partial introduction of responsible government in the field of provincial administration;

(*iii*) Non-introduction of responsible government at the Centre but enlargement of the Indian Legislative Council and more representation of Indians in it; and

(*iv*) Relaxation of the control of the parliament and the Secretary of State to the extent popular government was introduced in the provinces.

These recommendations were given a statutory shape under the Government of India Act, 1919.

(a) **Introduction of Dyarchy :** The most important feature of the Act was the introduction of dyarchy (from the Greek words *di* meaning two, and *archia* meaning rule—double government or government by two rulers) in the provinces.

The scheme of dyarchy necessitated demarcation of subjects of administration between the Central Government and the Provincial Governments which was done through Devolution Rules framed under the Act. The Central List included subjects (like Defence, Foreign Affairs, Coinage and Currency, Customs, etc.) where uniformity of legislation and administration for the whole country was desirable and the Provincial List (like Local Self-Government, Education, Medical Administration, Agriculture, etc.) wherein diversity of administration of suit different needs of provinces might be desirable.

The Provincial List was further divided into two parts—*Transferred* subjects (like Local Self-Government, Education, Hospitals, Industries, Agriculture, etc.) whose administration was to be entrusted to popular ministers, and *Reserved* subjects (like Law and Order, Police, Finance, Land Revenue, Labour, etc.) which were still to be administered by Executive Councillors (officials) in an autocratic fashion as before.

The Provincial Legislative Councils were enlarged and roughly 70% of the members were elected. The franchise was extended by lowering the property qualifications, raising the number of voters to 5.5 million. Unfortunately, the system of 'communal electorates' was not only retained by further extended and even the Sikhs, Europeans, Indian Christians and Anglo-Indians got separate representation.

The Governor was the head of the executive government in the province and was expected to play a vital role in the new set-up. For the *Reserved* subjects he was responsible as before to the Governor-General and the Secretary of State. Even in the administration of *Transferred* subjects the Governor was not a mere constitutional head. He could override the advice of popular ministers if he considered such a course desirable in the interest of the safety and tranquillity of the province, advancement and social welfare of backward classes or minorities or in the interest of public services, etc. Further, the Governor enjoyed extensive legislative powers. He could veto any bill; any bill rejected by the provincial legistature could be deemed to have been passed by the Governor's *power of certification*; he could issue ordinances; he could dissolve the legislature at any time or extend its term for one year. Provision was also made in the Act, in case of breakdown of constitutional machinery, for the Governor to take over the entire administration in his hands and administer the *Transferred* subjects as *Reserved* subjects.

Changes at the Centre. At the Centre the Government of India continued to be autocratic as before and in theory responsible only to the British Parliament.

Enlargement of the Central Legislature was carried out by making it bi-cameral. The Council of State, the upper house, was to comprise 60 members, of whom 34 were elected on high property qualifications and 26 nominated. The Legislative Assembly was to consist of 145 members, out of which 104 were elected and 41 nominated. Voting qualification was lower for the Legislative Assembly than for the Council of State but was tied to ownership of a house, payment of income tax or land revenue of a particular amount. Women were given the vote for the Assembly. The duration of an Assembly was 3 years, that of the Council of State 5 years.

No changes of fundamental nature were provided in the Central Executive under the Act. The powers of the Governor General already very extensive were further added to. For the first time, the Governor-General-in-Council got the powers of restoring cuts, certifying bills and promulgating ordinances. However, the strength of the Executive Council was increased to 8 and representation of Indians in it was increased from 1 to 3 members.

Appraisal of the Act and its Working. Unfortunately, the Government of India Act, 1919, was never given a co-operative trial. Right from the beginning the Indian National Congress condemned it as "disappointing and unsatisfactory". The Congress made it clear that dyarchy in the provinces would be tolerated only if it was also introduced at the Centre forthwith; it further demanded a statutory guarantee that full responsible government would be introduced within 15 years. Unable to get these assurances and reacting sharply to the oppressive policies of the Government, the Congress launched 'non-violent non-cooperation' movement in 1920 for the attainment of *Swaraj* or self-rule. In 1923 the Congress Swarajists contested election to the councils, not with a view to working the constitution but wrecking it from within the legislatures.

All the same, the first elections under the new Act were held in 1920. Dyarchy functioned in all the 9 Governors' provinces uninterruptedly from 1921 to 1937 excepting in Bengal and Central Provinces where it had to be suspended during 1924-27 and 1924-26 respectively.

The scheme of Dyarchy was 'cumbrous, complex, confused system, having no logical basis and rooted in compromise' and was foredoomed to failure. But the experiment was not altogether barren of results. Popular ministers turned their attention to the reform of local bodies, education and social legislation. The Bihar and Orissa Village Administration Act (1922), the Bombay Local Boards Act (1923), the Calcutta Municipal Act (1923), the Bombay Primary Education Act (1923), the Madras State Aid to Industries Act (1923), The Madras Religious Endowment Act (1926), etc., deserve mention. Further, the achievements of dyarchy, however limited, knocked the bottom out of the myth sedulously built up by the British that Indians were not fit to stand on their own legs. In addition, Indian leaders for the first time got some administrative experience in a constitutional set-up which was both exciting and stimulating.

SELECT REFERENCES

1. Appadorai, A. : *Dyarchy in Practice.*
2. Curtis, L. : *Dyarchy.*
3. Ilbert and Meston : *The New Government of India.*
4. Keith, A.B. : *Speeches and Documents of Indian Policy,* vol. ii.
5. Prasad, Bisheshwar : *The Origins of Provincial Autonomy.*

43

THE ROAD TO RESPONSIBLE GOVERNMENT—II

The Government of India Act. 1935

> We are provided with a car, all brakes and no engine.
>
> —*Jawaharlal Nehru*
>
> The progress of constitutional advance in India is determined by the need to attract Indian collaborators to the Raj.
>
> —*B.R. Tomlinson*

Circumstances leading to the passing of the Act. The Congress considered the Montagu-Chelmsford Reforms to be "inadequate, unsatisfactory and disappointing", but while urging the Government to speedily establish full responsible government in accordance with the principle of self-determination, it resolved to work them "so far as may be possible" with a view to bringing about at an early date the desired type of government.

Rowlatt Acts and Jallinwala Bagh Tragedy. But fate proved too strong for such good intentions. Justice Rowlatt's Committee produced a Report on the basis of which two Bills were introduced in the Imperial Legislature in February 1919 and passed, in spite of popular opposition, with the help of the official majority commanded by the Government. Gandhiji thereupon asked the people to use the weapon of *Satyagraha* against these iniquitous laws. Accordingly, *hartals* were observed throughout the country, resulting in disturbances at a number of places, the imposition of the Martial Law in the Panjab, the Jallianwala Bagh tragedy in which about 400 people of Amirtsar were killed and 1,200 wounded by General Dayer's machine-gunning a peaceful and unarmed crowd.

Khilafat Agitation. Meantime, the Muslims were full of resentment against the severity of the terms of the Treaty of Sevres, imposed by the victorious Allied Powers on the defeated Turkey. Gandhiji espoused their cause and launched a non-violent and non-cooperation campaign for the redress of the *Khilafat* wrongs to establish *Swaraj*. The impact of the war, the tragedy at Amritsar, the Khilafat Movement which temporarily bridged the gulf between the Hindus and Muslim—all these created a new situation and demanded a complete reorientation of policy and methods of the Congress. The fundamental change in the policy and methods of the Congress was reflected in Article 1 of the Constitution adopted in 1921 : "The object of the Indian National Congress is the attainment of *Swarajya* by the people of India by all legitimate and peaceful means." In other words, self-government within the British Empire was no longer to be attained solely through 'constitutional' means; unconstitutional means, provided they were 'legitimate and peaceful', might also be employed. This change in the fundamental character of the Congress came in the very year (1921) of the inauguration of the Montford Reforms and boded ill for its successful working.

The Swaraj Party. With the passage of time the opposition to the Act of 1919 became strong and more effective. Even the Moderates, for all their readiness to co-operate with the Government, found the Reforms inadequate and unsatisfactory. Some of the Congress leaders, especially Motilal Nehru and C.R. Das, formed the Swarajist Party with the avowed object of "wrecking the legislatures from within" and pledged to a policy of "uniform, continuous and sustained obstruction with a view to making government through the Assembly and the Council impossible." In the elections of 1923 the Swarajists won an absolute majority in the Central provencies Council and constituted the single largest party in Bengal and some other provinces. By its tactics it exposed the official hypocrisy behind the dyrchical scheme of government.

The Simon Commission, 1927-30. The British Government virtually recognised the failure of the Reforms of 1919 by appointing the Simon Commission in November 1927, two years before such a Commission was due. One ostensible reason suggested for this haste was the agitation in India, but the fact is that the Conservative Government of Lord Birkenhead felt sure that the next General Elections in Engalnd would return a Labour Government to power, and the Conservatives, therefore, did not like to leave the appointment of the Commission to such a successor government. This is proved by a private letter of Lord Birkenhead to Lord Reading, the then Viceroy, which letter also reveals another motive—to use the appointment of the Commission as a bargaining counter and thus to disintegrate the Swarajist Party.

The Simon Commission was to enquire "into the working of the system of government, the growth of education and the development of representative institutions in British India and matters connected therewith" and to report "as to whether and to what extent it is desirable to establish the principle of responsible government or to extend, modify or restrict the degree of responsible government then existing therein, including the question whether the establishment of Second Chambers of the local legislatures is or is not desirable." During the enquiry the Commission "was increasingly impressed by the impossibility of considering the constitutional problems of British India without taking into account the relations between British India and the Indian States." Therefore, the subject of these relations was also added to the purview of the Commission. No Indian was included in the Commission and its all-White composition was condemned by all shades of Indian public opinion and completely boycotted by the Congress. Lord Birkenhead justified the exclusion of Indians by asserting that in so far as the Commission was appointed by Parliament its personnel had to be confined to members of Parliament. But it was a very lame excuse.

A general *hartal* was observed all over the country on the day of the ill-starred Commission's landing in India and the Commission was everywhere greeted with black flags and cries of "Simon, go back". The Central Assembly was invited to form a Joint Committee to co-operate with the Commission, but it refused to do so.

The Nehru Report, 1928. While the Simon Commission was carrying on its work in isolation from Indian public opinion, the leading Indian political parties were trying to forge a common political programme. An All-Parties Conference, presided over by Dr. M.A. Ansari, was convened at Bombay on May 19, 1928 and appointed a Committee under Motilal Nehru's Chairmanship to consider and determine the principles of a constitution for India. The Committee consisted of Sir Tej Bahadur Sapru, Sir Ali Iman, M.S. Aney, Mangal Singh, Shuab Qureshi, G.R. Pradhan and Subhas Chandra Bose and its Report (submitted on August 10, 1928), says Dr. Zacharias, is "a masterly and statesmanlike one", while another commentator says that it "deserves to be read and studied in all its detail, as it sheds light on every subject it touches and displays a practical commonsense, which never loses itself in doctrinaire utopias, but which equally spurns to shelter itself behind enunciation of mere platitudes." The recommendations were unanimous except as to the basis of the constitution. While the majority favoured Dominion Status as "the next immediate step", it gave liberty of action to all those groups and parties which had the goal of complete independence as their aim. The Report confined itself to British India, as it envisioned a future link-up of British India with the Indian States on a federal basis. As regards the thorny communal problem, the report wisely recommended joint electorates with reservation of seats for minorities (except in the Panjab and Bengal) on population basis with the right to contes additonal seats. Full protection was afforded to the religious and cultural interests of the Muslims, and even "new provinces on linguistic basic were to be created with a view to the planning of Muslim-majority provinces." Nineteen Fundamental Right were also suggested for inclusion in the proposed statute. The Report suggested the the Indina Parliament should consist of (*a*) the Senate elected for 7 years,, containing 200 members elected by the Provincial Councils and

(b) the House of Representatives with 500 members elected for five years through adult franchise. The Governo-General (to be appointed by the British Government but paid out of Indian revenues) was to act on the advice of the Executive Council which was to be collectively responsible to the Parliament. The Provincial Councils were to be elected, on the basis of adult franchise, for five years and the Governor (to be appointed by the British Government) was to act on the advice of the Provincial Executive Council.

On December 2, 1928, the All-Parties Conference met at Calcutta to consider the Nehru Report, and Mr. Jinnah, on behalf of the Muslim League, moved a number of amendments to those portions of the Report which dealt with communal matters of which three were lost but one to the effect that the constitution should not be amended unless both Houses of Parliament separately passed it by a four-fifths majority, and a joint session of both the Houses approved it unanimously, was accepted.

On December 31, 1928, the Congress at its annual session adopted a resolution welcoming the All-Parties Conference Report and affirming that if this constitution was in its entirety approved by the British Parliament within a year, that is by December 31, 1929, the Congress would accept it but if it was rejected or not accepted by then, then it would organise a compaign of non-violent non-cooperation, non-payment of taxes, etc. Three months later, the Subjects Committee of the Muslim League approved of the Nehru Report subject to a number of stipulated safeguards (which Mr. Jinnah had put forward at the Calcutta Convention). But the open session of the Muslim League meeting at Delhi on March 31, 1929, rejected the Nehru Report and affirmed Mr. Jinnah's celebrated "fourteen points" being the minimum condition acceptable to the Muslims for any political settlement.

Meantime, there was a change in the complexion of the British Government. The Labour party, under the leadership of Ramsay Macdonald, acceded to power and this gave rise to a great many high and even exaggerated hopes in Indian quarters. The Viceroy paid a flying visit to England, and made the announcement when he returned on October 31, 1929, that he was authorised to make it clear on behalf of the British Government that "in their judgment it is implicit in the Declaration of 1917 that the natural issue of India's constitutional progress as there contemplated is the "attainment of Dominion Status". He added that the Government had accepted the suggestion of the Simon Commission that after the publication of the latter's Report and before its examination by the Joint Parliamentary Committee, a Conference should be called of the representatives of the British Government, of British India and of the Indian States, in order to seek the greatest possible agreement for the final proposals later to be submitted to Parliament.

This ill-timed declaration left the unfortunate Commission in the air, and stole its thunder. Also "Dominion Status" was unhappily capable of being variously interpreted. Moreover, the Congress leaders were not satisfied with the limited purpose and scope of the proposed Round Table Conference. What they really wanted was the convening of a Constituent Assembly. However, an interview took place between the Viceroy and Gandhiji but led to no fruitful agreement, and the Congress meeting at Lahore under the Presidentship of Jawaharlal Nehru, resolved to boycott the Round Table Conference, declared the nation's aim to win complete independence and authorised the All-India Congress Committee to launch a Civil Disobedience Movement, which was actually started in March 1930. Gandhiji started his historic march to Dandi Beach, thousands of volunteers courted arrest by breaking selected law ; there were *lathi* charges and ordinances were issued in quick succession, newspaper editors and printing-press keepers were taken to task, and there seemed to be a complete break between the Government and the nationalists.

The Round Table Conference, 1930-32. As announced by the Viceroy on behalf of the Government of England on October 31, 1929, a Round Table Conference was convened in London (November 16, 1930, to Janurary 19, 1931). The Congress leaders being behind the prison bars, 'safe' men of other parties, communities and services were nominated by the Government to represent India, as well as men like Sir Mirza Ismail, Sir Akbar Hydari and the Maharaja of Bikaner to represent the Indian States. After lengthy discussions, three basic principles were agreed to by the Conference, and accepted by the British Government : (1) the form of the new Government of India was to be an All-India Federation ; (2) the Federal Government, subject to some reservations would be responsible to the Federal Legislature, and (3) the Provinces were to enjoy autonomy. On the conclusion of the conference, Ramsay Macdonald, the British Prime Minister, made the momentous declaration : "The view of His majesty's Government is that responsibility for the Government of India should be placed upon legislatures, Central and Provincial, with such provisions as may be considered necessary...and also with guarantees...required by minorities."

The absence of Congress representation in the First Round Table Conference led to the decision to have a second one in which, it was hoped, that Congress representatives would take part. Efforts in that direction by Sir Tej Bahadur Sapru and Sir M.R. Jayakar led to the famous Gandhi Irwin Pact, being signed in March 1931, by which all political prisoners were released and the Civil Disobedience Movement called off. Gandhiji was appointed the sole representative of the Congress to the Second Round Table Conference (September 1 to December 1, 1931), but in spite of his having given a *carte blanche* to Mr. Jinnah, no settlement could be arrived at to solve the communal problem due to the latter's intransigence secretly supported by British statesmen like the Secretary of State for India, Sir Samuel Hoare. His mission having been unsuccessful, Gandhiji left for India in disgust, and was arrested on his arrival in the country.

Ramsay macDonald announced that in default of an agreed settlement as regards the respective quanta of representation of different communities the British Government would have to adjudicate their claims. Accordingly, he gave on August 4, 1932, his infamous "Communal Award" which related to representation in the provincial legislatures. However, Ramsay MacDonald's Communal Award was a little later partially modified by the Poona Pact which was accepted by the Hindu leaders as a result of Gandhi's fast to prevent a political breach between the so-called 'Caste Hindus' and 'Scheduled Castes'.

After another Round Table Conference (the third) in London (November 17 to December 24, 1932), a White Paper was issued in March 1933, which gave details of the working basis of the new constitution of India—dyarchy at the Centre and responsible government in the provinces. In February 1935, a Bill was introduced in the House of Commons by the Secretary of State for India which when passed became the Government of India Act, 1935.

Among the principal sources from which the Act drew its material were : (*a*) the Simon Commission Report ; (*b*) the Report of the All-Parties Conference (the Nehru Report ; (*c*) the discussions at the three successive Round Table Conferences ; (*d*) the White Paper ; (*e*) the Joint Select Committee Report ; and (*f*) the Lothian Report which determined the electoral provisions of the Act.

The Provisions of the Act. The Act was a lengthy and elaborate document, dealing as it did with a highly complicated type of federal constitution and seeking to provide legal safeguards against misbehaviour of Indian ministers and legislators.

The three main features of the Act were provisions for (*a*) an all-India Federation; (*b*) responsible government with safeguards and (*c*) separate representation of communal and other groups.

Proposed All-India Federation. The Act contemplated the establishment of an all-India Federation in which Governors' Provinces and the Chief Commissioners Provinces and those Indian States which might accede to be united, were to be included. In the the case of the States, accession to the Federation was voluntary, and the Federation could not be established until (*a*) a number of States, the rulers whereof were entitled to choose not less than half of the 104 seats of the Council of State and (*b*) the aggregate population where of amounted to at least one-half of the total population of all the Indian States, had acceded to the Federation. The terms on which a State joined the Federation were to be laid down in the Instrument of Accession.

The Federal Executive. Dyarchy, rejected by the Simon Commission, was provided for in the Federal Executive. Defence, External Affairs, Ecclesiastical Affairs and the Administration of Tribal Areas were Reserved in the hands of the Governor-General to be administered by him with the assistance of a maximum of three Councillors to be appointed by him. The other Federal subjects would be administered by the Governor-General with the assistance and advice of a Council of (not more than ten) Ministers to be chosen by him and to hold office during his pleasure (but to include representatives of Indian States and Minorities as laid down in an Instrument of Instructions to the Governor-General, and to be responsible to the Federal Legislature. The Governor-General had 'special responsibilities' regarding certain specified subjects (*e.q.*, the prevention of any grave menace to the peace and tranquillity of India or any part thereof); in respect of these subjects he had full freedom to accept or to reject the advice of the Ministers. K.T. Shah has rightly criticized the position assigned to the Council of Federal Ministers as follows ; "It is ornamental without being useful, onerous without ever being helpful to the people they are supposed to represent ; it had responsibility without power position without authority, name without any real influence." He goes on : "It seems extremely doubtful if the popular ministers of the Federation will have any real opportunity to inaugurate constructive schemes of economic betterment of social reconstruction...if the communal curb upon ministerial enthusiasm does not prove quite effective, there are the enormous powers of the Governor-General as protector and champion of the vested interest and imperialist exploitation which are bound to be employed to impede or frustrate too enthusiastic ministers. There are specific provisions in the Constitution as those relating to any discrimination against British vested interests...which will hamper the work of the ministers. The ministers' own internal difficulties—want of solidarity, etc., may prevent them from achieving anything beneficial to the people."

The Federal Legislature. It was to have two chambers, the Council of State and the Federal Assembly. The Council of State was to be a permanent body with one-third of its membership being vacated and renewed triennially. It was to consist of 156 elected members of British India and *not more than* 104 from the Indian States (to be nominated by the rulers concerned). The Federal Assembly whose duration was fixed for five years was to consist of 250 representatives of British India and *not more than* 125 members from the Indian States. The British Indian members in the case of the Federal Assembly were to be elected, not directly by the people as was to be the case in regard to the Council of State but indirectly by the members of the Provincial Legislative Assemblies on the system of proportional representation with the single transferable vote. The members from the States were to be nominated by the Rulers.

The following comments are called for in respect of the Federal Legislature :

1. In the Upper House the election was to be direct while in the Lower and theoretically more popular House it was to be indirect, a feature deviating from the general practice.

2. The princes were to nominate one-third of the representatives in the Lower House and two-fifths in the Upper House.

3. As regards the extent of Federal and Provincial laws, the Federal Legislature was to have power to make laws for the whole or any party of British India or for any federate State while a Provincial Legislature was to make laws for the Province or any part thereof. As regards the subject-matter of Federal and Provincial laws, there were three lists, the Federal Legislative List, the Provincial Legislative List and the Concurrent Legislative List. Residuary legislative powers were vested in the Governor-General to decide in his sole discretion as to under which list a particular subject fell.

4. The powers of the legislature were "cribbed, cabined and confined". Certain subjects were specially excluded from the purview and jurisdiction of Federal and Provincial Legislatures (*e.q.*, laws affecting the British Sovereign or the Royal Family, or matters concerning the Army Act, the Air

Force Act, or the Law of Prize Courts, or any amendment to the 1935 Act, etc.). Discriminatory legislation against British commercial or other interests was banned. Besides, there were many subjects of importance on which legislation could not be initiated without the previous sanction of the Governor-General (in case of the Federal legislature) or of the Governor-General and the Governor (in case of Provincial legislature). Non votable items in the Federal budget constituted about four-fifths of its total. Rejected by the Federal Assembly, any bedget items could still be placed, by the direction of the Governor-General, before the Council of State. In case of disagreement between the two Houses, the Governor-General could summon a joint sitting thereof, and even if a Bill was passed by both the Houses, he could veto it or sent it back for reconsideration, or reserve it for His Majesty's consideration, while even Acts assented to by the Governor-General could be disallowed by the king-in-Council.

Responsible Government with Safeguards. Another significant feature of the Act of 1935 was the provision of responsible government with safeguards. This feature of the Act has to be examined in (*a*) the Federal structure and (*b*) the Provinces.

The Federal Structure. The Act made the Governor-General the pivot of the entire constitution of India. It was he who gave unity and direction to its diverse and often conflicting elements and who was expected to keep the ship of the state on an even keel. He acted in three different ways or capacities : (*i*) He was normally to act on the *advice* of his Ministers, (*ii*) He could act in his individual judgement. In connection with his Special Responsibilities, he could and did act in his *individual judgment*, consulting but regarding or disregarding ministerial advice. His special responsibilities were in regard to (*a*) safeguarding the financial stability and credit of India, (*b*) the prevention of any grave menace to the peace or tranquillity of the country, or of any part thereof, (*c*) the protection of the legitimate interests of the minorities, the public servants and their dependents, (*d*) the prevention of commercial discrimination against goods of British or Burmese origin, (*e*) safeguarding the interests and the dignity of the rulers of the Indian States, and (*f*) securing of the due discharge of his own discretionary powers ; (*iii*) There was a third category of matters in which he did not even consult his Ministers, but acted *in his discretion*. Such matters were, *inter alia*, (*a*) the Reserved Departments of Defence, External Affairs, Ecclesiastical Affairs and Tribal Areas (to help him in his work he appointed three Councillors), (*b*) appointment and dismissal dismissal of the Council of Ministers, (*c*) ordinance-making and enacting Governor-General's Acts, (*d*) control over non-votable items, comprising about 80% of the budget, (*e*) issuing of instruction to Governors which were to be the latter's special responsibility, (*f*) powers of summoning a joint sitting of both Houses, of addressing the Legislatures, of sending them messages about a certain bill or bills, (*g*) according sanction to certain types of bills sought to be introduced in the Federal and Provincial legislatures and using his authority to stop discussion in any legislature at any time of any bill or to withhold his assent to any bill passed or to reserve the same for His Majesty's consideration.

Apart from these 'Departments' and 'Safeguards'—they were a legion indeed, the other departments were to be administered by the Governor-General with the aid and advice of the Council of Ministers. But in cases where the Governor-General was empowered to exercise his individual judgment, he might disregard ministerial advice. The ministers would be chosen and summoned by him in his discreation and would hold office during his pleasure. It was in this very limited way that 'responsibility' was to be introduced at the Federal Centre by the Act of 1935.

Provincial Autonomy

Provincial Executive. As in the case of the Federation, the Executive authority of a province was vested in a Governor appointed to represent the crown in the province. His position was largely modelled on that of the Governor-General.

The administration of the provincial affairs was to be ordinarily carried on by a council of Ministers appointed by the Governor from among the elected members of the provincial legislature and responsible to that body. The ministers held office during the Governor's pleasure and as such they carried on the administration with a double sense of responsibility. The Governor, like the Governor-General, did not only act as the constitutional head of the province merely acting on the advice of the Council of Ministers. He had "special responsibilities"regarding certain specified subjects (*i.e.,* the prevention of menace to the peace or tranquillity of the province or any part thereof), while in the case of particular provinces like the C.P. and Sind, circumstances necessitated a special rider to his such responsibilities. In the discharge of his 'special responsibilities', he was authorized to act in several matters *in his discretion* without consulting his ministers, in others he exercised *his individual judgment,* after considering the advice given to him by his ministers. If a question arose as to the capacity in which the Governor had to act to a particular case, whether as the constitutional head or in his discretion or in his individual judgement, his decision on the question *in his discretion* was to be final. In other words, the field of ministerial responsibility with respect to any particular matter was as wide or as narrow as the Governor might choose to make it.

There is no doubt that the Governor under the Act had enormous powers (which included many legislative powers as well as over non-votable items, comprising about 40% of the budget). The Governor could and in several cases actually did dismiss the ministers. He could also by a proclamation take the entire or partial governmet of the province into his own hands (in the first instance for six months) if he was satisfied that the government of the province could not be carried on in accordance with the normal provisions of the Act.

It might appear that the provisions in the Act of 1935 regarding the discretionary functions and special responsibilities of the Governor (as well of the Governor-General) were such as might be utilised to reduce responsible government to nullity. In this connection it must be remembered, as Keith points out, that all such provisions were included in the Act "in the hope that they will be accepted by Indian opinion as not intended to be effective and by British opinion as securing all that is requisite." The official theory or view of the relations between the Governor and his Council of Ministers was explained by Lord Zetland, "Let it not be supposed that the field of government is to be divided into two parts, in which the Governor and the Misistry operate separately at the risk of clashes between them. The essence of the new constitution is that the initiative and responsibility for the whole of the government of a province, though in form vesting in the Governor, passes to the Ministry as soon as it takes ofice". Sir Maurice Halectt, Governor of the U.P., expressed it thus : "After all, the relations of a Governor and his Ministers were not those of a master and his servant ; rather they are partners in a common enterprise—the good government of the province".

There is no gainsaying the fact that the provincial ministers under the 1935 Act were certainly superior in power to their predecessors under the 1919 Act. For one thing, now there were no "Reserved" departments in the provinces. The other ministers were to be appointed on the advice of the Chief Minister (who was to be such as commanded the confidence of the legislature) though the Governor had to see that monorities were duly represented in the ministry. The Governor, moreover, had to encourage collective responsibility. In actual functioning, several factors (*e,g.,* the ministerial party's strength in the legislature and the personality of the ministers as also that of the Governor) governed the actual position of the ministry, and as always in such cases, the personality equation was perhaps the most important one.

The Governor under the Act of 1935 seems to resemble that familiar figure of Greek tragedy *deus ex-machina* which literally means "a god out of a machine" and is usually used for a person or thing that saves the situation. This was a favourite stage-trick of the Greek tragedian Euripides. Whenever the plot of the play seemed hopelessly involved some divine person was introduced, borne down from above to clear up all difficulties.

Provincial Legislatures. The composition of Provincial legislature naturally varied from province to province. In all Provincial Legislative Assemblies all members were directly elected by the people. But in six provinces (Madras, Bombay, Bengal, the U.P., Bihar and Assam) there was a bicameral Legislature consisting of a Legislative Council and a Legislative Assembly and in each of these Legislative Councils a few seats were filled by the Governor through nomination.

The number of seats in the various legislative Assemblies was : 50 in the North-West Frontier Province, 60 each in Orissa and Sind, 108 in Assam, 112 in the Central Provinces, 152 in Bihar, 175 each in the Panjab and Bombay, 215 in Madras, 228 in the United Provinces and 250 in Bengal.

The separatist system of representation by religious communities and other groups—instead of representation by the general mass of the people usual in modern democracies—was a prominent feature of the Act of 1935. The electoral provisions of the Act were governed by the communal award of the British Government, as modified by the Poona Pact in respect of the Scheduled Castes. Under it, seats in the ligislatures were divided among various communities and groups. Besides, there were separate constituencies for General, Muslim, European, Anglo Indian, Indian Christian and Sikh communities. All qualified electors who were not voters in a Muslim, European, Anglo-Indian, Indian Christian or Sikh constituency were entitled to vote in a General constituency. Some of the General seats were reserved for the Scheduled Castes. All the members of the Scheduled Castes who were voters in a General constituency were to take part in a primary election for the purpose of electing four condidates for each reserved seat. The four persons, so elected, were to be candidates for election by the General electorate. Except in Assam, seats allowed also were divided among various communities. Moreover, there were separate constituencies for Labour, Landholders, Commerce and Industry, etc.

This communal award of the British Government accentuated the communal dissensions in the country, which paved the way for the eventual partition of India.

Other Provisions of the Act of 1935. (*a*) The Act provided for a Federal Court, with original and appellate powers, to interpret the constitution, but even in this respect the last word remained with the Privy Council in London.

(*b*) The new constitution was rigid, the sole authority competent to amend it being the British Government. On this point, we may cite S.M. Bose : "The Indian Legislatures have only been given the powers to express by resolution to His Majesty's Government their intention of a constitutional change in respect of the matters specified in this section. But the actual power of modifying the Act has been placed by the Act in the hands of His Majesty's Government by the Order-in-Council laid in draft before the two Houses, as provided in Section 309. In other words, no amending legislation by the Parliament will be required. In respect of those matters specifically mentioned in the Act variations may be made by Orders-in-council."

(*c*) Though the introduction of Provincial Autonomy and of partial Responsible Government at the Centre did diminish "Home" control over Indian affairs, yet where the Governor-General or the Governors acted in their individual judgment or discretion, they were made strictly responsible to the Secretary of State.

(*d*) Apart from the control given to the Federation by the Instrument of Accession, the right and obligations of the Crown in respect of the Indian States remained unaffected. These rights and obligations were left in charge of the Crown Representative. The combination of the offices of Governor-General and Crown Representative was allowed.

(*e*) Instead of the India Council of the Secretary of State (which was abolished by the Act) he was given advisers who might or might not be consulted or whose advice followed or not, except in respect to the Services. The Council was abolished because of much agitation in India against its persistent anti-Indian policies.

The Act Operation. The Government of India Bill received the Royal assent in August 1935. The British Government decided that Provincial autonomy would be introduced on April 1, 1937, leaving the Federation in abeyance–in fact the federation as visualized in the Act of 1935 never came into being. The electoral provisions began to operate on July 3, 1936 and the provisions for Provincial autonomy on Aprial 1,1937.

Pending the establishment of the Federation, the Central Government was to operate in accordance with the "Transitional Provision" read with the Ninth Schedule to the Government of India Act, 1935. Under the latter, certain provisions of the Act were continued in force with amendments. The amendments were necessitated by the introduction of Provincial autonomy. The powers conferred by the Act of 1935 of the Federal Legislature would be exercised by the Indian Legislature. The Governor-General-in-Council and the Governor-General would be under the general control of the Secretary of State for India and would comply with such directions as might be given by the Secretary of State. The members of the India Council were substituted by the Secretary of State's 'advisers'.

Even though the Federation was not established, the Federal Court came into existence to hear and determine constitutional cases.

The operative part of the Act of 1935 remained in force till August 15, 1947, when it was ammended by Independence of India Act, 1947.

The Working of Provincial Autonomy

After the first general elections under the new Act held in the winter of 1936-37, the Congress found itself in absolute majority in the Legislative Assemblies of five provinces (Madras, C.P., U.P., Bihar, Orissa). In Bombay, the Congress, along with two or three pro-Congress groups, could command a majority while in the N.W.F.P. and in Assam it emerged as the largest single party. But the Congress High Command wanted to have prior assurances of non-interference by the Governors in the day-to-day administration of the provinces before they would permit Congress Ministries to be formed. Things hung fire till Lord Linlithgow gave the required assurance on June 22, 1937, which resulted in the formation, next month, in the provinces of the N.W.F.P., the U.P., the C.P., Bihar, Bombay, Madras and Orissa, of Congress Ministries which during their two years tenure did a fair amount of creditable work notwithstanding the many handicaps they were working under. They concentrated on nation-building activities and perhaps their great achievement was their new and sympathetic approach to the people, their regarding themselves as servants of the people and the confidence they inspired in the masses that the interests of the latter were safe in the hands of the former. But the Muslim League during this period carried on an intensive propaganda against the Congress, that the rights and interests of the Muslims were jeopardised under the Congress regime.

The Congress Ministries, however, gave up office in October 1939, over the issue of India's having been dragged, or dragooned, into the Second World War, and of the failure of the British to clearly and categorically stating their war aims, especially including therein the treatment of India as a free nation. On the resignation of the Congress Ministries, the administration of the provinces concerned, except Assam, was taken over by the Governors under section 93 of the 1935 Act. The Governors appointed advisers, generally two or three, from among senior officials in their provinces. Thus there was no responsible government nor any vestige of provincial autonomy in a large part of British India (in the Provinces of Bombay, Madras, U.P., Bihar, C.P.) till the restoration of the Congress Ministries there in 1946.

In the N.W.F.P., a Muslim League Ministry was formed but it was replaced by a Congress Ministry in 1945. In Orissa Coalition Ministries were formed, but the Congress came back to power in 1946. In Assam a League Ministry was formed; it was replaced by a Congress Ministry in 1946. In Sind and Bengal the rule of the League was consolidated. The Panjab remained under the rule of the Unionist Party till the formation of a Congress-Sikh-Unionist Coalition Ministry in 1945.

Observations on the Act of 1935. The scheme of Federation, as envisaged by the Act, left much to be desired in view of the fact that an attempt was made therein to bring together two disparate elements—Indian States mostly under the autocratic rule of the Princes and British Indian Provinces enjoying responsible government to some extent. The grouping of these two heterogeneous elements could not but result in squabbles hindering the smooth working of the system. Moreover, the process prescribed for the formation of the Federation was ill-conceived and illogical. The Federation could not be brought into being unless a number of States had acceded to it. Accession to the federation was entirely voluntary on their part whereas it was s compulsory on the part of the provinces of British India. In order to induce the Princes to join the Federation, they were given preferential treatment in several ways—unduly large representation under a system of nomination by rulers. The Princes were expected to be retrogressive and reactionary factors and checks upon the nationalists.

An important part of the Act provided elaborate safeguards—which amounted to vital subtraction from the principle of self-government. Besides, the restrictions on the law-making powers of the legislatures, the Governor-General and Governors were empowered to override ministers and legislatures in certain circumstances. In the event of what a General might consider a breakdown of the Constitutional machinery, he could even assume absolute dictatorial powers.

Dyarchy, though thoroughly condemned, was still proposed at the Centre. Certain important departments like Defence, which got the lion's share of the budget and External Affairs were kept as Reserved.

India's constitutional status as a dependency, did not improve as powers of constitutional amendment and responsibility for Indian administration still remained with the British Parliament. Moreover, the Secretary of State retained his control over various All-India Services.

Separate representation of communal and other groups was certainly iniquitous and scandalously unreasonable.

Importance of the Act. The basic conception of the Act of 1935 was that the Government of India was the Government of the Crown, conducted by authorities deriving functions directly from the Crown, in so far as the Crown did not itself retain executive functions. This conception familiar in Dominion constitutions was absent in earlier Acts passed for India. The Act of 1919 indeed began by providing that the Government of India was vested in the Crown. But it proceeded straightway to devolve upon the Secretary of State's competence alike to control administration in India and to commit there or elsewhere acts of administration on his own motion. In latter sections it clothed the Governor-General-in-Council with powers of superintendence, direction and control over the civil and military administration, and it enabled a Provincial Government to be invested with functions by devolution rules made by the Governor-General-in-Council.

The whole of the 1935 Act rested upon a negation of this system of devolution and re-devolution. It resolutely turned its back upon the constitutional devices of the past. Accordingly, it set out by explicitly resuming to the Crown all rights, authority, and jurisdiction appertaining or incidental to the Government of His Majesty's territories in India.

Lord Linlithgow, Governor-General, speaking of the scope of the new Reforms said : " By the joint statesmanship of Britain and India there is about to be initiated an experiment in representative self-government which, for breadth of conception and boldness, is without parallel in history. These changes connote a profound modification of British policy towards India as a member of the Commonwealth. They involve nothing less than discarding old ideas of imperialism for new ideas of partnership and co-operation."

Indian Reaction to the Act of 1935. The Congress rejected the new constitution out of hand. In the course of a press statement, Jawaharlal Nehru, the then Congress President, reminded the country of April 1, 1937—the day when the "unwanted, undemocratic and anti-national" constitution as adumbrated in the Government of India Act, 1935, would be forced upon the country against the wholehearted and unanimous will of the country." On another occasion Pandit Nehru declared that the new constitution was "a machine with strong brakes but no engine."

Another critic affirmed that the Act "tests to the full Indian capacity for administration and government exactly as a man's capacity for swimming is tested...by throwing him into a river with his hands and feet tied." To call the new constitution "an edifice of self-government is a grim joke which the joker may enjoy but on those at whose expense it is crecked." "Remember, the new Federal structure has got to be fought tooth and nail. It is difficult to find suitable language to characterise it. It is disgusting, poisoning and offensive."

Pandit Malaviya's reaction was : "The new Act has been thrust upon us. It has a somewhat democratic appearance outwardly, but it is absolutely hollow from inside." C. Rajagopalachari called the new constitution "worse than dyarchy", and Mr. Jinnah characterised it as "thoroughly rotten, fundamentally bad, and totally unacceptable."

Sir Shanmukham Chetty opined : "It is indeed a far cry between the Government Act (of 1935) and Dominion Status...India has control neither in the internal nor in the external affairs......The safeguards, reservations, special powers of the Governor-General and the Governors, the weakness of the Indian Legislatures, and the Ministers in the Federal and Provincial Governments with no Central responsibility and weak provincial autonomy, the Communal Award, the States' representation bought at the expense of British Indians, the financial and other economic drawbacks, half measures of the Indianisation of the army with no control over the Defence—all these things show...not...Dominion Status."

Mr. Fazal-ul-Huq, Premier of Bengal, declared that under the Act, there was to be neither Hindu *raj* nor Muslim *raj.*

Sir Shafaat Ahmad Khan wrote : "The Legislature (Federal) is so curiously composed and its procedure is so ingeniously contrived that it will find it difficult to function freely and independently. It will be destitute of organic unity, will lack the momentum of a common allegiance and national solidarity and may resolve itself into congeries of inconsistent and even destructive sections lacking the rudiments of leadership and team work."

RESUME
Salient Features of the Government of India Act, 1935

The Government of India Act of 1919 provided for a review of the political sitution in India every ten years. In 1927 the process of review was set in motion by the appointment of the all-White Simon Commission. The All Parties' Conference submitted the Indian viewpoint in the famous Nehru Report (1928). The Simon Commission Report was discussed in the Round Table Conferences held in London during 1930-32. The British Government proposals were published in a White Paper which provided the basis for the Act of 1935.

Provincial Autonomy : Under the Act, the Governor's Provinces were given a new legal status and broadly freed from 'the superintendence direction and control' of the Government of India and the Secretary of State except for specific purposes. The provinces derived their power and authority directly from the British Crown.

Dyarchy in the provinces was replaced by Provincial Autonomy. The distinction between Reserved and Transfered subject was abolished and full responsible government was established subject to certain safeguards.

Provincial Legislatures were further expanded. Bicameral legislatures were provided in the six provinces of Madras, Bombay, Bengal, U.P., Bihar and Assam, the other five provinces retaining unicameral legislatures. The franchise was lowered though it still remained tied to property qualifications. Unfortunately, the principles of 'communal electorates' and 'weightage' were further extended.

The Governor was the head of the Provincial Executive and was expected to be guided by the advice of the popular ministers. However, the Act gave arbitrary powers (under the phraseology of 'safeguards' and 'special responsibilities') to the Governor to act 'in his discretion' in matters like summoning of the Legislature, appointment of Ministers, giving or withholding his assent to bills passed by the Legislature, etc., or 'exercise his individual judgment' in wideranging matters like prevention of grave menace to peace and tranquillity of the province, safeguarding legitimate interests of minorities, prevention of administrative discrimination against British commercial interests. Further, the Governor was invested with legislative authority to issue ordinances valid for six months or enact 'Governors' Acts.

Proposal for a Federation of India. The Act also provided for setting up of the Federation of India comprising British Indian Provinces and Indian States. However, entry into the Federation was compulsory for Indian Provinces but optional for Indian States. The Federation was to come into existence if certain conditions were fulfilled.

Dyarchy abolished in the provinces was proposed for the Federal Centre. The *Reserved* subjects includered Foreign Affairs, Defence and Ecclesiastical Affairs to be administered by the Governor-General through Counsellors appointed by him and responsible only to him. The *Transferred* subject were to be administered by the Governor-General on the advice of popular minister answerable to the federal Legislature.

The Federal legislature was to be bicameral comprising the Council of State having 156 representatives of British India and not more than 104 of Indian States. It was to be a permanent body subject to renewal of 1/3 of its members every third year. The Federal Assembly was to have 250 representatives of British India and not more than 125 of the Indian States. The normal tenure of the Assembly was to be five years.

The proposed federation had many odd features. While the representatives of Indian Provinces were to be elected, those of Indian States were to be nominated by the ruling princes. Further, the Indian States constituting merely 24% of the total population of India were given 40% of the seats in the Council of State and $33\frac{1}{3}$% of the seats in the Assembly. Even in Indian Provinces, the distribution of seats was not made on the basis of population but on the basis of their political importance. Another odd feature was the provision of indirect election for the Lower House (Federal Assembly) and direct election for the Upper House (Council of State). Worst of all, the vicious system of communal and class electorates was further extended to include not only General (*i.e.*, Hindus and Scheduled Castes), Muslims, Sikhs, Europeans, Indian Christians and Anglo-Indian electorates but also women (General), Sikh women in Punjab, Mohammedan women, Indian-Christian women in Madras, Anglo-Indian women in Bengal, besides electorates for Commerce and Industry, Londlords, Labour, University, backward areas and tribes, etc.

The Federation of India was not intended to be a sovereign legislature. It could not amend the India Constitution, which right remained with the British Parliament. Besides, the range of its legislative activities was limited in that it could not enact legislation affecting anyway British suzerainty over India or even the armed forces maintained in India. 80% of the budget was non-votable by the Federal Legislature. The Governor-General's powers to issue ordinances or enact Governor-General's Acts further circumscribed the legislative authority of the proposed Federal Legislature.

Appraisal of the Act of 1935. The proposal for setting up the Federation of India did not materialize and the Central Government in India continued to be governed by the provisions of the Act of 1919. However, the Federal Bank (The Reserve Bank of India) and the Federal Court were established in 1935 and 1937 respectively. The other parts of Act, particulary Provincial Autonomy, came into force on 1 April, 1937.

The hotch-potch of Authoritarian and Responsible government, called the Act of 1935, fell far short of Indian national aspirations. British imperialism still determined to maintain its stranglehold over India looked for new safeguards in communal and reactionary elements. The 'ifs' and 'buts' provided in the Act were so numerous as to elicit from Jawaharlal Nehru the cryptic remark that it provided 'a machine with strong brakes but no engine'. Even M.A. Jinnah described the scheme as 'thoroughly rotten' fundamentally bad and totally unacceptable". The shock of another world war and another round of non-cooperation movements were necessary to bring about a real change of heart in the imperial rulers of Britain.

SELECT REFERENCES

1. Banerjee, A.C. : *Indian Constitutional Documents* (1961 edition), vol. iv.
2. Chintamani and Masani : *Indian's Constitution at Work* (1940).
3. Coupland, R. : *Indian Politics* (1936-42).
4. Gwyer and Appadorai : *Speeches and Documents on the Indian Constitution*, 2 vols.
5. Joshi, G.N. : *The New Constitution of India* (1946).

44

THE TRANSFER OF POWER

> Our time in India is limited and our power to control events almost gone. We have only prestige and previous momentum to trade on and they will not last long.
>
> —*Lord Wavell, Oct. 1946*

Immediately after the Titanic Monster of the Second World War jumped upon the world stage early in September 1939, the British Government without any reference to Indian public opinion and even without formal reference to the Central Legislature, declared India a belligerent state. This was strongly protested against by the Congress Working Committee, which issued a statement on September 14, 1939, expressing its views on the situation created by the war. It said that "the issue of war and peace for India must be decided by the Indian people...The Committee cannot associate themselves or offer any co-operation in a war which was conducted on imperialistic lines and which was meant to consolidate imperialism in India and elsewhere...The Committee invited the British Government to declare in unequivocal terms what their war aims are in regard to democracy and Imperialism and the new order that is envisaged, in particular, how these are going to apply to India and to be given effect to in the present. Do they include treatment of India as a free nation whose policy will be guided in accordance with the wishes of her people ?"

Dominion Status after the War. The assurances the Congress sought from the Government were not forthcoming—only vague half-hearted phrases and pious platitudes were offered instead. Hence seven Congress Ministries tendered their resignations, and the administration of those provinces except Assam was taken over by the Governors under Secion 93 of the Act of 1935. Mr. Jinnah made the occasion a 'day of deliverance' and thanks-giving, as a mark of relief that the Congress regime had at least ceased to function. Only in Sind, Punjab and Bengal did popular ministries continue to function. To allay the resulting discontent, the Viceroy (Lord Linlithgow), in January 1940, declared that "Dominion Status of the Westminster variety as soon as possible after the War" was the goal of British policy in India. So what had been denied by the Act of 1935 was to be conceded after the war. But the Congress like old Omar Khayyam wanted "the cash in hand', and so 'let the credit go' by unlamented.

The 'August Offer' 1940. On August 8, 1940 (on the eve of "the Battle of Britain") came out a new declaration of policy, called "the August Offer"—*viz.*, a statement by the Viceroy on behalf of the British Government to the effect that (*a*) notwithstanding differences amongst political parties, the expansion of the Governor-General's Executive Council and the establishment of an Advisory War Council should no longer be postponed ; (*b*) the Government reaffirmed their desire to give full weight to minority opinion : (*c*) subject to the fulfilment of their obligations (*e.g.*, questions like Defence, Minority Rights, the Treaties with the States, and the position of the All-India Services), the British Government concurred that the framing of the new constitution should be "primarily the responsibility of Indians themselves, and should originate from Indian conception of the social, economic and political structure of Indian life" ; (*d*) as it was not possible to settle constitutional issues at a moment, "when the Commonwealth is engaged in a struggle for existence", the British Government "will most readily assent to the setting up after the conclusion of the war with the least possible delay of a body representatives of the principal elements in India's national life in order to devise the framework of the new constitution and they will lend every aid in their power to hasten decisions on all relevant matters to the utmost degree" ; (*e*) in the interval, it was hoped that all parties and communities in India would co-operate in India's attainment of free and equal partnership in the British Commonwealth of Nations.

This declaration marked an important advance over the existing state of things, in as much as it recognised at least the natural and inherent right of the people of the country to determine the form of their future constitution, and explicitly promised Dominion Status. However, the Congress rejected this offer, and Gandhiji even went so far as to declare that the declaration widended the gulf between nationalist India and the British rulers while Jawaharlal Nehru said in no uncertain terms that the whole conception of Dominion Status for India was "dead as a door-nail". The Muslim League, however, welcomed that part of the offer which the Congress had condemned, and the "clear assurance...that no future constitution, interim or final, should be adopted by the British Government without their approval and consent." The League went on to say that "the Partition of India was the only solution of the most difficult problem of India's future constitution." As can be imagined, the offer remained infructuous. Mr. L.S. Amery, the Secretary of State believed that "the constitutional deadlock today is not between a consentient Indian National movement asking for freedom and a British Government reluctant to surrender its authority, but between the main elements of India's national life."

The Cripps Mission, 1942. The stalemate continued, while the war went on in all its fury. In December 1941, Japan entered the war on the side of the Axis Powers and its spectacular successes during the early months of 1942 forced the British Government to make an earnest effort to resolve the deadlock in India. On March 11, 1942, Mr. Winston Churchill (the Prime Minister) announced that the War Cabinet had reached a unanimous decision on Indian policy, and that the leader of the House of Commons, Sir Stafford Cripps, would proceed to India as soon as possible to explain the decision and "to satisfy himself on the spot, by personal consultations, that the conclusions upon which we all are agreed and which we believe represent a just and final solution, will achieve their purpose." The Lord Privy Seal who had volunteered for the task was also, said Mr. Churchill, "to strive to procure the necessary measure of assent, not from the Hindu majority, but also from those great minorities amongst which the Muslims are the most numerous and on many grounds, prominent." Soon after reaching India, Sir Stafford communicated the Draft Declaration to the members of the Executive Council (on March 23, 1942) and two days later to the Indian leaders. On March 29, these proposals were made public at a Press Conference. The subsequent negotiations took a fortnight to conclude unfruitfully, working as Cripps did against heavy odds. Gandhiji called the Declaration "a post-dated cheque" to which some one added the words, 'on a failing banks.'

The Draft Declaration of the British Government contained the following proposals :

(*a*) "Immediately upon the cessation of hostilities steps shall be taken to set up in India in the manner pescribed hereafter an elected body, charged with the task of framing a new Constitution for India.

(*b*) "Provision shall be made for participation of Indian States in the constitution-making body."

(*c*) "The British Government undertook "to accept and implement forthwith the constitution so framed, subject only to : (*i*) the right of any Province of British India that is not prepared to accept the new Constitution to retain its present constitutional position, provision being made for its subsequent accession if it so decides. With such non-acceding Provinces, should they so desire, the British Government will be prepared to agree upon a new Constitution giving them the same full status as the Indian Union, and arrived at by a procedure analogous to that here laid down, (*ii*) the signing of a Treaty which shall be negotiated between the British Government and the Constitution-making body covering all necessary matters arising out of the complete transfer of responsibility from British to Indian hands ; it will make provision...for the protection of racial and religious minorities; but it will not impose any restriction on the power of the Indian Union to decide in the future its relation to the other member-states of the British Commonwealth.

Whether or not an Indian State elects to adhere to the Constitution, it will be necessary to negotiate a revision of its treaty-arrangements so far as this may be required in the new situation."

(d) The Constitution-making body would be elected by the members of the Lower House of the Provincial Legislatures by the system of proportional representation.

(e) Until the new Constitution could be framed, the British Government would remain responsible for the defence of India, but they "desire and invite the immediate and effective participation of the leaders of the principal sections of the Indian people in the counsels of their country, of the Commonwealth and of the United Nations. Thus they will be enabled to give their active and constructive help in the discharge of a task which is vital and essential for the future freedom of India."

The main features of the Draft Declaration so far as the future was concerned were : provision for Dominion Status with the right of secession for the provinces for a possible partition of the country and for a treaty providing for the transfer of power and safeguards for minorities. Until the new constitution could be framed, Defence was to be the sole concern of the British Government and the Governor-General was to continue with all his powers as before. As Jawaharlal Nehru put it : "The existing structure of Government would continue exactly as before, the autocratic powers of the Viceroy would remain and a few of us will become his liveried camp-followers and look after canteens and the like."

Observations on the Draft Declaration. The Declaration marked a further notable advance, even over the August Offer, in so far as it (a) granted the right of secession from the British Commonwealth ; (b) said that the making of the new constitution would be, now *solely* (and not only *mainly* as before) in Indian hands ; (c) proposed a plan for a Constituent Assembly ; (d) was an improvement in respect of the interim system of Central Government. Further, the people of India were asked to take part in the highest counsels not only of India, but of the Commonwealth and United Nations also.

However, these merits could not secure for the Declaration immunity from criticism. Each political party picked holes in it for reasons of its own and rejected the proposals. The Congress objected not so much to the long-term proposals as to the interim arrangements. The proposed arrangement about Defence was unacceptable to the Congress. Besides, the Congress had demanded, but did not receive an informal assurance that Governor-General would act as a constitutional head on the advice of the National Government consisting of Indian leaders. The rock on which the negotiations between Cripps and the Congress founded was the veto power of the Viceroy. In regard to the long term proposals, the Congress was opposed to the novel principle of non-accession of the provinces to the Union which seemed to be an axe applied to the very roots of the conception of Indian unity. This was the view of the Hindu Mahasabha too (which regarded the communal basis of the elections as obnoxious) as of the liberals like Sir Tej Bahadur Sapru and Mr. Jayakar, who said : "The creation of more than one Union, however consistent in theory with the principle of self-deter-mination, will be disastrous to the lasting interests of the country and its integrity and security". The Sikhs also opposed the proposals because there was provision for separation of provinces and declared their determination to fight tooth and nail any possible separation of the Panjab from the All-India Union. The "Depressed" classes felt strongly the non-inclusion of safeguards necessary for their interests.

The Muslim League opposed the creation of a single Union, the machinery for the creation of the constitution-making body and the method and procedure for ascertaining the wishes of a province as to accession. They, in brief, found the scheme unacceptable as it did not unequivocally concede Pakistan and seemed to deny the right of self-determination to the Muslims.

Apart from the criticism of the proposals by the political parties there were undoubtedly certain shortcomings in the Plan. The reiteration of the offer of August 1940 and the explanation added thereunto that "the present declaration is intended—not to supersede, but to clothe these general declarations with precisions..."also evoked suspicion as whether the British were really prepared to part with power on a substantial scale.

Further, the procedure of determining the wishes of a province in the matter of accession to the Union was not at all defined. According to Cripps, a province should reach its decision by a vote in the Legislative Assembly on a resolution that the province should join the Indian Union and that if the Majority for accession was less than 60%, the minority would have the right to ask for a plebiscite of the adult male population which would then determine the matter by a simple majority. This weighed the scales decisively against the Hindus succeeding in possible combination with other political fellow travellers in securing an accession to the Union in the case of either Bengal or the Panjab.

Besides, as to the treaty "covering all necessary matters arising out of a complete transfer of responsibility from British to Indian hands" it was not clear as to who was to be responsible for the enforcement of its terms, or as to who had the right of interpreting them.

The whole plan with which the name of Cripps came to be inextricably associated smelt more of a sop offered to Indian political leaders, in order to bring about active participation in the war effort on the part of all sections of the population, than a genuine attempt to solve the Indian impasse. Prof. Laski expressed his opinion on the proposals thus : "The one bright spot in the whole record was the mission of Sir Staffod Cripps for the preparation of which, let it be said with emphasis, Mr. Attlee deserves great credit. But the Mission came too late, it looked more like a counter-move against Japan than a recognition of Indian claims...it was carried out far too hurriedly...And it had about it...something of the British habit which Mr. Kingsley Martin has well described as the art of forgiving generously those we have grievously wronged. It was psychologically disastrous for Sir Stafford to go to India in a "take it or leave it" mood and his return practically announce that we washed our hands of the offer. This was bound to make it look as though our real thought was less the achievement of Indian freedom than of a *coup de main* in the propagandist's art among our allies who contrasted American relations with the Philippines against British relations with India."

The Cripps Mission is usually written off as a complete failure but on the war being won, "the failing bank" of the famous phrase weathered the storm and so "the post-dated cheque" was ultimately honoured.

"Quit India Resolution" and the August Revolt, 1942. After the failure of the Cripps Mission, there was a feeling of frustration among all sections of the people. The Congress which had done nothing so far to embarrass the British Government apart from demanding a Constituent Assembly to frame a new constitution for the country could no longer sit on the fence when the Japanese were virtually knocking at the doors of the country. Gandhiji now started his campaign for 'orderly British withdrawal' from India. He began his campaign late in April 1942. In his views, "whatever the consequences...to India her real safety and Britain's too lie in an orderly and timely British withdrawal from India." The phrase 'Quit India' to denote this move somehow came into vogue and it caught on.. On May 10,1942, he wrote in the *Harijan* : "The presence of the British in India is an invitation to Japan to invade India. Their withdrawal removes that bait." A fortnight later he wrote in the *Harijan* : "Leave India in God's hands, or in modern parlance, to anarchy. Then all parties will fight one another like dogs, or will, when real responsibility faces them come, to a reasonable agreement."

The Congress Working Committee on July 14, 1942, in a resolution demanding withdrawal of the British power from India, said : "Should this appeal fail, the Congress cannot view without the gravest apprehension the continuation of the present state of affairs involving a progressive deterioration of the situation and the weakening of India's will and power to resist aggression. The Congress will then be reluctantly compelled to utilise all the non-violent strength it might have gathered since 1920...for the vindication of political rights and liberty. Such a widespread struggle would inevitably be under the leadership of Mahatma Gandhi." The All India Congress Committee meeting at Bombay on Aughst 8, 1942, while approving of and endorsing the resolution of the Working Committee, expressed the opinion that "events subsequent to it have given it further justification and have made it clear that immediate ending of British rule in India is an urgent necessity both for the sake of India and for the success of the cause of the United Nations. The continuation of that rule is degrading and enfeebling India and making her progressively less capable of defending herself and of contributing to the cause of world freedom."

As a consequence, early next morning (August 9, 1942) Gandhiji and all members of the Working Committee were arrested and the All India Congress Committee and the Provincial Congress Committees were banned. But the people did not take this action of the Government lying down. There were numerous acts of violence and destruction of or damage to public property and in quite a number of places, there was a breakdown of Government machinery and dislocation of normal life and communications. Though the Congress leaders disclaimed any responsibility for this outbreak of violence, it is hard to believe that all of them were ignorant of such large-sacle planning by the extremists. On the Government side, severe repression went on and hundreds were put to death or thrown in prison.

The general policy of the Government was to suppress the disturbances in the country and also to detain the Congress leaders until they gave a definite assurance and guarantee of a different line of conduct. While the deadlock between the Congress and the Government was allowed to continue, the Muslim League observed on March 23, 1943, the "Pakistan Day". Mr. Jinnah sent a message to the Muslim population of India stating that the scheme of Pakistan was the final "national" goal of Muslim India. The League in a resolution on April 26, endorsed this view.

The Rajagopalachari Formula and the Desai-Liaquat Formula. In March 1944, Mr. C. Rajagoplachari evolved a formula with the "full" approval of Gandhiji for Congress. League co-operation on the basis of Pakistan. The scheme emboyding the formula was : (1) The League would endorse the demand for independence and co-operate with the Congress in forming a provisional government for the transitional period ; (2) At the end of the war a plebiscite of all the inhabitants in the Muslim-majority areas in the north-west and the north-east would decide whether or not they should form a separate state ; (3) In the event of separation, agreements would be made for Defence, Communications and other essential matters ; (4) These terms were to be binding only in case of transfer by England of full power and responsibility for the Government of India. Mr. Jinnah wrote to Gandhiji for elucidation of various points of detail in "the Rajapalachari formula". Gandhiji in offering the clarifications sought, added that the Lahore Resolution of the League being indefinite, "Rajaji had taken from it the substance and given it a shape", but Mr. Jinnah in reply claimed that Rajaji had mutilated that substance. And so the wordy exchange continued and ended in smoke as it was bound to, because of the radical differences of approach and objective between the Congress and the League. Mr. Jinnah was contending that the Muslims of India, as a separate nation, had the right of self-determination, and the Muslims alone were to be entitled to vote for partition and not the whole population of the disputed areas. In other words, the right of self-determination which he claimed for the Muslims was to be denied to the non-Muslims in those areas. Gandhiji refused to accept this position or the postulate of a separate nationhood. The Congress was concerned with the achievement of independence, and to that end, was prepared to pay the necessary price for Muslim co-operation and support, but the League cared nothing for the independence of the whole county, and wanted the Congress to agree to the two-nation theory and partition without any plebscite of the whole population. Mr. Jinnah was also opposed to a common Centre concerned with Defence, Commerce, Communications, etc.

Effort nevertheless continued to end the deadlock and Mr. Bhulabhai Desai, leader of the Congress Party in the Central Legislative Assembly, met Mr. Liaquat Ali Khan, Deputy Leader of the Muslim League Party in that Assembly, and gave him the draft of a proposal for the formation of an Interim Government at the Centre, consisting of (a) equal number of persons nominated by the Congress and the League in the Central Legislature, (b) representatives of minorities, and (c) the Commander-in-Chief. But no settlement could be reached between the Congress and the League even on these lines. But the fact that a sort of parity between the Congress and the League was decided upon had, as we shall see, far-reaching consequences.

While, in India, the constitutional deadlock continued, the war in Europe came to an end on May 1,1945 and General Election in England was in the offing.

"The Wavell Plan", 1945. Lord Wavell who had succeeded Lord Linlithgow as Governor-General in October, 1943 now made an attempt to resolve the deadlock in India. In March 1945, he went to England for consultations. The result of his consultations was soon revealed. On June 14, he broadcast to the people of India the proposals of the British Government to resolve the deadlock in India. On the same day, Mr. Amery, Secretary of State for India, made a similar statement in the House of Commons : "The offer of March 1942 stands in its entirety without change or qualification." He proposed the reconstruction of the Governor-General's Executive Council pending the preparation of a new constitution. With the exception of the Governor-General and the Commander-in-Chief (who would retain his position as War Member) all other members of the Executive Council would be nominated from amongst leaders of Indian Political life.This Council would have "a balanced representation of the main communities, including equal proportions of Muslims and caste Hindus. It would work, if formed, under the existing constitution. Though the Governor-General's veto would not be abolished, it would not be used unnecessarily. The portfolio of External Affairs (other than those of Tribal, and Frontier matters which had to be dealt with as part of the defence of India) was to be transferred from the Governor-General to an Indian member of the Council. A conference of representatives chosen by the Viceroy was to be convened with a view to obtaining from the leaders of the various parties a joint list, or failing it, separate lists of worthy people to constitute the new Executive Council. It was expected also "that provincial ministries in Section 93 Provinces would resume office and that there would be coalitions."

The members of the Congress Working Committee were let out of jail, and high hopes prevailed on all sides as invitations for the proposed Simla Conference went out to the leaders including Gandhiji. Meeting on June 25, 1945, the Conference was adjourned after three days of discussion. On July 11, Mr. Jinnah had a short interview with the Viceroy, during which he seems to have made it clear to the latter that the League, wishing to be regarded as the sole representative of Indian Muslims, was firmly opposed to the inclusion of any non-Leaguer Muslims in the Viceroy's list. But the Viceroy could not agree to this point of view. Three days later Lord Wavell wound up the Conference by declaring a failure of the talks.

The responsibitity for the failure lies partly on Lord Wavell himself and partly on Mr. Jinnah. At a Press Conference, Mr. Jinnah stated : "On a final examination and analysis of the Wavell Plan, we found that it was a snare...this arrangement by which...we would have signed our death warrant. Next, in the proposed Executive we would be reduced to a minority of one-third. All the other minorities such as the Scheduled Castes, Sikhs and Christians have the same goal as the Congress. On the top of this came the last straw.. that even about the five members of the Muslim bloc which were allotted to communal-wise...the Muslim League was not entitled to nominate all the Muslim representatives. But we finally broke as Lord Wavell insisted upon his having one non-Leaguer, a nominee of Malik Khizr Hyat Khan, representing the Panjab Muslims."

The Congress President (Maulana Azad) put the responsibility for the break down squarely on the shoulders of Mr. Jinnah. Lord Wavell, however, cannot escape the responsibility either. Lord Wavell's procedure could have been easily improved upon. He should have taken the leaders into confidence as regards the composition of his own list of members of the Executive Council. Possibly the Congress leaders might have been persuaded to accept that list either as a whole, or with minor modifications mutually agreed upon. Then, he should not have allowed the League practically to veto the whole plan and thus alone to block the path of progress. (Gandhiji, on whom the Cripps Proposals had fallen flat, felt that the Wavell Plan was sincere in spirit and contained the seeds of independence).

It must be noted in this connection that the Viceroy had assured the Congress President that "no party to the conference could be allowed to obstruct settlement out of wilfulness", but it seems that as in the parallel case of Cripps, Wavell's hands were stayed at the last moment. One tangible result of the failure of the Simla Conference was to strengthen the position of Mr. Jinnah and the Muslim League which was clearly manifested in the Elections of 1945-46.

Unkind critics suggest that the Simla Conference was due to the threat to the Conservative Party by the Labour Pary in the Elections in England in July 1945, or alternately "to Russian pressure, as the Cripps Mission was due to American pressure."

The Elections of 1945-46. The failure of the Simla Conference naturally added to the sense of frustration in the country but soon a silver lining was discernible in the clouds, for the new Labour Government of Britain (formed on July 10, 1945) installed an old friend of India, Lord Pethick-Lawrence, as the Secretary of State for India. The course of British policy towards India also changed due to other causes. The increasing international complications which followed the cessation of hostilities in Europe were one of them. Then the trial of some of the officers of the I.N.A. by British Court Martial in the historic Red Fort in Delhi in 1945-46 fired the popular imagination, the Congress "fully identifying itself with the ideals and interests of those valiant soldiers", resulting in increased Congress popularity among the people of India.

Shortly after Lord Pethick-Lawrence assumed office, Lord Wavell was summoned to England for consultations. On August 21 after a special emergency meeting of the Executive Council, the Viceroy's decision to hold elections to Central and Provincial Legislatures in India and to go to London was announced. On September 19, 1945, the Viceroy immediately on his return announced that after the elections in India, a Constitution-making body would be convened and that his Executive Council would be reconstituted with the support of the main Indian political parties. He also expressed the hope that ministerial responsibility would be accepted by political leaders in the provinces.

On the same day (September 19,1945), Prime Minster Attlee reiterated the announcement of the Viceroy, adding that the 1942 (Cripps) offer still stood "in all its fullness and purpose" and that the Government was "acting in accordance with its spirit and intention". This was followed on December 4 by a statement in the House of Lords by the Secretary of State for India regretting that the full significance of the proposals had not been properly appreciated in India and unjustified suggestions had gained wide currency, to the effect that the preparatory discussions would be a fruitful source of delay. He made it clear that the British Government regarded the setting up of the Constitution-making body as a matter of urgency. He thought that the misunderstanding would be removed by personal contact between members of Parliament and leading Indian "political personalities", and announced the sending to India of a Parliamentary delegation under the auspices of the Empire Parliamentary Association. He made it clear, however, that the delegation would have no authority to commit Britain to any policy.

Lord Wavell on December 10, 1945, addressing the annual meeting of the Associated Chambers of Commerce, said : "Quit India' will not act as the magic 'sesame'" and appealed for good-will, co-operation and patience.

Central and provincial elections were held in India about this time (winter of 1945-46). The Congress captured almost all non-Muslim seats in all the Provinces, the majority of the Muslim seats in the N.W.F.P., and some Muslim seats in U.P., C.P., Bihar and Assam. Though the Muslim League had captured an overwhelming majority of Muslim seats taken together, yet it could form ministries only in Sind and Bengal. The Congress assumed office in Assam, Bihar, U.P. N.W.F.P., Bombay, Madras, C.P. and Orissa. In the Panjab, though the Muslim League was the largest single party, it could not form a Government. A Coalition Ministry, composed of Akali Sikhs and Unionist Hindus and Muslims—all parties except the Muslim League—was formed there under Malik Khizr Hyat, leader of the Unionist Party.

The Parliamentary Delegation visited India in January 1946, during the course of the Elections and collected first-hand information about the political situation in the country.

The Cabinet Mission Plan, 1946. On February 19, 1946, Lord Pethick-Lawrence made an important announcement in the House of Lords that a special mission of Cabinet Ministers consisting of the noble Lord himself, the President of the Board of Trade (Sir Stafford Cripps), and the First Lord of the Admiralty (Mr. A.V. Alexander) would go to India to seek in association with the Viceroy an agreement with Indian leaders of the principles and procedure relating to the constitutional issue. In a debate on the above statement, held on March 15, Prime Minister Attlee declared in the House of Commons, "We are very mindful of the rights of minorities and minorities should be able to live free from fear. On the other hand, *we cannot allow a minority to place a veto on the advance of the majority.*" The words in italics were taken in India to indicate a change in the traditional policy of the British Government towards the Muslim League.

The Cabinet Mission reached Delhi on March 24, 1946, and had prolonged discussions with Indian leaders of all parties and goups. As the Congress and the League could not come to any agreement on the fundamental issue of the unity or partition of India, the Mission put forward their own plan for the solution of the constitutional problem. This plan was given in a joint statement, issued by the Mission and Lord Wavell on May 16, 1946.

As regards the long-term scheme, they rejected the Muslim League's demand for Pakistan on several grounds : First, the establishment of Pakistan would not solve the problem of communal minorities because the percentage of non-Muslims living in the north-west zone of Pakistan would be 37.93% and those living in the north-eastern zone 48.31% of the total population. Moreover, there was no justification for including within Paskistan, The predominantly non-Muslim districts of Bengal, Assam and the Panjab. According to them every argument that could be used in favour of Pakistan could equally be used in favour of the exclusion of the non-Muslim areas from Pakistan. There was no virtue in creating a smaller Pakistan involving a division of the Panjab and Bengal because, according to them, it would be against the wishes and interests of a very large proportion of the inhabitants of these provinces. Secondly, it would be injurious to disintegrate the transportation as also the postal and telegraph system of India. Thirdly, to divide the armed forces of India would 'entail the gravest dangers'. Fourthly, the Princely States would find it difficult to join one or the other Union. Lastly, "there is the geographical fact that the two halves of the proposed Pakistan State are separated by some 700 miles and communications between them both in war and peace would be dependent on the goodwill of Hindustan." These were very cogent arguments indeed against the partition of the country. So the Mission suggested that there should be one Central Government controlling at least some specified subjects. The Mission might have at the back of their minds when they made this suggestion the *anschluss* of 1876 resulting in the formation of the Dual Monarchy of Austria-Hungary. It is Just a speculation of the present writer but there is such a closensess between the terms of the *anschluss* and what the Cabinet Mission suggested.

The Mission recommended that the Constitution of India should take the following basic forms :

"(1) There should be Union of India, embracing both British India and the States, which should deal with the following subjects : Foreign Affairs, Defence and Communications ; and should have the powers to raise the finances required for the above subjects.

"(2) The Union should have an Executive and a Legislature constituted from British India and States' representatives. Any question raising a major communal issue in the legislature should require for its decision a majority of the representatives present and voting of each of the two major communities as well as a majoriy of all the members present and voting."

"(3) The provinces would enjoy full autonomy, for all subjects other than the Union subjects and all residuary powers should vest in the provinces.

"(4) Moreover, "provinces should be free to form Groups with Executive and Legislatures, and each Group could determine the provincial subjects to be taken in common.

"(5) The six Hindu majority provinces *viz.*, Madras, Bombay, C.P., U.P., Bihar, and Orissa would form Group A. The Muslim Majority provinces in the north-west (the Panjab, the N.W.F.P., Sind) would form Group B. Bengal and Assam would form Group C. Of the Chief Commissioners' Provinces three (Delhi, Ajmer-Marwara, Coorg) would join Group A and one (Baluchistan) would join Group B. The 'full autonomy' of the provinces and the provision for grouping were meant to give the Muslim League if not the form, the 'substance of Pakistan. It was obvious that Group B and C would be under absolute control of the Muslims."

The intention of the Cabinet Mission was to set in motion a Constituent Assembly—the machinery whereby a constitution could be settled by Indians themselves. The Constituent Assembly would, according to the scheme, be elected by the Provincial Legislative Assemblies, adult suffrage having been ruled out as it would involve delay in the making of the Constitution. The members of each Provincial Legislative Assembly would be divided into there groups— 'General', Muslims and Sikhs—and each group would elect its own representatives to the Constituent Assembly by the method of proportional representation with the single transferable vote. The number of representatives allotted to each province and community was to be proportional to its population, roughly in the ratio of one to a million. This procedure applied to eleven Governors' Provinces. Different arrangements were made with regard to the four Chief Commissioner's Provinces. The Table of representation for British Indian provinces is given below.

Group A

Province	*General*	*Muslim*	*Total*
Madras	45	4	49
Bombay	19	2	21
United Provinces	47	8	55
Bihar	31	5	36
Central Provinces	16	1	17
Orissa	9	0	9
	167	20	187

Group B

Province	*General*	*Muslim*	*Sikh*	*Total*
Panjab	8	16	4	28
N.W.F.P.	0	3	0	3
Sind	1	3	0	4
	9	22	4	35

Group C

Province	*General*	*Muslim*	*Total*
Bengal	27	33	60
Assam	7	3	10
	34	36	70

Grand Total : 292

To these 292 members were to be added four members from the four Chief Commissioners' provinces and not more than 93 members from the Indian States whose selection would be 'determined by consultation'.

The Constituent Assembly, thus formed, would be divided into three Sections (Section A corresponding to Group A and so on). Each Section would settle the constitution for its own provinces and also decide whether a Group constitution should be set up. The three Sections and the representatives of the States (that is, the entire Constituent Assembly) would jointly settle the Union Constitution. There was to be an Advisory Committee on the rights of citizens, minorities and tribal and excluded areas.

The Constitution of the Union and of the Groups would "contain a provision whereby any province could, by a majority vote of its Legislative Assembly, call for a reconsideration of the terms of the Constitution after an initial period of ten years and at ten yearly intervals thereafter." Moreover, the provinces were given the power to opt out of their respective Groups by a decision of their Legislatures after the general elections under the new constitution.

The Constituent Assembly would conclude a treaty with Britain "to provide for certain matters arising out of the transfer of power."

As regards the Indian States, the Cabinet Mission declared that when the new Constitution comes into force the British Government would cease to exercise the powers of Paramountcy. In that case, all the rights surrendered by the States to the Paramount Power were to return to them. Political arrangements between the States on the one side and the British Crown and British India on the other will thus be brought to an end. The void will have to be filled either by the States entering into a federal relationship with the successor-Government. The Governments in British India, or failing this, entering into particular political arrangement with it or them.

The Cabinet Mission contemplated the setting up of an Interim Government in which all the portfolios, including that of the War Member, were to be held by Indian leaders having the support of the major political parties.

Merits and Demerits of the Cabinet Mission Plan. The chief merit was that the Constitution-making body was to be constituted on the democratic principle of strength of population, the principle of 'weightage' being totally given up. Also, the democratic methods of deciding communal issues by simple majority (subject to provision of safeguards for minorities), was followed. Furthermore, the idea of Pakistan was completely discountenanced and all-India Union envisaged. Also, neither the British Government nor even non-official Europeans in India were to have any member in the Constituent Assembly, and the European members of the Provincial Assemblies were to absent themselves at the time of voting. (On the insistence of Gandhiji that the Europeans should have no vote, the latter made a statement that they would refrain from voting for themselves but would vote for electing Indian representatives. Gandhiji was bitterly against that too. Later on, the Europeans of Assam and Bengal did not take part in the election of the members of the Constituent Assembly but those of U.P. did.) Within the framework of the scheme, the Constituent Assembly was to be a perfect mistress in her own house, without any let or hindrance from the British Government or any Indian official.

Now to take the defects of the scheme: (1) While the Muslim minority was amply provided for, no such protection was afforded to other minorities, like the Sikhs in the Panjab. (2) The part of the porposals concerned with province-wise grouping was capable of being, and was actually, interpreted differently. The Muslim League took the compulsory grouping of provinces to be the corner-stone of the whole edifice of these proposals, and would not even talk or think of a compromise on that issue. But the Congress thought that the making of groups was optional for the provinces, and that the latter was free to join or not to join any group. Finally, however, the British Government decided in favour of the League's view on this point. (3) The order in which the Union and Sectional assemblies were to meet and work and draft their constitutions was ridiculous—first, to form the constitutions of the Groups and the Provinces, and then to frame a constitution for the Centre or the Union was indeed to put the cart before the horse.

The Constituent Assembly Elections and Formation of the National Government.

The Cabinet Mission Plan was accepted by the Congress and the Muslim League though with mental reservations. (The objection of the Congress to the Plan was mainly its provisions of grouping, that of the League to the rejection of its demand for a sovereign state of Pakistan.) The Cabinet Mission, in a statement issued before leaving India, expressed satisfaction that Constitution-making would proceed with the participation of the major parties, but regretted that certain difficulties prevented a multi-party Interim Government being formed, hoping that such a Government might come into existence after the elections to the Constituent Assembly. This decision to postpone the formation of the Interim Government displeased Mr. Jinnah, who accused the Viceroy of having gone back on his promise. Another shock was in store for Mr. Jinnah. The elections to the Coustituent Assembly took place in July 1946. The Congress captured 205 seats including all the 'General' seats but 9 and the League 73 out of 78 'Muslim' seats. As four other seats were captured by the Sikhs a little later, the Congress could count upon the allegiance of 209 members in an Assembly of 296. Mr. Jinnah was greatly disturbed and alarmed at the overwhelming majority at the command of the Congress and at the possibility of his and his League being totally eclipsed in the Constituent Assembly. On July 29, 1946, the Muslim Legue in a huff resolved to withdraw its acceptance of the Cabinet Mission Plan—the League, in fact, went further to register its annoyance by passing the "Direct Action" resolution, which started with condemning both the British Government and the Congress for their bad faith, and declared that the time had come for resort to Direct Action for the achievement of Pakistan. The Working Committee of the League was authorised to prepare a programme for such action at once and August 16, 1946, was fixed the 'Direct Action Day'.

On the 'D' Day began the 'Great Killing' in Calcutta, and the city then under a Muslim League Government was reduced to 'bloody shambles'. In October 1946, the Muslims of Noakhali and Tipperah (in Bengal) perpetrated untold atrocities on the Hindu population of those districts. As a reaction communal riots broke out in some parts of Bihar and U.P. and in Bombay. A movement for the partition of Bengal into two halves—one consisting of the Hindu-majority areas—was set on foot as the Hindus of the Province feared that they would be ground under the heels of a Muslim majority.

In the meantime the Viceroy invited the President of the Congress (Jawaharlal Nehru) to form the Interim Government which assumed office on September 2, 1946. The Muslim League kept out despite an offer made to it to join the Government. So the Interim Government consisted in the first instance of Congress nominees only—Pandit Nehru, Sardar Patel, Dr. Rajendra Prasad, Mr. Rajagopalachari, Dr. John Mathai, Sardar Baldev Singh, Sir Shafaat Ahmad Khan, Mr. Jagjiwan Ram, Syed Ali Zaheer, Mr. C.H. Bhabha, Mr. Asaf Ali and Mr. Sarat Chandra Bose. Though Mr. Jinnah had refused to co-operate, the Viceroy resumed his negotiations with him, as a result of which on October 13, the Muslim League decided to join the Interim Government to safeguard the interests of the Muslims and other minority communities and "for other very weighty grounds and reasons which are obvious". On October 26, five nominees of the League—Mr. Liaquat Ali Khan, Mr. Ghazanfar Ali Khan, Mr. Abdul Rab Nishtar, Mr. I.I. Chundrigar and Mr. Jogendra Nath Mandal (Scheduled Caste) joined the Interim Government. Two seats were already lying vacant and three nominees of the Congress, namely, Mr. Sarat Chandra Bose, Syed Ali Zahir and Sir Shafaat Ahmad Khan resigned to make room for the League nominees. The new Interim Government was, as was only expected, a house divided against itself with the Congress and the League blocs pulling in different directions. Pandit Nehru openly declared that 'the League pursued their aim to enlist British support and tried to establish themselves the King's party."

Even though the League had joined the Interim Government it peristed in its refusal to join the Constituent Assembly.

The Constituent Assembly with the Muslim League remaining aloof met for the first time on December 9, 1946, at New Delhi. On December 11, this Assembly elected Dr. Rajendra Prasad as its permanent President and only two days later Jawaharlal Nehru moved his famous "Objectives Resolution" (passed on January 22, 1947) which declared the Assembly's firm and solemn resolve that India would be an "Independent Sovereign Republic."

Mr. Attlee's Announcement, February 20, 1947. The next step on the fateful road to India's destiny was the important announcement by the British prime Minister, Mr. Clement Attlee, on February 20, 1947, in which he referred in no uncertain terms to the pronounced differences amongst Indian political parties hampering the functioning of the Constituent Assembly according to Plan and rendering it not fully representative of India's variegated population pattern. He went on to make the momentous declaration: "The present state of uncertainty is fraught with danger and cannot be indefinitely prolonged. His Majesty's Government wish to make clear that it is their definite intention to take necessary steps to effect the transfer of power to responsible Indian hands by June, 1948." If the League continued to boycott the Constituent Assembly, the British Government would then have "to consider to whom the powers of the Central Government in British India should be handed over, on due date, whether as a whole to some form of Central Government for British India, or in some areas to the existing Provincial Government or in such other way as may seem most reasonable and in the best interests of the Indian people." Thus the statement fixed the deadline (June 1948) by which the British would quit India and envisaged a partition of the country which the Cabinet Mission had completely discountenanced. In other words, the British Government in this respect fell back on the Cripps Proposals.

The publication of this statement was followed by a tearing, raging campaign by the League to bring about at any cost the partition of the country. Things in India were at a bad pass. The League resorted to unabashed violence in Calcutta, Assam, Panjab and the N.W.F.P., with a view to replace the non-League Ministries in the Panjab, Assam and N.W.F.P. (The statement had clearly declared that power might conceivably be transferred, in some cases, to Provincial Governments. The League, therefore, made a vigorous attempt to install League Ministries in all the areas covered by Pakistan). The League by its tactics of attrition, bringing about chaos or near-chaotic conditions, succeeded in dislodging the anti-League Ministry in the Panjab where the Governor's rule under Section 93 was introduced. In Assam and the N.W.F.P., the League, however, failed in its strategy.

It was now becoming increasingly clear to the veriest tyro in politics that in the new circumstances—the psychosis of hatred and fear–Indian unity was impossible to keep unimpaired.

The Mountbatten Plan, June 3, 1947. The announcement that Lord Wavell was to be replaced by Lord Mountbatten as Viceroy was followed by the latter's speedy arrival in India. The new Viceroy, a man of tact, energy and determination, did not let the grass grow under his feet, and almost immediately declared his intention to complete the transfer of power into Indian hands within a few months. To this end he consulted Indian leaders. The Qaid-i-Azam, intransigent as ever, would not yield an inch in his demand priniciple of Pakistan but insisted on a partition of the provinces affected in order to avoid compulsion if Pakistan was unavoidable. Shortly after this Lord Mountbatten paid a visit to London for consultations in May 1947.

On June 3, 1947, Lord Mountbatten published a statement outlining his solution of India's political problem. Some important portions of that statement are here reproduced: "It is not the intention of His Majesty's Government to interrupt the work of the existing Constituent Assembly... it is clear that any constitution framed by this Assembly cannot apply to those parts of the country which are unwilling to accept it. His Majesty's Government are satisfied that the procedure outlined below embodies the best practical method of ascertaining the wishes of the people of such areas on the issue whether their constitution is to be framed—(*a*) in the existing Constituent Assembly ; or (*b*) in a new and separate Constituent Assembly consisting of the representatives of those areas which decide not to participate in the existing Constituent Assembly. When this is done it will be possible to determine the authority or authorities to whom power should be transferred." The Provincial

Assemblies of the Panjab and Bengal were to meet in two parts, one representing the Muslim majority districts and the other representing the rest of the Province, and "the members of the two parts of each Legislative Assembly sitting separately will be empowered to vote whether or not the Province should be partitioned. If a simple majority of either part decides in favour of partition, partition will take place and arrangements would be made accordingly." The Legislative Assembly of Sind was to take its own decision at a special meeting. A decision of referendum was provided for in the case of the N.W.F.P., the Muslim-majority district of Sylhet was also to decide by means of a referendum as to whether it would join East Bengal or remain in Assam.

The Plan also made provision for the setting up of a Boundary Commission to demarcate boundaries in case partition was to be effected. The statement concluded with these words: "His majesty's Government propose to introduce legislation during the current session for the transfer of power this year on a Dominion Status basis on one or two successor authorities according to decisions taken as a result of this announcement. This will be without prejudice to the right of the Indian Constituent Assemblies to decide in due course whether or not the part of India in respect of which they have authority will remain within the British Commonwealth."

In essence, the Plan of 3rd June which formed the basis of the Indian Independence Act, 1947, was a further adaptation of the Cripps offer of 1942 with the two major modifications : the 3rd June Plan proposed to transfer power without the slightest delay, while the Cripps Proposals contemplated such transfer in an uncertain future. Again, the cessation of British sovereignty by the Indian Independence Act was not fettered by any provision for safeguarding the interests of minorities, while such a condition was an essential feature of the Cripps Proposals.

Partition of India. The Plan of 3rd June was accepted by all the political parties in the country. The Muslim League was jubilant because it had, after all said and done, got their 'homeland' though it was 'truncated and moth-eaten'. The Congress accepted the partition of the country because it was unavoidable under the cricumstances. The Sikhs gave in though grudgingly. The Plan was put into effect without the slightest delay. The Legislative Assemblies of Bengal and the Panjab decided in favour of partition of those provinces. East Bengal and West Panjab joined Pakistan ; West Bengal and East Panjab remained within the Indian Union. The referendum in the Sylhet resulted in the incorporation of that district in East Bengal. Two Boundary Commissions one in respect of each province were constituted to demarcate the boundaries of the new Provinces. The referendum in the N.W.F.P. decided in favour of Pakistan, The Provincial Congress refraining from the referendum. Baluchistan and Sind threw in their lot with Pakistan.

The Indian Independence Act, 1947. The British Government went ahead with its promised legislation, the Indian Independence Bill was introduced in Parliament on July 4, 1947, and the Indian Independence Act was enacted after a fortnight on July 18. The Act did not provide for any new constitution of India. It was only an Act "to enable the representatives of India and Pakistan to frame their own constitutions and to provide for the exceedingly difficult period of transition." In other words, the Act merely formalized and gave legal effect to the promise made by Lord Mountbatten in his 3rd June Plan.

The Act provided for the Partition of India and the establishment of the two Dominions (India and Pakistan) from the appointed date *viz.*, August 15, 1947 and for the legislative supremacy of these Dominions. The British Government divested itself of all powers and control over the affairs of the Dominions after the 15th of August. Pending the adoption of a new constitution for each Dominion, the existing Constituent Assembly would be Dominion Legislature, and either Dominion and every Province would be governed by the provisions of the Government of India Act, 1935. Each Dominion was enpowered to modify this Act, through its Governor-General up to March 31, 1948, and thereafter by its Constituent Assembly.

The King's right to veto laws or to reserve them for His Majesty's pleasure was given up and each new Governor-General was given the right to assent in His Majesty's name to any Bill Passed by the Dominion legislature of his country. The Act also terminated the suzerainty and paramountcy of the British Crown over the Indian States and all treaties, agreements, etc., between the two were to lapse on August 15. But existing arrangements between these States and the Government of India were to continue pending detailed negotiations between these States and the new Dominions. Similarly, agreements with the tribes of the North West Frontier of Indian were to be negotiated by the successor Dominion. The office of the Secretary of State for India was abolished and his work was to be taken over by the Secretary for Commonwealth Affairs. As a mark of transfer of power to Indian hands, the words "Emperor of India" and "India Imperator" were dropped from the Royal style and titles. Both the Dominions would have full powers and right to go out of the British Commonwealth of Nations should they so desire.

In short, the Act converted India from a dependency of the Crown into two independent Dominions within the British Commonwealth of Nations. The word 'independent' emphasised freedom from control of the British Parliament and Whitehall.

Truly did Mr. Attlee say during the second reading of the Indian Independence Bill in the House of Commons: "It is the culminating point in a long course of events... the Act of 1935, the Declaration at the time of the Cripps Mission, the visit of my Right Hon. Friends to India last year, are all steps in the road that led up eventually to the proposals that I announced to the House on 3rd June last. This bill is designed to implement those proposals."

The Indian Independence Act, 1947, was the swan song of the British power as far as India was concerned and was acclaimed as "the noblest and greatest law ever enacted by the British Parliament." The Act of 1947 not only closed a chapter, it also at the same time opened a new and glorious chapter of free India.

SELECT REFERENCES

1. Coupland, R. : *The Costitutional Problem in India* (1944).
2. Cross, Colin : *The Fall of the British Empire* (1968).
3. Johnson, Campbell : *Mission with Mountbatten* (1951).
4. Mansergh, Nicholas (Ed.). : *Transfer of Power*, 1942–47.
5. Menon, V. P. : *The Transfer of Power in India* (1957).
6. Philips, C. H. : *The Evolution of India and Pakistan*, 1858–1947.
7. Prasad, Rajendra : *India Divided* (1946).

45

GROWTH OF COMMUNALISM AND THE PARTITION OF INDIA

One communalism does not end the other; each feeds on the other and both fatten.
— *Jawaharlal Nehru*

The British were neither the foes of the Hindus nor friends of the Muslims. They set up Pakistan not as a gesture of friendship towards the Muslims, but under the compulsion of their international policies.
— *Wali Khan*

To look upon the communal problem in India merely as the Hindu-Muslim question or of religious antagonism between the Hindus and the Muslims is misleading. The communal problem at its base was more politically-motivated than religiously oriented. Apart from the Hindus and the Muslims there was a third party in the communal triangle; the British rulers interposed themselves between the Hindus and the Muslims and thus created a communal triangle of which they remained the base.

The strongest arm of the communal triangle was the British rulers. They were neither the true friends of the Muslims nor the foes of the Hindus; they were the true friends of British Imperialism and acted on the tested and tried maxim of *Divide et Impera*. Lord John Elphinstone, Governor of Bombay (1853–60), wrote in a minute, "*Divide et Impera* was the old Roman motto and it should be ours". Sir John Strachey, another eminent British civilian, wrote: "The existence, side by side, of hostile creeds among the Indian people is one of the strong points in our political position in India." Until the seventies of the 19th century it suited the Imperial interest to support the Hindus and they did it. The early British economic and educational policies benefited the Hindus more than the Muslims. The British looked upon the Muslims as chief conspirators in the Revolt of 1857. The Wahabi movement confirmed their suspicion. The British Government deliberately adopted the policy of suppressing the Muslims. However, a change in British policy is perceptible towards the 1870s. The Hindus, politically more advanced than the Muslims, demanded more share for Indians in higher services, agitated for grant of political rights, introduction of representative government, etc. The Hindu posed a serious menace to the stability of British rule in India than the politically, economically and educationally backward Muslims. This marked the beginning of a change in British policy towards the two communities. The Anglo-Indian bureaucracy which worked at the grass-roots of British administration in India worked for a change in British policy. W. W. Hunter's book, *The Indian Mussalmans* (published in 1871) described 'the Muslims too weak for Rebellion' and pleaded for a change of official attitude towards the Muslim community. Mr. Theodore Beck, the first British Principal fo the newly-started M. A. O. College at Aligarh played a notable role in mobilising Muslim opinion and influencing British policy towards the Muslims.

Sir Syed Ahmad Khan: Drift from Nationalism to Communalism. The utterances and changing policies of Sir Syed Ahmad Khan clearly indicate the strong political undertones of the communal problem. Syed Ahmad started as an advocate of a united Indian nation and preached Hindu-Muslim unity but later changed his views to become a staunch opponent of the Indian National Congress; he fell into line with the British Imperialists.

Syed Ahmad Khan started his political career as an advocate of Hindu-Muslim amity. He described the Hindus and the Muslims as "two eyes of a beautiful bride, *i.e.*, India." In a speech delivered in 1884 he said, "Do you not inhabit the same land? .... Remember that the words Hindu and Mahomedan are only meant for religious distinction—otherwise all person, whether Hindu or Mahomedan, even the Christians who reside in this country, are all in this particular respect belonging to one and the same nation." Addressing a Panjabi Hindu audience Sir Syed said that every inhabitant of India is a Hindu and added, "I am there fore sorry that you do not regard me as a Hindu". In a speech delivered at Gurdaspur in 1884 Sir Syed said, "We should try to become one heart and soul and act in unison. If united, we can support each other; if not, the effect of one against the other would tend to the destruction and downfall of both".

Contrast with this Sir Syed's speech at Meerut on 16 March 1888 where he maintained that the Hindus and Muslims were not only two nations, but as two warring nations who could never lead a common political life, should ever the British quit India. Why this sudden change in Syed Ahmad's outlook and policy ? The Muslim demand for separate electorates almost synchronized with the introduction of the system of election in the constitution of local bodies. Speaking in the Central Legislature in January 1883 on Ripon's Bill for establishment of local self-government in the Central Provinces, Syed Ahmad Khan referred to the vital difference between different Indian races and different religions, the unequal or disproportionate progress of education among different sections of the population and expressed the fear that any system of election, pure and simple, would result in the larger community overriding the interest of the smaller community. A true devotee of the Muslim cause, Syed Ahmad Khan was fully aware of Muslim backwardness in the fields of education and politics and came to the conclusion that India was not fit for the introduction of Western political institution like representative or responsible government, for his community could not get its due share in it. This fear took the form of Hinduphobia and loomed large in all subsequent Muslim political thinking.

The Anglo-Indian administrators were quick to work on Muslim apprehensions and strove to drive a wedge between the Hindus and the Muslims. The three English Principals of the M.A.O. College, Beck[1], Morrison[2] and Archbold[3], gave the pro-British and anti-Hindu bias to the Aligarh Movement. The Aligarh Movement worked to instil into the minds of the Muslims a spirit of loyalty towards the British Crown and worked consciously and deliberately to keep them away from the main stream of Indian political life. In August 1888 Syed Ahmad Khan set up the United Indian Patriotic Association with the avowed object of countering the Congress propaganda and policy in England and in India and to wean away people from the Congress. This was followed a few years later (1893) by the exclusively sectarian Muhammadan Anglo-Oriental Defence Association of Upper India to keep the Muslims aloof from political agitation and to strengthen British rule in India.

Communalism in writing of Indian History.[4] British writers on Indian history also served the Imperial cause by initiating, developing and emphasizing the Hindu-Muslim approach in their study of Indian history and development of Indian culture. This communal approach to Indian history, also imitated by Indian scholars, fostered the communal way of thinking. For example, the ancient period of Indian history was described as Hindu Period and the medieval period labelled as Muslim Period of Indian history, implying thereby that religion was the guiding force behind politics during

---

1. Theodore Beck joined the College in 1883 and became its Principal and continued there till he died in 1899. Beck was essentially a politician and his real mission at Aligarh was to forge an Anglo-Muslim alliance. In an obituary note the London *Times* lamented the passing away of an empire-builder who died at his post.
2. Theodore Morrison (1863–1936) joined the staff of the M.A.O. College, Aligarh, in 1889; Principal of the College, 1899–1905 Morrison worked like a British Resident accredited to the court of an Indian prince. He was member-secretary of Secretary of State's Council, 1906–16.
3. William A. J. Archbold (1865–1929) Principal of Aligarh College, 1905–8 and later of the Government College, Dacca, and the Muir Central College, Allahabad; played a notable role in organising the Muslim Deputation which waited on the Viceroy, Minto at Simla, 1 Oct. 1906.
4. For an excellent analysis of this aspect see R. Thapar, H. Mukhia and B. Chandra, *communalism and the Writing of Indian History.*

the whole of the Medieval period. True, both the rulers and the ruled, not unoften used religious slogans to suit their material and political ambitions, but it was certainly a distortion of history to infer—as was done by these writers—that all Muslims were the rulers and all Hindus were the ruled. In fact the Muslim masses were as poor, if not more, as the Hindu masses and were thoroughly oppressed and exploited by the Muslim rulers and their Hindu collaborators. All the same, this communal approach to Indian history did foster divisive communal tendencies in Indian politics in the last quarter of the 19th century and first half of the 20th century.

Communal side-effects of Religious Reform Movements. The religious reform and revival movements—both Hindu and Muslim—of the 19th century contained some mutually contradictory aspects. These movements were launched to purge Hinduism and Islam of irrational and obscurantist tendencies but these generated some unhealthy tendencies. The Wahabis' crusade against all non-Muslims and aim to establish *Dar-ul-Islam* (the world of Islam) was as odious to Hindus as Dayanand's slogan of Aryanisation of India and aim of *Shuddhi* (conversions of non-Hindus to Hinduism) were unpalatable to Muslims. Even Vivekananda's references to ancient Indian achievements as constituting the real Indian spirit—popularized to give a sense of Pride and National Identity to a demoralised nation—created a reaction in the Muslim mind who turned to Western Asian history for a tradition and identity.

New Hero-myths and Communal overtones. Similarly the militant nationalists of the early 20th century in their search for 'national heroes' and 'hero-myths' referred to Maharana Pratap, Shivaji and Guru Gobind Singh as national heroes and the Muslim rulers like Akbar, Shahjahan and Aurangzeb as 'foreigners'. The straight logic was that Pratap, Shivaji or Gobind Singh were nationalists because they were Hindus, and Mughal emperors were foreigners because they were Muslims. Besides, it was too much to assume that nationalism of the modern type existed in the medieval period of Indian history.

True, Tilak, Lajpat Rai, Aurobindo and later Gandhiji were strong believers in Hindu–Muslim unity, but in their writings and speeches they often employed a language, imagery and symbolism derived exclusively from Hindu sources (*e.g.* the slogan of Ram Rajya popularized by Gandhiji) had a religious tinge and did create a reaction in the Muslim mind. True, the references to Hindu theology were intended to involved the politically inert masses into the nationalist struggle by explaining to them nationalism couche in a language within their comprehension, *i.e.*, religious phraseology, but it did have the undesired effect of rousing Muslim communal susceptibilities—feelings cleverly exploited by the British rulers.

Patronage in Government Services used to Foster Communalism. In the absence of any avenues of gainful employment in trade and industry, the British Indian Government remained the biggest employer to which the educated youth hopefully looked for their means of livelihood. This enormous patronage—in higher and subordinate services—was cleverly used by the rulers to promote rivalry and discord among different sections of society. Our nationalist leaders were fully aware of the mischievous character of this bait, but the hunger—rather compulsion—for loaves and fishes blinded them to its dangerous potentialities. Jawaharlal Nehru explained then, "This enormous patronage was exercised to strengthen the British hold on the country, to crush discordant and disagreeable elements, and to promote rivalry and discord amongst various groups anxiously looking forward to employment in government service. It led to demoralization and conflict and the government could play one group against the other."[5]

The Simla Deputation (1 October, 1906) and Acceptance of the Principle of Communal Electorates. The Imperial administrators right from the Secretary of State in England to the District Officer in India, all were convinced that adequate 'counterpoises' to the growing strength of the

---

5. Jawaharlal Nehru: *The Discovery of India*, p.307.

Indian National Congress must be found, if the British rule in India was to be stable. One such counterpoise thought about was the official acceptance of the principle of separate Muslim electorates, *i.e.,* reservation of seats for the Muslim community and election to such seats to be made by separate Muslim electorates. The opportunity presented itself because a new scheme of constitutional reforms was being considered.

Inspired by Principal Archbold of M. A. O. College, Aligarh, H. H. the Aga Khan waited in a deputation on Lord Minto at Simla on 1 October, 1906. The Deputation was described by Maulana Mohammad Ali as a 'command performance'. Mr. Archbold prepared the draft of the Muslim Address, acted as a liaison between the Government and Muslim leaders and saw to the success of the Deputation to the last detail. The Deputationists expressed sentiments of loyalty to the British Crown, showed grateful appreciation of the British Government's policy of introducing further reforms, but expressed the apprehension that if the principle of 'election' was introduced without conceding reservation of seats for the Muslims it would prove detrimental to their interests. The Deputationists demanded the reservation of seats for the Muslim Community not only on the basis of their population but on the basis of their political importance and their services in the defence of the Empire. Lord Minto gladly accepted the Muslim demand for separate communal electorates. He earned a pat from Lord Morley, the Secretary of State, who wrote on 5 October, 1906, "Your address was admirable alike in spirit, in the choice of topics and in the handling .... It has been thoroughly appreciated here by the Press and the people...It seems as if all had gone excellently....".

Foundation of the Muslim League, 30 December 1906. In the wake of the fateful Simla Deputation the Muslim leaders mooted the idea of a Central Muhammadan Association to look exclusively after the interests of the Muslim community. The All–India Muslim League was formerly inaugurated on 30 December 1906 with the following aims and objects:

(*a*) To promote among Indian Moslems feelings of loyalty towards the British Government and to remove any misconception that may arise, as to the intentions of the Government with regard to any of its measures:

(*b*) To protect the political and other rights of the Indian Moslems and to place their needs and aspirations before the Government in temperate language; and

(*c*) So far as possible, without prejudice to the objects mentioned under (*a*) and (*b*), to promote friendly relations between Moslems and other communities of India.

Thus, from its very inception the Muslim League was a communal body established to look after the political rights and interests of the Muslim community alone. This character is more or less retained till 1947.

The true political ideas of the League are apparent from Nawab Waqar-ul-Mulk's speech delivered at Aligarh. The Nawab said, "God forbid, if the British rule disappears from India, Hindus will Lord over it; and we will be in constant danger of our life, property and honour. The only way for the Muslims to escape this danger is to help in the continuance of the British rule. If the Muslims are heartily with the British, then that rule is bound to endure. Let the Muslims consider themselves as a British army ready to shed their blood and sacrifice their lives for the British Crown".

For About a decade after 1913 the Muslim League came under the influence of progressive Muslim leaders like Maulana Mohammad Ali, Maulana Mazhar-ul-Huq, Syed Wazir Hussian, Hasain Imam and M. A. Jinnah (then a nationalist). From 1920 to 1923 the activities of the Muslim League remained suspended. However, the appointment of the Simon Commission (1927–30) and the Round Table Conferences at London (1930–32) that followed again brought the Muslim League into activity. By 1934 M. A. Jinnah, now a communalist, became its undisputed leader. The Communal Award (1932) of the British Government further widened the gulf between the Hindus and the Muslims.

Congress Ministries and the Muslim League, 1937–39. The first elections for the provincial legislative councils under the Government of India Act 1935 were held in 1937. The Muslim League contested the elections to various legislative bodies but achieved moderate success. Out of the 485 reserved Muslim seats, the League could capture only 110 seats. Even in the Muslim-majority provinces of the Panjab, the North-West Frontier Province, Bengal and Sind the League was trounced by rival Muslim parties. The Congress party gained an absolute majority in Bombay, Madras, U.P., Bihar, Orissa and the Central Provinces and was the largest single party in the N.W.F.P. The Congress decided to accept office in July 1937. The Muslim League hoped to form coalition ministries with the Congress in provinces like Bengal, Assam and the Panjab and desired the Congress to take Muslim League ministers in U.P. and Bihar. The Congress, consistent with its principles and policies and being proud of its non-communal outlook and policies—liberation of the country and a melioration of the condition of the masses—advised Muslim League members to sign the Congress pledge and become its members, if they desired to accept responsibilities of office.

Mr. Jinnah interpreted these moves of the Congress as a calculated policy against the Muslim League. He levelled 'sweeping and fantastic' allegations against the Congress ministries, dubbed the Congress a Hindu organisation out to crush all minorities. He came to the conclusion that the Muslims could expect neither justice nor fairplay from the Congress ministries. In 1938 the Muslim League appointed a committee under the chairmanship of the Raja of Pirpur to report on the oppressions of the Muslims in what it called "Hindu Congress Provinces". The Pirpur Report fabricated cases of alleged horrible atrocities perpetrated on the Muslims by the Hindus. The Report also observed: "The conduct of the the Congress Government seems to substantiate the theory that there is something like identity of purpose between the Congress and the Hindu Mahasabha... We Muslims feel that, notwithstanding the non-communal professions of the Congress and the desire of a few Congressmen to follow a truly national policy, a vast majority of the Congress members are Hindu who look forward, after many centuries of British and Muslim rule, to the re-establishment of a purely Hindu Raj". The general attitude towards the Congress was, "The Muslims think that no tyranny can be as great as the tyranny of a majority".

The Muslim League observed a 'Day of Deliverance and Thanks-giving' when the Congress ministries resigned in October 1939 over the war issue.

The Two-Nation Theory and the Pakistan Movement. The poet and political thinker Mohammad Iqbal is thought to be the originator of the idea of a separate Muslim State for the Indian Muslims and is believed to have given the necessary emotional content to the movement. Inspired by the spirit of Pan-Islamism Iqbal declared at the Allahabad session of the All-India Muslim League, held in 1930, "I have no hesitation in declaring that if the principle that the Indian Muslim is entitled to full and free development on the lines of his own culture and tradition in his own Indian homeland is recognised as the basis of a permanent communal settlement... I would like to see the Panjab, North-West Frontier Province, Sind and Baluchistan amalgamated into a single State. Self-government within the British empire or without the British empire, the formation of a consolidated North-West Indian Muslim State appears to me to be the final destiny of the Muslims, at least of North-West India".

The idea of a separate homeland for Muslims to be called Pakistan took a definite shape in the mind of a young under-graduate at Cambridge, Rahmat Ali. He visualized the Panjab, N.W.F.P. (also called Afghan Province), Kashmir, Sind, and Baluchistan as the national home of the Indian Muslims and he coined the word Pakistan in 1933. The word Pakistan was formed by taking the initials of the first four and the last of the fifth. Rahmat Ali maintained that the Hindus and Muslims were fundamentally distinct nations. He wrote, "Our religion, culture, history, tradition, literature, economic system, laws of inheritance, succession and marriage are fundamentally different from those of the Hindus. These differences are not confined to the broad basic principles. They extend to the minute details of our lives. We, Muslims and Hindus, do not interdine; we do not intermarry Our national customs and calendars, ever our diet and dress are different."

The most unequivocal declaration of the Hindus and Muslims as separate nationalities was made by M. A. Jinnah at the Lahore session of the League in March 1940, "They (Hindus and Muslims) are not religions in the strict sense of the word, but are, in fact, different and distinct social orders, and it is a dream that Hindus and Muslims can ever evolve a common nationality.. The Hindus and Muslims belong to two different religious philosophies, social customs, literatures... To yoke together two such nations under a single State, one of a numerical minority and the other as a majority, must lead to growing discontent and final destruction of any fabric that may be so built up for the government of such a State."

Demanding the partition of India, the Muslim League passed the resolution: "It is the considered view of this session of the All-India Muslim League that no constitutional plan would be workable in this country or acceptable to the Moslems unless it is designed on the following basic principle, *viz.*, that geographically contiguous units are demarcated into regions which should be so constituted with such territorial readjustments as may be necessary, that the areas in which the Moslems are numerically in a majority, as in the North-Western and Eastern zones of India, should be grouped to constitute 'independent states' in which the constituent units shall be autonomous and sovereign..." This resolution did not specify the areas in the proposed state of Pakistan. In 1942 Mr. Jinnah explained to Professor Coupland that Pakistan would be "a Moslem State or States comprising N.W.F.P., the Panjab, and Sind on the one side of India and Bengal on the other". He did not mention Baluchistan and Assam, nor did he claim Kashmir and Hyderabad. However, in a Memorandum to the Cabinet Mission on 12 May, 1946, the Muslim League demanded "the six Muslim provinces (Panjab, N.W.F.P., Baluchistan, Sind, Bengal, Assam) shall be grouped together as one Group".

Thus the Lahore session of the Muslim League gave it an Ambition and a Programme. Henceforth the demand for Pakistan became as much an article of faith for the Indian Muslims as their holy book, the Koran.

The Hindu Mahasabha. British imperial policies in India provided a congenial climate for the emergence, growth and popularity of communal organisations. A communal organisation though primarily organised to promote the interests of a particular community also indirectly promoted British imperial interests apart from serving the personal ambition of opportunistic leadership. This was not only true of the Hindu Mahasabha but also of the Muslim League, the Akali Dal and the All-India Depressed Classes Federation.

The genesis and early history of the Hindu Mahasabha are clouded in obscurity. In 1910 the leading Hindus of Allahabad decided to organise an All-India Hindu Mahasabha. In 1911 the Panjab Hindu Mahasabha organised a Hindu Conference at Amritsar. The Hindu Mahasabha set up its headquarters at Hardwar and used to organise the Akhil Bharatiya Hindu Conference at Hardwar on the occasion of important Hindu fairs.

The communal riots particularly in the Malabar coast and Multan that followed the suspension of the first Non-cooperation Movement in 1922 caused heavy losses to the Hindus both in human lives and property. A section of the Hindus decided to organise the Hindus in self-defence. Explaining the rationale of the Hindu Mahasabha, Pt. Madan Mohan Malaviya explained that the Mohammedans and the Christians had been carrying on proselytizing activities for centuries; the majority of the Muslims of India were converts from Hinduism, he added. To check this process, it was necessary to organise a Hindu Mission. Malaviya further explained that as a countermove to the Muslim League putting forward exaggerated claims for Muslim representation in the elected bodies, it was necessary to organise the Hindus to get a fair deal for their community. Thus *Shudhi* and *Sangathan* became the watchwords of the Hindu Mahasabha in the early years of its existence. Malaviya also emphasised the socio-cultural mission of the Hindu Mahasabha. The Indian National Congress being a political organisation, Malaviya added, it could not deal with social, cultural and non-political spheres. The Hindu Mahasabha was organised to remove the social abuses in Hindu society like child-marriage, casteism, untouchability etc. As such, Malaviya emphasised, that the Hindu Mahasabha did not in any way clash with the Congress but was planned to supplement and strengthen the Indian National Congress.

The tall claims of the Hindu Mahasabha as a socio-cultural organisation were hardly less hypocritical than similar claims put up by the Muslim League, the Akali Dal and other communal organisations. Under the leadership of V. D. Savarkar who became the President of the Hindu Mahasabha in 1938 and was re-elected again and again, the Mahasabha developed a political programme. Sore at the Muslim appeasement policy of the Indian National Congress, Savarkar popularized the concept of Hindu Rashtra. Savarkar maintained that India was a land of Hindus having only one nation i.e. the Hindu nation. The Muslims must accept their position as a minority community in a single Indian State, of course being promised just treatment and equal political rights on the basis of 'one man, one vote.' On the question of a national language, Savarkar upheld that according to democratic parctices the language of the majority must prevail.

After the death of V. D. Savarkar, Dr. S. P. Mookerji became the leader of the Hindu Mahasabha and imparted it a more nationalist outlook.

The Hindu Mahasabhas never gained that popularity witht the Hindu Masses as the Muslim League did with the Muslims in India. All the same, against the Muslim Leaguess demand for Pakistan, it raised the slogan of Akhand Hindustan.

The Hindu Mahasabha's propaganda of a Hindu race, Hindu culture, Hindu civilisation and Hindu Rashtra in India did harden the Muslim League's attitude and made it more suspicious and more determined to demand Pakistan. It must, however, be siad, in all fairness that the Muslim League was the first ever communal organisation to come into existence; the communal poison proved infectious and the Hindu Mahasabha and other communal organisations came into existence as a counterpoise to one another.

The Second World War and Furtherance of the Pakistan Plan

The August Offer, 1940. In response to the Congress offer for co-operation with the British Government conditional on its declaration of "the full independence of India" and formation of a Provisional National Government at the Centre, Lord Linlithgow in August 1940 offered the plan of setting up a constitution-making body after the war but assured the minorities that the British Government would not agree to any system of government whose authority was directly denied by large and powerful elements in India's national life. The Muslim League welcomed this part of the August Offer and passed the resolution, "The partition of India is the only solution of the most difficult problem of India's future constitution".

Cripps Mission (1942) and Encouragement to Separatist Forces. The Cripps Plan (March-April 1942) carried further the Muslim League's demand for the partition of India. The Draft Declaration of the British Government contained the provision for acceptance of the new constitution of India to be framed after the end of the war, subject to the condition:

"Any province of British India might refuse to accept the new Constitution and choose to retain its existing constitutional position, provision being made for its subsequent accession to the Indian Union if it so decided.

"With such non-acceding Provinces, if they so desired, the British Government would be prepared to agree upon a new Constitution, giving them the same fulll status as the Indian Union."

The Muslim League rejected this Cripps Plan and reiterated the demand for Pakistan.

Wavell Plan (1945) and the Communal Impasse. Mr. Amery, the Secretary of State, announced in the House of Commons on 14 June 1945, "The offer of March 1942 stands in its entirety without change or qualification" The re-constitution of the Governor-General's Executive Council was proposed to be done by nominating all of them except the Commander-in-Chief from amongst leaders of Indian political life. The Executive Council was to have "a balanced representation of the main communities, including equal proportions of Muslims and Caste Hindus." Lord Wavell called a conference at Simla in June-July 1945 to sort out an agreement between the Congress and the Muslim League. The Congress proposed to include two Congress Muslims out of its quota. Mr. Jinnah insisted that all Muslim members of the Council Must be nominated by the League. Lord Wavell announced the breakdown of the conference, giving the general impression that Mr. Jinnah had been given the veto to torpedo all constitutional advance in India.

The Cabinet Mission (1946) and the Communal Tangle. In the elections of 1945-46 the Muslim League captured an over-whelming majority of Muslim seats in all the provinces except the N.W.F.P. The Muslim League secured 75% of the total Muslim votes. The Congress party formed government in all the Hindu majority provinces and the N.W.F.P., while the League came in power in Bengal and Sind. In the Panjab a Unionist ministry was formed although the Leauge was the single largest party. The elections demonstrated that the Muslim League was a strong political party in the country.

The Cabinet Mission comprising Lord Pethick Lawrence (Secretary of State), Sir Stafford Cripps (President of the Board of Trade) and Mr. A.V. Alexander (First Lord of the Admiralty) reached India in March 1946. Meanwhile Prime Minister Attlee announced in the House of Commons that a minority could not be allowed to put a veto on the advance of the majority.

The Cabinet Mission rejected the demand for Pakistan and suggested instead a Central Government in charge of Foreign Affairs, Defence and Communications. It, however, conceded the Muslim League's demand half-way by grouping provinces in three groups (*viz.*, Hindu-majority provinces of Madras, Bombay, C.P., U.P., Bihar and Orissa to form Group A; Muslim-majority provinces of Panjab, N.W.F.P. and Sind to form Group B; and Bengal and Assam to form Group C). The "full autonomy" to the provinces and the provision for Grouping gave to the Muslim League "the substance of pakistan".

Further, the Cabinet Mission plan laid down procedure for the election of a Constitution-making body. In the election to the Constituent Assembly, the Congress won 199 of the 210 General seats, the League bagged 73 of the 78 Muslim seats. Mr. Jinnah maintained that the Congress having support of 211 members out of the total strength of 296 of the Constituent Assembly would place the Muslims at their mercy. He, therefore, demanded two Constitution-making bodies, one for the people of India and one for Pakistan.

Direct Action and Communal Riots, 1946–47. The Muslim League withdrew its acceptance of the Cabinet Mission Plan and observed 16 August, 1946 as 'Direct Action Day'. Direct Action was not directed for wresting Pakistan from the hands of the unwilling British Government but was directed against the Hindus. The League engineered communal riots in Bengal, U.P., Bombay, the Panjab, Sind and the N.W.F.P.

In the Interim Government formed on September 2, 1946, under the leadership of Mr. J. L. Nehru, the Muslim League refused to join, later agreed to join on 26 October 1946, not 'to work it but to wreck it' from inside. All the same the Muslim League refused to join the Constituent Assembly.

Attlee's Statement, 20 February 1947: Divide and Quit Policy. Prime Minister Attlee announced in the House of Commons the "definite intention" of the British Government "to effect the transference of power to responsible Indian hands by a date not later than June 1948". In the absence of the Muslim League's co-operation the British Government would have "to consider to whom the powers of the Central Government in British India should be handed over, on due date, whether as a whole to some form of Central Government for British India, or in some areas to the existing Provincial Governments, or in such other way as may seem most reasonable and in the best interests of the Indian people". Thus the British Government's decision to maintain some sort of unity of India underwent a change and it veered round to the possibility of setting up Pakistan.

Mountbatten Plan of Partition of India, 3 June 1947. Lord Mountbatten who succeeded Lord Wavell as Viceroy of India in March 1947 offered a plan for the partition of India in his 3 June 1947 announcement. The plan provided for referendum in the N.W.F.P. to decide whether the province would join India or Pakistan. A referendum was to be held in the Muslim-majority district of Sylhet (Assam) to decide whether the district would join East Bengal or remain part of Assam. The Legislative Assemblies of Bengal and Panjab were to meet each in two sections or parts (one representing the Muslim majority districts and the other the rest of the province) to decide by a simple majority whether the province was to be partitioned or not. The Hindu members of the Panjab and Bengal Assemblies decided in favour of partition of those provinces. East Bengal and West Punjab decided to join Pakistan while West Bengal and East Panjab joined India. The referendum in Sylhet district of Assam went in favour of Pakistan. The N.W.F.P. decided to join Pakistan.

The Indian Independence Act and Partition of India. The Indian Independence Act passed by the British parliament in July 1947 provided for the setting up of two independent dominions of India and Pakistan with effect from 15 August 1947.

Was the partition of India Inevitable and Unavoidable? The answers of these questions differ widely with the nationality of the writer—Indian, Pakistani or British.

In India the partition of the country is considered a tragedy. It is projected as the logical culmination of the long-standing British policy of Divide and Rule and the Muslim League's ideology of communalism and separateness. The two worked together and forced the Indian National Congress to agree to the partition of India. Indian writers largely place the blame at the door of the Congress leaders and agree that if they had shown adequate understanding, tact and boldness, the partition of the Motherland could be avoided. In Pakistan, however, the partition is considered as quite logical and inevitable and the growth of Muslim nationalism is traced in the depth of Indian history. Among the British scholars there is no unanimity of opinion about the rationale of the partition of India and there is difference of opinion among historians and those writers who served the *raj* in India.

Whatever the verdict of history, credit must be given to Mr. M. A. Jinnah for his adroit handling of the political situation.[6] He was a very shrewd politician and often dodged his political rivals by clever somersaults. He rose from strength to strength and earned the epithet of the Qaid-i-Azam (Great Organiser). Jawahar Lal Nehru attributes the growth of Muslim communalism to the delay in the growth of a strong Muslim middle class; this enabled the League to work up the psychology of fear among the emotionally excitable Muslim masses. The cry of 'Islam in Danger' brought the Muslim masses under the banner of the League and Mr. Jinnah stood forth as the political Messiah. All said, the acts of omission and commission on the part of the Hindu Mahasabha further fanned the fanaticism of the Muslim League. Mr. V. D. Savarkar, the president of Mahasabha, advocated 'an uncompromising doctrine of Hindu ascendancy' and openly announced that 'the only way to deal with the Hindu-Muslim schism was to insist that all India was Hindustan and that the Muslims must reconcile themselves to the status of a minority community in a democratic state which orders life by majority rule.'

SELECT OPINIONS

Jawaharlal Nehru. I suppose it was the compulsion of events and the feeling that we wouldn't get out of that deadlock or morass by pursuing the way we had done; it became worse and

---

6. Jinnah once remarked that he alone with the help of his Secretary and his typewriter won pakistan for the Muslims.

worse. Further a feeling that even if we got freedom for India with that background it would be very weak India, that is, a federal India with far too much power in the federating units. A larger India would have constant troubles, constant disintegrating pulls. And also the fact that we saw no other way of getting our freedom—in the near future I mean. And so we accepted it and said, let us build up a strong India. And if others do not want to be in it, well how can we and why should we force them to be in it?

Sardar Vallabhbhai Patel. I felt that if we did not accept partition, India would be split into many bits and would be completely ruined. My experience of office for one year convinced me that the way we have been proceeding would lead us to disaster. We would not have had one Pakistan but several. We would have had Pakistan cells in every office.

C. H. Philips. The growing division of opinion between the Congress and Muslim League produced a deadlock which throughout the war remained unbroken despite successive British offers, notably in the Cripps plan of 1942 and in the three-tiered proposal 1946. At this stage the British Government, placing its emphasis on responsible rather than strictly representative government, and on the maintenance of the unity of India, failed to carry the Congress and Muslim League with it Indians were concerned rather with the struggle for effective power and, on the Muslim League's side, with the implications for them of representative government. Alarmed by the fact that with the weakening civil and military resources in India it could no longer guarantee the maintenance of law and order, the British Government declared in February 1947 that the transfer of power must be composed by June 1948. The final, headlong rush to independence and partition was in fact completed by 15th August 1947.

Harold Laski. But as long as every vested interest in India is, like the Moslem interest, encouraged, openly or secretly, to believe that it will get better terms for independence from us than from a real attempt at accommodation with other interests, of course agreement between them is not forthcoming... in the same way, though more subtly is the Conservative party has long patronised the separation of Ulster, and with the same evil consequences.

Allan Campbell-Johnson. The time-limit (set by Lord Attlee for transfer of power, *i.e.*, June 1948) was in effect the logical conclusion of the policy decision of the British Government early in the war to cease recruitment for the Indian Civil Service. The normal complement of the Service was never much more than eleven hundred; by November 1946 it had fallen to five hundred and twenty British officers in senior positions, with the remainder Indians... The tremendous bureaucratic growth of work coinciding with the decline in the number of British senior officials made it clear, quite apart from other considerations, that it was going to be virtually impossible to hold on to India administratively beyond 1949. It is doubtful whether the police establishment was strong enough by 1947 to enforce any policy opposed by both major parties, and it is fair to say that any large military commitments in India to maintain the Raj would have been wholly unacceptable to the British Government or people.

SELECT REFERENCES

1. Bahadur, Lal : *The Muslim League.*
2. Campbell-Johnson, A. : *Mission with Mountbatten.*
3. Coupland, R. : *The Constitutional Problem in India.*
4. *History of Freedom Movement of Pakistan,* 4 vols.
5. Mehta and Patwardhan : *The Communal Triangle.*
6. Moon, P. : *Divide and Quit.*
7. Philips, C. H. and Wainwright M. D. (eds.) : *The Partition of India.*
8. Symonds, R. A. : *The Making of Pakistan.*
9. Wali Kahn : *Facts Are Facts.*

46

INDIAN ECONOMY UNDER COLONIAL RULE

> Our system acts very much like a sponge, drawing up all the good things from the banks of the Ganges, and squeezing them down on the banks of the Thames.
>
> —*John Sullivan*, President, Board of Revenue, Madras
>
> Britain and India's economic interests conflict all along the line.
>
> —*Jawaharlal Nehru*

Indian Economy on eve of British Conquest

Economic Disruption. The disintegration of the Mughal empire in the 18th century inevitably brought about economic fragmentation and disruption. The continuous conflicts and wars between a host a rival Indian princess disrupted economic activity. New agencies of pillage and plunder sprang up. Cultivation was adversely affected. Roads became unsafe and excessive demands for customs and other tolls hampered trade and commerce. European trading companies dabbled in politics and profited from the administrative and political confusion.

Self-Sufficient Village Communities. The most outstanding feature of the Indian village economy was the existence of self-sufficient and self-governing village communities. Indian villages functioned as little worlds of their own, having very little to do with the outside world. Village economy was self-subsisting, providing the foodstuffs it needed except perhaps a few necessities like salt and iron. Another marked feature was the union of agriculture and handicraft industry. The family of the peasant undertook spinning and weaving as a secondary activity and produced the cloth needed for the family. The other economic needs were also provided by village craftsmen like the carpenter, the goldsmith, the potter, the black-smith, the oil-presser, etc., who in effect were servants of the village and received a customary share in the village crops for their services. The basic land relationships in the village were governed by custom and usage. The concept of private property in land, as understood in the modern sense, did not develop. The land in the village belonged to the cultivating community, each family having its share of arable land. Since population was small and land more plentiful than at present, land was not an article of free purchase or sale *i.e.*, it did not become a commodity. Karl Marx described this communal ownership of land as the Indian form of communism.

The village communities were self-governing. The village panchayat administered the village affairs, settled disputes and administered justice. The village Headman was its leader in dealing with the government. The local chief or the distant subahdar did not interfere in village affairs except claiming a share in the village crops varying from one-sixth to one-half. Political convulsions did not disturb the placid life of village communities and Marx had these village communities in view communities in view when he referred to the "unchangeableness of Asiatic societies". It has been aptly said that the village communities "lasted when nothing else seemed to last".

There was a dark side to the stability and isolation of village communities. The ideal of self-sufficiency acted as a barrier to the creation of a wider market for Indian handicrafts. The closed and caste-bound socio-economic structure permitted little horizontal, vertical or spatial mobility of labour. It cramped human mind, stifled spirit of enterprise and became an instrument of socio-economic stagnation. Further, the indifference to political affairs outside the village militated against the emergence of national consciousness.

The urban economy of India presented a better picture. Indian handicrafts enjoyed worldwide renown. The cotton manufactures of Bengal (Dacca), Gujarat (Ahmedabad) and Masaulipatam; the silk fabrics of Murshidabad, Lahore and Agra; woollen shawls and carpets of Agra, Lahore and Kashmir were in demand both in India and abroad. Besides, gold and silver jewellery, metal work, fancy ivory items, arms, shields, ships etc. enjoyed a rare reputation of excellence. India had also developed her own banking system with *shroffs* and *mahajans* at the lower level and *Jagat Seths*, *Nagar Seths* and *Chetties* at the top. India also had a very favourable balance of trade and enjoyed the reputation of being the 'sink of gold and silver'. It seems that the preconditions for a rapid capitalist growth existed. However, certain socio-economic constraints like the law of escheat and the existence of feudal classes worked as a deterrent. Prof. Raychaudri has attributed India's economic backwardness in the 18th century to the absence of "any scientific and geographical revolution" and to the inability of society to respond positively to opportunity.[1]

Karl Marx[2] on Britain's Dual Rule in India

As a London-based correspondent of the *New York Daily Tribune*, Karl Marx wrote a series of articles on Indian affairs in 1853. The occasion was the impending parliamentary debates on the question of the renewal of East India Company's character.

Marx referred to England's dual role in India: one *destructive* and the other *regenerative*. He summed up the pre-British situation in India as characterized by permanent stagnation and unchangeableness[3]. As such Marx did not expect any progress to come forth out of Asiatic society itself. This was in sharp contrast to European society where progress was brought by the dynamics of its own contradictions from ancient society through feudalism to capitalism. England's destructive role in India lay in the destruction of the economic basis of the village communities, which caused a great social revolution in India. According to Marx, destruction of the old socio-economic system was a necessary step in the way of India's progress on modern lines.

England's regenerative rule in India began when it brought political unity in India, built a native army, developed means of transport and communications, introduced property rights in land, introduced freedom of press and created the new educated class imbued with European science. Through these policies, Marx hoped, England had introduced a dynamic element of Western civilization and laid the material foundation of Western society in India.

Marx's assessment of the colonial situation in India in the middle of the 18th century suffered from many limitations. He had never visited India and his sources of information were rather limited. He also shared the contemporary conviction about European superiority. Further, European imperialism was still expanding and Marx could not exactly project its later developments which started operating after Marx's death. All the same, his dialectical approach and conviction about socialist universalism gave him a rare insight. For example, he projected that the fruits of developments in India could not be enjoyed by the Indians till the British bourgeoisie had been supplanted by the industrial proletariat at home or the Indians themselves will have become strong enough to liberate the country from British rule.

---

1. Kumar, Dharma : *Cambridge Economic History of India*, Vol, II, p. 33.
2. See Marx's two articles in Appendices A and B.
3. Recent researches have exploded the myth of 'the unchanging India'. Forces of change—though slow—were at work before British rule, although the pace of change accelerated in the 19th century under Western influences (see Judith Brown, *Modern India*, p. 12)

Three Phases[4] of Economic Exploitation

R. P. Dutt, a Marxist dialectician and scholar has analysed three periods in the history of imperialist rule in India, *viz.*,

    (*i*) Period of Merchant Capital (Mercantilism)—from 1757 to the end of 18th century;

    (*ii*) Period of Industrial Capital (Free Trade Capitalism)—developed during the 19th century; and

    (*iii*) Period of Finance Capital—from the closing decade of 19th century to 1947.

Dutt rightly points out that each stage developed out of the conditions of the earlier stage and the different modes of colonial exploitation overlapped; old forms of colonial exploitation never entirely ceased but got integrated into new patterns of exploitation.

The Mercantilist Phase

From 1757 (the British victory in the battle of Plassey) began the special phase of Company's trade-cum-plunder of Bengal. The dominant economic doctrine of the times was that of Mercantilism. Mercantilist ideas which were very popular during 16th-18th centuries were an integrated part of the old colonial system.

Mercantilism was the economic counterpart of the spirit of aggressive nationalism. The basic idea was that of regulation of all economic activity in the interst of strengthening the nation. As far as overseas trade was concerned, it was sought to be regulated through chartered trading companies and the twin aim was (*a*) to have a favourable balance of trade (exports should be more than imports (*b*) to promote flow of bullion into the home country.

The Merchant companies aimed at a large profit-margin. This could be possible through three methods:—

---

4. **The impact of British rule on Indian Economy under the East India Company (1755–1857)** may be viewed under the following heads :

    (a) **Impact on Indian Agriculture.** The East India Company's authorities introduced new land tenures like Permanent Zamindari Settlement, Ryotwari, Mahalwari system etc., the State's land revenue demand was excessive; under Ryotwari and Mahalwari systems there was periodical upward revision of land tax; emergence of new social classes like landlords, money-lenders and land-speculators in the rural sector; rural indebtedness increased; Indian cultivator was driven below the poverty line. (For details see Chapter XIX

    (b) **Decline of Indian Cottage Industries.** British rulers used the political power of the state to strangle Indian handicrafts; machine-made products of England flooded the Indian markets and drove unemployment and misery among weavers, artisans etc. (see the sub-heading on Deindustrialization).

    (c) **Colonial manipulation of Indian trade and commerce.** A qualitative change came in the character of Indian foreign trade. To suit the interests of industrialized British economy, India's exports mostly consisted of food-stuff and raw materials and her imports largely of manufactured goods. British Agency Houses exercised great control over India's internal and foreign trade.

    Preferential tariffs upto 1858 provided that imports into India of non-British countries were subjected to double the rate of customs duty as compared to goods imported from Britain *e.g.*, in 1852 British cotton cloth, silk piecegoods, woollens, metals etc. paid 5% duty as compared to 10% duty charged on these items imported from non-British countries; similarly, British cotton yarn paid 3.5% duty as opposed to 7% leviable on non-British imports; books imported from Britain were allowed duty-free while non-British goods were charged 3% duty etc. etc.

    (d) **Drain of Wealth from India.** It was a logical corollary of Britain's discriminatory economic policies (for details see the sub-heading on Drain of Wealth)

(a) Monopoly control over trade and elimination of all possible rivals;

(b) Purchase of goods at cheap rates and sale of commodities at very high rates; and

(c) The above objectives could be achieved if they could establish political control over the countries they traded with.

The English East India Company's struggle with other Merchant companies in India, *viz.* the Dutch Company and the French Company, was aimed at elimination of all European rivals from the Indian trade. The various wars that the East India Company fought against Indian princes—the conquest of Bengal, Anglo-Mysore wars, the Anglo-Maratha wars and wars against other Indian powers were all directed towards control of political power over various parts of India. The political power that the Company acquired was used to control the economy of India—to control the very sources of Indian wealth and the internal and external trade of India. Indian merchants were prohibited not only from buying commodities directly from the producers (which were monopolised by the English) but the agents of the Company forced their goods on the Indian merchants at a price higher than the prevailing market price.

The Period of Colonial Plunder, 1757–72. The character of the East India Company underwent a change after 1757. It was no longer merely a trading company. Henceforth, it played the role of a commercial-cum-military-cum-political body in Bengal. It assumed the role of king-maker, changing nawabs of Bengal at will. No wonder, the Governor and members of his council engineered three quick revolutions in Bengal (revolutions of 1757, 1760 and 1764) because each new nawab offered fabulous presents to the Company's civil and military officers. The servants of the Company were infected with the spirit of making a 'quick buck' (referred to by the British poet William Cooper (1731–1800) as the 'get-rich quick mentality'). The Directors and shareholders of the Company wanted higher dividends. Even the British government wanted a share in the new mine of gold (*i.e.*, India) which the Company had found. Inevitably began, in the words of a British historian, a period of "open and unashamed plunder" of Bengal. R. C. Dutt has estimated that during 1757–65 the Company's servants exacted about £6 million (nearly four times the total annual revenue of Bengal), from the province of Bengal alone. Besides, while 'farming out' the revenue of Bengal to zamindars, the Company's officials received presents from the zamindars. By the sale of unauthorised *dastaks* (passchits) the Company's agents received bribes. The oppression of artisans was another form of plunder; the Company's agents compelled the weavers to sell cloth to them at low and dictated prices. The Company's servants even monopolised the raw material needed by artisans and charged a high price for them. William Bolts, a contemporary wrote that "the roguery practised in this department is beyond imagination but all terminates in the defrauding of the poor weaver........." The English indigo planters of Bengal took their pound of flesh from the cultivator. Above all, the Company appropriated the surplus revenue of Bengal which alone amounted to nearly £4 million during 1764-1771.[5] Adam Smith referred to the unilateral outflow of goods and treasure of India to Britain as "plunder" and in the context referred to the Court of Proprietors as the Court "for the appointment of plunderers of India".

The Drain of Wealth

The constant flow of wealth from India to England for which India did not get an adequate economic, commercial or material return has been described by Indian national leaders and economists as 'drain' of wealth from India. The drain of wealth was interpreted as an indirect tribute extracted by imperial Britain from India year after year.

Concept of Economic drain. In the mercantilist concept an economic drain takes place if gold and silver flow out of the country as a consequence of an adverse balance of trade. In the 50 years before the battle of Plassey (1757), the East India Company had imported bullion worth £ 20

---

5. For detailed calculations see R.C. Dutt, *Economic History of India*, vol. i, p. 46.

million into India to balance the exports over imports from India. British mercantilists were highly critical of the trade policies of the Company. Even the British government adopted a series of measures to restrict or prohibit the imports of Indian textiles into England. Apart from other measures, in 1720 the British government forbade the wear or use of Indian silks and calicoes in England on pain of a penalty of £ 5 for each offence on the weaver and of £ 20 on the seller.

After Plassey the situation was reversed and the drain of wealth took an outward turn as England gradually acquired monopolistic control over the Indian economy. After the East India Company extended its territorial aggression in India and began to administer territories and acquired control over the surplus revenues of India, the shape of drain underwent a change. Henceforth the Company had a recurring surplus which accrued from (*a*) profits from oppressive land revenue policy, (*b*) profits from its trade resulting from monopolistic control over Indian markets, and (*c*) exactions made by the Company's officials. All this 'surplus' was used by Company as an "investment" *i.e.* for making purchases of exportable items in India and elsewhere. Against the exports of goods made out of this 'investment', India did not get anything in return. This system was brought to an end by the Charter Act of 1813 when the territorial and commercial revenues of the Company were separated.

From 1813 onwards economic drain took the form of 'unrequited' exports. Barring a few exceptional years, favourable balance of trade had been the normal feature of our foreign trade till the outbreak of World War II. The focal point of the Drain Theory was that a portion of the national product of India was not available for consumption for her people or for capital formation, but was being drained away to England for political reasons—and India did not get an adequate economic return for it.

Constituents of Economic Drain

The imperial rulers used thousand and one methods to skin the Indian cat. The Indian administration was in British hands and was conducted in a manner to subserve the interests of England. The drain mainly consisted of the following:—

1. Home Charges. Home charges refer to the expenditure incurred in England by the Secretary of State on behalf of India. Before the Revolt of 1857 the Home charges varied from 10% to 13% of the average revenues of India. After the Revolt the proportion shot up to 24% in the period 1897–1901. In 1901–02, the Home charges amounted to £ 17.36 million. During 1921–22, the Home charges sharply increased to 40% of the total revenue of the Central Government. The main constituents of Home charges were:

(*a*) **Dividend to the shareholders of the East India Company.** The Charter Act of 1833 provided for an annual dividend of £ 630,000 to be paid to the shareholders of the Company out of the Indian revenues till 1874. In 1874 the loan of £ 4.5 million was raised to redeem the stock at a premium of 100%.

(*b*) **Interest on Public Debt raised abroad.** The East Indian Company had piled up a public debt of £ 70 million (mostly incurred by the aggressive wars waged by the Company) to dislodge Indian rulers from their principalities. By 1900 the public debt had risen to £ 224 million. Part of the debt was raised for productive purposes *i.e.*, for construction of railways, irrigation facilities and public works.

Sir Theodore Morrison in his lectures on "Economic Transition in India" has drawn attention to the aspect that railway investment brought into existence in India a new industry, generated employment and became the harbinger of industrial prosperity to India. Similarly, foreign capital investment for development of irrigation brought more areas under irrigation and brought immense advantages. And, Morrison adds, India got loans at low rate of interest. It must be pointed out that railways, irrigation works were designed and worked for the benefit of England. Because of England's tight control over the Indian economy, the railways did not bring about industrialization for India (for railway stores were purchased in England). Nor did it create employment opportunities; rather it created unemployment by destroying Indian weaving industry, thereby creating lot of unemployment. In this matter even Karl Marx proved to be a wrong prophet.

(*c*) **Civil and Military charges.** These included payments towards pensions and furloughs of British officers in the civil and military departments in India; expenses on India Office establishment in London; payments to the British war office etc., etc. All these charges were solely due to India's subjection to foreign rule.

(*d*) **Store purchases in England.** The Secretary of State and the Government of India purchased stores for the Military, Civil and Marine Departments in the English market. The annual average expenditure on stores varied from 10% to 12% of the Home charges between 1861–1920.

2. Interest on Foreign Capital Investments. Interest and profits on private foreign capital were another important leakage from the national income stream. Finance capital entered the Indian market in the 20th century. During the inter-war period the payments on this account roughly varied between Rs. 30 crores to 60 crores per annum. It must be pointed out that foreign capitalists were the least interested in industrial development of India; rather they exploited Indian resources for their own benefit and infact thwarted indigenous capitalist enterprise by fair and foul means.

3. Foreign Banking, Insurance and Shipping Companies. For banking, insurance and shipping services India had to make huge payments. Apart from constituting a drain on Indian resources, unrestricted activities of these foreign companies stunted the growth of Indian enterprise in these spheres.

Estimates of Economic Drain

Scholarly estimates about the drain of wealth from India widely differ depending on the period under review and the method of calculations employed. Writing in 1859, George Wingate estimated the drain at £ 4,221,611 p.a. for the seventeen years between 1835–1851 or a total of £ 71,767,387. In 1901, William Digby estimated the total drain from 1757 to 1815 to have been somewhere between £ 500 to £ 1000 million. Writing in 1948, an American scholar, Professor Holden Furber, put the annual drain figure for the period 1783–93 at £ 1.9 million. It should be kept in view that during the period under review the Company ruled over very limited territories in India. Indian nationalists like Dadabhai Naoroji, G.V. Joshi, D. E. Wacha, R.C. Dutt, etc. gave their own calculations. Dadabhai gave various estimates and often revised the basis of his calculations. He put the drain figure from the beginning of British rule down to 1865–66 at a total of £ 1500 million. In 1897, he reckoned the drain at Rs. 359 crores for the ten years 1883–92. In 1901, D. E. Wacha put the average drain from 1860 to 1900 at Rs 30 to 40 crores p.a. The same year R. C. Dutt calculated the drain at nearly £ 22 million p.a. Prof. C. N. Vakil calculated that the drain from 1834 to 1924 was anywhere between £ 394 to £ 591 million. Writing in 1963, V. I. Pavlov estimated that in the 1930's the British colonists squeezed India of £ 130 to £ 140 million in pure tribute alone and concluded, "With this amount India could annually construct three plants of the Bhilai type, each of which would exceed in capacity the country's iron and steel industry in the colonial period".[6]

Economic Consequences of the Drain

Dadabhai Naoroji described the drain of wealth as the "evil of all evils" and the main cause of Indian poverty. He maintained that Britain was "bleeding India white". In a letter to Sunderland in 1905, Naoroji wrote, "The lot of India is a very sad one. Her condition is that of master and a slave; but it is worse; it is that of a plundered nation in the hands of constant plunderers with the plunder carried away clean out of the land. In the case of plundering raids occasionally made on India before the English came the invaders went away...The British invasion in continuous and the plunder goes right on". Comparing the plundering raids of medieval rulers with the British methods of colonial plunder,

---

6. Pavlov, V.I.: *Economic Freedom versus Imperialism* (New Delhi, 1963), p. 7.

another critic has pointed out that the old time plunder had to restrict itself to richmen's houses and godowns where the wealth was accumulated; it was not worthwhile ransacking very little hut and little village. In contrast, the colonial plunder could reach the most lowly, the most humble and the most remote. Thus, British methods of exploitation though less painful were more thorough and resembled the blood-sucking leeches.

The drain of wealth checked and retarded capital accumulation in India, thereby retarding the industrialization of India. Indian products and treasure drained to England without adequate return was of great help in creating conditions in that country conducive for the growth of British factory industry in the early stages of the industrial revolution. What is worse is that part of the British capital entered India as Finance Capital and further drained India of her wealth. Naoroji complained, "British India's own wealth is carried out of it and then that wealth is brought back to it in the shape of loans, and for these loans she must find so much for interest, the whole thing moving in a most vicious and provoking circle". The drain had an immense effect on income and employment potential within India. R. C. Dutt quoted the Indian poet as saying that taxation raised by a king is like the moisture of the earth sucked up by the sun, to be returned to the earth as fertilising rain. Dutt lamented that the moisture raised from the Indian soil under colonial rule descended as fertilising rain largely on England and not India.

Naoroji also referred to the 'moral drain' which, according to him, consisted in the exclusion of Indians, from positions of trust and responsibility in their own land. He wrote, "All the talent and nobility of intellect and soul, which nature gives to every country is to India a lost treasure. There is, thus a triple dwarfing or stunting of the Indian race is going on under the present system of administration". Recently some scholars have questioned some of the presumptions of the Drain theorists. Ranade's emphasis on sociological causes of economic backwardness has been reiterated. Morris D. Morris has emphasised the "gestation" theory and Britain's role of "a night watchman, providing security, rational administration and a modicum of social overheads on the basis of which economic progress was expected to occur". Indian scholars have referred to the malutilisation and under-utilisation of foreign capital and colonial administration's deliberate policy of "guided underdevelopment".

In the historical perspective, the Drain of wealth theory high-lighted the foreign and exploitative character of British rule in a language within the comprehension of the average Indian. During our Freedom Struggle the Drain theory became a convenient slogan for any damnation of British colonial rule in India.

Deindustrialization: Decline of Indian Handicrafts

During the first half of the 19th century or even upto 1880 India's economy witnessed a strange phenomenon. While Western countries were experiencing industrialization, India suffered a period of industrial decline. This process has been described as 'de-industrialization'.

India's traditional handicraft industry decayed beyond recovery. The period of decline of Indian handicrafts was contemporaneous with the firm foundation of the Industrial Revolution in England and England's tight control over the strings of Indian economy.

Western scholars like Morris D. Morris and A. Thorner are never weary of emphasising the point that the decline of handicraft industries was inevitable and was a worldwide phenomenon and was a logical outcome and integral part of the Industrial Revolution and the coming of the factory system.

The peculiar situation in India–very different from the developments in European countries and North America–may be summarised thus :

(a) Nineteenth century India witnessed a steep decline of handicrafts, a process which continued well into the 20th century, and

(b) Unlike European countries India was not compensated by a sufficient rise of modern industry.

As a result of (*a*) and (*b*) there was a net decline in the number and proportion of the Indian population engaged in industry.

The 19th century was the period of Industrial Capital *i.e.*, Britain's rising industrialists and trading interests launched a new economic offensive based on the principles of free trade against India. Their persistent propaganda and lobbying resulted in the abolition of the Company's monopoly of Indian trade by the Charter Act of 1813. A change came in the character of Indo-British trade. So far India had been chiefly an exporting country; now onwards it became an importing country. English twist and cotton stuffs flooded Indian markets, spelling ruination of Indian weaving industry. The government of William Bentinck noted in 1834, "The misery hardly finds a parallel in the history of commerce. The bones of the cotton weavers are bleaching the plains of India". In a similar vein, Karl Marx, a shrewd contemporary observer, remarked, "It was the British intrude who broke up the Indian handloom and destroyed the spinning wheel. England began with depriving the Indian cottons from the European market; it then introduced twist into Hindustan and in the end inundated the very mother country of cotton with cottons'. Dr. D. R. Gadgil[7] has mentioned three principal causes which operated in the first half of the 19th century in bringing about a rapid decline in the artistic excellence and economic importance of Indian handicrafts. These were : (1) The disappearance of native Indian courts which patronised fancy arts and handicrafts and often employed the best craftsmen on a regular salary basis. (2) The establishment of an alien rule, with the influence of the many foreign influences that such a change in the nature of government meant. New classes rose after the establishment of British rule, namely the European officials and the new Indian educated professional class. The European bureaucracy normally patronised English–made products and the Indian Western-educated professional class imitated European standards and poured scorn on everything Indian. (3) The competition of a more highly-developed form of machine-industry. Another writer, Major B. D. Basu puts more emphasis on the use of political power by England to strangle Indian handicrafts.[8] He lists the imperial methods thus: (*i*) the forcing of British Free Trade on India, (*ii*) imposing heavy duties on Indian manufactures in England, (*iii*) the export of raw materials from India, (*iv*) the transit and custom duties, (*v*) granting special privileges to the British manufactures in India, (*vi*) compelling Indian artisans to divulge their trade secrets, (*vii*) holding of exhibitions, and (*viii*) building railways in India.

This is general agreement among scholars that the decline of Indian handicrafts was not universal "for the periods differed from one part of the country to another". Rajasthan, for example, was opened by railways after 1911, hence the decline occurred after that. Further, despite heavy odds the Indian handicrafts could not be completely wiped out. The rural population steeped in poverty and tranditionalism continued to purchase comparatively cheaper khadi cloth and village-made iron and wooden agricultural ploughs and other implements. The Swadeshi movement in the beginning of the 20th century popularised indigenous products on patriotic grounds and thus created some market for khadi in the urban areas. In the Gandhian era, village industries received encouragement and popularization of khadi kept alive Indian handicrafts.

The rise of capitalism and machine-made industries which heralded the Industrial Revolution in England and European countries gave a big jolt to handicraft industry—the price for industrialization—in all parts of the world but the unfortunate situation in India was that unlike the European development the decline of indigenous handicrafts in India was without the compensating development of modern machine industry.

Even after the rise of modern industry, in India after World War I, the process of de-industrialization of India continued *i.e.*, there was a fall in the percentage of workers in industry and

---

7. Gadgil, D. R. : *The Industrial Evolution of India in Recent Times* (Delhi, 1973) p. 38.
8. Basu, B. D. : *Ruin of Indian Trade and Industries*, pp. 10-11.

increase in the percentage of the agricultural working force. A reputed economist, Colin Clark, compiled a table indicating that from 1881 to 1911 the proportion of the working force engaged in "manufacture mining and construction" fell by half, from 35% to 17%.

Recently some Western scholars like Morris D. Morris have challenged the 'imperial exploitation thesis' put forward by Indian national writers and publicists[9] and instead argued that colonial rule "probably stimulated economic activity in India in a way which had never been possible before"[10] and that "the handloom weavers were at least no fewer in number and no worse off economically at the end of the period than at the beginning" and possibly "absolute growth occurred"[11] A. and D. Thorner have compared the census data for 1881 with that for 1931 in respect to workers engaged in Agriculture and Manufacture respectively and come to the conclusion that "the industrial distribution of the modern working force from 1881 to 1931 stood still"[12]. All the same, they concede that probably (?) the major shift from industry to agriculture happened sometime between 1815 and 1880[13].

A recurrent theme of national writers of all shaded of opinion—Moderates, Extremists and Gandhites—was that Britain developed those aspects of Indian economy—like railways, ports and irrigation developments—which subserved the economic interests of industrialised Britain and ignored and even thwarted the growth of modern industry within India. During our Freedom struggle the slogans of 'de-industrialisation' and Britain's callous indifference to Indian industrial development became a rallying slogan in the anti-colonial struggle.

Ruralization of Indian Economy

With de-industrialization, Indian economy tended to become more and more agricultural. Millions of manufacturing classes in industrial towns like Dacca, Murshidabad, Surat and other places were rendered jobless and drifted from towns to villages for a livelihood. This increasing dependence of the population on agriculture for subsistence and slant of the Indian economy on production of agricultural goods and raw materials—to the neglect of industrial development—has been described as a trend towards ruralization or peasantization of the Indian economy. British writers of the 19th and 20th centuries took pride in describing India as traditionally an agricultural country.

A close examination of the British economic policy towards India makes it abundantly clear that Britain deliberately adopted such policies which ruined the competing handicraft industries of India; it then helped develop the agricultural resources of India to make it "an agricultural farm" of industrialised Britain. As early as 17 March 1769 the Court of Directors desired the Company's agents in Bengal to encourage the manufacture of raw silk and discourage manufactured silk fabrics; this objective was to be achieved by forcing the silk-winders to work in the Company's factories and prohibit them from working in their homes. Commending this policy of compulsion-cum-encouragement, a Select Committee of the House of Commons in 1783 desired a perfect plan of policy "to change the whole face of that industrial country, in order to render it a field of the produce of crude material subservient to the manufactures of Great Britain". R. C. Dutt has rightly pointed out that this resolution settled policy of England towards India till 1833 and Later. "It effectively stamped out many of the national industries of India for the benefit of English manufactures". [14]

---

9. J. L. Nehru wrote, "Foreign political domination led to a rapid destruction of the economy India had built up... without anything positive or constructive taking its place" causing "poverty and degradation beyond measure". *Discovery of India*, 4th edition. pp. 36, 283.
10. Morris D. Morris *et al* : *Indian Economy in the 19th Century*, p. 8.
11. *Ibid* p. 9.
12. A. and D. Thorner, *Land and Labour in India*, p. 77.
13. *Ibid*.
14. Dutt, R. C., *Economic History of India* (London, 6th edition) Vol. I, p. 46

The Industrial Revolution had brought about a change in the pattern of England's economic development; its expanding textile industries needed raw material for its factories and markets for the sale of her industrial products. These developments called for a change in methods of British colonial exploitation in India and the need was felt to replace mercantile capitalism by free-trade capitalism. The abolition of the Company's monopoly of trade with India (by Charter Act, 1813) and winding up of its commercial business (by Charter Act, 1833) should be viewed in the backdrop of these developments.

Industrialised Britain desired the development of the vast potential of India's agricultural resources. However, a possible snag was the poor quality of Indian raw material. To make good this deficiency, the British nationals needed to be given permission for free entry and settlement in India. The Charter Act of 1833 removed all restrictions on European immigration and acquisition of landed property in India. And British capital flowed to develop India's plantation industry—in tea, coffee, indigo and jute cultivation. The Government of India provided adequate facilities. The Assam Wasteland Rules provided for the grant of extensive tracts of land up to 3000 acres per holder as freehold property exempted from land tax on payment of fixed sums. The tea planters of Assam used force and fraud to recruit labour for work in tea estates. The Government of India provided the legislative umbrella by legalising their exploitation. Act XIII of 1859 and Inland Immigration Act of 1882 made breach of contract a criminal offence and authorized the tea planters to arrest a run-away labourer without any warrant.

Alice and Daniel Thorners have rightly guessed that a major shift from industry to agriculture in India happened between 1815 and 1880. Unfortunately, no statistical record is available before the first census of 1881. R. P. Dutt, after a close examination of the census from 1891 to 1921, has calculated the increase in the percentage of the population dependent on agriculture thus :[15]

Year	Percentage of population dependent on agriculture
1891	61.1%
1901	66.5%
1911	72.2%
1921	73.0%

The census of 1931 put the figure of the population engaged in "agricultural and pastoral pursuits" at 61.1%. Vera Anstey ascribes this decline in number as "illusory... to be accounted for by a change in classification, not of occupation".

The over-pressure on agriculture created serious distortions in Indian economy apart from creating serious problems in the agrarian sector. The increase in the number of persons in agriculture did not mean increase in agricultural production, but impoverishment of the rural masses. A number of factors—historical, political, economic and social—blocked the modernisation of Indian agriculture and worked as a 'built-in depressor'. The 'stagnation' in Indian agricultural production amidst increasing population accounted for recurring famines and increasing poverty in the 19th and first quarter of the 20th century.

Commercialization of Indian Agriculture

In the latter half of the 19th century another significant trend in Indian agriculture was the emergence of the commercialization of agriculture. So far agriculture had been a way of life rather than a business enterprise. Now agriculture began to be influenced by commercial consideration *i.e.* certain specialised crops began to be grown not for consumption in the village but for sale in the national and even international markets. Commercial crops like cotton, jute, groundnuts, oilseeds, sugarcane, tobacco, etc. were more remunerative than foodgrains. Again, the cultivation of crops like condiments,

---

15. Dutt, R. P. : *India To-day* (Calcutta, 1979), p. 203.

spices, fruits and vegetables could cater to a wider market. Perhaps, the commercialization trend reached the highest level of development in the plantation industry *i.e.* in tea, coffee, rubber, etc. which were all produced for sale in a wider market.

A number of factors encouraged specialisation and commercialization of the new market trend. The spread of money economy, the replacement of custom and tradition by competition and contract, the growth of internal and external trade, the emergence of a unified national market (facilitated by expansion of railways and road transport) and the boost to international trade given by entry of British Finance Capital etc.

For the Indian peasant, commercialization seemed a forced process. To meet the excessive land revenue demand of the state and the high rates fo interest charged by the moneylender, the cultivator perforce had to rush a part of his harvest into the market and sell it at whatever price it fetched. Many poor cultivators had to buy back after six months part of the crop they had sold away at low prices at harvest time. Further, Indian agriculture began to be influenced by widely-fluctuating world prices. The cotton boom of the 1860s pushed up the prices but mostly benefited the host of intermediaries, while the slump in prices in 1866 hit the cultivator the most—bringing in its turn heavy indebtedness, famine and agrarian riots in the Deccan of the 1870s. Thus, the cultivator hardly emerged better from the new commercialization development.

Nor did modernisation lead to increase in agricultural production. A number of factors—historical, economic and social—served as a 'built-in depresser' and kept low the total agricultural output. Daniel Thorner rightly speaks of the 1890–1947 decades as a period of agricultural "stagnation".

Entry of British Finance Capital in India

In modern times underdeveloped and developing countries welcome an inflow of capital, enterprise, technology, etc. from advanced countries to supplement domestic resources and initiate the process of economic development. The unfortunate development with India in the colonial era was that foreign capital entered India in a big way but was used by the colonial administration not for development of colonial economy but for fuller exploitation of Indian resources. Capital inflow thus became another instrument of Indian exploitation.

Parliamentary papers connected with the East India Company make it abundantly clear that there was no investment of British capital in India till 1833 *i.e.* throughout the period the Company traded. The flow of British capital into India became significant only after 1857, penetrated into diverse economic fields in the latter half of the 19th century but tightened its tentacles over India in the 20th century in the form of finance capital. Finance capital became the new most powerful mode of colonial exploitation.

Forms of Investment. British capital investment in India normally took two basic forms :

(*i*) Loans raised in England by the Secretary of State on behalf of Indian Government and by semi-public organisation mostly for investment in railways, irrigation, developments of ports, hydro-electric projects etc.

(*ii*) Foreign business investments in India.

It has been estimated that before 1914 nearly 97% of British capital investments in India were diverted towards completion of economic overheads (mainly railways, road transport, merchant shipping, etc.), mining industry (coal and gold mining), development of financial houses (banking, finance, insurance, etc.)—towards promotion of auxiliaries calculated to fuller commercial exploitation of India's natural resources. British capital went into activities that were complementary to British industries and was in no way planned for industrial development of India.

British capitalists retained a dominant control over Indian banking, commerce, exchange and insurance and with their capital resources and official patronage dominated industrial sectors in

India's economy. According to an estimate, in 1913 foreign banks held over 3/4th of the total bank deposits while the Indian banks could attract only 1/4th of the deposits. An Indian industrialist complained that racial and political discrimination were made in the matter of credit advances and Indians usually did not receive in matters of credit the treatment that their assets entitled them to, while, on the other hand, British businessmen were frequently allowed larger credit than, what on ordinary business principles, they ought to have got.

Estimates of Foreign Capital Investment in India. Various estimates have been made of foreign capital in India. Some of the estimates are:

Source	Year in question	Amount (£million)
1. Edgar Crammond	1896	294
2. George Paish	1909-10	365
3. H. E. Howard	1911	450
4. G. D. Birla	1929	1000
5. Findlay Shirras	1929	500
6. V. K. R. V. Rao	1929	637.5
7. B. R. Shenoy	1939	829.79

The above estimates may not be taken as very accurate, but only as a broad indication. For example, Crammond's and Paish's estimates include British investments in India, Ceylon and Burma. The other estimates suffer from some conceptual and statistical flaws.

During the Second World War there was a large repatriation of foreign capital. India had a large balance of payments surplus mainly due to massive wartime purchases of Indian goods by the British government for war purposes. A Reserve Bank survey put India's gross foreign liabilities in June 1948 at about Rs 474 crores.

Many multinationals operated their subsidiary companies in India and penetrated deep into almost every sector of Indian economy—like Imperial Chemical Industries, Hindustan Lever Ltd., Dunlop, ITC, GEC, GKW, Union Carbide, Ashok Leyland and numerous pharmaceutical companies. Even after Independence, these companies are doing good business. In spite of the Monopolies and Restrictive Trade Practices Act (1969) and Foreign Exchange Regulation Act (1973), the multinationals are maintaining their hold on the Indian market.

Rise of Modern Industry:
Colonial Situation and State Policy

The British rulers of India did not conceive of an industrialized India, much less plan for her industrialization. Rather, the British rulers deliberately followed policies to 'de-industrialize' India and convert it and preserve it as 'an agricultural farm' of industrialized Britain. However, compulsions of maintaining imperial control over the country and its thorough economic exploitation led Britain to construct roads, railways, posts and telegraph lines, develop ports, irrigation works, banking, exchange and insurance facilities etc.—developments which provided the material basis for the beginning of modern industry in India. "The railways", wrote Lord Hardinge in 1846, "were planned for the prevention of insurrection, the speedy termination of war or the safety of the Empire". Lord Dalhousie touched on the commercial benefits from railway construction when he wrote in 1853, "England is calling aloud for the cotton which India does already produce in some degree, and would produce sufficient in quality, and plentiful in quantity, if only there were provided the fitting means of conveyance for it from distant plains to the several ports adopted for its shipment. Every increase of facilities for trade has been attended, as we have seen, with an increased demand for articles of European produce in the most distant markets of India". All the same, the construction of railways in India stimulated the growth of a number of other industries. The same year Dalhousie penned his minute on Railways. Karl Marx, gifted with a rare insight into historical developments, wrote for the *New York Daily Tribune* on 22 July, 1853: "When you have once introduced machinery into the locomotion of a country, which possesses iron and coal, you are unable to withhold it from its fabrication. You cannot maintain a net of railways over an immense country without introducing all those industrial processes necessary to meet the immediate and current wants of railway locomotion, and out of which there must grow the application of machinery to those branches of industry not immediately connected with railways. The railway system will therefore become, in India, truly the fore runner of modern Industry."[16]

Rise of Indian National Bourgeoisie. Indian traders, money-lenders and bankers had amassed some wealth as junior partners of English merchant capitalists in India. Their role fitted in the British scheme of colonial exploitation. The Indian money-lender provided loans to hard-pressed agriculturists and thus facilitated the state collection of land revenue; the loans also made possible the marketing of agricultural products. The Indian trader carried imported British products to the remotest corners of India and also helped in the movement of Indian agricultural products to the ports for export to the European market. The indigenous bankers helped both in the process of distribution and collection.

British capitalism did not permit Indian enterprise to compete with it and whenever necessary thwarted its natural growth. The colonial situation retarded the development of a healthy and independent industrial bourgeoisie. Thus Indian capitalism had a weak growth in an unhealthy environment and its development was different from other independent countries like Germany and Japan.

Growth of Indian Capitalist Enterprise. The textile industry first attracted the attention of the Parsi and Gujarati entrepreneurs. Bombay had the necessary raw materials, moist climate, availability of cheap labour and even a ready market for textiles. Hence a beginning in textile industry was made in Bombay in the 1850s. The boom in cotton prices resultant from the American Civil War (1861–65) and the subsequent depression adversely affected the growth of the industry. The industry recovered in the 1870s and number of mills rose to 56 by 1879, touched the figure of 266 by 1904-5 employing nearly two lakh workers. However, the Indian cotton textile industry faced many challenges *viz.* (*i*) competition from Lancashire and Manchester textile products, (*ii*) hostility from Indian colonial administration through discriminatory tariff and excise policies, (*iii*) removal of duties on cotton goods during 1879-82, (*iv*) absence of long-term credit facilities from European-owned and European-dominated banking industry, (*v*) expansion of railway system and concessional freight rates favouring movement of goods with port towns against linkages between inland centres, (*vi*) dependence on imported plant and equipment, and (*vii*) absence of state protection from the colonial administration.

In spite of the heavy odds, the Indian industrialists stood their ground by their ingenuity and cost reductions (including exploitation of labour). The Swadeshi Movement of the early 20th century gave some impetus to textile industry by popularising the use of Indian-made goods. The moral of these developments was that indigenous industrial developments was bound up with India's Freedom Struggle. From this time onwards we find the Indian capitalist class wooing and supporting the leadership in the Indian National Congress and financing some of its programmes and policies.

A significant development was the setting up of the first ever Tata Iron and Steel Company at Jamshedpur by Jamsedji Tata in 1907. It produced pig iron in 1911 and steel by 1913.

The 1850s and 1860s also witnessed the growth of plantation industries (*i.e.* indigo, tea, coffee, rubber etc.), jute mills and coal mines. Around 1880 twenty jute mills and 56 coal mines were working, increasing by 1895 to 29 jute mills and 123 coal mines. However, most of the industries were started and managed by British capitalists under encouragement from the Government of India.

---

16. For details of Marx's views on *The Future Results of the British Rule in India* see Appendix B.

Impact of First World War. The First World War proved a boon for Indian industrialists and gave Indian industries some sort of a protection against foreign competition. Foreign imports fell to a very low level while there was increase in Government purchases for war purposes. Further, exports of raw material became less which kept down their prices to the advantage of Indian industrialists. Again, wages did not rise much. All these advantages made possible fabulous profits during the war.

Another impact of the war was the quickening in the pace of political awakening and the Indian demand for protection of Indian industries out of patriotic considerations. The Government response was somewhat favourable though mainly guided by the twin objectives of (*a*) search for more revenue, and (*b*) strategic necessity for developing some degree of economic self-sufficiency. In 1915, Lord Hardinge announced, "After the war India will consider herself entitled to demand the utmost help which her Government can afford, to enable her to take place, so far as circumstances permit, as a manufacturing country." As a first step, the Government appointed an Industrial Commission in 1916 to report on possible openings for Indian capital enterprise in industry and commerce and to suggest the manner in which Government could help industrial development.

As a conciliatory gesture, in April 1917, the Government established the Indian Munitions Board which recommended a policy of purchase of stores for the army inside India and of setting up new plants in India for production of such stores.

Protection During Inter-War Period (1918–39). The end of the war in 1918 brought in focus the question of protection of Indian industry. Foreign competition strained their resources and shook some industries. Some remedial measures became inevitable and were willy-nilly adopted by the Colonial administration. Among the measures adopted were :—

(1) In December 1919 the Government appointed a Stores Purchase Committee which recommended the need for providing Indian industry with guaranteed minimum orders for Goverment purchases.

(2) The Montagu-Chelmsford Reforms favoured a policy of fiscal autonomy for India, and it was broadly agreed that "the Secretary of State should, as far as possible, avoid interference (in fiscal matters) when Government of India and its Législature are in agreement".

(3) In October 1921, the Government appointed a Fiscal Commission under the Chairmanship of Sir Ibrahim Rahimtoola. In its report submitted in 1923, the Commission recommended a policy of protection for industries in the initial stage of development or in cases where industries faced unfair competition. It laid down a Triple Formula for industries claiming fiscal protection, *viz.*,

(*a*) The industry in question should possess natural advantages such as sufficient supply of raw material, labour, cheap power and a ready home market.

(*b*) The industry cannot develop without protection or as rapidly as is desirable in the interests of the country.

(*c*) The industry must be able to eventually face world competition without protection.

The Commission also recommended the establishment of a Tariff Board to consider applications for fiscal protection. Though the Indian opinion was critical of the Triple Formula, yet under the new policy protection was granted to steel industry (1924), tinplate industry (1924), paper industry (1925), match industry (1928), cotton textile industry (1930), heavy chemicals industry (1931), sugar industry (1932) and silk yarn and piece-goods industry (1934), Some Indian industries like cement, glass and petroleum-refining were denied protection. The Government of India also accepted the system of Imperial Preferences (consolidated by the Ottawa Imperial Conference of 1932) based on concessional tariffs among members of the British empire. Since the system did not work in the interests of India, it was not renewed in 1936.

Despite the negative aspects of the over-valued rupee- £ exchange ratio of 1. s. 6 d. (after 1926), the Great Depression of 1929–30 and the imposed Imperial Preference System, Indian industry made significant progress during 1923-39.

Industrial Development, State Policy and Indian Capitalist Class (1939–47). The Second World War brought a period of scarcity and famine conditions for the general population but a period of super profits for the Indian businessman. The near stoppage of industrial imports amidst large-scale war requirements created specially favourable circumstances for the growth and consolidation of Indian capitalism. The unscrupulous producers and traders added to their profits through speculation, hoarding and black-marketing.

During the war the existing capitalist enterprises did not expand much nor new enterprises came into existence for the necessary plant and equipment could not be imported from abroad. All the same, war-time extraordinary profits helped the Indian capitalist to considerably expand his activities in various directions. Indian big business houses sponsored new Joint Stock Companies, promoted new banks (and utilized the bulk of their credit), floated life insurance companies (and used their profits). Another significant development was the growing collaboration between Indian and Foreign capitalists as was evident in a number of joint Indo-British ventures as Managing Agencies and joint industrial enterprises. Still a new trend was the Indian Big Business policy of diversification into factory industry, banks, insurance, trading, service agencies, speculation in commodities, bullion, stocks and shares, etc. All such developments made big business houses bigger still before the war ended in 1945.

In 1945, the Government set up a new Tariff Board to examine claims of industries for protection. The Board laid down new and more liberal guidelines *viz*:

(1) The industry seeking protection should have been established and conducted on sound business lines, and

(2) Either the industry in question should have natural and economic advantages and have potential to develop and function without protection within a reasonable time,

(3) Or the industry should deserve protection in national interest and the probable cost of such protection to the community was not excessive.

Although the above recommendations were more liberal than the Triple Formula laid down in 1923, yet it was considered insufficient, for the Tariff Board was authorised to recommend protection or assistance for not more than three years. It may be said that the rise of modern industrial enterprise in India has strengthened the Indian capitalist class. The Capitalist class drew strength from the nationalist movement and in turn sustained it by financial assistance. On the eve of independence, the Indian capitalist had struck roots and became a significant socio-economic force with the potential to influence political decisions.

British Legacy of Poverty and Under-developed Economy

A century and half of British rule in India has left behind a legacy of extreme poverty and economic backwardness both in the agricultural and industrial sectors. When the British withdrew from India in 1947 they left behind the world's most refractory land problem—hierarchy of land rights, insecurity of tenure, primitive techniques of cultivation, low per acre yield, fragmented agricultural holdings, money-lenders in control of credit and marketing of crops, investment in agriculture very shy. In short, the spectre of famine stared the country and India, 'one of the granaries of Asia, had been converted into a land of perpetual scarcity and famine'. The industrial sector presented an equally unhappy picture—lop-sided development of Indian industries, low production techniques, poor lot of the industrial worker and, above all, the continuing strangle-hold of British finance capital.

The British left behind a poor people with a low per capita income. Dadabhai Naoroji was the first Indian who attempted an estimate of Indian national income. Using rough and ready methods he estimated the average per capita income for 1867–68 to be Rs. 20 per annum. The official estimate calculated by Major Evelyn Baring and David Balfour put the average per capita income for 1882 at Rs. 27. In 1901, Curzon's government calculated the per capita income at Rs. 30 for the year 1897–98. The same year William Digby put the average per capita income for British India at Rs. 18 for the year 1899 *i.e.*, 43% less than that of Curzon for 1898–99. Dr. V.K.R.V. Rao used more sophisticated methods to assess the national income of the whole of India for the year 1931–32 and settled the per capita income at an average of Rs. 62 plus or minus 6%. Shah and Khambata, who also published their findings about national income estimate in 1924, commented, "The average Indian income is just enough either to feed two men in every three of the population, or give them all two in place of every three meals they need, on condition that they all consent to go naked, live out of doors all the year round, have no amusement, or recreation and want nothing else but food, and that the lowest, the coarsest and the least nutritious".

Thus when Britain quit India in 1947, it left behind an economy reeling under centuries of colonial exploitation and guided underdevelopment.

SELECT REFERENCES

1. Anstey, Vera : *Economic Development of India.*
2. Digby, William : *'Prosperous' British India.*
3. Dutt, R. C. : *Economic History of India*, 2 vols.
4. Gadgil, D. R. : *The Industrial Evolution of India in Recent Times.*
5. Kumar, Dharma (Ed.) : *Cambridge Economic History of India*, vol. II.
6. Morris D. Morris (Ed.) : *Indian Economy in the Nineteenth Century.*
7. Pavlov, V. I. : *The Indian Capitalist Class : A Historical Study.*
8. Singh, V. B. (Ed.) : *Economic History of India, 1857–1956.*
9. Tomlinson, B. R. : *The Political Economy of the Raj, 1914-47.*
10. Tomlinson, B. R. : *The Economy of Modern India 1860–1970* (New Cambridge History of India).

47

THE CONSTITUTION OF THE INDIAN REPUBLIC

> Many people hastily assume that the working of the Constitution has revealed its grave shortcomings, whereas the truth of the matter is that it is a noble Constitution which has been worked in an ignoble spirit.
>
> —*N.A. Palkhivala*

The Constitution of India was finalised by the Constituent Assembly on November 26, 1949 and came into force on January 26, 1950.

The Indian Constitution is a very long and elaborate document. It originally contained 395 Articles arranged in twenty-two parts and Twelve Schedules. Since then additions have been made by numerous amendments and some provisions have been repealed.

The Preamble. The Preamble to the Constitution reads:

We, the people of India, having solemnly resolved to constitute India into a Sovereign Socialist Secular Democratic Republic and to secure to all its citizens:

JUSTICE, social, economic and political;

LIBERTY of thought, expression, belief, faith and worship;

EQUALITY of status and of opportunity;

and to promote among them all

FRATERNITY assuring the dignity of the individual and the unity of the Nation;

In our Constituent Assembly this twenty-sixth day of November, 1949 do hereby adopt, enact and give to ourselves this Constitution.

Thus, the sovereign authority in India is vested in the people. The four essentials of democracy–Justice, Liberty, Equality and Fraternity–are the principal objectives of the Constitution. The chapters on Fundamental Rights and Directive Principles of State Policy contain elaborate provisions for giving practical shape to these basic principles.

Fundamental Rights. The rights which a constitution guarantees to the citizens are usually known as Natural Rights or Fundamental Rights. Democracy means the government of the majority party. Fundamental Right aim at preventing the government in power and the legislature from becoming totalitarian; in so doing Fundamental Rights afford the individual an opportunity for fuller self-development. Fundamental Rights are justiciable and any citizen can move the Supreme Court for their enforcement. The Supreme Court can declare all laws inconsistent with or in derogation of the Fundamental Rights as void. However, the Fundamental Rights are not absolute and the State is allowed to impose limitations on them in case of necessity. The 42nd Constitution Amendment Bill (1976) has upheld the power of the Parliament to amend the Fundamental Rights.

Part II of the Constitution provides for six broad categories of Fundamental Rights[1] viz., (*i*) *Right to Equality* including equality before the law, prohibition of discrimination on grounds of religion, race, caste, sex, or place of birth and equality of opportunity in matters of employment; (*ii*) *right to Freedom* of speech and expression, assembly, association or union, movement, residence,

---

1. The 44th Amendment to the Consitution, 1978 removed the Right to Property from the list of Fundamental Rights. Now the Right to Property is a legal right and Article 300A provides that "no person shall be deprived of his Property, save by authority of law"

and the right to practise any profession or occupation subject to the security of the State, friendly relations with foreign countries, public order, decency and morality; *(iii) Right against Exploitation*, prohibiting all forms of forced labour, child labour and traffic in human beings; *(iv) Right to Freedom of Religion* and free profession, practice and propagation of religion ; *(v) Cultural and Educational Rights* to minorities to conserve their culture, language and script and to recieve education and establish and administer educational institutions of their choice ; *(vi) Right to Constitutional Remedies* for the enforcement of Fundamental Rights.

Directive Principles of State Policy. While the Fundamental Rights are enforceable through law courts, the Directive Principles of State Policy are not enforceable by any court of law. These principles are in the nature of extra-legal instruction issued to the Legislature and the Executive for their guidance. The principles have been described as "fundamental in the governance of the country and it shall be the duty of the State to apply these principles in making laws" (Articles 37).

The Constitution declares India to be a democratic republic, but mere political democracy is not of much value unless it is accompanied by social and economic democracy. These principles lay down that the State shall strive "to promote the welfare of the people by securing and protecting as effectively as it may a social order in which justice, social, economic and political, shall inform all the institutions of the national life". The principles further require the State to direct its policy in such a manner as to secure the right of all men and women to an adequate means of livelihood, equal pay for equal work, and within the limits of its economic capacity and development to make effective provision for securing the right to work, education and public assistance in the event of unemployment, old age, sickness, disablement, etc. The State shall also secure for the workers humane conditions of work, a decent standard of life and full enjoyment of leisure and social and cultural opportunities.

In the economic sphere, the State is required to direct its policy in a manner as to secure the distribution of ownership and control of the material resources of the community to subserve the common good and to ensure that the operation of the economic system does not result in the concentration of wealth and means of production to common detriment.

Some Directive Principles are meant to promote and realise the Gandhian principles like organisation of village panchayats, promotion of cottage industries, enforcement of prohibition, betterment of educational and economic interests of Scheduled Castes and Scheduled Tribes, etc.

Another group of Directive Principles emphasizes provision of free and compulsory education for children below 14 years of age, separation of the judiciary from the executive and the promotion of inter national peace and security and honourable relations between nations, respect for international law and treaty obligations and settlement of international disputes by arbitration.

Fundamental Duties. The 42nd Amendment (1976) has enumerated a set of ten Fundamental Duties for citizens, namely, *(i)* to abide by the Consitution and respect its ideals and the institutions, the National Flag and the National Anthem, *(ii)* to cherish and follow the noble ideals of the national struggle for freedom, *(iii)* to uphold and protect the sovereignty, unity and integrity of India, *(iv)* to defend the country and render national service, when called upon to do so, *(v)* to promote harmony and the spirit of common brotherhood among all the people of India, *(vi)* to preserve the rich heritage of our composite culture, *(vii)* to protect and improve the natural environment, *(viii)* to develop the scientific temper, humanism and spirit of enquiry and reform *(ix)* to safeguard public property and abjure violence and *(x)* to strive towards excellence in all of individual and collective activity.

The Union Executive. The Union Executive consists of the President, the Vice-President and the Council of Ministers with the Prime Minister at its head.

The President is elected by an electoral college consisting of the elected memebrs of both Houses of Parliament and the elected members of the legislative assemblies of the States in accordance with the system of proportional representation by means of the single transferable vote. The term of the office of the president is five years and he is eligible for re-election. The President must be a citizen of India, not less than 35 years of age and eligible for election as member of the House of the People. He is entitled to a rent-free official residence and a monthly salary of Rs. 50,000 besides prescribed allowances. The President can be impeached for any violation of the Constitution and can be removed from office in accordance with the prodecure laid down in Article 61.

The President, in his capacity as head of State, is empowered to make appointments, summon, prorogue, address, send messages to Parliament and dissolve the House of the People ; issue ordinances when the Parliament is in recess, make recommendations for introducing or moving money bills and give assent to bills ; grant pardons, reprieves, respites or remissions of punishment and suspend, remit or commute sentences in certain cases. The executive power of the Union vested in the President is exercised by him either directly or through officers of the Government in accordance with the Constitution.

The Vice-President. The Vice-President is elected by the members of both Houses of Parliament in accordance with the system of proportional representation by means of the single transferable vote. He must be a citizen of India, not less than 35 years of age and eligible for election as a member of the Council of State. His term of office is five years. The Vice-President is the *ex-officio* Chariman of the Council of States and acts as President when the latter is unable to discharge his functions due to illnes, absence or any other cause, or till the election of a new President in case of a vacancy. The Vice-President can be removed from office by a resolution of the Council of States by a majority of the members of the Council of States (i.e. total members of the House, vacant seats excepting) and approved by the Lok Sabha (i.e. of the members present and voting).

Council of Ministers. The Council of Ministers with the Prime Minister at the head aids and advises the President in the exercise of his functions. The Prime Minister is appointed by the President who also appoints other Ministers on the advice of the Prime Minister. The Council of Ministers is collectively responsible to the House of the People. It is the duty of the Prime Minister to communicate to the President all decisions of the Council of Ministers relating to the adminstration and legislation and to furnish such other information as the President may call for.

The Union Parliament. The legislature of the Union also called Parliament, consists of the President and the two Houses known as Rajya Sabha (Council of States) and Lok Sabha (House of the People).

The Rajya Sabha. The Council of States consists of not more than 250 members, 12 of whom are nominated by the President and the rest are elected. It is a permanent body not subject to dissolution, but one-third of the members retire at the expiration of every second year. The elections to the Cuncil are indirect, the quota of seats allotted to each State is provided in the Fourth Schedule to the Constitution. The elected members of the Legislative Assemblies of the States elect members for the Council of States in accordance with the system of proportional representation by means of the single transferable vote. The representatives of the Union Territories are chosen in such a manner as Parliament by law prescribes. The nominated members are persons having special or practical experience in literature, science, art and social service.

The Lok Sabha. As per Act 18 of 1987 the House of the People consists of not more than 530 members directly elected from territorial constituencies in the States and not more than 20 members to represent the Union Territories. The number of seats for each State is so allocated that the ratio between the number and the population of the State is, so far as practicable, the same for all population of the State is, so far as practicable, the same for all States. Up to 2000 the President may nominate two Anglo-Indian members to the House of the People. Unless dissolved earlier, the term of the House is five years from the date of its first meeting.

Functions and Powers of Parliament. The main functions of Parliament are to make laws for the country and to find finances for the running of the Government. All legislation requires to be passed by both Houses of Parliament. Delegated legislation is also subject to review and control by parliament. A Money Bill can only be introduced in the House of the People on the recommendation of the President. The Council of ministers is collectively responsible to the House of the People which also votes the salaries and allowances of Ministers and can force the resignation of the Council of Ministers by refusing to pass the budget or any other major legislative measures or by adopting a vote of no-confidence.

The power to amend the Consitution including the Fundamental Rights rests solely in Parliament. The Parliament can impeach the President, ask for removal of Judges of the Supreme Court and High Courts, the Election Commissioner and the Comptroller and Auditor-General in accordance with the procedure laid down in the Constitution.

Parliament can appoint Parliamentary Committees to assist in its deliberations. The committees fall under three groups : those concerned with the organisation and power of the Houses, those assisting the Houses in their legislative functions and those dealing with financial functions.

The Supreme Court of India. The highest court of the land is the Supreme Court. It consists of a Chief Justice and not more than twenty six Judges appointed by the President. The judges hold office till the age of 65. The salaries of the judges of the Supreme Court are fixed by the Constitution itself. A Judge of the Supreme Court cannot be removed from office except by an order of the President passed after an address by each House of Parliament supported by a majority of the totral membership of the House and by a majority of not less than two-thirds of the members of that House present and voting has been presented to the President in the same session asking for his removal on the ground of proved mis-behaviour or incapacity.

The Supreme Court has both original and appellate jurisdiction. It has exclusive jurisdiction in all disputes between the Union and one or more States or between two or more States *inter se*. It also has extensive original jurisdiction in regard to enforcement of Fundamental Rights. Its appellate jurisdiction extends in all cases from every High Court involving question of law as to the interpretation of the Constitution. In civil cases, the right to appeal to the Supreme Court has been provided where the amount or value of the subject matter of the dispute is not less than Rs. 20,000 or of property of like amount (this value test was abolished in 1972) or where the High Court certifies that the case is a fit one for appeal to the Supreme Court. In criminal cases, an appeal is possible to the Supreme Court if the High Court (*a*) has, on appeal, reversed an order of acquittal of an accused person and sentenced him to death ; (*b*) has withdrawn for trial before itself any case from any court subordinate to its authority and has in such trial convicted the accused person and sentenced him to death ; or (*c*) certifies that the case is a fit one for appeal to the Supreme Court.

Government of the States. The system of government in the States closely resembles that of the Union. The governor assisted by a Council of Ministers with the Chief Minister at its head constitutes the executive. The Covernor is appointed by the President of India for a term of five years and holds office during his pleasure. The Chief Minister advises the Governor in the exercise of his functions except in so far as he is required by and under the Constitution to exercise his functions in his discretion. The Chief Minister and the Council of Ministers are collectively responsible to the Legislative Assembly of the State. In the case of the breakdown of the constitutional machinery in a State the governor takes the administration into his own hands in the name of the President.

Each State has a Legislature which consists of the Governor and two Houses, or only one House called the Legislative Asembly, Parliament can, by law, provide for the abolition of an existing Legislative Council or for the creation of one where one does not exist if the proposal is supported by a resolution of the Legislative Assembly concerned.

The Legislative Council of a State comprises not more than one-third of the total number of members of the Legislative Assembly of the State and in no case less than 40 members. The Legislative

Assembly of a State should consist of not more than 500 and not less than 60 members chosen by direct election from territorial constituencies in the State. The State Legislature has exclusive powers over subjects enumerated in List II of the Seventh Schedule to the Constitution and concurrent powers over those enumerated in List III. All money bills originate in the Legislative Assmbly.

An Overview of the New Constitution. (1) It is said that the Indian Constitution is an assemblage of the political systems of Great Britain, the U.S.A., Canada, Ireland, etc. Again, a good part of the Government of India Act 1935 has been reproduced in the new Constitution. Some have accused the constitution-makers of large-scale plagiarism. True, the makers of the Indian Constitution have borrowed freely from the working-constitutions of the world. The idea all along was not to evolve an orignial or purely indigenous system of government but to adopt a good and workable system suited to the needs of the country. And the constitution-makers have succeeded admirably in that objective.

(2) The Indian Constitution is fedral, but the term federation has not been used anywhere in the constitution document ; instead the word Union has been employed all through. The word Union has been used deliberately ; it emphasizes unity and integrity of the country more than the word 'federation'. Some Indian jurists have described the Indian Constitution as a 'co-operative federation'. Dr. Ambedkar explained why the Drafting Committee preferred the word Union to Federation. He said. "We wanted to make it clear that though India was to be a Federation, the Federation was not the result of an agreement by the States to join in a federation and that the Federation not being the result of an agreement, no State has the right to secede from it. The Federation is a Union because it is indestructible".

(3) It is maintained that the Fundamental Rights as listed in the Constitution are illusory and not real. The Parliament has the right to amend any part of the Constitution including Fundamental Rights. True, the Supreme Court has the right to sit in judgement over the validity of the laws passed by the Parliament and to declare as void any law or part of it which infringes Fundamental Rights. However, the Parliament has the right to abridge Fundamental Rights through amendments to the Constitution. And it is not for the Supreme Court to go into the merits of such amendments The 42nd amendment to the Constitution (1976) has upheld the right of the Parliament to amend all parts of the Constitution and put such amendments above judicial review. President Roosevelt's remarks on the Role of Judicial Review in the U.S.A. have relevance to Democratic India. The President said : "The Court...has improperly set itself up as a third House of Congress—a super legislature...reading into the constitution words and implications which were never intended to be there...We have therefore reached the point as a Nation where we must take action to save the Constitution from the court and the court from itself. We want a Supreme Court which will do justice under the Constitution—not over it".

(4) Critics maintain that the Directive Principles of State Policy as enshrined in the Constitution are pious platitudes, since these are not enforceable in any court of law. Dr. Ambedkar justified the Directive Principles by comparing them to the Instrument of instructions issued to the Governor-General under the Government of India Act. No Government in power, he maintained, can ignore them. The Government may not have to answer for their breach in a court of law, but will certainly have to answer for them before the electorate at election time.

It is held that Fundamental Rights are meaningless today to millions who have no economic means to enjoy them and it is the Directive Principles that are meant to set this right in the long run. Thus there is an unmistakable relationship between Fundamental Rights and Directive Principles. Chief Justice Bhagwati explains that the Directive Principles impose an obligation on the State to take steps to create an egalitarian social order which can ensure socio-economic justice and individual liberty to all. Thus the Fundamental Rights are intended to operate in the larger socio-economic framework, envisaged in the Directive Principles. It is obvious therefore that if anything has to give way, it will be the so-called Fudamental Rights and not the Directive Principles.

(5) The appointment of Mr. A.N. Ray as the new Chief Justice of India in April 1973 in disregard of the recommendations of the retiring Chief Justice, Mr. S.M. Sikri, and in supersession of the claims of Justice J.M. Shelat, Justice K.S. Hegde and Justice A.N. Grover has evoked comments from many quarters. While the Government has described this appointment in accordance with the recommendations of the Law Commission of 1958, the Opposition has described the appointment as "politically motivated". However, there is much weight in the comments of Shri Jayaprakash Narayan that "if the appointment of the Chief Justice of India remained entirely in the hands of the Prime Minister...then the hightest judicial institution of this country cannot but become a creature of the Government of the day".

(6) Critics maintain that the Emergency powers given to the President, particularly those under Article 359 giving him the right to suspend the right to enforce Fundamental Rights, was the "grand final and crowning glory of the most reactionary chapter of the Constitution" and "arch of autocratic reaction". In this context it is relevant to quote the pronouncement of the U.S. Supreme Court in ex-parte Miligan case, "No doctrine involving more pernicious consequences was ever invented by the wit or man, than that any of its (Bill of Rights) provisions can be suspended during any of the great exigencies of the Government."

(7) It is also maintained that the powers given to the President (actually to the Prime Minister) to supersede the government of a State in case of failure of constitutional machinery in the State are very wide and open to misuse. At the time of adoption of this Article, Pt. Hriday Nath Kunzru had warned, "The electors (of the State) must be made to feel that the power to apply proper remedy, if any mismanagement occurred, rested with them. It depended upon them to choose their representatives who would be capable of working in accordance with their best interest. If the Central Government or Parliament were given power to interfere, there was a danger that whenever there was a dissatisfaction in a State, appeals would be made to the Central Government to come to their rescue. The State electors would throw their responsibility on the shoulders of the Central Government. It was not right to encourage this tendency". The events in Kerala, U.P., West Bengal, etc., have proved how correct Prof. Kunzru was!

(8) Eminent Indian jurists believe that Parliament is only a creature of the Constitution and as such does not have the power to destroy the basic structure of the Constitution. A.N. Palkhivala contends that parliament cannot overthrow the supremacy of the Constitution to make itself supreme. However, there is no consensus among legal luminaries as to what constitutes the 'basic structure' of the Constitution. All the same, Palkhivala asserts that the supremacy of the Constitution and the limited amending powers of Parliament constitute the basic structure and fundamental features of the Constitution. These ensure the identity of the Constitution. The debate seems unending.

SELECT OPINIONS

K.C. Wheare. Just as in Canada the federal principle was modified by unitary elements in the form of control by the central government over the provincial government, so also in the Indian Constitution–but much more so–the Central Government is given powers of intervention in the conduct of the affairs of the State Governments which modifies the fedral principle. The Constitution does not indeed claim to establish a federal union, but the federal principle has been introduced into its terms to such an extent that it is justifiable to describe it as a quasi-federal constitution. Whether in its onerations, it will provide another example of federal government remains to be seen...The new Constitution...establishes indeed a system of government which is at most quasi-federal, almost devolutionary in character ; a unitary state with subsidiary federal features rather than federal state with subsidiary unitary features.

Allan Gledhill. To say that the new Constitution is not truly federal is not to criticise it adversely. 'Federalism is not necessarily good government ; it is at most a device which may secure good government in some cases'. That the Founding Fathers realised that they were not creating a federal government seems clear from their choice of the word 'Union' to descibe the aggregate of States...The essence of federalism is the existence of a sphere in which units can exercise executive and legislative authority free of central control...We have seen how on a Proclamation of Emergency or on the breakdown of the constitution in a State, or on disobedience of Central executive directions by a State or in a financial emergency, the Indian Constitution provides for the encroachment upon or supersession of State sovereignty, and even, in the last resort, for the annihilation of a State. Possibly these provisions may wither from lack of use, but when they inserted them in the Constitution, the Founding Fathers had not forgotten the emergencies which had arisen in the past, and which were likely to recur in the future...The results of their labours have been to establish a more unitary form of government than that contemplated by the Act of 1935.

Ivor Jennings. The Constitution...is essentially British in its texture. There is responsible government on British principles not only in the Government of India but also in the governments of the States. Though India is described as 'Sovereign Democratic Republic', and the description is wholly accurate, it might also be described as constitutional monarchy without a monarch ; for the functions of the President are essentially the same as those of the King or, in a Dominion, the King and the Governor-General combined...The details of the relations between the Union and the States seem to have been influenced by Australian experience, particularly in the sphere of trade and commerce between the States. Even the fundamental liberties of the Bill of Rights, other than those arising out of racial and caste discrimination, derive mainly from the experience of English constitutional history, though there are also echoes of controversies in the United States of America.

SELECT REFERENCES

1. Alexandrowicz, C.H. : *Constitutional Development in India.*
2. Basu, D.D. : *Commentary on the Constitution of India.*
3. Gledhill, Allan : *The Repulic of India.*
4. Jennings, Ivor : *Constitutional Laws of the Commonwealth.*
5. Wheare, K.C. : *Federal Government.*
   India's New Constitution Analysed.
6. Pylee, M. : *Constitutional Government in India.*

THE IMPACT AND LEGACY OF BRITISH RULE IN INDIA

> The most obvious fact is the sterility of British rule in India and the thwarting of Indian life by it.
> — *Jawaharlal Nehru*

> 'As India must be bled', the bleeding should be done judiciously.
> – *Lord Salisbury, Secretary of State for India, 1874-78*

The 'Balance-Sheet' Debate. The polemical debate about the nature of British impact on India started in the second half of the 19th century and continues even today. Nationalist writers like Dadabhai Naoroji, R.C. Dutt, D.E. Wacha, S.N. Banerjee began the task of assessing the merits and defects of British rule in India and developed the theme that Britain was exploiting India and draining away her wealth. Such writings and the challenge of Indian nationalism put the British historians on the defensive. To counter this nationlist viewpoint, administrator-historians like J.F. Stephen, John Strachey, Alfred Lyall, W.W. Hunter developed the theory of 'paternalism and trusteeship' and dwelt at length on the 'civilising mission' of Britain in India, ignoring altogether its impact on Indian society and the Indian response to British policies.

The shock of the First World War, the growing popularity of the nationalist movement and the wider appeal of the anti-imperialist slogans after the Russian Revolution of 1917 brought some change in the complexion of the 'balance sheet' debate. Though British writers like Ramsay Muir, P.E. Roberts, H.H. Dodwell *et al* still not tired of recounting, 'the immeasurable services to the peoples of India', 'the priceless gifts of Britain to the Indian people', yet some of them, P.E. Roberts for example, admitted 'the inherent reasonableness of India's claim to manage her own affairs'. Indian nationalist writers like Tilak, Lajpat Rai, Gandhi, Rajendra Prasad, Nehru *et al* became increasingly critical of Britain's 'negative role' in India and held her responsible for most of the ills of Indian society and economy.

In the post-independence period English writers like Percival Spear, Percival Griffiths, Philip Woodruff[1], Micheal Edwards *et al* have endeavoured to strike a balance between the plundering and constructive role of Britain in India. Woodruff, for example, finds the ultimate justification of British rule in the reaction it provoked which in turn stung political life into India. Edwards dwells on Britain's scaffolding of Free India and Pakistan and points out that out of exploitation came a unity of purpose and out of tyranny a sense of nationhood. Philips Mason in a somewhat comic style likens the Anglo-Indian association to a forced marriage between the masculine John Bull and the docile Indian girl which ended in divorce on 15 August 1947 ; now in a reminiscent mood both parties have some pleasant memories and some regrets and have decided to forgive and forget and be friends on equal terms.

Nature of British Conquest. It cannot be denied that the British conquest of India was of an essentially different and infinitely more intensive kind than India had known before. All the earlier conquerors–the Arabs, the Turks, the Mughals–who overran India, by an eternal law of history, were greatly influenced by the superior civilisation of the Hindus. Britain was in the vanguard of Eropean material civilisation when it conquered India and was thus less likely to be influenced by Hindu civilisation.

Unlike the earlier conquerors of India, the British did not settle in India but utilised India's economic resources for the benefit of their motherland *i.e.* Great Britain. Dadabhai Naoroji referred to

---

1. Philip Woodruff is the pseudonym of Philip Mason, I.C.S., who was Joint Secretary, Government of India.

this special characteristic of British conquest when he wrote to J.T. Sunderland in 1905, "The lot of India is a very sad one. Her condition is that of a master and a slave ; but it worse; it is that of a plundered nation in the hands of constant plunderers with the plunder carried away clean out of the land. In the case of plundering raids occasionally made on India before the English came the invaders went away and there were long intervals of security during which the land could recuperate and become again rich and prosperous. But nothing of the kind is true now. The British invasion is continuous and the plunder goes right on, with no intermission and actually increases and the impoverished nation has no opportunity whatever to recuperate".

Comparing the earlier invasions of Hindustan with that of the British invasion, Karl Marx wrote, "There cannot, however, remain any doubt but that the misery inflicted by the British on Hindustan is of an essentially different and infinitely more intensive kind than all Hindustan had suffer before... All the civil wars, invasions, revolutions, conquests, famines, strangely complex, rapid and destructive as the successive action in Hindustan may appear, did not go deeper than its surface. England has broken down the entire frame-work of Indian society..." The earlier conquerors of India left untouched the social and economic basis of Indian society and most of them eventually became a part and parcel of the Indian structure. The British conquest, on the other hand, knocked the bottom out of Indian socio-economic base and remained a foreign force, acting from outside and withdrawing its tribute.

Whatever developments–political, administrative, economic, social or intellectual–India witnessed during two centuries of British rule here were not planned by the colonial rulers out of any philanthropic mission for the good of India, but were merely offshots of the imperial rulers' larger aim of keeping firm their hold over India or for promoting the political, economic or material interests of their own country. It may be even more correct to say that political and social changes came in spite of the British or as an incidental or unexpected consequence of their activities. Jawaharlal Nehru has rightly commented that "changes came to India because of the impact of the West, but these came almost inspite of the British in India... They succeeded in slowing down the pace of those changes".

Karl Marx on Britain's Role in India. In a series of well-written articles contributed to the *New York Daily Tribune* in 1853 Marx made an excellent analysis of the problems of Asiatic society, especially in India and China, in the larger background of the rise of British capitalism in its frantic search for a colonial policy and a world market. With a rare insight Marx portrayed (*i*) an analysis of the pre-colonial Indian situation–social, economic and political (*ii*) assessed the impact of British rule and European capitalism upon it till the middle of the 19th century, and (*iii*) projected into the future and prophesied the future results of British rule in India.

Regarding the *destructive* role of Britain in India, Marx referred to Britain's wanton destruction of indigenous society with the comment that England was 'actuated by the vilest interests, and was stupid in her manner of enforcing it'. England's economic role in India was a crude plundering of India's wealth and its parasitic battening on Indian economy. Referring to Britain's *regenerative* work in India, which had just begun to transpire and whose essence lay in the reversal of those specific characteristics that lay at the root of Asiatic stagnation, Marx noted in 1853 the following signs :

(*i*) the unprecedented consolidation of the political unity of India, strengthened by the newly-laid telegraph lines ;

(*ii*) the development of railway lines ending village isolation and the introduction of steamships linking India so closely to Europe that 'that once fabulous country will thus be actually annexed to the Western World' ;

(*iii*) the economic development of India in the interests of the English millocracy, the railway system being the forerunner of modern industry ;

(*iv*) the rise of modern industry which would dissolve the hereditary divisions of labour ;

(v) the introduction of private property rights in lan—a great desideratum of Asiatic society;

(vi) the emergence of a free press and a class of educated Indians imbued with European science and endowed with the requirements for government.

Marx expected these developmets to fulfil Britain's positive and constuctive historic mission in "laying of the material foundations of western society in Asia". Unfortunately, Britain's role in modernizing India has turned out to be different from what he prophesied.

The impact of British rule may be summarised under the following heads :

Political. Political unification of India under one centralised government was perhaps the most significant development under British rule. The inexorable logic of imperialism worked a full circle till the whole of India from the Himalayas to Cape Comorin and from Chittagong to the Khyber Pass passed under British control. If the British Indian provinces were under 'direct' British rule, Indian States came under 'indirect' imperial rule. The British could rightly take pride that the British empire encompassed more extensive territories than the Mauryan or Mughal empires ever did.

Britain also gave to India—what British writers are never weary of emphasising—the Blessings of Peace. She maintained a strong army both for external defence and maintenance of internal security. Britain also organised a strong police for maintenance of law and order—all at a heavy expense to the Indian taxpayer.

Jawaharlal Nehru made a pertinent observation that the British undoubtedly rescued India from chaos and anarchy—that chaos and anarchy which was partly at least due to the aggressive and ambitious policy of the East India Company and their respresentatives in India. Further, the British used the strong military and police forces not for maintaining peace in the country but also for suppression of popular movements.

Another impact of British rule was the emergence of the spirit of Indian nationalism and the growth of the Indian nationalist movement. If political necessities compelled the imperial rulers to have a single administrative set-up for the whole of India, considerations of military defence and economic exploitation goaded them to develop the means of transport and communications through a network of roads and ralways and efficient organisation of the post and telegraph systems. These developments gave India the appearance of unity and fostered the spirit of one-mindedness. The emergence of an English-educated middle class intelligentsia and the development of the modern press fostered the modern concepts of nationalism, nationality, political rights etc. which in turn cleared the ground for the formation of an all-India political organisation like the Indian National Congress.

Enlightened imperialists like A.O. Hume, William Wedderburn, George Yule, Alfred Webb, Henry Cotton *et al* tried to keep the Indian National Congress as a 'loyal and innocuous' organisation in the beginning and even used its official platform for pro-British and anti-Russian propaganda. The Indian National Congress came to age in the beginning of the 20th century and started questioning the very moral right of Britain to rule India. The demand for Swaraj followed.

The development of Indian nationalism was never to the liking of British rulers of India. They used a thousand and one methods to weaken the movement. The Anglo-Indian bureaucracy which looked upon the Congress as a Hindu organisation worked hard to keep the Muslim community away from political agitation. The introduction of the system of reservation of seats for different cummunities in the Central Legislative Council, Provicial Legislative Councils and even Local Bodies ; the principle of reservation of the police, in the army and other services– were all calculated to hinder the development of a healthy political and social outlook on national issues. The British also regimented the Indian Princes as a Third Force in Indian politics. The policy of 'counterpoises' roped in not only the Indian princes, but also the big zamindars and even the Scheduled Castes among the Hindus. Thus, British policies struck at the very root of the solidarity of Indian nationalism. Before Britain quit India in 1947, it partitioned India into two independent states of India and Pakistan and left the Indian princely states a potential source for mischief. The fear of Balkanization stared India in the face. Thus the Indian National Congress' goal of a strong undivided free India was shattered, mainly due to the machiavellian policies of imperial Britain. The British who had always claimed credit for creating a strong unified India left behind a divided and weak India. Truly, had Karl Marx prophesied that Britain's role in India was 'swidish' and it would 'Irelandize India.'

Britain also claimed to have introduced in India a parliamentary system of government with the larger ideal of a democratic setup for the country. British writers are never weary of reiterating the existence of oriental despotism from the earliest times down to the Mughal times, particulary emphasising that no other system of government had been known in the country. Britain, it is claimed, inherited the autocratic system of government, but decided to introduce a liberal scheme of administration. The origin of democratic political ideals is traced since the governor-generalship of William Bentinck. A beginning towards the introduction of a representative system was made by the Indian Councils Acts of 1861, 1892 and 1909. It is also claimed that a concious direction to British policy India Act, 1919 and extended by the Government of India Act, 1935 through the introduction of dyarchy and provincial autonomy. Sir Verney Lovett, writing in 1919 and extended by the Government of India Act, 1935 through the introduction of dyarchy and provincial autonomy. Sir Verney Lovett, writing in 1919, reiterated, "Britain is pledged to establish a democratic system of government over two-thirds of India" and yet the British system of government in India remained despotic till its end in 1947.

True, British despotism succeeded oriental despotism. The colonial rulers cloaked British despotism in a constitutional garb and made it a 'constitutional autocracy'.

Law and Administration. Perhaps the most abiding impact of British rule has been in the field of law and administration. The British rulers introduced the Rule of Law in their territories. Even the meanest subject enjoyed personal liberty. For example, the principle of *habeas corpus* provided that no person could be arrested or kept in prison without a written order from the local executive-cum-judicial authority, even if the Viceroy desired otherwise. Even Government servants, for acts done by them in their official capacity, could be sued in the law courts. A natural corollary to the principle of rule of law was the principle of Equality before the Law. This certainly was a novel feature in a caste-ridden society. Furhter, the British rulers carried out a Codification of Law. The Code of Civil Procedure (1859), the Penal Code (1860) and the Code of Criminal Procedure (1861) laid down in clear, precise and exact language the law applicable to all citizens, high and low irrespective of the caste, creed or religious professions of the parties involved. The British also set up a gradation of courts, civil and criminal, for the trial of petty to heinous crimes with the right to appeal to High Courts and even an appeal to a Committee of the Privy Council in civil suits.

The legal system introduced by the British was not without its shortcomings. It was complicated and beyond the comprehension of the common man. It was very expensive and the rich had the opportunity to wear out the poor and the uneducated. Falsehood, chicanery and deceit paid high dividend. The inordinate delay in the decision of cases was another negative feature of the system. The lawyer class had vested interest in prolonging cases and pleading for clients who could afford to engage them. Even the government of the Free India has not been able to remove these deficiencies from the legal system. Perhaps, the worst aspect of the legal system in British times was the special procedure laid down for trial of Europeans in criminal cases. The Ilbert Bill highlighted the injustice involved in racial discriminations in judicial matters but provided no remedial measures.

The organisation of an Indian Civil Service which worked according to set rules and with machine-like efficiency and impartiality was another striking feature of the administration in contrast to the personal rule of the monarch or his governors as the case might have been in pre-British times.

The I.C.S. officers worked as Collectors, Magistrates and Judges and maintained a high standard of impartiality and integrity unmindful of the likes or dislikes of the Governor General or even the Prime Minister of England. Prof. B.B. Mishra writes, "Among the contributions of British rule in India the creation of the Indian Civil Service is one of the most remarkable. It constituted in fact the spine of the Indian body-politic, and to it the people generally looked for the protection of person and property, of life and liberty"

The much-praised I.C.S. was not without its drawbacks. In spite of repeated resolutions of the British parliament and announcements by the British monarchs about recruitment to the I.C.S. on the basis of competitive examination irrespective of racial considerations, the I.C.S. remained a close preserve of Europeans, Various subterfuges–like holding the examination in London alone, keeping low the maximum age limit for enterance, drawing the syllabus to suit English boys, interview evaluation, riding tests–were used to keep the Indians out of these services. Further, the much-praised virtue of efficiency became a vice because it was, as Rabindranath Tagore put it, 'untouched by hand' i.e. they became insensitive to the feelings of the people and to the new currents of thought and never bothered to gain the goodwill and co-operation of the people whom they despised. Worst still, the I.C.S. developed a cult of its indispensibility for India and unconsciously developed the sense of identifying India with their own interests. As Jawaharlal Nehru has put it, "They ran India, they wore India and anything that was harmful to their interests must of necessity be injurious to India". Indian nationalists rightly resented the fabulous salary and liberal allowances and still lavish pensionary benefits paid to I.C.S. and interpreted these as a big channel in the drain of wealth from India. Dadabhai Naoroji described the I.C.S. as 'leeches' which sucked Indian blood.

Today the I.A.S. officers are advised not to be guided by the old imperial tradition, but to accept new social responsibilities and work as useful limbs in the working of a democratic set-up.

Education, Oriental Studies and Indian Renaissance. Intellectually 18th century India presented the picture of a stagnant society. The traditional system of education had greatly suffered during the political instablility of the period. The new Renaissance spirit of scientific enquiry, scepticism, humanism and aggressive materialism which was rapidly transforming the West had not reached India. The political confusion of the 18th century which European intervention further accentuated delayed the infiltration of progressive ideas into India.

The Christian missionaries of Serampore–Carey, Ward & Marshman–with the Cross in their hands were the first to open schools for Indian children. Their educational endeavours were just a means for their higher aim of proselytization. Compulsion of administrative organisation, commercial penetration and need for cheaper clerks to man the lower rungs of the administration goaded the British government to provide in the Charter Act of 1813 a clause requiring the East India Company to annually set apart a sum of one lakh of rupees on the improvement of education in India. Some progressive Indians like Rammohun Roy urged the government to spend this fund on instructing Indians in mathematics, natural philosophy, chemistry, anatomy and other useful sciences. The Company's authorities dilly-dallied for two decades before a final decision was taken by the Committee of Public Instruction in 1835 under Lord Macaulay's charimanship and adopted by William Bentinck's government to spend the allocated amount for "English education alone". Macaulay's aim was, in his own words," to create a class of persons who would be Indians in blood and colour but English in tastes, in opinions, in morals and in intellect", apart from banishing idolatry in India.

Some painstaking British scholars devoted themselves to the study of Sanskrit, philology, Indian culture and Indian history. Sir William Jones indentified Chandragupta Maurya with Sandrokottus of Greek historians and this proved a landmark in Indian chronology, James Prinsep and Henry Masser deciphered the Brahmi script translated the Asokan incriptions and many texts of Buddhist literature. This opened a new chapter in the history of ancient India. Further, the efforts of

William Jones, founder of the Bengal Asiatic Society, Jonathan Duncan and other orientalists rekindled interest in the study of ancient Indian literature.

English writers take credit for England having heralded the Indian Renaissance. Percival Griffiths writes, "Whatever else of good or evil Britain may have achieved in India, she may justly claim to have brought about the grreat Indian Renaissance". It is hard to believe that modern political thought and scientific advances of the 18th and 19th centuries would not have reached India but for the British imperial rule in India. From times immemorial India had followed an open-door policy and even during the age of primitive means of transport and communications had maintained effective trade and cultural links both with the East and the West. Thus the wind of new ideas from the West would have reached India even without British rule. Jawaharlal Nehru rightly puts it, "Some beneficent changes came in spite of them or as an incidental and unexpected consequence of their activities". Rather, it would be more correct to say that British imperial rule diluted the beneficent impact of world progressive developments in India.

The British over-emphasis on education through the English medium and faith in the 'infiltration theory' limited the spread of education to an elite class and neglect of the education of the masses, thus creating a gulf between the English-educated and the masses. The Government turned its face even against the spread of higher education towards the last quarter of the 19th century when it found its spread working against imperial interests. Further, the over-emphasis on liberal education and utter neglect of technical education produced the phenomenon of educated unemployed.

The British pattern of liberal education and educational policies contained some inner contradictions. The emergence of modern political consciousness, political organisations and political agitations were as much a result of British educational policies as a reaction to imperial policies. It was a section of the English educated intelligentsia which exposed the true nature of imperial rule and provided leadership to modern political movements. Taken in this light the Macaulayan scheme of education proved beneficent to it.

Social and Cultural Impact. Westen impact has been all-pervading in the fields of Indian social life, has greatly influenced art, architecture, painting, literature, poetry, drama, novels and even Indian religions and philosophy. The pace-setters in these fields have been English public servants and men of letters and the carriers were largely the English-educated class who dominated the few professions of journalists, teachers, lawyers, doctors, etc. It was this Indian intelligentsia who spearheaded most of the social and political organisations in the country.

Western models–or better still modern world models–in social etiquette, dress, eating habits, dwelling units, furniture designs, better awareness about private and public hygiene, new modes of entertainment have penetrated deep into Indian life though traditional Indian-ness is writlarge in the countryside.

Change is a continuous process and India certainly would have witnessed social changes with or without British contact. Even after the British have quitted India, world currents in social outlook, dress, food habits, movie styles and even fashions and hair styles are penetrating deep into Indian life just as Indian models in some spheres are influencing world models.

The British rulers built town-halls after the Renaissance *palazzi* style, railway stations in the Gothic cathedral style, government buildings and secretariat offices in the western style with an admixture of traditional Mughal models. The Western-educated class copied these models in their private buildings and personal residences. In the field of painting Ravi Verma, Abanindranath, Gogonendranath, Jamini Ray and Amrita Sher-Gil were greatly influenced by the Western style. In the field of literature Rabindranath Tagore, Aurobindo Ghosh, Sarojini Naidu, Mulk Raj Anand, R.K. Narayan–to mention only a few names–were influnced by the English pattern. In 1913, Rabindranath Tagore's talent was recognised by the award of a Nobel Prize for Literature.

English words and idioms have penetrated into vernacular languages. Words like station, railway, cinema, hospital, vote, election, restaurant, hotel, union, etc., are understood even by the illiterate living in remote villages of India. Similarly, phrases like Government's responsibility, right to work, right to food, shelter and social security, right to organise the workers, right to equality before the law, right to freedom of speech, debate, movement etc. etc. have become common-place idioms in Indian life.

Economic Impact. Since the main motivation behind British intursion and subsequent domination of India was commercial and economic, the British impact in the economic sphere has been the most deleterious and devastating. Britain used the most sophisticated methods to exploit India's vast and rich economic potential. If even after two centuries of the most close contact and complete control of Indian economy by the British–technologically the most advanced nation in the world–India in 1947 presented the picture of an economically underdeveloped nation with hunger, poverty, low national income, the responsibility must lie squarely on the shoulders of the British imperial rulers.

Indian agriculture received the maximum care under the East India Company primarily because the main source of state income was land revenue. The Company tried various experiments to maximize the land revenue by resort to the method of 'open auction to the highest bidder'. The system of farming of land revenue did not work. Cornwallis introduced the Permanent Settlement of Land Revenue in Bengal, Bihar and Orissa in 1793. Subsequent administrators introduced the Ryotwari system in Bombay Presidency and most parts of the Madras Presidency, the Mahalwari system (a variation of the Zamindari system) in U.P. and with some further variations in the Punjab. The Zamindari system encouraged absentee landlordism and created a host of intermediaries between the state and the cultivator–all working to the misery of the cultivator. Even in the Ryotwari tracts, the excessive land revenue demand–periodically revised upwards–bought in the money-lender as an important factor in rural India. Rural indebtedness, backward methods of cultivation, inadequate irrigation facilities resulted in pauperization of the rural masses. Famines visited frequently claiming a heavy toll of life. In the later half of the 19th century 24 famines, modest and severe, scouraged India and claimed an estimated toll of 3 crores of the population.

Indian industry suffered the maximum at the hands of the British intruder. The superiority and extensive sales of Indian handicrafts in Europe and even in the British markets was anathematic to the interests of the commercial East India Company. The Whig government of the early 18th century imposed heavy duties on Indian textile imports in Britain. However, after the Napoleonic wars, the Indian markets were increasingly thrown open to British industrial products. The same British government which had earlier excluded Indian cotton goods from English markets by high protective legislation, now permitted British machine-made goods to be poured into India duty free or at nominal duties. This policy of *one way* free trade which ruined Indian handicrafts was the price India had to pay for the loss of her freedom. Even a British writer, H.H. Wilson has conceded, that Britain "employed the arm of political injustice to keep down and ultimately strangle a competitor with whom he could not have contended on equal terms." Karl Marx, writing in 1853 commented, "It was the British intruder who broke up the Indian handloom and destroyed the spinning wheel. England began with depriving the Indian cottons from the European market; it then introduced twist into Hindustan and in the end inundated the very mother country of cotton with cottons". Even Willliam Bentinck wrote in 1834, "The misery hardly finds a parallel in the history of commerce. The bones of the Indian weavers are bleaching the plains of India". Thus Indian handicrafts declined in the 19th century.

Could Indian handicraft industry stand the challenge posed by rising capitalism and Industrial Revolution? The capitalist mode of production and bourgeoisie commerce had destroyed handicraft industries in European countreis too. While in Europe the destructive process had been accompanied by a corresponding growth of new forces of industrial production, the peculiar unhappy situation in the Indian economic scene was that the loss of the old world was without the emergence of a new world. The process of industrial regeneration did not start in India because of British imperial policies in India.

Far from not planning the industrialisation of India, the imperial rulers deliberately followed policies to 'de-industrialize' our country. Britain's interest lay in converting and preserving India as an 'agricultural farm' of industrialised Britain. Thus, the British rulers deliberately carried out the policy of 'ruralization' and 'peasantization' of Indian economy. Whatever few Indian industries developed under the situation created by World War I and the economic depression of 1930s suffered from another disability that these were mostly controlled by British finance and capital. True, textile, cement, jute, paper, sugar, pig iron industries started in India, but the country lagged behind in the development of iron and steel, heavy engineering and metallurgical industries.

The 'gestation theory' popularized by modern Anglo-American scholars does not hold good even after a casual scrutiny of facts and figures. England's role in India was imperial, the Englishman's mission in India was economic exploitation, the 'Whiteman's Burden' was the burden of wealth that the whiteman carried out of India.

Undoubtedly, British rule has left behind indelible marks, for good or for bad, on almost every aspect of Indian life. European ways of thinking and European patterns have taken firm roots among urbanites who control the strings of India's destiny. The rich legacy of difficulties, particulary in the economic field, are an ever present reminder of the exploitative character of European imperialism in India. If at all there were some traces of modernization on the Western model, the British imperial rulers took care to deprive the people of India of a significant share in the benefits.

Free India cannot at one stroke write off the deep influences of two centuries of British imperial rule in India. The British rulers created a new structure of colonial institutions, a colonial economy, a colonial society and even a colonial idealogy. The institutions of landlordism, politically-loaded casteism, communalism, regionalism etc. etc., which were encouraged by imperial rulers to perpetuate their rule are evils defying easy eradication. Further, 'distorted modernisation' has created new problems. Thus, Britain left behind in 1947 a bleeding polity, a ruined economy, a sick society and above all, the ever present danger of neo-colonialism lurking all around.

Select Opinions

Ramsay Muir. The British power has...rendered three immeasurable services to the peoples of India. In the first place, it has given them a firmly organised political unity, which they never in all their history possessed before. In the second place, it has given them an extraordinary period of unbroken peace......And in the third place, this Empire has given to the Indian peoples for the first time impartial and unvarying justice ; under its guardianship the Reign of Law, which is the foundation of healthy political life has taken the place of the arbitrary will of innumerable despots. (*The Making of British India*)

Percival Griffiths. Whatever else of good or ill Britain may have achieved in India, she may justly claim to have brought about the great Indian Renaissance....It was primarily in Northern India that Hinduism, stagnant as it was at the beginning of the nineteenth century, was purified and revivified by its contact with Western thought, while simultaneously Western influence created a class of Indians who were neither Hindus nor British in their outlook–a class of which Nehru is perhaps the outstanding example. (*Modern India*)

Percival Spear. The British were the harbingers of the West. At times unconsciously, at times with optimistic zeal, and at times with reluctance or dislike, they were the vehicles of Western influence in India. That is why their influence in India has proved creative, and why their period will be looked back on as formative for the India that is yet to be. The British provided the bridge for India to pass from the medieval world of the Mughals to the new age of science and humanism. (*The Oxford History of Modern India*)

Jawaharlal Nehru. The British Government had also stood in the past, in theory at least, for Indian unity and democracy. It took pride in the fact that its rule had brought about the political unity of India, even though that unity was one of common subjection. It told us further that it was training us in the methods and processes of democracy. But curiously enough its policy has directly led to the denial of both unity and democracy.....The brief period during which the Congress governments functioned in the provinces (1937-39) confirmed our belief that the major obstruction to progress in India was the political and economic structure imposed by the British........Any kind of democracy in India was incompatible with the British political and economic structure and conflict between the two was inevitable. (*The Discovery of India*)

Bipan Chandra. As a result of British rule, India was transferred by the end of the 19th century into a classic colony.........Indian economy and social development were completely subordinated to British economy and social development. Indian economy was integrated into the world capitalist economy in a subordinate position and with a peculiar international division of labour. During the very years after 1760 when Britain was developing into the leading developed capitalist country of the world, India was being developed into becoming the leading backward, colonial country of the world. (*Freedom Struggle*)

SELECT REFERENCES

1. Dutt. R.P. : *India To-day.*
2. Edwards, Michael : *The Last Years of British India.*
3. Edwards, Michael : *British India.*
4. Griffiths, P.J. : *The British Impact on India.*
5. Hutchins, G.H. : *The Illusions of Permanence.*
6. Mason, Philips : *The Men who Ruled India.*
7. *Moral and Material Progress Reports*
8. Strachey, J. : *India* (London, 1888).
9. Strachey, John : *The End of Empire* (London, 1959).

NEHRUVIAN ERA : FIRST PHASE OF INDEPENDENCE, 1947-64

Nehru dominated India as completely as De Gaulle did France.........it could be said of him, as Louis XIV of France said of himself, *'L'etat, c'est moi'*.[1]

—Percival Spear

Nehru has a certain enigmatic quality, defying analysis......by temperament at once a democrat and a dictator........it is impossible to be with him without realizing his greatness and his singleness of purpose.

—Percival Griffiths

The Partition of India into two states of India and Pakistan in 1947 was a political development, which created a host of political and economic problems apart from flaming the fire of communal hatred in both the states.

The Indian Independence Bill, 1947, was rushed through the Parliament in a short period of twelve days (4th July to 16th July) and received the Royal Assent on 18th July, 1947.

The Indian Independence Act, 1947

The Indian Independence Act provided for the transfer of power on the basis of grant of Dominion Status to two successor states of India and Pakistan. Each Dominon was to have a Governor General, a Legislature with full powers to make laws for its Dominion. The Act also provided for the lapse of all treaties, agreements etc. between His majesty's government and the rulers of Indian Princely States.

The British authorities seemed to have rushed with the plan of transfer of power to the successor Dominions of India and Pakistan. From the Mountbatten Plan of 3rd June, 1947 to 15th August, 1947 was a gap of only 72 days. The deteriorating communal situation and spread of violence seemed to have prompted Mountbatten to transfer power at the earliest and escape all responsibilities for the near lawless situation in the country.

The Viceroy's Chief of Staff Ismay's remarks that "1947 was too late, rather than too early" should be read in this context. The Congress President, Acharya Kripalani pertinently pointed out to Mountbatten that the British could assert their authority, but did not care to.

The 3rd June, Partition Plan was a victory for M.A. Jinnah and the Muslim League but it was willy-nilly accepted by the All India Congress Commitee because of political compulsions and frustration. Mahatma Gandhi who had at one time declared that partition could only be effected over his dead body yielded only to the importunities of his topmost disciples out of sheer despair and sense of helpleless.

For the Hindu and Sikh population of Punjab it was a bolt from the blue. Even Maulana Abdul Kalam Azad pointed out that it is 'an occasion for mourning' in contrast to the feeling in the Congress Committee.

Inauguration of Indian Independence

15th of August, 1947 marked the end of the British Imperial **raj** and the beginning of India's independence. In a special function held in the Constituent Assembly at the midnight of 14th/15th August, Jawaharlal Nehru made his historic speech claiming the end of 'a period of ill-fortune' and

---

1. *L'etat, c'est moi* (Fr) = The state, it is I.

expressed the hope that India would rediscover her true self. He said : "Long years ago we made a tryst with destiny, and now the time comes when we shall redeem our pledge, not wholly or in full measure, but very substantially. At the stroke of the midnight hour, when the world sleeps, India will awake to life and freedom. A moment comes, which comes but rarely in history, when we step out from the old to the new, when an age ends, and when the soul of a nation, long suppressed, finds utterance. It is fitting that at this solemn moment we take the pledge of dedication to the service of India and her people and to the larger cause of humanity."

End of British Paramountcy over Indian Princely States and Integration of States

The Indian Independence Act, 1947 contains the following provision regarding Indian States. "All treaties, agreements etc. between His Majesty's Government and the rulers of Indian States shall lapse. The words 'Emperor of India' shall be omitted from Royal Style and Titles. The Indian States will be free to accede to either of the new Dominion of India or Pakistan".

In the National Provisional Government Sardar Vallabhbhai Patel headed the States Department. Patel and his chief aide, V.P. Menon appealed to the sense of patriotism of Indian Princes and urged them (i.e. used the tactics of Persuasion-cum-Pressure) to join the Indian Union on the basis of the surrender of three subjects of Defence, Foreign Affairs and Communication. On his part, Lord Mountbatten played a very positive role when he threw the weight of his personality and office behind the policy of Patel. By 15th August, as many as 136 jurisdictional States acceded to the Indian Union. Kashmir's Maharaja Hari Singh signed the instrument of Accession on 26th October, 1947 and the Nizam of Hyderabad in 1948. Judith M. Brown comments: "The truth was that within a short time after independence the new Government of India was the paramount power on the subcontinent, whatever the pre-independence assurances of the British and of Vallabhbhai Patel himself."[2]

The integration of the States into new India's political and administrative structure was the next logical step. Many small States which were too small for a modern system of administration were merged with adjoining provinces i.e. 39 states of Orissa and Chhattisgarh became part of either Orissa or Central Provinces. For geographical and administrative reasons Baroda and Kolhapur were made parts of Bombay province; Gujarat States were also merged with the Bombay province. A second form of integration of 61 states was the formation of seven centrally administered areas. In this category came the states of Himachal Pradesh, Vindhya Pradesh, Tripura, Manipur, Bhopal, Bilaspur and Kutch. A third form of integration of states was the Kathiawar, United States of Matsya, Union of Vinidhya Pradesh, Madhya Bharat, Patiala and East Punjab States Union (PEPSU), Rajasthan and United States of Cochin-Travancore.

The unification of India was still incomplete without the French and Portuguese enclaves. The French authorities were more realistic when they ceded Pondicherry and Chandernagore to India on 1 November, 1954. However, the Portuguese Government maintained that since Goa was part of the metropolitan territories of Portugal, it could in no way be affected by the British and French withdrawal from India. Indian authorities, however, maintained that Goa was one of the remaining outposts of colonialism. When negotiations and persuasions did not move the Portuguese Government, units of Indian Army had to be mobilized and Goa, Daman and Diu were liberated on 19th December, 1961.[3]

The Fall Out of Muslim League's Rejection of Cabinet Mission Plan

The Muslim League rejected the Cabinet Mission Plan on 16th August, 1946 and gave the call for 'Direct Action'. In fact, it was a call for anti-Hindu riots. The Muslim League Government in Bengal engineered the 'Great Calcutta killing' where the Hindus were the victims. The reaction was the outbreak of violence in Bihar, U.P., Bombay, Punjab, Sind and N.W.F. Province. A near civil-war situation had developed in many provinces.

---

2. Brown, Judith M., *Modern India*, p. 346.
3. For Reorganisation of terriories of India provinces and states on linguistic basis see chapter XXVII of this book.

The state of Punjab passed through very disturbed times. The three major communities–the Muslims, the Hindus and the Sikhs–were nearly balanced; the Muslims with a population of about 16 millions had a slight edge over the combined Hindu-Sikh population of 12 millions. However, in other sectors–wealth and education, services and professions–the Hindus and Sikhs were more prominent in the public life of Punjab and had made a larger contribution to its economic development than the Muslims. More so, they were conscious of their contribution in the building of Punjab and were proud of it.

In March, 1947 communal riots had disturbed many parts of north – western Punjab particularly Rawalpindi, Multan, Lahore and Amritsar. According to Penderal Moon, the casualties numbered 2049 killed and 1103 injured. The Sikhs were the worst sufferers. Migration of Hindu-Sikh population had started though on a small scale. Even the imposition of Governor's rule under section 93 of the Government of India Act 1935 could not maintain law and order in the Punjab.

Early Problems of Independence

Both the states of India and Pakistan faced the consequences of partition. The Indian Independence Act mentioned the procedure for settlement of three major problems, namely, the settlement of boundaries between the two states; the division of apparatus and personnel of I.C.S. and some other services and the division of military assets and formations.

Radcliffe's Boundary Award and the Punjab Carnage

As per the Partition Plan the Legislative Assemblies of Punjab and Bengal met each in two sections or parts (one representing the Muslim majority districts and the other of the rest of the province) and decided by simple majority in favour of the partition of the two provinces. As such, the boundaries of the two provinces had to be demarcated.

A Boundary Commission under the Charimanship of Sir Radcliffe was appointed to make the demarcation of boundaries on the basis of ascertaining the contiguous majority areas of Muslims and non-Muslim but was also to take other factors into account. Unfortunately, the Commission worked under serious limitations. Justice Radcliffe had "no knowledge about India". Further, the Commission was required to draw the boundaries and decide disputed points within a period of six – week deadline. Percival Spear comments, "With limitations of time, knowledge and understanding, it was virtually impossible to deal adequately with the often vital accessories of a boundary line – such as the location of the canal head waters in relation to the canals themselves, communications by road and rail, the fate of mixed or isolated populations and such 'invisible' problems as the location of pasture lands in relation to villagers's flocks and herds".[4]

After 15th August, 1947, violence broke out on both sides of the boundary line in the Punjab. It is very difficult to establish as to who began the orgy of murder. The Sikhs blamed the Muslims and the Muslims blamed the Sikhs and the Hindus. In fact, violence invoked counter-violence. Before long the cities of the Punjab were in flames, where armed bands of Sikhs and Muslims roamed the cities and the countryside committing unbelievable murders. District officers found themselves powerless as members of the Boundary Force refused to fire on their co-religionists.

The horror and brutality of the month of August, 1947 convinced the common man that nothing could put an end to their horrors except the physical separation of the Hindus, Sikhs and the Muslims. Thus began one of the greatest and almost mass migrations of history. A Government of India report gives a vivid description of the movement of refugees:

"Fleeing from towns and villages close to the Indo-Pakistan border, non-Muslims began to enter India in large numbers in small disorganized parties towards the end of August and early part of September, 1947. Later, when the Indian army began to help them, huge foot convoys each 30,000 to

---

4. Spear, Percival : *The Oxford History of India* p. 404.

40,000 strong, started upon a 150 – mile march from the fertile colonies of Lyallpur and Montgomery districts. Thus, in forty – two days (September 18th to October 29th), twenty four non-Muslim foot columns, 849,000 strong, with hundreds of bullock – carts and herd of cattle had crossed the broder into India.

"The movement of these columns raised problems of baffling complexity. When the supply of food failed, the Government of India had to drop cooked food as well as food grains by R.I.A.F. planes which flew from Amritsar and Delhi to Jaranwala, Lyallpur, Churkhana, Dhabhasinghwala, Balloki head – works and Bhai – Pheru. Drugs, vaccines and doctors were rushed by air and motor transport. A field ambulance unit was sent to Raiwind to inoculate refugees before they crossed the border. On the way the columns were often attacked and sometimes suffered heavy casualties. Women and children were abucted and unauthorized search deprived them of the few valuables they carried. The Columns suffered at hand of not only man but also nature. Exposure and devastating floods thinned their ranks. Nevertheless, the determined carvan moved on"

The railways played a notable role in the evacuation of refugees from Pakistan Punjab to India and Muslim refugees from India to Pakistan. According to one estimate, the railways carried 2,300,000 refugees inward or outward across the Indo – Pak frontier. By November, 1947 the movement of refugees almost came to an end it was estimated that almost 80 lakh refugees had crossed the border.

After the Punjab carnage, both governments of India and Pakistan had to face unprecedented problems of feeding, clothing, rehabilitation and, above all, finding occupations for town – dwellers as well as landless peasants and rural labourers. Lakhs and lakhs of Punjab refugees found shelter in Delhi. The Government of India set up a Department of Rehabilitation and planned a number of new colonies and markets in Delhi. The huge influx of Punjabi refugees into Delhi has given a new complextion to the social, cultural, economic and ethic life of the mega city of Delhi and even neighbouring states of Harayana and Western U.P.

Problems connected with Division of Resources of Civil Government

To resolve the problem of division of assets and personnel of civil Government a Partition Council, consisting of two representatives each of India and Pakistan and presided over by the Governor General, was set up. At the operational level a Steering Committee of two officials, H.M. Patel and Mohammad Ali attended to the details, to the satisfaction of both the parties. The committee offered all civil servants to give their option about the Dominion they would prefer to serve. Nearly 1,60,000 employees opted for tranfer from India to Pakistan or from Pakistan to India.

As far as the Indian Civil Services were concerned, a distinction was made between the European and Indian members. The European members could continue in service in India on their existing pay, leave, pension rights etc. However, if they decided to retire they were entitled to special compensation and early retirement. In the case of Indian members of Indian Civil Services they were to continue in service in their country i.e. India/Pakistan on the existing scale of service. The question of division of cash balances as well as allocation of Public Debt created great controversy. Pakistan demanded a quarter share of total cash balances of the Government of undivided India, but the Indian representatives maintained that only a small portion of the cash balances represented the real cash needs of the country and the rest was maintained only as an anti-inflationary measure.

However, Mahatma Gandhi, moved by his inner conscience took up the cause of Pakistan and wanted more cash payment to be made to Pakistan. To pressurize the Congress leadership in office, he began a fast upto death and made to Pakistan. In spite of some disputes, both India and Pakistan continued with common currency and coinage till Pakistan set up its own State Bank in 1948.

Problems Arising Out of Division of Military Forces and Equipment

A division of military personnel and arms and ammunitions evoked even a greater controversy than the problem of Civil Services. A Joint Defence Council with Auchinleck as its Supreme Commander was set up and assigned the duty of completing the division of the armed forces and their plant, machinery, equipment and stores. As a first step, it was decided that Muslim-majority units were to be transferred to Pakistan and non-Muslim units to India. Serious differences arouse and break down of talks was recognized and post of Supreme Commander was abolished. Both sides accused each other of serious discrimination. The British troops started their withdrawal from India on 17th August, 1947 and the process was completed on 28th February, 1948.

Murder of Mahatama Gandhi

Gandhiji was disillusioned with the partition of India but he still believed in the ideal of Indian nationhood in secular terms i.e. where members of all communities. Hindus, Muslims, Christains, Sikhs had equal rights in the land of their birth.

When communal riots broke out in Bengal during 1946-1947 he went there as 'one-man' army to help and salvage the Hindu community in Calcutta, Noakhali and Tipperah districts. After that he arrived in Delhi during the autumn to find the Muslim cummunity threatened with extinction from the city.

Quite a few lakhs of Hindu refugees from West Punjab, Sindh and N.W.F. Provinces had been shunted out lock, stock and barrel from their homes during the communal riots in these states and their mass migration to East Punjab, Western UP and Delhi they had lost many members of their families and almost all their belongings. These refugees brought with them tales of oppression committed on them not only by the Muslims fanatics but also by the new Pakistan authorities in these states. These refugees put up their own tents in the city, some found shelter in newly set-up government camps but a few found shelter in many mosques in Delhi. In this surcharged, atmosphere communal tension was inevitable. Some Muslim families vacated their houses in panic and some decided to migrate to West Punjab.

Gandhiji arrived in Delhi at this jucnture to look after the interests of the Muslim community. He started his daily prayer meetigs at the Birla mansion on 30 January, Marg, New Delhi.

The partition of India was a victory for the Muslim League and its followers, but by and large an unprecedented tragedy for the Hindu community. The Hindu Mahasabha and the R.S.S. fundamentalist organisations (which were the counterpart of The Muslim League fundamentalists) always maintained that Hindustan was primarily the land of the Hindus where they could practise their prevailing religious traditions without contamination caused by Muslim or European culture. It was further maintained that non-Hindus in India "must learn to respect and hold in reverence Hindu religion, must entertain no ideas but those of glorification of Hindu race and culture" and could only stay in India if they "wholly subordinated to the Hindu nation claiming nothing, deserving no privileges, far less any preferential treatment".

The Hindu fundamentalist organisation believed that the Indian National Congress leaders including Gandhiji were responsible for the 'vivisection' of the Holy Motherland and must be labelled as traitors. It was in this surcharged atmosphere of psychological and physical agony that Nathuram Godse shot dead Gandhiji on 30th January, 1948. Gandhi's murder gave a big shock and jolt to the nation, particularly the Congress party leaders. lakhs of Delhiites joined the funeral procession on the bank of the river Jamuna. Later, in a address to the nation on the All India Radio, Jawaharlal Nehru summed up the mood and spirt of the time, "The light has gone out of our lives and there is darkness everywhere.....the father of the nation is no more........ The best prayer we can offer him and his memory is to dedicate ourselves to truth and to the cause for which the great countryman of ours lived and for which he died".

Emergence of Nehru as the Undisputed Leader

The death of Mahatma Gandhi, the father of the nation, created a sort of political vacuum in the Congress Party and the national politics. The revulsion of public opinion discredited Hindu extremist organisations. Even Sardar Vallabbhai Patel (a champion of Hindu idelology, a realist in politics and supporter of big business and the political boss) and Jawaharlal Nahru (an idealist, secular-minded, semi-mystic and the Harrovian aristocrat with a dictatorial temperament) came together to work for the solidarity and welfare of the masses of India. Both Patel and Nehru were the idols of the masses and human models for patriotic Indians. There were other stalwarts like Purshottamdas Tandon, Prof. Ranga and other apostles of Socialism. In fact, the Congress Party had two wings as far apart as the Socialist and Conservative parties in England. The decks for Nehru's leadership in the Congress party were cleared with death of Patel (December, 1950) and Tandon (1951). Since no other political party worth the name had emerged which could offer an alternative government at the centre, Jawaharlal Nahru worked as Prime Minister till his death on 27th May, 1964.

Since Jawaharlal Nehru became the first Prime Minister at the incipient stage of Independent India and continued in office for 17 long years; his political thinking, economic planning and vision of socio-cultural sectors have left an indelible imprint on the developments and progress of Free India.

Parameters of Nehruvian Socialism

Nehru's political orientation began in 1920s when he proceeded on extensive tour of Europe and the World. He was impressed by the Russian model of Socialism but before long felt disillusioned with too much regimentation in its organisation and denial of human rights to the citizens. During the Non-Cooperation Movement (1920-22) he got ample opportunities to visit rural areas of U.P. He acquired first hand information about the exploitative nature of landlordism and money lenders at one end and the unhappy plight of the small cultivator and agricultural labour at the other end. In fact, he became aware of the state of entrenched poverty of the rural masses.

Nehru drew his inspiration from Marxism and Democratic Socialism stood for anti-imperialism, Nationlism and Socialism. Though Leftist in sentiment Nehru was tied by a silken thread to the Right under Gandhi's influence. In fact, Nehru looked to Gandhi as his mentor and guru and the people at large considered him as Gandhi's heir. A western historian has commented. "It was only in 1947 with the premiership of Free India before him on the one hand and the stark horror of civil war on the other, that Nehru broke with this mentor on the issue of partition."

There was a wide specturm of ideologies for the regeneration of Indian society. At one end were the Gandhians who believed in a non-violent revolution, leading to decentralization, relatively self-sufficient village communities without an artificial proliferation of wants and minimal resource to modern technology. The Socialists both within and outside the Congress, argued that removal of inequalities was as important as growth and stood for land reforms, greater public ownership and strict regulation of the private sector as a means of achieving greater equality. The Swatantra[5] Party which had many adherents within the Congress appeared, what they called, excessive emphasis on redistribution, considered land reforming as violation of fundamental rights to property, huge taxation and controls as inimical to incentives and public sector as inherently incapable of efficient management.

After independence, the Congress party under the leadership of Jawaharlal Nehru attempted a compromise between the above mentioned viewpoints – a compromise which leaned towards Socialism in declared intent but afforded the conservatives ample opportunities to resist implementation of Socialist policies.

---

5. The Swatantra Party was founded in 1959 by C. Rajagopalachari, the last Governor General of India (1948-50) and M.R. Masani of Bombay.

The constitutional framework seems to have been deliberately designed to include the Socialist zeal in practice. The Preamble to the Constitution which is the true index of the aims and aspirations of the people resolved to constitute India into "a Sovereign Democratic Republic" (the world Socialist was deliberately omitted)[7].

Part IV of the Constitution (containing Articles 36-51) listed the Socialist content under the heading "Directive Principles of State Policy" but made it very clear under Article 37 that "the provisions contained in this part, shall not be enforceable by any court." However, it mentioned that the articles were fundamental in the governance of the country and it was the duty of the state to apply the principles in making laws. It must be mentioned that the implementation of the Directive Principles has been very tardy till date and the new policy of liberalization, privatization and globalization has put further brakes as their implementation.

Economic Dislocation

The partition of India adversely affected the economy of India particularly in the matter of foodgrains and agricultural products. West Pakistan provinces were surplus in wheat and rice as 68% irrigated area of undivided India went to Pakistan. According to C.N. Vakil, yields of rice and wheat in India were only 750 Ibs and 650 Ibs per acre respectively as against 900 Ibs and 850 Ibs per acre in Pakistan; as such India with a slightly larger population in proportion to area than Pakistan, and with a much larger urban population, found herself with a greater shortage of foodgrains than had been experienced by undivided India. Almost a similar situation prevailed in regard to livestock since the better milk yielding cattle in India were in Sind and West Punjab.

An equally unhappy situation faced independent India in the matter of textile industry. While almost all the jute mills were located in Free India territory, nearly 80% of the raw jute was grown in East Pakistan (now Bangaladesh).

The situation of cotton textile industry was also unhappy. While most of the textile mills were located in India nearly 40% of the raw material, including some of the best varieties of American-type medium staple was cotton produced in Pakistan.

As far as the general industry was concerned, India's resources were largely unimpaired. Almost all the resources like coal, iron ore, manganese and mica were located in India.

All the heavy chemical plants, all paper mills, glass factories, cement, paint and matches factories were located in India.

The shortage of foodstuff was a big problem before the government of Free India. Extensive foodstuff imports created a serious balance of payments problem with great lowering of India's £ sterling reserves.

British economists point out that even before Independence India had a number of experienced industrialist and financers who could be expected to undertake great schemes of development. Also, the banking, insurance and managing agency systems were well developed.

Planning For All-Round Development

Jawaharlal Nehru wrote in 1946 "Nearly all our problems to-day have grown up during British rule and as a direct result of British policy: the prices; the minority problem; various vested interests, foreign and Indian; the lack of industry and the neglect of agriculture; the extreme backwardness in the social services; and above all, the tragic poverty of the people."[6]

As early as 1938 the Indian National Congress appointed a National Planning Committee under the chairmanship of Jawaharlal Nehru. The committee considered all aspects of planning in details. Nehru commented:

---

6. Nehru, Jawaharlal, *The Discovery of India* p. 284.

"The original idea behind the Planning Committee had been to further industrialization – the problems of poverty and unemployment, of national defence and of economic regeneration in general cannot be solved without industrialization. As a step towards such industrialization a comprehensive scheme of national planning should be formulated. This scheme should provide for development of heavy key industries, medium scale industries, and cottage industries ....

But no planning could possibly ignore agriculture, which was the mainstay of the people: equally important were the social services..... The more we thought of this planning business the vaster it grew in its sweep and range till it seemed to embrace almost every activity".[7]

Besides the National Planning Committee eight industrialists drew up "A Plan of Economic Development" which was popularly known as the Bombay Plan. Shriman Narayanan prepared Gandhian Plan. M.N. Roy, a revolutionary formulated the Peoples' Plan. However, these plans were of historical importance because they were only paper plans, which were never implemented.

In 1950 the National Planning Commission appointed with Prime Minister Jawaharlal Nehru as its Chairman and key ministers as its members. "The convention that financial sanctions for payments were contingent on the Planning Commission's clearance gave it considerable scope to shape investment decisions. More importantly, it played a major role in reconciling the competing claims of states and ministries and insuring that their programmes fitted into a coherent national plan."[8]

The objectives of Planning had a Socialist orientation and drew sustenance from the Directive Principles of State Policy mentioned in the Constitution. Four long-term objectives of the Planners in India were :

1. to increase production to the maximum possible extent so as to achieve higher level of national and per capita income;

2. to achieve full employment;

3. to reduce inequalities of income and wealth.

4. and to set up a socialist society based on equality and justic and to ensure absence of exploitation.

The objectives of Economic Planning were to be achieved through 'Mixed Economy' i.e. where Public and Private sectors were to co-exist and even some industries may be jointly owned and managed by the state and private enterprise. In the Public sector were listed steel plants, oil and its products, machine making, electrical works, aircarfts, ship building etc. In the Private sector textile, engineering, motor manufacture, cement etc. were mentioned.

First Five-Year Plan (1951-56)

After independence India faced three major problems – rehabilitation of refugees, severe food shortatge and inflationary pressure on economy. Thus the First Plan accorded the highest priority to agriculture including irrigation and power projects. About 44.6% of total outlay of Rs. 2069 crores in the public sector (later raised to Rs. 2378 crores) was allotted for its development. During this period the work on the Bhakra – Nangal Dam project near Ropar at the head of the Sutlej Himalyan valley was started. The great power and irrigation projects of Damodar valley and Hirakund valley were also started.

The total investment on the development of basic industry including small scale industry

---

7. *ibid.*, p. 373.
8. Kumar, Dharma (Ed), *The Cambridge Economic History of India*, vol. II, p. 950.

and mineral development was listed at 173 crores. Even though the initial emphasis was laid on increasing production, the plan did not limit itself to achieve material progress only and therefore, it provided for investment in the development of human resource also. A total expediture Rs. 240 crores was provided for social services, (Rs. 52 crores for education, Rs. 100 crores for medical and public health services, Rs. 49 crore for housing, Rs. 29 crore for backward classes and nearly Rs. 7 crore for labour and labour welfare, Rs. 4 crore for volunatary social organisations).

The plan also aimed at increasing the rate of investment from 5 to 7 per cent of national income.

Second Five-Year Plan (1956-57 to 1960-61)

The Second Plan was conceived in an atmosphere of economic stability. The targets fixed in the First Plan were broadly achieved particularly in the field of agricultural development. Henceforth, a forward thrust was planned for development of heavy and basic industries. Furhter, the Industrial Policy Resolution of 1956 accepted the establishment of a socialist pattern of society as the goal of economic policy. The objectives of Second Plan were :

1. an increase of 25% in the national income;

2. rapid industrialization with special emphsis on the development of basic and heavy industries;

3. large expansion of employment opportunities;

4. reduction of inequalities in income and wealth and more even distribution of economic power.

The total outlay on social services was originally placed at Rs. 945 crores, but later reduced to Rs. 180 crores. The plan laid special emphasis on development of educational and medical facilities as well as on the advancement of industrial labour, displaced persons and other under-privileged classes.

An allotment of Rs. 120 crores was made for housing schemes, but later reduced to Rs. 84 crores at the time of the re-appraisal of the plan.

The Plan also visualized additional employment of 7.9 million outside the agricultural sector and about 1.6 million in the agricultural sector. As the main target of the Plan was on industrialization, three great steel plants of over million tons capacity each were established at Rourkela, Bhilai and Durgapur.

Though all the targets of the plan werer not achieved, the Second Plan marked another significant milestone in the country's onward march towards prosperity.

Third Five-year Plan (1961-62 to 1956-66)

The third Plan was launched in 1961. The approach of the plan was basically a continuation and an implementation of the First and Second five-year plans. It envisaged a development outlay of Rs. 7250 crores in the Public Sector.

The plan aimed at increasing the national income by about 30 per cent from Rs. 14,500 crores in 1960-61 to about Rs. 19,000 crores by 1965-66 (at 1960-61 prices) and per capita income by about 17 per cent from Rs. 330 to Rs. 385 during the same period.

Nehru's death, May 1964

The achievements of the first two plans were great. Nehru played a vital role in the socio-economic development of India. It has been estimated that during this period the national income rose by 42 per cent and income per head by 20 per cent. However, during the last two years of the Third Five-year Plan the progress considerably slowed down. The situtation created by the Indo-Pakistan conflict (1965), two successive years of severe drought, general rise in prices, mounting debt obligations to the International Monetary Fund, the devaluation of the Rupee (June 1966) caused great anxiety and even delayed the formulation of the Fourth Five-year Plan.

Foreign Policy of Non-Alignment

The basic parameters of India's Foreign Policy were explained by Jawaharlal Nehru in September, 1946 when he declared :

"We propose, as far as possible, to keep away from the power politics of groups aligned against one another, which have led in the past two World Wars and which may even lead to distress on an even vaster scale. We believe that peace and freedom are indivisible and the denial of Freedom anywhere must endanger freedom elsewhere and lead to conflict and war. We are particularly interested in the emancipation of colonial and dependent countries and peoples and in the recognition in theory and practice of equal opportunities for all races........ We seek no domination over others and we claim no privileged position over other peoples".

In the late forties of the 20th century a bi-polar political world emerged. The two big world powers, the U.S.A and Russia had developed nuclear weapons and demonstrated their military might over weaker states. In Eastern Europe the pan-Slav movement gained popularity and Soviet influence over Hungry, Rumania and Bulgaria became paramount. To counter Russian influence in the north-east the U.S.A extended liberal economic and military assistance to Greece and Turkey and kept them out of the orbit of Soviet Union. In Western Europe, both greater and lesser states turned their eyes towards the U.S.A.

Nehru's main contribtion to the evolution of India's foreign policy was the acceptance and implementation of the concept of Non-alignment. Non-alignment meant taking independent decisions on international issues without being tied to any particular country or group of countries. Thus, Nehru and India's subsequent foreign policy has been in favour of peace and disarmament, racial equality and international co-operation for the peaceful resolution of international disputes.

Nehru's policy of Non-alignment was amply demonstrated during the Korean Crisis. During World War II, U.S.A. occupied South Korea and Russia North Korea. At the Postdam Conference, the 38th parallel of latitude was recognized as the line of control between north and south Korea. In 1950 Inida warned against the danger of expansion of conflict if the armies of one side were moved closer to the northern border of other. India's impartial approach recieved recognition when an Indian was chosen chariman of the United Nations Repartriation Commission to deal with the issue of prisoners of war. Again, India struck to the policy of Non-alignment during the prolonged political crisis in Vietnam, Cambodia and Laos. At the same time India opposed the aggresssive attitude and action of the colonial powers. India took a bold stand when in 1856 the Anglo-French forces invaded Egypt over the Suez Canal crisis. India's moral support to Egypt, both within and outside the UNO, greatly helped in the withdrawal of foreign troops from the Egyptian territory and recognition of Egypt's sovereignty over the Suez canal.

The first Non-aligned conference was held at Belgrade in 1961 in which 25 countries took part. The assembled delegates emphasized the need for periodical consultations among Non-aligned countries. The popularity of the Non-aligned movement attracted more and more countries to join it and at one time about 100 countries were actively associated with it. All along, the main focus of the movement was on Independence, Peace, Disarmament and Economic development.

Relations with Neighbour – States

Pakistan

Indo–Pakistan relations have been strained right from the day of the partition of India on 14 – 15th August, 1947. Mohammad Ali Jinnah, the chief architect of the Pak Plan was disappointed with the Mountbatten Partition Plan because it meant the wreckage of his all India plans and gave the Muslims a solution which left the remaining Muslim minority in India unprotected, divided the Muslim majority provinces of Punjab and Bengal and produced not only a north – eastern Pakistan but kept the western segment of Pakistan a thousand miles distant from the eastern segment (now Bangladesh). The Partition Plan also shattered the Hindu dream of Azad Akhand Bharat. Congress working committee leaders like Jawaharlal Nehru and Patel, however, felt that Indian independence could not materialize without the linked corollary of Partition of India. Many Hindu organisations felt that India and Pakistan could be united once again after the British imperial rule was withdrawn from India. It may, however, in this context be mentioned that the Muslim Fundamentalist groups in Pakistan enjoyed greater popularity and had more say in the formulation of Pak policies as compared to Hindu Fundamentalist organisations in India whose influence was very marginal.

Nehru followed a liberal policy of promoting conciliation and reducing tension in mutual relations with Pakistan. All post – Partition problems connected with division of civil and military resources of undivided India were settled through negotiations. The Government of India even agreed to supply an undiminished quantity of canal water to Pakistan Punjab pending a long-term engineering solution of the problem recommended by the World Bank. Unfortunately for India, Pakistan's response was not positive. Just two months after independence, on 22nd October, 1947 the Pathan tribesmen from the north – west led unofficially by Pak army officers marched towards Srinagar, the capital city of Kashmir. In panic, Maharaja Hari Singh of Kashmir, on 24th October, appealed to India for military help. On the advice of Governor General Mountbatten, Nehru informed the Maharaj that under international law India could send its troops to Kashmir only after the State's final accession to India. On 26th October, the Maharaja signed the 'Instrument of Accession' to India as also on Nehru's advice agreed to install Sheikh Abdulla as the Prime Minister of the State.

In view of the grave military situation in Kashmir, on 27th October, nearly 100 planes airlifted Indian troops and weapons to Srinagar to check the invaders from advancing towards Srinagar. Many battalions of Indian troops reached Kashmir by land routes. Within days the Pak – aided invaders were driven out of the valley, though they still controlled western parts of the state.

Apprehending a full – fledged war between India and Pakistan, Lord Mountbatten advised Nehru to refer the Kashmir Problem to the Security Council of the United Nations seeking a vacation of pak aggression. Nehru sent a request to this affect to U.N. on 30th December, 1947.

At the Security Council, the U.S.A. and Britain, for strategic reasons of propping up Pakistan as a frontline state against the USSR, supported Pakistan's line of argument. Ignoring India's complaint about Pakistan's direct involvement in the 'Kashmir question' the Security Council under U.S.A. – British influence listed the problem as "India – Pakistan Dispute". It passed many resolutions the upshot of which was a suggestion of ceasefire along the Line of Control (L.O.C.) which both India and Pakistan accepted on 31st December, 1948.

Ever since the ceasfire became effective, Pakistan controls the other side of L.O.C. which comprises northern and western portions of Kashmir covering an area of about 84,160 sq km. Pakistan has set up a shadow Kashmir Government with capital at Muzzaffarabad which toes the line of Islamabad. Pak – occupied Kashmir provides a foothold to Islamic fundamentalists and terrorist groups to indulge in cross – border violence.

Pak authorities have so often harped on the U.N. Resolution of August, 1948, which contains provision for holding of plebiscite in Kashmir about the 'Accession Decision' but forget to mention the two pre-conditions for holding a plebiscite, namely,
1. Pakistan should withdraw its forces from the state of Jammu and Kashmir, and
2. the authority of Srinagar administration should be restored over the whole state.

Since Pakistan never accepted the above two pre-conditions, a plebiscite in Kashmire could not be held. In the meantime, a Constituent Assembly was elected in Kashmir, which voted for Kashmir's final accession to India. After this, Kashmir elected its own Legislative Assembly and also participated in all subsequent General Elections for the Parliament in New Delhi.

Critics blame Nehru for his utopian liberalism and being too much under the spell of Mountbatten's advice when he announced that he was in favour of holding a referendum on 'Kashmir's accession' decision once peace and law and order were restored in the valley. Before long, Nehru himself was disillusioned with the partisan posture of the great powers dominating the Security Council. In a very pensive mood he wrote a letter to his sister Vijaylakshmi in February, 1948," I could not imagine that the Security Council could possibly behave in the trivial and partisan manner in which it functioned. These people are supposed to keep the world in order. It is not surprising that the world is going to pieces. The United States and Britain have played a dirty role, Britain possibly being the chief actor behind the scenes".[9] It, must, however, be admitted that Nehru's rushing to the U.N. and open declaration of holding a plebiscite on the issue of Kashmir's final accession to India gave an international complextion to the Kashmir problem and also gave a *locus standi* to Pakistan in the Kashmir tangle.

Even in the post Nehru era Indo – Pak relations continue to be hostile. The Indo – Pak wars in 1965, 1971 and May – June, 1999 (Kargil crisis) have furhter aggravated bilateral relations. Pakistan continues its proxy war against India by training and financing military groups across the Line of Control and even in other parts of India. Many militant organisations describe the war against India as a *Jehad* and propagate that in Islam, politics is just a subsidiary activity of their religion. On the other hand, India's approach is that the Kashmir question is not a religious issue but an administrative and political matter.

Kofi Annan, United Nations Secretary General, during his visit to India in March, 2001 gave a severe jolt to the Pak leaders when he explained that U.N. Resolution of 1948 was no longer 'relevant' because Pakistan did not withdraw its troops from P.O.K. (Pak Occupied Kashmir) which was a pre-condition for a plebiscite. According to Annan, only UN resolutions adopted under chapter 7 were "self enforcing" ones. He advised both countries to exercise restraint and resort to bilateral talks. He said "Pakistan and India should take constructive steps and exercise restraint and show wisdom to reduce tension in the region".

China

Both India and China had suffered from Imperial rule. India became independent in August, 1947 and Communist China became a Republic in 1949. Nehru believed that both countries with common experience of exploitation at the hands of the colonial powers and common experience of exploitation at the hands of the colonial powers and common problems of under-development and poverty would join hands to earn a respectable place in the world. Both countries subscribed to the policy of Non–alighment and Non–aggression. When Nehru visited China in 1954, both the countries signed the Panch Sheel i.e. five principles (of co-existence) viz;

1. Mutual respect for each other's territorial integrity and sovereignty;
2. Non-aggression;
3. Non-interference in each other's internal affairs.
4. Equality and mutual benefit, and
5. Peaceful co-existence.

An unhappy legacy of World War II was division of the world into two hostile power blocks, one led by U.S.A. and Western powers and the other led by the Soviet Union. Thus emerged organisations like the Baghdad Pact, the Manila treaty, SEATO and CENTO which made countries of West and East Asia appendages to the Western Power Bloc. These Power Blocs looked askance at India's policy of Non-alignment and neutrality and staying out of military blocs. John Foster Dutles,

---

9. Letter quoted in S. Gopal : *Jawaharlal Nehru–A biography,* Vol. II, pp.-27.28.

US Secretary of State, dubbed indian policy of Non-alignment which he called "Immoral Neutrality". It is common knowledge that U.S.A - Britain led power Bloc invariably supported Pakistan in almost all Indo - Pak problems, and for their own strategic considerations.

India had a long frontier with China from the Karakorams to Burma with a gap for Nepal. One meeting point was from Chinese Tibet to Sinkiang; the second stretched eastward to Sikkim and the third was the stretch of territory from Sikkim to Burma covered by the NEFA (North-Eastern Frontier Agency). In the first section lay Aksai Chin plateau where the border between India and China had never been agreed, rather never surveyed even. The third line was most volatile because it stretched from Lhasa to Tibet.

In 1950 China gave a jolt to India's hand of friendship by forcibly occupying Tibet without even informing India. An official protest was lodged with the Chinese authorities, but it was rejected by the Chinese. In 1954 India recognised China's sovereignty over Tibet. In 1955. Nehru stretched long his hand of friendship by projecting China and Chou En – lai at the Asian – African Conference at Bandung in Java.

In 1959 the Tibet situation worsened when the Dalai Lama – a religious leader much respected by the Hindus – fled from Tibet against China's mal-treatment. The International Commission of Jurists confirmed the ruthlessness and brutality of the Chinese against Dalai Lama. The Indian Government gave shelter to Dalai Lama but refused to give him permission to set up a government-in-exile. The Chinese authorities objected to the shelter given to the Dalai Lama and in retaliation against India moved its troops near the Kongka Pass in Ladakh, killing a dozen Indian policemen. The Indian Government wrote a latter of protest to China but recieved no satisfactory reply. The Indian intelligentsia urged Nehru to take firm action but Nehru's approach was to narrow the area of dispute and to maintain friendly relations with China.

The Chinese Attack, 1962

Nehru's ambition of Asian leadership and world reputation collapsed when in October, 1962 the Chinese army launched an attack and overran many Indian posts in the eastern sector in NEFA (later called Arunachal Pradesh). The Indian army commander in sheer panic withdrew leaving the door wide open for the Chinese army to walk in. Emboldened, on 20th October, the Chinese army advanced in the western sector and captured thirteen forward posts in the Galwan valley and even threatened the Chushul airstrip. A general sense of panic gripped the people and it seemed that the Indian army had left the door wide open for the Chinese to occupy Assam and many other parts in the plains.

On 9th November, Nehru wrote two letters to the U.S. President Kennedy describing the situation on the Indo-Chinese border as "really desperate" and requesting for military help. He wrote to Britain also for help. Apprehending military confrontation with the Western Bloc, the Chinese declared a unilateral withdrawal of their troops from advanced positions on the Indo-Chinese border.

The long borders between India and China have still not been delineated even forty years after the Chinese invasion of 1962. In 1964, the Chinerse authorities announed the establishment of the Tibet Autonomous Region. However, even today the place of Dalai Lama in the socio-political set up of tibet remains ambiguous.

Nepal, Burma and Sri Lanka

Nehru took special care to keep friendly relations with Nepal, Burma and Sri Lanka. In 1950 a special treaty of Peace and Friendship was signed with Nepal which recognized Nepal's total sovereignty over its territories apart from providing to Nepal's foreign trade all possible commercial transit facilities through India. As far as Burma was concerned, Nehru had close personal relations with U Nu, even though Indian businessmen in Burma were looked upon as commercial rivals. The relations with Sri Lanka too were cordial although the problems of Tamil settlers created occasional tensions.

Nehru's Achievements and Failures : An Overview

Jawaharlal Nehru started his political-cum ministerial career as de facto head of the Interim Government on 2 September, 1946 and later as first Prime Minister of Free India on 15th August, 1947 with all the adulation of a hero of India's Freedom Struggle. The first few years in office were a period of gestation and great expectations on the part of the people. However, as the period of implementation of ambitious policies began to be assessed the euphoria disappeared.

Nehru played a notable role in the consolidation of Indian independence and promoting national integration. He refused to play second fiddle to any of the two Power Blocs. Instead, with his vision of a free world, he propagated the policy of Non-Alighnment and five principles of peaceful co-existence (Panch Sheel). His efforts were rewarded when in 1961 he stood with Nasser of Egypt and Tito of Yugoslavia at Belgrade and gave a call to the world for nuclear disarmament and peace.

Nehru realized that the strongest pillars of independence were economic development and self-raliance. In 1950 the Government appointed a Planing Commission to prepare a blueprint for rapid economic development and removal of endemic poverty, social injustice and oppression. The first two Five-Year Plans of 1951-56 and 1956-61 yielded eccouraging results but the third Five-Year Plan ran into serious trouble because of debacle on the Indo-Chinese border and all round slump in the economy.

Nehru had committed himself to democracy and a parliamentary system of government in India. He played an important role in the framing of the New Indian Constitution. In the first session of the Constituent Assembly, Jawaharlal Nehru moved the Objectives Resolution which spelt out the fundamentals of the constitutional structure. The very first sentence of the Objectives Resolution reads: "The Constituent Assembly declares its firm and solemn resolve to proclaim India as an Independent Sovereign Republic". Our constitution became effective from 26th January, 1950.

Nehru fought three National General Elections. The functioning of the democratic set up revealed certain deficiencies and Nehru's government sponsored and Parliament approved 17 Constitutional Amendments Acts to cope with the changing eco-social scenario. Nehru must deserve credit for nurturing the spirit of democracy which has really taken roots in the Indian psyche. During the past period of half a century democracy has worked effectively in India whereas most of the countries in our neighbourhood like Pakistan, Bangladesh, Myanmar, Indonesia etc. have hopped between democracy and military dictatorship.

Unfortunately, Nehru did not prove to be a good party organizer or reformer. Nehru himself was conscious of the unhappy working of the Congress party. Even as early as 1948 he wrote : "It is terrible to think that we may be loosing all our values and sinking into the sordidness of opportunistic politics". Later in 1957, he addressed the Congress Members of Parliament, "The Congress Party is weak and getting weaker.... Our strong point in the past. Unless we get out of our present rut, the Congress Party is doomed. Following a further slump in the Congress vote bank in the General Elections of 1962, Nehru with the help of K. Kamraj (Chief Minister of Madras) made a desperate effort to revive the credibility of the Congress Party. Under the Kamraj Plan, it was decided to motivate six Union Ministers and six Chief Ministers (including Kamraj himself) to resign from their ministerial positions and take up responsibility for strengthening the Congress Party. On 24th August, 1963 six senior Cabinet Ministers; namely, Morarji Desai, Lal Bahadur Shastri, Jagjivan Ram, S.K. Patil, B. Gopala Reddy and K.L. Shrimali submitted their resignations, Six Chief Minister including Kamraj also resigned. In January, 1964 Kamraj was elected as President of the Congress Party. Unfortunately, no tangible improvement was witnessed in the party scenario, as the ousted ministers continued to resort to political manoeuvers to control political influence and patronage. Nehru himself, because of ill health (he suffered a stroke in January, 1964) had neither the energy nor the will to take up any corrective measures.

Perhaps, Nehru's greatest failure was in international relations. He started off his foreign policy with a bang but it ended with a whimper. He heedlessly complicated the 'Kashmir Question' by going to the UN and offered to hold a plebiscite on the question of 'accession of Kashmir' after the return of peace. Whether on this issue he acted on his emotional instinct or under the advice of Lord Mountbatten, the responsibility restes on his shoulders. Similarly, on the question of Indo – China border clashes whether Nehru was guided by his outcome was disastrous for India and even fatal for his own reputation. In sum, in matters of foreign policy Nehru left behind a legacy of difficulties for India which is still reeling under its impact.

In any assessment of Nehru's place in history one must take into account the British legacy of extreme poverty and economic backwardness both in agricultural and industrial sectors. In fact, the British rulers had created a structure of colonial institutions, a colonial economy, a colonial society, and even a colonial ideology. The institutions of landlordism, politically-loaded casteism, communalism, regionlism etc. along with 'distorted modernization' were also a legacy of the British Rule. The world political scenario of two opposing Power Blocs was another challenge.

In the given circumstances, Nehru tried his best but his achievements were not up to the mark. Unfortunately, in the international field too, India lost the halo of moral authority bequeath by Mahatama Gandhi.

In Indian history, Nehru still occupies the place of a hero. He was pace-setter in the field of social reforms especially equality for all citizens in respect of class, caste and gender. Above all, Nehru laid foundations upon which his successors have been trying to build a prosperous and happier India.

SELECT REFERENCES

1. Nehru, Jawaharlal : *An Autobiography*
2. Nehru, Jawaharlal : *Glimpses of World History*
3. Nehru, Jawaharlal : *The Discovery of India*
4. Gopal, Sarvepalli : *Jawaharlal Nehru : A Biography*
5. Collins and Lapierre : *Freedom At Midnight*
6. Nanda, B.R. : *Indian Foreign Policy. The Nehru years*
7. Bipan Chandara : *Ideology and Politics in Modern India*
8. Dharma Kumar : *The Cambridge Economic History of India Vol. II (1857 - 1970)*

LITERARY, ARTISTIC AND CULTURAL MOVEMENTS IN MODERN INDIA

However grave and calamitous might have been the impact of British imperial political and economic policies in India, it cannot be denied that British rule and English language broadly became the media for India's contact with the Western civilization and Western advances in the fields of science, technology and even Western political thought, cultural and social developments.

After the Revolt of 1857 the Macaulayian scheme of education through the medium of English language received a new stimulus when the Government of India set up in 1857 three universities of Calcutta, Bombay and Madras. University education made possible a wide diffusion of Western knowledge through lectures and books. Thus, in the three Presidency towns a newly—educated middle class grew up which became conversant with Western concept of political nationalism and also liberal—radical thought of writers like Milton, Shelley, Bentham, Rousseau, Voltaire and even Karl Marx. Percival Spears sums up the developments with the remarks: "The new middle class was a well—integrated all—India class with varied background but a common foreground of knowledge, ideas and values.... It was minority of Indian society, but a dynamic minority... It had sense of unity of purpose and of hope". This new middle class proved to be the new soul of Modern India and in due course infused the whole of India with its spirit. This English—educated middle class mooted the idea of an all—India political organisation like the Indian National Congress and later provided leadership to the Congress in all stages of growth—and even after Indian independence.

Since there was no other Indian language in which the educated elite could converse or communicate with one another, English language became the *lingua franca* of the English—educated classes in India. Knowledge of English language had an additional advantage because it could provide employment in Government services as also opportunities in professions of lawyers, doctors, teachers, engineers etc. In the last decades of the 19th century a number of English language periodicals began to be published followed by the publication of newspapers in English language.

Another noticeable trend in the new Indian literature was that of emphasis on patriotism and the ardent hope for India's Freedom. Writers in all Indian languages composed songs condemning British exploitation of India's resources and wrote in praise of Indian history, culture and heritage.

Bengali Literature: The impact of Western thought and literature was noticeable in the field of Bengali literature. In Indo-English poetry two young Bengali women, Aru Dutt and Toru wrote poems which were English in form though Indian in subject matter. Toru's collection of *Ancient Ballads and Legends* vindicated her talent of poetic utterance in English language. Romesh Chandra Dutt a great Congress leader and once President of the Indian National Congress (session held at Lucknow in December 1899) published translations of the Ramayana and Mahabharata in English. Dutt's book entitled *Economic History of India* in English, 2 Volumes received great recognition.

The 19th century also witnessed a veritable rebirth of Bengali intellect. Thoughtful Bengalis closely scrutinized the country's past and found that many old beliefs and practices were no longer of any use and needed to be discarded. At the same time they also discovered that many aspects of India's cultural heritage were of intrinsic value not only for Indians but also for humanity in general. Thus, the concept of an amalgam of the best of Western and Eastern ideas gripped the imagination of Bengali intellectuals. This trend was reflected in literary writings of Bengalis. Raja Ram Mohan Roy (1774–1833) was a great innovator in Bengali literature. Other notable scholars were Ishwar Chandra

Vidya-sagar (1820–1891), Madhu-sudan Datta (poet, 1824–1873), Bankim Chandra (novelist and essayist, 1838–1894), Sarat Chandra Chatterji (novelist, 1876–1938) and, above all, Rabindra Nath Tagore (1861–1941) and Aurobindo Ghose (1872–1950).

In the field of Anglo-Indian literature mention may also be made of Western scholars who drew inspiration from India's past literature. In this category the names of Williams Jones, Max Muller, Edwin Arnold and Anthony Hope are noteworthy.

Hindi Literature : During the 19th century Hindi literature also made notable progress. Instead of *Braja Bhasha and Avadhi Hindi*, and Khadi Boli Hindi became the popular medium of expression. Bharatendu Harish Chandra (Dramatist, poet and essayist, 1846–1884) earned popularity as the father of modern Hindi literature. Prem Chand (novelist and short-story writer (1880–1936) Surya Kant Tripathi Nirla (poet), Jaya Shankar Prasad (poet, dramatist), Ramchandra Shukla (critic) earned great reputation as Hindi writers. The writings of 20th century writers like Sumitra Nandan Pant, Mahadevi Verma, Ram Kumar Verma, and Jainendra Kumar are read with great interest even today.

In Bhojpuri, Manoranjan's forthnight poems caught the imagination of even the common man. His poem फिरंगिया became very popular.

फिरंगिया	BHOJPURI
	The British Colonialist
सुन्दर सुधर भूमि भारत के रहे रामा । आज इहे भइल मसान रे फिरंगिया ॥	Oh the British Colonialist! The beautiful and attractive land of India has become today a cremation ground.
अन्न धन जन बल बुद्धि सब नास भइल। कौनो के ना रहल निसान रे फिरंगिया ॥	The grains, wealth, people and power, all have been destroyed and now there is not even a sign of any of them.
सब विधि भइल कंगाल देस तेहू पर । टेकस के भार ते बढौले रे फिरंगिया ॥	The nation has been impoverished in all respects. Still you have loaded us with fresh taxation.
दुखिया के आह तोर देहिआ भसम करी । जरि–भूनि होइ जइबे छार रे फिरंगिया ॥	The sigh of the oppressed people will burn your body and you will be completely consumed and turned into ashes.
जुलुमी कानून ओ टेकसवा रद कइ दे । भारत के दे दे तें स्वराज रे फिरंगिया ॥	Withdraw the draconian laws and taxes and give India its freedom.
नाही तइ सांचे-सांचे तोरा से कहत बानी । चौपट हो जाई तोर राज रे फिरंगिया ॥	Otherwise your entire empire will be swept away by the waves of the tears of thirty-three crore people.
तैंतीस करोड़ लोग अंसुआ बहाई ओमें । बहि जाई तोर समराज रे फिरंगिया ॥	

Manoranjan

Urdu Literature: Urdu poetry and literature also developed during the modern times. Sir Sayyid Ahmed Khan (1817–98) who founded Mohammedan Educational Congress in 1886 (renamed as Anglo-Oriental Educational Conference in 1890) played a notable role in encouraging Urdu writers to reorient Urdu literature along modern line. Poetical gatherings gave a new incentive to Urdu language. Till the end of 19th century Urdu poetry was mainly a reflex of Persian poetry. The most notable figures were Asadullah Khan Ghalib (1806–1869), Altaf Hussain Panipati popularly known as Hali (1837–1914), Akbar Allahabadi (1846–1921), Brij Narain Chakbast (1882–1926), Pandit Ratannath Sarshar and Mohammad Iqbal (1873–1938).

Tamil Literature : Among the Tamil writers the names of Kuppuswami Mudaliyar (novelist), R. Krishnamurti (short-story writer), Chakravarti Rajagopalacharya (essayist short-story writer) and, above all, Subrahmanya Bharti (poet, philosopher and nationalist, 1882–1946) are the most conspicuous writers.

Telegu Literature : The Telegu literature which had for centuries centered round religious themes was influenced by modern political and economic themes during the later half of the 19th century. Rao Bahadur Viresh Lingam Pentulu (1848–1919), a poet, dramatist, novelist and critic) became the trend—setter of modern Telegu literature. Other outstanding writers were Nanduri Venkata Subbarao, M.O. Rama Rao and Garimella Satyanarayana. Satya Narayana's poem 'We Don't Want The White British Rule became very popular: It reads:

మాకొద్దీ తెల్లదొరతనము

పల్లవి : మా కర్థి తెల్లదొరతనము రవ
మా కర్థి తెల్లదొరతనము॥

అనుపల్లవి : మా ప్రాణాల్పై సంచిమాసాలు చరియంతె ॥మా కర్థి॥

చరణములు

పస్సిండు దేశాలు పండుతున్నాగాని-వడ్డన్నమై రావు పండి ।
ఉప్పు। ముట్టుకుంటె దోషమండి।
నోటి మట్టకొట్టి పారాడండి।
అయ్యో! కక్కుర్లో పోరా-టారు పెంటామై ॥మాకర్థి॥

వర్తకమునస్వప్ప-పట్టణములు పట్ల-రాజ్య మొక్కటి అర్థినాడు
దాష్పి। రాణ కర్మంచినాడు।
రావు। వ్రతమ్మ పంచేసినాడు।
ఈ ఎశ్వరమేశ్వర్-శక్తస్థానంబారు ॥మాకర్థి॥

కర్తులంటూ పెట్టి-పార్టీలు పట్టి-చె స్నేహభావము పంచినాడు ।
ద్రవ్య। దాహము కర్పించినాడు।
తెల । రూపాలు కడు పెంచినాడి
మా । ఆశ్రయముల ద్రుంచి-రహా- యునిపంచారు ॥మా కర్థి॥

పన్నెరజమురోదా-స్వేచ్ఛావధూటణ-కారాగృహమున వేచి
యుండి
పూల సర్వ్యములసు దార్చియుండి
మీకు ముచ్చటలను తెల్పుటండి
ఈ చప్పు రాజ్యముఎ దరగ వైలుకరండి ॥మా కర్థి॥

We Don't Want This White Rule

We don't want this white rule—Oh God
We don't want this white rule
That ambushed our lives and
robbed us of our honour.
We don't want this white rule....

Lands here yield plenty of crops
Yet not a morsel of food for us to eat,
Even to touch salt is a crime.
Miies away he runs, throwing
    dust into our mouth.
And lo! We are to fight with street
    dogs to have a share of our food!
We don't want this white rule....

He established law courts and created many a group,
Only to destroy our comradeship,
Encouraging greed, ill-will and undesirable ideas,
He left us behind to starve and cry all along.
We don't want this white rule....

Here at the gates of jail,
The bride—freedom—is waiting
With bunches of flowers in hand,
Only to welcome you and cheer you up.
Come, enter the jails straightaway
To discard, to condemn this moribund rule.
We don't want this white rule....

Garimella Satyanarayana

Marathi Literature : In the 19th and 20th centuries the theme of Marathi literature centered round romanticism, liberalism and nationalism. The establishment of a number of universities in Marathi-speaking areas helped in the development of Marathi language as well as research in various fields. The outstanding literary figures in the 19th and 20th centuries were M.G. Ranade (1842–1907), K. J. Telang (1850–93), V. S. Chiplankar (1850–82), R.K. Gopal Bhandarkar (1834–1925), V. S. Khandekar (novelist), G.T. Madhkolkar (poet and novelist) and H. D. Salgarkar (poet) whose poem is reproduced below :

Literary, Artistic and Cultural Movements in Modern India

तयाला तुरुंग भिवविल किती ?

मातृभूमिच्या उद्धारास्तव देह दिला करवतीं ।
तयाला तुरुंग भिवविल किती ? ॥ धृ ॥
शुभमालेसम लोहशृंखला मानित जो सर्वदा ॥
तयाला काय करिल कायदा ॥
प्राण पणाला लावुनि प्रेमें राजकारणीं उडी ।
घेइ जो सत्याचा सवंगडी ॥
स्वार्थत्यागी विषयविरागी मर्द मानधन असा ।
शत्रुला शिर नमविल तो कसा ॥
देशास्तव सर्वस्व समर्पिन ध्येय जयाचें निकें ।
तया गृह कारागृहसारिखें ॥
कलाकुशल कल्पनाविलासी प्रयत्नवादी मुनी ।
जनाच्यां स्तुतिसुमनांचा घनी ॥
अंतरी श्रीहरी सदोदीत करितो मज प्रेरणा ।
म्हणे लव गर्व न ज्याच्या मना ॥
त्रस्त जिवाच्या मुक्त भावना व्यक्त करुनि दाखवी ।
प्रतापी हा पुण्यात्मा कवी ॥
स्वातंत्र्यस्फूर्तिचें सिंचुनि अमृतकण ।
मृत मानवतेला आणितसंजीवन ।
तो सेनापति कवि साहिल का बंधन ?
अरिशिबिरीं क्षण विश्रांतीस्तव जात सुखें संप्रती ।
तयाला तुरुंग भिवविल किती ? ॥

How Can the Prison Walls Frighten Him?

How can the prison walls frighten him (a patriot)
Who has knowingly dedicated his self unto his motherland?
How can the laws (of foreign rulers) deter him
Who always regards iron chains as flower garlands?

He who is the lover of truth who takes a leap (into freedom movement) caring little for his own life.
He who is selfless and brave and has given up lust
Will he bow down ever to the enemy?

One whose pure aim is to devote everything to the motherland
To him, iron bars are like a sweet home.

A dreamer of dreams yet exerting like a saint.
People shower praises on him.
'What I do is inspired by God', says he.
For he never boasts.

Like a poet, he gives expression to peoples's predicament.
He inspires them with thoughts of freedom.
He awakens them from their slumber.

Will such lieutenant (people's leader) ever accept any restrictions?
He is going to the enemy-camp for a while to rest.
How can the prison walls frighten him?

Harihar Gurunath Salgarkar
'Kunjavihari'

Punjabi Literature : A group of writers belonging to Singh Sabha became very prominent in the later half of the 19th century. Their theme of discussion centered on socio — religious matters. Bhai Vir Singh (poet), Rana Surat Singh (poet), Puran Singh (poet, essayist), Mohan Singh (poet), Amrita Pritam (poetess, novelist and short-story writer), Kartar Singh Duggal (novelist and short-story writer), Balwant Singh Gargi and Rajendra Singh Bedi (both short-story writers and novelists) were the most outstanding personalities in the list of modern Punjabi writers.

Broadly speaking, the wind of change and ferment of ideas were visible in all parts of India and these developments were amply reflected in the literature of all Indian languages. We find a synthesis of the Western and Eastern values and cultures both in subject matter and style in Indian literary writings. Many notable Western literary works ranging from the writings of Shakespeare, Tolstoy, Victor Hugo, and T. S. Eliot to George Bernard Shaw were translated in many Indian languages.

Art and Architecture

The early European settlers in India brought with them European designs of architecture particularly in the construction of their churches and fortresses. Under the British East India Company's rule in India, the administrators showed no or very little dislike for Indian arts, architecture, religion or life-style.

After the British success in the Revolt of 1857, the British ruling class in India developed a racial superiority complex towards India and everything Indian. *The Punch* cartooned the Indians as a sub-human creature, half gorilla, half Negro who could be kept in check by superior force only. The neo-British imperialism was justified by the slogan of 'Whiteman's Burden' and the 'Civilizing Mission' of England in India. All the same, historical researches in ancient Indian history conducted by European scholars like Max Muller, Monier Williams, Roth etc. opened new vistas of India's rich cultural heritage. The researches in Medieval Indian art, architecture (monuments like Qutab Minar and Taj Mahal), music and painting revealed rich legacy. Emotions apart, gradually a new trend in Indian arts and architecture emerged which was a blend of the best of the West and best of the East.

In the field of architecture an Indo-British style of architecture popularly known as Victorian style developed. Even a change was perceptible in the architectural designs of churches. The churches of Kolkata and Chennai, the cathedrals of Lahore and Simla had the touch of Victorian style.

The Museum building of Jaipur reflects an amalgam of the prevailing Rajput style adapted to modern requirements. In the beginning of the 20th century G. Wittel designed the architectural design of Gateway of India and the Prince of Wales museum at Bombay.

The architectural plan of New Delhi was designed by Sir Edward Lutyens and Sir Edward Baker. The structural design of Parliament Houses, Rashtrapati Bhawan, North Block, South Block buildings and even residential buildings for government employees give an impression of a coherent whole without any disturbing or ill-fitting element anywhere.

Film Industry

The first indigenous silent feature film named *Raja Harishchandra* was produced by Dada Sahib Phalke. It was released on 3rd May 1913 at Coronation Cinema, Bombay.

The film industry took its modern shape in the 1920s. The first Indian talkie was named *Alam Ara* and was produced by Ardesher in 1931. The model of talkie films became popular in Bengal and South India. *Jamat Shasthi* was the first Bengali talkie, *Bhakta Prahlad* the first Telegu talkie, while *Kalidas* was the first Tamil talkie. The film versions of these talkies were produced in many other Indian languages like Kannada, Malayalam, Marathi, Gujarati, Oriya, Assamese and Punjabi.

Bimal Roy produced many popular films like *Do Biga Zamin*, *Devdas* and *Madhumathi* Similarly Raj Kapoor of Bombay produced films named *Boot Polish*, *Shri 420* and *Jagte Raho*. V. Shantaram shot into fame with the production of *Do Ankhen Bara Hath* and *Jhanak Jhanak Payal Baje* film Director Mehbood produced *Mother India*.

The films made by the commercial film companies of Bombay and Madras can be classified into two categories namely, 'mythological' and 'social' to which a third category can be 'historical' films which gave exaggerated images of great men and women of India from Chandragupta Maurya to Rani of Jhansi.

The most popular segment of films in the category of 'social' films have been more popular because they deal with contemporary and near contemporary social life. The theme centres round tear-jerking partings and reunions, the hero or heroine (or both) are saved from a dreadful fate at the last moment, the regular interpolation of songs and dances etc. Such films have been attracting large crowds. In Indian film songs the melody retains its Indian character and the singer often uses traditional vocal ornaments, although the accompanying orchestra shows a great deal of Western influence and may include Western instruments of all types. Of late, Western popular music with all its lively rhythms, single harmonic structures and emphasis on tune, has greatly influenced Indian film music.

Theatre Associations

The evolution of the system of popular theatre plays can be traced in the history of South India. The theatre plays had various aspects like musical plays, ballets and *ragakavayas* from the last of which the modern forms of *Kathakali* developed. Later the modern *bharatanatyam* took shape in which the dancer does not wear costume but impersonates in nine various characters in story. Meanwhile the system of Street plays developed in Andhra and Karnataka.

In northern India, Calcutta witnessed the birth of modern drama. The first stage-play in Bengali language was produced in Calcutta by a Russian indologist, Lebedev in 1795. It was an adaptation of the English comedy *The Disguise* (written by Richard Paul Jodrell). The actors and actresses used mixed English-Bengali to cater to the needs of a mixed audience.

The first play in Bengali written by Pandit Ramnarayan was named *Kulin Kulasarvarana* which was a social satire against the practice of polygamy among upper caste brahmins. Another popular play of Ramnarayan was *Ratnavali*. Another notable dramatist was Madhusudan Dutt who wrote a number of popular plays.

Dinbandhu Mitra (1827–74) shot to fame with the publication of his play *Nil Darpan* (published in 1860) which highlighted the atrocities of the British Indigo planters in Bengal Presidency. The play created a political sensation in the nationalist circles in India. Even the government was alarmed and appointed an Indigo Commission in 1860. The recommendations were incorporated in Act VI of 1861. The Bengal Indigo planters developed cold feet and gradually moved out of Bihar and U.P. Other notable playwrights were Jyotirindranath, Manmohan Basu, Dwijendralal Roy and Grishchandra Ghosh. Rabindranath Tagore's plays though very thoughtful did not catch the popular imagination of the common man in Bengal.

Prithviraj Kapoor was another notable playwright. He set up the Prithvi Theatres, which was the first professional Hindi Theatre group with a permanent staff. Prithviraj believed that popular plays could provide good entertainment and also reform Indian society. His most popular plays were Shankuntla, Dewar (wall), Pathan, Ghaddar (traitor), Kalaakar (artist), Paisa (money), Kissan (farmer) and Ahuti (offering).

Other theatre organizations in India were Theatre Unit (Bombay), Anamika (Calcutta), Three Arts Club, Indraprastha Theatre, Little Theatre Group and Delhi Arts Theatre. The establishment of the National School of Drama in Delhi was another landmark in the development of Theatre Organizations.

The latest trend in the field of Theatre Organization is to attempt a workable synthesis of the traditional Indian and Western style and techniques regarding issues and problems facing humanity in general both in the East and the West.

Writers' Organizations

A salutary effect of the widespread literacy and cultural activities in India in the 19th and 20th centuries was the establishment of many Writers' Organizations.

A group of intellectuals in Andhra Pradesh founded the Sahiti Samiti. Mr Srivasankra popularly known as the Anna Guru (Elder Brother) was its first President. Many short-story writers, poets and painters associated themselves with the organization. Later, they also started the publication of a journal called *Sahiti*.

The literary stalwarts of Maharashtra organized the Ravikiran Mandal (popularly called Sunday Club) in 1923. Poets and musicians patronized the Mandal. The most popular poets associated with it were Girish, Yashwant and Madhav Juabin. Similar associations were organized in different cities in Maharashtra.

The intellectuals of Orissa organized the *Sabuja*. Stalwarts like Saratchandra Mukerji, Baikuntha Nath Pattanayaka, Kalindicharan Panigrahi and Harshandra Badala, Vishvanatha Kara, the editor of journal *Utkala Sahitya*, were closely associated with the organization.

LITERARY LUMINARIES
Rabindranath Tagore (1861–1941)

Rabindranath was born at Calcutta on 7 May 1861 as the fourteenth child of Devendranath and Sarda Devi.

The Tagore family was amongst the leading families of Calcutta when the Indian Renaissance movement started in Bengal under the pioneering leadership of Rammohan Roy. The family supported Roy's analysis that the progress of India lay in a proper blend of the best of the West and the East. One of Rabindranath's brothers, Satyendranath Tagore was the first Indian to be selected for the I.C.S. in 1864.

Rabindranath was a widely travelled person and toured Europe and America many times and came into contact with a wide spectrum of personalities in the literary and political fields.

In the early decades of the 19th century Tagore did much to popularize the Swadeshi movement. He believed that self-help and self-respect should form the true foundation of Swadeshism.

He stood for a national scheme of education. He was convinced that the mother tongue should be the medium of instruction, that in any system of real education there should be a link-up of learning and living in an atmosphere of freedom. In 1901, a school was established at Shanti Niketan which finally developed into the world famous University of Visva-Bharati in 1918.

Tagore inherited the love for poetry and song from his family. His works include more than a thousand poems and over two thousand songs in addition to a large number of short stories, novels, dramatic works and essays on diverse topics. In 1913, his selection of poems in *Gitanjali* was selected for the Nobel Award in Literature. In 1912, Tagore composed *Jana Gana Mana* (now India's National Anthem) which conveys the message that India stood for unity amidst diversity. Besides, Tagore was a painter of unusual merit; he painted some 3000 pictures. In 1915, Tagore was awarded Knighthood by the British monarch George V.

Tagore came in close contact with Gandhiji. He raised his voice against oppression in all parts of the world. He expressed his unhappiness at the outbreak of the Second World War. In April 1940, he questioned Britain's intentions towards India's struggle for independence in a write-up entitled *Crisis in Civilisation*.

Tagore was a versatile genius. He made notable contributions to religion and educational thought, crusaded for social and economic reforms for a just political order in the world. Indeed, he was one of the greatest sons of India and his message is for the betterment of the entire mankind.

C. *William Radice writes*

Were there two Rabindranath Tagore? Or rather, was there one Rabindranath and one Tagore? I've been wrestling with this question for years. It underlies a maddening problem of nomenclature. In writing about India's greatest modern writer, which name should we use? In Bengali he is known as Rabindranath. As such, he is the supreme Bengali poet. The solar imagery of the name has been irresistible to many of the lesser Bengali poets who have written poems about him. He is the sun : they, at best, are the planets circling round him. Rabindranath himself could not have been unaware of this when he wrote, in a brief poem:

"*How easy it is*
To mock the sun:
The light by which it is caught
Is its own."

That is the translation of Radice, not his Bengali words; but the personality it expresses – proud, sensitive to criticism, fearless of truth, conscious of greatness – is that of the Bengali

Rabindranath. The same voice spoke when a huge delegation came to Santiniketan by a special train on November 23, 1913, to felicitate him on the Nobel Prize, and he turned them away with bitter irony, castigating the hypocrisy of those who had attacked him beofore and were congratulating him now.

Yet can we deny that "Tegore" existed too? The Nobel Prize for Literature was awarded to Tagore, not to Rabindranath. The books that the prize made famous, which were translated into the world's major languages, were all by Tagore, not Rabindranath. India outside Bengali knew him more through those books than through his Bengali writings. When Bangladesh adopted *Amar Sonar Bangla* as her national anthem, she chose a song by Rabindranath; but when *jana-gana-mana* became the national anthem of India it was because Tagore had written:

> 'Where the mind is without fear and the head is held high;
> Where knowledge is free;
> Where the world has not been broken up into fragments by narrow domestic wall...
> Into that heaven of freedom, my Father, let my country awake."

True, Rabindranath towards the end of his life often expressed regret that he had done the English versions that had made him world-famous: they were, as he said in a letter to Amiya Chakravarty, "self-mockery"; and to William Rothenstein he wrote that his western fame had been "an accident" and that he felt "almost ashamed that I whose undoubted claim has been recognised by my countrymen to a sovereignty in our own world of letters should not have waited till it was discovered in its own true majesty and environment". The image that those translations had projected, reinforced so indelibly by W.B. Yeats in his well-intentioned but deeply ignorant Introduction to *Gitanjali*, became a terrible burden. It cramped the free poetic spirit in him, the Rabindranath whose Bengali writings in prose and verse could be deft and witty and charming in a way that his Western admirers could never imagine. To his friend Charles Freer Andrews, Rabindranath wrote in 1921 from New York :

> "When the touch of spring is in the air, I suddenly wake up from my nightmare of giving 'message" and remember that I belong to the eternal band of good-for-nothings; I hasten to join in the vagabond chorus. But I hear the whisper around me; "This man has crossed the sea', and my voice is choked."

Yet Tagore and Rabindranath were not entirely separate entities. Rabindranath would not have wished to disown the Tagore who resigned his knighthoood in protest at the Amritsar massacre of 1919; who spoke at the very end of his life of the crisis in civilisation that World War II had brought; who engaged in passionate debate with Gandhi; who, far more than by his personal predicament, could feel choked by evil and injustice.

Prashna (1932) is one of his greatest Bengali poems, but its voice is Tagore's as well as Rabindranath's:

> "My voice is choked today; I have no music in my flute:
> Black moonless night
> Has imprisoned my world, plunged it into nightmare. And this is why,
> With tears in my eyes, I ask:
> Those who have poisoned your air, those who have extinguished your light,
> Can it be that you have forgiven them ? Can it be that you love them?"

Above all, in Visvabharati–the creation that meant more to him than any other, though it brought him most heartache–Tagore and Ranindranath came together. Sensitive visitors to Santiniketan will encounter that dual spirit. They will sense the Rabindranath who brought up his family there-alone, after his wife died in 1902; whose many gifted relatives linked him to the leading trends of the Bengal Renaissance; who taught the children of his school under mango trees; who preached eloquent

Bengali sermons in the glass-panelled Prayer Hall; who drew and painted; who sang his songs; who shuttled sleeplessly between the various houses of Uttarayan. But they will also feel the presence of Tagore, whose fame attracted famous foreign scholars to teach at Santiniketan; who received, in extreme old age, a doctorate conveyed to him by representatives of Oxford University; who left to the archives of Rabindra Bhavana a vast international correspondence.

If elsewhere the two aspects–and the two names–seem less in synchrony; whether when reading, say, reviews of his English books in the western press, which are seldom informed by any knowledge of his Bengali background; or, at the other extreme, when listening to Rabindrasangeet or recitations of his poems in Bangladesh, a country that has little need of English and only knows Rabindranath, not Tagore; that is because of his *purnata,* the completeness with which he embodied the entire subcontinent and its modern involvement with the West. If East and West are sometimes in conflict in his name, as well as in unity, that is true of the subcontinent as a whole.

Yet the fact that the two did come together, in that name, offers hope. That was his real prophetic role: to point us towards a new, post-twentieth century *purnata,* reconciling not so much East with but poetry with prose, art with morality, idealism with realism, religion with science.

This promise was expressed in another brief poem. It is by Rabindranath, certainly; but in its restless aspiration, Tagore is present too:

"Tumultuous days
Rush towards night.
Seas are the goal
Of streams in full spate.
Impatient spring-flowers
Long to be fruit."
Restlessness strives
To be calm and complete."

PREM CHAND

Prem Chand his original name was Dhanpat Rai Srivastava born in July 31, 1880, at Lamati, near Varanasi, Indian author of numerous novels and short stories in Hindi and Urdu who pioneered in adapting Indian themes to Western literary styles.

Prem Chand worked as a teacher until 1921, when he joined Gandhi's Non-co-operation Movement. As a writer, he first gained renown for his Urdu-language novels and his contributions to Urdu journals. Except in Bengal, the short story had not been an accepted litetary form in Northern India until Prem Chand's works appeared Best-know for his works in Hindi, Prem Chand did not achieve complete fluency in that language until his middle years. His first major Hindi novel, *Sevasadana* (1918; "House of Service"), dealt with the problems of prositittution and moral corruption among the Indian middle class. Prem Chand's works depict the social evils of arranged marriages, the abuses of the British bureaucracy, an exploitation of the rural peasantry by money-lenders and officials.

Much of Prem Chand's best work is to be found among his 250 or so short stories, collected in Hindi under the title *Manasarovar* (The Holy Lake"). Compact in form and style, they draw, as do his novels, on a notably wide range of nothern Indian life for their subject matter. Usuall they point up a moral or reveal a single psycholigical truth.

Professor Alok Rai Writes

Prem Chand, a writer and a cultural phenomenon on whom no special claims could be made, but to whom, by the same token, no special honour was owed. This was much harder for my father than for myself. I grew up feeling cheated by the famous ancestor who died a full 10 years before I was born. So it is Prem Chand that is my theme, and not my thoughtless grandfather.

Writing about Rudyard Kipling, Orwell struggled to reconcile his obvious distaste for the brash poet of imperialism with his recognition of Kipling's creative vitality, both as a story-teller and as a poet many of whose lines had acquired the ultimate accolade of popular, unattributed curency, like folksongs: "It takes great vitality even to become a byword; but to remain one, that is genius."

Munshi Prem Chand, a hoary icon, a sometime sentimentalist from a bygone age, firmly established in the dubious immortality of a curricular classic, poses a similar challenge. For he, too, has become a byword, the familiar and rubbed down currency of our social imagination.

Embalmed in textbooks, routinely rehearsed in classrooms Prem Chand is obviously dead. Here he is the author of a few stories that are universally known, even though they have been rendered innocuous by being made part of the hypocritical tedium of the education system. One may just feel a pang of affiliation for the little boy who buys a chimta for his grandmother; for Gangi who dies, thirsty, turned away from the Thakurs' well; for the farmer who is almost gradeful that with his harvest reduced to ashes, he will no longer have struggle to keep awake guarding it in the cold winter night-but little survives outside the lethal parentheses of school.

The idealistic tales in which, after a clear-eyed depiction of the horrors of his (and alas, our) society, assent is sought for improbable and "Gandhian" changes of heart cannot speak any more to our cynical selves. The icon "Prem Chand" seems almost complicit with the establishment that honours him, like a distant ancestor who is both remembered and, in the very act of remembering, forgotten.

And yet, as an old song has it-he's dead, but he won't lie down! His books continue to be printed. When the copyright fell into public domain, dozens of publishers in the depressed and depressing, literate and semi-literate Hindi world, got into the business of doing reprints. Clearly, he still speaks to a large number of readers. My subject is precisely this curious, this amazing, this alarming persistence.

Party, of course, this has to do with the persistence of certain shameful realities–this voice from the past can still sound vibrant with a relevant anger. The brutalised landless labourers of *Kafan* are still with us, in ever greater numbers; traditional caste oppression against the Dalits is still rife, albeit now sometimes in an updated OBC version; the middle class still struggles to reconcile its vaunted ideals with the shabby compromises of its everyday existence; the contempt for politicians finds an echo in contemporary vigilante fantasies......

But I suspect there is more to it than just that. When Stephen Dedalus sallies forth into the future in James Joyce's *Portrait of the Artist as a Young Man,* he intends, famously, "to forge, in the smithy of my soul, the uncreated conscience of my race". Similar young men dominate the modern traditions of many of India's languages–encyclopaedic Renaissance men (not many women, alas, for all the well-known reasons), towering and formative individuals whose cultural influence goes far beyond their considerable achievements and competencies. What unites these masters of conscience is the fact that they enlarged the range and reach of the social imagination by making a greater proportion of the marginalised life of their times available to the imagination for being given narrative shape, and so form the basis for a moral order.

'It is arguable whether it is the sluggishness of our contemporary reality that cripples poets and writers, singers and artists, whose social function it is to reinvent and reconfigure our experience;

or whether it is our imaginations that have failed to rise to the challenge, so that we remain trapped in the narrative constructions of these powerful, old men ? On both counts, the persistence of Munshi Prem Chand is alarming.

But there is one final respect in which he still lives-this writer who died too young ever to become an old man. Prem Chand was a school-teacher; he had two little children, and the third, my father, wasn't born until later that year. His wife was literate even articulate, in her rough rustic fashion, but no more. he had no private wealth to fall back upon. Because a passing Mahatma gave a call for non-cooperation, he threw himself into the national movement, leaned once into the wind and simply let go, this no-longer-young man on the flying trapeze. It seems scarcely credible now.

SELECT REFERENCES

1. Chaudhri, B. M. (Ed.) : Homage to Rabindranath Tagore (Tagore Centenary Celebration Committee, Kharegpur)
2. Dutt, R. C. : The Literature of Bengal
3. Majumdar, R. C. (Ed.) : History and Culture of the Indian People, II vols.
4. Radhakrishnan, S. : East and West
5. Rahbar, Hansraj : Premchand, Jiwan and Krititva
6. Singhal, D. P. : India and World Civilization 2 vols.
7. Tagore, Rabindranath : My Reminiscences
8. Ward, B. : India and West

APPENDIX I
KARL MARX ON THE BRITISH RULE IN INDIA[1]

...Hindustan is an Italy of Asiatic dimensions, the Himalyas for the Alps, the Plains of Bengal for the Plains of Lombardy, the Deccan for the Apennines, and the Isle of Ceylon for the Island of Sicily. The same rich variety in the products of the soil, and the same dismemberment in the political configuration. Just as Italy has, from time to time, been compressed by the conqueror's sword into different national masses, so do we find Hindustan, when not under the pressure of the Mohammedan, or the Mughal or the Briton, dissolved into as many independent and conflicting States as it numbered towns, or even villages. Yet, in a social point of view, Hindustan is not the Italy, but the Ireland of the East. And this strange combination of Italy and Ireland, of a world of voluptuousness and of a world of woes, is anticipated in the ancient traditions of the religion of Hindustan. That religion is at once a religion of sensualist exuberance, and a religion of self-torturing asceticism; a religion of the Lingam and of the Juggernaut; the religion of the Monk, and of the Bayadere.

I share not the opinion of those who believe in a golden age of Hindustan, without recurring, however, like Sir Charles Wood, for the confirmation of my view, to the authority of Khuli-Khan.[2] But take, for example, the times of Aurangzeb ; or the epoch, when the Mughal appeared in the North, and the Portuguese in the South; or the age of Mohammedan invasion, and of the Heptarchy[3] in Southern India ; or, if you will, go still more back to antiquity, take the mythological chronology of the Brahmin himself, who places the commencement of Indian misery in an epoch even more remote than the Christian creation of the world.

There cannot, however, remain any doubt but that the misery inflicted by the British on Hindustan is of an essentially different and infinitely more intensive kind that all Hindustan had to suffer before. I do not allude to European despotism, planted upon Asiatic despotism, by the British East India Company, forming a more monstrous combination than any of the divine monsters startling us in the Temple of Salsette. This is no distinctive feature of British colonial rule, but only an imitation of the Dutch, and so much so that in order to characterise the working of the British East India Company, it is sufficient to literally repeat what Sir Stamford Raffles, the English Governor of Java, said of the Old Dutch East India Company.

"The Dutch Company, actuated solely by the spirit of gain, and viewing their subjects with less regard or consideration than a West India planter formerly viewed a gang upon his estate, because the latter had paid the purchase money of human property, which the other had not, employed all the existing machinery of despotism to squeeze from the people their utmost mite of contribution, the last dregs of their labour, and thus aggravated the evils of a capricious and semi-barbarous

---

1. Published in the newspaper *New York Daily Tribune* of 25 June 1853.
2. Reference to a speech delivered in Parliament on June 3, 1853, by the British Minister Wood. Marx's remark is levelled at Wood's tendentious attempts to represent British rule in India as "progress" in comparison with the poverty prevailing in Hindustan in the past, particularly when it was conquered by Nadir Shah (Khuli Khan).
3. The *Heptarchy* (Seven Governments); designation of the seven Anglo-Saxon kingdoms (sixth to eighth century). Marx by analogy uses this term here to denote the dismemberment of the Deccan before its conquest by the Mohammedans.

Government, by working it with all the practised ingenuity of polticians, and all the monopolizing selfishness of traders."

All the civil wars, invasions, revolutions, conquests, famines, strangely complex, rapid and destructive as the successive action in Hindustan may appear, did not go deeper than its surface. England has broken down the entire framework of Indian society, without and symptoms of reconstitution yet appearing. This loss of his old world, with no gain of a new one, imparts a particular kind of melancholy to the present misery of the Hindu, and separates Hindustan, ruled by Britain, from all its ancient traditions, and from the whole of its past history.

There have been in Asia, generally, from immemorial times, but three departments of Government: that of Finance, or the plunder of the interior ; that of War, or the plunder of the exterior; and, finally, the department of Public Works. Climate and territorial conditions, especially the vast tracts of desert, extending from the Sahara, through Arabia, Persia, India and Tartary, to the most elevated Asiatic highlands, constituted artificial irrigation by canals and waterworks the basis of Oriental agriculture. As in Egypt and India, inundations are used for fertilizing the soil of Mesopotamia, Persia, etc.; advantage is taken of a high level for feeding irrigative canals. The prime necessity of an economical and common use of water, which, in the Occident, drove private enterprise to voluntary association, as in Flanders and Italy, necessitated, in the Orient where civilization was too low and the territorial extent too vast to call into life voluntary association, the interference of the centralizing power of Government. Hence an economical function devolved upon all Asiatic Governments, the function of providing public works. This artificial fertilization of the soil, dependent on a Central government and immediately decaying with the neglect of irrigation and drainage, explains the otherwise strange fact that we now find whole territories barren and desert that were once brilliantly cultivated, as Palmyra, Petra, the ruins in Yemen, and large provinces of Egypt, Persia and Hindustan; it also explains how a single war of devastation has been able to depopulate a country for centuries, and to strip it of all its civilization.

Now, the British in East India accepted from their predecessors the department of finance and of war, but they have neglected entirely that of public works. Hence the deterioration of an agriculture which is not capable of being conducted on the British principle of free competition, of *laissez-faire* and *laissez-aller*. But in Asiatic empires we are quite accustomed to see agriculture deteriorating under one government and reviving again under some other government. There the harvests correspond to good or bad government, as they change in Europe with good or bad seasons. Thus the oppression and neglect of agriculture, bad as it is, could not be looked upon as the final blow dealt to Indian society by the British intruder, had it not been attended by a circumstance of quite different importance, a novelty in the annals of the whole Asiatic World. However changing the political aspect of India's past must appear, its social condition has remained unaltered since its remotest antiquity, until the first decennium of the 19th century. The hand-loom and the spinning-wheel, producing their regular myriads of spinners and weavers, were the pivots of the structure of that society. From immemorial times, Europe received the admirable textures of Indian labour, sending in return for them her precious metals, and furnishing thereby his material to the goldsmith, that indispensable member of Indian society, whose love of finery is so great that even the lowest class, those who go about nearly naked, have commonly a pair of golden earrings and a gold ornament of some kind hung round their necks. Rings on the fingers and toes have also been common. Women as well as children frequently wore massive bracelets and anklets of gold or silver, and statuettes of divinities in gold and silver were met with in the households. It was the British intruder who broke up the Indian hand-loom and destroyed the spinning-wheel. England began with depriving the Indian cottons from the European market ; it then introduced twist into Hindustan and in the end inundated the very mother country of cotton with cottons. From 1818 to 1836 the export of twist from Great Britain to India rose in the proportion of 1 to 5,200. In 1824 the export of British muslins to India hardly amounted to 1,000,000 yards, while in 1837 it surpassed 64,000,000 of yards. But at the same time the population of Dacca decreased from 150,000 inhabitants to 20,000. This decline of Indian towns celebrated for their fabrics was by no means the worst consequence. British steam and science uprooted, over the whole surface of Hindustan, the union between agriculture and manufacturing industry.

These two circumstances—the Hindu, on the one hand, leaving, like all Oriental peoples, to the central government the care of the great public works, the prime condition of his agriculture and commerce, dispersed, on the other hand, over the surface of the country, and agglomerated in small centres by the domestic union of agricultural and manufacturing pursuits—these two circumstances had brought about, since the remotest times, a social system of particular features—agricultural the so-called *village system*, which gave to each of these small unions their independent organization and distinct life. The peculiar character of this system may be judged from the following description, contained in an old official report of the British House of Commons on Indian affairs:

"A village, geographically considered, is a tract of country comprising some hundred or thousand acres of arable and waste lands; politically viewed it resembles a corporation or township. Its proper establishment of officers and servants consists of the following descriptions : The *potail*, or head inhabitant, who has generally the superintendence of the affairs of the village, settles the disputes of the inhabitants, attends to the police, and performs the duty of collecting the revenue within his village, a duty which his personal influence and minute acquaintance with the situation and concerns of the people render him the best qualified for this charge. The *kurnum* keeps the accounts of cultivation, and registers everything connected with it. The *tallier* and the *totie*, the duty of the former of which consists in gaining information of crimes and offences, and in escorting and protecting persons travelling from one village to another; the province of the latter appearing to be more immediately confined to the village, consisting, among other duties, in guarding the crops and assisting in measuring them. The *boundaryman*, who preserves the liimits of the village or gives evidence respecting them in cases of dispute. The Superintendent of Tanks and Watercourses distributes the water for the purposes of agriculture. The Brahmin, who performs the village worship. The schoolmaster, who is seen teaching the children in a village to read and write in the sand. The calendar-Brahmin, or astrologer, etc. These officers and servants generally constitute the establishment of a village ; but in some parts of the country it is of less extent; some of the duties and functions above described being united in the same person; in others it exceeds the above-named number of individuals. Under this simple form of municipal government, the inhabitants of the country have lived from time immemorial. The boundaries of the villages have been but seldom altered; and though the villages themselves have been sometimes injured, and even desolated by war, famine or disease, the same name, the same limits, the same interests, and even the same families, have continued for ages. The inhabitants gave themselves no trouble about the breaking up and divisions of kingdoms; while the village remains entire, they care not to what power it is transferred, or to what sovereign it devolves ; its internal economy remains unchanged. The *potail* is still the head inhabitant, and still acts as the petty judge or magistrate, and collector or rentier of the village."

These small stereotype forms of social organism have been to the greater part dissolved, and are disappearing, not so much through the brutal interference of the British tax-gatherer and the British soldier, as to the working of English steam and English Free Trade. Those family-communities were based on domestic industry, in that peculiar combination of handweaving, hand-spinning and hand-tilling agriculture which gave them self-supporting power. English interference having placed the spinner in Lancashire and the weaver in Bengal, or sweeping away both Hindu spinner and weaver, dissolved these small semi-barbarian, semi-civilized communities, by blowing up their economical basis, and thus produced the greatest, and to speak the truth, the only *social* revolution ever heard of in Asia.

Now, sickening as it must be to human feeling to witness those myriads of industrious patriarchal and inoffensive social organizations disorganized and dissolved into their units, thrown into a sea of woes, and their individual members losing at the same time their ancient form of civilization, and their hereditary means of subsistence, we must not forget that these idyllic village communities, inoffensive though they may appear, had always been the solid foundation of Oriental despotism, that they restrained the human mind within the smallest possible compass, making it the unresisting tool of superstition, enslaving it beneath traditional rules, depriving it of all grandeur and historical energies. We must not forget the barbarian egotism which, concentrating on some miserable path of land, had quietly witnessed the ruin of empires, the perpetration of unspeakable cruelties, the massacre of the population of large towns, with no other consideration bestowed upon them than on natural events, itself the helpless prey of any aggressor who deigned to notice it at all. We must not forget that this undignified, stagnatory, and vegetable life that this passive sort of existence evoked on the other part, in contradistinction, wild, aimless, unbounded forces of destruction and rendered murder itself a religious rite in Hindustan. We must not forget that these little communities were contaminated by distinctions of caste and by slavery, that they subjugated man to external circumstances instead of elevating man to be the sovereign of circumstances, that they transformed a self-developing social state into never changing natural destiny, and thus brought about a brutalizing worship of nature, exhibiting its degradation in the fact that man, the sovereign of nature, fell down on his knees in adoration of *Hanuman,* the monkey, and *Sabbala,* the cow.

England, it is true, in causing a social revolution in Hindustan, was actuated only by the vilest interests, and was stupid in her manner of enforcing them. But that is not the question. The question is, can mankind fulfil its destiny without a fundamental revolution in the social state of Asia? If not, whatever may have been the crimes of England she was the unconscious tool of history in bringing about that revolution.

Then, whatever bitterness the spectacle of the crumbling of an ancient world may have for our personal feelings, we have the right, in point of history, to exclaim with Goethe :

> *"Sollte diese Qual uns qualen,*
> *Da sie unsre Lust vermehrt,*
> *Hat nicht Myriaden Seelen*
> *Timur's Herrschaft aufgezehrt?"*[4]

---

4. *Should this torture then torment us*
   Since it brings us greater pleasure?
   Were not through the rule of Timur
   Souls devoured without measure?
   From Goethe's *Westostlicher Diwan, An Suleika.*

APPENDIX II
KARL MARX ON THE FUTURE RESULTS OF THE BRITISH RULE IN INDIA[1]

... How came it that English supremacy was established in India? The paramount power of the Great Mogul was broken by the Mogul Viceroys. The power of the Viceroy was broken by the Mahrattas. The power of the Mahrattas was broken by the Afghans and while all were struggling against all, the Briton rushed in and was enabled to subdue them all. A country not only divided between Mohammedan and Hindu but between tribe and tribe, between caste and caste; a society whose framework was based on a sort of equilibrium, resulting from a general repulsion and constitutional exclusiveness between all its members. Such a country and such a society, were they not the predestined prey of conquest? If we knew nothing of the past history of Hindustan, would there not be the one great and incontestable fact, that even at this moment India is held in English thraldom by an Indian army maintained at the cost of India? India, then, could not escape the fate of being conquered and the whole of her past history, if it be anything, is the history of the successive conquests she has undergone. Indian society has no history at all, at least no known history. What we call its history, is but the history of the successive intruders who founded their empires on the passive basis of that unresisting and unchanging society. The question, therefore, is not whether the English had a right to conquer India, but whether we are to prefer India conquered by the Turk, by the Persian, by the Russian, to India conquered by the Briton.

England has to fulfil a double mission in India : one destructive, the other regenerating—the annihilation of old Asiatic society, and the laying of the material foundations of Western society in Asia.

Arabs, Turks, Moguls, who had successively overrun India, soon became *Hinduized,* the barbarian conquerors being, by an eternal law of history, conquered themselves by the superior civilization of their subjects. The British were the first conquerors superior, and, therefore, inaccessible to Hindu civilization. They destroyed it by breaking up the native communities, by uprooting the native industry, and by levelling at all that was great and elevated in the native society. The historic pages of their rule in India report hardly anything beyond that destruction. The work of regeneration hardly transpires through a heap of ruins. Nevertheless it has begun.

The political unity of India, more consolidated and extending farther than it ever did under the Great Moguls, was the first conditions of its regeneration. That unity, imposed by the British sword, will now be strengthened and perpetuated by the electric telegraph. The native army, organised and trained by the British drill-sergeant, was the *sine qua non* of Indian self-emancipation, and of India ceasing to be the prey of the first foreign intruder. The free press, introduced for the first time into Asiatic society, and managed principally by the common offspring of Hindu and Europeans, is a new and powerful agent of reconstruction. The *Zemindar* and *Ryotwar* themselves, abominable as they are, involve two distinct forms of private property in land—the great *desideratum* of Asiatic society. From the Indian natives, reluctantly and sparingly educated at Calcutta, under English superintendence, a fresh class is springing up endowed with the requirements for government and imbued with European science. Steam has brought India into regular and rapid communication with

---
1. Published in the newspaper *New York Daily Tribune of* 22 July, 1853.

Europe, has connected its chief ports with those of the whole south-eastern ocean, and has revindicated it from the isolated position which was the prime law of its stagnation. The day is not far distant when, by a combination of railways and steam vessels, the distance betwen England and India measured by time will be shortened to eight days, and when that once fabulous country will thus be actually annexed to the Western world.

The ruling classes of Great Britain have had, till now, but an accidental, transitory and exceptional interest in the progress of India. The aristocracy wanted to conquer it, the moneyocracy to plunder it and the millocracy to undersell it. But now the tables are turned. The millocracy have discovered that the transformation of India into a reproductive country has become of vital importance to them, and that, to that end, it is necessary, above all, to gift her with means of irrigation and of internal communication. They intend now drawing a net of railways over India. And they will do it. The results must be inappreciable.

It is notorious that the productive powers of India are paralysed by the utter want of means for conveying and exchanging its various produce. Nowhere, more than in India, do we meet with social destitution in the midst of natural plenty, for want of the means of exchange. It was proved before a committee of the British House of Commons, which sat in 1848, that "when grain was selling from 6s. to 8s. a quarter at Kandesh, it was sold at 64s. to 70s. at Poona, where the people were dying in the streets of famine, without the possibility of gaining supplies from Kandesh, because the clay-roads were impracticable".

The introduction of railways may be easily made to subserve agricultural purposes by the formation of tanks, where ground is required for embankment, and by the conveyance of water along the different lines. Thus irrigation, *sine qua non* of farming in the East, might be greatly extended, and the frequently recurring local famines, arising from the want of water, would be averted. The general importance of railways, viewed under this head, must become evident, when we remember that irrigated lands even in the districts near Ghauts; pay three times as much in taxes, afford ten or twelve times as much employment, and yield twelve or fifteen times as much profit, as the same area without irrigation.

Railways will afford the means of diminishing the amount and the cost of the military establishments. Col. Warren, Town Major of the Fort St. William, stated before a Select Committee of the House of Commons:

"The practicability of receiving intelligence from distant parts of the country in as many hours as at present it requires days and even weeks, and of sending instructions with troops and stores, in the more brief period are considerations which cannot be too highly estimated. Troops could be kept at more distant and healthier stations than at present, and much loss of life from sickness would by this means be spared. Stores could not to the same extent be required at the various depots and the loss by decay, and the destruction incidental to the climate, would also be avoided. The number of troops might be diminished in direct proportion to their effectiveness."

We know that the municipal organization and the economical basis of the village communities have been broken up, but their worst feature, the dissolution of society into stereotype and disconnected atoms, has survived their vitality. The village isolation produced the absence of roads in India, and the absence of roads perpetuated the village isolation. On this plan a community existed with a given scale of low conveniences, almost without intercourse with other villages, without the desires and efforts indispensable to social advance. The British having broken up this self-sufficient *inertia* of the village, railways will provide the new want of communication and intercourse. Besides, "one of the effects of the railway system will be to bring into every village affected by it scuh knowledge of the contrivances and appliances of other countries, and such means of obtaining them, as will first put the hereditary and stipendiary village artisanship of India to full proof of its capabilities, and then supply its defects." (Chapman, *The Cotton and Commerce of India*).

I know that the English millocracy intend to endow India with railways with the exclusive view of extracting at diminished expenses the cotton and other raw materials for their manufactures. But when you have once inroduced machinery into the locomotion of a country, which possesses iron and coal, you are unable to withhold it from its fabrication. You cannot maintain a net of railways over an immense country without introducing all those industrial processes necessary to meet the immediate and current wants of railway locomotion, and out of which there must grow the application of machinery to those branches of industry not immediately connected with railways. The railway system will therefore become, in India, truly the forerunner of modern industry. This is more certain as the Hindus are allowed by British authorities themselves to possess particular aptitude for accommodating themselves to entirely new labour, and acquiring the requisite knowledge of machinery. Ample proof of this fact is afforded by the capacities and expertness of the native engineers in the Calcutta mint, where they have been for years employed in working the steam machinery, by the natives attached to the several steam engines in the Hardwar coal districts, and by other instances. Mr. Campbell himself greatly influenced as he is by the prejudices of the East India Company, is obliged to avow "that the great mass of the Indian people possesses a great *industrial energy*, is well fitted to accumulate capital, and remarkable for a mathematical clearness of head, and talent for figures and exact sciences." "Their intellects'" he says, "are excellent" Modern industry, resulting from the railway system, will dissolve the hereditary divisions of labour, upon which rest the Indian castes, those decisive impediments to Indian progress and Indian power.

All the English bourgeoisie may be forced to do will neither emancipate nor materially mend the social condition of the mass of the people, depending not only on the development of the productive powers, but of their appropriation by the people. But what they will not fail to do is to lay down the material premises for both. Has the bourgeoisie ever done more? Has it ever effected a progress without dragging individuals and peoples through blood and dirt, through misery and degradation?

The Indians will not reap the fruits of the new elements of society scattered among them by the British bourgeoisie, till in Great Britain itself the now ruling classes shall have been supplanted by the industrial proletariat, or till the Hindus themselves shall have grown strong enough to throw off the English yoke altogether. At all events, we may safely expect to see, at a more or less remote period, the regeneration of that great and interesting country, whose gentle natives are, to use the expression of Prince Saltykov, even in the most inferior class, "*plus fins et plus adroits que les Italiens*," whose submission even is counterbalanced by a certain calm nobility, who, notwithstanding their natural languor, have astonished the British officers by their bravery, whose country has been the source of our languages, our religions, and who represent the type of the ancient German in the Jat and the type of the ancient Greek in the Brahmin.

I cannot part with the subject of India without some concluding remarks.

The profound hypocrisy and inherent barbarism of bourgeois civilisation lies unveiled before our eyes, turning from its home, where it assumes respectable forms, to the colonies, where it goes naked. They are the defenders of property, but did any revolutionary party ever originate agrarian revolutions like those in Bengal, in Madras, and in Bombay? Did they not, in India, to borrow an expression of that great robber, Lord Clive himself, resort to atrocious extortion, when simple corruption could not keep pace with their rapacity? While they prated in Europe about the inviolable sanctity of the national debt, did they not confiscate in India the dividends of the *rayahs*, who had invested their private savings in the Company's own funds? While they combated the French revolution under the pretext of defending "our holy religion", did they not forbid, at the same time, Christianity to be propagated in India, and did they not, in order to make money out of the pilgrims streaming to the temples of Orissa and Bengal, take up the trade in the murder and prostitution perpetrated in the temple of Juggernaut? These are the men of "Property, Order, Family, and Religion."

The devastating effects of English industry, when contemplated with regard to India, a country as vast as Europe, and containing 150 millions of acres, are palpable and confounding. But we must not forget that they are only the organic results of the whole system of production as it is now consituted. That production rests on the supreme rule of capital. The centralisation of capital is essential to the existence of capital as an independent power. The destructive influence of that centralization upon the markets of the world does but reveal, in the most gigantic dimensions, the inherent organic laws of political economy now at work in every civilized town. The bourgeois period of history has to create the material basis of the new world—on the one hand the universal intercourse founded upon the mutual dependency of mankind, and the means of that intercourse; on the other hand the development of the productive powers of man and the transformation of material production into a scientific domination of natural agencies. Bourgeois industry and commerce create these material conditions of a new world in the same way as geological revolutions have created the surface of the earth. When a great social revolution shall have mastered the results of the bourgeois epoch, the market of the world and the modern powers of production, and subjected them to the common control of the most advanced peoples, then only will human progress cease to resemble that hideous pagan idol, who would not drink the nectar but from the skulls of the slain.

APPENDIX III
KARL MARX ON THE INDIAN REVOLT[1]

The outrages committed by the revolted Sepoys in India are indeed appalling, hideous, ineffable—such as one is prepared to meet only in wars of insurrection, of nationalities, of races, and above all of religion; in one word, such as respectable England used to applaud when perpetrated by the Vendeans on the "Blues,"[2] by the Spanish guerrillas on the infidel Frenchmen, by Servians on their German and Hungarian neighbours, by Croats on Viennese rebels, by Cavaignac's Garde Mobile or Bonaparte's Decembrists on the sons and daughters of proletarian France. However infamous the conduct of the Sepoys, it is only the reflex, in a concentrated form, of England's own conduct in India, not only during the epoch of the foundation of her Eastern Empire, but even during the last ten years of a long-settled rule. To characterise that rule, it suffices to say that torture formed an organic institution of its financial policy. There is something in human history like retribution; and it is a rule of historical retribution that its instrument be forged not by the offended, but by the offender himself.

The first blow dealt to the French monarchy proceeded from the nobility, not from the peasants. The Indian revolt does not commence with the Ryots, tortured, dishonoured and stripped naked by the British, but with the Sepoys, clad, fed, petted, fatted and pampered by them. To find parallels to the Sepoy atrocities, we need not, as some London papers pretend, fall back on the middle ages, nor even wander beyond the history of contemporary England. All we want is to study the first Chinese war, an event, so to say, of yesterday. The English soldiery then committed abominations for the mere fund of it; their passions being neither sanctified by religious fanaticism nor exacerbated by hatred against an overbearing and conquering race, nor provoked by the stern resistance of a heroic enemy. The violations of women, the spittings, of children, the roastings of whole villages, were then mere wanton sports, not recorded by Manda rins, but by British officers themselves. Even at the present catastrophe it would be an unmitigated mistake to suppose that all the cruelty is on the side of the Sepoys, and all the milk of human kindness flows on the side of the English. The letters of the British officers are redolent of malignity. An officer writing from Peshawar gives a description of the disarming of the 10th irregular cavalry for not charging the 55th native infantry when ordered to do so. He exults in the fact that they were not only disarmed, but stripped off their coats and boots and after having received 12d. per man, were marched down to the river side, and there embarked in boats and sent down the Indus, where the writer is delighted to expect every mother's son will have a chance of being drowned in the rapids. Another writer informs us that, some inhabitants of Peshawar having caused a night alarm by exploding little mines of gunpowder in honour of a wedding (a national custom), the persons concerned were tied up next morning, and "received such a flogging as they will

---

1. Published in the newspaper *New York Daily Tribune* of September 16, 1857.
2. *Vendeans*. Participants in the counter-revolutionary revolt which the French royalists engineered in the Vendee (Western France) in 1793, with the support of the English, against the French Republic.

    The "*Blues*": This was what the soldiers of the republican army and in general all adherents of the Convent were called during the French Revolution of the end of the eighteenth century.

not easily forget". News arrived from Pindee that three native chiefs were plotting. Sir John Lawrence replied by a message ordering a spy to attend to the meeting. On the spy's report, Sir John sent a second message, "Hang them." The chiefs were hanged. An officer in the civil service, from Allahabad, writes: "We have power of life and death in our hands, and we assure you we spare not." Another, from the same place: "Not a day passes but we string up from ten to fifteen of them (non-combatants)." One exulting officer writes: "Holmes is hanging them by the score, like a 'brick'." Another, in allusion to the summary hanging of a large body of the natives: "Then our fun commenced." A third: "We hold court-martials on horseback, and every nigger we meet with we either string up or shoot." From Benares we are informed that thirty zamindars were hanged on the mere suspicion of sympathizing with their own countrymen, and whole villages were burned down on the same plea. An officer from Benares, whose letter is printed in the London *Times*, says: "The European troops have become fiends when opposed to natives." And then it should not be forgotten that, while the cruelties of the English are related as acts of martial vigour, told simply, rapidly, without dwelling on disgusting details, the outrages of the natives, shocking as they are, are still deliberately exaggerated. For instance, the circumstantial account first appearing in the *Times*, and going the round of the London press, of the atrocities perpetrated at Delhi and Meerut, from whom did it proceed? From a cowardly person residing at Bangalore, Mysore, more than a thousand miles, as the bird flies, distant from the scene of action. Actual accounts of Delhi evince the imagination of an English person to be capable of breeding greater horrors than even the wild fancy of a Hindu mutineer. The cutting of noses, breasts, etc., in one word, the horrid mutilations committed by the Sepoys, are of course more revolting to European feeling than the throwing of red-hot shell on Canton dwellings by a Secretary of the Manchester Peace Society,[3] or the roasting of Arabs pent up in a cave by a French Marshal,[4] or the flaying alive of British soldiers by the cot-o'-nine-tails under drum-head court martial, or any other of the philanthropical appliances used in British penitentiary colonies. Cruelty, like every other thing, has its fashion changing according to time and place. Caesar, the accomplished scholar, candidly narrates how he ordered many thousand Gallic warriors to have their right hands cut off. Napoleon would have been ashamed to do this. He preferred dispatching his own French regiments, suspected of republicanism, to St. Domingo, there to die of the blacks and the plague.

The infamous mutilations committed by the Sepoys remind one of the practices of the Christian Byzantine Empire, or the prescriptions of Emperor Charles V's criminal law, or the English punishments for high treason, as still recorded by Judge Blackstone. With Hindus, whom their religion has made virtuosi in the art of self-torturing, these tortures inflicted on the enemies of their race and creed appear quite natural, and must appear still more so to English, who only some years since still used to draw revenues from the Juggernaut festivals, protecting and assisting the bloody rites of a religion of cruelty.

The frantic roars of the "bloody old *Times*", as Cobbett used to call it—its playing the part of a furious character in one of Mozart's operas, who indulges in most melodious strains in the idea of first hanging his enemy, then roasting him, then quartering him, then spitting him, and then flaying him

---

3. Reference to John Bowring, one of the leaders of the Peace Society and other Free-Trader organisations in England. In the fifties, while occupying the post of British Consul at Canton and of commander-in-chief at Hongkong, he proved to be a cruel and rapacious coloniser. In October 1856 he provoked a conflict with the Chinese authorities because the latter had attacked a ship carrying contraband while flying the British flag. He ordered Canton to be bombarded, an act which served as a prelude to war with China (1856–58).

4. During the suppression of an insurrection in Algeria in 1845, General Pe'lissier, subsequently a Marshal of France, ordered a thousand Arab rebels to be driven into mountain caves and choked to death by lighting campfires at their entrances.

Appendix III

alive[5]—its tearing the passion of revenge to tatters and to rags—all this would appear but silly if under the pathos of tragedy there were not distinctly perceptible the tricks of comedy.

The London *Times* overdoes its part, not only from panic. It supplies comedy with a subject even missed by Moliere, the Tartuffe of Revenge. What is simply wants is to write up the funds and to screen the Government. As Delhi has not, like the walls of Jericho, fallen before mere puffs of wind, John Bull is to be steeped in cries for revenge up to his very ears, to make him forget that his Government is responsible for the mischief hatched and the colossal dimensions it had been allowed to assume.

---

5. Reference to the air sung by Osmin, the Majordomo of a rich pasha, in Mozart's opera, *Die Entf-iihrung aus dem Serail*.

APPENDIX IV
THE ROLE OF CLASSES DURING THE REVOLT OF 1857

Marxist scholars have delved deep into the literature on the Revolt of 1857–58 to ascertain the role of the different classes of Indian society during the struggle. Talmiz Khaldun characterizes it as an uprising of "the Indian peasantry fighting desperately to free itself of foreign as well as feudal bondage"[1] and blames the propertied class for betrayal of the national cause. He particularly underlines the setting up of the Mutiny Court or the Military and Civil Management Committee[2] with General Bakht Khan as President (*Sahib-i-Alam Bahadur*) early in July 1857; this Administration Court is interpreted as symbolic of the emergence of a democratic spirit among the soldiers and reinforced with large-scale peasant participation in the revolt gave it a solid mass basis and a popular character. Another Marxist scholar, P.C. Joshi, views the establishment of the Administration Court as embodying "a pattern of soldier-peasant democracy... within the framework of a constitutional monarchy"[3].

Hard pressed for finances, the Administration Court put the rich merchants and bankers of Delhi to levy and forced them to advance loans to the Mughal Government. On 4 June the bankers of Delhi were persuaded to subscribe a lakh of rupees for the war effort. The army's monthly pay bill for August 1857 estimated at Rs. 573.000[4] could not be paid and the banias and shopkeepers showed resistance in supplying provisions for the army on credit or deferred payment basis. This infuriated the sepoys and they indulged in looting.[5] In this surcharged atmosphere the commoners looked upon the propertied classes as enemies of the revolution and freely looted them, seized the account books of zamindars and moneylenders and burnt them. All this put the upper classes on the defensive and they complained of indiscriminate loot and plunder. The bankers complained that they had paid four lakhs of rupees and still were being harassed. A particular target of the sepoys' wrath was the rich servants of the company, particularly when their loyalty was suspect. The upper classes began to fear victory more than defeat in the rebellion. Such circumstances goaded the feudal and propertied class to betray the popular cause. The zamindars, the merchants, the moneylenders, the educated middle class and the native officials—all sided with the British or observed sullen neutrality as demanded by the circumstances. Khaldun concludes that though originally organised to restore the old, outmoded and pre-British economy, the rebellion of 1857–58 "ended as a peasant war against indigenous landlordism and foreign imperialism".[6] P.C. Joshi doubts if the rebellion could be described as a

---

1. P. C. Joshi (Ed.), *Rebellion 1857* (New Delhi, 1957), p. 52.
2. S. N. Sen has produced a facsimile copy of the constitution of the Mutiny Court in his book *Eighteen Fifty-Seven* with the comments that the said Court was set up under the influence of Western ideas and English institutions but adds that the court could not make its power felt either over the army or over the civil officers of the government and anarchy and disorder continued as before. (S.N. Sen, *Eighteen Fifty-Seven*, New Delhi, 1957, pp. 75–76).
3. P. C. Joshi, *op. cit.*, p. 192.
4. C. T. Metcalfe, *Two Native Narratives of the Mutiny in Delhi*, p. 143.
5. R. C. Majumdar makes copious references "to greed of the sepoys which led them to plunder Europeans and Indians alike and caused bitter wranglings among themselves over the share of the loot". (*British Paramountcy and Indian Renaissance*. Vol. IX, pp. 508–13). Unfortunately, Majumdar's information is mostly based upon the diary of Munshi Jiwan Lal, an affluent citizen of Delhi. Jiwan Lal was put to levy and had to shed Rs. 50,000 and part of his jewellery. Jiwan Lal's narrative could not but be influenced by such misfortunes.

'peasant war'. On the basis of the study of District Reports he contends that the wrath of the peasantry was not directed against the landlords as a class but only against that section of the landlords (non-cultivating zamindars and moneylenders turned zamindars) who had been created by the British regime (after dispossessing the peasant cultivators). Joshi underlines the fact that the peasantry accepted the leadership of the traditional landlords. He comes to the conclusion that the revolt of 1857–58 was a broadbased national uprising in which the Indian peasants made a compromise with the traditional landlords in the interest of the common struggle. All the same, he blames the landlords—who fearing the revolutionary completion that the struggle was assuming—for playing the traitor to safeguard their narrow class interests. He rightly blames the 'feudal betrayal' as a big factor in the failure of the national uprising. Mohit Sen, another Marxist scholar, underscores the shortsightedness of the rebels for relying too heavily by the primitive vigour of peasant democracy; hence the disunity, the lack of organisation, the parochialism, the failure to sustain the feudal betrayal Sen concludes: 'The defeat of the 1857 uprising showed that while the peasant was no longer a primitive rebel, he was not able to produce that independent power and projection with sufficient attractive force of an alternative future system that could bring down the industrial colonialism of the West."[7]

---

6. P.C. Joshi, *op. cit.*, p. 52.
7. Mohit Sen, *The Indian Revolution* (New Delhi, 1970), p. 4.

APPENDIX V
LIST OF GOVERNORS, GOVERNORS-GENERAL AND PRESIDENTS

GOVERNORS OF BENGAL

Clive (First Adminstration)	1757-60
Holwell (officiating)	1760
Vansittart	1760-65
Clive (Second Administration)	1765-67
Verelst	1767-69
Cartier	1769-72
Warren Hastings	1772-74

GOVERNORS-GENERAL OF BENGAL
(Regulating Act of 1773)

Warren Hastings	1774-85
Sir John Macpherson (offciating)	1785-86
Earl (Marquess) Cornwallis	1786-93
Sir John Shore	1793-98
Sir A. Clarke (officiating)	1798
Richard Wellesley, Earl of Mornington	1798-1805
Marquess Cornwallis (Second Administration)	1805
Sir George Barlow (officiating)	1805-7
Earl of Minto I	1807-13
Marquess of Hastings (Earl of Moira)	1813-23
John Adams (officiating)	1823
Lord Amherst	1823-28
William Butterworth Bayley (officiating)	1828
Lord William Bentinck	1828-33

GOVERNORS-GENERAL OF INDIA
(Charter Act of 1833)

Lord William Bentinck	1833-35
Sir Charles Metcalfe (officiating)	1835-36
Earl of Auckand	1836-42
Lord Ellenborough	1842-44
Sir Henry (Viscount) Hardinge	1844-48
Earl of Dalhousie	1848-56
Lord Canning	1856-58

GOVERNORS-GENERAL AND VICEROYS

Lord Canning	1858-62
Lord Elgin I	1862-63
Sir Robert Napier (officiating)	1863
Sir William T. Denison (officiating)	1863
Sir John Lawrence	1864-68

Appendix V

Earl of Mayo	1869-72
Sir John Strachey (officiating)	1872
Lord Napier of Merchistoun (officiating)	1872
Earl of Northbrook	1872-76
Baron (Earl of) Lytton I	1876-80
Marquess of Ripon	1880-84
Earl of Dufferin	1884-88
Marquess of Lansdowne	1888-94
Earl of Elgin II	1894-98
Lord Curzon	1899-1904
Lord Ampthill (officiating)	1904
Lord Curzon	1904-5
Earl of Minto II	1905-10
Baron Hardinge of Pensnurst	1910-16
Baron Chelmsford	1916-21
Earl of Reading	1921-25
Lord Lytton II (officiating)	1925
Lord Irwin	1926-31
Earl of Willingdon	1931-34
Sir George Stanley (officiating)	1934
Marquess of Linlithgow	1934-36

GOVERNORS-GENERAL AND CROWN REPRESENTATIVES
(Act of 1935)

Marquess of Linlighgow	1936-37
Baron Brabourne (officiating)	1938
Marquess of Linlithgow	1938-43
Lord Wavell	1943-47
Lord Mountbatten	1947-48
C. Rajagopalachari	1948-50

PRESIDENTS OF THE INDIAN REPUBLIC
(THE NEW CONSTITUTION)

Dr. Rajendra Prasad	1950-62
Dr. S. Radhakrishan	1962-67
Dr. Zakir Hussain	1967-69
V.V. Giri (officiating)	June-July 1969
M.M. Hidayatullah (officiating)	July-August 1969
V.V. Giri	August 1969-August 1974
Dr. Fakhruddin Ali Ahmed	August 1974-February 1977
B.D. Jatti (officating)	February-July 1977
Neelam Sanjiva Reddy	1977-82
Giani Zail Singh	1982-87
Ramaswamy Venkataraman	1987-92
Dr. Shankar Dyal Sharma	1992-97
K.R. Narayanan	1997-2002
Dr. A.P.J. Abdul Kalam	2002-2007
Pratibha Patil	2007-2012
Pranab Mukherjee	2012-2017
Ram Nath Kovind	2017-Present

APPENDIX VI
CHRONOLOGY OF PRINCIPAL EVENTS

1707	Death of Aurangzeb at the age of 89.
	Accession of Prince Muazzam to the throne with the title of Bahadur Shah I (1707-12).
1708	Shahu becomes the Chhatrapati of the Marathas (ruled, 1708-49).
	Death of Guru Gobind Singh and Banda Bahadur assumes leadership of the Sikhs in the Panjab (Banda executed in 1716).
1712	Jahandar Shah's acession to the throne (ruled, 1712-13).
1713	Farrukhsiyar becomes Emperor (ruled, 1713-19)
	Balaji Vishwanath appointed as Peshwa.
	Abdulla Khan appointed as Wazir and Hussain Ali as Commander-in-Chief of Mughal Empire.
1717	Farrukhsiyar grants a *firman* to the English Company exempting their trade in Bengal from payment of duties in return for a lumpsum payment of Rs. 3,000 per annum. *Jizya* reimposed (abolished in 1719).
1719	Assassination of Farrukhsiyar.
	Accession of Muhammad Shah (ruled, 1719-48).
1720	Baji Rao I appointed as Peshwa.
	Fall of the Saiyyid brothers.
1724	Saadat Khan appointed Nawab of Oudh.
	Asaf Jah declares himself a virtually independent Nizam in the Deccan.
1737	Baji Rao's raid on Delhi.
1739	Nadir Shah's invasion of Delhi.
	The Marathas take Salsette and Bassein.
1740	*Appointment of Balaji Baji Rao as Peshwa.
	Alivardi Khan becomes Nawab of Bengal, Bihar and Orissa.
	Dost Ali, Nawab of Carnatic, killed in a battle with the Marathas.
1742	Dupleix appointed French Governor of Pondicherry.
1744-48	First Anglo-French Carnatic War.
1746	La Bourdonnais, French Governor of Mauritius, captures Madras.
1748	Treaty of Aix-La-chapelle and restoration of Madras to the English Company.
	Accession of Ahmad Shah as Mughal Emperor (1748-54).
1749	Death of Shahu and accession of Raja Ram (grandson of Raja Ram I and Tara Bai) as Chhatrapati.
1750-54	Second Anglo-French Carnatic War.
1751	Clive's capture of Arcot and its successful defence against Chanda Sahib.
1754	Dupleix's dismissal.
	Alamgir II becomes Mughal Emperor (ruled, 1754-59).
1756	Death of Alivardi Khan, Nawab of Bengal.
	Accession of Siraj-ud-daula as Nawab of Bengal.
	Sairaj-ud-daula captures Calcutta and the Black Hole Episode.
1757-63	Third Anglo-French Carnatic War.

Appendix VI

1757	Ahmad Shah Abdali invades Delhi and Agra.
	Battle of Plassey.
	Mir Jaffar installed Nawab of Bengal.
	Clive appointed Governor of Fort William, Bengal (First term, 1757-60).
1758	The Marathas overrun the Panjab.
1759	Ali Gauhar, son of Emperor Alamgir II, revolts against his father and invades Bihar.
	Ghazi-ud-din murders Alamgir II.
1760	The English win the battle of Wandiwash.
	Marathas win battle of Udgir against the Nizam.
	Mir Kasim becomes Nawab of Bengal (ruled, 1760-63).
1761	The Third Battle of Panipat between the Marathas and Ahmad Shah Abdali.
	Pondicherry falls to the English.
	Shahzada Ali Gauhar becomes Mughal Emperor Shah Alam II (ruled, 1761-1806).
	Madhava Rao assumes charge as Peshwa (ruled, 1761-72).
1763	The English Company deposes Mir Kasim and reappoints Mir Jaffar as Nawab of Bengal (1763-65).
1764	Battle of Buxar.
1765	Najm-ud-daula recognised as Nawab of Bengal.
	Clive's Second Governorship of Bengal (1765-67).
	Shah Alam II grants the *Diwani* of Bengal, Bihar and Orissa to the English Company.
1766	The English Company granted the Northern Circars.
1767-69	The First Anglo-Mysore War.
1770	A severe famine in Bengal.
1771	The Marathas escort Emperor Shah Alam II to Delhi.
1772	Warren Hasings assumes office as Governor of Bengal.
1773	The regulating Act passed by the British Parliament.
1774	The Rohilla war between the Rohillas and the Nawab of Oudh supported by the Company.
	Warren Hastings becomes the first Governor-General (1774-85).
	The Supreme Court established at Calcutta.
	The trial and execution of Nand Kumar.
1775-82	The First Anglo-Maratha War.
1780-84	The Second Anglo-Mysore War.
1782	Death of Haider Ali.
1784	Pitt's India Act passed by the British Parliament.
1786	Cornwallis assumes office as Governor-General (1786-93, again 1805).
1790-92	The Third Anglo-Mysore War.
1793	Permanent Settlement of Bengal announced.
	Charter Act of 1793 passed by the British Parliament.
1794	Death of Mahadaji Sindhia.
1795	The Battle of Kharda between the Nizam and the Marathas.
1798	Zaman Shah (grandson of Ahmad Shah Abdali) invades India.
	Lord Wellesley assumes charge as Governor-General (1798-1805).
1799	The Fourth Anglo-Mysore War.
	Death of Tipu Sultan.
	Ranjit Singh captures Lahore.

1800	Death of Nana Fadnavis.
1801	Wellesley annexes Carnatic.
1802	Treaty of Bassein between Baji Rao II and the English.
1803-05	The Second Anglo-Maratha War.
1805	The Company's forces fail to take Bharatpur.
	Recall of Wellesley.
1806	Vellore Mutiny.
1808	Malcolm's mission to Persia and Elphinstone's mission to Kabul.
1809	Treaty of Amritsar between Ranjit Singh and the Company.
1813	The Charter Act of 1813 passed by the British Parliament.
1814-16	The Anglo-Nepal War.
1817-18	Military operations against the Pindaris.
	The Third Anglo-Maratha War.
1819	Elphinstone appointed Governor of Bombay (1819-27).
1820	Munro takes over as Governor of Madras (1820-27).
1824-26	The First Anglo-Burmese War.
1827	Malcolm takes charge as Governor of Bombay.
1828	William Bentinck takes over over as Governor-General (1828-35).
1829	*Sati* declared illegal
1830	Raja Rammohan Roy visits England (died there in 1833).
1831	Ranjit Singh meets William Bentinck at Rupar.
	Bentinck deposes Raja of Mysore and the Company takes over the administration of Mysore.
1833	The Charter Act of 1833 passed ; abolition of the Company's trading rights.
1834	Bentinck annexes Coorg (Southern malabar coast).
1835	English adopted as the official language by the English Company.
1838	Tripartite treaty between the Company, Ranjit Singh and Shah Shuja.
1839	Death of Ranjit Singh.
1839-42	The First Anglo-Afghan War.
1843	British annexation of Sind announced.
1845-46	The First Anglo-Sikh War.
1848	Lord Dalhousie assumes charge as Governor-General (1848-56).
1848,49	The Second Anglo-Sikh War and annexation of the Panjab.
1848	The annexation of Satara by the Doctrine of Lapse.
1852	The Second Anglo-Burmese War.
1853	First Railway line between Bombay and Thana opened.
	Annexation of Nagpur.
	The Charter Act of 1853 passed by the British Parliament
1854	Dalhousie annexes Jhansi.
	Charles Wood's Despatch on Indian Education.
1855	The Santhal Insurrection.
1856	The annexation of Oudh.
1857	Establishment of Universities at Bombay, Calcutta and Madras.
	Outbreak of the Mutiny, Revolt and First War of Indian Independence

Appendix VI

1858	Queen Victoria's Proclamation (1st November).
1861	The Indian Councils Act, 1861 passed by the British Parliament.
	Enactment of the Indian Civil and Criminal Code.
	The Indian High Courts Act passed.
1863	Death of Dost Mohammad, the Afghan Amir.
1865-66	The Orissa Famine.
1865	Telegraphic communication with Europe opened.
1869	Opening of the Suez Canal.
1872	The Kuka revolt in the Panjab.
1874	The Bihar Famine.
1875	The trial and deposition of the Geakwar of Baroda.
	The Prince of Wales visits India.
1876	The Royal Titles Act made Queen Victoria Kaiser-i-Hind.
1876-77	The Delhi Durbar organised by Lytton.
1876-78	The Great Decan Famine.
1878-80	The Second Afghan War.
1878	The Vernacular Press Act passed.
1880	Lord Ripon assumes charge as Governor-General.
1881	First Factory Act passed in India.
1882	Appointment of the Hunter Commission on School Education.
1883	The Ilbert Bill Controversy.
	First Indian National Conference meets at Calcutta.
1885	The First Indian National Congress meets at Bombay.
	Bengal Tenancy Act passed.
	The Third Anglo-Burman war.
1889	The Maharaja of Kashmir forced to abdicate.
	Second visit of the Prince of Wales.
1891	The Age of Consent Bill passed.
	Manipur Rebellion.
1892	The Indian Councils Act passed by British Parliament.
	Split in the Arya Samaj.
1893	Organisation of the Muhammedan Anglo-Oriental Defence Association of Upper India.
	Mortimer Durand's Mission to Kabul.
	Tilak celebrates the Ganapati Festival.
1895	Tilak organises the Shivaji Festival.
1896-97	The Great Famine in India.
1897	Murder of two Englishmen, Rand and Ayerst at Poona.
1899	Curzon becomes Governor-General of India.
1899-1900	Another Great Famine in India.
1904	Younghusband Mission to Lhasa.
	Indian Universities Act passed.
1905	Foundation of the 'Servants of India Society'.
1906, October	The Partition of Bengal comes into force.
	Lord Minto receives the Agha Khan Muslim Deputation at Simla.

December 31	The Muslim league formed at Dacca.
1907	Anglo-Russian Entente signed.
	Lala Lajpat Rai and Ajit Singh deported to Mandalay.
1908 April 30	Execution of Khudiram Bose.
July 22	Tilak sentenced to six years' trnasportation on charges of sedition.
1909	The Indian Councils Act passed.
	Madan Lal Dhingra shoots dead Curzan Wyllie in London.
	S.P. Sinha appointed Law Member of Viceroy's Executive Council.
1911	The Coronation Durbar at Delhi
1912	Delhi becomes the new capital of India.
December 23	Bomb thrown at Lord Hardinge on his state entry into Delhi.
1913	Gandhi starts his Satyagraha in South Africa against Asiatic Law Amendment Act.
November 1	Ghadar Party formed at San Francisco to organise a rebellion in India to overthrow British rule.
1914 June 16	B.G. Tilak released from jail after long imprisonment.
August 4	Outbreak of World War I.
September 29	*Kamagata Maru* reaches back Budge Budge, Calcutta.
1915	Death of G.K. Gokhale and P.S. Mehta.
	Formation of Home Rule League by Mrs. Annie Besant.
1916	Foundation of Benares Hindu University.
	Tilak organises Home Rule League at Poona.
1917 April	Gandhi launches the Champaran campaign in Bihar to focus attention on grievances of indigo planters.
June	Madras Government interns Mrs. Besant.
August 20	Montagu's announcement regarding introduction of Responbsible Government in India.
1918	Indians declared eligible for King's Commission in the Indian Army.
	Trade Union movement begins in India.
	All India Depressed Classes League formed.
1919 April 6	Call for All-India hartal against Rowlatt Bills.
April 9	Deportation of Dr. Satyapal and Dr. Kitchlew ; trouble begins at Amritsar.
April 13	Jallianwala Bagh-tragedy at Amritsar.
	Government of India Act 1919 passed.
1920	First meeting of the All-India Trade Union Congress.
	Foundation of Aligarh Muslim University.
	Hunter Commission Report on Jallianwalla Bagh Massacre published.
	First Non-cooperation Movement launched by Gandhiji.
1921	M.N. Roy's attempts to organise the Communist Party of India at Tashkent.
1921 August	Moplah rebellion on the Malabar coast.
1922 Feb.	Violent incidents at Chauri Chaura and Gandhiji calls off the Non-Cooperation Movement.
1924	The Communist Party of India organised at Kanpur.
1927	Appointment of the Simon Commission.
1928	Nehru Report recommends principles for the new Constitution of India.
1929	Sarda Act passed prohibiting marriages of girls below 14 and boys below 18 years of age.
	Meerut Conspiracy case against the Communists.

Appendix VI

April 8	Bhagat Singh and his friend throw a bomb in the Imperial Legislative Assembly.
December 31	The Congress adopts the goal of Complete Independence for India.
October 31	Lord Irwin's announcement about Dminion Status as the goal of British policy in India.
1930 Jan. 1	Jawaharlal Nehru hoists the tricolour of Indian Independence on the banks of the river Ravi at Lahore.
February 14	The Congress passes the Civil Disobedience Movement Resolution.
March 12	Gandhiji begins Dandi March (12 march-5 April) to manufacture illegal salt.
1931 March 5	Gandhi-Irwin Pact signed.
1932	Ramsay MacDonald announces the Communal Award (modified by the Poona Pact, 24 September).
1935 Aug. 4	The Government of India Act passed.
1937 July	Congress ministries formed in the provinces.
1939 April	Subhas Chandra Bose resigns the Presidentship of the Congress.
October	Lord Linlighgow declares Dominion Status as the ultimate goal of British policy in India. Congress ministries resign in the provinces.
December 12	The Muslim League celebrates Deliverance Day.
1940 March	The Muslim League adopts the Pakistan Resolution.
August	The Viceroy declares British policy towards India's constitutional problem (August Offer).
October	The Congress starts the Individual Civil Disobedience Movement (suspended in December).
1941	Death of Rabindranath Tagore (1861-1941).
1942 Feb.	Japanese bombardment of Rangoon. Singapore falls.
March-April	Cripps Mission visits India.
July 14	Congress Working Committee adopts the Quit India Resolution.
August-September	The Revolt of 1942.
1943 June	Subhas Chandra Bose reaches Tokyo.
October 21	Bose announces the formation of Provisional Government of Free India.
1945 June	Wavell call the Simla Conference in a bid to form the Executive Council of Indian political leaders.
1946 Feb.	Mutiny of naval ratings at Bombay.
March-June	Cabinet Mission visits India.
July	Elections for the Constitutent Assembly held.
September	Jawaharlal Nehru heads the Interim Government.
December 9	Indian Constiuent Assembly meets at New Delhi.
1947 February 20	Lord Attlee announces Britain's decision to transfer of power to Indian hands before June 1948.
June 3	Lord Mountbatten announces transfer of power in August 1947.
July	Indian Independence Act passed by the British Parliament.
August 15	India becomes Free.
1948 January 30	The Death of Mahatma Gandhi.
1949 November 26	Adoption of the new Indian Constitution.
1950 January 26	The Constitution of the Indian Republic comes into force. Dr. Rajendra Prasad becomes the first President of India.
1951	First Five-Year Plan inaugurated
1951-52 Oct.-Feb. 1952	First National General Election
1956	States Reorganisation Act passed. Second Five-Year Plan inaugurated.

1957	Second National General Election
1961	Third Five-Year Plan launched
1962	Third National General Election
1964, May 27	Death of Jawaharlal Nehru
1965	Indo-Pakistan War
1966, Jan. 20	Mrs. Indira Gandhi becomes Prime Minister
1967	Fourth National General Election
1969	Fourth Five-Year Plan launched
1971	Fifth National General Election
Dec. 8	War with Pakistan
1974	Fifth Five-Year Plan inaugurated.
1975, June	State of Emergency declared.
1977	Sixth National General Election.
1980	Seventh National General Election; Indira Gandhi assumes office as Prime Minister; Sixth Five-Year Plan inaugurated.
1984, Oct. 31	Assassination of Indira Gandhi. Rajiv Gandhi sworn in as Prime Minister.
1984, Dec.	Eighth National General Election
Dec. 31	Rajiv Gandhi assumes office as Prime Minister of India
1985, Feb.	The 52nd Constutional Amendment Act bans floor crossing by members elected on party tickets to Parliament/legislative bodies.
Oct.	The Cabinet approves the Seventh Five-Year Plan (1985-90).
1986	Union territories of Mizoram and Arunachal Pradesh get the status of States.
1987, May	Union Territory of Goa gets statehood.
1987 July	Following Rajiv-Jayawardene accord, an Indian Peace–Keeping Force reaches Sri Lanka.
Nov.	Sarkaria Commission submits its final report on Centre-State relations.
1987-89	The Bofors Guns Scandal and the Fairfax Agency issues rock the nation.
1989, March	The 61st Constitutional Amendment Act lowers the voting age from 21 to 18 years.
1990	The 62nd Constitutional Amendment Act extends the reservation of seats for S.C./S.T. in the Lok Sabha and State Assemblies up to 2000 A.D.
1990, Aug.	Prime Minister V.P. Singh accepts the Mandal Commission Report.
1990, Dec.	T.N. Seshan assumes charge as Chief Election Commissioner.
1991, May	Assassination of Rajiv Gandhi.
June	Tenth Lok Sabha Election held. P.V. Narasimha Rao assumes office as Prime Minister.
1994, Dec.	Madan Lal Khurana sworn in as Delhi Chief Minister.
1996, May	Eleventh Lok Sabha Election held. Atal Behari Vajpayee sworn in as the first B.J.P. Prime Minister.
June 1	H.D. Deve Gowda. leader of newly-formed 13 parties United Front, assumes office as Prime Minister.
1997, April	I.K. Gujral assumes charge as 12th Prime Minister of India.
1998, Mar. 19	Atal Behari Vajpayee sworn as Prime Minister of the first BJP-led coalition government at the Centre.
May 11-13	India conducts 5 Nuclear Tests in Pokhran range in Rajasthan.
1999, May-July	In the Kargil Crisis India won a convincing victory, while Pakistan suffered a humiliating defeat.
2000,	The Constitution (79th Ammendment Act) 1999 extends the reservation for SCs and STs in the Lok Sabha and State Assemblies for a further period of 10 years i.e. upto 25 January 2010.
2000, March 19	Bill Clinton, President of the U.S.A. arrives on a 5 days official trip to India.

Appendix VI

2000, Nov.	Creation of 3 new Indians States of Chattisgarh, Uttranchal and Jharkhand.
2001, Jan. 1	George W. Bush elected as 43rd President of the U.S.A
2001, Aug.	The Parliament passed a Bill increasing nearly three-fold the salaries, allowances and pensions of members of Parliament.
2001, Nov.	The Lok Sabha cleared the Constitution (91 Amendment) Bill seeking to extend the freeze on delimitation of Parliamentary and Assembly constituencies until 2026.
2001, Dec. 13	Pakistan-based terrorists attacked the Indian Parliament.
2002, Feb. 27	The Godhra massacre (engineered by Muslim Fundamentalist and Pakistan ISI agents?) took a toll of 58 lives. This triggered off communal riots in Gujarat.
2002, April 2	POTA (Prevention of Terrorism Act) passed by Parliament and received the President's assent.
2002, May 14	The Parliament passed the Constitution (93rd Amendment) Bill which makes Education a Fundamental Right for all children in the age group of 6-14 years.
2003, Dec	Parliament approved the Constitution (97th Amendment) Bill which disallows Defections in Parliament and state Legislatives and after limits the size of ministerial jobs to 15% of the strength of the legislature concerned.
2004, May	Membership of the European Union increased from 15 to 25 nations with a total population of 45 crores.
2004, May 22	Manmohan Singh elected leader of the Congress led U.P.A. coalition and sworn as the Prime Minister of India.
2005, July 18	Indo–U.S. Civil Nuclear Deal was signed under which U.S.A. will supply fuel and technology to India's civilian nuclear energy programme. The final approval of all concerned authorities is expected by the end of 2006.
2005, Sept.	The Hindu Succession (Amendment) Act 2005 removes gender discrimination and gives daughters equal rights with sons in inheritance of joint family property.
2005, Dec. 23	11 Members of Parliament were expected from the Houses of Parliament for the 'cash for-query scam' (i.e. these M.Ps raised questions in the Parliament after they recurred bribes from interested parties)
2006, Feb	National Rural Employment Guarantee Act (NREGA) ensures employment guarantee to residents of rural areas.
2006, July 11	The Mumbai serial bomb blasts in train's seem to have been planned and executed by foreign Islamic Terrorists in collaboration with Indian Terrorists.
2006, Dec.	George W. Bush signed the U.S.-India Peaceful Atomic Energy Co-operation Act, 2006. The U.S.A. Congress has approved the N-Deal. However, some differences about its implementation still exist.
2006	The Indian Parliament passed the 93rd Constitutional Amendment Bill enabling the Government to provide 27% Quota (Reservation for O.B.Cs students in Educational institutions like IITs, IIMs and other central universities.
2007, April	Physically 'disabled' candidates will henceforth be given 7 chances to sit in the I.A.S. examinations in place of the normal 4 chances.
2007, April	Babubhai katara a former Minister and some more M.Ps were caught in a human trafficking racket i.e., helping persons to migrate to U.S.A. with fake passports and other documents.
2007, July	Mrs. Pratibha Patil, the first Indian woman who took oath as president of India.
2007, Sept 19	All citizens over the age of 65 years and living below poverty line (B.P.L.) will be eligible for pension of Rs. 400 p.m.
2008, July 22	Increasing differences with the Left Parties over the U.S.–India Civil Nuclear Deal issue compelled Prime Minister Manmohan Singh to seek the confidence of the Lok Sabha. In the election that was held on 22 July 2008 the Prime Minister won the confidence of the majority of the Members of Lok Sabha.
2008, Nov.	The 26/11 Terrorist attack on Bombay city left 166 people dead.
2009, January	Asif Ali Zardari takes over as the new President of Pakistan.

2009, Feb.	Barrack Obama takes over as President of the U.S.A.
2009, April 2	The G-20 meeting was held at London to discuss the global economic downturn.
2009, May 18	V.P. Prabhakaran, founder of the LTTE was killed by the Lanken army.
2009, May 22	Manmohan Singh took the oath of office as Prime Minister of India.
2010, April 1	The Indian Government initiates The Right of Children to Free and Compulsory Education Act to provide free and compulsory education to all children aged between 6 & 14 years, making education a fundamental right for millions of children.
2010, Oct. 3	XIX Commonwealth Games, were held in Delhi, India from 3 to 14 October 2010.
2010, Oct. 3	Indian Rupee symbol got. Recognition (A Great Economic Development).
2010, March 12	Russia signs a nuclear reactor deal with India which will see it build 16 nuclear reactors in India.
2010, Sept 29	India launches a national identity scheme aimed at reducing fraud and improving access to state benefits.
2011, Jan 1	India & Pakistan exchange the annual lists of their nuclear installations and facilities under the Agreement on the Prohibition of Attack against Nuclear installations which was signed on December 31, 1988.
2011, April	Gandhian Crusader Anna Hazare began a non-violent protest against corruption in the country and the passing of the Lokpal Bill in the form of an indefinite hunger strike. Hazare started his fast on April 5th in Delhi and continued till April 9th.
2011, May	Mamta Banerjee was sworn in as the first woman and 11th chief minister of West Bengal.
2011, November	In Ludhiana India won the Kabbadi World Cup and brought glory to the nation in a sport other than cricket.
2011, October	The World's population passes the seven billion mark.
2012, March	NCPCR released Guidelines to Eliminate Physical Punishment in Schools.
2012, April 19	India successfully test fires 500 km range Agni-V ICBM
2012, July 22	Pranab Mukherjee is elected as India's 13th President.
2013, April 2	The Criminal Law (Amendment) Act, 2013—amendments to criminal law to sternly deal with sexual assault cases.
2013, May 3	Union Cabinet's approves the launch of NUHM as a sub-mission under the National Health Mission (NHM)
2013, July 14	India shuts down its public telegram service.
2013, Nov. 5	The Mars Orbiter Mission (MOM), was successfully launched into low earth orbit by the Indian Space Research Organisation (ISRO).
2013, Dec. 18	The Lokpal and Lokayukta Bill, 2013 was passed by the Rajya Sabha.
2014, May 26	Narendra Modi took oath as India's 15th Prime Minister.
2014, June 2	India's newest and the 29th State Telangana formed.
2014, Sept 5	India and Australia signed a deal under which Australia will supply Uranium to India for energy generation.
2014, Sept 24	India created history when Mangalyaan, our very own spacecraft reached Mars within first attemt.
2014, Sept 30	NASA and ISRO signed an agreement to collaborate on an earth-observing Satellite called NISAR and future Mars missions.
2015, Feb 14	Arvind Kejriwal of AAP became Chief Minister of Delhi.
2016, June 22	Indian Space Research Organisation (ISRO) launched 20 Satellites through a single rocket, breaking its 2008 record of launching 10 satellites in a single mission.
2016, Nov 8	Prime Minister Narender Modi announced the demonetisation of ₹ 500 and ₹ 1000 currency notes to check corruption.
2017, June 5	India's space agency, Indian Space Research Organisation (ISRO), successfully launched its most powerful homegrown rocket-a spacecraft GSLV Mark III. The country hopes will carry humans to space.
2017, July 1	GST (Goods and Service Tax) implemented.
2017, July 24	Ram Nath Kovind elected as India's 14th President.

APPENDIX VII
WHO'S WHO IN MODERN INDIA

1. *Abdul Ghaffar Khan* (1890-1987). Mohamadzai Pathan tribesman from North West Frontier Province (now in Pakistan); organiser, Khudai Khidmatgar Movement; participated in Congress campaigns for India's freedom; popularly known as Badshah Khan and also Fronties Gandhi.

2. *Aga Khan III* (1877-1957). Head, Bohra Ismaili Muslims; founder-member and President of All India Muslim League, 1906; 13 ; headed, Muslim Deputation to Lord Minto, October 1906 ; leader, Indian Delegation to League of Nations Assembly in 1932, 1934, 1935, 1936 and was elected its President in 1937; recipient of many titles from British Crown.

3. *Ambedkar, B.R.* (1891-1956). Mahar (Harijan) from Madhya Pradesh; leader, Depressed Classes of India; member, Bombay Legislative Assmembly, 1926-34; member, Governor General's Executive Council, 1942-46; chairman, Drafting Committee of Indian Constitution; Law Minister, Nehru's Cabinet, 1947-51.

4. *Ansari, DR. M.A.* (1880-1936). Sunni Muslim from U.P.; medical practitioner, Delhi; President, All India Muslim League, Indian National Congress, 1927 and All Parties Conference, 1928; participated, Civil Disobedience Movement; Chancellor, Jamia Millia Islamia, 1928-36.

5. *Attlee, Clement* (1883-1967). Leader, Labour Party in England; Prime Minister of Great Britain, 1945-51; piloted, Indian Independence Bill in British Parliament, August 1947 on the basis of which India was partitoned into independent dominions of India and Pakistan.

6. *Aurobindo, Sri* (1872-1950). Kayastha from West Bengal; qualified, I.C.S. but failed in riding test, 1890; leader, Bengali Extremists, 1906-10; retired to Pondicherry, 1910; editor, *Yugantar*

7. *Azad, Maulana Abul Kalam* (1888-1958). Born at Mecca of Indo-Arabic descent; eminent freedom fighter; Congress President, 1923, 1939-46; Education Minister in Nehru's Cabinet, 1947-58; author, *India Wins Freedom*.

8. *Banerjee, Surendranath* (1848-1925). Kulin Brahmin from Bengal; entered I.C.S., 1871; dismissed from I.C.S., 1874; President, Indian National Congress, 1895, 1902; Minister, Bengal Government, 1921-23; editor. *Bengalee*; author, *A Nation in Making*.

9. *Bonerjee, W.C.* (1844-1906). Brahmin from Bengal; President, Indian National Congress, 1885, 1892; member Bengal Legislative Council, 1894-95.

10. *Besant, Mrs Annie* (1847-1933). Anglo-Irish descent; came to India, 1895; President, Theosophical Society. 1907-33; founder Central Hindu College, Benares; organiser, Home Rule League, 1916; President, Indian National Congress, 1917; left Congress over Non-Cooperation Resolution. 1920.

11. *Bose, Subhas Chandra* (1897-1945) Kayastha from Bengal; resigned , I.C.S., 1920 President, Indian National Congress, 1938, 1939; escaped to Germany, 1942; organiser, Indian National Army, 1943; popularly known as Netaji.

12. *Chatterji, Bankim Chandra* (1838-94) Brahmin from Bengal; civil servant, Bengal Government; author *Anand Math* which contains the national song 'Bande Mataram'.

13. *Churchill, Winston* (1874-1965). Conservative leader of Great Britain; Prime Minister, 1940-45, 1951-55; organiser of English victory in World War II; diehard imperialist; opposed all concessions to India.

14. *Cotton, Henry* (1845-1915). Member, I.C.S., 1867-1902; KCSI, 1902; President, Indian National Congress, 1904; MP, 1906-10; author, *New India*.

15. *Cripps, Stafford* (1889-1952). Distinguished member of Labour Party of Great Britain; famous for Cripps 'offer', 1942, member, Cabinet Mission to India, 1946.

16. *Das, Chittaranjan* (1870-1925). Nationalist leader from Bengal; perticipated, Non-Cooperation Movement; President. Indian National Congress, 1922; founder, Swaraj Party; popularly known as Deshbandhu.

17. *Dayanand, Saraswati* (1824-83). Brahmin from Kathiawar Gujarat; great socio-religious reformer; founder Arya Samaj, 1875; author, *Satyartha Prakash*.

18. *Derozio, Henry* (1809-31). Anglo-Protuguese discent; poet and teacher, Hindu College Calcutta; leader, Young Bengal Movement.

19. *Dutt, R.C.* (1848-1909). I.C.S. 1871-97; President, Indian National Congress, 1899: author, *Economic History of India*.

20. *Dyer, Brigadier-General R. Harry*. Chief culprit, Jallianwalla Bagh Massacre; resigned, 1920.

21. *Elphinstone, Mountstuart* (1779-1859). Soldier and administrator; Resident at Poona, 1811; Governor of Bombay, 1819-27 author, *History of India*.

22. *Gandhi, Mrs Indira* (1917-84). Kashmiri Brahmin descent; Prime Minister of India. 1966-77, 1980-84; elected chairperson, NAM, March 1983; assassinated, 31 Oct 1984.

23. *Gandhi, Mahatma* (1869-1948). Vaisya-bania from Gujarat; in South Africa, 1893-1914; returned to India, 1915; apostle of Peace and Non-Violence; stellar role in Indian freedom Struggle; remembered as Bapu of the Nation.

24. *Gokhale Gopal Krishna* (1866-1915). Chitpavan Brahmin from Maharashtra; member Bombay Legislative Council, 1899-1901; member, Imperial Legislative Council, 1902-15; founder, Servants of India Society, 1905; typical Congress Moderate leader.

25. *Har Dayal* (1884-1939). Kayastha from Delhi; organiser, Ghadr Party in U.S.A.; radical socialist and revolutionary.

26. *Hume, A.O.* (1829-1912). Scottish descent; entered Bengal Civil Service, 1849; Secretary, Revenue and Agriculture Deptt, Govt. of India, 1870-79; retired, 1882; founder, Indian National Congress, 1885; General Secretary of Congress, 1885-1906; left India, 1894.

27. *Iqbal, Muhammad* (1876-1938). Kashmiri descent; peot and philosopher; President, All India Muslim League, 1930; propagated for separate homeland for Indian Muslims; his thinking oscillated between Pan-Islamism and nationalism; author, famous song '*Sare jahan se achha Hindustan hamara*'.

28. *Jinnah, M.A.* (1876-1948). Khoja Muslim from Bombay; President, Muslim League, 1916, 1920, 1934-48; organiser, campaigns for Pakistan; first Governor-General of Pakistan, 1947-48; popularly remembered as Qaid-i-Azam.

29. *Lajpat Rai* (1865-1928). Panjabi bania; author, lawyer and Arya Samaj leader; reputed Extremist leader; President, Indian National Congress, 1920; author, *Unhappy India*.

30. *Lakshmi Bai, Rani* (1827-1858). Maratha Brahmin descent; married Gangadhar Rao of Jhansi, 1842; resented, Jhansi's annexation by Dalhousie, 1854; reputed leader during Revolt of 1857; died fighting at Gwalior fort, June 1858.

31. *Liaquat Ali Khan* (1895-1951). Panjabi Sunni Muslim descent; settled in U.P; member, Central Legislative Assembly, 1936; General Secretary, All India Muslim League, 1937; Finance Minister, Nehru's Interim Government, 1946: first Prime Minister of Pakistan. 1947-51.

32. *Macaulay, T.B.* (1800-59). English poet, essayist, historian and politician; Law Member, Governor General's Council, 1834: advocate, English scheme of education in India; Chairman, Indian

Law Commission; author, *History of England, Historical Essays*.

33. *Malabari. B.M.* (1853-1912). Parsi from western India; editor, *Indian spectator, Voice of India*; social reformer; crusader for Age of Consent Bill.

34. *Morley, John* (1838—1923) British Liberal statesman and author; Secretary of State for India, 1905-10; remembered as co-author of Morley-Minto Reforms, 1909.

35. *Mountbatten, Lord Louis* (1900—1979) Great grand-nephew of Queen Victoria; naval officer and statesman; Supreme Commander of Allied Forces in S.E. Asia, 1943-6; last Viceroy of India, March-August, 1947; first Governor General of Free India, August 1947—June 1948.

36. *Muller, Friedrich Max* (1823—1900) German national; great Sanskrit scholar and philologist; translated into English *Vedic Hymns, Sacred Books of the East*.

37. *Naidu, Mrs Sarojini* (1879—1949) Bengali Kulin descent; married a Maharashtrian; poetess, politician and freedom-fighter; President, Indian National Congress, 1925; Governor, U.P. 1947-49.

38. *Nana Fadnavis* (—1800) Maratha Brahmin; celebrated Prime Minister of the Peshwas at Poona, 1774-1800; defender of Maratha interests against Tipu, the Nizam, and E.I. Co.

39. *Nana Saheb* (1825—1860) Maratha Brahmin; adopted son of Peshwa Baji Rao II; great hero of the Revolt of 1857.

40. *Naoroji, Dadabhai* (1825—1917) Parsi; journalist and businessman; founder, East India Association London, 1866; member, Bombay Legislature Council, 1885; member, British Parliament, 1892-5; President, Indian National Congress,1886, 1893, 1906; author, *Indian Poverty and the British Rule in India*.

41. *Nehru, Jawaharlal* (1889—1964) Kashmiri Brahmin descent; President Indian National Congress, 1929, 1936, 1937, 1946, 1946, 1951-54; First Prime Minister of Free India, 1947-64.

42. *Nehru, Motilal* (1861—1931) Kashmiri Brahmin; Advocate, Allahabad High Court; Founder-member Swaraj Party; President, Indian National Congress, 1919, 1928.

43. *Pal, Bipin Chandra* (1858—1932) Bengali Kayastha; prominent Brahmo Samaj leader and social reformer; author and journalist; prominent extremist leader; opposed Non-Co-operation Movement led by Mahatma Gandhi.

44. *Patel, Sardar Vallabhbai* (1875—1950) Gujarati lawyar and politician; leader, Kaira Satyagraha, 1918, Bardoli Satyagraha, 1928; President, Indian National Congress, 1931; First Deputy Prime Minister of India, 1947-50.

45. *Rajagopalacharia, Chakravati* (1879—1972) Tamil Brahmin; prominent freedom-fighter who often differed with Gandhi; Chief Minister of Madras, 1937-39; member, Governor General's Executive Council, 1947-46; First Indian Governor General of Free India, 1948-50; founder, Swatantra Party.

46. *Rajendra Prasad*, Dr. (1884—1963) Bihari lawyer and freedom-fighter; a true Gandhite; President, Indian Congress, 1934, 1939; President Indian Constituent Assembly, 1946-50; First President of Indian Republic, 1950-60.

47. *Ramakrishna Paramhansa*, (1836—86) Bengali Brahmin; priest Kali Mandir, Dakshineswar Calcutta; preached realisation of God through service of humanity; his teachings widely propagated by Swami Vivekananda.

48. *Ranade, Mahadev Govind* (1842—1901) Chitpawan Brahmin; great patriot and social reformer; awarded C.I.E., 1887; Judge, Bombay High Court, 1893-1901; author, *Essays on Indian Economics. Rise of the Maratha Power*.

49. *Roy, Rammohan (Raja)* (1772—1833) Bengali religious and social reformer; co-founder, Hindu College Calcutta, 1817; founder, Brahmo Samaj; awarded title of Raja by Mughal Emperor, 1830; remembered Father of Indian Renaissance.

50. *Syed Ahmad Khan* (1817—98) Born Delhi; entered service of E.I. Co., 1837 demonstrated loyalty to the British, during the Revolt of 1857; retired Sub-Judge, 1867; founder, Aligarh movement; political outlook was communal, not secular or nationalist; member, Imperial Legislative Council, 1878-83; Knighted, 1888.

51. *Tagore, Rabindranath* (1861—1941) Bengali Brahmin; poet and philosopher; awarded Nobel Prize for Literature, 1913; founder, Visva-Bharati University, 1921; composer, Jana Gana Mana, India's national song.

52. *Tantia Tope* (—1859) Deshastha Maratha: Nana Saheb's Chief Lieutenant during Revolt, 1857-1858; deserted by compartriots; executed, 1859.

53. *Tilak, Bal Gangadhar* (1856—1920) Chitpawan Brahmin from Maharashtra; teacher, journalist and fearless freedom-fighter; editor, Kesari, Maharatta; jailed for sedition, 1897-98 and 1908-14; author slogan, "swaraj is my birthright and I shall have it".

54. *Vidyasagar, Ishwar Chandra* (1820—91) Bengali Brahmin; prominent Sanskrit scholar and teacher; Principal, Fort William College, Calcutta; crusader for widow re-marriage and against polygamy.

55. *Vivekanand, Swami* (1863—1902) Bengali Kayastha; Vedantic Scholar and Hindu missionary; organiser, Ramakrishna Mission, 1897; author, *Karmayoga, Rajayoga, Bhaktiyoga, Prachya and Paschatya*, preached value of social service and self-sacrifice.

APPENDIX VIII
ACTIVITIES OF THE CHRISTIAN MISSIONS DURING BRITISH RULE

Christinity is reported to have entered India in the first century A.D. when St. Thomas landed on the Malabar Coast. By the third century A.D. the Syrian Christians had emerged as a body in the State of Kerala. During Akbar's reign, in 1580, a Baptist Christian mission was set up at Fatehpur Sikri and its missionaries participated in the religious discussions at the *Ibabat-Khana*. The Jesuit Missionaries are reported to have opened a Jesuit College at Agra in the times of Emperor Shah Jehan.

A new phase in East-West relations began when Vasco-da-Gama landed at Calicut in 1498. Vasco had explained the motive behind his visit thus: "We have come to seek Christians and spices". The Portugese Roman Catholic missionaries, like Francis Xavier and Robert-de-Nobili, did some notable work in the field of opening some elementary schools and some orphanges.

In the 17th and 18th centuries, the Directors of the English East India Company and the English authorities in India adopted contradictory postures, sometimes encouraging missionary activities and at other times limiting missionary activities in India. In the 18th century, in particular the English East India merchants and officials, looked upon the Salvation Army (Christian missionares) as a threat to their profits (they had in view the Mughal antipathy to the Portuguese Jesuits as a cautionary precendent) and put all sorts of restrictions on the entrance of missionaries in the Presidency towns.

The Serampur Missionaries

The Baptist missionaries from England-the trio, Joshua Marshman, William Carey and William Ward-wanted to start their activities from Calcutta. Loard Wellesley, the Governor General (1798-1805) considered them so "subversive", 'a menance to tranquillity', that they were banned from entering Calcutta', these missionaries were compelled to settle in the nearby Danish settlement at Serampur. The Serampur trio did some useful work in the field of education, setting up a printing press, translating the Ramayana and Mahabharata into English, besides attempting social reforms.

The Evangelical movement in England added to the missionary influence and their popularity in London; it did influence the thinking of the Company's Directors and the Members of Parliament. As a result, the Charter Act of 1813 lifted the Company's blanket ban on missionary activities in India, and missionaries from the U.K. could enter, reside and openly preach. The Charter Act of 1833 went a step further and threw open India to missionaries of the whole world, who are free to preach and even settle in India. Consequently, many German and much-funded American Protestant missionaries came to India. The Roman Catholic Missions also became more vigorous and their missionaries from all parts of the world poured into India.

Missionary Comments on Hindu Socio-religions practices

The primary motive of the Christian missionaries was to convert the Indians to Christanity. In particular, they decried Hindu religion and their religious parctices like idolatry and image-worship. To hammer their point, the Christian missionaries praised the tenets and practices of their religion. This evoked a sharp reaction in orthodox Hindu circles, though the missionaries did succceed in having some converts from the lower classes and in backward tribal and hill areas. All the same, the social and educational activities attracted the notice and praise of the newly Western-educated class.

The missionaries crusaded against the discrimination against women in Hindu society;

social evils like infanticide, child-marriage, polygamy, sati, forced widowhood, came under sharp condemnation. Practices like purdah, dowry system, the Devadasi practice (in Bengal) and denial of proper education to women, also received their attention.

The rigidity of the Caste system and untouchability were the other targets of the Missionarie's attacks. Though conversion amongst the lower castes were moderate, the inequality based on the Caste system received the careful attention of the leaders of the various socio-religious reformers.

The missionaries also turned their attention to the neglected and primitive tribes like Santhals in southern Bihar, the Marria-gonds in Madhya Pradesh and the numerous tribals in Garo Hills and other areas in North-eastern states. The missionary efforts did attain some success in conversions.

In the field of social service, the missionaries were very active, though their humanitarian approach was an adjunct to their primary aim of eonversions to Christianity. The missionaries opened many medical dispensaries, some hospitals and some medical Institutions to win the heart of the weaker sections of Indian society. Similarly, they opened some orphanges for the physically handicapped and the and blind. Service centres were also opened during epidemics, famines, droughts, floods,etc. The missinoaries won notable success in the field of education, production of vernacular literature, setting up printing presses and publications. In this field, the missionaries worked as pioneers, when they opened modern elemantary schools, made provision for teaching English language, set up teachers, training institutions, set up special schools for girls, which provided vocational education also. The missionaries did valuable work in the field of adult education and carried on novel experiments in rural education in their schools at Moga, Salem, Medak, Ankaleshwar, Dernakal and at several other places. During 1936-37, there were 14,341 missionary institutions of the types, with a total student-strength of 1,118,200 on their rulls. The total expenditure involved was over Rs. 38 million.

In the political field, the missionary activity, particularly in the fields of political awakening and development of national outlook was only marginal.

An Overview: Many Western scholars and apologists of missionary activities highlight the pioneering thrust of the missionaries in introducing the modern printing press in India, opening of Westernised type of schools,commenting on the rich cultural heritage of the Indian classics, focussing attention of socio–religious evils in the Indian set-up and popularising humanitarian values in society. The Missionaries' condemnation of deficiencies in Indian religious practices evoked reactions among Indian leaders, who earnestly turned their attention to socio–religious reforms in Indian society. Taken in this light—both in action and reaction–the missionaries become heralds of modernisation of India.

APPENDIX IX
Objective Type Information about Wars During Modern Indian History
Anglo-French Carnatic Wars

Name	Period	Result
1. First Carnatic War	1746-48	Ended by Treaty of Aix-La Chapelle in Europe. It was a drawn struggle.
2. Second Carnatic War	1750-54	It proved an inconclusive war, but the English had an edge over the French.
3. Third Carnatic War	1758-63	Ended by the Treaty of Paris. The British won a decisive victory over the French in India.

Anglo-Mysore Wars

Name	Period	Result
1. First Mysore War	1767-69	Ended by Treaty of Madras. Haider Ali had an edge over the English.
2. Second Mysore War	1780-84	Ended by Treaty of Mangalore, it was a drawn struggle.
3. Third Mysore War	1790-92	Ended by Treaty of Seringapatam. Tipu Sultan lost
4. Fourth Mysore War	1799	Tipu died in the War. Mysore lost its independence.

Anglo-Maratha Wars

Name	Period	Result
1. First Maratha War	1776-82	Ended by Treaty of Salbai. It was a drawn struggle.
2. Second Maratha War	1803-06	The Company concluded separate treaties with Scindia, Bhonsle and Holkar. The English had an edge over the Marathas.
3. Third Maratha War	1817-18	Maratha defeat was complete. Peshwa's territories annexed to British India.

Anglo-Burman Wars

Name	Period	Result
1. First Burman War	1824-26	Ended by Treaty of Yandaboo. The British annexed Arakan and Tenasserim.
2. Second Burman War	1852	The British annexed Rangoon and Lower Burma.
3. Third Burman War	1885	Annexation of Upper Burma. Burma lost its independence.

Anglo-Afghan Wars

Name	Period	Result
1. First Afghan War	1839-42	The invasion of Afganistan was a failure. Dost Mohammed became the new Amir of Afganistan.
2. Second Afghan War	1878-80	The British invasion of Afganistan was a failure. Abdur Rehman became the new Amir.

Anglo-Sikh Wars

Name	Period	Result
1. First Sikh War	1845-46	Ended by the Treaty of Lahore. The Sikhs lost territory and prestige also.
2. Second Sikh War	1848-49	The Sikh State collapsed. Punjab was annexed to British India.

APPENDIX X
THE PEOPLES' MOVEMENTS IN THE PRINCELY STATES

After Robert Clive's diplomatic victory at the battlefield of Plassey, it took the English East India Company about 50 years to establish British dominion over the whole of India. Under British imperial rule, India was broadly divided into two parts, (*a*) British India i.e. Indian Provinces and Chief Commissioners' territories under direct administration of the Governor General-in-Council, (*b*)Princely India or Indian States or Indian India under the administration of Indian rulers. According to an authorized list published by the Government of India in 1929 there were in all 562 States of Which 108 were Salute States, 127 were non-Salute States and 327 were small States and Jagirs. The size of the States widely differed: at one end of the scale was Hyderabad with an area of 82,700 square miles with population of 1.25 crores inhabitants and an annual income of about 7 crores of rupees, and at the other end of the scale minute States in Kathiawar limited to an area of few acres and in some cases with an annual income of an ordinary artisan.

The system of government in most of the Indian States was despotic where the ruler enjoyed absolute power in all spheres of administration. In fact, the vast majority of the States were bastions of political, economic and social backwardness. The rulers kept the people of States illiterate and deprived them of all civil laberties and subjected them to unchecked exploitation, including forced labour. Pt. Jawaharlal Nehru described the States as "sinks of reaction and incompetence".

Emergence of Political Consciousness in the Princely States

The early years of the 20th century marked the emergence of the Radical or National Party popularly known as the Extremist Party in the Indian National Congress. An accompanying development was the organisation of a Terrorist Revolutionary wing. The draconian legislation passed by the Government of Lord Minto drove the revolutionaries underground and many of them took shelter in the Princely States. These runaway terrorists became the agents of politicisation in the States. The overall result was the development of political consciousness in the minds of the people of Princely States. Further, the Khilafat Movement and the Non-Cooperation Movement (1920-22) put forward a model for political organisation and mass mobilisation before the people of the States. As a result, States 'Peoples' conferences were organised in Hyderabad, Mysore, Baroda, the Kathiwara States, the Deccan States, Indore and Nawanagar. The organisation of the All India States Peoples' Conference in December, 1927, was the next logical development. The conference held at Bombay was attended by 700 political workers drawn from different states.

The leaders of the AISPC like Balwantrai Mehta and Maniklal Kothari naturally looked upon the Indian National Congress for help and guidance in their struggle for representative type of government in the Princely States. On their part, the leaders of the Congress knew that the Princely States were 'legally' independent entities and this fact imposed understandable restraint on the merger of the popular movements in Princely States and British India. All the same, the Nagpur Congress (1920) passed a resolution calling upon the Princes to grant full responsible government in their States. Henceforth, the Congress allowed the residents of Princely States to become members of the Indian National Congress, but made it clear to the States' leaders that they should not initiate political activities in the states in the name of the Congress but must do so either in their individual capacity or as member of the States' local political organisations. In the 1927 Congress session the resolution of 1920 was passed again. In a significant departure Pt. Nehru at his Lahore Congress (1929) Presidential address declared: "The Indian States cannot live apart from the rest of India" but added that the "only people who have a right to determine the future of the States must be the people of these States".

Princely States' Role in the British Policy of 'Divide and Rule'

What was the motivation of the British authorities in keeping intact the Indian States and supporting the despotic rule of the Indian Princes? The Indian Princes had served as "breakwaters to the storm of 1857" and could henceforth serve as bulwark of the British Indian empire. The British Crown guaranteed the continued existence of the Princely States in return for unquestioned loyalty to the Crown. All the same, the Government of India exercised great interference and control over the rights of Indian Princes through the British Residents and Political Agents posted at the capitals of the Princely States. Lord Canning had referred to the rulers of the Indian States as "feudatories and vassals" and to the Crown as the unquestioned ruler and Paramount Power in India. The British authorities used the Princes as a divisive forced to checkmate the Freedom Struggle in India. In February 1921, the Chamber of Princes was set up to recognise the states as "an independent constituent of the empire". In fact, the Government of India and the Indian Princes formed a common front to preserve their "positions and privileges". Recognising the Indian Princes as a distinct political identity, the Indian Princes were invited at the Round Table Conferences held in London during 1930-32. The Federal Structure proposed for the whole of India by the Government of India Act 1935 proposed 33 $1/3$% seats for the States in the Federal Assembly and 40% of the seats in the Council of State. The mischievous element in the porposed Federal Legislative structure was that while the representatives of Indian provinces were to be elected those of Indian states were to be nominated by the ruling princes. Lee-Warner has pointed out the "steadying influence" of the Indian Princes in the proposed Federal set-up. He wrote, "With that influence in the federal legislature I am not afraid in the slightest degree of anything that may happen, even if the Congress managed to get the largest proportion of votes". The Indian National Congress and the AISPC clearly saw the imperialist manoeuvre and demanded that States' representatives in the proposed Federal set-up should also be elected by the people of the States. The British authorities reacted to this demand by encouraging the Princes not to give their consent for the formation of the federation. And All India Federation never came into existence!

People' Movements in Some States and Princes' Reactions

The first elections in the provinces under the Government of India Act 1935 were held in the winter of 1936-37, and Congress Ministries were formed in seven provinces. The appointment of popular ministries in British Indian provinces created a new sense of confidence in the people of the Indian States and the year 1938-39 witnessed the mushrooming of Praja Mandals in many States and political activity picked up in Rajkot, Jaipur, Patiala, Hyderabad, Mysore, Travancore, Orrisa States and even Jammu and Kashmir. At the Haripura Congress Session (February, 1938) it was demanded for the first time in unequivocal language that the Congress ideal of *Purna Swaraj* was applicable not only to British India but also to Princely States.

In Mysore State the AISPC launched a mass movement and demanded an elected Government and for acceptance of state Peoples' Conference as a legal body. In the district of Monar the police opened fire on a rally of hundred people causing thirty casualities. Sardar Patel mediated and a compromise was reached with Mirza Ismail, the Diwan of Mysore, on the basics of recognition of the Congress. As no general agreement could be reached on other issues, the movement was begun again in September, 1939.

In the Princely States of Dhenkanal, Talcher, Nilgiri, Ranpur in Orissa, the situation was far worse. Here, the *adivases* started a struggle with bows and arrows. The British authorities helped the States' authorities to suppress the movement brutally.

The Government in two Southern States of Travancore and Cochin faced a mass movement launched by the Socialists and the Communists. The Youth League organised by the Leftists started a mass struggle in September 1938. The Government banned the Youth League and meeting and demonstrations were prohibited. In spite of the ban, hundreds of *satyagrahies* entered Travancore. The Jatha from Malabar was led by the Communist leader A.K. Gopalan and the Jatha from Malabar was under the leadership of Pandyan. The police lathicharged and the firing killed Pandyan and grieviously injured Gopalan. The police brutalities on the people continued. The National Front newspaper in an article of 30 October 1938 wrote, "The advent of the State Congress, a political organisation demanding a responsible government under the aegis of the Highness, is the immediate cause for the reign of terror and ruthless repression that defaces the once blooming landscape, creates a regular inferno with all its horrors".

In February, 1939 Pandit Jawaharlal Nahru president over the all India States' Peoples' Conference held at Ludhiana. Nehru made it clear that the he had come to the meeting "not only because I am intensely interested in the freedom of people of the States, but as the bearer of the goodwill of the rest of India and with a pledge of our solidarity" Nehru referred to the majority of the States as "sinks of reaction and incompetence" and declared that the system in the states had been propped up and artificially maintained by British Imperialism and added, "That system has no inherent importance or strength, it is the strength of British imperialism that counts......Therefore, when conflict comes we must recognise who our opponent is". In very emphatic language Nehru declared, "The freedom of the People of the States is a big enough thing yet it is part of the larger freedom of the India".

The rulers of most of the Princely States were highly allergic to the organisation of political associations in their States and not unoften refused to recognise their existence and even unleashed a reign of terror and ruthless repression through the State police force. The Maharaja of Manipur refused to meet a deputation of Nikhil Manipuri Mahasabha in May 1939 and sent a message through his Private Secretary, "His Highness will not see you so long as that cap will remain on your head". The Maharaja of Patiala met a deputation of the Praja Mandal in August 1939 and in a typically dictatorial tone told the Mandal:

"My ancestors have won the state by the sword and I mean to keep it by the sword. I do not recognise an organisation to represent my people or to speak on their behalf. I am their sole and only representative. No organisation such as Praja Mandal can be allowed to exist within the state. If you want to do Congress work, get out of the state. The Congress can terrify the British Government but if it ever tries to interfere in my state it will find me a terrible resister. I cannot tolerate any flag other than my own to be flown within my boundaries....I advise you to get out of the Mandal and stop all kind of agitation, or else, remember, I am a military man; my talk is blunt and bullet straight".

World War II and States' Peoples' Participation in India's Freedom Struggle

The beginning of Second World War gave distinct turn to the Freedom Struggle in the Indian sub-continent. Popular Congress ministries in provinces resigned in October 1939 on the issue of India being dragged without the consent of the Indian people into the Second World War and asked the British Government to declare their war aims. After the failure of the negotiations between the Congress and the British imperial rulers, the Congress launched the Quit India Movement in 1942 and called upon the people of British India and Princely States to fight for India's freedom. Henceforth, the people of Princely States formally joined the Indian Struggle for Independence. All the same, the peoples' organisations in different States continued their struggle for introduction of responsible government in their States.

Appendix X

The Indian Independence Act, 1947, terminated the Crown's sovereignty and Paramountcy over British India and Princely States; all treaties and agreements etc. between the Crown and the Princely States lapsed with effect from 15th August, 1947. Thus, the Princely States became legally independent. However, Lord Mountbatten's Plan of 3rd June 1947 had emphasised that Princely States would be free to join Free India or Free Pakistan. The National Government of India and Home Minister Sardar Vallabhbhai Patel used various methods—persuasion, diplomatic pressure and even armstwisting to get Princely States rulers' agreement to join the Indian Union by the end of 1947, though Junagarh and Hyderabad signed the Instrument of Accession in 1948.

The States Reorganisation Act, 1956, brought about reorganisation of States boundaries on linguistic lines which resulted in the merger of many Princely States into neighbouring States of the Indian Union.

APPENDIX XI
SUBHAS CHANDRA BOSE AND THE I.N.A.

Subhas Chandra popularly known as Netaji was born in a respectable middle class Bengali family on 23 Januray 1897. Subhas's father, Jankinath Bose was a known public figure at Cuttack where he successively became the Chairman of the Cuttack Municipality and Government Pleader and Public Prosecutor. In 1912 Jankinath became a member of the Bengal Legislative Council and received the title of Rai Bahadur.

Subhas graduated from Calcutta University in 1919 with a First Class in Philosophy. The same year his parents sent him to England to compete for the Indian Civil Service. In 1920 he appeared for the I.C.S. and came out fourth in order of merit. However, Subhas did not complete the year of probation which every succesful candidate in the examination was required to undergo. The sequence of political developments in India beginning with the Jallianwala Bagh Massacre (13 April 1919), followed by the enactment of the Rowlatt Act and the Congress resentment with the launch of the Non-Cooperation Movment (1920-22) emotionally disturbed Bose and he decided to resign from the much-coveted I.C.S. in April 1921 explainning :

"I did not think that one could be loyal to the British Raj and yet serve India honestly, heart and soul".

At the Calcutta Congress Session (1928) Gandhiji himself moved the main resolution demanding a Dominion Status Constitution for India. Unsatisfied, Bose moved an amendment to the resolution demanding full independence for India. The Gandhiites joined hands to save the prestige of Gandhiji who had threatened to retire from the Congress if the Bose's amendment was carried out. The amendment was lost by 973 votes against 1350 votes.

In 1929, Subhas Chandra Bose was elected President of the All-India Trade Union Congress, the position which he held till 1931. In fact, by this time Bose had emerged as a prominent and influential leader of the Left Wing in the Indian National Congress. He gave a dynamic lead to the youth and the students of the country on a National scale, also rallying the support of the industrial workers by building up trade unionism on solid foundations.

In 1930 Subhas participated in the Salt Satyagrah Movement and the Government arrested him and lodged him in jail. On 5th March 1931 Gandhiji signed the Gandhi-Irwin Pact and suspended the movement. Subhas along with many others were set at liberty. However, Subhas protested against the Pact especially because patriots like Bhagat Singh and his associates had not been saved from the gallows.

During 1931 and 1937 Bose was arrested and jailed a number of times. However, the situation changed for the better when under the Government of India Act 1935. Provincial autonomy was introduced and in the first General Provincial Elections held in 1937 the Congress Party came in power in seven provinces out of eleven provinces.

At the Haripura Congress session in Gujarat (February 1938) Bose was unanimously elected the President of the Indian National Congress at the early age of 41. In his long Presidential address he stressed the revolutionary potentialities of the Congress Ministries formed in the seven Provinces. He spoke at length on the Fundamental rights of Indian citizens, talked about national problems relating to eradication of poverty, illiteracy and disease and adoption of system of scientific production and distribution along socialistic lines. Contrary to the popular notion that Pandit Jawaharlal Nehru

Appendix XI

was the first Congress leader who talked of Economic Planning, it was Bose, who in his Presidential Address in 1938 emphasized on the need of setting up a National Planning Committee and even emphasized that Planning Commission "will have to adopt a comprehensive scheme for gradually socializing our entire agricultural and industrial system in the spheres of both production and distribution" The All-India National Planning Committee was formally inaugurated by Bose at Bombay on 17 December 1938.

The Gandhiites did not like the functioning of Subhas Bose as Congress President during 1938. As such Bose faced stiff and organized opposition for the next Presidential Election. On his part, Bose announced his candidature on 21 January 1939. He also declared his support to "new ideas, ideologies, problems and new programmes" particularly his plans for an anti-imperial struggle against continuation of British rule in India. The Rightists, with the blessing of Mahatama Gandhi put up the name of Pattabhi Sitaramayya for the position of Congress President. In the election held at Tripuri (now Madhya Pradesh), Bose won by 1580 votes against 1377 cast in favour of Sitaramyya. In anguish Gandhiji declared that Sitaramayya's defeat was "more mine than of his". The election was followed by sensational developments culminating in the resignation of 12 out 15 members of the Working Committee headed by Sardar Patel, Maulana Azad and Mr. Rajendra Parsad, Pt. Jawaharlal Nehru did not formally resign but issued a statement, which led everybody to believe that he had also resigned.

Jawaharlal Nehru expressed his unhappiness with Bose's aspersions on his colleagues. Nehru also did not subscribe to the view that the election fight was between the left and the Right. In a letter to Bose on 4 Feb. 1339 he maintained :

"I do not know who you consider a Leftist and who a Rightist, The way these words were used by you in your statements during the Presidential contest seemed to imply that Gandhiji and those who are considered his group in Working Committee are the Rightist leaders. Their opponents, whoever they might be, are the Leftist. That seems to me, an entirely wrong description......If instead of these words, we talked about policies it would be far better."

There seems to have been a basic difference of policy and tactics between subhas Bose and the Gandhiites in the assessment of India's preparedness for Civil Disobedience movement and the favourable international scenario.

In his Presidential Address at Tripuri session of the Congress, in 1339, Bose said :

"I have been feeling for sometime past, namely that the time has come for us to raise the issue of Swaraj and submit our national demand to the British Government in the form of an ultimatum. The time is long past when we could have adopted a passive attitude and waited for the federal scheme to be imposed on us".[1]

Referring to the favourable political scenario, Bose said :

"The sanction that we possess today is mass civil disobedience or satyagraha. And the British government today are not in a position to face a major conflict like an all-India satyagraha for a long period......What more opportune moment could we find in our national history for a final advance in the direction of Swaraj, particularly when the international situation is favourable to us"[2]

---

1. Selected Speeches of Subhas Chandra Bose (Publications Division, Ministry of Information and Broadcasting, Govt. of India)p. 103.
2. *Ibid*, p. 104.
3. Rajendra Prasad : Autobiography, 1957.

Gandhi in an interview on 5th May 1939 declared, "Subhas Bose holds that we possess enough resources for a fight. I am totally opposed to his views. Today we possess no resources for a fight". Rajendra Prasad, later in his autobiography clarified that Gandhiji and the older leaders would not accept a situation where the strategy and tactics were not theirs but the responsibility for implementing them would be theirs"[3]. In sheer disgust Bose resigned as Congress President in April 1339.

In September 1939 the Second World War broke out in Europe. India was dragged into the imperialist war by an ordinance issued by the Governor General declaring India a belligerent country. The Congress ministries in seven provinces resigned in October 1939, but Mahatama Gandhi declared that he would not like to embarrass the British Government during the war.

Bose activated the Forward Bloc[3A] organization and an All India Forward Bloc meeting was held at Nagpur in June 1940. The Forward Bloc passed a resolution for the immediate establishment of a Provisional National Government in India.

In July 1940, the Bengal Government arrested Bose on the eve of Anti-Holwell Movement Satyagraha at Calcutta, and sent him to jail. In prison, Bose resorted to hunger strike and was released in December 1940. On 26 January 1941, on the historic "Independence Day", Bose escaped from police surveillance at Calcutta and via Peshawar and Russia reached Berlin. From January 1942 Bose began his regular broadcast from Radio Berlin, which aroused great enthusiasm in India.

Subhas Bose believed in the popular maxim, 'enemy's enemy is a friend' In other words, since Hitler and Mussolini (whatever their political ideology) were the enemies of imperial Anglo-French bloc, they were India's friends and could help India in uprooting British rule from India. Further, Bose realised that 'Britain's difficulty was India's opportunity'. In his broadcast from Berlin radio on Marcdh 1, 1943, Bose said :

"In the present case those who are trying to overthrow the British Empire are helping our liberation and, are therefore our friends and allies, while all those who are trying to save that empire are only attempting to perpetuate our slavery. But apart from this theoretical proposition, my personal experience as well as my interviews with Herr Hitler and Signor Mussolini have convinced me that in this struggle against British Imperialism, the Tripartite Powers are our best friends and allies outside India....

Victory is assured, time is working for us. Our allies abroad are ready to help us. What more one can desire ? Be confident that India is gong to be free, and that before long.

Down with British Imperialism ! Long live Free India ! Long live Revolution !"[4]

Organization of the I.N.A. (Indian National Army)

World War II served as a catalyst in India's struggle for freedom. Japan's attack on the American naval base at Pearl Harbour (7 December 1941) was followed by quick blows at French, Dutch and British colonial empires in the Far East. The British Army suffered humiliating defeat in Malaya and Singapore, leaving 45000 POWs in the hands of the Japanese. The credit of organizing an I.N.A. gose to Capt. Mohan Singh, an officer in the British Indian Army; he refused to retreat with the British army and instead contacted the Japanese authorities for help and co-operation in organizing an Indian National Army to liberate India from British colonial rule. The first division of the I.N.A. with

---

3A. In May 1939 Bose had announced the formation of the Forward Bloc within the congress for the democratisaion, radiolocations and reorientation of the Congress into an instrument of the profile's will to freedom.

4. Selected Speeches of Subhas Chandra Bose, ibid, pp 155-59.

16300 soldiers was formed on 1st September 1942. However, the project did not make much head way because serious differences developed between Mohan Singh and the Japanese authorities about the desired strength of the I.N.A. and its exact role in anti-colonial struggle.

The more vigorous phase of the I.N.A. began with the arrival of Subhas Chandra Bose at Singapore on 2nd July 1943. Bose set up the Azed Hind Government (The Provisional Government of Free India), adopted the Tri-colour flag and gave the slogan *Jai Hind* (Victory to India). Bose also reorganized the Azad Hind Fauj (I.N.A.). To the Indian recruits he offered : "You give me blood , and I will give you freedom". His war slogan was "Dilli Chalo" (On to Delhi). On 6th July 1944, Subhas made an appeal on the Azad Hind Radio, Singapore, to Gandhiji : "India's last war of Independence has begun......Father of our Nation ! In this holy war of India's liberation, we ask for your blessings and good wishes".

In May 1944 Battalion 1 of I.N.A. captured Mowdok, (outpost situated south-east of Chittagong) and hoisted the tricolour flag on Indian soil. Another battalion under Shah Nawaz Khan joined the Japanese army in their assault on Kohima in Nagaland. The next target was Imphal in Manipur to be followed by a rapid advance across the Brahamaputra into Bangal. The campaign achieved only limited success. Unfortunately, the fortunes of war turned against Japan and they had to withdraw from the Indo-Burma border to meet American threat in the South Pacific. The retreat of the I.N.A. began in the middle of 1944 and ended by mid 1945, resulting in surrended of I.N.A. troops to the British army.

Subhas Bose escaped from Singapore towards Japan and is reported to have died[5] in a plane crash over Taipeh, Taiwan (Farmosa) on 18 august 1945.

I.N.A. Trials. The British Government of India charged the captured I.N.A. soldiers of "waging war against the King". The trials were held in Delhi's Red Fort and the first three accused were Capt. P.K. sehgal, Capt. Shah Nawaz Khan and Gurbaksh Singh Dhillon (one Hindu, one Muslim, one Sikh.).

The Indian people looked upon Sehgal, Shah Nawaj, and Dhillon as India's freedom fighters and national heroes. Leaders of all political parties—the Congress, the Muslim League and the CPI– demanded the release of INA prisoners. The people of India joined in a big way by organizing protest meetings, taking out processions and issuing calls for hartals in the major towns of India. All these developments gave out the impression of a spontaneous mass upheaval. Bhulabhai Desai, T.B. Sapru, Jawaharlal Nehru and Asaf Ali worked as the Defence Counsel for the I.N.A. heroes. The Court Martial found all the three guilty but Lord Wavell, the Viceroy, sensing the mood of the nation, remitted their sentences on 1st January 1946. All the same, the Viceroy announced that the remaining trials will be restricted to such soldires who were accused of using brutal methods to force their fellow P.O.W. to join the I.N.A.

An Overview : The I.N.A. trials did not remain a question of right or wrong of I.N.A. men' actions but was looked upon by Indian leaders as a question of England vs. India. The basic question asked was : Did the British rulers have any moral right to decide questions exclusively concerning Indians ? Indians belonging to almost all political parties and diverse social classes and even sizeable segments of Government employees and men of armed forces looked upon I.N.A. men as national heroes. Shrewd British politicians and watchful administrators realised that the time to quit India had come.

---

5. There is no 'irrefutable proof' of Subhas's death in the air crash. The Government of India appointed a Commission of Enquiry under the Chairmanship of Justic Mukerjee to probe into the facts and circumstances relating to the disappearance of Netaji Subhas Bose. In May 2002, the term of the Enquiry Commission was extended by one year.

Assessment of Bose's Achievements : Bose was a prince among freedom fighters, a true revolutionary. He had no patience with slow methods of political agitation. He looked upon Gandhian methods of non-violence as impracticable. He was critical of the suspension of the Non-Cooperation Movement in 1922 and described it as "nothing short of a national calamity"; he described the suspension of the Civil Disobedience Movement in 1934 as "a confession of failure". He was an important member of the Congress Socialist Party and believed that some form of synthesis was possible between Communism and Fascism. His critics including Jawaharlal Nehru accused him of pro-Fascist and pro-Nazi sympathies. In fact, Bose's passion for Freedom and impatience for an early success goaded him to seek support of even Fascist powers. He was the hero of the youth and a firebrand. His name shines brightly in the galaxy of India's freedom fighters.

Select opinions

Jawaharlal Nehru : In February 1938 Subhas Bose was President of the Congress. He did not approve of any step being taken by the Congress, which was anti-Japanese or anti-German or anti-Italian. And yet such was the feeling in the Congress and the country that he did not oppose this and many other manifestations of Congress sympathy with China and the victims of Fascist and Nazi aggression. We passed many resolutions and organized many demonstrations of which he did not approve during the period of his presidentship, but he submitted to them without protest because he realized the strength of feeling behind them. There was a big difference in outlook between him and others in the Congress Executive, both in regard to foreign and internal matters, and this led to a break early in 1939. He then attacked Congress policy publicly and, early in August 1339, the Congress executive took the unusual step of taking disciplinary action against him, one of its ex-presidents. (*The Discovery of India,* p 499)

Jawaharlal Nehru : Matters came to a head in the Congress at the presidential elections early in 1939. Unfortunately Maulana Abul Kalam refused to stand and Subhas Chandra Bose was elected after a contest. This gave rise to all manner of complications and deadlocks, which persisted for many months. At the Tripuri Congress there were unseemly scenes........

Subhas Chandra Bose resigned from the Presidentship and started the Forward Bloc, which was intended to be almost a rival organization to the Congress. It petered out after a while, as it was bound to do, but it added to the disruptive tendencies and the general deterioration. Under cover of fine phrases, adventurist and opportunist elements found platforms, and I could not help thinking of the rise of the Nazi party in Germany. (*Nehru : An Autobiography,* p 606)

Micheal Edwards : Bose was perhaps the only genuinely reolutionary Indian nationalist leader and took a genuinely revolutionary road. He had no faith in gradualism or in parliamentary democracy as a system suited to economically and socially backward countries. He was deeply influenced by the romantic fascism of Nazi Germany, yet he represented the continuing achievement of religious and cultural nationalism. Though many of his political ideas came from Germany, Italy and the Soviet Union, his model for an independent India was based on the Turkey of Kemal Atarturk. When a strong central authority had solved the problems of social change, then, perhaps, the masses would be ready for democracy. (*British India :* 1772-1947, p 292)

APPENDIX XII
CONCISE ENCYCLOPEDIA OF INDIAN FREEDOM STRUGGLE

The Mutiny And Revolt of 1857

1857, March 29	–	Sepoy Mangal Pandey blew the trumpet of Revolt against the anti-emotional and anti-people policies of the British rulers in India when he fired at Lt Baugh, Adjutant of 34 N.I. at Barrackpur, Calcutta.
May 10	–	Mutiny of sepoys at Meerut.
May 11-12	–	Sepoys captured Delhi and proclaimed Bahadur Shah II as Emperor of India.
May-June	–	Mutiny and rebellion spreads through the Indo-Gangetic plain, Rajputana, Central India and parts of Bengal.
July	–	Mutinies and civil rebellions broke out at Indore, Saugar, parts of Panjab.
Sept.	–	The English recaptured Delhi.
Dec.	–	The English recaptured Kanpur.
1858 March	–	Lucknow recaptured by the English.
April	–	Jhansi surrendered to the English.
July-Dec.	–	English authority re-established in India.
1866	–	Dadabhai Naroji organized East India Association in London to focus public opinion on Indian questions. Soon after branches of the Association were formed in major Indian cities.
1867	–	Poona Sarvajanik Sabha formed.
1869	–	Surendra Nath Banerji disqualified for the I.C.S.
Oct. 2	–	Birth of M.K. Gandhi.
1870	–	Dadabhai Naroji published his first estimate of India's per capita income at 40 shillings p.a.
1872	–	**Kuka Movement in the Panjab**
		The Namdharis (also called Kookas) organized a public-spirited movement in the Panjab against the Muslim practice of cowslaughter and anti-people policies of the British administration in the Panjab. Guru Baba Ram Singh gave a call for Non-Cooperation by boycott of Government jobs, Law courts and even Western culture.
		In 1872 the Namdharis captured Malodh fort near Ludhiana. The government hit back by massive slaughter of Kookas and arrested and deported Guru Ram Singh.
1875 April 10	–	Swami Dayanand Saraswati laid the foundation of the first Arya Samaj at Bombay.
	–	Madame Blavatsky formed the Theosophical Society in the U.S.A.
1875 Sept.	–	India League founded at Calcutta.
1976 July	–	Indian Association established at Calcutta to work for the interests of the whole country.

1876-78	–	Great south Indian famine.
1877 Jan. 8	–	Lord Lytton laid foundation stone of Mohammadan Anglo-Oriental College at Aligarth.
1878	–	Lytton's government passed the Vernacular Press Act, the Arms Act and the Licence Act.
1879	–	Lytton's government abolished import duties on cotton goods imported from England.
1881	–	Tilak's two newspapers *Kesari* and *Maharatta* start publication.

Hume's Role in The Foundation of the Indian National Congress

A.O. Hume joined the I.C.S. in 1849. During 1857 he was working as District Officer at Etawah in U.P. where about 100 civilians were killed on charges of anti-British activities.

Hume's relations with his colleagues were never cordial and many of them complained about his egoism and eccentric behaviour. Even Viceroys Lytton and Dufferin had a poor opinion about his abilities. In 1882 he retired from service as a bitter and frustrated man. Gopal Krishna Gokhale and almost all contemporary Congressmen regarded Hume "as the real founder of The Indian National Congress."

1883 March	–	Hume addressed an open letter to graduates of Calcutta University.
Dec.	–	The Indian National Conference held its first session at Calcutta.
1883-84	–	Ilbert Bill controversy highlighted racial discrimination in the dispensation of justice in British India.
1884 May	–	The Mahajana Sabha founded at Madras.
Dec.	–	Theosophical Society held its annual session at Adyar, Madras
1885 Jan. 31	–	Bombay Presidency Association formed.
	–	Indian National Union founded.
Dec.	–	The Indian National Conference held its second session at Calcutta.
	–	First session of Indian National Congress held at Bombay.
1887	–	Indian National Social Conference founded at Bombay.
1888 Aug.	–	Principal Beck established United Indian Patriotic Association at Aligarh
Nov. 30	–	Viceroy Dufferin's St. Andrews Day Dinner speech castigated the Congress.
1889 July	–	British Committee of the Indian National Congress formed at London.
1891	–	The Age of Consent Bill (forbidding marriage of girls below 12 years of age) passed.
1892	–	Indian Councils Act passed.
1893	–	Muhammadan Anglo-Oriental Defence Association of Upper India formed at Aligarh.
1895 March 15	–	Tilak organized the Shivaji Festival as a National Festival.
1896-97	–	The great famine which affected almost all parts of the country.
1897	–	Plague epidemic in Bombay and Poona.
June 22	–	Chapekar brothers murdered the cruel Plague Commissioner Rand and Lt. Ayerst at Poona.
1898	–	Death of Sir Sayed Ahmed Khan.
1899	–	Death of Principal Beck of M.A.O. College, Aligarh.

Appendix XII

1899-1900	–	A devastating famine causes havoc in India.
1900	–	V.D. Savarkar start the *Mitra Mela* at Nasik.
1902	–	Madame Bhikhaji Rustom, K.R. Cama left India and settled in Paris.
	–	Swami Shraddhanand laid foundation of Gurukul Kangri at Hardwar.
1905 Feb. 18	–	Shyamji Krishnavarma set up the India House at London to work for India's freedom.
July 20	–	Publication of Government Resolution on Partition of Bengal.
Aug. 7	–	Public meeting at Town Hall, Calcutta adopted a resolution on Boycott and Swadeshi.
Oct. 16	–	Partition of Bengal became effective.
1906 Oct. 1	–	Lord Minto received the Muslim Deputation headed by Aga Khan.
Dec. 31	–	The Muslim League founded at Dacca.
1907 May 9	–	Lajpat Rai and Ajit Singh deported to Mandalay.
May 11	–	Vicroy issued an ordinance putting restrictions on holding of public meetings.
Dec.	–	Congress split into Moderates and Extremists at Surat session.
1908 April	–	The Congress under Moderate leadership adopted a new loyalist Constitution for the party.
April	–	Trial of Alipore conspiracy case; Khudiram Bose executed.
June 8	–	The Newspapers (Incitement to Offences) Act and Explosive Substances Act passed.
July 22	–	Tilak sentenced to six years' imprisonment on charges of inciting sedition.
Dec.	–	Revolutionary leader Aswini Kumar Datta and eight others deported.
Dec. 11	–	Criminal Law (Amendment) act passed.
1909	–	Depressed Classes Mission Society of Madras formed.
May 21	–	The Indian Councils Act passed.
July 1	–	Madan Lal Dhingra shot dead Curzon Wyllie in London.
1910	–	Aurobindo Ghosh retired to Pondicherry.
1911 Dec. 12	–	Coronation Durbar in honour of George V held at Delhi.
	–	Announcement about transfer of capital from Calcutta to Delhi.
1912 Dec. 23	–	Bomb thrown at Viceroy Hardinge while he was making his state entry into Delhi.
1913 March 14	–	Gandhi started his satyagraha campaign in South Africa.
Nov. 1	–	Ghadr Party formed at San Francisco, U.S.A.
1914 June 30	–	South African government passed the Indian Relief Act.
Aug. 4	–	First World War breaks out.
Sept. 29	–	*Kamagata Maru* incident near Calcutta.
1915	–	Indian Independence Committee formed in Germany.
January	–	Gandhi returned from South Africa to India.
Feb. 19	–	Death of Gopal Krishna Gokhale
June	–	Rash Behari Bose escaped to Japan.
Nov.	–	Death of Pherozeshah Mehta.
1916	–	Mohammad Ali and Shaukat Ali interned.

Home Rule Movement

April 28	–	Tilak forms the Indian Home Rule League
Sept. 1	–	Mrs. Annie Besant inaugurated another Home Rule League. The two Home Rule Leagues worked in close harmonious co-operation but retained their separate organizations.

The demand of Home Rule or Self Government for Indians was interpreted as : Legislative Councils to be elected by the people and Executive Councils to be responsible to Legislatives.

The Government took a tough stand and arrested Tilak in July 1916 and later Mrs. Besant.

The Home Rule Movement broadened the base of the National Movement and even women and students participated in its activities.

Dec.	–	Congress-League Lucknow Pact.
	–	Reunion of Moderates and Extremists achieved.
1917 April 18	–	Gandhi tried for Champaran Satyagraha.
June 15	–	Mrs. Besant interned by Madras Government.
July	–	Lord Montagu assumes office as new Secretary of State for India.
August 20	–	Montagu's announcement in British House of Commons about introduction of Responsible Government in India.
Dec. 10	–	Appointment of Rowlatt Committee to report on crimes connected with Revolutionary movement in India.
1918	–	Indians declared eligible to hold King's Commission in the army.
April	–	Rowlatt Committee submitted its report.
1919 Feb. 6	–	Government introduces two Rowlatt Bills in the Central Legislative Assembly.
Feb. 24	–	Gandhi formed Satyagraha Sabha.
April 6	–	Call for all-India hartal over the Rowlatt Acts.
April 9	–	Deportation of two Amritsar leaders, Dr. Satyapal and Dr. Kitchlew.
April 10	–	Firing at Amritsar & Lahor in connection with Rowlatt Act hartal.
April 11	–	Brigadier-General Dyer appointed Military Administrator of Amritsar.
April 13	–	Jallianwala Bagh Massacre.
April 15-24	–	Martial Law proclaimed at Amritsar and five districts of Panjab.
June 7	–	All India Congress Working Committee appointed a special Committee to enquire into Panjab happenings.
Oct.	–	Viceroy appointed Hunter Committee to enquire into Panjab developments.
Dec, 23	–	Government of India Act 1919 received royal assent.
1920 May 28	–	Hunter Committee Report published.
August 1	–	Death of B.G. Tilak.
August 1	–	The All India Khilafat Committee organized an All-India hartal under Gandhi's guidance.
1920-22	–	**The Non-Cooperation Movement**

It was a movement of organized protest against British policy of ruthless suppression after World War I

Appendix XII

Dec. 20	–	Nagpur session of Congress endorsed policy of Non-Cooperation. Congress demanded Swaraj (i.e. Self Government Programme of Non-Cooperation) :

(1) Surrender of Government titles and honours;

(2) Boycott of Government durbars and official functions;

(3) Triple boycott of : (a) Legislatures, Central and Provincial (b) Government courts (c) Government Educational institutions.

(4) Boycott Of Foreign goods.

1921	–	Gandhi surrendered his title of Kaiser-I-Hind to the Government Congressmen Boycotted State organized elections; Government courts, Government Educational institutions. Bonfire of Foreign goods was a common site in cities.

Assam-Bengal railway strike caused anziety to Government.

Jan 10	–	Duke of Connaught reaches India to inaugurate the new Constitution; a general boycott and hartal against the royal visit.
August	–	Moplah rebellion
Nov. 17	–	The Prince of Wales reaches Bombay; Congress gives a call for general protest and hartal.
1922 Feb. 5	–	Violent incident at Chauri Chaura villages of Gorakhpur district in which some police personnel was hacked to death by the mob.
Feb. 11-12	–	Meeting of Congress Working Committee at Bardoli and suspension of Non-Cooperation Movement.

The Non Cooperation Movement did not achieve its goal of 'Swaraj'. On the positive side, N.C.M. broadened the social base of the National Movement-peasants, workers, women and even students joined the struggle for Indian Freedom.

1923 March	–	Formation of Swaraja Party.
	–	Surendranath Banerjea as Minister amends the Calcutta Municipal Act (1899).
Aug.	–	The Hindu Mahasabha holds its session at Benares.
1924	–	C.P.I. starts its activities in India.
Feb. 4	–	Gandhi released on health grounds.
1925 June 16	–	Death of C.R.Das
Aug. 9	–	The Kakori train robbery committed.
Aug. 22	–	V.J. Patel elected the first indian President of the Central Legislative Assembly.
1926	–	Trade Union Act passed.
Dec. 23	–	Swami Shraddhanand murdered by a Muslim fanatic.
1927 Nov. 8	–	Appointment of Simon Commission announced.
1928 Feb. 3	–	Simon Commission reaches Bombay; All-India hartal agains the All White Commission.
Aug. 28-31	–	All Parties Conference deliberates on Nehru Report.
Sept.	–	Hindustan Socialist Republican Association founded.
1929 March 20	–	Arrest of Communist Party members followed by trial of Meerut Conspiracy Case 1929-33.

March 29	–	Jinnah's 14 Points published.
April 8	–	Bhagat Singh and his Associates throw bombs in the Central Legislative Assembly.
Sept. 13	–	Jatin Das, an under trial in the Lahore Conspiracy case died in jail after 64 days' hunger strike. Trial of Lahore Conspiracy case.
Oct. 31	–	Viceroy Irwin announces Dominion Status as the goal of constitutional advance in India.
Dec.	–	Congress session at Lahor declares Purna Swaraj (complete independence) as goal of the Congress.
1930 Jan. 1	–	J.L. Nehru unfurls the Tri-colour flage of independent India.
Jan. 26	–	'Independence Day' Pledge taken by nationalists all over India.

Civil Disobedience Movement, 1930-34

Non-Cooperation Movemen 1920-22 sought to pressurize the Government by withholding all cooperation in the running of civil administration. C.D.M. sought to paralyze the Government administration by open opposition to unjust Government acts and non-payment of taxes.

Feb. 14	–	Congress Working Committee passes the Civil Disobedience Resolution.
March 12	–	Gandhi starts his march from Sabarmati Ashram to Dandi beach.
April 5	–	Gandhi and his party reach Dandi beach.
April 6	–	Gandhites start boiling sea water to manufacture illegal salt.
April 18	–	Surya Sen, a Bengal revolutionary organized the Chittagong Armoury Raid and set up the provisional government of free India.
June 7	–	Simon Commission Report published.
Nov. 12-19	–	First Round Table Conference meets in London.
1931 March 5	–	Gandhi-Irwin Pact signed; suspension of C.D.M.
March 23	–	Bhagat Singh, Sukh Dev and Raj Guru executed.
Sept. 7-Dec. 1	–	Second Round Table Conference meets in London.
1932 Aug. 16	–	British Prime Minister Ramsay MacDonald announces the Communal Award extending separate electorates for Depressed Classes. (Scheduled Casts of to-day)
Sept. 24	–	Poona Pact signed which negated the Communal Award and kept the Depressed Classes into Hindu fold.
Nov. 7-24	–	Third round Table conference in London deliberates on Indian constitutional problem.
1934 May	–	C.D.M. totally withdrawn by the Congress
	–	C.D.M. did not achieve the Congress goal of Purna Swaraj but inaugurated new era of mass nationalism. Henceforth, Gandhi was the Congress and the Congress was Gandhi.
Oct.	–	Formation of All India Congress Socialist Party.
1935 July	–	Rahmat Ali, a Cambridge University student publishes a pamphlet on the Pakistan movement.
Aug. 4	–	Government of India Act 1935 receives royal assent.
1937 July 7	–	Congress Working Committee permits Congressment to accept office in Provincial Governments.

Appendix XII

1938 Feb. 19	–	Subhas Chandra Bose elected President of the Congress Party.
	–	V.D. Savarkar becomes the President of Hindu Mahasabha.
Nov. 15	–	Muslim League releases the Pirpur Report castigating Congress Ministries of discrimination against the Muslim community.
1939 January	–	Subhas Chandra Bose re-elected Congress President.
April 29	–	Subhas Bose resigns the presidentship of the Congress under pressure from Ghandhites.
Sept. 1	–	Germany invades Poland which marks the beginning of World War II.
Oct. 17	–	Viceroy Linlithgow declares Dominion Status as the goal of British policy in India.
Oct. 27-Nov. 15	–	Popular Congress Ministries in provinces resign over the war issue.
Dec. 22	–	Muslim League expresses jubilation over resignation of Congress Ministries by celebrating 'Day of Deliverance'.
1940 March	–	Lahore Session of Muslim League passes the Pakistan Resolution.
1940 May 10	–	Winston Churchill assumes office as Prime Minister of England.
July 2	–	Subhas Bose arrested under Defence of India Rules.
Aug. 8	–	Viceroy makes the August Offer, a declaration about British policy in India.
Aug. 18-22	–	Congress Working Committee rejects the August Offer.
Oct. 17	–	Congress starts Individual CDM; 25,000 persons court arrest.
1941 March 28	–	Subhas Bose reaches Berlin.
Sept. 9	–	Churchill declares that Atlantic Charter not applicable to India.
Dec. 7	–	Japanese bomb Pearl Harbour, Hawaii Islands, USA.
Dec. 8	–	Britain declares war against Japan.
1942 Feb. 15	–	Japanese occupy Rangoon; British Army Commander surrenders 40,000 Indian prisoners of war to Japanese Commander.
Feb. 15	–	Japanese occupy Singapore.
1942 March 23	–	Stafford Cripps brings new constitutional proposals to India.
March 28-30	–	Rash Behari Bose calls a Conference of Indians at Tokyo,
April 6	–	First Japanese air bombing of Indian territory.
April 10	–	Both the Congress and the Muslim League reject Cripps Proposals.
July 14	–	Congress Working Committee adopts the Quit India Resolution calling upon Britain to quit India immediately.
July 23	–	CPI declared a legal association.
August	–	40,000 Indian Prisoners-of-war in Burma join the I.N.A. under Captain Mohan Singh.
Aug. 9	–	Gandhi and top Congress leaders arrested.
Aug. 11	–	The popular Revolt of 1942 begins. Congress declared an unlawful organisation.
Sept., 1	–	The INA formally established.
1943 July 2	–	Subhas Bose reaches Singapore.
Oct. 21	–	Bose announces the formation of Provisional Government of Free India.
Nov. 6	–	Government of Free India receives Andaman & Nicobar Islands from the Japanese.

Dec.	–	Muslim League at its Karachi session adopts the slogan of 'Divide and Quit'.
1944 March 19	–	I.N.A. hoists the Tricolour Flag on Assam soil.
March 22	–	Japanese advance columns enter Manipur.
June 7	–	Japanese army retreats from Kohima.
1945	–	Labour Party wins General Elections in England.
May 7	–	Germany surrenders before Allied forces unconditionally.
June 14	–	Viceory Wavell calls Simla Conference to reconstitute the Viceroy's Executive Council.
Aug. 6-9	–	American Air Force drops Atom Bombs on Hiroshima and Nagasaki.
Aug. 10	–	Japan surrenders unconditionally.
Aug. 18	–	Subhas Bose reaches Taipei, Formosa.
Dec. 9	–	General Elections to Indian Central Assembly.
1946 Feb. 18	–	Mutiny of Indian naval ratings in Bombay against discriminntory policy against Indians.
May 16	–	Cabinet Mission announces two proposals.
1946 July 6	–	J. L. Nehru assumes office as Congress President.
Aug. 6	–	Viceroy Wavell invites Nehru to form an Interim Government.
Aug. 16	–	Muslim League launches 'Direct Action Day'.
Sept. 2	–	Indian Interim Government assumes office.
Oct. 13	–	Muslim League joins the Interim Government.
Dec. 9	–	Constituent Assembly meets and 'Objectives Resolution' moved.
1947 Jan. 31	–	Muslim League rejects Cabinet Mission Plan.
Feb. 20	–	British Prime Minister Attlee announces British plan to end British rule in India latest by Feb. 1948.
March 24	–	Lord Mountbatten assumes office as Viceroy of India.
June 3	–	Mountbatten announces the plan of Partition of India.
June 10	–	Muslim League accepts June 3 Plan.
June 14	–	Congress approves of June 3 Plan.
June 4	–	Indian Independence Bill introduced in British Parliament.
July 18	–	Indian Independence Bill receives royal assent.
Aug. 14	–	Pakistan comes into existence.
Aug. 15	–	India became free.

APPENDIX XIII
M.A. JINNAH AND THE MAKING OF PAKISTAN

Mohammed Ali Jinnah was born at Karachi on 25 December 1876 in a lower middle class family. His father Jinnah Poonja was a small hide merchant. The family were Khoja Muslims i.e. followers of the Agha Khan. Mohammed Ali received his early education at Karachi and Mumbai. In 1892 he went to England and qualified for the Bar in 1896. Jinnah's married life was unhappy. His first wife Amaibai died during his absence in England. He could not pull on with his second wife Ruttie Pettie, which resulted in divorce and death of Ruttie in the prime of youth. Unhappy married bonds left a marked imprint on his character and made Jinnah a bitter rather a callous person who became increasingly introvert and self-centered.

As a liberal thinker, Jinnah stood against bigotry and fundamentalism. He rarely went to a mosque to say his *namaaz* and had no compunction ignoring Islamic taboos on food and drink. One of his close friends, J.N. Sahni who often joined him for lunch at the Mumbai High Court mentions that Jinnah's Parsi wife often brought him ham-sandwiches which he relished with a sherry followed by a cigar.

Jinnah's public career may be divided into four distinct periods of unequal lengths :

(*i*) 1906-1920. During this period Jinnah was a fire-brand nationalist, a great Congress leader and worked for national unity on a secular basis. He showed no sympathy with the Aligarh Movement or the Khilafat Movement. He exhorted the people to separate religion from politics.

(*ii*) 1920-1928. This period witnessed Jinnah drifting away from the Congress. All the same he remained wedded to the ideal of a single Indian nation

(*iii*) 1928-1937. During this period Jinnah came under the influence of separatist ideology of the League.

(*iv*) 1937-1947. This period made Jinnah the chief spokesman of the Two-Nation theory and demand for a separate homeland for the Muslims.

Jinnah's first inspiration in nationalism came from the Liberal Congress leaders like Dadabhai Naoroji, Surendranath Banerjee, G.K. Gokhale and Pherozshah Mehta. He worked as Private Secretary to Naoroji at the Congress session at Kolkata 1906. About his debt to Surendranath Banerjee, Jinnah wrote, "I learnt my first lessons in politics at the feet of Surendranath Banerjee. The impact of Gokhale's personality on Jinnah is evident from his remark that he desired to be a "Muslim Gokhale".

Jinnah was elected to the Imperial Legislative Council in 1910, nominated in 1913, elected again in 1915, 1923, 1926 and 1934. Within the Council he earned the reputation of a mature politician, of sharp intellect and dauntless courage.

As a true national leader, Jinnah stood for freedom, constitutionalism and absence of factionalism in social or political life. He played a notable role in blunting the separatist tendencies of the Muslim League in 1913 he drafted a new constitution of the Muslim League which espoused the Congress ideal of self-government by constitutional means, emphasized the need for co-operation with other communities and, above all, promotion of national unity. He was greatly instrumental in bringing rapprochement between the League and the Congress which resulted in the Lucknow Pact (1916).

Jinnah was also associated with the Home Rule League and was also closely connected with the Congress-League joint scheme for constitutional reforms. In 1919 he showed his anger at the Rowlatt Act by describing it as the 'Black Act'.

The 1920-28 was period of self-exile from active politics for Jinnah. Maybe, Gandhi's emergence at the apex of the Congress leadership and mass nationalism inaugurated by the Non-Cooperation Movement did not suit the aristocratic temperament of Jinnah. Prof. Mohammad Habib believes that even among the Muslim community there could be no place for Jinnah at the top so long as Maulana Mohammed Ali lived, and he would accept no lower place. The death of the Maulana in 1931 opened the doors of Muslim leadership for Jinnah. Lesser politicians like Khaliquzzaman, Feroz khan, Fazlul Haq etc., willingly became his assistants and accepted his superior intellect and followed his imperious commands. Jinnah emerged as the Quaid-i-Azam (the Great Organizer).

This Muslim League under Jinnah's leadership successfully contested the Provincial Legislative Council elections of 1937 and won moderate successes in Muslim constituencies. When the Congress spurned Jinnah's offer for coalition ministries in the provinces, Jinnah's disillusionment was complete. As a successful politician, he launched a consistent propagands campaign against Congress rule which climaxed in the Pirpur Report (1938), Shareef Report on Bihar (March 1939) and Fazlul Huq's 'Muslim sufferings under Congress Rule' (December 1939). The Muslim League observed a "Day of Deliverance and Thanks-giving" when the Congress ministries resigned in October 1939 over the World War issue.

By 1940 Jinnah became the greatest advocate of the two-nation theory though he was not its author. He, however, gave an ideological content to the Muslim demand for a separate homeland. His slogan of *'Le Ke Rehenge Pakistan'* (we must win Pakistan) seemed to have clicked with the Muslim masses. Henceforth, Jinnah showed his diplomatic skill, torpedoed the Simla Conference (1945), the Cabinet Mission Plan (1946) triggered off communal riots and forced the hands of the Congress and the hesitant British government to concede the demand for Pakistan. Jinnah became the first Governor General of Pakistan.

A sharp drift towards the partition of India came when on 20th February 1947 British Prime Minister Attlee made an announcement in the House of Commons of his government's "definite intension" to effect the transfer of power to responsible Indian hands by a date not later than June 1948. This announcement was followed by the appointment of Lord Mountbatten as the new Viceroy of India in March 1947.

Lord Mountbatten's charismatic personality and machiavellian moves opened the gates for a political set-up in India ranging from a federation to a confederation, to plans about 'balkanisation' of the Indian sub-continent into a large number of semi-independent/independent Indian states.

Mountbatten had many rounds of informal talks with J.L. Nehru, M.A. Jinnah, Liaquat Ali Khan, Baldev Singh etc which opened the political 'Pandara box' about the nature of the proposed new Central Government, autonomy of Indian provinces and 'virtual independence' to 562 Princely Indian States.

Jinnah deserves credit for strategically compelling the Indian National Congress and Lord Mountbatten to accept a 'speedy' 'surgical operation' for the partition of India and creation of Pakistan. In short, the British policy of 'Divide and Rule' took a U-turn and assumed the shape of 'Divide and Quit' India. Unfortunately, the new political scenario in the Indian sub-continent is still reeling under the misconceived policies of the British imperial rulers.

An Overview

Jinnah stands out as one of the most 'enigmatic' and paradoxical figures in Indian history. Born in lower middle class family, he developed an aristocratic temperament; he was a typical product of Macaulay's dream of belonging to a class who were "Indian in blood and colour but English in tastes, in opinions, in morals and intellect". He showed scant interest in Islam or Islamic thought and yet became the most vocal advocate of Muslim community in India. He could not address the Muslim audience in Urdu, the only language it understood yet became the most popular leader of the Muslim masses. He had little interest in religion, yet made religion the basis for a separate Muslim state of Pakistan.

Jinnah was politician par excellence. In the game of politics, he outwitted Gandhi, Nehru, Patel or rather the whole Congress leadership put together. Gandhi was lucky in having a strong team of competent leaders to assist him, Jinnah, on the other hand, had to depend on second-raters. Jinnah planned all his moves and took decisions single-handed; in a humorous mood he once remarked that "he alone with the help of his secretary and his typewriter won Pakistan for Muslims".

Recent writers have argued that Jinnah embodied in his character all strong points and weaknesses of his class *i.e.* Muslim middle class. The young Muslim bourgeoisie class was working to have a separate state apparatus in its own hands. It used religion as the basis of politics but was not interested in an Islamic state. They were more interested in the political liberation of the Muslims than in the religio-socio-economic emancipation of the Muslim masses whose spokesmen they became. In a way, Jinnah showed callous disregard for the interest of Indian Muslims. When a group of Aligarh students asked him about the fate of Indian Muslims, he remarked, "I have written off the Mussalmans of India".

APPENDIX
XIV

THE NATIONAL SYMBOLS

MAKING OF THE INDIAN NATIONAL FLAG

(A) On 7 August 1906, S.N. Banerjee hoisted this Congress flag in Green Park, Calcutta. The flag had three horizontal stripes – deep green, deep yellow and deep red. The design also included eight white lotuses, words 'Vande Mataram' in Devnagri, a white sun and a white crescent-and-star.

(B) In 1907, Madame Cama, then in exile, hoisted this flag in Paris. This flag was similar to the first flag.

(C) In 1916, Dr. Annie Besant introduced this Home Rule flag. It has five red and four green horizontal stripes with a miniature Union Jack on the top-left corner with seven stars.

(D) In 1921, Mahatma Gandhi introduced this Congress Flag. It had Charkha printed on the flag composed of three horizontal stripes white, green and red.

(E) In 1931, the Congress Flag Committee suggested this design, which comprised a Charkha printed on a totally saffron-coloured flag. The Congress Working Committee disapproved this design.

(F) In August 1931, the All-India Congress Committee at Bombay accepted this flag which had three horizontal stripes with Charkha printed on it.

(G) On 22 July 1947, the Indian Constituent Assembly accepted the National Flag. The Charkha has been replaced by Dhamma Chakra of Emperor Ashoka.

DIMENSIONS OF THE NATIONAL FLAG

The National Flag is a horizontal tricolour of deep saffron (*kesaria*) (representing 'courage and sacrifice') at the top, white ('peace and truth') in the middle and dark green ('faith and chivalry') at the bottom in equal proportion. The ratio of width of the flag to its length is two to three. In the centre of the white band is navy-blue wheel which represents the *chakra*. Its design is that of the wheel which appears on the abacus of the Sarnath Lion Capital of Ashoka. Its diameter approximates to the width of the white band and it has 24 spokes.

The design of the National Flag was adopted by the Constituent Assembly of India on 22 July 1947.

GUIDELINES ABOUT HOISTING THE NATIONAL FLAG

- Wherever the National flag is displayed it should occupy the position of honour.
- A damaged or dishevelled flag should not be displayed.
- The Flag shall not be intentionally displayed with 'saffron' down or allowed to touch the ground or the floor or trail in water.
- The Flag shall not be dipped in salute to any person or thing.
- The Flag shall not be used as drapery in any form whatsoever or as a receptacle for receiving or carrying anything.
- The Flag shall not be used for commercial purposes.
- Paper Flags used by public on cultural and sports events should not be discarded or thrown on the ground after the event.

Insulting or showing disrespect to the National Flag is an offence punishable under the Prevention of Insults to National Honour Act, 1971.

(*Ministry of Home Affairs, Government of India*)

STATE EMBLEM

The State Emblem is an adaptation from the Sarnath Lion Capital of Ashoka (Emperor of Mauryan Empire, 273-232 B.C.). In the original, there are four lions, standing back to back, mounted on an abacus with a frieze carrying sculptures in high relief of an elephant, a galloping horse, a bull and a lion separated by intervening wheels over a bell-shaped lotus. Carved out of a single block of polished sandstone, the Capital is crowned by the Wheel of the Law (*Dharma Chakra*).

In the State Emblem, adopted by the Government of India on 26 January 1950, only three lions are visible, the fourth being hidden from view. The wheel appears in relief in the centre of the abacus with a bull on the right and a horse on left and the outlines of other wheels on extreme right and left. The bell-shaped lotus has been omitted. The words *Satyameva Jayate* from *Mundaka Upanishad,* meaning 'Truth Alone Triumphs', are inscribed below the abacus in Devanagri script.

Appendix XIV

NATIONAL ANTHEM

Rabindranath's *Jana-gana-mana*, composed originally in Bengali was adopted in its Hindi version by the Constituent Assembly as the National Anthem of India on 24 January 1950. It was first sung on 27 December 1911 at the Calcutta Session of the Indian National Congress. Playing time of the full version of the National Anthem is approximately 52 seconds.

Jana-gana-mana-adhinayaka, jaya he
Bharata-bhagya-vidhata.
Punjab-Sindh-Gujarat-Maratha
Dravida-Utkala-Banga
Vindhya-Himachala-Yamuna-Ganga
Uchchala-Jaladhi-taranga.
Tava shubha name jage,
Tava shubha asisa mange,
Gahe tava jaya gatha,
Jana-gana-mangala-dayaka jaya he
Bharata-bhagya-vidhata.
Jaya he, jaya he, jaya he,
Jaya jaya jaya, jaya he !

The following is Tagore's English rendering of the anthem :

Thou art the ruler of the minds of all people,
dispenser of India's destiny.
Thy name rouses the hearts of Punjab, Sind,
Gujarat and Maratha,
Of the Dravida and Orissa and Bengal;
It echoes in the hills of the Vindhyas and Himalayas,
mingles in the music of Jamuna and Ganges and is
chanted by the waves of the Indian Sea.
They pray for thy blessings and sing thy praise.
The saving of all people waits in thy hand,
thou dispenser of India's destiny.
Victory, victory, victory to thee.

NATIONAL SONG

The song *Vande Mataram*, composed in Sanskrit by Bankimchandra Chatterji, was a source of inspiration to the people in their struggle for freedom. It has an equal status with *Jana-gana-mana*. The first political occasion when it was sung was the 1896 session of the Indian National Congress. The following is the text of its first stanza :

Vande Mataram !
Sujalam, suphalam, malayaja shitalam,
Shasyashyamalam, Mataram !
Shubhrajyotsna pulakitayaminim,
Phullakusumita drumadala shobhinim,
Suhasinim sumadhura bhashinim,
Sukhadam varadam, Mataram !
Vande Mataram !

The English translation of the stanza rendered by Sri Aurobindo in prose is :

I bow to thee, Mother,

richly-watered, richly-fruited,

cool with the winds of the south,

dark with the crops of the harvests,

The Mother !

Her nights rejoicing in the glory of the moonlight,

her lands clothed beautifully with her trees in flowering bloom,

sweet of laughter, sweet of speech,

The Mother, giver of boons, giver of bliss.

NATIONAL CALENDAR

Under British rule, the Government of India followed the Gregorian Calendar based on the Christian Era.

The National Calendar based on the *Saka* Era, with *Chaitra* as its first month and a normal year of 365 days was adopted from 22 March 1957 along with the Gregorian calendar for the following official purposes : (*i*) Gazette of India, (*ii*) news broadcast by All India Radio, (*iii*) calendars issued by the Government of India, and (*iv*) Government communications addressed to the members of the public.

The months of the National Calendar, with their days and the dates of the Gregorian Calendar corresponding to the first day of the Saka Month are given below :

Saka	Gregorian
1 Chaitra 30/31 days	March 22/21
1 Vaishaka 31	April 21
1 Jyaistha 31	May 22
1 Asadha 31	June 22
1 Sravana 31	July 23
1 Bhadra 31	August 23
1 Asvina 30	September 23
1 Kartika 30	October 23
1 Margasira 30	November 22
1 Pausa 30	December 22
1 Magha 30	January 21
1 Phalgnua 30	February 20

Appendix XIV

NATIONAL ANIMAL

The magnificent tiger is a striped animal. It has a thick, yellow coat of fur with dark stripes. The combination of grace, strength, agility and enormous power has earned the tiger its pride of place as the National Animal of India. Out of eight races of species known, the Indian race, the Royal Bengal Tiger, is found throughout the country except in the north-western region and also in the neighbouring countries, Nepal, Bhutan and Bangladesh.

NATIONAL BIRD

The Indian peacock, the national bird of India, is a colourful, swan-sized bird, with a fanshaped crest of feathers, a white patch under the eye and a long, slender neck. The male of the species is more colourful than the female, with a glistening blue breast and neck and a spectacular bronze-green train of around 200 elongated feathers. The female is brownish, slightly smaller than the male and lacks the train.

NATIONAL FLOWER

Lotus is a sacred flower and occupies a unique position in the art and mythology of ancient India and has been an auspicious symbol of Indian culture since time immemorial.

The Lotus symbolises purity, beauty, majesty, grace, fertility, wealth, richness, knowledge and serenity and not to forget enlightenment. It is also a symbol of triumph, since the lotus is rooted in the mud and can survive to regerminate for thousands of years. It represents long life, honour and good fortune.

They are found in white and pink colours in general and they grow in shallow and murky waters. Some blue coloured flowers are also sighted.

Goddesses Lakshmi and Saraswati are associated with the flower lotus. Even Lord Siva, who wanted to escape the wrath of the Lord Saneeswaran, morphed himself into the shape of a bee and took asylum inside a lotus. Buddhists regard this flower as a sacred one. The plant is having various uniqueness attached to it. Though the large leaves of the plant are floating on the surface of the water, even a drop of water is not accommodated on top of the leaves. Perhaps, they are teaching the human beings to lead a life of non-attachment and avoid the worldly pleasures.

Untouched by the impurity, lotus symbolises the purity of heart and mind. Human beings are instructed by Indian scripture to live a life of non-attachment. The lotus holds additional significance for Hindus, as it is a symbol of God and used often in religious practices.

It was this depth of thought that made the founding fathers of modern India enshrine the Lotus in the Constitution as the National Flower.

Appendix XIV

Physical Map of India

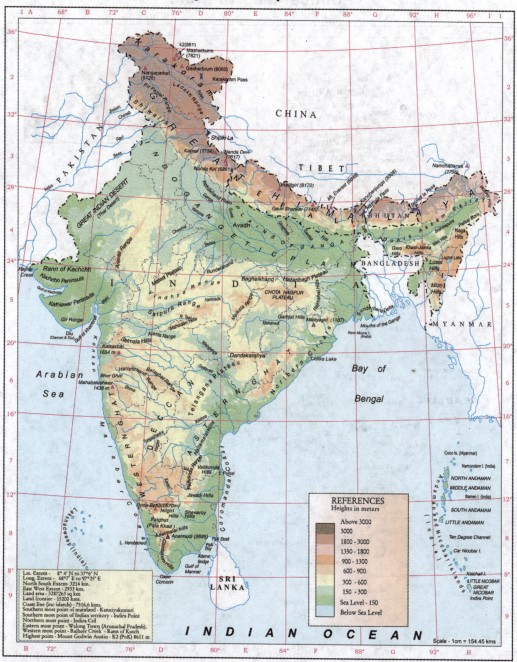

India is the 7th largest country in the world. It is located between 8°4' and 37°6' North Latitude and 68°7' and 97° 25' East Longitude. It measures 3,214 km from North to South and 2,933 km from East to West with a total land area of 3,287,263 sq. km.

Political Map of India

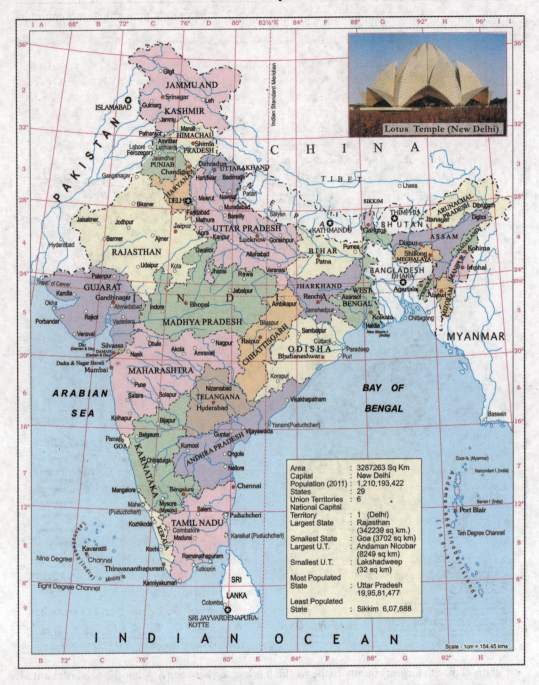

India is divided into 29 States, 6 centrally administered Union Territories and 1 National Capital Territory of Delhi.

APPENDIX XV
SHRAMEV JAYATE (MAY DAY, 2007)

On the occasion of the International Labour Day, the Government of National Capital Territory of Delhi offers its felicitations to the working class and rededicates itself to protect the interests of the working class. It is the workers who form the pivot of economic development of the country. It is the working class, which will ensure a place for India amongst the developed nations of the world. The workers of India are second to none in the world. The Labour Department, Government of National Capital Territory of Delhi, resolves to ensure dignity and prosperity to the workers in the society.

ON THE OCCASION OF MAY DAY, GOVERNMENT OF NATIONAL CAPITAL TERRITORY OF DELHI STRONGLY URGES THE EMPLOYERS :

- Not to employ Children who have not completed their 14th year of age. Employment of children below 14 years, even as domestic workers, is punishable. The Child Labour (Prohibition and Regulation) Act, 1986 prescribes fine upto Rs. 20,000/- and/or imprisonment up to 1 year.
- In case child-labour is found, inform Childline 1098
- Pay at least the statutory minimum wages fixed by the Government of the category of the workmen employed. The present minimum rates of wages w.e.f. 01.02.2007 for unskilled workmen are Rs. 3470.00 per month or Rs. 133.45 per day and for skilled Rs. 3894.00 per month or Rs. 149.75 per day. For Clerical and Non Technical Supervisory Staff. Non Matriculates Rs. 3663.00 per month or Rs. 149.90 per day, Matriculates but not Graduates Rs. 3918.00 per month or Rs. 150.70 per day and Graduates and above Rs. 4230.00 per month or Rs. 162.70 per day.
- Full details may be downloaded from the Website labour, delhigovt. nic.in Workmen are advised to file their claims before Dy. Labour Commissioner of the District, if minimum rates of wages are not paid to them.
- Issue appointment letters/leave cards to their workmen.
- Ensure the security of women employed in the light of the directions of the Hon'ble Supreme Court of India as contained the Vishakha v/s the State of Rajasthan case. Constitute Committee in the establishment.
- Accord top priority to the safety of workers working for their establishments.
- Ensure timely compliance of awards passed by the Labour Courts/industrial Tribunals.
- Pay a cess at the rate of 1% of the cost of construction, in respect of building or other construction, in respect of building or other construction works initiated by them as provided under the Building and other Construction Workers Welfare Cess Act, 1996.

The workers are urged to maintain the dignity of labour. They are called upon to ensure their commitment to duty in the task of nation building.

The workers engaged in building or other construction works are urged to enroll as beneficiaries of the Delhi Building and other Construction Workers Welfare Board. The Board extends several security schemes for its beneficiaries. For membership contact the Citizen Service Bureaus of the M.C.D.

LABOUR DEPARTMENT
Govt. of NCT of Delhi,
5, Sham Nath Marg, Delhi-110054

APPENDIX XVI

PRIME MINISTER'S NEW 15-POINT PROGRAMME FOR THE WELFARE OF MINORITIES AND ITS ACHIEVEMENTS

OBJECTIVES
- Enhancing opportunities for education
- Ensuring equitable share in economic activities and employment
- Improving the conditions of living of minorities
- Prevention and control of communal disharmony and violence

The new 15-point programme incorporates programme-specific interventions. The highlights of the programme are:

Enhancing Opportunities for Education

1. **Equitable availability of Integrated Child Development Services (ICDS)**

    A certain percentage of Anganwadi centres will be located in blocks and villages with a substantial minority population ensuring that the benefits of these schemes are available to them.

2. **Improving access to school education**

    A certain percentage of schools under Sarva Shiksha Abhiyan, Kasturba Gandhi Balika Vidyalaya Scheme and other similar government schemes will be located in villages/localities with a substantial minority population.

3. **Greater resources for teaching urdu**

    Central assistance for recruitment and posting of urdu language teachers in primary and upper primary schools.

4. **Modernizing Madarsa education**

    Area intensive and Madarsa Modernization Programme to be substantially strengthened and implemented effectively.

5. **Scholarships for meritorious students from minority communities**

    Pre-matric and post-matric scholarships for students from minority communities.

6. **Improving educational infrastructure through the Maulana Azad Education Foundation**

    Foundation to be strengthened and its activities expanded.

Equitable Share in Economic Activities and Employment

7. **Self-employment and wage employment for the poor**

    Earmarking of physical and financial targets of Swarnjayanti Gram Swarojgar Yojana (SGSY), Swarn Jayanti Shahari Rojgar Yojana (SJSRY), Sampurna Grameen Rojgar Yojana (SGRY) for minorities.

8. Upgradation of skills through technical training

A certain proportion now will be located in areas predominantly inhabited by minority communities and upgradation of some existing it is to 'Centers of Excellence' on the same basis.

9. Enhanced credit support for economic activities

Strengthening National Minorities Development & Finance Corporation (NMDFC) with greater equity support and earmarking a certain percentage of priority sector bank lending for minorities.

10. Recruitment to State and Central Services

Special consideration will be given to minorities in recruitment to Central and State police forces, Railways and nationalized banks and public sector enterprises. An exclusive scheme will be launched for minority communities for coaching in government and private institutions.

Improving the Conditions of Living of Minorities

11. Equitable share in rural housing scheme

A certain percentage of Indira Awas Yojana (IAY) will be earmarked for poor beneficiaries belonging to minority communities.

12. Improvement in condition of slums inhabited by minority communities

Ensuring benefits of Integrated Housing & Slum Development Programme (HSDP) and Jawaharlal Nehru National Urban Renewal Mission (JNNURM) flow equitably to the cities/slums predominantly inhabited by minority communities.

Prevention and Control of Communal Riots

13. Prevention of communal incidents

District and police officials of the highest known efficiency, impartiality and secular record to be posted in communally sensitive and not-prone districts.

14. Prosecution for communal offences

Special courts or courts specifically earmarked would be set up to try communal offences so that the offenders are brought to book speedily.

15. Rehabilitation of victims of communal riots

Victims of communal violence to be given immediate relief and prompt and adequate financial assistance for their rehabilitation.

EDUCATIONAL PROGRAMME FOR THE WELFARE OF MINORITIES

Scholarship for Minorities Students

Students belonging to the Muslim, Christian, Sikh, Buddhist and Parsi Communities, Notified as minority communities under Section 2(c) of the National Commission for Minorities Act, 1992 are eligible to apply for one of the following scholarships of the Ministry of Minority Affairs, Government of India

Scheme of pre-matric scholarship for minorities

- Scholarship will be awarded to eligible students of classes I to X in government/recognized private schools/institutes.
- Financial assistance includes admission/tuition fees and maintenance allowance.

- Students who have scored not less than 50% marks in the previous final examination, and whose parents'/guardian's annual income does not exceed ₹ 1 lakh, are eligible for the scholarship. 50% marks requirement will not apply to class I students.
- Those who were awarded the scholarship for 2008-09 and fulfill the conditions of the scheme may apply for renewal of scholarship for 2009-10.

Scheme of post-matric scholarship for minorities

- Scholarship will be awarded to eligible students of class XI upto Ph.D. in government/recognized private schools/colleges/universities / institutes including technical and vocational courses of ITIs/ITCs (affiliated with NCVT) of class XI and XII level and the courses other than those covered under merti-cum-means scholarship scheme.
- Financial assistance includes admission/tuition fees and maintenance allowance.
- Students who have scored not less than 50% marks in the previous final examination, and whose parents'/guardian's annual income does not exceed ₹ 2 lakh, are eligible for the scholarship.
- Those who were awarded scholarship for 2008-09 and fulfill the conditions of the scheme may apply for renewal of scholarship for 2009-10.

Scheme of merit-cum-means scholarship for minorities

- 20,000 new scholarship will be awarded to eligible students stuyding in technical/professional courses at under graduate and post-graduate levels.
- Financial assistance includes reimbursement of course fees and maintenance allowance.
- Full course fee is reimbursed for 70 listed institutes in the scheme. Course fee upto a maximum of ₹ 20,000/- is reimbursed for other institutes.
- The annual income of the parents or guardian of the student should not exceed ₹ 2.50 lakh from all sources.
- Those who were awarded the scholarship for 2008-09 and fulfill the conditions of the scheme may apply for renewal of scholarship for 2009-10.

In each scheme, 30% of scholarships are earmarked for girls belonging to the minority communities Details of the schemes, including application formats, are available on the website of the Ministry of Minority Affairs–www.minorityaffairs.gov.in.

ACHIEVEMENTS OF THE PROGRAMME

Education

- 68 Lakh Scholarships awarded.
- Constructed in areas having a substantial minority population :
  - 1770 Primary and Upper Primary schools under SSA.
  - 3530 New Primary and Upper Primary schools opened under SSA.
  - 60 existing ITIs upgraded into Centre of Excellence.
- Sanctioned under Multi-Sectoral Development Programme in Minority Concentrated Districts:
  - 22 Polytechnic institutions for construction / upgradation.
  - 24 ITIs for construction / upgradation.

- 10482 Additional Class Rooms approved.
- 658 School buildings approved.
- 123 Hostels approved.

Improvement in Living Conditions

- 10.84 lakh Indira Awas Yojana houses constructed.
- 1,70,629 habitations taken up in areas having a substantial minority population under National Rural Drinking Water Programme.
- Sanctioned under Multi-Sectoral Development Programme in Minority Concentrated Districts:
  - 27,077 Units of drinking water facility.
  - 2446 Units of Health Centres
  - 25515 Units of Anganwadi Centres.

Institutional Growth

- Maulana Azad Education Foundation Corpus Fund increased to ₹ 700 crore (paid up as on date ₹ 550 crore).
- National Minorities Development and Finance Corporation's authorized share capital enhanced to ₹ 1500 crore.
- Waqb Amendment Bill passed in Lok Sabha on 07.05.2010.
- Computerization and digitization of records of State Waqb Boards.

Employment and Economic Opportunities

- ₹ 1557.11 crore under term loans and Micro Finance distributed by National Minorities Development & Finance Corporation.
- 2458 Bank branches opened.
- Priority sector lending increased to ₹ 1,08,850.89 crore.
- Nearly 16,000 students imparted Free Coaching.
- Representation in Government jobs increased to 9.09%.

APPENDIX XVII

EDUCATIONAL AND SOCIO-ECONOMIC DEVELOPMENT OF THE MINORITY COMMUNITIES

- A new scheme **'USTTAD'** (upgrading the skills and Training in Traditional Arts/Crafts for Development) has been approved to preserve traditional arts/crafts of minorities and build capacity of traditional artisans/craftsmen.
- Another new scheme **'Hamari Dharohar'**, to preserve rich heritage of minority communities of India under the overall concept of Indian culture, has been approved.
- **'Cyber Gram Yojana'** for **digital literacy** of minorities mainstreamed under Jan Vikas Karyakram (Multi Sectoral Development Programme) CSC e-Governance Services India Ltd. of Department of Electronics and Information Technology engaged as Knowledge Partner. To start with, Sanction issued for development of 244 Cyber Madarsas in West Bengal.
- **"MANAS (Maulana Azad National Academy for Skills)"** established on 10.11.2014 under National Minorities Development & Finance Corporation (NMDFC) to upgrade Skills of minority youths and place them within India and overseas.
- MANAS signed MoU with National Skill Development Corporation and Sector Skill Councils of Health, Security, Logistics, Leather and Media & Entertainment. A Regional office of MANAS also opened at Chennai.
- **Direct Benefit Transfer** of Scholarships in the bank account of students has also been operationalized in respect of Post-Matric, Merit cum Means Scholarships and Maulana Azad National Fellowship from 2014-15.
- Where there are no accounts with the students, particularly for children studying in lower classes, bank accounts opened under **'Pradhanmantri Jan Dhan Yojana'** to be utilized.
- Under a new scheme of **'Seekho aur Kamao (Learn & Earn)'**, The Placement linked Skill Development Initiative for Minorities, sanction has been issued for training of fresh 16,270 minority youths in 24 States during 2014-15.
- Under **"Jan Vikas Karyakram (Multi-Sectoral Development Programme)"**, which is implemented through State Government/UT Administrations, sanction has already been issued for the Skill Development training programmes for 95,824 minority youths during 2014-15.
- **"Swachch Bharat Mission"** integrated with "Jan Vikas Karyakram (Multi-Sectoral Development Programme)" for construction of toilets for boys and girls in schools and public places.
- To provide an avenue to the students of madarsas for mainstream education, Ministry introduced a new scheme called **"Nai Manzil"** which bridges the gap between Madarsa

Appendix XVII

Education and the mainstream education. It provides trade basis skill training in four courses at the same time of formal education, in field of:
(a) Manufacturing
(b) Engineering
(c) Services
(d) Soft skills

- Ministry has approved coaching of 1150 minority students for Free Coaching for Engineering and Medical Entrance Examination during 2014-15 so far.

- **National Waqf Development Corporation (NAWADCO)** established in January 2014, has identified 77 waqf properties for commercial development.

- NAWADCO has signed an MoU with National Building Construction Corporation (NBCC) for developing properties on 08.09.2014.

- **"Nai Roshini"** the scheme for Leadership Development of Minority Women (Implemented in 2012-13), Training of 66,350 minority women sanctioned during 2014-15.

- **Padho Pardesh**–Scheme of interest subsidy on educational loans for overseas studies for the students belonging to the minority communities. Launched in financial year 2013–2014.

- **Nai Udaan**–Support for students for preparation of main examination who clear prelims conducted by UPSC/SSC, State Public Service Commission (PSC) etc.

APPENDIX XVIII

DEPARTMENT FOR THE WELFARE OF SC/ST/OBC/MINORITIES GOVERNMENT OF NCT OF DELHI

The Department is fully commited to the highest standard of excellence and transparency in providing the benefis to the people belonging to SCs/STs/OBCs/Minorities. The following schemes are being implemened by Govt. of NCT of Delhi for socioeconomic development of residents of Delhi belonging to SCs/STs/OBCs/Minorities (including Jain community):

1. Free supply of stationery for the students of classes I to XII of all Government/Aided/Recognized Public Schools affiliated to Directorate of Education/Kendriya Vidyalaya/National Open School/Schools affiliated to NDMC/Delhi Cantonment Board/East, North and South Delhi Municipal Corporations.
2. Merit Scholarship for the students of classes I to XII of all Government/Aided/Recognized Public Schools affiliated to Directorate of Education/Kendriya Vidyalaya/National Open School/Schools affiliated to NDMC/Delhi Cantonment Board/East, North and South Delhi Municipal Corporations.
3. Merit scholarship for college professional technical institutions students
4. Vocational and technical scholarships
5. Dr. B.R. Ambedkar Award for the students of each discipline at the graduation level.
6. Reimbursement of tuition fee for the students of public schools.
7. Hostel for boys students at Dilshad Garden studying in Class XII or above in Government/Recognized Schools or Colleges.
8. Hostel for girls students at Dilshad Garden studying in Class XII or above in Government/Recognized Schools or Colleges.
9. Pre-examination coaching to the aspirants of Group B and Group C (non-technical only) posts of different competitive examinations in Government/Semi-Government/Bank/Public Sector Undertakings.
10. Health, housing and others funding of 50% share by the Government towards development charges for electrification of un-electrified house sites colonies allotted under Twenty-Point Programme.
11. Institution of Dr. Ambedkar Ratan Award.

APPENDIX XIX
MAHATMA GANDHI NATIONAL RURAL EMPLOYMENT GUARANTEE ACT (MGNREGA), 2005 – 5 YEARS

National Rural Employment Guarantee Act was enacted on 5th September, 2005 and came into force w.e.f 2nd February, 2006. On 31st December, 2009 the Act was renamed by an Amendment as the Mahatma Gandhi National Rural Employment Guarantee Act 2005. It is now commonly referred to as Mahatma Gandhi NREGA.

THE RIGHTS TO DEMAND EMPLOYMENT
To exercise this right the rural household must obtain a Job Card

What is a Job Card ?

A Job Card is the basic legal document, which enables the registered household to demand guaranteed employment.

How is a Job Card Obtained ?

The applicant should apply orally or in writing to the Gram Panchayat. The Job Card is issued to the household as a whole. It will have the names and photographs of each registered member of that household.

A legal guarantee of 100 days of wage employment in a financial year to every rural household whose adult members volunteer to do unskilled manual work.

The entire registration process is free of cost

The registered household does not have to pay for a Job Card and the photograph

The Job Card will be issued within 15 days of the application. A complaint may be filed with the Programme Officer at the Block level or District Programme Coordinator in case of non-receipt of the Job Card A Job Card is a record of a worker's rights. It is a valid for five years.

3 Necessary Steps to Get Employment Under NREGA :

- Registering with the Gram Panchayat and obtaining a Job Card with unique registration number and photograph.
- Submitting a written application with the Job Card number for employment to the Gram Panchayat.
- Obtaining a dated receipt from the Gram Panchayat.

A Job Card guarantees the workers right to demand employment.

The Duties of a Job Cardholder

1. The Job card should necessarily remain in the custody of the wage earner only and not shared with anyone
2. The days of work and wages entered in the Job Card should be accurate.
3. In case of complaints regarding Job Card entries the Programme Officer/District Programme Officer may be contacted.

Employment guarantee is provided by Job Card only.

5 YEARS OF MGNREGA

- Employment provided to 4.1 crore households in 2010-11 upto December 2010.
- Persondays generated since inception 879 crore.
- Women participation: 410 crore persondays (47%)
- SC participation : 245 crore persondays (28%)
- ST participation : 214 crore persondays (24%)
- Total Central release since inception: ₹ 112861.16 crore.
- Total expenditure on wages since inception ₹ 74677 crore around 70%.
- Average wage per persondays increased from ₹ 65 in 2006-07 to around ₹ 100 in 2010-11.
- Total works taken up in 2010-11 are 68 lakhs : 50 % works related to water, 12% works on individual land owned by SC/ST/BPL/ Small and Marginal farmers and Land Reform and IAY beneficiaries, 21% works on Rural Connectivity and 13% works on land development.
- Over 10 crore bank/post office accounts of Mahatma Gandhi NREGA Workers have been opened, making Mahatma Gandhi National Rural Employment Guarantee Act the world's largest financial inclusion initiative.

ROAD AHEAD

- Transparency and Accountability : Effective Social Audit.
- Biometric enabled, ICT-based Mahatma Gandhi NREGA process for safeguarding worker's rights.
- Enhanced Productivity and Sustainable Development.
- Strengthening Gram Panchayats.
- Empowering Workers.
- National Electronic Fund Management (NEFM) introduced

TRANSFORMING RURAL LIVES THROUGH NEW INITIATIVES

- During 2014-15 and 2015-16 (so far) nearly 8 crore rural households have been given employment under MGNREGA. 42 lakh rural households have completed 100days.
- Focus on skilling of the MGNREGA workers; 18 lakh youth/households to be skilled in phases.
- Barefoot Technicians (BFT) to emerge from the MGNREGA workers; 10000 BFTs to come up in the first phase.
- ₹ 47936 crore earned as wages by rural workers employed under the programme, since April 2014 till Feb., 2016.
- Emphasis on women participation in MGNREGA: 57% of MGNREGA workers are women in 2015-16 (so far). This is the highest ever participation.
- Nearly 64% of total expenditure on assets in 2015-16 (so far) has been on activities related to agriculture and allied sector.
- The Government has ensured the highest ever persondays generation in the second and third quarter of 2015-2016 (so far) compared to the last 5 years.
- Highest expenditure on MGNREGA recorded by the Government in 2015-16 (so far).
- 94% of wages have gone directly to the accounts of the MGNREGA workers in 2015-16 (so far).

APPENDIX XX
1-2-3 OF THE NUCLEAR DEAL

1. At a time when India faces crippling energy shortages, and when our nuclear plants are short of uranium, the nuclear deal assures us the supplies we need to power the future. If we do not act now, our future energy independence is at stake.

2. The Nuclear deal ends the technological isolation we have suffered since Pokharan. It will lift the world's sanctions against us, allow our nuclear scientists to take their honoured place in the international community and grant us the status of a recognised nuclear power that will not sign the NPT but is respected as a non-proliferator. The deal restores our sovereign honour.

3. The nuclear deal will reduce our dependence on crude oil and gas, whose international price has crossed US $ 140 a barrel and continues to mount upward. It offers us an invaluable source of clean, efficient and safe energy to add to the variety of energy sources we need–coal, oil, wind, hydro, solar, biofuels and nuclear–as we seek to bring prosperity and hope to all Indians in the 21st century.

In Other Words :

The deal strengthens India's energy independence, sovereignty and autonomy. It ends the sanctions that have crippled our nuclear efforts. It invests in India's future.

Think of Tomorrow—Support the Agreement Today.

MINISTRY OF PETROLEUM AND NATURAL GAS
Government of India

APPENDIX XXI
STATEWISE ALLOCATION OF SEATS IN STATE LEGISLATURES

No.	States	Legislative Assemblies	Legislative Councils
1.	Andhra Pradesh	175	58
2.	Arunachal Pradesh	60	—
3.	Assam	126	—
4.	Bihar	243	75
5.	Chhattisgarh	90	—
6.	Goa	40	—
7.	Gujarat	182	—
8.	Haryana	90	—
9.	Himachal Pradesh	68	—
10.	Jammu & Kashmir	87	36
11.	Jharkhand	81	—
12.	Karnataka	224	75
13.	Kerala	140	—
14.	Madhya Pradesh	230	—
16.	Maharashtra	288	78
16.	Manipur	60	—
17.	Meghalaya	60	—
18.	Mizoram	40	—
19.	Nagaland	60	—
20.	Odisha	147	—
21.	Punjab	117	—
22.	Rajasthan	200	—
23.	Sikkim	32	—
24.	Tamil Nadu	234	—
25.	Telangana	119	40
26.	Tripura	60	—
27.	Uttar Pradesh	403	100
28.	Uttarakhand	70	—
29.	West Bengal	294	—

APPENDIX XXII
STATEWISE ALLOCATION OF SEATS IN PARLIAMENT

States & UTs	Rajya Sabha	Lok Sabha
Andaman and Nicobar Islands (UT)	—	1
Andhra Pradesh	11	25
Arunachal Pradesh	1	2
Assam	7	14
Bihar	16	40
Chandigarh (UT)	—	1
Chhatisgarh	5	11
Dadra & Nagar Haveli (UT)	—	1
Daman and Diu (UT)	—	1
Goa	1	2
Gujarat	11	26
Haryana	5	10
Himachal Pradesh	3	4
Jammu & Kashmir	4	6
Jharkhand	6	14
Karnataka	12	28
Kerala	9	20
Lakshadweep (UT)	—	1
Madhya Pradesh	11	29
Maharashtra	19	48
Manipur	1	2
Meghalaya	1	2
Mizoram	1	1
Nagaland	1	1
National Capital of Territory of Delhi	3	7
Odisha	10	21
Puducherry (UT)	1	1
Punjab	7	13
Rajasthan	10	25
Sikkim	1	1
Tamil Nadu	18	39
Telangana	7	17
Tripura	1	2
Uttar Pradesh	31	80
Uttarakhand	3	5
West Bengal	16	42
Nominated	12	2
Total	**245**	**545**

Rajya Sabha shall consist of 238 elected representatives of States and Union Territories and 12 members to be nominated by the President (Art. 80). The Council of States shall not be subject to dissolution but as nearly as possible one-third of its members shall retire, as soon as may be, after the expiry of 2 years. Elections to Rajya Sabha are indirect. Although the Constitution provides for 250 members it has now only 245 seats and of these, 233 are represented by the states and the UTs.

Lok Sabha The House of the People (Lok Sabha) shall consist of 552 members chosen by direct election from territorial constituencies : 530 members from States, 20 members to represent Union Territories and 2 are Presidential nominees from Anglo-Indian community (Art. 81).

The House of the People shall continue for 5 years (unless sooner dissolved) from the date of its meeting and no longer and the expiry of the said period of 5 years shall operate as dissolution of the House (Art. 83). The mandatory provision of dissolution may be extended for a year due to emergency.

APPENDIX XXIII
HIKE IN SALARIES AND ALLOWANCES OF MEMBERS OF PARLIAMENT

Cabinet approved a three-fold hike in salaries and doubled the allowances of Members of Parliament (MPs) w.e.f. August 2010.

	Existing	Recommended	Approved
1. Basic	1,92,000	9,60,000	6,00,000
2. Constituency Allowance	2,40,000	4,80,000	4,80,000
3. Office and Stationery Allowance	2,40,000	7,20,000	4,80,000
4. Daily Allowance (for 180 days)	1,80,000	3,60,000	3,60,000
5. Air Travel (Existing 34 trips. Recommended and approved 50 Trips)	9,51,320	13,99,000	13,99,000
6. Rail Travel (Unlimited First AC for Self and Spouse)	72,000	72,000	72,000
7. Rail Travel (Unlimited Second AC fare for attendant)	36,000	36,000	36,000
8. Telephone (Existing 150000 free calls Recommended and Approved 2,00,000)	1,50,000	2,00,000	2,00,000
9. Residence in Delhi	24,00,000	24,00,000	24,00,000
10. Broad band	18,000	18,000	18,000
11. Electricity (50,000 Units a year)	50,000	50,000	50,000
Total	45,29,320	66,95,000	60,95,000

Recommended by Joint Committee on Salaries and Allowances of MPs
Approved By the Cabinet
Annual Income in ₹

APPENDIX XXIV
DELHI MUNICIPAL CORPORATION ELECTIONS

Municipal Elections in Delhi in the year 2012, the Bharatiya Janata Party (BJP), popularly known as the Saffron Party, emerged victorious as the Congress Party fell way behind the Saffron Party in the civic body polls.

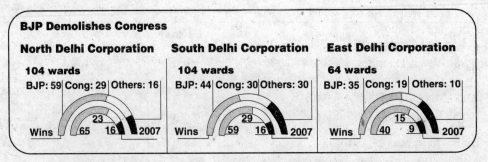

Graph Showing Comparisons of Municipal Poll Results–2007 and 2012

Delhi MCD Elections 2017

The Bharatiya Janata Party's long list of electoral successes continued as it notched up a massive victory in the Municipal Corporation of Delhi Elections. The BJP won 181 of the 272 seats, leaving the Aam Aadmi Party well behind of 49 seats with the congress suffering another dismal day. The BJP also swept all three corporations.

	BJP	AAP	Cong	Others
SDMC	70	16	12	6
NDMC	64	21	16	3
EDMC	47	12	3	2
	181	49	31	11

APPENDIX XXV

PROTECTION OF WOMEN FROM DOMESTIC VIOLENCE ACT, 2005

OBJECTIVES

To provide protection to women who are victims of violence of any kind occurring within the family.

WHO ARE COVERED BY THE ACT ?

Women who are or have been in a relationship with the abuser where both parties have lived together in a shared household and are related by blood, marriage or a relationship in the nature of marriage, or adoption.

WHAT IS DOMESTIC VIOLENCE ?
- Physical abuse, sexual abuse, verbal abuse, emotional abuse and economic abuse.
- Harassment to meet any unlawful dowry demands.

WHO CAN REGISTER A CASE ?
- The aggrieved woman herself
- Anyone who has a reason to believe that an act of domestic violence has been or is likely to be committed.

WHOM SHOULD SHE APPROACH ?
- Can approach the Magistrate directly
- Take the help of the Protection Officer (an officer appointed by the State Government as Protection Officer) or the Service Provider/Ngo (an organization registered as service provider under the Act) to file a case.

WHAT DOES THIS ACT PROVIDE FOR ?
- Right to reside in the matrimonial or shared household, whether or not she has any title or rights in the household by issuing a Residence Order.
- Prevent the abuser from entering a workplace or any other place frequented by the abused, attempting to communicate with the abused isolating any assets used by both the parties and causing violence to the abused, her relatives and others who provide her assistance from domestic violence by issuing a Protection Order.
- Temporary custody of any child or children to the aggrieved person.
- Breach of protection order by the respondent is a cognizable and non-bailable offence punishable with imprisonment up to one year or with fine up to twenty thousand rupees or with both.

REHABILITATION SERVICES
- The shelter home shall provide shelter to the aggrieved person.
- Person in charge of the medical facility shall provide medical aid to the aggrieved person.

RESPONDENT'S ACCOUNTABILITY
- Monetary relief is payable by the respondent with the period specified by the Magistrate.
- Respondent can be directed to pay compensation and damages for the injuries, Including mental torture and emotional distress caused.

MINISTRY OF WOMEN AND CHILD DEVELOPMENT
Government of India

APPENDIX XXVI
EMPOWERMENT OF WOMEN

NATIONAL MISSION FOR WOMEN EMPOWERMENT IN INDIA

National Mission for Empowerment of Women (NMEW) is an initiative of the Government of India with a view to empower women socially, economically and educationally.

It has the mandate to strengthen the inter-sector convergence; facilitate the process of coordinating all the women's welfare and socio-economic development programmes across ministries and departments. The Mission aims to provide a single window service for all programmes run by the Government for Women under aegis of various Central Ministries.

In light with its mandate, the Mission has been named Mission Poorma Shakti, implying a vision for holistic empowerment of women.

Progress of the Mission during 2012-13 :

- A Mission Directorate and a National Resource Centre for Women (NRCW) have been set up to operationalise the NMEW with the aim to achieve holistic empowerment of women
- Convergence Projects have been operationalized through Poorna Shakti Kendras set up in 150 Gram Panchayats in Pali District of Rajasthan
- Action research studies have been initiated on women centric programmes and services which impact women
- 27 State Mission Authorities (SMA) have been notified and 21 State Resource Centres for Women (SRCW) have been set up
- Thematic Convergence Projects in areas such as declining sex ratio, skill development, livelihood promotion, gender budgeting and mainstreaming, social inclusion of marginalized women, access to justice, behaviour change communication have been announced

LIST OF OTHER GOVERNMENT INITIATIVES FOR EMPOWERMENT OF WOMEN

- Support to Training and Employment for Women (STEP)-A scheme for marginalized women.
- National Credit Fund for Women-Rashtriya a Mahila Kosh (RMK) for providing micro-financing for the socio-economic upliftment of the poor & asset less women in informal sector
- 33% reservation for women in Gram Panchayats and Municipal Bodies
- Mahatma Gandhi National Rural Employment Guarantee Act (MGNREGA) - Ensuring 100 days of employment
- Sarva Shiksha Abhiyan-Universal education for all

Schemes Relating to Women Health Care

- Janani Suraksha Yojana-Safe Motherhood intervention
- National Rural Health Mission (NRHM) - Access to quality healthcare for all
- Indira Gandhi Matritva Sahyog Yojana (IGMSY)–A conditional maternity benefit scheme for pregnant and lactating Women
- Restructured Integrated Child Development Services (ICDS) for pregnant and lactating mothers
- Counselling, Referral and Rehabilitation Services from Family Counselling Centres
- Women Health Volunteers Accredited Social Health Activist (ASHA)-to create awareness among the community for health & hygiene issues

Appendix XXVI

Schematic Interventions for Protective Environment for Women
- UJJAWALA - Prevention, rescue, rehabilitation, reintegration and repatriation of trafficked victimes
- Swadhar Greh Scheme-Institutional Support for rehabilitation for Women in Difficult Circumstances
- Working Women's Hostel (WWH) - Safe & affordable hostel for working women & women being trained for employment

Initialives for Girl Children
- Rajiv Gandhi Scheme for Empowerment of Adolescent Girls (RGSEAG)-SABLA
- Rajiv Gandhi National Creche Scheme for children of working mothers for providing Day care facilities
- Integrated Child Development Services (ICDS) for Early Childhood Development of children in age group 0-6 years
- Dhanalakshmi Conditional Cash Transfer

Laws Pertaining to Women
- Dowry Prohibition Act, 1961-Prohibiting Dowry
- The Indecent Representation of Women (Prohibition) Act, 1986-Protecting the dignity of women
- Protection of Women from Domestic Violence Act, 2005-Protecting women from domestic violence
- Pre-Conception and Pre-Natal Diagnostic Techniques Act, 1994 (PCPNDT)-Upholding Girl Child's Right to be born
- Maternity benefit At, 1961-Securing Right to motherhood & employment
- Right to Education Act, 2009-Guaranteeing access to education of women
- Prohibition of Child Marriage Zct, 2006- Prohibiting early marriage of Girl Child
- Immoral Traffic Prevention Act, 1956-Safeguarding women
- Sexual harassment of women at Workplace (Prevention, Prohibition and Redressal) Bill, 2013
- Equal Remuneration Act, 1976-Equal Pay for Equal Work
- The Criminal Law (Amendment) Act, 2013- amendments to criminal law to sternly deal with sexual assault cases

    The Criminal Law (Amendment) Act, 2013 : is an Act further to amend the Indian Penal Code, 1860 the code of Criminal Procedure, 1973, the Indian Evidence Act, 1872 and the Protection of Children from sexual offences Act, 2012.

    The massive public anger and uproars following the December 16, 2012 Delhi Gang Rape forced the drafting and eventual passing of this Act. The incident generated widespread national and international coverage and was condemned by various women's groups both in India and abroad.

Empowered Women
Empowered Nation
- The 'Beti Bachao, Beti Padhao' Yojana launched on 22 Jan 2015 with initial funding of Rs.100 crore and has turned out to be a very successful campaign to erase the difference between son and daughter.
- ₹ 6,000 financial assistance to women for nourishment during pregnancy.

- Maternity leave increased from 12 weeks to 26 weeks (MB Amendment Act) from 1 April 2017.
- 33 lakh health check-ups conducted under Pradhan Mantri Surakshit Matritva Yojana.
- ₹ 11,000 crore deposited in more than 1 crore accounts to ensure bright future of daughters.
- More than 2 crore economically weaker women given gas connection.
- Out of the 7.5 crore loans sanctioned under Mudra Yojana, 70% was for women.
- Under stand up India; atleast one woman has benefitted through each bank, with loans ranging from ₹ 10 lakh to ₹ 1 crore.
- 30 lakh jobs being provided to women in the textile Industry.

APPENDIX XXVII

BHARAT RATNA AWARDEES

1954	**Rajagopalachari:** Last & only Indian independence activist, Governor-General of India.
	C.V. Raman: Nobel Laureate physicist (1930)
	Sarvepalli Radhakrishnan: Philosopher, India's first Vice-President (1952-62) and second President (1962-67)
1955	**Bhagwan Das:** Independence activist, author
	Mokshagundam Visvesvaraya: Civil Engineer, Statesman and Diwan of Mysore (1912-18)
	Jawaharlal Nehru: Independence activist, author and first Prime Minister of India (1947-64)
1957	**Govind Ballabh Pant:** Independence activist, first Chief Minister of Uttar Pradesh (1950-54)
1958	**Dhondo Keshav Kerve:** Social reformer, educator
1961	**Bidhan Chandra Roy:** Physician surgeon & second Chief Minister of West Bengal (1948-62)
	Purushottam Das Tandon: Independence activist, educator
1962	**Rajendra Prasad:** Independence activist, jurist, first President of India (1950-62)
1963	**Zakir Hussain:** Independence activist, second Vice-President of India (1962-67) and Third President of India (1967-69)
	Pandurang Vaman Kane: Indologist and Sanskrit Scholar
1966	**Lal Bahadur Shastri:** Independence Activist and Third Prime Minister of India. (1964-66)
1971	**Indira Gandhi:** Former Prime Minister of India (1966-77) (1980-84)
1975	**V.V. Giri:** Trade Unionist, first Acting President of India and Fourth President of India (1969-74)
1976	**K. Kamaraj:** Independence Activist and former Chief Minister of Tamil Nadu (1954-57, 1957-62, 1962-63)
1980	**Mother Teresa:** Catholic nun, founder of the Missionaries of Charity and Nobel peace prize laureate (1979)
1983	**Vinoba Bhave:** Independence activist, social reformer and Ramon Magsaysay Award laureate (1958)
1987	**Khan Abdul Ghaffar Khan:** Independence Activist
1988	**M.G. Ramachandran:** Film actor and former Chief Minister of Tamil Nadu (1977-80, 1980-84, 1985-87)
1990	**B.R. Ambedkar:** Chief architect of the Indian Constitution and Social reformer.
	Nelson Mandela: Leader of the Anti-Apartheid Movement in South-Africa and Nobel Peace Prize laureate (1993)

Year	Recipients
1991	**Rajiv Gandhi:** Ninth Prime Minister of India (1984-89)

Vallabhbhai Patel: Independence activist and first Deputy Prime Minister of India (1947-50)

Morarji Desai: Independence activist and sixth Prime Minister of India (1977-79)

1992   **Abul Kalam Azad:** Independence Activist

J.R.D. Tata: Industrialist and philanthropist

Satyajit Ray: Filmmaker

1997   **Gulzarilal Nanda:** Independence activist and two times interim Prime Minister of India.

Aruna Asaf Ali: Independence activist

A.P.J. Abdul Kalam: Aerospace and Defense Scientist, eleventh President of India (2002-07)

1998   **M.S. Subbulakshmi:** Carnatic Classical Vocalist

Chidambaram Subramaniam: Independence activist and former Minister of Agriculture of India (1964-66)

1999   **Jayaprakash Narayan:** Independence activist and social reformer

Ravi Shankar: Hindustani Classical Sitar player

Amartya Sen: Nobel laureate, economist (1998)

Gopinath Bordoloi: Independence activist, first Chief Minister of Assam (1946-50)

2001   **Lata Mangeshkar:** Playback Singer

Bismillah Khan: Hindustani Classical Shehnai player

2009   **Bhimsen Joshi:** Hindustani Classical vocalist

2013   **C.N.R. Rao:** Chemist

Sachin Tendulkar: Cricketer

2014   **Madan Mohan Malaviya:** Educationist, politician (President of Indian National Congress (INC) in 1909, 1918 and founder of Banaras Hindu University

Atal Bihari Vajpayee: Former Prime Minister of India (1996, 1998, 1999-2004), poet

APPENDIX XXX

EMPOWERMENT OF WOMEN

NATIONAL MISSION FOR WOMEN EMPOWERMENT IN INDIA

National Mission for Empowerment of Women (NMEW) is an initiative of the Government of India with a view to empower women socially, economically and educationally.

It has the mandate to strengthen the inter-sector convergence; facilitate the process of coordinating all the women's welfare and socio-economic development programmes across ministries and departments. The Mission aims to provide a single window service for all programmes run by the Government for Women under aegis of various Central Ministries.

In light with its mandate, the Mission has been named Mission Poorma Shakti, implying a vision for holistic empowerment of women.

Progress of the Mission during 2012-13 :

- A Mission Directorate and a National Resource Centre for Women (NRCW) have been set up to operationalise the NMEW with the aim to achieve holistic empowerment of women
- Convergence Projects have been operationalized through Poorna Shakti Kendras set up in 150 Gram Panchayats in Pali District of Rajasthan
- Action research studies have been initiated on women centric programmes and services which impact women
- 27 State Mission Authorities (SMA) have been notified and 21 State Resource Centres for Women (SRCW) have been set up
- Thematic Convergence Projects in areas such as declining sex ratio, skill development, livelihood promotion, gender budgeting and mainstreaming, social inclusion of marginalized women, access to justice, behaviour change communication have been announced

LIST OF OTHER GOVERNMENT INITIATIVES FOR EMPOWERMENT OF WOMEN

- Support to Training and Employment for Women (STEP)-A scheme for marginalized women
- National Credit Fund for Women-Rashtriya a Mahila Kosh (RMK) for providing micro-financing for the socio-economic upliftment of the poor & asset less women in informal sector
- 33% reservation for women in Gram Panchayats and Municipal Bodies
- Mahatma Gandhi National Rural Employment Guarantee Act (MGNREGA) - Ensuring 100 days of employment
- Sarva Shiksha Abhiyan-Universal education for all

Schemes Relating to Women Health Care

- Janani Suraksha Yojana-Safe Motherhood intervention
- National Rural Health Mission (NRHM) - Access to quality healthcare for all
- Indira Gandhi Matritva Sahyog Yojana (IGMSY)—A conditional maternity benefit scheme for pregnant and lactating Women
- Restructured Integrated Child Development Services (ICDS) for pregnant and lactating mothers

- Counselling, Referral and Rehabilitation Services from Family Counselling Centres
- Women Health Volunteers Accredited Social Health Activist (ASHA)-to create awareness among the community for health & hygiene issues

Schematic Interventions for Protective Environment for Women
- UJJAWALA - Prevention, rescue, rehabilitation, reintegration and repatriation of trafficked victims
- Swadhar Greh Scheme-Institutional Support for rehabilitation for Women in Difficult Circumstances
- Working Women's Hostel (WWH) - Safe & affordable hostel for working women & women being trained for employment

Initialives for Girl Children
- Rajiv Gandhi Scheme for Empowerment of Adolescent Girls (RGSEAG)-SABLA
- Rajiv Gandhi National Creche Scheme for children of working mothers for providing Day care facilities
- Integrated Child Development Services (ICDS) for Early Childhood Development of children in age group 0-6 years
- Dhanalakshmi Conditional Cash Transfer

Laws Pertaining to Women
- Dowry Prohibition Act, 1961-Prohibiting Dowry
- The Indecent Representation of Women (Prohibition) Act, 1986-Protecting the dignity of women
- Protection of Women from Domestic Violence Act, 2005-Protecting women from domestic violence
- Pre-Conception and Pre-Natal Diagnostic Techniques Act, 1994 (PCPNDT)-Upholding Girl Child's Right to be born
- Maternity benefit At, 1961-Securing Right to motherhood & employment
- Right to Education Act, 2009-Guaranteeing access to education of women
- Prohibition of Child Marriage Zct, 2006- Prohibiting early marriage of Girl Child
- Immoral Traffic Prevention Act, 1956-Safeguarding women
- Sexual harassment of women at Workplace (Prevention, Prohibition and Redressal) Bill, 2013
- Equal Remuneration Act, 1976-Equal Pay for Equal Work
- The Criminal Law (Amendment) Act, 2013- amendments to criminal law to sternly deal with sexual assault cases

The Criminal Law (Amendment) Act, 2013 : is an Act further to amend the Indian Penal Code, 1860 the code of Criminal Procedure, 1973, the Indian Evidence Act, 1872 and the Protection of Children from sexual offences Act, 2012.

The massive public anger and uproars following the December 16, 2012 Delhi Gang Rape forced the drafting and eventual passing of this Act. The incident generated widespread national and international coverage and was condemned by various women's groups both in India and abroad.

APPENDIX XXXI

BHARAT RATNA AWARDEES

1954	**Rajagopalachari :** Last & only Indian independence activist, Governor-General of India.
	C.V. Raman : Nobel Laureate physicist (1930)
	Sarvepalli Radhakrishnan : Philosopher India's first Vice-President (1952-62) and second President (1962-67)
1955	**Bhagwan Das :** Independence Activist
	Visvesvaraya : Civil Engineer, Statesman and Diwan of Mysore (1912-18)
	Jawaharlal Nehru : Independence activist, author and first Prime Minister of India (1947-64)
1957	**Govind Ballabh Pant :** Independence activist, first Chief Minister of Uttar Pradesh (1950-54)
1958	**Dhondo Keshav Kerve :** Social reformer
1961	**Bidhan Chandra Roy :** Physician surgeon & Second Chief Minister of West Bengal (1948-62)
	Purushottam Das Tandon : Independence activist, educator
1962	**Rajendra Prasad :** Independence activists lawyer, first President of India (1950-62)
1963	**Zakir Hussain :** Independence activist, second Vice-President of India (1962-67) and Third President of India (1967-69)
	Pandurang Vaman Kane : Indologist and Sanskrit Scholar.
1966	**Lal Bahadur Shastri :** Independence Activist and Third Prime Minister of India. (1964-66)
1971	**Indira Gandhi :** Former Prime Minister of India (1966-77) (1980-84)
1975	**V.V. Giri :** Trade Unionist, first Acting President of India and Fourth President of India (1969-74)
1976	**K. Kamaraj :** Independence Activist and former Chief Minister of Tamil Nadu (1954-57, 1957-62), 1962-63)
1980	**Mother Teresa :** Catholic nun, founder of the Missionaries of Charity and Nobel peace prize laureate (1979)
1983	**Vinoba Bhave :** Independence activist social reformer and Ramon Magsaysay Award laureate (1958)
1987	**Khan Abdul Ghaffar Khan :** Independence Activist.
1988	**M.G. Ramachandran :** Film actor and former Chief Minister of Tamil Nadu (1977-80, 1980-84, 1985-87)
1990	**B.R. Ambedkar :** Chief architect of the Indian Constitution and Social reformer.
	Nelson Mandela : Leader of the Anti-Apartheid Movement in South-Africa and Nobel Peace Prize laureate (1993)
1991	**Rajiv Gandhi :** Ninth Prime Minister of India (1984-89)

Vallabhbhai Patel : Independence activist and first Deputy Prime Minister of India (1947-50)

Morarji Desai : Independence activist and sixth Prime Minister of India (1977-79)

1992 **Abul Kalam Azad :** Independence Activist.

J.R.D. Tata : Industrialist and philanthropist.

Satyajit Ray : Filmmaker.

1997 **Gulzarilal Nanda :** Independence activist and two times interim Prime Minister of India.

Aruna Asaf Ali : Independence activist.

A.P.J. Abdul Kalam : Aerospace and Defense Scientist, eleventh President of India (2002-07)

1998 **M.S. Subbulakshmi :** Carnatic Classical Vocalist.

Chidambaram Subramaniam : Independence activist and former Minister of Agriculture of India (1964-66)

1999 **Jayaprakash Narayan :** Independence activist and social reformer

Ravi Shankar : Hindustani Classical Sitar player

Amartya Sen : Nobel laureate economist (1998)

Gopinath Bordoloi : Independence activist, first Chief Minister of Assam (1946-50)

2001 **Lata Mangeshkar :** Playback Singer

Bismillah Khan : Hindustani Classical Shehnai player

2009 **Bhimsen Joshi :** Hindustani Classical vocalist

2013 **C.N.R. Rao :** Chemist

Sachin Tendulkar : Cricketer

2014 **Madan Mohan Malaviya :** Educationist and politicians (President of Indian National Congress (INC) in 1909, 1918.

Atal Bihari Vajpayee : Former Prime Minister of India (1996, 1998, 1999-2004), poet.

APPENDIX XXXII

EDUCATIONAL AND SOCIO ECONOMIC DEVELOPMENT OF THE MINORITY COMMUNITIES 2014-15

- A new scheme **'USTTAD'** (upgrading the skills and Training in Traditional Arts/Crafts for Development) has been approved to preserve traditional arts/crafts of minorities and build capacity of traditional artisans/craftsmen.

- Another new scheme **'Hamari Dharohar'**, to preserve rich heritage of minority communities of India under the overall concept of Indian culture, has been approved.

- **'Cyber Gram Yojana'** for **digital literacy** of minorities mainstreamed under Jan Vikas Karyakram (Multi Sectoral Development Programme) CSC e-Governance Services India Ltd. of Department of Electronics and Information Technology engaged as Knowledge Partner. To start with, Sanction issued for development of 244 Cyber Madarsas in West Bengal.

- **"MANAS (Maulana Azad National Academy for Skills)"** established on 10.11.2014 under National Minorities Development & Finance Corporation (NMDFC) to upgrade Skills of minority youths and place them within India and overseas.

- MANAS signed MoU with National Skill Development Corporation and Sector Skill Councils of Health, Security, Logistics, Leather and Media & Entertainment. A Regional office of MANAS also opened at Chennai.

- **Direct Benefit Transfer** of Scholarships in the bank account of students has also been operationalized in respect of Post-Matric, Merit cum Means Scholarships and Maulana Azad National Fellowship from 2014-15.

- Where there are no accounts with the students, particularly for children studying in lower classes, bank accounts opened under **'Pradhanmantri Jan Dhan Yojana'** to be utilized.

- Under a new scheme of **'Seekho aur Kamao (Learn & Earn)'**, The Placement linked Skill Development Initiative for Minorities, sanction has been issued for training of fresh 16,270 minority youths in 24 States during 2014-15.

- Under **"Jan Vikas Karyakram (Multi-Sectoral Development Programme)"**, which is implemented through State Government/UT Administrations, sanction has already been issued for the Skill Development training programmes for 95,824 minority youths during 2014-15.

- **"Swachch Bharat Mission"** integrated with "Jan Vikas Karyakram (Multi-Sectoral Development Programme)" for construction of toilets for boys and girls in schools and public places.

- To provide an avenue to the students of madarsas for mainstream education, Ministry is in the advance stage of formulating a new scheme called **"Nai Manzil"** which may bridge the gap between Madarsa Education and the mainstream education.

- Ministry has approved coaching of 1150 minority students for Free Coaching for Engineering and Medical Entrance Examination during 2014-15 so far.

- **National Waqf Development Corporation (NAWADCO)** established in January 2014, has identified 77 waqf properties for commercial development.

- NAWADCO has signed an MoU with National Building Construction Corporation (NBCC) for developing properties on 08.09.2014.

- **"Nai Roshini"** the scheme for Leadership Development of Minority Women (Implemented in 2012-13), Training of 66,350 minority women sanctioned during 2014-15.